1,000,000 Books

are available to read at

www.ForgottenBooks.com

Read online
Download PDF
Purchase in print

ISBN 978-0-282-03511-2
PIBN 10840841

1 MONTH OF
FREE
READING

at

www.ForgottenBooks.com

By purchasing this book you are eligible for one month membership to ForgottenBooks.com, giving you unlimited access to our entire collection of over 1,000,000 titles via our web site and mobile apps.

To claim your free month visit:

www.forgottenbooks.com/free840841

English
Français
Deutsche
Italiano
Español
Português

www.forgottenbooks.com

Mythology Photography **Fiction**
Fishing Christianity **Art** Cooking
Essays Buddhism Freemasonry
Medicine **Biology** Music **Ancient
Egypt** Evolution Carpentry Physics
Dance Geology **Mathematics** Fitness
Shakespeare **Folklore** Yoga Marketing
Confidence Immortality Biographies
Poetry **Psychology** Witchcraft
Electronics Chemistry History **Law**
Accounting **Philosophy** Anthropology
Alchemy Drama Quantum Mechanics
Atheism Sexual Health **Ancient History**
Entrepreneurship Languages Sport
Paleontology Needlework Islam
Metaphysics Investment Archaeology
Parenting Statistics Criminology
Motivational

FREDERIC P. WELLS.

HISTORY

OF

NEWBURY, VERMONT,

From the Discovery of the Coös Country
to Present Time.

WITH GENEALOGICAL RECORDS OF MANY FAMILIES.

By FREDERIC P. WELLS,

IN BEHALF OF THE TOWN.

ST. JOHNSBURY, VT.,
THE CALEDONIAN COMPANY,
1902.

PREFACE.

Seventy years ago, in the autumn of 1831, Rev. Clark Perry, then pastor of the Congregational church in this town, delivered an historical address embodying the results of the inquiries which he had made among the oldest people as to the early events of the settlement of the town, and the period of the Revolutionary War.

He lamented that all who had borne an active part in those events had been allowed to pass away without any pains being taken to gather from them the full particulars of those years, and that in consequence of that neglect, the time had passed when a complete history of the town could be written.

A period precisely equal to that which had elapsed since the first white men wintered in the Coös Country, to the date of Mr. Perry's address, has passed since his time, and it would seem useless to attempt, at this late date, what could not be properly done seventy years ago.

Yet the attempt has been made to gather the annals of the town, and the result is now submitted to the considerate judgment of those most interested in its history.

It is to Rev. Clark Perry that we owe the preservation of so much relating to our early years. He interested himself in the days of old, and imparted to others somewhat of his enthusiasm.

After Mr. Perry went away, Mr. David Johnson took up what was to him a most congenial task, that of collecting the papers of his father, Col. Thomas Johnson, and he thus preserved, incidentally, much of our early history.

Of the collections of Mr. Perry and Mr. Johnson, Rev. Grant Powers had the full use in preparing his historical sketches of the Coös Country, in 1846. Had Mr. Powers realized the interest which would one day be attached to all the memorials of those early years, he might have been more accurate in his statements, and have given honor to all to whom honor was due. But he allowed his own prejudices and those of others to influence the narrative; he neglected, for reasons well known to himself, to mention many of the most prominent men in Newbury and Haverhill, and, as a result, his work, while graphic and interesting, is unreliable as a history of either town, and is chiefly remarkable for what it does not say.

The present volume, made possible through the public spirit of the town as shown by its votes in the annual meeting of 1898, and the succeeding years, is an attempt to complete the work which Messrs. Perry, Johnson and Powers began. For the editor it has been the labor of many years, and many of the incidents which it relates were given him by people, now long dead, who could remember the Revolutionary War.

In its preparation all accessible sources of information have been drawn upon, and material enough for several such volumes has been found, so that the task has been one of selection and condensation.

That it is free from errors would be to claim what no history ever was or will be, and that its publication will bring to light facts which may modify some of its statements is probable. But it preserves much that would, otherwise, soon pass into oblivion, and its value will increase as the years go by.

It has been prepared amid the labors and cares of farm life, and at a distance from any reference library or collection of archives, and much more might have been gathered, had the editor more leisure for the task.

And for the absence of much that might be interesting in anecdote and reminiscence he may be allowed to plead his total loss, for almost thirty years, of the sense of hearing.

If this volume keeps the memory green of the noble men and women who have lived in Newbury; if it conveys to the present and future generations some idea of the trials and privations which their ancestors endured; if it makes clearer to them the struggles and self-denial through which the institutions of the town were built up, the labor and cost of its preparation will not have been in vain.

The study of those years past should make us more contented with the present. It is easy to view the past through rose-tinted spectacles; it is not so easy to comprehend the hard conditions of life in those days.

It is well for us if we can learn to say with Chaucer:

"It doth mine heart good,
That I have had my world as in my time."

The grateful acknowledgements of the editor and his readers are due to those citizens by whose influence the town was induced to undertake the publication of this volume, and to the various town officials who have aided in the work. A list of those in Newbury who have communicated a fact or a record would be a census of half its population.

The editor desires to mention several gentlemen whose kind assistance has been of great value in its preparation:

Acknowledgements are due to Hon. Albert S. Batchellor of Littleton, N. H., without whose aid no history of any town in the "New Hampshire Grants" would be complete; to Col. Henry O. Kent of Lancaster, N. H.; to W. F. Whitcher, Esq., of Woodsville;

to ex-Governor Farnham and Mr. Henry G. McDuffie of Bradford; to the late Mr. Edward Miller of Ryegate; to the late Hon. Lucius E. Chittenden of New York City; to Hon. E. E. Farman of Warsaw, N. Y., and Tours, France; to D. Farrand Henry, Esq., of Detroit. Also to Mr. Henry McFarland and the late Parker Pillsbury of Concord, N. H., to Messrs. Edwin A. Bayley, F. L. Bailey, and J. E. Chamberlin of Boston, and to Mr. Benjamin Hale of Newburyport, and to Hon. Ezra S. Stearns, now of Fitchburg. It is needless to mention that Miss M. J. Tenney of Haverhill, Mass., has greatly aided in the work.

Acknowledgements are also due to the town and church clerks in Newbury, Haverhill, Piermont, Bradford and Topsham; to the late T. W. Wood, and the late T. C. Phinney of the State and Historical Libraries at Montpelier; to Rev. N. F. Carter of the New Hampshire Historical Society; to Major Chase and his able assistants of the New Hampshire State Library; to Rev. L. H. Cobb, D. D., of the Congregational Library, Boston; to Mr. John Ward Dean of the New England Historic-Genealogical Society; to the officials of the Boston Public Library, and to the custodians of the state archives at Montpelier, Concord, Boston, Hartford and Albany. And last, but by no means least, to the publishers, the engravers, and the binders, through whose skill and care this history of Newbury is presented to its readers.

F. P. W.

NEWBURY, VT., January 6, 1902.

TABLE OF CONTENTS.

PART I.

CHAPTER V.

THE EARLY YEARS.

CHAPTER VI.

THE LAND DIVIDED.

CHAPTER VII.

EARLY DAYS IN NEWBURY.

CHAPTER VIII.

EARLY EVENTS.

CHAPTER IX.

THE NEW YORK CHAPTER.

CHAPTER X.

"WHEN WE WERE UNDER THE KING."

CHAPTER XI.

BEFORE THE REVOLUTION.

CHAPTER XII.

THE FIRST YEAR OF THE REVOLUTION.

CHAPTER XIII.

THE REVOLUTION—CONTINUED.

CHAPTER XIV.

THE REVOLUTIONARY WAR—CONTINUED.

CHAPTER XV.

THE TROUBLOUS TIMES.

CHAPTER XVI.

COL. THOMAS JOHNSON.

CHAPTER XVII.

THE END OF THE WAR.

CHAPTER XVIII.

NEWBURY IN THE VERMONT CONTROVERSY.

CHAPTER XIX.

NEWBURY IN THE VERMONT CONTROVERSY—CONTINUED.

CHAPTER XX.

AFTER THE WAR.

CHAPTER XXI.

THE NINETEENTH CENTURY.

CHAPTER XXII.

THE OLD MEETING-HOUSE.

CHAPTER XXIII.

A CHAPTER OF OLD THINGS AND NEW.

CHAPTER XXIV.

REMINISCENCES OF EARLY WELLS RIVER.

CHAPTER XXV.

THE FIRST CONGREGATIONAL CHURCH.

CHAPTER XXVI.

THE METHODIST EPISCOPAL CHURCH.

CHAPTER XXVII.

RELIGIOUS HISTORY — CONTINUED.

CHAPTER XXVIII.

RELIGIOUS AND EDUCATIONAL.

CHAPTER XXIX.

NEWBURY SEMINARY.

CHAPTER XXX.

NEWBURY SEMINARY—CONTINUED.

CHAPTER XXXI.

MONTEBELLO INSTITUTE AND OTHER SCHOOLS.

CHAPTER XXXII.

LITERARY NEWBURY.

CHAPTER XXXIII.

LIBRARIES—TEMPERANCE.

CHAPTER XXXIV.

METEOROLOGICAL.

CHAPTER XXXV.

A CHAPTER OF LOCAL HISTORY.

CHAPTER XXXVI.

MERCHANTS AND BUSINESS MEN OF NEWBURY.

CHAPTER XXXVII.

CEMETERIES—CARE OF THE POOR—THE MILITIA.

CHAPTER XXXVIII.

STAGES, INNS, AND POST OFFICES.

CHAPTER XXXIX.

CONNECTICUT RIVER.

CHAPTER XL.

HIGHWAYS AND RAILROADS.

CHAPTER XLI.

BANKS AND MONEY MATTERS.

CHAPTER XLII.

PROFESSIONAL MEN.—MISCELLANEOUS.

CHAPTER XLIII.

FRATERNAL SOCIETIES.

CHAPTER XLIV.

NEWBURY IN THE CIVIL AND SPANISH WARS.

CHAPTER XLV.

STATE, COUNTY, AND TOWN OFFICERS.

CHAPTER XLVI.

PART II.

PART I.

———

HISTORY OF NEWBURY,
VERMONT.

CHAPTER I.

GENERAL DESCRIPTION.

NEWBURY, Vermont, occupies the north-easterly corner of Orange county, and is separated by Connecticut river from Haverhill in the county of Grafton and state of New Hampshire. It is bounded on the south by Bradford and a small part of Corinth, on the west by Topsham, and on the north by Ryegate, in the county of Caledonia.

Speaking with more geographical accuracy, the parallel of forty-four degrees, north latitude, crosses the river about a mile below the southern extremity of the town. The meridian of seventy-two degrees, west longitude, passes through Haverhill at nearly the same distance from the most eastern point of Newbury.

It contains about 36,450 acres, comprising a great variety of soil—rich tracts of meadow, fertile upland, high hills and deep valleys, with some square miles of land whose broken and ledgy surface forbids cultivation.

A glance at the map of the town shows its principal streams, the location of its villages and post offices, and the highways and railroads which enable its inhabitants to communicate with each other, and the surrounding towns. But a more particular description is necessary toward the understanding of those natural features which so much influence the early development of a town and its subsequent history.

The longest settled, and best known parts of Newbury, are the meadows, or intervale lands, which border the Connecticut. These meadows have an average breadth of about one mile between the Newbury and Haverhill hills, and it is understood that the portion allotted by the river to this town is considerably the larger.

Through this intervale the river flows, with an average width of about five hundred feet, at times taking a straight course for some distance, then bending and doubling, touches the feet of the Newbury hills, now stretching away toward those of Haverhill. Midway of the town, it makes a circuit of nearly four miles, returning within a half mile of its starting point, enclosing a tract of wondrous beauty and fertility known as the Great Ox-bow. The scenery of the Connecticut valley has called forth the admiration of all who have beheld it. It would be easy to quote pages of description, which travelers from our own and other lands have written. One of the earliest, President Dwight of Yale College, wrote thus of the Ox-bow in 1803: "Its whole extent is one vast meadow, covered with the richest verdure, except a tract converted into arable ground, and it is scarcely possible for mere earth to exhibit a more beautiful surface."

The names of the several meadows, borne by them since the town was settled, beginning at the north, with their ancient limits, are: Upper meadow, from Stair hill at Wells River to the foot of Ingall's hill; Cow meadow, from the foot of Frye Bayley's hill to the ridge of land on which the houses at the Ox-bow are built; then the Ox-bow; next, Musquash meadow, which extends from the mouth of Harriman's brook to the point of rocks opposite the Dow or Keyes farm in Haverhill; Kent's meadow, from the point of rocks to White's cove, now Bailey's eddy; Sleeper's meadow, from the bend of the river to Bedell's bridge, and Hall's meadow, from the bridge to Bradford line.

The prospect of these meadows, with their alternating intervales on the Haverhill side, green with grass, interspersed with fields of corn and grain, through which the river winds, here hidden by the trees which bend over it, and there presenting its broad expanse to the sunshine, is one of loveliness and peace. Above and beyond, the hills of Haverhill with their farms and villages, the woods which clothe the higher elevations, the bulwark of Moosilauke lifting its bare and wind-swept top far into the sky, the attending and more remote mountains, present a scene of grandeur rarely surpassed.

Several points along the chain of rocky hills west of the meadows offer different aspects of the scene. The most noted view is along the road from Mr. Moore's house, passing over Mount Pulaski, behind Newbury village. Another prospect, scarce inferior, is from the heights in the rear of Ingall's hill.

In spring, or when great rains have fallen upon the country north of us, the scene takes on a new aspect. The winding channel of the river cannot carry away the water as fast as it is poured in by the swifter streams above us; the river overflows its banks; and the valley becomes a long narrow lake, with trees, buildings and the railroad embankment rising above the flood.

Could we know the history of these intervales, how they were formed in the course of long ages, the record would be more interesting than anything we can say about its human inhabitants. But the speculations and conclusions of geologists form no part of this history.

The course of ancient river beds is to be seen in many places on the meadows. The stream has, at several points, worn away acres of land from different farms. It has, moreover, changed its channel in more than one place, and detached portions of land from one town and annexed them to the other, without consulting the authorities of either Vermont or New Hampshire, or the wishes of those who imagined themselves the owners of the soil. An elm which is said to mark the spot where James Woodward in 1762 made his first pitch in Haverhill, now stands about ten rods from the river, on the Newbury side.

According to a statement of Gen. James Whitelaw in 1795, a line from the southeast to the northeast corner of Newbury would cut off about 2,040 acres lying east of it. The same line would take in a valuable part of Haverhill. The number of acres would be somewhat different now.

West of the meadows, and of the small tracts of plain which lie at the foot of the hills, for more than half the length of the town, extends a region which bears a striking contrast to that which we have been considering. Rising from the lower lands in precipices, or in pastures hardly less abrupt, extending back an average distance of about a mile, and stretching from Wells river to Hall's brook, is a region of hills which in some instances rise to a height of more than eight hundred feet above the river. Extensive ledges, bare or covered with shallow soil, are mostly clothed with woods, the second, third, and in some instances the fourth or fifth growth since the original forest was removed. It contains some tracts of good pasture, and in various parts farms were begun and abandoned. Wood roads wind about among the hills, and there is still some good timber growing on them. Two roads only from the west to the east part of the town cross this territory, and there is only one dwelling in the tract, which embraces fully one-tenth of all the land in town.

This wilderness, interposed between the villages along the river and the farms of the west part of the town, is a great disadvantage to Newbury. Had this section consisted of excellent farming land, the social, religious and political history of Newbury would have been very different.

Vermont is a land of hills, and Newbury has its full share. The wide and deep valley of Hall's brook bisects the town from northwest to southeast, drains about one-third of its area, and has furnished the power, at some twenty sites along the main stream and its branches, for mills of various kinds. It receives the waters of Hall's pond, which covers about three hundred acres, and lies a mile south of the geographical centre of the town. Round and Long ponds, which reflect the hills in the west part of the township, near the road from Newbury to Corinth, find their outlets in the same stream. Quite a large section of the town is drained by branches of Waits river in Bradford.

The hills south of Wells river rise high and steep, affording excellent pasturage. Jefferson hill, with its deep strong soil and long northern slope toward Ryegate, lies in the northwest corner of the town. Lime, burned to a small extent many years ago in a deep valley near the Topsham line, gave its name to the Lime-kiln neighborhood. Other local designations will be duly explained.

The railroad track where it enters Newbury from Bradford is said to be 375 feet above the sea-level. The highest cultivated land in town, long called the "Mountain Carter place," from which is a prospect of vast extent and variety, lies a mile or two northwest of the hamlet of West Newbury. A wooded hill behind this elevated farm, shares with two others, several miles from it and from each other, the claim of being the highest land in town.

Such a region of high hills, deep valleys and wide stretches of rolling upland, presents many fair prospects. Mount Mansfield and Camel's Hump may be seen on a clear day, to the northwest, from one or two hills, and Ascutney, far to the south. But the finest prospects are those of the Connecticut valley and the New Hampshire mountains. Moosilauke dominates the landscape in its direction. The "house on Moosilauke" can be seen from four out of five of the houses in Newbury, its elevation being 4,810 feet above the ocean and its distance from the river about nine miles as the bird flies.

Toward the south the mountains rise in lessening height. But east and north the Franconia and White Mountains stand like a wall beneath the sky. The long line of their summits, the intervening hills, and the peaks that rise far to the north are only seen in days of rarest atmospheric purity, and form a picture of which the eye seldom tires.

NOTE. Mount Washington is seen from the windows of about thirty houses in this town. From the house of Mr. Charles W. Eastman, near Wells River, and from a few points much lower than the house it is visible, and is the lowest spot in the Connecticut valley from which the highest peak in New England can be seen. At some points in the upper Coös the river is seen at high water from Mount Washington, but it must be remembered that the valley is there many feet higher above sea-level than at Newbury.

The height of Mount Pulaski has been ascertained by Prof. G. N. Abbott to be 379 feet above the fountain on the common, and 855 feet above the ocean. The ledge southwest is 70 feet higher. The summit of Wright's mountain in Bradford is 2,100 feet above the sea, and that of Blue mountain in Ryegate is 2,192 feet.

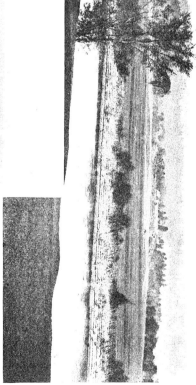

NORTHWEST FROM WRIGHT'S MOUNTAIN.

MUSQUASH MEADOW.
FARM OF F. E. KIMBALL, FROM HAVERHILL.

There are no natural curiosities worthy of especial notice in this town. The falls at Boltonville, down which the river pours over a succession of ledges, are picturesque at high water. Near the church at West Newbury, a small stream which comes down from the hills to the north, falls almost perpendicularly for about forty feet into a deep ravine, whose rocky walls, overhung by dense foliage, shut in a cascade well worthy of a visit when the brook is swollen by spring or autumn rains.

Such may serve for a general description of Newbury. Its hills have not yielded any mines of useful ore or precious metal. There are no quarries here to furnish the stone for the walls, or rich marbles for the costly adornment of great edifices in the cities.

No man of national fame was born in Newbury. It was never the birth-place of a President or even a Governor. It has not been the scene of any famous event. On the other hand we do not have to admit that any criminal whose evil deeds appalled the world, first drew breath here. It has never been the scene of any of the great crimes which have shocked humanity. But it has been the birth-place or residence of a great many men and women who helped make the world wiser and better. Not a few of them acted a modest part in great events. Its schools have trained thousands for the active work of life. Its churches have been ministered to by godly men. The farmers of its hills and valleys left to their children the legacy of honest, industrious lives. Their names and deeds are passing into oblivion. To chronicle the annals of the town, and to preserve their names and the records of their families in the town where they lived, and among the sons and daughters of Newbury who are scattered abroad, will be the scope of this volume.

CHAPTER II.

The Coös Country.

WHAT we now call Newbury, formerly comprised, with the portion of the Connecticut valley as far south as Orford, the "Lower Coös," and was still called by that name by the older people, within the memory of men yet living.

The name Coös, sometimes spelled Cohass and Cowass, was applied to two extensive tracts of land in the upper Connecticut valley, the other or "Upper Coös," being the broad intervales near Lancaster. The meaning of the appellation has been variously held to be, "a crooked river;" "a wide valley;" "a place of tall pines;" "a place of deer;" and "a great fishing place."

We will leave to special students the search among the confused mass of facts and theories concerning the various Indian tribes which, from time immemorial, dwelt or wandered here. It was, probably, neutral or disputed ground between large tribes, visited by various bands or families, for the purpose of fishing or cultivating the meadows.

It was, perhaps, the residence, for many years at a time, of some of these companies. But the testimony is so vague, and the time so distant, that nothing positive can be asserted. Those who have made a study of Indian relics are of opinion, from the examination of the stone arrow and spear heads and domestic utensils, that many of them came from far distant parts of the country, even from beyond the Mississippi, but whether through actual visits from those remote tribes, or by purchase, cannot be known.

The antiquity of these visits, or periods of habitation, is attested by these relics of the stone age, articles of greatest necessity, and therefore of greatest value in Indian eyes. These have been found upon all the meadows, and along the valley of Hall's brook. But the greatest quantity and variety, attesting their frequent visits, and long periods of residence, are found upon the Ox-bow and upon the ridge between it and Cow meadow. These consist of arrow and spear heads, axes, chisels, and domestic utensils. A stone mortar and pestle were found by the early settlers. The great Ox-bow seems to have been a spot beloved by the Indians. The remains of an Indian fort were found upon the Ox-bow by the settlers. These relics of a departed race possess a singular and mysterious interest.

Some mounds along the meadows in Haverhill have been thought to be the work of Indian hands. But the few who lingered here after the white men came were degenerate, and soon disappeared.

Almost equally uncertain is the time when the region was first visited by white men. In 1635, fifteen years after the landing at Plymouth, the first settlements began at Hartford, Connecticut, and Springfield, Massachusetts. From that date, in spite of Indian wars and the hardships of the wilderness, the frontier of civilization advanced up the river. Hadley was settled in 1647, and a few families ventured their lives in Northfield in 1673, whence they were, in a few years, driven by the Indians, so that a permanent settlement was not gained until 1713.

The first settlement in Vermont was made in what is now the southeast corner of Brattleboro, in 1724, when Fort Dummer was built to curb the Indians.

On the Merrimack, the progress was equally slow. In 1719, a colony from the north of Ireland, to which their ancestors had emigrated from Scotland about a century before, came over and began to settle at Londonderry, soon taking up land in the adjacent towns. From this remarkable body of people, known as the Scotch-Irish, came some of our best families. This colony was never molested by the Indians. Concord was settled in 1725, and a few families came to Boscawen and Canterbury before 1730.

For some years, the smoke from the log cabin of Ebenezer Webster, father of Daniel Webster, marked the outpost of civilization. Beyond, the country lay an unbroken wilderness to the French settlements along the Saint Lawrence. There, white men of another race, and another creed, had begun a civilization, which was, eventually, to measure its strength with the English race for the mastery of a continent. It is probable

that the first white men to view the Coös country were Catholic
missionaries or fur traders from Canada.

Future research may yet reveal the date and circumstances of
the earliest visits to this part of New England, which now lie
concealed among the archives of the Catholic missionaries. There
is reason to believe that the records of discovery exist, and, aside
from such probability of future confirmation from the recitals
which are contained among the records preserved at Montreal
and Quebec, are other considerations which favor the belief that
the first explorers of this valley were Frenchmen and not Englishmen. It is certain that the Kennebec valley was explored by the
Jesuit missionaries at a period which long antedates the first
recorded visits of white men to the Coös country. It can hardly
be supposed that these hardy and astute men who traced the
paths along the Kennebec to the English settlements by the sea,
overlooked the trails which passed down the Connecticut. Our
knowledge of the sagacity displayed by the Jesuit missionaries
and French soldiers, forbids us to suppose that the men who
explored the chain of the Great Lakes to the western extremity
of Lake Superior; who traced the Mississippi to its source and
followed its waters till they mingled with those of the Gulf of
Mexico; who planted their missions and trading posts along the
Missouri, would have left unvisited the Connecticut valley at
their doors.

So far as our present knowledge of the past reveals, the Coös
country emerges into the light of history about the beginning of
the eighteenth century,—two hundred years ago.

In the spring of 1704, (says Penhallow's "Wars of New England
with the Eastern Indians") word came from Albany that a band
of French Indians had built a fort and planted corn at Coös, high
up the river Connecticut. On this, Caleb Lyman with five friendly
Indians, probably Monhegans, set out from Northampton and
after a long march through the forest, surprised, under cover of a
thunder storm, a wigwam containing nine Indians, and killed seven
of them.

A tradition handed down from Col. Frye Bayley, and others of
the first settlers, relates that in the same year, one Capt. Wells
with a small force of men descended the Connecticut. At the
mouth of Wells river several of the men fell sick with the smallpox,
and the party spent the winter or a part of it there, building a
small log fort for their protection, subsisting by hunting, fishing,
and upon supplies purchased from the Indians. It is said that some
of the men died there, and that the river took its name from their
leader, who may have been Capt. Jonathan Wells of Deerfield.

This much is certain, that in 1725, Capt. Benjamin Wright of
Northampton, with a scouting party of sixty men, ascended the
Connecticut to the mouth of Wells river, which they followed, and

having passed several ponds, crossed the height of land, and descended Winooski river to Lake Champlain, returning by the same course. The journal of their expedition expressly mentions "the fort at the mouth of the Wells river." Many descendants of this Capt. Benjamin Wright are now living in Newbury.

Upon an ancient map, the name is spelled Weld's river. When Er Chamberlin, about 1770, began to clear land in what is now Wells River village, he found the remains of a log building, just above the mouth of that stream. Human bones have been dug up near that spot.

Other evidence of early visits to the Coös country is found in the narratives of those unfortunates who were taken captive by the Indians, and hurried through the wilderness from burning villages in Massachusetts and Connnecticut, who lived to recount their sufferings.

One of the best known of these was Rev. John Williams. He was minister at Deerfield, Mass., when the village was destroyed February 29, 1704, and one hundred and twelve prisoners, men, women and children, were carried off to Canada, by a party of three hundred and forty-two French and Indians. Mr. Williams lived to return and published a narrative of his sufferings called "The Redeemed Captive Returning to Zion." A copy of the first edition of this little volume is now worth more than its weight in gold.

He tells us that at the mouth of White river the company divided, and a part of the force, with some of the captives, went up that stream, while the remainder ascended the Connecticut and tarried some time at the Coös meadows. Their provisions giving out, they subsisted by hunting and fishing, and barely escaped starvation, two of their number, Jacob Holt and Daniel Hix, dying of hunger. Subsequently in his narrative he mentions Coös, as if the region was well enough known, even at that early day for its location to be understood by the mention of its name.

It would be easy to cite many similar involuntary visits to this part of New England. An ancient map, made about the time of the old French war, gives the correct course of both the Connecticut and Wells rivers, and says, "Along this route (up both these rivers), many captives have been carried to Canada."

Other Indian trails led up the Passumpsic, and by streams which descend from the heights near the source of the Connecticut. It is probable that most of these unhappy prisoners viewed the region with no favorable eye. Those who were hurried along with the prospect of a fearful captivity or a horrible death, were not likely to admire a country where each forward step made return more hopeless.

But there were others, hunters and adventurous spirits, who were capable of intelligent and leisurely observations and who saw the possibilities of the region as a desirable place for future settlement. By degrees it began to be generally known that, far up the great river, were fertile meadows waiting for the plow, and wooded uplands which could be turned into productive farms. But there was little to induce people to come here, and make new homes in the wilderness. There was still plenty of good land nearer the sea coast to be taken up. It was pleasant to be near the older towns which had become seats of wealth and culture. More than anything else, the fear of the Indians kept settlers out of Coös. From the breaking out of King William's war in 1689, till the surrender of Quebec, seventy years later, there was almost continual war. The line of the frontier was marked with fire and blood. Yet in spite of that, settlements advanced steadily into the wilderness.

On the 27th of February, 1709, Thomas Baker was taken captive at Deerfield, and was carried to Canada up the river, and over the carrying place to Lake Memphremagog. He remained among the Indians for a year, and learned much of the country, the rivers, and the passes through the mountains. In the spring of 1712, he raised a company of thirty-four men, with whom he reached the Coös in four days. They seem to have spent some time in exploring the locality, and having a friendly Indian for their guide passed through the trail along the Oliverian, and killed some Indians in what is now Rumney. They were pursued, but by a stratagem evaded their pursuers and reached Dunstable without the loss of a man. For this exploit they received by special resolution of the legislature of Massachusetts, a bounty of twenty pounds, in addition to their wages from March 24th, to the 17th of May.

This resolution, which is dated June 11, 1712, mentions Lieut. Baker as "commander of a company of marching forces in the late expedition to Coös, and from thence to the west branch of the Merrimack river, and so to Dunstable." From this man Baker's river in Warren, Wentworth, and Rumney is named. He died in Dover about 1763.

In 1748, settlements began at Charlestown, N. H., long called "Number Four," but were abandoned after several families had been carried off. After the erection of a fort at that place, a few of the settlers returned and cleared land under its protection. But it was hazardous, as Indians constantly prowled in the woods and assaulted the place ten times within two years. In April, 1747, while the fort was held by Capt. Phinehas Stevens, with thirty men, it was attacked by Boucher de Niverville with a large war-party of French and Indians, and sustained one of the most desperate sieges in the whole record of frontier wars. The assault lasted three days and two nights, and at the end of the third day, the enemy, having suffered great loss, withdrew to Canada. Richard Chamberlin, afterwards one of the first settlers of Newbury, was one of the garrison.

The settlement at Charlestown had now acquired a firm hold, and people began to think of settling the Coös country. In the summer of 1751, several hunters came up the river and examined the land on both sides as far as the highlands at the mouth of the Ammonoosuc.

In the following year, Capt. Symes of North Hampton made application to Governor Wentworth for charters of four towns six miles square at Coös, to be granted to four hundred men, who proposed to settle there. On the 22d of November, he again wrote to the Governor that three hundred and forty men were already engaged in the service, and prayed that fifty of them might be in the pay and maintenance of the province. These men were mainly from New Market, Rye, North Hampton, East Hampton and South Hampton. It further appears from the petition that several of them had been to Coös in the summer, and were favorably impressed with the country.

In his message to the General Court, Wentworth favored the design, and alluded to "previous grants and promises of land at Coös" being forfeited. It would thus appear that this was not the first attempt to settle the country. He also recommended that these four hundred men be formed into a regiment, one hundred men in each town. Their plan was to cut a road along the river from Charlestown and lay out towns on each side. They were to erect a stockade in each town, large enough to enclose a blockhouse and the dwellings of the settlers. Thus it was to be, not only a settlement, but a military post.

The project made some stir, and tidings of it reaching Canada, a deputation of French and Indians appeared at Charlestown, and remonstrated against it, using language not to be misunderstood, and the plan came to an end. So little is known of the scheme that we have no record of the names of the adventurers, or whether any of them were among the settlers of either Newbury or Haverhill ten years later.

In the spring of the same year, 1752, John and William Stark, Daniel Stinson, and Amos Eastman, while hunting in Rumney, were surprised by the Indians. Stinson was killed, William Stark got away, while John Stark and Eastman were taken to Canada. The party encamped the first night where Haverhill Corner now stands, and passed directly through the Coös meadows, and on their return in the summer passed through them again.

In the spring of 1753, a committee was appointed by the General Court, to go up "and view the Coös Country." This consisted of Col. Zaccheus Lovewell, Maj. John Talford, Capt. Caleb Page, a surveyor, and sixteen men, with John Stark as their guide. The celebrated Robert Rogers was one of the party. They came up the Pemigewasset and Baker's rivers, and marked out a road, cutting out the fallen trees, reaching the Connecticut river at

Moose meadow in Piermont.   They passed but one night in the valley, returning the way they came.   Grant Powers, following the the biography of General Stark, gives the year of this expedition as 1754, but the state archives show that it was in the previous year. It is supposed that they discovered traces of a large force of Indians, and made a timely retreat.

Meanwhile, the first mutterings of the storm which was about to burst began to be heard, and the great contest which was to decide forever whether North America was to be ruled by Frenchmen or by Englishmen, opened in the forests of Pennsylvania.

In the spring of 1754, Governor Wentworth, hearing reports of a French advance into the Connecticut valley, sent Capt. Peter Powers of Hollis, a brave and experienced soldier, with a company of men, of which James Stevens was lieutenant, and Ephraim Hale was ensign, who came up the Pemigewasset and Baker's rivers, and reached this valley at Piermont.   They seem to have followed the path marked out the year before by Lovewell and his men.

The journal of Captain Powers, now in the possession of the Connecticut Historical Society, is largely quoted by Rev. Grant Powers, who does not seem to have known what the real object of the expedition was.   In his message to the legislature of that year, Governor Wentworth says that he had sent Powers to see if the French had begun settlement at either Upper or Lower Coös, or had, as reported, built a fort at Northumberland.   Leaving Concord June 15, 1754, they came to the Hibbard place in Piermont on the 25th, and on the next day they went up as far as Horse Meadow, "above the cleared intervale."   On the 2d of July they reached Northumberland, but saw no signs of fort or settlement, but did find where the Indians had been making canoes, but who had probably fled on the approach of a force too strong to molest. On their return they crossed into Newbury at the mouth of the Ammonoosuc, and went through the cleared intervale, crossing into Haverhill below the Ox-bow.   They seem to have reached Concord safely with the Indians following close behind.   Captain Peter Powers was the father of Rev. Peter Powers, the first minister of Newbury and Haverhill.   Hundreds of his descendants have lived in the valley which he explored in 1754.

Five years later there passed through this valley an expedition to which there attaches a melancholy interest.   In 1759, Major Robert Rogers, whom we have met before as one of Lovewell's company of explorers, was sent by General Amherst from Crown Point, with about one hundred and fifty men, to destroy the Abenaki village which was situated upon the St. Francis, a few miles above its junction with the St. Lawrence, and was the residence of the most cruel tribe of Indians in Canada.   After leaving Lake Champlain, Rogers, finding himself pursued, and fearing that his retreat would be cut off, took the bold resolve of out-marching his pursuers, destroying St. Francis, and returning by Lake Memphremagog and the Connecticut. He accordingly sent men back to Crown Point to request General Amherst that provisions should be sent up the river from Charlestown to meet him as he came down.

The Indian village was surprised in the night and set on fire. Two hundred of the savages were killed. They found several captives, and nearly seven hundred scalps. Rogers's men, some of whom had suffered from this cruel tribe, gave no quarter, but inflicted a blow which struck terror to all the Indian tribes, from Lake Ontario to the Penobscot. The victors at once began their return through the wilderness, closely followed by the enemy. Near Lake Memphremagog their provisions gave out, and Rogers divided his men into small parties, the better to sustain life by hunting. Several of the band fell into the hands of the Indians, but most of them reached the great river, at one place or another, between the Nulhegan and the Passumpsic. But when the foremost came to the place where relief was to meet them, they found, to their horror, fires burning, but those who had made them were gone. Lieutenant Samuel Stevens had been sent up the river with boats and abundant provisions, but when he came to the place which had been appointed, finding no one there, he waited two days and returned. For this outrageous conduct he was dismissed the service.

It has never been clearly demonstrated where this spot was. Some of the survivors stated that Round island, in the mouth of the Passumpsic, which is separated by a deep and narrow channel from the railroad, a little below East Barnet, is the place where they found the fires burning. Others insist that the mouth of the Ammonoosuc is the place, which is the one specified by Rogers himself. The fact seems to be that the unfortunate men were so overcome with hunger and despair, that they did not know where they were, and were never able afterward to tell, with certainty, where they came out upon the river. The late David Johnson, Esq., who had personally known several of Rogers's men, was told by them that when they came to the mouth of Cow Meadow-brook, they found the smouldering embers of a fire, but no one with it, and that they were so much overcome by hunger and despair that some of them died. The first settlers, three years later, found the remains of men at various places upon the Ox-bow and the high ground near it, who were believed to be some of Rogers's expedition, and there may be still a few old men who can point out the spots where the bones of these unfortunate men were found.

Rogers, with three men, made his way with great peril down the river on a rude raft, and sent back boats with provisions to the men, as they could be found along the banks. Some of the survivors made their way through the woods to the settlements on the Merrimack.   Of the one hundred and forty-two men who had left St. Francis, forty-nine perished in the wilderness, or were tortured to death by the Indians.   Robert Rogers served under the king during the revolutionary war, and made his appearance in Newbury several times during the struggle.

The expedition of Rogers was one of the most dramatic episodes of the French and Indian war.   The story of the long march through the wilderness; the night attack; the burning village; the terrible tale of the retreat through the wilds of Canada; the famished men struggling through the pathless woods, and the fearful deaths of so many, thrill the imagination.   There has been much controversy over different portions of the narrative. Rev. Grant Powers, in his "Historical Sketches of the Coös Country," treats as fabulous the account of the relief expedition of Stevens. It appears that he had not seen Rogers's journal of the expedition. He made no mention of the statements which Mr. Johnson had obtained from the lips of some of the survivors, several of whom were living in this vicinity in his younger days.   But Mr. Powers was anxious to believe that his ancestor was the first to explore the country where so many of his descendants were to live, and put aside all evidence of previous discoveries.   Several men who afterwards attained considerable distinction in the revolutionary war were of Rogers's party.   One of them, Capt. Benjamin Wait, from whom the town of Waitsfield, where he settled and died, is named, is memorable.   And Waits river in Bradford was also named for him. The Indian name of this river—Mahounquamossee—is given upon the map of 1760.

CHAPTER III.

THE FIRST YEAR.

WITH the close of the French and Indian war the history of
Newbury begins, and practically that of Vermont. Before
that time a few settlements along the river, in the
southeast corner of the state, had been held only by the intrepidity
of the settlers. All the rest of it lay a wilderness, save only a few
spots of cleared land like the Ox-bow, or where the woods had been
removed for military purposes along Lake Champlain. But the
constant passing of troops and small companies through the state
had made the resources of the country generally known, and, at the
close of the war, civilization, whose outposts had been Charlestown
on the Connecticut, and Salisbury on the Merrimack, advanced
into the wilderness by leaps and bounds.

With the surrender of Montreal, on the 8th of September, 1760,
the empire of France in the New World, which had been so gallantly
held, passed away. The French in Canada settled quietly down
under English rule. There was no longer any one to stir up the
Indians against the settlers of New England. All that came to
them of the struggle in which they bore so great a part, had
been their own destruction. They saw their hunting-grounds pass
into the hands of their enemies, and were too feeble even to protest.
The army which had conquered Canada was disbanded, and the
victors sought their homes in the older settlements. Among those
who returned through the Connecticut valley from the surrender

of Montreal, were four officers who had served in Goff's regiment during the decisive campaign, and whose influence is felt in Coös to this day. They were Lieut.-Col. Jacob Bayley, Capt. John Hazen, Lieut. Jacob Kent, and Lieut. Timothy Bedell. As Jacob Bayley's name will occur in these pages more frequently than any other, and as there were several other officers named Bayley in Coös, to distinguish him from the others, he will be spoken of as General Bayley, although he did not attain the title until seventeen years later. We do not know whether either of the four had ever passed through here before. It is not known whether there were any others in the party. But we do know, from written statements made long after, by both Bayley and Kent, that they remained some days in the place, and carefully examined the surrounding country. They decided that it was a desirable place to settle in, the gateway to a vast country above, a central point which should command the trade of the region.

On their return to Hampstead, these four men, being prompt and resolute, set themselves at once to the work of obtaining charters of two towns at Coös, taking measures to secure their friends in the enterprise. Bayley and Hazen stood high in the estimation of the colonial government, as they had done efficient service in the late war, and both had influential relatives, whom Governor Wentworth was anxious to please. Hazen was aided by his brother, Moses Hazen, while Bayley received the advice and powerful support of his brother-in-law, Moses Little. These had been officers in the late war, and were to be still more distinguished in that of independence. As the result of their combined efforts, the charter of Newbury was granted, May 18, 1763, to Jacob Bayley, John Hazen, Jacob Kent and Timothy Bedell, with seventy-two associates. The charter of Haverhill was granted on the same day to the same men, John Hazen's name being first, with a number of partners equal to that of Newbury. But, before that time, a great deal had been done at Coös, and quite a number of families had begun to make homes here. Bayley and Hazen came up in the summer of 1761, and made their plans. The former went on to Crown Point, while the latter returned to Hampstead, by way of Charlestown, and engaged several men to come to Coös, cut and stack hay on the great and little Ox-bows. Col. Thomas Johnson says that they secured about ninety tons of excellent hay. Meanwhile, Col. Moses Little had been gathering cattle for himself, Bayley and the Hazens, mostly young cows and steers, with which John Pettie, Michael Johnston and Abraham Webb left Hampstead about the middle of August, and reached Coös the last of October. They came by way of Charlestown, then called Number Four, and followed a line of spotted trees along the river bank. They spent the winter here, feeding the hay to the cattle, and breaking the steers, subsisting mainly on provisions which had been brought up in boats from Charlestown. Dr. Bouton, in his history of Concord, N. H., says that the winter was unusually long and cold, and it would seem that the time must have dragged heavily to the men in their rude shelters on the Little Ox-bow. But spring came at last, and Johnston and Pettie, being relieved, started for home down the river. Their canoe was upset at a point now called Olcott Falls, and Johnston was drowned. He was a brother of Col. Charles Johnston of Haverhill, and of Col. Robert Johnston of Newbury. The next year, Abraham Webb, who was partly mulatto and partly Indian, was drowned in the river at Newbury, and was the first man buried in the cemetery at the Ox-bow.

In the spring of 1762, Capt. John Hazen came up and began to build a sawmill at the falls in North Haverhill. In February came the first family into Newbury, which consisted of Samuel Sleeper and his wife from Plaistow, or Hampstead, by way of Charlestown. They came up on the ice in a rude vehicle, half sleigh and half sled, which conveyed the family and a few necessaries for their primitive housekeeping. He lived for some time, says Rev. Clark Perry, in a rude hut which stood about where Mr. Doe's brick house now stands, at the Ox-bow, but later took up land where the Kents long lived, in the south part of the town. According to Rev. Grant Powers, Sleeper was a Quaker preacher, whom Bayley had sent on to take possession of the land for him, but none of the letters which are preserved, that passed between Bayley and Col. Little, mention Sleeper at all. Mr. Powers says further, that Sleeper made himself obnoxious to the people by disturbing the services of the Sabbath in the meeting-house, and interrupting the sermon by obtruding his dissent from the doctrines of the minister. For this untimely exercise of the right of free speech, he was imprisoned for awhile in a cellar upon Musquash meadow. Later he removed to Bradford where he became quite prominent, but died before 1771.

With Sleeper came Glazier Wheeler from Shutesbury, Mass., and his brother Charles, who had started on a hunting trip, fallen in with Sleeper, and established themselves at Newbury. Wheeler was a practical genius, whose skill in the use of tools made him invaluable on the frontier, but whose misdirected ingenuity was destined to get him into trouble. He engaged, some years later, in making counterfeiter's tools, and in the manufacture of base coin, and, according to the custom of the time, had his ears cropped. Later in life, he is said to have been employed in the mint at Philadelphia, on account of his remarkable skill as an engraver.

The second family was that of Thomas Chamberlain and wife from Dunstable, N. H., who settled on Musquash meadow, near the river, but later removed to the Ox-bow, where he built a house which afterwards became the parsonage. A depression in the ground, in the newest part of the cemetery, at some distance from the road, marks the cellar. He had been here before, more than once, as a hunter and as chain-bearer for Joseph Blanchard when he marked the bounds of the towns along the river in the winter of 1760–61. In June, "one day about noon," came Richard Chamberlin and wife, being the third family, from Hinsdale. N. H., in boats. Seven of their thirteen children came with their parents, the rest afterward. Before night they had erected a rude hut of posts and bark, in which they lived three months. A large stump in the middle, covered with a board, served for a table. He settled upon Musquash meadow, and kept a ferry between Newbury and Haverhill for many years. At the same time with Richard Chamberlin, says Mr. Perry, came Benoni Wright, and associated himself with Sleeper. For some strange doctrines which he preached and for his way of making himself obnoxious, the elders of the settlement condemned him to receive ten lashes, "well laid on." After this gentle reminder of public disapproval was carried out, Wright removed to Bradford, and dwelt for some time in a cave on the mountain which still bears his name.

According to Mr. Perry, Noah White, the first of seven brothers and sisters to settle in Newbury, came in 1762, but Mr. Powers says he came in the next year. In the former year came John Hazeltine, from Hampstead, and settled on the Ox-bow. In the same spring came Simeon Stevens, Joshua Howard, and Jaasiel Harriman, and were the first of the settlers to come up by way of the Pemigewasset and Baker rivers. They employed an old hunter to guide them, and came in four days. Stevens settled in Newbury, Howard on an island which still bears his name, now a part of the Grafton county farm, while Harriman, who was a blacksmith, lived a few years in both Newbury and Haverhill, but became one of the first settlers of Bath. Thomas Johnson arrived in the same year, and boarded awhile in the family of Uriah Morse, in Haverhill. Joshua Howard came as agent or hired laborer of Gen. Bayley, being an enlisted soldier in his company, but whose services not being needed, was sent here to take care of his cattle. In the fall came Jacob Kent, who was employed with Johnson by those who proposed to become proprietors, to examine the land, and make boundaries, preparatory to the town being chartered. In the summer, Gen. Bayley also came to see what was being done in the region to which he expected to remove, and from that time forth was the master spirit of the new colony. It would appear that there were five or six families in Newbury before it was chartered, who were here without any special leave to settle, or title to the soil, but who probably expected that when the town was chartered they should, with others, become proprietors, which, with most of them, was the case.

According to Col. Thomas Johnson, neither of the Chamberlains was in the interest of Bayley and Hazen, but Thomas came here to take possession in behalf of his neighbor at Dunstable,

Capt. Joseph Blanchard, under whom he had served in the late war, and who hoped to obtain a charter for a town in Coös. Richard and his sons were in the interest of Oliver Willard, a merchant and land speculator of Northampton, who also hoped to secure a charter, by virtue of possession; but Bayley and Hazen seem to have easily persuaded the Chamberlains to cast in their lot with them, as both Thomas and Richard, with Joseph and Abiel, sons of the latter, all became grantees under the charter. It is said that Willard was so mortified and angry at being thus supplanted by Bayley and Hazen, that he threatened that if he could ever catch the latter outside the settlement, he would flog him to his heart's content. The two men afterwards met at Charlestown, and, upon endeavoring to carry out his threat, Willard found Hazen much more than his match.

It was the testimony of the first settlers who still survived when Rev. Clark Perry collected the materials for his historical discourse in 1831, that good corn was raised on the Ox-bow in 1762, but lower down, on Kent's meadow, the first seed did not prove good, and it was so late before good seed could be had from Charlestown that it was not ripe before frost came. This corn, carefully dried, pounded up, and made into puddings with a little milk, was the chief food of the settlers. After this year, corn and wheat were both good and plenty. Mr. Perry says that potatoes were grown in that year from seed brought through the woods from Concord. Salmon were plentiful in the river, and trout in the brooks. Deer were not unfrequently found and bears were often killed, which, in the absence of beef and pork, formed a welcome addition to the larder; but it was several years before domestic animals could be spared for food, and during the earlier years their meat was seldom tasted at Coös.

Could we return for an hour to the primitive life at Newbury, one hundred and thirty-eight years ago, we should find little to remind us of the present aspect of the scene. The Connecticut flowed through a dense forest, broken here and there by Indian clearings of a few acres in extent. A heavy growth of pines covered the plain on which Newbury village now stands. Moosilauke overlooked a mighty forest which stretched away as far as the eye could reach; but a closer observation would discern tokens of a coming change. The sound of the settler's axe was heard by the river bank. In a few places, a rude trail, the precursor of the present river road, wound through the woods. The sun shone into new clearings here and there, and the smoke from a few log dwellings rose in the primeval forest, for the settlers had come. What was there here for that handful of adventurers in the Coös country in that far off winter of 1762-63? What was their manner of life in the rude huts which only partially sheltered them from the northern blasts? When we remember that there were no roads, no schools, no churches; that there was no physician nearer than Canterbury or Charlestown; that there was no habitation of white men within sixty miles of them, and that the woods were full of savage beasts, and that the dread of the Indians had by no means passed away, we wonder how the people endured it. One of the sons of Richard Chamberlain related in his old age, that they seldom arose in the mornings of that long winter, without seeing the tracks of bears and wolves in the snow around their cabin on Musquash meadow. Few of the cabins had doors, for as yet there was no sawmill, but a coverlid suspended over the entrance kept out some of the cold. Sometimes wolves would lift this curtain, and thrust in their heads. The cattle had to be shut in pens built strongly enough to resist the attacks of bears. Yet the people seem to have got through the winter very well. No one died, and we do not know that any went back in the spring disheartened to the older settlements. The men worked hard, at healthy, vigorous labor in the open air, chopping, and clearing land and hunting. They seem to have had plenty of food; they were all young, and took their privations as a matter of course. Richard Chamberlin was the only man past forty-five, and he was accustomed to pioneer life.

It is probable that there were several additions to the settlement during the winter. We know that Jacob Kent and Joseph Harriman came in January, for the former tells us this in his journal. They probably came from Concord on snow shoes, carrying their packs, each with his trusty gun, camping out at night, beneath such shelter as they could make. People thought little of such things then. How welcome must have been their coming to the settlers. We may be sure that the tidings of their arrival were not long in reaching every cabin on the Little Ox-bow and Musquash meadow, and the Great Ox-bow, and how the settlers must have flocked around the newcomers to hear the news! In these days when we have instant communication with all parts of the world, we cannot comprehend what the coming of an old acquaintance meant to these people, in this far-off nook of civilization; what feasts from their rude plenty would be set before the weary travelers. Such excitement must have been to the hardy settlers and their wives, what a brisk walk in the wintry air is to a man in perfect health, which sets every nerve and fibre in a glow. Still, make the best of the winter as they might, how welcome was the approach of the spring of 1763! How glad the people must have been to see the days grow longer; the snow banks settle; the bare ground once more appear; the river break up, and the cleared lands emerge from the snow. Col. Frye Bayley said, in his old age, that maple sugar was made in Newbury in that year. It is quite probable, however, that the hardships and privations which the people had to suffer were too much for two feeble frames, for in the spring two women at Coös died of consumption.

FROM THE HEIGHTS WEST OF COW MEADOW.

Showing Horse Meadow, Cow Meadow, the Great Oxbow, the Little Oxbow, and Musquash Meadow

Photo. by Corliss.

CHAPTER IV.

THE CHARTER.

NEWBURY, in England, is a municipal borough on the river Kennet, in Berkshire, near the border of Wiltshire, fifty-three miles west of London. "It owes its origin to the Roman station Spine, now represented by the modern village of Speen." Several centuries ago, a portion of the village, on the other side of the Kennet was called the New Borough, which became the market town of Newbury—that is New Borough—now having some ten or fifteen thousand inhabitants. Two battles were fought there during the civil war, in 1643, and 1644.

In 1635, certain emigrants, whose minister, Rev. Thomas Parker, had for some time preached in the English Newbury, settled at the mouth of the Merrimack in New England, and complimented their pastor by giving the name of Newbury to the new town. Our forefathers in Coös, when they applied for a charter to this town, gave it the name of Newbury, whence most of them originated, as their ancestors had given the name of the English town to the New England settlement.

No one knows what became of the original charter of Newbury, signed by Governor BenningW entworth on the 18th day of *May, 1763, and countersigned by Theodore Atkinson, his junior

---

* Powers says March 18, 1763, but May 18th is the correct date.

secretary. It is believed that Gen. Bayley carried it to New York
when he went there to obtain the charter from the Governor of
that state, in 1773, and it may be still in existence at Albany.
But the charter is on record at Concord, in the office of the Secretary
of State, in the second of the folio volumes of town charters. In
these volumes, the body of each charter is printed; in form and
conditions they are all alike, but the particular description of each
town is written in. The charters of Newbury and Haverhill are
precisely alike, except in the written parts. The following is the
particular description of this town as written:

"Beginning at a Tree marked   standing on the Bank of
the Westerly side of Connecticut River opposite to the mouth of
Amonusock River so called, and from thence Southerly, or South
Westerly, down Connecticut river til it comes to a Tree there
standing marked with the Figures   and is about seven miles
in A Strait Line below the Mouth of Amonusock afores[d] from
thence running North fifty-nine degrees West Six Miles and one
Quarter to a stake and stones, from thence North twenty Degrees
East Six miles & one half Mile to a stake and stones, from thence
to the Marked Tree on the Side of the River, the Bound first
mentioned."

Newbury, in common with other towns, was granted the
privilege of holding fairs and markets. The conditions of a grant,
were, in brief, as follows:

1st. Each grantee must cultivate, within five years, five acres for
each fifty acres which he possessed, under penalty of forfeiture.
2nd. All white pine was reserved for the royal navy.
3rd. A tract of land near the center of the town was reserved for
town lots, each grantee to have one acre.
4th. For this an ear of Indian corn should be presented when required
during two years.
5th. After December 25, 1773, each proprietor must pay one shilling
annually, Proclamation Money, for each hundred acres which
he held.

These conditions do not seem to have been very hard, but
before the rent became due, the charter granted by Wentworth
was superseded by that of the Governor of New York, and Newbury
became a part of that province. *By the terms of the charter, the
town was divided into eighty-one shares; one to the Church of
England; one to the Incorporated Society for the Propogation of
the Gospel in Foreign Parts; one for the first settled minister in
town, and one for the benefit of a school in the town. In addition
to these reservations, a tract of five hundred acres, counting as two
shares, was reserved for Governor Wentworth, and was called the
Governor's farm. This land includes most of what is now called

---

*Both town charters will be found in full in the appendix.

Wells River village, and the corresponding reservation in Haverhill embraces Woodsville.

The charter also provided that the first meeting for the choice of officers should be held on the second Monday in June, 1763, and that Jacob Bayley, Esq., should call the meeting and be moderator thereof. The conditions of the Haverhill charter are identical with those of Newbury, and the first meeting of the proprietors was to be held on the day following that of Newbury, the meeting to be called and presided over by John Hazen, Esq.

A glance at the map of the state will indicate that Newbury is a very large town in area, much larger than any of its neighbors, in fact there is only one larger town in the state. It may now be proper to explain how it came to be so large. In the year 1807, the town of Bradford, whose inhabitants had always considered themselves unjustly deprived of a portion of their territory by this town, applied to the legislature of that year, to have a strip of Newbury, one mile and sixty-eight rods wide, annexed to Bradford. Their claim was supported in a paper drawn up with great care by John McDuffee, Esq., of Bradford, a noted surveyor of his time, in which their side of the case was presented.

It will be noted by reference to the charter, that the south corner of Newbury was appointed to be about seven miles below the northeast corner, which would be near the southwest corner of Bedell's bridge. In reality, the corner of Newbury and Bradford is one mile and sixty-eight rods south of that point. According to their claim, Thomas Blanchard of Dunstable was employed in 1760 by Wentworth, to make a survey of Connecticut river—from Charlestown to the mouth of the Ammonoosuc, which latter place the Governor fixed upon as a point from which to establish the bounds of the towns above and below it. Between these two places, he was to erect a boundary, or mark a tree, at the end of every six miles, these boundaries being the north and south limits of the towns on the river. Blanchard chose Thomas Chamberlain as his assistant, and they made the north limit of the ninth pair of towns on the Connecticut river, now Bradford and Piermont, to be near the southwest corner of Bedell's bridge, and, finding that there still remained seven miles between that point and the island at the mouth of the Ammonoosuc, this was made into one town on each side of the river, one mile longer than the town below it.

The strength of the Bradford claim was in their belief that when Caleb Willard and Benjamin Whiting, under the direction of the proprietors of Newbury and Haverhill, surveyed the bounds of each town, in 1763, they, acting under private instructions from Bayley and Hazen, as they went down the river from the mouth of the Ammonoosuc, disregarded the boundary which Blanchard had made three years before, and kept on into the ungranted and unsettled land below them, and made a new bound, one mile and sixty-eight rods below the previous one. Thus doing, they had enriched Newbury and Haverhill, at the expense of Bradford and Piermont. The settlers upon the river road, south of Bedell's bridge, attended town-meeting in Mooretown, now Bradford, and paid taxes there, for some years before 1778. But in that year, Newbury reasserted its claim, and has held it ever since.

In rebuttal, Col. Thomas Johnson, with the assistance of Gen. Jacob Bayley, still in the full possession of his faculties, drew up a paper, stating the claim of Newbury to the strip in question, which is, in substance, as follows:

In 1762, Governor Wentworth, desiring a new survey made, sent Gen. Jacob Bayley, with Mr. McNeal, the King's surveyor, to make new bounds to the towns above Charlestown, and they proceeded up the river about thirty miles above the mouth of the Ammonoosuc. In that summer there was a road marked out from Canterbury, and, in some degree, made passable. In the same summer, Maj. Joseph Blanchard made application for himself and friends for a charter of what is now Newbury, and so did Oliver Willard, but Bayley and Hazen had claims upon the Governor for their services in the late war and had friends whom it was for his interest to oblige. He therefore promised the charter to Bayley and Hazen. But when they appeared before the Governor, Wentworth insisted that he should add the names of twenty of his friends to those who had been decided upon by Bayley and Hazen. To this the two latter naturally objected, representing that they had already been at considerable expense in surveying the town, and opening a road, and that it was unjust to them to admit twenty other proprietors, thus reducing the value of each of the shares—dividing the land among eighty proprietors instead of sixty. Wentworth was but following the custom of the time. The colonial governors were in the habit of rewarding their friends for their support, either by making direct grants of land to them or by placing their names among the grantees of new towns. The governments were poor in money, but rich in land which had an indefinite prospective value, and thus the royal governors could enrich their favorites without costing themselves anything. So Bayley and Hazen were told that the twenty names must go in, but that they should be allowed to take from the ungranted lands south of them enough to make up for twenty additional shares. Accordingly, the survey of Newbury, by Bayley, in 1763, cut out of the ungranted lands south of it a strip one mile and sixty-eight rods wide. The map, or plan, of Newbury, upon the back of the recorded charter gives the south-east corner of Newbury exactly where it is now. Therefore their claim that this addition to Newbury was by direct permission and authority of Governor Wentworth was admitted by the legislature, and Bradford lost its case. But Haverhill was less fortunate, or Piermont more persistent, as in 1784 the former town was compelled to divide with the latter a similar disputed strip along its south side.

In 1803, Newbury was compelled to relinquish to Topsham a strip one mile in breadth, which it had claimed, along the east side of that town, which in old deeds, is called "Topsham Gore." It was the opinion of the late Richard Patterson, who had carefully surveyed the town lines, that Newbury gained a little at the expense of Ryegate. The truth seems to be, that Newbury and Haverhill were settled when the land around them was ungranted, and the proprietors made the towns as large as they could.

The town of Newbury was granted to the following persons as proprietors, the spelling of their names being that of the charter:

Jacob Bayley, Esq.	John Hazzen
Ephraim Bayley	Ephraim Noyse
Jeremiah Allen	Enoch Thurstin
David Flanders	John Beard
Samuel Stevens	Joshua Copp
Abner Sawyer	John Ingalls
William White	Joshua Bayley
John Goodwin	John Hasseltine
Noah White	Simeon Goodwin
Edmond Morse	Joshua Hayward
Moses Little	Jesse Johnson
Simeon Stevens	Peter Page
Abner Bayley	Jacob Kent
Jaasiel Harriman	Abner Newton
Hayns Johnson	John Hugh
Joseph White	Samuel Hobart
Zacheus Peasley	Ebenezer Eaton
Thomas Danforth	John White, Jun.
James King	Caleb Johnson
William Holden	Timothy Beadle
Ebener Mudgett	Moses Hazzen
Joseph Chamberlain	Asa Foster
Richd Chamberlain	Daniel Appleton
Thomas Chamberlain ·	Abiel Chamberlain
Samel Johnson	Jonathan Broadstreet
Saml Stevens, Esq.	Wm Haywood
Benjn Emerson	Jacob Eaton
Nathnl Martan	Peter Morse
Joshua Hains	Archelaus Miles
Frye Bayley	Edward Bayley
Martin Severance	Col Willm Symes
Theodore Atkinson	Hon. John Temple
Mark Hunkg Wentworth	Benj Winn
Mark Temple	Samuel Cummius
Elnathan Blood	John Cummins
Col. Clement Marsh	Elias Alexander
Coll John Goffe	Capt. Marquand

Governor Benning Wentworth was counted as holding two rights, or shares.

Of the above grantees of Newbury the following became actual settlers: Jacob, Ephraim, Frye, and Joshua Bayley, Thomas, Richard, Joseph, and Abiel Chamberlain, William, Joseph, and Noah White, Caleb and Haynes Johnson, John Hazeltine, Simeon Stevens, Jacob Kent, Benjamin Emerson, Samuel Harriman, John Goodwin, and Moses Little. A few of these remained only a short time, but most of them made their homes here.

Jacob and Ephraim Bayley, John Hazeltine, Jacob Kent, and Simeon Stevens, who settled in Newbury, were grantees also of Haverhill, while John Hazen, Joshua Howard, Timothy Beadle (Bedell), and Simeon Goodwin, who settled in Haverhill, were also proprietors of Newbury.

The following were proprietors of Haverhill only, but settled in Newbury, although some of them did not remain here long: Aaron Hosmer, Nathaniel Merrill, Thomas Johnson, John Mills, Benoni Wright, Josiah Little, John Taplin, and Nehemiah Lovewell. The remaining grantees soon sold their rights to persons who became actual settlers.

The first meeting of the proprietors of Newbury was held at the inn of John Hall in Plaistow, N. H., Monday, June 14, 1763, at which the town was duly organized, and which seems to have been attended by several of the grantees. Jesse Johnson was chosen clerk; Caleb Johnson, constable; Benjamin Emerson and Capt. John Hazen, selectmen. This organization was made before any of the grantees present had removed to Newbury, and was merely in accordance with the terms of the charter, as a formal act. At the same time and place was held the first proprietors' meeting, which was the first town-meeting of Haverhill, at which Jesse Johnson was chosen clerk; Stephen Knight, constable; Capt. John Hazen, Jacob Bayley, Esq., and Maj. Edmund Morse, selectmen.

The town machinery, thus put together and set running at the inn of John Hall at Plaistow, on the 11th of June, 1763, and transported to Newbury in the next year, still continues, after the lapse of one hundred and thirty-seven years, by being wound up on the first Tuesday in March of each year, to do its regular work with very little change in its most important parts. There were then, as now, a moderator, clerk, selectmen, and an overseer of the poor. The constable still, as "when we were under the King," collects the taxes, and arrests evil doers. The highway surveyor of those and later times is represented by the road commissioner. But the real official labor of the town, is done by officers bearing the same titles at the close of the nineteenth century, as their predecessors bore at its beginning.

During the first thirty years of our history there were two

separate organizations, the Town of Newbury and the Proprietors of Newbury. All the male citizens of the town, who took "Freeman's Oath," could vote in town-meeting, and hold office, but only the grantees or those holding land immediately under them, could vote in the proprietors' meeting.

For some years the proprietors or grantees under the crown, owned the whole town, and divided the land among themselves, held their own meetings, and raised taxes upon the real estate. The Proprietors' Book, one of the most valuable of those preserved in the town clerk's office, records the proceedings of the proprietors' meetings, and the original divisions of the land among the grantees. These proprietors' meetings were held only when warned by the clerk at the call of a certain number of members. But when the land was all divided and many of the grantees had died or moved away, the meetings seem to have been held only at long intervals, (the last one recorded was in 1791), and the proprietary seem to have passed out of existence without any special vote to dissolve on the part of its members. But in Haverhill the proprietors seem to have exercised authority in the town, held their meetings regularly, and controlled public affairs. The last meeting of the proprietors of Haverhill was held August 22, 1810, almost twenty years after the Newbury proprietary had ceased to exist.

At the meeting held June 13, 1763, a committee consisting of Joseph Blanchard, Edmund Mooers, and Edmund Morse, was chosen to audit the accounts of Bayley and Hazen, and assess the amount of their expenses in procuring a charter, surveying the town, making a road from Canterbury, and other necessary expenditures, upon the proprietors' shares, with two and a half dollars upon each right, to defray the expense of laying out the town into lots. They also voted that the committee should select responsible men to assess and collect this tax. At that time the only legal residents of Newbury were the proprietors, so that this meeting was, in fact, the first legal town-meeting of Newbury, although held more than one hundred miles from it. It was also voted at this meeting that Jacob Bayley, John Hazen, Jacob Kent, Ebenezer Mudgett, and Lieut. Harriman should be authorized to bound the town, and lay out one lot to each proprietor in the intervale or meadow, and a house lot on the higher land, these lots to be of size according to their estimated value. For his services rendered to the town, Jacob Bayley was authorized to select five intervale lots, where he should choose, "provided that his taking so many does not incommode the settlement of the town."

Another meeting of the proprietors was called for September 26th, which adjourned to October 1st, at the same inn of John Hall, at which Jacob Bayley was chosen Proprietors' clerk, Edmund

Capt. John Brown, Lieut. Benjamin Emerson, assessors, and Caleb Johnson, collector. They

 e rights whose owners had failed to pay their

Mooers, moderator, Capt. John Hazen, Lieut. Benjamin Emerson, and Jesse Johnson, assessors, and Caleb Johnson, collector. They voted:

1st.   that "the rights whose owners had failed to pay their equal share of the expenses," should be sold at public vendue.

2d.   That allowance should be made to those who have already settled at Newbury.

3d.   That each proprietor should choose his intervale lot and receive the same, when he should improve by tillage three acres on each lot, and that they should pitch, in the order of their making improvements, each paying his share of the assessed expenses.

They also provided that if more than one person should pitch upon the same tract, they should draw lots and the loser should pitch elsewhere.

4th.   They voted to make half the road through Haverhill toward Portsmouth, with the proprietors of Haverhill, and chose Jacob Bayley, John Hazen, and Jacob Kent a committee to prepare such a road.

It will be understood that as early as 1763 there were no settlements between Canterbury and Haverhill, and whatever was to be done, must be by the settlers at Coös. A road of some kind must be had, yet we shall find that they did not intend to build the whole road alone.

5th.   They voted to lay out a fifty-acre lot of equal value, to each right, as near it as possible.

6th.   They chose Capt. Moses Little, Lieut. Moulton, and Jacob Bayley a committee to lay out one hundred acres to each right, "this fall, if there be time," and that these lots should be drawn.

Finally, they voted "to pay a preacher, with the proprietors of Haverhill to preach at s^d town, two or three months this fall or winter." On the same day, and at the same place, the proprietors of Haverhill met, and made similar regulations, and voted "to join with Newbury one or two months this fall in paying for preaching."

On the 1st day of March, 1764, another proprietors' meeting was held at the house of William Marshall, in Hampstead, which at once adjourned to the former place of assembly at Plaistow, where it was voted to sell at public vendue the mills which had been built at Haverhill by the proprietors of both towns. They voted, also, to give eighty acres of land to the man or men who should build a sawmill on Hall's brook, under certain conditions, the grant including the mill privilege. This meeting adjourned to William Marshall's house, in Hampstead, where it was voted that the proprietors assist Haverhill in laying out a road to meet the road from Portsmouth, and that Benjamin Whiting should be a committee to lay out the lands voted last fall.

The mills which had been built in Haverhill were sold at

auction April 2d, and were bid off by Jesse Johnson, John Hazen, and Jacob Bayley, for two hundred and ninety-seven dollars. When we speak of *dollars* in those early days, it must be understood that Spanish dollars are meant. Many of the older deeds on record in the town clerk's office mention the consideration to be a certain sum in "Spanish milled dollars."

The last meeting of the proprietors, held out of town, passed a vote about supplying the town with preaching, and adjourned to "Col. Jacob Bayley's att Newbury, Coös, on the 15th of October next."

CHAPTER V.

THE EARLY YEARS.

CONDITION OF COUNTRY.— INDIAN TRAILS.— HALL'S POND, BROOK AND MEADOW.— JACOB KENT.— JOHN FOREMAN.— THE FIRST WHITE CHILD.— THE FIRST MARRIAGE.— THE FIRST DEATH.— REV. SILAS MOODY.— HARDSHIPS OF THE SETTLERS.—NEW-COMERS IN 1763.— REV. PETER POWERS.— THE LOG MEETING-HOUSE.— THE FIRST SAWMILL.— THE MILL-CRANK AND ITS HISTORY.— SAW-MILL ON HARRIMAN'S BROOK.— THE FIRST GRIST MILL.— SETTLEMENT OF LANCASTER.— AT BATH.— CULTIVATION OF POTATOES.

WHILE the proprietors of the town were settling its concerns more than a hundred miles away from it, hardy and resolute men and women were making themselves homes in Coös. It is probable that there were quite a number of families here before the end of 1763, whose names have not come down to us. Mr. Powers and Mr. Perry seem only to have mentioned those who remained in Newbury. There were others who staid here a few years and then went on into newer lands or back whence they came. In the early records recur names of families which disappeared before the revolution.

Little but tradition informs us as to the condition of the meadows before their settlement. It is certain that a large part of the Great Ox-bow, in Newbury, and the Little Ox-bow in Haverhill, had long been cleared and cultivated by the Indians in their rude fashion. Of the other meadows little is known, but it is supposed that they were covered with woods among which lay a great mass of fallen timber amidst which tall weeds and tangled vines made, in many places, thickets which were almost impenetrable. But there were cleared places on most, if not all, and on Horse meadow was quite a large field.

There were several Indian trails; the location of most has long been lost, but of a few the general direction is known. The great trail, from the Merrimack to Lake Memphremagog, came up through Warren in a course, which, says William Little, in his history of that town, is followed very nearly by the railroad. Another came up the Connecticut, and at Wells River sent a branch up that stream. Indian Joe, the famous scout, used to point out a number of paths through the woods, which were made by his dusky brethren. The first road, which was marked by spotted trees from Charlestown to Coös, followed one of these trails. In various places in this town, where the woods have never been cut down, are paths which may be clearly discerned for long distances, which were here when white men came to Coös and are believed to be sections of pre-historic trails. The settlers used these woodland paths in their journeys and they gradually became public roads.

The settlers who came in 1762, made small clearings, both for the planting of corn for food, and with the expectation of thus establishing a claim to the lands upon which they wished to settle. Early in 1763, people began to come into both towns in quite large numbers. James Woodward and John Page came into Haverhill, and settled on the farms where they passed the rest of their lives. Noah White came to Newbury, and settled upon Kent's Meadow, but afterwards removed to Bradford where he became prominent.

In May came Daniel Hall and his sons in a boat from Northfield, Mass. They reached the mouth of a brook in Bradford after dark on a Saturday evening. On the morrow he refused to proceed on his journey, upon the Sabbath, and remained at the mouth of the stream till the next day. That brook—Hall's brook, Hall's pond and Hall's meadow perpetuate his name, says Rev. Clark Perry.

In November came Col. Jacob Kent from Plaistow and settled on Kent's meadow, where he built the first framed house in town. Later, not being able to buy as much of that meadow as he desired, he removed to Sleeper's meadow, where his descendants long lived. In the same month, and perhaps in the same company with Kent, James Abbott of Concord, and Ebenezer White of Plaistow, with their hardy sons and daughters, moved into Newbury. About the same time came Frye Bayley, then young and unmarried. Thomas Johnson moved over from Haverhill and located at the Ox-bow. These were men of superior character—the best possible material for a new settlement, and their influence extended over many years. Mr. Powers says that James Abbott's family was the twelfth in both towns. There were several young men who boarded in these families, clearing land, and doing other work.

In that year, John Foreman and two others, who had been soldiers for several years in the British army, left it at Quebec, and made their way to Coös. Foreman settled in Newbury, married a daughter of Richard Chamberlin, and after the war removed to Bath. Of him and his descendants a more particular account will be given later.

On the Ox-bow, April 4, 1763, was born the first English child,

Betsey, daughter of John Hazeltine. She married Capt. Nehemiah Lovewell, whom she outlived nearly half a century, and died November 19, 1850. A few weeks later the first white male child was born to Thomas Chamberlain and his wife, and was called Jacob Bayley Chamberlain. He settled in Canada after the war, and died there. His mother, says Mr. Perry, received a grant of one hundred acres from the proprietors, as a bounty. In the spring of the same year the first white child was born in Haverhill, but it died in a few days.

In Haverhill also was the first death among the settlers, Polly Harriman, of consumption, aged eighteen. Some weeks later "the Widow Pettibone" died in Newbury, the first death, and Abraham Webb was drowned.

It is believed that Aaron Hosmer and Susanna Chamberlain were married in that year, the first marriage at Coös.

Bayley and Hazen visited Newbury at least once in 1763, and made preparations for removal hither and Mr. Silas Moody, a relative of the Littles, who had recently graduated at Harvard, was engaged by the proprietors to come and preach, which he did, and remained several weeks, preaching in both towns.

It would seem that the year 1763, saw considerable progress in the settlement. A sawmill was in operation in Haverhill, and the rude huts of the previous year gave place to log houses with some semblance of domestic convenience. The forests began to fall before the axe, and the smoke rolled up from many a clearing in the autumn sunshine. According to Col. Little, a road was made passable for ox teams for two or three miles south from the Ox-bow. Carpenters and blacksmiths had come to Coös, and, although their tools were few and their conveniences rude, necessity stimulated the invention of many useful contrivances.

The season had been a fruitful one, and there seems to have been a good crop of potatoes, corn and wheat, with hay for the cattle. The latter were all young, and it was desirable to preserve them for their increase and labor, so it is not probable that much beef was killed in that year. We do not learn how early sheep and swine were brought to Coös. But the woods abounded in game, the rivers and brooks swarmed with fish. Those who had been here long enough to clear land and raise crops, had a plenty, although not a great variety of food. Still their way of living must have been very primitive, when sixty miles of wilderness separated the settlers from their nearest neighbors. But the hardy men and women thought little of these things; every nerve was strained to better their condition. Many of the necessities of life were hard to be had. Dr. Samuel White said in his old age that he had seen ten bushels of wheat exchanged for one of salt. Tea and coffee were rarely tasted at Coös in those early years. The herbs of the field were medicine for the sick. Their farming tools were rude and

RESIDENCE OF RICHARD DOE—BUILT 1820.
THIS HOUSE OCCUPIES THE SITE OF GENERAL BAYLEY'S HOUSE.

heavy, and much strength was wasted in handling the implements of their toil. A carpenter's tool of any kind was a treasure not to be valued in money. One man was the fortunate owner of a saw, another of an auger, while a third had a broad-axe, and the mutual exchange of these articles made kindly feelings, while their loss or injury was hardly to be forgiven.

Books were few, and schools were not yet, but there were men and women of intelligence who gave a tone to the settlement. The Bible was in every house, and was the one book which every one knew. All were poor except in land, with willing hearts and strong arms to win a sustenance from the soil.

The year 1764 was a year of increase to both towns. Dea. Jonathan Elkins, Col. Timothy Bedell and Hon. Ezekiel Ladd moved their families into Haverhill. In October General Bayley came with his family, although it would appear that his son Ephraim preceded him by several months. His house was already built, which stood where Mr. Richard Doe's brick house now stands at the Ox-bow. Water is still drawn from a well which was dug in that year, a few feet from the north-west corner of the house. "He had been," says Mr. Powers, "the principal mover in every proceeding, and now he had come to bless himself, and to save much people alive, in the approaching struggle between Great Britain and her colonies." In the same year, probably, Col. John Taplin came, and his son John. He seems to have lived about where the Spring Hotel once stood, and the library stands now. The proprietors who had not been able to persuade Mr. Moody to return and settle at Coös, addressed themselves to Rev. Peter Powers, who had returned to Hollis, after being settled a few years at Newent, now Lisbon, Conn., who was well known to most of them. He came in June to look the ground over, preached acceptably in both towns, and a mutual liking between him and the people led to his acceptance of the call made by the proprietors of the towns. The Congregational church was organized at Hollis in September of that year, and a log meeting-house was built, says Grant Powers, south of General Bayley's house, between it and the foot of the hill. After the erection of a better house of worship, it was used as a schoolhouse for some years.

In the same year, the frame of a sawmill on the lower falls of Hall's brook was raised. Everything about it except the saw, and the crank which propelled it up and down in the frame, could be made here, but the latter could only be procured at some larger place. One was engaged at Concord and in the winter time several men, who had prepared a sled which they thought would answer for its transportation, went down after it. They returned on snowshoes, drawing the sled, which had very wide runners, after them. The snow was deep, the weather extremely cold, and their progress was slow. When they were crossing Newfound lake, being very tired they made a halt, and sat down upon the sled to rest, but one of the party, John Page, arose and went some distance after water.   When he returned he found his comrades fallen into a sleep, which would soon have been death, had he not, after great effort, aroused them to a sense of their danger.   "But the same party," says Grant Powers, "came near perishing when they had arrived in sight of Haverhill, and had it not been for James Woodward to perform for Page, what Page had done for them upon the pond, they would have given up the ghost."   This crank, which so nearly cost the lives of six men, was placed in the first sawmill built in this town, which stood where Mr. Knight's upper dam is now, at South Newbury, in which it did service some twenty years.   Somewhere about 1790, David and Samuel Tucker and Jonathan Johnson built a mill at the outlet of Hall's pond, to which they transferred this crank where it outlasted several successive mills, until about 1871, this mill, the last survivor of the old "up-and-down" sawmills in this region, went to decay.   The old crank is now carefully preserved by Mr. S. S. Tucker, and is good for another century or two.   It weighs one hundred and seventy-five pounds.   A few weeks after this old crank began its work on Hall's brook, a sawmill was completed at the falls west of Newbury village, where several successors have been built.   In the fall of 1765, a grist mill went into operation, which stood at the foot of the hill below the saw-mill, but above the bridge.   This was the first grist mill in Orange county.

Haverhill and Newbury were not long allowed to remain the last setlements on the river.   In 1763, David Page, who had been dissatisfied with the division of land in Haverhill, resolved to begin a settlement at Upper Coös.   Lancaster was incorporated July 5, 1763, and in the following autumn, David Page, Jr., and Emmons Stockwell went there, built a camp, and wintered some cattle.   In 1764, David Page and others moved into that town, separated from Newbury by forty miles of wilderness.   Other towns in that region were soon occupied.

In 1765, Jaasiel Harriman, whom we have seen coming to Newbury in 1762, began to clear land near the great rock, south of Bath village, and on that rock his daughter raised the first vegetables in town.

Some of the early settlers, probably all who had families and household goods, came upon the ice, which furnished a level road from Charlestown, or in the open season, in boats.   For the safety and comfort of those who traveled directly by way of Plymouth, rude shelters of logs, with chimneys of stone, were erected at intervals of ten or fifteen miles.

Rev. Grant Powers has preserved many anecdotes of the early settlers, and their hardships, which without his painstaking would have, long ago, been forgotten.   It is not the intention of this volume to supplant the work which he did. His sketches should be in every house in Newbury. But he never intended his book to be considered a complete history of the Coös country. All he desired was to secure from oblivion some of the tales which still continued to be told when he preached in Haverhill seventy-five years ago. The Coös country owes a debt to Mr. Powers for his care, and we will not detract from the interest of his volume by telling his tales over again. He did not attempt to recount the real history of the times, and there is enough that he did not say to more than fill one volume.

It has before been stated that potatoes were raised in Newbury in 1762. It would seem by this that the use of the potato had, within a few years of the settlement of Newbury, become general. Potatoes were introduced into New England by some emigrants from the north of Ireland in 1719, and were first raised in the garden of Nathaniel Walker of Andover, Mass. The first mention of them in Newbury, Mass., was in 1732. In 1737, Rev. Thomas Smith of Portland, Me., says in his diary that there was not a peck of potatoes in the whole Eastern country. "So late as 1750," says Coffin's history of Newbury, Mass., "should any person have raised so large a quantity as five bushels, great would have been the inquiry among his neighbors, in what manner he could dispose of such abundance." They were first raised in beds, like onions. Yet little more than ten years later their use had come to be general.

CHAPTER VI.

THE LAND DIVIDED.

IN the fall of 1763, Benjamin Whiting, a noted surveyor of his
time, laid out the meadow lots, house-lots, and fifty-acre lots,
and made a plan of them, which was accepted June 14, 1764.
The several meadows were divided into sections containing from
eighteen to thirty acres each, according to their supposed value.
With each meadow lot was "coupled" a "house-lot" which lay
upon the upland along the river road, and which had from one to
five acres, and a "fifty-acre lot" lying back or west of the main road.
When a proprietor had made certain designated improvements
upon his "pitch," and had paid his share of the proprietors' expenses,
he received a title deed from Gen. Bayley, on behalf of the grantees,
of his meadow lot, with the house-lot and fifty-acre lot which
belonged to it. The meadows were divided into as many lots as
there were grantees. The rest of the town lay unsurveyed, except
that the boundary lines were ran out, until 1768. By that time
all the land on the meadows had been taken up, and there began to
be a demand for land in the back part of the town, for settlement.

The proprietors employed Dudley Coleman of Newbury, Mass.,
a graduate of Harvard College in 1765, who afterwards became
a noted officer in the revolutionary war, to come here and lay out
what are called the "hundred-acre lots." But before he began this
division, the proprietors, on the 27th of April, 1768, conveyed by
deed to Benjamin Whiting, for two hundred pounds, all that part
of Newbury which lies west of a line drawn from a point five and

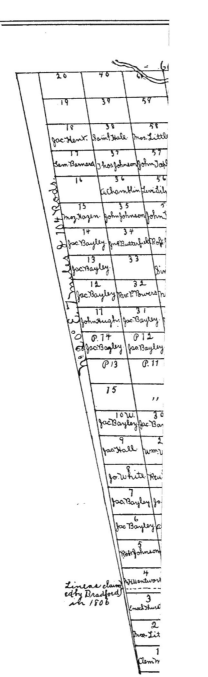

2 0	4 0	6 0
1 9	3 9	5 9
1 8 Jac. Hunt.	3 8 Saml. Hale	5 8 Mos. Little
1 7 Saml. Barnard	3 7 Thos. Johnson	5 7 John Taft
1 6	3 6 A. Chamblin	5 6 Levi Lily
1 5 Moz. Hazen	3 5 John Johnson	5 John
1 4 Jac. Bayley	3 4 Jno. Butterfield	Robt.
1 3 Jac. Bayley	3 3	Div
1 2 Jac. Bayley	3 2 Rev. P. Bowers	
1 1 John Hugh	3 1 Jac. Bayley	
P. 74 Jac. Bayley	P. 12 Jac. Bayley	
P 13	P. 11	
15	,,	
1 0 W. Jac. Bayley	3 0 Jac. Bar	
9 Jac. Hall	2 Wm.	
8 Jo. White	Rev	
7 Jac. Bayley	Jo.	
6 Jac. Bayley		
5 Robt. Johnson		
4 J. Wentworth		
3 Enoch Hurd		
2 Thos. Lit		
1 Clem.		

2 Miles & 104 Rods

Lineas claimed by Bradford in 1806

WHITING'S MAP OF NEWBURY.

Showing the whole town except Whiting's Gore, or the "Half-mile Strip." Made by Benjamin Whiting, 1769.

three-quarters miles from the southeast corner of the town along the Bradford line, to another point, the same distance from the northeast corner of the town, along the Ryegate line. This tract, which lies between the Topsham line and the west line of the "hundred-acre lots," is seven miles, one hundred and four rods long, and one-half mile wide, and is called to this day the "half-mile strip," or "Whiting's gore." It contains above two thousand acres, and may have been deeded to Whiting to pay him for his work in surveying the east part of the town. At the north end of this strip, and in the extreme northwest corner of the town, is the "glebe" which long paid rent to the Episcopal church.

This deed is signed by the proprietors of Newbury, in 1768, whose names were as follows, in the order of their signing, Whiting the grantee being expressly mentioned as one of them:

Jacob Bayley	John Taplin
Jacob Kent	Joseph Chamberlin
Moses Thurston	Enoch Thurston
Samuel Hale	Thomas Johnson
John Hugh	Peter Powers
Thomas Chamberlain	Abial Chamberlin
Jacob Hall	Richard Chamberlin
Gideon Smith	Robert Johnston
Abner Fowler	Levi Silvester
Joseph White	Simeon Stevens
Noah White	Benjamin Emerson
Robert Hunkins	Jacob Fowler
John Haseltine	Reuben Foster
Jonathan Butterfield	Leonard Whiting
John Hazen	Uriah Chamberlin

When we compare this list of the proprietors of 1768, with that of the grantees upon the charter of 1763, it will be seen that great changes had already taken place in the ownership of the town. Of the seventy-five names which are on the charter, only thirteen are attached to this deed, while seventeen new names are added. As several others of the grantees became actual settlers, it may be that they had not, in 1768, complied with all the conditions of the charter and received title deeds to their land. Of those seventy-five, about forty never settled here or obtained a full title to their land, but sold their claims. In those days men speculated in Vermont lands, just as rich men now invest in Western land, or in stocks and bonds. Men who had influence could get their names inserted in the charters of new towns, and would sell the rights thus obtained as soon as the land came into demand, while others dealt in rights and shares of wild land. By various means some men became owners of whole townships, either by buying out the actual grantees, or by means of inserting a great number of fictitious

three-quarters miles from the southeast corner of the town along the Bradford line, to another point, the same distance from the northeast corner of the town, along the Ryegate line. This tract, which lies between the Topsham line and the west line of the "hundred-acre lots," is seven miles, one hundred and four rods long, and one-half mile wide, and is called to this day the "half-mile strip," or "Whiting's gore." It contains above two thousand acres, and may have been deeded to Whiting to pay him for his work in surveying the east part of the town. At the north end of this strip, and in the extreme northwest corner of the town, is the "glebe" which long paid rent to the Episcopal church.

This deed is signed by the proprietors of Newbury, in 1768, whose names were as follows, in the order of their signing, Whiting the grantee being expressly mentioned as one of them:

Jacob Bayley	John Taplin
Jacob Kent	Joseph Chamberlin
Moses Thurston	Enoch Thurston
Samuel Hale	Thomas Johnson
John Hugh	Peter Powers
Thomas Chamberlain	Abial Chamberlin
Jacob Hall	Richard Chamberlin
Gideon Smith	Robert Johnston
Abner Fowler	Levi Silvester
Joseph White	Simeon Stevens
Noah White	Benjamin Emerson
Robert Hunkins	Jacob Fowler
John Haseltine	Reuben Foster
Jonathan Butterfield	Leonard Whiting
John Hazen	Uriah Chamberlin

When we compare this list of the proprietors of 1768, with that of the grantees upon the charter of 1763, it will be seen that great changes had already taken place in the ownership of the town. Of the seventy-five names which are on the charter, only thirteen are attached to this deed, while seventeen new names are added. As several others of the grantees became actual settlers, it may be that they had not, in 1768, complied with all the conditions of the charter and received title deeds to their land. Of those seventy-five, about forty never settled here or obtained a full title to their land, but sold their claims. In those days men speculated in Vermont lands, just as rich men now invest in Western land, or in stocks and bonds. Men who had influence could get their names inserted in the charters of new towns, and would sell the rights thus obtained as soon as the land came into demand, while others dealt in rights and shares of wild land. By various means some men became owners of whole townships, either by buying out the actual grantees, or by means of inserting a great number of fictitious names in the charters. In most of the Vermont towns not one of the grantees became an actual settler. It was very fortunate for Newbury and Haverhill that so many of their grantees were men already well known to each other, and that the plans for local government were so fully matured before much settlement had begun. The advantage gained by mutual acquaintance was still further secured by the fact that all, or nearly all, who came into either town from the lower portion of the Merrimack valley, were bound, in one way and another, by ties of common ancestry. All these aided to form a close union of common interests between Newbury and Haverhill, and helped to give the towns the strong and united position which they held before, and especially during, the revolutionary war.

Coleman and his men began their survey in September, at the southeast corner of the "half-mile strip," and ran eight parallel lines from Bradford to Ryegate. The last of these lines is often spoken of as the "east line of the hundred-acre lots." They then began at the Bradford line and laid out seventy-two lots, by running cross lines, and then began at the Ryegate line and laid out seventy-eight lots—all these between the half-mile strip, and the "east line," above mentioned. These one hundred and sixty lots are called the hundred-acre lots, and are numbered from one, up. They vary much in size. Mr. Patterson used to tell of a hundred-acre lot from which one hundred and fourteen acres were sold, and there were one hundred and twelve acres left. The survey was made in a pathless wilderness, with all the obstacles of hills, precipices, swamps, and fallen timber, and was far from accurate, yet has answered the purpose of sub-division for one hundred and thirty years.

Between these divisions, there remained a tract which they divided into lots which vary in size, and are known as P lots—"P 1 in the fourth range," and so on. There are fifteen of these lots. There still remained a strip of land called "The Gore," which is of unequal width, and extends from the east side of the half-mile strip to the east side of the hundred-acre lots, through the centre of the town. The town house stands on the north edge of the gore, which is sometimes half a mile wide. The "east line of the hundred-acre lots," crosses the road between Newbury and West Newbury, a short distance west of Joseph Johnston's house, and crosses the brook road, in front of the Chalmers sawmill. Between this and the fifty-acre lots lay an irregular and rocky tract which was unsurveyed for twenty years, when Gen. James Whitelaw was employed to complete the survey, and the land was divided among such of the grantees as still remained, giving them about thirty-four acres each. After 1800, Benjamin Baldwin of Bradford laid the half-mile strip out into lots.

It will be seen that the owner of each of the eighty shares was entitled to a meadow lot, with its appendage of house lot and upland, and two of the hundred-acre lots, besides an equal share of what still lay undivided, no inconsiderable quantity of real estate.

Before Coleman finished his survey, he laid out into seventy-eight lots a strip one mile wide, on the east side of what is now Topsham, but then claimed by Newbury. This was the land which Newbury had to give up to Topsham in 1803. It would seem that Gen. Bayley paid Coleman for his labor, and had to wait a long time for his own pay, as witness the following among the Johnson papers:

"NEWBURY, April 14, 1790.
The Proprietors of Newbury to Jacob Bayley, Esq., Dr.,
for money paid Capt. Dudley Coleman for laying out
the hundred-acre lots, £13.7.9
To 20 days work in assisting in laying out s^d lots at
4 shillings per day, 4.0.0
Interest on account, 20.9.4
£37.16.1

Received of the Proprietors by an order on Col. Frye Bayley, Collector of the Proprietors' tax, £37.16.1, which is in full of all betwixt me and the Proprietors of Newbury for all services done by me, and for notes, debts, dues, and demands preceding this date, and also for Mr. Moody's preaching in this town.
JACOB BAYLEY."

It would appear by the Proprietors' book that the first division of hundred-acre lots was made soon after Mr. Coleman completed his survey of the town. The proprietors drew the lots by numbers, one lot to each share. Some owned several shares, and drew as many lots. Few of the proprietors held more than one share. At the first drawing of lots, seventy-five were taken. The Proprietors' Book does not give the date of either the first or second drawing of lots, but it is evident that several years elapsed between them, as changes in the number of shares are given, new names are mentioned, and some of the former ones are not on the second list. At the second drawing seventy-eight lots were taken, making one hundred and fifty-three in all. There remained a considerable portion of the hundred-acre lots, which was not yet assigned.

The map of the one hundred-acre lots, made about 1774, gives 1200 acres as owned by John Pagan and John Witherspoon, which lay in a body east of the half-mile strip, and about midway between Bradford and Ryegate. East of this lay a tract of 600 acres owned by George Clinton. John Pagan was a merchant at Glasgow, who afterward held some public office in London; John Witherspoon was president of Princeton college, and of him we shall have more to say. George Clinton was governor of New York for some years.

In 1783, Dr. Witherspoon commissioned James Whitelaw and Alexander Harvey to sell and convey his lands in Newbury and elsewhere in Vermont. Deeds, on behalf of the proprietors, were granted by Jacob Bayley as early as the fall of 1763, but none were recorded for several years. The only offices in New Hampshire at that time, for the registry of deeds, were at Exetér and Portsmouth. As the control of that province over Newbury ended in 1764, it is not probable that any were sent away to be recorded.* Neither is it likely that many were sent away for record while this town was under the jurisdiction of New York, or that the authorities of that province established any offices for the recording of conveyances in what is now Vermont. The third session of the General Assembly of Vermont, sitting at Bennington, in February, 1779, passed a law that all deeds or conveyances of houses or lands should be recorded by the clerk of the town in which the land lay, or that of the nearest organized town, if there was no organization. It would seem that the town authorities procured a blank book, which bears the name of the First Volume of Land Records, in which the first recorded deed was given August 26, 1779, and received for record by Jacob Kent, town clerk, August 23, 1781. This volume, and the second of the series, also contains the record of deeds of land in Ryegate, Peacham and Topsham.

Vermont is the only state in the Union in which the record of deeds is kept by the clerk of each town, instead of an officer who keeps the records for the whole county, at the county seat.

In 1764, Newbury passed under the government of New York, and in 1765, Alexander Colden, Surveyor General, made a new survey of the boundaries of the town, at the request of Benjamin Whiting and the proprietors, and fixed the southwest corner at the present northwest corner of Bradford. This did not please the people of Newbury, and a petition for himself and twenty-five others of Newbury, was presented to Governor Clinton in December, 1766, by Whiting, which stated that the west line of the town, as laid down by Colden, did not include all the lands which had been granted by Governor Wentworth, and that the west line of the town lacked ninety-six chains and fifty links to bring it up to the town of Topsham. It was ordered in council that the Surveyor General should make the return of Newbury "according to the ancient bound," as prayed for by the petitioners.

---

*NOTE. Since this was written, it has been discovered that several deeds of land in Newbury, made in colonial days, are on record at Exeter.

WATERFALL ABOVE WELLS RIVER VILLAGE.

FROM WATER STREET LOOKING WEST.

CHAPTER VII.

EARLY DAYS IN NEWBURY.

THE first local town-meeting was held at Gen. Bayley's house, on June 12, 1764. Jacob Kent was chosen town clerk, an office which he was to hold till the end of the century; Jacob Bayley, Jacob Kent, and James Abbott, were selectmen; John Hazeltine was chosen constable; Maxi Hazeltine and Thomas Johnson were surveyors of highways; Richard Chamberlin and Simeon Stevens were tything-men; John Hugh was hog reeve, and Levi Sylvester was appointed field-driver. These latter titles with that of deer reeve, who was chosen the next year, sound strangely to our ears.

Tything-men were a sort of local police, the name being of Anglo-Saxon origin, which once meant the chief man of a tything or parish. In New England it was their duty to inspect taverns, keep an eye upon strangers and suspicious persons, and they could arrest, without a warrant, offenders against the laws. It was their duty to detain travelers upon the highway on the Sabbath, keep order in public assemblies, particularly in the meeting-house on the Lord's Day. When on duty the tything-man carried a wand or staff five feet long. In Massachusetts the tything-men were appointed by the selectmen, but here they were always chosen in town-meeting. There was but one for a number of years, but as the town grew, two or more were chosen from different parts of the town. A number of duties which are now performed by other officers were then attended to by the tything-men; thus the office was considered very important, and only the most staid and substantial citizens were elected to it.   The last tything-men were elected in 1850, but had not been chosen before for several years.   There are those living who can remember the tything-men in the old meeting-house walking about during sermon, and keeping a vigilant eye on the small boys.

Hog-reeves were charged with the oversight of swine that ran at large, to see that they were yoked and ringed.   They were to enforce the law against the owners of unruly hogs.   In the course of time their duties extended to the care of the town pound, and the taking up and detention of stray and quarrelsome cattle.   They were often called hog-wards, and their office still nominally survives under the title of pound-keeper.   Sometimes this official was called "hog-constable," and a few amusing stories are told concerning the election of various individuals to the position.

Many years ago the legal voters of Peacham laid themselves open to a keen thrust of the wit of their minister, Rev. Leonard Worcester, by nominating him for hog-constable.   He arose and thanked his fellow townsmen for the honor they proposed to do him, and said that if elected he would certainly accept, and for the same reason that he accepted the call to become their minister. "For," said he, "I came among you as a shepherd to his flock, but if you have so far degenerated as to become a herd of swine, it is fitting that I should be hog-constable!"   He was not elected.

We have not so good a story to tell upon that topic, but there is one which will do to relate.   In 1824, Dr. Calvin Jewett was moderator of town-meeting in Newbury, and when in the course of the proceedings it was necessary to choose a hog-constable, several persons declined the nomination.   Whereupon the doctor lectured the voters upon their delinquency, by telling them that the office was an important one, prescribed by law, and that some one ought to be willing to fill it, to which appeal the meeting responded by electing *him*.   He probably thought it rather more of a joke than anything else, but it could hardly have seemed one when about midnight he was awakened by several of his neighbors, who informed him that the office being important and prescribed by law, it was equally important that there should be no vacancy, and a justice of the peace who was present swore him in!

While the country was yet new, the woods abounded in deer. Both the skin and flesh of these animals were valuable to the settlers, and in 1741, a law was passed in New Hampshire making it a crime to kill a deer between January 1st and August 1st. It was the duty of the town to choose, annually, one or more deer-reeves, or deer keepers, who were to see that the law was observed, and to prosecute its violators.   But before the century ended, the deer had passed away, and the office with them.

For many years after the settlement of Newbury most of the unimproved land was unfenced, and the rights of the owners lay in common. It was the duty of the field driver to impound all animals running at large upon the public roads, or upon the common lands, without the consent of the land owners. For such services he received one shilling each, for cattle and horses, and three-pence each for sheep and swine, to be paid by their owners before being taken from the custody of the officer.

The first pound was made in 1766, and was a little north of the residence of William H. Atkinson. As the town grew, and domestic animals increased, Wells River was made into a "pound district," and one was built at West Newbury. These have long since disappeared. The only remaining pound stands upon the town farm, and is about fifty feet square. It was surrounded by a strong wall six feet high, now fallen down, and a heavy beam lay along the wall, on the four sides. A strong door, secured with a padlock, admitted the offending quadrupeds to an enclosure which has not been used for its intended purpose for thirty years.

The same town-meeting which voted to build a pound for the detention of unruly animals having four feet, voted also to erect a pair of stocks for the correction of such offenders as had but two. This terror to evil-doers was built by Joseph Chamberlin, and stood near his house on the "little plain." The stocks consisted of a platform about five feet from the ground, upon which was a bench on which the culprits sat, with their ankles inserted in holes of a convenient size, which were made in a frame in front of them. This was constructed of two beams, one above the other, which were hinged at one end, and holes, half in the upper and half in the lower timber, were made, of sizes to suit large and small people. The upper beam being lifted, the offender's feet were placed in the holes on the upper side of the lower one, and the corresponding upper half being brought down, it was secured by a padlock. The legs of the culprit were stretched out level, the bench had no back, and in that most uncomfortable position the unlucky malefactor had to sit from one to ten hours, according to the duration of the sentence, in full view of all who passed. For public information the culprit's name and offence were set forth upon a board placed above his head. Upon the frame work of the stocks was a sign board to which all public notices were affixed. The law of 1779 prescribed a penalty of twenty shillings a month upon any town which failed to provide stocks, and keep them in repair. The machinery of justice was expected to be always ready for work.

The Newbury stocks disappeared before 1810, but the whipping-post is well remembered by the oldest people, and stood, as late as 1836, a little north of Mr. Farnham's garden, a few feet back from the street. Small thefts, idleness, profanity, and a host of other offenses were punished by fines, by sitting in the stocks, and in aggravated cases, by whipping. Jails were few, and insecure; there was no state prison, and people could not afford to support criminals at public expense. So the offender was made a public spectacle in the stocks, or the rod of correction was faithfully applied at the whipping-post. There is evidence that both means of punishment were often used in Newbury in those early days.

Mr. Perry tells us that in 1764, or 1765, a man named Neal was supposed to have murdered an Indian at the Upper meadow. Both had been drinking and were heard quarrelling. They set out on the river in a boat, but Neal reached the Haverhill side alone. The body of the Indian, in a mangled state, was washed ashore on Howard's island. Neal was tried for the murder, and imprisoned at Portsmouth, but did not suffer death. Mr. Perry has also handed down the legend that an English officer was once murdered upon a rock by the river just above the outlet of Harriman's brook.

For some years after the settlement, detachments of the St. Francis tribe of Indians annually visited the place, and spent some time in hunting and fishing. A very few domesticated themselves among the settlers. Occasionally one of them would lay claim to a farm or a piece of land, which he would give up before witnesses, for some small article. Tradition asserts that the Indian title to several farms was extinguished in this way. The settlers never seem to have had any fear of them, but Rev. Mr. Powers in a letter written about 1767, describes them as a miserable crew, to whom there seemed little hope of doing any good. They, however, soon became extinct, but there is still a strain of Indian blood in more than one family in Newbury.   .

Mr. Perry tells us that the first store in Coös was opened at the Little Ox-bow in Haverhill, as early as 1765, perhaps before. From a letter in the handwriting of Col. Thomas Johnson it would seem that a school of some kind was kept in Newbury in that year.

Newbury and Haverhill had now come to be considered established settlements, with a society which attracted a valuable class of residents. Dr. Smith and Dr. Samuel Hale had established themselves in the practice of medicine. The talents and piety of Mr. Powers induced people to settle under his ministry.

All the traditions of those early days tell us that the first settlers of Newbury and Haverhill had to go down the river to Charlestown to mill for some years. If that was the case, it would seem that the gristmill which had been built on Poole brook in Haverhill by the proprietors in 1762, either did not go into operation, or proved ineffective. It may be that it only ground grain coarsely, and there was no mill which could make bolted flour any nearer than Charlestown.

It is hard to distinguish the precise facts in the meagre and faded records of those early days. Our ancestors were not given to the easy use of the pen, and seem never to have thought or imagined that a time would come when the smallest details of their life at Coös, would interest their successors. So they passed away, and only a very few of them left any written memorials. It is from the scanty remains of these that we gather a few particulars of their labors.

The first mechanics which come into a new settlement, are those whose trades supply the most immediate necessities of the settlers. People must have clothes, and shoes; next there must be carpenters and coopers, who can work in wood, and blacksmiths, who can work in iron.

The first houses being mere huts, which furnished a rude shelter from cold and storm, were soon replaced by more substantial habitations, made of logs. There was not much exercise in them for the skill of the carpenter. Log houses are warm, when well built, and when well cared for, will last many years. The last log house built by an actual settler, on newly cleared land, in this town, was abandoned about 1873, and was occupied for many years. The present generation of young people know log houses only by pictures. The first roofs were covered with bark, which soon gave place to shingles, split and shaved. As soon as there was a saw-mill to furnish boards, many conveniences of domestic comfort could be easily made. Before that, people learned to split boards from wide and perfectly straight blocks. The ancient desk in the town clerk's office, made by Col. Jacob Kent, is said to be of boards split and hewed with an axe. Shingles, until within about fifty years, were split and shaved. Being of selected timber, straight and clear of sap, they lasted about three times as long as the best of the sawed shingles do now. The shingles on the north side of the roof of the Johnson house at the Ox-bow, remained nearly a century before they were replaced. When framed dwellings are built, men who make the building of houses their trade, settle in a new community. There were good carpenters among the early settlers, and the pains-taking workmanship of some of the oldest houses, testifies to their skill.

Jaasiel Harriman, sometimes called Joseph Harriman, from whom Harriman's pond and brook are named, is said to have been the first blacksmith who came to Newbury. Tradition says that his first anvil was a particularly hard stone, laid on a stump. Harriman soon removed from town, but Joseph Chamberlin was a blacksmith, and carried on the trade for many years.

Nails were made by hand then, and for about forty years afterwards, as machines for making cut nails did not come into use till after 1800. In all the houses in this town built before 1805, the nails originally used were made by hand. Before machines were made for the manufacture of cut nails it was quite common, although, perhaps never in Newbury, for farmers to have a small forge built in a corner of their great kitchens, at which they made nails in stormy weather, or in the long winter evenings. The state records of New Hampshire show that bounties were paid men who could produce satisfactory evidence that they had made 100,000 nails within a specified time. Iron was first brought by boats up the river, from towns in Massachusetts, where it had been for many years mined and worked. Some years after the revolutionary war, iron of an excellent quality began to be made at Franconia.

Maxi Hazeltine, who lived at different times in Newbury, Haverhill and Bath, was a very skillful blacksmith, and some fine specimens of his workmanship, in the shape of locks and hinges, still exist. He made the lightning rod for the "old meeting-house" in 1788. When nails were thus made they were sold by number and not by weight, and hence came our modern designation of nails as four-penny, ten-penny, etc. There are many old bills extant in this town, which mention a certain number of nails.

On account of the scarcity of iron, and before machines were invented to work it readily, many utensils, now made of metal, were then made of wood. Consequently coopers were in demand, but now the trade has almost fallen into disuse. Wood for staves and hoops was plentiful, and there was a great demand for all the products of the cooper's art. It is related that John Mann, a cooper of Orford, made pails and tubs, which he drew to Newbury on a hand sled and exchanged for corn, about 1765.

We do not know how early brick were made in Coös, but certainly before 1770. Before that time chimneys were constructed of rough stone, laid up in clay. The first brick-yard is said to have been at the Ox-bow, where Mr. Doe's barn now stands, on the west side of the road.

We do not know when the first tannery was built at Coös. There was one in either Newbury or Haverhill as early as 1768, and one Eaton was a tanner in one town or the other, in 1777. Later tanneries are mentioned elsewhere.

CHAPTER VIII.

EARLY EVENTS.

THE FIRST ROADS.— PETITION FOR A ROAD TO PORTSMOUTH.— HARDSHIPS OF THE
SETTLERS.— TRAINING FIELD.— MILITARY COMPANY.— DARTMOUTH COLLEGE
IN HAVERHILL.— ORIGIN OF THE COLLEGE.— SITE SELECTED.— NEWBURY LANDS
PROMISED TO THE COLLEGE.— LOCATION AT HANOVER.— COUNTIES.

THE settlements at Coös had attracted attention all through
the older part of New England. It was considered a great
enterprise in those days, for Bayley, Hazen and their
associates to have pushed sixty miles into the wilderness. Their
example was followed by a great immigration. The roads opened
up the Merrimack and the Connecticut, caused the towns in the
upper part of both valleys to become settled several years before
they would otherwise have been. With Newbury and Haverhill as
their base of supplies, settlements began in the upper country.
Not only were Newbury and Haverhill becoming settled, but they
already had something to send to market, and having something
to sell, the inhabitants, naturally, wanted a road to get to market
upon. Then and for many years later, the only direct road to
Concord and Portsmouth, was by a way which could only be
traversed by pack-horses. It came up over the heights from Warren
by Tarleton pond, and entered Haverhill Corner by what is now
called the "old turnpike" into Court street. Those who travel over
that hilly road at the present day, may well wonder what its
condition could have been when it could only be traversed on
horse-back. It was not passable for an ox-cart for several years.
But in winter, when the snow lay deep, and streams and swamps
were frozen over, it was not so hard getting along. Even as late
as 1772, there were tracts of woods fifteen miles long on the road
from Concord to Haverhill, without a house or a clearing. We
may well understand why the settlers petitioned for aid in the
building of a road. Within a month after the granting of the

charter, Bayley and Hazen petitioned the General Court on behalf
of the proprietors of both towns, for aid in building a road from
Dover "through Barrington, Barnstead, Gilmantown, to cross
Winnepesocket Pond at the Wares, through Salem Holderness,
the Four Mile Township, and Romney to Haverhill."

On Christmas Day, 1764, Bayley again wrote, urging the
importance of a road as an aid to the settlement of the upper
part of the state, and said that since the previous spring, goods
to the amount of a thousand pounds, lawful money, had been
brought into Newbury, paid for chiefly in furs. The settlers
expected within a few years to have grain, live stock, wool, sugar,
butter, cheese, pelts and hides, pot and pearl ashes, to sell, and
would want roads to get them to market. Portsmouth was an
important market for some years, as it lay in a long-settled
community, and possessed much wealth and foreign commerce.
When Lake Winnipiseogee was frozen over, its straight and level
sheet of ice was a welcome change to the men and teams which
had traversed the hill roads for several days. It is probable that
in the second or third winter after the settlement people began to
go to market with their own teams.

The history of Hollis, N. H., tells us that during the first years,
many of the settlers at Coös returned to their old homes to spend
the winter, but this would not have continued after society had
become in some measure established. When there were schools,
and the ministrations of the gospel, so highly valued by our
forefathers, were had, people became more contented in their new
homes. There were people who in their old age told a younger
generation, that all which kept them in Coös was the terror of
the passage back to the places whence they came. Many a man
and woman came all the way from Concord alone, the woman
riding a horse and the husband walking by her side, carrying a
few indispensable articles, camping out under the trees at night.
Many cattle were lost upon the road by falling from precipices,
or by sinking in the swamps.

The first houses were mere shelters from the wind and storm,
without windows, lighted only by an opening in the wall which
must be closed to keep out the cold. Sometimes oiled paper was
used as a substitute for glass, which permitted a dim light to struggle
through. This state of things did not last more than two or three
winters, in this vicinity, but was repeated in newer towns for
some years, as they became settled. People hardly seem to have
minded much about their privations, but took them as necessary
preliminaries to the subjugation of the wilderness. But in their
old age, those of the pioneers who survived to tell of the settlement
of the country, to those who were young seventy years ago, were
wont to dwell with affectionate reminiscence upon those days of
privation. Seen through the long vista of years the harsh features

of the scene had faded away. Their fireside tales were less of disaster, of fear, and of want, of the danger from wild beasts and savage men, than of the many things that cheered them, of neighborly ministrations, of the kindly hands which had always a little to share, even in poverty, with their neighbor, of the intimacy which bound the few families at Coös in those early years. Their golden age was in the past, and the comforts of their later years had no zest like those first successes in their new homes. There is something in pioneer life which has a peculiar fascination, and there have been men and women who were never happy except when upon the verge of civilization, or a little beyond it.

Ever since the settlement of New England, military organizations had been carefully kept up as an aid to protection against the ever-dreaded Indian, and our forefathers in Newbury were not long in associating themselves for military defense. In the fall of 1764, the first military company at Coös was organized, and continued in existence down to the revolutionary war. The commission of Jacob Kent, as "Captain of an Independent Company of Militia, which Company is to consist of all the Inhabitants by Law obliged to do Military Duty in Haverhill and Newbury, in this Province respectively," is still preserved in the Kent family. It is dated September 6, 1764, and was one of the first, and certainly one of the very last military commissions granted by Benning Wentworth to any inhabitant of the New Hampshire Grants. The first training field was on the plain "east of Robert Johnston's tavern," where R. J. Hibbard now lives, and was so employed for many successive years.

Few are aware how near Haverhill once came to becoming the seat of one of the foremost colleges in the country, in which case the history of Newbury as well as of that town would be very different from what it is.

In 1740, Rev. Eleazer Wheelock was pastor of a Presbyterian church at what is now Columbia, Conn., and to eke out his small salary kept a private school. To this, in 1743, was admitted an Indian named Sampson Occum, who became a preacher of considerable fame, both in this country, and in Great Britain. In 1765, Joshua Moor, a farmer of Mansfield, Conn., gave a small property "for the foundation, use and support of an Indian Charity School," and additional funds for its maintenance were gathered in the colonies, and in England and Scotland. For many reasons it was desirable to remove the school to a new site, and Governor Wentworth secured its location in New Hampshire, and granted a charter for an institution of learning, which, in honor of the principal benefactor, was called Dartmouth College. But as yet no site had been fixed upon for its location, and Haverhill was one of several towns which made efforts to secure so desirable an acquisition, a place which seems to have been preferred by

Wentworth himself. The prominent men of Newbury and Haverhill at once saw what a great advantage it would be to Coös to have the new college located there, and engaged in the laudable attempt to secure it, with a public spirit which might well be emulated by the present generation. Newbury as a site was out of the question, as the town had passed under the authority of New York, by that time, but a spot was selected just above North Haverhill, on the plain, directly opposite the eastern extremity of the Ox-bow. They employed Elijah King, a surveyor, to lay out the land, and started a subscription paper, to which Jacob Bayley and John Hazen subscribed 1000 acres each, and Timothy Bedell 500 acres. Bayley went to Connecticut and laid their plans before Dr. Wheelock, and to Portsmouth to secure the cooperation of Wentworth. He gave a bond to convey to the college, if located in Haverhill, a part of the Ox-bow, which is now the east end of the farms of James Lang, Henry W. Bailey and Richard Doe. Colonel Asa Porter, a graduate of Harvard College, who had recently settled upon Horse Meadow, offered a valuable part of what is now called the Southard place. It was also agreed to sell to the college, at the cost of the improvements, the whole of the Little Ox-bow in Haverhill, on which was a framed house and a large barn. Dr. Witherspoon was appealed to, and responded with an offer of 1000 acres in Ryegate. In all about 6000 acres of the best lands in Newbury, Haverhill, Ryegate and Bath were promised. Mr. Powers exerted his influence with the people to promote the good cause. Gen. Bayley also agreed to put up the frame for a building two hundred feet long, to begin with. He went to Newburyport and enlisted the aid of the Littles in the enterprise.

Governor Wentworth wrote to Dr. Wheelock his express desire that the college should be located either at Haverhill, or at Landaff, which had been granted to it. There is nothing in our town or proprietors' records to show that any action was taken by either, in behalf of the college, but Haverhill took action by its proprietors in voting a mill lot to the college, in North Haverhill, and fifty acres of adjacent land. These negotiations lasted through several months, and the Haverhill party believed the prize already within their reach, when in August, 1770, they were astounded to learn that Wheelock had decided to locate the college at Hanover. The disappointment of the people at Coös was great, and so was it at several other places which had hoped to secure it. But his disappointment did not prevent Gen. Bayley from writing Wheelock a very kind letter.

We can only conjecture what might have resulted to Newbury had Dartmouth College been placed so near its bounds. In many respects the Haverhill location is superior to the one at Hanover. It has been said, and probably is in a measure true, that Dr. Wheelock feared the influence of certain men at Coös would weaken the personal control which he wished to establish over the institution. But there is no reason to suppose that he acted dishonorably in any way. It was certainly not the fault of the chief men of Newbury and Haverhill that Dartmouth College was not established in the latter town.

Before 1771, New Hampshire was all one county, and when its division into five counties was made, Vermont had become part of the province of New York, and Albany county extended its jurisdiction over all that is now Vermont. In 1768, Cumberland county, which comprised the present counties of Windsor and Windham, with part of what are now Rutland and Washington counties, was formed, and in 1770, Gloucester county, which was to include all the east half of the state, north of Cumberland, was erected.

On the 4th of April, 1772, an ordinance was passed by the Council of New York, directing the courts of Common Pleas and General Sessions of the Peace to be held at Newbury, on the last Tuesday of February and August, "during the space of seven years." The first session of the General Assembly of Vermont, 1778, merged the two counties of Cumberland and Gloucester into one, bearing the former name. But in February, 1781, what had before 1778, been Gloucester county was formed into Orange county, and Newbury was made the shire-town. In 1792, Essex and Caledonia counties and a part of Orleans county were taken from Orange county. In 1810, several other towns were taken from it, to form Washington county. The county-seat was removed to Chelsea in 1796.

Courts for Grafton county were established at Haverhill and Plymouth in February, 1773. Col. John Hurd, of Haverhill, was Chief Justice, and Col. Asa Porter, an Associate Justice. The first court-house stood upon the plain above North Haverhill, on the site which, a short time before, had been selected as the location of Dartmouth College.

In 1793, a court-house was built at Haverhill Corner, and the courts were held there, but the old building at North Haverhill was standing as late as 1820.

CHAPTER IX.

THE NEW YORK CHARTER.

WENTWORTH GRANTS.— THE KING'S ORDER IN COUNCIL.— NEW YORK OPPRESSIONS.— "THE GREEN MOUNTAIN BOYS."— GEN. BAYLEY IN NEW YORK.— THE NEW CHARTER.— ITS CONDITIONS.— THE GRANTEES.— DEED TO GEN. BAYLEY.— APPREHENSION OF INHABITANTS.— "DAVID JOHNSON vs. HARRISON BAYLEY."

IN the Proprietors' Book is the following: "May 1, 1765, The Proprietors met to consult what measures to take in consequence of the King's Proclamation Declaring the West Bank of the Connecticut River the Dividing Line between New Hampshire and New York." They voted, "To send Agents to New York to acknowledge their jurisdiction," and that "Jacob Bayley, Moses Little, and Benjamin Whiting should be the agents to act together or singly as occasion served, consistent with each other." This is the first mention on our records of a great controversy, which lasted twenty-seven years, out of which came the state of Vermont.

Up to the year 1764, the authorities of the province of New Hampshire had supposed the western boundary of their province to be a line drawn from the northwest corner of the province of Massachusetts Bay, to the southern extremity of Lake Champlain, thence up the middle of the lake to Canada. On the 3d of January, 1749, Governor Wentworth chartered the first township in what is now Vermont, that of Bennington. This action brought on a correspondence between Wentworth and the New York authorities, who claimed that the eastern line of their province, north of Massachusetts, was the west bank of Connecticut river. Wentworth insisted on his right, and in 1750, granted Halifax. In the next year he granted two towns, in the next, seven, and so on, till by the end of 1764, he had made grants of one hundred and eighty towns between Lake Champlain and Connecticut river. This in despite of the continual remonstrance of New York.

In 1764, the conflicting parties, by their agents, laid their claims before the King in Council. The representations, or the influence of the representatives of the New York claimants, proved the stronger, and on the 20th of July an order was made declaring the west bank of Connecticut river from the province of Massachusetts Bay to the 45th parallel of north latitude, *to be* the boundary line between the provinces of New York and New Hampshire, and a proclamation to that effect was issued. The people on the New Hampshire Grants were surprised but not alarmed at this order, which they regarded as merely extending the jurisdiction of New York in future over their lands, and had no apprehension that it could, in any way, affect their title to them. They continued to settle and cultivate their farms as before. But in the two little words *to be* lay a great deal of mischief. "The government of New York contended," says Mr. Slade, "that the order had a *retrospective* operation, and decided not only what should hereafter be, but what had always been, the eastern boundary of New York, and that, consequently, all the grants made by the Governor of New Hampshire were void." The settlers in the Grants were called upon to surrender their town charters, the authority under which they held their lands, and re-purchase those lands under grants from New York. "New grants of those who refused were made to others, in whose name actions of ejectment were commenced in the courts at Albany." These measures met with determined resistance, and a convention was called which chose Samuel Robinson to go to London, and lay their grievances before the King. Mr. Robinson plead their cause so well that a second Order in Council charged the Governor of New York, under penalty of His Majesty's displeasure, not to make any grant of any part of the land described in the report until further orders.

William Tryon became Governor of New York, and, notwithstanding this express prohibition, continued to make grants and writs of ejectment. When these actions came to trial, the settlers were not allowed to plead the royal order made to the Governor of New Hampshire, or of the charters made in pursuance of them, in defense. It is hard to see how Tryon dared to venture upon such a proceeding, in defiance of the royal order. But he was a tyrant by nature, and as the troubles between the crown and the colonies had begun, he was able to venture upon actions which, in quiet times, would have cost him his place. Besides, he was avaricious, and the fees, which were considerable, received for the charter of each new town, enabled him to accumulate wealth very rapidly. In addition to the fees, each charter secured to Tryon the five hundred acres in each township, which had been reserved before to the Governor of New Hampshire. Thus he might, in a few years, roll up an immense fortune, and there were plenty of people who did not scruple, under cover of law, to eject settlers and possess themselves of the farms upon which they had expended years of toil.

There was nothing left for these settlers on the Grants, who were forbidden any legal redress, but to resist by force, and officers sent to carry out the orders of New York were seized and "chastised with the twigs of the wilderness." This resistance was met by still further oppression, and armed bodies of troops were sent into the Grants to dispossess the settlers. They met with determined opposition, and military associations of men were formed, who called themselves the "Green Mountain Boys," whose exploits will forever be associated with the name of the state. Ethan Allen, Seth Warner, Remember Baker, and others, became very famous for their exploits, and impressed such terror that few New York constables had the temerity to venture into the region. A state of almost civil war raged in the southwest part of the state, which put a stop to its development for some years.

Of course all these things looked, and still look, very different from the New York side, and Mr. McMaster may not be far wrong in saying, "For seven years their treatment of each other would have delighted two Indian tribes on the war-path. Their history during this time is a shameful record of wanton attack and reprisals, of ambuscades laid in the dead of night, of murder, arson and bloodshed."

The settlers at Newbury probably felt no great alarm for several years, as they then had only little intercourse with the towns west of the Green Mountains. But reports came to them of the violent measures which were being taken against those who had not complied with the demands of the New York authorities. Blood had been shed; settlers had been ejected from their homes; families had been driven into the wilderness. Rumor magnified the danger, and the people believed that their farms were soon to be taken from them also. So great was the anxiety, that Gen. Bayley, after consultation with the principal men, went to visit the scene of the troubles and had an interview with Allen and the other leaders. Allen wanted Bayley to join with them in resisting the encroachments of New York. But he thought it best to go on to New York and find if there were any terms on which he could obtain security for the people at Newbury. They were, he said, few and poor, far from aid, and could not well, from their remoteness, act in concert with the people in the southwest part of the state.

It would appear that Allen and his associates were satisfied that it was Bayley's duty to secure peace if he could, as there is no record of any remonstrance made by them to the course taken by him and the proprietors of Newbury. At New York, Bayley met with Dr. Witherspoon, whose influence was great, and with Clinton, whom he had known in the French war. He was assured that he could obtain upon favorable terms a new charter, which would secure to the proprietors all the rights and privileges which they had held under Wentworth. With this assurance he returned home, and laid the matter before the proprietors, and was commissioned by them to return to New York, and act for them in the best manner he could. In New York, therefore, on the 6th of February, 1772, he presented a petition, as agent for the proprietors of Newbury, praying for the grant of a new charter. We have no account of the motives that were urged by Bayley and his advisers, before the Governor and Council, but he was successful. On the 19th of February, 1772, he received the new charter, which may be seen at the town clerk's office. It is written on parchment, and a leather case was made to keep it in. The specifications and conditions of the New York charter do not greatly differ from that which had been granted by Wentworth. It sets forth that the tract of land which had been granted to Jacob Bayley and others, by a charter from the Governor of New Hampshire, whose bounds had been fixed by the order in council made upon the petition of Benjamin Whiting and others, was re-granted to the following persons:

Jacob Bayley	John Taplin
Stephen Little	Samuel Stevens
Joseph Blanchard	Nathan Stone
Waldron Blaan	James Cobham
Joseph Beck	Samuel Bayard
John Wetherhead	William Williams
James Creassy	John Bawler
John Grumly	Marinus Willett
Richard Wenham	John Kelly
John Shatford Jones	James Downer
Samuel Bayer	John Keen
John Lewis	Crean Brush
John Taylor	

It reserved for religious and educational uses, and for the Governor's benefit, similar tracts of land to those which had before been allotted to them. The proprietors were to pay a yearly rent of two shillings and sixpence sterling on Lady Day of each year, for each hundred acres. There are regulations for the choice and succession of town officers, and for the preservation of the standing pine in the township. This charter is recorded in the Book of Patents, No. 16, page 195 etc., at Albany.

It would appear that New York laws required that there should be no fewer than twenty-five grantees to each charter, and so it runs to Jacob Bayley and twenty-four associates. It is not known, or supposed, that more than five of them—Bayley, Little, Taplin, Stevens, and Blanchard, ever visited Newbury, or had any interest here. The latter four may have been in New York when the charter was granted. The others were all New York men, who probably allowed their names to be used, upon solicitation. Some of them afterwards became active upon one side or the other, in the revolutionary war. It is a curious circumstance that a son of Marinus Willett, was, many years later, professor of Biblical Literature in the theological department of Newbury Seminary.

Before the charter was signed, the grantees gave a bond to the King of £2,000 New York currency, binding themselves to convey to each proprietor under the New Hampshire charter, a deed of the land he held, or was interested in, upon the payment of fees. On the next day but one, these twenty-four grantees executed a trust deed to Jacob Bayley of all their rights as grantees, he assuming the conditions of the bond. This deed was recorded in the office of the Secretary of State at New York, March 31, 1772, and delivered to Jacob Bayley. The latter kept the document in his own hands for sixteen years, when he left it with Col. Jacob Kent, the town clerk, to be recorded. The paper was mislaid, and was not found again until 1803, thirty-one years after its execution, when it was finally recorded here in Newbury by Isaac Bayley, town clerk at that time.

The expense of the New York charter is not known, but it is believed to have cost Gen. Bayley quite a sum. In his testimony before a master in chancery in a case which will be adverted to later, Isaac Bayley, his son, testified that a short time before the death of the General, a claim of between three and five hundred dollars came on from New York for the expense of procuring that charter, which the witness paid himself. Neither is it known what was paid to those who were influential with the council, but the fact that Clinton, about that time, became the possessor of six hundred acres of Newbury land, which had been ungranted, is suggestive. From that time until his death in 1815, Gen. Bayley, as agent under the new charter, gave quit-claim deeds to all who applied for them, who held lands under the old charter. But many neglected to do this, and after his death there arose, in some manner, a rumor, or apprehension, that the grantees of the new charter still held claim over those lands upon which a deed of confirmation had not been passed by him.

It is within the recollection of some yet living, that people sometimes acquired a title to their own farms, by allowing them to be sold for taxes, and then bidding them in, and paying the tax, received a deed from the collector. But in 1843, a decision of the Supreme Court settled the matter forever, in the following case. At the first division of one hundred-acre lots, No. 55 fell to John Hugh, who in 1770 sold it to Dr. Samuel Hale, who sold it to Col. Thomas Johnson in 1779. At the latter's death, it came into the hands of his son, David Johnson. Gen. Bayley died in 1815, but no administration was made of his estate till 1832, when Tappan

Stevens obtained license to sell whatever land still remained in his name. It was discovered that this lot was one of the few pieces of land left, upon which no deed had passed under the New York charter. After some years Harrison Bailey obtained a quit-claim deed from Mr. Stevens, against the latter's advice, giving his note for fifty dollars, hoping to make his claim good against Johnson. This he expected to do on the plea that the new charter made the old one void, and that no title under the New Hampshire charter was of any value, unless confirmed by a deed under the later one, and began to carry out his purpose by cutting timber upon this lot. Johnson at once secured an injunction to prevent Bayley from removing any more lumber, and commenced a suit for ejectment. The case was heard before a master in chancery, and came before the Supreme Court at the March term of 1843. The decision was, that Johnson's claim to the land upon which he had always paid taxes, never having been abandoned, was a legal claim, and that the New York charter only confirmed the one which had been given nine years before by Benning Wentworth. This ended all the troubles about the charters.

CHAPTER X.

"When we were under the King."

OF the period which intervened between 1769, and the breaking out of the revolutionary war, only a few scanty records survive. But from such annals of the time as have escaped destruction, we may obtain an idea of the condition of the people which may not be very far from the truth. By the year 1770, it is probable that the meadows and much of the upland or plain had been cleared, and the soil brought forth abundantly. A class of people had come into both Newbury and Haverhill, and made their homes, who possessed considerable education and some wealth. Several had seen service in the French war. Three or four possessed the advantage of a college education—Rev. Peter Powers, Col. Asa Porter, Col. John Hurd and perhaps others. Many were well known through the older portions of New England, and gave a certain rank and dignity to the new settlement, causing it to be known far and wide. Frame houses were replacing the log habitations of the pioneers. The towns above and below them were being settled, and, as Newbury and Haverhill had depended upon the settlements sixty miles away for their supplies, in their first years, so the new towns which sprang into existence after they had become established, came, in their turn, to depend upon Haverhill and Newbury, for seed and cattle with which to begin new farms. There was a ready sale for all the grain and cattle which could be spared. Mr. Whitelaw says that in 1773, the price of wheat was four shillings a bushel, rye about the same, and corn about three shillings. Beef and mutton were about two pence a pound, pork five pence, butter six pence, and cheese four and a half pence. Apple trees had been planted in both towns in the year 1763, and by 1770, their fruit had become quite plentiful, while as yet there were no trees in bearing elsewhere, nearer than sixty miles.

Workmen of all kinds had established themselves at Coös. Young men came, some unmarried, others whose families waited in the older settlements until homes could be prepared for them. Many of these paid for land in work. People were pleased with the country and persuaded their friends to come here and settle. Families which had been related, or previous to their coming, had been acquainted, saw intermarriages among their children. We do not know how many marriages were solemnized in Newbury in those days. Such occasions were generally made much of. The pension application of the widow of Thomas Hibbard, in 1837, mentions the guests at their wedding in 1772, by which it would seem that all the principal people in the neighborhood attended the ceremony. But it was no place for frail people, and the stern conditions of a new country, with the care of the large families of those days, bore hard upon women. Our annals make mention, only too frequently, of many wives who died within a few years after marriage. Only the strong survived, but those who reached middle age commonly lived beyond three score and ten.

We have no precise means of knowing the population of the town in those early days. Haverhill, by the census of 1767, returned one hundred and seventy-two inhabitants, of whom only one was over sixty years of age, and forty-three were under sixteen. In 1773, Haverhill reported three hundred and eighty-seven residents, all under sixty but one. There were at that time in that town one hundred and seven boys under sixteen. Probably Newbury had as many, and the united population was not under three hundred and fifty at the former, and at least seven hundred and fifty at the latter date. In 1767, Orford had seventy-five, and Hanover ninety-two inhabitants, who had increased to two hundred and twenty-eight, and three hundred and forty-two, respectively, at the latter date.

In 1770, a list of heads of families was returned to the Governor of New York, which gives us approximately the whole number of people who were here at that time, and is in many ways a valuable list.* They are as follows:

Jacob Bayley	Sylvanus Heath
Ephraim Bayley	Robert Hunkins
Frye Bayley	Samuel Hale
Samuel Barnet	Thomas Johnson
Jonathan Butterfield	Elihu Johnson
Thomas Chamberlain	Haynes Johnson

*Documentary History of New York, Vol. iv. p. 209.

Richard Chamberlin

Joseph Chamberlin

Abiel Chamberlin

Nathaniel Chamberlin

Uriah Chamberlin

Er Chamberlin

Ezekiel Colburne

Abner Fowler

Abner Fowler, Jr.

Jacob Fowler

Jonathan Fowler

John Foreman

Jonathan Goodwin

John Haseltine

Robert Haseltine

Daniel Hall

Enoch Hall

Robert Johnston

Jacob Kent

Nehemiah Lovewell

John Mills

Stephens McConnell

John Nutting

Peter Powers

Simeon Stevens

Ephraim Spafford

Gideon Smith

Levi Sylvester

John Taplin, Jr.

Daniel Tillotson

Moses Thurston

David Weeks

Ebenezer White

Joseph White

As families were large in those days, and there were many young men boarding in these forty-six households, an average of eight to each would give the population as about three hundred and fifty in 1770. All of these lived along the river road, or in houses reached directly from it. Mingled among the settlers, and not probably enumerated, were several Indians, who, although not worth much for steady work, gladly caught fish or hunted game, which they exchanged for the white man's grain and potatoes, and too often for the white man's fire-water. A few of them proved very efficient in the coming war.

In 1770, was the visitation of the army worm, whose ravages are so graphically described by Grant Powers. This pest destroyed all the corn and wheat between Northfield, Mass., and Lancaster, N.H. They were "millions upon millions," covering acres, completely hiding the walls and roofs of buildings over which they passed. About the first of September they suddenly disappeared, and not even the carcass of a worm was seen. Their description, as recorded by Rev. Dr. Burton of Thetford, tallies exactly with that of a similar pest which committed great depredations around Northampton and Springfield, Mass., a few years ago.

In that year or the next, settlements began in the back parts of the town, says Mr. Perry; a Mr. Kelly began to clear land not far from where the Union meeting-house stands at West Newbury. About the same time George Banfield, Edmund and John Brown began a clearing on the road that runs northwest from the school-house on Rogers's hill. Just before the revolutionary war broke out, Samuel Hadley and Samuel Eaton settled on the farm which Col. John Smith and his descendants have owned for more than a century. Up to this time all the settlements in Newbury were along the river, and the opening of farms in the back parts of the town was retarded and made difficult by the range of hills and broken country, of which mention is made in the first chapter of this volume. Had this tract, a mile or more in width, consisted of good farming land, gradually rising from the meadows, settlements would have spread back among the uplands. But the wilderness intervened, and the first settlers had to go four miles back from the river to find suitable land for farms. This range of hills has been a great obstacle to the development of the social, religious, and commercial prosperity of Newbury. The town has suffered by reason of the physical conditions which have prevented the establishment of a central village which should be a center of the common interests.

About the time that settlement began at West Newbury, Er Chamberlin commenced operations at Wells River. The ground now occupied by that village was then covered by a dense thicket of trees and fallen timber, through which Wells river found its way to the Connecticut by several channels. After a few years, having cleared some land, he built a dwelling-house and a sawmill. This part of Newbury is in the tract of five-hundred acres, reserved by Governor Wentworth, and called the "Governor's farm," to which, or a part of it, Chamberlin acquired a title.

The log meeting-house which had accommodated the settlers in their day of small things had now become too contracted, and perhaps the people felt that they were able to have something better. The warning for March meeting in 1770, contained an article "to see where the town will agree to meet on the Sabbath the spring and summer ensuing." There is no record of any action being taken, In 1771, the town was requested "to see if it will do anything to the meeting-house." No action is on record about that. It is believed that a meeting-house, or the frame of one, was put up in 1771, a little above Mr. Farnham's house on the "Little Plane," but the location being unsatisfactory, it was taken down, and set up opposite the cemetery on the Ox-bow. There is much obscurity connected with this building, both its location and uses have been the subject of dispute. At a special town-meeting, May 18, 1773, it was voted "to finish the meeting-house that is now raised, the owner giving in what is done." The meaning of this is not clear. It was also voted "that the notes that were given to build a meeting-house be given up, Captain Hazen giving up a bond which Haverhill took of Newbury for building the same." It is probable that these notes were payable in labor and materials, and that, the conditions being fulfilled, they were given up. The bond referred to seems to have been to the proprietors of Haverhill, as security for money advanced by them toward the building.

The old records of the county court tell us that in 1773, the August term of the Court of Common Pleas was held at Robert Johnston's Inn, and that, on the third day they adjourned to inspect "the building intended for a Court-House and jail in this township."

It goes on to say that the court-house was a frame building, with a tenement for the jailer, but the jail was of logs. The court seems to have been pleased with what had been begun, and appointed (whether to be raised by tax, or by subscription is not stated), £400, to finish the building in part, and for other purposes "not to be over nice in doing it." The court-house and the meeting-house, appear to have been one and the same structure, and is sometimes called in the town records "the State-House," sometimes "the Court-House" and once at least, as the "Meeting-house."

There is extant a bill of Thomas Johnson's against the town, dated February, 1773, in which some of the items are for shingles and for timber of various dimensions. If we suppose that this timber was used in the construction of the meeting-house, its size would seem to have been about forty feet by fifty, and fourteen feet in height of post.

The town had voted on the 14th of May, 1773, "To build a gaol 28x14 feet, one story high." Very little is known about this building, but it is believed to have stood back of the court-house, on the brow of the hill. One which was constructed in another part of the state about that time, was built with an inner, and an outer wall of logs, the space between the walls being filled with earth and stone. This jail seems to have been little used and fell into decay, as at the June term of Orange county court, held at Thetford in 1783, Abner Chamberlin, sheriff, represented that for want of a "Common Gaol" he was under an "intolerable burthen" for lack of a place to safely keep the persons committed to his custody. It was also represented to the court "that there is at Newbury in this county an ancient building which was formerly occupied by this county when under the jurisdiction of New York as a Common Gaol." The county records go on to say that it being represented that this "ancient building" might be obtained, the sheriff was directed to repair to Newbury, and agree with its owner for the building, which he was to put in proper repair for a "Gaol" at the expense of the county. It seems that it was put in proper repairs as in Spooner's Vermont Journal sometime in October of that year a reward was offered for the apprehension of one James Marston of Fairlee, who had "broken out of the Gaol at Newbury." This jail, or a successor, was standing and used for the purpose of a prison as late as 1794, for the autobiography of Mrs. Asa Bayley mentions it as containing prisoners in that year.

It appears that the meeting-house was not completed for some years, as on May 27, 1776, the town voted "To build pews and seats in the meeting-house on the vacant ground." It seems that some had built pews at their own expense, but that a large part of it was seated with benches, as the old one had been. It was voted "to sell the pews and seats when built, at vendue," and Ephraim Webster, Jonathan Goodwin, Jacob Kent, Simeon Stevens, and Dudley

NEWBURY VILLAGE—LOOKING SOUTHEAST.

[FROM NEWBURY SEMINARY SOUVENIR.]

Carleton were chosen a committee to perform the same. It was also voted "that Haverhill shall have opportunity to bid off the pews and seats if they shall think fit." This building, the second of the town and church, was used as a place of public worship about fifteen years, until the building of the "Old Meeting-house" in 1788. In it met the legislature for the October Session of 1787. It continued to be used for a court-house until the county-seat was removed to Chelsea in 1796, after which a school was held in it at one time. It was taken down by Col. Thomas Johnson in 1801, and the materials used in the construction of a building commonly spoken of as "the old court-house," which stood near the present schoolhouse in the Ox-bow district. The old people used to say that in this early meeting-house, the men were seated on one side, and the women on the other. On one occasion Mr. Powers was disturbed by some whispering which was going on, and, pausing in his sermon, rebuked the brethren for their unseemly conduct in the house of God. Whereupon one of the deacons arose, and informed the minister that the whispering was not on their side of the house, but came from the women's side. "Ah, then," sighed the good man, "it is of no use for me to say anything," and went on with his discourse. It will be observed that our forefathers never used the word *church* to designate the building employed for religious worship. It was always the "meeting-house," and the *church* was a body of religious believers which met in it.

The warning for town-meeting in March, 1798, contains the following article, "To see if the town will repair the Old Court-House, so that it may be of some advantage to the inhabitants, and take some method to do the same." It was voted, "To choose an agent to take care of the Old Court-House, and receive a lease of the land on which it stands from Gen. Jacob Bayley, for the use of the town and that Daniel Farrand, Esq., be agent." It was also voted "that said agent lay out a sum not exceeding fifteen dollars in making necessary repairs in and about said house." There is nothing to show that any work was done upon the building, and a few years later it was taken down.

Rev. Grant Powers tells us that, in one of the earlier years, the proclamation for Thanksgiving did not reach Newbury till after the appointed day had passed. The people, however, decided to keep the feast, but it was discovered that there was no molasses in the settlement. A supply being expected from Charlestown, the day was postponed to await its arrival, but, after waiting several weeks, the desired article not having appeared, Thanksgiving was kept without it.

CHAPTER XI.

BEFORE THE REVOLUTION.

A GATHERING of farmers and artisans at Inchinan, in far-off
Scotland, on the 5th of February, 1773, was destined to
have unforeseen consequences upon the future welfare of
Newbury. The most important event, affecting this town, between
its own settlement and the revolutionary war, was the colonization
of Ryegate. The latter town, settled by the Scotch, shares with
Barnet, the honor of being the only towns in Vermont established
by colonies from beyond the Atlantic. So large a proportion of
our Newbury people are of Scotch descent, that a particular
account of this enterprise seems to be a part of our history.

This Association, called the Scots American Company, which
is sometimes spoken of as the Inchinan colony, was formed for the
purpose of purchasing land for settlement in North America. At
this meeting, articles of agreement were signed, and two men,
James Whitelaw and David Allen, were selected to go to America,
and examine, and purchase land. Mr. Whitelaw, in after years
one of the most prominent men in Vermont, was well educated, a
surveyor, a man of rare judgment, business ability, and good sense.
David Allen was a farmer, then thirty-three years of age, Whitelaw
being only twenty-four. They left Glasgow March 25, 1773, and
arrived in Philadelphia on the 23d of May. They were met by
Alexander Semple, whom they had known in Scotland, who
introduced them to Rev. Dr. John Witherspoon. This gentleman,

whom we have mentioned before, was one of the most distinguished men of his time. He was born in Scotland in 1722, and became president of Princeton College, in New Jersey, in 1768. In 1776, he was a member from New Jersey of the Continental Congress, in whose debates he took a prominent part, and was a signer of the Declaration of Independence. He visited Newbury several times, and preached here more than once.

Dr. Witherspoon informed Whitelaw and Allen that he owned a township of land on Connecticut river, in the province of New York. This he would sell them, on favorable terms, but advised them to see all they could of the country before purchasing anywhere. Whitelaw and Allen visited the Mohawk valley, and crossed this state to Charlestown, N. H., where they saw Mr. Church who was joint owner of Ryegate, with Dr. Witherspoon, and arrived at the latter place on the 25th of June. They spent several days in examining the land, then returned to New York, and spent about three months in traveling through the middle and southern colonies, going as far south as the interior of North Carolina.

On the first of October they purchased the south half of Ryegate, for which place they set out, and reached Newbury November 1st, where they conferred with Gen. Bayley about their purchase. A week later, they were joined by James Henderson, a carpenter, who had been sent on by the Scots American Company. At that time there were no settlers in Ryegate, except Aaron Hosmer, who had moved across the line from Newbury. John Hyndeman, from Scotland, had already reached the place, and by the end of January they had two houses up and finished. In May there arrived from Scotland, David Ferry, Alexander Sym and family, Andrew and Robert Brock, John and Robert Orr, John Wilson, John Gray, John Shaw, and Hugh Semple. "In August, David Allen set out to return to Scotland and all the colonists attended him to Gen. Bayley's in Newbury, and James Henderson went along with him to Newburyport, where he took leave of him," says Whitelaw's journal.

In October came John Waddell, James Nelson, Thomas McKeith, Patrick Lang and family, William Neilson and family, David Reid and wife, Robert Gemmell and son, Robert Tweedale and wife, Andrew and James Smith. On the 22d, two weeks from their arrival, Andrew Smith died, the first death in Ryegate.

Mr. Whitelaw tells us that by the beginning of December all the settlers had houses built for themselves, on their lots, and were well pleased with their situation. Most of these first settlers located near what is now Ryegate Corner, or in the Whitelaw neighborhood, and as a great many Newbury people are descended from them, their names, and the time of their coming are here given.

In January, 1775, Mr. Whitelaw purchased of Jacob Bayley, all that part of lot No. 120 in Newbury, that lies north of Wells

River, in what is now Boltonville, with one-half the mill privilege, and James Henderson began to frame a sawmill and a grist-mill. In August, the frames of the grist-mill and the first framed house were raised, and about the beginning of October the frame of the sawmill was put up. On October 28th, the grist-mill was set going but the sawmill did not begin work until the middle of July afterward.

The first marriage was that of James Henderson and Agnes Symes, and eight days later that of Robert Brock and Elizabeth Stewart.

This settlement of Ryegate by the Scotch, was of untold value to Newbury, and the whole state, as it introduced into the New England community a new element, possessing to a remarkable degree the qualities of thrift, energy, and profound religious convictions. The early colonists were followed by others, many of whom settled in Newbury. The first comers endured many hardships, but they proved themselves equal to any emergency. The soil of Ryegate and Barnet is of the very best in Vermont, and in a few years the colonists attained a reputation as skillful husbandmen, which their descendants continue to hold at the present day.

Already, some of the first comers were selling out in Newbury, and moving into new towns. In 1770, Daniel, Jacob and Elijah Hall, with Jonathan Fowler, began to clear land in Barnet. In the same year the chief proprietors of that town engaged Col. John Hurd, of Haverhill, to build a saw-mill and a grist-mill, receiving for the work one hundred acres of land, which included most of what is now Barnet village. In 1774, settlers from Scotland, under the leadership of Col. Alexander Harvey, began to come into that town. Gen. Bayley, in a letter written about 1770, says that the whole country was rapidly filling up with a very desirable class of settlers, and what had, ten years before, been a howling wilderness was fast being turned into fruitful farms. All these newer settlements depended upon Newbury as their market and base of supplies. In 1774, or perhaps the year before, Col. William Wallace came from Scotland, and opened a store in a building which stood very near where Mr. Henry W. Bailey lives, on the Ox-bow. Before that time all purchases from the older towns had been made by people who went to the distant markets with their own teams, and brought up goods for their neighbors. Mr. Wallace was trained to mercantile pursuits, and soon did a very large business, which extended with the progress of settlements, almost to Canada.

Mr. Perry says that the first tavern in Newbury was opened by Col. Thomas Johnson after he built his new house in 1775, but it is certain that Col. Robert Johnston kept an inn three or four years before that time.

The first road in town was, of course, along the meadows, but the present river road does not follow the old path very closely. The earliest settlers built their houses upon the meadows, from which they were driven by the great freshet of 1771. Their first efforts as a community, were to make such roads as they could, by which the inhabitants could communicate with each other. A path followed by the settlers toward Bradford, gradually became passable for ox-teams, and was formally surveyed and accepted by the town, June 14, 1773. At the same time the road to Wells River was surveyed, and the record reads curiously to the present generation. "From a certain brook [the tavern brook at the top of Ingalls' hill] near the upper meadow near where a road was marked by the committee for highways, near where Nathaniel Chamberlin lives, thence northeast about four rods east of said Chamberlin's house as we have marked, having Mr. Er Chamberlin for our pilot, to Wells River, about fifty rods below said Chamberlin's mill." This road, through which the selectmen had to have a guide, turned off from the present river road at the top of Ingalls' hill, went west of the first range of low hills, and came out upon the present river road at the freight depot yard. The old houses along the river road were moved down from that ancient highway, which can still be traced. This river road, from Bradford to Wells River, was the only one laid out and accepted by the town, before the revolutionary war began.

Richard Chamberlin settled by the river bank, on Musquash meadow, and there kept a boat on which he ferried men and teams to and from the Haverhill side. The road which went to the "Old Ferry," and to the first bridge across the river, is the same which descends to the meadow, on F. E. Kimball's farm. It may be that some infringement upon his monopoly caused the town to vote June 1, 1773, "That Mr. Richard Chamberlin take care of the ferry that is by his house acrost Connecticut river and receive the profits of his ferrying for three coppers per man and horse, and one copper per man, and allowing the use of his boat on the Sabbath for Haverhill and Newbury to pass and repass to the public worship of God the boat being made good, this vote to continue till further orders." This was not the first trouble which Chamberlin had about the ferry. Some time, not far from 1770, Col. Asa Porter was granted, by the legislature, the sole right to keep a ferry within three miles, in a straight line, from the Little Ox-bow. He then resorted to some measure not now known, to make trouble for Chamberlin. In 1772, Thomas Johnson appeared before the General Court at Portsmouth, with a petition from Richard Chamberlin for a continuance of the ferry, "which he had maintained ever since the settlement of Newbury and Haverhill." A committee was appointed to investigate the matter, and found that Chamberlin's ferry was of convenience, and accomodated a different part of Haverhill from that of Col. Porter. So the petition was granted. The action of the town may have been in regard to some phase of the ferry dispute, but Chamberlin and his sons maintained and kept the ferry, until the bridge was built in 1796. At a town-meeting, May 28, 1776, it was voted, "To lay a rode to the river nigh the potash, through Dudley Carleton's land, after Haverhill has laid out a rode against it to the river." This is the farm road that passes through the Ox-bow.

By the year 1775, several frame houses had been erected. From what can be gathered, it is probable that there were, at that time, more houses between "the narrows" as the ridge where the railroad arch now is, was then called, and the mouth of Cow Meadow brook, than there are now. But life and property were exposed to dangers in those days, from which both have long been free. Children, and sometimes older people, were lost in the woods, and everybody had to turn out and hunt after them. Most farmers suffered an annual loss by the ravages of wild beasts. Wolves prowled about the farms, and were constantly on the watch for sheep. Men were living thirty years ago, who could remember when the sheep on the meadows had to be gathered at night into secure yards near the dwellings, to keep them out of reach of these rapacious but cowardly animals. Bears came down from the hills and devoured swine. One Sunday, three bears came into Col. Kent's house while the Colonel was gone to meeting, but out of respect for the day, or for the lady, who was alone, departed quietly.

One of Richard Chamberlin's girls, who had been across the river in her father's boat, returned in the dusk of the evening, and, after pushing the boat into the stream, found that an animal in the further end, which she had supposed to be a dog, was a young bear. The girl screamed, and the bear leaped over the side of the boat and disappeared with a great splash. Which was most alarmed, the girl or the bear, is not known. A bear seen on Kent's meadow was pursued by several men, who followed his trail out to what is now called Wallace Hill, where he took refuge in a great tree, completely screened by the dense foliage and gathering dusk. Desirous to secure his skin with as few bullet holes as possible, and, at the same time to save their powder, the men decided to watch the tree all night. They sent one of their number for refreshments, and kindled a fire, beside which they passed the night. In the morning they proceeded to dispatch the bear, but found that Bruin, desirous to keep his skin for his own use, had contrived to depart unheard in the darkness! The remarks of the hunters are not preserved.

In the early days, a bounty was placed upon the heads of bears, wolves, and wild cats. Bears were not so much dreaded as wolves. They were slower, and were not dangerous when not hungry. In winter they were out of the way. The meat of a fat bear was no

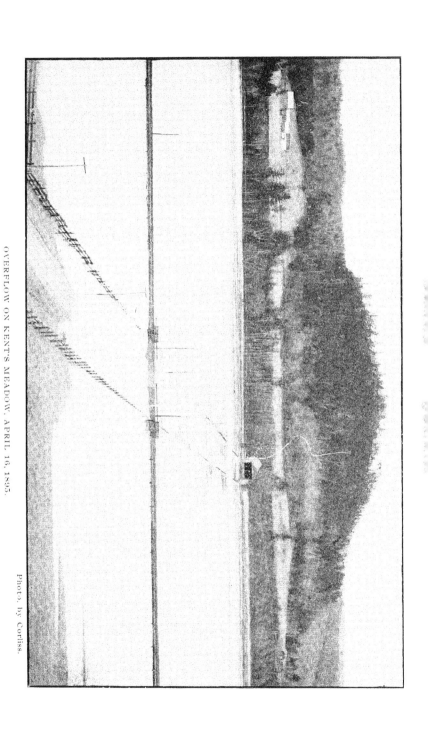

OVERFLOW ON KENT'S MEADOW, APRIL 16, 1895.

Photo. by Corliss.

bad substitute for pork, and not infrequently, when a bear had devoured a farmer's swine, the farmer took some satisfaction in eating the bear. Then there was his skin, and the bounty. Sometimes a cub was caught, and tamed, but who ever tamed, or wished to tame, a wolf? Bears have been seen in Newbury within a few years, and are not infrequent in the White and Franconia Mountains, but the wolf disappeared long ago. In 1776, a bounty of ten dollars was offered for the head of each wolf killed in town.

In those days everybody went to church. Haverhill people came on foot, crossing by Chamberlin's ferry at the Dow farm, or from the Porter place. Mr. Perry tells us that both men and women came on foot from Bradford, to the meeting-house at the Ox-bow. It was not uncommon for companies of a dozen or more to come, all the way from Ryegate Corner, on foot, carrying children, and when they came to Wells river, the women would take off their shoes and stockings and "trip it through as nimbly as the deer." We must not suppose, however, that it was altogether religious fervor which drew people to church. The natural desire of men and women to see each other, was fully realized, for the meeting-house was the one place in all the region where everybody saw everybody else, and where every bit of local gossip was in circulation. The long nooning was given up to argument and conversation. We may be sure that in the years which preceded the revolution, there was no place where the issues of the hour were more fully discussed, than at the meeting-house on the Sabbath, between services.

But there was an element in this, like every other frontier region, which was turbulent, and hard to keep under control. Offenses against morality were very common, not so much among the pioneers themselves, as in a floating class who are always found on the confines of civilization. Acts of violence were not unknown. In 1772, a tenant of Col. Little's, named Ryan, who lived on Musquash meadow, was ordered off the place by Dr. Porter of Haverhill, who had set up a claim to the land. Ryan refused to comply, and one night his house was broken open by a gang of lawless men acting under Porter's orders, the family was turned out of doors, the dwelling pulled down, and the farming tools thrown into the river. Next day, the Newbury people came to the aid of the Irishman, put him up a new house and sent a message of defiance to Porter. The appearance of Col. Little himself upon the scene, having opportunely come up to Coös, restored order.

During these, and many later years, Glazier Wheeler was engaged in the making of counterfeit money. He had a blacksmith shop in Newbury, but was associated with others, who had a log hut concealed in the woods in Haverhill, where they carried on operations. They made Spanish dollars of 1760, and crown pieces of 1752, and other coins, using an alloy containing one-half the legal quantity of silver. Later they became more bold, and still further adulterated the metal. Some of these coins were found in circulation as far south as Philadelphia, but several years passed before their real origin was suspected. Those who circulated them took good care not to have too many in one locality But in 1772, a man who was caught passing one of these coins, and had been under some suspicion before, to escape the gallows, implicated Wheeler, and officers were sent both from New York and from Massachusetts to take him, but he evaded capture. A letter from Governor Tryon to Governor Wentworth, brought a sharp reprimand from the latter, to the authorities of Haverhill, intimating that if the local constables could not suppress the unlawful proceeding, some more effectual means would be used. During a a number of years the good name of the region suffered from the operations of this gang. They conducted themselves with so much prudence that no evidence could be obtained to convict them. In 1772, Mr. John Munro was sent from New York to find out about Wheeler, and his whereabouts, and in a letter to Governor Tryon, on November 24th, graphically described Coös, as "a place up back of New Hampshire."

CHAPTER XII.

THE FIRST YEAR OF THE REVOLUTION.

MR. PERRY says that the frame of Col. Thomas Johnson's house on the Ox-bow, was raised the day the news of the battle of Lexington reached Newbury, and that on the same evening Nehemiah Lovewell, Peter Johnson, and Silas Chamberlin started for the seat of war. That was probably about the end of April, 1774. Our town records are strangely silent upon the subject of the revolutionary war. No one, who will take the trouble to go through the pages of the first volume of town proceedings, which record the actions of the town, from 1774, to 1783, would suppose that anything particular was going on in the world, least of all, that the town clerk, Col. Jacob Kent, was himself acting no small part in a great revolution. The actors in those scenes seem never to have imagined that they were doing anything remarkable, and have left very little to guide us during that long struggle. Our chief authorities for that period are Gen. Bayley's correspondence, as preserved in the New Hampshire state papers, the Documentary History of New York, the Washington correspondence, and "Governor and Council." There also remain certain letters of Col. Charles Johnston, Gen. Moses Dow, and Col. Ebenezer

Webster. The journal of Col. Frye Bayley, in 1776, the fragmentary diary of Col. Jacob Kent, the journal of Col. Thomas Johnson while a captive in Canada, and a few letters of his, give some idea of the times. The historian of Dartmouth College has given us many letters from the treasures of that institution. The state of New Hampshire has published all its revolutionary rolls and other papers. Our state has yet to do a similar work. Many years ago, David Johnson, Esq., with reverent care, copied all the correspondence of his father, and Gen. Bayley, which could be found. There are many unpublished papers in the possession of the New Hampshire Historical Society, which have been of great aid in the preparation of this history. From all these sources, aided by what can be locally obtained, some idea of what the revolutionary war was, here in Coös, has been prepared. These chapters should have been written a century ago. But better now than never.

The settlements at Coös were exceedingly patriotic. Even the Scotch settlers of Ryegate, fresh from Great Britain, were for the American cause, to a man. There were, in all the settlements, many who had seen service in the French and Indian war. It was reported to New York, in 1773, that nearly all the heads of families in Mooretown, now Bradford, had "been out" in that struggle. Of the Newbury men, the following are known to have served in one or more campaigns of that war: Jacob Bayley, Thomas Chamberlain, Richard, Joseph, and Abiel Chamberlin, John Foreman, Jonathan Butterfield, Jacob Kent, Simeon Stevens, John Mills, Robert Johnston, Abner Fowler, Nehemiah Lovewell, John Taplin, and John Taplin, Jr., Jonathan Goodwin, Robert Hunkins, and John Hazeltine. There were probably others. The value of their experience, especially that of Jacob Bayley, Jacob Kent, John Foreman, and Robert Johnston, was very great.

Haverhill was equally fortunate in having men of experience and tried courage. John Hazen was now dead, but Charles Johnston, Timothy Bedell, and others, had military experience, and some knowledge of Canada.

Before the winter of 1774–5 had passed, Councils of Safety and Correspondence had been formed, and the sentiments of every man were known. But the country was in a defenceless state. Although all the able-bodied men knew something of military discipline, there were few weapons. On January 30, 1775, the town of Haverhill voted, "to furnish the town with a sufficient stock of powder, flints, and lead as soon as may be." The Coös country lay in the direct pathway from Canada to Massachusetts, and was most likely to suffer from a northern invasion.

In June, Capt. Charles Johnston wrote the provincial congress: "As to position of defense, we are in difficult circumstances; we are in want of both arms and ammunition. There is but very little, or none worth mentioning—perhaps one pound of powder to twenty men, and not one-half our men have arms. We look upon ourselves as in imminent danger of the enemy, and in no capacity for defense."

One special cause for alarm is given in a letter from President Wheelock, written from Hanover, March 22d, to Governor Trumbull:—"Your Honor well understands what a feeble and defenseless state these frontier towns are in, how near to the Canadians, and what an easy prey we may be to such a northern army of savages, etc., as we are threatened with. We hear of preparations making for an invasion, and that some of the warriors among the Indians were in high spirits to engage on the one side or the other, in the present controversy; and if they shall not be secured in our interest, they will likely join on the other side."

General Bayley, who had by his humane treatment of the Indians acquired a great influence over them, invited many of their chief men to come to Newbury, where he engaged several of them to act as scouts, and keep watch through the woods toward Canada.

On the 23d of June, 1775, Gen. Bayley prepared an address to the Northern Indians, which is here given in full.

"NEWBURY, Coos, June 23, 1775.

The present war is only between the King and a part of the Lords, and America. The Lords say all Americans shall become slaves, or servants to them shall plow no more than they say; eat nor drink nor war nor hunt but only by their leave; shall not kill deer, moose, beaver, or any other thing, but by their consent. Americans say they will, and that the King, by the Lords advice has sent redcoats to kill us, if we will not be subject to what they say. And we have thirty thousand men, with guns, great and small, to fight in our defense; we only want to live as we have lived, here-to-fore. We do not want to fight if they would let us alone.

You are as much threatened as we are, they want you to kill us and then they will kill you, if you do not serve them. Dreadful wicked men they be; they do not think there is any God that will punish them bye and bye. If you have a mind to join us, I will go with any number you shall bring to our army, and you shall each have a good coat, blanket, etc., and forty shillings per month, let the time be longer or shorter. If you will go to *Canada*, and gather what intelligence you can, and bring it to me, at any place you shall set, I will meet you myself, and pay you well; further if you are any way afraid of the Regulars, you and all those tribes shall have protection here, as we will fight for you in your own country if wanted; but if you, or the French or any other Indians fight against us, we know your country and shall be troublesome to you. You know how we could fight, last war. But I know you will be friendly, and you may depend upon us. We will pawn all we have for the most strict observance of any agreement with you. We are all now heathen, and we will be so with you, and we must all meet before God in a little while.

JACOB BAYLEY."

When, where, and to whom, this unique address was delivered is unknown. In the possession of the New Hampshire Historical Society, is a paper, drawn up by Col. Timothy Bedell, which is somewhat similar, and on the back of it is a statement that it was

*New York Archives, 4th series, Vol. II., Col. 1070.

probably delivered at a Council held on the Saint Francis. Perhaps Bayley's address may have been presented at that, or a similar gathering. It probably had some effect, as it is certain that the Indians gave Coös very little anxiety during the war. Its entire authorship is equally uncertain. The sentiments are Bayley's, and the general form of the address, but the style bears no resemblance to that of his letters which are extant. It is probable that his first draft was revised, and received its final polish from some abler hand, perhaps that of Rev. Peter Powers.

On the 15th of June, a letter from the New York Provincial Congress came to Newbury, desiring that a delegate should be sent from Newbury to attend that body, and enclosing articles of association which it was desired that all should sign, in behalf of a Congress of all the colonies. A town-meeting was called, and Jacob Bayley was chosen, "to send to York." No copy of the signatures to the association is to be found, but it is believed to have been signed by nearly all the men in Newbury. Bayley did not, however, attend the Congress, but, on the 29th of June, wrote to that body, giving as his reason for non-attendance, the state of the frontier, and the alarming intelligence from Canada. This letter, which is quite long, says that he could raise two or three hundred men for the defense of the frontier, from the neighboring towns, but that they needed at least two hundred guns, powder and flints. The letter was sent by Col. Harvey of Barnet.[*]

On the 16th of May, a company of minutemen was formed, of which Thomas Johnson was captain, Simeon Stevens, lieutenant, and Joseph Chamberlin was ensign. This company numbered forty-six men, six of whom were from Barnet. Later, it was reorganized, and numbered fifty-one, of whom nine were named Chamberlin. The records at Montpelier show that the men were in service from six to twenty days, and received two shillings a day. It is not probable that all the men were in service at once, but that they were called upon to stand guard, or go on scout, in turn, as many as were needed. It was eleven years before they were paid.

The common danger that the river towns were in, and the necessity that there be a commanding officer over all the militia, was now apparent. The military experience, ability, and patriotism of Jacob Bayley were well known and fitted him for the command, and it being intimated to him that it was the general desire, he was, later, appointed brigadier general by the New York authorities. The following paper, on the last page of the Proprietor's book, is not dated or signed, but is in his handwriting, and was probably written about the end of 1775. It

*Am. Archives, 4th series, Vol. II., Col. 1134.

seems to be the first draft of a military order to the companies along the river:

"Whereas it appears that many of the People on this River being Destitute of a Regular Command Desire that I should take the Command as Brigadier Gen'l and whereas it is of Necessity that it should be known who are ready for Action and who will command the several Regiments and Companys, you will therefore call upon each Colo on each side of Connecticut River, as far as the line of Massachusetts Bay for a return of their several Companies, specifying those who command and the number ready to turn out at a minute's warning and to order each Colo to make their Regiments ready for Action. You are not to regard what state or Convention the officers are commissioned from, and that each Company have an Alarm Post appointed and in case of an alarm to wait at the Post for orders, as it is not known where the Enemy will attack. Doubtless the Enemy will make a feint in some place of which I could wish People will be aware. I could wish each man will equip themselves with snow-shoes by the returns to be made to me or Colo Bellows, or Hunt, and whereas it is my opinion that if the Enemy make an attack on us this winter it will be at Otter Creek and Coos, the Reg't below Windsor and west of the River, if an attack is made to march to Rutland, Windsor, and Hartford, to look well to the Passages into the upper part of Windsor and Hartford."

It will be remembered that several months before the actual breaking out of hostilities, there was an alarm of an immediate invasion from Canada in order to put an end, at once, to the disaffection in New England. This was the first of many alarms which vexed the frontier during eight years.

It is probable that there were sixty or seventy men in Newbury, between the ages of sixteen and sixty, able to bear arms. A military company was organized in Bath. A few of the men had guns, the rest carried cornstalks to deceive the Indians.

During the entire war, parties of scouts, numbering from two or three to a score, were constantly patrolling the woods, watching the mountain passes, the river fords, and the islands at the outlet of Lake Champlain. Some journals of these expeditions are still preserved.

Bayley seems to have succeeded in getting some ammunition for the town, as a receipt from Alexander Harvey of Barnet, about the end of November, is for two pounds of flints from the Newbury stock. On the 15th of July, Col. John Taplin wrote to the president of the New York Congress, that "the country seems well united and the people fixed to one another in the cause of liberty." There were, however, a few men in Coös who had little confidence in popular government, and supported the cause of the Crown. The most prominent were, Col. Asa Porter, and Andrew S. Crocker, of Haverhill. The former, from his ability, his education, and his wealth, was particularly dangerous, and his house was believed to be the resort of the leading tories, and emissaries from Canada. A road near North Haverhill, and a piece of woods close by it, are often called the "tory road," and the "tory woods," to this day.

In the first week of September, 1775, several men from Newbury marched from Haverhill with a part of Bedell's regiment which was ordered to Canada. It is not known who they all were. Frye Bayley, and John Foreman were among them. The former was an ensign. It is probable that one of the Chamberlins and John Seagel were of the company. These men returned before winter. The invasion of Canada, which resulted so disastrously to the American cause, promised success for some time, and the belief was entertained that the whole of Canada would join with the colonies, and declare independence of Great Britain. But the American forces were repulsed at Quebec, and the advantages which had been gained were soon lost. Four hundred men of Bedell's regiment were disgracefully surrendered at a place called The Cedars. The American army was forced to retreat from Canada, and the condition of the troops was unfortunate. To prevent the total destruction of the army, troops were sent from the southern part of New England to join the forces and cover the retreat. The first men were sent by way of Charlestown, and the military road which was opened across the Green Mountains during the French war.

Washington being desirous to learn if a shorter route to Canada could not be made, Gen. Bayley, then with the army before Boston, informed the commander-in-chief that a much shorter road lay through the Coös country, and that he could find men who could go through the wilderness and mark out a road. Capt. Thomas Johnson was selected as the man to undertake this enterprise.* He was to take two or three men, and an Indian guide, and mark a road by blazed trees to St. Johns, and when the first troops reached that place he was to return, and make report of the time, and points of compass. He took with him Frye Bayley, Abial, and Silas Chamberlin, and John McLean. They left Newbury on Tuesday, March 26, 1776, the advance guard following several hours behind. Johnson's journal says that they "lodged that night with the last inhabitant"—probably in Peacham. They marched on snow-shoes, the snow melting, and the rivers breaking up, and they had to wade through the streams which they reached. On Sunday, the party reached Mr. Metcalf's on the Missisquoi, whence Frye Bayley returned to report progress. On Friday they reached St. Johns, about one hundred miles from Newbury. The expenses of the party amounted to twenty pounds, which was paid in 1786, as appears in a certificate at Montpelier. Along the path which had then been marked out, several regiments passed to Canada on show-shoes.

It was found that troops could be sent to Canada by way of

---

*Johnson's Journal. Johnson to Maj. Stark, 1804. Johnson in Spooner's Vt. Journal in reply to charge of Toryism.

Coös, about ten days quicker than by way of Lake Champlain, and this fact led the Continental authorities to begin a military road from Newbury to St. Johns.   James Whitelaw and a party of men were sent in advance to make a location, who were followed by Gen. Bayley, with sixty men and many teams, to cut down trees, build bridges, and lay corduroys across the swamps.   The road was partly completed to a point about six miles beyond Peacham, when scouts came in with tidings that Canadian troops were advancing down the path which Johnson had marked out, to capture the party who were building the road, and destroy all the settlements on the river.   Bayley and his men made a hasty retreat, and the road was abandoned.   Bayley was apprehensive for the safety of Whitelaw and his men, who were some distance in advance of the main body.   But the wily Scotchman was not caught napping, and made good his retreat, striking through the woods to the Connecticut river at Barnet.   On the 24th of June the committees of safety from Bath, Haverhill and Bradford met at Gen. Bayley's house, to concert measures for their common protection.   Messengers were sent to warn all the people up the river.   The alarm was great, and fear magnified the small party of Canadians who had actually followed Johnson's trail to the borders of Peacham, into an army.   Nearly all the settlers at the Upper Coös came to Haverhill, and some continued their flight to Concord.   The few inhabitants of Peacham came to Ryegate, and all Ryegate and Peacham came together to Newbury.   Joseph Chamberlin was sent with a scout of ten men to discover the whereabouts of the invading army, but finding no trace of them, returned.   The alarm soon died away, and the Ryegate and Peacham people found their homes undisturbed on their return.

In May, Capt. Frye Bayley was sent to the army in Canada, with dispatches from Washington, and remained with it until it reached Crown Point.   His journal, still preserved in this town, gives us a vivid picture of the sufferings of the men, and the difficulties which attended the retreat.   It will be found later in this volume.

With the return of the army from Canada, and the transfer of the seat of war to the Hudson river the immediate danger of invasion passed away.   It was succeeded by an alarm of a still more terrible nature.   Some soldiers returning by way of Coös, were taken with the smallpox.   A building was erected for their accommodation, which stood in the woods above the first railroad crossing north of the Newbury depot, and some portions of it remained when the railroad was built, in 1848.   A daughter of Col. Frye Bayley, who died in 1863, said that several men died there, and were buried in the woods.   Their names are unknown.

CHAPTER XIII.

The Revolution—Continued.

ON the 5th of July, 1776, the Committees of Safety from all the towns in the valley, met at College Hall in Hanover, to devise measures for the protection of the frontier. Gen. Jacob Bayley, of Newbury, Col. Charles Johnston, of Haverhill, and Col. Peter Olcott, of Norwich, were chosen a committee to direct and order the affairs of the Newbury department. Two hundred and fifty men were raised, under the command of Capt. Woodward, of Haverhill, to "scout and guard," with headquarters at Newbury.

The disasters which had befallen the army in Canada, had caused the tories in this part of the country to believe that the cause of liberty was about to fail, and they began to concert plans for the overthrow of the new institutions. A few men who had hitherto been counted upon the American side, now allied themselves with the supporters of the crown. Communications were opened with the Canadian authorities. Some of these messages were intercepted by Bayley's scouts. It was determined by the committees at College Hall to strike a blow at these enemies to the public safety.

In November, 1775, Major Robert Rogers came into Newbury under circumstances which excited alarm to all who knew the character and present relations of the man. He had chosen a time when Bayley, Kent, and others who might know him were away, and made himself friendly to the American cause, mingled intimately with the people, and found out all he could about the resources of the country. It was discovered that several Indians were lurking in the woods at the same time, and that Rogers had visited Col. Porter, and other prominent tories. Bayley returned somewhat unexpectedly, and knowing that Rogers held a command in the British army, sent to arrest him, but he had made his escape, disguised, it is said, as an Indian.

One of the first acts of the session at College Hall, was a resolve to strike a blow at the tories. On the 7th of August, Col. Porter, Col. John Taplin, David Weeks, and Jacob Fowler were arrested and brought before the Committee of Safety. After a hearing, Taplin, Weeks and Fowler were allowed to go on bail, but Col. Porter was sent to Exeter under guard, and confined in jail for some time. These resolute measures alarmed the tories, and suppressed, for a time, their machinations.

In September, 1776, several men from here enlisted in regiments from other states, which were sent to the Hudson. One of these was Peter Powers, the minister's eldest son, who died at New York on the 30th of that month, and is buried there.

In December, a number of men who belonged to Chase's regiment were sent to New York, to re-inforce Capt. Joshua Howard's company, in Gilman's regiment.

It will be understood that during the whole war, there were frequent calls for men on short terms of service for particular purposes. Many of the militia were upon the rolls of Bedell's regiment, and remained at home, except when called into actual service, when they were transferred to some company on the field. In Capt. John G. Bayley's company, "guarding and scouting," in Col. Peter Olcott's regiment, from April, 1777, to May, 1779, there were eighty-five men, and their terms of actual service, in that company, ranged from twenty days to two months and nine days, during the two years. But in the course of those two years, the great majority, perhaps nearly all, of that company, served in one or more campaigns, as members of other companies and regiments, in actual service. Several of them, like Nehemiah Lovewell, Robert Johnston, Frye Bayley and Jacob Kent, were enrolled as privates in the "home guards" (to borrow a modern phrase) while, at the same time, holding commissions and executing them, as officers, in regiments on the field. This dual connection renders the computation of the actual service of many revolutionary soldiers almost impossible.

At the beginning of 1777, the British ministry determined to crush the insurrection in America in one decisive campaign. Gen. John Burgoyne was ordered to assemble an army in Canada, advance by way of Lake Champlain and the Hudson, while Gen. Clinton was to ascend the river from New York with an overwhelming force, and thus sever New England from the other colonies. The campaign was well planned, and had it been as skilfully carried out, the war might have ended. It was known months in advance that great preparations were going on in Canada for an invasion of New England. It was believed at first, that the expedition was intended to march to Boston by way of Coös. The Committee of Safety sent urgent messages to the authorities imploring men and ammunition.

On February 26, Gen. Bayley wrote to the president of the New York Provincial Congress as follows,—

"NEWBURY, February 26, 1777.

Sir—We have lately sent scouts to St. Francis and Missisquoi, and find by the former that the enemy in Canada determine to survey the passes to this country, at least soon. From Missisquoi that General Carleton has confined Mr. Metcalf to Montreal, who has moved his family and moveables from Missisquoi. I suppose that Lieut. Hoisington's men should be ordered to duty under some commander. I am continually employed in the Service, but have no Pay, and am willing as long as I can live without Begging—the time is now come.

I had in Pay 60 men from the 1st of July to the 10th of September at ten Dollars per month and supplied them, which were the only soldiers in this Quarter. During this time I was Desired by Committees of this and Neighboring States to do this Service (they were men I had hired to make the road to Canada.) I must Desire you to consider my Case—and grant me relief by paying the roll offered you by my clerk, Mr. William Wallace, as I cannot do justice to the American Cause without. The militia are now on their march from this County. I am obliged to advance Marching Money and I am

Gentlemen, Your Most Obedient Humble Servant,
JACOB BAYLEY*."

On the following day, February 27, says Col. Frye Bayley's journal, "an express came from Gen. Schuyler to take every fifth man in the militia to go to Ticonderoga." This was on Saturday. On Monday the militia met at Robert Johnston's inn, where the draft was made and on the next day the men were mustered in and set out. No record of their names can be found.

On the 28th of May, the Council of Safety, at Kingston, N. Y., sent a message requesting Gen. Bayley to order a company of rangers from Gloucester and Cumberland counties, to march to Kingston, in Ulster Co.† On the 14th of June, Bayley wrote to the Council, in remonstrance to this order, as stripping the frontier of men and arms, which were much needed for present defense, and there was no money to advance to the men.‡ On the 29th of June, Burgoyne arrived at Ticonderoga, with a brilliant army of eight thousand British and Germans, besides many Canadians and Indians. He there issued a proclamation in which he promised rewards to those who joined his army, protection to those who remained quiet, and extermination to all who resisted. He threatened to unloose all the northern

---

*Documentary Hist. of N. Y., I. 641.
†N. Y. Archives, I., p. 153.
‡*Ibid, p. 156.*

Indians, many of whom had joined his army, upon the settlements. This proclamation was circulated throughout the country. On Sunday morning, July 7, one of them was found nailed to the door of the meeting-house in Newbury. In many places, the tories were exultant, and gave people much trouble. In Strafford and vicinity about thirty went over to the enemy. But in Coös the vigorous measures which had been taken by the Council of Safety had over-awed the disaffected. Joseph White and his son and perhaps one or two more, disappeared for a few months, and were supposed to have been in the enemy's camp. The threats of an Indian war, instead of terrorizing the people, produced the opposite effect, and aroused all New England to resistance. But it took time to gather the militia and meanwhile Burgoyne pursued his way unchecked to the Hudson. On the 6th of July, Ticonderoga was evacuated, and all its stores fell into the hands of the enemy, and the retreating forces were routed with great loss at Hubbardton. Skenesborough, now Whitehall, fell, and the British reached the Hudson on the 29th of July. Fort Edward was abandoned, and the Americans fell back to Saratoga, and then to Stillwater, at the mouth of the Mohawk.

Burgoyne believed himself secure and expected in a few days to form a juncture with Clinton. But being in need of supplies, he sent Col. Baum with two pieces of artillery and eight hundred British and Hessians, with a body of Canadians, Indians and tories, to sieze the military stores at Bennington. We all know the result of that expedition. The records are so incomplete that we do not know how many Newbury men were at Bennington. Nehemiah Lovewell was there, and probably one or two of the Chamberlins, as some of that family usually contrived to be on hand where any fighting was going on. Bayley was at Castleton on that day, but arrived soon after. So did others from Newbury, who helped guard the prisoners. Dr. Samuel White served as surgeon, but is not believed to have reached the field till the next day. Several men who fought at Bennington settled here afterwards, notably Thomas Mellen, whose narrative of the battle is one of the best accounts of it which we have. There were also some men from Newbury, who were in Capt. Thomas Johnson's company at Mount Independence, and who enlisted in other companies, and did service later in the campaign. Their muster roll is lost.

The shortness of the terms of service for which many, perhaps most, enlisted, was a great source of weakness to the American cause all through the war. Many of the New Hampshire men enlisted for only a month, their terms expired after the battle, and the men went home to secure their crops. Some of them returned to join the army at Saratoga.

6

The battle of Bennington has been considered the turning point of the revolutionary war. But work remained to be done before the capture of Burgoyne was accomplished. Money was very scarce, and the means for the equipment of the army were furnished by private citizens. John Langdon, of Portsmouth, pledged all his property. Jacob Bayley, of Newbury, mortgaged his farm. Hardly a town in New England, settled at that time, but has its patriotic incident connected with the Burgoyne invasion.

Mr. Perry says that nearly all the able-bodied men of Newbury went to the seat of war. Col. Thomas Johnson, who was serving as aid to Lincoln, was in command of most of the Newbury men at the capture of Ticonderoga and Mount Independence. After the surrender of the latter, Col. Johnson was in command of an escort of troops which was to take about one hundred prisoners to Charlestown, which he did, treating them with great kindness. Among the officers was a Mr. Spardain, whom he afterwards met while himself a prisoner in Canada.

Meanwhile, the investment of Burgoyne was proceeding and troops were being hurried to Saratoga. Gen. Bayley was active and untiring in his efforts to secure men and supplies. On the 21st of September, he wrote from Castleton, "We request that all the militia above Charlestown and eastward march with horses, bringing flour and beef to serve one month. I think every man of spirit will turn out. Pasturing good and plenty." Col. Jacob Kent was sent to Coös to engage the militia. His diary says that his regiment left Coös on September 25th, Thursday, reached Pawlet on Monday, and Saratoga on Wednesday, September 31st, and was present at the surrender of Burgoyne, October 17, 1777. It is not certain how many Newbury men were at Saratoga. The muster roll of Capt. Frye Bayley's company is given in the Appendix. This company served from September 23d, to October 27th. Their travel was two hundred and seventy miles.* It does not appear that any men were lost from this company. It did good service, however. One of its exploits was the capture of fifteen boats loaded with supplies for Burgoyne's army. These boats had passed down the Hudson, and had moored for the night on the further side of the river. Bayley determined to capture the boats, and called for volunteers. Bartholomew Somers, of Ryegate, and a man from New Hampshire, swam the river, secured one of the boats unobserved, and re-crossed the river. Bayley and as many men as could get into the boat, crossed the Hudson, and found that the men in charge, suspecting no danger, had gone on shore to eat their suppers. The boats were secured without alarm being given, and were all safely brought to the American side of the river.

---

*Muster roll at Montpelier.

Had this history been written, as it should have been, seventy years ago, it would have collected many personal reminiscences of that campaign, from the lips of men who marched from Newbury, and had their part in that memorable affair. David Johnson gathered a few anecdotes in his lifetime, which he transmitted to Rev. Grant Powers. One of them, the exploit of Ephraim Webster, and another, in swimming across Lake Champlain with dispatches, is well known, and is mentioned elsewhere in this volume. This is not the place to give a detailed account of the expedition of Burgoyne. Our narrative mainly concerns itself with those who were left behind. It is said that at one time there were but six able-bodied men left in Newbury, and these included the minister and Dr. Smith. The women did the field work, and had to bear the suspense as they could. It must have been ten days before the great news came to Coös, how that Burgoyne had been hemmed in at Saratoga, and had, after fighting bravely, been compelled to surrender.

The battle of Saratoga is considered by historians, as one of the decisive battles of the world. Before that event it was believed that the Americans would struggle to little purpose against Great Britain. But in a few months it was known all over Europe, that the great expedition of Burgoyne had met with disaster, and that, in the backwoods of America, a British army had been compelled to deliver up its arms. We all know what followed. It should be a matter of local pride that in that remarkable series of events, the men of Newbury bore a commendable part.

CHAPTER XIV.

The Revolutionary War—Continued.

A Time of Quiet.— Progress of Settlement.— Corinth.— Topsham.— Bayley, Lovewell, and Powell.— Alarms.— Tories.— Bedell's Journey to Canada.— Store-Houses.— The Hazen Road.— The Story of Tamalek.

IT seems probable that a comparative degree of peace and prosperity existed at Coös for two or three years after the surrender of Burgoyne. The disastrous failure of that expedition secured peace upon the frontier for a short time. The British in Canada were in no condition to renew the attempt to invade New England. Burgoyne had set out upon his expedition with a well-trained and fully-equipped army, and had been completely overthrown. A second invasion, though often threatened, was never begun. The interval of comparative peace enabled the inhabitants to establish themselves more securely in their possessions, and to extend the bounds of the settlement.

We have seen that clearings had been begun on several farms at West Newbury before the revolutionary war. By the year 1780, it is believed that some thirty families had settled in that part of the town, all away from the river road. It is probable that between 1777, and 1780, Col. Robert Johnston built a sawmill on his mill lot, a tract of one hundred acres, granted him as a bounty for building a mill at the falls, where the road to West Newbury from the village crosses Hall's brook. This lot lies east of, and adjoining, the hundred-acre lots.

About that time, certainly before 1780, Jonathan Butterfield built a grist-mill on Hall's brook at the same falls where Mr. Runnels' mill is now, but on the other side of the stream.

In the summer of 1777, Ezekiel Colby, from Newbury, began a settlement in Corinth, where his family was soon joined by others. Col. John Taplin and his sons removed thither, and became citizens of influence.

Reuben Page, a younger brother of John Page of Haverhill, who had served five terms in the revolutionary war, settled near the corner of Newbury, in Corinth, about 1780. In that year, the first sawmill was built in that town. Col. Thomas Johnson states that there were about forty families in Corinth in 1782.

In 1781, Thomas Chamberlain removed from the Ox-bow to a part of Topsham, then, and for some years later, claimed by Newbury. He was soon joined by Thomas McKeith, from Ryegate, and Samuel Farnham. The road from the river in Newbury to these remote settlements was the one that passes the schoolhouse on Rogers' hill. The part beyond the late Harrison Cheney's was abandoned many years ago, but this was the only outlet which the first settlers in Topsham and Corinth had for some years.

But although the country seemed peaceful, the leading men were apprehensive that hostilities would break out again, and they were soon reminded that it was only a truce and not a permanent peace.

In December, 1777, Capt. Frye Bayley and Capt. Nehemiah Lovewell, of Newbury, and John Powell, of Strafford, were sent from Newbury to Montreal, to escort one Capt. Singleton, who had been here to negotiate for an exchange of some prisoners. They took but three days' provisions, expecting by that time to reach settlements. They were overtaken by storms, their provisions gave out, and they suffered greatly from cold and hunger during their journey, which lasted ten days. On their arrival, their flag was disregarded, and they were thrown into prison where they remained several months. Bayley returned to Boston by way of Halifax, October 8, 1778.

During the years which followed 1777, the frontiers were kept in a state of continual and increasing alarm. This was in accordance with the policy of the authorities in Canada, which had several motives. One of them was to prevent the enlistment of men from Coös for service elsewhere; another, to keep people from settling here, and a third, to make the inhabitants think that their security lay in making peace with Canada.

The tories in Newbury and Haverhill plotted ceaselessly, but were restrained from actual violence by the wiser heads among them. Some of them were idle and dissolute persons who went as far as they dared without putting themselves in actual danger. Their number was very small, compared with those who embraced the patriot cause, and they confined themselves to the perpetration of a multitude of petty annoyances. It was common for some of them to go about after dark and frighten any solitary family by unearthly noises in the night. Another device was to go upon the hills behind Cow Meadow and raise the Indian war-whoop. The settlers lived in constant dread of their lives from these lawless people, and feared that they would gain courage from such cowardly actions as frightening women and maiming cattle, to murder and arson. Really nothing of the kind ever occurred, and no one was murdered, and no house was burned by the tories at Coös, so far as we know. It is probable that much of this immunity was due to the influence of Col. Asa Porter. His sympathies were with the royal cause, but his humane and liberal views forbade any violence, and he knew how to lay a strong hand upon the lawless.

It was believed by Gen. Bayley and the other leaders at Coös, that the time was favorable for another invasion of Canada, and that there would be no peace on the frontier, as long as the tories were sustained by hope from that quarter. On the 13th of October, 1778,* he instructed Col. Bedel to go to Upper Coös, and take proper men to go into Canada, and bring back all the intelligence which they could gather. The points upon which he solicited their inquiries were:—What forces were in Canada; the condition of the garrisons; the general sentiments of the people, and of the clergy toward the American cause; the disposition of the Indians, and whether there had been good or bad crops that season. They were also to buy all the moose skins, moccasins, and snow-shoes they could collect, and to engage the Indians to bring to Newbury all the skins and moccasins they could obtain, when the fall hunt was over. The information obtained inspired the belief, that if a sufficient force was sent into Canada to insure protection, the inhabitants would rise and throw off the British yoke. Preparations began at once for another invasion of Canada. A large storehouse was built at Haverhill, and a great quantity of military stores was collected there.† Cattle were bought and killed, their meat salted down, and the hides taken to the tan-yard. Many Indians came to Newbury, with skins to sell, and the more expert of them were employed in making snow-shoes. Military stores were brought to Newbury, and quantities of shoes, blankets and the like, were placed in a building which stood where Dea. Sidney Johnson's barn now stands, on the Ox-bow. The medical stores and more valuable goods were deposited in the southwest corner room in Col. Thomas Johnson's house, and in the chamber above it. In December, a party of men was sent to Peacham, to begin where Bayley left off in 1776, and open the road to Canada.

In April, 1779, Col. Hazen was directed to move his military stores to Peacham, and sent a letter to the selectmen of all the towns along the river, whose purport will be understood by the following extract from the town records:—"At a meeting held at the State House in Newbury at the request of Colo. Moses Hazen to see if the town of Newbury will repair the old Rode to

* New Hampshire War Rolls, IV., 276.
† Bedel Papers, p. 93.

Ryegate, or look out a new one, and also provide carriages to move his military stores to Peacham," it was voted, "that Colo. Moses Little, Thomas Chamberlain, Thomas Johnson, Robert Johnston, Josiah Page, and Colo. Lovewell be a committee to look out and lay a rode from Gen. Bayley's mill on Harriman's brook, to Wells River, at or below Whitelaw's mills, and make a return to the selectmen immediately." This road which was then made through the woods, was the "old road" which turned to the right at the top of the "saw-mill hill," and may easily be followed, until it comes out on the present road near where Henry G. Rollins now lives. It afterward became a public road, and was abandoned about 1842, when the road was laid out near Harriman's Pond. The road which Bayley had begun in 1776, was continued by Hazen through the towns of Cabot, Walden, Hardwick, Greensboro, Craftsbury, Albany, and Lowell, to a notch in the mountain in Westfield, still called Hazen's Notch.

A large portion of Bedel's regiment was ordered to Peacham to construct this road, which also built blockhouses at Peacham and other places, which were garrisoned during the war. Work was discontinued on the military road the last of August, the reports of forces being dispatched from St. Johns to capture the constructing party, hastening the abandonment. The road was never of any use from a military point of view, but it greatly aided the settlement of the towns through which it passed, and the road is called the Hazen Road to this day. There was never any intention of invading Canada at that time, and the whole affair of building the road and accumulating supplies was only a strategem to deceive the Canadian authorities and prevent their sending any troops from Canada to New York. Notwithstanding the failure of this expedition to Canada, Gen. Bayley and the other leading men at Coös believed that the proposed invasion was only postponed, and exerted themselves to persuade Washington and his generals that the only safety for New England lay in the subjugation of Canada, and until that should be accomplished, in the stationing of a strong and well-drilled force at Coös to guard the frontier.

There exist among the Washington papers many letters from Bayley, conveying the information gathered by his spies in Canada, regarding another expedition forming there and urging immediate action. By the beginning of 1780, the Coös country had become populous, and the great meadows yielded abundantly. The plunder of such a region offered a great temptation to the British in Canada, and it seemed a matter of common prudence to secure the safety of the Connecticut valley. But the British were never able to form another expedition in Canada, strong and well enough equipped, to promise success after the failure of Burgoyne.

Mr. Powers devotes considerable space to the narrative of an Indian feud, to which he assigns no date, but which is believed to have occurred about 1779. As his account differs in many particulars from those of Mr. Perry and David Johnson, it is only worth our while to give the main facts. Toomalek, whom Johnson calls Tamalek, a son of the wife of Captain Joe, was one of the Indians employed as scouts by Bayley, and who seems to have displayed traits of courage and fidelity, possessed some of the worst Indian characteristics of cruelty and revenge. He murdered a young Indian girl, the wife of one Mitchell, at the foot of the hill where the river turns north, at the upper end of the Ox-bow. A few years later he quarrelled with Mitchell and killed him. For both these he was acquitted by the Indian court, under the influence of one John, a savage Indian who had domesticated himself at Coös. Later he murdered Pial, son of John, in Haverhill. For this last crime he was condemned by Indian law, and shot in the court-house at Newbury, John being the executioner. His body was buried by Joe and Mary. About twenty-five years ago, the skeleton of an Indian was dug up near the site of the old court-house, which was believed to be that of Tamalek.

CHAPTER XV.

THE TROUBLOUS TIMES.

ALARMS.—BURNING OF PEACHAM.— THE "GREAT ALARM."— BENJAMIN WHITCOMB.—
A NIGHT OF TERROR.— THE BURNING OF ROYALTON.— MR. POWER'S TORY
SERMON. — ITS CONSEQUENCES. — "THE HALDIMAND CORRESPONDENCE."—
AZARIAH PRITCHARD.— CAPTURE OF COL. THOMAS JOHNSON.

THE change of plans which led to the abandonment of the
expedition to Canada brought trouble upon the people at
Coös, and the later years of the revolutionary war were full
of alarms. There were certain men upon whose heads a price was
set in Canada, and the hope of obtaining the offered rewards made
some of the tories concert plans for the capture of these men,
among whom were Gen. Bayley, Col. Thomas Johnson, Capt. Frye
Bayley, Col. Robert Johnston, Capt. John G. Bayley, Robert
Hunkins, and others. But all these were brave and resolute men
whom it would be no easy matter to kidnap, and great danger
attended any attempt at abduction, in a thickly-settled country,
among people accustomed to alarms. In August, 1779, some
children who had gone after blackberries in a clearing, back of
where E. B. Chamberlain now lives, discovered several men lurking
in the woods. The children ran to the houses and gave the alarm,
upon which guns were fired to call in the men who were at work in
the meadows. The smoke from clearing land in Ryegate and the
shouts of the strong-voiced Scotchmen urging their oxen were seen
and heard in Newbury, and were magnified by apprehension into
a massacre of the inhabitants, and the burning of the settlement.

We, who live in these times of instant communication and rapid
travel, can scarcely form any idea of the terrors of those days.
People who lived near the river kept boats and rafts hidden where
they could be quickly reached, by which they might escape into
Haverhill, the east bank of the Connecticut being considered safest.

Several families moved over to Haverhill about that time for greater security.

In 1780, houses were burned in Peacham, along the Hazen road, and the inhabitants carried to Montreal. On the 9th of August, a party of twenty-one Indians came into Barnard and made prisoners of three men, whom they bore off to Canada. In October, came the "Great Alarm," the burning of Royalton by a party which had been sent from Canada to destroy Newbury, in revenge for the murder of Gen. Gordon of the British army.

In July, 1776, Benjamin Whitcomb, whose home then, and for some years after seems to have been at Newbury, and who was in command of a scout on the river Sorel, had mortally wounded Gen. Gordon, as he was riding between Chambly and St. Johns, and had taken from him his watch and sword. Several attempts had been made to capture Whitcomb, but without success, when it was learned, in 1780, that he was living here. Some months preceding the invasion, one Hamilton, who had been taken prisoner with Burgoyne, and had been released on parole came to Newbury and remained sometime. He made himself friendly with people, and learned all he could about the situation and resources of the settlement. Later, he went to Hanover and Royalton, and under pretence of surveying land in the northern part of the state, went directly to the enemy in Canada.

In October, Capt. Nehemiah Lovewell, of Newbury, who had been sent with a company of rangers to garrison the blockhouses in Peacham and Cabot, and guard the Hazen road, was, with a small scout, near the Lamoille river, when he discovered a party of armed Indians, nearly three hundred in number, making their way south through the woods.* They were under the command of one Horton, a British lieutenant, with a Frenchman named La Motte as his assistant, and with Hamilton for their guide. Lovewell sent his fleetest men to warn the inhabitants. The alarm was sent to all the towns as far south as Charlestown. By the time the tidings reached Hanover, terror had magnified the invading force into an army. All the militia from Bath to Charlestown turned out. The people of Newbury, who lived below Harriman's brook, left their homes and fled to Haverhill. So many crowded upon a raft which left the Newbury side at Sleeper's meadow, that it began to sink, when Robert Hunkins and others lightened the frail craft by swimming ashore. The alarm reached Newbury after dark, and that night was one the like of which this town has never seen since. People left their homes as they were, the fires burning, their bread in the ovens, their suppers untasted, and fled for their lives. Some few retained presence of mind enough to secrete their most valuable possessions. The wife of Capt. John G. Bayley lowered all her

---

* Mrs. Lovewell's written statement in 1837, now in the N. H. Hist. Soc.

crockery and silver spoons into the well. Mrs. Ebenezer Eaton, who lived near where William U. Bailey has long resided, hid her spoons and her husband's knee-buckles so well that she was never able to find them again. In the morning the militia came in, the day passed without alarm, and people began to return. It was a day or two before the facts became known.

When the party under Horton came near the present site of Montpelier, they found Jacob Fowler of Newbury, and one or two others, who were hunting. Fowler was accounted a tory, and Horton acquainted him with their plans, but was informed by him that Newbury had received the alarm, and that the militia had gathered in considerable force. They next determined to assault Hanover, which had, since the establishment of Dartmouth College, become the largest place above Charlestown. But not daring to cross the river, at that time very high, they passed through Barre, Washington, and Chelsea, into Tunbridge, where they remained over Sunday, October 15th. On the following day they fell upon Royalton, killed several of the inhabitants and carried twenty-five persons to Canada.* They burned one house in Tunbridge, several in Randolph, twenty-one in Royalton; sixteen new barns filled with hay and grain, slaughtered about one hundred and fifty head of cattle, and all the sheep and swine they could find, and destroyed all the household furniture they could not carry away, taking about thirty horses laden with the spoil of the settlement. An untimely snow storm which fell that day, increased the dreariness of the situation. So fell upon Royalton the blow which had been intended for Newbury.

The troubles incident to life upon the frontier in time of war, were heightened by an act of indiscretion on the part of the minister, Mr. Powers. On the Sabbath, September 10, 1780, he preached two sermons from Judges v. 23, which were a scathing and intemperate review of the part which had been taken by the tories since the war began. The substance of these discourses was printed at Hanover, under the title "Tyranny and Toryism Exposed." Their deliverance gave mortal offense to the persons at whom it was directed, and tended to increase the hard feelings between the two parties at Coös. Mr. Powers' life was threatened by means of anonymous letters, and his name was added to those upon whose heads a reward had been placed. He became greatly alarmed for his safety, and moved with his family to Haverhill, into Col. Charles Johnston's house, leaving his son Stephen in his own at Newbury. This offended many of the whigs, as the patriots were called, especially some of the Bayleys and Col. Robert Johnston. They felt that they had endured much more

---

*Narrative of Zadoc Steele. Halls Eastern Vt.

for the cause of liberty, and had far more at stake than he had, and that, having by his utterances increased the ill will of the tories against them, he had left them to get out of the trouble as best they could. They succeeded in shutting up the meeting-house against him, and the rest of his preaching in Newbury was held in houses and barns, and in the open air.

In order to comprehend more fully the perplexities which beset the leaders at Coös during the last years of the revolutionary war, we must now advert to a phase of the history of Vermont which has been the perplexity of four generations of historians.

In October, 1780, certain men who had been prominent in the American cause, entered into negotiations with the Canadian authorities, which continued through nearly three years, and are known in history by the name of the commanding general in Canada, as the "Haldimand Correspondence." "This negotiation," says Dr. Williams, who wrote while the authors of it were still living, "consisted on the part of the British of constant attempts and endeavors to persuade the leading men of Vermont to renounce their allegiance to the states of America, and become a British province. On the part of the gentlemen of Vermont, the correspondence consisted of evasions, ambiguous, general answers and proposals, which had for its object a cessation of hostilities, at a time when the state of Vermont, deserted by the continent, and unable to defend herself, lay at the mercy of Canada."

It would be useless, in a town history, even to give a general idea of these negotiations which fill several thousand manuscript pages. There were only eight men in Vermont who were in the secret of this correspondence: Thomas Chittenden, Moses Robinson, Samuel Safford, Ethan Allen, Ira Allen, Timothy Brownson, John Fassett and Joseph Fay. They succeeded in making the British authorities in Canada believe that Vermont could be easily detached from its adherence to the American cause and annexed to Canada. They persuaded them to agree to a truce, by which the British troops were to be withdrawn from Vermont, while the militia of this state was disbanded. There is a great deal in this correspondence which has never been fully explained, and to read some of the letters of the Allens to the authorities in Canada, it would be believed that they were ready to sell Vermont to the British. How Gen. Haldimand and his officers allowed themselves to be thus duped, passes wonder. Indeed, it must be admitted that throughout the whole negotiation, Haldimand seems to have been actuated by a benevolent desire to avoid further bloodshed and bring the colonies, by kindly measures, back into the control of the crown.

No one on the east side of the state was admitted to the secret of these negotiations, but it was not long in coming to the knowledge of the leading men in the Connecticut valley, that something suspicious was going on in the west part of the state. It was known to Gen. Bayley that certain men living near Bennington had been to Canada; that Canadian agents had visited Vermont, and that a correspondence was going on along Lake Champlain. It was not long before an attempt was made by the British to secure an emissary on this side of the state.

Azariah Pritchard, a Connecticut tory, who was ambitious to secure a commission in the British army, had visited Canada, and was given to understand that he could bring himself into favorable notice, by seizing some prominent man in the Connecticut valley, and taking him into Canada as a prisoner. He secured a list of the men upon whose heads a price was set, and engaging a small company of lawless men, he came down to Coös, and learned all he could about the principal citizens. But the serious risks involved in taking a man out of a populous locality, deterred his attempt. He learned that Col. Thomas Johnson, who had entered into a contract with James Bayley of Peacham, to build a gristmill in that town, had started with Josiah and Jacob Page, and two ox teams, for Peacham with the mill stones, on Monday, March 3d, 1781. On Wednesday night, while Johnson and Page were staying at the house of Dea. Jonathan Elkins in Peacham, Pritchard and his men surrounded the house, and carried Col. Johnson, Jacob Page, and Jonathan Elkins off to Canada. Rev. Grant Powers, with his usual inaccuracy, says that Page was sent down the river and never heard from afterwards. As a matter of fact, he was exchanged, and returned to Newbury, settling finally in Ryegate, where he is well remembered by old people.

Jonathan Elkins was sent to Quebec, where he suffered greatly from cold and hunger. In the fall, he was carried to England and confined in Mill prison, and was not exchanged for a year and a half from the time of his capture, when he was but nineteen years of age. Hon. Henry K. Elkins, a prominent business man of Chicago, is a son of Jonathan Elkins.

Johnson was, on the contrary, treated with a leniency and courtesy in marked contrast to the harsh treatment which was the lot of Elkins. He was well known, personally, to many of the British officers in Canada, and was considered by the authorities as a fitting man to represent Canadian interests on the east side of the Green Mountains, where, as yet, they had no partisan of influence or station.

To their inquiries respecting the views and feelings of the people upon the New Hampshire Grants, he affected indifference, and appeared to have grown lukewarm in the cause of the colonies. They gradually made him acquainted with the negotiations which were going on between the Canadian authorities and the leaders in south-western Vermont, and he was informed that if he would serve their cause at home, he would be permitted to return to Newbury. Accordingly, upon his promise to inform them of what was being said and done at Coös, which would be of value to them, he was given his parole, at St. Johns, October 5, 1781, and reached home on the 12th of the same month.

During his captivity, he kept a diary which, for the first time, is published in this volume.

CHAPTER XVI.

COL. THOMAS JOHNSON.

His Unfortunate Situation.— Tidings of his Capture.— The Alarm.— Capt. Webb.— Riot at Col. Johnson's.— The Last Two Years of the War.— Blockhouses.— Bliss and Sleeper Killed by the Indians.— Sherwood and Smythe.— Their Report.— Plans to Capture Gen. Jacob Bayley.— Robert Rogers again.— Pritchard's Attempt to Take Bayley.— Shem Kentfield.—The Attack.—Sarah Fowler.

WHETHER the capture of Col. Thomas Johnson was planned in Canada, or whether Pritchard's exploit had placed in the hands of the British a man whom they believed could be wrought upon to serve their purpose, cannot be determined.

The war which Great Britain had carried on with the colonies, had now been conducted nearly six years, yet with all their resources of men and money England had little to show in the way of results. A new policy was now to be inaugurated, and the troubles between Vermont and New York were used by the British to weaken the attachment of the former state to the federal union, and finally draw it back to the Crown. With a similar result in view, but by various means, they hoped to win the revolted colonies, one by one, back to their allegiance.

The journal of Col. Johnson, while in Canada, shows that he was treated with a consideration greatly disproportioned to his rank as lieutenant-colonel in the colonial militia. But if the British expected much from him, they were disappointed, while at the same time his connection with them drew many troubles upon his head, here in Newbury. He had been very prosperous since he came to Coös, and as, by 1781, financial difficulties had overtaken Gen. Bayley, Johnson was probably much the wealthiest man in Newbury, and his fine house still attests the style in which he lived.

This prosperity had its drawbacks. He had made a few enemies, and as the worst charge which could be made against a

man in those days was that of toryism, there were those who had
not scrupled to say that he was at heart a tory, and had underhand
dealings with Canada. There had not been, for some time, the best
of feeling between him and Gen. Bayley, which arose out of some
transactions, between Johnson, and two of the latter's sons.
Probably no man in Coös was placed in a more difficult situation
during the later years of the war. His enemies averred that his
capture in Peacham was arranged beforehand, and that he had
gone there expressly to be thus taken, and when the tidings of his
capture reached Newbury, there was quite a riot at his house.

Mrs. Johnson had gone with her children to spend the day with
her sister, Mrs. Wallace, when, about ten o'clock, a messenger came
from Peacham, with the news of her husband's capture. It was
supposed that his captors were but the advanced guard of an
invading army, and the alarm was sent out to all the towns as far
south as Hanover. The first officer to arrive was Capt. Webb with
a few men. Between Webb and Johnson there had been trouble, in
some long forgotten manner, and the former took possession of the
house with his men.

At that time there was a considerable quantity of rum, brandy,
and other stores in the south-west front room, and the chamber
above it. Webb demanded the keys of Ebenezer Whitaker, the hired
man, and on his refusal, broke open the doors, and helped himself
and his men liberally to the spirits, using abusive language toward
Johnson. The men were becoming dangerous, when Capt. Jeremiah
Hutchins came over from Haverhill with his company, and restored
order.

When Johnson returned home, he found trouble awaiting him.
There were men who had returned from the Canadian prisons, in
which they had suffered from cold and hunger, who reported that
at a time when they were allowed only enough to keep soul and
body together, Johnson seemed perfectly at liberty, walking about
at his leisure, dining with the officers, and having a good time,
apparently. These rumors were seized upon by his enemies, and
colored to suit their purposes, and Johnson was exposed to no
small danger. But it does not appear that his loyalty was
doubted by Gen. Bayley, Col. Kent, or the more considerate men
on both sides of the river.

The last two years of the war were the most trying of all to
the people at Newbury. There was a constant succession of
alarms, and considerable bodies of troops were employed in
guarding the frontier. A blockhouse was built in Corinth, another
in Cabot, and a third in Barnet. There were several blockhouses
along the Hazen road, and others were built at Upper Coös, and
during some months of 1781, and 1782, a daily patrol was kept
up between these posts. Capts. Nehemiah Lovewell, of Newbury,
and James Ladd, of Haverhill, were stationed at Peacham. In the

summer of the former year, Constant Bliss, of Thetford, Moses Sleeper, of Newbury, Nathaniel Martin, of Bradford, and a fourth whose name is not preserved, were sent to take possession of a blockhouse on the west side of Caspian lake, in the town of Greensboro. In an unguarded moment, when at a distance from the house, they were attacked by a party of Indians. Bliss and Sleeper were killed and scalped, the others were carried to Quebec, and confined as prisoners.

People in these days who suppose that the revolutionary war ended with the surrender of Cornwallis in October, 1781, will be surprised to know that at no period in the war did the patriot cause seem more hopeless to the people in Coös, or their own situation more dangerous, than in the two years mentioned.

Col. Thomas Johnson had learned enough of the negotiations that were going on between the leaders on the west side of the state and the Canadian authorities, to make him anxious for the result. He took Gen. Bayley into his confidence, and laid before him what he had learned. The latter was not long in finding out much more, and, not being in the secret of their plans, they believed that Ethan Allen, and Ira Allen, Thomas Chittenden, and Jonas Fay, were engaged in a conspiracy to hand Vermont over to the British. It could not long escape observation that while the eastern part of the state was kept in constant alarm, there was peace and quiet west of the mountains. There were others besides Bayley and Johnson who knew that something mysterious was going on, and there were those on both sides of the river who entered into correspondence with Canada, in order to secure to themselves some share in whatever might be in the future.

Both Bayley and Johnson addressed themselves to Washington, laying before him such information as they had obtained. Some of their letters are given in this volume.

It had been agreed by Johnson, as one of the conditions of his parole, that he should give the British information of the movements of the Americans, with shelter and provisions to the British scouts, and that he should repair at once to any place to which he should be called. Early in 1782, he received a letter from Canada by the hand of Levi Sylvester. After that the correspondence became quite frequent, and he was closely pressed concerning the movements of Gen. Bayley and others. But the British in Canada were not long in finding out that their scheme for detaching Vermont from the American cause was making no progress, and having no apparent suspicion that they were being deceived by the Allens and their associates, sent, in September, 1781, Mr. George Smythe and Capt. Sherwood into Vermont to find out the cause of the delay.

These commissioners reported at Quebec on the 30th,* that they

---

* Haldimand Papers.

were "fully of the opinion that Messrs. Chittenden, Allen and Fay, with a number of the leading men in Vermont, are making every exertion in their power to endeavor to bring about a re-union with government, and that at heart one-third part of the people sincerely wish for such a change. But Congress are much alarmed, and have lately at great expense employed a number of emissaries in Vermont to counteract underhand whatever is doing for government. The principal of these are General Bayley, Colonel Chas. Johnston, Morey, Brewster, and Major Childs, on Connecticut river. This junto, of which General Bayley is the soul, are endeavoring to set the populace against the present leaders by insinuating that they are tories, and intend to sell Vermont to the British," etc. Gen. Bayley being the chief obstacle to their schemes, it was desirable to get him out of the way, and several plans were contrived for his capture.

Long after the war, a man confessed to Bayley that he with others lay in wait for him all one day, beside the road into the Ox-bow, and that he came near them several times, but each time turned back before they could seize him.*

Later, one Abel Davis, who lived in Peacham, and worked on either the British or the American side, as he found it to his advantage, came down to the home of Er Chamberlin, who lived at the mouth of Wells river, and feigning to be lame engaged Chamberlin to go to Gen Bayley and tell him that he had important intelligence to communicate. The General was about mounting his horse, when Capt. John G. Bayley came in and advised as a precaution, that he should accompany him, and that they should cross the river, and go up on the Haverhill side. Arriving opposite Chamberlin's house, they hailed Davis, and directed him to come over to them, which he did, but had nothing important to tell. Davis returned, and as his boat touched the Vermont shore, several armed men sprang out of the bushes and seized upon a man who chanced to be in the boat with him, supposing him to be Bayley. So he escaped their hands.†

In May, 1782,‡ Major Robert Rogers came into Coös with a strong force, and encamped among the hills back of where Bradford village now stands, and held communication with certain men of doubtful loyalty to the American cause, Col. Bedell, Davenport Phelps, Col. Taplin, Isaac Patterson, and others, sending for Johnson to come to him, but he contrived not to do so. Gen. Bayley obtained information of this, and a strong guard was stationed at his house every night for some time.

---

* Exeter News Letter.

† Johnson Papers.

‡ Johnson Papers.

THE COL. THOMAS JOHNSON HOUSE.
1775.

THE "DAVID JOHNSON HOUSE,"
NOW THE RESIDENCE OF MRS. L. F. WHEELER.

In June, another attempt was made, which is related at some length by Grant Powers, whose account differs in many particulars from those which still exist in the handwritings of Johnson, Bayley, Dow, Johnston, and others. Powers states that the date was June 17, 1782, while those who were engaged in the affair give it as the 15th, which was Saturday. Johnson's own account is, that on Friday, June 14th, Col. John Taplin came in from Corinth, and told him that there was a party in from Canada to take off some of his neighbors, but he replied that they must take care of themselves. The next morning Levi Sylvester came, and told Johnson that Capt. Pritchard, and Capt. Breckenridge, were in with a party of men and were encamped about two miles back from the Ox-bow. Johnson went with Sylvester, and held a long conversation with them upon the plans of the British respecting Vermont, now fully matured. These were, that Vermont should become a province of Canada, and all who opposed their plans were to be distressed and destroyed as fast as possible. They informed him that Gen. Bayley was the man who was thwarting the plans which promised so much, and that they had come to take him prisoner. Johnson left the men, and returned home by a circuitous route, determining at all hazards to give Bayley some warning.

The only plan which promised any success with safety, was the one which he adopted. Bayley, with two of his sons, was plowing on the Ox-bow, near sunset, when Johnson gave his brother-in-law, Dudley Carleton, a slip of paper on which he had written, "Samson, the Philistines be upon Thee." Carleton rode into the meadow, crossed the field where the General was plowing, and dropped the paper at some distance from the team, near the furrow. Bayley picked up the paper, read it, plowed round once or twice, and directed his sons to turn out the team. He remained upon the Ox-bow until the danger was over, and then crossed to Haverhill.

Gen. Bayley lived at that time in a one-story wooden house, with a gambrel roof, which stood where Mr. Doe's brick house now stands, on the Ox-bow. The guard at the house, which had been kept there for some time during nights, consisted of Capt. Frye Bailey, Ezra Gates, Joshua and Jacob Bayley, Jr., and Samuel Torrey, two of the General's youngest sons, and Thomas Metcalf. It had become well known that danger was imminent, but from what source was not understood.

In that same week one Shem Kentfield was hanged as a spy at Albany, and in his dying confession revealed the plot to capture Gen. Bayley. An express was sent to Newbury from Albany to warn Bayley of his danger. This warning reached him a few hours before the intimation from Johnson, so that he was on his guard. The attack was made "at early candlelight," by eighteen men, of whom three, Joseph White and Joseph White, Jr., and Levi Sylvester were from Newbury, Henry and David Cross were from the Upper

Coös. The rest, excepting Pritchard and Breckenridge, were unknown. Torrey was standing guard at the door, and the rest had stood their guns in a long hall which ran across the house from the front door, and opened into the ell part behind.

The attacking party rushed across the road from Cow Meadow and were not seen or heard until within a few feet of the house. Torrey was taken prisoner, and all the inmates of the house, save a young girl, Sarah Fowler, made their escape through doors and windows. *Ezra Gates was wounded in the arm as he was running from the house. This was the only occasion during the war, in which a hostile gun was fired, or blood shed, in Newbury.

The attacking party might easily have been cut off had the people showed any presence of mind, but the only persons at the Ox-bow who seem to have had their wits about them that evening were Mrs. Thomas Johnson, who loaded and fired several guns to give the alarm, and Sarah Fowler, who was the only person who remained in the house, and repeatedly blew out the candles which the soldiers had lighted to search for the General's papers. She was in charge of a young child of Mrs. Ephraim Bayley's. This young girl married Capt. Joseph Perkins, and they became early settlers of Shipton, P. Q., where she exemplified, during the privations of a frontier life, the same undaunted courage which she showed on that evening here in Newbury.

---

* Ezra Gates was a Connecticut soldier, who was left at Newbury sick, by one of the expeditions which was passing through. He settled in this town, and kept the toll bridge at Wells River for some years. He also lived a long time in Bath, where he is buried, although he died in this town, in 1844, aged 85. His right arm was always lame from the wound he received at General Bayley's. Many of his descendants live in towns near here.

CHAPTER XVII.

THE END OF THE WAR.

PRITCHARD'S RETREAT.— JAMES BAYLEY.— TRIAL OF JOHNSON AND CHAMBERLAIN.— JOHNSON'S JOURNEY TO HEADQUARTERS.— INTERVIEW WITH WASHINGTON.— PEACE.— SUMMING UP.— NEWBURY'S SERVICE IN THE REVOLUTION.—"GUARDING AND SCOUTING."— JOSEPH BRANT.— RESOLUTION AGAINST THE TORIES.— SIMILAR ACTION OF HAVERHILL.— REFLECTIONS.— FORTS AND BLOCKHOUSES.— FORT AT THE OX-BOW.

PRITCHARD did not remain long in Newbury. He knew very well that an hour or two would bring a force together which could easily cut his men off, and began a retreat, taking with them Torrey and Pike, the latter being Bayley's hired man. A little south of the cemetery, the party met James Bayley returning from his father's sawmill, bare-headed and bare-footed. Him they took prisoner, and carried to Canada in that condition. They also took Peletiah Bliss, who, although an old soldier, had the adroitness to feign terror, and they let him go. They stopped at the house of Andrew Carter, who lived at or near the "old Buell place," at West Newbury, and drank up all the milk the old lady had, and ate all the bread they could find. In passing through Corinth, they forced the inhabitants to swear allegiance to the King.

They were followed, about an hour later, by a force of thirty or forty men who had been called together by the alarm, and which went on their trail as far as Topsham, where they surrounded the house of Thomas Chamberlain, and brought him and his son Jacob prisoners to Newbury. About five o'clock on Monday morning, Johnson was arrested, in his own house, and taken before the Council of Safety at Haverhill, to answer to the charge made by Capt. John G. Bayley, that he had planned the attempt to capture Gen. Bayley. The latter appeared before the Council, and without revealing the fact that he had been warned by Johnson, contrived to get him off. Chamberlain, who had lately fallen under the influence of Col. John Taplin, was induced to tell what he knew, and was allowed to go home.

Capt. Absalom Peters, with a strong company, was ordered to Newbury, and remained in camp until the end of the war, himself acting as aid to Gen. Bayley. There were no further attempts to molest any men at Coös. But Johnson's troubles increased. He was reported to Canada by the tories, as having warned Bayley of his danger, and by certain patriots in Newbury was charged with being himself a tory and a spy. Some of the scouts who returned to Canada with his answers to communications from there were waylaid, and the contents of his letters made public.

It appears, also, that Gen. Bayley, to whom he had intrusted important secrets, was not as cautious as he should have been, and he was obliged to appear suspicious of Johnson in order to hide the facts, and to connive at the measures which were taken. A guard was posted around Col. Johnson's house for several weeks, day and night. This was made up of men who did not belong here, a piece of caution which averted much friction. Gen. Bayley drew up a letter to Washington in which he set forth the unfortunate position of Col. Johnson, which he sent by Capt. Frye Bayley. It was desired to effect his exchange, in order that he might be free to reveal the plots of Chittenden and the Allens. For, at that time, and for a year or two at least afterwards, both Bayley and Johnson were firmly persuaded that the dangers to which both were exposed, and from which they had suffered, were the work, not of the British in Canada, but of Ethan and Ira Allen, Thomas Chittenden, and Jonas Fay.

Bayley did not scruple to say that in his opinion Ethan Allen was as great a traitor as Benedict Arnold, and that there would be "no peace till five or six rascals were hanged." Johnson was threatened on both sides, and his life and property were in great danger. There still exist, in various libraries and archives, a great number of letters written by Bayley, Johnson, Gen. Moses Dow, Charles Johnston, Ebenezer Webster, father of Daniel Webster, and others, to various individuals in high positions, which set forth the unhappy state of the times. Almost every man of any consequence in Newbury seems to have been involved in the troubles of the time, with the single exception of Col. Jacob Kent, whose name is never mentioned in the correspondence. He was probably completely occupied with his own affairs, and in the faithful execution of the public offices which he held.

Johnson finally decided to lay his case before Washington in person, and on the 20th of November set out for Newburgh, going via Exeter to solicit the advice of the leading men in that region. On December 4th, he reached Newburgh, and had a very satisfactory interview with the commander-in-chief. Washington could not then directly aid him, but assured him of his sympathy, and acknowledged the value of his services. Johnson returned home on the 12th of December. Meanwhile the British in Canada were preparing an expedition to occupy Vermont, but it was too late, for the war was fast hastening to its close. Active hostilities had ceased more than a year before. It was only along the frontiers that any strife remained.

In a few months, peace was restored, the colonies became a nation, and the people of Newbury and the rest of Vermont, were at liberty to cultivate their farms, clear land, and build themselves houses without any danger of molestation from tories or Indians.

The question has been often asked, how it was that the Coös country, so exposed to attack, so tempting a prey to the rapacity of the British in Canada, the Indians and the tories, so often threatened during almost eight years, yet escaped all serious disaster? With the slight exception of the attack on Gen. Bayley's house, not a hostile gun was fired in Newbury during the whole war, nor, so far as we know, was a dollar's worth of property destroyed. Yet at various times the danger was so grave that it seemed the country would have to be abandoned. We have no record of the number of alarms which were given here in Newbury, but at Lancaster, there were ten alarms in which the militia were called out.

Fergurson's History of Coös County says, "the number of of days spent in guarding and scouting by men of Lancaster during the war was four hundred and fifty-seven. One man was carried away captive from Lancaster in 1780, and two in 1782. In 1775, there were eight families in Lancaster, comprising sixty-one people." We have no means of knowing precisely how much time was spent by Newbury men in guarding and scouting during those eight years, but we can form some estimate from the records which still remain of one or two of several companies which were employed in that work.

In Capt. John G. Bayley's company, "guarding and scouting," from April, 1777, to May, 1779, as appears from the records at Montpelier, there are enrolled the names of eighty-five men, whose entire time of service is given as 2,862 days, an average of thirty-four days each. The custom was that when an alarm was given, or when it was advisable to watch a pass or a ford, or guard a blockhouse, a number of men were called out for the purpose by the captain, and this was so arranged that each man should have about an equal share of the work.

It must be remembered that in the time mentioned, Burgoyne's expedition and capture occurred, and nearly all the men enrolled in Capt. Bayley's company saw actual service in that campaign in other companies, notably those of Capt. Thomas Johnson and Capt. Frye Bayley. But the campaign of Burgoyne was the only one when the militia of Newbury were all called to the field, at the time when the New Hampshire Grants arose as one man to hunt the enemy down.

Capt. Frye Bayley was in command of a company, also employed in guarding and scouting, from January, 1781, to the end of the war, in which about seventy men were enrolled, whose time of service was from fourteen to fifty days. Taking these two companies as a basis of calculation, it would seem that, on the average, four or five men were, taking one month and one year with another, on guard during the whole war, from this town. This leaves wholly out of account the service of Newbury men in the active campaigns, in which there were always several engaged. To their constant care, and close observation of what went on in the northern wilderness, the settlements owed much. The danger incurred by these rangers and guards was very great. They were often sent, two or three at a time, through the wilderness, to see what was going on along the St. Lawrence, to observe the Indians on the Richelieu, or to inspect the fortifications at Isle Aux Noix. Yet in that hazardous service it is believed that not more than two or three Newbury men perished.

The words, "guarding and scouting," cover the records of various service. Prisoners were often sent here, for safe keeping, or to await an exchange, and, in the latter case, men were detailed to escort these to the Canadian lines. Men were also employed in guarding the military stores deposited here, or in Haverhill, and, in case of alarms, to protect the houses of the more prominent citizens, or watch the roads.

There were no mails or post-offices in Vermont then, so that all dispatches had to be sent by special messengers.

Only the most hardy and discreet men were sent in the dangerous service of ranging the wilderness between here and the Canadian settlements.

But the great cause, under Providence, for the exemption of the Coös country from being the scene of such horrors as desolated Wyoming, was the powerful influence of Joseph Brant, the great chief of the Mohawks. He was educated by President Wheelock at his Indian school, and when the war broke out, Wheelock is said to have interceded with Brant for the protection of the Coös country, and that the latter threatened vengeance if the Connecticut valley was ravaged.

The last entry of the few in our town records which relate to the war, shows the feeling toward the tories. At a town-meeting held June 3rd, 1783, it was voted: "No person that hath joyned the Enemy shall have any abidence in this town and any person that shall harbor or feed them shall get the Displeasure of the town by so doing." It was also voted, "that Samuel Barnet, John Haseltine, Reuben Foster, Gideon Smith, Silvanus Heath, Frye Bayley and Joshua Bayley be a committee to deal with all such persons." Such actions on the part of towns seem to have been common, for the records of Haverhill give an article in the warning for town-meeting September 16, 1783, as follows: "To pass some votes as said inhabitants shall think fit concerning tories, absentees or persons who have left the United States of America, and voluntarily taken residences within the lines of the enemies of such states, and have returned or may return into this town." It was voted "That Jonathan Ring, Joseph Hutchins, Nathaniel Merrill, Thomas Miner and Ephraim Bayley be a committee to take care that no such persons mentioned be suffered to reside in this town."

Whether any action was ever taken against the tories by the Newbury resolution is not known. Significant, however, is the circumstance that certain families cease from our annals about that time. But many, perhaps most, of these men, settled quietly down under the new government, and by industry and kindly bearing soon won back the good will of their neighbors, and in a few years all bitterness passed away.

So ended, happily in the main, the great struggle for independence, and out of it Newbury had emerged almost uninjured. Of all its residents who had served in it, not more than five or six, so far as we know, lost their lives. The hardships of the campaigns seemed slight to these pioneers. Men accustomed to the severe toil and exposure of those days, were already inured to the dangers of the wilderness. The hardest part of the war fell upon those who did not share its exciting scenes, but upon whom fell the burden of waiting at home, the wives and the mothers. How fared they, these women of Newbury, when all the men in the settlement who could march, had gone to the army? Tradition says that at one time of danger, when all the able-bodied men of Newbury went after Burgoyne, there were but six men left in this town. We wonder how they lived through those scenes who remained at home. Perhaps people were less nervous then than now. When a man left home to go on a scout, his wife did not expect to hear from him again till he returned.

Mention has been frequently made of forts and blockhouses. It must not be supposed that regular fortifications were meant by the former term. They were, usually, no more than very strongly built houses, commonly of logs, which, when held by a few resolute and wary men, could resist the attacks of a considerable force. Such were farm houses which stood at some distance from any others, in new clearings. The log houses of those days were easily made secure from bullets. Frame houses were more open to attack, as the walls were not thick enough to stop bullets, and the windows were larger. For the defense of such, a stockade, so called, was constructed of posts a foot or more in size, and eight or ten feet long, standing on end close together, around the house, at a distance of ten or fifteen feet from it, secured by a strong gate. Such a stockade was built around Col. Robert Johnston's house, which is now a barn, standing at the south end of the village, and some of the posts remained till after 1800. The house of Maj. Nathaniel Merrill, now owned by W. F. Eastman, next north of the cemetery at Horse Meadow, was surrounded by a stockade, as was that of Col. Charles Johnston, at Haverhill Corner, the older part of the house in which Mr. William Tarleton now lives.

In the records preserved at Montpelier, mention is made of sums of money and labor expended in building a "fort" at Piermont.

Blockhouses were not made for dwellings, but for defense, and were built very strongly of logs, and placed at strategic points. Some of these were small buildings which could shelter a few men, and several were built along the Hazen road in Peacham and Hardwick. Sometimes they were large enough to shelter a considerable garrison. There was one such on a hill near Corinth Centre, which was garrisoned by forty men at one time, and was a central point whence scouting parties were sent out.

Mention is found in old records of a fort at Newbury, and there has been some discussion as to where it stood. Mr. Frye Bayley, in 1836, pointed out to Dea. D. T. Wells, who died in 1899, the location and general plan of that building, which stood on the narrow summit of the ridge at the left hand, beyond the cemetery, going toward the Ox-bow. The traces of two parallel ditches may still be seen, and forty years ago a few brick and cinders remained on the spot. No mention is made of it in the town records, and it was probably built, not by the inhabitants, but by some of the many bodies of troops which were continually passing through the valley, and was large enough to furnish barracks for one or two companies. Capt. Absalom Peter's company, which was stationed here during the summer of 1782, was probably quartered in it. Miss Sally Bayley, who died in 1867, remembered the building, which was taken down when there was no further use for it.

CHAPTER XVIII.

Newbury in the Vermont Controversy.

THE year 1777, is memorable as the "Bennington Year," and as
also the year in which the country between Lake Champlain
and Connecticut River was formed into a new state. But
fourteen years were to pass, and many complications arose, before
Vermont became a member of the Federal Union.

Our limits forbid, and the scope of this history does not require
a full account of these complications, but as the town itself, and
some of its citizens by themselves, took a small part in these
operations, it is necessary to give some account of them. We have
seen that Newbury was settled under a charter granted by the
governor of New Hampshire, but that in 1764, by the King's order
in Council, what had been known as the New Hampshire Grants,
was declared to be part of the territory of New York.

Now it did not make very much difference to the settlers which
government they were under, if they were not molested in their
lands, if the results of their toil were secured to them, and the laws
were faithfully administered. But in 1770, the New York courts
repudiated these New Hampshire charters, and declared all
proceedings under them to be of no effect. The governor of New
York proceeded to make new grants of lands which had been settled
and cultivated for a number of years, to persons from that colony,
and many of the settlers along the western side of the state, were
driven from their homes, and strangers reaped what they had sown.

The inhabitants of several towns west of the Green Mountains, chose Committees of Safety, "whose business it was to attend to their security and defense against the New York claimants." We have also seen that the proprietors of Newbury secured themselves from molestation by procuring a new charter from the governor of New York.

The committees of towns which lay near each other, met from time to time to devise measures for their protection, and when the revolutionary war broke out, all these committees were called to convene at the inn of Cephas Kent, in Dorset, on the 26th of July, 1775, to devise measures for the common safety. This convention accordingly met, and took action concerning the raising of troops for the invasion of Canada, and appointed a committee, with authority to call another convention when it should seem necessary. This second convention met at the same place as the first, on January 16, 1776, transacted some business, and appointed a committee of three, with power to call a general meeting of all the committees in the Grants.

A third convention met at Dorset, July 24, 1776, which was attended by delegates from thirty-one towns, all west of the mountains. This body devised means, both offensive and defensive, against the British in Canada, and measures of common protection against the authorities of New York. This convention, having adjourned to the 26th of September, met at the same place, and was attended by delegates from twenty-five towns west of the mountains, and from eight on the east side, Windsor being the most northerly. In this convention were fifty-six delegates, representing thirty-six towns on the Grants, who took measures for separation from New York, and for defense against the British in Canada. They also voted that Col. Jacob Bayley, and Col. Jacob Kent, should be, with Capt. Abner Seeley, a committee to lay the proceedings of the convention before the inhabitants of the County of Gloucester.

At that time both Bayley and Kent were holding offices under New York. Kent was assistant judge of the inferior court of common pleas, while Bayley had been, as previously stated, elected a deputy from Newbury for the session of the New York Congress in 1775, but did not take his seat. This convention remained in session four days, and adjourned to the 30th of October, at Westminster. At this last mentioned session, no delegate appeared from any town above Norwich, and it does not appear that any one from Newbury was present, as Solomon Phelps was instructed to write a letter to General Bayley, asking his assistance. Adjourned to the 15th of January, 1777, this convention met again at Westminster, adopted a Declaration of Independence, and chose a committee of five to present the proceedings of the meeting to the Continental Congress. Of this committee Gen. Bailey was to be one, and Col. Thomas Johnson was made one of a Committee of War. This convention declared the New Hampshire Grants to be an independent state under the name of "New Connecticut."

It would seem that the convention felt some anxiety as to the course Newbury would take, this town having no special reason to separate from New York. Indeed at that time, General Bayley was attached to New York, and on the 19th of February, 1777, addressed the New York Convention, in a letter* which he probably intended should represent the state of affairs, and the sentiments of the people in Gloucester County, but which instead, faithfully indicates his own mental perplexity as to what ought to be done. This was written while Burgoyne's invading army was getting ready in Canada, and displays his fears at the impending danger, and his solicitude that the setting up of Vermont as an independent state at that time, would make it easy to be conquered from Canada. He therefore opposed any separation, until the public safety was more assumed. His letter, is in some particulars very obscure and perplexing, although his general meaning is clear. But in the course of the next four months Bayley changed his mind, and on the 14th of June again addressed the New York authorities, and informed them that whereas before the people of Gloucester were opposed to any separation, they were now to a man, violent for the change. This sudden action on Bayley's part laid him open to the charge of inconsistency, but was due to the fact that those who were working for the new state took care to circulate copies of the New York constitution throughout the Grants.

At that time the New York assembly consisted of seventy members, apportioned to counties; New York city and county having nine, Albany city and county ten, Dutchess seven, and the others in like proportion. Vermont was divided into three counties and allowed only nine members as follows: County of Charlotte four, Cumberland three, Gloucester two. The Senate had twenty-four members, of whom three were apportioned to the Vermont counties.† When Gen. Bayley and the other leaders in this part of the territory had read this constitution, and perceived the unfairness which gave to Albany County alone, a larger representation than the whole of Vermont, they were convinced that the common interest of the Grants compelled the formation of a new state.‡

On the fourth of June the convention met at Windsor, at which seventy-two delegates representing forty-two towns were in attendance. The minutes of the convention give "Mr. John G. D. Bailey, and Capt. Robert Johnson" as the delegates from Newbury.

---

*Documentary Hist. of N. Y. Vol. 4, p. 560—561. Gov. and Council I, p. 373, 4.
†Governor and Council, p. 1, p. 54.
‡Hon. L. E. Chittenden's letter, Sept. 7, 1898.

They were, without doubt, John G. Bayley and Capt. Robert Johnston. But there is nothing in our town records to show that any meeting to choose delegates to this convention was ever held. This is probably owing to the neglect of the town clerk, Col. Kent, to record the warning and the proceedings of the town meeting. That both these men attended, is certain. It having been discovered that the name, New Connecticut, had been given to a district on the Susquehanna, the convention unanimously voted that the New Hampshire Grants should thereafter be called and known as Vermont. The towns were directed to hold meetings on the 23d of June, to choose delegates to a convention to be held in the meeting-house at Windsor on the 2d of July. Accordingly, at a town meeting duly warned, of which Reuben Foster was moderator, it was voted, "To be separate from the state of New York, and formed into a state by name of Vermont." Also "To accept of the independence voted in the convention held at Westminster on the 15th of January, with the amendments, and that Col. Jacob Bayley and Reuben Foster be delegates."

"Of the proceedings of that convention," says Mr. Walton, "no complete account exists." Even the names of the delegates are not all known. The reason is, that at that time Burgoyne was on his march, all New England was in alarm, and the proceedings of the convention passed unobserved. But the members remained at their posts until the 8th, adopted a constitution, and chose a Council of Safety, which should administer the affairs of the state until a government under a constitution could be organized. Of this famous council, Jacob Bayley of Newbury was one, and was chosen, says Hon. L. E. Chittenden, in a letter to the editor of this volume, at the personal solicitation of Thomas Chittenden, who represented to the convention the importance of having the strongest man east of the mountains, upon the board. The only source of authority in Vermont, from August, 1777, to March, 1778, was this council, which prescribed the conduct of the war, raised troops, appointed officers, and exercised all the duties which commonly fall to the executive. The records of this Council of Safety fill 121 pages of the first volume of "Governor and Council."

The constitution, which was very nearly a copy of that of Pennsylvania, provided for a Governor, Deputy Governor, House of Representatives, and a council of twelve members instead of a Senate. The convention then adjourned, and before it came together again, Burgoyne had met his fate.

The first General Assembly of Vermont convened in the meeting-house at Windsor, March 13, 1778, and organized the new state, the Newbury minister, Mr. Powers, preaching the election sermon. It seems probable that Col. Jacob Kent represented Newbury. We have no record of the election of anyone. On the opening of the Assembly, a committee from sixteen towns on the east side of

Connecticut river appeared, and presented a petition praying that these towns might be admitted to become part of the new state. There were the river towns between Cornish and Littleton and six lying back from the river.*

Foreseeing that to grant their request would involve the new state in trouble with New Hampshire, and yet unable to dismiss the petition without offending the river towns on the Vermont side, with whom the proposed union was popular, the Assembly hit upon the expedient of referring the subject to the freemen of the several towns, to be decided according to the instructions which they should give their representatives, at the next meeting of the assembly.

The town-meeting held in Newbury upon the above matter, agreed to leave the whole subject for fuller consideration. Nothing appears on our town records as to such later action, but from the sequel we infer that the delegates, Reuben Foster and Jacob Kent, were instructed to declare in favor of receiving these towns, and others which wished to join the new state.

The Assembly met at Bennington in June, when these sixteen New Hampshire towns were received by vote. This was called the "First Union." On the 8th of October, 1778, the Assembly met again at Windsor, when the representatives from the west side of the mountains, who were called the Bennington party, and who had opposed the union with the New Hampshire towns because it threatened to disturb the supremacy which they wished to hold in the new state, brought forward, upon the second day, a protest from President Weare of New Hampshire, against an action which threatened to dismember that state. They also produced representations which they had secured from members of the Continental Congress, to the effect that Vermont could not be admitted into the union as a state, unless it relinquished its claim upon these New Hampshire towns. The Bennington party, although not strong enough to dissolve the union by a direct vote, succeeded in passing a series of resolutions, which were calculated to cause uneasiness among the delegates from the towns on both sides of the river.

All the actions of the Assembly are not known, but the course taken was such as to cause twelve members from each side of the river, with Lieut.-Gov. Marsh, two members of the Council, and the clerk of the House, to withdraw from the Assembly. These seceders met and called a convention to meet at Cornish, N. H., on the 9th of December. The remaining members of the Assembly adjourned to Bennington on the 12th of February 1779, where they dissolved the union without opposition.

At a town-meeting held in Newbury, on December 7th, 1778,

---

*These towns were:—Cornish, Lebanon, Dresden, (Hanover,) Lyme, Orford, Piermont, Haverhill, Bath, Lyman, Apthorp, (Littleton,) Enfield, Canaan, Cardigan, (Orange,) Landaff, Gunthwait, (Lisbon,) and Morristown, (Franconia.)

General Bayley being moderator, the town approved of the action of its representatives in withdrawing from the Assembly, and chose Col. Thomas Johnson and Dr. Gideon Smith to represent the town in the Cornish convention.

There were now three well defined parties which desired to exercise authority over what is now the state of Vermont. They are known as the Bennington party, of which the Allens and Thomas Chittenden were leading spirits, which strove to erect a new state between the Connecticut river and Lake Champlain. The second party, called the New Hampshire party, desired to re-annex the Grants to that state. The third, called the New York party, asserted the claim of that state over what is now Vermont. It seemed probable that the two last parties would effect a compromise, and divide Vermont between them, along the ridge of the Green Mountains.

To these parties was now added a fourth, smaller than either of the others, but which commanded attention, from the ability of its leaders. This party, sometimes called the "college party," because its head-quarters seemed to be at Dartmouth College, had for its prime object, the union, under one jurisdiction, of the towns on both sides of Connecticut river. It grew out of the common interest of the valley towns, which were much more intimately connected with each other, than with those which lay beyond the mountains to the east, or the west of the valley. This party determined to keep these towns together, either by a union of them with New Hampshire or with New York, or, failing to make favorable terms with either, by erecting a new state, in the Connecticut valley, to be composed of the towns on both sides of the river.

"The struggles of these four parties," says Professor Chase in his History of Dartmouth College, "for six years kept New Hampshire and New York, as well as the new state itself, in an unceasing turmoil, that involved even the Continental Congress, and threatened not only civil war at home, but, at one stage, through the unscrupulous tactics of one of the parties, the surrender of the disputed territory to the British."

CHAPTER XIX.

Newbury in the Vermont Controversy—Continued.

The Convention at Cornish.—Manifesto of Bayley, Payne and Woodward.— Town Meetings.— Vermont in an Unfortunate State.—Action of Newbury—Of Haverhill.—The Charlestown Convention.—The "Second Union."—The New York Towns.—The Vermont Legislature Meets in New Hampshire.— Civil War Threatened.—Washington's Letter.—Dissolution of the Union.—The Thetford Convention.—Town Meetings.—Reconciliation.—Admission of Vermont into the Federal Union.

BEFORE the convention assembled at Cornish, three of the seceders, Jacob Bayley of Newbury, Elisha Payne of Orange, N. H., and Bezaleel Woodward of Hanover, issued from Spooner's press at the last mentioned town, a pamphlet, dated December 1, 1778, entitled, "A Public Defense of the right of the New Hampshire Grants on both sides Connecticut River to associate together and form themselves into an Independent State."*

This, which is but one of several appeals which made their appearance at the time, was undoubtedly prepared by Mr. Woodward, and occupies fourteen closely printed pages of the fifth volume of Governor and Council. The pamphlet itself, is exceedingly rare.

The Cornish convention passed a number of resolutions containing the reasons for their action, looking toward a union of the river towns in Vermont with the state of New Hampshire, in case they failed to unite the river towns in New Hampshire, with the state of Vermont. General Bayley and Davenport Phelps were appointed a committee to present the action of the convention to the New Hampshire legislature, and at Newbury, on the 17th of

*Vt. Gov. and Council, Vol V, p. 525. N. H., State Papers, Vol. X, p. 287.

March, 1779, they drew up a definite proposition addressed to that body.

Bayley and Phelps, with Lieut.-Gov. Marsh, repaired to Exeter, and presented their case before the legislature. Ira Allen appeared in the interest of the Bennington party. The legislature voted to appeal the matter to the Continental Congress, which was done, but nothing seems to have come of their action.

The freemen of Newbury were warned to meet in town-meeting on April 6th, 1772, "to take into consideration a letter sent into the town by Col. Peter Olcott, the substance of which is to see if the town, with the other towns lying on the Connecticut river, will petition to Congress not to confirm the state of Vermont, until we should have an opportunity to give our reasons why it should not be confirmed, and to consider the form of such a petition." This meeting, of which Ephraim Webster was moderator, voted, "that a petition be laid before the Continental Congress, representing the arbitrary, unjust, and unconstitutional proceedings of the state of Vermont, so called."

The protest of Nehemiah Lovewell, against this petition, "as being erroneous, and very unfortunate," may still be seen in the first volume of Town Proceedings. Nothing, however, came of the petition to Congress.

Vermont was now in a very embarrassing situation. New York claimed the whole territory on one side, and New Hampshire on the other, while Massachusetts put in a claim for a strip along the southern border. Congress seemed indifferent, and it appeared that the new state would be divided up among its neighbors, or fall a prey to the wiles of the British in Canada. This was in the very midst of the revolutionary war, when politics ran high, party spirit was bitter, and the alarms kept the country in a constant state of anxiety.

During a space of two years our town records are silent upon the controversy, but on the 22d of March, 1781, a town-meeting was called by order of the General Assembly, "to see if they would accept of the union of the people on the east side of the river, to be with the Grants on the west side." Voted in the affirmative, and that Jacob Kent and Josiah Page represent the town at Windsor.

It will appear that a great change had taken place since the First Union was so summarily rejected, and we shall have to go back several months to understand the cause.

We must bear in mind, however, that the whole history of these proceedings is very obscure, and many interfering interests add to our perplexity. The action of the town of Haverhill, on March 31, 1781, was similar to that taken by many other towns east of the river.* "To agree to the articles of union between the state of

---

*Haverhill Town Records.

Vermont and the New Hampshire Grants," and chose Timothy Bedell, and Joshua Howard representatives to the General Assembly at Windsor." It is not necessary for us to consider the grievances which led the towns in the western part of New Hampshire, to desire a separation from the rest of that state, and annexation to Vermont.

A convention of delegates from the towns in Cheshire County, held at Walpole, November 17, 1780, determined that "matters lately agitated with respect to the New Hampshire Grants, render a union of territory absolutely necessary."

They sent out a printed circular, calling a convention from all the towns within the Grants, to meet at Charlestown, on the third Tuesday in January, 1781. This convention was attended by delegates from forty-six towns, and passed resolutions looking toward a second union of the towns on the east side of the river with Vermont. A committee was appointed to confer with the Vermont legislature, which was to convene at Windsor in February, and the convention adjourned, to meet at the same time, at Cornish, on the opposite side of the river.

This session of the Assembly met on the third of February, and on the 10th received the committee of the convention. After consideration of an elaborate report, articles of union were agreed upon, to take effect when ratified by two-thirds of the interested towns.

On the fifth of April the convention and the Assembly met at the same places as before, and, the returns being favorable, members from thirty-five towns east of Connecticut river were admitted to seats in the legislature of Vermont.* This is known as the "Second Union." For the first time for several sessions of the Assembly, Newbury was represented, as we have stated, by Col. Kent and Josiah Page. Col. Bedell and Capt. Joshua Howard were the members from Haverhill. Thirty-six Vermont towns favored the plan of union, seven dissented, and six made no return.

In June, the Assembly met again, this time at Bennington, and at that session the representatives from eleven towns near Hudson river, now within the limits of the state of New York, were admitted to seats, on terms similar to those which had been given to the towns in New Hampshire. These New York towns were brought into the union through the contrivance of the Bennington party, in order to balance the increase of territory on the east side of the state. Newbury does not appear to have been represented at this session.

---

* These towns were:—Hinsdale, Walpole, Surry, Gilsum, Alstead, Charlestown, Acworth, Leinster, Saville, Claremont, Newport, Cornish, Croydon, Plainfield, Grantham, Marlow, Lebanon, Grafton, Dresden, Hanover, Cardigan, Lyme, Dorchester, Haverhill, Landaff, Gunthwaite, Lancaster Piermont, Richmond, Chesterfield, Westmoreland, Bath, Lyman, Franconia and Lincoln.

This Assembly sent delegates to the Continental Congress, applying for the admission of Vermont to the Federal Union. These delegates were informed by that body, that it was indispensable for admission, that Vermont relinquish all claim to territory east of the Connecticut, and west of a line drawn from the north-west corner of Massachusetts, to the southern extremity of Lake Champlain. This was precisely what the Bennington party wished to bring about.

On the eleventh of October, 1781, the Vermont legislature met at Charlestown, in the state of New Hampshire, when Elisha Payne of Lebanon, in that state, was chosen Lieutenant-Governor of Vermont, in default of an election by the people. Members were present from thirty-six towns east of the river, and from sixty-six west of it. This Assembly passed some resolutions concerning the terms prescribed by Congress, and regulated the courts of the towns east of the river. It was not to be expected that the authorities of New Hampshire would stand idle, and allow the state of Vermont thus to detach a portion of its territory and hold a session of its legislature within its borders.

In most of these towns which had been thus annexed, this new union was strenuously opposed by a minority. Disturbances broke out, the authority of Vermont was defied in its new possessions, and armed collisions took place in Cheshire County.

The Governor of New Hampshire ordered a draft of 1000 men, to proceed to the scene of disturbance. The commander of the Vermont troops prepared to hold the new territory by force of arms. Civil war seemed imminent, and great anxiety prevailed, while disinterested spectators wondered what would come next.

It was at this period that the tories and the British in Canada were most active and most hopeful, for they expected and desired that the dissensions should increase, and the state of the Grants become such that the people would return to their allegiance, as their only refuge from anarchy. But this was not to be. Wiser counsellors were at hand. Vermont was not to become a province of Canada, neither was the Connecticut valley to be the scene of civil war. At this critical period, Washington, who had been observing these proceedings with deep anxiety, threw the weight of his vast influence into the scale. In a letter to Gov. Chittenden, he pointed out the danger to the general welfare of the country, if any state could, at will, seize upon and annex a portion of another state. He made an earnest appeal for immediate submission to the will of Congress as the only condition for the admission of Vermont into the Federal Union.

In February, 1782, the Vermont legislature met at Bennington, when few of the representatives from the eastern side of the state could be present, and dissolved the union with the New Hampshire towns by a formal vote.

It does not appear that either Gen. Jacob Bayley, or Col.

Thomas Johnson had anything to do with this Second Union. Indeed, during much of the time when it was in existence, Johnson was a prisoner in Canada. The deep-seated distrust which both held toward Ethan Allen and his associates madeit impossible for them to concur in any scheme which would put the river towns into the control of the Bennington party. In their view the interests of these towns were identical, and they wanted to have all the territory drained by the Connecticut, north of the Massachusetts line, under one government. It does not appear, either, that they opposed the plan, probably thinking it would come to nothing.

General Bayley wrote to President Weare at Exeter: "I am determined to fight for New Hampshire and the United States as long as I am alive, and have one copper in my hands."*

Several of the river towns in Vermont were not willing to give up the matter without another trial, and a convention was called to meet at Thetford in June, to which Newbury was invited to send a delegate. Our town records are silent as to this invitation, and any action which came from it, but in the state archives at Concord is a paper in the handwriting of Col. Kent, which is as follows:——

"NEWBURY, May 31, 1782.

At a Legal Meeting of sd Town, on said Day being a full meeting voted to be under the Government of the State of Newhampshire at the same time chose Gideon Smith to meet a Convension of members from towns who should be of our Opinion at Thetford in Order to make application to sd State of Newhampshire.

But two men Voted in the Negative, who were William Wallis and Levi Silvester.

JACOB KENT, Town Clerk.

It would certainly seem that at this time, Newbury people had little wish to join the new state of Vermont. The other towns which sent delegates to the convention at Thetford, were, Bradford, Thetford, Norwich and Hartford. This convention chose Abel Curtis of Norwich, agent, to present the application of these five towns to the New Hampshire legislature, and that body entered into a correspondence with the authorities of New York, which insured some protection to the frontier. Very little is known concerning either this correspondence or its result. But a second paper in the New Hampshire Archives shows that something was done:

NEWBURY, November 7, 1782.

Whereas Application was made to the State of Newhampshire at their Session at Concord in June last by Mr. Curtis, Agent for five Towns, and Incouragment given for Jurisdiction and Protection, and we are Sensiable that protection has been afforded from sd State for which we return sd State thanks in the Name of this Town, and now Desire said state would Extend Jurisdiction over Said Town in its fullest Extent as it is the Desire of the Town in General.

SYLVANUS HEATH, ⎫ Selectmen
JOSHUA BAYLEY, ⎬ of
FRYE BAYLEY, ⎭ Newbury.

---

*N. H., State Papers, Vol. VIII. p. 281.

The precise meaning of this paper we do not at this distance of time, know.

It may be that prominent men in New Hampshire interceded with the Bennington party, now successful, on behalf of the towns which still held out. Certain measures of that party provoked an appeal to Congress, which drew from that body, December 7, 1782, an order forbidding any resort to coercive means.

But the troubles gradually subsided; the river towns, one by one, recognized the authority of the new state, till Norwich and Newbury were left alone in opposition. Two years later a complete change was wrought. Newbury sent two representatives, Jacob Bayley and Ebenezer White to the Vermont legislature, and in 1786, Jacob Bayley was again elected a councillor, and took his seat at the board under Governor Chittenden, whom he had a few years before, denounced as a traitor. Vermont looked for immediate admission into the Federal Union, but the influence of New York was strong enough to keep it out for several years.

Meanwhile the state was being peopled by an industrious and thriving class of emigrants, new towns sprang up, taxes were light, and the new state was, evidently, doing so well alone, that it became desirable to admit so prosperous a commonwealth into the Union.

Political reasons demanded its admission to balance the entrance of Kentucky; sufficient influence was brought to bear upon New York to give up its claims upon the payment of a sum of money, and at a convention which met at Bennington, January 10, 1791, in which Daniel Farrand represented Newbury, and took an important part, the state of Vermont assented to the Constitution of the United States.

The act for the admission of Vermont into the Union was approved by Washington February 18, 1791, and on the fourth of the following March it became the first of thirty-two states to be admitted to the Federal Union.

CHAPTER XX.

AFTER THE WAR.

THE REVOLUTIONARY WAR AS IT NOW APPEARS.—THE TORIES.—A FAMILY FEUD.—
HALF-HEARTED PATRIOTS.—DEPRECIATED CURRENCY.—THE LAW OF 1787.—
AN OLD BILL.—"THE CRITICAL PERIOD IN AMERICAN HISTORY."—GENERAL
DISTRESS.—SHAYS' REBELLION.—HENRY TUFTS.—COUNTERFEIT MONEY.—THE
BUSHEL OF WHEAT.—LUMBERING.—MASTS.—VISIT OF PRESIDENT DWIGHT.

IT is now a century and a quarter since the revolutionary war began, and it is possible to view, dispassionately, the whole course of events. Yet the precise measure of either praise or blame which should be allotted to each actor in those scenes cannot be awarded now, but the Americans were not all disinterested patriots, neither were all the British tyrants.

One class of men has received scant justice at the hands of posterity. Seventy years ago the name of Tory was so obnoxious that it was hardly possible to offend a man more than to call him by a name which implied that either he or his immediate ancestor had taken the unpopular side in the great struggle. Many years ago the word "Tory," was found scratched upon the stone in the Ox-bow cemetery, which marked the grave of a certain revolutionary officer, whose situation during the war had made him the object of much annoying criticism from his enemies. The culprit was discovered, and a bitter feud resulted between two families which out-lasted that generation.

It has been asserted, with considerable probability, that the war for independence was the work of a minority of the people of the colonies, and that, had the result depended upon a ballot, the colonies would have adhered to the crown. Fortunately for us and for the world, the contest was decided in favor of popular government, but much obloquy has fallen upon certain men in Coös, which they never deserved.

Colonel Asa Porter, Col. John Taplin and others, were men of education and influence who had held office under the crown, and who honestly believed that the sort of goverment which was intended to be set up would bring about, in the end, worse evils than those which the country before suffered. Thence they declined to cast in their lot with men like Bayley, Johnson and Bedell, and in consequence of their prominent position, they were held to be guilty, in popular belief, of instigating a thousand plots and deeds of which they were both innocent and ignorant.

There were men in the Coös country who took advantage of the disordered state of the times to gratify private malice, and there were also those who profited by underhand dealings with the enemy. There were others, officers in the Continental service, who kept up a secret correspondence with Canada. There were those also in Coös, who were locally active in the plot to supersede Washington by Gates. But the outcome of the war so signally resulted in making Washington pre-eminent above all other Americans, that those who had striven to overthrow him, made haste to remove the traces of their hostility.

Still, all was not destroyed, and the pride of many families would be wounded could they know what the Canadian archives can reveal. But these were few; the great majority of the people in the Connecticut valley were true and loyal to the patriotic cause. Among the troubles which grew out of the war, and which the Coös country had to share with the older portions of the colonies, was the disturbance to business which arose from the depreciation of the currency. Successive issues of paper money, which could not be redeemed in coin, were still further shorn of their value by numerous counterfeits. The bills issued by the order of the Continental congress were so poorly executed that it was very easy to counterfeit them, and even the genuine soon became of little value. In these days of a stable currency, we find it hard to imagine the state of things which would result, if a man could not know what the dollar bill which he received today will be worth tomorrow or next week. Business security is only assured when a man knows that the dollar of today will be worth just one hundred cents next week or next year, or five years hence.

But the continental currency depreciated so rapidly in value, that the General Assembly of 1787 found it necessary to fix by law the value of paper money expressed in contracts made at different times after September, 1777, when the Continental dollar began to fall below the Spanish milled dollar, which was the chief coin in circulation. By that law, the value of the Spanish dollar was that of two paper dollars in 1778; by the September following it was worth three dollars, and ten months later the Spanish dollar was valued at ten paper dollars. In all contracts dated January 1, 1780, one dollar in silver was held to be equal to twenty paper dollars; by the first of the next September the ratio was 72 to 1 and kept on rising. Money was never so plenty as when it was almost worthless, because when a man received any of the currency, he made haste to spend it as soon as possible, to get as much out of it as he could.

There were men ruined by this fall in values. John Hugh, who owned a farm on the Ox-bow, sold it, receiving his pay in Continental currency, with which he intended to purchase new land in the north part of the state, but before he could invest the money, it had become almost worthless.

The following bill, preserved among the Little papers, has interest in this connection:

> "Dr.——The United States of America to Moses Little. On express from General Bayley to his excellency, General Washington, being 350 miles from Coös to Morristown, February 28, 1781.
>
> To my expenses on the road to headquarters, $ 946
> To my expenses on my return,   1146
> To my time, 31 days, at $81 per day,   2345
>   ————
> $4437."

This formidable bill, when reduced to coin, shrinks to the modest sum of $63.44.

The years which passed between the end of the war and the adoption of the Federal constitution were, to the country, generally, years of distress and uncertainty. This time was what Prof. Fiske has so well entitled, "The critical period of the American republic." The new nation was only a league between the states; there was no central authority, no head to the new government. It seemed doubtful, even to the wisest and most patriotic, if the new nation would long endure.

There was great distress in all parts of the country. Many had become impoverished by the war; many had left the country. A few had seized upon the opportunities of the time to acquire wealth. The continental currency had become so worthless that no one would take it, and disappeared from circulation. Taxes were high, and money was scarce. Those who were so unfortunate as to have all their property in wild land, saw it worth so little as hardly to sell for enough to pay the taxes upon it. Those who had money, made haste to invest it in real estate, taking advantage of the dire necessities of their neighbors. Our town records show how many farms, and tracts of wild land, came into the hands of a very few men about that time.

In Massachusetts a formidable rebellion broke out in 1786, under the leadership of Daniel Shays. There were outbreaks in different parts of New Hampshire and Vermont. At Rutland a mob prevented the sitting of the court. Here in Newbury, one Henry Tufts, who was always in mischief somewhere, appeared at the court-house on the day of the opening of the court, made an inflamatory speech, displayed a gun, and called on the people to follow him, and turn out the judge, lawyers and jury, who were, he declared, the authors of all the misfortunes which the country suffered. Tufts was, however, at once disarmed, and put in jail, after which, being compelled to sit in the stocks, he decided to leave the town. Some years later, he wrote from Maine, under an assumed name to Col. Johnson, trying to recover the gun which had been taken from him. This was that Henry Tufts, who, later, published an autobiography of which Thomas Wentworth Higginson gave some account in Harper's Magazine for March, 1888, under the title, "A New England Vagabond." Tufts died in Maine in 1831. He married one of his numerous wives in this town.

The evils which were caused by a depreciated currency were augmented by the great amount of base coin which was in circulation. When we speak of the money of those days, two things must be remembered—that there were no banks in this country until after the revolutionary war, so there were no bank-notes—and that the United States did not begin the coinage of gold and silver until 1792, consequently all the coin which circulated was of foreign countries. At the present time it is rare to see a foreign coin in circulation, except Canada silver, but in 1787, an account of money, amounting to one hundred pounds sterling, sent to New York, enumerated coins of five nationalities. Here in Newbury, the records of the First Congregational church show that it was voted, June 6, 1788, "that each member should leave a pistareen with the minister for the purpose of purchasing the wine for the communion service."

In these days, counterfeiting is about as dangerous business as a man can engage in, but in those days of slow communication, the occupation was comparatively safe and lucrative. It was much easier and safer to counterfeit the coins of some distant country, whose money was little known, than it was to imitate the coin of the United States, had any been made then.

Glazier Wheeler, whom we have met before, had fallen into the hands of men who obliged him to make for them Spanish dollars and "Half Joes," which contained only one-fourth as much pure metal as the genuine. The money which he had been making, contained one-half the usual amount of gold and silver. Wheeler was caught in the act of making dies, was made to stand one day upon the pillory at Haverhill, have one of his ears cropped, and be imprisoned one year. He complained bitterly over his treatment by those who had profited by, and then abandoned him. He had served with credit in the war, and later, is said to have retrieved his fortune by his skill as an engraver in the mint at Philadelphia.

At this time, and for many years before and after, the standard of value, in local trade, was a bushel of wheat, the staple product of the farms, the one for which there was the most steady demand, and most equable value. The bushel of wheat paid taxes; upon it was computed the minister's salary, and the laborer's wages. The great meadows produced, annually, thousands of bushels for export, and the hill farms were beginning to contribute to the supply. At present a field of wheat is hardly seen on the meadows from Ryegate to Hanover.

The years which passed between the end of the war and the beginning of the century, were, on the whole, very prosperous ones in Haverhill and Newbury, for those who had been here long enough to have established themselves, or those who came here with money enough to purchase improved farms. The country between Haverhill and Concord had become settled, and the roads were better every year. The whole north country from here to Canada line was filling up with an industrious and thrifty population. Newbury being at the head of boat navigation on the river, had the great advantage of situation, and there were some very enterprising men in this town in those days, who were quick to seize upon the opportunities then offered.

They made it for the interest of people about to settle above here to purchase their supplies in Newbury, instead of bringing them from the places whence they came. In turn Newbury was a convenient market, and the merchants had much trade with all the upper country.

The circumstance of the courts being located here, brought many people into the place, and caused it to be well known. Some of our older houses, twenty or more, were built in that period. Haverhill academy was opened in 1793, and soon made its influence felt. One evidence of the prosperity of the time is shown by the enterprise of the people in building roads, and making it easier to market the produce of the farms.

In 1796, the town suffered a considerable loss in the removal of the county seat to Chelsea. For nearly twenty-five years Newbury had received all the benefit which in every newly settled country attends the possession of the seat of justice. Several lawyers, some of whose names have not come down to us, made their home here, and it was from that removal, that Newbury ceased to be the most important place in the east part of the state, above Windsor. The close of the century left the town in a prosperous condition, when we take its position into consideration. The distance of the nearest market, and the condition of the highways, prevented the development of the resources of the country. Only live stock, and the more portable products of the farm went to the distant markets.

When we consider that a century ago there were no manufacturing towns, and that there were, in all New England, not more than ten places of as many thousand inhabitants, and those along the coast, we may well wonder that there was any market at all, not already supplied by towns nearer the sea-ports. There was, however, a growing export trade, and those products of the farm which were in greatest demand were those which were required to supply this trade. These were butter, cheese, wool, maple sugar, dressed meat, salts, (i e., pot and pearl ashes,) and grain. Lumber was floated down the river, either in the log, or in boats, usually the former. Timber for ship-building, especially for masts, was in demand. It is said that during the wars of Napoleon, trees were cut in this town to supply masts for the French navy, and which were floated down the river.

There are huge pine stumps four feet and over in diameter, still remaining in the woods in Newbury, from which the trees were removed a hundred years ago, and which bid fair to outlast another century, and which may have furnished masts for Napoleon's ships.

The sale of trees for masts began soon after the revolutionary war, and was continued for many years. Some of the accounts of sales of these still exist. Dr. McKeen thus states regarding similar transactions in Bradford: "Pine trees were then plenty and money scarce. Sticks of timber sixty feet long were estimated by their average diameter at the rate of twenty-five cents an inch. According to this rule a mast sixty feet long and thirty inches in diameter would come to but seven dollars and a half. One giant mast 116 feet long, and forty inches in diameter was thus delivered. This large pine trunk, at the above rate, would be estimated at not quite twenty dollars." These facts are given to show how hard people had to work in those days to get a little money.

Another business which was quite important was that of building flat-bottomed boats for the conveyance of lumber to market, and bringing up cargoes of salt, rum, iron and other heavy articles of merchandise. There were several builder's yards in this town. One, and perhaps several, were at Wells River. Boats were also built near the mouth of Harriman's brook, and near the present site of Bedell's bridge. Sometimes, for lack of a return cargo, the boat was sold for its lumber, and the men who had gone down with it, returned on foot. The men who went down with rafts usually returned in this way, and there are still old men who have often walked back from Hartford, or Northampton, after going down with their load. Many, and perhaps most of the older men who were living twenty years ago, had spent considerable time upon the river in their younger days, just as many of the older men of the present day used to be teamsters between here and Concord before the railroad was built.

There are none left who can tell what Newbury was at the close of the century, the exact location of homes, or precisely what parts of the town had been cleared. Boltonville and the farms around West Newbury, were settled much earlier than any other sections back from the river. John Wilson, who came to Bradford in 1795, and settled west of Wright's Mountain, stated in writing in his old age, that at the date mentioned, the only road from Corinth to Newbury was the one which goes past the Rogers hill schoolhouse. About 1788, John C. Foster bought land, and began clearing on the farm which, two years later, he sold to William Peach. Not much later, settlement began on the farm long owned by William Wallace, and about the same time, by Thomas Mellen, where J. C. Leavitt now lives, south of the town house. These were the first settlements in that part of the town. In 1796, President Dwight of Yale college, made the first of three journeys which included the Connecticut valley. In this year he mentions the fine apple orchards along the river road, the finest he had ever seen, but wheat, he said had been blasted upon the meadows for some years. Dr. Dwight was a very close observer, and some of his remarks are worth quoting:

"October 7, Crossed the river at the ferry above the Great Ox-bow. The boat was managed by two children smaller than I had ever seen entrusted with such employment. But the expedition and safety with which we crossed the river, proved their perfect competency for their business, and convinced me that we generally estimate the capacity of children beneath the truth. The houses of the place are moderately good in size and structure, but not being painted have an unpleasant appearance.

About 1782, a spring was discovered, which ceases, it is said, to flow for some time once in every two or three years. When its waters are left to settle they are covered with a yellow pellicle, and emit a strong sulphurous odor."

He again visited Newbury in 1803, and 1812, noting many improvements at each visit.

CHAPTER XXI.

THE NINETEENTH CENTURY.

IN 1799, a recruiting station for the United States army was
opened at Newbury, and it would seem from certain bills which
remain among the Johnson papers, that a company of soldiers
from the regular army was stationed here. They mention
"barracks," and a "hospital". Capt. Andrew McClary was
the officer in command, and J. V. Glen was Adjutant. The
bills are in a handwriting which is a marvel of beauty.

Near the close of the century many citizens of France sought
refuge in this country from the troubles and dangers of their own
land. Upon the heads of some of them, a price was set, and they
made their way, for security, to the remote villages. Several of
these, both men and women came here, and remained some time.
They did not mingle with the townspeople, as only one or two
spoke English, but kept entirely to themselves. They do not
appear to have taken their exile much to heart. Some of them
had rooms at the Ox-bow, and others were quartered lower
down in the village. One evening these latter went up to
Moses Johnson's tavern, where they made merry, returning long
after midnight. At that time there was a very tall and large
tree standing on the west side of the road, south of where
Dea. Sidney Johnson now lives. The moon, then low in the
west, cast its broad shadow across the white, dusty road, and
when the merry party came to the place they imagined that the
shadow was a stream of water, and came to a standstill. They
debated for some time how to cross without falling in and getting

wet, when one of the party, less tipsy than the rest, wrenched a board from the fence, which he placed across the chasm, and the party, holding each others hands for security, tip-toed safely over. Augustus de St. Pot, one of them, taught dancing school a term or two here in Newbury, and afterward went to Maryland. There was considerable gossip about these people at the time, but they were soon forgotten.

The news of Washington's death reached Newbury about the end of January, 1800, and appropriate religious services were held in the meeting-house. According to the recollections of Reuben Abbott, a procession was formed at Lovewell's tavern, now the Sawyer House, which comprised the military companies in the neighborhood, and the veterans of the war, and marched, with military music, to the meeting-house, where a sermon was delivered by Rev. Mr. Lambert, and a funeral anthem, composed by Mr. Ingalls, was sung. The pulpit and galleries were hung with black, and the services made a great impression.

In 1801, John Peach, Noyes and Joshua Bayley went out to Jefferson Hill, then covered with an unbroken forest, and began to clear land. John Peach built the first log house, near the present residence of his son, A. M. Peach, and Joshua Bayley the second. They were joined, later, by Merrill, James, Jacob, Ephraim and John Bayley.

Dr. Samuel White came about 1806, and later comers settled around them. James Bayley settled at the top of the hill, at the south, where Thomas P. Bailey now lives, and that house, the oldest on the hill, was built in 1827. James Bayley moved to St. Lawrence Co., N. Y., in 1833, and died there.

Dr. White lived near the present schoolhouse, his farm being on that side of the road. Then came the farm of John Peach; his son, James, afterward owning the northerly part. Merrill Bayley's place was where Albert Wright lives, his brother, Ephraim, settling south of him. The buildings erected by Ephraim are gone. Joshua Bayley's farm was north of the cross-road, and his brother, Noyes, lived where Mr. Randall does now, and the log schoolhouse which stood till 1847, was on the north side of the road, opposite the burying-ground.

John Bailey's farm was that now owned by George W. Bailey, and Jacob settled where Andrew Wylie now lives, but later, bought out his brother James. James Waddell settled on the present farm of Henry Randall, and John Waddell on that now owned by Robert Lackie.

Archibald Hunter came from Scotland, and cleared the place where Andrew Arthur lives; Nathan Avery, Jr., built the house, and lived on the farm now owned by the widow of Alvah James, and Aaron Morse lived west of him, a little way from the road. These were later comers. James, son of John Peach, was the first child born on the hill, in 1803, and Mrs. Joseph Fuller, in 1833, was the youngest child of the first settlers. A bridle road, whose location is almost forgotten, led up through Scotch hollow to the east side of the hill. The first public road from the hill went to Boltonville, and was surveyed by Nathan Avery, July 1, 1810.

For many years this neighborhood was somewhat isolated from the rest of the town, and the people formed a community of their own. Later, and especially since the building of the railroad, its interests are more with South Ryegate, than with the rest of Newbury.

Mention is elsewhere made of the legislative session of 1801, and of other things, in connection with particular periods of local history. In 1805, an event occurring in Haverhill has a place in the annals of Newbury. On the 18th of December, Josiah Burnham, a prisoner in the jail at Haverhill Corner, murdered, under circumstances of peculiar atrocity, two fellow prisoners, Hon. Russell Freeman, and Capt. Joseph Starkweather. Burnham lived here in Newbury a number of years, and was a signer of the New York petition of 1770. He was, by turns, farmer, horse-dealer, school-master, and vagabond. He was also a very good surveyor. His trial took place at Plymouth, and his defense was Daniel Webster's first plea. This latter circumstance gives the murder an historic interest. Burnham was hanged August 12, 1806, the gallows being erected on the hill-side north of the Corner. It was estimated that 10,000 persons, the largest crowd that had ever gathered in this part of the country, witnessed the execution. A remarkable sermon was preached on that occasion by Rev. David Sutherland of Bath. Burnham had sold his body to the surgeons for rum, and after the execution, it was brought over to Newbury, and placed in Dr. McKinstry's office, in the Col. Johnson house. The same evening it was dissected in a small building which stood where the east end of James Lang's barn now stands, at the Ox-bow. One of the doctors, from up country, brought a large cleaver, such as is commonly used by butchers, as his share of the dissecting instruments. The skeleton of Burnham is in the anatomical museum at Hanover.

From the opening of the century down to the breaking out of the southern rebellion in 1861, there is little in the annals of the town which does not find a more appropriate place in the history of the various institutions of Newbury. A few things, however, do not seem to have a proper position in any of these.

The first two decades of the century do not seem so prosperous as those which preceded and followed them. The population, which had been 873 in 1790, and 1304 in 1800, showed a gain of only 59 in the first ten years, and only 160 in the second decade. This, despite the fact that in those years many farms were opened, and large sections of the town came into cultivation,

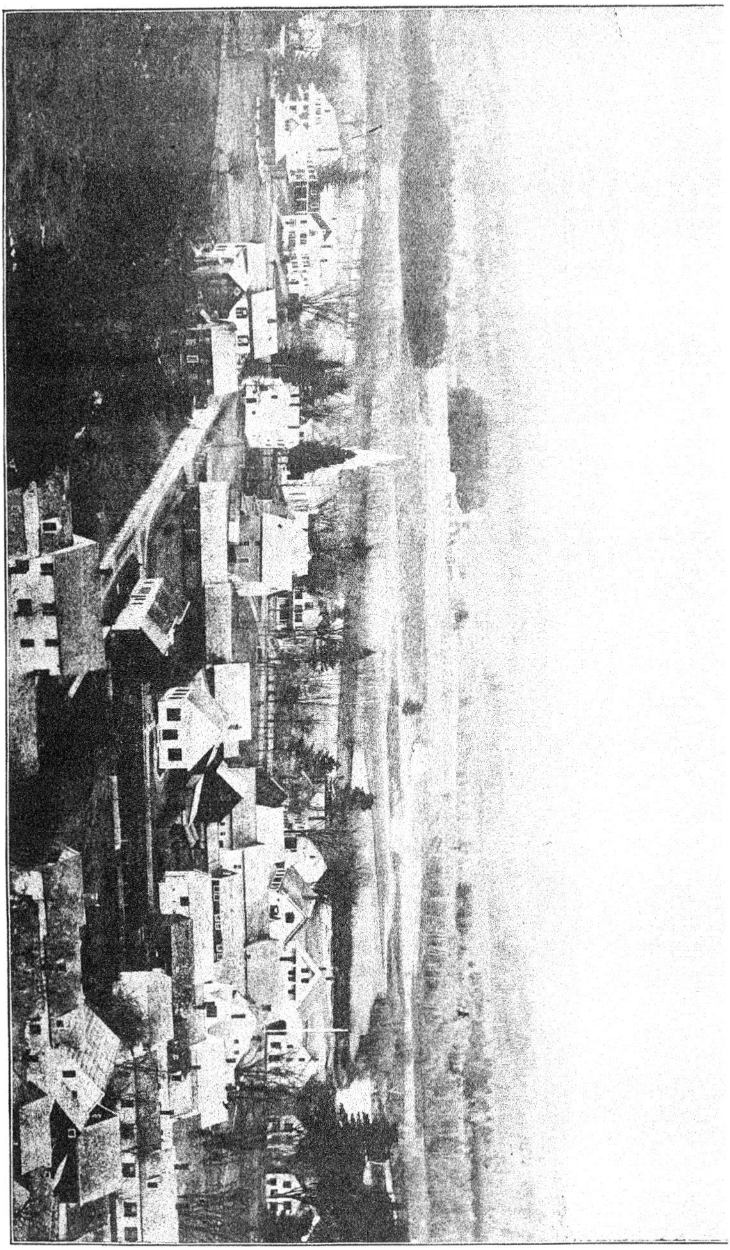

and, also the records of families, which show that many people came here to settle in those years, and the natural increase of population was quite large.

As early as 1800, there was a considerable immigration, and many families went up to the north part of the state and the southern townships of Canada, and took up land. About that time it begun to be complained that the young men were "going west," which meant the valley of Lake Champlain and the Mohawk valley. Several, before 1810, had gone to Ohio, the frontier of civilization.

There seems also to have been a shifting of population within the town. It has been stated, on good authority, that there were about fifty houses in 1800, between the mouth of Cow Meadow brook and Col. Robert Johnston's tavern, where Mr. Hibbard now lives. Any one who will take the trouble to count those now standing which were built subsequently to 1830, will see that most of those standing in 1800 have disappeared. It is probable that, in spite of the growth of the village, there were more residents between the upper curve of the Ox-bow, and Bradford line, a hundred years ago than there are now. Those who came to settle here in the first twenty years of the century, made their homes in the back parts of the town.

The war of 1812 was not popular in this town, which was no longer in the place of danger, as it had been in the struggle for independence, a generation before. The embargo which President Madison had laid upon commerce bore heavily upon New England, even in these remote quarters. A clause in the warning for a special town-meeting in July, 1809, ran as follows: "To see what money the town will raise for the payment of this town's quota of Soldiers from the time they march to the time of their discharge, in addition to what is allowed by the United States."

Voted: "That this town do not think it expedient or proper to raise any money for the payment of any soldiers which may be called into service by authority of Congress."

"That if Congress suppose it necessary to call for the militia for the purpose of carrying into effect or enforcing such laws as are by them made, and more particularly a host of acts laying EMBARGO, which are considered by us as oppressive and unconstitutional, they will provide means for the payment and support of such militia."

Voted: "That it is the sense of this town that if there are any persons therein who are in favor of the present measures of the General Government, and especially the late acts laying an Embargo, these people are in duty bound, and will, undoubtedly lend their aid and assistance into carrying into effect those laws, with whatever compensation the United States see fit to provide."

These terse and vigorous resolutions were probably drawn up by

Benjamin Porter Esq., who, it is said, sat with his brother-in-law, Mills Olcott, of Hanover, in the Hartford convention. It would seem, however, that the town took some measures for defense, as at a special town-meeting held in September, 1810, it was voted, "To raise $150. to purchase ammunition to furnish the Town Magazine." This magazine, commonly called the "old powder house," was a small brick building which stood among the pines on the summit of Montebello. It was standing forty years ago, and traces of it may, perhaps, still be seen. The first powder house was built in 1809. It was struck by lightning and destroyed while empty and rebuilt in 1836.

For a special town meeting in September, 1812, the warning ran; "To see if the town will raise any money in addition to the present wages of the men detached from the militia in this town, if they are called into actual service, and if so, how much." (Voted: not to raise any money for that purpose.)

"To see if the town will give said soldiers a bounty when they are called to march, if so, how much, and vote to raise the same." (Voted: Not to give any bounty.)

Voted: "To raise $100 to defray the expense of procuring equipments for those soldiers who are not able to equip themselves."

There is only one further record of action or want of action of the town which was at a special meeting, July 6, 1813.

"To see if the town will raise money to pay sundry contracts made by the selectmen the year past for provisions, equipment, etc., for the drafted militia." (No record of any action.)

It would seem, notwithstanding these, that the town did its duty in the matter, and a considerable number of men enlisted and served for longer or shorter periods. The records of the war of 1812, at Washington, are not now accessible, and no attempt has been made to collect the records of soldiers of that war. A company of detatched militia, under Capt. Levi Rogers, served in Col. Fifields' regiment of state troops. Several men were from this town.

Wells River was made a depot of supplies for the army, and great numbers of cattle were brought and dressed there, as Mr. Leslie relates in his chapter upon that village. In those years, also, nearly all the famous men of the early settlement and the war of independence, passed away. James Abbott died in 1803; Jacob Kent in 1812; Jacob Bayley in 1815; and Thomas Johnson in 1819. Only Robert Johnston and Frye Bayley, of the more distinguished remained in 1820. In Haverhill, also, their contemporaries were nearly all gone at the latter date. John Hazen died before the revolutionary war; Timothy Bedell in 1787; Charles Johnston in 1813; Moses Dow in 1814; Asa Porter in 1818.

On the 19th of February, 1819, died Indian Joe, or "Joe Indian," as he is often called, the last of the Coösuck Indians, of whom not much but tradition remains. He was considered a remarkable man, and rendered services to the early settlers, and to the American cause, whose nature and extent cannot now be ascertained. He served in Capt. John Vincent's Co., of St. Francis Indians in 1777-'78, and was often employed as a scout by Gens. Bayley and Hazen. He knew, thoroughly, all the country between Coös and Canada, and the value of his services was very great. He evidently was held in high estimation by the settlers, and as he grew old there appears to have been no difficulty in obtaining a pension for him from the state. This pension, at first small, was increased at different times, until, for several years before his death the state appropriated seventy dollars, annually, for his support. Col. Frye Bayley was made his guardian, and after Col. Bayley's removal to Chelsea, his son was appointed in his stead. It was at the latter's house that he died. He lay out one night when hunting, on the 1st of February, and froze both his feet, and was nearly exhausted when discovered by the party which was in search of him. Most of the principal men in town attended his funeral, and his gun, which was found loaded, was discharged over his grave. "He was," says David Johnson, "remarkably amiable and pleasant in his disposition when sober, and even when intoxicated was never known to quarrel with any one."

Many amusing stories used to be told about Joe, and Molly his wife. "Molly's Pond" in Cabot, and "Joe's Pond," which is partly in Danville and partly in Cabot, are named for them. The remains of a log canoe, made and used by Joe, were to be seen, a few years ago, on the shore of Round Pond in this town. Joe and Molly once visited Washington at his headquarters at Newburgh, N. Y., and were introduced to the General and dined at his table, after the officers had withdrawn. They were gratified by the marked attention paid them, and it was the great event of his life. "He was" to again quote Mr. Johnson, "a shrewd man, and a close observer of men and manners. He praised his friends with genuine warmth, and reproached those who used him ill with the bitterest terms of sarcasm which his imperfect knowledge of the English language could supply." A few years ago, his grave in the Ox-bow cemetery was suitably marked.

CHAPTER XXII.

The Old Meeting-House.

CONSIDERABLE space is given in these pages to the erection of this structure, as it was a very important building in its day, and many details of its construction still remain. These indicate many of the customs of the time, and incidentally show the cost of the labor and material employed.

Soon after the war there arose a demand for a larger and more suitable building for religious worship than the one which served the double purpose of a church and court-house. This matter was for several years dismissed by the town, but at a special town meeting held August 14, 1787, the work was taken up. Two of the articles of warning read as follows: "First, to see if the town will fix on a place to build a meeting-house; second, to see if the town will build a meeting-house, if so, how large, and where; to choose a committee to prosecute said business, and also what measures will be most expedient to prosecute and facilitate the same." At this meeting it was voted to build a meeting-house on the "little plain," the material for which should be provided by the first of the ensuing May.

Thomas Johnson, William Wallace, Dudley Carleton, Robert Johnston and John Haseltine, were chosen the committee, to whom were afterward added, Jacob Kent, John Mills, Remembrance Chamberlain, and Frye Bayley. A plan of the meeting-house seems to have been prepared, and at an adjourned town-meeting held September 6, 1787, they "proceeded to sell the Pew Ground to the highest bidder."

In order to understand the proceedings, it will be well to give some idea of the completed building. It stood on the west side of the street, and very near it, about half way between Mr. Farnham's and Mrs. Catharine Atkinson's, with the side of the building toward the street. On the south end was a tower, about twelve feet square, which projected its full width from the end of the building, and rose several feet above the apex of the roof, supporting the belfry, which was not quite as large, and open on all sides. Above the belfry rose the tapering steeple, surmounted by a gilded weather cock, which was about eighty feet from the ground. This was the first steeple erected in Vermont. At the foot of the tower was one of the entrances, a door which opened into the body of the church, and stairs which gave access to the galleries above. On the opposite end of the building, next to Mrs. Atkinson's, was a similar projection, with entrance doors, and stair-cases, but which did not rise above the roof. The main entrance, "the front door," was on the east side next the street, exactly in the middle, and from it ran the "broad aisle" to the pulpit, which was on the west side of the house. A narrower aisle, which crossed this precisely in the middle of the church, extended the whole length of the house, between the doors at the ends. The galleries were built around three sides of the house, that over the main entrance being reserved for the singers.

The pulpit was high, that the minister might see his hearers in the galleries; it was reached by winding stairs, and above it hung the "sounding-board," suspended from the ceiling by an iron rod. In front of the pulpit was an elevated seat for the deacons, and before them was a wide board which was hung on hinges, and formed a communion table. The pews were about seven feet square, each having its door; there were seats on three sides of each pew. These seats were hung on hinges, and were raised against the sides of the pews when the congregation stood up during the long prayer, and were let down again at its close with a clatter which sounded like the discharge of small artillery. There was a row of pews around the sides of the house, called the "wall pews," and in front of them ran a narrow passage, crossing each of the intersecting aisles. The rest of the pews, considered the most desirable, were called the "body pews," and opened either into one of the main aisles, or into this narrow passage. Above the partitions of the pews ran a rail, supported by many small turned posts which were the delight of children to twirl in sermon time.

There were three windows on each side of the main door, and seven in the upper part, which lighted the galleries, on the east side. There were as many on the west side, and several at each end, so the church had plenty of light. Some of these windows, with their many small panes, may still be seen in Mr. Farnham's building. The meeting-house was a dignified, substantial edifice, painted white and considered one of the best church buildings in rural New England in its day. At this sale the pews upon the ground floor of the projected house, forty-eight in number, were sold at auction, and realized £495, 7s. or $1,650.00. Four of them brought more than fifty dollars each and were bid off by Thomas Johnson, John Mills, Jacob Bayley and Joshua Bayley.

The sale of the pews seems to have realized a sufficient sum to justify the committee in proceeding to build, and on the 1st of January, 1788, they agreed to "certain regulations for the purpose of building a meeting-house in Newbury and for finishing the same," which were as follows:

*Art 1. That each holder of a pew shall have the liberty of turning in One Thousand of Good Merchantable White Pine Boards to be delivered on the little Plain where said House is to be Built, By the first Day of April next. Also each Pew is taxed with Four Bushels of wheat and Three Bushels of Ingian Corn, and as much more as is found convenient for each Person to turn in. The wheat for the lower end, and back part of the town, to be Delivered at Col. Robert Johnston's; and the Middle and Upper District to Deliver their Wheat at Col. Thos. Johnson's.

The whole Wheat and Corn to be delivered by the first of February, and as there will be considerable Pork wanted for carrying on the Building, such persons as choose to, pay in Pork. Beg that they will give Timeous Notice of the Same, or turn it in at the aforesaid place and Time, and the two shillings on the pound that is to be paid in cash are Requested to pay it Immediately, or Give information what of each article they will procure.

Good Rye will be accepted at four shillings per bushel; Wheat at five shillings; Corn at three shillings; Clear Salt Pork at eight pence per pound; By the Hogg, Fresh at five pence per pound; Seasoned Boards at 20 shillings per 1000; Clapboards 42 shillings per 1000, and short shingles at 9 shillings per 1000."

The committee had already fixed upon a carpenter of approved skill, in the person of Levi Webster, of Enfield, N. H., whom they agreed to pay five shillings a day, in wheat or neat stock, who came about the middle of March, and seems to have found the lumber on the ground, and labored with such skill, and good assistance, that the frame was raised on the 25th of June, 1788. It is said that every able-bodied man in both Newbury and Haverhill was at the raising, and the town seems to have provided a sumptuous dinner, the bills for which are still in existence. Veal was 3p. per lb., pork 8d., butter 8p., cheese 7p., bread 2p. per lb., and rum 4 shillings a gallon.

It seems that the house was not completed at once, as the bills for plastering are dated August 27, 1790, and specify the various portions of the interior which were plastered, aggregating 659 square yards, at 3d. per square yard. The ceiling contained 2,668 square feet, which gives us an approximate idea of the size of the house, which was probably about 45x60. The bill of Maxi Haseltine, a blacksmith, includes "two and one-half days work of

---

*Johnson Papers.

myself drawing the lightning rod, at 6 shillings a day, making five pr. of hinges at two and sixpence each, making pulpit hinges and fixing Brass for the Door 8 shillings, and putting up the rod, one shilling." The meeting-house was painted in eleven days by Joshua Ward at 6 shillings a day, which was done in November, 1790.

On the 21st of September, 1789, the gallery pews, thirty-five in number, were sold at auction, to be paid for in wheat, and brought from twenty to forty-five bushels, according to location, the town receiving therefor 903 bushels, valued at £228, 7s. 6d. The amount received from the sale of all the pews was about $3,250. and as Col. Thomas Johnson stated in 1806, that the house cost between five and six thousand dollars, that left $2000, or more to be raised by tax. According to receipts still extant, it seems that the "meeting-house tax" was paid mainly in material, supplies and labor.

A large square door stone, which required four yoke of oxen to draw from the Catamount in Haverhill, was placed in front of the main entrance by Capt. Jacob Bayley. The completed meeting-house was regarded with commendable pride by the people of Newbury, who possessed for some years the best building of the kind in the state, and the contracts for building more than one church in this vicinity stipulated, that it should be "equal to the one at Newbury." It was a large building and, with its wide galleries, would seat nearly 1000 people. In pleasant weather it was well filled, as it was for many years the only place of worship on the Sabbath in town. Now there are seven or more places where Sabbath services are held. There is no record of its dedication. It was occupied as a place of worship by the First Congregational church for fifty-two years. In it were held the commemorative services upon the death of President Washington, and in it the election sermon was preached before the General Assembly in 1801. In that house were ordained Rev. Nathaniel Lambert, Rev. Luther Jewett and Rev. Clark Perry and Rev. George W. Campbell was installed. The building was also occupied for town-meetings and other large gatherings. In 1801, the year in which the bell was cast for the Ladd street meeting-house in Haverhill, Col. Thomas Johnson and Col. William Wallace contracted with a bell-founder at Hartford, Conn., for a bell weighing 600 lbs., and were notified that it would be ready by June. What became of that bell is unknown. A bell was purchased and hung about 1828, Dea. Swasey thinks. This bell was removed to the "new meeting-house" in 1840.

There was no provision for warming the house until about 1816, and it must have been a cold place, in its exposed location, on a winter's day. But cold or heat made little difference with the attendance. The introduction of the stoves met with considerable opposition. They were inadequate to heat the great building, with its many loose windows. The late Dea. George Burroughs used to remark that at best, it "wasn't quite so chilly." One man was heard to say that they did more harm than good, for they "drove the cold into the back seats, so it was colder there than before." In 1791 the town voted "that John Foster have twenty shillings if he take care of the meeting-house, and keep it well swept for one year." In 1792, Joseph Chamberlin was voted one pound for similar service.

For the March meeting in 1794, Article 7 in the warning reads: "To see if the town will appoint a Chorister or Choristers to lead the singing, also what encouragement they will give Masters to teach the art of singing in the town, and give directions how often to meet for that purpose." Jeremiah Ingalls, Jacob Bayley and Simeon Stevens were chosen.

In 1795, it was voted "to sell so much of the ground as to make one pew on each side of the Broad Alley," and William Wallace was chosen to sell the ground for two pews for no less than thirty pounds for the ground, for each pew.

In March, 1802, it was voted, "not to allow Mr. Joseph Chamberlin anything for the ground where the meeting-house stands."

We may well wonder how the people endured the two long services in that building in the cold winter days. But Mr. Farnham's house was then an inn, and the people who could not go home at noon, warmed themselves at its hospitable fireside, or at those of the other houses which were near. Such repairs as were necessary were made by the town for many years, but in 1828 it was repainted and reshingled by subscription.

About that time began an agitation in favor of a new meeting-house. The Methodist society, then rapidly increasing in number, had laid claim to the use of the house a part of the time, a few years before, and there arose some contention about the relative shares held in it by the town and the Congregational church.

On the 14th of February, 1840, a meeting of the Congregational society was held in Judge Berry's office, at which the report of a committee previously chosen to inspect the condition of the meeting-house, and estimate the cost of re-modeling and refitting it, and of ascertaining upon what terms the claims of the town and individuals could be secured to the society, was heard. The report was adverse to the further retention of the house. Certain pew-owners, who were no longer connected with the society, declined to sell their shares except upon exorbitant terms, and the society decided to build a new church, and James Brock, Freeman Keyes, William Bailey, A. B. W. Tenney, Joseph Atkinson and William Burroughs were chosen a committee to build a new meeting-house.

The last service was held in the house on the 8th of November, 1840, and the new church was dedicated on the Friday following.

Thus abandoned, the building stood for eight years, occasionally used for public gatherings. Its end was inglorious enough. In 1848, the town sold it to the Connecticut and Passumpsic Rivers Railroad Company to be made into a depot, the windows and pews were taken out, and an attempt was made to lower the great building, steeple and all, down the high bluff in its rear, an undertaking which would be considered rather formidable even in these days. In getting it down the hill, some of the rigging employed in the operation, gave way, and the whole structure fell with a great crash. It has been thought that there were those who were opposed to having the old meeting-house turned into a railroad station, who contrived its downfall. In its day it was the most important building in town, and a landmark of the Connecticut valley. It was considered a fine building, but no picture was ever made of it, and there is nothing to show where it stood.

One to whom every memory of the old house is dear, has kindly communicated the following brief reminiscence:—

I hardly know how to convey the memories which are mine of "the Old Meeting-house." My first recollection was being taken there Sundays—winter and summer. In summer time, of women in gay attire carrying cinnamon roses and caraway sprigs, according to age. In winter, of a bitter cold atmosphere, two box-stoves, one at each end of the longest aisle, which was from north to south, and of the "foot-stoves" which individuals brought to their pews—only the wealthier ones had these—there was none for our pew, much to my sorrow.

In later days, after a new church was built, where the Congo' stands at the present time, the "Old meeting-house" was the "play-house" of the neighborhood children. We climbed the rickety stairs to the belfry—swung on the "lightning-rod," which descended from that to the ground, just within our reach—played meeting in the body of the house—sung in the "singing-seats"—sat in the "deacons-seat"—marched up the broad aisles, of which there were two, from north to south, and from east to west—entered the grandest pews, which differed from others only in having a three cornered shelf for the hymn books—sat in the seat of the deacons—and grandest of all, ascended, with all dignity and solemnity, as we had seen done, to the pulpit and "preached" under the "sounding-board" with the ornament on its top decorated with red, white and blue and gold stripes. I never could understand why it did not fall. I really expected it would.

Nothing would give me greater pleasure than to be able to sketch all these pictures as they live in my memory, but it seems to me that there are many in our land and on foreign shores that must remember just how it all looked.

In later years, I cannot give the date, there was a revolt among the students of Newbury Seminary, and the disaffected ones got up an independent "exhibition" there, on a large stage erected for the occasion; the "Witches cauldron" boiled—"Clan Alpine's" hosts were marshalled—"Roderick Dhu"—"Lochiel" was enjoined to "beware." A few weeks since I met one of these heroes—there must be others—but alas many, many, are, I know not where.

MRS. L. J. PEASLEE.

Before 1808, when Montpelier was fixed upon as the capital, the General Assembly met in the more considerable towns in different parts of the state. Between the first session, in March, 1778, and that of October, 1808, a period of thirty years, there were forty-seven sessions of the legislature, fifteen being held at Windsor and eight at Bennington.

The October session of 1787 was held at Newbury, from October 11th to the 27th. It convened in the court-house, opposite the cemetery on the Ox-bow. Thomas Chittenden was Governor; Joseph Marsh of Hartford, Lieutenant Governor; Joseph Fay of Bennington, Secretary; Gen. Jacob Bayley was one of the council; Capt. John G. Bayley was sheriff; Rev. Lyman Potter of Norwich, preached the election sermon, and Gideon Olin was speaker of the House of Representatives. There was a review of all the militia, in the field behind Col. Robert Johnston's house, and a troop of cavalry escorted the Governor to the place where the election sermon was delivered. Most of the prominent men in the state were in attendance, but nothing very important was transacted. Chittenden county was organized at that session, and a proclamation was issued by the governor, announcing the completion and publication of the statute laws.

It is said that after the Assembly adjourned, Gov. Chittenden started for his home in Colchester, on foot and alone, but, somewhere, between here and the Winooski valley, got lost in the woods, and was compelled to pass the night under a fallen tree.

The second session held here, was the most important event which had taken place in the history of the town, and was brought about, mainly, through the efforts of Col. Thomas Johnson. For this, great preparations were made, land was bought by what we should now call a syndicate, and a building was erected for the purpose of convening the assembly and council. This land was the narrow strip on part of which the Ox-bow schoolhouse now stands; it was bought of Rev. Mr. Lambert by William B. Bannister, and by him conveyed to Col. Thomas Johnson and others. A building, known by tradition to the present generation, as the "Old Court-House," was erected on that spot, the previous court-house, opposite the cemetery being taken down, and the material used in its construction. It contained one large room, fitted up with desks for the House of Representatives, which had a small gallery at one end, over the entrance, and at the other end of the building was a "council chamber" for the governor and council. There were several smaller rooms.

The building was erected by subscription, Col. Johnson's share of the expense being about $400. Jeremiah Harris of Rumney was the master-workman, and it was, if tradition be correct, the first building in this part of the country to be erected by the "square rule."

The assembly met on the 8th of October, Isaac Tichenor of Bennington being Governor, and Paul Brigham of Norwich, Lieutenant Governor, and Amos Marsh, Speaker.

"Election day," was the great event of the session in those days. On that day the governor was officially notified of his election, and took the oath of office, which was afterward administered to the council. Then His Excellency, escorted by all the militia in the vicinity rode in state to the meeting-house, where the "Election Sermon" was delivered.

One curious feature of the day must not be forgotten. Some months before the time, notice was given in the public prints that an original ode would be sung on that occasion, and the poets of the day were urged to prepare their strains in competition for the honor of producing the song, to which music would be composed by Mr. Ingalls. Col. Thomas Johnson, William B. Bannister, and James Whitelaw were the committee to pass upon the merits of such productions as should be offered. When the time came for the decision, the committee found themselves unable to decide which of the effusions submitted by two gentlemen from Peacham, Mr. Ezra Carter and Mr. Barnes Buckminster, was the superior, and it was finally agreed that Mr. Ingalls should compose music for both; that one, to be sung before sermon should be called the Election Ode, and the other, to follow the discourse, should bear the title of the Election Hymn. Both were accordingly sung, and Mr. Ingalls drilled a large choir, consisting of all the best singers in the vicinity during several weeks before the great day. Both productions are preserved in Mr. Ingalls' singing-book, the "Christian Harmony."

Reuben Abbott, who died about twenty-five years ago in Maine believed himself to be the last survivor of that large band of singers. The election sermon was preached by Mr. Lambert to as many of the people as could crowd into the meeting-house. After the services, the governor and council, with all the clergymen who were in attendance, repaired to a tavern, and dined at the expense of the state.

In those days, and for many years after, it was customary for members of the legislature, from distant parts of the state, to come on horseback to the place where the assembly met, hire pasturage, and turn their horses out to grass till the end of the session.

Gov. Tichenor boarded at the house of Col. William Wallace, the building, which, afterward enlarged, became the Spring Hotel, using the south front parlor as a reception room. There are still preserved in town articles of furniture which are associated with the session of the legislature in 1801.

Thomas Tolman of Greensboro, one of the most prominent men of the state in his time, was clerk of the House, and the following letter from him preserves for us some of the usages of the period:

"GREENSBORO, July 16, 1801.

COLO. THOS. JOHNSON, Dear Sir:

I desire you to procure from Boston a Ream of the best paper, fine, thin and soft for the pen, and also one dozen skins of vellum, or good parchment for the handsome and fine writings of the legislature. Your account shall be paid, and also your trouble. If I may depend I will not make any other application. Add ¼ hundred the very best Holland quills. One thing more. I depend on you, if you please, to make a provision for a convenient place for my office and quarters. It must be near the legislature, contain a fireplace or stove, and if convenient a bed, as for a considerable part of the time I shall write at unseasonable hours, it would be agreeable if I could sleep in the same room. Excuse this trouble. My regards to Mrs. Johnson and to your sons. I am, with consideration,

Your friend and humble servant,

THOS. TOLMAN.

No important legislation was accomplished at this session, which adjourned on the 6th of November.

In 1806, a strong effort was made to secure another session for Newbury, but without avail, and whatever hopes had been indulged of securing the permanent location of the state capital at Newbury came to no result. The building itself proved a most unfortunate investment for those who built it. It was erected by subscription, and the legislature was hardly out of it before a suit began between Col. Johnson and Asa Tenney, and before it was tried, Mr. Harris, the contractor, brought suit against Johnson, Tenney and Col. Wallace for his pay. In the end, between 1801 and 1853, it has been said that ten law suits grew out of that unlucky building. The last of these was decided by the Supreme Court in 1852, and was occasioned by the erection of the schoolhouse now standing there. Joseph Atkinson and others were the respondents, and it was held that by the terms of Mr. Bannister's deed, the land could not be used for any other purpose than as a common, which must remain unfenced, and is the property of the town. This decision was doubtless in accordance with the law, but something should be done to improve this property, which lies in a beautiful part of the village, and might be made a very attractive spot.

The building is well remembered by the older people. It stood nearly forty years, before it was finally taken down. It was uncertain whether the town or anyone really owned it, and occasioned a good deal of ridicule from the people of other places.

In 1806 the town voted: "That the selectmen provide and fix proper bars and locks to all the rooms in the State or Town house which lead to the Assembly Room or Gallery, at the town's expense." Later, the town voted the use of the building for a high school. It was used for all sorts of purposes, and the last years of its existence were melancholy enough. It stood, gloomy and dark; windows and doors gone; the roof fallen in; the stairs hanging from the gallery; the floors covered with broken plaster; children were forbidden to go inside of it; and the nervous dreaded to pass the ruinous old building after nightfall. Strange and uncanny sounds came from it on windy nights, and superstitious folks persuaded themselves that the place was haunted. At last, about 1839, the old building was taken down. Sundry doors and windows from it, which may have served their turn in its predecessor, are still in use in town.

Mr. Perry hints that the absence of public spirit which prevailed in Newbury during the first two or three decades, at least, of the century, originated in the troubles which grew out of the old court-house. There may be those who will think that the amount of ardent spirits consumed in the construction of the building had something to do with its misfortunes. Col. Thomas Johnson's bill for liquors furnished the workmen was about fifty dollars.

TENNEY MEMORIAL LIBRARY.

Photo. by Corliss.

CHAPTER XXIII.

A Chapter of Old Things and New.

THE year 1800, may be considered as a time when a great change came over the town. The old men, the first settlers, who had made their homes here in the wilderness, and had carried the Coös country safely through the struggle for independence, were passing off the stage of active life. New men, new measures, came to the front. Before that time the town-meeting settled the affairs of the town. It hired and dismissed the minister; regulated the schools and the highways; and was the source of authority for the little commonwealth. Life was simpler then than now, and bore little resemblance to the complexity of modern existence.

Before considering, in detail, the institutions of the town, we will glance at some of the changes in domestic life, which took place during the earlier half of the century.

Mr. Perry says that the first wheeled carriage was brought into Newbury by Rev. Mr. Goddard, who came to preach after Mr. Powers went away. This was in 1783. Ox carts only, were used before that time. The first chaise was not owned in town until after 1790. There was rapid improvement in the public roads about the end of the century, and by 1800, several of the well-to-do farmers had bought some kind of vehicle for driving. Mr. Sutherland states, however, that there were no wheeled vehicles in Bath, until several years after his settlement there, in 1804. Men and women rode on horseback, wives riding behind their husbands on "pillions." The first chaise was brought into Bath in 1807, and the first wagon in 1811.

One of the Chamberlins was a wheelwright, and probably began to make and repair carts and sleds very early. Sleds were all made with two runners, which were, sometimes, very long and awkward to turn. Traverse sleds were not invented till after 1825. Swings for shoeing oxen came into use about 1810. Before that time, oxen were usually thrown down upon the ground and their legs secured, when they were shod. Oxen were sometimes trained to stand still and be shod, as horses are. They were used entirely for farm work, and road work; horses were used for driving and riding, and every man who owned a horse, owned also a saddle, an article seldom seen in use now. The raising and breaking of steers, and the sale of fat oxen, formed a large portion of the work of the farm. There were many men in this town forty years ago, who contrived to turn off a yoke of fat oxen every fall, replacing them with the next younger pair from the farm stock, thus keeping several pairs of oxen and steers on hand at a time.

There are few oxen now in use in this town, but before the introduction of farm machinery, they were more profitable than horses. They worked better among the rocks and stumps with which the farms were covered, and were thus well adapted to pioneer life, and the uses of the farm, down to a late day. There were men, and quite extensive farmers too, in this town, who did not keep horses, but did all their work with oxen, relying upon exchange with some neighbor for the rare events when a horse was indispensible. At a cattle fair held in Orford, in 1850, there were exhibited four hundred yoke of oxen in one team; one hundred and fifty pairs of them were owned in that town.

Sheep were kept on every farm, sometimes two or three hundred, but the introduction of imported breeds did not begin till a little before the civil war, and the fleeces were lighter than afterward.

Cloth of all kinds, was homemade; the wool carded, dyed, spun, woven, and made up at home. When wanted for pantaloons, coats and the like of a more durable kind, and more stylish appearance, the web was taken from the loom, and sent to a "fulling-mill," where it was subjected to a process which compacted the cloth, and made a smooth surface. This was called "fulled" cloth, and was one of the chief products of the farms, and one which never failed of a ready sale, when taken to the market towns. There were tailoresses in those days, who visited, in regular succession, certain farms, and fabricated the garments for the men and boys. The clothing thus patiently constructed, had an enduring quality wholly unknown to the present generation. A young man received a "freedom suit" on arriving at his majority, and it was an even chance which would last the longest, the man, or the clothing which he wore. Instances are on record where a man wore his wedding suit on the fiftieth anniversary of his marriage, the garments little the worse for the Sunday wear of fifty years. A man's outer garment was a frock of homespun, colored blue, and nothing was warmer, or more convenient. Such, in the earlier decades of the nineteenth century, were worn to meeting. Dr. Lyman Beecher, father of Henry Ward Beecher, used to be fond of exchanging with Rev. Leonard Worcester of Peacham about once a year, and one Sunday on returning to his Boston church after one of these visits, told his congregation, that on the Sunday before when he stood up to offer prayer in the Peacham meeting-house, "half an acre of blue frocks rose up before me, with an honest heart under every one of them!"

Flax has not been raised in this town to any extent, these forty years, yet, formerly its cultivation was general. On some of the farms which have been in the same hands for several generations, the "flax-brake," the "swingle", the "hetchel," instruments by whose means the rough fibre was prepared for spinning, may still be seen. The "flax-wheel," or "little wheel," with its accompanying distaff, is one of the things most highly prized by collectors, and there are few left in Newbury. Linen, however, of fine quality and beautiful texture, was formerly made in this town, and it was once considered the proper thing for a young woman about to be married, to be able to show her entire wedding outfit, spun and woven with her own hands. The invention of the power loom has supplied the country with an inferior quality at a cheaper price. A "freedom suit" was one given to a young man upon attaining his majority, and was usually stipulated for in indentures, when a boy was "bound out."

One of the earliest accounts preserved in town is one of Col. Frye Bayley's, which reads as follows:—

"1768, Col. Jacob Bayley, Dr. to one Coat and Waistcoat, and Breeches, with Buttons and Trimmings for John Beard's Freedom Suit. £6. 8. 0."

The custom of giving a "freedom-suit" survived to a late day. The process of "binding out" boys and girls was very common, down to within about fifty years, and there have, possibly, been a few instances since that time. In earlier days, when families were very much larger than now, it often happened that a man died, leaving a large family of helpless children. It was then the duty of the poor masters, or selectmen, to find homes for such children, and apprentice them to learn the "art, mystery, trade, and calling," as the indenture read, of a husbandman, cordwainer, or blacksmith, as the case might be. A "bound out boy," as such an one was, is often alluded to, in the literature of the present day, as hardly more than a slave. In reality, scarcely anything better could happen to a homeless child, than to be placed in a good family where he would be well fed and clothed, taught industrious habits, given the rudiments of an education, and sent regularly to meeting. Some of the best men and women ever reared in Newbury were brought up in that way.

Minors and indentured children were often allowed to "buy

their time," i. e., by the payment of a certain sum, one, two, or three years before attaining their majority, the obligations between them and their parents or guardians, was dissolved.

Cochran's History of Antrim, N. H., states that the "square rule" in framing timber, came into use in that town about 1812. There is a tradition that it was used in this town first, in the building of the "old court-house," so called, in 1801. If any of the timbers in that building are extant, it would be possible to find if it was so framed. Before that time the "scribe rule," was the only one in use. By that rule instead of cutting all the posts, all the braces, and all the beams of a barn to an exact length, each piece was fitted to the place where it was to go. In some place, near, if not in, Newbury, it is said that the framing of the first barn by the new method was ridiculed by all the carpenters in the region, who declared that a building so framed in defiance of the prescribed rule could never be raised. When the time came, however, the new frame went together with marvelous ease, and the new way of framing timber soon superseded the old.

The first sawmills were of the vertical, or "up and down" kind, and no farther back than 1855, there were no fewer than twelve in operation in this town. Their construction was very simple, and the whole outfit of the mill, with the exception of the saw and the crank, could be made by the local carpenter and blacksmith. The crank, which was of iron, and weighed about 175 pounds was firmly imbedded in the end of the water-wheel axle, and an arm from this crank reached to the frame directly above it, which held the saw, and propelled it up and down between two straight posts. The carriage on which the log lay, passed between these upright posts and was so contrived by means of a ratchet-wheel—commonly called a "rag-wheel"—that as the saw came down, the carriage moved forward about three-eighths of an inch, remaining stationary while the saw went up. A "spring-pole," fastened above was so arranged, as, partially, to counter-balance the the weight of the saw and frame. When well built, with a good head of water, these mills did excellent work, and would sometimes make 150 strokes to the minute. The manner of securing the log to the carriage was clumsy, and it often took longer to set the log for each board, than to saw it. A smaller water-wheel was employed to reverse the carriage. Even after the introduction of circular saws, both kinds would sometimes be seen in the same mill, the circular saw used for the smaller logs, while the larger were sawed in the old way. It was a vast log indeed, which could not be mastered by the up-and-down saw. But in a few years they all disappeared, and the young people of the present generation have little idea how they were built.

There has been a grist-mill at Boltonville, continuously, for a century and a quarter, longer than upon any other site in town.

Grist-mills at Wells River are mentioned elsewhere by Mr. Leslie. At South Newbury, there has, at various times, been a run of stone in the successive mills which have stood at the two water privileges owned by Mr. Knight. A grist-mill was built very early at the same falls where Mr. Runnels' mill now stands, but on the other side of the brook. The same mill, or a later one, was owned by Benjamin Atwood. The present brick grist-mill was built in 1834, and was burned to the walls in 1863. It formerly contained two sets of bolting machinery. The present proprietor would have no use for them, as there is not a bushel of wheat raised in this town now, for home consumption. There have been several mills at South Newbury, near the present grist-mill, and various manufactures were carried on there.

On June 12, 1851, a fire broke out which consumed five dwelllings, and some of the mills. Ransom R. Aldrich, who had carried on quite an extensive business there in the manufacture of articles of wood, and had there introduced the first board planing machine in Orange county, was burned out, and removed his business to Bradford. Mackerel kits, and other wooden wares, were long made in a two-story building, which stood very near the site of Mr. Davis's beehive factory.

Just above Mr. Runnels' mill, but on the other side of the brook, in the sharp angle at the bend of the stream, stood a wooden building in which Eber J. Chapin carried on the carding and cloth-dressing business. This building was burned about 1856, and there is no trace of it remaining. In front of the house in which his son, A. A. Olmsted now lives, Isaac H. Olmsted had a large building in which he made chairs. This was one story high, beside the road, but in the rear had several stories. This was carried away by the great freshet of 1869. There was long a sawmill, owned at first by Mr. Atwood and later by the Tuttles, at the falls near where the old road from West Newbury comes down.

The brook road formerly crossed the stream below the present grist-mill, and, passing through Mr. Abbott's field, crossed the present road in front of his house, and following the brook, came out to the West Newbury road on the east side of the brook, at the falls near Joseph Johnston's house. At these latter falls, Capt. James Johnston erected two sawmills, and two grist-mills. The first mills were burned. The sawmill was near the bridge, the grist-mill at the falls, lower down. The latter went out of business in 1837, or 1838, but stood until it fell to pieces. The sawmill was in operation till the dam was carried away by the freshet of 1869, but the mill stood for a few years afterward. He also built a carding mill on the east side of the brook, below the sawmill, which he operated from 1814, to 1822. Near the bridge was a blacksmith shop, in which was a trip-hammer.

Before the Chalmers brothers erected their first mill on the

10

present site, there was a building which had been used as a bobbin mill. A short distance above it, at a deep cleft in the rock, was a shop in which Thomas Abbott, a wheelwright, made wagons and sleighs of a very substantial kind, some of which are still in use.

Not far from 1820, Dea. William Burroughs built a sawmill at the falls near his house, where a ledge of rocks made a natural dam. This sawmill, owned by himself, later by his sons George and William, and afterward by the former and Nathan Bartlett, who succeeded William Burroughs in the ownership of what is now the town farm, did a good business until the circular mills came into use, when it went into decay, and was carried away by the freshet of 1869.

Near the town house, at the foot of "Meader hill," a Mr. Cook erected, about 1835, a blacksmith shop, which was fitted up with a trip-hammer, and other machinery, in which he made edge tools of a superior quality, during some years. All trace of these works has long disappeared. The buildings are standing on another site. About half a mile above the town house, close by the road, in a deep ravine, stood a mill which was fitted up with machinery for several operations. This mill did not stand long or do much business. The machinery was made by local carpenters and blacksmiths. The water-wheel was a huge, upright one, with "buckets" along its rim, the weight of the buckets when full of water, causing the wheel to revolve. Its motion was not very regular. This mill had several owners, and went to decay about 1858.

The "Fleming sawmill," next above it, was built by Joseph Prescott and Samuel Gibson, and operated by Alonzo Fleming many years. It went away in a freshet, June 5, 1872. The stream which comes down from Round and Long ponds has turned two mills. About 1858, Thomas Corliss put a circular saw into a building which he had erected a few years before, in which he did business, in the spring and fall for about twenty years. John and Thomas Corliss, Sr., and Solomon Jewell, erected, about 1820, a sawmill on the farm of the former, which was operated till about 1865, and fell in ruins in June, 1877. Somewhere about 1790, Jonathan Johnson, Samuel and Jonas Tucker, built a mill at the foot of Hall's Pond, which, several times rebuilt, was in operation till 1871, the last of the old "up and down" mills, and using the crank placed in the first mill in town. A part of the mill still stood when the present dam was built for storage, about 1883. In 1841, Capt. Samuel Eastman erected a building at the falls on Vance brook, near the Union Meeting-house, in which he carried on a starch factory for two years. This ends the list of mills on Hall's brook and its branches.

Harriman's brook and pond, were formerly called Taplin's brook, and Taplin's pond. There have been several mills along that stream. Gen. Jacob Bayley built a distillery at the place sometimes called "the old tannery." This is called in old deeds "Gen. Bayley's malt house." Later, probably about 1790, it passed into the hands of Rasmus Jonson, a native of Sweden, who built the quaint house now owned by N. Lupien. He was called "Stiller" (distiller) Jonson. The making of whiskey was in those days thought to be as reputable a business as any other. The buildings afterward passed into the hands of Freeman and Henry Keyes, who converted them into a tannery. Since then they have been put to various uses under several owners. A grist-mill formerly stood at the foot of the falls, above the bridge. The mill at the top of "sawmill hill," was first built by Gen. Bayley, and after him was owned by several persons. In 1838, Joseph Atkinson sold it to Austin Avery, who kept it in operation till a short time before he died, after which it went to decay. It was rebuilt in 1882, and has since been in use, when there was water to run it. At the "dry sawmill" the mill was abandoned about 1855.

There have been mills on Scott's brook, nearly down to South Ryegate, of which no particular account has been received, and there have been a few elsewhere. The first steam sawmill was erected by the Scotts, at Ingalls' hill, near the "Tavern brook," "about the time the railroad was built." Of later portable mills, it is not worth while to attempt any history. They have nearly stripped the town of its timber.

It is believed that the first stove in this part of the country was one set up in the house of Rev. David Goodwillie, in Barnet, about 1790, by his brother, who was a tinsmith in Montreal. Stoves for heating were certainly in use in Newbury by 1800, but cooking stoves did not come till after 1820. Before that time all cooking was done at the fireplace, which, in the larger houses, filled more than half of one side of the great kitchen. Wood was more than plenty, it was an object to get rid of as much of it as possible, and the great fireplaces were sometimes eight feet long, five feet high, and three feet or more deep. To build a roaring fire in one of these caverns was a work requiring considerable skill. First, the "back-log," of maple or birch, two feet or more thick, and as long as the fireplace, is drawn into the kitchen by a horse, or pair of steers, and rolled by the farmer and his boys to its place at the back side of the chimney, where it will defy the heat for days, sputtering and giving out clouds of steam and smoke. In front of it, is a structure of various kinds of wood, green and dry, with pine knots, burning like torches, and sending out a resinous smell. The andirons support the burning mass, and on long, cold winter nights, enough wood is consumed to heat a modern house a week. Such a blaze we moderns never know. The fire illumines every corner of the room and the great chimney roars defiance to the blast. Half the heat goes up its huge throat, and the draft draws in the cold outer air through every crack and crevice of the room. Before the fireplace stands the "settle," a long, wide seat, whose high back shuts out all draught, and when the wind rages outside, and the snow drives against the panes—

"The house-mates sit,
Around the radiant fireplace, enclosed
In a tumultuous privacy of storm."

Kettles, large and small, hang by "hooks and trammells," from the "lug-pole," a green stick, which is suspended from hooks along the roof of the fireplace. This gave place, about 1785, to the iron crane, by means of which the kettles could be swung out into the room.

Later, when wood grew scarce, fireplaces were made smaller, as we see them now. Some of the older houses had four, and even more fireplaces, built on the ground floor, and in the chambers, around the chimney, which was the core, about which the house was constructed. On one side of the fireplace, nestling against the great chimney, with an opening into the kitchen, was the brick oven, which was, commonly, about four feet long, three or more in breadth, and two feet high, with an arched roof, and a small opening into the chimney. To heat the oven, a fire of light, dry wood was made in it, and kept up until the bricks were thoroughly heated, when the fire was withdrawn, the oven swept, and the interior filled with loaves of bread, pots of beans, joints of meat, pies and cakes, and closed up. The oven gave out a steady even heat, and it is a waste of time and breath to try to convince any one, who has ever tasted the flavor of the baked beans and bread, which the old-fashioned brick ovens turned out, that any modern range, however marvelously constructed, can produce anything which approaches their delicious flavor. There are still a few houses in this town, in which the brick oven is occasionally used.

Friction matches were not invented till about 1834, and before that time the only way of starting a fire was by "flint and steel," which consisted in striking a spark by their means into "tinder," which was prepared in various ways. It was a matter of domestic economy not to let the fire on the kitchen hearth ever go out, but this sometimes happened, and there are a good many people left in this town who can remember being sent to the next neighbors, to "get some fire."

Candles were, next to the firelight, the only means of illumination which our predecessors possessed, and were made by being run in moulds, or by "dipping." By the last named process, a great many candles were made at a time, and "candle-dipping," was one of the annually recurring labors of the farm.

It is not possible to tell when the first oil lamps were brought into town. Mr. Livermore is "not prepared to deny that there

ON WELLS RIVER.

OLD BLACKSMITH SHOP
IN WELLS RIVER.

FIRST SAWMILL CRANK IN TOWN.

may have been, in 1820, one or two oil lamps," in Haverhill Corner, and they were, probably, introduced here about the same time. Kerosene came in 1859, and was preceded by a number of illuminating compounds, one of which, called "camphene," gave a brilliant light, but was dangerously explosive. Whale oil was used in most families before kerosene came into general use. Candles were made of tallow, and sometimes other substances, animal and vegetable, were mixed with it which hardened them, and improved the quality of the light.

Watches were brought into town before clocks, and came with the first settlers. Col. Kent's diary mentions selling a watch to Abiel Chamberlin in March, 1763. The watches of those days were called "bull's eyes," and had two cases, an outer and an inner, which were detachable.

No fewer than seven families claim the honor of having brought the first clock into Newbury, and it is impossible to decide the precedence. A clock owned by Dea. Sidney Johnson, is believed to be one of the oldest in town, and was owned by his grandfather, the Colonel. The works were imported, but the inner case bears the name of a jeweler at Newburyport. There is a family tradition that some years after being brought here it needed cleaning and a local clock cleaner took it to pieces and accomplished the task. But he could not put it together again, nor, it seems, could the united skill of the settlement accomplish the feat, and the works were taken to Haverhill, Mass., on horseback, put together, and brought back in the same way. Its tall upright case was made by Michael Carleton.

Most of the houses had their "noon marks," which indicated when the sun had reached the meridian. The custom of placing noon marks upon houses continued down to 1860, at least, and the late Richard Patterson stated that he had marked more than a hundred such. In the absence of clocks, people were often very skillful in telling the hour of the night by the progress of the heavenly bodies, and there were men who could tell the time by the stars, with surprising accuracy. When the sky was overcast, this resource of the watcher failed, and some amusing mistakes are chronicled. A woman whose husband was from home, arose from her sleep, and supposing it to be near morning, thought that she would spin till it was time to arouse her children. She accordingly kindled a fire, lighted her candle, and got out her wheel. She spun on and on, but the day did not break. She continued her task, but it was not until she had accomplished more than a usual day's "stint," that the light began to glow over the eastern hills. With the daybreak came her brother, who lived about two miles away, in plain sight, who inquired anxiously after the health of the family. They had seen her light burning all night, and thinking some one of the household must be ill, he had come over to ascertain the cause.

When the bell was placed in the meeting-house on Ladd street, in Haverhill, it was rung at morning, noon, and nine o'clock in the evening, and the same custom was continued by the Newbury bell, when hung in the belfry of the "old meeting-house," in 1828.

The first town clock in this region, north of the college clock at Hanover, was placed upon the brick meeting-house at Haverhill Corner, about 1840. There is no record of the opening of any shop for the repair of clocks and watches here before 1830; there was one in Haverhill before 1810.

In earlier days, and down to the middle of the third decade of the century, there were but three vocations open to women— domestic service, nursing and teaching. For the first, there was little demand and small pay. Families were large, and there were apt to be many girls in them, for whom there was no outside employment. Seventy-five cents a week was considered very good pay, for a strong woman, whose daily task began before daylight, and continued during the evening. One dollar a week, in special cases, was thought very high pay. Housekeepers of the present day must almost sigh for those early days, when there was a surplus of domestic help. It was not uncommon for a woman who had worked nine months in a family, for seventy-five cents a week, to continue through the winter on board wages.

Nursing was a precarious employment, and hardly better paid than domestic service. In 1815, two dollars a week was received by a very skillful woman who had the care of the wife of David Johnson.

Teaching was about the most poorly paid of all woman's labors. Masters were usually employed in winter, and that left only a few months, when a young woman might secure a school, for a dollar a week and board.

With domestic service may be classed the work of tailoresses, who went from house to house and made up the men's garments. Such were quite important personages in their time, and a woman who "went out sewing," and had skill with the shears and needle, received fair pay, which was often in produce or home made cloth.

With the opening of the cotton mills in Lowell and elsewhere, there came a great change. There was a steady and increasing demand for female labor, in the mills, and in the other employments which soon opened in the growing manufacturing towns. Thousands of bright, resolute, capable young women flocked to the cities, and often found homes for themselves there. Instead of a surplus of domestic help there began to be a scarcity, and a consequent rise in wages of the few employments open to women, in this part of the country.

In these days, when every farmhouse draws upon distant

regions for the supply of its daily needs; when our flour comes from beyond the Mississippi; when our homes are lighted by oil from Pennsylvania; when our shoes are made in one part of the country, and our coats in another; when luxuries and conveniences of which our fathers, seventy years ago, never even dreamed, are found in the remotest dwellings among the hills, it is hard, even impossible, for us to put ourselves in their places. The expenses of a healthy family were very small, when every farmhouse was a hive of industry, where butter and cheese, woolen and linen cloth, and many other articles of commerce were manufactured.

At the sixtieth wedding anniversary of Nathaniel Roy and wife, of Barnet, about twenty-five years ago, it was stated that this couple, although well-to-do, and hospitable, had not, in that time, bought a pound of meat, a pound of flour, or a pound of sugar. Many of the families in Newbury of that era could say as much. The actual, unavoidable cash expenses of a healthy family a century ago, hardly exceeded twenty-five dollars. People commonly worked out their taxes, and store bills were paid in produce. Nearly every man had some trade at which he could work, and exchange the skilled labor of his hands, with some other man, equally skillful in some other employment. Sometimes, and often, a man was master of two or three trades. There were men in this town who made their own shoes, of hides furnished by their own cattle, and converted into leather at the local tannery, formed upon lasts carved out by their own hands, sewed with linen thread made upon their farms, with "waxed ends," furnished with bristles from the backs of their swine, and soled by pegs made by themselves. The same men, could, probably, shoe a horse, lay up a chimney, or make tables and chairs. An old account book, kept by Jonas Tucker, shows that he did all these, and more, and there were many like him.

All farm work, except plowing, harrowing and hauling was done by hand, and with the aid of tools which a man would not now accept as a gift. The iron plow did not come into use till after 1820; the plow of earlier date was of wood, except the point, which was of iron, and fastened on by bolts, and plates of iron were attached to the wing and share, where the most wear came. With plows like these were the great meadow farms tilled, eighty years ago. Harrows were made of the crotches of trees, into which the teeth were placed. Our complicated variety of modern apparatus for pulverizing the soil, was then unknown. It is only within fifty years that cultivators began to come into use.

Grain was reaped, the only way in which it could be gathered, on newly cleared land. A good reaper could cut about an acre in a long August day, laying it in "gavels." Cradling came next, and a man could cradle an acre rather quicker than he could mow one. The occupation required a peculiar deftness of arm, and a good cradler was paid about forty cents a day, more than the wages of a mower, in 1820. Grain was threshed entirely by the flail, and cleaned by hand by the help of a "fan." This was made of thin boards, and shaped much like the letter D, the semi-circular side being next to the operator. It was about four feet long, on the straight side, and around the circular part ran a thin board, set on edge, and fitted with handles like those of a basket, on each side of the man who held it. About a peck of uncleaned grain was poured into the fan at a time, and it was shaken up and down in a peculiar way, by the handles, with a sound that went "swish," "swish," "swish." The exercise was varied by shaking the fan, to bring all the grain to the front, and the chaff and dust was expelled by the breeze created by the motion of the fan, and the falling grain. The process was considerably hastened by working in the wind. A man could clean up about thirty bushels in a day, "if his back-bone was made of iron."

Winnowing mills came into use about 1815, and threshing-machines twenty years later. The first machines only threshed the grain, the cleaning was done afterward, by the hand-mill.

Mowing was all done by hand, down to about 1855, when mowing machines came slowly into use. There were men in this town who made a business of mowing, hiring out to mow on the great meadow farms, keeping up a steady swing from morning till night. Such men had great strength and endurance, qualities aided by liberal draughts of New England rum. Some of these could mow very rapidly. There is a story of a man who could mow faster than he could ordinarily walk, and when he wanted to go anywhere quickly, he took a scythe and mowed his way along. Such tales illustrate to us the prowess of our ancestors! The bent scythe snath came into use about 1810. Before that time they were all straight, and many old people clung to the straight snath, as long as they lived. Worn out scythes were made into horseshoes by the blacksmiths.

The first mowing machines were brought into town and sold by Dea. George Swasey. They bore little resemblance to the machines now in use, which are the result of many years of experiment. They had only one wheel, the cutter-bar extended at right angles to the machine, and could neither be raised nor lowered. The only way of stopping the scythe when the machine was moving was to take it out. In a short time the hinged cutter-bar came into use, and other improvements, one after another. Yet the vital principle of the machine, the knives attached to a bar of steel, moving swiftly back and forth between immovable fingers, was the same at first as now. The many and various improvements consist in the more ready application of the power to the knives, and in the manner by which the cutter-bar is adjusted to the conditions of the grass, and the inequalities of the surface.

The horse-rake is of modern invention, the first mention is of one on Long Island in 1826. This consisted of a beam of wood about eight feet long, into which wooden teeth were fastened, and which had handles like those of a plow. The teeth slid under the hay, and when full, the horse was stopped and backed, the man drew out the rake, and, bearing down upon the handles it was made to pass over the windrows when the process was repeated. Later, some genius put teeth on both sides of the head, and, by means of a lever on the handles, the rake was made to turn over when full. This was called the "revolving rake," and there may be a few still in use in this town. Another rake had wire teeth, and was much like the present rakes, but had no wheels, and the man walked behind, holding by a pair of handles. When full, it was lifted up by main force, and the hay was discharged. This kind of rake was called the "man-killer," and no man who ever followed one, behind a fast-walking horse, over a five acre field, on a sultry July afternoon, ever doubted the applicability of the name. In 1857, Charles P. Carpenter, of St. Johnsbury, invented a rake which went on wheels, and was one of the first predecessors of the wheel-rakes now in use.

Maple sugar began to be made in the second or third spring of the settlement of Newbury. Its manufacture has steadily increased, and the capital invested in the business probably exceeds in value that of all the farm implements and machinery in use, seventy years ago. In earlier years, sap was caught in wooden troughs, and boiled in kettles hung from poles in the open air. Sugar-houses with arches and set pans came into use about 1857, and evaporators ten years later. The industry may be completely revolutionized by discoveries and inventions sure to come within a few decades.

The wages of a farm laborer have steadily increased. In 1800, Isaac Waldron hired out to Col. Frye Bayley for one year for eighty dollars. Eight dollars a month, at the beginning of the century, and long after, was the ordinary pay. The few living yet whose memory runs back to the '30s declare that this sum was the common pay of a hired man in those days. But eight dollars a month meant something then, and he saved enough in a few years to buy a good farm. Very few save anything now. Wages were higher along the seacoast, where the young men went to sea, and it was common for young men in this part of the country to start off on foot, in April, for Salem or Marblehead, work there all summer, returning in the fall. The number of occupations in which a young man could engage in those days was very small. But with the opening of the railroads, the requirements of manufacturing cities, and the westward migration, laborers became scarcer, and wages rose. During the civil war wages rose to a high figure, and the introduction of farm machinery had hardly begun. At the present time comparatively little farm work is done by hand, but machinery has not yet come to the aid of the farmer's "chores."

An industry which has wholly passed out of existence in this part of the country, was the manufacture of "salts" as pot and pearl ashes were called. The manufacture of these began early. There was a "potash" in 1768, at the foot of the hill below Mr. Lang's barn, on the Ox-bow. There was always a great demand for these products and "salts" were one of the very few things which always brought cash. They were formerly made quite extensively around West Newbury, and in different parts of the town there are places which resemble the sites of abandoned houses, and which the old people will say "is where they used to make salts."

In early days grain was the staple product of the farms, and thousands of bushels of corn, wheat, rye, oats and barley, were exported. Some farmers went to Salem, the wheat market for the export trade, several times in each year. About 1800, the blight came upon the wheat which grew on the meadows, and it soon became unprofitable there.

The raising of fat cattle for market was profitable. The Boston markets were mainly supplied from Vermont and New Hampshire. Immense droves of fat cattle were collected by buyers in this part of the country every year, and driven to market. Young cattle were also brought in herds from northern New York, and sold to the farmers along the Connecticut valley.

During the civil war, the price of wool rose to seventy-five cents and even one dollar a pound, in the depreciated currency of the time, and every one rushed into the wool business. With the return of peace, and a plentiful supply of cotton, wool declined, and sheep became unprofitable in their turn.

Dairying has always commanded a large share of the farmer's labor, and was never more skilfully conducted than at present. Formerly, the butter season began with the turning out of the cows to pasture in the spring, and ended when they were brought to the barn in the fall. Few fed grain to cows in winter, except to one or two which were allowed to go farrow, for a supply of milk.

All the butter and cheese making was done by hand, and with most of the farmers, butter was stored away in the cellars to await cool weather and the higher prices which came with it. The burdens of the dairy were heavy on the women of the family, and many a housewife wore her life out in this work. The introduction of the creamery system and the invention of the cream separator, has changed all this. With improved systems of dairying came the silo, for preserving corn-fodder, and a great change in farming. Instead, as formerly, of exporting great quantities of grain, vast amounts of western feed are brought into Newbury to supply the dairy farmers, and the acreage of corn, now larger than ever, is all consumed in town.

The wages of carpenters in 1820, were $1.25 per day for a skilled workman, and seventy-five cents for an apprentice. The bricklayers on the seminary building, in 1833, received $1.25 per day.

John Mills is understood to have burned the first kiln of brick at South Newbury, at the foot of the hill, north of Mr. Doe's. There have been two other brick-yards in that part of the town, one east of the brook, near the grist mill, and the other north of the mill-pond. George Eastman leased the latter yard, and its appliance for brickmaking, of Benjamin Atwood, for every tenth brick; his father, Seaborn Eastman, also made brick there.

Beside the tanneries mentioned elsewhere, and that of Webster Bailey, one was conducted at West Newbury by Oscar Blake, on the farm now owned by W. C. & D. Carleton. One of the old barns on that farm was one of the tannery buildings.

The house in which Joseph Sawyer lives at West Newbury, was built for a chair factory, by two brothers by name of Caswell.

The question is often asked, Was there more wealth in Newbury sixty years ago than now? It cannot be precisely answered. Wealth has a relative rather than a positive value. The changes of the last half century have been so great and so various that the measure of value which served in 1840, hardly answers the purpose now. Still the changes of the intervening time are rather with individuals than with the whole community. There are families in this town whose habits and manner of life differ very little from those of their predecessors here seventy years ago.

But the comforts and conveniences within the reach of the farmers of moderate means in Newbury at the present time are far greater in number and variety now than then.

Life is what people make it for themselves, and the study of past conditions is of value if it makes us more content with the world as we have it in our time.

NOTE. Mr. Swasey thinks that he brought his first mowing machine into town in 1854. It was a Ketchum mower, of the kind described on page 152, and sold for $100. The year before, Mr. Edward Hale, on the upper meadow, used something resembling a mowing machine. The cutter bar was of wood, two inches thick, and could cut only tall grass.

The late Deacon Wells helped start the first revolving horse rake in town, about 1836, on Col. Tenney's farm. They were afraid that the horse would take fright and run away, so the Colonel grasped the handles, Timothy Haseltine held the horse firmly by the head, while Mr. Wells took a strong grip on the reins. The rake revolved, and came down with a clatter, the men braced themselves for the catastrophe; the horse stopped, put down its head and took up a mouthful of hay. "Oh, if that's the way you are going to act," says the Colonel, "we'll stop and put the boy on!"

CHAPTER XXIV.

REMINISCENCES OF EARLY WELLS RIVER.

BY HON. CHARLES B. LESLIE.

WELLS RIVER Village is in the northeastern corner of the town of Newbury and also the county of Orange, on the Governor's right. Five hundred acres were granted to Governor Benning Wentworth, which right came into the hands of Er Chamberlin by purchase, and he built the first grist-mill.

The village is at the head of boat navigation. The boats spoken of and once used on the Connecticut river, would carry about twenty-five tons of merchandise, and they went down the river loaded with lumber, that is clapboards and shingles, etc., and brought back heavy goods like iron, salt, rum, molasses, and that class of goods. They could not come any farther up than Stair Hill, at the lower side of the village, where they unloaded. These boats were built for the use of square sails, set in the middle of the boat. They had a crew of seven men to propel them up the river, six spike pole men who worked three on a side, by placing one end of the pole on the river bottom, the other end against the boatman's shoulder and walking back about half the length of the boat, pushing on the pole. The captain steered with a wide bladed oar at the rear. Rafts of lumber were made up here, to be piloted

MT. LAFAYETTE   WOODSVILLE   MOOSILAUKE   CONNECTICUT VALLEY   WELLS RIVER

WELLS RIVER VILLAGE FROM THE "LEDGE"

CONNECTICUT VALLEY   WELLS RIVER LOOKING WEST FROM BACK OF RAILROAD STATION   THE LEDGE

to Hartford, Conn., in boxes sixty feet long, and thirteen feet wide, just the right size to go through the locks at the falls on the river, singly. There was a sawmill at Dodge's falls, where timber was sawed, and floated down through the narrows, to Ingalls' eddy, where they put six boxes together, making what was called a "division." The boxes could not be floated by this village, except at high water, because of the sand bars.

About 1835, a Transportation Company was formed for propelling these boats up stream by means of steam-tugs, which were built with a stern-wheel; these tugs were too large to pass through the locks, which necessitated a boat between each lock. One steamboat too big to pass through the locks was built here, near where the Henderson block now stands, and was used as a passenger and tow boat as were those previously mentioned. This last boat operated between Wells River and White River Falls. This boat was called the Adam Duncan, and finally blew up one fourth of July at White's Eddy just below the bridge at Newbury street. One Dr. Dean, of Bath, was on board, and jumping overboard, he was killed by the paddles or was supposed to have been. After the explosion the boat floated down stream to White River Falls, where it lay till it rotted. Before these longer boats were put on the river, one boat small enough to pass through the locks, called the John Ledyard, came up from Hartford, making one trip as far as Wells River.

Prior to the building of high dams on the river, salmon used to run up as far as Wells River and were caught here. Undoubtedly the Indians used to come by way of Wells River from Lake Champlain and fished here for salmon in the Connecticut river, and probably met Indians of other tribes who came down the Connecticut river from the north part of the state. Their arrowheads and flints have been found on the hills north of Wells River Village, back a little from the Connecticut river.

Before the days of railroads, Wells River was quite a junction for the stage roads and market routes. The writer has seen as many as fifty loaded two-horse teams in the streets of Wells River, at one time. The highway going north turned off at the top of Ingalls' hill and kept back just on top of the hill till it came out on the meadow up here at Stair hill, and all farm buildings below Stair hill were on the hill. From Stair hill the road passed through Wells River, and up the paper mill road to the willow tree just below William Buchanan's house, where the old grist-mill was. The road then crossed the Wells River, going to Ryegate. There was no road west of the paper mill. The road ended at the paper mill, until about sixty years ago, but the road to Leighton hill went up the high hill just opposite the house of Mr. William Buchanan, and all persons traveling that way were obliged to climb this immense hill. About sixty years ago a Spanish doubloon, (about twenty dollars), was picked up on land now owned by Mrs. Moore. Doubtless this coin was lost there by some one in one of the military expeditions which was on the way to Canada.

The first hotel was kept by Mr. Benjamin Bowers, I think, who came here before 1796. He died, and was buried in the field near where Mr. Newton Field now lives. The hotel was on the spot where the Baldwin block is situated. It was a small house, and after Joshua Hale succeeded Bowers, it was used as an ell to the front which Hale put up, which was just like the house now kept by Johnson, called the Wells River House. This last named house was also erected by the Hales, for Mrs. Hale's sister, Mrs. Barstow. The Hales kept the hotel for many years, and accumulated a good property. After the Hales, the same hotel was kept by various persons—one Pickett, Justus Gale, Jesse Cook, Simeon Stevens, Young and Hobbs, Sawyer and Chaplin, Jacob Kent and Harry B. Stevens.

The Coössuck House was situated where the new hotel now is and was kept by Jacob Kent, Henry F. Slack and William R. Austin and by Slack alone. After Slack quit the Coössuck House he kept one situated on the land north of S. S. Peach's present dwelling. This house is now gone, having been destroyed by fire some years since, and while Slack owned it he leased it to one John A. Bowen. Slack went back into the Coössuck House and kept it till he died, having bought it of Colonel Kent. It has been kept by one Hartshorn, and by Durant & Adams and by one Fry, and was burned down in 1892 and the present one built on its site. This hotel was built by Col. Kent.

The early general merchants were: Josiah Marsh, who became quite a land owner in the village of Wells River. I am very sure he came from Connecticut. He traded in the south end of the building, now called the Bachop block, but formerly known as the Hutchins & Buchanan store, and which they enlarged by adding about half of its present size on the north end of it, about forty-five years ago. Mr. Marsh had a large trade, and must have come before the war of 1812. The land records in Newbury will tell when he first became a land owner. Mr. Marsh had a large storehouse on the west side of Main street, opposite his store, standing where the present Hale's Tavern stands. It was built for storing heavy merchandise.

In the war of 1812 there were many army supplies furnished from Wells River, to wit: Beef from cattle slaughterd here—there were two slaughter-houses—one opposite the house now occupied by Dr. J. F. Shattuck, and upon the same side of Wells River that his house stands; the other was down on the bank of Connecticut river, and near where Richard Henderson's house now stands. The flour was ground in the grist-mill, which stood near the large willow tree back of Mr. W. G. Buchanan's dwelling-house, just above the present dam across Wells River. The dam which furnished the power to that grist-mill, was above Mr. Buchanan's house and nearly opposite to Hon. E. W. Smith's residence. This dam turned the water into a canal which was thus taken to the grist-mill. The site of this canal is now visible. This grist-mill doubtless was built by Er Chamberlin. Probably Mr. Marsh was engaged in the slaughtering of cattle and grinding flour, and furnishing them to the American army. Mr. Marsh gave to the town the old burying ground, but which ceased to be used for burial purposes a few years since, the bodies interred there having been removed to the new cemetery.

Those merchants who occupied the Marsh store were: Samuel Hutchins, and his son Samuel, from Bath, N. H. The firm name was Samuel Hutchins & Son. This firm was succeeded by Hutchins & Goodall. This firm was composed of the above named Samuel Hutchins, Jr., and one Alexander Goodall. Then there was a younger Hutchins came into the concern by the name of William. He stayed only a short time and went West. Then Mr. Samuel Hutchins took in the late Moses Buchanan, and they did business under the name of Hutchins & Buchanan. Afterward Col. James Buchanan, a brother of Moses, having been a clerk for Hutchins & Buchanan, was taken into the firm, and I think the firm name of this company was Hutchins, Buchanan & Co. Afterwards Moses Buchanan sold out to his younger brother, William G. Buchanan, Mr. Hutchins having gone out of the firm, and the Buchanan's did business under the name, style and firm of J. & W. G. Buchanan. The Hutchinses, Goodalls, and Buchanans, one and all, were good sharp and well trained business men, did a large business, and accumulated large properties. Those who have occupied that store since are W. G. Buchanan and Gilbert Child—Buchanan & Child; Then came Mr. Archibald Bachop, who married a sister of the above named Buchanans, and he took in as a partner, Mr. A. S. Farwell. This last named company failed, and Mr. Bachop, by trusting irresponsible customers lost his property.

There came here from Connecticut, about the same time Marsh did, Mr. G. A. Burbank, a relative of Peter Burbank, who also was a merchant. He built the dwelling-house which has since been rebuilt and remodeled, and is now the fine residence, owned and occupied by Colonel Erastus Baldwin. His store was a little east of Colonel Baldwin's dwelling-house and abutted on the highway leading to McIndoes Falls. It was removed many years ago. The writer hereof remembers the store, and his first pair of boots, being trimmed with red morocco, and a hat to match, were purchased for him of one Averill, who was the proprietor of, or a clerk in, said store. After the store building ceased to be used as a store, it was used in manufacturing from cattle's horns, horn combs, to be worn in those days by women, and afterwards the building was used for a dwelling-house.

Another merchant came here early from Northumberland, N. H., by the name of William Eames. He traded in the store which until very lately stood where W. G. Foss' dwelling-house stands. It was customary in those days for country merchants in this section of the country to take of their customers and debtors, in the fall of the year, neat cattle, and take them afoot to Brighton market. This was done by the merchants hereabout, Mr. Eames, Hutchins & Son, Hutchins & Goodall, and Hutchins & Buchanan, and Mr. Eames went to Brighton with a drove of cattle and was taken sick there and died. I well remember the time, and that his death was greatly lamented, he being highly esteemed here. Mr. Eames was in company in the tailoring business with Stephen Meader, the father of the late A. S. Meader, the long-time tailor here. This copartnership did not include the store trade at all. The tailor's shop was in the second story of the store which was reached by a flight of stairs, out-of-doors, on the south side of the store. J. L. Woods settled the Eames estate. After the death of Mr. Eames, the store was occupied by Moore & Shurtliff for a while, then a firm, Baxter & Hunter traded there and this firm was succeeded by Timothy Shedd and Hiram Tracy, under the firm name of Shedd & Tracy. After a year or two Shedd & Tracy moved out of the Eames store into Mr. Shedd's large building, which Mr. Shedd had used as a shoe and leather store, which stood on the west side of main street, and just south of the street now leading from Main street to the creamery. This has been removed and is the same now occupied by F. Deming. Since Shedd & Tracy moved out of the Eames store, it has been occupied by Mr. A. S. Farwell for sale of dry goods and also tailoring business, carried on by Mr. Farwell. Shedd & Tracy traded in the Shedd store for many years. Finally Mr. Tracy traded there alone, succeeding the firm of Shedd & Tracy, but he became badly involved, and failed. Mr. Tracy came here as early as 1828 from Woodstock, Vt., and for his first wife married a daughter of Mr. Shedd.

After Mr. Tracy ceased trading, Timothy Shedd and his son, William R. Shedd, went into business in trade, and also milling business, remodelling the bark mill into a grist-mill. They did business under the firm name of T. & W. R. Shedd and they moved the store, which had till then always been the property of Mr. Shedd, to its present situation, where it is now owned and occupied by Mr. F. Deming, and where Mr. Deming has traded for 40 years, having during that time, had one partner for a short time, viz: the late A. T. Baldwin, and has within the present year associated with him, S. E. Clark.

Timothy Shedd came to Wells River from Rindge, N. H., at an early date of its settlement. He was a tanner by occupation and by his great industry and energy, accumulated a good estate. He was man of large stature, and capable of doing the work of his occupation, at first alone, which, as we all know, is of a very laborious nature. He was of abstemious habits, as well as very close in his dealings. He was an influential member of the Congregational church, first at Newbury, and later at this place. His first work, he told the writer, was done under a shed near the present grist-mill, and his bark house was at the mouth of the canal, through which the water passes, which carries the grist-mill. I well remember the old bark house. After it ceased to be used, he erected the building which has since been remodelled and made into the present grist-mill, and in which were stored large quantities of hemlock bark, and therein ground up to be used in vats, to tan the hides with. In my early boyhood Mr. Shedd had so extended and enlarged his tannery business, that he had not only a large number of vats at the mill where he ground the bark as aforesaid, but he had, also, a large number near where the store, now occupied by Mr. Deming now stands. These vats were out-of-doors and uncovered. The rear part of Mr. Deming's store, which is now used for a back-store and barn, the lower story was then used for limeing and beaming hides, to take the hair off, and run over the flesh on them, and had vats therein, in which the hides were limed, and also to soften and remove the ill effects of the limeing, by putting them into a vat, containing hen manure. The upper part of this building, over the tannery, was used for the finishing of leather. Where the front part, or salesroom of Deming's store is, was used as a dwelling. (Probably used by Mr. Shedd when he was first married). Mr. Shedd also manufactured harnesses and boots and shoes, keeping several men at work making them. The *modus operandi* of tanning sole leather was this: After the hair was taken off they were fulled in a fulling-mill, and then put into vats, a layer of bark and then a hide, and then bark and hides, alternately, till filled, then filled with water and allowed to remain six or eight months, when they were taken out, dried and rolled with a brass roller heavily loaded down, and which was propelled by water, back and forth over the hide, which had become leather, until it was made hard and compact, when it was ready for market.

Mr. Shedd also during his busy life was engaged in the lumber business, owning and operating a sawmill on the north end of the present dam across Wells River, in this village. The country here-abouts was, at the the time of the early settlement of Wells River village, heavily timbered with large pine trees, hemlock and spruce as well as hardwood. The pine, hemlock and spruce was much of it sawed into lumber, but a considerable quantity was floated in the log, down the Connecticut river. At first, hemlock and spruce was not valuable timber, but have become so since the pine has been cut off.

Peter Burbank was the first lawyer who located at this place.

11

He came from Somers, Connecticut. He was a strong and well read lawyer, endowed with a great memory and strong common sense, which means that he was broad minded, and could apply his knowledge in a manner to influence judges and jurors in his favor. He was a careful and wise counsellor and looked cases well over before commencing a suit, and when his suit was begun he left no means unemployed to carry his cause to a victory for his client, and the same was true of his efforts if he was called to defend a cause. His office was a building about 15x15, and stood pretty near where Robert Nelson's store and dwelling-house now is. Mr. Burbank did a large and successful law business, and was a hard antagonist in the trial of suits. He was in politics a Jeffersonian and Jackson democrat and was elected to the legislature of the town of Newbury in the years 1829 to 1831. He was untiring in his law practice. He procured the charter to be granted of the Bank of Newbury while a member of the legislature in the latter year, and was its first president. He was fifty-five years old when he died, January 13th, 1836, at his home in Newbury near South Ryegate, which he called "The Hermitage", and is the same place occupied by the descendants of the late William Nelson. Mr. Burbank liked farming pursuits, was a lover of good horses, and owned the Morgan stallion called the Woodbury horse and afterwards the Burbank horse. This horse made the best appearance under the saddle of any horse in the country.

Gustavus Grant Cushman was born in Barnet, Vt., Nov. 6, 1804. At the age of twenty years he entered the office of Messrs. Paddock & Stevens, at St. Johnsbury, and finished his legal education with Peter Burbank, and was admitted to the bar at Danville, April, 1827, and began practice at Wells River, and I am quite sure, as a partner with Mr. Burbank, and in 1829 he removed to Bangor, Me. He held various public offices there up to the time of his death about 1875.

Hon. Abel Underwood was born in Bradford, Vt., April 8, 1799. He determined early to have a liberal education, and he was graduated from Dartmouth College in the class of 1824. He read law with Hon. Isaac Fletcher, at Lyndon, Vt., and was admitted to the bar, at Danville, in 1827. He was, for a short time, in company with Mr. Fletcher when he came to Wells River, and located in the practice of his profession. In 1828 clients were not numerous for the young lawyer, with Peter Burbank, who was then considered a giant in the practice of the law, as a competitor, and so he went to Dexter, Me., but his clients there were not numerous, and he came back to Wells River, after a short residence in Maine, and made Wells River his final abode till his death, which occurred April 22, 1879. After his return to Wells River, his old antagonist, Peter Burbank, had ceased to practice, and Mr. Underwood began to have clients in plenty, and in a few years had a lucrative business. He held various offices, representing Newbury in the legislature in 1861 and 1862. He was also state's attorney for Orange County in the year 1839, which office he filled for two years. He was United States District Attorney for Vermont in the years 1849 to 1853. He was a Judge of Circuit Court from 1854 to 1857. He was also a Register of Bankruptcy under the bankrupt law, and held various offices of trust both in his profession and out of it. He was of industrious habits, and persevering and determined in the prosecution of his business, whatever it was, and conscientious and honest in all of his relations in business intrusted to his care. He was president and director of the Bank of Newbury for many years.

Elijah Farr, lawyer, was born in Thetford, Vt., August 14, 1808, but his parents, soon after his birth, removed to Bradford and he always called that town his home. He was a remarkably tall man, being six feet, five inches in height and of a very slim build. His education was acquired in the common schools of the town and Bradford Academy, preparatory to the study of the law. His law preceptor was Hon. J. F. Redfield, of Derby, Vt., and who was for many years, twenty-five I think, a judge of Supreme Court of Vermont and for a large part of that time its chief justice. He was admitted to the bar in Orleans County, June 3d, 1835. He came immediately to Wells River, and entered into copartnership with Peter Burbank, the copartnership being dissolved by the death of Mr. Burbank. Mr. Farr was one of the executors of Mr. Burbank's will. He was a good lawyer, an eloquent and powerful advocate. He was in politics a democrat and was state's attorney for Orange County in 1839 and 1841 and state senator for the years of 1843 and 1844. He was postmaster at Wells River under several administrations. His law practice was extensive and he was successful therein. He died July 2nd, 1845. He had the year before, taken into copartnership, a young man, who had read law with him, the present writer, who was admitted to the bar in December, 1843, at the Orange County Court, which copartnership terminated by the death of Mr. Farr, and I took the firm's business and helped settle his estate.

Isaac W. Tabor, a Bradford man, practiced law at Wells River, from 1830 to 1833. He was a good lawyer but his business was not large here. He removed to Houlton, Aroostock County, Me., where he took a high position as a lawyer and man. He represented Houlton in the legislature and died there, January 23, 1859.

D. Allen Rogers was born in Columbia, N. H., September 11, 1828, and died at Wells River, July 11, 1881. He was a son of Rev. Daniel Rogers, who died at Stewartstown, N. H., many years ago, but subsequent to his son coming to Wells River. Mr. Rogers was a good academical scholar. He read law with Lyman T.

Flint, Esq., at Colebrook, N. H., and was admitted to the bar of Coös County at the May term, 1854. He held the office of postmaster at Colebrook, for some years. Mr. Rogers sold out his practice at Colebrook and bound himself not to practice there, under the expectation of going into the law practice with Cornelius Adams, Esq., at Washington, D. C., but Mr. Adams soon after died and that ended his high aspirations. He was forced to leave Colebrook and go to St. Johnsbury, Vt., where he remained about one year, when he became a partner with the writer, in January, 1860, and removed to Wells River where he lived until his death. Mr. Rogers was state's attorney for Orange County in 1876, and for two years, which office he so well filled that the presiding judge, who was holding court at Chelsea, during the session of the Republican convention, held during Mr. Rogers' incumbency of that office, recommended that he be nominated again, he having filled the office so well that the county and state would be benefitted by his being again nominated and elected, but the office-seekers prevented that being done. Mr. Rogers was elected to represent the town of Newbury in the General Assembly for the biennial session, 1872, and held the office of selectman of Newbury for two years, and filled all of these trusts well. He was an excellent Biblical scholar and was the superintendent of the Sabbath school at Wells River for many years. Being well read in the word of God he was an able and pleasing instructor and so beloved by the scholars that they placed a granite monument at his grave.

There have been other lawyers of later years who have been ornaments to the profession, one of whom I will speak of because of his successful conviction of a man who called himself "Dr. W. H. Howard," namely, Charles C. Dewey, then state's attorney for Orange County. Howard had performed a criminal operation upon a young woman at Bradford, Vt., and she died from its effects. Mr. Dewey was a very well read and strong lawyer, and by his management of the Howard case so successfully, he was brought into prominence as a lawyer. He went to Rochester, N. Y., from Wells River, but soon came back to Vermont and located at Rutland, and died there of softening of the brain.

The first paper-mill was erected on the south end of the same dam and privilege that supplies the water that propels the machinery in the present mill. "Bill" Blake, as I understand it, came up from Bellows Falls, Vt., and built the mill, and afterward Samuel and Stephen Reed, brothers, and natives of Rindge, N. H., came here from Bellows Falls, and succeeded Mr. Blake in the ownership of the mill. They manufactured writing and wrapping paper, and after a few years they formed a copartnership with Captain Ira White, and finally sold out to Mr. White and moved away. These brothers had four sisters that came to Wells River, one after the other, from Rindge, N. H., where the Hales came from, to work in the hotel kept by Joshua Hale. Pretty soon after one of the girls came she would get married, and Mrs. Hale would send for another of the sisters until they were all married. One married Timothy Shedd, one Captain Ira White, one Emory Gale, and the other Charles Hale, the only son of Joshua Hale, and Mrs. Charles Hale was the grandmother of Charles Hale Hoyt, the celebrated playwright.

Capt. White was born in Swansey, N. H., in the year 1789, and when he was twelve years of age went to Surry, N. H., to live with Judge Lemuel Holmes* during the rest of his minority. Upon his arriving at the age of twenty-one years, March 22, 1810, Judge Holmes gave him a nice recommendation as to his faithfulness and honesty. In April, 1810, Mr. White went to Bellows Falls, Vt., where he lived five years, when he came to Wells River to live in 1816, being then twenty-six years old. After he bought out the Reeds, he increased the paper-making business greatly. Writing paper and brown wrapping was manufactured by him and by the Reeds too. The manner of manufacturing paper in those days was very much different from what it is now and the quality poorer. The rags were brought to the mill by Mr. White's peddlers, several of them sent out over the northern part of Vermont and New Hampshire, where they gathered cotton and linen rags, bought by way of a barter trade and delivered at the paper-mill where they were assorted and cut up by female help, and then ground into paper pulp, the white ones for writing and the colored ones for wrapping paper. In some of the wrapping paper straw was mixed with the rags. After the rags were beaten into pulp, in two great beaters, the pulp was put on to a wire sieve, made the size of the sheet of paper, and shaken to even it on the sieve, when it was put on to woolen felt cloth. The felt and pulp were used alternately, till the pile was of the proper size, when the mass was put into a larger press, capable of giving great pressure, and after the proper time, was taken from the press and the paper removed from the felting and dried in a room in the second story of the mill, having sliding pieces of boards, so that the air had free access to dry the paper. After the paper was sufficiently dried it was finished by having first, all the lumps picked out of the paper and it was callendered so as to make it smooth and fit to write on, whether it was in the sheet, or in a blank or account book. Of course, it would be hard to use steel pens upon it, but in those early days, the quill was what the pen was made of. Mr. White had a store, two rooms, in the south end of the second story of the Hutchins & Goodall store. The stairs by which the rooms were reached were on the outside of the building. Mr. White afterwards erected the

*Judge Holmes afterward came to Newbury, and died here.

building now used by Mr. Sheldon as a jewelry store and tenement. Here Mr. White had on the lower floor, his store, or salesroom, in front, and in the rear was a part of his book-bindery, a portion of the second story being also used as a book-bindery. The rest of the second floor was used as a printing office.

Mr. White was the first man to introduce a printing-press into Wells River.' The first one was what was called a Ramage press, and after that he got a newer and better pattern of a press. He printed spelling-books and testaments. He finally went to work and dug the canal to take water from the pond to the present mill, and it proved to be so costly that it failed him. There was a grist-mill in the old paper-mill, which was used to grind unbolted meal, after the grist-mill that stood just below the willow tree near William G. Buchanan's dwelling-house, ceased to be used. Captain White was a man of strict integrity, and of good habits, and lived to be ninety-eight years and eight months old. His children were three; one son and two girls. One of the girls is the wife of William G. Buchanan, and the other married a Mr. Fay of Boston and died there a few years since. The son, Henry K. White, was a natural trader and peddled all of his business life. He died at Toronto, Ont., leaving a widow and daughter. After Mr. White's failure the paper-mill property went into the hands of his bondsmen, Timothy Shedd and Charles Hale. They let Captain White's son, Henry K. White, take it into his hands and operate it for a short time, and finally Durant & Adams bought it and did a larger business. This firm was succeeded by Adams & Deming.

One of the early settlers of Wells River was John L. Woods, Esq. He came from Corinth, Vt., and soon became the possessor and owner of a large part of the land in and around the village. The records of the town will show when he came and the lands he owned. He owned and lived in a house which stood where Mrs. Samuel A. Moore's house is and was engaged in farming and lumbering, and also to a limited extent in brick-making, having kilns on the field which Mrs. Moore now owns and one where Jerry Sullivan lives. He administered upon the estate of William Eames, who has been before spoken of, and· a large amount of litigation grew out of its settlement, which Mr. Woods put into the hands of the late Judge Underwood, who had just come back from Maine, and for whom Mr. Woods took a liking. Doubtless more lawsuits were had than were really necessary and the estate was insolvent in consequence. Mr. Woods became the owner of the sawmill located at the mouth of the Ammonoosuc River, in Woodsville, where the dam now is, and went over there and built a dwelling house and store near the sawmill, where he lived until his death. His grave is in a little lot, just large enough for it, just south of the public highway, leading under the railroad bridge in that village. At the time Mr. Woods went to Woodsville to reside, there were but two dwelling houses there, one of which was a large two-story house, called the Brock house, situated at the northeasterly end of the village, and the other a farmhouse, then occupied by Cyrus Allen, and now owned by Joseph Willis, situated at the southwesterly extremity of the village, which is named for Mr. Wood, and which has come to be, by railroading and court-house, an important center of business. Mr. Woods was a good hearted man and friendly to the poor, whom he helped. He was a man of good judgment as to values of properties and of first-class business tact and integrity.

One of the early industries in Wells River was the cloth-dressing business. John W. Leslie and his younger brother, George R. Leslie, came from Bradford, Vt., in 1818. John bought the clothing works and took his brother, George R., who was by trade a clothier, into company with him, and John W. engaged in the lumbering business quite extensively, and to a limited extent carried on farming. In those days cloth-dressing was an important trade. Woven cloth was home-made, both for men's and women's wear, and brought to the cloth-dressing shop, where it was fulled in a fulling-mill, to make the fabric thick and close in fibre. It was then colored and a knap raised by teazles, and then sheared and pressed, and much of the cloth when finished was fine looking and made handsome suits. Girls, until they became of age, wore dresses made of flannel, colored red and wine color, which were warm and comfortable. The clothier's shop was situated on the bank of Wells River, on the premises now occupied by Mr. Graves. The water privilege was granted by Er Chamberlin to one Quimby and by Quimby to one Felch, I think, and then to the Leslie's. The land title records will show as to this.

The parents of the Leslies were Alexander Leslie and Lucy Warner Leslie, who raised ten children—five sons and five daughters. They are of Scotch descent and can trace their genealogy back to the reign of James I., under whom they held important offices. John W. was the father of the writer, as has been hereinbefore stated, and George R., the father of the late George Leslie, who was for many years the able cashier of the Bank of Newbury, both while it was a state bank and when it became a national bank. It is one of the best banks in the state, its officers, one and all, having been conservative and first-class business men. The cloth-dressing and wool-carding business ceased under the management of George R. Leslie, it having ceased to be of any importance because of the great woolen manufacturers' establishments at Lowell and Lawrence, Mass., and other places.

The old blacksmith shop, now standing on Main street, is not the original one that stood there. The first one was burned down some time prior to 1830, and the present one, now called the "Old Smithy," was erected on the same site. It was owned by the Wells's when burned and they built the "Old Smithy," but were not the first blacksmiths that plied their trade in the village, one John Sly and one Williams, examine the land records for Mr. Williams' full name and the time he came here and left.

Abel Wells and his sons came quite early in the settlement of the village. I have understood they came from Peacham, Vt. Abel's wife was a Morse, if I remember aright. His sons were Waterman, Jared, Hiram, Augustus, and Horace Wells, and there was one daughter, a Mrs. Mack. The old folks resided in a house which stood where Mrs. Lucinda C. Baldwin now lives. Waterman was the first one who was married, his wife being a Miss Sleeper, and they lived in the south half of a double house standing on the ground now occupied by C. B. Leslie's dwellings. Jared married a sister of the late Abner B. White and lived in the old homestead of his father, the same doubtless being the property of the sons. The father, Abel Wells, was driving a horse and carriage on the hill near Mr. C. W. Eastman's present residence, when he met a peddler, whose cart was loaded with rags and sheep skins, which frightened Mr. Wells' horse and he ran away. Mr. Wells was thrown out and killed, his neck being broken. The Wells's made cow-bells. The bells were put into clay mortar, heated to a great heat, and when sufficiently brazen, cooled gradually by throwing them about with pitchforks.

The first physicians came early in the settlement of the village, from Lancaster, N. H. Their names were Samuel Carter and a Dr. Burnside. They did not stay here long. The next one was Enoch R. Thatcher, who came from Woodstock, Vt., about 1827, and practiced here with good success for a great length of time.

Emory Gale and his brothers, Leonard and Justus, came here early, from Guilford, Vt. Emory married one of the Reed sisters, hereinbefore spoken of. He was the father of a large family, among whom now living are Mrs. A. B. White, Miss C. A. Gale, and Mrs. Carlos M. Morse of Plymouth, N. H. Mr. Gale was engaged in lumbering and farming, and was a good citizen. Leonard Gale was never married. He was a mechanic and owned the building now occupied by Sherwin & Son, which had water power under it to propel the necessary machinery used by Mr. Gale, who manufactured various articles. The most important were shingle machines, to saw out short shingles, which were used all about the country. The other important branch of his manufactory was a machine used in manufacturing writing paper. He was a nice man, accumulated considerable property, and died here at a ripe old age. Justus kept the hotel for a short time and went west.

Charles J. Scott and Cyrus J. S. Scott, sons of John Scott, who married a Miss Johnston, at one time owned the farm on which

Peter Burbank lived and died, called "The Hermitage," near South Ryegate in Newbury. This farm they exchanged with Mr. Burbank for land in Wells River village. They immediately after went into the lumbering business here. They were shrewd business men and accumulated quite a property. Cyrus, the younger, married a daughter of Timothy Shedd, and was a scholarly man. Their lumber business was large and that of Cyrus extended into the state of Michigan. Mrs. Susan Colby, of Woodsville, is a daughter of Cyrus Scott.

In the early days of state banks they were obliged to keep a place of redemption of their circulation, which, for this section of New England was in Boston, Mass. Each bank was under the necessity of redeeming its own bill, by the bills of other banks or by gold and silver coin, and the way they got their money to and from Boston was by way of stage drivers, who were common carriers for that purpose. The bank here put into the hands of one John Hawes, a large sum of money, to be taken to Haverhill Corner, N. H., to be then delivered to another driver. It was in the summer of 1842, or thereabout, and when Mr. Hawes reached Haverhill he looked for the money put into his care, and it could not be found. The passengers were searched but nothing came of it, and men were immediately sent back with rakes, who raked the highway from Haverhill to Wells River without success. The bank took measures to at once bring suit against the stage company for the money, and it so happened Farr & Underwood were both out of town. The writer ventured to bring the suit and the claim was secured. Nothing more was heard of the money until the making of repairs on highways the next year, while repairing a small bridge at Stair hill, the package was found all safe, which was a great relief to Mr. Hawes, whose honesty never was doubted.

About the year 1828, in September, there came a great flood, and the village of Wells River, as well as all sections of the country were inundated and flooded. The people at the north end of the village went on to the hill back of Baldwin's block and staid there all day until the waters receded. At this time the sawmill on the north end of the dam, before spoken of, was torn down sufficiently to relieve the great body of water that came down Wells River, from further flooding the village, the water being from four to six feet deep in the upper end of Main street. The water broke around the south end of the dam, which was badly gutted, so as to necessitate building a part of the present dam of stone. At the time of the first grist-mill, just below the willow tree, before spoken of being in use, of course the present dam had not been built, and the public highway bridge crossed the river just below the grist-mill and above the dam. When the dam was erected, the bridge across the river was then put at the head of Main street, where it has been ever since—for ninety years, more or less.

After the cessation of the mill at the "willow tree," the dam being washed away that brought the water into the flume, the machinery was taken up to the paper-mill, and there used till the Shedds built the present mill.

It was taken to the paper-mill probably about 1812, and used for grinding supplies for the army, and the custom grinding for the farmers about. There was for many years a bolt in it, and it did a large amount of business.

FIRST CONGREGATIONAL CHURCH

CHAPTER XXV.

THE FIRST CONGREGATIONAL CHURCH.

NEXT to the town organization itself, the oldest institution in Newbury is this church. We can only mention here the chief events in its long and honorable record. At the third meeting of the proprietors of Newbury held at the inn of John Hall in Plaistow, N. H., on the 3d of October, 1763, it was voted, "To pay a Preacher with the Proprietors of Haverhill, to preach at s^d towns two or three months this fall or winter."

On the same day the proprietors of Haverhill held a meeting at the same place, and voted, "To join with Newbury in paying for preaching one or two months this year." In September Mr. Silas Moody, a relative of the Littles', who had recently graduated at Harvard College, was induced to come to Coös, with the expectation that if he and the people were mutually suited, he was to become their pastor. According to an old receipt signed by him, it would seem that he preached three Sabbaths in Newbury, and two in Haverhill, being paid by each town in proportion. Mr. Perry seems to think that he came again in the spring of 1764, and preached, and it would seem that he gave satisfaction, as the proprietors at a meeting at Hampstead on the 1st of March, instructed Jacob Bayley, "To apply to Mr. Moody, or elsewhere to preach at Coös next summer." He did not see fit to settle here, but after teaching a few years, became pastor of the Congregational church at Arundel, now Kennebunkport, Me., where he died, after a ministry of forty-five years. Professor Moody of Bowdoin College is his great-grandson, and he has other well known descendants.

Mr. Moody not being available, General Bayley made a most fortunate choice in Rev. Peter Powers, who had returned to his native town of Hollis, after a pastorate at Newent, now a part of Lisbon, Conn., of six or eight years. He came to Coös at the end of May, 1764, and preached in houses and barns, to the settlers in both towns. Mr. Powers and the people were mutually pleased and on his return to Hollis, a church was organized in September, consisting of members who had settled, or were about to settle, on each side of the river. This was the second church formed in Vermont, the one at Bennington, two years earlier, being the first. Mrs. Asa Bayley's autobiography tells us that there were fifteen original members, eight of whom were present at Hollis, at its organization. There has been some discussion as to whether this was a Congregational or a Presbyterian church. General Whitelaw, writing home to Scotland in 1773, speaks of it as Presbyterian, and Mr. Powers was a member and clerk of the Grafton presbytery. The early records are lost, yet it seems safe to infer that it bore resemblance to both systems of church government, but that, after some years, it became entirely Congregational, without any particular vote to that effect, on the part of its members.

On the 24th of January, 1765, the town tendered Mr. Powers a formal call, and the selectmen, Jacob Bayley, Jacob Kent, and James Abbott, who were deacons of the church as well, were appointed to wait upon him, and receive his answer. They were also instructed, "To apply to the town of Haverhill, and to the propriety of both Haverhill and Newbury, to see what assistance they will give us toward getting the gospel and supporting the same." It will thus be seen that there were five distinct bodies uniting in the settlement of the minister—the church, the two towns and the proprietors of each town.

In those days the minister was settled by the town, and supported by direct tax. Such usage, however repugnant to our ideas of the independence of church and state, was in accord with the law and custom of the time, and worked well enough when the people were all of one mind in their religious views.

On the 1st of February the town met, and received Mr. Powers' acceptance of the call, and directed that the installation should be on the last Wednesday of the month. It voted also that Rev. Abner Bayley of Salem, N. H., Rev. Daniel Emerson of Hollis, Rev. Henry True of Hampstead, Rev. Joseph Emerson of Pepperell, Mass., and Rev. Joseph Goodhue, should be a council for the installment. It was also voted that Jacob Bayley, Esq., should represent the town of Newbury at the council, which was to be held "down county, where it is tho't most convenient." There being no church of any kind within sixty miles, the council was most conveniently held in one of the older towns, where there were churches and people. We have no record to show that the church itself was represented by a delegate at the installation of its own minister, but as Jacob Kent was present, he may have attended on its behalf. Mr. Powers preached his own installation sermon which was afterwards printed, from Matt. 22 : 8, 9. He moved his family to Newbury about the end of March, several men and teams going down to Charlestown, to bring his goods up on the ice, which, before their return had become unsafe.

On the third Tuesday in April a town meeting was held, at which it was voted that James Abbott, Capt. Fowler and Dr. Smith should be a committee to provide the materials for Mr. Powers' settlement. He was to receive seventy-five pounds lawful money, six shillings to the dollar, paid semi-annually, and thirty cords of wood, carried to his house, yearly. He was also to receive $450, as settlement money, $200 to be paid in cash and the remainder in labor and material to build a house, all this to be paid within ten months of his acceptance.

The Haverhill town records show that Mr. Powers received from that town for the first three years £89. 5s. 6d., and that after 1771, the proportion of Haverhill was £35 until 1777, when its share was £37. 6s. Mr. Powers' labors were not confined to Newbury or Haverhill, but it does not appear that any other of the towns in which he labored, contributed to his support. He was, for several years, the only minister in this part of the Connecticut valley, and was called upon to preach, solemnize marriages, and bury the dead, all the way from Hanover to Lancaster. He is said to have preached the first sermon in twenty-seven towns in this vicinity, and organized several churches, on a Presbyterian platform. For twenty years at least, the meeting-house at the Great Ox-bow, in Newbury, was the only church building within many miles, and people came there to meeting from Mooretown, now Bradford, from Ryegate Corner, and from Bath, on foot, both men and women. It is probable that in pleasant weather, all the settlements from Thetford to Peacham were represented in the meeting-house at Newbury.

It was fortunate for the settlements at Coös, that they were able to secure, for eighteen years, the ministrations of a man so able and earnest as Rev. Peter Powers. But it must not seem strange that during the Revolutionary war his salary fell into arrears, and there was friction between him and the town. However, in the course of time, his dues seem to have been paid. He removed to Haverhill in 1781, in consequence of the troublous times, and the town considered that in so doing, he had withdrawn from the agreement made when he was settled in 1765. After some correspondence between him and the authorities of Newbury, his pastorate terminated, and Newbury and Haverhill, grown larger and stronger, became separate parishes, and it does not appear that

Haverhill, as a town, contributed afterwards to the support of preaching at Newbury. Of Rev. Peter Powers and his descendants a more complete account appears in another part of this volume.

From 1782 until 1788, the church was without a pastor, and part of the time without regular preaching. The pulpit was supplied by several individuals, whose periods of service cannot be given, or the names of all. Rev. Ebenezer Cleveland, who preached some years at Bath and Landaff; Rev. Abishai Colton; Mr. Jeremiah Wilkins, afterwards a merchant at Concord, N. H.; Mr. Goddard, Mr. Tolman, and Rev. Lyman Potter, were among them, as appears by receipts for sums paid them for preaching.*

On the 11th of April, 1787, Mr. Jacob Wood, a native of Boxford, Mass., and a graduate of Dartmouth College in 1778, who was for three years preceptor of Moors' Indian Charity School, at Hanover, began preaching, receiving twenty-four shillings a Sabbath. He was ordained and installed January 7th, 1788. Mr. Wood was a learned and faithful minister, and greatly beloved during his ministry. A passage in the "Life and Times of Elder Ariel Kendrick," describes him as a gloomy preacher, who dwelt more upon the terrors of the law, than upon the persuasions of the gospel. He was taken ill and died, February 10, 1790, in his thirty-second year. During his illness, it is said, he talked in Greek, being deprived, at intervals, of the use of his reason. He also made some rhymes which were long remembered. Mr. Wood's funeral was attended by all the ministers in the region, who were entertained by the town, which also assumed the expenses of his illness and burial. He was buried at the Ox-bow, and is the only one of all the ministers of the three Congregational churches in this town, who is buried in Newbury. Some articles of furniture, once owned by him, and a few books that were his, are still preserved here. His salary was £84, paid in wheat, rye, corn, beef, butter, cheese and wool. In lieu of "Settlement" the town purchased for a parsonage, Thomas Chamberlain's house, whose site is marked by a depression of the surface in the newest part of the cemetery, at some distance from the road. The "old meeting-house" was built†

*Mr. Tolman was the same gentleman whose letter is given on p. 139. Rev. Mr. Potter emigrated to Ohio, and was one of the earliest ministers of that state.

†As the first three meeting-houses were built by the town, a more particular account of their erection is previously given. Some facts which have come to light since the earlier chapters of this volume went to press, deserve mention. The committee to build a meeting-house in 1768 were, on the part of Newbury, John Taplin, Jacob Kent and Jacob Fowler; on the part of Haverhill, Timothy Bedell and Ezekiel Ladd. Rev. Grant Powers states that a framed meeting-house was erected near where the "old meeting-house," was afterwards built, but as there was dissatisfaction with its location, it was taken down, and rebuilt west of the cemetery. He does not seem to have known the cause of the dissatisfaction. At that time the vicinity of what is now North Haverhill was the principal part of that town, and the people there did not like the location of the meeting-house, thinking it too far south for their convenience, so it was taken down, and relocated and became both church and court-house.

during his ministry and the minister taxes of those who had settled in the south-west part of the town were remitted.

On the Sabbath which followed Mr. Wood's death, Mr. Nathaniel Lambert, a graduate of Brown University, began his ministry, and on the 29th of May, received a formal call from the town, and on November 17th, was ordained and installed. The ordination sermon, which was printed, was preached by Rev. Ebenezer Bradford, of Rowley, Mass. His salary was to be ninety pounds the first year, with an annual increase of five pounds, until the third year, when it was to remain at one hundred pounds, with the use of certain lands owned by the town. The parsonage where Mr. Wood had lived was sold, and new quarters were found for the minister in the house now owned and occupied by Mr. J. B. Lawrie.

Just what led the town to vote in 1794, "that Jacob Bayley, Esq., Simeon Stevens and Jeremiah Ingalls should be choristers to lead in singing," we may never know. It is possible that there was a want of harmony in the choir, in more than one form. Mr. Lambert was dismissed by council April 4, 1809, but resided here, and continued to preach for two years more. The cause of his leaving was the delinquency of the town in paying his salary, and he only obtained what was due him by a suit against the town. With his ministry, closed the union of the town and the church, to the advantage of both. Mr. Lambert was a very able preacher, widely known and esteemed, and preached the election sermon before the legislature in 1801. In his theological views he was of the Hopkinsonian school of Calvinism. He died at Lyme in 1838.

From Mr. Lambert's dismission to 1821, the church was supplied by several ministers. Its business affairs, which had before been conducted by the legal voters of the town of Newbury, were now managed by a society, formed among those who were interested in its welfare. For some years after 1816, Rev. David Sutherland of Bath, was moderator of the church. On January 1st, 1821, Rev. Luther Jewett, of St. Johnsbury, was called by the church and society, and ordained on the 28th of February. He was dismissed on account of ill health in February, 1828. Mr. Jewett was a native of Canterbury, Conn., and a graduate of Dartmouth College. He was a member of Congress from 1816 to 1819, and a man of talent, promptness and energy.

Rev. Clark Perry became pastor on June 4, 1828, and was dismissed June 15, 1835. He graduated at Harvard College in 1823, and at Andover Theological Seminary in 1826. Those yet living, who remember Mr. Perry, always speak of him with peculiar affection. Inquiries made by him into the early history of the town, resulted in an historical discourse, delivered in 1831, which preserved for later generations much which would certainly have otherwise been lost. Mr. Perry died at Gorham, Me., July 22, 1843.

Rev. Geo. W. Campbell was installed in January 1836, and dismissed July 9, 1851. The old meeting-house had grown dilapidated and was, besides, not owned by the church, and a new church building was erected on the site of the present one, at a cost of about $3,000, and dedicated November 13, 1840. In 1843, the present vestry building was erected, by subscription, and has since been enlarged and altered. Mr. Campbell died at Bradford, Mass., in 1869. The council which dismissed Mr. Campbell, installed Rev. Artemas Dean as his successor.

On Sunday, January 13, 1856, the church edifice was burned. The sexton had made the fires in the stoves, rang the first bell, and gone home. A driving snow storm was going on with a high northwest wind, and little was saved. The steeple remained standing for some time after the east end of the building had fallen in, and the west end being undermined by the fire and shaken by the wind, the bell began to toll, and kept on tolling until the tower fell over into the flames.

The society at once set about the work of building a new church, and the present edifice was erected in the summer of 1856, Archibald Mills being the master workman. While the work was going on services were held in the Seminary Hall, which was offered for the use of the church by the trustees. Every part of the new building was constructed with the thoroughness which characterized the work of Mr. Mills, and it was first opened for public worship on the Sabbath before its dedication, which was September 23, 1856. Mr. Dean was dismissed March 31, 1857. He was a very earnest preacher, direct and fearless. His resignation was demanded by the state of his health. He is now retired, living in New York City.

Rev. Horatio N. Burton, was installed December 31, 1857, and dismissed in March, 1869. A particular account of Dr. Burton and his family is elsewhere given. From his dismission to the coming of Rev. S. L. Bates, a period of two and a half years, the church was supplied by Rev. George B. Tolman, and Rev. A. T. Deming, both now deceased. Mr. Bates came here in November 1871, and was installed, January 16, 1872. He was a fine musician, and did much toward the development of musical taste in the community. He was dismissed January 28, 1890. Rev. W. A. Bushee supplied the church most of the time from his dismission till the coming of Rev. J. L. Merrill, in 1891, who has entered upon the tenth year of his pastorate.

The First Congregational church of Newbury has always been one of the strong churches in the state. Its ministers have ranked among the abler men in the Connecticut Valley. While it has never had among them, any one who could be named among the eminent divines of New England, they have been men of culture, well trained for their work. It is the mother church of all the northern portion of the valley, and there is hardly a church of the

Congregational order, and of many others as well, north of Hanover, which does not number, among its earlier members, some one from the Newbury church, and fourteen ministers have gone from the parish. Its mission has largely been to train its sons and daughters for other fields. It has sent out three colonies: One in 1829, when seven members were set off to form a church in Topsham; twenty-four in 1840, as a nucleus of the church at Wells River; and twenty-one in 1867, to begin the church at West Newbury. Owing to the loss of the earlier records, and the neglect to record all the names of those who have joined it, the precise number of the members cannot be given. They are probably, about 1,400, in all. Representatives of seven generations, from more than one of its earlier members, are found upon the roll of this ancient church, and those which have sprung from it, in this town.

"The children of thy servants shall continue, and their seed shall be established before thee."

The following have served as deacons.

*Jacob Bayley,	1764–1815	David T. Wells,	1853–1868
*James Abbott,	1764–1803	*Freeman Keyes,	1853–1871
*Jacob Kent,	—— 1812	*George Burroughs,	1869–1887
*Thomas Brock,	—— 1806	*Joseph Atkinson,	1872–1883
Jeremiah Ingalls,	1803–1810	Henry H. Deming,	1872–1883
*William Burroughs,	1812–1835	*Daniel P. Kimball,	1883–1895
*John Buxton,	1819–1864	Sidney Johnson,	1883
*James Brock,	1835–1855	George Swasey,	1883
*Jonas Meserve,	1853–1869		

A Sunday School has been connected with the church since about 1816.

In 1797, James Andrew Graham, LL. D., published in London a volume of "Letters from Vermont," in which he says: "Newbury has the most elegant church in the state, with a large bell, the only bell in the state." What basis this latter statement rests upon, is not known. It is not believed that there was any bell here at that time. The first bell in this part of the country, north of the college bell at Hanover, is believed to be the one which formerly hung in the Ladd street meeting-house at Haverhill, and which, now cracked, hangs in the schoolhouse near by, and bears the inscription, "Wm. Doolittle, Hartford, 1802." Arthur Livermore characterizes it as "the sweetest bell ever heard." Rev. J. L. Merrill says that a considerable sum in silver was contributed by the citizens of Haverhill and cast into the bell metal, which accounted for its silvery tone. Deacon George Swasey thinks that the first bell upon the meeting-house was bought in 1828. This

---

*Died in service.

12

bell was removed to the new meeting-house, and melted when that church was burned in 1856. The present bell, cast by Jones & Hitchcock of Troy, N. Y., was bought in 1857, and first used April 12th, of that year.

The history of the choir would fill a small volume. Jacob Bayley and Simeon Stevens first "took the lead of the singing"; then came Jeremiah Ingalls, who trained what was then considered a wonderful choir. It is said that travelers would plan to stop in their journeys over Sunday, in Newbury, to hear the fine singing. It is not certain who succeeded Mr. Ingalls. Jacob Kent 3d, was leader in 1829, and probably for some years before and after; then came P. W. Ladd, for about twenty years; H. N. Burnham was leader for some years, and E. K. Prouty, at two periods, the last, more than fifteen years, ending in 1866. The later leaders have been: N. B. Stevens, Joseph Atkinson, E. H. Farnham, E. J. Robinson and others. The present chorister is M. A. Gale. According to the recollections of Reuben Abbott, Mr. Ingalls introduced the bass viol into the old meeting-house, which was afterward played by William B. Bannister, and later, by one or more of the Kent family.

In the church which was burned there was a small instrument called a "seraphine." In 1857, a pipe-organ which had been used in a church at Lowell, Mass., was purchased for $300. Miss Fanny Johnson, Miss Ellen Jewett and Miss Joanna A. Colby were organists in its time. In 1877, the present organ, costing about $1,500 was placed in the church. Mr. Henry K. White, Miss Fanny Bailey, Prof. David A. French, Mrs. J. B. Lawrie, Miss Caroline Lang, Miss Rosamond Chamberlin and others, have played this organ. Miss Mae B. Ford, a graduate of the Conservatory of Music, Boston, has been the organist for several years, when in town.

The communion service used by the church has an interesting history. We do not know what utensils were used during the first years. On June 28, 1792, the church voted:—"That each brother pay three shillings to the treasurer of the church for the purpose of procuring certain furniture, or certain utensils, for the sacramental table." With this money, "two Flaggons" were purchased. In 1799, Dr. Gideon Smith died, and left fifty dollars by will, to purchase articles for the communion service. This money was loaned for a time, and in 1811, six silver cups, and a flagon, were bought with it, which are inscribed with his name. In 1872, Mrs. Charles Atkinson gave two flagons, two plates and a baptismal bowl. Other gifts to the church have been made from time to time.

In 1893 the interior of the church was completely remodelled— new pews put in, the old windows replaced by memorial glass, and many other improvements made, at a cost of $3,300. Windows were placed in the church in memory of the following persons:

Freeman and Emeline C. Keyes, Charlotte Butler Shedd, Belle Hibbard, Hanes and Phebe Johnson, Lavinia, wife of Rev. Dr. J. J. Owen, Harry C. Bayley. The vestry has several times been enlarged and fitted for the social uses of the society.

Mr. Powers lived in his own house, which was a little north of Mr. Doe's brick house at the Ox-bow and Mr. Wood in one which stood in the present cemetery. In Mr. Lambert's time, the town bought the house where Mr. Lawrie now lives, which was the parsonage for many years. Mr. Dean lived in a house which stood where Mr. James George's now stands, at the south end of the village, and which was burned in September 1855. In that year Deacon James Brock died, and left by will $500 as a parsonage fund, to which enough was added to purchase the present building, then a one-story house, which had been a grocery, and a tailor shop, and remodeled it into its present appearance. It is understood that Mr. Powers kept a book, in which he recorded the names of members received to the church, baptisms administered, marriages solemnized, and funerals attended by him. He carried this to Maine, but it long ago disappeared. Reference was made to it as far back as 1810, and in 1830, Rev. Clark Perry caused search to be made among the Powers families for it, but in vain. In 1845, David Johnson tried to find it, as did the editor of this history in 1896. It has, probably, been destroyed, as none of Mr. Powers' descendants know anything about it. If it could be found, it would be invaluable to the town and church. Nathan Goddard signed his name as "clerk" March 19, 1784, and kept the records till 1791.

Rev. Nathaniel Lambert,	acting clerk,	April 3, 1791-June 29, 1811
Webster Bailey,	acting clerk,	June 29, 1811-Dec. 30, 1816
William Burroughs,	clerk,	Dec. 30, 1816-March 5, 1821
Rev. Luther Jewett,	clerk,	March 5, 1821-Feb. 3, 1825
William Burroughs,	clerk,	Feb. 3, 1825-May 2, 1828
Rev. Clark Perry,	acting clerk,	May 2, 1828-June 15, 1835
Joseph Berry,	clerk,	June 15, 1835-Jan. 3, 1836
Rev. G. W. Campbell,	acting clerk,	Jan 3, 1836-Jan. 26, 1851
Freeman Keyes,	acting clerk,	May 3, 1851-Feb. 27, 1858
Rev. H. N. Burton,	acting clerk,	Feb. 27, 1858-July 11, 1862
L. Downer Hazen,	acting clerk,	Nov. 11, 1862-Feb. 6, 1866
Rev. H. N. Burton,	acting clerk,	March 3, 1866-Feb. 1, 1868
E. H. Farnham, Jr.,	clerk,	Feb. 6, 1868-Feb. 5, 1870
George Swasey,	clerk,	March 26, 1870

It is not possible to give the entire list of Sunday school superintendents. The following are recalled: George Ropes, in the early '30s, P. W. Ladd, Dea. Freeman Keyes, 1846-'71; H. H. Deming, 1871-82; Sidney Johnson, 1882.

CHAPTER XXVI.

The Methodist Episcopal Church.

THE researches of Rev. A. L. Cooper D. D., show that, from the year 1788, appointments in the adjoining towns of New York and Massachusetts, included preaching stations in the extreme southwest part of Vermont. The list of appointments, down to 1826, is from Dr. Cooper's pamphlet. In 1796 Rev. Nicholas Sneathen, a native of Long Island, at the solicitation of John Langdon of Vershire, came to that town to preach, and formed what was known as the Vershire circuit. There seems reason to suppose that he preached in this town at least once in that year. Mr. Sneathen, afterward attained distinction, and was chaplain of the House of Representatives at Washington, and, later, one of the founders of the Methodist Protestant church. He died in 1845.

A "circuit" embraced a number of preaching stations, each too small to support a minister alone, which were visited by the pastor, in regular order. The biographical notice in this volume, of Rev. Solomon Sias, will give some idea of the labors of these itinerant ministers. It is probable that from the first, the Vershire circuit included an occasional appointment in Newbury.

In 1797, Ralph Williston was appointed upon this circuit, and in 1798, Joseph Crawford. In the winter of 1798-'99 a class of five members was formed in Bradford. In 1799, this circuit was called the Vershire and Windsor circuit, and in that year the first Methodist church building in Vermont was erected in Vershire, Revs. Joseph Crawford and E. Chichester being the appointees upon this circuit.

In 1800, the New England conference was formed, and the Vershire circuit, which then included all of Orange County, was transferred to it from the New York conference, to which it had previously belonged, and Timothy Dewey was appointed to the charge. In 1801, Solomon Langdon and Paul Dustin were appointed. In that year a class was formed in Newbury, at the house of Joseph Prescott, where N. C. Randall now lives, by Revs. James Young, Elijah Sabin and John Broadhead. There were eleven in this class, but the names of Joseph Prescott and wife, Ashbell Buell and wife, and Stephen Powers are the only ones which are preserved.

In 1802, the Vershire district became a part once more of the New York conference and Samuel Draper with Oliver Beale were sent to it. From 1804 to 1826, this part of the state was called the Vermont district of the New England conference, and the following were the appointments to the Vershire circuit: In 1804, John Robertson and D. Goodhue; 1805, Oliver Beale; 1806, Elijah Hedding, afterwards bishop. The biography of Bishop Hedding states that the circuit embraced ten towns, and the work was so arranged that he was to pass through these towns, and preach from one to three times daily, within the limits of each, every two weeks. In 1807, B. F. Lombard was in charge; 1808, Eleazer Wells, who spent his last days here; 1809, Joel Steele; 1810, N. W. Stearns; 1811, W. Bannister; 1812, Erastus Otis; 1813 and '14, B. R. Hoyt, afterward long a resident, and financial agent of Newbury Seminary. In 1815, Amasa Taplin was the appointee; in 1816, Jonathan Worthen; 1817, Samuel Bates; 1818 and '19, Solomon Winchester; 1820, Eleazer Wells, (supply); 1821-'22, Joel Steele; 1823, Joel W. McKee and C. D. Cahoon; 1824, John Lord, Joseph B. White, John Foster; 1825, Isaac Barker and N. W. Scott.

In 1826, the continued growth in numbers and financial ability of the Vershire circuit, which had been marked in 1823 by the appointment of two preachers to the charge, instead of one, is further shown by setting off Bradford and Newbury as a separate station, in the Danville district, and Paul C. Richmond was appointed over it. In 1827-'28 A. H. Houghton was in charge. In 1829, the New Hampshire and Vermont conference was organized, and C. W. Levings was sent to Newbury. In 1830,-'31, this church was in the Plymouth district, and Schuyler Chamberlin and R. H. Spaulding were in charge in 1830; William D. Cass, and F. T. Daily in 1831. In 1832, the conference name was changed and called the New Hampshire conference; Newbury was put into the Danville district again with C. Cowen and W. Nelson on the circuit. In 1833, the western half of the territory was called the Vermont district and Richard Newhall and C. Cowen were the pastors.

In 1834, Newbury Seminary was opened and an era of great prosperity began for the church, with a house of worship of its own, and the full service of a pastor. During the next thirty-four years, no church in the conference was more important, or better equipped for service. Some of its best ministers were stationed at Newbury, and their labors were shared by the seminary professors, and by a number of ministers of the same order, who had taken up their residence here, where their experience and advice were of great value with those students who had the ministry in view. The pastors in charge were: For 1834, S. Kelley and N. O. Way. In 1835 this was called the Barnard district, and S. Kelley continued in charge. In 1836, it was included in the Chelsea district, with E. J. Scott, the appointee, and in 1837-'38, John G. Dow. In the latter year Newbury was put into the Danville district, where it remained for some years.

The appointments since 1838 were: In 1839, William M. Mann; 1840, J. Templeton; 1841-'42, L. D. Barrows; 1843, Alonzo Webster; 1844, supplied from the seminary; 1845, Moses Chase; 1846, E. Pettingill; 1847, Haynes Johnson; 1848-'49, S. P. Williams; 1850-'51, H. P. Cushing; 1852-'53, E. Copeland; 1854, J. G. Dow; 1855, Haynes Johnson; 1856-'57, P. P. Ray; 1858-'59, S. Quimby; 1860, A. G. Button; 1861-'62, W. D. Malcolm; 1863, D. Packer; 1864-'65, E. C. Bass; 1866-'67, H. A. Spencer; 1868-'69.-'70, Z. S. Haynes; 1871, J. W. Cline; 1872, S. B. Currier; 1873-'74, G. M. Tuttle; 1875-'76-'77, P. N. Granger; 1878-'79, J. McDonald; 1880-'81-'82, Leonard Dodd; 1883-'84-'85, J. H. Winslow; 1886-'87-'88, N. W. Wilder; 1889-'90-'91, Thomas Trevillian; 1892-'93, A. G. Austin; 1894-Oct. '95, John L. Tupper; Oct. 1995-'96, A. W. Ford; 1897-'98, W. H. White; 1899, W. C. Johnson; 1900, F. D. Handy. These are the ministers whose appointments were from conference. We must not omit mention of most valuable service rendered by the seminary professors, by resident clergymen, and by students who had the ministry in view. These faithfully supported the pastors and found their way into all parts of the town. Many a successful minister, between Maine and California, looks back to his first sermon preached in the Leighton hill schoolhouse, or in district No. 12.

There was another class, now long passed away—men not in active service, but occasionally preaching in the intervals of business, and others, not attached to any circuit, but who traveled about on horseback, preached in sparsely settled neighborhoods, and assisted at protracted meetings, or took for a time, the place of some disabled minister. Many of these, when past labor, published brief but interesting narratives of their experiences. Such a one is that of "Father Newell,'" who came to Newbury now and then. A more pretentious work was the autobiography of Rev. Dan Young, who lived in Lisbon, and had a leaning toward political life. He preached in Newbury a great deal. On one occasion he baptized a number of converts in a deep

JOHN STEVENS, M.D.

pool on Hall's brook, near the present residence of Mr. Andrew Knight. A bridge spanned the stream, at some height above the water, and many of the throng gathered upon it to witness the ceremony. Mr. Young observed the weakness of the structure, and begged the persons upon it to come away, but to no purpose. In the following night when no one was near, the bridge fell into the stream. Mr. Young was able but eccentric, and his book is shorn of half its value by the lack of an index, and by his total omission of the dates of the events which he records.

The present church building at Newbury village was erected in 1829, on land given to the society by Rasmus Jonson. Timothy Morse, John Atwood, and Dr. John Stevens, were the building committee. At the time of its erection the members preferred to speak of it as the Methodist Chapel, and it is sometimes called "The Chapel," to this day. According to the custom then, the pulpit was in front of the gallery, the pews facing the entrance doors. Somewhere about 1845, the pews were turned around, and a pulpit built at the other end of the house. During the days of the old seminary, from 1834 to 1868, the church was in term time completely filled. Those were the prosperous days of the church, when the Newbury appointment was second to none in the state. The parsonage was built in 1838, principally through the efforts of Rev. J. G. Dow.

The Seminary Hall and one of the class-rooms were used for devotional meetings. There was generally, in those days, one Sabbath in each month, when the pastor preached at West Newbury, and seldom one, when there was not some religious service in the back part of the town, conducted either by the pastor, or by some of his numerous assistants. In those days several families were identified with the church, who composed most of its permanent membership and from whom came its principal support. The families of Col. John Bayley and those of his sons and daughters, and their connections the families of Dr. John and Ephraim Stevens were prominent. The family of Timothy Morse, and those of the Atwoods, Carletons, Joseph Prescott, Ross Ford and his sons, Paul McKinstry, E. C. Stocker, the Rogers families, Stephen Powers' and Hutchins Bayley's, Clark Chamberlin's, and Andrew Grant's, the George and Leighton families, with many others of whom not a single representative remains, were the substantial people who shared the burdens and the privileges of the society.

Dr. John Stevens was the leader of the choir for many years, and others of the family played the bass viol. A small instrument called a seraphine was placed in the gallery in the early fifties, and was usually played by the music teacher from the seminary. After Dr. Stevens retired the chorister was commonly the teacher of vocal music in the seminary, and the choir, during term time, received accession from many sweet and fresh young voices.

A Sunday school was established early, and for many years the superintendent was the principal of the seminary and the classes were taught by the teachers from that institution.

We have mentioned that a class was formed at West Newbury in 1801, but the time when such were commenced at the village, and on Leighton hill is not known. During term time, there were one, and sometimes two classes, sustained for and by the students.

The New Hampshire Conference met at Newbury in June, 1842, Bishop Hedding presided, and James M. Fuller was secretary. The Vermont Conference has twice held its session here. The first of these was in June, 1856. Bishop Baker presided, and Rev. A. G. Button was secretary. In April 1867, it met here again, with Bishop Scott presiding, and Rev. R. Morgan, secretary.

The removal of Newbury Seminary to Montpelier was a blow to the church from which it has never recovered. It was attended with the departure of several families, and followed by the death of members who were sorely needed. Its field, embracing nearly the whole town, must now be cultivated by the pastor alone, without the abundant aid which supplemented the labors of his predecessors in the old seminary days. Since 1866, the pastor preaches at the village in the forenoon, and then drives out five miles to West Newbury, or the town house to a second service. It is a laborious charge, one in which the virtues of patience, fortitude and self-denial are fully cultivated.

The history of the church since 1868 chronicles few prominent events. In 1876, the house of worship was repaired; the gallery, then disused, was partitioned off for a small vestry; a raised platform for the choir was built at the left of the minister; the sombre desk was replaced by a set of pulpit furniture, the gift of the brothers Ford, and other changes were made. In 1887, Freeman J. and Dr. Orlando W. Doe of Boston presented the church with a bell, weighing 2000 pounds, in memory of their parents. A tower, which bore no sort of resemblance to the modest design of the main structure was erected by subscription, and attached to the east end of the church, in which the bell was placed. In 1899 this tower was taken down, and a new belfry, as near like the original one as could well be made, in pleasing harmony with the rest of the building, was built, and the bell placed in it. At the same time the old windows were removed, and new ones of stained glass were put in.

Windows were placed in the church in memory of the following persons: Joseph Prescott, by Miss Belle Prescott; Rev. Solomon Sias, by his daughter; Ephraim B., and Dr. John Stevens; Maria Nourse George, by her children; Ebenezer C., and Mary M. Stocker, by their daughters; Mrs. Lydia Rogers Bolton, by her children; Charles W. Leighton, by Mrs. Leighton; John S., and Mary Jane George, by F. W. George; principals of Newbury seminary, by subscription. Upon the memorial window, behind the pulpit, are inscribed the names of the principals of Newbury Seminary. Services of rededication of the church and reunion of the students of the seminary were held September 19, 1900. An historical address was delivered by Hon. Horace W. Bailey, sermon by Rev. J. O. Sherburne, prayer by Rev. J. A. Sherburne, remarks by Prof. Solomon Sias of Schoharie, N. Y., and others. Letters from several former pastors of the church, principals of the school, and early pupils were read.

The church has sustained other losses than those occasioned by death or removal. In 1888 a number of members withdrew, and connected themselves with an organization now known as the Free Christian church. In 1896 the conference saw fit to establish a new Methodist church in Newbury, called the Newbury Centre and Boltonville church, transferring to it a number of members from the village church, without, in some cases at least, consulting their wishes in the matter. George C. McDougall was appointed to this new charge, preaching at the town house, and at the depot hall, in Boltonville. This project, of dividing what was already weak, resulted in failure, and after three years, Mr. McDougall was given a new appointment, and the village minister again supplied at the town house.

Mention must not be omitted of various charitable and missionary societies which have been supported by the congregation. In 1835, there was founded the "Dorcas Society," which was, in time, superseded by the "Woman's Foreign Missionary Society," and the "Woman's Home Missionary Society." Much, of which no record is kept, was done by the former, in aid of indigent students who had the ministry in view.

Such is the imperfect record of a church which has a most worthy place, both in local history and in the annals of Methodism, and of it may be hoped that, grand as its past has been, its best work is yet to be done.

CHAPTER XXVII

RELIGIOUS HISTORY—CONTINUED.

THE first record of religious service at Wells River is found in a vote of the town on March 25, 1805, "that Mr. Lambert preach every second Sabbath in each three months of the time, at Wells River, so-called." Of what previous religious privileges that part of the town had, we know nothing, but many of the people in the region from which the membership of the present Wells River church is drawn, were members of, or attendants at, the churches at Newbury, Horse Meadow, or Bath.

From the funeral discourse of Rev. Samuel R. Thrall, published in 1874, some facts relating to the religious history of Wells River are gathered. The time alluded to was in the late thirties, when the older men like Joshua Hale had passed away, and before any religious organization was gathered there.

"In those days Wells River was pre-eminently a missionary field. The village was a noted stopping place for stage-drivers, and as noted for its utter lack of religious character. In all the village there was not one man, and only one woman, who could be expected to attempt offering a prayer at the bedside of the dying. There were very few men that could not be counted upon not to swear like pirates upon any shadow of provocation. Two men, neither of whom was a professing Christian, one day asked each other why they could not have a church, and after a little talk together set about the work of building one."

In 1838, a Meeting-house Society was organized, on the 24th

SCHOOL BUILDING AND CONGREGATIONAL CHURCH, WELLS RIVER.

of May, and Charles Hale, Emory Gale and Jacob Kent, Jr., were chosen a committee to select a site for a church. They decided upon a piece of land owned by Timothy Shedd, which was bought for $150. Charles Hale, Emory Gale, and Timothy Shedd were the building committee, and upon this lot the present house, now greatly enlarged, was built, at a cost of $2,650, and the building then consisted only of an audience room, which was on the ground floor. The house was heated by stoves. There were 58 pews, which brought at the auction sale, February 1, 1840, $2,701.14, three pews remaining unsold. The highest price was brought by pew No. 2, which was bid off by C. J. S. Scott for $70. The subscriptions were repaid from the avails of the sale, and the building became the property of the pew-owners. It was, at first, a union meeting-house, and each pew-owner had a right to name a minister whose sentiments agreed with his own, such part of the year as his share in the house bore to the whole. It is not known that the privilege was ever exercised, and the Meeting-house Society gave place, many years ago, to the Congregational Society.

The church was dedicated January 28, 1840, the sermon being preached by Rev. George W. Campbell, of Newbury. Rev. David Sutherland, of Bath, offered the prayer of dedication. On the 14th of April, 1840, twenty-four members of the Newbury church, who lived in the vicinity of Wells River, were organized, by a council, into a branch church, under the oversight of Rev. Mr. Campbell, and the Newbury church. This branch became an independent church, by act of a council which met Jan. 12, 1842. At the public services held the next day, a discourse was delivered by Rev. David Merrill, of Peacham, author of the celebrated "ox sermon." On the 13th of the following April, Rev. Samuel R. Thrall, who had been preaching since January 24, 1841, was ordained and installed. He was dismissed March 16, 1847. His salary was $400, and the use of the parsonage. Of his somewhat remarkable family, and of Rev. J. D. Butler, who succeeded him, an account is elsewhere given.

Mr. Butler, then a professor in Norwich University, and afterwards its president, began to preach April 11, 1847, was ordained October 14, of that year, and dismissed in 1850. For some time he resided at Norwich, driving to Wells River on Saturday and returning on Monday. Mr. Butler afterward became eminent as a linguist, traveler and teacher. He is still living at Madison, Wis., connected with the University and the Historical Society of that state, and in 1898, at the age of eighty-five, was chaplain of the Wisconsin senate. In his time, and mainly through his exertion, the bell was purchased, which was hung February 29, 1848. For some years it was rung at six a. m., noon, and nine p. m. The sum received as damages caused by the building of the Passumpsic railroad was applied to painting and repairing the church.

Rev. S. M. Plympton was ordained and installed, May 8, 1851, and resigned May 5, 1861. He was born at Sturbridge, Mass., in 1820, was graduated at Amherst College in 1846, and at Andover Theological Seminary 1849. After leaving Wells River, he was chaplain of the 4th Vermont, in the Civil War, and died at Chelsea, September 14, 1866. His salary was $500 and the parsonage.

Rev. William S. Palmer was ordained and installed pastor, February 19, 1862, and closed his services September 14, 1874, to become pastor of the Second church at Norwich, Conn. Mr. Palmer was born in Orford, N. H., August 6, 1827, was graduated at Dartmouth College in 1849, and Andover Theological Seminary in 1852. Before coming to Wells River he was a teacher. He was widely known, and often called upon to deliver sermons and addresses upon public occasions. In 1869, the church building was enlarged to give room for twelve additional pews, and thoroughly repaired at a cost of about $2000. Rev. John Rogers, "a good preacher and a ripe scholar," preached some months after Mr. Palmer left. He died soon after leaving Wells River. Rev. Eugene J. Ranslow was called, October 11, 1875, and continued in office till 1888. He is now pastor of the church at Swanton. Mr. Ranslow was graduated at Vermont University, and served in the navy during the Civil War.

Rev. Rufus C. Flagg, a graduate of Middlebury College, was called December 11, 1888, and recognized by council January 22, 1889. He resigned January 21, 1897, to become president of Ripon College, Wisconsin. A call was extended to Rev. Rolla G. Bugbee, June 19, 1892. He was pastor till January 21, 1897. In 1894 the church edifice was thoroughly repaired, and, to some extent, remodelled. An addition was made behind the pulpit to contain the organ, new pews were put in, electric lights introduced, and many other improvements made, at a cost of $6,500. Mr. Bugbee resigned January 21, 1897, and after the pulpit had been occupied by several individuals, Rev. George H. Credeford of Winthrop, Me., was tendered a call, April 19, 1898, and entered upon his ministry.

Mr. Credeford married April 4, 1899, Miss Ella M. Bixby of Newbury, and is the only one of the twenty-six ministers of the three Congregational churches of Newbury who has taken a wife in this town.

The deacons have been:

Dudley C. Kimball, 1842–1847	C. O. Penniman, 1873
Moody Powers, 1844–1863	A. M. Whitelaw, 1877
A. B. W. Tenney, 1863–1873	H. W. Adams, 1890
F. Deming, 1894	

The whole number of members whose names were on the roll to January 1st, 1900, was 510.

The first parsonage was the house next north of the

school building, built by Silas Chamberlin in 1792. The present parsonage was erected in 1876. The organ was put into the church by the Ladies Society in 1872, at a cost of about $1,200. The organists in their succession have been Miss Ellen Underwood, George B. Fessenden, Mrs. Anna D. Leslie, and at present, Mrs. E. W. Smith. The leaders of the choir, from the early '40s have been Leonard Gale, then A. T. Baldwin about twenty years. The present leader is Hon. E. W. Smith. The first communion service of the church was of Brittania metal, and was presented to it, June 1, 1842, by Mr. Timothy Shedd, and was, by the church, given to the one at West Newbury, August 1, 1867. The present service was presented in 1867; the silver pitchers were given by Edward Hale, the goblets by A. T. Baldwin, and Franklin Deming, and the baptismal urn by the Ladies Aid Society.

There are six memorial windows in the church, in memory of the following persons: Dea. A. B. W. Tenney and wife, by Miss Martha J. Tenney; Rev. Salem M. Plympton, by Mrs. F. Deming; Daniel A. Rogers, by Mrs. F. Deming; Mrs. Lucy W. Whitelaw, by her children; Anna J. Kimball, and Helen S. Kimball Hubbard, by their father, Dea. J. P. Kimball; and one dedicated to the Sabbath School by the pupils of the school.

The Wells River church, which draws its membership and audience from four towns, three counties, and two states, has been, for about forty years, one of the largest and strongest in the state.

We have seen that Newbury was settled by people of the Congregational order, and that, according to the law and custom of the time the minister was supported by tax. At first, when all the people lived along the river, the meeting-house at the Ox-bow was a central place. But settlements spread, and in the course of twenty-five years the heavy woods in the south and southwest parts of the town were broken by little clearings, in the midst of each of which was a log house, and in most cases, a family of children. By 1785, there were settlements in the south part of the town all the way to Topsham line, and the settlers felt it a hardship that they should be taxed to support preaching at a part of the town, miles away, along trails which could only be travelled on foot, or on horseback. The town seems to have been considerate and in 1788, Joseph Harriman, William Pettie, Josiah Pratt, Israel Putnam, John Sly, Jonathan Ladd, James Heath, and Moses Winn and son, were exempted from paying their minister tax. Some of these lived in what is now Topsham, eight or ten miles from the Ox-bow. In 1790, it was voted to release those that lived west of Wright's mountain. But in the next year these dwellers far away considered that they ought to have preaching and united in the following petition:

Whereas, we whose names are underwritten live at such a distance from the place of public worship that we cannot attend without much trouble and difficulty, we therefore pray you would take it into consideration and grant unto us our proportionable part of preaching according to what the back part of the town pays, etc.

John Vance	James Vance	John Haseltine
Otho Stevens	John Johnson	Joseph Kent
Tarrant Putnam	Moses Johnson	Samuel Butterfield
John Vance, Jr.	Peletiah Bliss	William Kincaid
James Dodge	Paul Ford	Robert Lovewell
Samuel Hadley	Moses Chamberlin	Benjamin Akin
Samuel Tucker	Jacob Pratt	Abraham Brickett

It was voted to request Mr. Lambert to preach at Capt. John Haseltine's such a proportion of the time as the list of said subscribers bears to the list of the whole town. This arrangement continued during some years, but was not quite satisfactory to the people beyond the mountain, as in 1794, Nicholas White, Timothy White, John Sawyer, John Sanders, Joseph Sleeper, Ephraim Metcalf, Robert Lovewell, James Thompson, Nathaniel Dustin, and Jonas Chapman were released from their tax. But in 1801 the town decided not to release the settlers beyond the mountain, but ordained instead that Mr. Lambert should preach the last Sabbath in each month at Mr. Tarrant Putnam's. In 1804 the town voted to continue this arrangement, and also voted that Mr. Lambert should preach the second Sabbath in each three months, near Mr. Zaccheus Dustin's. This is where Hale Bailey now lives.

With the dismission of Mr. Lambert the union between church and state passed away, but by that time there were members of his church in every school district in town, and they were not neglected in the pastoral ministrations. Preaching was held much of the allotted time at Jonas Tucker's and at the schoolhouse "near Mr. John Doe's," as runs the record of various meetings by Rev. Clark Perry. Along the valley of Hall's brook "the schoolhouse near Mr. Peach's," was selected as a religious gathering place, and meetings were held on Jefferson hill.

Methodism was at first more strong at West Newbury than elsewhere, the first class meeting in town being held at Joseph Prescott's. Its earlier services were held in farm-kitchens and the schoolhouse on Rogers hill. But none of these could contain the multitudes that thronged to revival services which were held in 1827, in a barn which stood opposite the present residence of the late Oliver B. Rogers. Camp meetings were held once and again on Jefferson hill.

Members of the Carter and Haseltine families with others, were connected with a Baptist church in Bradford, whose meeting-house, a century ago, adjoined the cemetery on the upper plain. This society became extinct, and a Free-Will Baptist church was organized, which on October 21, 1809, withdrew from the Free-Will Baptist connection, and adopted tenets commonly held by the religious body which designates itself by no other title than that of Christian, but adopting the name of Christian Baptists. This

WEST NEWBURY.

UNION MEETING HOUSE, WEST NEWBURY.

Photo. by Corliss.

society, at one time very flourishing, built, in 1834, a church building, now lately repaired, in that part of Bradford called "Goshen," just across the Newbury line.

There were several attempts to build a church at West Newbury, one as early as 1810, but the matter was delayed many years. It was not easy to fix upon a site. There were influential people in the part of the town which adjoins Topsham, who wanted it to be built near the present-residence of R. S. Chamberlin.

On February 16, 1832, an association was formed and on the 18th the first meeting of the Union Meeting-house Society was held at the dwelling-house of David and Elijah Tucker. This meeting, of which Levi Rogers was president, and Daniel Putnam clerk, chose John B. Carleton, David Haseltine, Dudley Carleton, Jr., Nathaniel Niles, and Jonas Tucker, a committee to build a meeting-house which should contain not fewer than fifty, nor more than fifty-six pews. The subscriptions to the house were payable, one-third in money, and one-third in neat stock and grain. The site was given by Col. John Smith and the timber was hewed by Dudley Carleton, Jr. Archibald Mills was the thoroughly capable master workman, and the church, whose exterior has been little altered, was erected on a sightly eminence, where it is a conspicuous landmark, and one of the most pleasing church edifices in this region. It is strange that no trees have ever been set out around it. In the fashion of the time, there was a gallery for the singers above the vestibule; in front of it was the circular pulpit, supported on posts, as high as a man's head, and attained by stairs behind; the body pews faced the pulpit, and the front doors. There were fifty-six pews, forty of which were in front of the pulpit, and sixteen at the right and at the left. A pipe organ, built by Robert McIndoe was placed in the gallery. At the sale of pews the sum realized was $1,452.75, which more than paid the cost of the building. The pew-owners were Presbyterians, Congregationalists, Methodists, and Baptists, and were entitled to the use of the house by ministers of each order, such part of the time as the number of pews held by each party bore to the whole number. In 1843, the organ was sold and removed. In 1854, the building was repainted and newly shingled, at a cost of $250. In 1873, the house was thoroughly repaired, new windows put in, and new pews; the aisles were carpeted, the gallery was closed in, and made into a vestry, and the pulpit which had been in the Congregational church at the street was placed at the west end of the house. Oliver B. Rogers, John Smith, William C. Carleton and Levi L. Tucker were the committee.

The house was rededicated September 11, 1873, by special services, at which sermons were preached by Rev. Isaac McAnn, the presiding elder, and by Rev. William S. Palmer, of Wells River. At this meeting a subscription for a cabinet organ was started, which was purchased and used for the first time on Thanksgiving day.

The entire expense of the repairs was about $2,000. In 1891, the building was repaired and repainted. In the spring of 1892, a bell weighing one thousand pounds was presented to the society upon certain conditions, by Bradley D. Rogers of Buffalo, and Mrs. Angelina P. Webster of Plymouth, N. H., son and daughter of Levi and Betsey Rogers, and in their memory. Repairs and alterations were made upon the belfry, and on July 4th of that year the new bell was hung and dedicated with appropriate services. The bell was presented by Mr. Rogers, and accepted by Rev. C. H. Coolidge; a dedicatory prayer was offered by Rev. J. L. Merrill, and a sermon was preached by Rev. A. G. Austin. Brief addresses were delivered by others.

The present committee of the society are John Smith, Dudley Carleton, and Joseph Sawyer, and in its existence of nearly seventy years it has had but three clerks, Daniel Putnam, 1832-'59; Thomas L. Tucker, 1859-'87; Byron O. Rogers, 1887.

It is creditable to the people of West Newbury that two religious societies have occupied the same building for such a long period in harmony, and it is also creditable to the successive committees of repairs that they have preserved intact, the belfry and tower, which are so well adapted to the building, and harmonize with the landscape in which the church has stood so long. Services were held with considerable regularity for over thirty years by the pastors of both churches at the village, and by others. Since 1865, regular alternate services have been held by the pastors of the Congregational church, organized in 1867, and the pastor of the Methodist church whose field includes nearly all of the town. In the earlier years, Moses Brock, Sr., led the singing, and Thomas L. Tucker played the organ. Later, Mr. Tucker became chorister and under his leadership of about thirty years, the choir was considered the best in town. His son, S. S. Tucker has long been the chorister, and Mrs. Joseph Sawyer the organist most of the time since the instrument was purchased.

In 1839, the town house was built as near the geographical centre of Newbury as possible, the location being selected as about equally inconvenient to all sections of the town. It has been used as a substitute for a church building in that locality since its erection, and, since 1866, services by ministers who alternate there and at West Newbury have been regularly held. It accommodates a part of the town which is several miles from any church, and a congregation of fair size gathers there. Dea. A. McAllister was superintendent of its Sunday-school for nearly twenty-four years. About fifty families are nearer the town house than to any church edifice.

For many years the pastor of the Congregational church at the village, held one service in the month at West Newbury, and many members of the church lived in that part of the town. Somewhere about 1860, this practice was discontinued, and the

Congregationalists at West Newbury were left without preaching. During several years the people engaged preaching for a few months at a time, but no minister remained there long enough to make much impression. In the summer of 1865, Rev. David Connell came to the place and began services, and under his preaching a Congregational church of twenty-one members was formed, on February 13, 1867. All of these were from the Newbury church. The church was organized by a council held in the Union Meeting-house, of which Rev. Silas McKeen, D. D., was moderator, and Rev. John K. Williams was scribe. Dr. McKeen preached the sermon, and other parts were taken by Revs. H. N. Burton, J. K. Williams, William S. Palmer and J. D. Emerson. Mr. Connell lived for one year in the house which E. Minard now owns and occupies. In 1866, he moved into the present parsonage, then owned by H. K. Wilson, which was, in 1868, purchased by Freeman Keyes, James Abbott and O. C. Barnett, and by them conveyed to the church under conditions which provide for its becoming the property of the Vermont Domestic Missionary Society, should the church become extinct.

Mr. Connell resigned his charge in 1869, and removed to the north part of the state. He was born in Edinburgh, Scotland, February 15, 1815, and was graduated at Glasgow University, and at the Theological Seminary connected with it. He was an able man, of large information and wide acquaintance, and well equipped for the ministry, but was not able to avoid trouble in the parish. His ministry was unfortunate, and he left the community in a divided condition. Mr. Connell died at Portsmouth, N. H., November 11, 1895. Mrs. Connell was also from Scotland, and in many respects a remarkable woman. They had a large, and somewhat unusual family. Their oldest son, William, is a lawyer in Omaha, Neb., and was a member of Congress for one term; another son is a physician there; James is a jeweler in Portsmouth, N. H., another also lives in Omaha, and of the daughters, Lillian married Rev. H. M. Tenney, D. D., another is a widow, and a third is a teacher.

A very different man from Mr. Connell, was Rev. Robert D. Miller, who in January 1870, came to West Newbury, and entered upon his labors with the church. Few men coming into a place so torn with dissension could have managed such a work of reconciliation as Mr. Miller, and that, not by argument, but by the force of his own exemplary life, and winsome personality. Mr. Miller was born in Dummerston, Vt., September 23, 1824, was graduated at Amherst College in 1848, and at Hartford Theological Seminary in 1853. Under his ministry the church prospered, and it was largely through his influence that the Union Meeting-house was repaired in 1873. In March 1875, he resigned his charge, to the great regret of the whole community, and, it is believed afterward of his own. He is still living at Malden, Mass. During his ministry, his son, Charles, a fine young man, met his death by drowning, at Gill, Mass. His only surviving son, John C., a graduate of Middlebury College, is in business in Boston.

In June, 1875, Rev. Amzi B. Lyon took charge of the church, and remained here thirteen years. He was born of a long line of clerical ancestry, at Brownhelm, O., March 22, 1831, was graduated at Oberlin College, 1854, and Andover Theological Seminary in 1857. He was a man of quiet, studious habits, and a good citizen, faithful in his calling. Mr. Lyon was married, for the third time, while at West Newbury, to Miss Clara E. Palmer of Concord, N. H., long a teacher at Abbott Academy at Andover, Mass. She was the daughter of Hon. Dudley S. Palmer, a prominent citizen of Concord, who spent his last years at the parsonage, dying there May 1886. Mr. Lyon went into missionary work in Spearfish, S. D., and he died, at Chadron, Neb., March 3, 1890. He left a daughter, Emma, who was graduated at Abbott academy, and married Rev. Charles E. Rice, and a son, now in Colorado.

In the fall of 1888, Mr. Edward W. Smith came here from Brooklyn, N. Y., and was acting pastor two years, and was ordained an evangelist in the Union Meeting-house, November 13, 1889. Mr. Smith was sincere, but ill-equipped for the ministry, and his brief pastorate was not a success.

Rev. Chalmer H. Coolidge, a native of Peru in this state, who had taken a partial course at Oberlin College, was acting pastor from May, 1892, to May 1896. Mr. Coolidge represented this town in the legislature of 1894. He was a man of ability, extensive information, and great industry. He resigned to become pastor of the church in Piermont. In June following Mr. Coolidge's departure, Mr. Ralph H. Abercrombie, from Lawrence, Mass., a graduate of Bangor Theological Seminary came, and was ordained and installed pastor of the church, November 6, 1896, the only settled minister the church has ever had. He was dismissed by council August 23, 1898, and became pastor of the Brookfield church. Mr. Abercrombie was a fine musician, a man of genial nature, who did much good and made many friends.

The church was without a minister till October, 1899, when Rev. George A. Furness came here from Wardsboro, and still remains. The minister preaches at the church at West Newbury, and at the town house. The members are widely scattered; those who live in this town receive their mail at six different post-offices. It has always been small in numbers and weak financially, and has been sustained only by much self-denial on the part of a few, and by aid from the missionary society. But it has been a means of good, and may yet see great prosperity. Connected with this small church are a Ladies' Missionary Society, and a Ladies' Aid Society, and a flourishing society of Christian Endeavor.

The deacons have been:

*James Abbott,	1867–1870	*Moses Brock,	1867–1874
*David T. Wells,	1868–1899	*Archibald McAllister,	1868–1899
Maurice H. Randall,	1896 ——	Jonas Tucker,	1896–1900
Albert N. Kendrick,	1900 ——		

†The Free Christian church, the youngest religious society in Newbury, had its origin in a tent meeting held near Newbury village in September, 1888, by Rev. H. C. Holt, and a society was formed of individuals who held similar views with his, most of whom had previously been connected with the Methodist church. They at once set about building a meeting-house of their own at Newbury village, which was begun December 6, 1888, and completed February 6, 1889. This building, usually spoken of as the Adventist church, cost about $700 not counting the value of much labor which was freely given. The cost of the land was $175. This building was dedicated February 6, 1889. This society was not formally organized into a church till March 22, 1892, but sustained regular preaching, both in the church building, and in other parts of the town. In the fall of 1890, Mr. Holt held a series of tent meetings in John Buchanan's sugar orchard, near the Centre, which were attended by great numbers of people.

The Free Christian church was organized March 22, 1892. The number of original members was thirty, and fourteen have since been added. The articles of belief held by the church include repentance and faith; baptism by immersion; personal holiness; the near approach of the advent of Christ; the literal resurrection of the dead; the destruction of the ungodly; the renewed earth, the home of the saints; and that death ends the opportunity for conversion. Rev. H. C. Holt was chosen pastor April 6, 1892, and held the office till his death, August 27, 1896. He was born in Hartland, Vt., October 16, 1844, began preaching 1879. He was pastor of the Advent church at Bridgewater, Vt., several years, then engaged in evangelistic work until he came to Newbury.

Rev. George H. Temple was chosen pastor of the church, December 25, 1897. He was born in Warren, Vt., March 17, 1847, began preaching in 1886; pastor one year of the Advent church in Warren, then engaged in evangelistic work until he came here.

The present officers are: John B. Brock and W. E. Marston, deacons; W. E. Marston and O. W. Brock, elders; O. W. Brock, clerk and treasurer; O. W. Brock, superintendent of Sunday school. The members of this church are scattered over town, and some of the most regular attendants live seven miles and more from the place of worship.

---

*Died in service.

†Prepared by Mr. J. B. Brock.

In the second chapter of this volume we have mentioned the probability that the first white men who visited the Coös country were Catholic missionaries from Canada. But so far as is now known, there were no families here of the ancient faith till the building of the railroad in 1847, when a multitude of Irishmen and their families came here, and received the occasional ministrations of a priest. After the railroads were completed a few Catholic families remained, and were visited from time to time by a clergyman of their order. It was not for many years that a church was gathered.

St. Ignatius's Catholic church was organized and built in 1874 by Rev. J. S. Michaud of Newport, Vt,. the first pastor and who continued as paster until about 1880. Since that date the church has been supplied with pastors as follows: Rev. D. J. O'Sullivan; Rev. R. F. Higgins, Rev. J. Whitaker, White River Junction, Vt., Rev. J. A. Boissonnault of St. Johnsbury, Vt.; Rev. J. Paquet, and Rev. J. Pontbriand, Lyndonville, Vt., the present pastor. The church has about eighty communicants. Residents of Newbury, Groton and South Ryegate also attend this church, which is at Wells River.

CHAPTER XXVIII.

Religious and Educational.

IN an early chapter of this volume it was pointed out that the town owed much of its early prosperity to the fact that so many of its grantees became actual settlers, and their previous acquaintance and concerted action placed the new settlement in a very strong position. This was no less true of the church. The grantees who became settlers, were, almost without exception, favorable to the system of church government established here, and before a single framed house had been built in town, "The Church of Christ at Newbury and Haverhill, in Coös," as the old records run, had been placed on a firm footing. In towns where all the settlers were persons who had bought out the original proprietors, and were in general, strangers to each other, it was many years, usually, before a church was formed, as there was apt to be such a diversity of opinion that no one society became strong enough to support a minister, until the early years had passed away.

By the old colonial law the majority of voters decided the form of worship, and there was no exemption from tax, of those who differed from it. But in 1780, an act of the legislature enabled any person who differed from the established order, to escape being taxed to support it, on presentation of a certificate, duly attested, that such person belonged to some other church, and contributed to its support. In 1801, a further act enabled any person who presented to the town clerk a declaration in writing, that he did not agree in religious opinion with a majority of the inhabitants of the town, was released from taxation for the support of the church. It is significant that while in Bradford the number of certificates presented under these acts was about 150, here in Newbury there were but eighteen, thirteen of which related to members of the Baptist church at that town.

The foregoing account of the churches of this town gives but a meagre idea of the religious history of Newbury. To narrate the small beginnings of each society; to give the names and succession of their pastors; to describe the various edifices which have been consecrated to religious worship; to merely mention the channels through which the benevolence of the churches has reached its sharers, is about all that we can do.

But when we have said all this, and even more, we have not begun to tell what its churches have been to the town. There have been many men and women here in Newbury, to whom the church of their choice, which, in their view, realized most nearly the divine ideal, was the dearest thing on earth. The churches of Newbury have been built up and fostered by the self-denial and loving care of several generations of devout men and women. It is to these, the business men of our villages, the farmers of our hills and meadows, rather than to the ministers of the gospel who have labored here, devout men as they have been, to whom belongs the honor of maintaining the Christian religion in this town. Making all possible allowance for the mixture of human frailty with the worthiest aspirations, the fact still remains that the Christian religion, has been, during all these years, the strongest power here in Newbury. It is easy to deny this, and to point out that a spirit of wordliness has entered the churches and weakened their influence; that faith is not as of yore upon the earth. Yet it may well be asked, whether, had Newbury been settled by men who cared nothing for these things, if no church spire had ever pointed toward Heaven; if the sound of the church-going bell had never floated over these hills; if there had been no godly ministry here; if, had there been none in Newbury who loved the house of God, would there have been anything in the history of the town worthy of remembrance?

The religious history of Newbury would not be complete if we failed to note that a large number of its families, during more than 127 years, have been connected with the Presbyterian churches in Ryegate. By request, the following brief account of these, prepared by the late Edward Miller, Esq., is inserted here:

The first settlers of Ryegate attended church at Newbury, and occasionally received the ministrations of its minister, Rev. Peter Powers. Not far from 1779, the first church in that town, the Associate Presbyterian, was formed. This is often called the "Seceder" church, and was an offshoot from the General Associate church. In 1858, the seceders united with two other bodies and formed the United Presbyterian church. This church was joined with one at Barnet Centre, till 1823. Rev. David Goodwillie, and his son, Rev. Thomas Goodwillie, D. D., occupied the pulpit of the church at Barnet Centre for a period of eighty years. They were among the most prominent ministers of the state. The Ryegate church erected one of the finest church buildings in this vicinity, at the Corner, a few years ago.

The Reformed Presbyterian church at Ryegate Corner, generally called the Covenanter church, was organized in 1799. Rev. James Milligan was its pastor from 1817 to 1840; Rev. James M. Beattie from 1844, till his death in 1882. Their house of worship at the Corner, was burned August 16, 1899. This church has always had a considerable representation in Newbury. The members consider the taking of oaths to support a temporal power as unscriptural, and do not vote or hold office.

The Reformed Presbyterian church at South Ryegate was formed in 1843, and the present church edifice built in 1849. This church differs from the Covenanters in that its members use the elective franchise. Many of this congregation live in Newbury.

These three churches use a version of the Psalms in meter, at their Sabbath service.

The youngest Presbyterian church in Ryegate is called the "First Presbyterian church," and was organized, says Mr. Samuel Mills, by a commission from Boston Presbytery, November 12, 1875, with fifty-three members. Its membership on January 1, 1900, was 160. Many of this number live in Newbury. Since its organization this society has built a church, vestry and parsonage, costing about $7,000 at South Ryegate. Rev. William Wallace is its fifth and present pastor, installed January 1, 1900. "The Presbyterian form of religious worship is founded on the word of God as expressed in the confession of faith, catechisms, larger and shorter, with the form of church government agreed upon by the Assembly of Divines at Westminster, and practiced by the church of Scotland." These four churches have had several hundred members in this town.

We conclude the religious history of Newbury, by presenting a picture of a Sunday in Haverhill Corner, eighty years ago. It was written by Hon. Arthur Livermore, now past ninety years of age, residing in England. Those who remember the times say that with a few changes of names, it would describe a Newbury Sabbath in those days, and have asked for its insertion here.

On Sunday mornings in summer, we were sent to our chambers, each with a tract, to await the hour of preparation for the more serious business of the day, and the familiar hail at the foot of the stairs: "Now boys, you may lay aside your tracts and go into the garden and gather your carraway, and then it will be time to set out for meeting." That sort of nosegay was deemed to be the thing for the holy hour, and to say the truth, it has to this day, the odor of sanctity to my nostrils. We were called to meeting by the sweetest bell ever heard, which old Mr. Cross made to swing in the steeple of the meeting-house on Ladd street, with a strongly religious air, which no other bell ever had, nor could any but the same old man draw forth from that one.

Grant Powers expounded the doctrines to a congregation that knew not the infelicity of doubt, and with the air of one who did not doubt either his own dogma, or his hearers' acceptance of it. The system of faith conserved in that church did certainly prevail. Those who resisted were marked. Those who regarded the matter objectively none the less believed, and looked for the day when that belief should be informed with life, and bear fruit in the heart.

Following the afternoon meeting was the Sunday school, held in a schoolhouse at the Corner. For this the boys and girls prepared by committing to memory such hymns and scriptures as they pleased, for which they received payment at the rate of one cent for each hundred verses so committed. The tally was kept by the issue of tickets of the denomination of one cent and one mill, all of which were redeemed in cash at the end of the quarter. If the mammon of the world appeared to some to have been unwarrantably thus drawn into the service of religion, it may be remembered that much scripture was thus impressed upon memories at a period when such memories were more impressible, and retentive.

Conference came in the evening "at early candle-lighting," at which the minister was not ordinarily present, but left to the deacons, and other gifted members of the church, the conduct of that somewhat diversified scene of exhortation, psalmody, mutual encouragement and prayer.

"Early candle-lighting," the formula used by the minister to denote the time for the conference to meet, denoted also the absence of clocks in some of the houses that could be depended upon as unerring timekeepers. I like to dwell upon any of the tokens of manners more primitive than our own, when the flight of the hours was marked by the movements of the heavenly bodies, when the cock announced the beginning of the day's labor, and the twilight its close. This gloaming of Sunday never failed of light sufficient to guide the pious steps of dear Mrs. Webster to the conference. She bore in a brass candlestick, a tallow candle, to help in the imperfect illumination of the scene. If she ever wearied of the clumsy exhortations, of the prayers that painfully dragged for the devout orator to frame a wish, or to imagine a want not already more than supplied by the bountiful source of all good; if she failed to be wakened to ecstacy by the singers grouped around the candles, and holding their books in a manner to receive their very dim light, she took up arms against the perception of such weariness, because the conference was a means of grace, and it was her duty, and should be her privilege, to attend with regularity. And she did so. Twenty years at least, later, the same candle was represented by its like, conveyed in the same candlestick, by the same figure, scarcely changed, though moving with steadiness somewhat impaired by age.

Seventy years ago the kitchen clock in Mrs. Webster's house was wound on Saturday evenings, because the winding was not counted a work of necessity or mercy permitted to be done on Sunday.*

Mention was made in the last chapter, of the "Goshen Meeting-House," which stands just over the line in Bradford. After that chapter was printed, the contracts, and other papers relating to its construction came to light, and were placed in the editor's hands, that the particulars of its erection might be preserved. They cast some light upon the usages of the time, as both the church at Wells River and the one at West Newbury, were contracted for in a similar manner.

This meeting-house is the only one left, in this vicinity, in which the pulpit is in front of the gallery, and the pews face the entrance doors. Not only the church at West Newbury, and the Methodist church at the village, but the brick church at Haverhill Corner, were built in that way.

---

*NOTE. Mrs. Webster was the wife of Hon. Stephen P. Webster, an old-time lawyer of Haverhill Corner. He lived in a large two-story house on the north side of Court street.

The Christian Baptist church, once very flourishing, is nearly extinct, and the building was falling into decay, when measures were taken, in 1899, for its preservation. It is now seldom used. The interior containing forty pews, is very quaint and plain.

In October, 1832, a committee was appointed by the Goshen society to superintend the building of a meeting-house, which met once each month at the store of F. & H. Keyes, that stood on the line between Newbury and Bradford. The committee were: Henry Keyes, clerk, David Manson, Levi Colby, E. B. Rollins, Simeon Chase, Jr., William Heath, Nicholas S. Chadwick, and Levi Carter.

The society erected the frame and boarded it, with roof and cupola, and then, by their agent, Richard Aldrich, conveyed it to this committee, who furnished the capital for completing the church. Those who did the work and those who furnished the material, were paid one-third in cash, and the rest in grain or neat stock. When the house was finished the committee received the pews, forty in number, which they were to sell at such prices as would repay them.

George W. Prichard, Israel Willard and William Burroughs were the referees who certified as to the quality of the work and estimated its cost, and the first named, with Ellis Bliss and Moses Chamberlain, were the committee who appraised the pews. The house was completed in June, 1834, and, the contract being fulfilled, the committee dissolved. This account of the building of the Goshen meeting-house is given because it was largely built by Newbury people, and many families from this town regularly attended there. The late Nicholas Chadwick told the editor of this volume, that the building would have been placed upon the town line, had there been a level spot large enough for it.

The town-meeting of March 12, 1769, took the first recorded action regarding education, by voting fifteen pounds for the support of a school. It is probable that during the previous years, something was done, and there were private schools, of some kind, as there were several who were well qualified to teach, among the settlers, and the children were not allowed to grow up in ignorance. The town continued ever after to aid the cause of education by increased appropriations. The first schools were held in private houses, and in the log meeting-house. Chance has preserved the name of one of the pioneers of education in Vermont. In a letter to some gentlemen at Newburyport, dated at Newbury, Coös, September 28, 1772, *Col. Moses Little writes to recommend one James Hicks, who had taught school in Newbury, with great

---

*Little papers.

success, the preceding year.   This James Hicks was, the letter said, well educated in the school of London.   How he came to have wandered into this wilderness, we shall never know.   He seems to have gone to the Barbadoes, intending to return to England.

There was only one school in town for many years, for the people were poor, and had a hard struggle to get along.   We know very little about either schools or text-books.   Probably all the instruction was from the Testament, and the New England Primer. These were in every house.

Among the Johnson papers are preserved sundry agreements which relate to early schools in this town.

"NEWBURY, Novr 8th, 1781.

We the subscribers being met for the Purpose of Hiring a schoolmaster, have agreed to give a suitable person Ten Bushels of Wheat per Month, if one cannot be hired for less and found, have chose Thos. Johnson, Capt. John G. Bayley, Wm. Wallace, a Comity to Regulate sd school, and to tax and rate sd district, agreeable to the Number of Scholars that shall be in sd school, and if there is Thirty scholars in sd district, we the Proprietors, agree that no scholars shall be advertised to be taught in sd school, out of the District, the above to be binding for three months only.

ELIHU JOHNSON	WILLIAM WALLACE
THOS. JOHNSON	JOSEPH CHAMBERLIN
PELETIAH BLISS	BENJAMIN MUZZEY
EBENR WHITE	JOHN G. BAYLEY.
EPHM BAYLEY	

Evidently the desired man would not be paid in wheat, as the following relates to the same school.

NEWBURY, Nov. 15, 1781.

"We the subscribers do here-by promise to pay Samuel Hopkins seven pounds, four shillings, by the 12th day of February next, to be paid in hard money, and hard money only, provided he teach a school three months according to the Directions we have given him of equal date herewith, if not then paid, then Interest till paid. Witness our hands.

THOMAS JOHNSON.
JOHN GD BAYLEY.
WILLIAM WALLACE."

Mr. Hopkins seems to have done his best, as the paper is endorsed:

"NEWBURY, Feb. 5, 1782.

We the subscribers do hereby acknowledge that the within named Samuel Hopkins has performed his part of this Oblegation, and we are in Duty bound to pay the same.

THOMAS JOHNSON
JOHN G. BAYLEY."

The following is of later date, and more precise in specifying the qualifications of the master.

"NEWBURY, Sept. 18, 1786.

We, the subscribers, do each of us agree to Pay our equal Proportion in Produce for the board and support of a good schoolmaster, Qualified to teach English, writing and Arithmetic in the midle District school and to find our Proportion of wood at sd school, Provided there is a sufficient number of subscribers, not less than

Twenty, The Schoolmaster to be immediately agreed with for two or three months.

John Beard	Jacob Bayley, Jun.
Ephᴹ Bayley	Joshua Bayley
Frye Bayley	Jacob Bayley
John McLane	John G. Bayley
Dudley Carleton	Thos. Johnson
Joseph Chamberlin	William Wallace
Jacob Tressell	John Mills.

We can read much between the lines of this agreement. The desire to have the children taught the fundamental rules of business, the scarcity of money, but the plentitude of produce, and above all, their earnest desire to do the best they could for their children.

The town was divided into four school districts in 1782, and in 1789 into seven. In 1796 there was dissatisfaction with the master in the Ox-bow district, and Colonels Johnson and Wallace applied to President Wheelock at Hanover, to send them a young man who could teach a satisfactory private school. William B. Bannister was sent, and was so acceptable that he drew away nearly all the pupils from the regular district school, and the master resigned. On October 25, 1796, the district voted that Mr. Bannister's school should be considered the district school, and Rev. Mr. Lambert, Colonel Johnson, and Dr. Kinsman should be a committee to fix a rate and attend to the interests of the school. Mr. Bannister afterward became a prominent citizen of this town. The rate bill of that school is preserved, and the cost was assessed, "one-half on the Grand List, and one-half on the scholar." A similar mode of providing for the expenses was common in many districts in town within twenty years.

In 1801 the General Assembly established a Grammar school in Orange County, and a special town-meeting was held at which Asa Tenney, and William B. Bannister were chosen a committee to meet the county committee, and see upon what terms the school could be established at Newbury. Nothing came of this, as the school was located at Chelsea.

In 1811, the law assessed a tax of one cent on the dollar in support of schools, and the town voted that the tax might be paid in good wheat at one dollar per bushel, good rye at seventy-five cents; and good Indian corn at fifty cents.

In 1818, there were 603 children, between the ages of four and eighteen, in the sixteen districts, as follows: Wells River, 36; Upper Meadow, 23; Ox-bow, 78; Village, 56; Martin, now Kendrick, 18; Rogers' Hill, 43; West Newbury, 43; Brock, 45; Powers district, 22; Grow district, 37; Doe district, 39; Lime Kiln, 20; Jefferson Hill, 28; Wallace Hill district, 28; Boltonville, 29; South Newbury, 73. Before the change to the town system there were twenty-one districts. In some of these, no school had been maintained for years. In 1823, the number of pupils reported was 691, and the following year, 707.

In 1825, the citizens seemed to have awakened to some sense of the backward condition of the schools, and the town passed the following resolution, in which the terse and vigorous diction of Rev. Luther Jewett is plainly seen:

"Resolved,—That a committee of seven be appointed by the town, whose duty it shall be to examine the several school districts in town, twice in the season, once near the commencement of each term, and once at the close of the same, and make report at the next March meeting, of the best scholars in each district, and of those who may make the greatest improvement; likewise to make report of each master who should excell in the work of instruction and government of said school, and designate those, if any, whom they may judge deficient in literary accquirements or injudicious or improper mode of governing their schools."

Dr. Calvin Jewett, David Haseltine, A. B. W. Tenney, Ephraim B. Stevens, Alfred Nevins, James Bayley 2^d and Haynes Johnson 2^d were the committee. This excellent resolution was better made than kept.

The school district system began with the settlement of the town, and endured till it was swept away by the acts of the General Assembly which supplanted it by one which placed the schools under a more direct control, and more efficient supervision. Each district was a little independent commonwealth, with certain well defined boundaries, which built and owned its own schoolhouse, raised and collected its own taxes, and on the last Tuesday of March, in each year, the voters settled its momentous concerns with a formality which copied, on a small scale, the proceedings of the annual town-meeting. Each district had its board of officers, school district politics ran high, and the system was the occasion of more local quarrels than anything else in town. Too often the sole qualification of the school committee was his ability to hire a teacher on lower terms than anybody else. Schools have been taught in Newbury, and large schools too, for seventy-five cents a week, and even as low as fifty cents, with board.

Often, and, in early days, usually, the teacher boarded around, going from house to house, here a day and there a week, her sojourn under each roof being regulated by the proportion of pupils furnished from the family, or by the share of the general tax which was paid by the head of the household. The former was called "boarding by the scholar," and the latter "boarding by the Grand List." It was not altogether the worst of systems. The teacher and the pupil were brought close together; the former had the opportunity to estimate more accurately the influences which surrounded the latter, and many a famous teacher owed much of her after success to the occasion for insight and study of her pupils, which was afforded by "boarding around." Nor was the value all to the teacher and the pupil. The advent of a gentle, refined, teacher into a lonely farmhouse, was an event. For such an one the best room was prepared, the house took on an unwonted cheerfulness, and her gentle influence was remembered there for years afterward. The teacher was thus brought into closer relations with the pupil and the parents than now. Somewhat of good passed forever away with the old system.

The first schoolhouses were of logs. The log meeting-house of the first settlers, was, after its disuse for that purpose, and perhaps before, used for a schoolhouse. The last log schoolhouses, on Jefferson hill, and Leighton hill, were burned in 1847. The second generation of schoolhouses were nearly square; at one end was the door, and at the other, the teacher's desk. The rude benches and desks were at the right and left of the teacher, facing the stove, which occupied the middle ground between the teacher's desk and the door. Two such edifices, now falling into decay, still stand on the county road, one near Long pond, and the other in the "Doe neighborhood." The latter was mercilessly ridiculed by Rev. H. N. Burton in his report as superintendent of schools, nearly forty years ago.

"This school is certainly in pursuit of knowledge under difficulties. The terms are short; the numbers few; the pupils tardy and irregular; the wood is usually green and buried in the snow; the schoolhouse old and rickety, stuck in a side-hill, between two roads, among the rocks, in the edge of the woods, over a brook. We add that the scholars and teachers must have been pretty good, or they would have made no progress at all."

The kind of schoolhouse built fifty years ago, is represented by one still standing in the town house district.

The district schoolhouse was the place where were held singing and spelling schools, prayer and class meetings, lawsuits, justice trials, lyceums and lectures. Around these old-time buildings cluster a thousand memories.

We have better schoolhouses, and greater facilities for acquiring a common school education, but more commodious and more healthful school-rooms and all that can be taught therein, will not give the world a better class of men and women than were trained in these rude old schoolhouses in Newbury sixty years ago. It is easy to ridicule them, and the old systems of teaching, but there were other lessons taught than from books. In them were learned the lessons of self-denial, of fortitude, of the value of time, of honesty, of individual responsibility, and out of them came men and women who have been an honor to our town.

The terms of school were usually two, winter and summer, of ten or twelve weeks each, and it was not until about twenty years ago that the back districts had a fall term. The opening of Newbury Seminary was of vast benefit to the schools of this town. It sent a class of trained teachers out among the district schools and furnished a ready means of education for the best scholars. The wages paid teachers were very low. A dollar a week and board, was a common price for the school mistress sixty years ago, and twenty years ago the salary (if such it could be called) had hardly doubled. Winter terms were taught by masters, at twelve or fifteen dollars a month, and board. The master usually held his position of command "by the dynamic reasons of larger bones." Some schools bore a hard name, and disgraceful rows in them were all too common. Others were dominated by a few bad boys, who were upheld by their fathers, of whom teacher and committee stood in fear. These evils passed away with the district system.

The cost of maintaining the schools in Newbury under the old system, cannot be ascertained, for the reason that the districts managed their own financial affairs and raised the taxes necessary for their maintenance, or part of them. It was easy for a few penurious men to combine, and force the district to limit the term of its school to the briefest period which the law would permit, and fix the compensation at the lowest possible price at which a teacher of the most meagre qualifications could be engaged.

The decay and depopulation of more than one neighborhood in this town is the result of a niggardly policy toward its schools. It was a long step forward when the town assumed the care of its school system. Under the old law, a district composed of intelligent people who knew what a school should be, and were determined to have a good school, always had one, while those localities where ignorance and penuriousness ruled, was always burdened with a school whose inefficiency was worse than no school at all.

In 1830, a select school was opened in a building called the "old Porter office," which had been the law office of Daniel Farrand and after him of Benjamin Porter, and which stood near, and a little east of, Henry W. Bailey's house at the Ox-bow. In their day it was customary for country lawyers to have their offices in separate buildings, standing near, but not connected with, their residences. Such may still be seen at Bath Upper Village. This building is now the kitchen part of Silas Leighton's house. This edifice was secured by Hon. Joseph Berry and David Johnson, and fitted up for a school-room. These gentlemen became financially responsible for the success of the school. Their first teacher was Harriet Newcomb from Keene, and her letter of acceptance of their offer to engage her to teach, gives some idea of what was expected of a lady teacher seventy years ago.

Keene, April 27, 1830.

Joseph Berry Esq.,
    Dear Sir:

On receiving your favor of the 24th I have decided upon leaving Keene sooner than I had at first intended and will take the stage on Friday next. Answering your inquiry as to the text-books which I prefer to use I will mention: "The National Reader," Murray's or Putnam's Grammar, preferring Greenleaf's, Woodbridge's Ancient and Modern Geography, Smith's Arithmetic, Blake's Conversations on Chemistry and Philosophy. I am sorry to say that I do not understand Algebra well enough to teach it, but can teach German and French.   *   *   *

Harriet Newcomb.

It would seem that it was not considered necessary for a young lady to know algebra, as Miss Newcomb came and taught a term of thirteen weeks, from May 3, to July 31, having seventeen pupils who paid twenty-five cents per week, and twelve and one-half cents for use of books. In the fall she taught a second term of twelve weeks, having twenty-eight pupils. She seems to have been succeeded by Miss Charlotte Foxcroft, who taught two terms in 1831, for three dollars per week and board, receiving extra for languages and ornamentals. Her receipts for the two terms were ninety-five dollars, quite a large sum in those days for a woman to earn. She must have been a very popular teacher, as several children were named for her. The names of fifty-nine pupils are preserved, of whom only one is now living in this town. Caroline B. Gibson of Leominster, Mass., was preceptress from September, 1833 to June, 1834.

This school was incorporated in 1830, and kept in operation till the opening of Newbury Seminary, when it was discontinued. In 1843, owing to some dissatisfaction which arose about that time with the management of the Seminary, it was revived under the care of Miss Abigail Williams of Kennebunk, Me. In the fall of 1843, an extension of corporate privileges was granted, and the school was remodelled, with a department for young men, and called "Newbury High School." The session was held in the Congregational vestry, then a new building containing two school-rooms, one of which was in the chamber.

David Johnson was president of the board of trustees and William Atkinson was treasurer. The catalogue for 1844 gives ninety-five names, with an aggregate attendance of 130. Jonathan Tenney was the principal, Nancy C. Johnson, preceptress, Miss Ellen Gregory, teacher of music, painting and drawing, and Edward P. Kimball was assistant. It would seem the causes of dissatisfaction with the Seminary were removed, as the school was discontinued not long after 1844.

CHAPTER XXIX.

Newbury Seminary.

NEWBURY village was, for thirty-four years, the home of a school somewhat remarkable in its way, and now that a period almost equal to that of its existence here has passed since its removal, and those trained within its walls have acted such part, little or great, as they have in the world, it is possible to consider the institution itself, and its place in the educational history of New England, much more accurately than ever before.

The academies in this part of the country which preceded it, were children of the communities in which they were placed. They came slowly into existence to meet, in some measure, the needs of the young people, who were anxious to obtain somewhat more of learning than the meagre teaching of the district schools. Newbury Seminary was the creation of a religious body which selected the village as a convenient place for its denominational school, and by the same organization it was removed.

Along some lines of educational work it was the pioneer, and the ideas which had their unfolding here, were developed by other and richer institutions. Some of its experiments in education have been rejected by the experience of time, but it accomplished a work which seems greater as the years pass. It had its origin as one of the earliest institutions of learning in a denomination of Christian

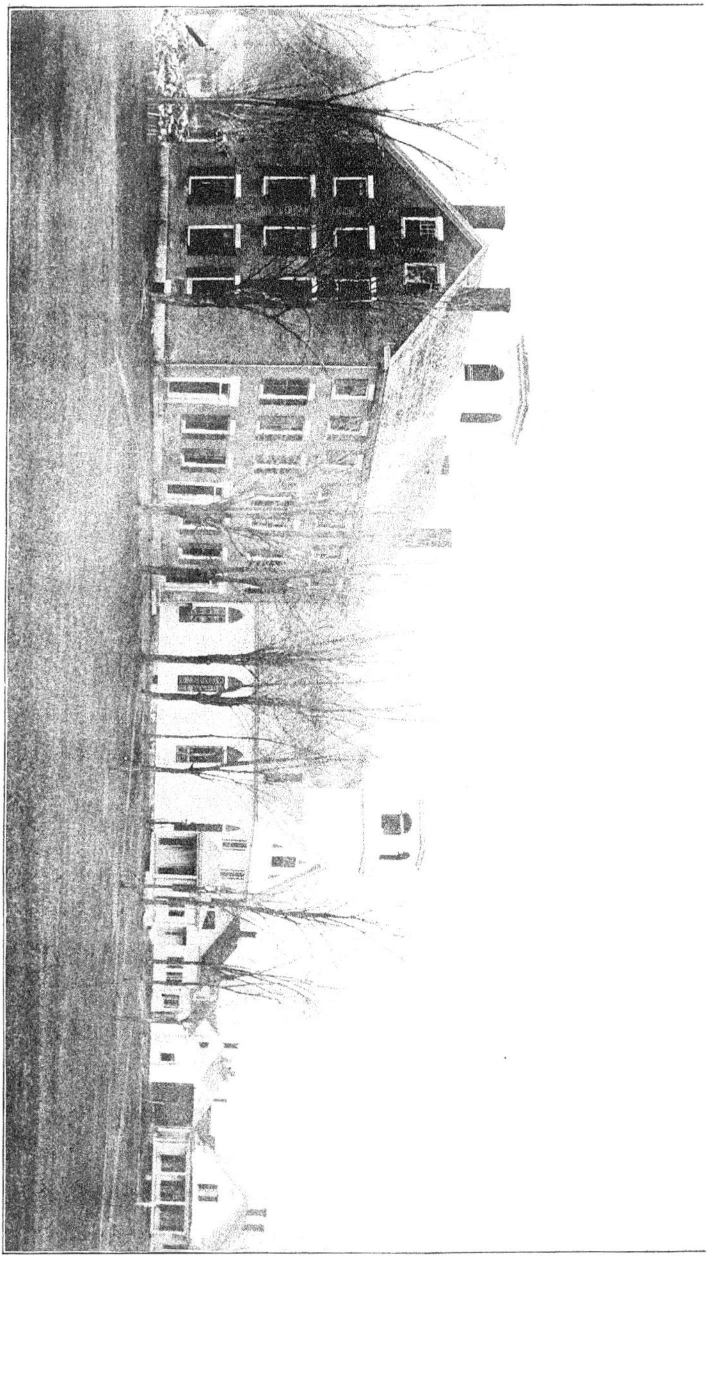

people, then small in numbers and weak financially, but which is now the largest in the land, and numbers its schools by hundreds. It had no endowment; it was only by the closest economy that it was carried on, but "there were those who loved it," and gave freely of whatever means or talents they had. Its history deserves something more than a chapter in the annals of the town in which it was placed.

At the session of the New Hampshire conference of the Methodist Episcopal church, held at Lyndon, in this state, in 1832, a committee, of which Rev. Solomon Sias was chairman, was appointed to consider the subject of founding and maintaining a literary institution within its borders, which then included the territory now embraced by the Vermont conference. This committee, after due consideration, recommended that a committee of seven be appointed to consider propositions from such towns as should offer inducements, with discretionary power to locate such a school, make contracts, purchase lands, and enter into any necessary arrangements to carry the contemplated object into effect. At the session of conference held at Northfield, N. H., in 1833, this committee reported that among the towns which had made proposals for the location of such a school, Newbury had been selected because of its central location, and local advantages.

The sum of $6,000 had been pledged on condition that the school should be located here, a larger sum than had been offered by any other place. This sum was also pledged on condition that the conference should raise an equal amount, which, by much self-denial on the part of many of its members, was done.

The old Lovewell farm and tavern-stand, then owned by William Bailey, were bought, the purchase including nearly all the present common, most of the land west of the present Sawyer House to the ridge of Mt. Pulaski, south to the present farm of D. Y. Ford, including a part of Musquash Meadow, and some necessary pasture. Proposals for the erection of the present Seminary building were advertised in the Democratic Republican at Haverhill, in March, 1833, by Benjamin R. Hoyt, John W. Hardy, and Timothy Morse, according to a plan which could be seen at Morse & Burnham's store. They called for a brick building, three stories in height, forty feet by seventy on the ground. In reality it falls a few inches short of those dimensions in both length and breadth. The building was begun in the spring of 1833, and the exterior was completed, as it now stands, before cold weather. The brick were made at the yard of Benjamin Atwood, near the grist-mill at South Newbury, and delivered on the spot, it is said, for three dollars per thousand. So little was the science of ventilation then understood, that a height of ten feet, three inches, between floor and ceiling, for the lower floor, nine feet, nine inches, for the second, and eight feet, five inches for the third, was deemed amply sufficient space for a school of more than two hundred pupils.

At that time Benjamin Kelley lived on what is now the common, nearly opposite the present residence of James B. Hale. The town bought his place, removed the buildings, and added the land to the portion of the seminary farm which had been set apart for a common. At the same time a deep "gulley" across the common, which had been caused by a terrible storm in 1795, was filled, at an expense of about $700, and the bounds of the common were made about as they now are.

The Seminary building, when completed, contained two large rooms on the ground floor, for the male and female departments, and two or three smaller rooms. The second floor had a large lecture hall, a library room, and a number of small rooms for various purposes. The third floor was divided into a number of study rooms. The entire cost of the building and its simple furniture, was about $4,100. The boarding-house, formerly the old Lovewell tavern, now the "Sawyer House," contained about forty rooms for students, and cost, including the land, and necessary alterations upon the building, not far from $6,500.* The long wing of that edifice, which now extends in the direction of Mt. Pulaski, was then two stories in height, and stood at right angles to the main, or front part, of the house, extending toward the common.

Newbury Seminary was chartered by the General Assembly of Vermont in 1833, its control being vested in a board of thirteen trustees. This body, says Rev. A. L. Cooper, was a close corporation, electing its own officers and filling its own vacancies, the conference having no immediate control beyond recommending a course to be pursued. Of this body, Timothy Morse was resident agent, and oversaw the construction of the building.

In the spring and summer of 1834, the machinery of the new institution was put together, and on Monday, September 15, the school opened with prayer in the chapel, and an introductory address by Mr. Baker.† The initial catalogue of the seminary was of the first term only, and contains the names of 122 pupils, the number of young men being eighty-one.

The principal, or as he was then styled, the preceptor, was Rev. Charles Adams, born at Stratham, N. H., in 1808, and a graduate in 1833, of Bowdoin College. He was, says Mrs. Twombly, of medium height, robust and impulsive. In school he was considered arbitrary, but just toward all, a man feared and respected, rather than loved. He was highly esteemed in town, both as a preacher

*Democratic Republican, August 6, 1834.

†Democratic Republican, September 19, 1834.

REV. CHARLES ADAMS.
1834 39.

BISHOP BAKER.
PRINCIPAL 1839-44.

REV. HARVEY C. WOOD.
1845-46.

REV. SIMEON F. CHESTER.
PRINCIPAL 1867-68.

and as a citizen. In 1839 he left Newbury, and was connected with Wilbraham Academy four years; was two years professor in Concord Biblical Institute, and ten years president of Illinois Female College, but closed his active career as a clerk in the dead letter office at Washington. He died at above eighty, about ten years ago. Mr. Adams built and occupied the house now the residence of Deacon George Swasey.

In the catalogues of 1834 and 1835, Rev. John G. Bennett's name appears as a teacher in English. Mr. Adams' assistant was Mr. Osman C. Baker, a native of Marlboro, N. H., and a student for three years at Wesleyan University. He was, says Mrs. Twombly, tall and large in stature, very kind, but firm in the school-room. In society he was retiring, but able to give a good account of himself when called upon. In 1844, he was elected a professor in the Theological Institute at Concord, N. H., and in 1852, was chosen a bishop in the Methodist church, in which office he died, December 20, 1871. He was the author of several works upon the polity and discipline of the Methodist Episcopal church.

The first preceptress of the Seminary was Miss Elsey French, who afterward married Joel Cooper, of Rochester, Vt. The school began with only a limited course of study, which was enlarged from time to time, as the interests of the pupils demanded, and money to pay more teachers could be had. Music was not taught until the fall of 1837. In those primitive days, board at the boarding-house including washing, fuel and lights, was only $1.25 per week, and tuition was very low. The school year at first was forty-eight weeks, in two terms, but after a year or two the year was divided into four terms of eleven weeks each.

"The financial condition of the school," says Rev. J. A. Sherburne, "through nearly its whole history, was an occasion of much anxiety and perplexity to its friends, who were often before the public, asking for aid. One means of raising funds was by the sale of scholarships. One hundred dollars constituted a scholarship and entitled its holder to the privilege of sending a student free of tuition. As the money for these scholarships was used up in the current expenses instead of being invested, they were a constant financial embarrassment to the school."

The seminary farm had been purchased with the idea of affording needy students a chance to pay part of their expenses in labor upon it, but not meeting expectations, it was afterward sold. The establishment of the seminary was, in many ways, a great advantage to Newbury, and made the village widely known, while the coming of families drawn hither by its advantages, caused a demand for more houses, of which about forty were erected during the ten years which followed the opening of the school, while some of the older dwellings were enlarged to meet the demand for tenements and rooms.

Among those who, from time to time in the earlier years, were drawn hither by Newbury Seminary, were a number of Methodist ministers, who came here to educate their children, or who, being retired from active service, found congenial society with the brethren of their persuasion. Among these may be mentioned Rev. N. O. Way, and Rev. B. R. Hoyt, who occupied, successively, the house where the Farnham family have long lived. The latter clergyman had several sons, who became somewhat distinguished. Others were Revs. Solomon Sias, Orange Scott, Calvin Granger, G. F. Wells, men of honorable distinction in their day, who aided greatly in giving a high tone to the society of the village, and in whose families were young people possessing rare qualities of mind and heart.

The first steward was Mr. Lewis B. Tebbetts, who had been a merchant in Dover, N. H., and who was induced to come here and open a store for the sale of school books, stationery, and other essentials for the student. He afterwards acted as secretary for the trustees. Mr. Tebbetts built and occupied the house in which Mrs. Nelson Bailey now lives.

The coming of so many bright, earnest young men and women to the staid village, brought new life; the young people of the place came into contact with young men and maidens who were, commonly, the best and most advanced scholars in the place where their homes were; and opportunity of acquiring a more thorough education was brought to the doors of the young people of this town.

The catalogue of the summer and fall terms of 1836, gives 249 students, besides thirty-one in a primary department—the young men still outnumbering the young women about two to one. In the spring term of that year Miss Jane Z. Morrison, who had been connected with the school at Newmarket, N. H., became preceptress. She was the daughter of Dr. Moses Morrison, who once lived on the "old McIndoe place," at West Newbury; "a man," says Mrs. Webster, "of much learning but little thrift," who afterward removed to Bath. She married Rev. Alexander Nelson, a native of Ryegate, who taught here at one time, and who afterward became president of a western college. Miss Betsey Dow became preceptress in 1837, and was succeeded two years later by Miss Calista H. Johnson. Miss Dow married Rev. J. H. Twombly and is still living.

Mr. Baker's assistant was Mr. Clark T. Hinman, who in 1844, succeeded Mr. Baker in his turn. Mr. Hinman was born in Kortwright, Delaware County N. Y., August 3, 1819, and graduated at Wesleyan in 1839. He resigned in 1846, to become principal of Wesleyan Seminary at Albion, Mich., and on June 23, 1853, was elected the first president of Northwestern University, at Evanston, Ill. He died while on a journey east, at Troy, N. Y.,

October 21, 1854, from typhoid fever, the result of overwork. He had made a profound impression upon a considerable portion of the public, and his loss to the university was almost irreparable. Mr. Hinman received the degree of D. D., from Ohio Wesleyan University. He is buried at the Ox-bow, with his wife, who was a daughter of Hon. Timothy Morse of this town. He occupied the house, built by Mr. Morse, in which S. L. Swasey now lives. A very poor portrait of Dr. Hinman appeared in the Northwestern Christian Advocate for August 31, 1898.

During the administration of Messrs. Baker and Hinman, J. Harrison Goodale taught Latin in 1841, and in 1842, Rev. Henry W. Adams taught Hebrew, Latin and mathematics; Miss Rachel Smith was preceptress from 1841, (succeeding Miss R. H. Corliss, who had held the position for part of the year 1840,) until her sudden death, March 27, 1844. Miss Smith was the only teacher ever connected with the Seminary, who died while in service. The catalogue for 1845 gives 329 different students for the year and six teachers.

During the administration of Mr. Hinman, probably in 1842, a colored girl presented herself for admission. At that time it was held by a large portion of the public, to be a sin and a crime to teach a colored person to read and write, a view endorsed generally by the clergy and the religious press, who ranged themselves on the popular side. Her coming made some sensation and there were those who advised her exclusion from the school, and the steward was inclined to refuse her a place at the boarding-house. But the preceptress insisted that she should come, and gave her a seat next her own at the table, to the great disgust of some, who predicted the ruin of the school. Miss Allyn, now Dr. Rachel Allyn, who furnishes this reminiscence, shared her room with the colored young lady, and no calamity came upon the institution for this action. We can hardly comprehend in these days a state of affairs which make this act one of moral heroism. But only a few years before, Noyes's Academy, in Canaan, N. H., which had opened it sdoors to a few colored pupils, was, for that cause, in a legal town-meeting, condemned as a nuisance, and on the 20th of August, 1835, 500 men, embracing some of the most substantial and respected citizens of Canaan and other towns, aided by a string of ninety-five yoke of oxen, hauled the offending building out of town, where it was soon set on fire and burned.

The relations between the trustees and the faculty, and between the latter and the pupils were generally harmonious, but Prof. G. N. Abbott recalls a circumstance which shows that the course of things did not always run smoothly. "It was customary at the end of each fall term to have an exhibition, which of course attracted a great deal of the students' interest and attention, with a profit of doubtful value. Somewhere about 1842, the corporation voted to have no exhibition at the end of the fall term. Some of the students rebelliously persisted in getting up an exhibition, and were expelled."

Mr. Hinman's chief assistant was Rev. Harvey C. Wood, a graduate of Dartmouth College in 1844, who, on the resignation of the former, became his successor, being the third assistant who attained to that office. Mr. Wood is yet living, a resident of Aurora, Neb., hale and hearty at eighty-three. In the fall of 1846, Rev. Francis S. Hoyt, who had fitted here for college, and graduated at Wesleyan University, became principal, but resigned after two terms, to take charge of Wesleyan Seminary at Springfield, Vt., which opened its doors March 2, 1847. In the fall of the latter year Mr. Wood, who had been his predecessor at Newbury, succeeded him at Springfield. Mr. Hoyt afterward filled a professor's chair in Ohio Wesleyan University, and, later, became editor of the Northwestern Christian Advocate. He is still living at Berea, Ohio. He was succeeded by Rev. Joseph E. King, who had been his assistant and who was principal from 1848, to 1853. Under his administration the school attained its highest prosperity, and widest influence.

In the fall of 1847, smallpox broke out in the school and village, which caused great excitement. Many of the students went home, and a few died.

The catalogue for 1847-8, gives 241 different students, with an aggregate attendance of 338. For the first time the young women outnumbered the young men.

Dr. King writes, that his salary for the first year, as assistant, was $350, board at that time being $1.50 per week. As principal he received $400, at first, which was increased $50 annually. Mr. King induced the versatile and accomplished James E. Latimer, to come from Wesleyan University, and act as his assistant, at a salary of $350. Mr. Latimer was afterward principal of New Hampshire Conference Seminary, and later, became professor of Historic Theology in Boston University. Miss Dyer was preceptress in 1847-8. She afterward became Mrs. Cushing. The next year the number of students had risen to 346, with aggregate attendance of 604. In the latter year, Mr. Jabez Brooks, who was soon called to a professor's chair in a western college, taught Greek and mathematics. In that year the interior of the seminary building was remodeled into the form which it retained until again made over for the graded school, in 1887. This made a hall and one recitation-room on the ground floor, four recitation-rooms and a reading-room on the second floor, and a small hall was made across the north end of the third story.

In 1849, the Female Collegiate Institute was chartered, which went into operation in 1850. Mr. F. D. Hemenway came into the faculty in the latter year, to become, after four years, a professor at Evanston. In 1850, Miss Caroline J. Lane became preceptress,

REV. JOSEPH E. KING, D. D.,
FIFTH PRINCIPAL OF NEWBURY SEMINARY.

who was succeeded in 1852 by Miss Jane P. Chase. In 1850 also Mr. George N. Abbott, lately deceased at South Newbury, who had been assistant while a student in 1844, and again in 1847, while in college, came into the faculty, as teacher of science and mathematics. In 1852, Miss Sarah E. King succeeded Miss Chase as preceptress. She afterward, as Mrs. Ames, became a noted teacher in New England and New York.

In the last two years of Prof. King's administration, the institution reached high-water mark, the whole number of different students being 534, the aggregate attendance 878, and in the fall term of 1851 there were 320 pupils. There were nine teachers, three of whom were in the music and ornamental departments. Professors King, Noyes, Cushing and Abbott with Miss Chase and Miss Calef were the working faculty. Dr. King gives us an insight into the financial working of the institution at that time. He says: "The revenues for maintaining so large, and really so able and accomplished a faculty, were all derived from tuition fees ranging from $3.25 to $4.50 per term. The boarding-house paid its own way, keeping teachers and students comfortably, if not handsomely at $1.50 per week. Out of the surplus from these modest revenues the buildings were kept in the best of repair, and several valuable improvements were made; we were out of debt, and there was money in the treasury at my resignation in November, 1853. There was a nominal treasurer, and an actual auditor, the venerable 'father' Solomon Sias, who received two dollars annually for going through the accounts and the vouchers. The treasurer had no function but to read the report put into his hands. The work was all done by the principal."

In November, 1853, Mr. King announced to the resident trustees, that he had received an offer to become the principal of a new institution, about to be opened, under favorable auspices, in the state of New York. He would gladly have remained in Newbury, but after waiting four days and receiving no word from that body he telegraphed his acceptance. When it was known that he was about to leave, the trustees and citizens, with a zeal and unanimity which came too late, offered him almost any terms if he would stay. Had their offer been earlier, he would have remained and built up in Newbury, such an institution as that at Fort Edward, of which he has long been the head. Dr. King married a daughter of Amherst Bayley, and an account of his children will be found among the annals of that family.

The seventh principal was Henry S. Noyes, born December 24, 1822, at Landaff, N. H., and a graduate of Wesleyan in 1848. Mr. Noyes sustained the character which the school had attained and was supported by an able faculty, Charles W. Cushing, Jonathan Johnson, F. D. Hemenway, and Jasper Tenney, being his assistants, with Mrs. Noyes as preceptress, and five other teachers—eleven in all. Mr. Noyes was principal but one year, when he resigned to become professor of mathematics in Northwestern University, of which he was acting president, from 1860 to 1867. He died there May 24, 1872.

From 1855 to 1858, Rev. Charles W. Cushing, who had been connected with the school as assistant for eight years, was principal. In 1858 there were thirteen teachers, Mr. Henry Lummis being his lieutenant two years, while Miss Azubah C. Edson was preceptress during Mr. Cushing's administration. Mr. Cushing was the only principal who never attended college, and owes his position and fame entirely to his own exertions. He was afterward principal of Lasell Female Seminary.

There are many who will recall Mr. Charles Gobeille, the French teacher for several years. He was deformed, but very polite and agreeable. In 1858, Rev. Fenner E. King, who had been assistant for three years, became principal, and held the office four years, after which he entered the ministry, and died March 30, 1869, at Carydon, Iowa. He was a relative of Rev. J. E. King, and married a Miss Nelson, of Ryegate. Cambridge, N. Y., was his birthplace in 1826, and he graduated at Wesleyan in 1854. During his administration the patronage fell off somewhat; other academies drew students away; money for needed repairs, and the purchase of more modern apparatus was not forthcoming; and the breaking out of the war called away many young men, ten enlisting at one time. The number of different pupils fell to 267. A military department was added during the first years of the war.

When Mr. King resigned in 1862, the traditional policy of the school was followed by placing his assistant, Rev. George C. Smith, at its head. Rev. J. C. W. Coxe, afterward principal at Montpelier, was his associate for some time. Under Mr. Smith's administration the school regained somewhat of its former patronage, and there were 415 different pupils in attendance in 1863. He was born at St. Johnsbury, in 1830, graduated at Wesleyan in 1859, and, after leaving Newbury, at the end of the winter term, in 1866, was at the head of Drew Female Seminary at Carmel, N. Y. He died in 1871. His wife was Miss Newhall of this town.

Miss Emeline B. Chapin was preceptress from 1858 to 1863, when Miss Betsey M. Clapp held that position two years. Rev. Silas E. Quimby succeeded Mr. Smith, both as assistant, and as principal, giving place at the end of the fall term of 1867, to Simeon F. Chester, A. M. Rev. Charles W. Wilder was associated with Mr. Quimby, and Mr. Chester, and Miss Kate S. Jewell was preceptress. At the end of the spring term of 1868, the seminary was closed, and Mr. Chester became the first principal at Montpelier. He has been, for many years, the honored master of the high school at Springfield, Mass.

Mr. Augustus Pond was, in 1837, the first music teacher; in

1838, Miss Martha Morse, who became Mrs. Hinman, taught until 1846. Mr. Thomas A. Cutter, in that year, was followed in the next by C. S. Harrington; Miss Lucia M. Stevens, now Mrs. Peaslee, and her sister, who became Mrs. Ladd, taught the science from 1847 to 1855. Two of the Cheney brothers, and Mr. E. K. Prouty taught vocal music at various times. In 1855 L. B. Harrington taught music; Mr. Joshua Gill in 1857, and in 1859, David A. French, who was connected with the school excepting two years, during which Mr. Solon G. Smith conducted that department, until the school closed. Several others assisted from time to time.

Connected with the seminary were two other institutions which had a separate legal existence, but which were, actually, under one management, and shared a common purse. One of these was called "Newbury Biblical Institute," and was designed to train young men for the ministry. Mrs. Twombly tells us that the beginning of this department was on this wise: At the opening of the winter term of 1837, (she, then Miss Betsey Dow, being preceptress), five or six young men solicited the principal to form a class in Mental Philosophy. This class was formed, but for want of time on the part of Messrs. Baker and Hinman, was given to her.

"At the annual examination in 1838, the class and its teacher received special commendation from the board of visitors for the manner and thoroughness of the work accomplished." Miss Dow continued to hold the class while she remained in the school, when it was taken by Mr. Baker, who added studies of a theological character. During some years before this the desirability of a theological school in which to train young men for the Methodist ministry had been agitated, and the proposal had met with some rivalry and jealousy among the conferences, and the institutions which desired to secure such a theological department as an addition to their own courses of study.

On the 11th of August, 1841, the seminary trustees announced in Zion's Herald, that, following the recommendation of the annual conference held in Dover the preceding June, a department of sacred science would be opened immediately, in connection with Newbury Seminary, "to meet the wants and conditions of those who were called of God to the work of the ministry, until more complete provision could be made." Rev. W. M. Willett, a learned man, and fine Hebrew scholar, became president of this department, and with him was associated Rev. John Dempster, D. D.

Dr. Willett was born in New York city in 1803, and lived to be past ninety, dying a few years ago, having filled a chair in Drew Theological Seminary for some years. He came of a noted Dutch family and was son of Col. Marinus Willett, a noted officer in the revolutionary war, who was one of the grantees of Newbury under the New York charter. He lived in the brick house built by Timothy Morse, where the Leslie family have long resided and was quite a wealthy man.   He edited and published the "Newbury Biblical Magazine."

At the end of the spring term of 1846, Newbury Biblical Institute closed its work here, and was merged into the General Biblical Institute at Concord, which, about twenty years later, closed its work there and the theological department of Boston University was opened in its stead.   Thus the oldest and most important Theological Seminary of the Methodist Episcopal church in the United States, had its humble origin in a class in Mental Philosophy taught in 1837 by Miss Betsey Dow, in Newbury Seminary.   "Honor to whom honor is due."

The establishment of a theological department at Newbury Seminary was an experiment little favored by the great majority of the Methodist clergy of that day.   Before this time the ministers of that order were, generally, men who had obtained only a limited education.   Many of them had never attended even a district school for a whole year altogether, but had acquired their training in the arduous work of the itinerarcy, and the continued study of the Bible and Wesley's sermons.   They regarded with distrust, and, perhaps, with a little jealousy, any attempt at systematic training of the clergy.   But there were those who took a more comprehensive view, and saw that if the Methodist church would attain the eminence and permanency which they desired, it must have an educated ministry.   But the failure to secure an endowment, and to erect a suitable building for the accommodation of its students, caused the discontinuance of the Biblical Institute.

The "Female Collegiate Institute," was chartered in 1849, and became a department of Newbury Seminary, having however, a separate board of trustees, and special courses of study for the higher education of young women.   It went into operation in the fall of 1850.   No endowment was ever provided, and tuition fees of both institutions were kept in a common purse, all bills being paid by the treasurer of the seminary, who was, during most of the time, the principal.   During the eighteen years of its existence, 118 young ladies were graduated, and received diplomas.   This institution was transferred with the seminary to Montpelier, and has still a legal existence.

There were several private societies connected with the seminary, which deserve passing mention.   Mrs. Twombly says that she organized, in the fall of 1837, "a literary society, composed of young ladies only, for the benefit of the more advanced, many of whom had taught in the district schools, and which was the first society of the kind formed in any academy in the country. This fact was elicited by those who opposed these separate organizations. They wrote to the different schools, asking if such societies existed and hoped to silence the young ladies by proving to them that they were going beyond their sphere, being bold and

presumptuous in assuming what belonged to gentlemen only.'
The "Aesthetic Society" was formed in 1852, and at first included
only such young ladies as were pursuing their studies at the
institute. The Band Society of young men was organized in 1856,
and the Adelphi Society in 1857. The Ladies Literary Society came
into existence in 1861. The two former of these shared a hall upon
the third floor, and the two latter held their meetings in a room
finished off for them in the attic. These societies still exist at
Montpelier. Other organizations were formed from time to time,
which existed for months or years. Rev. J. A. Sherburne recalls
that in his time, the early '40's, a paper was edited by the students
and printed by Mr. Rand, for some time, but its very name is now
forgotten. A public debating society called the Pulaski Lyceum,
met at stated times, and furnished opportunity for the cultivation
of public speaking. Exhibitions were held once or more during each
year, and lectures were provided by the faculty or by the literary
societies.

The more advanced students scattered through Newbury and
the adjacent towns, as teachers in the district schools, and those
who had the ministry in view, exercised their talents in the
schoolhouses among the hills, and were prominent in the prayer
and class meetings which were regularly held in the seminary
building. Much less, in those days, was required than now, by
way of training for the Methodist ministry, and many young men
entered active service with no further preparation than a few terms
at this institution. The great majority of the non-resident students
attended the Methodist church and assisted in its services. The
religious life of the school was always earnest and carefully fostered.
Scarcely a term passed without a measure of religious interest, and
revivals, which embraced most of the pupils, are remembered.

We may not close this retrospect of the institution, without
making mention of a class of men and their wives, who in a humble
sphere aided essentially in the general prosperity. These were the
stewards, who, usually, but not always, kept the boarding-house,
and received a meagre share of the praise when all went well, and
were sure to have a full measure of blame when things went ill.
Much depended upon the tact, good humor, and adaptablity of
those who had the oversight of the boarding-house, and a morose,
crabbed steward was certain to be the object of all the pranks
which a band of mischievous students could invent. The stay of
such an one was short. Mr. Lewis A. Tebbetts, Royal B. Waldo,
E. B. Stevens, were among the earlier of the stewards. Mr. and
Mrs. O. B. Rogers, still living at West Newbury, kept the
boarding-house back in the early 50's.* Wealth was not
accumulated by any of the stewards while engaged in the office.

*Mr. Rogers has died since this was written.

"Old Newbury Seminary"came to an end many years ago   The methods of instruction have so changed since its day, and the advances in natural science have been such, that its course of study, and its apparatus of illustration would now be condemned in any backwoods graded school. But in its time it was not behind the age in which it flourished. Its teachers had the enthusiasm of youth, and, with few exceptions, the art of imparting their own ardor to their pupils. It was a working school, and drew its students, almost entirely, from families of farmers and mechanics, young men and women trained to labor, who knew the narrow limits of their opportunities, and made the best of them. Newbury was an ideal place for such a school. There was little to distract the attention of the student. Baseball, football, lawn-tennis and the like amusements were unknown. There was no need of any gymnasium, or class in physical culture. The young people of that day were brought up to work, and knew very well how to obtain exercise and the means of support at the same time.

A conservative estimate, derived from a careful study of the catalogues, gives the number of students who attended the institution from 1834, to 1868, at about 7000. Of these, some remained but one term, or even less; others spent years within its walls, and obtained from the institution all it had to give. Comparatively few entered college. The vast majority of the pupils, here received all the education which they ever had, beyond the district school. To give even the names of all, in the various ranks of life, who received, in that plain brick building, some of the training which enabled them to attain honorable mention above their fellows, would occupy many closely printed pages of this volume. No human arithmetic can compute the value rendered to the world by "Old Newbury Seminary."

While its poverty forbade its attaining a rank as one of the great schools of the country, it was highly successful as a factor of education in this part of New England. Much of its energies were engrossed in the struggle for existence. During its earlier years a heavy debt rested upon the institution, and it was only by great self-denial on the part of some of its friends that it was kept from actual bankruptcy. The salaries which it could pay were so meagre that it could not retain its teachers after they had won, within its walls, reputations which commanded elsewhere a fair compensation. It trained its own teachers for other institutions. Great schools are built up by great instructors, and no one of the principals of Newbury Seminary remained long enough to impress the stamp of his own individuality upon it during many years. For its teachers, it was but a stepping stone to better positions. Of the twelve principals, and as many others who were their chief assistants, four became college presidents, and all but three were, after leaving Newbury, at the head of some college or academy.

REV. F. S. HOYT.
PRINCIPAL 1847.

REV. CHARLES W. CUSHING.
PRINCIPAL 1855-58.

GEORGE CROSBY SMITH.
PRINCIPAL 1862-66.

REV. SILAS E. QUIMBY.
1866-67.

Miss Elsey French, and her successors, with their associates, were no less honored in their own after life, although not in positions so conspicuous.

The great work which Newbury Seminary accomplished was, to vary slightly the language of one of the greatest of English critics when speaking of our smaller American colleges: "It got hold of a multitude of young men and women who might never have resorted to a distant place of education. It set learning before them in a visible form, plain indeed and humble, but which accomplished for those who came to it, a work which a richer and more stately institution might have failed to do."

The name of Miss Calista H. Johnson, who was preceptress in 1837, was accidentally omitted in this chapter. Few of the under teachers remained long, and it was not thought worth while to give their names.

NOTE. The editor wishes to acknowledge not only the aid received from residents of the town in the preparation of this chapter, but especially the kind assistance of Rev. J. A. Sherburne, Rev. A. L. Cooper, Rev. Dr. J. E. King, Rev. C. W. Cushing, and Mrs. B. Dow Twombly and that of Rev. J. W. Merrill, D. D., who has deceased since it was written in 1898.

CHAPTER XXX.

NEWBURY SEMINARY—CONTINUED.

A REMINISCENCE BY PROF. G. N. ABBOTT.—WHY THE SCHOOL WAS REMOVED.—REV. A. G. BUTTON.—SALE OF PROPERTY.—SUPREME COURT DECISION.—LATER SCHOOLS.—REV. S. L. EASTMAN.—TOWN CENTRAL SCHOOL.—OBSERVATIONS.

THE memory of the writer of this reminiscence reverts to a time when the brick walls of the seminary building were about breast high (to a man) and when a multitude of carts and men were engaged in filling up "the gully" which an immense shower had washed out on a memorable occasion in the past, just where the seminary common was destined to be. But the doors of the seminary did not open to him till more than seven years later, when the institution was fully under way, with a full board of instructors and a large patronage.

The spring term of 1841, brought to him the unspeakable privilege, as then regarded, of reciting English grammar and algebra to Rev. Mr. Hinman, and natural philosophy and chemistry to Principal Baker. The classes in these subjects were large, made so by volunteers; for at that time there was no set course of study, each student being allowed to choose his own studies so long as there was any chance to presume his fitness to enter upon them. Chemistry was taught by recitations and experiments, and its study was evidently pursued by students of both sexes, for pleasure as well as for profit. Years later it seemed strange to the writer to see a majority of his college classmates showing by their conduct a willingness that the chemistry hour might be relegated to the

---

NOTE. It was the expressed preference of Professor Abbott, that this reminiscence should be given only as, "By a former pupil," or some such title. But, since his decease, it has seemed to the editor, that we have so very little of the work of this learned and excellent man, that the public would desire that his authorship of this paper should be declared.

period of diurnal slumber. This apathy of the college class was not properly attributable to any fault in the instruction, which was indeed excellent, but on the other hand, Mr. Baker, of the seminary, had an uncommon genius for making a recitation-room agreeable; and he could make it doubly interesting when any branch of natural science was the topic, for to his mind nature was never commonplace.

It is to be remembered that the time now referred to was before the invention of the telegraph had thrilled the world with a sense of the practical possibilities of nature's forces—before the Darwinian hypothesis had roused an absorbing interest in the question of man's kinship to nature; and that hence this unpretentious teacher's enthusiasm in natural science might have been in a sense anticipatory of its future achievements. Already, however, geology, with its eons of pre-Adamic life, had made its revelations, which were taught in this seminary before being put into the curriculum, of at least some of the New England colleges. The seminary could not then well be said to be behind the times, whatever else might be said of it.

As regards the manner of conducting recitations, it was similar to that of a college. In general an hour was allowed for each recitation, so the whole lesson could be discussed. The work of the class was not interfered with by the presence of other scholars—the studying being done for the most part in the private rooms of students, as if they had been students in a university. The changes of occupants of recitation rooms at the end of each hour were accomplished with as much quietude and decorum as prevails at the entrance and exit of a church congregation.

The writer's acquaintance thus begun, with the internal working of the institution, lost nothing of its delightful character during its continuance for more than three years, in which time preparation for college was acquired. It always seemed easy to study in Newbury, as if, there, some pre-"Roentgen rays" were helping to deeper and easier insight. This was possibly not entirely due to the existence of the seminary. It was possibly something more than a pleasant joke, when an old resident of the place, after speaking of the lack of bustle and business, said, however, it was a good place for meditation. But the seminary had the advantage of this—so to speak—meditative atmosphere. At any rate the apparent facility with which students' attention could be drawn to the instruction of book or teacher, whatever the reason for such facility, made an impression on the writer, which time and comparative observation have only served to deepen. Of course not all those students were geniuses; but their respective talents, whether five, two, or one, were almost without exception devoted to honest work.

During the period covered by this narration thus far, there were other teachers than the two before mentioned, no doubt also highly worthy of mention; but this being designed to be simply a personal reminiscence, those with whom no intimacy was had, can not well be remembered better than they were ever known. There should be named, however, one other teacher, Rev. Henry W. Adams, who was instructor in Latin for a time. He is pleasantly remembered, but his continuance was not long enough to give his pupils the full benefit of his acquaintance.

It would be interesting in connection with one's personal reminiscence to refresh one's memory of all those honored instructors, who well nigh two generations ago, used to appear every week-day morning at prayers, in the old seminary, by the help of truthful portraits. No such portraits have come to the writer's knowledge. He has, to be sure, seen as a magazine frontispiece, what purports to be a picture of Rev. Dr. Clark T. Hinman, who died at the age of thirty-five, the president of Northwestern University; but to one who for years often witnessed the vivacity, the earnestness, the energy, displayed in the ruddy countenance of the living Dr. Hinman, or on fit occasions his sunny smiles of enjoyment and pleasantry, this picture affords little satisfaction, except as it may truthfully represent his fine head of hair, and the mere geometrical symmetry of his features, while the expression is utterly wanting. It was probably copied from a faded daguerreotype. The live, unfaded physiognomy of the man himself, was faultless in expression and exceptionally agreeable to contemplate, besides being truthful to the inner man. A beholder naturally did not feel that his eyes were on a man who looked one thing and thought another. Of course such a physiognomy indicated less of reserve than some wise men affect. A readiness to speak out his thoughts was characteristic of the man. Of this he was conscious, as appeared from a remark of his on a Greek passage in a reading lesson, which represented Simonides as saying that he had often regretted having spoken but never having kept silent. The teacher's comment was to the effect that he had more often regretted not having spoken. In the remembrance of Dr. Hinman there is only brightness without an unpleasant shadow.

Of Principal Osmon C. Baker, afterward Bishop Baker, it may certainly be said that he presided with rare dignity over the assembled students. His presence meant a voluntary prevalence of order and propriety. If an uncommonly daring student ventured for once to disturb the quiet ongoing, he suddenly found that discipline was not wanting. On one well remembered occasion, a young man thought to attract attention by a verbose answer to his name at public roll-call. Quick came the words, "That is not a proper answer, Mr. ———— : call at my room at 12 o'clock." Had a flash of lightning darted through the assembly room, the effect could hardly have been more startling. Bishop Baker can be remembered only to be honored and revered.

Another instructor also, though not strictly belonging to the seminary board of teachers, yet comes up distinctly in these recollections. Prof. William Marinus Willett came to Newbury to·assist in starting the projected theological school called the Biblical Institute. Being of a generous disposition and having abundant private resources, he offered to give instruction in Hebrew, gratis, at his own private house, to seminary students desiring it, irrespective of their connection with a theological class. The writer was one of a small number who availed themselves of this privilege, and he still most gratefully remembers its enjoyment.

At the beginning of the fall term of 1847, a teacher was wanting, owing to some failure of an engagement. The trustees requested the writer to fill the vacancy for a single term—he then being an undergraduate in the University of Vermont. The acceptance of this offer gave him an opportunity to make the familiar acquaintance—as roommate—of Rev. Joseph E. King, who was then just entering upon his connection with the seminary. From that brief association the writer learned, among other things, that the born gentleman has some marked advantages over the artificially educated one. Success was assured to Mr. King from the very beginning of his career in Newbury. During this very busy term little intimacy was had with other teachers, of whom Rev. Francis Hoyt was the principal.

During an interval of four years, following the last mentioned date, some changes were wrought. The number of students was materially increased. The Female Collegiate Institute was created and associated with the seminary. This brought the young women to the front, giving them a chance to prove, if they could, the fallacy of the old theory of their mental inferiority. It was a pleasant change, enjoyed apparently by the young men as well as by the young women. The increased number of recitations seemed to make it necessary to abbreviate them somewhat—the plan apparently being to make up by increased animation the loss in time. At any rate the shortening was a stimulus to both pupil and teacher to come to the recitation with lesson prepared. In the same interval Rev. J. E. King had become principal of the seminary and president of the Collegiate Institute; Mr. Henry S. Noyes and Rev. Charles Wesley Cushing, instructors—or, according to the newer student dialect, professors; Miss Caroline J. Lane preceptress, who was later succeeded by Miss Jane P. Chase, and the latter by Miss Sarah Etta King.

A further connection of the writer with the institution, as a teacher, introduced him into these new associations. Though the usual intercourse between fellow teachers may appear freer and less constrained than that between teacher and pupil, yet in their efforts for an exact mutual understanding, the teacher and the fairly intelligent pupil may get a deeper insight into each other's mental substratum, than is likely to come from an exchange of many learned conventionalities between persons acting the agreeable. Accordingly, it is easy to imagine the writer better acquainted with his own teachers, previously mentioned, than with those just now named. Still most persons, and especially persons of such demonstrative habits as teachers are by the requirements of their profession, will be likely to manifest to ordinary observation, some, if not all, of their own peculiar traits. Among possible traits, may appear in a given case, a marked ability to read character. Any one can see how valuable an ability this would be for an educator, or for the head of an institution, who has much to do with differing characters of both students and teachers.

Of the persons just above named, President King could hardly fail to be seen as possessed in an eminent degree, of the faculty for discerning the inner man of any one coming under his observation. Such a faculty, used mostly often in discovering the best side and best possibilities of another's character, is likely to effect friendly relations. One who finds himself seen in a better light than that in which he sees himself, should at least be thankful for a revelation of his own better capabilities. As used by Mr. King, the faculty in question cannot fail to have been of great service both to himself and to many others.

Prof. Noyes was characterized by great aptitude for acquiring knowledge and readiness in communicating the same. With all his facility of communication, however, he did not fail to impress his pupils with the importance of utilizing their own faculties in the process of making knowledge their own. He did not propose to do all the students' studying and reciting. The recitations of his classes meant business, and it was easy for him to hold the respect of those whom he taught.

Of Prof. Cushing, among other things, may be mentioned his unusual versatility, adapting him almost equally to the chair of the scientific instructor, to the pulpit, or to almost any rostrum for popular enlightenment. Much valuable talent, no doubt, practically runs to waste for want of adaptation to any existing forum. If a man really has something to say to his fellowmen, it is of no small consequence that he be able to say it on any fit occasion.

In institutions of the grade of the one now considered, teachers. are not the only recognized educational agencies. Self-education must supplement the instructor's work, or the result will be too little substantial. To give themselves a field for mental self-exertion students generally form literary and debating societies, and these societies come to be regarded as a part of the institution's machinery. In the present instance there were such societies in a state of healthy activity during the whole time covered by this sketch. In the last of the periods referred to, they were more in

PROF. GEORGE N. ABBOTT.

H. N. CHAMBERLIN.

HON. ABEL UNDERWOOD.

number and certainly not less prosperous, than in the earlier period. Their literary character was more pronounced—that is, they presented more written work—in the later time, though the oral discussion of questions was vigorously continued. These societies occasionally gave public performances—open, that is, to all students and to any others desiring to be present. Into their preparation for such entertainments they were wont to put a considerable amount of creditable brain-work.

Should any reader of this sketch note an omission of higher titles, in connection with some of the names which have appeared, he may understand that such omission—where it occurs—was intentional, the object being to "modernize" as little as possible. This brief reminiscence has been written at the request of persons desiring to perpetuate the memory of Newbury Seminary (this name popularly including the whole institution) as it imaged its own character in the mind of an observer familiarized with its ongoings. It is as such observer that the writer has spoken, only desiring that, in so far as these few words can serve to transfer to other minds, the picture which is in his own, their effect may be to help keep in lively view a bright spot in the history of Newbury.

It may well be asked how it came to pass that this school, for which thirty-four years of successful operation had given a prestige among the educational institutions of New England, and which had been conducted at a minimum of expense, with such a maximum of result, was removed from Newbury. This is not a part of the history of this town which is pleasant to tell, as it is a portion of it not creditable to the honesty or sagacity of those who conspired to bring about the removal.

Among the various ambitions which inspired Rev. Amasa G. Button, long a resident of Newbury, and president of the board of trustees of Newbury Seminary, was the desire to represent the town in the state legislature. To this end he was presented as a candidate for town representative, during several years. But it being well understood by the leaders of the republican party that a large section of the party would not support Mr. Button, they contrived to set him aside at the caucuses. But in 1865, he made a personal canvass for the office, and caused it to be made known that unless he was elected, he would have the school removed from Newbury. No one paid much attention to his threat, but he would probably have been elected had he conducted his canvass with fairness and courtesy. But the course which he unfortunately took, and the intemperate language used by a noisy individual, who claimed to speak for him at the caucus, whose utterances Mr. Button made no attempt to check, gave great offense to many, and while Mr. Button's friends presented his name, his opponents nominated Mr. L. D. Hazen. There ensued the most sharply contested Freeman's meeting ever held in this town, and the contest was prolonged till nearly nine o'clock in the evening, without any sign of yielding on either side.

At that late hour, a few republicans who had hitherto supported Mr. Hazen, by an agreement with some of those who had voted for Mr. Button, presented the name of W. W. Brock, who received about twenty votes. At the last ballot, both Mr. Button, and Mr. Hazen were dropped, and Mr. Brock was elected. Mr. Button, deeply mortified at the result, lost no time in carrying his threat into effect, and at the next session of conference he was ready with his schemes. He was a man of much financial ability, a ready and fluent speaker, with a plausible manner, and a great force of will, and having some wealth, and a thorough knowledge of the members of the conference, had no trouble in securing the appointment of a committee to his liking, whose duty should be, to investigate the conditions of Newbury Seminary. This committee made precisely such a report as Mr. Button would have written, which was to the effect that the interests of the conference required the removal of the school to a more central place, and one "where the local influences would be more favorable." There were many plausible reasons for such a removal, which were adroitly urged by Mr. Button and his friends.

Newbury Seminary was founded under the auspices of the New Hampshire conference when it included nearly all the territory now controlled by the Vermont conference, and at that time Newbury was the most central place. The division of the territory left Newbury on one side of the newly-formed Vermont conference. At the same time there were academies at Springfield and Fairfax, which, as well as Newbury Seminary, were under the auspices of conference. It was not very difficult to make the brethren believe that the educational interests of the conference required the consolidation of these three institutions into one, which should be near the center of the state, and which they expected would become to the Vermont conference all that the seminary at Tilton is to the New Hampshire conference. They failed to consider the difference which unalterable geographical conditions imposed upon an institution located at Tilton, and one at Montpelier. Neither did they observe that the students of Newbury Seminary came chiefly from the Connecticut valley above Orford, and from the towns which were drained by the upper branches of the river, and that few students from these localities would cross the hills to Montpelier.

Another reason had also great weight. The old seminary building needed thorough repairs and remodelling. This was just after the close of the civil war, when education was making wonderful advances, and new ideas were controlling the minds of men. To those who had seen some of the splendid school buildings which were springing up all over the country, the plain old brick building, with its inconveniences, seemed mean and meagre. It were better to take the building down. Better still to erect a new one at Montpelier, which place bid the highest for the location of the new institution.

There was a great deal of talk about doing something to retain the school here, and had a wise and far-sighted public spirit prevailed in Newbury, the school would never have been moved away. A few public meetings were held and that was about all. In short, had there been one man as resolute to keep Newbury Seminary here as Mr. Button was to move it away, it would be here still, and Newbury would now be one of the great educational centers of New England. It is probable that $20,000 could have been raised to keep the school here, had people been alive to their own interests. But, looking back, people seem to have felt a strange apathy regarding the whole matter.

At the close of the spring term of 1868, the school was closed, and in the fall the term began at Montpelier, in buildings which had been used as a hospital and barracks during the war. In a few years a building more costly and pretentious was erected, and the institution, at first chartered as the "Vermont Conference Seminary," then re-christened "Vermont Methodist Seminary," and now simply "The Montpelier Seminary," still exists. It has been a heavy load for the conference to carry. Newbury Seminary was, practically, self-supporting; Montpelier Seminary is always running behind, financially, and every few years a desperate effort has to be made to raise the debt, and keep it from closing its doors. The attendance is hardly one-third that of the old seminary at Newbury in its best days. Among the means to which conference resorts to keep the school going, is a system of assessments which compels the hard-worked, and under-paid ministers of the Vermont conference to contribute a sum equal to two per cent of the nominal salary of each to the Montpelier Seminary. Truly Mr. Button did the educational interests of the conference little service when he succeeded in removing Newbury Seminary to Montpelier. But of Montpelier Seminary itself, nothing but praise can be said.

The conference, at the annual session, in 1868, granted the trustees of Newbury Seminary, the right to sell the property of the institution, and transfer the proceeds to the new seminary at Montpelier. They at once sold the real estate at Newbury to Mr. A. J. Willard, one of the trustees, and about the same time the seminary and boarding-house were stripped of everything which could be carried away, and Mr. Willard received a deed from the trustees, of the whole property. The matter was not allowed to be thus settled. Suit was brought against Mr. Willard and the trustees, by Mr. Tappan Stevens, and other gentlemen, which was entered in the court of chancery for Washington county, at the September term of 1868. Upon hearing, Judge Peck, the chancellor, ordered that A. J. Willard should convey the real estate back to the trustees, placing the title where it was before he received the deed, and the defendants were enjoined from selling or disposing of the property, and from using the same, otherwise than in the use and support of Newbury Seminary. The case was carried to the Supreme Court, and was argued at the general term, 1869. Judge Poland and C. W. Willard argued the case in behalf of A. J. Willard, T. P. Redfield being counsel for the plaintiff. The decree of the Court of Chancery was affirmed by the Supreme Court, and the trustees were enjoined from selling the property, and using the proceeds of an institution chartered by the name of Newbury Seminary, which had long existed at Newbury, for the use and support of another institution located at Montpelier.

During these legal proceedings a school had been maintained in the old building. In the fall of 1868, Rev. John M. Lord, a Congregational clergyman, and a graduate of Dartmouth College, who had retired from the ministry, opened a school, with the assistance of his wife, in two rooms of the seminary building, which he conducted for two or three terms. Mr. Danforth, a student from Dartmouth College, with one or two assistants, taught a select school in the building in 1870, and was followed by Mr. Arthur W. Blair.

In the fall of 1871, the trustees authorized Rev. Samuel L. Eastman, a native of Newbury, and a graduate of Northwestern University in the class of 1857, to re-open Newbury Seminary under the old name, with a competent corps of assistants. The institution re-opened with a very fair attendance, and there seemed some prospect for a time, that Newbury Seminary would again attain its former fame.

Had Mr. Eastman possessed the personal magnetism of Dr. King, or the power of arousing enthusiasm in his pupils, which belonged to Professor Cushing, and others, who had been at the head of the old institution, he might have built up a school which would have proved a formidable rival to the one at Montpelier. Wholly lacking in these indispensible qualifications for successful administration, the qualities of good scholarship, energy and perseverance, which he certainly had, availed him little, and attendance soon began to fall off. The opening of Montebello Ladies' Institute drew away the pupils from the most well-to-do families in town. Mr. Eastman complained to the trustees that the school did not pay expenses and received from them a mortgage deed of all the real estate, which, after some years, he foreclosed.

Mr. Eastman labored with great energy to keep the school going, but to no avail; the attendance dwindled away to a handful, and the experiment of a new Newbury Seminary ended in melancholy failure. In the spring of 1887, he did the town a good service by selling the property to Dr. Hatch, from whom the village school district bought the old seminary building, which, in time, passed into the ownership of the town, and is now occupied by a graded school. From time to time one portion of the interior, after another, has been remodelled, and it is now better adapted to the purposes for which it was originally intended, than ever before. What there may be in the future for this structure which has borne so noble a share in the cause of education, time only can tell.

In June, 1884, the semi-centennial of Newbury Seminary was held within its walls, and was attended by a large number of its former pupils, from all parts of the country. Addresses were made by many who had been connected with the institution during nearly every term of its existence, and the plain old "Seminary Hall" seemed once more as of old. The reunion was tinged with sadness, as the former pupils wandered through the old rooms, and marked the decay which had begun to fall upon the structure. There still exists a corporation known as "The Trustees of Newbury Seminary," which meets at stated times, elects its officers, and dissolves, without having any duties whatever to perform, funds to administer or affairs to direct.

Before we close these chapters upon this institution, it is well that we consider, for a moment, what would have been the result, both to the school itself and the town in which it was placed, had it never been removed. The old seminary was the work of an earlier and simpler day. When it began its part in the educational work of the century, the religious body which founded it, was itself struggling for recognition. During the thirty-four years of its existence, the Methodist church had passed the period of experiment, and had come to be the largest religious organization in the land. Some of the best and brightest minds in the church had entered the walls of this institution as teachers. It was one of the very earliest of its schools of learning, and contributed to an extent not to be estimated, to the development of the denomination. When it was organized, the common school system, if system it could be called, was crude, and its results unsatisfactory. In those early days there was an academy in nearly every larger town, an institution entirely separate from the district schools. At the present day, the common school system has so changed, and the sphere of its labor so enlarged, that the graded schools have supplanted the academies. The teacher of seventy years ago, if placed in a modern school-room would helplessly contemplate the apparatus of instruction.

If the old seminary still existed, its patronage would represent a different class of pupils from those who flocked to its doors fifty years ago. An examination of its catalogues shows that the majority of the students came from places where no academies existed. In most of those localities at the present time, the curriculum of the graded schools embraces most of the studies which were then taught here. An institution which should hold the rank in the educational system of today, that Newbury Seminary did in its prime, would require a costly endowment, and new methods of instruction. The school had fallen behind in the march of intellect, when it came to an end in 1868. Its methods and apparatus were those of an earlier day, and but two courses were left to choose for it—either to reorganize the school on a new basis with a munificent endowment, or remove it elsewhere. The people of Newbury most unwisely permitted its removal, and naught remains of it, save the old building and the memories which cluster around it.

It is idle to speculate upon the degree of usefulness to which the institution might have been brought here in Newbury, or its influence upon the town. It had its day and ceased to be, but its influence will continue to be felt long after all who were connected with it have passed away.

CHAPTER XXXI.

MONTEBELLO INSTITUTE AND OTHER SCHOOLS.

IN 1873, Rev. William Clark purchased the property known as the Newbury Sulphur Springs and Bathing Establishment. The buildings were enlarged and improved by him, and school-rooms were finished off in them which were intended as temporary accommodations for the school, which he opened in the fall of that year, under the name of Montebello Ladies' Institute. It was hoped by him and his associates, that an endowment would be secured for the institution, and permanent buildings erected.

Mr. Clark was born in Barre, Vt., July 6, 1819, graduated at Dartmouth College in 1842, and after teaching for a few years, was ordained a Congregationalist minister, and from 1852 to 1859, was a missionary in Turkey, and founder of a seminary at Babek, on the Bosphorus. Much of his life was spent abroad, several years of it as U. S. consul at Milan. The institute derived its name from the place of his residence in Italy. During his long sojourn in Europe he gathered a small, but invaluable collection of authentic paintings by the old masters, which he brought to Newbury. Among them were The Holy Family, Van Dyk; Christ in the Garden, Correggio (formerly owned by the empress Maria Louise); The Village Festival, Teniers (probably); Christ Preaching in the Desert, Rembrandt. Mr. Clark greatly improved the premises, and laid out walks on what had before been known as Powder-house Hill, and made a very attractive place of it.

The principal of the institute was Miss Mary E. Tenney, who was assisted by several other teachers, and the school, founded and conducted by them, was of a much higher rank than any which had been opened here. No one of all the teachers of Newbury

Seminary had enjoyed the advantage of foreign travel, or had more than a limited acquaintance with modern languages. At Montebello, German, French and Italian were in daily use among the members of the family. Of the institute and its principal, the following was prepared by Miss Genevieve Clark:

In the autumn of 1873 was opened a boarding and day-school for young ladies at Montebello—then the property of Rev. William Clark. The school was named the Montebello Ladies' Institute, and afforded superior facilities for mental and moral culture. The institution was select and homelike, and no efforts were spared to render it in its discipline, in its teaching, and in its entire influence, worthy of patronage and confidence. Mr. and Mrs. Clark had the care of the family arrangements of this institution, and to the young ladies placed under their care furnished a refined Christian home.

The principal of the school was Miss Mary Elizabeth Tenney, who, for three years before coming to Newbury, had been the preceptress of Glenwood Ladies' Seminary, West Brattleboro, Vt. In 1867 after completing the course of study in one of New England's seminaries, Miss Tenney had for two years the advantages of foreign travel and study, giving special attention to the languages and music.

At Montebello Miss Tenney had with her five teachers, who in each and every department required the pupil to not only understand, but master the studies pursued. The number of boarding pupils was limited to twenty-five, these were from New England, and the Middle States. The day pupils numbered sixty-five, all that the building could accommodate.

Regarding the character and standing of this institute, Rev. S. L. Bates, in a memorial sermon preached in Newbury, February 15, 1880, said, "The name of Mary Elizabeth Tenney will always be spoken with profound reverence and with tender affection by all who knew her excellence and were observant of her life-work Her relations to this community were such as to awaken in us all special admiration and thankfulness for what she was and what she did. To her, teaching was not merely a calling, it was a life. The one thought and desire of her soul evidently was to fulfil the grand purposes of her existence in her chosen work. It is not too much to say that her influence and labors in this place were of incalculable value, not only to those who received her instructions but to the community at large." Owing to the promise and hope of less care and responsibility, Miss Tenney resigned her position at Montebello, in the summer of 1879, and accepted a professorship in Smith College, Northampton, Mass. She entered upon her duties there in October of the same year, but her health was unequal to the position, and she left the college two months later, for her father's home in Westborough, Mass. Here she died in February, 1880. In

MARY E. TENNEY.

the Vermont Chronicle soon after, appeared the following tribute written by Rev. Mr. Bittinger of Haverhill, New Hampshire:

Many hearts are saddened at the early death of this accomplished Christian lady. Her noble and winning character, and the high hopes which she inspired, made her the center of a large circle of personal friends and admirers. None that knew her doubted the brilliant career which lay before her in her chosen profession. Just entered upon her duties as professor of French and history in Smith College, her health yielded to the long strain of overwork in study and teaching. Her work at Newbury, Vt., was as thorough and conscientious as any educational service with which the writer is acquainted, and would stand the severest tests of genuine training. She possessed wonderful powers over her pupils—a natural born leadership—not of official position, but of character and excellence. Her mind was enriched by varied opportunities of foreign study and travel, which her fine culture combined with her rare natural endowments gave her a foremost place among educators.

Trained in one of New England's best Christian families, the daughter of Erdix and Elizabeth Hamilton Tenney, her father, Dr. Tenney, for thirty-five years the esteemed pastor of the church in Lyme, N. H., she breathed from the first, a religious atmosphere, and this rarest of inheritances she never lost.

It was a young life that went out February 12, only turned of 35, but this comfort is kept, it was faithful, good and true. In the death of this gifted young woman not only a great loss is sustained by her immediate friends, but the college and education share in the bereavement.

Some time before Miss Tenney left Newbury, Mr. Clark returned to Europe, and resided abroad, in teaching and in business, till 1889. He died at Westboro, Mass., February 8, 1894, in his seventy-fifth year. Mrs. Clark was a sister of Mrs. Joseph Atkinson.

In the fall of 1879, the institute opened under the management of Mrs. Isaac Bridgman of Northampton, Mass., and her son, Mr. John Bridgman, who conducted it for one year. They were excellent teachers, but did not secure the attendance which had been drawn to it by Miss Tenney; the property of Montebello was at that time somewhat involved, and no endowment having been secured, and no one being ready to assume the financial responsibility for the school, it was discontinued. Its day pupils were drawn from the best families in Newbury and its vicinity, and the influence exercised by the school and its teachers was of great value.

During the spring of 1880, a paper called "The Montebello Critic," was published by the pupils, as an organ of the institute. The first number of this bright little sheet was issued April 5, and the last of five bi-weekly issues, on June 9. It was printed at the "Globe" office, Lisbon, N. H.

For the following sketch we are indebted to Mr. W. H. Buck:

Early in the seventies, the people of Wells River, perceiving that in order to keep abreast of the times, a more commodious school building was necessary, began agitating this question and persistently continued doing so until this important subject assumed definite form, and out from the smoke of the conflict, there stands today, in our village, a large and commodious school building, light and airy and well supplied with school paraphernalia.

Since its completion in 1874, the educational work of the Wells River Graded School has been of a high order and the students who have gone out from this institution have taken high positions of trust and honor in our land. Lawyers, doctors, inventors, mechanics and farmers are among its alumni. Mrs. Quimby was the first principal, remaining a year. In the spring of 1876, W. H. Buck was elected principal. Under his management, with an able corps of assistants, the school came rapidly to the front, and was soon recognized as one of our leading educational institutions. During his five years of hard and unremitting labor, the school was thoroughly organized and well graded, and on his retirement in 1881 it was in a flourishing condition. Then followed a year of unsuccessful work.

In 1882 the trustees secured the services of Principal E. W. Goodhue, who remained at the head of the school for six years. Mr. Goodhue was a thorough instructor and under his management the school was brought to a high standard of scholarship. From this time on, the trustees were unsuccessful in obtaining efficient principals, necessitating frequent changes, which necessarily retards educational progress, until in 1890 Miss Edna Stewart, a lady of high intellectual and executive ability, was elected principal. Under her instruction the standard of scholarship was raised. During her term of service two classes were graduated, the graduates taking high rank in the colleges to which they were admitted, which was a very strong testimonial of excellent work well done and she leaves a record which has not been excelled in the history of the school.

During the next four years a number of changes were made in the working force of the school. In the fall of 1898, Professor H. S. Richardson, a graduate of Dartmouth, was elected principal. Miss Carr in the primary room, Miss Dunlap in the intermediate, and Miss Munsell in the grammar, are his able and efficient assistants.

The present corps of teachers are all experienced and thorough instructors and we feel that the future of our school promises great results. Our people take a just pride in our school and nothing that is essential to its upward and onward progress is withheld. In 1886 our school was incorporated by an act of the legislature under the name of the Wells River Graded School, and it will be the aim of our people to ever make it one of the leading educational institutions of our state. The following are the teachers who have seen long service in the school: Mr. and Mrs. W. H. Buck, five years; E. W. Goodhue, six years; Miss Edna Stewart, three years; Annie (Clark) English, five years; Louise (Whitney) Bailey, six years; Miss Ella A. Dunlap, ten years.

The laws which have sought to provide schools and regulate them, have been so many, so various and so often altered, that it is not worth while to attempt following the changes they have caused. In early days the school districts were left much to themselves, as far as the conduct of the schools was concerned, receiving a certain or uncertain portion of the taxes according to their proportion of pupils, or to the aggregate of attendance.

At the annual town meeting of 1825, the following resolution was adopted:

Voted: That a committee of seven be appointed by the town whose duty it shall be to examine the several district schools in the town of Newbury twice in the season, once near the commencement of such school, and once at the close of the same, and make report at the next March meeting of the best scholars in each district, and of those who may make the greatest improvement, likewise to make report of each master who shall excell in the mode of instruction and government of such schools, and designate those, if any, whom they may judge deficient in literary acquirements, or injudicious or improper mode of governing their schools.

Provided, that the said committee shall not be obliged to visit any school unless the clerk or committee of such school district shall furnish the chairman of the Town School Committee with a written notice of the time when their district school commences, and the time of terms to be kept, one week previous to the commencement of said school. Chose Calvin Jewett, David Haseltine, A. B. W. Tenney, Ephraim B. Stevens, Alfred Nevers, Jas. Bayley 2d and Hanes Johnson 2d, be the committee.

It is pretty safe to say that if Rev. Luther Jewett wrote the first half of this extraordinary resolution, somebody else wrote the last half. Like many other resolutions, it was, probably, better made than kept, as we hear no more of it.

There is no record of any superintendent of schools being chosen, or any one having the general oversight of them, till 1846, and not till much later, that any examination of teachers was had, or attempt made to assure their qualifications for the position. But gradually, and in spite of much opposition, the schools were brought under closer oversight, and the standard of the qualifications of their teachers was raised. A century ago, about all that was required of the master was that he could read and write, and "cipher" as far as the "Rule of Three." People were poor, and few young men received any more "schooling" than one or two months, in winter, when work was not driving. They had but little time to learn, and what little they had time for, must be very practical. To read well, to write a legible hand, to keep such simple accounts as a farmer needed, was all they tried to learn. And there were scores of men here in Newbury, whose early education was as meagre as this, but whose hard, practical common sense and determination, made up for deficiencies; men who conducted the town affairs, and did the town honor in the General Assembly. A noted Englishman visited Montpelier about 1832, and spent several days listening to the proceedings of the House of Representatives. He declared that he had never heard purer English, more solid, sensible, concise arguments, or

statements which went more directly to the root of the matters in
question, than came from those farmers and business men, very few
of whom had ever seen the inside of a college or academy.

Some of the farmers in this town became great readers,
especially of history and philosophy; with others their studies took
a mathematical turn. Bancroft Abbott, grandfather of the late
Professor Abbott, with the aid of a few old text-books, completely
mastered algebra and geometry. Simon Carter, a farmer who
lived just across the Topsham line, and died in 1868, acquired so
thorough a knowledge of mathematics that he was frequently
appealed to as authority in hard problems.

Two men, one of whom was a college graduate, were discussing
an abstruse point in mathematics. One of them declared that he
must be correct because he was told so at college. The other
replied, "I am sure I am right, for Simon Carter told me so."
"Well," replied the other, "if Simon Carter said so, it must be so."

When there were few books, people read those that they had
over and over, and the faculty of memory was more fully cultivated
than now. There were several men in Newbury sixty years ago,
who could repeat the whole of the New Testament and most of the
Old. One of the Renfrews could render the entire Pilgrim's Progress
word for word. Some of the Scotch Presbyterians could repeat the
Westminister Assembly's Shorter Catechism, questions and answers,
and the references. Such men were not easily worsted in argument.
Jeremiah Boynton, a farmer well remembered, and a regular
attendant at church, would, after his return home, repeat to his
wife, an invalid confined to her room and bed, the greater part of
both sermons.

When we speak of the schools of those times it must be borne in
mind that people were poor, and these schools were the best they
could provide. They had only what they could pay for. The era
of municipal extravagance had not begun sixty years ago.

The school lands comprise certain lots which were set apart
by both charters of the town for religious and educational
purposes. These are: One of the eighty-one shares into which the
proprietorship of the town was divided, was granted to the Church
of England, one to the Society for the Propagation of the Gospel in
Foreign Parts, and one for the benefit of a school. Portions of
certain farms on Leighton hill, and others in the north-western
corner of the town, comprise these lands. The farm near South
Ryegate, once called the Scott place, later "The Hermitage" of Hon.
Peter Burbank, and now owned by the heirs of William Nelson, is
on the glebe or church lands. These lands formerly paid rent to the
Episcopal church, and Hon. C. B. Leslie recalls the fact that in his
early days of practice, he used to carry the rents from Mr. Nelson,
to an agent of the Episcopal church at Chelsea. Later a law was
passed, not without opposition, which took these revenues from the

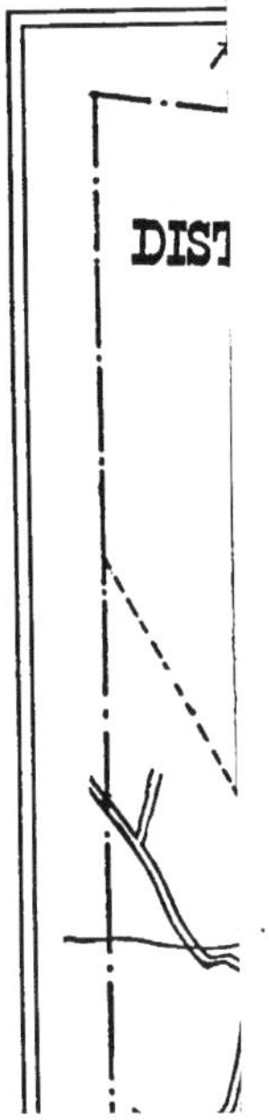
DIST

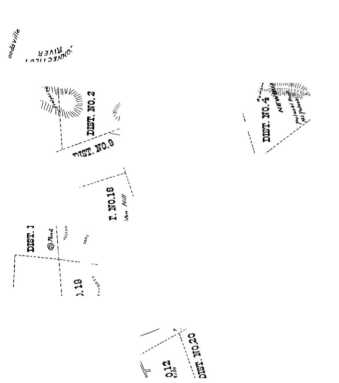

Goodville

CONNECTICUT RIVER

DIST. NO. 2

DIST. NO.9

DIST. NO.18

Van Hill

DIST.]

Pond

D. 19

DIST. NO.20

0.12

DIST. NO.4

NEWBURY

Mt. Pulaski Road

DIST.]

Rogers

Glverton Brook

Boscawen Bridge

Episcopal church, and gave them for the support of the schools. These tracts are known as "leased lands," and conveyance of title in them is by lease and not by deed. The income from the school land was $104 in 1899.

These lands have caused the town some trouble from time to time. Sometimes tenants failed to pay the rents, and once or twice there was suspicion that these sums were diverted from the town treasury. In 1827 Asa Tenney was appointed agent for the school lands in town, and such an agent is still annually chosen. The following particulars regarding various schoolhouses are worth preserving:

The first schoolhouse at Wells River was near the upper bridge on the main street. The one which was removed to make way for the present brick building was a one-story building, having two school-rooms.

In the Ox-bow district schoolhouses have stood upon several different sites. For some years the schoolhouse was near Mr. Farnham's house. The present building, now disused for some years, was built in 1851. In 1779, Col. Robert Johnston conveyed land to District No. 4, (the village district) as a site for a schoolhouse. The brick schoolhouse, now used as an office by Horace W. Bailey, Esq., was built in 1839, at a cost of $475.

There was, formerly, a schoolhouse on what is now Mr. Greer's land, near Mr. Kimball's line, on the east side of the road. The one on Rogers hill was built in 1862, and took the place of one standing before 1820. In 1827, a schoolhouse of brick, and of very peculiar internal arrangement, was built at the foot of the hill, below William Putnam's, at West Newbury, taking the place of one which was burned. This building gave way, in 1871, to the one now standing there, for some years disused.

The schoolhouses on Jefferson Hill, at the Lime Kiln and at Boltonville, are elsewhere mentioned. The first one in "Scotch Hollow," now the Center, stood at the top of the hill above Mr. Buchanan's. The second one, on the "school road," was built in the early fifties. The first one on Leighton hill, was a log house, burned in 1847, and stood on the road from the present one to M. B. Abbott's at the top of the long hill. The second one stood on the same site, and was demolished in 1873. The first school in the town house neighborhood was taught in 1823 in the "square room" of William Peach's house, by Adeline Gibson. In 1824 a schoolhouse was built below his house, which was removed about 1845, to the road which goes to Hall's pond, near the main road. In 1850, one was erected near the lily pond, which was in use just fifty years.

In January 1869, the schoolhouse near Mr. John Kendrick's was burned, and a new one built in that year. In the winter of 1862-63, the schoolhouse near Harriman's pond burned so quietly

Episcopal church, and gave them for the support of the schools. These tracts are known as "leased lands," and conveyance of title in them is by lease and not by deed.   The income from the school land was $104 in 1899.

These lands have caused the town some trouble from time to time. Sometimes tenants failed to pay the rents, and once or twice there was suspicion that these sums were diverted from the town treasury. In 1827 Asa Tenney was appointed agent for the school lands in town, and such an agent is still annually chosen.   The following particulars regarding various schoolhouses are worth preserving:

The first schoolhouse at Wells River was near the upper bridge on the main street.   The one which was removed to make way for the present brick building was a one-story building, having two school-rooms.

In the Ox-bow district schoolhouses have stood upon several different sites.   For some years the schoolhouse was near Mr. Farnham's house.   The present building, now disused for some years, was built in 1851.   In 1779, Col. Robert Johnston conveyed land to District No. 4, (the village district) as a site for a schoolhouse.   The brick schoolhouse, now used as an office by Horace W. Bailey, Esq., was built in 1839, at a cost of $475.

There was, formerly, a schoolhouse on what is now Mr. Greer's land, near Mr. Kimball's line, on the east side of the road.   The one on Rogers hill was built in 1862, and took the place of one standing before 1820.   In 1827, a schoolhouse of brick, and of very peculiar internal arrangement, was built at the foot of the hill, below William Putnam's, at West Newbury, taking the place of one which was burned.   This building gave way, in 1871, to the one now standing there, for some years disused.

The schoolhouses on Jefferson Hill, at the Lime Kiln and at Boltonville, are elsewhere mentioned.   The first one in "Scotch Hollow," now the Center, stood at the top of the hill above Mr. Buchanan's.   The second one, on the "school road," was built in the early fifties.   The first one on Leighton hill, was a log house, burned in 1847, and stood on the road from the present one to M. B. Abbott's at the top of the long hill.   The second one stood on the same site, and was demolished in 1873.   The first school in the town house neighborhood was taught in 1823 in the "square room" of William Peach's house, by Adeline Gibson.   In 1824 a schoolhouse was built below his house, which was removed about 1845, to the road which goes to Hall's pond, near the main road. In 1850, one was erected near the lily pond, which was in use just fifty years.

In January 1869, the schoolhouse near Mr. John Kendrick's was burned, and a new one built in that year.   In the winter of 1862-63, the schoolhouse near Harriman's pond burned so quietly one night, as not to be observed by its nearest neighbors, and in the summer following a new one, now disused, was built.

In 1857 schools were held in twenty-one districts in Newbury. In several of these there are not now children enough to make a school, and the few there are sent elsewhere. Two, and in some cases three, districts, have been consolidated, and a new house built which should accommodate all. At present there are twelve schools in town, and there are seven old schoolhouses, either vacant, or turned to other uses.

In 1887, the village district purchased the old seminary building, and began its interior reconstruction. In 1892, the Ox-bow and village districts were made one. In 1893 the town central school was begun, and is a graded school with free tuition to residents of the town. Its principals have been:

Elmer E. French, 1890-93,	Tufts College, Mass.
Fred E. Prichard, 1893-95,	Dartmouth College.
Ethan A. Shaw, 1895-97,	Norwich University, Vt.
Charles L. Orton, 1897-98,	Vermont University.
Gay W. Felton, 1898-90,	Vermont University.
Geo. D. Osgood, 1900,	Vermont University.

The following is a list of college graduates who were natives of Newbury. It is not assumed that this list is by any means complete, but it includes all the names which could be gathered.

Abbott, George N.	Vermont University, 1849,	Teacher.
Abbott, William T.	Dartmouth, 1882,	Lawyer.
Atkinson, Frances M.	Vermont University, 1895,	Librarian.
Bates, Mary E.	Vermont University, 1894,	Librarian.
Bayley, John M.	Unknown, 1816,	Merchant.
Boyce, Nathaniel S.	Michigan University, 1854,	Physician.
Brickett, Harry	Dartmouth, 1840,	Teacher.
Chalmers, Edward E.	Dartmouth, 1887,	Lawyer.
Chamberlain, Remembrance	Middlebury,	Minister.
Chamberlin, Preston S.		Physician.
Dean, Samuel H.	Harvard,	Teacher.
Doe, Orlando W.	Harvard,	Physician.
Eastman, Samuel L.	N. W. University, 1859,	Teacher.
Eastman, Horace T.	Vermont University, 1871,	Business.
Farwell, Julia H.	Mt. Holyoke,	Teacher.
Johnson, Haynes	Dartmouth, 1822,	Minister.
Johnson, Moses	Dartmouth, 1834,	Business.
Johnson, Alexander G.	Dartmouth, 1837,	Editor.
Johnson, Edward C.	Dartmouth, 1840,	Merchant.
Johnson, Jonathan	Wesleyan,	Lawyer.
Keyes, Henry W.	Harvard,	Business.
Keyes, Charles W.	Harvard,	
Keyes, George T.	Harvard,	
Ladd, John J.	Dartmouth, 1852,	Teacher.
Leslie, Charles E.	Dartmouth, 1877,	Lawyer.
McIndoe, George J.	Dartmouth, 1895,	Business.

McLeod, Robert D.	Michigan, 1888,	Lawyer.
Olmsted, Perley A.	Vermont University, 1876,	Business.
Powers, Jonathan	Dartmouth, 1787,	Minister.
Powers, John Hale	Wesleyan, 1869,	Business.
Porter, Timothy O.	Dartmouth, 1822,	Editor.
Porter, George	Dartmouth, 1831,	Editor.
Quimby, Carl	Wesleyan, 1889,	Optician.
Rogers, Edwin A.	Harvard,	Lawyer.
Ruggles, Henry E.	Dartmouth, 1845,	Minister.
Smith, Raymond U.	Norwich University, 1894,	Lawyer.
Shurtleff, William S.	Yale,	Lawyer.
Spencer, John W.	Boston University, 1891,	Minister.
Swasey, Samuel	Dartmouth, 1828,	Lawyer.
Tewksbury, William A.	Middlebury, 1865,	Lawyer.
Tucker, George	Beloit, 1853,	Minister.
Wallace, John	Dartmouth, 1808,	Lawyer.
Watkins, Harris R.	Dartmouth, 1888,	Physician.

The following were at some college for a longer or shorter time but did not graduate:

Carleton, John H.	Wesleyan,	Business.
Cargill, Charles G.	Norwich,	Physician.
Clark, Carrie	Oberlin,	Teacher.
Lang, Caroline H.	Women's College, Baltimore,	Teacher.
Powers, Mathew	Dartmouth,	Farmer.
Ropes, Arthur,	Dartmouth,	Editor.
Scott, Orange W.	Wesleyan,	Minister.
Tenney, A. B. W.	Dartmouth,	Business.
Wallace, Dudley C.	Dartmouth,	Physician.
Wason, Thomas,	Dartmouth,	Died in colle

CHAPTER XXXII.

LITERARY NEWBURY.

THE first settlers of this town compared favorably in intelligence with those of any other, but they could not have had many books, still, doubtless, every family, not wholly indigent, owned a Bible, and it was thoroughly read and studied. It took time to accumulate in the whole settlement as many volumes as any intelligent farmer will now have. The few treasured books and pamphlets which have come down to us from the pioneers, are, generally, of a semi-theological character, dealing with the most abstruse subjects upon which the human intellect can exercise its powers of inquiry and inference. Some of these works, which our fathers loved, are of so profound a character that few of us, shallow moderns, possess resolution enough to sit down and resolutely grapple with their contents. The mental giants of those days produced volumes whose intelligent study calls for their comprehension, the concentrated attention of all the mental faculties which their readers possess. One of these works, "An Inquiry into the so-called Freedom of the Human Will," written by a New England clergyman in a country parish, before the revolutionary war, is considered one of the masterpieces of the human intellect. Upon such books, and by sermons modeled upon them, were our forefathers trained.

The first settlers of Newbury were illiterate, if we consider illiteracy to consist in poor spelling. Of all the men who were in Newbury before the revolution, counting out certain Scotchmen, there were, probably, not three, besides the minister, who could write a short letter without making mistakes in orthography. General Bayley could not, nor Colonel Johnson, nor Colonel Kent. It is easy to laugh at their letters, but one of their descendants, who should undertake to hold an argument with his ancestor, would have little reason to laugh. The men who carried the Coös country safely through the revolutionary war, had found little time to learn the niceties of spelling, but they did know the whole subject of the controversy with Great Britain, to the last particular.

Newspapers began to be taken in town as early as 1768, but their reception could have been only at irregular intervals, as some one happened to come up from the seacoast. A newspaper was a treasure in those days, and was passed from hand to hand, and from family to family. One reason why so few papers from the early days survive, is, that they were worn out with reading. Many of the pamphlets against tyranny printed between 1770, and 1775, found their way here, and a very few originated in the Coös country. After the war the circulation of papers increased, and all the wealthier families took at least one.

In 1794, Nathan Coverly, Jr., came here from Salem, Mass., and started the first printing office in the Connecticut valley, north of Hanover, in a building since burned. It stood on the other side of the road from the dwelling of the late Miss Swasey, at the Ox-bow. He did a considerable amount of printing, including a few small books, in a creditable manner. Of one of these, Flavel's "Token for Mourners," a few copies are still owned in this vicinity. He carried on a store for the sale of books and stationery in the front part of the building, the printing office being at the rear. In 1796, probably in May, he began the publication of a newspaper called the "Orange Nightingale and Newbury Morning Star." A part of No. 15, of the date August 25, is preserved. It was well printed, carefully made up, appears to have been Federalist in politics and bore the motto: "Here truth is welcome—Candour guides the way." It had the latest news from London, dated June 1st, and speaks of the French victories in Italy under Bonaparte. There is very little local news. A criticism upon the proceedings of a church council, which was held to adjust some difficulties between the churches of Newbury and Haverhill, an account of a woman killed by a bear in St. Johnsborough, (St. Johnsbury) and a poem upon the death of a daughter of Josiah Page of Ryegate, are about all.

This paper was short-lived for want of funds and patronage, and Mr. Coverly closed out his business here, and returned to Salem, where he was living in 1808. The type and fixtures were sold to Farley & Goss of Peacham, where they were used in the publication of a paper called the "Green Mountain Patriot." This paper came to grief in its turn, and the materials of the office were taken to Danville and used in starting the "North Star," in 1804. No further attempt was made to publish a paper here in Newbury for more than fifty years, as far as can be learned. Ira White, however, had a printing office at Wells River, where he did a great deal of miscellaneous printing, and published school, and other books. For some years after 1840, when Newbury Seminary was at its highest prosperity, there was a printing office at Newbury village. Hayes & Co., were printers, succeeding a Mr. Rand, who later became the publisher of Zion's Herald.

When the theological department of the seminary was established, it was believed that there was sufficient encouragement to warrant the starting of a magazine, devoted to reviews, essays, and general religious intelligence, and which would, it was hoped, find its way into the more cultured circles of the Methodist church, in the country generally. The "Newbury Biblical Magazine" was begun in May 1843, and issued on each alternate month. Professor William M. Willett was the able editor, and the other professors seem to have been contributors. The first number was a pamphlet of forty-eight pages, which was afterwards enlarged, and in its general character compares well with other reviews of the time. It was singularly free from controversy and some of its critical essays were very profound. It may be questioned if the Methodist church possesses, even at this day, a more able publication, when we consider that it was conducted in a small and remote country village, far removed from any large library, such as is indispensable to the critical student, and that its editor and chief contributor was engaged in labors which would seem enough to keep one man busy. The magazine came to an end with the twelfth number, that of March, 1844. The reasons for its discontinuance as given by the editor, are the great amount of labor which it imposed upon a man not strong in health, and want of financial support. From a bound volume of this excellent production, owned by the late Andrew Grant, much that is valuable regarding Newbury Seminary was obtained. The first six numbers of the Biblical Magazine were printed by Hayes & Co., and the remainder by L. J. McIndoe.

"The Christian Messenger" was commenced March 12, 1847, and was edited by the seminary professors, and resident ministers, and was, for many years, the religious organ of the Methodist church in Vermont. Its stay, however, in Newbury, was short, as after a little more than a year it was moved to Montpelier. It was discontinued a few years ago.

In 1848, an anti-Catholic paper, called "The Northern Protestant and American Advocate," was started, but its life, at least in Newbury, was brief. In 1845, Lyman J. McIndoe removed his printing office from Haverhill to Newbury, and in April, 1848, began the publication of the "Aurora of the Valley," a semi-monthly literary publication, which soon became very popular, and which he enlarged. It did not collect much news at first, and depended mainly upon contributions to its columns from local

LYMAN J. McINDOE.

writers. Some of its short stories and essays were very good. It was, later, changed to a weekly newspaper, still possessing a literary character, and supported the Whig, and afterward, the Republican party. D. B. Dudley was its assistant editor for a time. About 1857, the paper was removed to Bradford, and later, to Windsor, where it was merged into the Vermont Journal.

Mr. McIndoe was an able editor, who was successful financially, and his paper was a great benefit to the town. A literary taste displayed in the selection of stories for the Aurora caused its introduction into many families, and was the medium whereby much valuable literature was brought into the homes of Newbury people. Mr. McIndoe had his first printing office in the "old depot building," and afterward in a two story structure with a high basement which stood between James B. Hale's house and his store. In this he did an extensive business, printing religious books and tracts. He also kept an excellent book-store, which was continued by his brother David, till about the time of the removal of the seminary. During the existence of that institution, several papers were sustained by the students at different times, which had their little day and expired. A small publication was conducted by the pupils of Montebello Ladies Institute for a short time. It was called "The Montebello Critic," and was published in the spring of 1880.

At Wells River an eight-page weekly paper was commenced in 1878 by W. S. S. Buck, called "The Riverside," but was discontinued after some time. A monthly paper in the interest of the Congregational church at that place, edited by Rev. R. C. Flagg, was begun in March, 1889. It was called "Church and Home," and was published by F. Sherwin and Son. Its existence was two years, the last number being published in February, 1891. Mr. Sherwin and his son are the sole representatives of the printer's craft in this town.

Mention should be made of two or three Haverhill papers which had a large influence and circulation in Newbury. The "New Hampshire Post and Grafton Advertiser," was begun in 1827 and continued till 1848. Its politics were Whig, and it had several owners. In 1828, Hon. John R. Reding began the publication of the "Democratic Republican," which was continued by his brothers till 1863. He married a sister of Hon. Isaac Hill of Concord and the paper, which was ably edited, was the strenuous advocate of the principles of the Democratic party, as represented by Andrew Jackson. A bound volume of this paper, which contains most of the numbers from January 9, 1833, to February 22, 1837, has been of much value in the preparation of this book. It is owned by Joseph C. Johnston. The first daily paper taken in town is believed to have been the "Boston Daily Atlas," in 1848. Col. O. C. Hale began to take it about the time the railroad was built. The breaking out of the civil war caused a great increase in the number of both daily and weekly papers taken here, and daily papers were first sold on the trains about that time.

The first religious paper was the "Boston Recorder," and it was taken as early as 1818 by one family and perhaps by others. Some post office bills which remain among the Johnson papers show that among the papers taken here just one hundred years ago (1800) were "The Boston Centinel," "Portsmouth Chronicle," "Worcester Spy," and the "Connecticut Courant." The Centinel was, long ago merged into the "Boston Advertiser." The others are still published. There were three copies of "The Museum" taken, a paper which the editor cannot identify, also the "Cabinet." The "Worcester Gazette" had two subscribers.

In these days, when every family receives many requests to subscribe for newspapers every year, it is hard to comprehend the difficulty our ancestors had in subscribing for a paper at all. When in 1795, Hon. Thomas Tolman of Greensboro, whom we have mentioned before, and General Crafts, of Craftsbury, who afterwards became governor of the state, decided to take a paper printed at Philadelphia, they did not know how to obtain it, and addressed the following letter to Colonel Thomas Johnson:

GREENSBORO, Mar. 21st, 1795.

DEAR SIR:—

It having been agreed to take 2 or 3 newspapers from the other states, thro' your hand as Postmaster, and from Newbury to be conveyed in the best manner to this Town and Craftsbury. will you be so kind as to take the trouble of contracting (thro' the mail) with Mr. Bache of Phila. for his General Advertiser. printed twice a week, for one year. for me. and direct them enclosed under cover and directed "Thomas Tolman, Greensborough, by the Newbury mail, Vermont," or something like it, with the terms conveyed in the first conveyance, for which if you will make yourself accountable to him, I will to you.

I am, Dear Sir,
Your obed't and humble servant,
THOS. TOLMAN.

It had been intended to give a list of all books printed in Newbury, but it was found to be impossible. No record was kept of them, and only a few copies remain. Ira White printed school books, and several religious works, including an edition of the New England Primer. A small volume entitled, "The Female Wanderer, Written by Herself," bears his imprint. Hayes & Co. printed small volumes, biographies, and reprints of English classics. In addition to several works which bear his name, L. J. McIndoe printed a number of Sunday school books for Rev. Orange Scott, which bear the imprint of the Wesleyan Association.

How many books Mr. Coverly, our first printer, published, is unknown. , The complete titles of the following are here given:

THE POOR MAN'S COMPANION,
OR
MISCELLANEOUS OBSERVATIONS CONCERNING PENAL AND SANGUINARY LAWS,
THE MODE AND NATURE OF EVIDENCE,
AND
AN INQUIRY INTO THE PROPRIETY AND POLICY OF PUNISHMENT.

BY JOHN YOUNG, ESQ.,
OF NEWHAMPSHIRE IN NEW ENGLAND.

NEWBURY, VERMONT,
PRINTED BY NATHANIEL COVERLY,
AND SOLD AT HIS BOOK-STORE NEAR THE COURT HOUSE.

This formidable title ushers in some observations upon the duties and privileges of the citizen. John Young lived in Haverhill at one time, and in his life played many parts in many places. This little volume is a curiosity. It consists of one hundred pages, measuring six inches by four, and is bound, literally, in boards, thin sheets of wood, covered with paper, forming the covers. The type is clear, and the edges of the leaves are untrimmed. A copy is owned by Hon. Horace W. Bailey.

A TOKEN FOR MOURNERS.

BY JOHN FLAVEL.

PRINTED BY NATHANIEL COVERLY
AT
NEWBURY, VERMONT,
NEAR THE COURT HOUSE, 1796.

A copy owned by Mr. Sherwin, at Wells River, has 132 pages. What follow are missing. There is a complete copy in the library of the Vermont Historical Society at Montpelier.

HYMNS.

SILAS BALLOU, UNIVERSALIST.

NATHANIEL COVERLY,
NEWBURY, VERMONT, 1797.

This title is furnished by Hon. Albert S. Batchellor.

The following bibliography gives, by authors' names, the titles of all books or pamphlets written by natives of Newbury, as far as they could be ascertained; of all addresses delivered in this town, or elsewhere by persons residing in Newbury at the time of delivery, with a few which do not come under either of these heads:

ABBOTT, GEORGE N. Essays and Reviews. (A short time before his death, Prof. Abbott had begun to collect the titles of his works, which consisted mainly of contributions to such publications as the "University Magazine," "The Mercersburg Review," and the like. They were upon topics which appealed to scholars like himself. A few were printed separately.)
  "The Christologic Problem." An essay read before the Winooski Association, January 8, 1867, Andover, Mass., 1869, 20 pp.
ADAMS, REV. HENRY W. Discourse delivered before the preachers of the Danville district, in the Methodist church at Newbury, March 24, 1843. Newbury, Hayes & Co. pp. 43.
ATKINSON, REV. GEORGE H., D. D. Biography.

BAILEY, HORACE W. Report as superintendent of schools, 1886. Catalogue of the
    Library and Philosophical apparatus of Dr. Cutting of Lunenburg.
BAYLEY, MRS. ASA, (Daughter of Dea. James Abbott.) Memoir. By herself, edited
    by Rev. Ethan Smith, 1815, pp. 207.
BATES, REV. S. L. Sermon. On the death of Miss Mary E. Tenney, February 15,
    1880, pp. 13.
    Sermon. Before the General Convention, 1888, (In Vermont Chronicle.)
    "The Days of Old." An Historical Discourse, upon the 125th, anniversary of
    the First Congregational church, September 29, 1889.
BOLE, REV. JOHN. Sermon. At funeral of Mrs. William Reid. (In published volume
    of sermons, 1860.)
BRADFORD, REV. EBENEZER. Sermon, at ordination of Rev. Nathaniel Lambert,
    November 17, 1790.
BROWN, CHESTER. Shepard Family, (of Newbury and Hardwick.) Montpelier,
    Argus & Patriot Office, 1894, pp. 16.
BURTON, REV. H. N. Report as Superintendent of Schools, 1860, '61, '62.
    "Go Forward." Discourse delivered at the semi-centennial of the Vermont
    Domestic Missionary Society, at St. Johnsbury, June 17, 1868. Montpelier,
    Freeman Office, pp. 16.
BUTTON, REV. A. G. Report, as Superintendent of Schools, 1863.
BUTLER, PROF. JAMES DAVIE. Address, on the Battle of Bennington, delivered before
    the legislature, October 20, 1848, while pastor of the church at Wells River.
    (Contains the narrative of Thomas Mellen.)
CAMPBELL, REV. GEORGE W. Republicanism. Sermon delivered at the dedication
    of the Congregational Meeting-house in Newbury, November 13, 1849,
    Haverhill. J. R. Reding, pp. 18.
    Sermon. February 20, 1847. At the Ordination of Rev. George H. Atkinson,
    Newbury. L. J. McIndoe, pp. 24.
CHAMBERLAIN, WRIGHT, Report, as Superintendent of Schools, 1875.
CHAMBERLIN, EVERETT, Chicago and the Great Conflagration, 1872.
    The Political Struggle of 1872.
    Chicago and Her Suburbs.
CHAMBERLIN, JOSEPH EDGAR, The Listener in Town, 1896.
    The Listener in the Country, 1896.
    John Brown, a Biography, 1899.
    Statement of Line of Descent of Chamberlin Families in Newbury, 1894,
    pp. 11.
CHALMERS, ROBERT, Description of Plans Submitted for the Garfield Monument,
    1881, pp. 4.
    Pamphlet upon Atmospheric Moisture in the Form of Fog and Dew, 1874,
    pp. 6.
CHURCH, FIRST CONGREGATIONAL. Covenant, 1823, pp. 4. Manual, 1876,
    Montpelier, J. Poland, pp. 24.
    Report Annual, 1877, and each succeeding year, except 1889, '90, '91.
    Wells River Congregational. Manual, 1842.
    Manual 1864, McFarland & Jenks, Concord, N. H.
    Manual 1890, Coös Steam Press, Woodsville.
DEMPSTER, PROF. J. The Benefit and Danger of Society.
    An Address to the Ladies' Mutual Improvement Society of Newbury
    Seminary, November 14, 1845. L. J. McIndoe, pp. 11.
FARRAND, DANIEL. It is not known that Judge Farrand published anything while
    living here. Several of his daughters wrote tales and sketches, poems and
    historical works, or were associated with others in the preparation of school
    and college text-books, But they left Newbury while young, and were not
    identified with the town in any way.
JOHNSON, NANCY, Letters from a Sick room.
    Simple Sketches and Plain Reflections, pp. 180.
    The Myrtle Wreath.
    Little Things.
    Peasant Life in Germany, Two Ed., pp. 426.
    Cottages of the Alps, pp. 401.
    Iroquois, (See Johnson Family—this volume.)
JOHNSTON, JANE, She is understood to have published several small volumes, or
    tracts, for children. One is remembered—An account of the life and death of
    Amaziah, son of Joseph Ricker, who died about 1815, at the age of twelve.

HASELTINE, SAMUEL, Religious Experience. By himself, with some account of his life and death, pp. 38, 1819.
HINMAN, CLARK T. Address before the Ladies Literary Society, November 17, 1841, pp. 33.
INGALLS, JEREMIAH, The Christian Harmony. A book of church music, 1805, pp. 201, Henry Ranlet, Exeter, N. H.
KEYES, DEA. FREEMAN, Memorial, 1872, pp. 27.
KEYES, HENRY, In Memoriam. Testimonial of the Vermont State Agricultural Society, 1870, pp. 4.
LAMBERT, REV. NATHANIEL, Election Sermon, delivered at Newbury before Governor Tichenor, October 8, 1801, pp. 21.
    Sermon, delivered about 1796.
MERRILL, REV. J. L. Historical address at the Centennial of Haverhill Academy, August 4, 1897. (In "Centennial Anniversary.") pp. 68-85.
MUNSELL, MRS. ANTHA M. "The Over Sixty Club," of Wells River, pp. 26, Sherwin & Son, Wells River, 1900.
NEWBURY SEMINARY. Catalogues. The first catalogue was of the fall term of 1834. Afterwards a catalogue was issued at the end of each academic year, except 1868. Triennial catalogues were published of the Collegiate Institute in 1867, and after removal to Montpelier.
    Catalogue, by Rev. S. L. Eastman, in 1875, '76.
    Newbury High School, 1844.
NEWBURY, TOWN OF. Town Reports, 1893, and each following year.
    Selectmen and Auditors, Report of the Financial Condition of the Town, February 1876.
    Report of the Committee appointed to Investigate the Financial Books of the Town of Newbury, March 1, 1877.
    Report of the Superintendent of Schools, by Rev. S. M. Plympton for March 1859. By Rev. H. N. Burton for 1860, '61, '62. By Rev. A. G. Button, for 1863. By Wright Chamberlain, for 1875. By Horace W. Bailey, for 1886. Of late years the school report has been printed with the town report, in the years 1894, et seq.
    Town Central School. Catalogue published in 1897, and each succeeding year.
    Village Library Association. Catalogue, 1881.
PATTERSON, RICHARD, On the Financial affairs of Newbury, May 1, 1877.
    Same subject, February 1, 1880.
PLYMPTON, REV. S. M. Report as Superintendent of Schools, 1859.
PORTER WILLIAM T. Timothy O., Benjamin and George, (See Porter family.)
    William T. Life of. By Francis Brinley 1860, pp. 273.
PUTNAM, ELDER BENJAMIN, Sketch of life of. By himself, 1821, pp. 216.
POWERS, REV. PETER, Sermon delivered at his installation in Hollis, N. H., February 27, 1765. "For the Towns of Newbury and Haverhill, at a Place Called Coös." Portsmouth, 1765.
    Sermon at the Funeral of Mrs. Frye Bayley, February 1, 1772. (This was one of the very earliest publications in Vermont.) Newburyport.
    Sermon preached before the General Assembly of the State of Vermont, on the day of their First General Election at Windsor, March 12, 1778, Newburyport, pp. 40.
    Tyrany and Toryism Exposed. The substance of two sermons preached at Newbury on Lord's Day, September 10, 1780. Westminster, 1781. (These were the sermons which were the occasion of Mr. Power's leaving Newbury.)
POWERS, REV. GRANT, Historical Sketches of the Discovery, Settlement and Progress of Events in the Coös Country, Haverhill, 1841, pp. 240, 2d edition, 1880.
SANBORN, PROF. E. D. Sermon at Funeral of Dea. Freeman Keyes, June 1871. (In "Memorial," also in Vermont Journal.)
SUTHERLAND, REV. DAVID, Christian Benevolence. A Sermon Delivered before the Washingtonian Benevolent Society in Newbury, July 4, 1812, pp 15.
TEMPERANCE, SONS OF, Constitution and by-laws of Pulaski Division Established at Newbury, April 23, 1849, pp. 24, Aurora of the Valley Press, 1849.
TENNEY, MARTHA J. The Tenney Family, 1891, pp. 370.
TENNEY MEMORIAL LIBRARY. Catalogue 1897, pp. 88, Opinion Print, Bradford.
    Catalogue Supplementary, 1900, pp. 34, Sherwin & Son.

THRALL, REV. SAMUEL L. Sermon. Valedictory, at Wells River, March 28, 1847.
WALLACE, JOHN, Oration before the Washington Benevolent Society, July 4, 1812,
  pp. 14, Windsor, Thos. M. Powers.
    Address delivered at Newbury, July 4, 1823, pp. 11, Haverhill, N. H., S. T.
  Goss.
WELLS RIVER VILLAGE. Annual Report 1898.
    Annual Report 1899.
WILLETT, REV. WM. Inaugural Address delivered before the Newbury Biblical
  Institute, 1843. In Biblical Magazine.
WOOD REV. H. C. On Reading. An address delivered before the Ladies' Literary
  Society of Newbury Seminary, 1845. Hayes & Co., Newbury, pp. 12.
WHITE, LYDIA E. (Miss White is not a native of this town, but of Topsham, yet is
  of Newbury ancestry, and spends much time here. As mention of her name and
  publications is not given in Gilman, they are recorded here for preservation.)
    "The Record of a Day." A paper published in October, 1864, under the
  auspices of the Christian Commission as a supplement to all the religious
  weeklies in New York, circulating in these and in pamphlet form, to the number
  of about half a million copies, besides being copied extensively by the general
  press. It proved exceedingly popular, being an account of a day spent in
  gathering hospital supplies. So true to life were its character sketches, that,
  although entirely fictitious, it everywhere passed for a bona fide narrative.
  Nothing else was produced during the war that gave so graphic an idea of the
  home work done for the army and navy, during those trying years. Later
  works of Miss White have been, "The Campaign at Widdletown," "Parish
  Notes," "Live Coals," "Success in Society." Her brother, Carlos E. White,
  published "Ecce Femina," and a younger brother, N. Byron White, has published
  certain agricultural works, the best known of which is "Thirty Years Among
  Cows."
WHITE, REV. PLINY H. Essay upon the Ecclesiastical History of Vermont.
  Delivered before the General Convention of Congregational Churches, held in
  Newbury, June 1866.

CHAPTER XXXIII.

LIBRARIES—TEMPERANCE.

BY the year 1800, several men had quite respectable collections
of books. Rev. Nathaniel Lambert, Mr. Farrand, Benjamin
Porter, Col. Thomas Johnson, and Col. Frye Bayley were
among these. The latter reported in 1805, that he had £50 worth
of books. Many of these were rare volumes, or were so by the
time the family became extinct in town, so that at the auction sale
of the property, in 1863, after the death of its last representative,
some of the rarer volumes were secured by collectors, and libraries
in the cities.

About 1796, certain gentlemen agreed to place in a convenient
room, such books as they could spare, for the common use of such
as acquired a title to the privilege by presenting a book. This
Library Association was afterwards incorporated, and was in
existence for many years.

The Congregational Sunday-school was organized about 1815,
and soon began a collection of such books as were then considered
proper for religious reading. The library of Newbury Seminary
was neither large, nor carefully selected, but contained many
valuable works. An agricultural library was started in February,
1864, by a number of farmers, who subscribed for shares, which
were five dollars each. This did not seem to arouse much interest,
and most of the shares were sold at a small portion of their cost.
The greater part of these volumes are now included in the Tenney
Memorial Library.

On October 10, 1868, a few ladies formed the "Newbury Village

Library Association," at the suggestion of Rev. Dr. G. H. Atkinson, who presented it with a number of volumes. Mrs. C. M. Atkinson was the first president, and Miss Julia Farnham was librarian. The books were kept in Mr. Farnham's house. In 1885, the library was moved to a suitable room in the Congregational vestry. In 1890 Miss Charlotte Atkinson became librarian, and in 1894, Mrs. J. L. Merrill succeeded her. An annual fee of one dollar was required of the persons using the library, and funds for the purchase of books were raised by means of entertainments. The first catalogue was printed in 1881. By June, 1897, the number of volumes had increased to about 1600.

In the autumn of 1895, Miss Martha J. Tenney, of Haverhill, Mass., made public her long cherished intention of erecting a suitable building for a library, in memory of her father, Col. A. B. W. Tenney, and the owners of the old Spring Hotel site promptly offered as much of that valuable location as she should desire for the purpose. A definite proposition was made by Miss Tenney to the town, to which the selectmen responded by calling a special town-meeting on January 28, 1897, which was well attended. A unanimous vote in favor of accepting the proposition was the result of the meeting, and upon the receipt of the telegram announcing the acceptance of her offer, Miss Tenney instructed Mr. H. M. Francis, an architect of Fitchburg, Mass., to prepare the plans for a building 40 x 45 feet, of brick and stone, for a library.

Mr. J. B. Littlehale of Fitchburg was the contractor; the work began in June, and was completed in January. The building is Romanesque in style, the basement is of Ryegate granite, the walls are of Longmeadow stone, and red brick. The roof is slated, and the construction of the building is very thorough. When completed the land and building were conveyed to the town, under the conditions set forth by Miss Tenney in her proposition to the selectmen. The building and its contents are under the care and management of a board of nine trustees, who are, in the order named by Miss Tenney:

F. P. Wells	Thos. C. Keyes
Horace W. Bailey	Erastus Baldwin
Byron O. Rogers	Mrs. W. H. Atkinson
Mrs. C. F. Darling	Rev. J. L. Merrill.
C. C. Doe	

This body of trustees is self-perpetuating. The present officers are: Rev. J. L. Merrill, President; Mrs. W. H. Atkinson, Secretary; Mrs. C. F. Darling, Treasurer; Byron O. Rogers, Auditor. Horace W. Bailey is chairman of the executive committee, and Miss Frances M. Atkinson has been the librarian since the building was opened. The town, by its acceptance of the deed of gift, must appropriate, annually, a sum of not less than $150 for its maintenance and enlargement. The building was first opened to public inspection on

MARTHA J. TENNEY.

the evening of March 17, 1897. It contains a reading and art room, and the library of the Newbury Village Library Association, with such additions as have been made to it. The village library contained about 1,600 volumes, to which some 600 were added before the building was opened. By gifts and by purchase the library has steadily grown, until on November 1, 1900, it numbers 3,535 volumes. The reading-room is furnished with the best magazines, and works of reference are accessible. It is open to the public on Wednesday and Saturday afternoons and evenings, and is free to all the inhabitants of the town. When opened, the library was without endowment, or other income, than the annual appropriation from the town, but liberal gifts have been made to it, and the income from the town and its invested funds, has paid all its expenses and provided for the purchase of new books. Within the past year, (1900) through the liberality of Miss Tenney, it receives the photographs and other publications of the Library Art Club.

The Tenney Memorial Library was dedicated June 10, 1897, the one hundred and second anniversary of the birth of Col. Abner Bailey White Tenney. The day was very rainy, but the Congregational church, in which the exercises were held, was completely filled. Rev. J. L. Merrill presided; prayer was offered by Rev. W. H. White, and a scholarly oration was delivered by Prof. Sanborn Gove Tenney. Hon. Horace W. Bailey testified the public appreciation of the gift by a well prepared address, and remarks were made by Hon. Henry O. Kent of Lancaster, N. H., Hon. F. W. Baldwin of Barton, Vt., Mrs. A. P. Webster of Plymouth, N. H., and others. Letters were read from Miss Tenney, Mrs. Sophia Tenney Hale, and Rev. Artemas Dean, D. D. The Mahogany Quartette of St. Johnsbury sang, and a Boston lady presided at the organ. At this gathering several hundred dollars were subscribed as the nucleus of a permanent fund. Miss Tenney, who is much of an invalid, has never yet seen the building which she has erected for the benefit of her native town.

The Wells River Library Association had its origin in 1849. Rev. James D. Butler, pastor of the Congregational church, who had traveled extensively in Europe, gave a course of lectures, the proceeds of which went for the purchase of books. These were the first lectures upon European travel ever delivered in this town. This library has steadily grown, and was, for some years, kept at the bank, Mr. Leslie, the cashier, serving as librarian. On May 30, 1892, Col. Erastus Baldwin conveyed to the village, and the association, the two-story building in which the library is now placed, in memory of his brother, Alvi T. Baldwin, and Ralph Baldwin, the latter's son. The rent of the tenement above is for purchase of books, of which there are now about 1,500. The present officers of the association are: Erastus Baldwin, President;

R. G. Brock, Vice President; Miss Addie K. Bigelow, Librarian and Treasurer, and the Executive Committee are: Dr. and Mrs. J. F. Shattuck, Mrs. E. Baldwin, Mr. J. F. Hale and Mr. N. H. Field. A membership fee of fifty cents annually entitles each member to take books from the library, under the rules. In 1899, arrangements were made for an exchange of volumes between the libraries at Wells River and Newbury village.

Several private libraries deserve mention. That of Hon. Benjamin Hale, most of it having been that of his father, President Hale, of Geneva College, was large and valuable. He lived in the brick house now owned and occupied by Mr. Richard Doe.

The First Congregational church has retained its pastors long enough for them to collect many books, and Rev's H. N. Burton, S. L. Bates and J. L. Merrill, the successive occupants of the present parsonage, have made it the home of libraries, by no means altogether theological. The same may be said of the pastors of the Wells River church.

The largest private library in town is that of Hon. Horace W. Bailey, which, somewhat miscellaneous in character, has many rare volumes, and is especially rich in publications relating to the early history of Vermont. The editor of this volume returns his thanks to Mr. Bailey, and to Rev. J. L. Merrill as well, for the free use of their collections of historical works.

The most valuable and best selected private library in Newbury, is that of Mr. George H. Moore, which contains fine editions of the English classics, many of which were imported by him. It is particularly strong in the departments of philosophy and history. Mr. Moore owns some of the earliest printed books known, and several of his volumes are so rare as to be almost unique. He possesses the only set of Hogarth's Plates in this vicinity.

"Of making many books there is no end," said the wise man, and the present inhabitants of Newbury have no reason to complain of a scarcity of reading. The young people of the present day have no comprehension how their predecessors sixty years ago, or even much later, hungered after "something new to read." They will never value books as people used to do when they were very few.

In early days the use of ardent spirits was universal. Everybody, practically, drank; only here and there was a man who did not drink at all. Intemperance, and all the evils that followed in its train, was regarded with indifference by most, with aversion by some, and with horror by a very few. Spirits were handed around at weddings and funerals. Every social gathering was marked by excesses. A glass of spirits was placed upon the pulpit, that the minister might refresh himself when fatigued by the delivery of his long sermon. Col. D. S. Palmer, who died at West Newbury in 1886, remembered hearing one of the most noted divines of New Hampshire preach a sermon upon the wrath to come, when too much under the influence of liquor to stand erect in the pulpit. It seems strange how little good men realized the extent of the evil, and their own share in extending it. Men in those days sold rum and whiskey, who would at the present time no more sell liquor, than they would poison their neighbors' cattle.

Cider was universally drank, and in some families was placed on the table at every meal. There was a cider-mill and often three or four, in every neighborhood. There were also several distilleries in town. The old farmers consumed an amount of the beverage which seems incredible. From twenty to forty barrels of cider were considered necessary to support a family through the winter, and some of this cider became hard, very hard indeed, before it was drank. Many, but by no means all, of the old cider-drinkers, acquired a taste for potato-whiskey and apple-brandy. But there were many men who drank cider daily who rarely tasted anything stronger. Indeed, it must be admitted that spirituous liquors did not, seventy years ago, have the deadly effect which they now produce.

The men of the early decades of the century were much more exposed to cold and storm and their toil was hard and in the open air. Their vigorous frames could readily withstand the effects of the stimulants. And there may be some truth in the remark of an aged lady that "folks didn't talk temperance till liquor got so bad it killed people."

Rev. David Sutherland, of Bath, has left the following record of the use of liquor in his early ministry, which began in 1804:

"During the first seven years of my pastoral life, I was sorely grieved with the prevalent use of intoxicating drinks. I could enter no house without encountering the rum bottle, or an apology for its absence. Intemperance was the bane, not only of the church of which I was pastor, but of all churches within my knowledge. I preached with great earnestness and plainness on the subject of intemperance. But the evil still continued. It occurred to me at last, that total abstinence must be the only check, for just as long as temperate drinking continued, intemperate drinking would. I immediately adopted the total abstinence principle, although, for ought I knew, I was alone in creation in adopting the principle. But I did adopt it, and not only published it in my own congregation, but in every congregation to which I had access, that I would never offer a drop of strong drink to any man, nor accept it from any man. And my resolution became so extensively known, that, except in one instance, I have not been asked to drink any intoxicating liquor these forty-two years." (This was written in 1853.)

Haying and sheep-washing were especial seasons of excess. People drank in summer because the weather was so warm, and in winter because it was so cold. It was not thought possible to raise a barn without spirits. As late as 1860 it was not uncommon to furnish liquor, but by that time it had begun to be thought a bad practice. At the raising of a barn in that year, the owner had promised that there should be no liquor. But when the help came together it was found that several men were under its influence, and the temperance men seeing the situation, went home. The owner was obliged finally to concede to the temperance sentiment, in order to get his barn raised at all.

The accounts kept of a distillery at West Newbury, from 1811 to 1813, reveal some curious things. A well known citizen, a pillar in the town and church, who kept a tavern, was credited to thirty-seven gallons of whiskey. In December, 1812, Daniel Lindsey began to work eight months for Daniel Eastman, for twelve gallons of whiskey a month. It is not probable that he drank any part of this. He simply took his pay in what was, in those days, an article of commerce, and no more was thought of it than if he had taken it in wheat.

There is a curious bill extant entitled:

"To sundry expenses against the commissioners of the estate of Peletiah Bliss, 1798.

	L.	S.	D.		L.	S.	D.
to one pint brandy,	0.	3.	0.	to five meals,	0.	7.	6.
to five meals,	0.	7.	6.	to ½ mug tod,	0.	0.	9.
to ½ pint brandy,	0.	1.	6.	to mug Cyder,	0.	1.	4.
to ½ mug Flip,	0.	0.	9.	to pint brandy,	0.	1.	6.
to three meals,	0.	4.	6.	to pint of wine,	0.	2.	0.
to ½ pint brandy,	0.	1.	6.	to four meals,	0.	6.	0.
to horses kept,	0.	6.	2.	to pint wine,	0.	2.	0.
Amounting to £2. 2s. 4d.							

William Wallace, Isaac Bayley and Asa Tenney were the commissioners, and the spirits were set before the people who had business with them. The bill rendered by Col. Thomas Johnson in 1801, against the committee who built the "old court house" included a charge of £9. 16s. 8d. for rum.

It was many years after that before the temperance reform began, and even as late as 1833, the New Hampshire Courier, speaking of the commencement exercises at Dartmouth College in that year says: "The most striking feature of this annual college celebration, and the one which appears most prominent in the eyes of a stranger, is the shocking extent to which vice and intoxication are carried on by the assembled crowd. The common was covered with a complete hurly-burly of peddlers, auctioneers, tippling booths and travelling shows. More than twenty different gambling establishments were to be seen in operation on the open common at one view."

The annual musters and June trainings were seasons of

drunkenness. At the muster in 1821, the bill for treating the regiment, of about 600 men, was $21.25—about one gallon of spirits to each thirty men. The handbill for an auction in Haverhill, in 1832, contains the announcement that a barrel of choice whiskey would be opened for the benefit of purchasers. Mr. David Eastman thinks that at a certain store at West Newbury, after 1841, a hundred barrels of rum were sold in ten years. It is by such facts as these that we may mark the progress and operation of the temperance reform, which began about 1840.

Mr. Livermore says that at Haverhill Corner in 1820, and for the next decade, there was more or less drinking among the members of the bar, and decanters of rum and brandy were always in evidence in the parlor of the boarding-house, and on the dinner table. There was an old lawyer named Moody, from Strafford county, whose invariable formula, after summoning the waiter, with a rap of his cane, to the foot of the stairs, was to order: "Waiter, bring a bottle of rum, a bottle of brandy, a pitcher of water, a bowl of sugar, four teaspoons, and a pack of cards!"

The earliest records that are preserved of the First Congregational church in this town, show very plainly how prevalent the vice was in those days, by frequent mention of prominent members being censured for drunkenness. The temperance reform was not altogether the work of churches or associations, or brought about by the arguments of reformers. People began to think for themselves upon the miseries which were wrought by the traffic, and their convictions made themselves felt in the form of laws, which should restrict and eventually forbid its sale.

The cause was half won when drinking became unpopular, when it was to a man's discredit that he drank, and loss of standing that he sold liquor. There is still liquor drank, and men who get drunk, and there are a few old men who were brought up when drinking habits were universal, and who take an occasional glass. But, generally speaking, the present representatives of the class of men who drank seventy years ago, are total abstainers now. Various temperance organizations have flourished for a time, in this town, of which no particular account has been obtained.

CHAPTER XXXIV.

METEOROLOGICAL.

DAVID JOHNSON'S JOURNAL.— COL. THOMAS JOHNSON'S JOURNAL OF THE SEASONS.— THE WINTER OF 1780.— SNOW STORMS.— FRESHETS.— THE CLOUD-BURST OF 1795.— COLD YEARS.— THE SNOW STORM OF 1834.— THE DARK DAY OF 1780.— THE YELLOW DAY OF 1881.— THE METEORIC SHOWER OF 1833.— THE COMET OF 1857.

MENTION of a weather chapter for this history to one of the oldest men in town elicited the remark, that "There has been a good deal of weather here in Newbury." No one will attempt to gainsay this, and the object of this chapter is to collect and preserve data regarding remarkable storms and other phenomena. There was an old farmer in this town, dead now these thirty years, who used to say that there had been no really good weather since Andrew Jackson's day. These have been gathered from a great variety of sources, old newspapers, diaries, town histories, memoranda in old account books, and the like. One unique record, consisting of notes made by Colonel Thomas Johnson is given entire. It is, probably, the earliest weather record ever made in this part of the country.

A still more remarkable register was kept by his son, David Johnson, from May 1, 1835, to January 1, 1859. In this he noted, daily, the height of the thermometer, at 6 A. M., noon, and 6 P. M.; the direction of the wind; the appearance of the clouds; the fall of rain or the depth of snow; the coming of the earliest birds. and the southward flight of the wild geese; the dates of opening and closing of the river; and any observations or comparisons which occurred to him. He also mentions the earliest date in the season when there was snow on Moosilauke; the time and appearance of the Aurora Borealis; the sight of comets, meteors and the like. When he was from home or ill, some one of the family made these observations for him. At the end of each year, he posted up the weather account, with as much care and method as he did those of his own business. One would suppose that Mr. Johnson had nothing else to do but look after the weather. Toward the end of his life, some of his observations were published, and attracted the attention and correspondence of scientific men.

Some facts communicated by him in January, 1857, to the New York Times, at the request of Lieutenant M. F. Maury of the Smithsonian Institute, seemed to him to call for a word of apology. "In conclusion it may be as well to observe that for the absence of scientific accuracy in these crude sketches, the writer may be allowed to plead, in excuse, that they were made by an unlettered old man, in the seventy-ninth year of his age, but who is blessed with eyesight to see to read and write without the aid of spectacles."

Had Mr. Johnson given his observations a wider range, with the flavor of reminiscence and anecdote, which he could have imparted, he might have produced something not unlike the "Natural History of Selborne." The following "Journal of the Seasons," is given without change or omission, but the spelling and use of capitals are modernized. A note in the hand-writing of David Johnson would imply that it was publshed in the Regent's Report of the state of New York for 1852.

In the year 1773 the wheat was headed out in June, 10th day.

June 10th. This night there was an uncommon great frost, killed a considerable part of the Indian corn so that it never grew again.

June the 11th. This night there fell a snow two inches deep.

November 13, 1782. This day began to fodder cattle. This night the river froze over in some places.

November 29. Very cold.

December 1st. Very warm weather.

December 6th. Cold sharp weather two days. Warm weather one week.

December 12th. Cold time.

December 30th. Snow fell this day.

February 2nd, 1783. This a very cold day.

February 17th. This day the great rain began and rained three days. This month more than common warm.

March 10th. This one of the coldest days that ever I knew.

March 29th. Three very warm days. This day heavy thunder.

March 30th. This day the river broke up. This night the frogs peeped.

April 16 and 17. Uncommon hot for the time of year.

April 25th. This day the apple tree blows out to be seen.

May 18th. This evening there fell the heaviest shower we ever knew. The river raised fifteen or sixteen feet, flowed the ploughed land.

August 9th. This day was the coldest that had been at that season for seventy-five years. The frost hath done great damage in many places killing almost all the corn and sauce—had it not been for the fog I think that we should have lost a great part of our corn.

September 10. The rain began at this time and continued till the 19th of October without giving us more than two days at a time of fair weather. Then there fell a snow at the height of land about knee deep with a most violent storm here—about three inches. The snow went off with a great rain which made a great freshet the 23rd of this month—October. Then we had one week of fair weather.

November 28. This day there fell a small snow and winter set in.

November 30. This day and night there fell a deep snow.

December 1. This one of the most blustering days that ever I knew.

Uncommon pleasant weather till the last of December.

January, 1784. Severe and still cold weather till the last of February. Then warm and pleasant. The middle of March the snow was all gone.

April 1. Pleasant weather. The 8th day the weather turned cold. Three days severe cold.

April 14 and 15. Rained steady, 16th, snowed all day. Snow fell one-half foot deep.

June 28. About this time the weather was exceeding hot.

July 15. A severe drouth about this time.

July 25. A great plenty of rain about this time.

October and November. The pleasantest weather that ever was known.

December 3. This day fell the greatest quantity of rain that ever I knew in the time. The river rose fifteen feet in one night. The winter set in late.

April 10, 1785. This day the snow was two feet deep in the Ox-bow.

The winter past hath been the most moderate, altho the snow hath been four feet.

April 20, 1785. The old snow not being gone, there fell a snow about six inches deep.

April 24. This day the river broke up and the ice went clear.

April 28. This day I went into the Ox-bow and the snow was so deep in the road that I could not ride in the road. Some places the drifts were three feet deep.

1785. This is a very cold summer.

October 17. This night was the first frost to kill anything.

October 23. This day the great freshet was at the height which covered all the meadows—swept all the fences off.

November 20. About this time the ground froze up.

December 4. This day the snow fell to make sledding.

March 22, 1786. This day the river broke up and the road began to settle.

March 26. This day the frogs began to sing.

April 2. This day there fell a snow one foot deep with the severest storm we had this winter.

June 8. Very hot weather.

June 17. This day finished molding.

August 23. The frost killed things on the high land. This month exceeding cold.

September 12. Gathered my apples. The last of September and the first of October as hot weather as any we have had this summer.

November 15 and 16. At this time the river shut over and winter set in without rain and the streams the lowest or as low as ever was known.

December 9. This day fell a deep snow and not one day that it thawed since the 15th day of November. The best sledding this winter. Went to Portsmouth with my slay (sleigh) and returned the last day of December. Went to Portsmouth for the second time and returned the 26th of January.

May 20. The river broke up at this time but did not clear out till the last day of March.

April 9. This day began to plow and sow.

April 18, 19, 20, 21. These days have been the coldest weather that ever we would know at that season of the year. One of the coldest summers that we would know. A warm fall as we know. The first cold weather that came this winter was the first week in January, 1788.

1788. This spring rather cold and backward.

July 2nd. About this time I began to mow. Have been about two weeks trying to get hay with five or six hands. Have got three loads in and about eight or nine more in the field rotting. If the forepart of the day is ever so clear and fair it don't fail of raining by three o'clock in the afternoon.

July 26. This day fell such a quantity of rain that on the next day the river flowed the low meadows so that the hay was floated.

May 21, 1789. This day turned out cattle to pasture but poor feed and but just planting. No apple-tree blows to be seen yet.

November 3, 1789. This day fell snow over shoes and good sledding.

November 11. The pleasantest weather you ever saw.

December 22, 1794. Good plowing at this time, good boating on the river till the first of January, 1795.

The winter of 1761-62, when the men employed by Bayley and Hazen wintered at Coös, was long and cold, and the snow had not all disappeared in the woods, on the first of May. In August, 1764, there was a heavy frost, which froze the leaves on the trees, but the corn on the meadows was shielded by a fog.

The winter of 1780 was long and cold, and for forty successive days, including the entire month of March, the snow did not thaw on the south sides of buildings, as far south as Haverhill, Mass. It lay four feet deep in the fields, and was so hard that teams could travel about upon it over the fences in every direction.

There seems to have been no freshet of any magnitude from the first settlement till 1771, and the inhabitants felt secure upon the meadows. But after that experience most of the settlers removed to higher ground. A few, however, clung to the idea that the flood of that year would never be repeated. Colonel Johnson's record closes in 1794, and there is little to guide us for several years. On the 19th of February, 1802, says President Dwight, in writing in 1813 of this part of the country, a snow-storm began which lasted a week, and it was estimated that more than four feet fell. This storm was general throughout New England, and as far south as Rhode Island the snow was as deep as here.

In 1807 there was a freshet, and another in 1812. This last carried away every bridge on the river above Orford. The former flood exceeded, in the estimation of old people, everything which had been experienced before, and a mark made upon a rock near Colonel Tenney's was not again reached by the water until 1876. These freshets appear to have been produced by rains and the melting of deep snows in the north, and did not cause the local injury which was made by one in 1828, which was not exceeded till 1869. Great damage was caused along all the streams, and at Wells River several buildings were carried away, or were destroyed to give a passage to the flood. At the March meeting in 1829, the taxes of many who had suffered by the freshet were abated.

In January 1839, after a period of fine winter weather, a heavy rain set in, the night of the 25th and continued about thirty hours. "The river flowed one-third of the Ox-bow, and one-half of Cow meadow. The ice broke up, but did not clear out round the Ox-bow. Vast quantities of ice came down from above, mixed with wood and timber; thirty or forty acres in Cow meadow were covered with a mass of ice, wood and timber."

Nearly every year the rise of the river causes a flood upon the meadows and railroad travel has, more than once, been suspended for several days. On the 28th of April, 1850, a rain set in, and the river rose higher than before since 1807. The railroad was under water from where Alfred Chamberlin now lives to Ingalls hill, and the water rose to the thresholds of the windows of Edward Hale's house on Upper meadow. The winter of 1861-62 was memorable for depth of snow, and in the spring the water was again very high, and Bedell's bridge was carried away. But all previous damage by flood in this town was exceeded by the "great freshet" of 1869. The summer had been very wet, and on the 2d of October, heavy rain set in, which lasted two days. All the brooks in town were swollen to rivers, bridges were swept away, and many pieces of highway washed out. A second freshet on the 12th destroyed most of the repairs which had been made upon the roads. A tax of fifty-five cents on the dollar, to repair damages, was voted at a special town-meeting, November 8th. On the meadows the loss was great. The corn was nearly all cut and shocked, and it stood under water for a long time. It was a great task to get it dry after the river had subsided, as the ears and stalks were soaked, and covered with sand.

In 1876, after this part of the Connecticut valley had become dry and people had begun planting, heavy rains and melting snows in the mountains, caused a flood in which the river rose about eight inches above the highest water-mark before reached. The water was six inches deep on the kitchen floor of the house in which Charles C. Scales now lives, on the Upper meadow. In 1895, the spring freshet was very high, railroad travel was suspended for a few days, and the water stood nearly three feet deep in the bridge between Newbury and Haverhill.

In June, 1795, there was a heavy shower—perhaps what we should now call a cloudburst—on the hills around Harriman's brook, and that stream, swelled to a torrent, broke around the mill-dam, west of Newbury street, poured down the hill, and across what is now the common, and washed out a deep channel which began about where the fountain is, or used to be, and caused the "gulley" north of Mr. Cobleigh's house. The gulley was as deep as it now is east of the street, for some way on the common. Before that time, the plain was unbroken at that place. James Wilson, who came to Bradford in that month, stated in a paper of reminiscence, which he drew up in his old age, that the water in the river was discolored by the mud from that wash-out for many miles.

A special town-meeting was warned to be held on the 1st of September: "To see if the town will bridge over the Gulley, or

turn the road back of Capt. Lovewell's barn." It was voted—
"That the road nigh Capt. Lovewell's shall continue where it was
always trod" and a bridge was built across the chasm. When the
seminary building was erected the part of the gulley upon the
common was filled in by the town, at a cost of $700.

In our northern latitude unseasonable storms are long
remembered. During several years, from 1812 to 1818, the
seasons were cold and the times were hard. The year 1816 was
known as the "cold year," and the "famine year." The season was
early, and planting was well advanced by the 15th of May. But
the summer was very cold and there was frost in every month.
Moosilauke was white twice in July and three times in August. On
the 5th of June, some masons who were building a brick house at
Bath Upper Village, were compelled to abandon their work until
the 10th as the mortar froze in the open air. Thermometers had
not then come into general use, but it was afterwards believed that
the temperature was not much above zero. The corn was entirely
destroyed in that year—only a few saved enough for seed by
maintaining fires around their corn fields. James Works of
Waterford went down to Connecticut and brought up a large
quantity of corn in a flatboat, to Newbury, which he sold for $2.50
per bushel, the common price at that period being about fifty
cents. Money was very scarce and provisions were so dear that
some people suffered from hunger. A daughter of Thomas Brock
was married in that year, and the family, although well-to-do, were
hard pressed to provide the young lady with a suitable outfit.

"May 15th, 1817," says an entry in an old account-book kept
by Robert Barnett, "snow fell three inches deep at the Upper
meadow, and in Orange it fell six inches deep, and so cold as to
freeze potatoes which were planted."

"June 16th there was a very hard frost which froze potatoes to the ground."

On the 15th of May, 1834, occurred the great snow-storm
which is a landmark in the memory of old people. An entry in an
account-book kept by Jonas Tucker of West Newbury is as follows:

"Snow fell from daylight to ten o'clock two feet deep, on higher land it fell two
and a half—had it not settled it would probably have been from two and a half to
three and a half deep. For about two hours it gained an inch in each ten minutes.
16th May. The earth was completely covered with snow all day.
17th, Bare spots appeared."

The season was an early one. Plum and apple trees were in
blossom before the middle of May, but on the 13th it grew suddenly
cold, and people along the river road planted corn with their
mittens on. The snow was damp and broke down trees badly. It
grew cold after the storm, and water froze hard in the houses, and
as far south as Concord, icicles two feet long, were formed. On the
heights, east of Haverhill Corner, over three feet of snow fell. At

Burlington the storm lasted about twenty-four hours. The stage from Burlington to Haverhill went all the way on runners. The stage from Montpelier to Danville stuck in the snow, and had to be abandoned. The third day was warm, and the snow was all gone before dark. The small streams were swollen to a great height, but the river was not much affected. In spite of the storm, 1834 was "a great fruit year."

There has not since, been such an untimely storm. Many anecdotes are remembered by aged people, of cattle and sheep lost and perishing in the snow, and, in not a few instances, men who went to search for them became bewildered, and relief parties had to be organized to find them.

The winters of 1843 and 1850 were extremely cold, as was that of 1854. There were twenty mornings in February of the latter year, when the mercury was below zero. July and August were very dry. There was a heavy fog nearly every morning, but no rain, and very little fell during the fall. Fire, started in the swamp on Leighton hill, east of the farms of J. F. George and Mrs. Wheeler, destroyed a large amount of timber, and all the men in the vicinity were called out to fight the fire, on the 22d, 23d and 24th of August.

The 5th, 6th, and 7th of February, 1855, were believed by the oldest people to be the coldest days known since the town was settled. The mercury fell to −36° at the Ox-bow, and, on the 7th, the highest point reached was −17°. The day was windy, and there were many sufferers by the cold. At Boston the thermometer indicated −20°, at New York −7°, at Philadelphia −6°, and at Washington −3°. The winter of 1874 was remarkable for its length. On the 1st of May, the snow was still deep, and people did not gather in their sugar tools till after the 10th, and there was sugar made in this town after the 15th. But if we have had long winters and untimely snow-storms, we have also had winters of unusual mildness, and, more than once, the ground has entirely thawed out, and people have done plowing in midwinter.

On the 18th of January, 1817, when the snow was very deep, there was a thunder-storm in the night which lasted two hours, and many buildings were burned by lightning, in different parts of New England. In the evening of March 14, 1850, there was a heavy thunder-shower. The snow was deep, and the previous day was the first mild day of the spring. Several buildings have been struck by lightning and burned in this town, but so far as known, no life has been lost from that cause.

It seems singular that Colonel Johnson makes no mention of the famous "Dark Day" which occurred May 19, 1780. For several days previous, the air was full of smoke, and on the morning of the 19th there was, here in Newbury, a light shower, with some thunder. About ten o'clock it began to grow dark, and before noon it became so dark that one could not see to read in the open air, and all visible objects assumed strange colors. Fowls went to roost, small birds flew into the houses, as if seeking the protection of men, and cattle came home from the pastures, uttering strange cries of distress. Candles were lighted in the houses, and in places where there were churches, multitudes flocked to them, thinking that the end of the world had come. In the afternoon it rained, and the water which fell was discolored, as if mixed with soot. By four o'clock, it was as dark as it usually is at midnight, when there is no moon, and candles and torches burned with great brilliancy. It was the night of the full moon, but it was so dark that a sheet of white paper, held before the eyes, was invisible. Very few people slept that night, but sat up, and "watched for the morning," which was remarkably clear, the sun rising in cloudless splendor. A great deal has been written about this occurrence, which is generally believed to have been caused by combined thick clouds and dense smoke. It did not extend much beyond the Hudson, and was darkest in southern New England. It was not as dark here in Newbury, but it was dense enough to be remembered as one of the remarkable events in the memories of old people fifty years ago.

November 2, 1819, another dark day occurred, which recalled that of 1780. Candles were lighted in many of the houses at noon, but the obscurity passed away before evening.

September 6, 1881, is celebrated in meteorological annals, as the "Yellow Day." This day was also very dark, and in houses and mills artificial light was used. The most remarkable feature was the strange colors which all objects assumed, yellow taking the mastery of all the rest, producing strange effects upon familiar objects. Kerosene and gas burned with intense brilliancy, like electric lights, and all outlines in the open air seemed to waver and grow indistinct. The air was very moist; the temperature about 75°; the wind was north, and blew moderately. Toward evening these appearances gradually passed away.

The meteoric shower of November 13, 1833, was one of the most wonderful sights ever witnessed. The night was perfectly clear, and about ten o'clock the display began. Thousands of meteors fell, some of them with dazzling brilliancy. The flashing was incessant, many at the same instant falling in all directions. People were awakened from sleep by the glare, and the superstitious thought that the end of the world had come. The comet of 1857 was hardly less wonderful. When most brilliant, the head of the comet was at the zenith, while the tail had not all risen over the northern hills, and was in breadth about equal to one degree of the horizon. It was so bright that one could easily read by its light, and the shadows of objects were cast southward. It also passed away, but to the ignorant it was an object of dread, portentous of some great calamity in the universe.

CHAPTER XXXV.

A Chapter of Local History.

Boltonville.—Whitelaw's Journal.—Mills.—Dea. Andrew Brock.—The Boltons.—Present Mills.—Residents There in 1832.—The Lime Kiln Neighborhood.—First Settlers.—Schools.—Lime Burning.—Religious History.—The Swamp Road Fight.—The Grow and Doe Neighborhoods.—Disappearance of Families.

THIS paper is compiled from an article upon Boltonville prepared several years ago by Mrs. Lydia S. Bolton; from a later paper by Mrs. N. Robinson; from information by Mr. Edward Miller, and from an account written by Mr. E. G. Parker upon the business men and farmers in Boltonville, in 1832.

The first mention of the place now called Boltonville is found in General Whitelaw's Journal, and is as follows:

"About the beginning of January, 1775, James Whitelaw purchased the part of lot 120 in Newbury that lies north of Wells River, with one-half the privilege of the river, to build milns for the company and James Henderson began to block out wood for building them. About the middle of August we raised the frame of the grist-miln and first framed house, and about the beginning of October we raised the sawmiln.

"Oct. 28, 1775. We set the grist-miln running.

"July 1, 1776. Alarm came of St. Johns being retaken by the regulars, and that Indians would be sent through to lay waste the country; all the people in Ryegate moved down to Newbury where they had more company, but after about ten days, and seeing no appearance of danger returned home. A few days later we set the sawmiln going, which answers its end very well."

This land, and water privilege, was bought by the Scots American Company which settled Ryegate, because they found they had, in that town, no stream of water sufficient for mills. The frame of the first sawmill stood where the grist-mill shed now stands.

BELOW THE FALLS,
BOLTONVILLE.

BOLTONVILLE.

James Ferguson was the first miller. The first dwelling-house was occupied by Dea. Andrew Brock. These were the first buildings in the place. This water privilege is the best on Wells River, the stream falling about sixty feet in the course of six or eight rods, the last fall being about thirty feet.

Later, James Smith bought of Josiah Little the remainder of lot No. 120, lying on the south side of Wells River, and built his house on the plain, back of where Mr. Sly's house now stands, and the first road to Jefferson hill passed by it, and went over the great hill to the present corner of the Jefferson hill, and Scotch Hollow roads.

On the 23d of May, 1787, the Scots American company sold the mills, with the land that lies in Newbury, and two lots adjoining, in Ryegate, with a reserve of the pine lumber for the company's use, to Dea. Andrew Brock, and at this time the name of "Brock's Falls" was given the place. In our earlier town records, it is called "Whitelaw's Mills."

About 1809 the grist-mill and sawmill were burned, but Deacon Brock at once set about rebuilding them, and soon had a new grist-mill completed, and set running. About 1812 there was a room finished off in the mill, and a carding machine put in.

About 1817 Deacon Brock died, and from his estate in March, 1820, John Bolton of Danville bought the grist-mill and carding-mill, and the land lying west of it in Newbury. The next month, William Bolton, then a young man, moved his family into the place. In the fall of 1820, John Bolton bought of Thomas Eames of Wells River, all the right he owned in the fulling-mill, which stood where the grist-mill shed now stands with the right of drawing water from the grist-mill flume. In the spring of 1826, John Bolton commenced erecting a building for carding and cloth dressing.

In the spring of 1827, the machinery was taken out of the grist-mill, removed to the factory, and Mr. Gardner carried on the business there. In the spring of 1829, the old Brock grist-mill was torn down, and the present one, built by John and William Bolton, at a cost of $4,000, was set running on the 29th of September the same year. In 1835, John Waddell bought of John Bolton the water privilege at the head of the great falls, erected a house and shop, together, for the manufacture of furniture and general repairing, and occupied it until his decease. In 1843 John Bolton died, and the property he owned in Newbury was, by will, left to his son, William, and the wife of his son Luther. In 1853 William Bolton took down the old house which Deacon Brock built in 1775, and built the one in which Mr. Robinson now lives, very near where it stood.

In 1863 H. K. Worthley bought the grist-mill owned by William Bolton, and kept it in his hands until December, 1887, when it was sold to Freeman P. Tucker. At the latter's death it passed into the hands of his brother, Samuel A. Tucker.

In the year 1831 a mail route was established from Wells River to West Topsham, through Groton, and a petition was sent to Washington for a post office at what had been known as Brock's Falls. At the suggestion of Mr. Robert Whitelaw, the name of the place was called Boltonville, and William Bolton was the first postmaster. He resigned the office in 1841, and Thomas Wasson was appointed in his place, which he held until the office was discontinued. In 1863 it was re-established, and H. K. Worthley, F. P. Tucker, and S. A. Tucker have since held the office. The carding-mill and farm are now owned by Charles S. Bolton. Thus far the narrative of Mrs. Bolton.

Mr. Parker tells us of the residents of Boltonville in 1832:—

John Waddell ran a wheelwright and carpenter's shop in the basement of the factory building, later he built the house and shop, (now owned by Mr. Sargent, and used as cider mill, etc.,) and continued the same business until his death. Jacob W. Sulham was the village shoemaker; he owned, and lived in a house where Mr. Sargent's house now stands. As was the custom, Mr. Sulham went from house to house with his "kit" of tools, fitting and repairing boots and shoes for each member of the family. He also took his fiddle for evening entertainment, where the neighbors were sure to form a merry group around the tallow candles, to hear the fiddle talk. Israel Sly, the blacksmith, lived in the basement of William Bolton's house, on nearly the same site where N. Robinson now lives. He built the shop now standing near the iron bridge. Later he built the house on the hill, where his son Edwin now lives, working in the shop, and farming until his death. Mrs. Sly, his wife, lived with her son, Edwin, until her death, November 23, 1899. Jacob F. Paige, carpenter and joiner, lived in the house now owned by Mrs. Mary Hadlock. His shop was in the back part of his house, but his business and family increased so fast he was obliged to build a house and shop on land now owned by N. Robinson, the buildings long since torn down.

Samuel Boyce lived in a log house a little south of where D. B. Reid now lives, and raised a family of five boys and three girls. Horatio Stebbins lived on nearly the same site where Alonzo Boyce resides, carried on a small farm, and did blacksmith work in a shop near his house. Enoch Nelson owned the farm, and lived in the house which Lewis Hill now owns and occupies. His brother, Stephen Nelson, owned a large farm at the end of the road, beyond where Mrs. Stephen Putman now lives. Mr. Nelson was a successful farmer, an honest and respected citizen. William Gardner owned the Vance farm, and lived in a log house south of where Mr. Vance now lives. John McLure lived—and cleared up the farm— and built a set of buildings near where his sons James and Charles, now live. Mr. McLure was a staunch Presbyterian, and deacon of the church for many years; a hard-working, industrious farmer, accumulating quite a property. James Henderson, senior, built, about 1806, the house in which James Gardner now lives; and his son James built that in which Edwin Henderson and his mother reside, selling the old house and part of the farm to Hugh Gardner, father of the said James. A Mr. Quint owned and lived on the farm on the hill, where his son Josiah now lives; he also built a mill at the Quint place, so-called, where barley was hulled and oatmeal was made, doing a large business, as that was the only mill of the kind for miles around. James Foresythe lived on the farm now owned by Mrs. Cole and formerly, by the late Duncan Ritchie. Michael Cross lived on a small farm on the main road, at that time, leading to Jefferson Hill, and made baskets. Charles Wheeler, better known as "Uncle Charlie," owned a few acres of land a little off the main road, and gained a livelihood by hunting, fishing and trapping. William Randall, father of Moses Randall, owned a farm and lived on the hill back of where Moses Randall now lives.

The Methodist society held meetings in the summer seasons, in a barn on William Gardner's farm, near where James Vance now lives; afterwards in the hall of the factory building; later in a schoolhouse standing on the site of the M. & W. R. R. station.

School was held in a log schoolhouse, near where James Vance's sugar house now stands. In 1834 it was burned, and for several years school was held in different places in the district; in a room over John Waddell's shop; in the hall of factory building; and in Jacob F. Paige's shop, until the district could agree upon a building lot, for the schoolhouse above mentioned.

Along the west side of the town, from Ryegate line south, lies a deep valley, shut in on the west by the massive Topsham hills, and on the east by Jefferson hill, and the heights west of the Center, and Long pond. The west line of the "hundred acre lots" passes for several miles along the bottom of this valley, and the west side of it lies mostly within the "half mile strip," or "Whiting's Gore." About midway lie two small ponds. The outlet from one of them, called Scott's brook, finds its way down the valley northward, to Wells river at South Ryegate. The water from the south of these ponds follows the valley southwest into Topsham, and Tabor branch of Wait's river, by a small stream called the Levi brook. The soil along the valley is of limestone formation, deep and productive. The farms which cling to the hills on the west, are among the best in town, and the locality is noted for its orchards, and its excellent pasturage.

This part of the town, once called the Nourse neighborhood, and often, District No. 12, is more generally designated as the "Lime Kiln." It was long somewhat isolated from the rest of the town, its only outlet, except through Topsham, being the road across the hills to Newbury village, seven miles away. Consequently it has a history and annals which are all its own, and somewhat of these have been gathered for this chapter, by Mr. Henry Whitcher, Mr. C. B. Fisk, and Mr. Thomas P. Bailey. There is material of tale and legend among the hills of this town to furnish a volume for a novelist.

The first settlers came about 1789, and made clearings in the dense woods. Among them were John McAlvin, Adam Salter, David Pulsifer, Stephen Chase, Mason Randall, and Josiah Newton. The first recorded deed was from Mason Randall to Jeremiah and David Nourse, May 9, 1803, and the second, September 5, 1803, from Stephen Chase to Josiah Newton, who conveyed, in July, 1815, to Robert Johnston, the same farm, which is now the homestead of Henry Whitcher.

Most of the families which were prominent there fifty years ago, came after residing some years in Ryegate or Groton. The Whitcher and Renfrew families came that way; the Eastmans from New Hampshire; the Nourse and Boynton people from Windham County. Some of the early families came over from Topsham.

For a few years the children of that locality attended school in Topsham, it being a union district, the schoolhouse standing on the edge of the lonely burial ground which lies high among the hills on the old Topsham road. In 1807, District No. 12 was established, and a schoolhouse was afterward built on the Nourse farm, near the small cemetery there. Later a schoolhouse was erected near Isaac Eastman's which was remodelled in 1889, at an expense of about $800, and is used also for religious meetings.

Some time near 1829, John Botten began the manufacture of lime, which was carried on later by Charles George, who did a large business until 1836 or '37, when he sold out to Isaac Eastman, who continued the work about twenty years, until competition from lime brought by railroad ruined the business, as the new quality was whiter. Mr. Eastman made, in some years, about 3,000 bushels of lime, which was used in all the region, and walls plastered with it sixty years ago are still firm.

Isaac Olmsted, in 1830, began the making of chairs, which he carried on some three years. Josiah Dow and Samuel Eastman were shoemakers. George Cook was a blacksmith for some time about 1841. David Chase, and his son-in-law, W. B. Stevens, were coopers. In 1846-8 William H. Nourse built a sawmill in the north end of the district, which did a good business for several years. In 1838 there were, in that part of the town set off as district No. 12, in 1807, seventeen families which embraced 115 persons, and sent thirty-four scholars to school. In the same region there are now twelve families and forty-five persons, with seven children of school

Photo. by Corliss.

NEWBURY TOWN HOUSE.

Photo. by Corliss.

IN THE LIME KILN NEIGHBORHOOD.

age. The present bounds of the district contain twenty-two families, with ninety-two inhabitants, and twenty children who attended school. Several well known teachers came from this locality, and two or three college graduates.

The religious history of this part of the town is somewhat peculiar, as it is remote, and no church was ever organized there. There have always been members of several churches in the vicinity who lived at the Lime Kiln, and religious services have been held a part of the time during the past eighty years. Rev. Daniel Batchelder from Corinth, who built up a large Free Will Baptist church in that town, labored there successfully about 1815, and later. Rev's Paul Richmond and William Peck gained converts to the Methodist church by their fervent preaching. Rev. Clark Perry, and others of the Congregational order, held many services there. After the opening of Newbury Seminary, the zeal of both professors and students led them to that valley, and stated services were long held, and a Sunday school was in very successful operation. There were always good singers in that neighborhood, and the fine singing drew encomiums from Bishop Baker. In 1842, an Adventist preacher by the name of Staples came, and held large grove meetings, predicting the exact time of the end of the world. But the date which he had set for the final consummation having passed with no manifest change in the operations of the universe, the excitement which he produced soon died away, and the preacher departed. Representatives of seven shades of doctrines reside in that neighborhood at the present time.

This fragment of local history must also include mention of a controversy called the "Swamp Road fight." This road, which begins at the old Burbank mill site on Scott's brook, near South Ryegate, follows this stream across a cedar swamp to a point on the Levi brook road near David Lumsden's, and was built in 1860. It is about two miles and three-quarters long. Before that road was built the residents there could get their produce to market only by the roundabout road through Topsham, Corinth and Bradford, or by choice of climbing over Jefferson hill, or the hills toward Newbury street. It took six years of struggle to get the much-needed road surveyed and built.

A petition with about 200 names attached, dated September 30, 1854, was presented to the selectmen, who were A. B. W. Tenney, John B. Carleton and Joseph Smith, praying them to lay out and build this road. This they refused to do, as did another board a year or two later, on the ground that the road would benefit Corinth, Topsham and Ryegate more than it would Newbury, and recommended that a Courts Commission be appointed, with power to assess those towns to help build the road. Accordingly a petition was presented to the court, and Stephen Thomas, A. H. Gilmore and John B. Peckett were appointed as a commission. They viewed the proposed route, and after holding several hearings, decided that the road should be built, and that Ryegate and Topsham should be assessed forty per cent of the cost. This decision aroused much opposition among the largest taxpayers of these towns, who were not much interested in the building of a road which lay in a remote corner of Newbury, and much more bitterness was engendered there than the affair would seem to have warranted. Seventeen meetings of the commission were held, at which the petitioners were represented by Hon. C. B. Leslie, assisted by Robert Ormsby and J. W. Batchelder. The towns employed counsel to oppose the building of the road, and many were bitterly opposed to it who knew little or nothing about the matter. But the petitioners were in the end triumphant, and Mr. Whitcher, who, with Thomas P. Bailey, managed their cause, were successful in stopping the opposition of Topsham, and Col. Horatio Brock being town agent in 1859, having satisfied himself of the necessity of the road, recommended the building of it. At that time, Ephraim Bailey, T. P. Bailey, and Charles H. George, lived on the line of the proposed road, and were not near anyone already built. He directed that the road should be built, which was done, and completed in November, 1860.

The building of the railroad through South Ryegate brought this locality nearer a market, and the swamp road is now one of the most travelled in town, and not expensive to keep in repair.

Before closing the account of this controversy it is proper to say that while there were plenty of people who were perfectly willing to do all the talking which was called for, and more, the financial load was carried by a few, and the survivors wish their names preserved. They were: Henry Whitcher, Ephraim Bailey, T. P. Bailey, James Peach, C. H. George, Isaac Eastman, John Peach, John Weed, Levi James, Nelson Renfrew, James Crawford, Thomas Wormwood and William Hunter of Newbury, George Hall, James White and J. B. Darling of Ryegate, S. F. McAllister, W. T. George, Lyman Batchelder and Valentine Weed of Topsham.

There was a prospect, at one time, that the Montpelier and Wells River railroad would be built up Scott's brook, thence to East Corinth, and through the vicinity of the copper mines, but nothing came of it.

Newbury is such a large town in area, that the Grow and Doe neighborhoods, in the southwestern corner, are more than twelve miles from Wells River by the nearest roads. Settlements, however, began in that part of the town much earlier than in other sections which are now more thickly settled. Settlements began in Topsham, just beyond the Newbury line in 1781, on what was soon known as Chamberlain hill, and is now oftener called Currier hill. Eighty years ago that locality, on both sides of the line, was quite densely populated; there was a store and a tavern on Currier hill, and trainings were long held on the old Chamberlain farm. The first settlers of Topsham were a fine race of people, and more than one man of national fame has come from that town. *In both the Doe and Grow neighborhoods, were early established several families of marked individuality, who were of good standing in the town, and acquired considerable wealth. Among these were the Grow, Putnam and Chapman families, of the first settlers, and the Fultons, Emersons and others, later comers. Doe, Clark and Corliss, were the most common names in the other school district, with the Renfrews, who came later. There was a fine Scotch element here, and some of the most prominent men in town affairs have lived in this locality.

This section of Newbury is drained by branches of Waits river, and its inhabitants receive their mail at East Corinth. Many families, which in the early decades of the century were prominent around West Newbury, have entirely disappeared before the end of it. The Carters and the Haseltines are all gone, and only one family keeps up the Rogers name.

If no other value belongs to the present volume, it will preserve the names and deeds of these, and other families—the substantial people of Newbury in their time.

---

*NOTE. President Gates of Iowa College is a native of Topsham, and Rev. Alvi T. Twing, D. D., secretary of the Missionary Society of the Episcopal church from 1866, till his death in 1882, was also born in that town.

CHAPTER XXXVI.

MERCHANTS AND BUSINESS MEN OF NEWBURY.

COL. WILLIAM WALLACE is understood by Mr. Perry to have opened, about 1775, the first store in Newbury, in a building which stood near Mr. Lawrie's house. A few years later he removed this building, which he considerably enlarged, to the site now occupied by the library. When he erected the house which afterward became the Spring Hotel, he removed this building to the other side of the street, where it still stands, the back part of the old "Newbury House."

Col. Thomas Johnson was a merchant as well as an innkeeper, and kept store in a building now used as a corn barn by Mr. Weed. He afterward fitted up a wing to his house for that purpose. This, long after removed, is the kitchen part of Mr. James Lang's house. His son David Johnson succeeded him in the business, which they had for some time carried on together, and built the brick building, now the residence of Mr. Southworth, in which he did business until within a year or two of his death. A clerk of Colonel Johnson's a century ago, named Tural Tufts, wrote a beautiful hand, and kept writing-school winters.

Of other than these, as traders, we have very little account. One John McLain is mentioned often in the early annals as a merchant, but who he was, or where he traded, are uncertain. He

---

NOTE. It was intended that this paper should follow that of Mr. Leslie upon Wells River. But many desired particulars could not be obtained then, and other chapters were substituted. It is to be regretted that some one, to whom the history of the village is as familiar as that of Wells River is to Mr. Leslie, had not prepared this chapter.

must have been here several years, a century and more ago. One Stickney, or, perhaps, two brothers of the name, carried on business here about the time of the war of 1812. There were, probably, others, whose names have not come down to us, who did a mercantile business in the earlier decades of the century.

In 1820, Dr. Luther Jewett had a drug-store in his house—the one under the great elm south of the cemetery. In the '90's Nathan Coverly, Jr., kept a book and stationery store in connection with his printing office, which was in a building nearly opposite where the late Miss Swasey lived. James Spear, who built and owned what is now Montebello House, was a hatter, and had a shop in a small building which stood near it, in which he kept the post office for some time. The present Congregational parsonage was a grocery in the early '30s, and afterwards became a tailor's shop. Hon. Joseph Berry is advertised in the Democratic Republican about the same time as keeping a book-store.

About 1830, Simeon and Austin Avery erected a large building for the Tyson Furnace Company of Plymouth, Vt. This was intended as a place for the storage and sale, for this region, of their plows and stoves, and was called the "Depot Building." Mr. Peter Wheelock was the Company's agent for some time. This building stood between T. C. Keyes's house and the town clerk's office; was very large, standing with its end to the street, and, in front was much like Keyes's store. The lower floor was divided by a hall which ran the whole length of the building, and there was another on the second floor. There were always several families living there, and a number of small stores were opened in it—and closed. Paul McKinstry carried on the stove and hardware business there, for many years. Hayes & Co. had their printing office in that building, and Mr. McIndoe began there the publication of the "Aurora." On the second floor Simeon Shepardson took photographs and ambrotypes, in the '50's and '60's. This building was burned in the fire of 1876.

Where the town clerk's office now stands, William K. Wallace had a small building in which he carried on the watch and clock business. Burnham Shepard succeeded him, who sold to S. L. Swasey, in 1875.

There was a building on the corner where James B. Hale's store now is, as early as 1810. Timothy Morse came here about 1815, and remained here till his death, nearly fifty years later. He built the store on the corner last mentioned, which was burned in 1876. He was a very active, energetic man, who always had several lines of business in his hands at a time. Mr. Morse was a brother of Robert Morse, a well known innkeeper at Rumney, and largely engaged in the stage business. Timothy Morse married a daughter of Cotton Haines of Rumney, the wives of Seth Greenleaf and W. W. Simpson, well known stage proprietors and drivers, being sisters of Mrs. Morse. Mr. Greenleaf was the first conductor on the old Boston, Concord and Montreal railroad, and was employed in that capacity till 1868. Mr. C. H. Greenleaf of the Profile House is his son.

Dennison R. Burnham came here about 1830, and his first partner, in the Morse building, was a Mr. Skinner. This partnership did not last long, for Mr. Morse bought Mr. Skinner out, and the firm became Morse & Burnham. James M. Chadwick, who had been their clerk, came into the firm, and they had a branch store at South Newbury, in the house now that of Mr. A. B. Rogers. Later Mr. Burnham removed to Plymouth, N. H., and kept the Pemigewasset House, until it was burned, in October, 1862. Carlos M. Morse, son of Timothy, bought out Mr. Chadwick, and had Anson M. Stevens as a partner for some two years. After carrying on the store alone about a year, Mr. Morse sold out to Henry H. Deming, in 1862.

Timothy Morse was one of the most active business men Newbury ever had. His plans embraced a great variety ot ventures, many of which were successful, and others were not. He owned the great meadow farm which is now that of Frank E. Kimball, and usually had some building operation going on. He built the brick part of the old Newbury House, the brick house in which the Leslie family live, that of S. L. Swasey and that of C. F. Darling, and others. He was largely influential in erecting the Methodist church building in 1829. There had been much controversy and some bitterness about the old meeting-house between the two religious societies, but Mr. Morse was far-sighted enough to see that it was for the interest of the Methodist society that it should have a house of worship of its own. The event proved his sagacity, as one of the motives which operated largely in securing the establishment of Newbury Seminary here was the fact that the society had a good church building.

Mr. Deming came from St. Johnsbury, and carried on that store till 1882. The later years, his son, Charles H. Deming, was his partner, and, before the store was sold to James B. Hale, in 1882, C. H. Deming had carried on the business alone. Mr. Hale has now been in trade on that corner eighteen years. About the time Mr. Deming came here, Mr. Chadwick erected a small building in front of his house, which was the one in which Mrs. Jacob Worthen lives, and in which he kept a general store till a few years before he died. This store is now the middle part of that in which Silsby & Knight have their grocery and feed business. After Mr. Chadwick, Ezra A. Day, now of Worcester, Mass., kept store there, the building being moved to the site of Silsby & Knight's store. Horace W. Bailey came into it a year or two after Mr. Day went away, and kept groceries and feed. He erected the front part of that building. Before the fire of 1876, there was a long, two story

RESIDENCE
OF
T. C. KEYES.

RESIDENCE OF MISS H. E. KEYES.   T C. KEYES'S STORE.

building, with a high basement, standing with its end to the street, between the house and the store of James B. Hale. It was an old building, and had many occupants. Deacon Swasey does not remember its erection or its builder. L. J. McIndoe had his printing office in it, after he went out of the depot building. He also had an excellent book-store, which his brother, Rev. David McIndoe, kept after him. Mr. James Smillie had his book-store there a few months in 1870-'71.

On the other side of the street, Col. William Wallace kept store in the back part of what is now called the "Old Newbury House," which, in 1834, his son, Moses Wallace, offered for sale, in the Democratic Republican. Timothy Morse built the brick part of that old hotel, and it was used for a tavern till about 1873. There was a brick blacksmith shop in those days, on the brow of the hill, back of Mr. M. A. Gale's house.

The business house now represented by Thomas C. Keyes, has existed longer than any other in this vicinity excepting, perhaps, that in Bradford of which J. B. W. Prichard is the present head, whose father, Col. George W. Prichard, began business there, in 1812.

Reed & Gould were general merchants in the building which is now the dwelling-house occupied by J. E. Worthen, and which then stood where Mr. Keyes's store now stands. In 1823, Freeman Keyes, then a young man of eighteen, came here from Vershire, as their clerk. In 1825, his brother Henry, then fifteen years old came, into that store. In 1829, Mr. Gould died, and Freeman was taken into the firm, which then became Reed & Keyes, and when Henry became of age, in 1831, the two brothers bought out Mr. Reed, and formed a partnership, under the firm name of F. & H. Keyes, which continued without interruption till 1854. During this time they built up one of the strongest mercantile firms in Orange county. From 1831 till after 1834, at least, the brothers conducted a branch store, in "Goshen," a few rods from the meeting-house. *The building was taken down about 1880. One of the brothers was usually in charge of this establishment, and it did a large business. It was called "Keyes's backstore." Mr. T. P. Hazelton was in charge of it at one time. In addition to their mercantile business they conducted other enterprises. After the death of Rasmus Jonson they bought the distillery, and converted the buildings into a tannery in which they did a fair amount of leather manufacture, making a market for hemlock bark.

In 1846, the Connecticut and Passumpsic railroad was begun. The firm commenced by subscribing $10,000 for stock, which was frequently increased as more money was needed. From that time

---

*Their first store was in Bradford, but they erected a building just on the Newbury side of the line. After some years they sold to William McDuffie.

Henry Keyes devoted most of his time to the railroad enterprise, leaving the management of the store to his brother. In 1854, the brothers dissolved partnership, Freeman taking the store, and Henry took the farm in Haverhill. This was the General Dow farm, which was owned by Mr. Dow and his heirs from 1785 to 1848, when it was sold to the C. & P. R. R. Co. to avert a suit for damages, threatened by the circumstance that the building of the embankment in the river, just above the point of rocks, on the Newbury side, had caused the river to wash away some part of the farm in Haverhill. This farm was bought by F. & H. Keyes in 1850. The firm was reconstructed under the name of F. & H. T. Keyes, the latter member being a younger brother, Horace T., who remained in the firm till 1872. In 1864, Thomas C. Keyes, son of Freeman, was admitted as a partner, the firm name being F. & H. T. Keyes & Co. In 1871, Freeman Keyes died, and, a year later T. C. Keyes assumed the management, which he still retains.

The present building was erected in 1840, and the old store was moved to its present site, the third building below the Keyes's store. The store was not closed during the moving of the building, but customers were let in and out of it by movable steps. John A. Meader was the master workman on the present building. The upper part was finished off for, and used as, a tenement.

The post office building was put up for a storehouse originally, with a hall above, which was used by the Sons of Temperance, "The Know-Nothings," and, later by the Masons, being called "Pulaski Hall." During the civil war this hall was used by the ladies who made supplies for the soldiers. During many years the upper part of the store was used for offices, tailor shops and the like, and the telegraph office was there till about 1862. In the long period—almost eighty years—in which the Keyes family has conducted the mercantile business in Newbury, a great many young men and boys entered their employment, and were trained toward the attainment of the success in business, which most of them secured.

Some particulars of clerkship are preserved which cast light upon the wages of the time:

In 1829 Royal Blake engaged to work one year in the store as clerk for $70, one-half cash and the other half goods at twenty-five per cent advance. In 1830, he left the store and went on the road, peddling goods for one-half the profits made after deducting the cost of freight, and all expenses. In 1845 Josiah Tilden came there to learn the business, and was to receive $35 the first year, and $10 in advance each following year. Several other young men entered the store from time to time, on similar terms.

About 1825, William Bailey bought the old "Lovewell Tavern stand," and with Dea. John Buxton as his partner, conducted a general store for some years.

Deacon Buxton was a harness maker, who, later, took his

apprentice, Ebenezer C. Stocker, into partnership.   Mr. Stocker carried on the business after Deacon Buxton retired, until he died, in 1892.

P. W. Ladd came from Haverhill in 1828, and after working many years at the blacksmith trade, went into the stove and tin ware business, in the building which Mr. Marcy uses for a carriage shop.

The building in which E. H. Farnham carries on the cabinet business, was built and after some years enlarged, by Mr. George Ropes, who came here about 1826, and married a daughter of John Johnson.   He did considerable business, and made many winnowing mills, some of which are still in use.

Evelyn H. Farnham made furniture and coffins, and did general repairing in that building, and his son, bearing the same name, is a cabinet maker, and has done a great deal of fine work in repairing and renovating antique furniture.

There has been no general store at South Newbury since the branch store of Morse & Burnham went out of trade.   Mr. Runnels has kept a grocery in his mill, since he came there, in 1881.   There was no merchant at West Newbury until Capt. Samuel Eastman began trade in 1841.   He built the store in which J. B. C. Tyler now trades.   In 1847* he built a starch factory near the Union Meeting-House.   Mr. Eastman failed in business, and was succeeded in the same building by Hazen K. Wilson, who took Horatio N. Carleton as partner, a year or two later.   In 1870 they built a new store where the creamery is now, and carried on a very large business.   In 1874 Mr. Carleton went out of the firm, and John N. Brock became partner with Mr. Wilson till 1877, when he sold out to Mr. Wilson, and removed to Bradford.   Mr. Wilson took his son George into trade with him, and conducted the business till the winter of 1882-'3, when he closed out and went to Florida.   David Brown, with a small capital, went into the building and did a little trade, and died there.   The Darlings of South Ryegate bought the building and put in a new stock of goods, a Mr. Adams, who had been in the store of A. T. Stewart & Co., New York, being their manager.   This store was burned while owned by the Darlings February 21, 1888.

John B. C. Tyler is the merchant at West Newbury now, in the old Eastman store.   A telephone line was constructed from South Newbury to West Newbury in 1897.   Samuel Gibson kept store, many years ago, in a wing of the tavern-house built by him, and afterward long owned by John Wood at the Centre.   In 1865 Thomas P. Bailey opened a general store, at the same place, which he kept till 1869.   In 1870, Nelson B. Tewksbury began trade in the same rooms, building his present store in 1871.   He has carried on a general mercantile business there for over thirty years.

---

*This date is incorrectly given in a previous chapter as 1841.

CHAPTER XXXVII.

CEMETERIES—CARE OF THE POOR—THE MILITIA.

THE oldest burial-ground in this town, and one of the very oldest in this state, is the Ox-bow cemetery, which has been in continuous use since 1763. Rev. Clark Perry, in 1831, states that the first person buried there was Polly Harriman, who died in Haverhill in the spring of 1763, whose remains were brought over to Newbury for burial. Mr. Perry twice repeats the same statement later in his discourse, which was delivered while there were several persons living, who might have attended her funeral. But Rev. Grant Powers, writing sixteen years later, states that she was buried near the meeting-house at Horse Meadow. The second person buried there was the first who died in this town—"the Widow Pettibone." The third was Abraham Webb, who was an half-breed Indian, and had been a slave of Gen. Jacob Bayley. To quote Mr. Perry's precise language: "Polly Harriman, the Widow Pettibone, and Abraham Webb, were the first three occupants of that plot of ground where most of the fathers and many of the children, and the stranger that came to sojourn among them, now sleep together in quiet silence." It is believed that it was, formerly, an Indian burial-ground, as human bones were exhumed in digging the earliest graves. Originally, the cemetery did not come up to the road, but there was once a house between it and the highway. This was removed long before the birth of any one living.

The town-meeting, held May 28, 1776, voted—"To clear and fence the burying-ground," by which vote it would seem that little

THE OX-BOW CEMETERY.

pains had then been expended upon the last resting place of the dead. There is no recorded action regarding the cemetery again till March 27, 1798, when the town voted—"To fence the two front sides of the burial-ground that is near the court-house with cedar posts, hard-wood rails tenanted in the posts, and boards nailed on s^d rails, with pickets sawed in top, the back sides to be fenced with cedar posts and rails." It will be remembered that there was then one house, and perhaps more than one, in what is now the newest part of the yard, and a lane ran along the south side of the old part. Additions have been made to the ground from time to time till it now includes several acres.

The older part had long been neglected, and had grown up to a thicket of pine bushes and poplar trees, which had, in some instances fallen, and broken down the ancient stones, few of which are now left. In 1870 these bushes were all cut down, and the ground cleared of the undergrowth. The oldest stone which can be deciphered bears the date of 1768—the name has crumbled away and no one knows whose dust has lain there all these years. Many of the older stones were made by a Mr. Risley, at Hanover, and paid for in wheat. Some of the bills are still in existence. The fine and well-preserved stone erected to the memory of "Mr. Peter Powers, son of Rev. Peter Powers, and Mrs. Martha Powers, his wife, who died at New York, in ye Continental Army, September 30, 1776, in his 19th year," was made by Mr. Risley in 1790, and cost twenty bushels of wheat. The one to Rev. Jacob Wood (now broken) cost eighteen bushels, and the one to Capt. Simeon Stevens cost the same amount. Many of the later slate stones were carved by Wyman Smith. The early headstones, with their quaint inscriptions and elaborate carvings are nearly all gone, and pains should be taken to preserve the few that remain, No record is known to exist of the number of burials in this village of the dead.

It is probable that, with one or two possible exceptions, no burial-ground east of the Green Mountains, in this state, contains the dust of an equal number of revolutionary soldiers. The late Col. Jacob Kent believed that about seventy-five were buried there. His estimate is probably under rather than over the real number. It also holds the dust of several men who were participants in the earlier struggle—the French and Indian war. Of many, the places of their burial can no longer be pointed out, and in a few years, more of these heroes' graves will have disappeared. It is the duty of the town, either of itself, or by acting through some patriotic society, to see that the graves which can be indicated, are provided with suitable headstones.

The following are the names of revolutionary soldiers who are buried here, whose graves, with very few exceptions, are known.

pains had then been expended upon the last resting place of the dead. There is no recorded action regarding the cemetery again till March 27, 1798, when the town voted—"To fence the two front sides of the burial-ground that is near the court-house with cedar posts, hard-wood rails tenanted in the posts, and boards nailed on s^d rails, with pickets sawed in top, the back sides to be fenced with cedar posts and rails." It will be remembered that there was then one house, and perhaps more than one, in what is now the newest part of the yard, and a lane ran along the south side of the old part. Additions have been made to the ground from time to time till it now includes several acres.

The older part had long been neglected, and had grown up to a thicket of pine bushes and poplar trees, which had, in some instances fallen, and broken down the ancient stones, few of which are now left. In 1870 these bushes were all cut down, and the ground cleared of the undergrowth. The oldest stone which can be deciphered bears the date of 1768—the name has crumbled away and no one knows whose dust has lain there all these years. Many of the older stones were made by a Mr. Risley, at Hanover, and paid for in wheat. Some of the bills are still in existence. The fine and well-preserved stone erected to the memory of "Mr. Peter Powers, son of Rev. Peter Powers, and Mrs. Martha Powers, his wife, who died at New York, in ye Continental Army, September 30, 1776, in his 19th year," was made by Mr. Risley in 1790, and cost twenty bushels of wheat. The one to Rev. Jacob Wood (now broken) cost eighteen bushels, and the one to Capt. Simeon Stevens cost the same amount. Many of the later slate stones were carved by Wyman Smith. The early headstones, with their quaint inscriptions and elaborate carvings are nearly all gone, and pains should be taken to preserve the few that remain, No record is known to exist of the number of burials in this village of the dead.

It is probable that, with one or two possible exceptions, no burial-ground east of the Green Mountains, in this state, contains the dust of an equal number of revolutionary soldiers. The late Col. Jacob Kent believed that about seventy-five were buried there. His estimate is probably under rather than over the real number. It also holds the dust of several men who were participants in the earlier struggle—the French and Indian war. Ot many, the places of their burial can no longer be pointed out, and in a few years, more of these heroes' graves will have disappeared. It is the duty of the town, either of itself, or by acting through some patriotic society, to see that the graves which can be indicated, are provided with suitable headstones.

The following are the names of revolutionary soldiers who are buried here, whose graves, with very few exceptions, are known.

The titles given are those which indicate their rank as commissioned officers, in the Continental service.

Bancroft Abbott	Jacob Fowler
Nathan Avery	Abner Fowler
Gen. Jacob Bayley	Jonathan Goodwin
Capt. Jacob Bayley	Nehemiah Hadley
Major Joshua Bayley	Jonathan Hadley
Capt. Frye Bayley	Sylvanus Heath
Capt. John G. Bayley	Capt. Lemuel Holmes
James Bayley	Col. Thomas Johnson
James Bayley sd	Joe (Indian)
John Barnett	Col. Robert Johnston
Thomas Brock	Col. Jacob Kent
Peletiah Bliss	Jacob Kent. Jr.
Joel Carbee	Capt. Nehemiah Lovewell
Richard Chamberlin	Peter Martin
Lieut. Abiel Chamberlin	Thomas Mellen
Lieut. Joseph Chamberlin	John Mills
Benjamin Chamberlin	John Mills, Jr.
Moses Chamberlain	William Peach
Remembrance Chamberlain	Gideon Smith
Asa Coburn	Capt. Simeon Stevens
William Doe	Peletiah Watson
John Eaton	William Wallace.

The absence of any memorials to mark the last resting place of so many of the patriotic dead of the revolution is easily understood by any one who calls to mind the poverty of the country in the early days, the destruction by time of so many of the rude stones, and the fact that many of these veterans died very poor, and

"Lie here by poverty distressed no more."

Few of the men of the revolution survived when the country grew rich enough to pension its heroes, but in that place of graves lies the forgotten dust of many a brave man. There should be some organization to preserve the memorials which remain.

Of the soldiers of the war of 1812, the following are known to be buried there:

Col. John Bayley	John Bayley	J. Amherst Bayley
Michael Bayley	Edward Rollins	Ross C. Ford
Simeon Stevens	George Avery.	

Soldiers of the civil war:

George Bailey	William O. Moulton
George Chalmers	Alvin G. McKinstry
Henry E. Dunbar	James A. Newell
Samuel A. Eastman	Edwin M. Noyes
Charles W. Greenleaf	Owen O'Malley
W. W. Johnston	Orvin C. Temple
Joseph Kent	C. S. Wallace
Edward P. Keyes	Emery J. Webster.
Thomas F. Kelley	

This cemetery has, of late years, received the oversight of an association which has expended considerable labor and money in

"The Old Haseltine House," West Newbury, built about 1807, by Capt. David Haseltine, in which he died, and in which his son, David, lived after him. This house has been repaired since this photograph was taken.

CEMETERY AT WEST NEWBURY, NOV. 1900.

Photo. by Corliss.

the care of the grounds. While much has been done, much is needed—the building of a receiving tomb, the introduction of a water supply, and many lesser conveniences for the proper care of a large cemetery.

Next in age to that at the Ox-bow is probably one in the extreme southwest part of the town, in what was long called the Grow neighborhood. This cemetery has a sunny location, with a southwesterly slope, and is believed by Mr. D. S. Fulton to contain about 200 graves, only a part of which are marked. Reuben Page, who saw several years' service in the Revolutionary war, Benjamin Muzzey, who was in local service, and Daniel Stevens, who was a teamster in the army at 17, are buried there. This cemetery contains one or two of the quaintly carved stones which were common about 1800. The burial-ground near the Rogers hill schoolhouse, is on land conveyed to the town by Daniel Eastman, in 1801, and the interments there are estimated by Mr. David Eastman at above 200. John and David Haseltine, Thomas Eastman, Paul Ford and Joseph Olmsted, were revolutionary soldiers, whose remains rest there, and probably others. The ground, being wet, was not well adapted for a cemetery, and in 1835 a new one was opened near the church, on land given by Col. John Smith, and to this latter, some of those interred in the older one were removed. Most of the older settlers of West Newbury are buried in one or the other of these cemeteries.

In the new cemetery are buried: Col. John Smith, Israel Putnam, Stephen Powers, and Dudley Carleton, who served in the war of independence, and Colonel Smith, David Haseltine, Nathaniel Niles, Ware McConnel, John Corliss, and Col. Levi Rogers of the war of 1812. Soldiers of the civil war: Stillman Jenne, Joseph M. Nason, Edwin C. Niles, Robert F. Smith, and Thomas L. Tucker. George King served in the Crimean war.

There is another cemetery at West Newbury, a sort of family burying-ground, on the "old Putnam place." Some ten or twenty are believed to have been buried there. The graves of only six are marked in any way. The place had grown up to timber, but was fenced by the town in the year just passed.

The old cemetery at Wells River, which was in the village, was first used about 1801, and was in use till after 1863, and there were occasional later burials. These ceased after the opening of the one near Mr. Eastman's, in 1867, and in 1890 leave was obtained to remove the dead therein buried to the new enclosure. This was done, and the ground given over to other uses. It is said that several veterans of the old wars were buried there, but of these the name of Joshua Hale is alone recalled, of the revolutionary war; Charles Hale and others are of the last war with England. Loren Vance, Edward B. Wright, Joshua Kendall and William Wallace were soldiers of the civil war.

The cemetery at Boltonville is of late enclosure, and contains many graves—the earliest burial was in 1842. Lieut. John Whitcher, John and Stephen Putnam, and Carlos Chamberlin, of the civil war, rest here.

The first burial in the cemetery on Jefferson hill was about 1848. The location of this yard is very pleasant. Jacob and Joshua Bailey and William White were soldiers of the war of 1812; George Lumsden and William Wheeler of the civil war. Dr. Samuel White must not be forgotten, as he was a surgeon in the revolutionary war, and attended the wounded from the Battle of Bennington. There are two other small cemeteries on Jefferson hill, each containing a few graves. One is on the "Jewell place," and the other in the Tenney pasture. These have lately been enclosed.

On the "Nourse place," in the Lime-Kiln neighborhood, is a small burial ground, containing perhaps fifty graves. George Banfield, of the revolutionary war lies here, also Aaron Fisk, Daniel Stevens and Edwin Tuttle, of the civil war. On the Orrin Heath farm is a small enclosure, in which the Clark and Renfrew families, with a few of their neighbors are buried. The locality is very retired. The cemetery at the town house is on land given by Charles George, and the first burial was that of his daughter, in 1839. Many families bury their dead here. A new yard was enclosed south of the town house in 1884. Wells Goodwin and Thomas Corliss, soldiers of 1812, are buried here, and John Wells, a "Plattsburgh Volunteer." Horace D. Eastman, Ephraim E. Fleming, Edmund E. Hix, Amos Meserve, Ephraim Rowe, Jonas W. Tuttle, and Milo C. Bailey, of the civil war, are here buried. Amos Meserve was the only Newbury soldier killed in battle, whose remains were brought home. There are a few unmarked graves in other parts of the town, but the custom so common in many parts of New England, of burial upon farms, never prevailed here.

Funeral customs have changed considerably since 1763. About 1785, the town purchased a "burying-cloth," in accordance with the usage of the time. This was made of heavy black goods, with a gilt fringe and tassels, and was large enough to cover the coffin, while it was being borne to the grave on a bier. The burying-cloth was owned by the town, and a small fee was charged for its use. In early days coffins were not bought ready-made, but were ordered of the local carpenter when wanted. It was not uncommon in many places, although perhaps not in Newbury, for people of some wealth to have their coffins made while they were yet living, and upon such, considerable expense was sometimes lavished. The custom, now universal, of enclosing the coffin in an outer box for burial, came in about the opening of the civil war, although occasionally observed before.

The cemeteries in town are pleasantly located, and, generally, quite as well looked after as those of other towns. One thing, however, should be no longer neglected. The inscriptions upon all the older stones should be carefully copied, and recorded. It sometimes happens that the date of some person's death is of great importance.

The poor and unfortunate we have always had with us, and the money expended for their support would amount to a larger sum than people suppose. The town had not been long settled before there were people needing aid, and in 1771, Jacob Bayley, Jacob Kent and John Haseltine were chosen "poormasters." Who were the objects of their care, or what the expense to the town, we do not know. It is probable that such aid was in the shape of provisions and medical attendance. The officers do not seem to have had much to do, as the same persons were also chosen as "supervisors," "commissioners," and the like for many years. Usually there is no mention of any overseer of the poor in the record of town-meetings. There were poor people, however, who had to be helped and bills and receipts preserved among the Johnson and Kent papers show that such public expense was much the same in its details as now—aid to the physically and mentally infirm, help in sickness, burial of the dead, and the care of orphan children.

There is a curious bill among the Johnson papers:

Feb. 12, 1790.

"The town of Newbury Dr. to Joshua Swan,
to Diging the Reverend Jacob Woods Grave, £0. 6. 0.
to Diging Jona Emersons Grave, 0. 3. 0.
0. 9. 0."

Why it cost twice as much to dig the minister's grave as the pauper's is among the "whys" which it is often very easy to ask concerning the town's affairs.

One Mr. Hearn, or Heron, is often mentioned, and the name is singular from the fact that he is always spoken of as *Mr.* Hearn, while other recipients of the town's bounty are called by their proper names. In some long-forgotten way the town became involved in a lawsuit about this Mr. Hearn. Poor man! his troubles were over in this world more than a hundred years ago.

No person is entitled to expect relief from a town unless he is a resident of it, and to determine what constitutes residence has always been a perplexing question, and has given rise to more lawsuits between towns than almost anything else, and various laws have been passed, and decisions of the Supreme Court handed down, which bear upon this question. There was, formerly, a law, in most of the New England states, which provided a way by which towns could prevent any newcomer, from gaining residence, and thus freeing the town from responsibility for support of such person. The process was called "warning out of town," and consisted in the reading in the hearing of such a person, by a constable, or by leaving a copy of a warrant, issued by the selectmen, of which the following is a specimen.

State of Vermont   }   To the first Constable of
Orange County, ss.   }   Newbury in s^d County.
    Greeting. By the authority of the State of Vermont, you are hereby required to warn A. B. and family, now residing in Newbury to depart s^d Town. Hereof fail not, but of this precept and your doings due return make according to law. Given under our hands this 27th day of December, 1814.

ASA TENNEY,   } Selectmen
JOSHUA HALE, }   of
JONAS TUCKER, } Newbury.

State of Vermont   }
               }   Newbury, Jan. 6, 1815.
  Orange Co. ss.   }
    I then served this precept by leaving a true and attested copy with the said A. B. and family. Attest, Abner Bayley, Constable.

      Fees
Travel 10 miles,   .60   Newbury Town Clerk's office
Copy,   .17   Jan. 10, 1813.
        ‾‾‾   Rec^d and recorded,
       .67   I. BAYLEY, Town Clerk.

    This thing was quite profitable for others, if rather unpleasant for the person who thus received a hint that his residence was not desired, as there was a fee for the selectmen who prepared the warrant, another for the constable, and another for the clerk. There are 112 such warnings recorded in the first book of town proceedings. The first is dated January 5, 1787; the second, July 20, 1806; and the last, November 12, 1816, when the law was repealed. One of these warrants includes twenty-four families.

    In 1823 it was voted, "not to build a poorhouse." It was the custom for many years to "sell the poor at auction," as it was called. The support of the homeless poor was set up at auction, in town-meeting and struck off to the lowest bidder. This was quite apt to be some sordid soul, who pinched and starved the unfortunate beings, who were thus at his mercy. This gave rise to some scandals, which may as well not be recalled.

    In 1837, the "surplus money," from the United States, was divided among the towns, and Newbury received $5,376.03, and with a portion of this the town bought the Simon Blake farm at West Newbury, for a town farm, Charles Hale, Moody Chamberlain and A. B. W. Tenney being the purchasing committee. This was the last earthly home of many unfortunates, during the twenty-nine years it was thus occupied. No record was ever kept of the deaths that occurred there. In 1846 there were eleven persons whose ages averaged 76 years. In 1866 the town sold that farm to William C. Carleton, and purchased the farm of O. C. Barnett, who bought it back the next year. Two persons died there while that was the town farm. The present farm was bought of Porter Watson in 1867, and the main part of the present structure was built, and the barns remodelled, in 1885, under the management of John S. George, the overseer. The deaths at the present farm have been forty. The system of herding all the helpless beings of a whole county under one roof never has been adopted in Vermont.

Before speaking of the militia system which prevailed after the establishment of the national government, it is well to consider why that system first became necessary. From the earliest settlement of New England down to the close of the War of Independence, the fear and dread of the Indian entered, as one of the conditions of existence, into every-day life. It was necessary for self-preservation, that there should be some system of military training among the settlers, that men might know what to do, and where to resort, in case of attack, and under whose orders to place themselves. The militia system was brought from England, and adopted to meet new conditions in America. In every new settlement, one of the first things which the settlers attended to was the formation of a military company for self-defense. Thus we have found that in 1764, while the settlements at Coös were hardly two years old, the able-bodied men were formed into a company of militia, of which Jacob Kent was made captain. When the revolution came on, all these military companies were of vast service, as furnishing men for the field, who already knew a little of military discipline.

Soon after the war began, all the able-bodied men between the ages of sixteen and fifty were enrolled in the "train-bands." These bands met for regular drill, and when there was a call for men, as many as were needed were sent out from these bands. Besides these, was the "alarm list," in which were enumerated all the men between fourteen and sixty-five, who were liable to be called upon in an emergency. At two or three times of peril during the war the alarm list was resorted to. One of these was during the last weeks of the campaign of Burgoyne, when all the stronger men went to the seat of war, while the old men and boys kept watch and ward at home. After the war, and down to about 1847, all the able-bodied men between the ages of eighteen and forty-five years were, with few exceptions made by law, enrolled in the militia, and required to do military duty. Every man was obliged to keep himself constantly provided with such arms and equipments as were necessary for actual service, and, for so doing, his poll was exempt from taxation. The military force of the state amounted to about 25,000, and was divided into four divisions, ten brigades, and thirty-five regiments, with from eight to twelve companies each.

Belonging to most of the regiments was also one company of cavalry, one of artillery, one of light infantry, and in many cases, more than one, of each. Each division was commanded by a major-general, with a division inspector, a division quarter-master and two aids; each brigade by a brigadier-general, with a brigade inspector, brigade quarter-master, and one aid; each regiment by a colonel, lieutenant-colonel and major, with the customary staff; and each company by a captain, lieutenants and ensign, with the usual non-commissioned officers. The major and brigadier-generals were appointed by the legislature. The field officers were chosen by the commissioned officers of their respective regiments, and the several companies chose their own officers. Such was the military system of our fathers, and it had both its good and evil effects. It constituted an organized force, which acquired some knowledge of military discipline, and which, when the war of 1812 came on, was immediately effective. It was also of value, as teaching an erect bearing and an alert air to those who took pride in military evolutions. In the course of years it came to pass that those who were fond of military display formed themselves into crack companies, which were composed of picked men, and which, while computed in the regular militia, were enrolled as independent companies. These were uniformed, and their equipments were superior in quality. These companies frequently met for drill and inspection; their officers were men of wealth and standing in the community; the men took a great deal of pride in their organizations; and these companies, whether of cavalry or infantry, in their handsome uniforms, presented, by their correct evolutions and military bearing, a marked contrast to the regular companies, who were not uniformed. These latter, which included all not otherwise enrolled, between the ages of eighteen and forty-five, were derisively termed the "floodwood companies."

The select companies generally adopted some designation, the "Washington Guards" or the like, while the regular companies were made up of men who had not time, money, or perhaps inclination to join the expensive select organizations. Still a captain was a captain, and a colonel was a colonel; the title once won, usually attached itself to a man's name through life, but more than one man in this town was ruined by the self-conceit which the accession to the "little brief authority," gave to an inferior personality.

The militia were ordered out to training in June, and in the fall the brigade met for "general muster." The first training field was that in the rear of R. J. Hibbard's house, but after many years the militia living east of Hall's brook met at the upper meadow, or on the hill back of Wells River. Those west of the brook drilled at West Newbury. General muster was held on the "old parade ground" at East Corinth, where fairs are now held, and that plot of ground has seen more military display than any other piece of land in this county.   There was an artillery company in Topsham and a company of cavalry, wholly or partly made up in this town.   The Newbury militia were long attached to the first regiment, second brigade, and fourth division of the state militia.   In 1821, Moody Chamberlin was colonel; James A. Bayley, Dudley Carleton, and James Wallace were captains; A. B. W. Tenney was captain of a company of cavalry which numbered forty men; there were ten men in the band and each company had its drum corps.   The rank and file on parade numbered 590 men.

One of the good results of the old militia system was its fostering of the love and practice of martial music, and there were several fine bands in this county which are now forgotten.   The West Newbury drum corps is the legitimate successor of one of these old organizations, and some of the young men in it are grandsons and great-grandsons of its members, eighty years ago. Great were the days of "June training," and nothing could eclipse the glories of "annual muster," and if any of the present generation want to hear some good stories, let them go to some of the few who remain, who "used to train."

It would require more time than the editor of this work can command to ascertain the names of captains in the old militia; the colonels before 1800, were, some of them, Frye and Joshua Bayley, Nehemiah Lovewell, Jacob Kent, father and son, and Robert Johnston.   Later, and of a younger generation, were Waterman Wells, A. B. W. Tenney, Charles Hale, John Bayley, Amherst Bayley, Jacob Kent (grandson), Horatio Brock and Levi Rogers.

There was, however, another side to the old militia system. Many men, especially the officers, expended much more money than they could well afford, and the trainings and musters were seasons of riot, drunkenness and fighting.   Among the thousands who flocked to the parade ground were many hard characters. Gambling and vice were unblushing, and the prevalent custom of "treating" led to evil results.   It was the custom for a company to assemble at the captain's house, and fire a salute, when that officer appeared and treated the crowd.   The late Ezekiel White of Topsham, was one of the first to substitute a good dinner in place of a "treat," and the custom was often adopted as temperance sentiments began to prevail.

The militia system fell into disrepute in the early '40's.   It had become unpopular with the rank and file to whom the loss of time, and the expense incurred was considerable; it was many years since there had been a war; the whole system was felt to be an unnecessary burden; temperance sentiment was not in harmony with the excesses which attended it, and public opposition was strong enough, about 1847, to abolish all the militia laws. The volunteer companies generally maintained their organization for some years. After the civil war the militia system was revived for a few years, but soon fell into disfavor, and was, in its turn, abolished. The military organizations now connected with the state militia are wholly voluntary.

CHAPTER XXXVIII.

STAGES, INNS, AND POST OFFICES.

FIRST STAGES.—QUEBEC AND BOSTON STAGE.—STAGE LINES.—TAVERNS.—THE SPRING HOTEL.—THE NEWBURY HOUSE.—THE LOVEWELL TAVERN.—OTHER INNS.—POSTAL ROUTES.—FIRST POST OFFICE.—POSTAGE.—PRIVATE CARRIERS.— NEWBURY· OFFICES.—OFFICIAL LIST SINCE 1832.

THERE was no public conveyance for passengers between here and Concord until after the century began. In 1805, a charter was obtained for a turnpike from Haverhill corner to Baker's river, which was finished in 1809, and soon after, the mail carrier, Silas May, drove a wagon along the route, in which he carried the mail, and any chance passenger. This turnpike went over the hills from Haverhill to Warren. The road through Oliverian Notch was not built till 1826.

In the New Hampshire Patriot for December 25, 1810, appears the following advertisement:

"NEW LINE OF STAGES FROM BOSTON TO QUEBEC.

Public notice is hereby given that there is a regular line of stages erected, to run from Quebec through Craig's Road to Boston, and will commence on the fourteenth of January next, and will be regularly kept up by the subscribers, the proprietors of the said line. Will run as follows: Start from Quebec and Boston on Monday of each week, meet at the line of 45 degrees of north latitude at Stanstead on Wednesdays and arrive at Boston and Quebec on Saturday of each week.

JOSHUA STILES.
JOHN GRIFFIN.
R. W. GOOLD.
*JONA. SINCLAIR.
JAMES GARDNER.
*HENRY STEVENS.

Newbury, Vt., Dec. 17, 1810."

This notice has called out some speculation, and there have been doubts expressed if the enterprise ever began. Certainly it could

---

*Mr. Sinclair was of Haverhill, Henry Stevens of Barnet.

not have continued long. The war came on soon after, and would have put an end to the business, had it survived till that time. Little's History of Warren says there was a line of stages begun in 1811, which soon failed up. This may be the same.

In 1814 a line of stages began to run from Haverhill to Concord, which kept up till the railroad was opened in 1848. In the same year, a stage line went into operation down the river, and connected to New York. There were many enterprising men in Haverhill Corner in those days, and it became the centre for a number of stage lines, and the place where the stages laid up over night. This gave occupation to a large number of taverns, and, in the busy season, it was not uncommon for from 150 to 200 travelers to pass the night there. There were lines to Plymouth, Hanover, Lancaster, Danville, St. Johnsbury, Montpelier and elsewhere. In 1832, a stage left Haverhill three times a week, at six a. m., for Albany via Chelsea and Royalton, where it lodged, and left at five a. m., the next day for Poultney or Fort Ann, where it lodged again, reaching Albany on the third day, in season for the afternoon boat to New York. The fare was six dollars.

Stage drivers were great men in those days; hardy, tough (they had to be), men of energy, with fertility of research to meet the exigencies of their exacting occupation. It was a hard life, and stage drivers were rough, but kindly. Mr. Harry B. Stevens, of Bradford, is an old stage driver, one of the last who are left, and he could fill a good-sized volume with recollections of his experience.

Mr. Livermore says that in 1820, the eastern stage left Haverhill on Tuesdays and Fridays at four o'clock in the morning, taking breakfast, "which seemed late," at Morse's inn in Rumney, and arriving at Concord at six in the evening, "unless detained by adverse conditions of weather, spring and autumn mud, and the like." Two days were spent in going to Boston. In 1835, the traveler had choice of several routes between Concord and Boston.

"Old stage times," a title which denotes an era long passed away, denotes also one of hospitality, of good cheer in the old taverns, belated travelers, and much stir and bustle. People could travel easier, but there was still no easy way of marketing produce. Farmers went to market in winter with their own teams, carrying the more valuable and portable products of the the farm. Most farmers went, at least once, in the winter, "down below." Many of the old "pungs" in town, have made the journey time and again, long before their present owners were born. Pungs were built to last, they never wore out. Old residents of Concord say that they used to see strings of teams, a mile long and more, of farmers from up country, on their way to market, their teams walking as close behind each other as they could go. There were men who made a business of teaming from Concord to the north country, driving four, six, or eight horses.

THE SPRING HOTEL AS IT APPEARED IN 1865.

THE SPRING HOTEL IN 1878.

When all the travel went along the public roads, taverns were common. Mr. Leslie has given an account of early inns at Wells River. Nearly all the taverns in Newbury were on the river road. In 1800, Jeremiah Ingalls built a large house at the top of what is now called Ingalls hill where he kept a tavern called Ingall's Inn, about ten years. The old Johnson house on the Ox-bow was opened as an inn in 1775, and was long a noted tavern, kept by Colonel Johnson, and by his son, Moses. The town records show that Col. William Wallace was an innkeeper as early as 1785, whether in the house which afterwards became the Spring Hotel or not, is not known. In 1800 he kept the latter tavern. It was then a square, two-story house, much like the old Bliss tavern at Haverhill Corner, in which Mr. Leith lives. In 1810 Mr. Edward Little owned it, enlarging it, and adding a third story. Barnard Brickett succeeded Mr. Little, and in his time it was called Brickett's Inn. Peter Wheelock, from 1833 to 1836, was succeeded by Joseph Atkinson, who gave place to Tappan Stevens, in whose hands it remained until nearly the end of his life. Judge Stevens, as he was called, enlarged the building. During much of its history the Spring Hotel was run in connection with the sulphur springs. These springs were discovered about 1782, and there is a record of their being resorted to for curative purposes in 1804. What is now called Montebello House was built by James Spear—the front part of it—and was enlarged from time to time and bathrooms added. Little can be accurately learned about its various proprietors. It was remodelled and enlarged to its present appearance in 1873, by Rev. William Clark.

The Spring Hotel was kept by Nelson B. Stevens after his uncle, Judge Stevens, retired from it. This hostelry was one of the noted inns of the north country, and always enjoyed the reputation of being a well-kept hotel, with a good run of custom, and was a popular summer resort in connection with the sulphur springs. About 1868, it came into the hands of Samuel L. Kendall, who added, in 1869, a fourth story with a French roof and cupola, and a wing containing thirteen rooms. He introduced gas, manufactured upon the premises. The main building then contained about forty rooms, was painted white, and was a very conspicuous landmark. In that house, as originally constructed, there was a secret apartment, known only to the proprietor, reached by a winding passage around one of the great chimneys, and fitted up with huge chests for the concealment of smuggled goods. After Mr. Kendall the house was owned by John E. Chamberlain, and while kept by his son, R. W. Chamberlain, was entirely destroyed by fire, September 5, 1879. Its site remained vacant until the library building was erected there, seventeen years later. According to family records, the house in which Mr. E. H. Farnham and his sister live, was opened as a tavern in 1788, by Joseph Smith, and kept by him till his death.

The old Newbury House was built by Timothy Morse, about 1834, the brick part of it, and was an addition to the wooden part, which was owned as a store by Moses Wallace. This tavern often changed hands, and the name of all its proprietors cannot be given. Nelson B. Stevens kept it for several years, also Hiram Hill, and from 1854 to 1856, Ezekiel Sawyer.

The oldest part of what is now the Sawyer House was built soon after the revolutionary war, by Capt. Nehemiah Lovewell, who kept tavern there till his death in 1801, and his widow succeeded him, keeping it till 1825. This was, originally, a two-story house, the third story being added later. In 1833, it was purchased for a seminary boarding-house. Mrs. Lovewell had trouble with Col. Thomas Johnson over a barrel of rum, which she bought of him, and which she averred was more than half water. The colonel stoutly affirmed that it was rum, and nothing but rum, when it left his premises. The affair made much talk, and the colonel sued the widow for slander. It came out in the trial that the barrel had taken a whole night to travel the mile which lay between the two taverns, a circumstance which Mrs. Lovewell's hired man, and two others, were very backward about explaining. But peace was restored.

At South Newbury, Col. Remembrance Chamberlain, and his son Col. Moody Chamberlain, kept tavern on what is now called Riverside Farm, for many years. The house was burned in February, 1876. Col. John Smith opened, about 1804, a tavern, on the farm now owned by his grandson, the present John Smith, at West Newbury. The old tavern sign is preserved by the latter. Gideon Tewksbury kept tavern for a long time, on what is now called the Cunningham place, near the Bradford line. At the Centre, Samuel Gibson built and occupied for a tavern, the house in which the late John Wood lived, and which was burned in March, 1899. Other houses in town were used as taverns at one time, or another. In days when people went to market with their own teams, they usually carried their provisions with them, and grain for their horses, sleeping at night on the bar-room floors. Ten cents was usually charged for lodging, in this manner. The principal revenue of the inn came from the bar.

During the time that Wells River was the terminus of the railroad, there were lines of stages from there to Littleton, St. Johnsbury, Danville and other points. Hotel business was thriving; a few made money; others lost about all they had. Several went into the business there who were not adapted to the occupation, and failed in consequence.

Before the revolutionary war there was nothing resembling a postal service, conducted by the government, in this part of the country, and all the letters which came to Coös were brought by private hands. In those days it was considered the proper thing, if a man was going to a distant place, to let his neighbor know his intention beforehand that they might send any letters which they wished, by him. There were merchants in Salem and Boston who made themselves popular with their customers up this way by caring for letters left with them, and any one from Coös going to such places was expected to call at their stores and get such letters as were to come this way, and bundles of newspapers were among the most desired freight of a sleigh returning from market in winter.

In 1776, for military purposes, the council of safety appointed a post-rider to go from Portsmouth to Haverhill, once in two weeks, by way of Dover and Plymouth, and return by way of Hanover and Keene. This was primarily intended for the conveyance of military information, but the carrier, John Balch, was allowed to carry private letters for a small sum.

In 1783, the first mail route was established in Vermont, from Bennington to Albany, once in two weeks, and two years later the service was extended to Rutland, Brattleboro, Windsor and Newbury. The carriers went once a week, and received two pence a mile, hard money, between Brattleboro and Newbury. When, in 1791, Vermont entered the Federal Union, the general government assumed the mail service, but for some reason the northerly portion of the route was discontinued, and Hanover remained, for some years, the last post office on the river.

In February, 1791, a resolution to establish four post routes and riders in New Hampshire, was carried by only one majority in the legislature, there being thirty-four votes for, and thirty-three against it. In June of that year these routes went into operation, the rider going once each week from Concord by way of Boscawen and Plymouth to Haverhill, returning via Hanover and Canaan, receiving £12 for each six months. In 1795, the federal government took possession of the mail routes, and extended the river route from Hanover to Newbury, and Thomas Johnson was made postmaster at Newbury, and Capt. Joseph Bliss at Haverhill. For about five years these places were the post offices for all the country north of them, as far as settlements extended. September 1, 1799, a mail route went into operation from Newbury through Ryegate and Peacham to Danville, once each week. Gen. James Whitelaw was the first postmaster in Ryegate, Samuel Goss at Peacham, and David Dunbar at Danville. A few months later, however, Mr. Dunbar resigned the Danville post office and one or two small appointments which he held under government, alleging that they were not, altogether, "as profitable as a good farrow cow." In 1810, a route was established from Danville to Derby and return once in two weeks.

In 1807, the following routes, which included Newbury and Haverhill, were in operation:

"From Portsmouth by Dover, Rochester, Middletown, Ossipee, Moultonborough, Centre Harbor, and Plymouth, to Haverhill and Newbury, Vt., and from Newbury, by Haverhill, Plymouth, New Hampton, Meredith, Gilmantown, Nottingham, and Durham to Portsmouth once a week." The rider was to leave Portsmouth on Tuesday, at 2 p. m., and arrive at Newbury by 7 p. m., on Friday.

"From Hanover by Orford to Haverhill, once a week." This left Hanover on Fridays and connected with the Portsmouth mail at Haverhill.

"From Montpelier by Berlin, Barre, Washington, Corinth, Bradford, Newbury, Ryegate, Barnet, Peacham, and Danville to St. Johnsbury, once a week." The rider left Montpelier Thursday noon, lodged at Newbury Friday night, reaching St. Johnsbury at 5 p. m., Saturday. There was a route from Haverhill to Guildhall once a week.

Examination of the proposals for carrying the mail in 1807 shows that a mail left Boston twice a week, Tuesday and Friday, at 3 a. m., and, remaining at Francestown over night, reached Windsor at 2 p. m., on Wednesday and Saturday. There the mail was transferred to another rider, reaching Hanover about nine o'clock of the days last mentioned. As there was but one mail a week above Hanover, and that left on Friday morning, the letters which left Boston on Friday, remained at Hanover several days before they went along. A more direct route, however, went by way of Salem, and Haverhill, Mass., to Windsor, and connected there with the Hanover mail. Letters were from a week to ten days coming from New York, and, in that year a letter which came from Ohio took six weeks to reach Newbury.

Rates of postage were so high as to be almost prohibitive. The postage upon letters was computed, not upon their weight, but upon the number of sheets which the letter contained. The postal rates were eight cents for all distances under forty miles, increasing to twenty-five cents when more than five hundred. If there were two sheets, the letter paid twice these rates, and so on. Newspapers were carried for one cent each, and one and a half cents when the distance was over one hundred miles. Even as late as 1816, letter postage to Boston was one shilling, or seventeen cents. Very few letters were prepaid; the person addressed had to pay the postage, but was not compelled to take the letter from the office. Persons whose standing was good were allowed to let their postage bills run several months.

From an old account book kept by David Johnson, who succeeded his father as postmaster in 1800, some interesting particulars are gathered. It will be remembered that in 1800 postal service had been extended to Peacham and Danville, but Newbury was still the post office for a considerable territory. For the quarter ending April 1, 1801, the amount collected for unpaid letters received through the mail was $14.12½; the postage upon letters prepaid at the office was $4.82½; and the amount collected from newspapers was $1.57. A few sundry items brought the receipts of the Newbury office to $20.12½.

Mr. Johnson's commission—thirty per cent of the amount collected from unpaid letters, and fifty per cent of the sum paid upon newspapers, all amounting to $5.64 was not a magnificent salary. Postmasters, however, were privileged to send their own letters free through the mails, and this to a man with large correspondence, like Mr. Johnson, was no small matter.

The net receipts of the Newbury office in 1806 were $49.61½, and Mr. Johnson's salary amounted to $29.15. One hundred and twenty free letters were received. The average postage on letters received at Newbury for September, 1824 was fifteen cents.

Among the Johnson papers are many like the following:

Newbury, Oct. 1, 1803.

Ben Porter, Esq., Dr.
To postage on letters received since July 1, $2.24
Do. newspapers,   .39
$3.63

Allowing him the low average of ten cents on each letter, it would give him only twenty-two letters in three months, probably only a small part of those which he actually received. The fact was that on account of the high postage most letters were sent by private hands. Ingenious people contrived to evade postage by means of dotted words and letters in newspapers, which passed through the mail for one cent each. These letters and words when read consecutively, conveyed information. Another way, still remembered by many elderly people, was to send a blank sheet of paper, made up like a letter. Peculiarities in the address, or in the form of the letters used, understood by the sender and the receiver, conveyed information as to the writer's health and circumstances. The person addressed would receive the letter, examine it, and return it to the postmaster, professing inability to pay the postage, having, meanwhile, obtained information of the writer, without expense. When the postage on a letter was twenty-five cents or more such evasions were very common. There was something wrong in a system which drove people to cheating in order to gratify their natural desire to hear of each other's welfare.

In 1820 the lowest rate of postage on a letter was six cents; above thirty miles, ten cents; above eighty miles, nine pence; and so on, till letters going more than 400 miles, paid twenty-five cents. In 1840, the efforts of Rowland Hill and others, in the face of great ridicule and opposition, effected the reduction of postage in Great

Britain from one shilling to one penny. Six years later in this country, postage was reduced to five cents for 300 miles, or less, and ten cents between places more distant. Postage was later reduced to three cents between all offices in the country, without regard to distance. In 1883, the present rates for letter postage were adopted. Postage stamps were invented in 1847, and adopted by the American government in 1852. Postal cards were introduced in 1873.

Owing to the high rates of newspaper postage, country papers found it for their advantage to have their papers distributed among their patrons by private carriers. In 1796 "The Orange Nightingale and Newbury Morning Star," then published in this town, advertised its carriers in the following manner:

"NEW POST.

Phillip Rawlins proposes riding as Post thro the towns of Riegate, Barnet, and Peacham, in each of which towns any person who wishes to become a subscriber for the 'Orange Nightingale' will be supplied at the moderate price of ten shillings per annum. In Duesburg (Danville), Cabot, Walden and Hardwick at Twelve Shillings, and through Greensboro and Craftsborough for Fourteen Shillings per annum. Those persons who will please to favor him with their commands, may depend on having their business strictly attended to.

Newbury, August 25."

The last sentence alludes to the fact that these carriers conducted a sort of express business, carried small packages, executed commissions and the like. Files of old newspapers from the earlier third of the century have many such notices. There may be people still living who can remember when the Danville "North Star" was distributed by carriers.

The first postmaster at Newbury was Col. Thomas Johnson, 1785-1800; David Johnson, 1800-1812. The office was in their store, at the Ox-bow. Joseph Smith succeeded Mr. Johnson, and kept the office in his tavern, where Mr. Farnham now lives, till his death in 1815. The next postmaster was James Spear, Jr., who lived in what is now Montebello House. He was a hatter, and the office was in his shop, a small building near his house. Mr. Knight kept the office in his house, the brick house north of the old Newbury House. Since his time the office has been in the Keyes store, in the building which stood where Mr. Hale's store stands, at three different periods in its present location, and from 1891 to 1897, in the store of Silsby and Knight.

Isaac W. Tabor was postmaster at Wells River before Mr. Burbank, but whether he was the first one at that place, is not known. In April, 1871, a postal route was put into operation between South Newbury and Newbury Centre, and offices were established at the latter place and West Newbury. Before that time there had been an arrangement by which some one went from West Newbury to South Newbury, daily, for the mail. After 1866, by a similar arrangement, the mail was brought to the Centre from Newbury on Tuesdays and Fridays.

The following official list, procured for this volume by Mr. Horace W. Bailey, from the Post Office Department at Washington, gives the date of appointment of each occupant of the offices in town since 1832. It will be remembered that before Mr. Worthley's appointment at Boltonville, in 1865, the post office there had been discontinued during several years.

NEWBURY

James Spear, Jr.,	appointed,	About 1815
Prentiss Knight,	"	November 14, 1831 `
Freeman Keyes,	"	December 15, 1845
William B. Stevens,		February 24, 1849
J. M. Chadwick,		April 9, 1849
Daniel Peaslee,		May 23, 1853
Simeon Stevens, Jr.,		March 31, 1854
Jedediah C. Woodbury,	"	July 31, 1858
H. B. Morse,		August 2, 1861
Thomas C. Keyes,		June 9, 1875
R. W. Chamberlin,		September 23, 1885
William H. Silsby,		June 11, 1891
M. C. Knight,		April 6, 1893
G. L. Andrews,		April 15, 1897
Susie S. Sawyer,		October 1, 1900

WELLS RIVER.

Peter Burbank,	appointed,	December 12, 1832
Elijah Farr,	"	January 28, 1836
Hiram Tracy,	"	June 12, 1841
Charles B. Leslie,		December 26, 1844
William R. Shedd,		February 6, 1850
A. S. Farwell,		December 23, 1852
C. B. Leslie,		May 12, 1853
Seneca Dickey,		October 4, 1853
A. S. Farwell,		April 5, 1856
Franklin Deming,		May 4, 1861
Edgar C. Graves,		February 23, 1886
John Bailey,		May 14, 1889
A. H. Bailey,		March 30, 1893
William G. Foss,		May 22, 1897

BOLTONVILLE.

William Bolton,	appointed,	January 15, 1833
Thomas Wasson,	"	April 14, 1841
H. K. Worthley,	"	April 17, 1865
Freeman Tucker,		January 13, 1888
H. C. Sargent,		June 1, 1895
Sarah Tucker,		August 13, 1895
Samuel A. Tucker,		January 27, 1899

SOUTH NEWBURY.

Thomas J. Doe,	appointed,	June 23, 1838
William W. Brock,	"	October 21, 1862
James Gage,	"	September 21, 1865
William W. Brock,		September 20, 1869
Miss A. A. Doe,		March 14, 1871
Edson Doe,		March 26, 1872
George N. Renean,		December 26, 1879
W. H. Child,		September 20, 1880
Clarence A. Butler,		March 7, 1883
A. J. Knight,		February 20, 1886
Henry W. Heath,		September 1, 1886
A. J. Knight,		September 24, 1887
George Franklin,		January 12, 1895
A. A. Olmsted,		October 2, 1895
P. D. W. Hildreth,		August 5, 1897

WEST NEWBURY.

H. N. Carleton,	appointed,	April 5, 1871
Dudley Carleton,	"	July 8, 1874
Hazen K. Wilson,	"	July 22, 1874
Dudley Carleton,		February 23, 1883
J. B. Darling,		January 8, 1887
Hector Haseltine,		March 31, 1888
J. S. Buttenworth,		July 9, 1890
E. A. Minard,		July 6, 1891
J. B. Tyler,		July 25, 1896

NEWBURY CENTRE.

Nelson B. Tewksbury, appointed,   April 5, 1871.

CHAPTER XXXIX.

CONNECTICUT RIVER.

THE census of 1840, gives twenty-seven men as employed upon the river. Before the railroad was built, boating was an occupation which employed many men. The boats in use, and the mode of their operation, are described by Judge Leslie elsewhere in this volume. In these days, when anything but a mill log is seldom seen upon the Connecticut, it is not easy to realize that a large commerce was once carried upon that stream.

Boating began upon the river with the first settlements along its banks, and the commerce extended as the country opened. After the revolutionary war, when the nation was in prospect of a long peace, internal improvements were demanded, and among others, some way of passing the falls and rapids along the channel of Connecticut river. As early as 1785, and probably before that time there were men who were constantly engaged in the business of transporting passengers and merchandise on the river. Many of the early settlers of the town came that way, especially of the Scotch emigrants of this town, Ryegate and Barnet.

The records, from 1809 to 1816, of a storage ware-house at

NOTE. This chapter was prepared after the preceding chapters were printed, at the request of many who desired that all the particulars which could be gathered, of the early navigation of Connecticut river, and of the bridges which cross it, should be thus preserved. Thanks are due to the several gentlemen who have furnished the necessary data, and, especially, to the secretary of state at Concord, and to Messrs. Chester Abbott, of Woodsville, and Arthur K. Merrill of Haverhill, for their kind assistance in collecting data concerning the bridges.

Wells River, show that a great amount and variety of goods were received there, and that merchants and others, from towns sixty miles north of here, had their goods brought in that way. About one-third of the storage charges were for ardent spirits, and the downward freight seems to have consisted mainly of hides and ashes, besides lumber.

The following characteristic letter is in the handwriting of its author:—

NEWBURY, 23d October, 1816.
MR. THOMAS K. BRACE, Dear Sir:

The unbounded goodness of Providence having visited the country adjacent to Connecticut River with plentiful showers of Snow and Rain, I presume you will soon see at Hartford again the Boats from Coös. If Mr. Warren Evans should arrive at Hartford with a Boat, you may put on board two tierces T. I. Salt, & 30 or 40 lbs Lorillard's Snuff. I enclose Thirty-two Dollars on Account.

DAVID JOHNSON.

It must be remembered that at this time the development of the western country had hardly begun, the Mohawk valley was the western limit of civilization, and the growing towns on the seacoast drew their supplies for local use, and for the export trade, within the bounds of New England itself. Consequently there was rivalry between the business men of the sea-port towns of Massachusetts, and those of Hartford and Springfield, for the control of trade from northern New England, and between these last-mentioned towns, and New Haven and New York, which also sought for the Vermont trade.

Boston capital built the Middlesex canal, from that city to Lowell, which was opened in 1803, and the great advantage to all northern New Hampshire soon began to be felt. By the aid of locks, boats could come up the Merrimack to Concord without breaking bulk, and in a very short time merchants at the cities on this river found that they were losing trade. They, in their turn, sought to improve the navigation of the Connecticut, so that boats could pass from Hartford to Barnet. The falls which were the chief obstacles to navigation were those at Enfield, South Hadley, Turners Falls and Bellows Falls. There were others, such as White River falls, Water Queechy and the like, but these were less. It was necessary to construct canals around these falls and rapids. The first one opened was that at South Hadley, in 1795. When completed, it was two and one-half miles long, and had eight locks. That at Turners Falls was three miles long, and had ten locks. The Enfield canal was opened in 1829, and was six miles long; the one at Bellows Falls was short and had eight locks. There were shorter canals constructed at White River and Water Queechy.

Boats were built, as Mr. Leslie says, just wide enough to pass through the locks at these falls, and they saved all the labor and time required before, to unload each boat, and transport the merchandise around the rapids by teams. There was a charge for lockage at each fall. In 1823, the tariff of tolls at Bellows Falls canal shows that each boat passing through the canal paid $2 toll, and eighty cents for each ton it carried. The boxes of lumber which were to pass through the canals were not to exceed fifty-four feet in length and seven in width and to draw not more than three feet of water. As there were three other long canals to be passed through, besides two or three very short ones, it will be seen that the canal tolls alone amounted to, at least, four dollars per ton. In the same year the rates of freight charged by a boating company between Concord, N. H., and Boston, via the Middlesex Canal, were seven dollars per ton from Concord to Boston, and ten dollars per ton from Boston to Concord. The Boston people sought to gain the trade of the north country by constructing a canal from Pemigewasset river in Wentworth to Connecticut river in Haverhill, after improving the channel of the river as far as Wentworth. John McDuffee, Esq., of Bradford, surveyed the route in 1825, and made an elaborate report. This canal would have followed, generally, the present line of the railroad, from Warren to Haverhill. The difficulty of getting water at the height of land was the chief obstacle. The merchants of Haverhill Corner, which, eighty years ago was the most important place in the north country, were not in favor of river navigation, their interest lying in the Coös turnpike, which was largely built by Haverhill capital, and which, in its turn, built up Haverhill Corner. This turnpike, which went out through Court street, and passed between the Tarleton lakes in Piermont to Warren, was then the most traveled road in all this region. There was a tavern about every two miles, and often 200 teams passed over it in a day. One may now travel for miles along that road without meeting a team, and what was then a prosperous community, east of Tarleton Lake, has not now a solitary inhabitant. But the passage of boats along the river was slow, and some plans were formed by which their time could be shortened. It took twenty-five days to go from Wells River to Hartford and return.

Steamboats were constructed to carry passengers and freight, and take boats in tow. In 1826, one called the Barnet was built in New York for service on this river, but it never got above Bellows Falls. In that year a convention, of which Hon. Moses P. Payson of Bath was president, was held at Windsor to determine plans for the improvement of the river navigation as far as Barnet, or, as Mr. Livermore puts it, "to legislate Connecticut river into the list of navigable streams, and to order the removal of obstacles."

The Connecticut River Navigation Co. issued a pamphlet containing the reports of the president and directors, and that of Mr. Hutchinson, its civil engineer. He recommended the construction of dams at suitable points along the stream, by means of which the water could be raised high enough to make navigation easy, these dams to be passed by canals. Two of these were to be in this town, the upper one below the rapids at Wells River, costing about $32,000 which was intended to enable the boats to cross the bar, and pass through the narrows; the other at the upper curve of the Ox-bow, which also included the cutting of a canal across its narrowest part, thus shortening the distance by several miles. This would cost $56,000. The estimated cost of these dams and canals between Hartford, Conn., and Barnet was over $1,000,000. It was expected that when these improvements were completed, small steamboats would ply upon the river, each drawing a small fleet of boats. The project was feasible, and had no railroads ever been built, something of the kind would have been carried out. The latter part of the report discusses the comparative cost of transporting freight at four miles an hour on the river, and at an equal speed upon a railroad, it not being believed then that trains could be made to go faster than six or eight miles an hour, at the utmost.

In 1830, a small steamboat called the John Ledyard, was built, and was taken through the locks by the falls on the river, from Hartford to Wells River. Hiram Wells of the latter place, an experienced river-man, was the pilot. Its arrival at Wells River was announced by the firing of cannon, and a large crowd assembled to see the wonder. A poem, by some forgotten writer, commemorated the great occasion, the closing stanza of which is preserved:

> " 'Tis gone. 'tis gone, the day is past,
> And night's dark shade is o'er us cast;
> And further, further, further still,
> The steamboat's winding through the vale,
> The cannon roar, o'er hill, through dale,
> Hail to the day when Captain Nutt
> Sailed up the fair Connecticut."

But the expectations of those who hoped that its advent would usher in an era of prosperity were not realized. The boat was taken through the narrows, a short distance above the mouth of the Ammonoosuc, to a bar in the river. A long rope was attached to it, and a string of river-men and others, wading, tried to haul the boat over the bar. But to no purpose. The John Ledyard went back down the river, and never returned.

In the fall of that year the Connecticut River Valley Steam Boat Company issued stock for the building of several boats. One certificate, which is preserved, reads as follows:

No. 628.

THIS CERTIFIES, that Henry Keyes of Newbury, in the County of Orange and State of Vermont is the owner of one Share of Capital [SEAL.] Stock in the Connecticut River Valley Steam Boat Company, transferable according to the form subjoined.

WITNESS the Corporate Seal of said Company at Windsor, this 16th day of March, A. D. 1831.

J. W. HUBBARD. *Clerk.*   JONA. H. HUBBARD, *President.*
Shares, No. 1174.

On the back of this certificate is the pencilled memorandum: "Paid $12.50 March 21, 1831."

In that year five boats were built, and put upon the river, at different sections between Hartford and Wells River. The Adam Duncan, of which Mr. Leslie speaks, and which was built just above the mouth of Wells River, cost about $4,700. It was sixty feet in length, on the keel, with a breadth of beam of twelve feet, the guards projected over the sides to an entire width of nineteen and one-half feet, and it drew twenty-two inches of water. The cabin was ten by twenty-four feet, and was divided into two parts by a movable partition. Four boilers, each fifteen feet long by one foot in diameter, propelled this leviathan of the deep. Horace Duncan of Lyman was the captain of the boat, and Hiram Wells was its pilot. The company issued tickets, which were printed in sheets, and were two by four inches in size. At the left end of each was a figure of the Goddess of Plenty, with agricultural implements at her left, and a mill in the distance on her right; at the top was the picture of a steamboat, and in the vacant space was printed:

"This ticket entitles the bearer to Twenty miles travel on board the Boats of the Connecticut River Valley Steam Boat Company.

J. W. Hubbard, *Clerk.*

Windsor, Jan. 20, 1831."

The Adam Duncan made a trial trip, it seems, and on its second trip, which was a Fourth of July excursion to Hanover, the connecting pipe between the boilers burst, letting the steam and water escape. There can be few, besides Mr. Leslie, surviving, who were on the boat at the time. "Several of the passengers," he says, "were in the fire-room, but no one was injured except Dr. Dean of Bath, who jumped overboard, and was drowned." This ended the career of the "Adam Duncan" which was taken to Olcott Falls and stripped of its machinery.

The steamboat company did not long survive the Adam Duncan. There were many obstacles to successful navigation of the river; the rates of freight were high; the enterprise did not pay expenses; assessments were called for, and in 1832 the company failed. Steamboat service was, however, continued down the river, below Turners Falls, till the railroad was built. The canals which had been constructed with such expense around the various falls are still, most, if not all of them, used for some purpose. The Enfield canal is owned by a corporation called the Connecticut River Co., and is still kept open for the passage of boats, and quite a revenue is collected from mills which extend for about a mile along its banks, and receive water from it. The old canal at Holyoke, which is on the Hadley side, furnishes power for several mills, and the same may be said of that at Bellows Falls.

In 1825, the war department sent an engineer to Barnet, who made surveys of three separate routes for a canal from that place to Canada. The same season, the Connecticut River company employed Holmes Hutchinson, an expert from the Erie canal, who made a survey of the river from Barnet to Hartford. His report as to the feasibility and desirability of the scheme was accepted by the company. But nothing was ever done in the practical work of constructing a canal, although, had no railroad ever been built, such a canal would have been made. But the first charter for a railroad in Vermont was granted in the same year in which the steamboat company went to pieces, and the era of railroad building set in. Within a few years the canals which had been constructed at such an expense, and with such expectations, the Middlesex, and the New Haven and Northampton Canal, were disused. The former was, practically, discontinued in 1846, and the last boat passed through it in 1852. Traces of this former highway of commerce may still be seen, beside the railroad, in Billerica and Wilmington.

We have considered the means by which our fathers sought to utilize the river for transportation; our narrative now concerns itself with the bridges which have spanned the stream since 1795.

For the first thirty-five years after the settlement of Newbury and Haverhill, all public travel across Connecticut river, in the open season, was by ferry. Charters for ferries were sometimes granted by the New Hampshire legislature, and sometimes the towns on both sides of the river permitted some one to keep a ferry during a limited period, at a place not covered by any charter. The first ferry was kept by Richard Chamberlin, and after him by his sons. He had no charter, but kept the boat for the public convenience. In 1772, the legislature of New Hampshire approved his title to keep a ferry, and in the next year a town meeting in Newbury confirmed his right, and fixed the rates of toll.

The ferry of Col. Asa Porter was by charter, which gave him the exclusive right to maintain one between his farm and the Ox-bow, his right extending for three miles up, and as many down, the river. At Wells River, Er Chamberlin began to keep a ferry, about 1772, for which, after some years, he obtained a charter. At South Newbury, it is said that Uriah Stone, a native of Germany, who came to Haverhill in 1763 or 1764, and settled very near the present site of Bedell's bridge, carried people across the river in a boat which he made himself, hewing out the planks. Later, he removed to Piermont where he settled on what is now called the Hibbard place, where he kept a ferry to Mooretown, now Bradford. He died in 1819. The late President Chester A. Arthur was his great-grandson.

Moody Bedell kept a ferry a little above the present bridge called by his name, and in 1801, the town of Haverhill granted him the right to maintain one between his farm, which was below the mouth of the Oliverian, and that of Remembrance Chamberlain, in Newbury. The "ferry house" was on the Newbury side. The right to maintain a ferry from Colonel Porter's farm, now called the Southard place, on Horse Meadow, to the Ox-bow, still remains in the farm.

Ferry-boats were flat-bottomed, and were wide enough, and long enough, to convey a loaded wagon with horses or oxen. Usually two or more boats were kept at the ferry, one for foot passengers, and a larger one for teams. When a traveler came to the river side opposite the "ferry house," if he saw no one with the boat, he proceeded to "hail the ferryman."

The first bridge across Connecticut river was built at Bellows Falls, in 1785, by Col. Enoch Hale, father of Joshua Hale, long so prominent at Wells River. It consisted of a single span, 365 feet in length, and extended from a ledge of rocks on one side of the river, to one on the other side. This bridge was of much value to the surrounding country, but proved a financial loss to its owner. In 1797 there were thirteen bridges across the river. Newbury and Haverhill being the principal towns in this part of the valley, and lying on the great road from the market towns to the north country and Canada, the principal men in both towns early saw the advantage which a bridge between them would be, locally, and also what an impetus it would give to the increasing traffic from the growing towns to the north, if there was a bridge here by which the river could be quickly and safely crossed at all seasons.

The first charter for a bridge between Newbury and Haverhill was granted January 14, 1795, to Col. Asa Porter, "and Associates," who were styled the "Proprietors of Haverhill Bridge."* This was to be erected, as near as might be, upon the boundary between Haverhill and Bath, near the northerly end of the ridge upon which the railroad engine house is built, at Woodsville, a few rods north of the present bridge. The middle pier of it was to be built upon the small island in the river there, which was ceded to the proprietors of the bridge, and they were granted the exclusive right between the south end of what is now called Howard's Island, and a point two miles above the mouth of the Ammonoosuc. Four years were allowed for completion, a time which was in 1797, extended three years. No bridge was ever erected there.

The second charter for a bridge at Wells River was approved, December 27, 1803, and the incorporators were: Er Chamberlin, Ezekiel Ladd, James Whitelaw, Moses Little, Amos Kimball, William Abbott, and their associates.† The charter granted to Colonel Porter having lapsed, the new enterprise was given the privileges which had belonged to that one. It was to be placed

---

*N. H. Manuscript Laws, Vol. IX., p. 77.

†N. H. Manuscript Laws, Vol. XIV., p. 285.

where Er Chamberlin had kept a ferry for about twenty-five years. One share in the bridge was reserved to the latter, to recompense him for the loss of his ferry, and the right to maintain one reverted to him, upon the discontinuance of the bridge. This bridge was built in 1805, and stood below the present one, and above the mouth of Wells River, "at the ledge of rocks." The records of the Wells River Bridge Corporation show that in 1806 the shares of the bridge sold at their par value of fifty dollars, which proves that it was profitable. The rates of toll as fixed by the charter were: For each foot passenger, one cent; for a horse and rider, three cents; each chaise or two-wheeled carriage drawn by one horse, ten cents; one-horse wagon or cart drawn by one beast, eight cents; by two beasts, ten cents; each four-wheeled carriage or coach, twenty-five cents, and two cents for each horse more than two; two cents for each animal, except sheep and swine which were one cent each. These rates differ slightly from those of the Porter charter. It is not thought that this was a covered bridge, but that it was built upon wooden piers.

In the spring of 1807, this bridge was carried away by a freshet, and was rebuilt in that year. Between 1807 and 1812, when it was again carried away, it underwent considerable repairs. From 1812 to 1820, there was no bridge, and the ferry was conducted as before, by Chamberlin, who, in 1817, conveyed all his rights therein to John L. Woods.* The New Hampshire legislature in January, 1813, passed an act to allow the proprietors to rebuild and complete the bridge within two years after the following September.† An extension of two years time was granted in 1815, and a further extension of three years from November 1, 1817, was granted by the legislature, in the preceding June.

In 1820, a new bridge was constructed at a cost of about $3,000. This stood below the mouth of Wells River, and the abutment, on the Woodsville side can still be seen. This bridge, says Mr. J. P. Kimball, was originally an open bridge, and was built on "horses" or wooden piers, there being several of these under the bridge. Some time after it was built a sort of temporary roof was constructed over it. This bridge was carried away by the freshet of 1850. In the course of that summer a new bridge was erected there, which stood till the present one was completed, and then it was taken down.

In 1853, the Boston, Concord and Montreal Railroad Co. secured an entrance into Vermont by inducing the owners of this last bridge to erect a new one, a short distance below the mouth of

---

*Bridge Records.

†1. N H. Manuscript Laws, Vol. XX., p. 46. 2. Ib. XX. p. 288. 3. Ib. XXI. p. 48.

the Ammonoosuc, granting them the privilege of laying their tracks along the roof of the bridge, where they still remain. When it was built, and for many years after, locomotives and cars were constructed very much lighter than they are now, and traffic was also light, but in later years the increasing weight of rolling stock, and the increase also of traffic has compelled the repeated strengthening of the structure, which has narrowed the roadway until it is hardly wide enough for two teams to pass. The frequent passage of heavy trains, and shifting engines along the roof, render it a dangerous place, yet no serious accidents have yet occurred there. A new highway bridge, of modern construction, between Wells River and Woodsville, is greatly demanded.

The journal of the New Hampshire House of Representatives for the session of 1794, states that among the business brought before the house on December 30, was the following: "Whereas, Benjamin Chamberlin of Newbury, Vermont, proposes building a Bridge over Connecticut river, at, or near the place where he and his fathers have kept a ferry ever since the settlement of the town, which is the best and oldest road for passing between the states to the north and Canada, prays to be allowed to build and tend said bridge for toll." The principal subscribers to the enterprise, on the Haverhill side, were: Moses Dow, $400; Ezekiel Ladd and John Montgomery, each $100; and on the Newbury side: Thomas Johnson, $300; Benjamin and Nathaniel Chamberlin, and Josiah Little, each $100. The Haverhill subscriptions amounted to $1,000, and it was stated that as much had been promised from Newbury, but owing to the high water and floating ice prevailing at the time, the man with the Newbury subscription was unable to cross the river. On the 7th of January, 1795, the same day on which Colonel Porter presented his petition for a bridge at Wells River, a petition similar to that offered by Chamberlin, was presented in behalf of Simeon Goodwin and Robert Johnston.

Ebenezer Brewster of Hanover, Peter Carleton of Landaff, and Capt. John Mann of Orford, were appointed a committee to view the river from the lower end of Howard's island to the south line of Haverhill, and select a site for a bridge. This committee reported at the June session of 1795, in favor of locating the bridge about thirty rods below Chamberlin's ferry. The charter was granted June 18, 1795, to Benjamin Chamberlin, Ezekiel Ladd, Moses Dow, Thomas Johnson, William Wallace, John Montgomery, and associates as "Proprietors of Haverhill Bridge."* Their charter rights extend "from the extreme point of the little Ox-bow, to the southwest corner of Ezekiel Ladd's farm, a little above the mouth of the Oliverian." The rates of toll were nearly like those of the Wells River bridge. A bridge was built there in 1796, and stood for

---

*N. H. Manuscript Laws. Vol. IX., p. 164.

some time. It was, probably, an open bridge. Among the Johnson papers there is a copy, in his own handwriting of a letter from Colonel Johnson to General Chase, which casts some light upon the construction of that bridge, and its fate.

NEWBURY, April 19, 1797.

SIR:

You have no doubt heard of our misfortune as to losing our Bridge, it was owing to two things: 1st the ambition of some of the proprietors wanting to have. the longest arch yet built; 2d the workman was not equal to so great a peice of business.   One abutment stands good, also the little Bridges with very little repairing are good, our Plank with a considerable part of the timber on hand.   The main thing we want is a workman that understands building a Peer in the middle of the river, we have no man in this part of the Country that ever helped build one, or knows anything about it.   As you went through the business for us last year, I ask as a particular favor in behalf of the Proprietors, that you would recommend to us a suitable man to undertake to build a Peer.   *   *   Our stone are all within ten rods of the river bank, and our timber within ¾ of a mile.   One Peer will want to be twenty-five feet high.   In this case I wish you would make a brief guess what the cost would be to build such a peer.

Yours, etc.,

THOS. JOHNSON."

That some kind of a bridge was reconstructed there seems evident from the recorded action of the selectmen in 1798, who placed the south limit of highway District No. 2, which "runs down on the river as far as the north abutment of the bridge across Connecticut river." This bridge is mentioned elsewhere. But it did not stand many years, evidently, as the records of the present bridge corporation, beginning January 1, 1805, state that on that day a meeting of the Haverhill Bridge Company was held, at which Charles Johnston, Samuel Ladd, Joseph Pearson, John Montgomery, Jeremiah Harris and Asa Tenney were appointed a committee to make estimates for building a bridge similar to the "Federal Bridge" over the Merrimack river at Concord, and to determine the best place to build said bridge. This committee reported, May 4, 1805, that the bridge be built "from land of Mr. Phineas Ayer in Haverhill, to that of Col. Robert Johnston in Newbury," i. e., where the present bridge is. Some time between that date and 1809, a bridge was built. The records are meagre, and nothing is said about this bridge being carried off, but on April 3, 1822, Ephraim Kingsbury, the clerk, sold all the shares in the corporation to Asa Tenney and Josiah Little for one cent a share. It would seem there was nothing left of the bridge.

There is no further record till August 18, 1833, when Josiah Little petitioned for a meeting to be called on September 10, at which stock for a new bridge was subscribed.

In the Democratic Republican for September 19, 1833, Ephraim Kingsbury, clerk, advertises for proposals for building the present bridge, and for furnishing stone, and erecting the abutments and a pier, which was built in 1834. No record of the cost is preserved, but it is understood to have been about $9,200. It is believed to be the oldest bridge on Connecticut river, yet it is still called the "new bridge" by old people. The thoroughness of its construction is attested by its having withstood all the freshets of nearly seventy years, although the water has, several times, been three feet deep along its driveways, and great quantities of logs crowded against it from above. It has a double passage-way for teams and is believed to be the only bridge of that manner of construction left on the river. Repairs have been made upon it from time to time, and in 1895, about $2,000 was expended upon it. The structure was strengthened by means of arches, a feature not known, or not employed in this part of the country, at the time it was built.

On April 1, 1898, it was voted to call in all the old stock, and issue new, which consist, of ninety-two shares of one hundred dollars each. It is all owned by eleven persons. The present directors are: W. H. Atkinson, H. E. and R. W. Chamberlain. Arthur K. Merrill is clerk and treasurer.

The charter for a bridge between South Newbury and Haverhill was granted, June 16, 1802, to Moody Bedell and others, to be built within the limits of Bedell's ferry.* The first meeting of the stockholders was held May 9, 1805, at the inn of Asa Boynton in Haverhill. There were one hundred shares of stock, Moody Bedell holding thirty-five. Twenty-three shares were held on the Vermont side, Capt. William Trotter of Bradford, holding fifteen. Moody Bedell conveyed for $900, his rights in the ferry, to the bridge company. The first directors were William Trotter, Moody Bedell, Asa Boynton, and Gideon Tewksbury. On the 24th of June they contracted with Avery Sanders to build a bridge for $2,700. This was an open bridge, resting on wooden piers. General Moody Bedell, for whom that bridge and its successors were named, was a son of Col. Timothy Bedell, who visited Coös with Bayley, Hazen, and Kent, in 1760, and was himself a revolutionary soldier, and a distinguished officer in the war of 1812. He died in 1841. How long this bridge stood is not precisely known. President Dwight speaks of crossing it in 1812. In that year the shares held by General Bedell were sold to Hon. Moses P. Payson of Bath. In 1821, September 4, a meeting was held to see about rebuilding the bridge, by which it seems that it had been wholly or partly carried away. It appears that much of the timber and plank were saved. On June 16, 1824, the report of the committee which rebuilt the bridge was presented, which showed that the cost had been $2,585.61 exclusive of what was paid the committee for their services. It would appear that this bridge stood till 1841, as on February 11th the directors were instructed to use every effort to secure the bridge. But, three days later, the stockholders voted "not to rebuild," by which vote it seems that the bridge had been carried away in the meantime.

---

*N. H. Manuscript Laws, Vol. XIII., p. 136.

There was no bridge from that time till 1851, when an open bridge, supported by wooden piers, and with heavy timbers crossing the driveway overhead, was built. Col. Moody Chamberlain, J. R. Reding and Asa Low were the building committee. This was carried away by the high water of the spring of 1862. In the fall of that year the middle pier of the present bridge was constructed, and the next year a covered bridge was built. C. G. Smith, Johnson Chamberlain and Nathaniel Bailey were the building committee. This bridge was of very light construction, and in 1865, the directors were instructed to strengthen it by putting in arches. This structure was very narrow, and was demolished by a gale, July 4, 1866. The present bridge was built in that year.

In 1812, a law was passed equalizing the tolls on the three bridges between Newbury and Haverhill, as follows: Each foot passenger, one cent; each person, except the driver, on any team, one cent; each one-horse team six and one-fourth cents; each chaise or other carriage, twelve and one-half cents; each team drawn by three horses, fifteen cents; four-wheeled carriage drawn by two horses, twenty-five cents, and three cents for each additional horse.*

In 1809, a charter was granted to Asa Tenney, Thomas, John, Moses and David Johnson, and William B. Bannister of Newbury, and eighteen others, resident elsewhere, for a bridge between Horse Meadow and the Ox-bow, at some place between one-half mile above, and one-half mile below Colonel Porter's ferry.† The proprietors were to build a road "from Colonel Porter's ferry house, to the main road in Haverhill." It is not known that any action was ever taken about building a bridge at that place.

---

*N. H. Manuscript Laws, Vol. XIX., p. 299.

†Ib., Vol. XVIII., p. 278.

ELM TREE AND RESIDENCE OF THE LATE HORATIO BROCK,
NOW OWNED BY JAMES A. BROCK.

THE KENT HOUSE, SOUTH NEWBURY.
BUILT BY COL. JACOB KENT 1ST. CLARK KENT STANDS AT THE LEFT OF THE
DOOR AND COL. JACOB KENT, 3D TO THE RIGHT OF IT. MISS RELIEF KENT

CHAPTER XL.

HIGHWAYS AND RAILROADS.

THE first volume of town proceedings contains the certified surveys of eighty-four roads or alterations of roads, which included all the highways which were laid out, and formally accepted by the town, to the year 1837. The earliest of these is the present river road, "beginning at the town line as was formerly," to Wells river—the stream, not the village. This return only gives the general course of the road, which, in several instances, departs from that of the "old" road. The second road accepted by the town, was one from "Mr. John Mills'es," (now Doe's Corner,) "to the town line near James Heath's," and is the road which passes out by the Rogers hill schoolhouse, and the old Haseltine place, through the Grow neighborhood, to the Corinth line, in what is now Topsham. John Wilson of Bradford stated in writing in his old age, that in 1795, this was the only road from Corinth to Newbury. A portion of this road, has been discontinued. It was surveyed by Aaron Shepard in 1785, and the courses are marked by trees. At the same time the road from Ebenezer White's, now Warren Bailey's, to the place at West Newbury where the late John Wilson long lived, and thence past the cemetery to the Rogers hill schoolhouse, was accepted.

It must be understood that these dates do not show when these roads first began to be trod, but when they were accepted by the town, which thenceforth assumed their maintenance. Before the time of such survey and acceptance, the roads were merely paths through the woods, and were kept in such repair and improvement as the people who lived on them were able to give, which was not much. The first roads were merely passages through the forest, through which people could find their way by "blazed" or spotted trees. The first settlers in the back parts of the town had no better roads than these during the first years, which were not passable by wheeled vehicles. The road to West Newbury, thus surveyed and accepted in 1785, had been traveled some fifteen years by that time.

The road that leads from Newbury Street to East Corinth, called the "county road," and which is one of the roads laid out by a county commission of which Col. Frye Bayley was a member, about 1797, has undergone more changes in its general course than any other, except the river road. It begins to be mentioned in 1788, and formerly left the present road behind the house of H. D. Gamsby, about half a mile from the top of "sawmill hill," and may be followed till it came out a little west of the highest point of land, between the village and the town farm. This old road was, except for the long, hard hill at the east end of it, very straight and level, and the road which comes from Leighton hill, was continued into the woods where the two joined. This old road was discontinued in 1841, when the present road was made, and the road east of Harriman's pond was laid out about the same time. The old county road again left the present road where there is a bend near a small brook, at the top of the last hill east of the town farm, and took a straight course over the hill, coming out at the great willow on the Peach farm, where F. G. Howland now lives. Later, the west end of it was brought down south of, and near Mrs. Demeritt's house, coming upon the present road a little west of it, where the schoolhouse once stood. This road was discontinued in 1824. The distance from the Peach farm to the street was about one-third less by these old roads than by the present one, and both are still used as foot-paths. There was no road past the present town farm till 1827, but the highway left the county road near the Lilly pond, half a mile east of the town house, and went south, past where Levi Whitman now lives, (that farm was not cleared then,) and came out to the one which now ends at the old Boynton place, now part of the Chalmers farm. The cellars of six houses which formerly stood on, or near that road, may still be seen.

At the top of the hill, beyond L. W. McAllister's, near Round pond, the old road took a straight course west and south of the present one, which it did not touch again till it came out and crossed it at the "four corners," where the late Davis Cheney lived, in a large, two-story house. Thence it followed the road which goes toward Currier hill, about half a mile, and turning abruptly, passed through the west side of what is now J. E. Currier's field, joining the present road near the ruinous schoolhouse in the Doe neighborhood.

There are many miles of such disused roads in this town, and the precise location of some is not now remembered. Somewhere about 1840, the road along Wells river, from the paper mill to the four corners was made. Before that time all travel went up an old road from the paper mill to the "Ben Chamberlin place."

The road through Cow meadow gave the town considerable trouble, as appears from many recorded actions in town meeting. At one time the river washed away a section of it and the selectmen laid out a new road a little further from the bank of the river, but the abutting landowners refused to accept the damages awarded by the town for the land taken to set it further back, erecting gates across the road, which were not all removed till after 1805. This road formerly kept close along the river-bank, all the way from the Ox-bow to the foot of the Frye Bayley hill. The north end of it was altered to run west of the railroad, when the latter was built, in 1847.

In 1830, after several years of agitation, and determined opposition, a road was laid out around the base of Ingalls hill. Tappan Stevens was the leader of the agitation for this road, and David Johnson, who then owned the Ingalls farm, was the no less resolute leader of the opposition. A great deal of extravagant language was used, both by those who favored, and those who opposed the undertaking, and several appeals to the county court were had. But it was finally built, and was of great help to the heavy teaming of those days.

Formerly the highway tax was worked out, and only unsatisfactory results, in most cases, came from the labor. After heavy winter storms the roads were broken out, all the men and oxen in a neighborhood turning out to the task. With the use of road machines, snow rollers, and a more efficient oversight, the highways have steadily improved.

The first iron bridge in town was built at Wells River in 1880. There are now three over Wells river, and three over Hall's brook.

The railroad was opened from Boston to Concord in 1842, and it was determined by the ruling powers in New Hampshire at that time, that the road should not be extended beyond that point, and the legislature of that year passed a law, by a vote of 136 to 84, that no railroad should be constructed until the corporation should first pay to the owner of lands which they proposed to cross, whatever he should exact for the privilege. This put a stop to railroad building in that state for several years, and the attempt to secure a charter for a road from Franklin to Orford failed. But in a few years the agitation for railroads in the north part of the state became so formidable as to threaten to overturn the party in power, when charters were secured for the Northern railroad from

Concord to the mouth of White River, and for the Boston, Concord and Montreal, from Concord to some point on the Connecticut river in Haverhill.

The Connecticut and Passumpsic Rivers railroad was first chartered November 10, 1835, but no work was ever done under this charter, which became void. The second charter was secured October 31, 1843. The road was to commence at some point on the Massachusetts line, near the Connecticut river, run up that river and the Passumpsic, to some point on the Canada line, in Newport or Derby.

In 1845, the right was secured to divide the route at the mouth of White river, the northerly portion to be called the "Connecticut and Passumpsic Rivers Railroad." The road was organized at Wells River, January 15, 1846, with Erastus Fairbanks as president. The survey was commenced in April following, and ground was broken on the 7th of September. Miller Fox was the chief engineer, and brought his family to this town. A steam shovel was brought up and set to work on William U. Bailey's farm, and multitudes flocked to see the strange machine. The ledge at Ingalls hill was considered the most difficult part of the work between White River Junction and Wells River. The men employed at that time in railroad construction were mostly Irishmen, and a horde of men, women and children of that nationality invaded the town, where their brogue and actions excited aversion and fear. Many of their cabins stood along the foot of the hill south of where Mr. Learned now lives, then called the "Frye Bayley hill."

Several years before, the town had, at great expense, built a road around the base of Ingalls hill, close to the river, which may still be traced, in places, and which was of great help to the heavy travel which, in those days, went along the river road.

There was not, however, room enough around the base of the ledge for both railroad and highway, and the railroad was obliged to purchase of the town the road which it had constructed around the foot of the hill.

·A short time after work began on the ledge at that place, a riot broke out among the Irishmen, which ended in a tragedy. There was a bitter feud between the men who came from the county of Connaught, in Ireland, and those who came from the county of Cork. The latter, who were called the Corkonians, had driven the former, who were known as the Fardowners, from their work on the Northern railroad. The Connaught men came up to work on the Passumpsic railroad, and when the Northern road was completed, the Cork men came to work on this road, and there was soon trouble between the two gangs. Most of the men employed in the great cut at Ingalls hill were Cork men, and in the night of the 21st of September, 1847, a party of the Connaught men went in a body to the shanties of the Cork men, threatening their lives.

and attempting to break in upon them. But the Cork men had firearms, and kept their assailants at bay, who went away, threatening to return in a week with re-enforcements. The next day, which was Monday, Michael Kelley, who was in charge of the work at Ingalls hill secured warrants against several of the rioters, and, with Leander Quint as deputy sheriff, arrested three of them, took them to Newbury and returned after others. On entering a shanty at the south end of Ingalls hill Kelley pointed out Patrick Gallagher, who was arrested, when a gang of six or eight men assaulted Kelley and Quint. Kelley retreated backward, was shot through the neck and instantly killed. Quint escaped. Kelley's body was stripped of his watch and money. The rioters escaped to the woods. The affair produced great excitement, the country was roused, the roads and bridges were watched, and some of the men were taken.

At a court held at Wells River, Michael McGinty was committed to jail without bail and three others in default of it. Some of the rioters were sent to the state prison, but no one suffered death, as it could not be proved by whom the fatal shot was fired.

The railroad was opened to Wells River, November 6, 1848, the terminus being where the freight depot now is. Work began on the railroad above that point December 17, 1849, and trains began to run to McIndoes October 7, 1850. The road was completed to St. Johnsbury November 23, 1850; and regular trains began to run from that place November 28th. Meanwhile the Boston, Concord and Montreal railroad was slowly making its way up the Pemigewasset valley, and the building of that road was regarded with hostility by the projectors of the Northern and Passumpsic roads, for both were after the business of the north country. Late in the fall of 1849, the road was opened to Plymouth, and May 25, 1851, the cars came to Warren. Cutting through the great ledge at Warren Summit took a year and a half, and cost $150,000. The road was opened to East Haverhill in the fall of 1852, and in May of the next year to Woodsville.

The building of the bridge across the Connecticut at Wells River was the occasion of a railroad war. Of this Judge Leslie, who probably knows more about that affair than any one else living, may be allowed to speak in his own words:

"I was attorney for over thirty years for the Boston, Concord, and Montreal Railroad, and the White Mountains Railroad, and had legal charge of their affairs hereabouts during that time. The facts were these: There was a strife between the New Hampshire roads and the Connecticut and Passumpsic railroad, as to the control of the White Mountain travel, and as the roads approached this place, there was a big war between them. The C. & P. went to work to prevent the N. H. roads from coming into Vt., and as a part of the program, laid out the spur road from the present passenger depot at Wells River to the prospective bridge across Connecticut river intending thereby to reach the White Mountains R. R., not caring to have any connection with the B. C. & M. R. R. But the men who were at the head of the latter road were in good friendship with the White Mountain people, but could not reach and extend its road into Vt. without a charter granted to it from the legislature of Vermont, and this the Passumpsic people would not permit, and the N. H. roads were able to prevent the Vt. road to obtain a right by charter to build a bridge into N. H., and as attorney for the N. H. roads I advised that land be bought in Vt. and build the abutment of the bridge upon that land in Vt. and so was given the power to buy eight acres of land for that purpose.

Then the Passumpsic people took another course, and undertook by way of an injunction, to prevent the putting and building of a bridge abutment upon the land so purchased, but failing in this, tried to confiscate this land to the state, claiming that the B., C. & M. R. R., being a foreign corporation, could not hold land in it, but the court held that it could, and decided the matter in favor of the B., C. & M. R. R. Then, to stop further litigation, I advised the B., C. & M. people to make a trade with the Wells River toll bridge Co., whose bridge was below the village of Wells River, and whose charter gave it the exclusive right to build a bridge within a certain distance, by which trade the public travel could be taken through the railroad bridge, which was done, and the toll bridge was taken down, which ended the war.

When the B., C. & M. reached Woodsville there was a great celebration of the event, with speeches by Asa M. Dickey and Mr. Quincy, the president of the road, and the first train was saluted by the firing of cannon and cheers from the assembled multitude.   This ended the great railroad fight."

There was much done, however, which Mr. Leslie does not mention, and at one time one company employed a small army of men in constructing the "dump," west of the bridge, while the other had a crew, equally large, busily engaged in digging it away. There was much rivalry between the roads for a time, and in the summer of 1853 the Boston, Concord and Montreal railroad ran a stage from Newbury to Haverhill depot, and carried passengers from Newbury to Concord, and below, for less than was charged by the Passumpsic railroad, directly from Newbury.   The stage thus mentioned, was driven by Mr. Thomas Johnson, still living in this town.

A charter was obtained in 1849, for a railroad from Montpelier to the Connecticut river in Newbury, called the "Montpelier and Connecticut River Railroad Co."   There was a plan to have the Boston, Concord and Montreal railroad cross the river at South Newbury, and pass up the valley of Hall's brook, to South Ryegate, but nothing was ever done under that charter.   The present Montpelier and Wells River railroad was chartered in 1867; work was begun upon it in the summer of 1871, and it was completed to Montpelier in November, 1873.

The first telegraph line was erected in 1851, and called the "Vt. and Canada Telegraph Co."   The wire, a single one, passed along beside the river road, and had no connection with the railroad; the idea of employing the telegraph in the operating of trains was not thought of then.   The first telegraph office at Newbury village was in the building which is now the Congregational parsonage. Jerry N. George was the first operator at Newbury, or one of the first.   The office was soon after removed to a tailor's shop in the second story of Keyes's store.   It was not till about 1861 that the office was removed to the depot, and the line carried along beside the railroad.   A single wire sufficed for all the business up to about 1870.   The telegraph line from Plymouth to Wells River was constructed in November, 1862. Mr. Farwell was the first operator at Wells River.

Railroading was new business fifty years ago, and some of the early regulations for the running of trains seem curious now. In 1851, trainmen were instructed not to run after dark in bad weather. The depots at South Newbury and Newbury are the ones which were built when the railroad was. The first depot at Wells River was below Stair hill, and the second was south of the parsonage. The present station was built in 1888. When Mr. Allison, the agent there, entered the office in 1862, all the work was done by him, with the aid of a boy. It now requires nine men to carry on the work at that important railroad centre.

The distance along the railroad from Bradford line to Ryegate line, is 9 miles, 2371 feet. The amount of land damages was $16,034.19. Freight rates were very high at first—$1.50 per 100 lbs. on first class freight to Boston.

The mail train south has always passed Newbury at about the same time for fifty years, but reached Boston at seven, instead of four, as now. Except for the first two or three years, this was the only passenger train. The accommodation train was put on for a few months in 1865, and made permanent in 1871. The road hardly paid its running expenses for some years, and shares sold at one time as low as five dollars. But, under the energetic management of Hon. Henry Keyes of Newbury, it was brought into a paying condition, and is the only road in the state which has ever paid a dividend to its stockholders.

The Connecticut and Passumpsic Rivers railroad was leased to the Boston and Lowell railroad Jan 1, 1887, and on the 27th of October in the same year, the latter began to be operated by the Boston and Maine railroad. The Boston, Concord and Montreal railroad was almost bankrupt for awhile, but under the management of Mr. J. A. Dodge, it became a good property. Up to 1870 a single passenger train, which had only a baggage car and a passenger car, accommodated all the travel, above Plymouth, except in summer. Up to 1870, during most of the year, one engine did all the work, above Woodsville. The "air line" trains, between Boston and Montreal, were put on in 1874.

CHAPTER XLI.

Banks and Money Matters.

WE have seen that there were no banks in the colonies before the revolutionary war, and it was not until near the close of the struggle that the first private bank in the country, the Bank of North America, was, in 1781, established at Philadelphia. In 1784, the first bank in New England, the Massachusetts, was established at Boston.

In New Hampshire, the New Hampshire bank at Portsmouth, was established in 1793, and no more were put in operation till ten years later, when another bank was chartered for Portsmouth, and banks were established at Exeter, Keene, and Haverhill. The opening of the Coös bank at Haverhill at that early day is significant, not only of the enterprise of the business men of Grafton County, but, also, of the growing wealth and financial importance of the Connecticut valley. At that time, and for many years after, there was no other bank within one hundred miles of Newbury, and a vast amount of business from the west side of the river was transacted there. The persons named in the act of incorporation of the Coös bank were: John Montgomery, Moses P. Payson, Peter Carleton, Moor Russell, Daniel Smith, Nathaniel Barlow and Timothy Dix, Jr.

George Woodward, a lawyer, who built and occupied the fine old mansion at the south end of the common at Haverhill Corner, was the first cashier, and the bank vault, a structure which would make a modern burglar laugh, may still be seen in the Merrill building. For about twenty-five years, that bank, and its successor, the Grafton bank, was the only bank in Grafton county. The old Coös bank failed, disastrously, after about twenty years. The fact that in 1820 its bills in circulation amounted to nearly $175,000, while the capital stock actually paid in was only $97,700, had something to do with its failure. Many Newbury people were embarassed by the catastrophe, but the winding-up of its affairs was intrusted to Mr. John Nelson, a lawyer of ability and integrity, who discharged his trust with great credit to himself, and to the satisfaction of those concerned. Mr. Nelson built and occupied the house where Mr. P. W. Kimball now lives, on the east side of the common at the Corner. The Grafton bank was kept in the brick house south of the brick block, where the vault still remains.

In Vermont, prior to the year 1817, in which year the first charter for a bank was granted by the legislature, a large majority of the people were opposed to the establishment of banks, or the issue of paper money. The experiment of a state bank, with branches in the larger towns, proved a failure, and came to an end, and this fact tended to heighten the popular distrust of similar institutions. In 1803, charters for banks at Windsor and Burlington were granted by the House of Representatives, but the governor and council refused to concur, on the ground that the issues of paper money would drive specie out of the country; would introduce an extensive and dangerous credit; would facilitate hazardous and unjustifiable enterprises; would tempt debtors to borrow money to discharge their debts instead of paying them; would tend to centralize the wealth of the state in the hands of a few; would make it hard for a poor man to borrow money except upon exorbitant terms; and because the governor and council considered that government was not designed to open new fields of speculation, or protect the property of individuals. These were the opinions of Gov. Isaac Tichenor and his advisers.

Other bank charters met a similar fate during several years, and it was not till 1818, that the first charters were granted for private banks in Vermont, which were at Burlington and Windsor. Banks were chartered at Brattleboro in 1821; Rutland in 1824; Montpelier, Danville and St. Albans, in 1825; Vergennes in 1826; Chelsea and Bennington in 1827; Woodstock, Middlebury and Bellows Falls in 1831; at Manchester, Newbury, Irasburgh and Guildhall in 1832.

The act incorporating a bank in Newbury was passed November 7, 1832, and William Atkinson, Peter Burbank and Timothy Morse of Newbury, William Barron and Asa Low of Bradford, Jonathan Jenness and James Petrie of Topsham, Daniel Cook of Corinth and Jesse Stoddard of Fairlee, were named in the act, and of these, Messrs. Atkinson, Morse, Petrie, Stoddard, Barron and Burbank were commissioners to receive subscriptions. Mr. Morse was clerk.

The amount of stock was $100,000, the number of shares to be subscribed for was limited to four to each person, and ten per cent was required to be paid with the subscription. The books were opened February 5, 1833, at the Spring Hotel, at Newbury, and on the 15th of the same month, the required number of 2000 shares having been subscribed, they were closed. The shares were subscribed for by 1032 individuals, but when the time arrived for the first meeting of the stockholders it was found that the shares had been absorbed by 85 persons. The first meeting of the stockholders was held at the Spring Hotel, March 8, 1833, when William Barron, James Petrie, Timothy Morse, Samuel Hutchins, Ebenezer Brewer, Epaphas B. Chase, and Peter Burbank, were elected directors. The number of shares voted upon was 1949.

To the great disappointment of Newbury village it was found that the majority of votes was in favor of Wells River as the place of location. This is said to have been brought about by the adroit management of Peter Burbank. William Barron and Timothy Morse declining to serve, Jesse Stoddard and Erastus Fairbanks were chosen directors in their places and Peter Burbank, president. On May 22, 1833, Stephen Haight, bank commissioner, authorized the bank to begin business, one-half of the stock being paid in, with Benjamin F. Moore, cashier. Until the completion of the bank building, its business was done in the south front room of the house in which the Leslie family long lived, now owned by Mrs. Graves, an adjoining closet serving as a vault.

On June 6, 1834, the first dividend, of five per cent was declared. The land on which the bank stands was bought of Samuel Hutchins, and the older part of the present building was erected in 1834. January 13, 1835, Timothy Shedd and Ephraim Chamberlin, Jr., were chosen directors, in place of Fairbanks and Chase, and Zabina Newell was elected cashier, and Ebenezer Brewer was elected president. In January, 1836, Levi P. Parks was chosen a director in place of Stoddard, and in February, William Wheeler in place of Burbank, deceased. The pressure of the panic of 1837, forced the bank to suspend its dividend for the semi-annual distribution in June. In 1838, Alexander Gilchrist succeeded as director, Dr. Petrie, who had lately died, and in September, a fourth assessment of $10 on each share was made. In 1839, A. B. W. Tenney became a director, in place of Mr. Brewer, and Samuel Hutchins was elected president. In 1841, Mr. Newell became a director and president, and Oscar C. Hale was chosen cashier, his salary at first being $300 which was gradually increased to $800 by 1846. In the former year, the bank paid a dividend for the first time since the panic of 1837. During those years much real estate must have been taken, as it appears many times in votes to sell. In 1843, Colonel Tenney was elected president, and Josiah Hale a director. In 1846, Mr. Gilchrist, who had deceased, was succeeded by Robert Harvey.

OSCAR C. HALE.

In 1842, the bank voted to destroy, for the first time, by burning, its mutilated notes to the amount of $48,287.50, and unused fractional blanks to the amount of $3,615.57. Before that time the bank had issued fractional currency, a practice afterwards discontinued. In 1845, Messrs. Tenney and Hutchins were authorized to employ an agent to attend the legislature, and procure a renewal of the charter.

October 28, 1847, it was voted to accept the provisions of the new charter, and an assessment of $5 per share was ordered. The board of directors stood for 1848: A. B. W. Tenney president, Samuel Hutchins, Robert Harvey, Timothy Shedd, E. B. Chase, Asa Low, and Charles Hale, the latter becoming director in that year. April 13, Abel Underwood was elected a director to succeed Mr. Low, and on April 27 Ephraim Chamberlin succeeded Mr. Chase. August 31 an assessment of $7.50 on a share was voted, and on December 14, the capital was reduced to $75,000. In 1850, Mr. Chamberlin was succeeded by Nathaniel Bailey, who gave place the next year to Oscar C. Hale. September 27, 1849, a committee consisting of Samuel Hutchins, Robert Harvey, A. B. W. Tenney, and Charles Hale, destroyed by burning $234,800 in mutilated bills. In 1851, Robert Harvey became president, and in 1853, William R. Shedd succeeded his father as director. In 1856, $228,700 in redeemed bills was destroyed, and in 1857, $14,300. In 1858, O. C. Hale resigned the position of cashier, and a set of resolutions was adopted by the directors, in appreciation of his long and faithful service, and $100 was appropriated with which to purchase a silver pitcher to be suitably inscribed, and presented to him. Mr. George Leslie succeeded Mr. Hale, and Isaac N. Hall was chosen a director. In 1859, Samuel Hutchins and Charles Hale were succeeded by R. M. Bill and George Leslie. In 1860, D. W. Choate was elected in place of Mr. Bill. January 14, 1862, it was voted to sell $3,500 of Rutland and Washington railroad stock. This was sold to Jay Gould, and the bank has the correspondence about them in Mr. Gould's handwriting. It was one of his first purchases.

At the opening of the civil war, July 1, 1861, the assets and liabilities of the bank were $373,324.78, the amount of outstanding notes being $267,300, the capital at the time being $75,000. Mr. Underwood became president in 1861, and the same board of directors managed the affairs of the bank during the war. It became a national bank June 24, 1865. In 1866, John Farr became a director in Mr. Leslie's room. In 1867, Mr. Choate was succeeded by John W. Batchelder. In the next year Mr. Leslie was again placed on the board, in the place of Mr. Batchelder. In 1870 and 1871, William R. Shedd was president, and was succeeded in 1872 by A. B. W. Tenney, who died September 13, 1873, having served the bank as director thirty-three years. Franklin Deming succeeded Colonel Tenney as president, and Mr. Harvey gave place, as director, to W. H. Cummings, who became president in 1874. In June, 1875, the capital stock was increased to $300,000, and the number of directors was reduced to five. In 1878, John Bailey, Jr., succeeded Mr. Underwood, and Mr. Hall gave place to Alexander Cochran, in the next year. The board of directors remained without change till 1891, when Mr. Cummings died, and was succeeded as director by John N. Morse, and Mr. Deming became president. November 21, 1893, Mr. Leslie died, after a long and faithful service of thirty-five years, in which he had discharged the duties of cashier to the entire satisfaction of the directors and the public. Nelson H. Bailey was chosen cashier on the following day. In 1894, Mr. Shedd deceased, and was succeeded by Erastus Baldwin. In 1898, Mr. Morse died, and E. Bertram Pike became a director.

It will be seen that the bank owes much of its stability to the long connection with it of its cashiers and directors. Mr. Hale and Mr. Leslie were entrusted with its funds for fifty-three years; Colonel Tenney was associated with it as director thirty-three years; William R. Shedd, forty-one years; Abel Underwood, twenty-eight years, while of the present board, Mr. Deming has been in service since 1874, Mr. Bailey since 1878 and Mr. Cochrane since 1879. The bank has, in common with all monetary institutions, had its losses, and in times of financial distress, it has required much skill on the part of its managers to avert misfortune but it has ever received the confidence of the business public, and in the days of the old state banks, its bills often commanded a premium. Several attempts have been made to rob the bank, without success. In 1900, an electrical alarm was placed upon the building.

The Wells River Savings Bank was incorporated in 1892, and opened for business March 7, 1893, in the rooms of the National bank. The deposits have steadily increased, until, at the close of the year 1899 there was due to the depositors nearly $370,000. At that date the trustees were: James Johnston, George Cochran, J. R. Darling, D. S. Fulton, Ora Bishop and E. W. Smith. The officers were: James Johnston, president, D. S. Fulton and J. R. Darling, vice presidents, Samuel Hutchins, treasurer. A few months later Mr. Johnston died, and was succeeded by John Bailey, both as trustee and president. Certain business conditions under which our predecessors in the early part of the nineteenth century had to labor, may well be mentioned here.

The years which followed the panic of 1837, were "very hard times," and were due, largely, to distrust of the monetary system, or want of system, which prevailed. The supply of farm produce exceeded the demand; it was hard to get it to market, and when there it scarcely brought enough to pay the cost of transportation. Money was very scarce, and many farmers hardly received ten

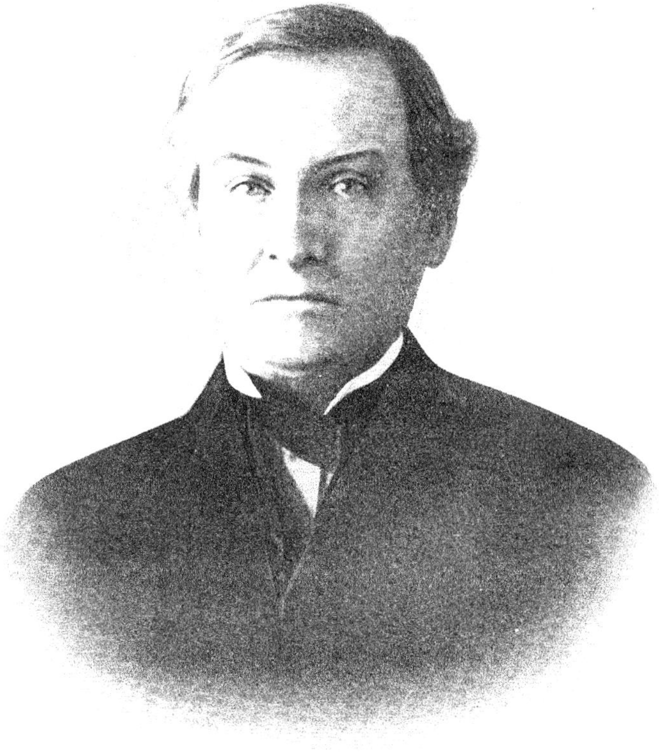

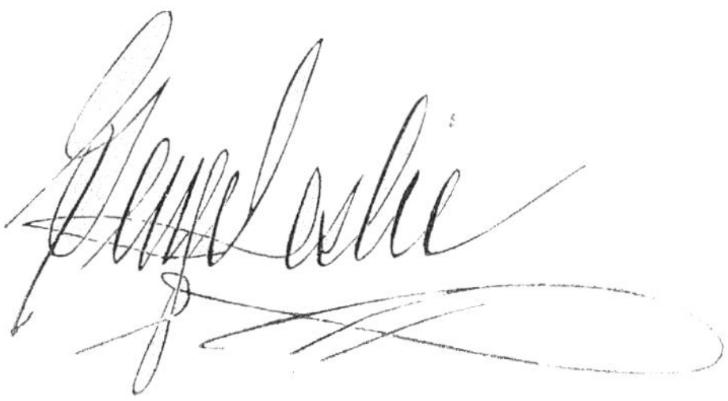

dollars in cash for the whole year. Mr. Henry Whitcher relates the following: "A Mr. Carruth, a hard working farmer of Topsham, in the hard times of 1841, took his butter, a large quantity, to Wells River to sell. He was offered eight cents a pound, but said that he must get more than that, and went to the other merchants, but could get no offer, at any price, so he went back to the man who had offered him eight cents, and sold him the butter, expecting to receive a part of it in cash. But he was told that he must take it all in store pay. 'But I must have some money,' said he 'for I have a letter which has been in the post office for six months, because I have not had twenty-five cents to get it out.' He was given twenty-five cents, and went home." Compared with distress like this, what do we know in these days about hard times and scarcity of money?

One of the evils under which the country labored, was the uncertain value of the money which was in circulation. Whatever may be the faults of the national banking system, it assures absolute protection to the holders of its bills. The five dollar bill which a man receives in Newbury, will be worth exactly that sum anywhere in the country, and even if the bank which issues the bill should fail, the bank note is just as good as before. So that it makes no difference to the holder what bank issues the note. But before the exigences of the civil war forced the present system upon the country, this was very different. The value of a bank note depended upon the ability of the issuing bank to redeem it. If the bank failed, the note was worthless. There were hundreds of banks in the country, and prudent people took only specie, or the bills of such banks as they knew were solvent. People were also careful about taking the bills of banks at a distance. Bills of western banks suffered a discount in the east, because of their insecurity, while bills of New England banks commanded a premium in the west. There were brokers who dealt in bank bills, exchanging the bills of distant banks for those near home for a percentage, which was often very large.

There was also much counterfeit money in circulation. The receipts from an auction held in this town in 1856, amounted to about $1,100 in cash, of which nearly $100 proved to be counterfeit. At present counterfeit money is so rare that Mr. Bailey, the present cashier of the bank of Newbury, has seen but two bad bills in his long connection with that institution. But in those days, each bank had a different plate for its bills, so that there were thousands of different bills in circulation, and it was easy to pass counterfeits of distant banks. There were also bills in circulation purporting to be of actual banks, but which had no existence whatever.

Sometimes the imitations of a bank's bills were better engraved than the genuine, as the counterfeiters could command better skill than the banks themselves. The process of making a bank-note paper which cannot be imitated was not then known. Gangs of counterfeiters infested the country, carrying on operations in remote hamlets, or in Canada. These associations were often wealthier than the banks whose money they imitated, and were able to evade punishment either by keeping out of the reach of justice, or, in many cases, by bribing a jury. To protect themselves, the banks combined in associations intended to detect and punish counterfeiting.

Our neighboring town of Groton, was, at one time, the locality of a gang of counterfeiters. In January, 1849, some dies for engraving were stolen from the office of W. W. Wilson of Boston, one of his employees, named Christian Meadows, an engraver and printer, disappearing about the same time. This man came to the bank at Wells River one day, and was recognized by Mr. Hale, the cashier. Later he was seen in company with a man who registered at the hotel as "W. H. Warburton, Groton, Vt." The latter, who was an Englishman, was a burglar and bank robber, generally known as "Bristol Bill," from his connection with a bank robbery at Bristol, R. I. Detectives were put upon the case, and from the evidence secured, Col. Jacob Kent, sheriff, with a party of men, went to Groton on the evening of March 5, 1849, and arrested Warburton, and a woman named Margaret O'Connell, a counterfeiter from Boston. On the premises they found a complete set of burglar's apparatus. At Groton Village they found a "transfer press," weighing about 1,500 pounds, a copper plate printing press, and blank copper plates. Several men in Groton were implicated in the affair, and were arrested. Under the bee house of one Ephraim Low were found three boxes marked "axes," containing 135 dies for vignettes, names of banks, etc., being most of the lot stolen from Mr. Wilson, and a set of engraver's tools.

Between the robbery of Mr. Wilson and the Groton affair was a burglary on Long Island, in which Warburton, Meadows and the O'Connell woman were implicated. The latter person was well educated; an accomplished and daring woman. She was taken to New York to testify in the Long Island case. Warburton, Meadows, Ephraim Low, McLane, Marshall, and Peter M. Paul were taken to Danville jail. Paul turned state's evidence, Low died in jail. Warburton (Bristol Bill) and Meadows were sentenced to state prison for ten years. After sentence was passed upon Warburton, he sprang upon Mr. Davis, the state's attorney, and, with a knife which he had contrived to secrete, inflicted a dangerous, but not fatal wound, in his neck. After the expiration of his sentence he was taken back to Caledonia county, and there sentenced to six more years of imprisonment for his attack upon Mr. Davis. Meadows was pardoned by Governor Fairbanks, at the solicitation of Daniel Webster, this being one of the last acts of the latter's life, and was afterwards employed in the engraving department of the treasury at Washington.

Among other usages of a sterner age, which have completely passed away, was that of imprisonment for debt, a practice defended by many excellent people upon grounds which a more humane era condemns as both cruel and impolitic. Sometimes the law was of real value, but it oftener inflicted punishment upon men whose misfortune was made to be a crime. Any creditor could, upon failure to meet an obligation, have the unfortunate debtor sent to jail till the debt was paid. This power was a terrible weapon in the hands of a bad man. Our town records contain several articles like the following in the warnings for annual meetings: "To see whether the town will do anything for the relief of A. B., now confined in Chelsea jail for debt." Once or twice, but not often, the selectmen were instructed to see what could be done. There were but two ways of release, either by paying the debt and costs of imprisonment, or by taking "poor debtor's oath." Sometimes men languished for years, in jail, for debt. One man was thus confined in Danville jail fourteen years. A slight alleviation of the evil permitted a man whose reputation for honesty was good, upon giving sufficient security, to obtain employment, if he could get it, within a certain distance of the jail, returning to imprisonment at night. These bounds were called the "jail limits," and persons whose liberty was thus restricted were styled "jail birds." It is fortunate for many men now living in Newbury that imprisonment for debt has long been abolished.

NOTE. In early chapters of this volume, mention is made of Glazier Wheeler, and his counterfeiting schemes, and the statement that he is said to have afterwards been employed as an engraver in the mint at Philadelphia. Mr. Bittinger makes this statement in his history of Haverhill, and it is made elsewhere. Since those chapters were printed I have seen the autobiography of Stephen Burroughs, which if it may be relied upon, casts some doubt upon this. Wheeler and Burroughs were associated in schemes of counterfeiting in the year 1787. He says thus of Wheeler:

"He was a man tottering under the weight of years, having long since, to all appearances, been a presumptive candidate for the grave. He was a man of small mental abilities, but patient and persevering in any manual pursuit, to admiration. Credulous in the extreme, which subjected him to the duplicity of many who had resorted to him for his work; inoffensive and harmless in his manners, simple in his external appearance, and weak in his observations on men and manners. He had spent all his days in the pursuit of the knowledge of counterfeiting silver so as to bear the test of assays. He had always been unfortunate and always lived poor."

Burroughs and Wheeler were sentenced to three years in the House of Correction, and confined on Castle Island, in Boston harbor. After their arrival at that place Wheeler is not again mentioned. One other circumstance related in this autobiography deserves notice: While a student at Dartmouth College Burroughs had for a roommate, Jacob Wood, who afterward became the second minister of this town, and for whom he entertained considerable dislike. Stephen Burroughs was the only son of Rev. Eden Burroughs, D. D., of Hanover, and his book of some 400 pages, is the history of a woefully ill-spent life. But he was a man of talents, and his narrative possesses considerable historical value. Late in life he reformed, and taught school in Canada with great success. He died at Three Rivers, P. Q., in 1840, aged eighty-five years, a member of the Catholic church. Several editions of his book have been published.

CHAPTER XLII.

Professional Men.—Miscellaneous.

MOST of the physicians who were in practice here long enough to be remembered, either belonged to families already settled in this town, or founded families of their own, and are mentioned at more length elsewhere. But, for convenient reference, the names of those who practiced here for some years are given place.

Dr. Gideon Smith and Dr. Samuel Hale were the earliest. Dr. Samuel White came in 1773, and died in 1848. At the opening of the century, Drs. Kinsman and McKinstry, with Dr. White, were in active practice. The former removed to Portland, Maine. Drs. Stevens and Jewett were here in the '20's. The former passed his entire life in this town. In the last half of the century Drs. Watkins and Watson were successful in practice; the former was widely known. Since 1885, Dr. Hatch has practised here much of the time, and Dr. Russell and Dr. W. M. Pierce are the latest practicioners.

Wells River had no settled physician for some time after it became quite a village. Dr. Enoch Thatcher was the first who staid long. He died in 1850, aged 45. Dr. John McNab lived there at intervals after 1825, and had a large practice. Dr. Daniel Darling and Dr. Bugbee were there in the early '50's, also Dr. McNeice and Dr. Blood. The former died in 1859. Dr. A. H. Crosby, of a family famous in the annals of surgery, was located there for some years before the civil war; Dr. Ira Brown and Dr. J. R. Nelson, in the '70's. The present physicians are Drs. Lee and Shattuck.

At West Newbury, a Dr. Merrill was in practice, in some form, long ago, and a Dr. Morrison, who removed to Bath. Dr. Carter

E. V. Watkins

practised there many years before he went to Bradford. Dr. Samuel Putnam was there early, but lived, much of the time, in "Goshen." In dentistry, Dr. Dearborn was here as early as 1852, and had an office in the Keyes building. Dr. Newton was here in 1857, and Dr. Gibson in 1858, and subsequently. He also had an office at Wells River. One Dr. Wood practised in the later '60's, and Dr. Buxton began a practice in 1880, which he transferred to Kansas.

At. Wells River, Dr. H. D. Hickok was for some years in the "art preservative of teeth," but removed to Malone, N. Y. Dr. Munsell came in 1880, and still remains. He also has an office at Harwich, Mass., which he occupies during some months of each year.

The medical history of the town has not much of interest. The biographical notice of Dr. Samuel White gives some idea of what was demanded of doctors in old days. Of all diseases the smallpox was most dreaded, and we may infer from repeated actions of the town, that it broke out every few years. In 1776, it was brought here by soldiers on the retreat from Canada. It again visited the town in 1783 and 1792. In the latter year, an article in the warning for town meeting read thus:

"To see if the town will open a pest house in some convenient place in s^d town."

The town voted "That the meeting recommend to the selectmen to give liberty to have a House for noculation of the smallpox opened in this town, and under such regulations and restrictions as shall prevent its spreading."

In 1803, the disease raged in all the Coös country, and again broke out in 1810, but was not so severe here as in Corinth, where many died. Robert McKeen, a brother of the first president of Bowdoin college, came down with it, and chose to be taken to a solitary habitation, where he died, attended by an old man. In 1847, the disease broke out among the students at the seminary. There were many cases and several died. Among these was a daughter of Barron Moulton, of Waterford, the wife of Dr. Stevens, and the wife and three children of Rev. S. P. Williams, the pastor of the Methodist church. The alarm produced was very great. Hardly any one could be found to attend the sick, and there was some suffering from want of care. It was at the time of the building of the railroad, and it was supposed that it was brought here by the laborers, but it proved to have come otherwise.

Capt. James Wallace left his farm, and for many days and nights took care of the sick. For this he refused any compensation, saying that he had done no more than was his duty to do by his neighbors in trouble. At the town meeting in March, 1848, he was publicly thanked by the town for his attention to the sick during the excitement. There were a few mild cases in town in 1862 and one or two later.

In 1815, the "spotted fever" broke out, but was not so severe
here as in many other places. In Warren, N. H., whole families
were swept away, and entire neighborhoods were depopulated.
Persons seemingly in perfect health were stricken with the disease,
and died in a few hours. Dr. Lemuel Wellman, a noted physician of
Piermont, went to Warren to help care for the sick, took the
disease, and died in four hours. It is many years since any serious
epidemic has visited this town. This town has sent out a goodly
number of physicians; of most of them mention is made among .
the family records.

As with the doctors, so with the lawyers,—most of them were
connected with local families, and are particularly mentioned
elsewhere. Mr. Leslie has given sketches of several who were
located at Wells River, and well known to him. A still more
elaborate paper upon the "Bench and Bar of Orange County," by
Hon. Roswell Farnham of Bradford, occupies 136 pages of Childs's
Gazetteer of Orange County. Reference is made to it for a more
complete account of such as are mentioned here only by name. The
following lawyers, with their terms of practice here, are mentioned
by Governor Farnham:

Daniel Farrand,	1787–1796	Charles B. Leslie,	1843
Benjamin Porter,	1796–1818	Charles Story,	1850–1851
Wm. B. Bannister,	1800–1807	Timothy P. Fuller,	1848–1852
John Wallace,	1814–1826	Charles C. Dewey,	1854–1860
Peter Burbank,	1815–1836	David T. Corbin,	1859–1861
John Chamberlin,	1818–1822	Daniel A. Rogers,	1861–1881
Abel Underwood,	1828–1879	Benj. F. Burnham,	1861–1863
Joseph Berry,	1827–1852	Washington Patterson,	1871
Isaac W. Tabor,	1830–1833	E. W. Smith,	1872
Scott Sloan,	1884–1898		

The above list includes only those who were in active practice
here for at least a year, and more. There were several men, not in
regular practice, but who had extensive knowledge of law, and
were engaged on many cases. Among them the late Richard
Patterson should find a place. He was self-educated, but his
keenness of intellect, and wide reading, made him the master of
more legal knowledge than was usually possessed by men trained in
the profession. Of several of these lawyers particulars are given in
these pages which were not known to Mr. Farnham. But before
the removal of the county seat to Chelsea in 1796, there must have
been several lawyers here who are not enumerated by Mr. Farnham,
but whose names are preserved among various legal papers of the
time. Josiah L. Arnold was in practice here a short time in 1792,
and a Mr. Brown.

Since the retirement of Judge Leslie, and the removal to Woodsville of their office by E. W. Smith and Son, there is no lawyer in this town whose office is located here. Woodsville now attracts the profession as Haverhill Corner did formerly. This part of the country was a better field for lawyers a century ago than it is now. Whether it is that people have become more peaceable, or whatever the cause, it is certain that there was much more litigation then than now.

Rev. David Sutherland says that when he came to Bath in 1804, Esquire Buck held a justice court at Bath village every Monday morning, and was seldom without cases to try. The late Esquire Patterson stated that there were about four lawsuits when he came to Newbury in 1832, where there was one, sixty years later. This condition of more peaceful neighborhoods can be deplored by no one, except by that class of the legal fraternity who are never able to attain to anything higher in the profession than to help forward a neighborhood quarrel.

According to inquiries made by Rev. J. D. Butler in 1849, the oldest house in Wells River is the "old parsonage," now the residence of Dr. Munsell. It was built in 1792, by Silas Chamberlin, on part of the present site of the church, and removed to its present location by James Matthews about 1836. The kitchen part appears to be older than the rest of the house. The next oldest is the kitchen part of the George Leslie house, which was built in 1794. The next oldest is that of Mr. Adams, which was built by Simon Douglass, about 1805, probably. All the old houses between Stair hill and Ingalls hill, on the Upper meadow, originally stood on the old road, which ran upon the higher land, and were moved to the new, or present road, many years ago. The most northerly one was formerly called the Heath house, and is understood to have been built by Sylvanus Heath, who died about 1787. Mr. Scales's house was built by his grandfather, Charles Chamberlin, and is understood to have been built before 1800.

The age of the Colonel Tenney house in which Mr. McAllister lives, or its builder, are unknown. This was the Nathaniel Chamberlin farm, and may have been built by him, or by his successor, Jonathan Tenney. It was moved "down the hill" about 1800. The house of Mr. Learned is one of the very oldest in town, although little of the original structure, except the roof and timber remains. This was the Col. Frye Bayley house, and was begun by him in 1775, but the war came on, and nothing was done to it for several years. It was very little altered when remodelled by Mr. Learned a few years ago. That house saw a great deal of fine company in the best days.

The old Johnson home on the Ox-bow is believed to be the oldest in town, and the frame of it was raised, says Mr. Perry, the day that the news of the battle of Lexington reached Newbury, which was probably about the end of April, 1775.* The contract, still preserved, for doing the mason work, shows that the great chimney was built the year before. It was used as a tavern by Colonel Johnson and by his son Moses. Frank Johnson, the latter's son, owned it till his death, and his widow, who became Mrs. Duncan McKeith, lived there till 1863, when she sold it to Robert Nelson. Many interesting things could be told about this venerable mansion, which has long been a landmark of the valley. As before stated, a wing or addition to that house on the north side, is now the kitchen part of Mr. James Lang's house. According to Mr. Powers, the glass for the windows was brought from Concord on horseback, but it may be that this was for an earlier frame house, which stood a little north of it. The barns are older than the house; one of them is believed to be the oldest building in this town. A plan of these buildings, made by Colonel Johnson, while a prisoner in Canada, is preserved by Mr. T. C. Keyes.

The house of Dea. Sidney Johnson was built in 1800, by his grandfather, the colonel. There was formerly a wing to that house, on the upper floor of which was a ball room, used in connection with the tavern house. The David Johnson house, which Mrs. Wheeler owns, and occupies for a summer residence, was built in 1807. The kitchen part of the house opposite the cemetery, was formerly the kitchen half of the two-story house in which Col. John Bayley lived. The kitchen part of the Silas Leighton house was once the "old Porter office," and before Mr. Porter's time was used for the same purpose by Mr. Farrand. Afterwards, as before stated, it was used for a young ladies' school.

The house under the great elm was built, it is understood, by Mr. Bannister, about a century ago. The quaint old house in which the late Miss Swasey lived was built in 1797, by her father, Capt. Moses Swasey, and was intended to be the kitchen part of a larger house, which he did not live to build.

According to Miss Swasey, the house which Mrs. Miller owns and occupies was built by Col. Peter Olcott, for his daughter, who married Benjamin Porter. Colonel Olcott was one of the most distinguished men in this part of the country in his day, and is not supposed ever to have lived in Newbury, although he was chosen in 1776, a representative from this town to "York," with Gen. Jacob Bayley, but an old plan of the river road, preserved in the first volume of the town buildings, gives Esquire Farrand as living there, in 1795. This house often called the "Harry Bayley house," has been much altered from its original plan. The house of Mr. Henry

---

*A misprint in a former chapter gives the date as 1774.

RESIDENCE OF JAMES B. LAWRIE.

RESIDENCE OF HENRY W. BAILEY.

W. Bayley, was built by his grandfather, Isaac Bayley, Esq. Its age is unknown, but it is understood to be more than a hundred years old. General Bayley died in that house, and six generations of the family have lived in it.

The house owned by Dr. Hatch used to stand where Mr. Darling's now does. Its age or its builder are unknown to Dea. George Swasey. The "Bailey Avery house" was built in 1785, by his grandfather, Col. Joshua Bayley, his daughter, Sally, being ten years old when it was built. She was born in 1775. The house in which Mrs. Lupien lives was built by Rasmus Jonson, a native of Sweden, who came here about 1780.

Returning to the river road—Mr. James Lawrie's house was standing in 1785, and may be a few years older. It may have been built by Col. William Wallace, and was for many years the Congregational parsonage, and was occupied as such by Rev's Nathaniel Lambert, Luther Jewett, Clark Perry, and George W. Campbell. It formerly had two large chimneys, which were taken down in 1857.

The main part of Montebello House was built, according to information considered reliable, in 1795, by James Spear. The one next south of it, at the top of the hill, was built by Joseph Chamberlin, but its age is unknown. It is one of the oldest in town. Mr. Farnham's house was, according to family record, opened as an inn by Joseph Smith in 1788. It formerly had a square roof, like that of Henry W. Bailey's house. Mr. Atkinson's house was built by Horace Stebbins. The hotel called the Sawyer House, was built, as before stated by Capt. Nehemiah Lovewell, soon after the revolutionary war. A small volume could be written about that house, and its inmates, as it has been used as an inn, or as a boarding-house for the seminary students, for 115 years.

The house in which Robert J. Hibbard lives was built by his great-grandfather, Col. Robert Johnston, and is very old. It was formerly larger than now, and a part of it was taken down when it was remodelled. It had a square roof then. Mr. Jonathan Griffin's house was built by Thomas Burroughs who came here in 1790, and that of Mr. Kimball, by Levi Sylvester, before 1800. The "old Stevens house" is one of the oldest in town, and was built by Capt. Simeon Stevens, who died in 1787. Its great chimney was taken down a few years ago, and contained brick enough to build a modern cottage. Mr. John Heath's house was formerly that of Joseph Kent, and had a square roof. That of Robert Meserve is the original Col. Jacob Kent house, but its age is unknown. It is thought to have been built before 1780.

The house owned by C. C. Doe, at South Newbury, was built by Dr. Samuel White, before 1790. The house known as the Davenport house is one of the very oldest in town, and was built by John Mills very soon after the revolutionary war. After him, it became the property of Benjamin Porter, Esq., who enlarged it, so that it was formerly very much larger than now. It was remodelled and a part of it taken down by Mr. Davenport, about 1865. The Porters were a very aristocratic family, and that house has probably sheltered more distinguished men than any other in this town. Daniel Webster, Rufus Choate, Franklin Pierce, Jeremiah Mason and other eminent men have slept beneath its roof. It had, long ago, the reputation of being haunted, and stood empty for some time on that account. Mr. W. W. Brock's house was built in 1800, by his grandfather, Thomas Brock. This closes the list of century-old houses, on the river road.

There are not many as old as that in the back part of the town. The one on the "old McIndoe place" is one of them, and was built by Paul Ford. The old Haseltine house was erected by Capt. David Haseltine, some years before 1800, and is the oldest left standing in that part of the town. The old house, long unoccupied, opposite Joseph C. Johnston's, is supposed to be the oldest in the back part of the town, and was built by Capt. James Johnston. The house next south of the town house, owned by J. C. Leavitt, was built by Thomas Mellen, and was standing in 1802. The oldest in Boltonville is the James Gardner house, and was built, says Mrs. Agnes Gardner, by James Henderson in 1807. In the Grow neighborhood stands a very old house, thought to be a century old, and built by Jonah Chapman. It has been very little altered, inside or out, since it was built. Mr. James Eastman's house is believed by Mr. Whitcher to be the oldest in the Lime-Kiln neighborhood.

It may be well to give the derivation of many local names, although most have been given before.

Wells River, the stream, from which the village has its name, was named for one Captain Wells, who visited the locality in 1704. Harriman's pond and brook were formerly called Taplin's pond and brook. Joseph Harriman was one of the earliest settlers. Mount Pulaski was thus christened at a Sunday school celebration held there about 1825, at which Rev. David Sutherland delivered an address. It was, of course, named for the Polish nobleman, who fell in the revolutionary war.

Hall's meadow, brook and pond, are named from Daniel Hall, an early settler. Different parts of the brook have been called Whiting's brook, Chalmers brook, Peach brook, and the like. A group of houses along this stream at South Newbury, was given the name of Happy Hollow by James Bayley, who once lived in the Brock neighborhood. The appropriateness of the name has sometimes been questioned. A branch of Hall's brook, called Vance brook, which winds about among the hills at West Newbury, and falls into a deep ravine near the Union Meeting House, was so named from a family of early settlers in that locality.

Jefferson hill was settled during the administration of Thomas Jefferson, and was given the name, it is said, by John Peach. Boltonville was first called "Whitelaw's Mills," then "Brock's Mills." The present name was given when the post office was established. Scott's brook, in the northwest part of the town was named for John Scott, an early settler there. Levi brook, in the Lime-kiln neighborhood was named for Levi James, who came there in 1813. He was influential in getting the road built along that stream in 1830, and it was called "Levi James's brook," then "Levi's brook," and then simply Levi brook, as now.

The census of the town, since 1790, is as follows :

1790, 873.	1800, 1304.	1810, 1363.
1820, 1623.	1830, 2252.	1840, 2578.
1850, 2984.	1860, 2549.	1870, 2241.
1880, 2316.	1890, 2080.	1900, 2125.

In 1890 Wells River village had 525 inhabitants, and in 1900, 565. It will be seen by the above table that Newbury has shared in the depopulation of all hill towns in New England. There are more than 200 spots in town where houses once stood, and there are none now. The large farms have absorbed the smaller ones, and the causes of their abandonment are the same as of hundreds of other towns.

Family names, borne by several households seventy years ago, have entirely disappeared, and others have but one or two representatives. A new class, with ideas and aspirations very different from the founders of the town, has, in many cases, come to the farms which they tilled. There are some indications that the tide has turned and that the waste places of the town may again be built up. Better roads, a more liberal policy toward schools ; free mail delivery ; whatever will tend to render the farmer's lot more desirable, will bring about that result.

The following list contains the names of the revolutionary pensioners who were living in town in 1840, with their ages:

William Tice, 80	Asa Coburn, 83	Sarah (Ring) Ladd, 72
Daniel Heath, 76	Joseph Harriman, 85	John Smith, 82
Samuel Johnson, 77	Sarah Ladd, 79	Thomas Mellen, 83
Peter Bayley, 87	Nathan Avery, 81	

Before 1825, pensions were paid at Burlington, annually, for the whole state, and those who lived in distant parts of it had to get their money as best they could. It was common then for some one to go to Burlington and collect the pensions for those living in different localities, for a fee. There were instances known of men thus collecting money, and decamping with their ill-gotten gains. After 1825, pensions for the eastern part of the state were paid, semi-annually, at Windsor.

The last revolutionary pensioner who died in Newbury, was Simon Ward, at the house of Myron Abbott, January 5, 1858, aged 96 years, eight months, 23 days. He was buried at Hanover. The last revolutionary soldier in Vermont, was Jonas Gates, who died at Chelsea in 1864, in his 100th year. The last survivor of the war of 1812 in this town, and the last enlisted soldier of that war in this state, was Wells Goodwin, who died December 11, 1894, aged 100 years, 1 month, 2 days.

This list of nonogenarians is not claimed to be a complete one, but includes all whose names could be found. The year of death, age in years, and nativity are also given. Names joined by brackets are those of husband and wife.

Lydia (Bancroft) Abbott,	1850,	New Hampshire,	90
John Atwood,	1862,	New Hampshire,	95
William Bailey,	1866,	Massachusetts,	90
Sarah Bailey,	1867,	Newbury,	90
Martha (Powers) Bailey,	1880,	Newbury,	90
Beneiah Bowen,	1877,	New Hampshire,	94
Polly (Hilliard) Bowen,	1865,	New Hampshire,	95
Rebecca (Abbott) Brock,	1872,	New Hampshire,	91
Mehetabel (Barker) Carleton,	1842,	Massachusetts,	90
Dudley Carleton,	1879,	Newbury,	91
Euphemia (Fairfull) Chalmers,	1895,	Scotland,	90
Dennis Crummey,	1894,	Ireland,	95
Charlotte (Page) Coburn,	1852,		91
John Downer,	1863,	Connecticut,	92
Sarah (Sargent) Eastman,	1831,	New Hampshire,	90
Martha (Ellsworth) Farnham	1890,	Greensboro,	90
Alonzo Fleming,	1896,	Canada,	90
Elisha French,	1868,		96
Sarah (Towle) George,	1865,	New Hampshire,	93
⎰ Wells Goodwin,	1894,	Ryegate,	100
⎱ Lydia (Heath) Goodwin,	1887,	New Hampshire,	93
Phebe Goodwin,	1881,	Newbury,	101
Mrs. Susan Griner,	1866,	Massachusetts,	90
Judith (Dustin) Grow,	1886,	New Hampshire,	96
Amos K. Heath,	1891,	Newbury,	91
Hanes Johnson,	1878,	Newbury,	90
Ebenezer Kendrick,	1881,	New Hampshire,	96
Marvin Kasson,	1881,	Connecticut,	96

Mary (White) Kent,	1834,	New Hampshire,	97
Elvira (Morton) Knight,	1897,	Concord,	90
Col. John Kimball,	1867,	Haverhill,	94
Mrs. Mary Leighton,	1862,	New Hampshire,	92
Moses Morton,	1899,	Bath, N. H.	93
Thomas Mellen,	1853,	New Hampshire,	96
Mrs. Jane Parker,	1861,	New Hampshire,	97
∫William Peach,	1839,	Massachusetts,	91
∖Elizabeth (Bowden) Peach,	1839,	Massachusetts,	91
Samuel Powers,	1857,	Newbury,	91
Jean (Nelson) Renfrew,	1880,	Ryegate,	90
Mary (Nichols) Rogers,	1816,	England,	99
Mrs. Amelia Rogers,	1850,		90
∫Col. John Smith,	1851,	New Hampshire,	93
∖Sarah (Kincaid) Smith,	1854,	New Hampshire,	92
Dea. John Smith,	1894,	New York,	94
Jacob W. Sulham,	1896,		91
Simeon Stevens,	1858,	Newbury,	91
Michael Sullivan,	1890,	Ireland,	90
Mrs. Esther Truesdell,	1823,		90
Harmon Titus,	1890,		92
Dea. Selah Wells,	1842,	New York,	92
Mrs. Dolly White,	1887,	Vermont,	103
Simon Ward,	1858,	New Hampshire,	97
Dr. Samuel White,	1848,	New Hampshire,	97
Lucia (Kasson) Wallace,	1888,	Connecticut,	93
Jane Waddell,	1896,	Barnet,	92
Betsey (Manson) Willoughby,	1872,	New Hampshire,	90
Ira White,	1886,	New Hampshire,	97
Jabez Wheeler,	1887,	Province of Quebec,	91

Time and education have wrought the disappearance, almost complete, of a class of beliefs which, seventy years ago, influenced the minds of men to an extent little comprehended by the present generation. Still these notions have not wholly died out and there are farmers, yet in this town, who do not begin haying on Friday, or dress pork on the old of the moon. But in the early part of the century, the belief in witchcraft had not wholly died away. There was an old farmer at West Newbury, who affirmed that he had seen witches dancing along the crane in the fireplace at midnight, and believed that some malady which affected his cattle was caused by a woman in his neighborhood, whom he accused of being a witch. In despair of relief he resorted to a process, which, in more credulous times, was held to possess a mysterious power. With a mixture of tallow and beeswax he moulded what he considered to be an image of the offending woman, which he hung up before the fireplace. As the effigy slowly melted, he stuck it full of thorns from the thorn-apple, and at the same hour the woman who had cast an evil spell upon his cattle fell down stairs and broke her arm. When this old man was on his death bed he kept the family Bible under his head as a protection from witches. Dr. Carter, who attended his last illness, slyly took the Bible out, and put in a pile of old almanacs, a substitution which when discovered, came near sending the old man into another world several weeks before his actual departure.

There was once an Enoch Arden case in this town which did not terminate like that of Tennyson's hero. A farmer who lived near the Topsham line went away, and not being heard from for several years, his wife, believing him to be dead, married again, her second husband carrying on her farm. Some time after this the missing man returned, and came into the field where his successor was at work. The two men sat down on a rock and discussed the situation. They finally agreed that the lady, thus unexpectedly the possessor of two husbands, should decide which of them should abide with her. After some consideration she chose, and it would seem, wisely, the second. Whereupon the man who came home, "went his way, and she saw him no more."

After the chapter on post offices was printed, a small memorandum book came to light, which shows that in 1848 there were sixty different weekly papers taken through the Newbury post office. Of these the "Christian Messenger" had fifteen subscribers; "The Flag of Our Union," had twentyone; the "Vermont Watchman," sixteen; and the "Vermont Journal" fourteen. The "Boston Daily Atlas" was taken by Timothy Morse, the "Morning Post" by Henry Keyes, and the "New York Daily Tribune" by some one whose name cannot be made out.

CHAPTER XLIII.

FRATERNAL SOCIETIES.

MASONRY IN THE COÖS COUNTRY.—ANTI-MASONRY.—CHARITY LODGE.—PULASKI LODGE.—ODD FELLOWS.—BOUNTIES IN THE CIVIL WAR.—ELECTRIC LIGHTING.—EVENTS AT WELLS RIVER.—AT NEWBURY.—FARMS—NEWBURY CORNET BAND.

A FARMING town, with no large central village, is not a very good field for the development of those societies which flourish best in more densely populated localities, still Newbury has had a modest share in the benefits which such organizations are understood to confer.

The researches of Hon. A. S. Batchellor, show that the first Masonic lodge in the Connecticut valley, north of Massachusetts, was established at Charlestown, N. H., by a charter from the St. Andrew's Grand Lodge of Massachusetts, dated November 10, 1781. Col. Timothy Bedell, of Haverhill, was one of its charter members. This was called "the Vermont Lodge," the New Hampshire towns in this valley, then adhering to the State of Vermont. This lodge was removed, in 1788, to Springfield, Vt., and Faithful Lodge was chartered to take its place at Charlestown. Dartmouth Lodge was established at Hanover, in 1788.

In June, 1799, Union Lodge was organized at Haverhill. Col. William Wallace, of Newbury, was one of the charter members, and some of its communications were held at Newbury, and it seems probable that many members of that lodge lived in this town, as on one occasion, about 1805, a sermon was preached in the meeting-house before the Masonic bodies. In 1809, this lodge was removed to Orford, and, later, Grafton Lodge was established at Haverhill.

October 17, 1811, Charity Lodge was chartered at Newbury by the Grand Lodge of Vermont. John Ewen, John Bayley, Isaac Bayley, Moses Johnson, William Bailey, David Barnett and others were members. Moses Johnson was Master, William Barron was

Senior Warden, and William Bailey, Junior Warden, of this lodge. For nearly twenty years it was very active, and numbered some of the most prominent men in Newbury among its members. In 1829, the anti-Masonic controversy, one of the most remarkable manifestations of popular excitement, broke out, and was seized upon by adroit politicians, as a means of getting into public office. Dr. Spalding of Haverhill, in his "Reminiscences," speaks of it thus:

"The old federal party in Vermont, in consequence of their opposition to the war of 1812, had become so unpopular as to lose all political influence in the state, and therefore resolved to regain it by taking advantage of this excitement in New York. and were much encouraged by their success there. They induced the editor of the "Danville North Star," to renounce masonry, and publish an anti-masonic paper. The institution was not only attacked, but every mason, whatever his character might have been heretofore. was denounced as a liar and murderer, and unless he would renounce and denounce masonry, was unworthy of being a fit member of society. Some went so far as to proscribe masons in their business. and a few said they longed to see them ·put to the guillotine. Ministers were dismissed from their parishes, and some of the most worthy members of our churches were ex·communicated."

Vermont was the only state in the Union in which the anti-masons came into power. In 1830, William A. Palmer, of Danville, was the candidate of the party for governor, and this party was large enough to prevent an election by the people. Governor Crafts was re-elected, by the legislature. In 1831, Palmer and the anti-masons had the largest vote, but not a majority. He was elected by the legislature, after nine ballots, by a majority of one. The same thing happened the next year, and Palmer was re-elected by the legislature, after 49 ballots, by two majority. In 1833, Palmer was re-elected by the people. In 1834, the anti-masonic party had begun to go to pieces. A large portion of it joined with the Whig party, but Palmer was again elected by the legislature. But in 1835, although Palmer still led the popular vote, the Whig party, led by Horatio Seymour, was strong enough to prevent an election by the people, and defeat Palmer in the legislature, but not strong enough to elect any one else. After 63 ballots there was no choice for governor. The effort was then given up, and Silas H. Jennison, who had been elected lieutenant-governor, on the ticket with Palmer, had to take the governor's chair.

Thus ended one of the strangest chapters in the history of Vermont politics.

Newbury does not appear to have been carried away by the popular craze. In neither of these years did Palmer receive a plurality of the votes cast for governor in this town. In 1830, Palmer received 32 votes, against 182 for the two other candidates; in 1831, 49, against 118; in 1832, 92, against 210; in 1833, 129, against 187; in 1834, 79, against 156; in 1835, 82, against 195. There seems to have been a good deal of staying at home done about that time, on election day, as at Freemen's meeting in 1836, when the anti-Masonic party had gone out of business, the ballots cast for governor, which in 1835 had been 277, rose to 440, and in the next year to 482.

The subjoined account of Masonic and Odd Fellows lodges, and other fraternal societies at Wells River, gives an accurate account of the present status of those bodies. In addition, there have been organizations of Sons of Temperance, Good Templars and Patrons of Husbandry, which had their day of brief prosperity, and of decline. The present Farmer's Grange at Newbury, is of late origin.

*"A Masonic lodge was established at Newbury, Vermont, in 1811, by a dispensation from the Grand Lodge of Vermont, and the first meeting was held in the Moses Johnson hall, October 17. Moses Johnson was its first master and Isaac Bayley its first secretary. So far as I have been able to determine from the records, the last meeting of Charity Lodge was held on the second Monday of December, 1828. Later, I suppose this Lodge was moved to Bradford. January 19th, 1861, Philip C. Tucker, Grand Master of Vermont, granted a dispensation for the re-establishment of a Masonic lodge at Newbury, and appointed D. A. French the first master; A. W. Eastman, the first deacon, and Milo Dodge the first junior deacon. The first meeting of Pulaski Lodge was held at Brother Tappan Stevens'. At this meeting Ephriam B. Stevens was elected first treasurer and Henry L. Watson first secretary. A. W. Eastman contracted with Mr. Keyes for the use of his hall for $30 a year. At a meeting of Pulaski Lodge, held August, 7, 1871, it was voted to remove the lodge to Wells River, as soon as a suitable hall could be procured, and S. S. Peach and E. G. Parker, were appointed a committee to confer with Mr. Penneman, in regard to same. Soon afterwards Pulaski Lodge was finally and pleasantly established in its new quarters in Wells River, where it has been located for the past twenty-eight years. Pulaski Lodge has always maintained a high standard of excellence in its work among the lodges of the state. It has made many good men Masons within its walls. It has always dispensed charity to all worthy brothers of the order when called upon. It now numbers sixty-four members. Its present officers are: H. T. Baldwin, master; J. A. George, S. W.; R. U. Smith, J. W. Financially the lodge is in good condition, and has taken into its ranks, a good many of the leading young men of our town. At the present time it is dispensing its charity with a generous hand, and no worthy brother goes empty-handed from its doors. We wish for the lodge many years of prosperity, and may it ever be found on the side of right in the future, as it has been in the past."

†"Temple Lodge, No 10, Independent Order of Odd Fellows, was

---

*By W. H. Buck.

†By R. G. Brock.

organized March 23, 1881, with six charter members, namely,
Harry A. Holton, George P. Arthur, Samuel M. Chamberlin, Edgar
C. Graves, Frank L. Morse and James A. George. Its growth
from that time has been steady and healthful, and at the close of
this year has had 115 names on its roll. A large majority were
the young and middle-aged men of this town; men who have
been honored by their townsmen with positions of trust and
responsibility. Of this number eleven have died and many have
moved away, and transferred their connection to other lodges,
leaving the present membership about sixty. Since its organization
the lodge has paid to members and their families in sick and funeral
benefits, several thousand dollars, but greater, and more beneficial,
has been the kindly ministrations of the members to each other in
time of sickness or sorrow.

Corinthian Chapter No. 42, of the Order of Eastern Star was
instituted at Wells River, January 15, 1898, with twenty-five
charter members. This institution also is flourishing."

The events of the last forty years can be touched upon but
briefly. The civil war broke out in April, 1861, and the next four
years were times of anxiety, mourning families, sudden changes,
and the breaking up of old associations. With the close of the war
a new era was found to have begun. The frugal domestic life and
quiet manners of the early half of the century passed away, and
were succeeded by an era of inflated prices and more costly living.
City life and the attractions of the west, drew the young people
away. The panic of 1873 still further tended to discourage
agriculture. During the war, sheep raising had been very profitable,
and at one time wool brought one dollar a pound.

When the "hard times" of 1873 came on, many farmers were
deeply in debt, and with the low prices which prevailed, could not
obtain the comfortable support for their families, to which they had
become accustomed. Many farms were sold for what they would
bring, and the town was the poorer for the loss of families. But
our loss was the general gain; they carried the institutions of New
England to newer states, and the sons of Newbury made themselves
known wherever they went.

The changes in farming have been many and great, and those
who have adapted themselves to the successive changes, have
succeeded. Stock-raising, like sheep-farming, became unprofitable,
and was succeeded by dairying, which is now the principal
occupation of our farms.

In the second year of the civil war the town was obliged to
offer bounties as an encouragement to the enlistment of men to fill
the quotas allotted to the town. Newbury was, by a large
majority, in favor of the war for the Union, but there was a

considerable minority who opposed the war, and censured the administration of President Lincoln. At special town-meetings in the years 1862, '63 and '64' bounties, amounting usually, to about eight dollars a month, for the time the soldier was expected to serve, were voted. The war expenses of Newbury amounted in all to $42,622.07. From this came our town debt, which, it is hoped the year 1901 will see wiped away. In all probability the town has paid, not much less than $70,000, as its share of the expense of putting down the rebellion.

Later events at Wells River, not elsewhere mentioned, are as follows:

On July 21, 1870, the freight depot was burned and the old engine house, which had stood there since the railroad was built. In 1876, the old American House was burned. In 1888, the village was incorporated, with municipal officers of its own. On September 26, 1892, the largest fire which was ever in that village, was caused by lightning, which struck the hotel stable about 4 a. m., and the old "Coösuck House" and out-buildings; the Hatch building, used as a barber shop and tenement; the Smith Meader building, used as a tailor and shoe maker's shop; the Belodo building, occupied, as a store and tenement; Mrs. Badger's two-tenement house, D. W. Learned's house, barn and harness shop, and Mrs. Colby's house, were burned. The new buildings erected on the "burnt district" are Hale's Tavern, Mrs. Learned's and Mrs. Colby's houses.

Electric lighting was first introduced into Wells River from the Woodsville plant about September 1, 1891, some twenty street lights were installed, and Mr. Deming's house was wired and lighted, being the first house in town to have electric lights.

The electric and water works plant at Wells River, organized in the spring of 1896, is owned and operated by the village, for the purposes of street lighting and fire protection, and furnishes water for domestic and sanitary purposes, and electric current for lighting or power. The power and pumping station was built on Wells river, near a site known as "Scott's lower mill," where a granite dam was built for the station. The two turbine wheels have about one hundred and fifty horse power. The generator furnishes electricity for sixty-five incandescent street lights, and for about 1800 house lights. In the fall of 1900, wires were carried down the river to the farms of H. T. Baldwin and James G. Learned, and to the Grafton County farm buildings, on Horse Meadow in Haverhill. A power pump, with a normal capacity of three hundred gallons per minute was placed in the power house, and pumps water to a reservoir, on the hill west of the village, two hundred and thirty feet above the street. This reservoir, built of stone and cement, has a capacity of 270,000 gallons, the water being filtered. A ten inch main pipe conveys the water to the main street, supplying twenty hydrants at a pressure of about one hundred pounds to the square inch. The water is distributed about the village for house supply.

Nothing definite has been learned about the mills which have long stood at the several falls between Wells River and Boltonville. At the site known as the "box-factory," a large plant was burned in 1873. Its successor, a sawmill and basket factory, was burned in 1900. At the "Hadlock mill site," Mr. Andrew Aitkin is, in January, 1901, erecting a building for a sawmill and basket factory.

The Wells River Creamery Company was organized October 14, 1891, with a capital stock of $3,000, which was afterward increased to $5,000, and the number of shares to fifty. A building was erected in that year, but the plant was not ready for work till April 1, 1892. This creamery has a branch at Swiftwater, N. H.

In 1894. Col. Erastus Baldwin erected at Wells River, a windmill tower of which he gives the following account:

"In regard to the windmill I constructed:—To have the well bored, in 1894, we went down eighty feet, and struck a living spring of the purest water analyzed. The water came up to the top of pipe, (which is eight inch iron). I have pumped thirty gallons a minute for eight hours and only lowered the water seventeen feet in the pipe. The tower is made from southern pine and is 176½ feet high, twenty-five feet higher than any other windmill tower in the world. The tank the water is pumped into holds 1,013 barrels. Three years ago I began manufacturing sodas, and have shipped this season, and sold, 2,200 four dozen cases. Have used three tons of granulated sugar, beside the other extras. When in full working order I seal up, ready for shipment, 200 dozen per day. The water is used at my house and tenements."

In Newbury village the principal events have already been mentioned. On Sunday, August 13, 1876, fire, caused by children playing with matches in a barn, destroyed the Deming store, the "old depot building," the "old book store," and the drug and jewelry store of S. L. Swasey.

The Newbury village Creamery Association was organized in January, 1892, and the building erected in the following spring, with a branch, or skimming station, at West Newbury. The first creamery in town was the one at South Newbury, which began in 1884, and continued in operation till 1898, when it was consolidated with the one at Haverhill, by the Lyndonville Creamery Co., which controlled both plants.

Newbury has some of the largest farms in the state, and a very interesting volume could be written about our farms and their owners. Few of them are in the hands of the families which owned them a century ago. The largest in town, that of Frank E. Kimball, upon the Musquash meadow, has 165 acres in one field. This farm, and that of W. H. Atkinson, which lies south of it, were gathered by the Little family, by purchase or forclosure of mortgage, from the earliest settlers. The Kimball farm was purchased of Mr. Little, by Timothy Morse, who, in 1857, sold it to Lucius Hazen and sons. In 1865 the Hazens sold it to a Mr. Palmer, from whom, in the next year, it was purchased by° D. C. and D. P. Kimball. There were several large barns on this farm, which were removed, and the present immense barn built by the Kimballs. The fine residence on that farm was burned January 4, 1898. On the Upper meadow, no descendant of an original settler remains, except C. C. Scales and Alfred Chamberlain. The McAllisters own the Heath and Tenney farms; H. T. Baldwin the Hale farm, while the Dr. Smith and Ingalls farm is now owned by Mr. Learned and son, who also own that of Col. Frye Bayley. The farm of F. W. George is made up from the rights of several proprietors.

On the Ox-bow, Dea. Sidney Johnson and Henry W. Bailey are the only ones who own farms, which have come to them directly from their ancestors, the original proprietors. Mr. Doe owns most of General Bayley's farm, and a part of Mr. Lang's was that of Nathaniel Merrill. On Kent's meadow, Robert J. Hibbard is the only descendant of an original proprietor, who owns the same farm. M. E. Kimball's farm was that of Levi Sylvester, and others. A. Greer owns the Colonel Stevens farm. On Sleeper's meadow the three Kent farms are owned by John Heath, C. E. Brock and Robert Meserve; that of Dr. White by C. C. Doe, while the Colonel Chamberlain farm is at present called the "Glendower Stock Farm." That of W. U. Bailey was made up from several farms. On Hall's meadow, that of W. W. Brock has been in the family about 130 years; that of Jonathan Smith for half that time. The farm of James A. Brock, was, long ago that of Maj. Stevens McConnel. That between the two last mentioned, has been in the Chamberlain family for many years.

Lack of space forbids mention of many interesting particulars regarding the larger farms in the back part of the town. At West Newbury, the farm of John Smith has been in the family since 1790; that of W. C. and D. Carleton is made up of the farms of Capt. John G. Bailey, and a part of the "old Eastman place." It has one of the largest sugar orchards in the state, and their apparatus for sugar making is complete.

Newbury Cornet Band was organized in 1857 or 1858. Henry W. Bailey was chosen its leader, and continued as such during its existence. The first leader was Mr. C. H. Clark, a noted circus band leader. There were twelve members. During the civil war several of the members were in the army, and the band was broken up. In 1863, after the return of Mr. Bailey from the war, it was re-organized, and maintained till about 1880. A notable instance of its furnishing music was at the dedication of the Summit House on Moosilauke, where more than a thousand people had gathered, on July 4, 1860. Another memorable occasion was a flag-raising at the Ox-bow, in 1861, where the flag was raised by Capt. Hanes Johnson and David Johnson, Esq.,' the last surviving sons of Col. Thomas Johnson, both past eighty years of age at the time.

About 1868, an orchestra, composed of members from Newbury and adjacent towns, was organized, with Mr. Bailey as leader, which furnished music for all occasions till about 1886. The "Crafts Genealogy" claims that the first piano in Vermont was brought to Craftsbury, by the wife of Governor Crafts, in 1797. Mr. Livermore says that there were, in 1819, two pianos at Haverhill Corner; one was owned by the family of Gen. John Montgomery, and the other by the daughters of General Dow. It is believed that the first pianos in Newbury were purchased by David Johnson and Timothy Morse, for their daughters, about 1834.

In 1893, Mr. George H. Moore erected, about one and a half miles from Newbury village, on the road to West Newbury, the most costly residence in town. The site commands one of the loveliest prospects in the Connecticut valley, which it overlooks for many miles. The house is of colonial style, built of cobble-stone and native rock, laid in Portland cement. It is one of the finest private residences in the state.

President Dwight, in his "Travels in New England," a century ago, devotes several paragraphs in glowing description of the panorama of the valley and mountain scenery which was spread before him as he stood upon the spot now occupied by this mansion.

Some one has styled Newbury "the land of continuance." Its scenery has lost none of its loveliness in a hundred years. Men may come and men may go but the valley of the Connecticut remains forever.

CHAPTER XLIV.

Newbury in the Civil and Spanish Wars.

Soldiers Credited to this Town.—Col. Preston Post.—Col. Preston Relief Corps.—Veterans now Residing here.—Spanish War.

THE following list of soldiers from Newbury, who served in the Rebellion, with their regiment, rank, company and history, was furnished for Hemenway's Gazette by Hon. Henry W. Bailey.

FIRST REGIMENT. Three Months.

NAME	RANK.	CO.	MUSTERED IN.	REMARKS.
Avery, Nathan A.,	Priv.,	D	May 2, '61,	Mustered out Aug. 15, '61·
Brooks, James B.,	"		"	" "
Brock, Thomas A.,	"		"	" "
Chamberlin, R. W.,				
Clark, Fred Ezra,	"		"	
Howard, Emery A.,				
Johnson, George A.,				
Meserve, Robert,				
Page, Albert,	"			
Tucker, Thomas L.,	Mus'n,	D,		
Wilcox, Edwin A.,	Corp.,	D,		

THIRD REGIMENT. Three Years.

Avery, Frederic B.,	Priv.,	C,	July 16, '61	Died at Andersonville, March 13, '65·
Bailey, Henry Ward,	Band,		"	Discharged Aug. 9, '62·
Bailey, Charles F.,	Priv.,	C,		Promoted 2d Lieut., Nov. 25, '63· Mustered out July 27, '64
Bailey, Thomas P.,				Discharged Nov. 6, '62·
Bickford, Wm. J.,				Discharged Aug. 15, '62.
Bliss, Philetus,	"		"	Mustered out, July '27, '64·
Bowley, Addison,	"		Sept. 22, '62,	Died Feb. 27, '63·
Carruth, Robert B.,	Mus'n.,		July 16, '61,	Re-enlisted Dec. 21, '63· Mustered out July 11, '65·
Chamberlin, Cutler B.,	Priv.,	K,	Sept. 22, '62,	Mustered out June 19, '65·
Corbin, David T.,	Capt.,	C,	July 16, '61,	Discharged Sept. 12, '62·
Danforth, Samuel,	Priv.,	C,	Sept. 22, '62,	Mustered out June 19, '65·
Dunbar, Henry E.,	Corp.,	C,	July 16, '61,	Discharged May 4, '62·

Farnham, Evelyn E.,	Serg.,	C,	July 16, '61,	Discharged Nov. 4, '62·
Farnham. Frederic E.,	Priv.,	C,	"	Died April 10, '62·
Gardner, George H.,		"	Jan. 10, '62,	Re-en. Dec. 21, '63· Killed at Spottsylvania May 12, '64·
Gardner, Horatio W.,			"	Discharged June 4, '62·
George, James L.,		"	July 16, '61,	Mustered out July 27, '65·
Greig, James,		"	"	Re-en. Dec. 21, '63· Promoted Sergeant Jan. 1, '64· Killed at Cedar Creek Oct. 19, '64·
Heath, Everett K.,		"	"	Re-en. Dec. 21, '63· Promoted Corp. Dec. 18, '64· Mustered out June 19, '65·
Johnston, Erastus C.,			"	Dis. Dec. 1, '61· Re-en. 9th G. Mustered out June 19. '65·
Kelley, Walter M.,	Priv.,	·K,	Jan. 8, '63,	Lost one eye in the Wilderness. Discharged May 17, '65·
Kelly, Thomas F.,		"	Dec. 31, '63,	Mustered out July 11, '65·
Langmaid, Solomon S.,	Priv.,	C,	Apr. 12, '62,	Re-en. March 22, '64· Mustered out July 17, '65·
Little. Charles W.,	Priv.,	D,	July 16, '61,	Discharged sick.
Lumsden, George,	Priv.,	K,	April 12, '62,	Discharged July 9. '62·
Meader, Charles C. 2d,	Priv.,	C,	July 16, '61,	Mustered out July 27, '64·
Meserve, Amos,		"	"	Killed at Lewinsville, Sept. 11, '61·
Peach, George,			"	Re-en. Dec. 21, '63· Promoted Corp. Killed at Petersburg April 2, '65·
Ramsay, John W.,	Q'master,		"	Pro. 2d Lieut, Aug. 10, '61· Killed in action June 29, '62·
Stebbins, Horatio N.,	Priv.,	C,	Sept. 22, '62,	Tr. Invalid Corps. Died Nov. 20, '63·
Temple, Orvin,	Priv.,	G,	July 16, '61,	Discharged Jan. 22, '64·
Tuttle, Samuel M.,	Priv.,	C,	Sept. 22, '62,	Pro. Corp. Dis. May 17, '65·
Wallace, William, 3d,		"	"	Mustered out June 5, '65.
White, Charles,	Priv.,	G,	"	" " "
White, Charles K.,	Priv.,	K,	"	Pro. Corp. Nov. 1, '63· Mustered out June 19, '65·

FOURTH REGIMENT. THREE YEARS.

Avery, Ayers N.,	Priv.,	H,	Sept. 20, '61,	Died March 23, '63·
Bailey, Auburn F.,	Priv.,	F,	Dec. 31, '63,	Died at Salisbury, N. C., Jan. 22, '65·
Chapin, Charles C.,		"	Sept. 30, '62	Pro. 2d Lieut. Mustered out Jan. 13, '65·
Clark, Isaac,	Priv.,	G,	Dec. 31 '63,	Mustered out July 13, '65·
Dowse, Asa,		"	"	Mustered out June 29, '65·
George, Edmund H.,	Priv.,	H,	Sept. 20, '61,	Discharged.
Heath, William W.,		"	"	Re-en. Feb. 17, '64· Killed at Wilderness May 5, '64·
Halley, John S.,		"		Mustered out. Sept. 30, '64·
Stamford, Thomas N.,	Corp.,	D,		Reduced to ranks. Mustered out Sept. 30, '64·
Teel, Benjamin W.,	Priv.,	F,	Sept. 30, '62,	Mustered out June 19, '65·

SIXTH REGIMENT.

Dickenson, Elijah,	Priv.,	B,	Sept. 22, '62,	Tr. to inv. corps Oct. 1, '63·
Jenne, Stillman,		"	Oct. 15, '61,	Discharged Jan. 6, '63·
Jenne, Roswell C.,		"	"	" Nov. 24, '62·
Jenne, William S.,		"	"	Pro. Corp. Mustered out June 26, '65·
Martin, Moody C.,		"	Sept. 22, '62	Discharged Nov. 13, '62·
Meader, William,	Priv.,	G,	Sept. 22, '62	Tr. to inv. corps, Oct. 1, '63·

EIGHTH REGIMENT. THREE YEARS.

Atwood, William D.,	Priv., C,	Feb. 18, '62,	Mustered out June 22, '64·
Bean, George, N. M.,	Priv., D,	May 17, '64,	Mustered out June 15, '65·
Brown, George L.,	"	Jan. 9, '62,	Discharged July 5, '63, re-en. Died May 20, '64·
Bean, Richard C.,	"	May 17, '64,	Mustered out June 15, '65·
Burnham, Benj. F.,	Priv., F,	Dec. 31, '63,	Discharged Dec. 13, '64 for promotion in colored troops.
Danforth, George L.,	Priv., C,	Feb. 18, '62,	Re-en. Jan. 5, '64. Mustered out June 28, '65·
Evans, Walter D.,	"	"	Died June 25, '63·
Fleming, Freeman F.,	Wag., D,	Jan. 5, '64,	Mustered out June 28, '65·
Hemenway, F. W.,	Priv., C,	Dec. 31, '63,	Mustered out June 28, '65·
Kelley, Loren F.,	"	Feb. 18, '62,	Killed at Port Hudson, June 14, '63.
Meader, Horace E.,	Priv., ·D,	"	Died March 25, '63·
Morrison, George W.,	"	"	Mustered out June 22, '64·
Morrison, Hiram,	"	"	Re-en. Jan. 5, '64· Mustered out June 28, '65.
Noyes, Parker Jr.,	Priv., C,	"	Discharged Oct. 17, '63·
Noyes, James,	· "	"	Trans. La. Nat. Guards, Dec. 31, '62·
O'Malley, Owen F.,	Priv., D,	Dec. 26, '61,	Re-en. Jan. 5, '64· Tr. to V. R. C. Mustered out July 17, '65·
Page, Albert E.,	Serg., C,	"	Discharged Aug. 11, '63·
Prouty, Elijah K., Jr.,	Priv., G,	"	Discharged Oct. 1, '62, for pro'n in 2d La. Vols.
Smith, Robert F.,	Priv., D,	"	Discharged Oct. 17, '62·
Tuttle, Elias J.,	"	"	Mustered out June 28, '65·
Tuttle, George L.,	Priv., D,	Feb. 18, '62,	Re-en. Jan. 5, '64, Pro. Corp. Mustered out June 28, '65·
Waldron, Benjamin,	Serg., C,	"	Re-en. Jan. 5, '65· Died March 29, '65·
Waldron, John M.,	Priv., C,	"	Re-en. Jan. 5, '65· Mustered out June 28, '65·

NINTH REGIMENT. THREE YEARS.

Bailey, Hibbard H.,	Priv., G,	July 9, '62,	Deserted Jan. 13, '63·
Bolton, Carlos E.,	"	"	Mustered out June 13, '65·
Brock, Andrew,	"	"	Discharged May 14, '63·
Chamberlin, Amos J.,	··	"	Mustered out June 13, '65·
Flanders, Amos,	"	"	Discharged Jan. 15, '63·
Learned, Benj. F.,	Serg., G,	"	Discharged March 14, '63·
Learned, Seldon F.,	Priv., G,	"	Mustered out June 13, '65·
Learned, William A.,	"	"	Died June 21, '63·
Murry, George M.,	"	"	Mustered out June 13, '65·
Fuller, Joseph H.,	Priv., C,	Jan. 6, '64,	Mustered out May 13, '65·
Perkins, Jonathan,	Priv., E,	Dec. 31, '63,	Mustered out July 26, '65·
Putnam, John C.,	Priv., I,	Aug. 13, '64,	Mustered out Aug. 3, '65·
Wright, William T.,	Priv., C,	July 9, '62,	Tr. to inv. corps.

TENTH REGIMENT, THREE YEARS.

Bartlett, Alonzo F.,	Priv., G,	Sept. 1, '62,	Mustered out May 13, '65·
Bartlett, Oscar F.,	"	"	Pro. corp. Feb. 6, '65· Mustered out June 22, '65·
Damon, George B.,	Capt., G,	"	Pro. major Dec. 19, '64· Brev. maj. Oct. 19, '64· Mustered out June 22, '65·
Hadlock, James W.,	Priv., G,	Sept. 1, '62,	Mustered out May 13, '65·
George, Charles H.,	"	"	Mustered out June 22, '65·
George, Osman C. B.,	"	"	Died Dec. 2, '63·
George, James H.,	Mus'n, G	"	Pro. prin. mus'n May 1, '63· Mustered out June 22, '65·
George, Jno. N, ·	"	Sept. 2, '64,	Mustered out June 22, '65·
Haynes, Charles V.,	Priv., G,	Sept. 1, '62,	Killed in action, Nov. 27 '63·

McKinstry, Azro P.,   Priv., G,   Sept. 1, '62,   Mustered out June 22, '65·
Place, John C.,   "   "   Missing Sept. 19, '64· Dead.
Scruton, William C.,   Corp., G,   "   Died Sept. 19, '63·
Thompson, Charles,   Priv., G,   "   Mustered out June 22, '65·
Tuttle, Edwin,   "   "   Pro. corp. Nov. 1, '64· Must-
                                                         ered out June 27, '65·

ELEVENTH REGIMENT.

Sampson, Horace B.,   Priv., D,   Nov. 9, '63·   Died Feb. 6, '64·
Williams, John D.,   Serg., L,   June 27, '63·   Died of wounds Oct. 26, '64·

TWELFTH REGIMENT. NINE MONTHS.

Atkinson, William H.,   Priv., H,   Oct. 4, '62,   Mustered out July 14, '63·
Avery, Park,   "   "   "   "
Bailey, George,   "   "   "   "
Barnett. George B.,
Barrett, Charles G.,
Bartlett, Charles P.,
Bartlett, Daniel S.,
Bartlett, John M.,   ..
Bailey, Milo C.,   "
Bean, George N. M.,   "   "   ·"   "
Brock, Thomas H.,   Serg., H,   "   Pro. 2d Lieut. Co. H, March 10,
                                                         '63· Must. out July 14, '63·
Chamberlin, Joseph A.,   Priv., H,   "   Mustered out July 14, '63·
Chamberlin, R. W.,   1 Lt., H,   "   Resigned March 4, '63·
Eastman, Addison W.,   Corp., H,   "   Reduced to ranks Dec. 8, '62·
                                                         Mustered out July 14, '63·
Gage, Asa B.,   Priv., H,   "   Mustered out July 14, '63·
Greig, Thomas,   "   ..   "   "
Howard, Emery A.,   Serg , H,   "   "   "
Johnston, Joseph C.,   "   .
Keyes, Edward P.,   "
Leonard, Sidney S.,   Priv., H,   "   Died May 3, '63·
McAllister, Leonard W.,   "   "   Mustered out July 14, '63·
McKinstry, Alvin L.,   "   "   "
McKinstry, Henry,   "   "   "
Meserve, Robert,   Corp., H,   "   Pro. Serg. Nov. 4, '64· Must-
                                                         ered out July 14, '63·
Moulton, William O.,   Priv., H,   "   Died April 27, '63·
Nason, Joseph M.,   "   "   Died April 7, '63·
Newell, James A.,   "   "   Mustered out July 14, '63·
Peach, Jonathan J.,   "   "
Ricker Isaac M.   "   "
Rogers, Nelson J.,
Rollins, Henry G.,
Stebbins, Scuyler C.,   "   "
Stevens. Augustus B.,   "   Died March 12, '63·
Tewksbury, Nelson B.,   "   "   Mustered out July 14, '63·
Wallace, George W.,   "   "   Mustered out July 14, '63·
Wallace, James Jr.,   "   "   Discharged March 13, '63·
Wallace. William K.,   "   "   Discharged April 22, '63,
Whitman. Monroe D.,   "   "   Mustered out July 14, '63·
Woodward, Clark J.,   "   "   "
Wormwood, William,   "   "   "   "

FIFTEENTH REGIMENT. NINE MONTHS.

Aitken, Andrew,   Priv., D,   Oct. 22, '62,   Mustered out Aug. 5, '63·
Chalmers, George, Jr.,   Serg., D,   "   Discharged April 28, '63·
Chalmers, William W.,   Priv., D,   "   Mustered out August 5, '63·
Cowdry, Albert R.,   Corp. D,   "   "   "
Cowdry, Milo G.,   Priv., D,   "   "   "
Hunter, Nathan A.,   "
Jones, William B.,   "
Wheeler, William,   "

Webber, George,   Priv., D, Oct. 22, '62,   Mustered out Aug. 5, '63·
Webber, Russell L.,   "   "   Dis. at Brattleboro May 11, '63·

SEVENTEENTH REGIMENT.

Aldrich, William T.,	Priv., I,	May 10, '64,	Mustered out July 17, '65·
Cadue, John,	Priv., E,	Apr. 12, '64,	Tr. to V. R. C., Aug. 21, '64·
Chapman, John,	Priv., I,	July 6, '64,	Discharged Dec. 18, '64·
Jenne, Roswell C.,	"	Apr. 12, '64,	Discharged Oct. 13, '65·
Landers, Andrew,	"	May 10, '64,	Died Sept. 5, '64·
Riley, James,	"	Apr. 12, '64,	Mustered out July 14, '65·
Underwood, William H.,	"	May 10, '64,	Mustered out July 14, '65·
Wilson, Joseph,		"	Discharged May 27, '65·

FIRST CAVALRY REGIMENT.

Abbott, Horace N.,	Priv., D,	Dec. 31, '63,	Died in Gen. Hos. June 30, '64·
Bailey, Samuel P.,	Corp., H,	Sept. 16, '61,	Missing Oct. 11, '63· Died in Andersonville.
Bennett, John W.,	L. Col., D,	Nov. 19, '61,	Mustered out Nov. 18, '64·
Cook, George,	Priv., F,	Sept. 8, '64,	Mustered out May 30, '65·
Fleming, George H.,	Priv., D,	Dec. 31, '63,	Tr. to V. R. C. Apr. 25, '65·
Howland, Levi P.,	"	Sept. 22, '62,	Missing June 30, '63·
Leet, Charles Jr.,	"	Dec. 31, '63,	Mustered out June 1, '65·
Leet, Henry,	"	"	Mustered out Aug. 9, '65·
Mitchell, Harris B.,	Serg., D,	Nov. 19, '61,	Pro. capt. Mus. out Aug. 9, '65·
Marsh, Henry G.,	Priv., D,	Dec. 31, '63,	Deserted Dec. 26, '64·
Powers, John Hale,	"	Nov. 19, '63,	Mustered out Nov. 18, '64·
Sargent, Phineas L.,	"	Sept. 26, '62,	Mustered out May 29, '65·
Webster, Emery,	"	Dec. 31, '63,	Died Feb. 15, '64·
Webber, George,	Priv., I,	Aug. 12, '64,	Mustered out June 21, '65·
Webber, Philip,	"	"	Mustered out June 21, '65·

SECOND SHARPSHOOTERS.

Clark, Fred Ezra,	Priv., H,	Dec. 31, '61,	Discharged June 24, '62·
Whitman, Shepard B.,	Priv., E,	Nov. 9, '61,	Discharged Dec. 4, '62·

FIRST BATTERY.

Blodgett, Clark Perry,	Priv.,	Dec. 31, '63,	Tr. to 1st Co. Heav. Art. Mus. out July 28, '65·
Clark, Fred Ezra,	"	"	Tr. to 1st Co. Heav. Art. Dis. Feb. 13, '65·
Kasson, William W.,			Pro. 2d Lieut. Heav. Art. Mus. out July 28, '65·
Little, Dana D.,			Died Aug. 31, '64·
Pennock, Calvin,			Tr. to 1st Co. Heav. Art. Mus. out July 28, '65·

SECOND BATTERY.

Carbee, Henry C.,	Priv.,	Jan. 13, '64,	Mustered out July 31, '65·
Davidson, George B.,	"	"	Mustered out July 31, '65·
Greig, Thomas,	"	"	Died May 11, '64·
Smillie, John,			Pro. corp. Mustered out July 31, '65·

THIRD BATTERY.

Bailey, Milo C.,	Priv.,	Sept. 1, '64,	Mustered out June 15, '65·
Barnett, George B.,	"	Sept. 2, '64,	" "
Farnham, Frank E.,	"	Sept. 3, '64,	" "
Hardy, Sumner,	"	"	
Wormwood, William,	"	Sept. 2, '64,	" "

This list gives the enlistments only which were credited to Newbury. There were those from this town who enlisted in other states, in which they chanced to reside when the war broke out, but it was not possible to obtain their records.

†Col. Preston Post, No. 64, Department of Vermont, Grand Army of the Republic, was organized at Wells River, October 27, 1883, with twelve charter members, and up to the present time there have been enrolled eighty-four soldiers and sailors of the rebellion, forty-one of whom were residents of the town, and sixteen enlisted from Newbury. Of the fifteen past commanders, eleven have been from Newbury: James A. George, R. G. Brock, D. B. Reid, W. H. Munsell, Andrew Aitken, C. N. Paige, W. H. Goodwin, J. M. Waldron, S. L. D. Goodale, N. A. Hunter and Samuel Tuttle.

The Grand Army has for its object the keeping fresh the memory of those who have died, and the town has aided this object by liberal appropriations for the observance of Memorial Day. The organization has also been honored, its members having held every office in the gift of the town.

The following are members of the Post who were residents of Newbury. Those marked with a star have removed from town.

William P. Johnson,	Co. K,	10th Vermont Regiment.
*Cummings Priest,	Co. H,	8th New Hampshire Regiment.
William H. Goodwin, -	Co. H,	3d " "
Sergt. Russell Moore,	Co. C,	12th " "
William H. Munsell,	Co. L,	1st Vermont Regiment Cavalry.
David B. Reid,	Navy,	Monitor Monadnock.
Charles N. Paige,	Co. D,	4th Massachusetts Heavy Artillery.
James A. George,	Co. A,	1st New Hampshire " "
Corp. Robert G· Brock,	Co. F,	15th Vermont Regiment.
Andrew Aitken,	Co. D,	" " "
Corp. Daniel Taisey,	Co. D,	" " "
Corp. Charles F. Persons,	Co. D,	" " " Deceased.
Stephen Putnam,	Co. B,	6th New Hampshire Regiment, deceased.
*George Webber,	Co. D,	15th Vermont, and D, 1st Vermont Cavalry.
William H. H. Gardner,	Co. C,	3d "
*Rev. Eugene J. Ranslow,	Navy,	Sloop of war, Brooklyn.
Sergt. William H. Silsby,	Co. K,	8th Vermont.
John M. Waldron,	Co. E,	8th "
Henry G. Rollins,	Co. H,	12th "
*Lyman J. Brown,	Co. K,	10th "
*Nathan A. Hunter,	Co. D,	15th "
*Charles P. Bartlett,	Co. H,	12th "
Corp. Samuel Tuttle,	Co. C,	3d "
James L. George,	Co. C,	3d "
*Asa Dowse,	Co. G,	4th "
*S. L. D. Goodale,	Co. E,	2d "
Walter M. Kelley,	Co. K,	3d "
*Nahum E. Harvey,	Co. I,	3d "
Corp. Elias J. Tuttle,	Co. D,	8th "
Corp. George L. Tuttle,	Co. D,	8th "
Harvey D. Gamsby,	Co. E,	15th " and C. U. S. S. S.
Ephraim Rowe,	Co. B,	6th New Hampshire, deceased.
Joseph C. Johnston,	Co. H,	12th Vermont.
Albert A. Bowen,	Co. B,	15th New Hampshire.
Jonathan F. Geiffin,	Co. I,	39th Massachusetts.
*Charles H. Chase,	Co. I,	5th New Hampshire.
Clark P. Blodgett,		1st Vermont Battery.

†By R. G. Brock.

*Corp. Oscar B. Daniels,	Co. D,	8th Vermont.
*Samuel C. Stevens,	Co. I,	3d Vermont.
Lorin A. Vance,	Co. K,	2nd Massachusetts, deceased.
John L. Hanson,	Co. B,	27th Maine.
Sergt. Samuel E. Goss,	Co. I,	5th New Hampshire.
Capt. A. R. Hawley,	Co. E,	8th Vermont.
Kimball Marshall,		6th Massachusetts.

*Col. Preston Relief Corps No. 10, Department of Vermont, of Wells River, Vt., was instituted May 6, 1885, by Department Inspector, Mrs. Margaret H. Ide, of St. Johnsbury, Vt., with eighteen charter members. Sixty names, in all, have been enrolled. Five of the number have "fallen asleep." Sixteen have been transferred and discharged, leaving a present membership of thirty-nine. Mrs. Mary B. Goodwin was the first president of the corps. One hundred dollars and eleven cents has been expended in money, for relief; this includes the furnishing of a room in the Soldier's Home at Bennington, Vt. Quite a sum of money has been given to the Post, to aid in their relief work. Eighty-six dollars and fifteen cents is the estimated value of relief other than money, and the end is not yet; for, working as auxiliary to the G. A. R., and with the motto—Fraternity, charity and loyalty—the mission of this organization will end only when our last veteran is laid at rest, and the sons and daughters of veterans shall come to the front—shall assume our duties, and "Deck them with garlands, these soldiers of ours."

The veterans of the civil war who are members of Colonel Preston Post are given in the account of that organization. Those not given there, now residents of Newbury are:

W. H. Atkinson	Albert C. Fuller
A. A. Avery	Frank Fisher
George B. Barnett	E. H. Farnham
Thomas P. Bailey	Everett K. Heath
Robert Carruth	J. J. Hutton
R. W. Chamberlin	Hiram P. Kidder
Amos J. Chamberlin	Robert Meserve
E. J. L. Clark	Leonard W. McAllister
Isaac Clark	Nelson B. Tewksbury
Frederic Durant	Chas. H. Thompson
H. D. Davis	James Wallace
Joseph Fuller	Philip Webber

These two lists give the names of all the veterans of the civil war now residing here. Those who are buried here are mentioned in the accounts of the cemeteries in town.

The names of Newbury volunteers in the Spanish-American War as prepared by M. L. Brock are:

Moses L. Brock, 1st Lieut.
Charles F. Wilson, Q. M. Sergt.
Charles H. Jackson, Corp.

---

*By Mrs. A. M. Munsell.

Priv. Allard, Hal. H.
" Bailey, Elcena W.
" Bailey, Merton
" Bailey, Frank P.
" Bailey, Leroy F.
" Bailey, Edward T.
" Barrie, Norman
" Brock, John A.

Priv. French, Chas. B.
" Greenwood, Henry
" Hunter. William
" Lane, Alvah
" Lupien, Leon A.
" Mann, Arthur E.
" Silver, Charles L.
" Smith, John B.

"All the Newbury volunteers were members of Co. G, 1st Regiment Vt. Volunteer Infantry. They mustered into the U. S. service, May 16, 1898; started south the 23d day of May, going to Camp Thomas, Chickamauga Park, Ga., where they remained during the summer. Upon cessation of hostilities the regiment was sent back to Fort Ethan Allen, Vt., arriving there the 23rd day of September, 1898; were furloughed for thirty days, and mustered out of service the 28th day of November, 1898. While the regiment saw no active service, the long period of inaction in camp was a harder test of endurance than any active campaign, and the regiment was individually a skeleton of its former self, when it once more stood on good Vermont soil. The Newbury men all returned safely, though several were very seriously ill with typhoid and malarial fevers. Corporal Jackson, Privates Greenwood, Bailey and Hunter have re-enlisted, and are now in the Philippines doing service against the natives."

CHAPTER XLV.

State, County, and Town Officers.

IN the following lists are given the names of the principal town officers, and those who were residents of Newbury, while holding state offices. In Vermont, the town is the unit, and the county only an aggregation of units, convenient for the assembling of the people in courts. In the other states the county is the unit, and the towns merely a sub-division of it. Consequently, in Vermont, each town is a more independent commonwealth than in other states.

The speaker of the House of Representatives in 1798 was:

Daniel Farrand.

A member of the council in 1778, 1786, '87, '88, '89, '90 was:

Jacob Bayley.

The Senators were:

A. B. W. Tenney, 1836, '38
Timothy Morse, 1840
Tappan Stevens, 1841, '42
Elijah Farr, 1843, '44
Henry Keyes, 1847, '48

Joseph Atkinson, 1854, '55
Horatio Brock, 1860, '61
William R. Shedd, 1872
John Bailey, 1886
Horace W. Bailey, 1894

The Chief Justices of Orange County Court were:

Jacob Bayley, 1786, '87, '88, '89, '90,' 91.
Tappan Stevens, 1844.

The Sheriffs were:

John G. Bayley, 1786, '87, '88
Frye Bayley, 1789, '90, '91, '92, '93, '94, '95, '96
A. B. W. Tenney, 1834

Tappan Stevens, 1837
Jacob Kent Jr., 1842, '43

The Marshall in 1845-'49 was:

Jacob Kent.

The Fish and Game Commissioner was:
Horace W. Bailey, 1894-1900.

The Judges of Probate were:

Jacob Kent, 1786, '87, '88, '89, '90, '91   Charles B. Leslie, 1854, '56, '58
Daniel Farrand, 1796, '98, '99, '00   Henry W. Bailey, 1868-75

The Registers of Probate were:

Nathan Goddard, 1786, '87   Isaac Bayley, 1791-96
Daniel Farrand, 1788, '89   Joseph Berry, 1840
        Charles B. Leslie, 1850

The Judge of Circuit Court in 1855-'56 was:
Abel Underwood

The States Attorneys were:

Daniel Farrand, 1796, '98   Elijah Farr, 1839, '41
Abel Underwood, 1838, '40   Asa M. Dickey, 1850
        Charles C. Dewey, 1858

The Clerks of Courts were:
Isaac Bayley, 1801-1812
Joseph Berry, 1850

The following were Town Clerks:

Col. Jacob Kent, 1764-98   Joseph S. Gould, 1828   Simeon Stevens, Jr., 1839-41
Isaac Bayley, 1798-1814   Isaac Bayley, 1829-35   David Johnson. 1841-56
Moses P. Clark, 1814   Isaac A. Bailey, 1835-37   Henry W. Bailey, 1856-86
Isaac Bayley. 1815-28   David Johnson,1837-39   Horace W. Bailey, 1886-97
        Albert W. Silsby, 1897

The members of Constitutional Conventions were:

Daniel Farrand, 1791   James Spear, 1822   John E. Chamberlain, 1843
Jacob Bayley, 1793   Moody Chamberlain, 1828   Joseph Atkinson, 1850
James Spear, 1814   Tappan Stevens, 1836   Richard Patterson, 1869

The Delegates to Conventions before 1784, and Representatives to the General Assembly, were:

Col. Jacob Bayley and Col. Peter Olcott, Representatives to send to "York," 1776.
Col Jacob Bayley and Reuben Foster, Members of Convention at Windsor, 1777.
Reuben Foster and Col. Jacob Kent, Representatives at Windsor, 1778.
Capt. Thos. Johnson and Dr. Gideon Smith, Rep. to Convention at Cornish, Dec. 7, 1778.
John G. Bayley. 1779.
Jacob Kent. 1780.
Jacob Kent and Josiah Page. to convention at Windsor, March 28, 1781.
John G. Bayley, 1781.
Dr. Gideon Smith, to convention at Thetford, June, 1782.
Not represented, 1783.
Jacob Bayley, Ebenezer White, 1784.

John G. Bayley, 1785   Isaac Bayley, 1814   A. B. W. Tenney, 1841
Thomas Johnson. 1786   Isaac Bayley, 1815   Wm. H. Carter, 1842
Thomas Johnson, 1787   Benjamin Porter, 1816   Simeon Stevens, Jr , 1843
Thomas Johnson, 1788   Simeon Stevens. Jr., 1817   John Atwood, 1844
Thomas Johnson, 1789   Asa Tenney, 1818   James Buchanan. 1845
Thomas Johnson, 1790   Simeon Stevens, Jr., 1819   James Buchanan, 1846
Joshua Bayley, 1791   James Spear, 1820   Samuel Grow. 1847
Daniel Farrand, 1792   Levi Rodgers. 1821   Samuel Grow, 1848
Daniel Farrand. 1793   Charles Johnston, 1822   A. B. W. Tenney, 1849
Joshua Bayley, 1794   John L. Woods, 1823   A. B. W. Tenney, 1850
Thomas Johnson 1795   John L. Woods, 1824   Moody Chamberlain, 1851
Daniel Farrand, 1796   John L. Woods, 1825   Oscar C. Hale, 1852
Thomas Johnson, 1797   Charles Johnston, 1826   Oscar C. Hale, 1853

Daniel Farrand, 1798
Thomas Johnson, 1799
Thomas Johnson, 1800
Thomas Johnson, 1801
Joshua Bayley, 1802
Joshua Bayley, 1803
Joshua Bayley, 1804
Isaac Bayley, 1805
James Spear, 1806
James Spear, 1807
James Spear, 1808
Joshua Bayley, 1809
No Record, 1810
Benjamin Porter, 1811
Benjamin Porter, 1812
Asa Tenney, 1813

Timothy Shedd, 1827
Timothy Shedd, 1828
Peter Burbank, 1829
Peter Bu·bank, 1830
Peter Burbank, 1831
A.B. W. Tenney, 1832
A.B. W. Tenney, 1833
A B. W.Tenney, 1834
"Nine ballots and no elec-
tion, 1835" (see Fulton
family)
Simeon Stevens, Jr., 1836
Simeon Stevens, Jr., 1837
Moody Chamberlain, 1838
A. B. W. Tenney, 1839
A. B. W. Tenney, 1840

James M. Chadwick, 1854
Henry Keyes, 1855
A. B. W. Tenney, 1856
Andrew Renfrew, 1857
Andrew Renfrew, 1858
Henry W. Bailey, 1859
Henry W. Bailey, 1860
Abel Underwood, 1861
Abel Underwood, 1862
William R. Shedd, 1863
William R. Shedd, 1864
Wm. Wallace Brock, 1865
Wm. Wallace Brock, 1866
Robert R. Fulton, 1867
Robert R. Fulton, 1868
John Bailey, Jr., 1869

The Constitutional convention of that year recommended biennial sessions, and the change was made.

John Bailey, Jr., 1870
Henry W. Adams, 1876
Edgar W. Smith, 1882
Franklin Deming, 1888
Chalmer H.Cooledge, 1894
Hammond T. Baldwin, 1900.

Daniel A. Rogers, 1872
Levi L. Tucker, 1878
John Bailey, 1884
. A. Allyn Olmsted, 1890
Wm. H. Silsby, 1896

Ebenezer C. Stocker, 1874
Daniel P. Kimball, 1880
Thomas C. Keyes, 1886
A. Allyn Olmsted, 1892
Frank E. Kimball, 1898

So many local or personal issues effect the vote for town representative, that the ballot for Governor is believed to express, more nearly, the political opinion of the town.   The first record of votes is in 1795:

							Total
1795	Isaac Tichenor	30.	Thomas Chittenden	12,	Scattering	3,	45
1796	Isaac Tichenor	54,	Thomas Chittenden	6,			60
1797	Elijah Paine	23,	Isaac Tichenor	6,	"	1,	30
1798	Isaac Tichenor	54,					54
1799	No record.						
1800	Isaac Tichenor	61,				2,	63
1801	Isaac Tichenor	85,	Israel Smith	18,			103
1802	Isaac Tichenor	57,	Israel Smith	64,			121
1803	Isaac Tichenor	60,	Jonathan Robinson	69,			129
1804	No record.						
1805	Isaac Tichenor	62,	Jonathan Robinson	37,			99
1806	To 1812. No record.						
1812	M. Chittenden	106,	Jonas Galusha	103,	"		217
1813	and 1814 no record.						
1815	M. Chittenden	108,	Jonas Galusha	79,	"	5,	192
1816	Samuel Strong	118,	Jonas Galusha	107,			225
1817	Jonas Galusha	95,	Isaac Tichenor	67,			162
1818	Jonas Galusha	117,	Mark Richards	1.			118
1819	Jonas Galusha	115,	William C. Bradley	3,			118
1820	Richard Skinner	91,					91
1821	Richard Skinner	100,					100
1822	No record.						
1823	C. P. Van Ness	32,	Henry Olin	2,			34
1824	C. P. Van Ness	111,	Joel Doolittle	1,			112
1825	C. P. Van Ness	78,					78
1826	Ezra Butler	85,	William Hall	15,			100
1827	Ezra Butler	98,					98
1828	S. C. Crafts	163,					163
1829	S. C. Crafts	129,	Joel Doolittle	86,	Herman Allen	13,	228
1830	S. C. Crafts	91,	Ezra Murch	91,	Wm. A. Palmer	32,	214
1831	Heman Allen	82,	Ezra Murch	36,	Wm. A. Palmer	49,	167

1832	S. C. Crafts	117,	Ezra Murch	93,	Wm. A. Palmer	92,	302
1833	Ezra Murch	174,	Wm. A. Palmer	129,	Horatio Seymour	2,	305
1834	Wm. C. Bradley	99,	Wm. A. Palmer	79,	Horatio Seymour	67,	235
1835	Wm. C. Bradley	170,	Wm. A. Palmer	89,	Charles Payne	25,	284
1836	Silas H. Jennison	188,	Wm. C. Bradley	173,			361
1837	Silas H. Jennison	222,	Wm. C. Bradley	220,			442
1838	Silas H. Jennison	244,	Wm C. Bradley	238,			482
1839	Silàs H. Jennison	267,	Nathan Smith	242,			509
1840	Silas H. Jennison	284,	Paul Dillingham	243,			527
1841	Nathan Smilie	250,	Charles Paine	250,	Scattering	16,	516
1842	Charles Paine	239,	Nathan Smilie	252,	"	23,	513
1843	John Mattocks	241,	Daniel Kellog	266,	"	14,	521
1844	Wm. Slade	265,	Daniel Kellog	253,	W. R. Shafter	14,	532
1845	Daniel Kellog	228,	Wm. Slade	173,	W. R. Shafter	28,	529
1846	Carlos Coolidge	95,	Paul Dillingham	244,	O. C. Shafter	72,	511
1847	Paul Dillingham	228,	Horace Eaton	169,	L. Brainerd	50,	
					Scattering	13,	550
1848	Carlos Coolidge	195,	Paul Dillingham	244,	O. C. Shafter	72,	511
1849	Carlos Coolidge	278,	Horatio Needham	279,			557
1850	C. K. Williams	288,	L. B. Peck	252,	Scattering	2,	542
1851	C. K. Williams	262,	Timo. P. Redfield	260,			520
1852	E. Fairbanks	264,	J. S. Robinson	254,	"	33,	551
1853	E. Fairbanks	222,	J. S. Robinson	254,	L. Brainerd	30,	496
1854	Stephen Royce	267,	Merritt Clark	228,			495
1855	Merritt Clark	228,	Stephen Royce	188,	James M. Slade	60,	476
1856	Ryland Fletcher	298,	Henry Keyes	216,			514
1857	Hiland Hall	284,	Henry Keyes	236,	Scattering	2,	522
1858	Hiland Hall	284,	Henry Keyes	236,			520
1859	Hiland Hall	276,	John G. Saxe	235,			511
1860	E. Fairbanks	292,	John G. Saxe	193,	Robert Harvey	55,	540
1861	Fred. Holbrook	281,	Andrew Tracy	76,	B. H. Smalley	34,	
					R. Harvey	28,	419
1862	Fred. Holbrook	232,	B. H. Smalley	83,			315
1863	J. Gregory Smith	263,	T. P. Redfield	201,			464
1864	J. G. Smith	260,	T. P. Redfield	191,			451
1865	Paul Dillingham	267,	C N. Davenport	169,			436
1866	Paul Dillingham	287,	C. N. Davenport	148,			435
1867	John B. Page	248,	J. L. Edwards	156,			404
1868	John B. Page	271,	J. L. Edwards	160,			431
1869	P. T. Washburne	252,	H. W. Heaton	111,			363
1870	John W. Stewart	255,	H. W. Heaton	110,			365
1872	Julius Converse	289,	Abram B. Gardner	134,			423
1874	Ashael Peck	248,	W. H. H. Bingham	139,			487
1876	H. Fairbanks	297,	W. H. H. Bingham	177,			474
1878	Redfield Proctor	235,	W. H. H. Bingham	137,			372
1880	Roswell Farnham	304,	E. J. Phelps	188,	Scattering	23,	515
1882	John L. Barstow	233,	G. E. Eaton	119,	"	24,	476
1884	Samuel Pingree	272,	L. W. Redington	143,	"	5,	420
1886	E. J. Ormsbee	266,	S. C. Shurtleff	113,	"	21,	400
1888	W. P. Dillingham	262,	S. C. Shurtleff	132,	"	25,	419
1890	C. S. Page	276,	H. F. Brigham	143,	"	21,	440
1892	L. K. Fuller	272,	B. B. Smalley	146,	E. L. Allen	33,	451
1894	Urban Woodbury	262,	G. W. Smith	139,			401
1896	Josiah Grout	302,	J. H. Jackson	87,	Scattering	38,	427
1898	E. C. Smith	209,	T. W. Maloney	79,	"	22,	310
1900	W. W. Stickney	273,	J. H. Senter	85,	"	26,	384

Town meetings were held in houses and barns until the first
meeting house was built, in which, and its successors, they were
held for many years. In the '30s the town met frequently at Samuel
Gibson's tavern, where Oscar Renfrew now lives, at the Center.
There were several efforts to build a town-house, but they came to

nothing. The present town-house was built in 1839, at a cost of about $800. The land on which it stands was given by Charles George, who also gave the timber for the frame. It was repaired and painted in 1888. Several efforts have been made to remove the town-house to Newbury village or to West Newbury, but without avail.

The moderators of annual meetings are given in the following list, but not those of special meetings. After 1790, many of these latter were of little importance. In one year there were seventeen town meetings.

1767	No record	1827	Calvin Jewett
1768	Maj. John Taplin	1828	Peter Burbank
1769	Maj John Taplin	1829	Peter Burbank
1770	Col. Jacob Bayley	1830	Peter Burbank
1771	Col. Jacob Bayley	1831	Peter Burbank
1772	(Leaf torn out)	1832	Joseph Berry
1773	Col. Jacob Bayley	1833	Moody Chamberlain
1774	No record—Page blank	1834	Tappan Stevens
1775	" "	1835	Tappan Stevens
1776	Col. Jacob Bayley	1836	Moody Chamberlain
1777	Col. Jacob Bayley	1837	Tappan Stevens
	Reuben Foster	1838	Hiram Tracy
1778	Gen. Jacob Bayley	1839	Jacob Kent
	Reuben Foster	1840	Hiram Tracy
1779	Reuben Foster	1841	Hiram Tracy
	Ephraim Webster	1842	Jacob Kent
	Gen. Jacob Bayley	1843	Elijah Farr
1780	No record of annual meeting	1844	Charles Hale
	Col. Nehemiah Lovewell	1845	Tappan Stevens
	Ephraim Webster	1846	Jacob Kent
1781	Gen. Jacob Bayley	1847	Jacob Kent
	Dudley Carleton	1848	Jacob Kent
	Thomas Johnson	1849	Simeon Stevens, Jr.
1782	Reuben Foster	1850	Tappan Stevens
	Ebenezer White	1851	R. M. Richardson
1783	Jacob Bayley	1852	Jacob Kent
1784	Jacob Bayley	1853	John E. Chamberlain
1785	Jacob Bayley	1854	Jacob Kent
	Reuben Foster	1855	O. C. Hale
1786	Jacob Bayley	1856	O. C. Hale
1787	Ebenezer White	1857	C. C. Dewey
	Jacob Bayley	1858	J. E. Chamberlain
1788	Jacob Bayley	1859	C. C. Dewey
1789	Jacob Bayley	1860	Horatio Brock
	March 25, Jacob Bayley	1861	Horatio Brock
1790	Ebenezer White	1862	Lucius Hazen
	April 6, Jacob Bayley	1863	A. G. Button
	June 29, Ebenezer White	1864	A. G. Button
	July 22, Jacob Bayley	1865	Andrew Renfrew
1791	Ebenezer White	1866	William R. Shedd
1792	Ebenezer White	1867	William R. Shedd
1793	Ebenezer White	1868	John Bailey
1794	Ebenezer White	1869	Andrew Renfrew
1795	Jacob Bayley	1870	William R. Shedd
1796	Jacob Bayley	1871	William R. Shedd
1797	Ebenezer White	1872	J. E. Chamberlain
1798	Daniel Farrand	1873	William R. Shedd
1799	Thomas Johnson	1874	John Bailey
1800	Ebenezer White	1875	Andrew Renfrew
1801	Thomas Johnson	1876	John Bailey

1802	Thomas Johnson	1877	John Bailey
1803	James Spear	1878	A. T. Baldwin
1804	James Spear	1879	A. T. Baldwin
1805	James Spear	1880	A. T. Baldwin
1806	James Spear	1881	A. T. Baldwin
1807	James Spear	1882	E. J. Ranslow
1808	James Spear	1883	A. T. Baldwin
1809	Frye Bayley	1884	John Bailey
1810	James Spear	1885	John Bailey
1811	James Spear	1886	John Bailey
1812	Asa Tenney	1887	John Bailey
1813	Asa Tenney	1888	John Bailey
1814	Asa Tenney	1889	Andrew Renfrew
1815	Asa Tenney	1890	Andrew Renfrew
1816	Asa Tenney	1891	Andrew Renfrew
1817	Asa Tenney	1892	J. R. Weed
1818	James Spear	1893	J. R. Weed
1819	Asa Tenney	1894	J. R. Weed
1820	Asa Tenney	1895	J. R. Weed
1821	James Spear	1896	B. O. Rogers
1822	Jonas Tucker	1897	J. R. Weed
1823	Moody Chamberlain	1898	Horace W. Bailey
1824	James Spear	1899	Horace W. Bailey
1825	Charles Johnston	1900	J. R. Weed
1826	Charles Johnston		

The following is a list of the Selectmen:

1764 Jacob Bayley, Jacob Kent, James Abbott.
1765 John Taplin, John Haseltine, Jacob Kent, Benj. Whiting, Noah White.
1766 Jacob Bayley, Jacob Kent, John Taplin.
1767 Jacob Bayley, John Taplin, Jacob Kent.
1768 Jacob Kent, Dr. Samuel Hale, Robert Johnston.
1769 Jacob Fowler, Joseph White, Moses Thurston.
1770 Thos. Johnson, Simeon Stevens, Levi Sylvester.
1771 Dr. Smith, Joseph Chamberlin, Robert Hunkins.
1772 Not recorded.
1773 Robert Johnston, Simeon Stevens, Dr. Smith.
1774 No record.
1775 No record.
1776 Jacob Kent, Ephraim Webster, Simeon Stevens.
1777 Reuben Foster, Robert Johnston.
1778 Ephraim Webster, Joshua Bayley, Dudley Carleton.
1779 Dr. Smith, Thos. Johnson, John Haseltine.
1780 No record.
1781 Joshua Bayley, Nehemiah Lovewell, Remembrance Chamberlin, Josiah Page, Abiel Chamberlin.
1782 Frye Bayley, William Wallace, Jacob Bayley, Jr., Silvanus Heath.
1783 No record.
1784 Jacob Kent, Robert Johnston, Dudley Carleton, John Haseltine, Silvanus Heath.
1785 William Wallace, Frye Bayley, Ebenezer White, Thomas Johnson.
1786 Jacob Bayley, Jacob Kent, James Abbott.
1787 Thomas Johnson, Charles Bayley, Moses Chamberlin.
1788 Robert Johnston, Dudley Carleton, Remembrance Chamberlin, John Brown, Jacob Kent.
1789 Jacob Kent, William Wallace, Levi Sylvester.
1790 Thomas Johnson, Remembrance Chamberlin, Joshua Bayley.
1791 Dudley Carleton, Moses Chamberlin, Nehemiah Lovewell.
1792 John G. Bayley, Joshua Bayley, Samuel Tucker.
1793 Joshua Bayley, William Wallace, Daniel Farrand.
1794 Joshua Bayley, Remembrance Chamberlin, Nehemiah Lovewell.
1795 Joshua Bayley, Remembrance Chamberlin, Nehemiah Lovewell.
1796 Joshua Bayley, Ebenezer White, Peletiah Bliss.
1797 Ebenezer White, Thomas Chamberlain, Samuel Tucker.

1798 William Wallace, Joshua Bayley, Dudley Carleton.
1799 William Wallace, Dudley Carleton. Daniel Putnam.
1800 Joshua Bayley, Daniel Putnam, Benjamin Bowers.
1801 Joshua Bayley, Daniel Putnam. Benjamin Bowers.
1802 Joshua Bayley, Daniel Putnam. Benjamin Bowers.
1803 Joshua Bayley, James Spear, Gideon Tuxbury.
1804 Joshua Bayley, James Spear, Gideon Tuxbury.
1805 James Spear, Gideon Tuxbury, James Johnston.
1806 James Spear, Gideon Tuxbury, James Johnston.
1807 James Spear, Gideon Tuxbury. James Johnston.
1808 Joshua Bayley, James Spear. Jacob Kent, Jr.
1809 Joshua Bayley, Jonas Tucker, Josiah Marsh.
1810 Bancroft Abbott, Joseph Smith, Nathan Avery.
1811 Isaac Bayley, Jonas Tucker. Joseph Smith.
1812 Isaac Bayley, Jonas Tucker. Joshua Hale.
1813 Asa Tenney, Joshua Hale, Jonas Tucker.
1814 Asa Tenney, Joshua Hale, Jonas Tucker.
1815 Asa Tenney, Isaac Bayley, Jonas Tucker.
1816 Isaac Bayley, Abner Bayley, Josiah Little, Jr.
1817 Joshua Hale, William Bayley. John Bayley.
1818 Levi Rogers, Jonas Tucker, John Johnson.
1819 Levi Rogers, Timothy Shedd. John Bayley.
1820 Asa Tenney. Levi Rogers. John L. Woods.
1821 Joshua Bayley, Levi Rogers, Jonas Clark.
1822 Samuel Powers. Moody Chamberlin. Samuel Rogers.
1823 Moody Chamberlain, Samuel Powers, Samuel Rogers.
1824 Samuel Powers, Moody Chamberlin. Samuel Rogers.
1825 Moody Chamberlain, Charles Johnston, John Buxton,
1826 Levi Rogers, Simeon Stevens, James Carter, Moody Grow, Joseph L. Gould.
1827 A. B. W. Tenney, Moody Grow, James Brock.
1828 Moody Grow, John Atwood, James Bayley 2d.
1829 Moody Grow, John Atwood. James Bayley 2d.
1830 Moody Chamberlain, A. B. W. Tenney, Samuel Gibson.
1831 Samuel Gibson, Levi Carter, James Abbott.
1832 Levi Carter, Samuel Gibson, James Abbott.
1833 Moody Chamberlain, Charles Hale, Jonas Tucker.
1834 Moody Chamberlain, Charles Hale. James Abbott.
1835 Moody Chamberlain, Charles Hale, James Abbott.
1836 Moody Chamberlain, Charles Hale, John B. Carleton.
1837 A. B, W. Tenney, John B. Carleton, Samuel Rogers.
1838 A. B. W. Tenney, John B. Carleton. Levi Carter.
1839 Moody Chamberlain, Jacob Kent, Jr., Samuel Grow, Jr.
1840 John B. Carleton, James Wallace, Benjamin Atwood.
1841 John B. Carleton, Charles Hale, Benjamin Atwood.
1842 Charles Hale, Jonas W. Clark, Moody Chamberlin.
1843 Charles Hale, Moody Chamberlin, John Renfrew.
1844 Moody Chamberlain, John Renfrew, William Burroughs.
1845 Samuel Gibson, Levi Carter, Thomas Wasson.
1846 W. R. Shedd, Levi Carter, Simeon Stevens, Jr.
1847 W. R. Shedd, Levi Carter, Simeon Stevens, Jr.
1848 Jared Wells. John E. Chamberlain, John B. Carleton.
1849 John B. Carleton, John E. Chamberlin, Emory Gale.
1850 John E. Chamberlain, Tappan Stevens, W. R. Shedd.
1851 R. M. Richardson, John B. Carleton, Robert Renfrew.
1852 A. B. W. Tenney, John B. Carleton, Joseph Smith.
1853 A. B. W. Tenney, John B. Carleton. Joseph Smith.
1854 A. B. W. Tenney, John B. Carleton, Joseph Smith.
1855 John B. Carleton, Joseph Sawyer, Joseph Smith.
1856 James Abbott, Robert Renfrew, William R. Shedd.
1857 Andrew Renfrew. Horatio Brock, James Abbott.
1858 James Y. Prescott, Ezekiel Sawyer, Abiel Deming.
1859 Lucius Hazen, L. L. Tucker, James Wallace.
1860 Lucius Hazen, L. L. Tucker, William R. Shedd.
1861 William R. Shedd, John Atwood, Joseph Smith.

1862   William R. Shedd, John Atwood, Joseph Smith.
1863   William R. Shedd, Joseph Smith, L. D. Hazen.
1864   William R. Shedd, L. D. Hazen, Joseph Smith.
1865   William R. Shedd, L. D. Hazen, Joseph Smith.
1866   William R. Shedd, L. L. Tucker, Harrison Bailey.
1867   John Bailey, L. L. Tucker, H. G. Randall.
1868   John Bailey, L. L. Tucker, H. G. Randall.
1869   John Bailey, Richard Doe, E S. Tuttle.
1870   John Bailey, Richard Doe, J. R. McAllister.
1871   John Bailey, W. W. Brock, Richard Patterson.
1872   John Bailey, W. W Brock, John Smith.
1873   W. W. Brock, John Smith, D. A. Rogers.
1874   W. W. Brock, Richard Doe, J. B. Wilson.
1875   F. Sherwin, Richard Doe, J. B. Wilson.
1876   Richard Doe, L. L. Tucker, F. Sherwin.
1877   F. Sherwin, G. W. Chamberlain, L. W. McAllister.
1878   F. Sherwin, G. W. Chamberlain, L. W. McAllister.
1879   Henry W. Adams, J. J. Smith, John Reid.
1880   H. W. Adams. W. W. Brock, John Reid.
1881   W. W. Brock, John Reid, L. L. Tucker.
1882   John Reid, John S. George, Robert Lackie.
1883   Richard Doe, Robert Lackie. John S. George.
1884   D. P. Kimball. Henry Whitcher, W. W. Brock, Jr.
1885   D. P. Kimball, Henry Whitcher, D. B. Reid.
1886   W. G. Foss, D. B. Reid. J. F. Fulton.
1887   W. G. Foss, J. F. Fulton. D. B. Reid.
1888   D. P. Kimball, Robert Nelson, W. W. Brock, Jr.
1889   D. P. Kimball, Robert Nelson, W. W. Brock, Jr.
1890   Robert Nelson, G. W. Chamberlain, H. G. Rollins.
1891   Robert Nelson, H. G. Rollins, G. W. Chamberlain.
1892   Robert Nelson, H. G. Rollins, G. W. Chamberlain.
1893   H. T. Baldwin, A. Greer, William M. Rollins.
1894   H. T. Baldwin. A. Greer, William M. Rollins.
1895   H. T. Baldwin, A. Greer, W. M. Rollins.
1896   W. M. Rollins, O. C. Renfrew, C. H. McAllister.
1897   A. Greer, Moses L. Brock, Byron O. Rogers.
1898   M. L. Brock, B. O. Rogers, Albert H. Bailey.
1899   B. O. Rogers, W. Patterson, L. W. McAllister.
1900   B. O. Rogers, W. Patterson, L. W. McAllister.

Before 1776, the selectmen appear to have performed all the duties of Listers. After that year they are as follows:

1776   Jacob Bayley, Jacob Kent, Robert Johnston.
1777   Reuben Foster, Robert Johnston, (Illegible.)
1778   Joseph Chamberlin, Ephraim Webster, Dudley Carleton.
1779   Dr. Smith, Thomas Johnson, John Haseltine.
1780   No record.
1781   Joshua Bayley, Nehemiah Lovewell, Josiah Page.
1782   Frye Bayley, William Wallace, Edmund Brown.
1783   No record.
1784   Jacob Kent, Robert Johnston, Dudley Carleton.
1785   William Wallace, Frye Bayley, Ebenezer White.
1786   Jacob Bayley, Jacob Kent, James Abbott.
1787   Frye Bayley, Charles Bayley, Moses Chamberlain.
1788   Thomas Johnson, John Scott, Jonathan Goodwin.
1789   Nehemiah Lovewell, James Vance, Silas Chamberlin.
1790   Jabez Bigelow, Parrit Hadley, John Johnson.
1791   No record.
1792   Er Chamberlin, James Johnston, Simeon Stevens.
1793   Joshua Bayley, Jacob Kent, Jr., Otho Stevens.
1794   Asa Tenney, Moses Johnson. Jeremiah Ingalls.
1795   Samuel Butterfield, Paul Ford, Jeremiah Ingalls.
1796   Isaac Duffs, Moses Swasey, Jeremiah Ingalls.

1797 Josiah Rogers, Charles Chamberlain, Asa Tenney.
1798 Isaac Bayley, Samuel Tucker, Er Chamberlain.
1799 John Vance, John Bayley, Benjamin Bowers.
1800 A. McLaughlin, John Bayley, Jonathan Johnson.
1801 Nehemiah Lovewell, Asa Tenney, Dudley Carleton.
1802 Moses Swasey, A. McLaughlin, Jacob Kent.
1803 Isaac Bayley, Peter Preston, James Johnson.
1804 Asa Tenney, Benjamin Bowers, Jonathan Johnston.
1805 James Spear, James Johnston, Benjamin Porter.
1806 Samuel Lancaster, Joshua Hale, Ephraim Clark.
1807 Ephraim Clark, John Bayley, Moses Johnson.
1808 Joseph Smith, Joshua Hale, Nicholas White.
1809 Joshua Hale, Jacob Choate, Samuel Putnam.
1810 Gideon Tewksbury, Samuel Putnam, James Spear.
1811 David Johnson, Simeon Stevens, Samuel Powers.
1812 John Bayley, Timothy Shedd, Jonathan Russell.
1813 Charles Johnston, Charles Hale, Samuel Grow.
1814 Samuel Grow, Isaac Bayley, Charles Hale.
1815 Charles Hale, Charles Johnston, M. F. Morrison.
1816 Joshua Hale, Abner Bayley, Gideon Tewksbury.
1817 Isaac Bayley, Jonas Tucker, Charles Hale.
1818 George A. Burbank, John Buxton, John B. Carleton.
1819 Simeon Stevens, Daniel Putnam, Gideon Tewksbury.
1820 Charles Hale, Jonas Tucker, Abner Bayley.
1821 Jonas Tucker, Joseph Chamberlin, James Bayley 2d.
1822 John L. Woods, David Johnson, John B. Carleton.
1823 David Johnson, Charles S. Johnson, John L. Woods.
1824 Jeremiah Nourse, David Johnson, John B. Carleton.
1825 John B. Carleton, Jeremiah Nourse, Tappan Stevens.
1826 Isaac Bayley, John Atwood, James Abbott.
1827 Charles Hale, James Abbott, Abner Bayley.
1828 Peter Burbank, Charles Johnston, Jonas Clark.
1829 Peter Burbank, Charles Johnston, Jonas Clark.
1830 David Johnson, James Abbott, Levi Carter.
1831 David Johnson, Jonas Clark, Jacob Kent, Jr.
1832 Moody Grow, John Renfrew, James Wallace.
1833 David Johnson, James Abbott, Simeon Stevens.
1834 David Johnson, David Haseltine, Samuel Gibson, Jr.
1835 David Johnson, Waterman Wells, David Haseltine.
1836 David Johnson, Elijah Farr, David Haseltine.
1837 Levi Rogers, Moody Chamberlain, James Abbott.
1838 David Johnson, Charles Hale, Moody Chamberlain.
1839 Samuel Gibson, Jonas W. Clark, Moses Rogers.
1840 Oscar C. Hale. Josiah W. Rogers, Horatio N. Brock.
1841 Josiah W. Rogers, Jeremiah Nourse, Oscar C. Hale.
1842 Charles Hale, Jonas W. Clark, Moody Chamberlin.
1843 Clark Kent, Simeon Stevens, Jr., Samuel Grow.
1844 Clark Kent, Hiram Tracy, Moody Grow.
1845 Samuel Grow, Clark Kent, William R. Shedd.
1846 George Leslie, Joseph Berry, Joseph Smith.
1847 Charles Hale, Robert Renfrew, William Burroughs.
1848 Henry K. White, Robert Renfrew, William Burroughs.
1849 Leander Smith, Horatio Brock, Page P. Grove.
1850 David Johnson, William McDuffie, Richard Patterson, Johnson Chamberlain,
     Horace R. Hale.
1851 David Johnson. H. F. Slack, Enoch Wiggin.
1852 Robert Renfrew, Ezekiel Sawyer, Enoch Wiggin.
1853 Robert Renfrew, Ezekiel Sawyer, Enoch Wiggin.
1854 Horatio Brock, Robert Renfrew, Richard Patterson.
1855 Robert Renfrew, Horatio Brock, Ezekiel Sawyer.
1856 Johnson Chamberlain, John Renfrew, Jr., Joseph Atkinson.
1857 G. W. Sampson, L. L. Tucker, Johnson Chamberlain.
1858 Johnson Chamberlain, James S. Johnston, John G. White.
1859 Charles E. Benton, John Bailey, Jr., John Renfrew, Jr.
1860 William R. Shedd, Horatio Brock, John Renfrew, Jr.

1861   W. W. Brock, R. R. Fulton, John Bailey, Jr.
1862   W. W. Brock, J. Bailey, Jr., R. R. Fulton.
1863   E. Wiggin, R. R. Fulton, A. M. Peach.
1864   R R. Fulton, A, M. Peach, D. Y. Ford.
1865   W. R. Shedd, D. Y. Ford, L. L. Tucker.
1866   D. Y. Ford, W. R. Shedd, John S. Daily.
1867   R. R. Fulton, H. G. Randall, A. H Burton.
1868   R. R. Fulton, H. G. Randall, A. H. Burton.
1869   D. P. Kimball, A. H. Burton, C. E. Brock.
1870   W. R. Shedd, D. Y. Ford, John Smith.
1871   W. R. Shedd, D. Y. Ford, John Smith.
1872   John Reid, M. C. Bailey. H. A. Albee.
1873   George Swasey. John Smith, H. D. Haseltine.
1874   W. R. Shedd, J. J. Smith, J. Bailey, Jr.
1875   Andrew Renfrew, J. J. Smith. A. M. Peach.
1876   J. J. Smith, J. Reid, L. W. McAllister.
1877   J. J. Smith, A. M. Peach, Wright Chamberlin.
1878   W. R. Shedd, J. J. Smith, J. Reid.
1879   W. G. Foss, Henry Whitcher, J. J. Smith.
1880   W. G. Foss, Henry Whitcher, Horace W. Bailey.
1881   John Bailey, Henry Whitcher, J. J. Smith.
1882   W. R. Shedd, H. G. Rollins, H. Whitcher.
1883   H. Whitcher. H. G. Rollins. J. F. Fulton.
1884   Horace W. Bailey, J. F. Fulton, L. W. McAllister.
1885   Horace W. Bailey. J. F. Fulton. L. W. McAllister.
1886   F. Sherwin, J. Reid, L. W. McAllister.
1887   H. D. Hazeltine, A. M. Peach, L. W. McAllister.
1888   H. D. Hazeltine, L. W. McAllister, Moses Brock.
1889   H. D. Hazeltine, L. W. McAllister, Dudley Carleton.
1890   John Smith, F. Sherwin, David Lumsden.
1891   L. W. McAllister, D. Lumsden, Abner Bailey.
1892   Robert Nelson, H. G. Rollins, D. Lumsden.
1893   C. H. McAllister, J. F. George, M. L. Brock.
1894   F. Sherwin, J. F. George, O. C. Renfrew.
1895   C. C. Scales, M. L. Brock, J. F. George.
1896   F. W. George, J. R. Weed, H. G. Bailey.
1897   F. W. George. J. R. Weed. L. W. McAllister.
1898   D. S. Fulton, J. R. Weed, L. W. McAllister.
1899   J. R. Weed, D. S. Fulton, M. J. Randall.
1900   D. S. Fulton, M. J. Randall, M. H. Randall.

The First Constables, beginning with 1764, were:

1764	John Hazeltine	1807	Benjamin Brock
1765	Richard Chamberlin	1808	Abner Bayley
1766	Thomas Chamberlain	1809	Noyes Bayley
1767	Abner Fowler	1810	Simon Douglass
1768	Moses Thurston	1811	Merrill Bayley
1769	Robert Johnston	1812	Abner Bayley
1770	Abiel Chamberlin	1813	Frye Bayley
1771	Ebenezer White	1814	Abner Bayley
1772	No record.	1815	Nathan Avery
1773	No record.	1816	Abner Bayley
1776	Abiel Chamberlin	1817	Thomas R. Brock
1777	Thomas Johnson	1818	Nathan Avery
1778	Abiel Chamberlin	1819, '20	Tappan Stevens
1779	John Bayley	1821	Henry Doe
1780	No record	1822	Samuel Grow
1781	Jacob Bayley, Jr.	1823	Tappan Stevens
1782	Thomas Brock	1824, '25	Caleb Stevens
1783	No record.	1826	James A. Bayley
1784	Abiel Chamberlin	1827	Caleb Stevens
1785	Dr. Smith	1828, '29	Jacob Kent
1786	Silvanus Heath	1830, '31	Jacob B. Stevens
1787	Joshua Bayley	1832, '33	Caleb Stevens

1788	Charles Bayley	1834	Nathaniel Bayley
1789	Frye Bayley	1835	Robert Fulton
1790	Jonathan Goodwin	1836, '37	James Matthews
1791	John Johnson	1838	D. R. Burnham
1792,'93	Paul Ford	1839	E. B. Stevens
1794	Jacob Kent, Jr.	1840, '41	Peter Wheelock, Jr.
1795	James Johnston	1842, '43	John E. Chamberlain
1796	James Spear	1844-46	E. B. Stevens
1797	Asa Tenney	1847	Seth Ford
1798	Jeremiah Ingalls	1848, '49	E. B. Stevens
1799	Frye Bayley	1850	Henry F. Slack
1800	Moses Johnson	1851-61	Andrew Renfrew
1801	No record.	1862. '63	N. B Stevens
1802	Joseph Smith	1864-72	John Bailey
1803,'04	Simeon Stevens	1873, '74	H. G. Randall
1805	William Bailey	1875, '76	George W. Chamberlain
1806	Abner Bayley	1877-88	John Bailey
		1889-1900	John R. Weed

For the first years the selectmen seem to have had the care of the funds, but in 1779 the first treasurer was chosen. Not much is preserved regarding the receipts and disbursements of this official, and it is not alone of late years that the accounts of the town have fallen into confusion for want of a systematic manner of keeping them. In 1840, the financial affairs of the town had fallen into such a state that David Johnson was appointed a committee to investigate the matter, and at the March meeting of 1841, made the following very characteristic report.

"The committee appointed at the meeting of the town on the 2d day of March last, to investigate the financial situation of the town, has attended to the duties of his appointment, and after a tedious and laborious examination of Books, Town Orders, and Accounts. all involved in the most delightful confusion—having succeeded in reducing the chaotic mass of materials to a very remote approach to order and exactness—begs leave to lay the result of his labours before the town in the following report. * * *"

There was an utter lack of system in the business affairs of the town, which brought on this state of things. The publication of the town reports in printed form has compelled a reformation in the method of keeping accounts.

The Treasurers have been:

1779-87	Dudley Carleton	1837	Tappan Stevens
1787-92	Thomas Johnson	1838-41	James M. Chadwick
1772	Nehemiah Lovewell	1841	David Johnson
1793	Frye Bayley	1842-44	Tappan Stevens
1794	Daniel Farrand	1844-46	Joseph Atkinson
1795-98	William Wallace	1846	David Johnson
1798-1800	Asa Tenney	1847	Joseph Atkinson
1800-09	James Spear	1848	David Johnson
1809-14	David Johnson	1849	Joseph Atkinson
1814-21	Josiah Little	1850-55	J. M. Chadwick
1821	Jonas Tucker	1855-59	John Stevens
1822	Josiah Little	1860-64	E. C. Stocker
1823-27	David Johnson	1864	H. H. Deming
1827-31	E. B. Stevens	1865-78	Henry W. Bailey
1831-34	Freeman Keyes	1878-89	George Leslie
1834-36	James Spear, Jr.	1889-98	J. B. Hale
1836	William Atkinson	1898-01	A. W. Silsby

As far as can be ascertained, there was no person chosen as Superintendent of Schools till 1847, when Rev. G. W. Campbell was elected to that office. His successors have been:

1849	Rev. J. D. Butler	1867-70	Rev. Z. S. Haynes
1850-51	Rev. Elisha Brown	1871	Dr. I. T. Bronson
1852	Edwin A. Rogers	1872-74	Rev. R. D. Miller
1853-57	Rev. C. W. Cushing	1875	E. W. Smith
1858	Rev. S. M. Plympton	1876	D. S. Corliss
1859	Rev. H. N. Burton	1877	Wright Chamberlain
1860	Rev. F. E. King	1878	Rev. A. B. Lyon
1861	Rev. H. N. Burton	1879-81	Rev. E. J. Ranslow
1862-64	Rev. A. G. Button	1882-84	W. H. Buck
1865-66	A. H. Burton	1885-90	Horace W. Bailey

In this latter year a county board of education was established which continued two years.

1891	Rev. J. L. Merrill.
1892	W. H. Buck.

In 1893, the town system came into operation, a school board of three being constituted, one of whom is chosen each year. The board then chosen were:

Horace W. Bailey for one year.
J. J. Smith, two years.
L. W. McAllister three years.
1894   H. E. Cobleigh
1895   Rev. J. S. Tupper, who resigned in October and A. J. Whitcher was
          appointed to fill the vacancy.
1896   M. H. Randall.
1897   A. J. Whitcher.
1898   G. B. Barnett.

These last three constitute the present board.

The selectmen seem to have had the charge of the poor till 1821. In that year Daniel Putnam was made Overseer. Those who have held that office have been:

1821	Daniel Putnam	1845, '46	Daniel Putnam
1822	Isaac Bayley	1847, '48	Charles J. Smith
1823	Isaac Bayley	1849	Oliver B. Rogers
1824	James Brock	1850-57	Abner Chamberlin
1825	Asa Tenney	1858	Caleb Stevens
1826	John L. Woods	1859	Samuel Martin
1827-32	Tappan Stevens	1860	R. C. Sawyer
1833, '34	Caleb Stevens, Jr.	1861-66	O. B. Rogers
1835	Tappan Stevens	1867	The Selectmen
1836	Moody Chamberlain	1868	Richard Doe
1837	Abner Bayley	1869-76	Dan Y. Ford
1838	Charles Hale	1877	Harrison Bailey
1839, '40	Moody Chamberlain	1880-90	John S. George
1841	John B. Carleton	1891-95	John Reid
1842, '43	John E. Chamberlain	1896-99	John F. George
1844	Clark Kent	1900	John R. Weed

At the first annual meeting in 1764, it was voted that Maxi Haseltine and Thomas Johnson should be surveyors of highways. They voted also to make the road by a "rate" and to raise two thousand pounds "old tenor" to make the road, and that a man should be allowed four pounds a day for his work, and for a yoke of oxen, three pounds. In the depreciated currency of the time, a pound was probably worth about twenty-five cents.

In 1776, a man was "to receive six shillings, and oxen four shillings" for a day's work. In 1779, it was voted that in lieu of a day's work, a man should pay a bushel of wheat. In 1798, the town was divided into nine highway districts, each in charge of a "surveyor" or "path-master." The number of such districts was increased from time to time, and this imperfect and inconvenient care of the highways was continued till within a few years. People usually worked out their taxes, under the direction of men who had no technical knowledge of the science of road making. In winter the roads were broken out, all the people turning out with their oxen and sleds. This system, or want of one, continued till road machines and snow-rollers came into use, when the law placed the general oversight of the highways into the hands of the selectmen.

In 1892, the law was again changed and placed the roads and their care in the hands of one individual, styled the Road Commissioner, who has the charge of all outside the limits of Wells River village. These have been:

1893–95	Robert Lackie	1897	Robert Lackie
1896	Henry G. Rollins	1898–00	Warren W. Bailey

The accounts of the town began to be kept in dollars and cents, instead of pounds, shillings, and pence, or Spanish dollars, in 1798. In 1799, the town voted fifteen dollars, "for the purpose of making and erecting guide posts in the necessary places in s^d town."

CHAPTER XLVI.

REVOLUTIONARY AND MISCELLANEOUS PAPERS.—THE NEW HAMPSHIRE CHARTER.—
THE NEW YORK CHARTER.—DIARY OF GEN. JACOB BAYLEY IN THE OLD FRENCH
WAR.—JOURNALS OF COL. JACOB KENT.—COL. FRYE BAYLEY'S DIARY IN 1776.—
COL. THOMAS JOHNSON'S JOURNAL WHILE IN CANADA.—THOMAS MELLEN'S
NARRATIVE.—LETTERS.—REVOLUTIONARY MUSTER ROLLS.—NEWBURY LANDS IN
1808.—MISCELLANEOUS.

THE NEW HAMPSHIRE CHARTER.

Province of New Hampshire.

Newbury

GEORGE THE THIRD.

By the Grace of GOD. of Great Britain, France and Ireland, KING,
Defender of the Faith, &c.
To all Persons to whom these Presents shall come.
Greeting.

KNOW ye. that We of Our special Grace, certain Knowledge, and meer Motion
for the due Encouragement of settling a *New Plantation* within our said Province,
by and with the Advice of our Trusty and Well-beloved BENNING WENTWORTH, Esq;
Our Governor and Commander in Chief of Our said Province of NEW-HAMPSHIRE
in *New-England,* and of our COUNCIL of the said Province; HAVE upon the
Conditions and Reservations herein after made, given and granted, and by these
Presents, for us, our Heirs and Successors, do give and grant in equal Shares, unto
Our loving Subjects, Inhabitants of Our said Province of *New-Hampshire,* and Our
other Governments, and to their Heirs and Assigns for ever whose Names are
entred on this Grant, to be divided to and amongst them into Eighty one equal
Shares, all that Tract or Parcel of Land situate, lying and being within our said
Province of *New-Hampshire,* containing by Admeasurement   *Acres,*
which Tract is to contain Something more than Six Miles square; out of which an
Allowance is to be make for High Ways and unimprovable Lands by Rocks,
Ponds, Mountains and Rivers, One Thousand and Forty Acres free. according to a
Plan and Survey thereof, made by Our said Governor's Order, and returned into the
Secretary's Office. and hereunto annexed, butted and bounded as follows, *Viz.*
Beginning at a Tree marked standing on the Bank of the Westerly Side of
Connecticut River opposite to the Mouth of amonusock River so called, and from
thence Southerly or South Westerly down Connecticut River, as that runs til it
comes to A Tree there standing marked with the Figures   and is about Seven
Miles on A Strait Line below the Mouth of Amonusock aforesd from thence runing
North fifty nine degrees West Six Miles, & one Quarter of A Mile to A Stake &
Stones, from thence North Twenty degs East Six Miles, & one half Mile to a Stake
& Stones, from thence to the Marked Tree on the Side of the river, the Bound first
above mentioned—And that the same be, and hereby is Incorporated into a Township

by the Name of Newbury And the Inhabitants that do or shall hereafter inhabit the said Township, are hereby declared to be Enfranchized with and Intitled to all and every the Priviledges and Immunities that other Towns within Our Province by Law Exercise and Enjoy; And further, that the said Town as soon as there shall be Fifty Families resident and settled thereon, shall have the Liberty of holding *Two Fairs*, one of which shall be held on the   And the other on the   annually, which Fairs are not to continue longer than the respective   following the said

and that as soon as the said Town shall consist of Fifty Families, a Market may be opened and kept one or more Days in each Week, as may be thought most advantagious to the Inhabitants. Also, that the first Meeting for the Choice of Town Officers, agreable to the Laws of our said Province, shall be held on the Second Monday in June next which said Meeting shall be Notified by Jacob Bayley Esq who is hereby also appointed the Moderator of the said first Meeting which he is to Notify and Govern agreable to the Laws and Customs of Our said Province; and that the annual Meeting for ever hereafter for the Choice of such Officers for the said Town, shall be on the Second Tuesday of *March* annually, To HAVE and to HOLD the said Tract of Land as above expressed, together with all Privileges and Appurtenances, to them and to their respective Heirs and Assigns forever, upon the following Conditions, viz.

I. That every Grantee, his Heirs or Assigns shall plant and cultivate five Acres of Land within the Term of five Years for every fifty Acres contained in his or their Share or Proportion of Land in said Township, and continue to improve and settle the same by additional Cultivations, on Penalty of the Forfeiture of his Grant or Share in the said Township, and of its reverting to Us, our Heirs and Successors, to be by Us or Them Re-granted to such of Our Subjects as shall effectually settle and cultivate the same.

II. That all white and other Pine Trees within the said Township, fit for Masting Our Royal Navy, be carefully preserved for that Use, and none to be cut or felled without Our special Licence for so doing first had and obtained, upon the Penalty of the Forfeiture of the Right of such Grantee, his Heirs, and Assigns, to Us, our Heirs and Successors, as well as being subject to the Penalty of any Act or Acts of Parliament that now are, or hereafter shall be Enacted.

III. That before any Division of the Land be made to and among the Grantees, a Tract of Land as near the Centre of the said Township as the Land will admit of, shall be reserved and marked out for Town Lots, one of which shall be allotted to each Grantee of the Contents of one Acre.

IV. Yielding and paying therefor to Us our Heirs and Successors, for the Space of ten Years, to be computed from the Date hereof, the Rent of one Ear of Indian Corn only, on the twenty-fifth Day, of *December* annually, if lawfully demanded, the first Payment to be made on the twenty-fifth Day of *December*, 1763.

V. Every Proprietor, Settler or Inhabitant, shall yield and pay unto Us, our Heirs and Successors yearly, and every Year forever, from and after the Expiration of ten Years from the abovesaid twenty-fifty day of *December*, namely, on the twenty-fifth Day of *December*, which will be in the Year of Our Lord, 1773 *One shilling* Proclamation Money for every Hundred Acres he so owns, settles or possesses, and so in Proportion for a greater or lesser Tract of the said Land; which Money shall be paid by the respective Persons abovesaid, their Heirs or Assigns, in our *Council Chamber* in *Portsmouth*, or to such Officer or Officers as shall be appointed to receive the same; and this to be in Lieu of all other Rents and Services whatsoever.

In Testimony whereof we have caused the Seal of our said Province to be hereunto affixed. Witness, BENNING WENTWORTH, Esq; Our Governor and Commander in Chief of Our said Province, the 18th Day of May, In the Year of Our Lord CHRIST, One Thousand Seven Hundred and Sixty Three And in the Third Year of Our Reign.

B Wentworth

By His EXCELLENCY's Command,
With Advice of COUNCIL,
        Theodore Atkinson, Junr Secry
Province of New Hampr May 18,-1763
Recorded According to the Original Charter under the Province Seal
                        ċt T Atkinson Junr Secry

The Names of the Grantees of Newbury Viz

Jacob Bayley Esq
Eph^m Noyse
David Flanders
Joshua Copp
Joshua Bayley
John Goodwin
Joshua Haward
Moses Little
Simeon Stevens
Abner Newton
Hayns Johnson
Ebenezer Eaton
Thomas Danforth
Timothy Beadle
Ebenez^r Mudget
Dan^{ll} Appleton
Thomas Chamberlain
Willm Haywood
Benj^a Emerson
Archelaus Miles
Fry Bayley
Honble John Temple
Theodore Atkinson
Mark Hunk^g Wentworth
Willm Temple

John Hazzan
Jeremiah Allen
John Beard
John Ingalls
William White
Simeon Goodwin
Edmond Morse
Stephen Little
Jacob Kent
Jaasiel Herriman
Samuel Hobart
Zacheus Peasley
Caleb Johnson
William Holden
Asa Foster
Richd Chamberlain
Jonathan Broadstreet
Sam^{ll} Stevens Esq
Peter Morse
Joshua Hains
Coll Willm Symes

Ephraim Bayley
Enoch Thurstin
Samuel Stevens
Abner Sawyer
John Hasseltine
Noah White
Jesse Johnson
Peter Page
Abner Bayley
John Hugh
Joseph White
John White jun^r
James King
Moses Hazzan
Joseph Chamberlain
Abiel Chamberlain
Sam^{ll} Johnson
Jacob Eaton
Nath^{ll} Morton
Edward Bayley
Martin Severance

Benj^a Winn Samuel Cummins
John Cummins Elnathan Blood
Esq^{rs} Elias Alexander Coll Clem^t March
Capt Markquand of Newbury And
Coll John Goffe—

His Excellency Benning Wentworth Esq a Tract of Land to Contain five Hundred Acres as Marked B: W: in the Plan which is to be accoun'ed two of the within Sares—one whole Share for the Incorporated Society for the Propogation of the Gospel in Foreign Parts—one Share for A Glebe for the Church of England as by Law Established One Share for the first settled Minister of the Gospel and one Share for the Benefit of A School in Said Town

Province of New Hamp^r May 18th 1763
Recorded from the Back of the original Charter of Newbury under the Prov Seal.
⅋ T Atkinson Junr Secr^y

THE NEW YORK CHARTER.

Copy of Letters Patent To Jacob Bayley and Twenty-four other for 24,500 Acres of Land in the County of Gloucester, and erecting the same, together with 500 acres reserved to the Crown, into a Township by the Name of Newbury.

George the Third by the Grace of God of Great Britain, France and Ireland, King Defender of the Faith and so forth. To all to whom these Presents shall come, Greeting. Whereas our Province of New York in America hath ever since the Grant thereof to James Duke of York been abutted and bounded to the East in Part by the West Bank or Side of Connecticut River. And Whereas of late Years great Part of our said Province lying to the Westward of the same River hath nevertheless been pretended to be granted by divers Instruments under the Great Seal of the Province of New Hampshire as tho' the same Lands had then belonged to and were within the Bounds and Limits of the said Province of New Hampshire and within the Powers and Jurisdiction of the Government thereof. And Whereas among others the Tract of Land by these Presents herein after granted Part of our said Province of New York as aforesaid hath been so pretended to be granted and to be erected into a Township of the said Province of New Hampshire by the Name of Newbury. And Whereas our loving Subject Benjamin Whiting in Behalf of himself and others his Associates by their humble Petition presented unto our trusty and well beloved Cadwallader Colden Esquire, our Lieutenant Governor and then our Commander in Chief of our said Province of New York, and read in our Council for our said Province of New York on the Twenty-second Day of May, which was in the Year of our Lord, One Thousand, Seven Hundred and Sixty-five, did set forth, among other Things, in Substance, that there was a certain Tract of Land. Beginning at a marked Tree standing on the Bank of the westerly Side of Connecticut River opposite to the Mouth of Amonusock River, and from thence extending Southerly or Southwesterly down Connecticut River as it runs til it comes to a Tree standing there marked with certain Figures and which is about seven Miles on a streight Line below the Mouth of Amonusock River aforesaid, from thence running North fifty nine Degrees west six Miles and one Quarter of a Mile to a Stake and Stones; from thence North twenty Degrees East six Miles and one half Mile to a Stake and Stones and from thence to the marked Tree on the Side of the River the Place of Beginning. That the Petitioners conceiving the said Tract of Land to have been within the Province of New Hampshire had seated themselves and made actual Improvement thereupon under the pretended Grant of that Government, but finding by our Royal Order in Council of the Twentieth Day of July One Thousand seven Hundred and Sixty four that the said Tract of Land was within the Jurisdiction of our Province of New York, and the Petitioners who were the only Settlers thereon being willing to secure their Possessions and Improvements by our Grant under the Seal of our said Province of New York and to hold the same under our said Government of New York, the Petitioners did therefore humbly pray that our said Lieutenant Governor would be favorably pleased by our Letters Patent to grant unto them in equal Proportions the Tract of Land aforesaid containing about Twenty six Thousand acres on the like Terms on which Lands are usually granted within our said Province of New York. Which Petition having been then referred to a Committee of our Council for our said Province of New York, our same Council did afterwards on the same Day, in Pursuance of the Report of the said Committee, humbly advise and consent that our said Lieutenant Governor and then our Commander in Chief as aforesaid should by our Letters Patent grant unto the said Benjamin Whiting and the other Petitioners in equal Proportions the Tract of Land aforesaid under the Quit Rent, Provisoes, Limitations and Restrictions prescribed by our Royal Instructions. And Whereas our loving Subject Jacob Bayley by his Petition in behalf of himself and the Proprietors and Inhabitants of the said Tract of Land presented unto our trusty and well beloved William Tryon Esquire, our Captain General and Governor in Chief in and over our said Province of New York and the Territories depending thereon in America, Chancellor and Vice Admiral of the same, and read in our Council for our said Province of New York on the fifth Day of February now last past, did set forth, That he had been appointed by the Proprietors and Inhabitants of the said Tract of Land an agent for the Purpose of Obtaining our Letters Patent aforesaid to be granted under our said Province of New York for the same Tract and therefore he the said Petitioner did humbly pray that our Letters Patent might issue in the Names of the several Persons mentioned in the Schedule to his said Petition annexed, and that the same might be erected into a Township by the Name of Newbury. On due Consideration of which last recited Petition, our same Council did humbly advise, that instead of the Persons mentioned and intended as Grantees in and by the Report and Proceedings aforesaid, our said Letters Patent should issue in the Names of the several Persons mentioned in the Schedule aforesaid. And that the several Shares of the said Tract of Land which by the pretended Grant or Charter from the Government of New Hampshire were intended for public Uses be granted in Trust as follows, that is to say. One such Share for the Use of the Society for the Propagation of the Gospel in foreign Parts, a like Share as a Glebe for the Use of the Minister of the Gospel in Communion of the Church of England as by Law established for the Time being residing on the Premises, a like Share for the first settled Minister of the Gospel in the said Township, and one Hundred acres for the Use of a Schoolmaster residing on the Premises. That the Share of the said Tract of land formerly allotted to Benning Wentworth Esquire should remain vested in us, and that the whole of the said Tract of Land should be erected into a Township by the Name of Newbury, with the usual Privileges. In Pursuance whereof, and in Obedience to our said Royal Instructions, our Commissioners appointed for the setting out all Lands to be granted within our said Province have set out for the several Persons mentioned in the Schedule aforesaid, to wit, for Jacob Bayley, John Taplin, Stephen Little, Samuel Stephens, Joseph Blanchard, Nathan Stone, Waldron Blaan, James Cobham, Joseph Beck, Samuel Bayard, John Wetherhead, William Williams, James Creassy, John Bowles, John Grumly, Marinus Willet, Richard Wenman, John Kelly, John Shatford Jones, James Downes, Samuel Boyer, John Keen, John Lewis, Crean Brush and John Taylor. All that certain Tract or Parcel of Land situate, lying and being on the West Side of Connecticut River in the County of Gloucester within our Province of New York. Beginning at the Northeast Corner of the Township of Corinth, which said Corner is likewise the Northwest Corner of the Township of Mooretown, and this Tract runs thence along the North Bounds of the said Township of Mooretown South fi ty nine Degrees East five Hundred and fifteen Chains to Connecticut River ; Then up along the West Bank of the said River as it winds and turns to a Pitch Pine Tree marked with the Letters and Figures 1765 N B Y from which Tree the Mouth of Ammanoosick River bears South fifty three Degrees East, Then from the said Tree North sixty Degrees West four Hundred and seventy seven Chains, Then South Twenty Degrees West five Hundred and twenty Chains to the Place where this Tract began, Containing Twenty five Thousand Acres of Land and the usual Allowance for Highways. and containing exclusive of the five several Lots or Parcels of Land herein after described Twenty three Thousand and five Hundred Acres of Land and the usual Allowance for Highways. One of which said Lots or Parcels of Land distinguished by the Name of the fifth Lot is to remain vested in us, and is bounded as follows, that is to say, Beginning at the before mentioned Pitch Pine Tree marked for the Northeast Corner of the said larger Tract, and runs thence along the North Bounds of the said larger Tract North Sixty Degrees West eighty Chains ; Then South twenty Degrees West Seventy Chains ; Then South Sixty Degrees East Eighty two Chains to Connecticut River, and then up along the West Bank of the said River as it winds and turns to the Place where this fifth Lot began, containing Five Hundred Acres of Land and the usual allowance for Highways.   And also our said Commissioners have set out to be granted in Trust for the Uses and Purposes herein after mentioned the following four Lots of Land, Parts and Parcels of the said larger Tract so set out as aforesaid, that is to say, For the use of the Incorporated Society for the Propagation of the Gospel in Foreign Parts All that certain Lot or Parcel of Land distinguished by the Name of the first Lot, and which begins at the Northwest Corner of the said larger Tract of which this Lot is a Part and runs thence along the West Bounds of the said larger Tract South twenty Degrees West thirty two Chains ; Then South Sixty Degrees East one Hundred Chains ; Then North twenty Degrees East thirty two Chains to the North Bounds of the said larger Tract ; Then along the said North Bounds North Sixty Degrees West one Hundred Chains to the Place where this Lot began, Containing Three Hundred Acres of Land and the usual Allowance for Highways.—For a Glebe for the Use of a Minister of the Gospel in Communion of the Church of England as by Law established for the Time being Residing on the said larger Tract. All that certain Lot or Parcel of Land distinguished by the name of the second Lot, and which begins in the West Bounds of the said larger Tract at the Southwest Corner of the said first Lot and runs thence along the said West Bounds South Twenty Degrees West thirty two Chains ; Then South sixty Degrees East one Hnndred Chains ; Then North twenty Degrees East thirty two Chains to the said first Lot ; and then along the South Bounds of the said first Lot North sixty Degrees West one Hundred Chains to the Place where this Second Lot began, Containing Three Hundred Acres of Land and the usual Allowance for Highways.—For the first settled Minister of the Gospel on the said Larger Tract, All that certain Lot or Parcel of Land distinguished by the Name of the Third Lot, and which begins in the North Bounds of the said larger Tract at the Northeast Corner of the said first Lot, and runs thence along the East Bounds of the said first and second Lot South Twenty Degrees West Sixty four Chains ; Then South sixty Degrees East Fifty Chains ; Then North twenty Degrees East sixty four Chains to the North Bounds of the said larger Tract ; and then along the said North Bounds North Sixty Degrees West Fifty five Chains to the Place where this third Lot began, Containing Three Hundred Acres of Land and the usual Allowance for Highways.—And for the use of a Schoolmaster residing on the said larger Tract, All that certain Lot or Parcel of Land distinguished by the Name of the fourth Lot, and which begins in the North Bounds of the said larger Tract at the Northwest Corner of the said fifth Lot and runs thence along the said North Bounds North sixty Degrees West fifteen Chains ; Thence South twenty Degrees West Seventy Chains ; Then South sixty degrees East fifteen Chains to the said fifth Lot ; and then along the West Bounds of the said fifth Lot North Twenty Degrees East Seventy Chains to the Place where this fourth Lot began, Containing One Hundred Acres of Land and the usual allowance for Highways.

And in setting out the said larger Tract and the several Lots and Parcels of Land last described, our said Commissioners have had regard to the profitable and unprofitable acres and have taken Care that the Length of any of them doth not extend along the Banks of any River otherwise than is conformable to our said

Royal Instructions, as by a Certificate thereof under their Hands bearing Date the Eleventh Day of this Instant Month of March and entered on Record in our Secretary's Office for our said Province of New York may more fully appear. Which said Tract of Twenty Five Thousand Acres of Land and the usual allowance for Highways so set out as aforesaid according to our said Royal Instructions, We being willing to grant to the said Jacob Bayley and the other Persons mentioned in the Schedule aforesaid, their Heirs and Assigns forever (except as is herein after excepted) with the several powers and Privileges and to and upon the several and respective Use and Uses, Trusts, Intentents and Purposes, Limitations and Appointments, and under the several Reservations, Exceptions, Provisoes and Conditions herein after expressed, limited, declared and appointed of and concerning the same, and every Part and Parcel thereof respectively.

Know Ye that of our especial Grace, certain Knowledge and meer Motion, We have given, granted, ratified and confirmed, and do by these Presents for us, our Heirs and Successors, give, grant, ratify and confirm unto them the said Jacob Bayley, John Taplin, Stephen Little, Samuel Stevens, Joseph Blanchard, Nathan Stone, Waldron Blaau, James Cobham, Joseph Beck, Samuel Bayard, John Wetherhead, William Williams, James Creassy, John Bowles, John Grumly, Marinus Willet, Richard Wenman, John Kelly, John Shatford Jones, James Downes, Samuel Boyer, John Keen, John Lewis, Crean Brush and John Taylor, their Heirs and Assigns for ever, All that the aforesaid large Tract or Parcel of Land, set out abutted, bounded and described by our said Commisioners in Manner and Form as above mentioned (Except thereout as hereafter is excepted) and including All those the aforementioned several smaller Tracts or Lots of Land severally and respectively set out by our said Commissioners as Parts and Parcels of the same large Tract for the Use of the incorporated Society for the Propagation of the Gospel in Foreign Parts, For a Glebe for the Use of a Minister of the Gospel in Communion of the Church of England as by Law established. For the first settled Minister of the Gospel on the said larger Tract, and for the Use of a Schoolmaster residing on the said larger Tract. Together with all and singular the Tenements, Hereditaments, Emoluments and Appurtenances to the same and every Part and Parcel thereof belonging or appertaining; and also all our Estate, Right, Title, Interest, Possession, Claim and Demand whatsoever of, in and to the same Lands and Premises hereby granted and every Part and Parcel thereof; And the Reversion and Reversions, Remainder and Remainders, Rents, Issues and Profits thereof, and of every Part and Parcel thereof, Except and always reserved out of this our present Grant unto us, our Heirs and Successors for ever, All that the aforesaid certain Lot or Parcel of Land containing five Hundred Acres with the usual Allowance for Highways herein before mentioned to be set apart and remain vested in us, abutted, bounded and described as aforesaid, and distinguished by the Name of the fifth Lot as aforesaid, together with all and every the Appurtenances thereunto belonging, the same Lot being included within the Bounds and Limits of the larger Tract of Twenty five Thousand Acres of Land herein before described, and within the Township by these Presents herein after constituted. And also Except and always reserved out of this our present Grant unto us, our Heirs and Successors forever All Mines of Gold and Silver, and also all white or other Sorts of Pine Trees fit for Masts of the Growth of Twenty four Inches Diameter and upwards at twelve Inches from the Earth for Masts for the Royal Navy of us, our Heirs and Successors.

To have and to hold all and singular the said Lands, Tenements, Hereditaments and Premises by these Presents granted ratified and confirmed, and every Part and Parcel thereof with their and every of their Appurtenances (Except as is herein before excepted) unto them our Grantees above named their Heirs and Assigns for ever, To, for and upon the several and respective Use and Uses, Trusts, Intents and Purposes herein after expressed, limited, declared and appointed of and concerning the same, and every Part and Parcel thereof respectively, and to and for no other Use or Uses, Intent or Purpose whatsoever, that is to say,—As for and concerning All that the before mentioned small Tract, Lot or Parcel of Land so set out for the Incorporated Society, for the Propagation of the Gospel in Foreign Parts as aforesaid, being Part and Parcel of the said Tract of Land and Premises hereby granted, ratified and confirmed, and within the township by these Presents herein after constituted, and every Part and Parcel of the same Lot of Land with the Appurtenances to the same belonging (except as is herein before excepted) To and for the only proper and seperate Use and Behoof of the Society for the Propagation of the Gospel in Foreign Parts above mentioned, and their Successors for ever, and to and for no other Use or Uses, Intent or Purpose whatsoever.—And as for and concerning All that the before mentioned small Tract, Lot or Parcel of Land so set out as and for a Glebe for the Use of a Minister of the Gospel in Communion of the Church of England as by Law established, being Part and Parcel of the said Tract of Land and Premises hereby granted, ratified and confirmed, and within the Township by these Presents herein after constituted, and every Part and Parcel of the same Lot of Land with the Appurtenances to the same belonging (except as is herein before excepted) In Trust as and for a Glebe for ever, To and for the only proper and seperate Use Benefit and Behoof of the first Minister of the Gospel in Communion of the Church of England as by Law established having the Cure of Souls and residing on the said Tract of Land hereby granted and his Successors for ever Ministers as aforesaid for the Time being residing as aforesaid and to and for no other Use or Uses, Intent or Purpose whatsoever.—And as for and concerning All that the before mentioned small Tract, Lot or Parcel of Land so set out for the first settled Minister on the said Tract of Land hereby granted, the same Lot or Parcel of Land being Part and Parcel of the same Tract hereby granted, ratified and confirmed and within the Township by these Presents herein after constituted and every Part and Parcel of the same Lot of Land with the Appurtenances to the same belonging (except as is herein before excepted) In Trust to and for the Sole, proper and seperate Use, Benefit and Behoof of the first settled Minister of the Gospel that shall be settled and Officiating on the said Tract of Land hereby granted, his Heirs and Assigns for ever, And in Trust also that our said Grantees their Heirs or Assigns shall well and truly by good and sufficient Assurances in the Law convey the same last mentioned small Tract or Lot of Land with the appurtenances to such Minister of the Gospel as shall be first settled and Officiating as aforesaid his Heirs and Assigns for ever in Fee Simple as soon as may be after such Minister shall be settled and Officiating as aforesaid. and to and for no other Use or Uses, Intent or Purpose whatsoever. And as for and concerning All that other small Tract, Lot or Parcel of Land so set out for the Use of a Schoolmaster, being also Part and Parcel of the said Tract of Land and Premises hereby granted, ratified and confirmed, and within the Township by these Presents herein after constituted and every Part and Parcel of the same Lot of Land with the Appurtenances to the same belonging (Except as is herein before excepted) In Trust for ever, to and for the sole and seperate Use, Benefit and Behoof of the first public Schoolmaster of the Township by these Presents herein after constituted and erected officiating and resident in the same Township and his Successors schoolmasters as aforesaid for ever, and to and for no other Use or Uses, Intent or Purpose whatsoever.—And as for and concerning All the Rest, Residue and Remainder of the said Tract of Land, Tenements, Hereditaments and Premises hereby granted, ratified and confirmed, To have and to hold one full and equal Twenty fifth Part (the whole into Twenty five equal Parts to be divided) of the said Rest, Residue and Remainder, and every Part and Parcel thereof, with all and every the Appurtenances to the same belonging or in any wise appertaining (except as is herein before excepted) unto each of them the said Jacob Bayley. John Taplin, Stephen Little, Samuel Stevens, Joseph Blanchard. Nathan Stone. Waldron Blaau, James Cobham, Joseph Beck, Samuel Bayard, John Wetherhead, William Williams, James Creassy, John Bowles, John Grumly, Marinus Willet, Richard Wenman. John Kelley. John Shatford Jones, James Downes, Samuel Boyer, John Keen, John Lewis, Crean Brush and John Taylor, their Heirs and Assigns respectively, To their only proper and seperate Use and Behoof respectively for ever as Tenants in Common and not as Joint Tenants and to and for no other Use or Uses, Intent or Purpose whatsoever, All and singular the said Tract of Land and Premises hereby granted and every Part and Parcel thereof To be holden of us our Heirs and Successors in free and common Socage as of our Manor of East Greenwich in our County of Kent within our Kingdom of Great Britain, Yielding, Rendering and Paying therefore yearly and every Year for ever unto us, our Heirs and Successors at our Custom House in our City of New York in our said Province of New York, unto our or their Collector or Receiver General there for the Time being, on the Feast of the Annunciation of the blessed Virgin Mary commonly called Lady Day the yearly Rent of Two Shillings and six Pence Sterling for each and every Hundred Acres of the above granted Lands, and so in Proportion for any lesser Quantity thereof, Saving and except for such Part of the said Lands allowed for Highways as above mentioned in Lieu and stead of all other Rents, Services, Dues, Duties and Demands whatsoever for the hereby granted Lands and Premises, or any Part thereof. And we do of our especial Grace, certain Knowledge and meer Motion, create, erect and constitute the said large Tract of Land containing Twenty five Thousand Acres herein before mentioned and every Part and Parcel thereof a Township for ever hereafter to be, continue and remain, and by the name of Newbury for ever hereafter to be called and known. And for the better and more easily carrying on and Managing the Public Affairs and Business of the said Township, our Royal Will and Pleasure is, and we do hereby for us, our Heirs and Successors, give and grant to the Inhabitants of the said Township, all the Powers, Authorities, Privileges and Advantages hertofore given and granted to, or legally enjoyed by all, any or either our other Townships within our said Province of New York, and we also ordain and establish that there shall be for ever hereafter in the said Township Two Assessors, one Treasurer, two Overseers of the Highways, two Overseers of the Poor, One Collector, and four Constables elected and chosen out of the Inhabitants of the said Township yearly and every Year, on the Third Tuesday in May, at the most public place in the said Township by the Majority of the Freeholders thereof, then and there met and assembled for that Purpose; Hereby Declaring that wheresoever the first Election in the said Township shall be held, the future Elections shall for ever thereafter be held in the same Place as near as may be and Giving and Granting to the said Officers so chosen Power and Authority to excercise their said several and respective Offices during one whole Year from such Election, and until others are legally chosen and elected in their Room and stead, as fully and amply as any the like Officers have, or legally may use or exercise their Offices in our said Province of New York, and in case any or either of the said Officers of the said Township should die or remove from the said Township before the Time of their annual Service shall be expired, or refuse to act in the Offices for which they shall respectively be ehosen, Then our Royal Will and Pleasure further is, and we do hereby direct ordain and require the Freeholders of the said Township to meet at the Place where the annual Election shall be held for the said Township, and choose other or others of the said Inhabitants of the said Township in the Place and stead of him or them so Dying, removing or Refusing to act, within Forty Days next after such Contingency. And to prevent any undue Election in this Case, we do hereby ordain and require, that upon every Vacancy in the Office of Assessors, the Treasurer and in either of the other offices the Assessors of the said Towhship shall within ten Days next after any such Vacancy first happens, appoint the Day for such Election, and give public Notice thereof in Writing under his or their Hands, by affixing such Notice on the Church Door, or other most public Place in the said Township, at the least, ten Days before the Day appointed for such Election; and in Default thereof, we do hereby require the Officer or Officers of the said Township, or the Survivor of them, who, in the Order they are herein before mentioned shall next succeed him or them so Making Default, within ten Days next after such Default, to appoint the Day for such Election, and give notice thereof as aforesaid; hereby Giving and Granting, that such Person or Persons as shall be so chosen by the Majority of such of the Freeholders of the said Township as shall meet in Manner hereby directed shall have, hold exercise and enjoy the Office or Offices to which he or they shall be so elected and chosen from the time of such Election until the third Tuesday in May then next following, and until other or others be legally chosen in his or their Place and stead as fully as the Person or Persons in whose Place he or they shall be chosen might or could have done by Virtue of these Presents. And we do hereby will and direct, that this Method shall for ever hereafter be used for the filling up all Vacancies that shall happen in any or either of the said offices between the annual Elections above directed. Provided always and upon condition nevertheless, that if our said Grantees, their Heirs or Assigns, or some or one of them shall not within three Years next after the Date of this our present Grant settle on the said Tract of Land hereby granted so many Families as shall amount to one Family for every Thousand Acres of the same Tract; Or if they our said Grantees, or one of them, their or one of their Heirs or Assigns shall not also within three Years to be computed as aforesaid, plant and effectually cultivate, at the least, three Acres for every Fifty Acres of such of the hereby granted Lands as are capable of Cultivation; Or if they our said Grantees, or any of them, their or any of their Heirs or Assigns or any other Person or Persons, by their or any of their Privity, Consent or Procurement, shall fell, cut down, or otherwise destroy any of the Pine Trees by these Presents reserved to us, our Heirs and Successors, or hereby intended so to be, without the Royal License of us, our Heirs or Successors, for so Doing, first had and obtained, that then and in any of these Cases this our present Grant, and every Thing therein contained, shall cease and be absolutely void, and the Lands and

Premises hereby granted shall revert to and rest in us, our Heirs and Successors, as if this our present Grant had not been made, any Thing herein before contained to the contrary in any wise notwithtanding.   Provided further, and upon Condition also nevertheless, and we do hereby, for us, our Heirs and Successors, direct and appoint, that this our present Grant shall be registered and entered on Record within six Months from the Date thereof in our Secretary's Office in our City of New York in our said Province of New York, in one of the Books of Patents there remaining; and that a Docquet thereof shall be also entered in our Auditor's Office there for our said Province of New York; and that in Default thereof this our present Grant shall be void and of none Effect, any Thing before in these Presents contained to the Contrary thereof in any wise notwithstanding.   And we do moreover of our especial Grace, certain Knowledge and meer Motion consent and agree, that this our present Grant being registered, recorded and a Docquet thereof made as before directed and appointed, shall be good and effectual in the Law to all Intents, Constructions and Purposes whatsoever against us, our Heirs and Successors, notwithstanding any Misreciting, Misbounding, Misnaming, or other Imperfection or Omission of, in or in any wise concerning the above granted, or hereby mentioned or intended to be granted Lands, Tenements, Hereditaments and Premises or any Part thereof.

In Testimony whereof we have caused these our Letters to be made Patent, and the Great Seal of our said Province of New York to be hereunto affixed.   Witness our said trusty and well beloved William Tryon Esquire, our said Captain General and Governor in Chief in and over our said Province of New York, and the Territories depending thereon in America, Chancellor and Vice Admiral of the same, at our Fort in our City of New York, the Nineteenth Day of March in the Year of our Lord One Thousand seven Hundred and Seventy two, and of our Reign the Twelfth.

First Skin Line the Twenty third the Letters *cob* in the name *Jacob*, Line the forty fourth the Letters *se* in the Word *seven*, Line the fiftieth the Word *then*, and Line the sixty first the Word *the*, Second Skin Line the Twenty fifth the Word *with*, and third Skin Line the second the Words *at our*, all wrote on Rasures;   and second Skin Line the forty third the Words *for the Time being residing as aforesaid*, and third Skin Line the Twenty sixth the Word *such* interlined.   CLARKE.
                                                                  WM TRYON
New York Secretary's Office, 13th April 1772.   The within Letters Patent are recorded in this office in Lib: Patents No. 16 Page 195.
                                                       Geo Banyar D Sec'ry
New York Auditor General's Office 14th April 1772.   The within Letters Patent are Docqueted in this office.
                                                       Geo Banyar Depᵞ Audʳ.

PART OF THE JOURNAL OF CAPT. JACOB BAYLEY, IN THE OLD FRENCH WAR.

These fragments of General Bayley's journal are preserved among the Little papers at Newburyport, and were copied for the editor, by Hon. Benjamin Hale. They were in the form of letters addressed to Col. Moses Little. It is not known that any other portions of his journals remain.

A JOURNAL OF OUR EMBARKATION AND PROCEEDING DOWN LAKE GEORGE, AND SIEGE OF TICONDEROGA.

July 21, 1759.   We embarked from Lake George about sun-rise, on the west side of the Lake.   The whole army marched down the Lake in three columns, the Rangers, light infantry and Grenadiers went in front and the center column consisted of the artillery stores and Train, with Invincibles in front of them. Then we proceeded down the Lake, and around as far as the entrance of the first French narrows, about sunset.   Yᵉ wind being boisterous drove the soldiery on the artillery, which made it necessary to retreat.   Orders being given to that purpose we retreated.   But the wind blowing down the Lake made it difficult, and broke our ranks, but we retreated on the west side of the lake about a mile to a cove, where my company rid it out very well.

July 22. In the morning, about break of day, I drew off, and looked after the rest of the regiment, and found them about sunrise which was Sunday. We soon began to advance down the narrows in the same order as when we first embarked, and arrived and landed without any loss of position. The advance party joined by Col⁰ Willard, marched round the mountain and took possession of the sawmill, intrenched and got some cannon up—at the same time the regulars & Col⁰ Willard took the hill opposite the fort and built a breast-work.

July 23 The army took possession of the French breastwork without the loss of one man. They played smartly on us with the cannon and mortars, we intrenched 30 rods within their breastworks and got up the cannon and mortars.

Tues., 24. Nothing remarkable, only we intrenched very smartly and things looked "Serious."

Wed., 25. We again embarked for Fort George, left the army in good spirits and in good condition & situation, and arrived at yᵉ fort in the evening. From whence we took carriages for the regiment, and marched yᵉ 26th of July to Fort Edward, there lodged, and on Friday, July 27th marched to Saratoga, and on Saturday, July 28, embarked on board the Schows, and about 11 o'clock got to Stillwater—from thence to the Half-Moon and there lodged. From thence on the Sabbath, the 29th the men marched to Schenectady, and I went to Albany —lodged at Capt. Lansings.

Mon. 30th. Got stores and sent them to the men, and marched to the Mohawk. On Tues. 31st Lodged with the men. Wednesday August 1st loaded our battoes— sent them off and marched about four miles up Mohawk river; from thence on Thursday, 2ᵈ, we marched about six miles, to one Hares and lodged. From there we marched about twelve miles, on Friday to fort Hunter, & from there on Saturday to Canajoharie, about 20 miles. On the Sabbath tarried till the Battaux came up, which was about 10 o'clock. Marched about four miles to Fort Hendricks, from thence on Monday 6, marched by the little carrying place about nine miles from fort Hendricks, was obliged to go back to yᵉ carrying place to haul over the bateaux and baggage.

Tues. 7. set forward six miles and the next day went as far as Little Indian field, about 13 miles, had bad marching this day, but through as good land as men need to settle on. This was not the only good land we went through, for it was good all the way from Schenectady—five settlements on the German Flats, but all abandoned by the inhabitants, all ye way below we settled, and men lived finely.

Thurs. 9. We marched about 13 miles to Great Indian field—got there about 12 o'clock; met a number of Indian bateaux with three prisoners and 11 scalps. On the next day we met yᵉ first party of prisoners. There were about 600 of them. Tarried at this place this night. The bateaux did not come up until night.

Fri. 10 Marched to Fort Stanwix which was 12 miles, and arrived at yᵉ fort that night.

Sab. 12. We marched from yᵉ fort toward Oswego, Lodged in yᵉ wood about 4 miles from fort Stanwix.

Mon. 13. We marched to Oneida, about 10 miles. Fine land from yᵉ fort to Oneida. There we gave the Indians one ax, and they stole two or three more. Here they have two small block houses and other small houses, some of them quite handsome after their fashion. The inhabitants appear civil but are deceitful. Tarried there two hours then marched to Tuscarora, 5 miles, where we lodged. This town was very regularly built, about 8 houses on each side of y road, all the same height and length, and set even at yᵉ front.

Tues. 14. We marched to Canasadago, which was 16 miles, stayed a little there, then marched on Wednesday 16th to Onandaga, passed by on the right three miles further and camped. All this way was choice land—not one foot of bad —thousands of acres that we passed through were cleared and full of grass—all as far as we could see was so, on both sides of yᵉ path. Passed over Tucarara river, and Onandaga river. Our course was south by west.

Thurs. 16. We marched to the Three rivers about 16 miles acrost Onandaga river & a branch of the salt lake. This lake is quite salt & we found goose grass growing on the flats & it had yᵉ scent of yᵉ salt marsh. There is a very salt spring that boils up out of yᵉ ground as big as a great pot, & runs to yᵉ lake. Our course this day was about north.

Fri. 17. We marched thence over Seneca river & down Oswego river about 24 miles. Bad travelling—much tired.

Sat. 18. In the morning we marched about 7 miles to Oswego, the river here runs N. west by north.

Sab. 19. We had preaching at Oswego.

The company seemed to have remained at Oswego without special incident till Sept. 9.

Sun. 9. Five whale boats and 13 bateaux with 250 men, under command of the captain of ye Royals—upon an expedition toward Oswego Lake.

Mon. 10. Two French top-sail vessels appeared in sight of our incampment. Cruised some time, then tacked & stood from us.

Tues. 11. A Report in ye lake. In ye morning came in two whale boats from Capt. Parker, & brought in 4 French prisoners which they took on an Island in ye lake.

Wed. 12. All the pickets in camp are ordered to work on ye fort, which goes briskly on. Dies one of the French prisoners, brought in last night. * * *

Mon. 17. A very bad storm. Ensign Kent holds unwell. I was somewhat ill which made me think of home. Dies one Wingate of Capt. Berry's company.

Wed. 19. Made my return of the regiment which was—exclusive of the officers 210 and 62 sick and 15 with Capt. Goffe, and 13 with ye adjutant bateauxing.

Fri. 21. Cool but pleasant. About two o'clock in the afternoon dies Otho Stevens, [See Stevens Family.]

Sat. 22. Cloudy—wind south east—looked likely to storm—I had orders to go to Albany.

Mon. 24. Set out in ye morning for Albany & with a great deal of difficulty arrived at ye Great Falls with 50 men of our Regiment Including Mr. True and ye doctor, 7 of our company, viz.—Seargt Copp, Josiah Heath, Moses Hase, Jonathan Goodwin, William Landy, John Scribner and William Page.

Tues. 25. Died, Abijah Foster, very suddenly.

Wed. 26. Went up the river as far as ye Three Rivers, Incamped about dusk.

Thurs. 27. Set out about sun-rise and preceded up the river & arrived at the Lake about an hour by the sun. Set out to go over the Lake just before sun-set. Proceded up the Lake about 20 miles, stayed on ye north side of ye lake.

Fri. 28. Arrived at ye picket on Canada Creek about 2 hours by ye sun. This night died McKeen of Capt. Lovewells Co.

Sat. 29. Proceded toward Fort Stanwix—got this day about 20 miles & encamped.

Sab. 30. About sun rise set forward and arrived at fort Stanwix about noon, where we awaited the arrival of the batteaux.

Mon. October 1. Met with some difficulty to get bateaux for the sick but about 10 o'clock took a bateau & arrived at ye Little Indian Field about sunset. Went about a mile to another little field and encamped.

Tues. 2. Arrived at ye little carrying place about noon and stayed that day waiting for ye bateaux.

Thurs. 4. About 2 oclock bateaux for the remainder of our men came, and we set out & arrived at Flatter's about 8 miles from the Falls and lodged.

Fri. 5. Set out. (They reached Schenectady about 10 o'clock on Sunday.

Mon. 8. Set out with all the sick. Got to Mr. Onthank's, that night ye sick came. Tues. 46 more came. Wed. 10 and Thurs. 11 came 6 more.

Fri. 12. Sent off 18 and Mr. True.

Sabbath, 14. Sent off 18 men of the party.

Tues. Sent off 5 men.

The end of first fragment of diary.

ORDER FROM COLO. GOFFE.

To Capt. Jacob Bayley,
Portsmouth, May 18, 1760.

You are hereby ordered immediately upon sight of these to cause all men enlisted by you and your officers to march to Litchfield, to be at sd Litchfield on Thursday, 22d day of this instant May, without fail, in order to receive Billeting and thence proceed to No 4.

From Yours &c. JOHN GOFFE, Colo.

SECOND FRAGMENT OF CAPT. JACOB BAYLEY'S JOURNAL.

IN CAMP AT ISLE AU NOIX, AUG. 24, 1760.

To Colo Moses Little.

Sir:

I take this opportunity to inform you of our situation according to your request. I should have written before, but nothing worth communicating occured till now. I shall give you a short sketch of a journal from our embarkation at Crown Point to this day.

Mon. 11. Aug. Embarked in three columns, the Rangers for a front of ye whole. The right column consisted of Regulars, with a small bateau in the front, 2 columns of Rhode Island and New Hampshire with legionary (?) bateaux in their front. A large brig and 2 sloops were at Windmill Point at this time & near Isle au Noix. Proceded in this manner. Wind contrary. The 3d & last column were Massachusetts men, with another bateau in their front.

Tues. 12. We procede 8 miles, wind being contrary.

Wed. 13. Embarked early with an easy gale in our favor. The wind increased & blew very hard, so that the whole fleet was in danger, but we arrived at a good harbor about 12 in the afternoon. Several men were drowned this day by a boat breaking in two, 8 men drowned of 11 of which 3 were from our regiment. Several helmsmen were knocked overboard and drowned.

Fri. 15. Proceded with a good gale as far as to Windmill Point & encamped on Isle La Motte. Our brig and fleet joined us & our fleet looked formidable.

Saturday 16. Set out early and arrived at our landing about noon. We were met by the French with all the force they could make by water, but we forced them to retreat. We immediately landed without opposition and threw up breast-works, securing our Bateaux.

Sabbath 17. Cleared a Road within 500 yards of the French fort without disturbance. One bateau went close to the French, was shot upon by them, one of their shot took off 8 legs from 6 men. One was a captain of a train who lost both legs, and one man more, both died same day, the others are like to do well.

Mon. 18. Continued clearing the road, began our batteries which were within 400 yds. of the French, who fired smartly on us, but without effect. Some few were killed on both sides with small arms.

Tues. 19 Decamped, marched & encamped opposite to the island at about 500 yds. from it. Threw up a breast work the whole length of the island. Pretty smart fire this day, but none hurt. One deserter came in & informed us of the strength of the enemy—says they are about 1400. The French fired briskly on us in the afternoon but without effect.

Thurs. 21. Works went on well; exchanged several shots, they wounded several of our men. In the evening the French attempted a rally, but were scared back.

Fri. 22. Took 5 prisoners who informed us that General Amherst was at Isle La Galloa last Tuesday sennight & was besieging that place, which lies on the river about 80 miles above Montreal & Gen. Murray was at the mouth of the river Sorel, which is the river we are on, about 50 miles from us & about the same distance from Montreal.

Sat. 23. The Indians killed and scalped one of our men. Orders given for unmasking our batteries at 2 o'clock, which was done by the time appointed. The French kept up an incessant fire on our men with cannon, wall-pieces and small arms, but did us little damage, wounding only one man. At 3 o'clock the signal was given at which our cannon & mortars, royals & cohorns, consisting of about 30, fired five rounds successively with good effect, beating down all before them, continued all the afternoon & night; we endeavored to cut their boom that our vessels might pass. The French fired smartly upon us. * * *

Sabbath 24th. Began a new Battery within musket shot of the French. They played smartly upon us, especially in the night and killed one officer, and wounded another, and about 13 men. We did not complete cutting the boom, it being very strong. They have fastened 5 logs abreast with iron staples & links 1½ inches in diameter, the whole anchored every 10 ft. to ye ground. The length of the boom is about 80 yds. They defended it in the best manner, being sensible that if we got below them they could not go off, but must fall into our hands. The island is exceedingly strong, but they are short of ammunition. If we cannot get below the island, or be some time of the siege, they will hold their ground. There is no such thing as to storm the island on the upper side. It is picketed 2 rods into the water & a vast deal of boards thrown without the pickets but they must surrender or run away, sooner or later. If it is my fortune to survive, I will give you the whole. I remain your most humble servant,

                                                        J. BAYLEY.

EXTRACTS FROM THE DIARY OF COL. JACOB KENT.

In the possession of Col. Henry O. Kent of Lancaster, N. H., are several small pocket-books which were formerly the property of Col. Jacob Kent, the pioneer. The diary consists of notes made here and there among various accounts. Such of these as seemed likely to interest the readers of this volume, were transcribed for the purpose by the present owner.

May 31, 1760. This day marched from Plaistow, (N. H) for the campaign. Marched to Derry—and there met with Capt. March. Started from there about seven o'clock and lodged at Lieut. John Parkmans (?) at Litchfield. The next morning Ensign Harriman went out to care for his stallion—the horse being loth to be caught reared and struck Ensign Harriman on the elbow hurting him very much.

June 1. Marched to Monson, now Milford, there lodged at Hopkins and Monday morning got off for Peterborough. Travelled 6 miles to Timothy Pages, of Number Two—there dined and marched about 4 miles and stopped at Landlord Hailes of Shiptown and there drinkt a bowl of punch, then marched to Mitchells at Peterborough; the next day Tuesday marched to Keene, the next day went to Swanzey to press men and the next day I took the team and went to the Great Meadows (Westmoreland) and lodged there two nights, then sending the baggage by boats we marched to Major Bellows (Walpole) and from thence to Number Four (Charlestown) and there joined the regiment and there tarried until the 16th of June—when we marched over the river (Connecticut) and there camped and went to work upon the Road.
(The work given this Regiment was to cut a road through the primeval wilderness to the Green Mountains and repair Starks old road—the route being across the present State of Vermont, from Charlestown to Lake Champlain opposite Crown Point). (H. O. K.)

June 7. As I was marching into No. 4 with Ensign Harriman, E. Stevens and J. Gile we overtook a party of about 20 soldiers who told us there had been a family taken by the Indians, from a house about 60 rods forward not more than half an hour before—which we found to be true—the man and his wife and five children were taken and carried off—I took the other family with me—and we marched into No. 4 that night and there joined the Regiment. The next day was a Sabbath Day and we had preaching.

About the 10th of June Lieut. Beatel (Bedel) took 20 men, and is to follow scouting Ensign Harriman took 25 men with Sergeant Clement and went into the carpenters works. They are first to repair the old Fort at No. 4 and then in building Bridges and Block Houses on the Road.

June 10. I marched up the River three miles and crossed, encamped and built a block house by the river side, also built a large scow and a canoe—then going up on our road to Crown Point, returning every night till June 28, and then moved about 5 miles. The next day being a Sabbath Day we had one sermon and then Killed an Ox, drawing our allowance. The same night we heard the French had left Cowbeck (Quebec) and returned to their Quarters again with great loss by sea and land.

Tuesday July 2. Colonel Goffe came up with the Regiment. The sixth day we left our Encampments and marched over the North branch of Black River about 5 miles and camped on the Road—the tenth day we marched about 5 miles, the twelfth day about a mile and a half. A Sunday we had a sermon preached.

The same day Captain Lovewell, Willard and Hazen marched their companies for Otter Creek.

Thursday June 17, there came in two Rangers from Major Rogers to inform us that there was a party of the Enemy across the Lake near the mouth of Otter Creek that Major Rogers thought would fall upon our Regiment, whereupon we threw up a breast work and prepared for them.

June 19. There marched off 96 men with their arms and packs for home—four were taken and returned the same day. Another party were marching off—but by force of arms were brought back to the Quarter guard and their asked forgivness of the Colonel and were forgiven—the next day 12 of Captain Hazens deserters returned.

June 21. Sergeant Roe was confined for misconduct on parade and encouraging desertion—was tried by Court Martial and broken and reduced to the ranks.

June 24. Marched on about 5 miles.

July 27. Left our encampments and marched for Crown Point—marching 8 miles—the next day marched fifteen miles—the next day marched 15 miles our provisions growing short. There was a Recruit sent out to meet us, about 12 o'clock. The next day we marched 15 miles and went over Lake Champlain at Crown Point and into camp.

August 1. We recovered Crown Point and there tarried until the 7th, and then the Regiment joined the Army and went down the Lake for Canada all except the invalids and those detailed to work in the brick yards at Crown Point.

August 16. The army landed and the 28th the Isle au Noix was given up and the next day our people went forward.

Sept. 18, 1860. The Regiment returned back to Crown Point.

Oct. 21. At night there came a fall of snow.

Oct. 23. 80 invalids were marched oft to go through to No. 4.

Here the entries end abruptly.

(As a summary it appears that Goff's Regiment Marched from Plaistow near the N. Hamp. seaboard—June 1, reaching the Connecticut at Charlestown or No. 4 on the 16th, that they cut the military road—bridging streams and erecting block houses—to protect their line of communications—between June 16 and July 27—probably earlier, as the Regiment left its last cantonments on that day for a long march of 53 miles over the completed road to the east shore of the Lake. Crown Point was recovered August 1, the army going down the Lake toward Canada, in batteaux Aug. 7, landing at Isle au Noix Aug. 16, which was surrendered Aug. 28, opening the communications with Canada and returning to Crown Point Sept. 18. It would seem from the New Hampshire Rolls that the Regiment reached home and was mustered out in November, 1760. (H. O. K.)

CAMPAIGN OF 1777. BURGOYNE'S SURRENDER.

Newbury, September, the 23d, 1777. Then made a draft out of Newbury.

Lieutenant Nathaniel Morrill	William Johnson	James Gilchrist
Ensign Frye Bailey	Uriah Chamberlain	Ebenezer White
Enoch Brown	Thomas Brock	William Chappel
David Hasseltine	Jonathan Fowler	Joseph Taylor
Josiah Page	Thomas Chamberlain	Levi Sylvester, Jr.
Dudley Carleton		

Tuesday, 25th of September. I marched the regiment for the camps. Lodged at Colonel Gilbert's the first night. Marched the second day to Windsor, and there joined Colonel Marsh's (?) regiment and marched to Corfrine a Saturday. A Sabbath day marched to Whites of Shaftsbury and Monday we marched to Captain Maynards (?) at Tynmouth and Tuesday to Powlett and lay in camp till Saturday; then marched to White Creek about two miles; there lay until Monday; then marched to Cambridge about 15 miles. Tuesday marched nine miles and Wednesday marched over the River to Saratoga and went into Camp.

Thursday, August 8, marched back and to Fort Miller, and Friday marched back to Saratoga. (No date.) General Gates came up and engaged General Burgoyne and Saturday they continued the action, a Sabbath Day also. A Monday and Tuesday there was a cessation of Arms. Friday the 17th, their Army surrendered to General Gates.

DETACHED MEMORANDA.

June 17, 1760. James Chase, belonging to Captain Hazzou's company received a flogging of fifty lashes.

July 13, 1760. One George, belonging to Captain Tilton's company received a flogging of four score lashes for denying his duty.

July 16, 1760. Encamped on the Road about 20 miles from No. 4.

June 25, ye 1760. Colonel Goffe and Captain Small and Major Emery and Lieut. Stone rode up from No. 4 to the encampments by the river, with Widow Johnson and Miriam Willard and Abigail Willard. They had a very fine rain to go home in for their comfort, and it also was a great comfort to us to hear that they were so comfortably wet.

Date not given:—"Things that were passed into the Colonel's mess. 13 quarts of Rum and ¾ of pound of Tea."

1763. Col. Jacob Bayley Dr. for a horse, three hundred pounds, for a mair, two hundred pounds, for a pair of oxen, three hundred and fifty pounds and for one ox, one hundred and seventy pounds.

1771. Sowed winter wheat Sept. 6—except one piece harrowed in October 14th.

1762, December 28. This day got off (from Plaistow) for Coös with Lieut. Harriman.

1760, July 4. There came up a squad or party of 10 or 12 to our second encampment on the Roads—four were young women. The young men appeared very gay and sprightly, Mrs. Willard with her wig and all.

"1788. Provisions for raising the Meeting House.

Salt Pork,	17lbs.
Fresh Meat,	48lbs.
Bread,	40lbs.
Cheese,	6½lbs.
Rum,	One Gallon.
Beer,	One Barrell.

Jacob one day and a half with 4 Oxen and one day on the House and for 14 lbs. of Pork carried to Joseph Chamberlain and for 6½ lbs. Lamb and for cash paid to Mr. Wallace $1.00 and for five hundred of board nails and one thousand and a half of shingle nails paid to Mr. Wallace."

"January 1789. Mr. Spooner the printer Dr.

For 3 bushels of Wheat delivered to Mr Samuel Grow.
£. s. d.
0 15 0"

"Newbury, 1790. The Town of Newbury Detor. For boarding Mr. Nathaniel Lambert and keeping his horse 11 weeks and a half at two bushels of wheat per week 23 bushels—before he gave his answer, from the time he gave his answer, until he was ordained was 5½ weeks and 2 bushels a week, 11 bushels." The town of Newbury paid me for boarding the Rev. Nathaniel Lambert up to the 17th of Nov. 1790. From that date Mr. Lambert pays for his own board.

The Rev. Nathaniel Lambert got off for Rowley (near Newbury, Mass.) Jany 17, 1791 and returned back, February 7, 1791."

A FRAGMENT OF THE JOURNAL KEPT BY COL. FRYE BAYLEY DURING

THE REVOLUTIONARY WAR.

This portion of Col. Frye Bayley's journal was found among some old papers bought by the late Richard Patterson, at the auction held after the death of the last of the family in Newbury, in 1863. It fills the first four pages of an account book which is all in Col. Bayley's handwriting, and contains transactions with most of the prominent men at Coös from 1766 to 1790. The second and third leaves, which apparently contained the journal from August 10th to February 9th, are missing. Col. (then Ensign) Frye

Bayley was sent on several occasions, during the winter of 1775-6, to the army in Canada, by his uncle, General Bayley, and in May was sent to the army with dispatches from General Washington, and remained with it during its retreat to Crown Point. So much of the journal as relates to the army is here given. He kept a diary during the whole of the war, but this is all that is known to remain of it.

June 10 Day 1776. Provision Day, one man died at St. Johns with pain in his Breast. One man Died with the Small Pox in a Tent just by me.

11 Day. I made a Return of Sick and well. Col. Wait came in. The Small Pox goeth very hard with ye men.

12 Day. Veryyhot. Bad bad for ye sick. I drew a Gun. I heard Bad news from ye Three Rivers.

13 Day. Our Company drew nineteen Blankets and Six kettles.

14 Day. John Treble's clothing was vandued. I went to Chambly, one man died.

15 Day. Capt. Esterbrook died. Minchin set out to go to Sorrel.

16 Day, Sunday. I went on Fatigue to stop ye road to Laprarie.

17 Day. I went on Scout to guard the Battaux from Chambly.

18th Day. The army retreated to ye Isle au Noix.

19 Day. The Sick die Very Fast.

20 Day. I set out with Col°. Poore's regiment next for Crown Point. Lodge Isle Mott.

21 Day. Lodged on Skitton's Island.

22 Day. The wind being against us we were Forced on a small island by reason of wind—thereon three hours.

23 Day. We arrived at Crown Point about ten o'clock. Our capt. died at even.

24 Day. Capt. Wait came in this morning has been all day Drawing Provision and hath not got any yet.

25 Day. About noon I got my Provision and set out for ye Isle aux Noix. Lodged about fifteen miles from ye Point.

26 Day. I Set out Very Early the wind Being fair till five. In ye afternoon came up a Blow and I was obliged to run Before ye wind Five miles on a Small Island and Lodged there.

27 Day. We rowed to ye Isle of Mott where I met the army.

28 Day. I set out from there with ye whole army, the wind against us I landed on a small Island about midnight. The General came and ordered us off the Lake. Being exceding Rough and the wind very high we rowed five miles to the army. Quartering of ye wind through much Difficulty we Landed.

29 Day. We Lodged on Skilton's Island.

30, Sunday. We got to Giliners Creek.

July First, 1776. We arrived to Crown Point 2 Day. I pitched the tent 3 Day. I wrote a letter to my wife. Henry Eaton died.

4 Day. Nothing stiring today. 5. I made tent For Holiday.

6 Day. I made tent for myself.

7 Day, Sunday. People die very fast. Ten buried in a Day.

8 Day. Capt. Wilkins Died last night. I have been to the Burying. I saw 66 graves of New England people and two in some graves that Died within three weeks.

9 Day. I Set on court martial to try Joshua Bedle.

10. Passed Muster. Ebenezer Holiday died. His shoes his Nurse had.

11 Day. I saw eight men whipped.

12 Day. I was on Fatigue.

13 Day. Rain. Enoch Hall went from here.

14 Day, Sunday. I received Sixty five Dollars of Capt. Young of wages due to me. Let Robertson have one Dollar for washing; payed Moses Chamberlin Five Dollars for Note he Bought of me against Silas Chamberlin. I Bought one Quart of Rum, one Dollar.

15 Day. I embarked for Ticonderoga. I lodged five miles short of harbour.

16 Day. I arrived at said harbour. I bought one cake chocolate, one and six pence.

17 Day. I bought Pair of Shews ten and six Pence.

18 Day. I payed one Dollar for Vinegar and my Barber one and six pence. I settled with ye mess since I came to Crown Point to the 17th of this. I am indebted twenty two shillins.

19 Day. Col. Hazen had his trial.

20 Day. I bought Cow.

21 Day, Sunday. Luis Seaby confined.

22 Day. I Drank Bristor Beer. Luis Seaby whipped. Received letter from my wife.

23 Day. I Payed Major Wales five Dollars. Wrote letter to my wife.

24 Day. I am on Guard.

25. I was Relieved of main Guard.

26 Day. I went on Fatigue over ye Lake.

27 Day. I went over to ye mount to clear encampment.

28, Sunday. I removed over to ye Mount.

29. I went to the General. Mr. Weatherspoon came in.

30 Day. I received Letter from my wife Spent four shillings.

31 Day. I went over ye River. Sent Six Dollars to my wife by Weatherspoon.

August ye First, 1776. Hottest day has been. Lieut. White like to Bleed to Death. 20th Day of July my child died.

2 Day. I went on Fatigue. Split one mortar, one the day Before.

3 Day. Made a stop.

4 Day, Sunday. I wrote Letter to my wife.

5 Day. I brought my cow home. Settled with ye mess.

6 Day. I went to Capt. Carliles court martial.

7 Day. Leut Whitcomb came home.

8 Day. I wrote Letter to Joshua Bayley.

9 Day. Meigs died. Capt. Carlile came in. Wrote letter to my wife.

A part of Journal missing. August 9th to Jan. 2nd, '77, was then at home.

Feb. 19. I enlisted under Lieut. Taylor.

22 Day. An express came from Gen. Schuyler to take every Fifth man of ye militia.

24 Day. We drafted the men of this Town to go to Ticonderoga.

25. They passed muster.

26. They set out.

27. Capt. Taplin's company met at Robert Johnston's.

March 3. Capt. Taplin's Company met at ye State House. The old Officers gave up and chose new ones.

18 Day. The ground is almost bare.

April 19, 1790. Bill Seidgel began work for me and is to work six months for 18 Dollars.

April 22, 1790. John Smith came to work for me and is to work 8 months for 49 Dollars.

August 13, 1783. This Day payed Henry Lovewell his wages in full for scouting while under me, together with his brother, Nehemiah, the whole being Four pound, 17 shillings and four pence.

April 17, 1783. This Day Rec'd of Capt. Frye Bayley in full from the State of Vermont for services done in his Company in ye year 1777 in Colo Peter Olcotts Regiment, together with Ephraim Martin, Benjamin Martin, Patrick Kennedy, Ichabod Collins and John Osmore. Received by me,

BENJ. DAVIS.

JOURNAL OF THOMAS JOHNSON WHILE A CAPTIVE IN CANADA, 1781.

This journal is contained in two small and much worn pocket-books now in the possession of Mrs. A. G. Johnson of Watertown, Conn. The spelling and use of capitals are modernized.

March 5, 1781. This morning early went over to Haverhill for my mill stones with my teams. Returned before dinner, shod my oxen, took dinner. Set out for Peacham at 2 o'clock, little thinking the length of my journey before I would see my family again. This night put up at Orrs in Ryegate.

Tuesday 6th. This day being thawy and bad going, was obliged to leave one of my mill stones within one mile of the place where we lodged. This night arrived at Peacham with the other mill stones. Lodged at Mr. Elkin's.

Wed. 7th. This morning finding my oxen lame sent Mr. Josiah Page with 4 oxen home. Then hired Jonathan Elkins with his oxen and went back and took the other mill stone and returned to Peacham that night. Should have returned home that evening, but was a little unwell. Thought that I would go early next morning.

Thursday, 8th. This morning about 12 or 1 o'clock awakened out of my sleep—found the house beset with enemies—thought that I would slip on my stockings and jump out of the window and run, but before that, came in two men with their Guns pointed at me—challenged me for their prisoner, but did not find myself the least terrified. Soon found two of the men to be old acquaintances of mine. Soon found some motions for tying me, but I told them that I submitted myself a Prisoner, and would offer no abuse. Soon packed up and marched, but I never saw people so surprised as the family were. When wd came to Mr. Davis's I found the party to consist of eleven men, Capt. Prichare commanding them. Marched seven or eight miles. Daylight began to appear. I found that Moses Elkins looked very pale. I told the Capt. that he had better let him go back, for he was drowned when he was small, and that he would not live through the woods. He said that he would try him further, but on my pleading the pity that it was to lose such a youngter he sent him back. We halted soon for refreshment. To my great surprise I found John Gibson and Barlow in the party. Then marched about four miles—obtained leave to write a letter and leave on a tree. Then marched—I was most terribly tired and faint. Camped down on the River Lamoille this night.

Friday, 9th. This day marched down the River Lamoille about Twelve miles below the forks. One of the finest countries of land that ever I saw. Camped about Eleven o'clock at night.

Saturday, 10th. This day marched to the Lake. Underwent a great deal by being faint and tired. The Captain and men were very kind to us. Stormy and uncomfortable night.

Sunday, 11th. This morning went on to the Lake ten miles north of the River Lamoille. Marched fifteen miles on the Lake, and then crossed the Grand Isle, marched ten miles to the Point au Fer. Dinner being on the Table I dined with the Commandant of that Post and supped with him. Was well treated.

Monday, March 12th, 1781. This day marched to the Isle Aux Noix. Went into the Fort into a Barrack, got a cooking, but the Commandant ordered the Prisoners out of the Fort to a Block House but soon had sent me a good dinner and a bottle of Wine. Then Capt. Sherwood called on me to examine me. In the evening Captain Sherwood and Captain Prichard waited on me to Mr. Jones' where we drank a bottle of Wine. Capt. Prichard and I slept there.

Tuesday, 13. This day marched to St. Johns. Col. St. Leger took me to his house—gave me a shirt. Gave me refreshment which I much needed. Told me that I was to dine with him Major Rodgers and Esquire Marsh and others dined there. Then gave me my Parole, which I am told is the first instance of a Prisoner having his Parole in this Fort without some confinement. Went and lodged with Esq. Marsh.

Wednesday, 14th. This morning Esq. Marsh and I were invited to Capt. Sherwood's to breakfast. Then Capt. Sherwood took charge of me, and I lived with him. To my great satisfaction this evening came Mr. Spardain to see me who was a prisoner to me at Ticonderoga. He said on hearing that I was made Prisoner he went to inform him of the good he and others had from me while they were Prisoners to me. The Commandant sent him to my Quarters to inform of my good treatment to them much to my advantage.

Thursday, March 15, 1781. This morning not well. Dined with the commandant and other Gentlemen. Was carried home in the Carryall.

Friday, 11th. This day came Esq. Marsh and Major Rodgers to see me. Spent some time very agreeably.

Saturday, 17th. About this time a French church was burned with Lightning with Fifteen thousand Livres. Priests money.

Sunday, 10th. Low spirited.

Monday, 19th. This day dined with Col. St. Leger and a number of Officers. This day the River broke up here.

Tuesday, 20th. This day dined with Esq. Marsh and Major Rodgers and others at Mr. Holts.

Wednesday, 21st. This day nothing but time passing heavy.

25

Thursday, 22nd. This day came Orders from the General for me to go to the Isle aux Noix and there to live with Esq. Marsh.

Friday, 23rd. This day the wind blew so strong from the South that we could not go to the Isle Aux Noix. This evening Col. Peters spent with me—appeared to be very friendly to me—offered to lend me money, but at the same time, flung out something against me that I know to be false, though appearing to be all in good nature. Lodged with me.

Saturday, 24th. This morning embarked for the Isle Aux Noix, the wind fair—Three hours in passage. Found a very decent house prepared with fires made to receive us. Good Lodgings. Invited to dine with Major Dundas, Commandant. Very handsomely entertained.

Sunday, 25th. This day heavy hearted. A cold day.

Monday, 26th. This day being stormy spent in reading Madame Pompadour and other good Histories.

Tuesday, 27th. This day the Lake was almost frozen over again. Clear and cold.

Wednesday, 28th. This day being stormy spent it in reading the Tattler.

Thursday, 29th. This day pleasant at this time. I had the reading of the Charters of the Provinces of America, as given by the King.

Friday, 30th. A very pleasant day but a very foul stomach.

Saturday, 31st. This day idleness and laziness. Nothing but mud and mire out doors. Codfish and Potatoes for dinner.

Sunday, April 1st, 1781. This day being pleasant Laziness was the most intimate acquaintance. Dined at the mess and as this day was Sunday one bottle of Wine would not do for each man.

Monday, 2nd. This being stormy and I being a Prisoner confined. This day I arrived to the years of Thirty nine.

Tuesday, 3rd. This day being stormy and Esq. Marsh being sick made a long and tedious day.

Wednesday, 4th. This day being pleasant. My eyes tired of Reading. Laziness got the chief seat.

Thursday, 5th. A pleasant day but nothing to do nor nothing to say.

Friday, 6th. This day spent in reading agriculture.

Saturday, 7th. This day spent and many more on the Adventures of Roderick Random.

Sunday, 8th. This day dined at the mess. One bottle of Wine to a man. The whole method of Bundling to be repeated. This I was obliged to make Sunday's work.

Monday, 9th. This day spent in mending stockings and drinking some good Flip, and eating some of the worst of Canadian Beef.

Tuesday, 10th. This day Capt. Sherwood arrived here which gave me some pleasure as he procured better provisions and I got leave to go a gunning, which gave me a better taste for sleep. Esquire Marsh being unwell. This being an out Post, the season of the year being bad we lived something low for a few days. Mr. Marsh returned to St. Johns to procure new stores.

Wednesday, 11th. This day being stormy, time passes heavily.

Thursday, 12th. This day dined at the mess. One bottle of wine would not do to each man. The affair of Bundling comes over again.

Friday, 13th. This day nothing but a heavy heart and a distracted mind.

Saturday, 14. This is a cold snowy day. A large volume of Plays to read which helps roll off time.

Sunday, April 15. This day went over the River a gunning. Esq. Marsh returned to the Island again.

Monday, 16. This day Capt. Sherwood went to St. Johns again. Col. St. Leger and Major Dundas called on us to see how we did and how we fared.

Tuesday, 17. Dined with the mess. Most agreeable dinner. Last evening arrived Capt. Ancrum in three days from Carleton Island, which is two hundred and fifty miles.

Wednesday, 18. This is a pleasant day. Oh! the keen and cutting thoughts of my family and affairs at home.

Thursday, 19. This day went to see Mr. Jones. Had apples to eat. Had a most agreeable dish of coffee, and a very agreeable company.

Friday, 20th. This is a rainy day. Had the History of Alexander the Great to read. Spent several days.

Saturday, 21st. These long days and tedious nights.

Sunday, 22nd. This day dined at the mess. Drinked one and a half bottle Wine each, then drank Tea at Capt. Ancrum's, then drank Hot Punch with Major Dundas and others till eleven o'clock. Drunk enough.

Monday, 23. Oh my head—my head which forced me to go to bed.

Tuesday, 24th. This day drank coffee at Mr. Jones. Many walks around the Island.

Wednesday, 25th. This day had Thunder and Sharp Lightening. This day the Bays and Creeks broke up and the Ice cleared out.

Thursday, 26th. This day as well as many others spent in reading the Tattler. Pleasant weather.

Friday, 27th. This day went a gunning. Spent the most of the day.

Saturday, 28th. This day the last Snow and Ice disappeared from the Island. Sorrow and grief give no relief.

Sunday, 29th. This day dined at the mess. A very strong south wind. About this time I expect that the Freshet is carrying the fences off in Coos. I think that the Freshet must be very high.

Monday 30th. This day we got Greens or Nettles for dinner. What is Time? O Time thou art the cruelest monster that ever man be sensible of. When I walked round this Island many a time I begrudged the poor Frogs their happiness.

Isle Aux Noix, Tuesday, May 1st, 1781. This day dined at Mr. Jones. Very agreeably entertained. Disagreeable news from the General.

Wednesday, 2nd. This day received the following answer to my request that I made to the General for my liberty to go home on my Parole—"I am sorry that the frequent breaches of faith on the part of our enemies of which the last expedition furnished a recent instance which prevents my granting your request of returning upon Parole at least for the present." This instance of the breach of faith that the General refers to is one Capt. John Chipman, who got his Parole last fall on the Lake. He got it by the recommendation of several of his old acquaintances recommending him to be a man of honor and fidelity. He took a canoe on shore and was to send Doct Smith back in exchange for him in the same Canoe but as I am informed as soon as he got his liberty he got Dr. Smith closely confined and escaped those who recommended him and got his liberty, much to their disadvantage. Paid no regard to his honor that he had pledged all in the most solemn manner. Here we may see how much distress one unfaithful scoundrel brings on a large number of Prisoners left behind who are honest.

Thursday, 3rd. This day nothing to say, nothing to do, only to reflect on my captive estate—a fine comfort indeed.

Friday, 4th. This day read the Tattler till it hath almost Tattled my brains out.

Saturday, 5th. This day spent in Gunning and walking.

Sunday, 6th. This day a severe southwind. A bad headache.

Monday, 7th. This day Col. Allen came in with the flag from Vermont. This day Capt. Sherwood returned here. This evening orders were received that I must go to St. Johns tomorrow morning. But I had no liberty to speak to those of my acquaintance that came in with the Flag.

Tuesday, 8th. This day being rainy I did not return to St. Johns. This day three ships with their Tenders passed Island into the Lake. Oh the distress of my mind this day for my situation and the situation of my family.

Wednesday, 9th. This day returned to St. Johns. Col. St. Leger took me to his own house. Lived with him.

Thursday, 10th. This day had the History of the Conquest of Mexico and Peru and all that part of the world.

Friday, 11th. Col. St. Leger being lame he requested that Esquire Marsh should dine with us till he should recover.

Saturday, 12th. This day found another of my old Prisoners which was no damage to me.

Sunday, 13. This day had news that the shipping had arrived at Quebec. This day had news that there was to be an exchange of Prisoners this summer. God grant it may be true.

Monday, 14th. Sorrow and grief is caused for want of a prospect of relief.

Tuesday, 15th. This day the first ship arrived from England at Montreal with Goods.

Wednesday, 16th. This day dined with us Major Sumner, adjutant General from Quebec, a commissioner to treat with the Flag.

Thursday, 17th. This day had news that there was a number of Prisoners broke out of Jail at Montreal.

Friday, 18th. This day pleasant weather but O how tedious and long is time. O thou Time that rollest away like the irremmovable mountain.

Saturday, 19th. O thou precious Time that I could once more enjoy thee under my own vine and under my own Fig Tree and with my dear family.

Sunday, 20th. This day wrote letters home to my family but what an agravating pleasure is this.

Monday, 21st. O Patience! God grant thee to be my friend and companion while in this captive state.

Tuesday, 22nd. He that made Time gave an impatient mind.

Wednesday, 23rd. O the discontented mind that never can be confined.

Thursday, 24th. This day came in or was brought in about Forty people out of the country. This day dined at Mr. Holt's with a large number of Officers.

Friday, 25th. This day came in Abraham Wing who was a Prisoner to me, who treated me with neglect, and seems to try to do me all the hurt he can, gave some false reports concerning my conduct although I showed him twice the favors I did the rest of the Prisoners, and got him freed and set at liberty and sent home. This day the Flag left the Isle Aux Noix.

Saturday, 26th. This day came in twenty Loyalists. This day I heard that I am to return to the Island again. This day entertained with a new History—one point supported that I never heard before.

Sunday, 27th. This day very well entertained with company and good living.

Monday, 28. This day Col. St. Leger did me the favor to carry me in his Calash to Chamblee to see brother Page.

Tuesday, 29th. This day to the Isle Aux Noix again.

Wednesday, 30th. This day mosquitoes by the bushel. You may fight and scratch and still you will have your match.

Thursday, 31st. A distressed heart and a tormented mind proves very unkind.

Friday, June 1st. Providence hath ordered my fate To fall into this troublesome state.

Saturday, 2nd. This day returned to St. Johns again with Capt. Sherwood.

Sunday, 3rd. This day was meant to hear and get good. But we must go starving without such food.

Monday, 4th. This being the King's Birthday made it a great day for firing cannon and carousing. This day returned to the Isle again.

Tuesday, 5th. O tedious Time that never will be out of mind.

Wednesday, 6th. This day Capt. Sherwood moved all his things from this place. Left us nothing to cook with nor books to read. Dined at the mess.

Thursday, 7th. This day there fell some rain which there has not been these five or six weeks. O tedious time and a despairing mind.

Friday, 8th. This evening there was a Boat sent from St. Johns to carry us to St. Johns.

Saturday, 9th. This day returned to St. Johns again. The General sent me a Parole to sign and for me to go to the Three Rivers.

Sunday, 10th. This day at Twelve O'clock left St. Johns. Lodged within nine miles of Sorel.

Monday, 11th. This day came to the Three Rivers. Eighteen Leagues. Mostly a fine country if there was anybody to till it.

Tuesday, 12th. This day dined with Dr. Bar and a number of Gentlemen. Could get no place to board.

Wednesday, 13. This day spent lonely. No company till evening. Dr. Morenton invited me to drink Tea with him.

Thursday, 14th. This day there was a Roman Catholic procession. Their carrying God Almighty about the streets is something new to me. Their walks, their shows very entertaining.

Friday, 15th. This day took my lodgings at Mr. Veyssears-Frenchman, but an English Priest. An English wife.

Saturday, 16th. At Three Rivers. This is a pleasant Town for prospect, the vessels sailing close by the town, but all strangers, which makes it very lonesome.

Sunday, 17. This day nothing but lonesome and melancholy scenes.

Monday, 18. This day Lieutenant Tyler called on me, the first that I have seen that I knew since I came here.

Tuesday, 19. The night passed very sick. This day not able to keep about. A solitary day to me.

Wednesday, 20th. This day Capt. Sherwood and Capt. Prichard passed this town.

Informed me that Mr. Wing had given some very false accounts of my conduct towards the Prisoners at Ticonderoga. This account was given at Quebec which gave me some uneasiness.

Thursday, 21st. This day was the Grand Roman Catholic procession which was very entertaining. This day dined with us two Dutch majors. Major Picket had his wife with him, who was Governor Skeens daughter.

Friday, 22nd. The weather is most exceedingly cold for the time of year.

Finis.

The end of the first Journal kept by Thomas Johnson of Newbury, Coös while a captive in Canada, taken March 8, 1781.

SECOND JOURNAL.

THREE RIVERS, CANADA, JUNE 23, 1781.

Saturday, 23. This day 43 prisoners were brought back that broke jail three weeks ago. They had got almost to New England.

Sunday, 24. This day Major Rodgers and Capt. Brackenridge passed through the town which gave me some pastime.

Monday, 25th. Oh, how heavy is time to pass away. When I have nothing to do nor nothing to say.

Tuesday, 26th. This day went to the Grand Hospital with Doctor Morinton to see the sick and lame. There were seven men there who were taken at Royalton on White River. Their rooms, their bedding, their attendance, their provisions were all of the neatest and of the best kind.

Wednesday, 27th. This day felt the symptoms of Hell Torment, according to the Priests' account, that ever I was sensible of. This day I was in the King's Garden. Peas almost fit to pick. Beans full in the blow. They told me that they had cucumbers some days ago.

Thursday, 28th. This day is almost spent away. I am glad although it makes me mad that my time should be spent and to no better intent.

Friday, June 29th. At this time I had magazines in plenty to read which gave me some relief.

Saturday, 20th. This day hard work to keep my mind, my heart, my soul and my body all together.

July 1st. Sunday. Spent last evening very agreeably with Doctors Morinton and Cole only drank a little too much Chinny Toddy. This morning walked out on the Common. Saw two men coming, walking hand in hand. Soon stripped off their clothes and knocked on like hearty fellows. But a short battle.

Monday, 2nd. This day spent some considerable time in picking strawberries and walking.

Sunday, 3rd. This day very hot weather.

Wednesday, 4th. I think it is a curse to the land and a curse to their king to have such a miserable set of inhabitants as these Canadians.

Thursday, 5th. This day nothing but a perplexed mind.

Friday, 6th. O, the pleasant imaginations of the night visions. but the horrors of the despairing soul when awakened and capable of receiving the full torrent of the most miserable separation from Love's sweets, charms, happiness and enjoyments of the soul.

Saturday, 7th. About ten days since the worms began to be bad in this Province have increased till they have done great damage.

Sunday, 8th. This town is about three quarters of a mile each way and is settled thick. There is one large stone church, one stone nunnery about two hundred feet long and about thirty feet wide, three stories high. Another Stone Church or Nunnery, but now made a Hospital of about one hundred feet long and forty feet wide, and one large Stone Barrack. Colonel Jonincko has a large Stone House. He is the greatest man in this country among the French. He married an English captive for his wife. His family is large, very handsome and genteel.

Monday, July 9th. This day had Lord George Gordon's trial to read. The Buildings in this town make a very bad appearance on the outside but much better in the inside. The women in this Town are much fairer and much more delicate than in any town that I have seen in this Province, They are very polite. There are six young Women in this town to one young man.

Tuesday, 10th. This day news from the Colonies that General Phillips had had a battle with the Rebels and that he had killed three hundred and taken fifteen hundred, and that Lord Corn Wallis had had a battle with General Greene and that General Greene prevailed the first of the Battle, but that Corn Wallis prevailed the last of the battle, and that General Greene retreated with his Cannon, with considerable loss on both sides.

Wednesday, 11th. These Canadians are the most Ignorant, Superstitious, Idle, Careless set of people that can be thought of, spending half their time in Holidays and going to Mass. The Women wear a Riding Hood the hottest weather.

July 12th, Thursday. Very impatient to hear from home. A rumor of an engagement that the Rebels had with the Indians above Detroit, and that a number of the Indians were killed.

Friday, 13th. This day Col. Peters called on me. Tells me that Benjamin Patterson was at Quebec. Gave me an account of many things that happened since I left Coos, and that my Wife was as well as she had been of late. This day had the Second part of Lord Gordon's trial to read.

Saturday, 14th. This day went through the fields. I find their manure carrying out and spreading to lay all summer on the top of the ground. Their Indian Corn planted within one foot and a half, so that they cannot make any hill if they had a mind to.

July 15th, Sunday. This day very hot and a small thunder shower. This day dined with Dr. Morrinton.

Monday, 16th. This day a large number of English papers to read.

Tuesday, 17th. This day a fine shower and much wanted.

Wednesday, 18th. This day borrowed the Fourth Volume of the Spectator, much to my satisfaction.

Thursday, 19th. O the melancholy thoughts of the separation from my family and friends.

Friday, 20th. This day received a letter from Esquire Marsh, informing me that McGilbraith was come into St. Johns and that my family were well the last of May, and that there was another man at my house the 24th of June and that my family were well then. The unspeakable satisfaction that I received from this piece of news.

Saturday, 21. Without the enjoyment of my family I am as destitute of any real satisfaction and comfort as a Dog is of a Soul.

Sunday, 22nd. After a solitary day was invited to Sup at Mr. Fraziers on Salmon and baked Pigeons. Very agreeable.

Monday, 23. This day a terrible Thunder Storm.

Tuesday, 24. All the dreaming is not worth a mans notice in common state of business yet by them I get my chief consolation.

Wednesday, 25th. This day heard that Mr. McGilbraith had gone to Quebec. This evening heard that there was a man in Town who left word for me that he was at my house and that my Wife was confined the Sixth of July last, but when I came to inquire I found the man to be Benjamin Patterson and as he was within twenty Rods of my Quarters for some hours and did not send to me that all he told he knew nothing of.

Thursday, 26th. O the unspeakable torments of the mind when I reflect upon my situation.

Friday, 27. Post-day. O how often am I disappointed by waiting on the Post Office without the least consolation This day Col. Gordon passed the Town to be confined at Quebec for breaking his Parole at Montreal.

Saturday, 28th. This morning not well. This day dined with Doctor Barr and a number of other Doctors. This evening received my letters from home, but they had to go to Quebec before I could see them.

Sunday, 29. This day spent in writing to my friends. Hot weather.

Monday, 30th. This day spent in writing and perusing letters.

Tuesday, 31st. My morning vision was a fortnight old. This day sent off the following Letters:

List of Letters.

One to Mrs. Johnson	To Mr. Wallace
" Doctor Hopkins	" Col. St. Leger
" Esq. Marsh	" Brother Page
" Capt. Mathews, Quebec	" Mr. Gilbraith

This evening Esq. Marsh called on me on his way to Quebec.

Wednesday, Aug. 1st. Several days spent in reading a collection of Letters.

Thursday, 2nd. Nothing better than a perplexed mind.

Friday, 3rd. No consolation but all mortification.

Saturday, 4th. O how much do I fear the news that I may hear.

Sunday, 5th. I find myself nearly in Job's situation. All bad tidings.

Monday, 6th. Some time spent in reading Don Quixote de la Mancha.

Tuesday, 7th. O time. cruel time, that it is said passes like a vapour, but I think it moves like a millstone.

Wednesday, 8th. O, when shall I be freed from this captive state. God grant these days may be few and not great.

Thursday, 9th. This day dined with Dr. Barr and Doctor Morinton. Had some muskmelon.

Friday, 10th. This day getting a pair of Plow Irons made for Col. St. Leger.

Saturday, 11. Sorrow and distress is a great enemy to my breast.

Sunday, 12th. A distressed heart and a tormented mind prove very unkind. This evening received a letter from Doctor Hopkins, and that I had another opportunity to write to my friends again.

Monday, 13th. This day have spent in writing Letters home to my friends again. (Same list as before except to Capt. Atkinson and Brother Jesse Johnson.)

Tuesday, 14th. Sent off my Letters.

Wednesday, 15th. This day a Grand Holiday and a great mass. They say that they keep it because the Virgin Mary conceived that day, and it is but four months, to the time that they keep for our Saviour's birth.

Thursday, 16. This day hearing the Bells ringing, saw all the people running to wait on the Priest out of Town, some following bareheaded, some on their knees. All this Route because the Priest was going out of Town to give the Sacrament to a sick woman. When the Bells ring the people must drop their business altho' ever so urgent and agreeable and fall to praying or run after the Priest.

Aug. 17. This day three Prisoners who deserted from Quebec were taken and carried by the Town. This day at Four O'clock came by here four Prisoners. One was Naaman Powers and young Martin from Moretown. They tell me they are but eight days from Peacham. Distressing news from my family.

Saturday, 18th. This is a most melancholy day. This afternoon received a letter from Dr. Hopkins informing me that he was returning home without getting my last letters that I sent to him which gave me great uneasiness. Nothing but disappointments for me.

Sunday, 19th. Last month came into this Town a Judge of the Court for this Province. The Court was called after nine o'clock in the morning. They told me there was forty cases. I expected the Court was going to sit the most of the week, but to my surprise they were all tried. Judgment given and dismissed by twelve o'clock the same day, and the Judge left Town after dinner.

Monday, 20th. This day passed and came to anchor Eleven or Twelve Ships. I was looking on the Ships, Saw one of the Ships Boats overset. Spent this day in viewing the Ships and other Craft passing.

Tuesday, 21. This day received news that General Clark with the Fleet had arrived in the River. This day received a letter from Esquire Marsh that Brother Page was like to get some liberty if I would pass my word for him which gives me great satisfaction. This day had Codfish and new Potatoes. This afternoon had the present of a Pear made to me.

Wednesday, 22. This day the Canadians just got engaged in their reaping. This evening heard that there were one hundred and fifty Prisoners exchanged and gone over the Lake.

Thursday, 23. O, the length of the day when a heavy heart bears the sway.

Friday, 24. The French here think it a great favor from the Lord if he will take their children from them by death. For they think they are Saints always interceding for them until they go to them. If they are sick they give them little or nothing to take. They are as cheerly and as brisk as when they are born, and when they die they have some person to come and take them away and they trouble themselves no more about them.

Saturday, 25th. This day the Sergeant that took Naaman Powers to Quebec called on me and told me that he was not closely confined, but had liberty. This day had news that Twenty Ships of the fleet were arrived at Quebec.

Sunday, 26th. This day came by express the account that Fortyfive Ships of the

Fleet had arrived at Quebec. This evening received news that my Bills (of Exchange) were sold which gave me relief.

Monday, 27. This day news that the Fleet had nearly all arrived.

Tuesday, 28th. Were it not for Hope the Heart would break. This day at Twelve O'clock I received the account that I might return home on my Parole and that Capt. Bronson with some others would call on me in a few days.

Wednesday, 29th. This day such a strong South wind that I have no hopes of the Prisoners coming up the River.

Thursday, 30th. The south wind still continues to blow. This day walked about two miles up to the Ferry where I saw a new fashioned Bedstead which much pleased me.

Friday, 31. This day waiting very impatient for the Prisoners to come from Quebec.

Saturday, September 1st. The Southwind still continues to blow so that I can get no account of my fellow Prisoners.

Sunday, 2nd. This day passed very agreeably with a young Gentleman, a School-master from England.

Monday, 3rd. Rainy day and a south wind still continues to blow. I am waiting with great impatience for my fellow Prisoners.

Tuesday, 4th. This morning unwell, my patience worn out. This day spent in reading the Pamphlet entitled "Reflections on the Rise and Progress of the American Rebellion," showing the disposition of our Forefathers from the time that they left England and went to Holland and from that time to the time they came to Plymouth and their intentions till this war.

Wednesday, 5th. My distress is inexpressible, as I have been waiting as long a time as I might have been at home and can hear nothing from the Prisoners.

Thursday, 6th. O, the unspeakable distresses and torments of my mind this day.

Friday, 7th. This is a Rainy day, Horror and distress lies heavy on my breast.

Saturday, 8th. This day chiefly spent in seeing the shipping go by, and walking four or five miles up the River. O how unkind is a distressed and tormented mind. Last night there was a frost here.

Sunday, 9. Worn out with Laziness, Idleness, and a perplexed mind.

Monday, 10th. This day spent in settling my business and getting ready to go with the first Post.

Tuesday, 11th. This morning a bad Storm about two o'clock. This day went aboard Ship—went to Sorell.

Wednesday, 12th. This day wrote to St. Johns by Post.

Thursday, 13. This day came to La Prairies. Bad luck getting over the River.

Friday, 14th. This day came to Montreal. Took Lodgings at Mr. Thomas Busby's.

Saturday, 15th. This day spent in looking and walking.

Sunday, 16th. Montreal. This is a pleasant Town.

Monday, 17. The History of "Tom Jones" gives me some amusement.

Tuesday, 18th. This is a stormy day.

Wednesday, 19th. The old story, a heavy heart.

Thursday, 20th. Distress.

Friday, 21st. A distressed mind.

Saturday, 22nd. I have no disposition for writing at present.

Sunday. Nothing worth notice.

Monday, 24th. This day Col. Peters dined here.

Tuesday, 25th. This day came some Officers to see us.

Wednesday, 26th. I got Page out of Irons.

Thursday, 27. Last night a bad accident between me and my Bed-fellow.

Friday, 28. Company which passed time some better.

Saturday, 29th. This day some news that gave me some hopes that I should get away.

Sunday, 30th. This day dined aboard Ship. Captain Woodruff. Very handsomely entertained.

Monday, Oct. 1st. Time is still rolling with but little expectation of relief.

Tuesday, 2nd. O the distress, distress.

Wednesday, 3rd. This day finished the third volume of Tom Jones. Cold weather comes on. O the horrors of the mind.

Thursday, 4th. This day about four o'clock received an express for me to repair immediately to St. Johns. Had a great surprise by my Landlady. Had to travel all night.

Friday, 5th. Found Captain Bronson with about Fourteen Prisoners waiting for me. About Two O'clock this day left St. Johns. Camped about four miles from Isle Aux Noix.

JOURNEY HOME.

Oct. 6th, Saturday. This morning a contrary wind. Passed the shipping to Point Au Fer. The wind turned in our favor. Lodged on the Point O'Rush.

Sunday, Oct. 7th. This morning fair wind but when we came to Cumberland Bay the wind grew too high. Some danger. We put into the Isle of Belcho Nine O'clock. On a Stone wrote this, Passed the split Rock to Grog Bay. There met Col. Peters with families and Pattersons wife. He went back with us with the Flag. Lodged three miles above the split Rock.

Monday, 8th. Passed the Ship Carleton near Crown Point. Camped three miles above Mount Independence.

Tuesday, 9th. Came to Skenesborough at One O'clock. Lodged with Col. Walbridge.

Wednesday, 10th. This day came to Castleton at One O'clock. Could not get a Horse till night. Was very ill treated at the Creek by one John Bowman in Clarendon. Lodged in Clarendon.

Thursday, 11th. Dined at Coffins. Lodged at Cornish.

Friday, 12. Dined at Dresden. Came home in the evening.

THE NARRATIVE OF THOMAS MELLEN.

At the session of the General Assembly in 1848, Prof. James D. Butler, then pastor of the Congregational church at Wells River, was invited to deliver an address before that body, upon the battle of Bennington. The special occasion was the placing in the State House of the cannon captured at that battle, where they still remain.

Mr. Butler, learning that Thomas Mellen, a survivor of that battle, was living in Newbury, went to see him, and obtained from him an account of the battle, which is given in the pamphlet containing the address, and the proceedings of the occasion. The narrative is also reprinted in Major Caleb Stark's life of his father, Gen. John Stark.

Thomas Mellen was then living in the family of his son Robert, who owned the farm, and lived in the house which is now that of John Buchanan at the Centre. The late Mr. Edward Miller, then teaching school there, stated that Mr. Mellen had a room by himself, which was a small building behind the house, but within a few feet of it, where he spent most of his time, working and reading.

Dr. Butler writes the editor of this volume:

"Whatever I gathered from Thomas Mellen is specially worthy of preservation. It was a distinct addition to the history of the battle—the plain tale of a soldier—and probably the last one set down by an interviewer.

When I visited him, though upward of ninety-two years of age, he was so far from being bald or bowed down, that you would think him in the Indian summer of life. His dress was all of gray homespun, and he sat on a couch, the covering of which was sheep-skins, with the wool on. I have given his statements, so far as possible, in his own words:"

"I enlisted," said he, "at Francestown, N. H., in Colonel Stickney's regiment and Captain Clark's company, as soon as I learned that Stark would accept the command of the State troops; six or seven others from the same town joined the army at the same time. We marched forthwith to Number Four and stayed there a week. Meantime I received a horn of powder and run two or three hundred bullets; I had brought my own gun. Then my company went on to Manchester; soon after I went, with a hundred others, under Colonel Emerson, down the valley of Otter Creek; on this excursion we lived like lords, on pigs and chickens, in the houses of tories who had fled. When we returned to Manchester, bringing two hogsheads of West India rum, we heard that the Hessians were on their way to invade Vermont. Late in the afternoon of rainy Friday, we were ordered off for Bennington in spite of rain, mud and darkness. We pushed on all night, making the best progress we could; about day-break I, with Lieut. Miltimore, came near Bennington, and slept a little while on a hay-mow when the barn-yard fowls waked us; we went for bread and milk to the sign of the 'wolf,' and then hurried three miles west to Stark's main body.

Stark and * * * * * * rode up near the enemy to reconnoitre; were fired at by the cannon, and came galloping back. Stark rode with shoulders bent forward, and cried out to his men: 'Those rascals know that I am an officer; don't you see they honor me with a big gun and a salute.' We were marched round and round a circular hill till we were tired. Stark said it was to amuse the Germans. All the while a cannonade was kept up upon us from their breast-works; it hurt no body, and it lessened our fear of the great guns. After a while I was sent, with twelve others, to lie in ambush, on a knoll a little north, and watch for tories on their way to join Baum. Presently we saw six coming toward us who, mistrusting us for tories, came too near us to escape. We disarmed and sent them, under a guard of three, to Stark. While I sat on the hillock, I espied one Indian whom I thought I could kill, and more than once cocked my gun, but the orders were not to fire. He was cooking his dinner, and now and then shot at some of our people.

Between two and three o'clock the battle began. The Germans fired by platoons, and were soon hidden by the smoke. Our men fired each on his own hook, aiming wherever he saw a flash; few on our side had either bayonets or cartridges. At last I stole away from my post and ran down to the battle. The first time I fired I put three balls in my gun; before I had time to fire many rounds our men rushed over the breast-works, but I and many others chased straggling Hessians in the woods; we pursued until we met Breyman with 800 fresh troops and larger cannon, which opened a fire of grape shot; some of the grape shot riddled a Virginia fence near me; one shot struck a small white oak behind which I stood; though it hit higher than my head I fled from the tree, thinking it might be aimed at again. We skirmishers ran back till we met a large body of Stark's men and then faced about. I soon started for a brook I saw a few rods behind, for I had drank nothing all day, and should have died of thirst if I had not chewed a bullet all the time. I had not gone a rod when I was stopped by an officer, sword in hand, ready to cut me down as a runaway, who, on my complaining of thirst, handed me his canteen, which was full of rum; I drank and forgot my thirst. But the enemy outflanked us, and I said to a comrade, 'we must run, or they will have us.' He said: 'I will have one fire first.' At that moment, a major, on a black horse, rode along behind us, shouting 'fight on boys, reinforcements close by.' While he was yet speaking, a grape shot went through his horse's head; it bled a good deal, but the major kept his seat, and rode on to encourage others. In a few minutes we saw Warner's men hurrying to help us; they opened right and left of us, and one-half of them attacked each flank of the enemy, and beat back those who were just closing round us. Stark's men now took heart and stood their ground. My gun barrel was at this time too hot to hold so I seized a musket of a dead Hessian, in which my bullets went down easier than in my own. Right in front were the cannon, and seeing an officer on horse-back waving his sword to the artillery, I fired at him twice; his horse fell; he cut the traces of an artillery horse, mounted him and rode off. I afterward heard that the officer was Major Skene. Soon the Germans ran, and we followed; many of them threw down their guns on the ground, or offered them to us, or kneeled, some in puddles of water. One said to me, 'Wir sind ein bruder!' I pushed him behind me and rushed on. The enemy beat a parley, minded to give up, but our men did not understand it. I came to one wounded man flat on the ground, crying water or quarter. I snatched the sword out of his scabbard, and while I ran on and fired, carried it in my mouth, thinking I might need it. The Germans fled by the road and in a wood each side of it; many of their scabbards caught in the brush and held the fugitives till we seized them. We chased them till dark; Colonel Johnston, of

Haverhill, wanted to chase them all night. We might have mastered them all, as they stopped within three miles of the battlefield; but Stark, saying 'he would run no risk of spoiling a good day's work,' ordered a halt. and return to quarters.

I was coming back, when I was ordered by Stark himself, who knew me, as I had been one of his body guards in Canada, to help draw off a field-pieee. I told him 'I was worn out.' His answer was, 'don't seem to disobey; take hold, and if you can't hold out, slip away in the dark.' Before we had dragged the gun far, Warner rode near us. Some one pointing to a dead man by the road-side, said, 'Your brother is killed,' 'Is it Jesse?' asked Warner. And when the answer was 'yes,' he jumped off his horse, stooped and gazed in the dead man's face, and then rode away without saying a word. On my way back I got the belt of the Hessian whose sword I had taken in the pursuit. I also found a barber's pack, but was obliged to give up all my findings till the booty was divided. To the best of my remembrance, my share was four dollars and some odd cents. One tory, with his left eye shot out, was led in, mounted on a horse, who had also lost his left eye. It seems to me cruel now—it did not then.

My company lay down and slept in a corn field, near where we had fought—each man having a hill of corn for a pillow. When I waked next morning, I was so beaten out that I could not get up till I had rolled about a good while.

After breakfast I went to see them bury the dead. I saw thirteen tories, mostly shot through the head, buried in one hole. Not more than a rod from where I fought, we found Capt. McClary dead and stripped naked. We scraped a hole with sticks, and just covered him with earth. We saw many of the wounded who had lain out all night. Afterward we went to Bennington, and saw the prisoners paraded. They were drawn up in one long line; the British foremost, then the Waldeckers, next the Indians, and hindmost the tories.''[*]

This narrative is referred to by President Bartlett in his address at the Bennington Centennial, and by ex-Minister Phelps in his address at the dedication of the monument.

The following letters, selected from many which were available for use in this volume, give a better idea of the state of the Coös country, and the perplexities which beset the patriot leaders, than any mere description could do.

We know, what Bayley and Johnson themselves found out in no long time, that they were mistaken as to the real motives of the Vermont leaders. But these letters permit us to see the situation as they saw it.

GEN. BAYLEY TO COL. MOREY.

CASTLETON, 22d Septr, 1777.

Sr—Success attends us yet, in part, we have cut off their Communication—we have taken Tie Side [i. e. the outworks of Fort Ticonderoga] exeept the old fort hope soon to have all Lake George. Taken about 500 prisoners; we want help much; our Division is only 1500 men. General Lincoln's gone to join General Gates. You and all the militia Eastward must turn out and with Horses and one Month's Provisions which will, I hope, put an end to the dispute this way. Genl Arnold fought a Battle two days ago on the left of Genl Gates. Great numbers fell on both sides. He took 250 Prisoners and three pieces and the field. Pray turn out.

Yours, JACOB BAYLEY.[†]

---

[*]From Memoirs and Official Correspondence of Gen. John Stark. By Major Caleb Stark p. 66–69.

[†]N. H. State Papers, Vol. xviii., p. 136. Original in Hibbard Collection, Vol. 10, . 20.

JAMES LOVELL TO GEN. WASHINGTON.

BOSTON, March 11, 1782.

Sir:

A very high degree of jealousy possesses the breast of my correspondent concerning the insincerity of some of the Cabinet Council of Vermont in their present conduct towards Congress. The jealousy manifest in every conversation which I have had with him here should not, however, make me neglect to convey to your excellency such information as the enclosed which, if corroborated by other circumstances within your knowledge, will doubtless effect some of your arrangements for the ensuing campaign in which and through life I wish prosperity and honor may attend your Excellency.

And am Sir your most humble Servant,

JAMES LOVELL.*

This letter accompanied the following one.

JACOB BAYLEY TO GENERAL WASHINGTON.

NEWBURY, March 7th, 1782.

Sir:

You may remember that I mentioned the case of Captain Thomas Johnson to you, the necessity of his being exchanged in order to prove the treasonable conduct of a member of Vermont, &c. I told you Johnson had the confidence of the enemy in Canada and knew what had been transacted between them and Vermont. I am still further convinced as Captain Johnson has lately received a letter from Canada and answer demanded, which he complied with, otherwise he supposed his intent to make discovery to us would be suspected by the enemy. He showed to a friend of the United States what he received from and sent to Canada, which was from the enemy an enquiry whether an expedition to Canada was intended by us, or any preparations therefor, how the people stood as to a union with them in Canada, informing they intended an exhibition early to Albany, &c. Captain Johnson's return was that he heard nothing of an expedition by us to Canada and that affairs went on well with us in Vermont. In about a month doubtless other letters from General Haldeman will be sent to Captain Johnson. All letters and copies will be kept. Capt. Johnson wishes his exchange may soon take place. His situation is really critical, for without General Washington's particular directions he is exposed to the severest punishment. If he does not correspond the enemy will suspect him and be exposed, to be recalled to Canada, by which we shall lose his evidence in matters of the greatest importance. I send you this as no private correspondence with the enemy is admissible. It is come to my knowledge and I wish to convey the same to the Commander-in-Chief, which I dare not attempt by public post. I wish anyway, it may be transmitted to his Excellency, General Washington. The above answer arrived to me yesterday. I must leave the matter to your directions.

And am, Sir, your most obedient Humble Servant,

JACOB BAYLEY.†

NEWBURY, April 10, 1782.

Sir:

I delivered to General Lincoln some minutes to be made use of by your Excellency. The late revolution in Vermont has had such influence on the people respecting myself that I am more safe at home than for a year past. I now find that Capt. Johnson can and does correspond with General Haldeman, which correspondence is made known to me and two others. His reason for the correspondence is he says that he may not be suspected until he is exchanged or some other method is taken

---

*Addressed to General Washington. Volume 54, Page 305, of Washington correspondence.

†For James Lovell, Boston. Vol. 54, Page 305, of Washington correspondence.

that he may deliver what he knows relative to the enemy in Canada and our internal foes. The substance of the accounts from Canada are that if we do not go into Canada this year (which they enquire about) they shall pursue their plan early in May which was to go to Albany and then seat themselves, for the protection of Vermont. The last of this month or first of May another packet will be brought. We shall doubtless have it in our power to secure the bearer. I must think the correspondence of Vermont with the enemy is not to deceive them, but was actually designed to destroy the United States. Their present excuses are to deceive us until the enemy can seat themselves at some convenient point on the Grants which I am afraid will be early this Spring. There is not the least doubt but General Arnold's plan reached to Vermont and Canada, and if he had succeeded there would nothing have been said by Vermont about discovering the enemy or if provisions had not failed in Canada last season no excuse would have been made by the Traitors. Was not the Commander of Vermont troops in 1780 in council with the enemy at Crown Point? Was it not in his power to have defeated the enemy at Fort Ann, Fort George and Ballston that season? It was not for want of men. Vermont now says they did deceive the enemy last season, but they raised for something fifteen hundred men and kept them in pay all last summer when, by their own confession, there was no danger. The question, who did they mean to deceive, Congress or the enemy? Now they say the Enemy are undeceived and the number of men called for this campaign is three hundred where if the enemy have been deceived, there is the utmost danger. Doubtless Vermont is an asylum for all Continental deserters. Mr. Elijah Finman of Woodbury informed me today that he saw Sunday in Vermont as he passed through from Bennington to this River, that he knew who defied him taking them or anybody else. I wish for some orders to be given respecting Mr. Johnson; his case is critical. If he not correspond he is discovered. if he do it is in the face of the act of congress. Your excellency will pardon all mistakes, I doubt not, in this, also for giving so much trouble to you, as I cannot forbear until the matters are settled by Congress in this quarter, and permit me to subscribe myself

Your Excellency's most humble servant,
JACOB BAYLEY.*

NEWBURY, May 30, 1872.

Sir:

I sent your Excellency an account of the correspondence which might be carried on between Capt. Thomas Johnson and the enemy by General Lincoln, and also other matters relating to the transactions of the leading men in Vermont with the enemy &c, as those matters seem to be ripening off fast and expect they will soon put them into execution. I send Capt. Bayley with the letters and accounts from said Johnson who will give you other intelligence and as I am afraid we shall not be able to effectually oppose the Enemy wish your Excellency's directions respecting these matters. I shall not trouble your Excellency with any more than saying the enemy are doubtless fortifying at Crown Point. Major James Rodgers has been in here and has gone back satisfied that most of the leading men in Vermont will not oppose British Government. I believe he will not find it true tho' many are gone back. This town and some adjacent, stand fast. We expect trouble from Vermont and Britain connected. I wish for some directions and assistance if possible.

I am your Excellency's
Most humble Servant.
JACOB BAYLEY.†

---

*Addressed to Gen. Washington, Vol. 54, Page 202, of Washington correspondence.

†Addressed to General Washington, Volume 57, Page 15 of Washington Correspondence.

THOMAS JOHNSON TO GENERAL WASHINGTON.

NEWBURY, Coos, 30 May, 1782.

May it please your Excellency,

To suffer me to lay before you a brief yet imperfect narrative of my observations while a prisoner in Canada and how matters have since been conducted.

Some time in the month of March, 1781, I was surprised in the middle of the night at a house about twenty miles from home by a party of Enemy from Canada, consisting of ten men under the command Azariah Prichard formerly an inhabitant of Connecticut, who since the commencement of the present war, viz. in the year 1777 made his escape into Canada. I was immediately made prisoner as I was getting from my bed, and as I was going to said Prichard, (who was about four or five miles distant I concluded that no topic would prove more agreeable than that of a union of Vermont with Great Britain, and being previously persuaded that for a considerable time there had been an intercourse maintained between them I determined to make myself as intimate with * * * * on the subject as possible. Accordingly, soon after I got into conversation with my Captain, he told me that I was just such a man as he wanted, and before we got into Canada he gave me particular instructions concerning my behavior when I should come upon examination, and I approved myself accordingly and soon contracted an intimate acquaintance and conversation with leading men in that quarter and obtained a particular state of the affairs of Vermont and found that Ira Allen and others had twice been into Canada, and that two Flags had been sent from Canada into Vermont and that the outlines of a Treaty were then actually formed between them, viz: That Vermont should be a Charter Government similar in most respects to Connecticut yet more liberty on the side of the State that they should be protected by Government whenever necessary that Ira Allen was then daily expected in again to complete the matter. I found likewise that this plan was agreed upon with Ethan Allen before he left the British.

April. About this time several parties from New York City came in by whom we had information that General Clark with a considerable reinforcement was coming into Canada, the particular accounts from the Southward, Cornwallis's success, the taking of St. Eustatia, the situation of the American and British armies, &c. &c. These accounts gave a new spring to the British blood, and seemed to raise them superior to a negotiation with Vermont as a neutral state; nothing but a submission without further delay would answer on pain of displeasure. Everything was then pursued to carry on two expeditions, one against Schenectady and the other against Albany, hand barrows, wheel barrows, a new construction of Batteau very light and portable, artillery carriages, and light Trucks or hand waggons, fashioned so that six men would sit on a Batteau large enough to carry fifteen men and baggage and run with it three or four miles in an hour, and every other thing necessary to force a rapid march or retreat with the greatest expedition. Nothing now prevented their intended expedition but the want of provisions. But before that arrived information came that General Starke with a body of troops was marching towards Saratoga; this put them into great consternation.

July. At this time provisions were so scarce that they were obliged to distribute what little they had in very small quantities, by the barrel &c to every quarter. Wheat was now four dollars or upwards per bushel, Beef twenty coppers per pound, Butter, and Veal double that sum. The Officers often said that all the Prisoners must be sent out of the Province. One third part of their cattle died in the spring for want of forage; the worms devoured almost every green thing so that there was no prospect of wintering more than one third part of what cattle the winter had spared. During the carrying on the aforesaid expeditions it was agreed by the Allens &c on the part of Vermont that they would lay still and give them no trouble as the Officers had often told me. Thus Ethan Allen did at Castleton in the fall of the year 1780, when the British destroyed Fort George, Fort Ann and many of the Inhabitants in that quarter, and came round within one day's march of the place where Allen lay with near a thousand men and suffered them all to pass on unmolested, when at the same time I heard many of the Officers often say that Allen might easily have cut them off if he would but he had agreed to the contrary. The rehearsal of these actions of the infernal villians is enough to make my blood run cold in every vein. Now I was reduced to straight quarters and offered a commission of major on swearing allegiance to the King and taking part with them; otherwise they told me that I must be sent away with other prisoners and take my fate with them. Now I was obliged to deal on punctilios. I told them I had rather lay in gaol five years than lift my finger to shed the blood of my countrymen. But that everything in my power for peace I would invariably pursue. Notwithstanding all the plausible pretences of the Vermonters, the spirit of jealousy was high. They constantly kept Spies amongst them to watch their motions some of whom came in and said that some of the Inhabitants of the Grants were for fighting, but generally they were for neutrality or submission. In May one Major Lunneaux Adjutant General and a principal confidant of the General came up, who with Major Dundas and Captain Sherwood were appointed commissioners to treat with Ira Allen sole commissioner Plenipotentiary from Vermont, and upon examining commission found it only from Governor Chittenden and not from the authority of the state, and · therefore it was thought improper to proceed. But it was proposed between the parties that Vermont should raise six hundred men as standing troops, and another party sufficient to man a twenty gun Ship and all to be commanded by Officers of their own, commissioned by the king and set in conjunction with the British and should raise two thousand on an emergency. I was often asked if I thought Vermont was able to perform as much on their part and many other questions of the like nature. In June one George Smyth who had been taken up as a spy from the British army and put into gaol at Albany and it is thought would have been hanged but by the assistance of the Vermonters made his escape from gaol, and came into Canada and was immediately appointed a Commissioner to treat with the Vermonters. Likewise one Sergeant Smyth in character dress, and in company with a party of Indians went to Philadelphia or near thereabouts under the notion of treating for peace and there continued in such disguise until he had gotten all the intelligence of the situations of the armies proceedings of Congress, &c. &c., and then returned into Canada and gave so good an account of matters that the General gave him an Adjutant's commission and other presents. This I had from his own mouth in September. Seeing they had been disappointed in their campaigns for want of provisions and that a plenty had afterwards arrived, they determined to pursue the same as early in the spring as possible, with about three thousand effective men, which I think as many as they could anyway send out.

About the time I was coming out of Canada Captain Prichard told me that he kept a correspondence with one Davenport Phelps, a Gentleman educated at Dartmouth College on this River, and grandson of Doctor Wheelock the late President; that he was going over to see how matters were conducted, and when I got to Connecticut River I heard that Phelps was a member of Vermont General Court from Orford, a Town on the east of the River who immediately left the Court after they had transacted such matters as more immediately related to Prichard's business and went thirty miles up the River to Mooretown where Prichard was waiting to see him before he could return to Canada again. It may not be amiss to observe that as at first I determined in every shape to pursue such measures as would be most likely to gain an acquaintance with their secret movements and operations so that on my return home I might be able to render service to my country. Hence it will not appear strange that I should easily consent to continue a correspondence for a further benefit to the public. Upon the conclusion of this matter, General Haldimand sent me a seal to affix to all my letters of correspondence that I need not sign my name and so be in danger of discovery. In the month of October last one Levi Sylvester being in the woods hunting was taken prisoner carried into Canada and there entered into an agreement with Prichard as a carrier, to meet him at certain times and places in the woods and deliver and receive letters of intelligence. By him I received a letter from Prichard in January last, the first time that he came in and said that he made his escape but he is looked upon as an honest man in general, he likewise brought letters to several other persons, viz: to John Patterson and to Isaac Patterson from Benjamin Patterson a Refugee, and another from Prichard to Thomas Chamberlin and agreed to meet Prichard again at Onion River the last of February. At which time I sent a letter to General Haldimand and another to Prichard copies of which and my first letter are enclosed also the Newspapers containing the account of the surrender of Cornwallis. Sylvester likewise told me that he delivered to Prichard a letter from said John Patterson for his son Benjamin in Canada, and he brought me a letter from Geo. Smyth, (a copy enclosed,) and he delivered three other letters to me with orders for me to deliver them viz: One to Col. Bedel which was directed to "T. Mountene," one to John Patterson and one to Isaac Patterson which three last letters were opened, copied, sealed up and delivered to the wife of John Patterson (he not being at home) but said John told me afterwards that he had received them

1782
April

and delivered one to Bedel and the other to Isaac. A few days afterward I received a verbal message from said Bedel by William Wallace, that I must be more cautious and not deliver letters to women lest I should be found out.

May 13

Col. Bedel went to my house to see me but as I was not at home he waited till evening; and as he was returning I met him in company with said Wallace and Bedel told me that he had some business of importance to tell me, viz: That Major Rogers with a strong guard was then in Mooretown and wanted very much to see me; that I must go down that night and see him and gave me directions how to find him, but meeting with some disappointments I could not go that night. Said Bedel further told me that six hundred of the Enemy had come over the Lake with force, etc., and were fortifying there; that Rogers had had an express from New York within three weeks and the British were going to vacuate New York and Charleston, and to go with all their force to Canada, the ensuing campaign which they would maintain at all events.

14th. The next morning I went to see Bedel and told him that I had not been to see Rogers but would go the ensuing evening. Bedel said that he was not certain that I could find him as he might be moved. But John Patterson being there Bedel said he would send Rogers word if possible to meet me at the place appointed for last evening. I went but could not find him. Bedel likewise told me that there was another party at another place. He said Rogers' principal business was to enquire into the temper of the people in general and see as many as he could and get the opinion of as many of the leading men as he could in this part of the country and see if they are well disposed to Government and to continue to act up to former engagements. So that, if he could make a favorable return to the General it would not be likely that we should be treated any further at present. Bedel did not say directly that he had seen Rogers, but said that I might depend upon what he had told me; that he had his information direct and not from any second hands; that if I should see Rogers he would have me give a good character, and in as high and as favorable a light as he thought it would bear.

May 21st. Levi Sylvester came to my house and told me that Joseph White and another man by the name of Miller were or had been at or about Thomas Chamberlin's and had sent for him to come and see him, but as he sent him no tokens he did not go to see him, for his orders were not to have any thing to do with any persons without they had certain tokens.

But Sylvester told me that Chamberlin told him that he had seen White and White told him that Rogers was come in, and upon the same business as Bedel had said, and that the said White was sent as a Spy, to see how Rogers, Bedeld an others conducted, and to find out whether there were any signs of treachery to be observed. Thus I have given your Excellency a broken and unperfect account; yet I think I have hinted at the most material facts; and submit them to your candid perusal and beg leave to subscribe myself your Excellency's most devoted and most humble servant.

THOMAS JOHNSON.

GEN. JACOB BAYLEY TO GENERAL WASHINGTON.

NEWBURY, 16th Sept., 1782.

Sir:

Agreeable to your Excellency's directions I supported about Fifty Savages of the St. Francis Tribe from November, 1778, when in from hunting, which was at least half the time, to February, 1781, except the summer Colonel Hazen was here with his regiment. The parties sent here from Head Quarters, to gain intelligence from Canada I have supported, and also they wintered with me and returned in the spring. The Rations only will come to a considerable sum. I never had the command of any public provisions but supplied them out of my own. Where I have been assisted by any they now call. I have been obliged to move my papers, cannot exhibit an account. If it is consistent I wish some Gentlemen at Boston might be appointed to settle the account as it is very expensive for me to go to Philadelphia. Have nothing left but my Farm but what I have advanced for the public, even my time as much as though I had been the whole time in the Army since the present war. I have not received anything for my time (and I think it well spent if I have done any good) but little for my advancements. I should take it in the greatest favor if in your Excellency's power to give me some assistance by my Son who bears this. Your Excellency will lay the greater obligation on your Humble Servant,

JACOB BAYLEY.

To His Excellency, General George Washington.

NEWBURY, 19th September, 1782.

Sir:

Last night a man who I can depend upon returned from St. Johns in five days He was a week at that place. He was eight days since at Isle Au Noix and says he saw two thousand men embark at St. Johns and proceed up the Lake and when at the Island found them encamped there that the whole on the Island was between three and four thousand men, their destination was not public but supposed to take possession of Vermont, that a Flag from Vermont was eight days ago at the Island, that all the principal officers was gone to Quebec, that the Vessels at Crown Point was ordered to be down before the 10th of October that the General informed him by a message that he wanted him or some one to come to him from Coos at St. Johns before the 10th of October as after that time he could not direct where he could meet him that all the small parties and Indians were called in, I have sent off another man today who will doubtless see General Haldeman and obtain further intelligence. He is to be back in fifteen days. If any material occurs I will send immediately. From one who has made application for leave to go to Canada to her husband, am informed that she must be at Crown Point before the tenth of October, as the Vessels will be down the Lake at that time. I thought the above information of some importance and as I sent my Son three days ago by way of Exeter to your Excellency I send this after him and hope it will overtake him before he leaves Exeter. The Allens are with a number of armed men taking up, confining, judging and condeming those who do not adhere to them in Champlain County. They carry their Court with them and make short work. Mr. Johnson's line of intelligence seems to fail which makes me take another course for intelligence which is done without much loss as I make the Enemy hire them. My informant was hired to pilot a British Officer to Canada, whose name is Arraby, who passed this place undiscovered about twenty miles north at a Frontier house and applied to my old Pilot Davis who had got into favor with the Enemy while a prisoner the summer past, to pilot him to Canada, which he did by his Son and is now gone himself with instructions from me, who begs the favor to subscribe myself

Your Excellency's

Most humble Servant,

JACOB BAYLEY.*

His Excellency, Gen. Washington.

MOSES DOW OF HAVERHILL, TO HON. MESHECH WEARE, CONCORD, N. H.

Sunday Evening, June 16, 1782.

Hon. and much respected Sir:

Since I wrote you by Capt. Bailey two deserters have come in from Montreal who informed that the British were fortifying Oswego and were making Quebec very strong. That all the prisoners from Vermont were to be sent home immediately. Since which time a number have arrived who say that the others are generally coming, some say that they are exchanged, others that they are on parole, but they generally incline to say but little about affairs. Five or six days since a party of Indians came and took one Abel Davis out of his house, about thirty miles to the Northward, being the farthermost house on Hazen's road, pillaged his house and carried him off. Last evening just before dark a party of Eight or Ten made an attack upon Gen. Bayley's house, fired two or three guns by which one man had his arm broke in such a manner that 'tis much feared it will prove mortal, and two men taken prisoners out of his house and one of his sons was likewise taken at his own house about half a mile from the General's on their retreat, which immediately gave an alarm to both towns. A party of about 30 men were sent in pursuit of the Enemy 12 or 15 miles, but no purpose. Thomas Johnson was made acquainted with

*Volume 59. Page 174. Washington Correspondence.

Pritchard's being in and his designs about two hours before the attack, had just time to give General Bayley a hint by which means he made his escape but had not time to collect any force to oppose them until it was too late. Three or four had just met but were attacked before they were prepared to oppose them. On their retreat the Enemy made prisoners of a number of men in the back part of Newbury and in the Town of Corinth, who swore allegiance to the King of England and were dismissed. Yesterday morning Pritchard sent Levi Sylvester to Mr. Johnson to inform him that he wanted to see him, accordingly Mr. Johnson went into the woods at time and place agreed on and conversed with Pritchard and Capt. Breckenridge about one hour. Pritchard told him that Gen. Haldeman had just received a return from *this King* that Vermont was established a Province. That the Indians were not to be suffered to molest the Inhabitants any more, but that all who submitted to the Government of Vermont were to be used kindly and to enjoy all their lands and privileges, but that opposers were to be destroyed as fast as possible, that Doctor Smith and Capt. Sherwood were appointed commissioners to plan and control and Pritchard to execute the same. That Shem Kentfield and Vandike had sworn previously to Kentfield's execution that this Sylvester was a traitor and a Spy instead of a deserter as he represented, and had brought packets or correspondence from Canada to Tories here, that the intelligence was carried directly to Gen. Haldeman and would soon be here so that it was not safe for Sylvester to tarry here any longer, but must go to Canada with him. Pritchard further said that Governor Chittenden had received an account that all Newbury but three or four had voted to make application to New Hampshire to be received and protected, and that Gen. Bayley was very active in the matter and had sent the same by express to Gen. Haldeman and entreated him in the most earnest and pressing manner to send immediately and take Gen. Bayley off the Ground, as he kept this part of the country in a tumult and confusion and unless he was taken away he could not carry his plans into effect.

Johnson earnestly entreated Pritchard to forbear taking Gen. Bayley as it might be the means of his being suspected, taken up, and found out, but he said that there was no danger of that because Col. Bedel said when he was in before that he was not in the least mistrusted. but yet that should be the case that he would rescue him. That he should leave John Cross at Corinth under the care of Col. John Taplin so that if anything should turn up contrary to his expectation Cross would return into Canada in three days and give him information, and he would immediately come with a sufficient force to lay all that country waste, as he had 150 and as many more as he pleased at his command. Johnson told him that it would not do to destroy this country, as there were so many well disposed to Government, and that he avoid shedding blood, which he promised to do, at this time except in his own defence. Pritchard told Johnson that he was sorry that Davis was taken since Sylvester was obliged to go to Canada, he intended to have gone to Davis and engaged him to carry on the correspondence in Sylvester's place. That the Indians were sent out after the deserters and went contrary to their orders in taking prisoners but that he would send Sylvester to Davis and engage him and send him home immediately. This information of Mr. Johnson's may be depended upon as I had it from his own mouth and have it from under his hand and would mention many things more but have not time. Thus. Sir, you see our distressing situation, constantly watched by the Tories and exposed to their ravages and unable to help ourselves or render that service to the public which we are daily convinced it stands in need of at this day for want of a proper strength to check these growing evils which will soon prove intolerable and all that will not swear allegiance must quit their habitations or be butchered, and in less than one month we expect to be reduced to the sad alternative. Earnestly entreat your Honor's influence in General Court, at Congress, or with his Excellency the Commander-in-chief that we may be protected and the public cause supported. Suppose twenty or thirty persons may have sworn allegiance to the King at this time, and it may not be ten days before a large party may be in and raise the British Standard in our neighborhood and possibly amongst us. Last evening received an official account from Col. Tupper, Commandant at Albany of Kentfield, and Vandikes depositions. Had it been received six hours sooner we should have been able to have taken Sylvester, but he was entered Pritchard's party and was the man that broke the man's arm as within mentioned and is gone off. It is a great pity that intelligence of such importance should not be forwarded by an Express in the most expeditious manner.

Your Honor will please excuse the blunders, inaccuracy, etc., as we are in great tumult, hurry, etc., and receive these few broken hints and suffer me with all deference and esteem to subscribe myself your sincere friend and humble Servant.

MOSES DOW.†

P. S. Entreat that such parts of this letter as relates to Mr. Johnson's correspondence may be kept the profoundest secret, as his life character, and fortune all are hazarded upon it.

MUSTER ROLLS.

The following Muster rolls are of those companies which were raised in Newbury for the defense of the frontier, and to repel the invasion of Burgoyne.

They do not include the service which the majority of the men performed elsewhere, in New Hampshire and Massachusetts regiments. Where the record of such service could be obtained, it is given in the family record of such soldier, and it is also given in the case of men who served in the war before coming here.

For research the following volumes should be consulted: Vols. XIV., XV., XVI., XVII., of the New Hampshire State Papers; "Connecticut Men in the Revolution," and the series of volumes which contain, in alphabetical order, the record of each soldier or sailor who served in the revolutionary war from the state of Massachusetts.

MUSTER ROLL OF A COMPANY OF MINUTE-MEN UNDER THE COMMAND OF CAPT. THOMAS JOHNSON.

(Johnson Papers.)

NEWBURY, 16 May 1775.

Thomas Johnson, Captain
Joseph Chamberlin. Ensign
Elihu Johnson, Sergeant
Abiel Chamberlin, Sergeant
Jacob Hall, (Barnet), Sergeant

Simeon Stevens, Lieut.
Thomas Hibbard, Clerk
Joseph Wilson, Sergeant
Josiah Page, Sergeant

PRIVATES.

John Beard (Baird)
Jacob Bayley, Jr.
Asher Chamberlin
Moses Chamberlin
Richard Chamberlin, Jr.
Jacob Fowler
Jacob Gates
Elijah Hall (Barnet)
Daniel Hall (Barnet)
William Johnson
Henry Lovewell
James Mills
Jacob Page
Benjamin Rawlins
Moses Stevens
Timothy Sargent
Lemuel Webster

Peletiah Bliss, Jr.
Er Chamberlin, Jr.
Nathaniel Chamberlin
Silas Chamberlin
Samuel Eaton
Ward Thurston
Samuel Hadley
Moses Kelley
Amos Kimball (Barnet)
Nehemiah Lovewell, Jr.
Daniel Mills
John Merritt (Barnet)
Samuel Pearse (Barnet)
Peter Sylvester, Jr. (Barnet)
Levi Sylvester, Jr.
Mansfield Taplin
Jonathan Hadley

The service of these men was from eight to twenty days each.

---

†Hon. M. Weare, Esq., President, etc., Concord. Volume 57. Page 282. Washington Correspondence.

A PAY-ROLL OF A COMPANY OF MINUTE-MEN IN THE SERVICE OF THE COUNTRY, IN THE YEAR 1775, UNDER COMMAND OF CAPT. THOMAS JOHNSON.

(From the original at Montpelier.)

	Days in Service		Days in Service
Thomas Johnson, Captain,	20	Abiel Chamberlin, Sergeant,	20
Joseph Chamberlin, Lieut.,	20	Joseph Wilson, Sergeant,	20
Simeon Stevens, Lieut.,	20	Josiah Page, Sergeant,	20
Elihu Johnson, Sergeant,	10	Thomas Hibbard, Clerk,	20

PRIVATES.

John Baird,	12	Sylvanus Heath,	15
Jacob Bayley, Jr.,	15	Daniel Hall,	20
Joshua Bayley,	15	Jonathan Hadley,	8
James Bayley,	15	John Haseltine,	8
Ephraim Bayley,	10	William Johnson,	15
John G. Bayley,	20	Robert Johnston,	20
Benjamin Barnet,	12	Moses Kelley,	10
John Barnet,	12	Zaccheus Lovewell,	10
Samuel Barnet, Jr.,	12	Nathaniel Merrill,	23
John Brown,	6	James Mills,	8
Jonathan Butterfield,	10	John Minot,	12
Nathaniel Chamberlin,	20	Aaron Osmer,	15
Asher Chamberlin,	20	Benjamin Rollins,	10
Richard Chamberlin, Jr.,	8	Timothy Sargent,	
Er Chamberlin,	10	Moses Stevens,	8
Moses Chamberlin,	12	Levi Sylvester, Jr.,	15
Silas Chamberlin,	12	Gideon Smith,	12
Samuel Eaton,	20	Ward Thurston,	20
Abner Fowler,	30	Samuel Webster,	8
Jacob Fowler,	20	Ephraim Webster,	10
Jacob Gates,	8	Asa Webster,	6
Samuel Hadley,	21		

The amount of this roll was £62, 1. Approved and paid, October 26, 1786.

A Company of Independent Militia marched to Fort Ticonderoga, under the command of Captain Thomas Johnson, in 1777, and assisted in the siege of Mount Independence.

No muster roll of this company, or list of the men has been found, although search has been made for it at Montpelier, Concord, Boston and Washington.

The names of some of the men are known, and it is believed to have comprised very nearly the same men who, in September following marched to Saratoga under Col. Frye Bayley; Capt. Johnson then acting as an aid to General Lincoln.

After the capture of Ft. Ticonderoga this company was sent to escort some prisoners to Charlestown, N. H.

The following is among the Johnson papers:

NEWBURY, October 1, 1777.

The Expenses Paid by me for 72 prisoners and 26 of the guard from Castleton to Charlestown.

Paid for Provisions and ferige (ferriage), £6, 6, 7.

Please to Pay this Account to Gen'l Bayley or to Capt. John G. Bayley and you'll oblige your humble servant.

THOMAS JOHNSON, Captain.

To the Paymaster of the State of Vermont, £6, 6, 7.

PAY-ROLL FOR CAPT. FRYE BAYLEY AND LIEUT. NEHEMIAH LOVEWELL WHILE IN CAPTIVITY.

(Original at Montpelier.)

Sent under Flag by the Hon. Maj. Gen. Gates in December 1777.

Frye Bayley, Capt. 12 mo., £8 per month, £96, rations, £24. Total, £120.
Neh. Lovewell, Lt. 12 mo., £4 per mo., £48, rations, £12. Total, £60.
From the United States in January 1779 they received a part of this.
Ordered to be paid £24 and £12, respectively.

RUTLAND, Pay Table Office, Oct. 24, 1786.

March 1776.

State of Vermont to Thomas Johnson, Dr.

To 15 days on a scout from Newbury to St. Johns' by order of General Bayley,	£4, 10.
Abiel Chamberlin, 15 d,	3.
Silas Chamberlin, 15 d,	3.
John McLean, 15 d,	3.
Frye Bayley, 8 d,	1, 12.
Provisions for scout,	3, 8.
Expenses at St. Johns,	1, 10.
	£20.

Pay Table Office, RUTLAND, Oct. 26, 1786.

The within account examined and approved, and the Treasurer is directed to pay the sum to Thomas Johnson, or bearer, it being twenty pounds lawful money.

LEM CHIPMAN, TIMO BROWNSON, Com'rs.

Treasurer's Office, RUTLAND, Oct. 26, 1786.
Rec'd of the Treasurer the contents of the above.

THOS. JOHNSON.

MUSTER ROLL OF CAPTAIN FRYE BAYLEY'S COMPANY, IN COL. PETER OLCOTT'S REGIMENT, WHICH MARCHED TO SARATOGA, SEPT. 23–OCT. 27, 1777.

(Original at Montpelier.)

Frye Bayley, Captain
Nathaniel Merrill, 1st Lieutenant
Robert Hawkins, 2d "
Moses Chase, Sergeant
Robert Stevens, "
Sylvanus Heath, "

Stephen Rider, Sergeant
Bartholemew Somers, Corporal
Thomas Brock, "
Enos Sawyer, "
Duncan McClain,

PRIVATES.

Ephraim Bayley
James Bayley
David Beard
Peletiah Bliss
Enoch Brown
Uriah Chamberlin
Dudley Carleton
Ichabod Callen
Benjamin Dow
Jonathan Fowler
George Gregg
David Haseltine
William Johnson
Peter Johnson
Patrick Kennedy
Ephraim Martin

Benjamin Martin
Jonathan Martin
James McLaughlin
William Mitchell
John McClain
John Orr
Benjamin Orr
John Ormand
Josiah Page
David Reid
Tamereck (Indian)
Alexander Thompson
Joseph Taylor
David Whittier
William Wallace

MUSTER ROLL OF CAPT. JOHN G. BAYLEY'S COMPANY.

In Service, Guarding and Scouting from April, 1777, to March 6, 1779, in the Regiment under command of Col. Peter Olcott.

John G. Bayley, Captain,	1 mo.	Joseph Chamberlin, Lieut.,	1 mo.
Nathaniel Merrill, Lieut.,	1 mo. 14 d.	Thomas Hibbard, Sergeant,	1 mo. 28 d.

PRIVATES.

Jacob Bayley, Jr.,	1 mo.	Samuel Hadley,	1 mo.
James Bayley,	1 mo.	John Haseltine,	1 mo.

Ephraim Bayley,	1 mo. 3 d.	David Haseltine,	1 mo. 25 d.
Frye Bayley,	1 mo.	James Hunter,	1 mo.
Joshua Bayley,	1 mo.	Robert Hunkins,	20 d.
John Baird.	1 mo.	Robert Johnston,	1 mo.
Jonathan Butterfield,	1 mo.	Thomas Johnson,	1 mo.
John Barnet,	1 mo.	Elihu Johnson,	1 mo.
Amos Barnet,	20 d.	William Johnson,	1 mo.
Benjamin Barnet,	1 mo.	Jacob Kent,	1 mo.
Samuel Barnet,	2 mo. 4d	Nehemiah Lovewell,	19 d.
John Brown,	1 mo. 15 d.	Nehemiah Lovewell, Jr.,	20 d.
Peletiah Bliss,	25 d.	Henry Lovewell,	13 d.
Thomas Brock.	29 d.	Zaccheus Lovewell,	1 mo.
Edmund Brown,	1 mo.	Ephraim Lacy,	1 mo.
Er Chamberlin,	1 mo.	Benjamin Muzzey,	1 mo.
Nathaniel Chamberlin,	1 mo.	John Mills,	1 mo.
Asher Chamberlin.	1 mo.	John Mills, Jr.,	1 mo. 2 d.
Moses Chamberlin,	1 mo.	Aaron Osmore,	1 mo. 20 d.
Silas Chamberlin,	1 mo.	Josiah Page,	1 mo.
Remembrance Chamberlain,	1 mo. 29 d.	Jacob Page,	1 mo.
Uriah Chamberlin,	1 mo.	Simeon Stevens,	
Thomas Chamberlain,	28 d.	Samuel Stevens,	1 mo. 2 d.
Dudley Carleton,	1 mo.	Otho Stevens,	1 mo.
James Dodge,	18 d.	Timothy Sargent,	1 mo.
Samuel Eaton,	1 mo.	Gideon Smith,	1 mo. 25 d.
Jacob Fowler,	1 mo.	Levi Sylvester,	1 mo.
Abner Fowler,	1 mo.	Levi Sylvester, Jr.,	1 mo.
Jonathan Fowler,	28 d.	John Taplin,	18 d.
Jacob Fowler, 3d,	1 mo.	William Taplin,	1 mo.
Reuben Foster,	2 mo. 25 d.	Mansfield Taplin,	1 mo. 20 d.
John Goodwin,	1 mo.	Samuel Webster,	1 mo.
Willoughby Goodwin,	1 mo.	Ephraim Webster,	1 mo.
Jonathan Goodwin,	1 mo.	Ephraim Webster, Jr.,	1 mo.
Sylvanus Heath,	1 mo.	Asa Webster,	1 mo.
Jesse Heath,	1 mo.	William Wallace,	1 mo.
Samuel Heath,	1 mo.	Ebenezer White,	23 d.
James Heath,	1 mo.	Joseph White,	1 mo. 2d.

This Pay Roll, amounting to £193.17, was approved and paid July 9, 1785.

PAY ROLL OF CAPT. SIMEON STEVENS' COMPANY.

(N. H. State Papers.)

In Newbury from May, 1779, to May, 1781, of service done in guarding and scouting in the Sundry alarms, guarding prisoners, etc., under the command of Col. Peter Olcott.

Simeon Stevens, Captain	25 d.	Wright Chamberlin, Sergeant	
Joseph Chamberlin, 1st Lieutenant	25 d.	Henry Lovewell,	"
Dudley Carleton, 2d "	25 d.	Josiah Page,	"
Samuel Eaton, Sergeant			

PRIVATES.

Ephraim Bayley	Elihu Johnson
Frye Bayley	Samuel Johnson
Jacob Bayley, Jr.	Peter Johnson
James Bayley	Robert Johnston
Samuel Barnett	Thomas Johnson
John Barnett	Jacob Kent
Benjamin Barnett	Jacob Kent, Jr.
Amos Barnett	Amos Kimball
John Baird,	Moses Kelley
Edmund Brown	Ephraim Lacy
John Brown	Zaccheus Lovewell
Jonathan Butterfield	Jonathan Lovewell
Peletiah Bliss	Nehemiah Lovewell
Thomas Brock	Nehemiah Lovewell, Jr.

Er Chamberlin
Thomas Chamberlain,
Remembrance Chamberlain
Uriah Chamberlin
Nathaniel Chamberlin
Silas Chamberlin
Abiel Chamberlin
Moses Chamberlin
Silas Chamberlin
Nathaniel Chamberlin
Silas Chamberlin
Uriah Chamberlin
Remembrance Chamberlain
Andrew Carter
James Dodge
Samuel Fellows
Paul Ford
Jacob Fowler, Jr.
Jacob Fowler, 3d
Jonathan Fowler
Abner Fowler
Reuben Foster
Jonathan Goodwin
Willoughby Goodwin
Jacob Gates
John Haseltine
David Haseltine
Robert Hunkins
Sylvanus Heath
Jesse Heath
James Heath
Thomas Hibbard
William Johnson
Benjamin Sawyer, Jr.
Enos Sawyer
Levi Sylvester, Jr.
John Taplin
John Taplin, Jr.
Mansfield Taplin
William Taplin

Cornelius Morgan
Thomas McKeith
Duncan McLain
John Mills
John Mills, Jr.
Benjamin Muzzey
Aaron Osmer
Jacob Page
Stephen Powers
Jonathan Powers
John Russell
Otho Stevens
Isaac Stevens
Samuel Stevens
Gideon Smith
Levi Sylvester
Timothy Sargent
Aaron Shepard
Ashbel Shepard
Joseph Taylor
John Taplin
Mansfield Taplin
William Taplin
Thomas Thurber
John Vance
James Vance
Nicholas White
Ebenezer White
Joseph White, Jr.
Samuel Webster
Ephraim Webster
Asa Webster
William Wallace
Joseph Wilson
Joseph White
David Weeks
Zadoc Wright
Francis Wright
Oliver Willard

Each private's service was 19 days, excepting James Dodge who served 29 days, Robert Johnston, 57 days, Aaron Osmer, 32 days, Frye Bayley, 29, Abiel Chamberlin, 31, Jacob Gates, 39, and Amos Kimball, 8. Amount, £149, 7, 4. Paid July 9, 1785.

A Pay-Roll of a Party of Men Belonging to Col. Peter Olcott's Regiment Under the Command of Capt. Frye Bayley, Employed in Scouting.

Dated at Newbury, 8th May, 1781.

(Original at Montpelier.)

Frye Bayley, Captain
James Bayley, 1st Lieutenant

Thos. Chamberlain, 2d Lieutenant.

PRIVATES.

Jacob Bayley, Jr.
Joshua Bayley
Benjamin Barnet
Joseph Chamberlin
Abiel Chamberlin
Er Chamberlin
Samuel Eaton
John Gibson
Samuel Hadley

Samuel Johnson
John Lovewell
Nehemiah Lovewell
Henry Lovewell
Nathaniel Merrill
Jonathan Powers
Stephen Powers
Aaron Shepard
Levi Sylvester

David Haseltine   Asa Webster
Jesse Heath   Ephraim Webster
Thomas Johnson   Joseph White
    This service was done from October 1, 1780, to May 8, 1781. £57, 10, 7. Paid
February 20, 1783.

PAY-ROLL OF CAPT. FRYE BAYLEY'S COMPANY.

    In Newbury, from May, 1781, till the end of the war in scouting, guarding, etc.,
in Sundry alarms, under the command of Colo. Peter Olcott and Colo. Robert
Johnston.

(Original at Montpelier.)

Frye Bayley, Captain,	1 mo. 20 d.	Joshua Bayley, Sergeant,	1 mo. 20 d·
Remembrance Chamberlain, 1st Lieut.,		Samuel Eaton, "	16 d·
	1 mo. 2d.	Er Chamberlin, "	6 d.
John Russell, 2d Lieut.,	12 d.	John Brown, "	12 d.
Edmund Brown, Ensign,	16 d		

PRIVATES.

James Bayley,		James Johnston,	11 d.
Jacob Bayley, Jr.,	1 mo. 20 d.	Jacob Kent., Jr.,	11 d.
John G. Bayley,	1 mo. 2 d.	Moses Knight,	1 mo. 14 d.
Peletiah Bliss,	11 d.	Robert Kay,	1 mo.
Jonathan Barrows,	6 d.	Nehemiah Lovewell,·	12 d.
Thomas Brock,	11 d.	Cornelius Morgan,	11 d.
Samuel Barnet,	11 d.	Thomas McKeith,	11 d.
Samuel Butterfield,	6 d.	Benjamin Muzzey,	11 d.
John Canada, (Kennedy),	11 d.	Jonathan Powers,	15 d.
Nathaniel Chamberlin,	6 d.	Stephen Powers,	1 mo. 20 d.
Moses Chamberlin,	1 mo. 11 d.	Levi Sylvester, Sr.,	10 d.
Joseph Chamberlin,	1 mo. 14 d.	Reuben Sandborn,	6 d.
Uriah Chamberlin,	11 d.	James Spear,	11 d.
Abiel Chamberlin,	11 d.	Ashbel Shepard,	6 d.
Silas Chamberlin,	17 d.	Aaron Shepard,	11 d.
Dudley Carleton,	11 d.	Otho Stevens,	11 d.
Luther Eddy,	11 d.	Simeon Stevens,	25 d.
Paul Ford,	20 d.	Giden Smith,	11 d.
Samuel Fellows,	2 d.	John Sayer,	12 d.
Reuben Foster,	11 d.	James Taylor,	6 d.
Jacob Fowler,	11 d.	John Vance, Jr.,	11 d.
Jonathan Goodwin,	11 d.	Peter Wesson,	6 d.
Timothy Haseltine,	6 d.	James Wesson,	6 d.
Samuel Hadley,	15 d.	Aaron Wesson,	6 d.
Thomas Hibbard,	6 d.	Samuel Webster,	11 d.
Sylvanus Heath,	11 d.	Ephraim Webster,	12 d.
David Haseltine,	11 d.	William Wallace,	11 d.
Elihu Johnson,	6 d.	John Way,	11 d.
John Johnson,	11 d.		

    The amount of this roll was £91, 11. Paid July 9, 1785.

    The State of Vermont to the several officers and men hereinafter named for
service done by order of the commanding officer at Fort Wait, A. D. 1781. (Fort
Wait was in Corinth).

Lieut. Abner Fowler, 11 d. scouting,	£2, 6, 9.
Bracket Towle, 5 d. scouting,	1, 7, 3.
Serg. Zaccheus Lovewell, 22 d. scouting,	1, 15, 3.
William Taplin, 6 days,	8,
Benjamin Sanborn, 5 days,	6, 8.

    This may certify that the above is just and true.

                                                    JOHN TAPLIN.

    Paid March 3, 1784.

    Upon a Pay Roll for a number of militia under Capt. Robert Hunkins on an
alarm at Peacham, August 15, 1781, Seth Ford is credited to seven days.

MUSTER ROLL OF CAPTAIN JOHN VINCENT'S COMPANY OF INDIAN RANGERS.

In the service of the United States of America, belonging to the Saint Francis Tribe, enlisting for one year from May 1st, 1780. (Johnson Papers.)

John Vincent, Captain, Remarks   Swasin, Sergeant
John Sabattis, Ensign, died June 30, 1781   Louis, Sergeant

PRIVATES.

Joseph	Peal Susuph
Joseph Sabattist	Susuph Mohawk
Baziel Sabattist,	Joseph Squant, deserted March, 1781
Apom Sabattist,	Joseph
Peal Susupp, died December 10	John Battist
Tamenick, died December 10	Charles
Joseph Mally	

NEWBURY, 30th April, 1781.

These Mustered in Captain John Vincent's Company of Indians as specified in the above Roll. The Rolls to be made agreeable to this Roll, and the Remarks from 30th April, 1781.

JACOB BAYLEY.

(Original in the handwriting of Thomas Hibbard.)

The following men in Newbury were among the 400 signers from Gloucester and Cumberland counties, of a petition to the New York General Assembly, for a confirmation of their grants, and for the remission of one-half the usual fees. Their names were signed in the presence of Hon. Samuel Wells, a judge of the Court of Common Pleas. The petition is dated Jan. 26, 1773.

(Documentary History of New York, Vol. 10, pp. 449-500.)

James Abbott	Abner Fowler
Jacob Bayley	Abner Fowler, Jr.
Frye Bayley	Peter Fowler
Ephraim Bayley	Jonathan Fowler
Joshua Bayley	Joseph Fowler
Jacob Bayley, Jr.	Jonathan Goodwin
Samuel Barnet	John Goodwin
Samuel Barnet, Jr.	Samuel Hadley
Amos Barnet	Solomon Hall
Peletiah Bliss	Aaron Hosmer
Peletiah Bliss, Jr.	Daniel Hunt
John Beard	Thomas Hibbard
John Brown	Samuel Hale
Thomas Brock	Robert Hunkins
Josiah Burnham	Daniel Hunt
Edmund Brown	John Haseltine
Welbee Butterfield	Haynes Johnson
Thomas Chamberlain	Elihu Johnson
Richard Chamberlin	William Johnson
Richard Chamberlin, Jr.	Benjamin Muzzey
Joseph Chamberlin	Hugh Miller
Nathaniel Chamberlin	John Mills
Uriah Chamberlin	John Mills, Jr.
Abner Chamberlin	Henry Moore
Benjamin Chamberlin	Nathaniel Rix
Abiel Chamberlin	Stevens Rider
Er Chamberlin	John Skeele
Silas Chamberlin	John Sawyer, Jr.
Jonathan Farwell	

MUSTER ROLL OF A COMPANY OF VOLUNTEERS.

Enlisted under the command of Capt. Emerson Corliss, agreeable to an act of the Legislature of Vermont, passed on the 6th of November, 1812. Met at dwelling house of Gideon Tuxbury, in Newbury, on the 4th day of March A. D. 1813, for the purpose of choosing the officers to fill said company.

(Original owned by Hon. Henry C. McDuffie, Bradford).

Emerson Corliss, Captain
James Davis, 1st Lieutenant
Daniel Leslie, 2d Lieutenant
John McDuffie, Sergeant
Eben S. McFarlin,   "
Thomas Hilands,   "

Nathan B. Taplin, Sergeant
James McDuffie, Corporal
Benjamin Rowe,   "
Mannasser Leach,   "
Moody Grow,   "
Samuel Grow, Ensign

PRIVATES.

Ephraim Aldrich
Silas Aldrich
Isaiah Batchelder
John G. Bayley
Abner Bayley
John Bayley
Samuel Chapman
Jacob Colby
John Corliss
Nathan Colby
Timothy Corliss
John Carter
Nathl. H. Cunningham
Fenno Dean
Benjamin Duty
Timner Dodge
Nathan Dustin
Lemuel Fuller, Jr.
John Gaffield

James M. Hinds
Aseph Hyde
Elijah Howard
Timothy Heath
William Kinnard
William Ladd
Moses Mills
James Martin
John Martin
David Manson
Humphrey Nichols
Moses Page
John Putnam
Stephen Rogers
Billy Stearns
Peter Severance
Silas Sweet, Jr.
Jonas Taplin
William Wilson

BRADFORD, 5th March, 1813.

Honored Sir:—In obedience to your commission I have enlisted good and effective privates and have led them to a choice of officers, on the 4th instant, and all agree to stand ready at a moment's warning at the call of our country, and that no lines shall stop us if we are called either against foreign enemies or domestic traitors; and all agree to obey the orders of their superior officers according to the rules and articles of war. I have herewith sent you a copy of the enlistment and the names of the several persons enlisted, out of whom James Davis of Topsham was chosen first Lieutenant, Daniel Leslie of Bradford, second Lieutenant and Samuel Grow of Newbury ensign. All of them have accepted their appointments and if you would be so good as to send to each of them their commissions as soon as possible I should be pleased. This from your friend who will always endeavor to stand ready in obedience to your call.   JOHN McDUFFEE.

To his Excellency Jonas Galusha, Gov. of the State of Vermont.

N. B.—Please to direct the commissions, if forwarded, to the Post Office, Bradford.

This was a company of Minute Men which enlisted to be called upon in case of an emergency, but not having been needed it was discharged at the close of the war, in 1815.

The captain of the company, Emerson Corliss, was an old Revolutionary hero. He enlisted when he was only seventeen years of age, and was in the battles of Bunker Hill, Trenton, Princeton, Bennington, Stillwater, Saratoga and many others. He was twice wounded, and at the battle of Bennington, seven balls were shot through his coat and one through his hat. Mrs. P. S. Chamberlin of Bradford and Mrs. R. W. Chamberlin of Newbury are his granddaughters.

ELECTION ODE.

The following letter, in beautiful handwriting, is preserved among the Johnson papers, and relates to the ode which was sung after the Election sermon, before the General Assembly, in the old meeting house Oct. 10, 1801:

PEACHAM, V^t., AUG. 9th, 1801.

COL^o. THOMAS JOHNSON,

Sir: Through General Whitelaw I have received a polite request from you to furnish, in company with Mr. Carter and Mr. Goss, an ode for the ensuing election. For my own part I have undertaken the task with much diffidence, and have executed it by no means satisfactorily to myself. Such as it is, however, I enclose it to you, and you may be assured that I shall not be disappointed should it be rejected or too defective for so public an occasion.

I believe Mr. Carter has forwarded you a similar one by this mail; as far as I am interested you are welcome to make use of one, or both, or neither, as your judgement shall dictate.

I am, Sir, Respectfully your most o'b't Servt.,

BARNES BUCKMINSTER.

(The ode is copied from the Christian Harmony, pp. 163-165.)

1
Welcome the day from which our State,
Computes the era of its date,
This day a government began
Essential to the rights of man;
O may its blessings ne'er expire
Till time's extinct, the globe on fire.

2
Not fifty years have rolled away
Since savage foes spread wide dismay
Where now rich fields of yellow corn
Our vallies and our hills adorn
The maple, screen for Indian darts,
Now yields the wealth of India's marts.

3
Vermont, thy sons are more than blest,
In wealth increasing, public rest;
Thy rulers from the people's choice
Obedient to the public voice,
Possess the power, the goodness, will,
A people's interest to fulfill.

4
But most in him, the Chief who guides
The faction's waves of popular tides,
Whose patriotism none impeach,
Whose virtue no vile slanders reach,
To whom the graces long have paid
The homage of a patriot's aid.

OWNERS OF NEWBURY LANDS IN 1808.

(A list made by Asa Tenney.)

UPPER MEADOW FIFTY-ACRE LOTS.

1, 2, 3. Joseph Ricker
4, 5. (West ends) Edward Ricker
4, 5. (East ends) Charles Chamberlin
6, 7, 8, 9. Josiah Little
10. John Bayley and John Buxton

11. Uriah Chamberlin (sold to Asa Tenney)
12. Thomas Johnson
13. Dr. Smith & Jer. Ingalls

OX-BOW AND COW MEADOW FIFTY-ACRE LOTS.

1. Claimed by Col. Little and Col. Johnson
2, 3. Col. Johnson
4, 6. Josiah Little
5, 7. Frye Bayley

8, 9, 10, 11 and ½, of 12. Col. Johnson
½ of 12. Isaac Bayley.
13-22. Never laid out; between sawmill and No. 12 Musquash Meadow 50 acre lot.

Laid out to the meadow east of the road that goes to Chamberlin's ferry.

1, 2. Josiah Little
3, 4, 5, 6. Joseph & Benjamin Chamberlin

7. Col. Wallace
8. James Spear

MUSQUASH MEADOW FIFTY-ACRE LOT.

Laid out on the west side of the road to the ferry.

1. Col. T. Johnson
2. Col. R. Johnston
3. Samuel Lancaster
4, 5. S. M. Lancaster
6. Charles Bayley & T. Burroughs
7. Simeon Stevens
8. Col. Wallace
9. Ebenezer White
10. William Bailey

SLEEPER'S MEADOW FIFTY-ACRE LOTS.

1, 2, 3. Col. Kent
4, 5. Dr. Samuel White
6, 7. Col. Chamberlain

HALL'S MEADOW FIFTY-ACRE LOTS.

1, 2. Stephens McConnell
3. Jacob Fowler
4. Jonathan Goodwin
5. Thomas Brock
6, 7. John Mills
8, 9. John Mills Jr.
10. James Abbott
11. John Mills

HUNDRED-ACRE LOTS.

1 & 2. Asa Tenney, west half of each, east half sold to Mr. Metcalf
3. Col. T. Johnson
4. N. White (sold to Frost & Chapman)
5. Hadlock Morey
6. Mr. Ober
7. Edward Little
8. Stephen Rogers
9. Col. Little (claimed by Isaac Bayley)
10 & 11. S. Smith
12. Asa Tenney
13. A. Tenney & E. Little
14. N. Merrill
15. Josiah Little
16. Charles and James Bayley & Geo. Banfield
17. J. Little (sold to Dr. White)
18. Dr White (sold to Peach)
19 & 20. Part Public Lands
21. Jonathan Johnson
22. Jonah Chapman
23. Samuel Grow
24, 25. Josiah Little
26. Daniel Putnam
27. Josiah Little
28. Col. Rem. Chamberlain
29. N. White, Jr. (sold to Samuel Thompson)
30, 31, 32. New York Claim
33, 34. John Hazen
35. Josiah Little
36. Col. Little (sold to Joshua Bayley)
37. Col. Johnson ("   )
38. Col. Wallace ("   )
39, 40. Joshua and Isaac Bayley
41. Col. Little (sold to McDuffie)
42. Frye Bayley & Asa Tenney (sold to Coffran)
43. Col. Little
44. Thos. Chamberlain & Widow Putnam
45. Tarrant Putnam
46. James Scott
81. Gideon Tewksbury
82, 83. The Capt. Hazeltine farm
84, 85. Esq. Putnam's widow
86. R. Chamberlain & Brock
87. Col. Johnson
88. Stevens McConnell
89. Col. Frye Bayley & Nicholas White
90, 91, 92 Col. Little
93, 94. Isaac Bayley & Moses Johnson
95. John Bayley (sold to Porter)
96. Joel Machius
97. Col. J. Little
98, 99. Thomas Johnson
100. James Henderson
101. Josiah Rogers
102, 103. Thos. Eastman & Jas. Boyce.
104. Ortho Stevens & Montgomery
105, 106, 107. Samuel Tucker and others
108. Col. Little (sold to S. Tucker)
109. Col. Wallace (sold to J. & J. Johnston)
110. Col. Chamberlain
111. Stevens McConnell
112. Col. Johnson
113, 114, 115. School lots
116. Asa Tenney
117. Joseph Chamberlin
118. Josiah Little
119. J. Little
120. Widow Smith
121. Thos. Johnson, D. Carleton & Noah Stevens
122 Dudley Carleton
123. Rem. Chamberlin & Stephen Powers.
124. James Vance
125 James Boyce
126, 127. J. Little
128. A. Tenney & J. Tewksbury
129. Col. Johnson
130. Col. Little
131. A. Tenney

Birch

Mark of

Miles

Birch (top row)	47	46	45	44	43	42	41	40

33	34	35	36	37	38	39

N 61° W

17 Samuel Garnet	18 Jacob Kent	19 Glebe	20 Glebe	Range 1st
37 Enos Mudget to Jo Johnson	38 Jon'l Hale to W. Wallace	39	40 Glebe	Range 2nd
in Colin Little	58 Stephen Little	59	60	Range 3rd
76 John Haze to	78 John Taplin	79	80 Moses Little undivided land	Range 4th
81 John Taplin	98 Jacob Bayley to	99 Enoch Thurston Tho. Johnson	100 Edmond Moses to James Smith	Range 5th
101 Jacob Fowler	118 Clement March	119 Jacob Kent	120 Clement March	Range 6th
121 Jacob Bayley	138 Abner Little Fowler by	139 Thomas Johnson	140 William White	Range 7th
141 Joseph White to Thos Johnson	142 Edmund White to Thos Johnson	159	160 Wm White	Range 8th

N 60° W

were evidently written later.

COLEMAN'S MAP OF THE HUNDRED ACRE LOTS. The part beyond Whiting's Gore is now part of Topsham. This map was probably made about 1773. In the original, some of the names were evidently written later.

47. Col. T. Johnson
48. Col. Wallace
49. Col. Little
50, 51. Included in the Clinton Claim
52. Col. Wallace (Clinton Claim)
53. James Henderson
54. Col. Little
55. Col. T. Johnson
56, 57, 58. Col. Little
59, 60. Joshua & Isaac Bayley
61. J. Little, (sold to McDuffie)
62. J. Little
63. Josiah Platt
64. John Vance
65. Col. T. Johnson
66. Abraham Brickett
67. Col. T. Johnson
68. Col. Little (sold to Benj. Brock)
69. Benj. Porter
70. Isaac Bayley
71, 72, 73, 74. Col. J. Little
75, 76. Asa Tenney (sold to Mason Randall
77. Dr White & Joseph Chamberlin
78. J. Little (sold to John Strong)
79. Col. Johnson
80. James Henderson

132. N. Avery & Meader
133. Ebenezer Temple
134. Col. Johnson
135. Asa Tenney
136. Samuel Powers
137. Jona. and Jesse Johnson
138. Horace Stebbins
139. Col. Johnson
140. Noah White
141, 142. Col. Johnson
143, 144. Col. Johnson & Ben Porter
145. John Scott
146. James Johnston
147. Widow Lovewell
148, 149. Edward Little.
150. Josiah Little
151. J. Little & B. Porter
152. E. Little. Wm & Jas. Wallace
153. Col. J. Bayley
154. J. C. Jones (N. Avery)
155. James Wallace
156. Joel Carbee
157. Col. Wallace
158. Thos. Chamberlin
159. Col. T. Johnson
160. Noah White

P. 1 & 2 in 8th range, Col. Little.
P. 3 in 8th range, W. B. Bannister
P. 1 & 2 in 7th range, 3 & 4 in 6th range, J. Little
P. 5 in 5th range, Col. Little.

P. 7 & 8 in 4th range, B. Porter.
P. 9 & 10 in 3d range, Hon. G. Clinton
P. 11, 12, 13, 14, 15. Part of Witherspoon Tract

Undivided right of Col. Wallace, Abner Newton, John Hugh. Joseph White, Zaccheus Peaslee. James King, Asa Foster, A. Miles, Moses Hazen, John Temple.
Atkinson's 500 acres belong to Col. Little.
Governor's farm, 500 acres, all Wells River.

Poems enough to fill fifty pages were sent for insertion in this volume. Only one from these is selected for these pages.
The mill alluded to has since disappeared.

THE BROOK AND THE MILL.

On its rocky bed 'neath the frowning hill,
A relic of time, stands the quaint old mill.
In its every aspect it speaks decay
And little by little it crumbles away.
Here does it sway and there does it sink,
And its gable bows o'er the water's brink;
While its crazy walls by the winds do sway,
Proclaiming its fall at an early day,
But the brook is the same, all ragged and torn,
That I saw in the dew-time of life's young morn.
The stone-built dam in a rocky dell,
Where the water, a fleecy curtain fell;
Here a little cove where a minie mound
Of foam slow circled round and round;

47. Col. T. Johnson
48. Col. Wallace
49. Col. Little
50, 51. Included in the Clinton Claim
52. Col. Wallace (Clinton Claim)
53. James Henderson
54. Col. Little
55. Col. T. Johnson
56, 57, 58. Col. Little
59, 60. Joshua & Isaac Bayley
61. J. Little, (sold to McDuffie)
62. J. Little
63. Josiah Platt
64. John Vance
65. Col. T. Johnson
66. Abraham Brickett
67. Col. T. Johnson
68. Col. Little (sold to Benj. Brock)
69. Benj. Porter
70. Isaac Bayley
71, 72, 73, 74. Col. J. Little
75, 76. Asa Tenney (sold to Mason Randall
77. Dr White & Joseph Chamberlin
78. J. Little (sold to John Strong)
79. Col. Johnson
80. James Henderson

132. N. Avery & Meader
133. Ebenezer Temple
134. Col. Johnson
135. Asa Tenney
136. Samuel Powers
137. Jona. and Jesse Johnson
138. Horace Stebbins
139. Col. Johnson
140. Noah White
141, 142. Col. Johnson
143, 144. Col. Johnson & Ben Porter
145. John Scott
146. James Johnston
147. Widow Lovewell
148, 149. Edward Little.
150. Josiah Little
151. J. Little & B. Porter
152. E. Little. Wm & Jas. Wallace
153. Col. J. Bayley
154. J. C. Jones (N. Avery)
155. James Wallace
156. Joel Carbee
157. Col. Wallace
158. Thos. Chamberlin
159. Col. T. Johnson
160. Noah White

P. 1 & 2 in 8th range, Col. Little.
P. 3 in 8th range, W. B. Bannister
P. 1 & 2 in 7th range, 3 & 4 in 6th range, J. Little
P. 5 in 5th range, Col. Little.

P. 7 & 8 in 4th range, B. Porter.
P. 9 & 10 in 3d range, Hon. G. Clinton
P. 11, 12, 13, 14, 15. Part of Witherspoon Tract

Undivided right of Col. Wallace, Abner Newton, John Hugh. Joseph White, Zaccheus Peaslee. James King, Asa Foster, A. Miles, Moses Hazen, John Temple.
Atkinson's 500 acres belong to Col. Little.
Governor's farm, 500 acres, all Wells River.

Poems enough to fill fifty pages were sent for insertion in this volume. Only one from these is selected for these pages.
The mill alluded to has since disappeared.

THE BROOK AND THE MILL.

On its rocky bed 'neath the frowning hill,
A relic of time, stands the quaint old mill.
In its every aspect it speaks decay
And little by little it crumbles away.
Here does it sway and there does it sink,
And its gable bows o'er the water's brink;
While its crazy walls by the winds do sway,
Proclaiming its fall at an early day,
But the brook is the same, all ragged and torn,
That I saw in the dew-time of life's young morn.
The stone-built dam in a rocky dell,
Where the water, a fleecy curtain fell;
Here a little cove where a minie mound
Of foam slow circled round and round;

And the laughing cascade, where the stream with glee
Leaped into a miniature milky sea;
Next a shelving rock did the stream assail
And rippled down like a bridal veil,
Deep down in the shady pool below,
Where circled the whirlpool cups of snow.
Tortured and twisted, it onward falls,
With anger it lashes its rocky walls;
Rioting, roaring, with demon will,
And white with fury it reaches the mill,
Then passing the mill, in its headlong fray,
It rolls on the meadow serenely away,
Or idles about, 'neath the alders cool,
Like a tardy loiterer whipped to school.
How I watched its waters, that down did reel,
And like demon dashed at the trembling wheel;
Then, groaning with age and crazed with pain,
The old mill rushed to its work again.
Thus on did it toil, with a weakening will,
Till a sad day came to the poor old mill,
When, deaf to the water's taunt and roar,
The wheel stood still to be turned no more.
How oft, by the brookside I happily sat,
With seatless pants and with rimless hat,
And a worm on a bended pin did throw
To the trout, in the years of long ago.
Full oft, with that shattered rimless crown,
With water I filled up the pot-holes brown,
That the eddy of ages had worn adown,
How oft in the night, when the storm did pour,
Did I 'waken and listen to hear it roar,
As all white and ghostly it rushed adown
With a voice that the thunder scarce could drown,
Here the hill looks down with an aspect stern,
Beetling with bowlders, fringed with fern,
And the trees, 'mong whose branches and roots I played,
Still over the stream fling their grateful shade;
Resisting the flood's and the wind's rough shock,
Those giant claws, how they grasp the rock;
Triumphant o'er all, how they hold their place,
With foes fierce assailing both top and base.
Though old was the brook in the mill's young day,
Still young is the brook in the mill's decay;
The mill will pass as a fleeting dream
And the bridge drop piece-meal into the stream;
The bowlders, around which the waters play,
Will to pebbles be worn and swept away,
But the brook, without break in a single line,
Will sing its song till the end of time.

W. P.

November, 1888.

PART II.

BIOGRAPHICAL SKETCHES

AND

FAMILY RECORDS

Knox Mountain, Orange.

Wells River Valley.

Blue Mountain, Ryegate

Deltry's Mountain, Barnet

Connecticut Valley

Barnet Village.

Mount Gardner

Wells River.

Woodsville

Ammonoosuc Valley.

White Mo[untains]

PANORAMIC VIEW FROM KING'S HILL.

Biographical Sketches and Family Records.

THE following records have been prepared for this work by many persons, out of data derived from a great variety of sources. Some of them have been entirely the work of representatives of families, and appear under their names. Of others the data have been collected by different persons, and placed in my hands for completion and arrangement. With many more, the entire work has been done by me, others assisting as they could.

In the great majority of cases I could have no personal knowledge of the facts, and cannot vouch for accuracy in every case, but believe that they are, in the main, correct. To make them so, I have left no means untried. I have examined scores of town and family histories, and consulted town, church and family records not in Newbury only, but in other towns, and examined all the burial grounds within many miles.

In the necessary correspondence I have written more than 2000 letters, and have taxed the memories of the older people. All the information which I have sought has been given, where it could be given at all, most gladly.

Since I began this task, several of these aged ones who have told me of those who were the active men and women of Newbury when they were young, have themselves passed away. It is pleasant to think that they were spared thus to preserve the memories of so many who were otherwise in a fair way to be forgotten.

By way of explanation it may be well to say, that in the annals of the larger families, where the line of ancestry is given in brackets, and by connecting numerals, it is computed, in nearly every case, from the first of the name who settled in Newbury, and not from the emigrant ancestor. The line of ancestry, from the emigrant, to the first settler here, is indicated by large Roman numerals. In the records of the smaller families, which embrace only two generations from the first of the name who resided here, the plan followed is very simple, merely taking up each of the children in the order of their birth. But in those of the larger ones,

Biographical Sketches and Family Records.

THE following records have been prepared for this work by many persons, out of data derived from a great variety of sources. Some of them have been entirely the work of representatives of families, and appear under their names. Of others the data have been collected by different persons, and placed in my hands for completion and arrangement. With many more, the entire work has been done by me, others assisting as they could.

In the great majority of cases I could have no personal knowledge of the facts, and cannot vouch for accuracy in every case, but believe that they are, in the main, correct. To make them so, I have left no means untried. I have examined scores of town and family histories, and consulted town, church and family records not in Newbury only, but in other towns, and examined all the burial grounds within many miles.

In the necessary correspondence I have written more than 2000 letters, and have taxed the memories of the older people. All the information which I have sought has been given, where it could be given at all, most gladly.

Since I began this task, several of these aged ones who have told me of those who were the active men and women of Newbury when they were young, have themselves passed away. It is pleasant to think that they were spared thus to preserve the memories of so many who were otherwise in a fair way to be forgotten.

By way of explanation it may be well to say, that in the annals of the larger families, where the line of ancestry is given in brackets, and by connecting numerals, it is computed, in nearly every case, from the first of the name who settled in Newbury, and not from the emigrant ancestor. The line of ancestry, from the emigrant, to the first settler here, is indicated by large Roman numerals. In the records of the smaller families, which embrace only two generations from the first of the name who resided here, the plan followed is very simple, merely taking up each of the children in the order of their birth. But in those of the larger ones,

where the descendants of a common ancestor number several
families in each generation, a more elaborate plan is followed,
whereby the ancestry of each person may easily be traced. A
careful study of one of the longer records—that of the Abbott
family, for instance—will enable one to comprehend the system
which by a combination of Roman and Arabic numerals gives each
member his proper place, and connects him with the common
ancestor.

Our limits forbid more than a brief mention of each of many
thousand persons, and the records are often only—

"The short and simple annals of the poor."

But whatever their worldly circumstances, the people of
Newbury, here enumerated, have been, generally, a noble race of men
and women, well worthy of being thus kept in remembrance for
future generations.

F. P. W.

Abbreviations—b, born; d, died; m, married; c, child, children; res., residence;
rem., removed; q. v., whom see; 1st Ch., First Congregational Church; 2d Ch.,
Second Congregational Church; Meth. Ch., Methodist Episcopal Church; Pres. Ch.,
Presbyterian Church.

ABBOTT.

Most town genealogies begin with the name of Abbott, and Newbury has had
a fair proportion of persons bearing this widely spread name. The emigrant
ancestor, George Abbott, is understood to have come from Yorkshire, England, in
1640, and was one of the first settlers of Andover, Mass., in 1643, where he d.
December 24, 1681, O. S. He m. 1647, Hannah Chandler. Thirteen chil.

II. WILLIAM, (1657-1713); m. 1682, Elizabeth Gray; ten c.

III. JAMES, (1685-1787); m. Abigail Farnum; fifteen c.. He became one of the
first settlers of Concord, N. H., about 1737.

IV. JAMES, b. Andover, Mass., Jan. 12, 1717; d. Newbury, 1803. He removed
to Newbury in November, 1763, and settled on Lots 3, and 11, on the
Ox-bow, which he sold to Rev. Peter Powers, and removed to Haverhill,
where he was town clerk 1769-70, 1772-3, selectman and member of the
Council of Safety. He returned to Newbury, 1783, and bought the farm
still in the family, where his great-great-grandson, Irving A. Abbott,
resides. He and his wife and two children were original members of the
first church, of which he was one of the first deacons. All of his children
and many of his descendants were members of that church, and nearly all
have been more or less proficient in music. He m. Sarah, dau. Capt.
Samuel and Sarah (Lampson) Bancroft; b. Reading, Mass., Feb. 19,
1722; d.——.

Children:

i. Sarah, b. March 1, 1743; m. J. Walden of Warner, N. H.

ii. Abigail, b. Jan. 22, 1746; m. Maj. Asa Bailey. She published an autobiography, (See Bibliography of Newbury); d. Bath, N. H., Feb. 11, 1815; 17 c.

iii. Mary, b. Feb. 6, 1748; m. Oct. 27, 1772 Richard Minchin who died at
Crown Point, in the revolutionary war; 2d, Uriah Cross, and removed
about 1794, to near Lake Champlain.

iv. James, b. Oct. 18, 1750; m. 1780, Zylpha Smith, 2d, Mehetabel Hidden; removed to Ohio, 1809, served in the revolutionary war; died about 1814.
 v. Judith, b. Jan. 19, 1753; m. Dea. Thomas Brock, q. v.
2 vi. William, b. Apr. 24, 1755; d. June 14, 1804.
3 vii. Bancroft, b. June 4, 1757.
 viii. Ezra, b. Oct. 8, 1759, d. y.
 ix. Susannah, b. Mar. 3, 1763.
4 x. Ezra, b. June 2, 1765.

2 WILLIAM,[2] (James[1]) b. Concord, N. H., April 24, 1755; m. 1777. Mabel Whittlesey of East Guilford, Conn. They had eleven c., most of whom settled in Bath. Josiah settled in Groton, and was the father of Rev. Jacob J. Abbott, D. D.
5 Moses, eldest son of William, lived in Bath, near the mouth of the Ammonoosuc.

3 BANCROFT,[2] (James[1]) b. Concord, N. H., June 4, 1757; farmer on homestead 1783; m 1787, Lydia, dau. Ebenezer White, q. v. (Jan. 1, 1763-June, 1853); Ad. to 1st ch. 1822; served in rev. war in Bedel's regiment, and in local service; learned geometry, surveying, and navigation, without the aid of teachers; was proficient in mathematics; held town offices; d. Oct. 29, 1829.
 Children:
6 i. Thomas, b. June 8, 1788.
 ii. Merrill, b. Feb. 9, 1790; d. Apr. 12, 1794.
7 iii. James, b. Feb. 14, 1792.
 iv. Elizabeth, b. March 22, 1794; d. young.
 v. Mary, b. June 6, 1795; m. Feb. 10, 1816, Amos Bailey, her cousin; d. Oct. 24, 1834, Chicago, Ill.
8 vi. Ebenezer, b. Nov. 6, 1797.
 vii. Nicholas, b. Sept. 18, 1799; physician (Dartmouth Medical College 1827); m. Aug. 12, 1829, Mira Jewett of St. Johnsbury; rem. to Troy, O. 1834; two sons, and a dau. who m. Dr. Harter of St. Louis; d. Lafayette, Ind,, 1871.
 viii. Sarah, b. March 11, 1802; m. February, 1829, Marshall Southard, (b. Auburn, Mass., March 14, 1796; grad. Dartmouth College 1820; two years at Andover Theological Seminary; ordained Dec. 20, 1828; never settled, but occasionally preached; farmer where the late S. M. Rollins lived; rem. to Lyme, N. H., where he died March 12, 1857.) Six c.

4 EZRA,[2] (James[1]) b. June 2, 1765; m. 1786, Hannah Abbott; farmer in Newbury and Bath; revolutionary soldier; d. July 5, 1842.
 Children:
 i. Reuben, b. Dec. 26, 1786; m. about 1809; d. in Canton, Maine. From his recollections in 1869, many of the earlier incidents in this volume are given.
 ii. Hannah, b. Jan 24, 1790.
 iii. Ezra, b. Sept. 19, 1791; lived in Sutton, Vt.; five c.
 iv. Susan, b. Feb. 21, 1793; m. Thos. Martin of Bradford.

5 MOSES,[3] (William,[2] James[1]) m. 1802, Lucy Willis, (who d. July 13, 1842); 2d Aug. 17, 1844, Mrs. Lucy Wells; d. May 7, 1856.
 Children:
9 i. Myron, b. Apr. 24, 1803.
 ii. Adams, b. Aug. 7, 1804. Lived in Troy, Vt.; d. May 22, 1881.
 iii. Cynthia, b. March 5, 1806; m. Jonathan B. Rowell; d. in Ill. 1866.
10 iv. William B., b. Dec. 15, 1807.
 v. Lucy M,, b. Oct. 18, 1809; m. John C. Woods; d. in Ill.
 vi. Charity, b. July 7, 1811; m. B. F. Rowell of Ill.
 vii. Mabel, b. May 9, 1813; m. Moses Hastings; d. July 11, 1877.
 viii. Moses C., b. May 25, 1815, d. y.
 ix. Amanda, b. Feb. 9, 1817; m. Michael Bartlett; d. April 10, 1864.
 x. Moses, b. Dec. 27, 1818; d. July 31, 1889; lived in Bath. His son, Chester, is a prominent business man of Woodsville.
 xi. Sarah A., b. March 21, 1821; d. Danville, P. Q., March 17, 1882; m. March, 1845, Leonard Bishop of Landaff; lived in Newbury, 1865 till death; 5 c.

---

*Early dates from Abbott" Register. Prepared in part by Prof. G. N. Abbott.

xii. Albert L., b. Apr. 17, 1823. Still living in New Orleans.
xiii. Milo J., b. June 22, 1825; d. in Kansas.
xiv. Ira, b. Feb. 17, 1828; d. April 3, 1899.

6 THOMAS,[3] (Bancroft,[2] James[1]) b. June 8. 1788; m. 1st, Sept. 17, 1812 Anna,
    dau. Stephen Powers (b. May 12, 1792; d. Sept. 1, 1841); 2d, Dec. 23,
    1841, her sister Abigail (b. Sept. 7. 1797); farmer and wheelwright, his
    shop was on Hall's brook, a little above Chalmers sawmill, and his house,
    burned 1862, stood where A. A. Bowen's lower house is now; rem. to
    Cazenovia, N. Y., where he d.
    Children:
    i.   Emily, b. Nov. 16, 1813; died Jan. 15. 1844.
    ii. William C., b. July 4. 1815; rem. to Ohio.
    iii. Martha P,, b. Nov. 25, 1817; m. J. O. Wilkins of Sidney, O.; d. Dec. 24, 1894.
    iv. Mary, b. Dec. 20, 1819; m. Guy C. Kelsey of Sidney, O.; d. Oct. 16, 1895.
    v.   George E., b. Oct. 7, 1824; went to Sidney, O., but d. in Cal. while mining.

7 JAMES,[3] Dea., (Bancroft,[2] James[1]) b. Feb. 14, 1792; lived for some years where
    R. E. Barnett now lives, building that house in 1819; later he rem. to the
    homestead; dea. in Cong. Ch. at W. N.; was justice of the peace and held
    other town offices. He took an active part in the anti-slavery struggle;
    m. 1st July 6, 1820, Elizabeth W., dau. of Peter Martin (b. June 29, 1791;
    d. Dec. 2, 1863); 2d, April 18, 1865, Phebe dau. of Asher Hunkins,(b. Feb;
    1807); d. March 7, 1870.
    Children:
11 i.   George Nelson, b. Aug. 4, 1823.
    ii. Alonzo J., b. June 26, 1825; d. March 4, 1849.
    iii. Elizabeth Chastina, b. May 16, 1828; m. Charles W. Eastman, q. v.

8 EBENEZER,[3] (Bancroft,[2] James[1]) b. Nov. 6, 1797; m. June 11, 1829, Rebecca, dau.
    of Robinson Brock, who after his death m. Gilman Brown of Topsham;
    (d. Nov. 18, 1897); farmer on the homestead till 1839; rem. to Bradford,
    thence to Topsham; returned to Newbury and lived where Mr. Johnston
    does on Rogers Hill; d. April 11, 1873.
    Children:
    i.   Hazen, b. June 10, 1830; He lives in California.
    ii.   Charles, b. June 20; d. June 21, 1832.
    iii. James B., b. June 30, 1833; d. in California.
    iv.   Chloe Ann, b. Feb. 18. 1836; m. Thomas Chadwick of Bradford.
    v.   Mary B., b. May 21, 1838; m. Dr. Nathaniel S. Boyce of Guildhall, q. v.
    vi.   Julia F., b. July 29, 1840; d. Jan. 31, 1842.
    vii. Martha S., b. Dec. 2, 1843; m. David C. White of Topsham; d. Jan. 5, 1901.

9 MYRON,[4] (Moses,[3] William,[2] James[1]) b. Bath, Apr. 24, 1803; m. 1st, Apr. 22,
    1826, Clarissa Willis (b. Aug. 24, 1808, d. Aug. 21, 1865,) 2d, Jan. 21,
    1866, Martha, dau. of Loved Leach of Troy; lived in Albany, Vt., Bath,
    and, after 1854, in Newbury, near Hall's Pond; d. Bath, while visiting
    there June 3, 1883.
    Children; lived in Newbury, except the last.
    i.   Nancy W., b. Oct. 25, 1829 at Albany, Vt.; m. Dec. 6, 1848 Ira S. Bailey (b.
         Canada, Jan. 30, 1829; d. March 19, 1891 blacksmith;) d. June 28, 1896;
         no c.
    ii. Horace N., b. Bath, March 17, 1835; m. Apr. 9, 1857, Lydia, dau. Alonzo
         Fleming; c. Edwin, d. 1861; a dau. d. 1864; Cora Ada, b.——; m. John M.
         Goodwin, q. v.; enlisted Dec. 31, 1863 in Co. D. 1st Vt. Cav., was taken
         prisoner; d. in Gen. Hospital June 30, 1864; farmer in N.
    iii. Myron Birney, b. Bath, Dec. 18, 1840; m. Apr. 27, 1865, Ellen M., dau. John
         N. Brock (b. Oct. 5, 1846). C: (1) Harry E., b. June 14, 1866; m. Feb.
         22, 1888, Josie E. Weare of Woodsville; in trade at Woodsville, Littleton
         and Chester, Vt.; c: (a) Maurice J., b. Aug. 7, 1889; (b) Charles W., b.
         Feb. 19, 1892; (c) Elmer W., b. Oct. 25, 1895. (2) Elmer B., b. Sept. 27,
         1871, salesman, kicked by a horse at his father's house Aug. 1, and d.
         Aug. 3, 1894. (3) Willie M., b. June 27, 1873. (4 and 5). Twins, Horace
         M., and John N., b. and d. June 7, 1880.
    iv. Harriet, b. Aug. 6, 1844; d. 1850.

10 WILLIAM B.,[4] (Moses,[3] William,[2] James[1]) b. Bath Dec. 15, 1807; m. October, 1835, Mary Ann, dau. Phineas Chamberlin (b. Bath, July 16, 1813); farmer of Bath, removed to Wells River 1859, and was in company with Mr. Wilder in the grist mill; was a justice of the peace, and held various public offices; d. Newbury, April 30, 1870.
   Children all b. in Bath:
   i. Julia, b. Oct. 7, 1836.
   ii. Eunice, b. Nov. 24, 1837.
   iii. Phineas, b. July, 1839; d. Sept. 25, 1840.
   iv. Ellen, b. Feb. 23, 1842; m. Col. Erastus Baldwin, q. v.
   v. Solon, b. June 28, 1845; m. Dec. 1, 1868, Helen M. Pearson; rem. Winchendon, Mass; watchmaker and jeweler.
   vi. Orrin S., b. March 17, 1848; m. Sept. 4, 1867, Ella J., dau. of Levi Tabor; he was employed by A. T. Baldwin & Co., as salesman for several years, then went into the boot and shoe business at St. Johnsbury, where he now resides. C. all born in Newbury: (1) William Tabor, b. Feb. 1886; fitted for college at St. Johnsbury Academy; grad. Dartmouth College 1890; teaching some years; principal of Manchester N. H. High School; lawyer in practice at Peoria, Ill., went to Porto Rico 1899; in practice there. Mr. Abbott rendered very efficient service as a Republican campaign speaker in the presidential contests of 1896, and 1900, in the west. (2) Ethel, b. January 1877; took a course at the Boston Conservatory of Music; member of a church choir at St. Johnsbury. (3) Guy H., b. November, 1878; fitted for college at St. Johnsbury Academy; now in Dartmouth College. (4) Ellen M , b. October, 1880; grad. of St Johnsbury Academy. (5) Harold S., b. October, 1889.

11 *GEORGE NELSON,[4] (James,[3] Bancroft,[2] James[1]) one of Newbury's most scholarly men, was born August 4, 1823, in the west part of the town. He came of good English stock which settled early in Eastern Massachusetts. His early training was from his labors upon his father's farm and his attendance upon the common or district school as it is more frequently named in Vermont. He early showed an aptitude for mathematics and all studies that brought into full play his active reasoning powers. When seventeen years of age, the next year after his father moved to South Newbury and became the owner of the farm where both father and son died, George Nelson began his attendance upon Newbury Seminary with which he was for a long time intimately connected, both as pupil and instructor. Rev. O. C. Baker, afterward Bishop Baker was principal at the time Mr. Abbott entered the seminary. Principal Clark T. Hinman was at the head of that institution a part of the time while Abbott was a student there. Before he had left the common school our ambitious young friend had conceived the idea of obtaining a liberal education and entered the seminary with a purpose of fitting for college. Although a good deal hampered for want of means he entered the University of Vermont as a freshman in 1844 but did not graduate with that class because he was compelled to be out of college for a year to earn the means of paying his college expenses. During that year he was called to teach mathematics and the languages in Newbury Seminary and made a very decided impression upon the classes that came under his instruction. When he returned to college he entered the class that graduated in 1849. Among his classmates were Henry A. Burt, a leading lawyer in north western Vermont; Melvin Dwinell, an officer in the confederate army; Roswell Farnham, late Governor of Vermont; John O. A. Fellows, an eminent lawyer in New Orleans; Elnathan E. Higbee, President of Emmettsburg (Med.) College; McKendree Petty, for more than thirty years professor in the University of Vermont; William Robertson, Queen's counsel in Montreal; William G. Shaw, Judge of the City Court of Burlington; Charles C. Torrey, a Congregational clergyman and Edwin Wheelock, Congregational minister at Cambridge, Vermont, for more than forty years. From the first Mr. Abbott stood high in the estimation of his classmates as a scholar and a man and when places were

*By Hon. Roswell Farnham.

assigned to the members of the graduating class for commencement day Mr. Abbott had the post of honor next to the highest. Three years after his graduation he was honored with the degree of Master of Arts and was selected to deliver the Master's oration. He was also elected a member of the Phi Beta Kappa Society, an honor given only to the first third of each class. Immediately after his graduation he taught for a while in Pottsdam, N. Y., but was obliged to leave on account of failing health. After recuperating a time on the home farm he became one of the corps of professors at Newbury Seminary, where he remained for several years. It was while teaching at Newbury at this time that he became acquainted with his wife, who survives him, Miss Mary Ladd of Dalton, N. H., sister of Hon. William S. Ladd, later one of the Judges of the Supreme Court of New Hampshire. They were married Nov. 27, 1853. After leaving Newbury Seminary, Prof. Abbott continued to teach, his wife assisting him in a most helpful manner. He taught for several years in Mrs. Worcester's Young Ladies' Seminary at Burlington, Vermont. He also had private pupils in the city and taught Latin and Greek in the City High School. In 1871, he was offered the professorship of Logic and Psychology in Mercersburg College, Pennsylvania, and held that position till June, 1877. This institution was a school of the Reformed Church in America, once known as the German Reformed Church. How highly he was esteemed in those days we may learn from a letter written by Prof. John B. Kieffer of that same college but now of the Franklin and Marshall College, of Lancaster, Pa., in which he says. "We all had known him for many years, and had known only to respect him for his many noble traits. Indeed when he left Mercersburg I was but beginning to know him as he really was and our correspondence afterwards, as well as the testimony of such men as Dr. Buckham, confirmed the estimate I was then forming of his character and his ability." After leaving the college at Mercersburg, Prof. Abbott retired to the farm in Newbury where he had spent so many of his boyhood days. He carried however to the farm the characteristics and scholarly habits that were his when in the professor's chair. Every scholar who knew him was impressed with the fact of his scholarly ability and his indefatigable diligence in his search for absolutia erities on whatever line he attempted. He was an accurate mathematician, a careful, painstaking linguist and in the professorship which he filled in Mercersburg he kept quite abreast with the logicians and psychologists of the time by original work as well as study of the thought of workers in those sciences both in English and German. He was licensed to preach by the Orange Association of Congregational ministers in the spring of 1859 and wrote and delivered quite a good many occasional sermons from that time on as long as he was able to do so. He wrote for some of the leading reviews and periodicals, viz: Bibliotheca Sacra, the organ of Andover Theological Seminary; The Mercersburg Review, published at Philadelphia; Journal of Speculative Philosophy, published at St. Louis, Mo., and others of equally high literary standing. After he came to his old home in 1877, he still continued his scholarly habit and has left quantity of manuscript. Prof. Abbott was a practical surveyor and the farmers, his neighbors, realizing his absolute accuracy frequently called upon him to run obscure lines and to find obliterated corners and landmarks. He was also somewhat of a road builder. Prof. Abbott died Feb. 12, 1900, in the maturity of his remarkable mental powers and before any sign of the weakness of old age made its appearance. His widow and three children survive him.

Children:

i.   Irving, b. Chester, Vermont, Oct. 5, 1856; student at Mercersburg College some years; farmer on homestead and surveyor.

ii. Carl, b. Newbury, April 19, 1859; student at Mercersburg College but did not graduate; studied law with his uncle, Judge Ladd at Lancaster, N. H., and admitted to the bar; clerk in the Treasury Department in Washington; now in practice in Boston.

iii. Helen Maie, b. Burlington, June 24, 1867; studied for some years at the Conservatory of Music, Boston; teacher of music at a college in Springfield, Mo; then at New London, N. H. Academy; now at Perkins Institution for the Blind at South Boston.

ABBOTT.

ROYAL H., b. Andover, Maine, came to Newbury in 1868, and settled at Boltonville.
Children:
i. William H., d. in United States service.
ii. Elizabeth A., m. Nelson S. Forsyth; d. July, 1886.
iii. Martha, m. James Gardner, q. v.
iv. Edwin R., m. Ida, dau. of Valentine and Mary Morse of Haverhill; c., (1) Lewis W., b. Dec. 26, 1877. (2) Henry, b. Jan. 29, 1880. (3) Mary B., b. Feb. 3, 1886. (4) Frank G., b. June 22, 1888; d. Sept. 7, 1889.

ADAMS.

JOHN and ABIGAIL Adams were from Milton, Mass., who rem. to Wayland and are buried there.
JOSEPH, their son, b. in Milton in 1759; m. Aug. 14, 1793, Betsey Davis (b. New Bedford, 1765; d. Aug. 14, 1799); d. Concord, Mass., in 1830. They had five children, of whom Joseph, b. Littleton, Mass., May 2, 1796, d. June 1, 1863. He m. Roxalana, dau. of Daniel Hoar of Concord, probably of the same family as Senator Hoar (b. 1802, d. 1838.) Their son, Henry W. Adams, was b. in Concord, Mass., Nov. 17, 1825. When fourteen years of age he went to learn the paper trade at Cooperstown, N. Y., and in 1852, came to Wells River, and operated the old Ira White mill, in company with Union Durant, making straw paper. In 1856, they bought the new building east of the old mill, which, in 1857, they fitted up with new machinery for the manufacture of manila tissue, which has been their product in all these years since 1857. The reputation of their goods was very high, and their product always met with a ready sale being considered A No. 1, all the years operated by Durant & Adams, and by the Adams Paper Co. The partnership of Durant & Adams lasted thirty-seven years. In the meanwhile they owned and operated paper mills in West Derby, Bradford and Bellows Falls. This last mill was burned, with considerable loss, in 1866. They also owned and managed the Coösuck House, at Wells River, and the livery stable connected with it. In 1883, Mr. Durant died, and the mill was sold to Deming, Learned & Co. At the death of Mr. Learned the mill was sold to Franklin Deming and Henry W. Adams, who formed a partnership under the name of the Adams Paper Co. In 1895, the mill was sold to Warren Moore of Bellows Falls, but continues under the same name as before. While owned by Deming, Learned & Co. the mill was repaired, enlarged and equipped with more modern works, with great improvement in product and quality. On account of impaired health, Mr. Adams retired from his position as manager. He m. in Nashua, N. H., Aug. 31, 1848, Nancy Jackson, dau. of Abel and Varazina (Tower) Wright, b. 1828.
Children:
i. Flora Louise, b. Cooperstown, N. Y., July 6, 1851; m. Jan. 4, 1871, Oscar Cutler Hatch, now of Littleton, N. H., q. v.
ii. George Henry, b. Newbury, March 9, 1857; m. Martha Frances Sherman of Waltham. He has long held an important position in the American Watch Co., of Waltham, Mass., c., (1) George Harold, b. Oct. 31, 1879. (2) Roxalana, b. Aug. 2, 1883. (3) John Sherman, b. 1892. Mr. H. W. Adams has lived in Wells River since 1852, was town representative for the biennial term of 1876-77, has held most of the other town offices and was elected a deacon in the Congregational church in 1890.

AITKIN.

JOHN, son of Andrew and Margaret (Drummond) Aitkin; b. Star-Markinch, Fifeshire, Scotland, Dec. 3, 1813; m. 1842, Catharine, dau. of George and Janet (Patterson) Thompson; b. in the same parish, Dec. 11, 1811. They sailed for America, and came to Newbury, in the same year, living on the farm now owned by Samuel Tuttle. In 1848. he bought the retired farm, cleared by William Miller, on which he has since lived; farmer and stone-mason. She d. at Newbury, July 21, 1899.

Children, all b. in N:
i. Andrew, b. Oct. 14, 1842. Served in the Union Army. (See war record.) He m. 1st March 21, 1866, Mary L., dau. George Chalmers (b. Newbury, Dec. 12, 1842; d. Bradford, July 7, 1867), one son b. June 15; d. Aug. 20, 1867. He m. 2d, May, 13, 1873, Agnes J., dau. Walter Arthur, (b. Feb. 13, 1843; d. April 26, 1887). He m. 3d, Feb. 20, 1890, Nellie E., dau. of S. R. Hancock of Bath. Chil. (1) Oscar J., b. June 18, 1891; (2) Irma Gratia, b. July 24, 1892; residence, Wells River since 1868, excepting two years at East Corinth; carpenter and builder.
ii. George, b. June 4, 1844; m. Oct. 14, 1880, Agnes, dau. of William Middleton, of Washington, D. C.; residence, Los Angeles, Cal.; in mining business.
iii. William, b. May 20, 1846, m. Nov. 6, 1888, at Kingman, Arizona, Mary Regia Netier; residence, Truston Canon, on the Santa Fe & Pacific R. R.; farmer and fruit raiser.
iv. Janet, b. Oct. 18, 1848; m. June 5, 1879, James Arthur.
v. Margaret, b. Sept. 25, 1850; m. 1st, Jan. 23, 1880, Martin J. Hall, who d. Ryegate, Nov. 8, 1890; 2d, Nov. 5, 1895, John R. McLennan.
vi. Mary Ann, b. Oct 1, 1854; m. March 28, 1877, Wm. H. Berry; c. (1) Charles A., b. April 3, 1878; (2) George H., b. Aug. 12, 1880; (3) Ernest R., b. Sept. 10, 1881; (4) Josephine M., b. Ryegate, June 6, 1894.

ALLEN.

John, b. Glasgow, Scotland, Dec. 31, 1797. He m. Jan. 4, 1822, Mary Wallace, (b. Oct. 2, 1795; d. Newbury, March 25, 1882.) Their children were all born in Scotland. They left Scotland in March, 1841, their voyage across the Atlantic in a sailing vessel taking seven weeks and four days, coming to Newbury in May, 1841, and settling on the James Wallace farm. They lived in Topsham some years, but returned to Newbury. Both spent their last years with their daughter, Mrs. Cheney. He d. at N. March 22, 1873.
Children:
i. Mary, b. Nov. 29, 1823; m. R. A. Brainerd of South Hadley, Mass.
ii. John, b. June 11, 1825; d. Topsham, Aug. 14, 1845.
iii. William Wallace, b. Kilbride Parish, Scotland, April 11, 1827. Farmer on Leighton hill; m. Susan F. Willey of Topsham; (b. Newbury Jan. 3, 1833; d. Sept. 22, 1898.) (1) Clara Ada, b. May 23, 1857; m. Oscar Dickey of Orange, Vt. (2) William W., b. Nov. 3, 1858; in the West. (3) Nellie M., b. June 22, 1862; m. Charles McLure of Ryegate. (4) May Belle, b. Oct. 17, 1872; m. William George.
iv. James, b. Jan. 15, 1830; m. Elizabeth Arthur of Ryegate; d. Newbury, April 7, 1899.
v. Ann, b. Feb. 1, 1832; m. W. F. Kimball of Topsham.
vi. Agnes, b. March 18, 1834; m. Harrison Cheney of Newbury, q. v.
vii. Matthew, b. March 18, 1836; served nine mos. from Sept. 1862 in Co. F., 22d Conn; he m. Laura A. Magoun of Topsham.
viii. Elizabeth, b. June 28, 1838; d. Newbury, Nov. 18, 1841.

ALLISON.

Robert, b. Leslie, Fifeshire, Scotland, 1815; m. in 1839, Isabella, dau. of John and Isabella (Russell) Kinnaird, (b. Leslie, March 6, 1817, d. Newbury, July 8, 1895.) In the same year they came to America, being six weeks on the passage to New York, and up the Hudson and Lake Champlain to Burlington, thence to Newbury, and he obtained work at his trade, which was that of a currier, at Haverhill. About 1842, they removed to Piermont and in 1845 to Newbury, on the farm now occupied by their son John; d Newbury, 1845.
Children:
i. David R., b. Haverhill, 1841. In 1862, entered the employ of the Passumpsic Railroad at Barton, Vt., and in 1864, became station agent at Wells River, a position which he still holds. When he entered the station all the work was done by himself, with the assistance of a boy. It now requires nine men to carry on the work; m. 1871, Emma Carpenter, and has c. (1) Elsie Belle, b. 1876; m. Karl Morse of Jersey City, N. J. (2) Grace Carpenter, b. 1877.

ii. Isabella, b. Piermont, 1842; d. Jan. 12, 1888.
iii. John R., b. Piermont, 1844; farmer on homestead; unm.
iv. Robert B., b. Newbury in 1846; went west in 1867; railroad conductor in Missouri many years; now settled on a farm at Tina in that state; m. 1882, Carrie Barrett. Nine c.

ARTHUR.

WALTER, son of Robert Arthur, b. Johnston, near Glasgow, Scotland, Dec., 1813; m. 1838, Elizabeth Smith, (b. Port Helen, Islay, Scotland, Nov. 14, 1819; d. Newbury Aug. 23, 1878.) They came to America in 1839, lived a short time in Topsham, one year in Groton, in Ryegate till 1871, when they came to Newbury, and settled on Jefferson Hill, where their son Andrew lives. They were members of the Presbyterian church; d. Ryegate, March 28, 1883.
Children:
i. Robert, b. Scotland Mar. 20, 1839; res., Hudson, Black Hawk Co., Iowa.
ii. Agnes J., b. Ryegate, Jan. 13, 1843; m. Andrew Aitkin, q. v.
iii. Andrew, b. Ryegate, March 2. 1845; unm.
iv. James, b. Topsham, March 12, 1847; m. June 5, 1879, Janet, dau. John Aitkin; c., (1) William N., b. May 26, 1881. (2) Walter J., b. April 6, 1883.
v. Sarah Isabel, b. Ryegate Feb. 16, 1854; m. Jan. 13, 1875, M. F. McDonald of South Ryegate; d. at the Mary Fletcher Hospital, Burlington, July 12, 1894.

*ATKINSON.

I. JOHN, son of Thomas and adopted son of his uncle, Theodore Atkinson of Bury, Lancashire, Eng., was born in Boston, 1640, was in Newbury, Mass., 1663, and there in 1664 m. Sarah Myrich. He was a hatter by trade.

II. JOHN,[2] (John[1]) b. 1667; m. Sarah Woodman.

III. ICHABOD,[3] (John,[2] John[1]) 5th son of John, b. Aug. 13, 1714; m. Priscilla Bailey, 1733; d. 1803.

IV. AMOS,[4] (Ichabod,[3] John,[2] John[1]) 3d son of Dea. Ichabod and Priscilla Bailey, b. March 20, 1754; m. Anna Bailey 1778; d. Nov. 11, 1817.

V. WILLIAM,[5] (Amos,[4] Ichabod,[3] John,[2] John[1]) son of Lieutenant Amos and Anna Bailey Atkinson, b. at Newburyport, Mass., Nov. 13, 1779; m. Anna, dau. of Col. Josiah and Sarah (Tappan) Little, (b. Nov. 29, 1783; d. Nov. 13, 1866.) She inherited the sterling qualities of her ancestors and filled the various positions of life with marked fidelity. In early life Mr. Atkinson was a hatter and afterwards in the book trade with his brother-in-law, Edward Little. The family came to this town in 1830, occupying first the Spring Hotel and after a few years moved into the house then standing on the corner where Mr. C. Francis' Darling now resides. In 1844, by an exchange of property with Hon. Tappan Stevens, Mr. Atkinson became owner of and moved into the house built by Horace Stebbins on the "Little Plain" in which his grandson, William H. Atkinson, now lives. He held many town offices, was one of the persons named in the act incorporating the Vermont Central Railroad in 1832 and in that incorporating the Bank of Newbury. Mr. and Mrs. Atkinson observed their golden wedding, and ten years later, April 10, 1864, celebrated the sixtieth anniversary of their marriage. They lived two years after this and died within a few months of each other; d. April 25, 1866. Their c. were all born in Newburyport, Mass.
Children:
i. William, b. Oct. 11, 1806; m. Sept. 2, 1829, Charlotte Adeline Reed. He was in the marine insurance business in New York city where he d. Nov. 15, 1862.
ii. Charles, b. May 18, 1808; m. Ann Eliza Bates Jan. 4, 1830. They went to Illinois in 1835, and became interested in the industries and enterprises of a new country. He was one of the original founders of Moline, Ill., and it has been said there was hardly a business of any large proportion in the city that was not indebted to him for aid. He accumulated property, and

_____
*Prepared by Mrs. Joseph Atkinson.

at his death April 27, 1887, made generous bequests to schools, churches and colleges. The tankards, plates and baptismal bowl used at communion service of 1st ch. in Newbury, were a gift from Mrs. Charles Atkinson in 1872.

1 iii. Joshua Tappan, b. Feb. 9, 1810, q. v.
2 iv. Joseph, b. Feb. 15, 1812, q. v.
    v. Moses L., b. July 27, 1814; grad. Dartmouth College 1838, Harvard Medical school 1844; m. May 7, 1845, Catharine M., dau. of Edmund Bartlett, Esq., Newburyport, Mass.; practiced his profession at Lawrence, Mass., where he d. Jan. 18, 1852. In 1866, Mrs. Atkinson bought the house built by Joseph Chamberlin on the Little Plain, which the son and daughter, Edmund B. and Martha W., usually occupy during the summer.
    vi. Judith Tappan, b. June 25, 1817; m. May 18, 1837, Gideon D. Dickinson of Lebanon, N. H. They lived a few years in Maine and in Boston. In 1850, Mr. Dickinson went to California and after his return they resided in Chicago and Moline, Ill., where she d. Dec. 17, 1876. Their two daughters were both m. the same day, Sept. 16, 1862. (1) Anna C., b. May 6, 1838; m. William D. Hawley and went immediately with him to Alexandria, Va., where he had a position in the Union army. She soon became a regular visitor at one of the hospitals and spent many hours each week ministering to the comfort of our sick and wounded soldiers. Of a delicate constitution she soon fell a victim to the infection of the place and after a short illness d. Dec. 7 of the same year less than three months after her marriage. (2) Mary L., b. Aug. 9, 1841; m. Charles H. Deere, a wealthy plow manufacturer of Moline, Ill.
3 vii. George H., b. May 10, 1819, q. v.
    viii. Josiah L , b. Feb. 14, 1823; m. July 4, 1854, Isabella Clarkson who d. May 30, 1894; m. 2d, Mrs. Jennie Booth Champlin, Feb., 1896. He was engaged in farming in Vermont, lumbering and mining in California and since then has been a successful real estate agent in Portland, Ore.

1 JOSHUA TAPPAN,[6] (William,[5] Amos,[4] Ichabod,[3] John,[2] John[1]) b Feb. 9, 1810; m. Emeline Little of Campton, N. H., Nov. 1, 1831. They moved to Whiteside Co., Ill., in 1835 and began life as pioneers, enduring the hardships and privations incident to settling a new country. Mr. Atkinson built the first house in Union Grove township and it was here that the first religious services in town were held. His best efforts were always given for the public good and every worthy project found in him a friend and helper. In 1875, he removed to Geneseo, Ill., where he died May 28, 1894.
    Children:
    i. Anna E., b. at Union Grove, Whiteside Co., Ill., Nov. 26, 1836—the first white child born in that vicinity. Graduated at Knox College, Galesburg, Ill., in 1856. After teaching some time in Illinois she came to Newbury to reside with her grandparents and Nov. 3, 1863, m. Edward P. Keyes who d. Aug. 28, 1881. Mrs. Keyes was a woman of untiring energy and rare executive ability. She abounded in her ministrations to the aged, the afflicted and poor, and was greatly interested in all the benevolent and missionary enterprises of the time. Especially was this true of home missions. To this object she gave generously, not only of her means, but also of her time and influence. She d. suddenly at the home of her brother, Moline, Ill., Easter morning, April 15, 1900. Buried at the Ox-bow.
    ii. James W.
    iii. Sarah L., res. at Moline, Ill.
    iv. Josiah L.
    v. George L., deceased.

2 JOSEPH,[6] (William,[5] Amos,[4] Ichabod,[3] John,[2] John[1]) b. Feb. 15, 1812. Farmer in Newbury on Musquash Meadow and held various town and county offices. State Senator 1847-8. Delegate to the Constitutional Convention 1850; member of the 1st Cong. ch. 52 years, and before that of the 2nd Cong. ch. in Newburyport, Mass.; chosen deacon in 1871; m. 1st, Oct. 8, 1835, Charlotte, dau. of Moses and Elizabeth (Merrill) Swasey (b. June 3, 1814, d. Sept. 9, 1850); m. 2nd, June 4, 1851, Frances, dau. of

EV. GEO. H. ATKINSON, D. D.

JOSEPH ATKINSON.

Nathaniel and Fanny (Gould) Farrington of Walden. Vt.; d. suddenly Mar. 5, 1883, from heart failure, brought about by excitement caused by a fire which broke out in the church building the day before his death.
Children:

5　i.　William Hazen, b. Oct. 19, 1838, q. v.
　　ii.　George Little, b. May 28, 1842; d. Aug. 9, 1860.
　　iii.　Charles Henry, b. Aug. 13, 1845. Farmer in Illinois; m. Nov. 5, 1885, Mrs. Alice Little Hale, dau. of Capt. Joshua and Sophia C. (Tenney) Hale, Newburyport, Mass.; d. May 31, 1888.

3　GEORGE H.,[6] (William,[5] Amos,[4] Ichabod,[3] John,[2] John[1]) b. May 10, 1819. Fitted for college at Newbury Seminary and other academies, earning funds by teaching. Graduated at Dartmouth College 1843, Andover Theological Seminary 1846, appointed by the A. B. C. F. M. to do missionary work among the Zulus, So. Africa, but his health forbade his going to that climate. In 1847, he was commissioned by A. H. M. society to establish their first mission on the Pacific coast in Oregon, at that time our only territory there. He was m. Oct. 8, 1846, to Nancy Bates of Springfield, Vt. Ordained in the Cong. church, Newbury, Vt., Jan. 24, 1847, the ordination sermon preached by Rev. George W. Campbell being printed. In Oct. they sailed from Boston via Cape Horn and the Sandwich Islands for their mission. At Honolulu they had to wait three months for a vessel bound for Oregon, and did not reach the Columbia river till June 12, 1848. He settled in Oregon City where he organized the first Cong. church in Oregon, of which he was pastor for fifteen years. Pastor of the 1st Ch. Portland, Ore., ten years. Mr. Atkinson devoted all his leisure time to pushing forward the cause of education in the territory, and it was through his efforts that the public school system was established by the legislature in 1849. He was school superintendent at Portland and was efficient and active in building up the system of public schools established in that city. He founded in Oregon an academy which afterwards became the Pacific University of which he was one of the original incorporators and for more than forty years Secretary of its board of trustees. Received in 1865 the degree of D. D. from Dartmouth College. In 1872 he became general missionary for Oregon and in 1880 general Superintendent of Missions for Oregon and Washington. He lived to see the one church of Oregon grow into ninety-three, the result largely of his long continued and faithful services. During the last nine years of his life, his labors were more abundant than ever, his journeyings in the care of the churches averaging more than eight thousand miles a year. One of his last trips was to Tacoma, Wash., where he owned some lots and designed to give part of their value for a church building. Upon his arrival the need seemed to him so urgent that he gave the whole amount, $3,000, for the 1st Ch. of Old Tacoma. After his death it was incorporated as the Atkinson Memorial Ch.; d. Portland, Ore., Feb. 25, 1889.
Children:

　　i.　George H., b. Sept. 16, 1849; grad. Dartmouth College, 1871; Long Island Medical College 1873. He had an extended practice as physician and surgeon in Brooklyn, N. Y., and was popular in political and social circles. While operating upon a charity patient suffering from blood poisoning at L. I. Hospital, the poison entered his system through a scratch on his finger, causing the loss of his own life while saving that of his patient; m. Sept. 21, 1877, Clara, dau. of H. N. and Lamira Chamberlain, Newbury, Vt.; d. Dec. 27, 1884; one son George N., b. Feb. 18, 1881; d. Sept. 2, 1883.
　　ii.　Anna L. B., b. Oct. 24, 1851; grad. at Mills Seminary, Cal., 1869; m. Oct. 8, 1872, Frank M. Warren, who is the owner of salmon canneries, Columbia River, Oregon.
　　iii.　Edward M. L., b. Dec. 23, 1854; grad. Pacific University 1876; Columbia Law School, N. Y., 1879; lawyer at Portland, Oregon.

5　WILLIAM HAZEN,[7] (Joseph,[6] William,[5] Amos,[4] Ichabod,[3] John,[2] John[1]) b. Oct. 19, 1838. Farmer on homestead. Served in Co. H, 12th Vermont, in the civil war; m. Jan. 11, 1865, Ella, dau. of A. Hazen and Maria (Lang) Hibbard of Bath, N. H.; c., (1) Charlotte, b. Jan. 19, 1867; m. Oct. 12,

1892, Francis S. E. Gunnell; res. in Brooklyn, N. Y. (2) Frances M., b. Aug. 23, 1871; grad. Vt. University 1895. Librarian of Tenney Memorial Library. (3) Anna Isabel, b. May 15, 1878; grad. Bradford, Mass., Academy, 1898, and Pratt Institute, Brooklyn, N. Y., 1900.

ATWOOD.

The Atwoods were formerly quite prominent but they have long disappeared, and have left meagre records behind them.

1 JOHN ATWOOD, senior, and his family came here, probably, before 1830, as his certificate from the Orford, N. H., ch is dated in that year. He settled on and owned the farm now that of J. J. Smith. He d. in July, 1862, aged 95, and his wife, who was Mehetabel Gage, of Pelham, Mass., d. May 23, 1844, aged 77.
Children:
    i. Amos, no record.
2 ii. John, b. Jan. 15, 1796.
3 iii. Benjamin, b. August, 1797.
    iv. Mehetabel.
4 v. Hannah, b. Nov. 26, 1803.
    vi. Almira, b. 1806; m. Bailey White, (q. v.) ; d. April 7, 1839.
    vii. Mary Ann, b. 1810; m. I. H. Olmstead, (q. v.) ; d. March 10, 1842.

2 JOHN, JR.,[2] (John[1]) b. Jan. 15, 1796; farmer at W. N.; long a member, steward and class-leader in the Methodist church; town representative, 1844. He was also in business with his brother, Benjamin, at So. N He m. 1st, Feb. 12, 1829, Eliza, dau. of Levi Rogers, and widow of Bradley Doe, (b. May 4, 1807; d. Oct. 16, 1853.) 2d, Mary Ann Dow. 3d, Judith, dau. of Robinson Brock and widow of Wm. A. Boyce, (b. Feb. 23, 1808; d. Jan. 26, 1897). He d. March 3, 1883.
Children, all by 1st m.:
i. Amanda Rogers, b. April 13, 1830. She m. at Richmond, Ind., Oct. 10, 1855, Henry Clay Moore, who d. at St. Louis, April 13, 1889; res. Marietta, O., and afterward at St. Louis. She d. at St. Louis, Mo., Oct. 31, 1886. C., (1) Caroline A., b. Marietta, Sept. 23, 1856; d. Newbury, Aug. 23, 1864. (2) Henry Clay, b. Marietta, Sept. 27, 1858; d. St. Louis, Sept. 28, 1863. (3) John Atwood, b. St. Louis, Feb. 9, 1861. Graduated Yale College, 1883. In real estate business New York city. (4) Daniel Agnew, b. St. Louis, Dec. 4, 1864. Graduated Yale College, 1886; res. Pittsburgh, Pa.; president of the Pittsburgh Screw and Bolt Co. He m. Oct. 10, 1889, Nellie Card of Pittsburgh. C., Harriet D., b Feb. 19, 1892, and William C., b. June 25, 1893. (5) Paul, b. St. Louis, Aug. 26, 1867; d. Colorado, May 25, 1886.
ii. John. b. Aug. 8, 1831; d. March 29, 1854.
iii. George L. B., b. Aug. 2, 1833; d. Dec. 20, 1854.

3 BENJAMIN,[2] (John[1]) b. August, 1797. He was long in active business at South N., part of the time with his brother John, owning the saw and grist mill, and brick-yard. He made the brick of which the seminary building was built, and most of the brick houses at the Street, and S. N. The hamlet at S. N., after called Happy Hollow, was then known as Atwood's Mills. At the time of the famine in Ireland, large quantities of oat meal were ground there and sent to relieve the suffering. He built several of the houses in that place. His own, a two-story brick house, standing where George Tuttle's brick house now does, was burned in the fire of 1850. Benjamin Atwood was also prominent in the Methodist church, and so punctual and regular in his attendance that he was sometimes called the "Sabbath bell." He m. 1st. Aug. 19, 1819, Anna, dau. of William Doe, (b. Oct. 24, 1801 · d. Jan. 6, 1847). C., William D., and John. 2d. Mrs. Judith Richardson. C. (i.) Annie m. July 17, 1867, Rev. Alfred B. Drew of the New Hampshire conference. (ii.) Carrie. He died Feb. 10, 1854. William D. Atwood, carpenter and farmer in Newbury; served in the civil war (see soldier's record) and d. in the Soldier's Home, at Milwaukee. in 1893. He m. Sarah Louisa, dau. of Dea. John Buxton. (For account of herself and family see Buxton family.)

4 HANNAH,[2] (John[1]) b. Nov. 26, 1803; m. Feb. 14, 1832, Joseph Nason of Orford. They settled in Newbury, near Round pond, on the farm, and built the house

where Mrs. A. J. Bailey now lives. Later, they moved, and built the house in which Albert Kendrick lives, and carried on the saw mill. She d. June 9, 1887. Joseph Nason, b. Feb. 11, 1806; d. Nov. 5, 1890.

Children:

i. Atwood P., killed in his father's saw mill, March 25, 1860, aged 24 years, 7 months. He was rendered totally deaf in childhood by scarlet fever.

ii. Joseph M., served in Co. H, 12th Vt.; d. in service, April 17, 1863, aged 21 years, 6 months. Buried at W. N.

AUSTIN.

WILLIAM R., b. Upton, Mass., 1816; carpenter at Wells River, was also in the hotel, and other business at different times; came to Wells River 1839, or 1840; rem. to Wakefield, Mass., 1890; m. 1st Mrs. Sarah (Williams) Gage, who d. Sept., 1841, leaving one daughter, Sarah M.; m. 2d, Oct. 13, 1844, Hepzi E., dau. of Jonas Tucker, (b. July 4, 1811, d. Apr. 3, 1890); one son, W. G.; d. Wakefield, Mass., 1892.

1 SARAH MARIA, b. Newbury, Wells River, Sept. 2, 1841; m. Wells River, Jan. 1, 1867, Allen L. Dunshee; d. Wakefield, Mass., April 2, 1883.

Children:

i. Henry A., b. Wells River, Nov. 12, 1867; m. Malden, Mass., Nov. 12, 1894, Josie G. L. Scales.

ii. Carl E., b. Wakefield, Mass., Aug. 15, 1869; d. Lamanda, Cal., Feb. 24, 1897.

iii. Mark A., b. W. June 22, 1871; m. Chicago, Ill., Aug. 26, 1899, Emma C. Menardi.

iv. Sarah M., b. Nov. 23, 1873; d. Oct. 31, 1874.

v. William G., b. Feb. 13, 1875; d. July 24, 1875.

vi. Edgar L., b. Oct. 25, 1879.

vii. Edmund A., (twin to above) d. July 13, 1880.

viii. Dorothy E., b. May 31, 1882.

2 WILLIAM G., b. Sept. 18, 1851; d. Oct. 8, 1873. Teller in National Bank at Wells River. Cashier of Barre bank at time of death.

AVERY.

(Ancestry from the "Averys of Groton, Conn.")

I. CHRISTOPHER, b. in England about 1590. Came to America from Wiltshire, 1630-31. Lived in Gloucester, then in Boston, but settled finally, in New London, Conn., where he d. in 1679. His wife remained in England.

II. JAMES,[2] (Christopher[1]) b. in Eng. about 1620; came to America with his father; lived at first in Gloucester, where he m. Joanna Greenslade in 1643. In 1651, he became one of the first settlers of New London, Conn. In 1656, he built in Groton a house still standing; captain in the Narragansett fight and a prominent man in his time.

III. JAMES,[3] (James,[2] Christopher[1]) eldest son, b. Dec. 16, 1646; m. 1669, Rebecca Stallyan; d. Aug. 22, 1748, in his 102d year.

IV. EBENEZER,[4] (James,[3] James,[2] Christopher[1]) b. May 1, 1678; m. June 19, 1708, Dorothy, dau. of John Parke, who d. Nov. 6, 1732; d. July 19, 1752.

V. SIMEON,[5] (Ebenezer,[4] James,[3] James,[2] Christopher[1]) b. April 25, 1730; m. in Groton, Conn., Oct. 25, 1750, Sarah, dau. of Nathan Niles, (b. Oct. 23, 1732; d. Apr. 12, 1783); d. Sept. 18, 1790.

VI. NATHAN, b. Groton, Conn., March 31, 1759; enlisted in March, 1776 for nine months under Capt. Edward Mott and was in the battle of White Plains, Oct. 28, 1776. He also served three months at Fort Trumbull. He was one of the garrison at Fort Griswold when it was captured and most of the men were massacred, he being one of the few who escaped unhurt. After the war he came to Vermont and lived in Fairlee, and in Bradford, coming to Newbury in 1796. He settled on the farm where James Wallace now lives, and was a member of the Cong. ch.; m. in Hebron, Conn., Feb. 20, 1782, Anna Ayers, (b. March 31, 1758; d. May 22, 1840). He d. Jan. 16, 1841.

Children:
1	i.	Nathan, b. March 6, 1786; d. Aug. 21, 1845.
　　ii.	Nancy, b. March 17, 1788; m. Daniel Meader.
2	iii.	George W., b. Dec. 12, 1789; d. May 23, 1863.
3	iv.	Simeon, b. July 19, 1791; d. Feb. 19, 1858.
　　v.	Sarah A., b. May 7, 1793; d. unm. Aug. 21, 1817.
4	vi.	John A., b. Aug. 18, 1795; d. April 25, 1863.

1	NATHAN, b. Fairlee, March 6, 1786; m. 1st in Newbury, Sept. 29, 1808,
　　Sarah White (b. June 19, 1783; d. Oct. 22, 1841); 2d, 1843, Maria Virgin,
　　(b. 1805; d. Jan. 16, 1859). He lived many years on Jefferson Hill where
　　the late Alvah James long lived, building that house; farmer and surveyor;
　　d. Aug. 21, 1845.
　　Children:
　　i.	Eben, b. July 31, 1809; m. Aug. 14, 1836, Harriet Gould of South Reading,
　　　　Mass.; d. March 21, 1861, at S. Reading; one c. who d. Nov. 12, 1858.
　　ii.	Samuel Powers, b. Apr. 19, 1811; m. 1830, Lydia Crane of S. Reading, who
　　　　d. May 12, 1861; d. Feb. 21, 1859.
　　iii.	Mary Ann, b. April 7, 1813; m. James M. Avery. Both d. in Jan., 1883,
　　　　leaving two c., Osman who d. one week after his parents, leaving 4 c.;
　　　　Arthur H., now in Alabama, also one dau., Ella, d. y.
　　iv.	Sally, b. Aug. 12, 1815; m. Thomas Hunter; d. May 10, 1865, q. v.
　　v.	Nathan A., b. Oct. 6, 1844; served in Co. D. 1st Vt., 1861, and in Co. H, 4th
　　　　Vt.; d. in hospital March 23, 1863.

2	GEORGE W., b. Dec. 12, 1789; m. in Barnet Sept. 20, 1816, Vasti Virgin,
　　who d. Apr. 11, 1872. Served in the war of 1812, in Capt. Levi Roger's
　　Co. of detached militia, 5 mo. 27 d. Farmer on homestead; d. May 23,
　　1863.
　　Children:
　　i.	Mary Ann, b. Dec. 30, 1817; m. Luke Temple, q. v.
　　ii.	Park, b. Apr. 23, 1819, served in Co. H, 12th Vt. from Oct. 4, 1862, till went
　　　　out July 14, 1863; m. July 9, 1844, Jane, dau. of David Edwards; several
　　　　c., no record. Went to Kansas.
　　iii.	Charles, b. Dec. 26, 1821; d. Nov. 1, 1885, in N. H.
　　iv.	Peter, b. 1823; d. y.
　　v.	Margaret, b. March 7, 1828; m. John Edwards, q. v.
　　vi.	Harriet, b. May 20, 1830; m. June 14, 1864, Henry Boyce; d. Jan. 26, 1890.
　　vii.	Jane Wallace, b. March 23, 1832; m. James Edwards, q. v.
　　viii.	Caroline Kimball, b. July 10, 1834; m. Reed Virgin of Piermont.
　　ix.	Hannah, b. 1836; d. y.

3	SIMEON, b. July 19, 1791; m. July 14, 1814, Hannah, dau. of Col. Joshua
　　Bayley, (b. 　　1786; d. Oct. 1825)); 2d, Betsey Brown; 3d, Eleanor
　　Cochrane. He d. Feb. 19, 1858.
　　Children; 5 by 1st m., 3 by 2d:
5	i.	Austin Ayers, b. Oct. 11, 1814; d. April 18, 1888, q. v.
　　ii.	Simeon. He built the "Dr. Watkins house" at the village; afterwards went
　　　　west.
　　iii.	George W. He built the house south of the Dr. Watkins house; m. Jan. 2,
　　　　1848, Louisa, dau. of James Wallace; d. in Wisconsin.
　　iv.	Anna A.
6	v.	Bailey, b. Sept. 6, 1825; d. Oct. 9, 1883, q. v.
　　vi.	Fred, mustered into Co. C, 3d Vt., July 16, 1861. Taken prisoner and d. at
　　　　Andersonville, Ga., March 13, 1865.
　　vii.	Laura.
　　viii.	Dau., d. y.

4	JOHN AYERS, b. Bradford, Aug. 18, 1795. Came to Newbury with his parents
　　and fitted for college, at Haverhill Academy; grad. Middlebury 1826;
　　ordained a Congregational minister at Pomfret, Vt., Sept. 24, 1828;
　　missionary in this state four years; in the ministry 1832-46; editor of the
　　Religious Recorder 1847-55. This paper was afterwards merged into the
　　Evangelist. He m. Jan. 14, 1829, Emeline, dau. of Nathan G. Baldwin of
　　Monkton, Vt.; two c. of whom one is living; d. Syracuse, N. Y., April 25,
　　1863.

5 AUSTIN,[3] (Simeon,[2] Nathan[1]) b. Newbury, Oct. 11, 1814, on the farm now owned by John Allison. Lived a short time at Hartford, Conn., then returned to Newbury and bought of Joseph Atkinson the sawmill at Newbury Street, which he conducted many years, adding a small grist-mill; m. at Hartford. Conn., Dec. 18, 1836, Sarah Maria Hayes, who d. Aug. 26, 1871, aged 60 yrs, 1 mo., 16 days; d. April 18, 1888.

    Children, all but the 1st b. in Newbury :
- i. Sarah Amelia, b. Hartford, Conn., July 18, 1839; d. March 4, 1842.
- ii. Hannah Maria, b. July 16, 1841. Res. Boston.
- iii. Horace Ayer, b. Sept. 18, 1843; served in a N. Y. regiment in the civil war; m. Sept. 20, 1865, Clara A. Simmons; res. N. Y. City. C., (1) Edgar Leon, b. July 7, 1867; (2) Austin D., b. Nov. 25, 1869; (3) Joseph L., b. Feb. 3, 1871; (4) Clara May, b. 1873.
- iv. Herbert Allen. b. Jan. 16, 1846; m. Nov. 16, 1877, Addie A. Sumner, who d. Nov. 14, 1899, aged 54 yrs, 6 mo. 24 days; m. 2nd, Dec. 3, 1900, Mrs. Lupien: c., (adopted) Gertrude E., b. March 22, 1882.
- v. Marshall Johnson, b. March 18, 1848; m. Nov. 19, 1878, Della Perkins of Walden; res. Newbury; c., Clarence, b. Aug. 1881: d. Oct. 1882.
- vi. Lucy Graham. b. Jan. 22, 1851; m. 1879, Joseph LeMate; c., Sarah F., b. Sept. 4, 1879; Fred, Joseph and Marshall, the three youngest b. in Boston.
- vii. Etta Chapin, b. July 21, 1853; m. 1880, Henry Houseman; d. Boston, Mass., Sept. 1, 1882; c., Etta L., b. Boston, Jan. 15. 1882.
- viii. Herman Austin, b. June 28, 1855; m. in Jackson, Mich.. April 21, 1887, Mrs. Jennie D. Jones; res. Belmont, N. H.
- ix. Nelson Loyd, b. Dec. 15, 1860; d. Dec. 13, 1886.
- x. John Ely, b. Feb. 3, 1861; m. Oct. 27, 1892, dau. of Edward Stebbins; c., Gladys Hyacinth; b. Oct. 3, 1899.

6 BAILEY,[3] (Simeon,[2] Nathan[1]) b. Sept. 6, 1825. Carpenter. He was brought up by his aunt, Miss Sally Bayley, whom he cared for in her old age. Justice of the peace many years. Lived in the house built by his grandfather, Col. Joshua Bayley, for whom he was named, but he dropped the "Joshua" and was always known as Bailey Avery. He came to his death by the fall of a scaffolding at Mr. Garland's house. He m. Aug. 17, 1856, Persis A., dau. of John Wilson, of Bradford. He d. Oct. 9, 1883.

    Children, all b. in Newbury:
- i. Etheline E , b. Feb. 29, 1860; m. April 30, 1884, Frank W. Powers. One son, Frank K., b. June 19, 1888. She d. Oct. 4. 1891.
- ii. Elmer E., b. April 26, 1861. Farmer and house carpenter. Res. N. He m. April 7, 1886, Elizabeth A. Carter, of Waterloo, P. Q.
- iii. Byron F., b. Feb. 13, 1864. Res. Moline, Ill. Machinist. He m., 1st, June 22, 1887, Sarah A. Appleton, of Canada, who d. at Moline, June 24, 1890. One c., Persis, b. Moline, May 9, 1889. He. m., 2d, Oct. 30, 1894, Phebe Appleton. One c.. Elmer E.
- iv. Bertha Frances, b. June 26, 1866. Res. Moline, Ill.
- v. Delbert W., b. Feb. 14; d. Sept. 8, 1870.
- vi. Bailey W., b. Dec. 29, 1873; m. Frances Walter of Moline, Ill.
- vii. John Hibbard, b. Dec. 16, 1881.

BAILEY—BAYLEY.

Newbury seems to have been very attractive to persons bearing this name, as there were no fewer than seven men among the early settlers. who were the pioneer ancestors of Newbury families named Bailey. These were General Jacob Bayley, Col. Frye Bayley, Capt. John G. Bayley and Enoch Bayley, who were descended from John Bayley of England, and Salisbury. Mass.; James Bailey and Charles Bailey, whose emigrant ancestor was James Bailey of England. and Rowley, Mass.; and Webster Bailey who was a descendant of Richard Bailey of England, and Rowley, Mass.

Of these seven families, only the first and the last have living representatives here at the beginning of the 20th century who bear the name.

John of England and Salisbury, spelled his name Bayly, and this usage was continued for a generation or so, then an e was introduced in the final syllable, making the spelling Bayley. General Bayley and his sons spelled their name in this way, but, about sixty years ago, it began to be the fashion among their descendants to spell it Bailey. A few of the families adhere to the original spelling, and in this volume the usage of each family is followed.

There have also been individuals and isolated Bailey families whose ancestry is unknown.

I. JOHN[1], a weaver of Chippenham, Eng., m. Eleanor Knight. They had children, John, Robert, Joanna, and perhaps others; in 1635, the two Johns, father and son, and the daughter, sailed for America, on the "Angel Gabriel," which left Bristol June 4th. This vessel, which was a ship of 240 tons, was wrecked upon Pemaquid Island, in the "great storm" of August 14–18 of that year. John, senior, lived two years at Newbury, Mass., then became the first settler of Salisbury, where he d. in November, 1651. His wife died in England, never venturing to cross the ocean to join her husband, and he never dared trust himself to the mercy of the waves again. The daughter m. William Huntington.

II. JOHN[2] (1613-1691) m. Eleanor Emery and settled at Newbury, Mass.

III. ISAAC,[3] b. Newbury, Mass., July 22, 1654, m. June 13, 1683, Sarah, dau. of John Emery. She d. April 1, 1694; he d. April 26, 1740.

IV. JOSHUA[4], b. Oct. 30, 1685; m. Sarah, dau. of Stephen and Sarah (Atkinson) Coffin. She d. Nov. 27, 1768; he d. Oct. 6, 1760. Farmer of Newbury, Mass.

Children:
i.   Stephen, b. March 1, 1708; m. Hannah Kelley; d. July 2, 1797.
ii. Joshua, b. 1712; m. Elizabeth Morse; d. Sept. 29, 1786. Some of their children settled in Berlin, Vt.
iii. Abner, b. Jan. 15, 1715. Minister at Salem, N. H., 58 years. He m. Mary Baldwin, who d. Feb. 18, 1789. He d. March 10, 1798. Their dau. Mary, m. William White, q. v.
iv. Enoch, b. Sept. 10, 1719. He was the father of Col. Frye Bayley, q. v.
v.   Sarah, b. Feb. 15, 1721; m. Edward Tappan. Their dau. Sarah m. Josiah Little, q. v.
vi. Judith, b. Feb. 13, 1724; m. Stephen Little.
vii. Abigail, (twin to Judith), m. Col. Moses Little, q. v.
viii. Jacob, b. July 19, 1726; d. March 1, 1815.
ix. John, b. May 4, 1729; d. July 13, 1819

V. GENERAL JACOB BAYLEY[1], son of Joshua and Sarah (Coffin) Bayley, was born at Newbury, Mass., July 19, 1726.* His father was a farmer in moderate circumstances, and it is not supposed that the son received more than the rudiments of an education. He married, at the age of nineteen, Oct. 16, 1745, Prudence, daughter of Ephraim and Prudence (Stickney) Noyes, b. April 10, 1725. The name Prudence is said to have been indicative of her character. She was in the sixth generation from Nicholas Noyes of England and Ipswich, Mass., and in the 5th from William Stickney of Lincolnshire, Eng., and Rowley, Mass. Not far from 1747, they removed with others to a part, formerly, of the town of Haverhill, Mass., known as Timberland, or Haverhill district. This part of Haverhill, with a portion of Amesbury, was cut off from those towns by the state line of 1741, and became a part of New Hampshire. Jan. 12, 1749, these tracts were chartered into a town by the name of Hampstead. Jacob Bayley soon became prominent in town affairs, and in the militia. When the French and Indian war broke out, he saw service as a lieutenant, in 1756, in Capt. Alcott's Co., after which he raised a company, of which he was chosen captain, which became a part of Col. Meserve's regiment, and saw service on Lake George. During the siege of Fort William Henry his company comprised a portion of the garrison, and he escaped from the massacre which followed its surrender, Aug. 7, 1757, by running barefooted to Fort Edward, a distance of twelve miles, outstripping his Indian pursuers, who had destined him to run the gauntlet. For his losses at the capitulation, he was allowed the sum of £14, 11, 6, by the

*The Bailey Genealogy says in one place July 2, 1726.

provincial assembly. He remained in the army much of the time till 1760, and was connected with Amherst's expedition. In 1759, he was in command of a detachment which marched through the Mohawk Valley to Oswego. (See Journal). He was appointed lieutenant-colonel in Goff's regiment, succeeding him as colonel, and was present at the siege and surrender of Montreal. His after career, as relates to this town and the country, forms part of the history of Newbury, and is detailed in the chapters of this history which relate to its settlement and the revolutionary war, "All of which he saw, and part of which he was." The following is a concise account of the positions of trust held by him: Justice of Peace and Quorum for the whole of the New Hampshire grants by N. Y. Assembly, 1766; Representative to New York Congress, 1775; Commissioner to administer oaths of office, 1775; Judge of Inferior Court of Common Pleas, 1772-77; nominated Brigadier General for Gloucester and Cumberland counties, May 23, 1776; confirmed by New York Provincial Congress, Aug. 1, 1776; Delegate to Continental Congress to carry remonstrance and petition, presented April 8, 1777; Member of Convention to draft the constitution of the state, at Windsor, July 2-8, 1777; Member of Council of Safety appointed at this convention July, 1777; Member of first Council in 1778; Agent to Continental Congress, 1777; Member of the Council, 1778-79, 1784-94; Member of Constitutional Convention 1773, 1793; Member of Court of Confiscation, March, 1778; Commissary General of the Northern Department, under appointment from Washington, 1777, "These positions," says Joshua Coffin, in his History of Newbury, Mass, "involved great responsibilities, and subjected him to danger, difficulties and sacrifices of an extraordinary character, and many anecdotes might be related of his exploits, hair breadth escapes, encounters with the enemy, Indians and tories, his constant vigilance to escape the scouts sent from Canada to take him, for whom a reward of five hundred guineas had been offered dead or alive. By means of spies he acquired important intelligence of the movements of the enemy in Canada, and rendered great services with his purse, person and pen at and before the surrender of Burgoyne, where he was engaged with two or three of his sons. He made a treaty of friendship with the St. Francis Indians, and by his kindness to them won their attachment. Many of the tribe were of great service to the colonies during the revolutionary war. He sacrificed a large estate in the service of his country, for which he never received any compensation, and was equally distinguished for his talents, his patriotism, and his piety." It is understood that he commanded a brigade at Saratoga, at least, practically. It is believed that losses which he suffered by his services to the patriot cause amounted to about $60,000, for which, notwithstanding his applications to Congress, he received no return. He sacrificed all his estate to pay his debts, and died a poor man. He had great talents, and his usefulness to the American cause was very great. It is unfortunate for his fame that he took the course which he did regarding the motives and operations of the Allens, Governor Chittenden, and the other leaders of the Vermont cause. Had he understood their plans, and acted with them, his name would have gone into history second in fame to that of no man in Vermont. There has been considerable controversy as to the actual part which he took in the campaign which ended with the surrender at Saratoga. At that time he held the rank and discharged the duties of Commissary General, and Brigadier-General. From the meagre records which remain, it seems certain that he employed his whole time during the summer of 1777, in raising men and supplies for the army and sending them on, but when Burgoyne was invested and the men and supplies were on the ground, he took command in person, of the troops from Western New Hampshire and Eastern Vermont. Several certificates like the following are in existence:

"Headquarters, SARATOGA, Oct. 18, 1777.

This may certify that Col. Webster with a Regiment of New Hampshire

Volunteers have faithfully served in the Northern Army, until this date, and are discharged with honor.

By Gen. Gates' order,
JACOB BAYLEY, Brig-Gen.*

This certifies that Frederick Obrey (Aubrey) did duty as a surgeon in the Volunteer Company, and in the party under the command of Col. Brown, who was sent to Ticonderoga by order from General Lincoln.
JACOB BAYLEY, B. D. G., (Brigadier General)."†

"A return of the Men and Horses employed by Capt. Abel Marsh in carrying flour from Connecticut river to Battenkill for the use of the Northern Army by order of Jacob Bayley, B. D. G., 13 October, 1777."
On the back of the return is the following endorsement:
"This certifies that by direction of Gen. Lincoln I ordered the within supplies of flour which was delivered to the commissary at Battenkill at the time specified when the baggage horses were dismissed.
JACOB BAYLEY, B. G."‡

"General Bayley," says the late Hon. L. E. Chittenden, in a personal contribution to this volume, "is one of the neglected patriots of the Revolution." His last years were spent among his children; he continued to transact business until nearly the end of his life, and his memory which remained unimpaired, was replete with reminiscences of his long and eventful career, which he would relate with great minuteness. It seems strange to us, that of the many who listened to his narratives, not one of them all seems to have thought of putting them into writing. He has been well called "The Father of Newbury," and his services to the town and church can hardly be overestimated. He was admitted to the 2d ch. at Newbury, Mass., (now the 1st ch. at W. N.) in 1744, and was, May 31, 1752, with his wife, dismissed to form, with others, a church at Hampstead. In September, 1764, he became one of the first members of the 1st ch. in this town, and was, with Jacob Kent and James Abbott, one of its first deacons, holding that office during the rest of his life. In person he was about middle height, a stature not exceeded by any of his sons or grandsons, with a muscular, well knit frame, capable of great endurance. Mr. Reuben Abbott, who had known him well, said that he could easily trace the lineaments of his countenance, in all of his descendants whom he had met. His mind was not largely informed; he had lived a busy life from boyhood, without time for study, or general reading; he seems to have been well aware of this, and declined responsibilities where a trained intellect was required, but he appears to have possessed the qualities which inspire confidence and esteem, to an unusual degree. His influence with the Indians doubtless prevented many disasters to the frontier, and his sacrifices in behalf of the American cause contributed toward the establishment of our independence. His fame will always be great in this town; but to the present generation, even of his descendants, the services which he rendered are very imperfectly understood. His sphere of operations was narrow, but in it no man could have accomplished a more durable work; his loyalty to the patriotic cause was never questioned, and his course during the war has never needed apology or required vindication. His correspondence was very extensive. Many of his letters have been printed but large numbers of them remain in manuscript. The New York state papers and those of New Hampshire contain some of them, and, had space permitted, numbers of those, hitherto unpublished, would have found place in this volume. He d. March 1, 1815, in the house of his son, Isaac, in which the latter's grandson, Henry W. Bailey now lives, his wife having preceded him, June 1, 1809.

---

*Col. David Webster of Plymouth, N. H.   This certificate is owned by a descendant.

†Vol. II., Rev. War Rolls, (N. H.), p. 429.   Dr. Aubrey was from Bradford.

‡Vt. Historical Society-Collections.

Children :
1   i.   Ephraim, b. Oct. 5, 1746; d. July 7, 1825.
     ii.   Abigail, b. Jan. 16, 1749; d. y.
     iii.   Noyes, b. Feb. 16, 1751; d. y.
2   iv.   Joshua, b. June 11, 1753; d. July 3, 1841.
3   v.   Jacob, b. Oct. 2, 1755; d. June 28, 1837.
4   vi.   James, b. Oct. 1, 1757; d. Apr. 19, 1784.
     vii.   Amherst, b. Jan. 16, 1760; d. Jan. 6, 1783.
     viii.   Abner. b. Dec. 10, 1763; d. 1783.
5   ix.   John, b. May 20, 1765; d. July 26, 1839.
6   x.   Isaac, b. June 28, 1767; d. Aug. 30, 1850.

The ancestry of this family is computed from Gen. Jacob Bayley, and the descendants of each of the sons are mentioned in order of birth, i. e., the descendants of Ephraim are given first, then those of Joshua, et seq.

1   EPHRAIM,[2] (Jacob[1]), b. Newbury, Mass., Oct. 5, 1746. Served in the revolutionary war in several campaigns. Was in Capt. Frye Bayley's Co. at Saratoga. Captain in the militia. Lived with his father on the Ox-bow, and took a prominent part in the local events of his time. About 1790 he removed to Littleton, N. H., and settled upon the meadow below the village. Some years before his death he removed to Lyman where he d. July 7, 1825. He m., 1st, Hannah, dau. of Jacob and Betsey (Merrill) Fowler; b. South Hampton, N. H.; d. May 3, 1781. He m., 2d, Lucy, dau. of Nathan and Hannah (Morey) Hodges, b. Norton, Mass., Oct. 29, 1757; d. Sept. 10, 1836; c. by 1st m. seven, by 2d, four.
7   i.   Jacob, b. March 9, 1769.
     ii.   Abigail, b. Dec. 7, 1770; m. Solomon Mann., q. v.; d. July 11, 1849.
     iii.   Hannah, b. 1772; m. Col. Simeon Stevens, q. v.; d. April 21, 1817.
8   iv.   Abner, m. Hannah, dau. Ebenezer White, q. v.
     v.   Moses, m. Lucy Barker.
     vi.   Anna, b. Mar. 16, 1779; m. Jonathan Tenney, q. v., 2d, John Ellis; d. May 8, 1832.
     vii.   C. d. y.
     viii.   Lucy, b. June 16, 1782; m. Ezekiel Bailey, q. v.. d. March 1, 1870.
     ix.   Alanson, b. April 9, 1785; m. Abigail Hutchins of Bath, where he lived, but removed to Ill., where he d. March 16, 1849.
     x.   Myra, b. April 13, 1789; m. Eben W. Strong of Orford, N. H., and d. there August 22, 1861. 3 c.
     xi.   John Hayes, b. Littleton, April 4, 1793; m. Susan Farnsworth. Lived in Charlestown, Mass., and Philadelphia. No c.

7   JACOB,[3] (Ephraim,[2] Jacob[1]), b. March 9, 1769; m. Hannah, dau. of Uriah and Rachel (Colby) Chamberlain, b. Mar. 4, 1773. Lived in N., Haverhill and Littleton, but died in the West. She d. July 6, 1842.
Children:
     i.   Hannah F., b. March 19, 1792; m., 1st, Merrill Fowler, son of Jacob of Morristown; 4 c.; m., 2d, ——— Lothrop of Orange; 1 c; 3d, Abraham Gale.
     ii.   Simeon, b. Jan. 8, 1794; m. Mary Sawyer; res., Littleton, N. H., and Charleston, Vt.; d. 1861. Their descendants are numerous in Orleans County.
     iii.   Ephraim, b. 1796; d. about 1855; unm.
     iv.   Truman Mann, b. Littleton, May 17, 1798; m., 1st, Betsey Day, who d. 1834; m. 2d, Agnes, dau. of Robert and Agnes (Gray) Nelson; b. Lyman Aug. 26, 1809. Lived in Littleton, Lyman and Peacham, where he d. June 24, 1859. Nine c.
     v.   Betsey, b. June 12, 1800; m. James Lewis of Littleton and Rock Island, P. Q.; 10 c.
     vi.   Emeline, b. June 30, 1802; teacher; m., 1st, Samuel Eastman. (See Eastman family). 2d, Abial Chamberlin of Wells River. She d. Jan. 30, 1869.
     vii.   Uriah, b. Nov. 18, 1804; d. 1805.
     viii.   David W., b. April 21, 1807; m. Rebecca Christian. Lived in Dalton, N. H., but d. in California. 1 c.

ix. Sally M., b. June 13, 1809; m. late in life, Samuel Mann of East Haverhill.
x.   Jacob[6], b. April 10, 1812; d. unm. in Canada.
xi. Uriah, d. y.

8 ABNER,[3] (Ephraim,[2] Jacob[1]) ; lived in Newbury; d. in Topsham. He m. Hannah,
      dau. of Ebenezer White; b. June, 30, 1779.
      Children, all b. in N.:
      i.   Hazen, never married.
      ii.   Polly, m. William Lane of Orford.
      iii. Abigail, b. January, 1802; m., Jan. 26, 1823, Mark Sawyer, who d. March
            6, 1865. She d. Aug. 5. 1883. Their dau. m. Anthony Hood of N.
      iv.   Ruth. m. Thomas Kent of Orford.
      v.   Lydia, m. Samuel Putnam, son of Dr. Samuel Putnam, q. v.
      vi.   Hannah, m. Solomon Rider and went to Illinois. Two sons and a dau.
      vii. Anna, b. Aug. 30, 1805; m. Feb. 14, 1827, Benjamin Kelley; b. Feb. 14,
            1806. They were man and wife more than 70 years. Lived in Bradford.

2 COL. JOSHUA,[2] (Jacob[1]) b. June 11, 1753, at Hampstead. N. H. Served during
      several campaigns in the revolutionary war, in which he attained the rank
      of Major; was Colonel in the militia. Built about 1785, the house at
      Newbury Village long occupied by the late Bailey Avery. Town Represen-
      tative 1791-94, 1802-03. 04-09. He lived a few years with his son
      Ephraim on Jefferson Hill; m. Jan.,'1774, Anna, dau. Dea. Jacob Fowler,
      (b. June 22, 1754; d. May 15, 1837.) Member of 1st ch.; d. July 3, 1841.
      Children, all b. in Newbury:
      i.   Elizabeth. b. Nov. 6. 1774; m. John Wood; three sons, of whom John was a
            farmer at the Centre; (b. 1812; m. 1st, Sept. 9, 1842, Mary E. Tewksbury
            who d. Apr. 8, 1882; 2d, Mrs. Sally (Hutchins) Goodall, who d. Aug. 10,
            1900; he d. Apr. 25, 1896).
      ii.   Sally. b. June 8, 1776; d. unm., Feb. 21, 1867.
9   iii. Merrill, b. June 3, 1778.
10   iv.   Noyes, b. June 5, 1780.
11   v.   Joshua, b. Apr. 7, 1782.
12   vi.   James, b. June 9, 1784.
      vii. Hannah, b. 1786; m. Simeon Avery, q. v.
13   viii. Jacob, b. Apr. 17, 1789.
14   ix.   John, b. July 14, 1791.
      x.   Anna, b. Jan. 17, 1795; m. Dea. Moody Powers, q. v.
15   xi.   Ephraim, b. May 22, 1798.
16   xii. Benjamin Franklin, b. March, 1800.

9 MERRILL,[3] (Joshua,[2] Jacob[1]) b. Jan. 3, 1778. Settled on Jefferson Hill but
      rem. to Massena, N. Y., about 1833; m. July 24, 1804, Anna, dau. Dea.
      Moore of Thetford, (b. March 28, 1783; d. Nov. 19, 1856.) He d. July 30,
      1857.
      Children:
      i.   Cyrus B., b. July 24. 1805; m. Mary Sanborn of Salisbury, N. H.; d. 1879.
      ii.   Mahala, b. April 8, 1807; m. Thomas Bellamy of N. Y. He d. May 11, 1887;
            9 c.
      iii. Anna B., b. May 19, 1818; m. Feb. 14 1837, George Irwin; d. Dec. 27,
            1884. Three c. Their oldest son was Speaker of the House of Represen-
            tatives in New York and President of the New York Senate.
      iv.   William M., b. July 28, 1820; m. Feb. 15, 1849, Laura M. Felch; d. July
            11, 1894; five c.
      v.   Harriet B., b. Sept. 21, 1825; d. May 13, 1875.

10 NOYES,[3] (Joshua [2] Jacob[1]) b. Dec. 5, 1779. Lived on Jefferson Hill; rem. to
      Newbury Village 1860; m. Phebe, dau. William and Ruth (Johnston) Tice.
      (b. Ryegate, Feb. 24, 1787; d. Oct. 10, 1874); d. Aug. 27, 1863.
      Children:
      i.   Laura J., b. Jan. 17, 1812; d. May 30, 1888, unm.
      ii.   Harrison, b. Feb. 18, 1813; d. Nov. 25, 1886.
      iii. Mary Ann, b. Feb. 7, 1815; m. Enoch Wiggin, and, 2d, Harmon Titus; d. in
            Stockton, Cal., 1898.
      iv.   Ruth, b. Feb. 20, 1819; m. Henry E. Johnson, q. v.
      v.   Noyes, b. Dec. 12, 1819; went to California 1850; d. April 8, 1896,
            Stockton, Cal.

vi. Dan Y., b. Sept. 17, 1820; m. Dec. 23, 1857, Rachel Chamberlin; d. March 25, 185×.

vii. Andrew J., b. March 26, 1823; m. Charlotte Allen in California.

viii. Jacob, b. Aug. 21, 1827. Went to California.

ix. Jeremiah N., b. March 18, 1831. Went to California.

x. Sarah S., June 29, 1833.

xi. George C., b. July 25, 1837. Went to California.

11 JOSHUA,[3] (Joshua,[2] Jacob[1]) b. Apr. 7, 1782. Lived on Jefferson Hill; m. April 10, 1812, Sarah, dau. William and Ruth (Johnston) Tice, (b. Ryegate, Dec. 20, 1786; d. Feb. 14, 1873); d. Dec. 13, 1862.

Children:

17 i. William T., b. May 3, 1814.

18 ii. Azro Joshua, b. May 16, 1816.

iii. Sarah, b. July 2, 1818; d. y.

iv. Marion T., b. Dec. 8, 1820; m. Charles T. Henderson.

v. Robert, d. y.

vi. Robert T., b. July 18, 1824; m. March 1, 1853, Abby Henderson, (b. Aug. 15, 1828; d. Aug. 4, 1857). No c.

19 vii. Charles R, b. May 20, 1827.

12 JAMES,[3] (Joshua,[2] Jacob[1]) b. June 9, 1784. Served 5 mo. 27 d., in war of 1812; m. June 12, 1818, Sirena, dau. of Jabez and Elizabeth (Macintosh) Bigelow; (b. Ryegate, Dec. 19, 1796; d. Dec. 8, 1867); rem. to Massena, N. Y., Feb. 1838; d. July 7, 1859.

Children:

i. James P., b. Dec. 31, 1815; res. Massena, N. Y.

ii. Jabez B., b. April 27, 1818; res. Massena, N. Y.

iii. Sirena, b. Jan. 21, 1823; d. July 4, 1884.

iv. Eliza M., b. June 28, 1825; d. June 4, 1854.

v. Anna M., b. Dec. 15, 1827; d. May 23, 1849.

vi. Cynthia A., b. Feb. 16, 1831; m.

13 JACOB,[3] (Joshua,[2] Jacob[1]) b. April 17, 1789. Lived on Jefferson Hill, served 5 mos. 28 d., in Capt. Levi Rogers Co. in war of 1812. Was a member of the Meth. ch. He m. Nov. 23, 1815, Betsey, dau. William Peach, q. v., (b. Marblehead, Mass., June 12, 1790: d. Feb. 8, 1870); d. Aug. 10, 1850.

Children:

i. Elizabeth, b. Feb. 1, 1817; m. Obadiah C. Barnett, q. v.

ii. Mary, b. Jan. 15, 1820; m. David T. Henderson, q. v.

iii. Benjamin B., b. Aug. 13, 1822. Killed under log shed March 10, 1834.

20 iv. George W., b. Dec. 27, 1826.

21 v. Thomas P., b. May 18, 1829.

vi. Sarah Jane, b. Dec. 4, 1833; m. Joseph H. Fuller, q. v.

14 JOHN,[3] (Joshua,[2] Jacob[1]) b. July 14, 1791. Rem. to Jefferson Hill four years after his m. Served 5 mos. 28 d. in Capt. Levi Rogers Co. in war of 1812; m Jan. 23, 1819, Martha, dau. of Stephen Powers, q. v., (b. May 23, 1790; d. Sept. 14, 1880); d. Aug. 21, 1879.

Children:

i. Martha, b. June 11, 1820; m. 1st, Aug. 22, 1844, Edward Coolidge, grandson of Jonathan Hale, q. v. Mr. C. d. April 11, 1844; one son, d. y.; m. 2d, May 8, 1860, Andrew Nutter, who d. Oct. 14, 1893.

22 ii. John, b. Jan. 30, 1822.

iii. Mary, b. Dec. 20, 1824; m June 27, 1844, Calvin S. Matthews of Munson, Me. He went to California in 1852 and d. 1853; c., Martha, John H., d. y., Calvin H., b. April 28, 1851.

iv. Betsey, b. Jan. 28, 1827; m. Stephen Hicks of Haverhill; c., Nathan Davis, b. N., Nov. 24, 1860.

v. Abigail, b. May 20, 1830; m. Moses Brock, q. v.

vi. Almira Electa, b. June 19 1832; m. July 14, 1850, John M. Swain of Lowell, Mass. C., (1) Wellman Jenness, b. Sept. 14, 1853; (2) Mary Lizzie, b. Oct. 3, 1855.

15 EPHRAIM,[3] (Joshua,[2] Jacob[1]) b. May 22, 1798. Lived in N., except a few years after 1837 in Norfolk, N. Y. He m. Dec. 5, 1826, Mary, dau. of

Joseph Prescott. (b. April 25, 1806; d. Feb. 26, 1875.) He d. July 3, 1875.

Children:

i. Lucinda S., b. Newbury, Aug. 22, 1828; m. May 15, 1848, Henry E. Cook, blacksmith in Newbury; d. Castleton, April 17, 1875. C.. (1) Jennie I., b. April 14, 1850; d. Jan., 1868. (2) Lenora L., d. May 21, 1852; m. Milton Herring; res. Litchfield, Mich. One dau. (3) Harry H., b June 24, 1854; res. Castleton. (5) Edgar E.. b. June 20, 1856; res. also in Castleton. (6) Karl C., b. 1860; res. Medford, Mass. (7) Arthur B., b. Castleton, but lives in Maine.

ii. Joseph P., b. Dec. 31, 1830; res. Newbury; butcher; m. Dec. 21, 1872, Lucy R. Martin of Bradford. C., (1) Frank P., b. Ryegate, Jan. 8, 1874. (2) Leroy P., b. Newbury, March 31, 1875. (3) Mary M., b. April 1, 1877; m. Sept. 25, 1898. John H. Green; lives in Newbury. C., Charlotte M., b. Aug. 3, 1899. (4) Charles H., b. June 6, 1881; d. Oct. 1881. (5) Jesse Raymond, b. Oct. 25, 1882. (6) Charles C., b. May 24, 1885.

iii. Eliza V., b. May 7, 1833; m. (18) Azro Joshua Bailey, q. v.

iv. Lucy Ann Buxton, b. July 18, 1836; d. July 18, 1858.

v. Mary Jane, b. Massena, N. Y., April 17, 1840; m. Carlos E. Brock, q. v.

vi. Sophila George, b. Feb. 17, 1843; d. Mt. Holly, Vt., March, 1879; m. John Crawford.

vii. Amanda, b. July 20, 1848; d. April 17, 1849.

17 WILLIAM T.,[4] (Joshua,[3] Joshua,[2] Jacob[1]) b. May 3, 1814; farmer on Jefferson Hill. He m. September, 1853, Abi J., dau. of Jonas Tucker, q. v. (b. Dec. 24, 1816, d. May 4, 1893.) He d. March 23, 1883.

Children:

i. William E., b. April 4, 1854, farmer on homestead; m. Oct 26, 1888, Maria C. Stewart, b. Inverness, P. Q.. June 10, 1863. C., (1) Abi Mae, b. Aug. 26, 1889. (2) William S., b. June 24, 1891. (3) Livermore T., b. Dec. 23, 1893. (4) Margaret L, b. Dec. 3, 1897.

ii. Livermore T., b. July 25, 1860; farmer in Ryegate; m. May 7, 1891, Belle J., dau. of Pringle Gibson, b. Ryegate, Sept. 21, 1867.

18 AZRO JOSHUA,[4] (Joshua,[3] Joshua,[2] Jacob[1]) b. May 16, 1816. Went to Lower Waterford and kept hotel three years Ran carding mill at Boltonville two years; farmer till 1852. Jan. 10, he started for California via Panama, reaching San Francisco April 1, 1852, was there four years returning 1856. Kept hotel at Groton 1859-61. 1861-65 in California, Oregon and Idaho. Has since lived in this town. Farmer. He m., 1st, Sept. 13, 1840, Harriet, dau. of William Bolton. (b. Newbury Nov. 23, 1823; d. May 1, 1851). 2d, May 30, 1856, Eliza, dau. of Ephraim Bayley, (b. May 7, 1833; d. July 9, 1858). 3d, Jan. 13, 1859, Lydia Glover of Groton. He d. at Newbury, June 6, 1900.

Five c. by 1st m., seven by 3d.

i. Van Ness, b. Dec. 22, 1842; res. Grass Valley, California. Merchant.

ii. Alden B., b. March 18, 1844; res. La Grande, O. Machinist and railroad engineer. Married and has three c.

iii. Hibbard H., b. Jan. 1, 1846. Res. Steamboat Springs, Nev. Farmer. Four c.

iv. Ransom T., b. Oct. 20, 1847; res. San Francisco, Cal. Miner.

v. Hattie M., b. Aug. 30, 1849; m; res. Virginia City, Nev.

vi. Eliza A., b. Nov. 10, 1860; m. June 19, 1880, Osgood P. Wheeler, q. v.

vii. Fenton J., b. March 19, 1862; m. May 7, 1890, May Ambrose; res. Bisbee, Arizona. Miner.

viii. Chastena. b. July 4, 1868; res. San Francisco, Cal. Teacher.

ix. Clive A.. b. Dec. 17, 1869; res. Newbury. Carpenter.

x. Elcena, b. Dec. 5, 1872.

xi. Merton J., b. Feb. 7. 1873.

xii. Aldana, b. March 27, 1878.

19 CHARLES R.,[4] (Joshua,[3] Joshua,[2] Jacob[1]) b. May 20, 1827; m. Nov. 19, 1853, Myrilla J., dau. of John and Jane McClure, (b. Ryegate, July 1, 1832; d. Oct. 28, 1896); d. Sept. 28, 1873.

Children:

i. Sophronia M., b. Oct. 8, 1859; m. Jan. 12, 1892, Charles M. Libbey of Boston; res. Ryegate.

JOHN BAILEY.

ii. Charles R., b. July 20, 1867; m. July 27, 1892, Eva Adams of Chelsea, Mass.; res. Groton. Station agent and constable.

20 GEORGE W.,[4] (Jacob,[3] Joshua,[2] Jacob[1]) b. Dec. 27, 1826; m. March 6, 1866, Ann C. Felch, (b. Glover, Vt., Sept. 4, 1843). Farmer on Jefferson Hill.
   Children:
   i. Infant, b. June 21, 1868.
   ii. Herbert E., b. March 22, 1871; m. Grace H. Roberts. Went west, 1898; c. Elmer R.
   iii. George A., b. Dec. 28, 1872.
   iv. Mary E., b. Nov. 12, 1876; m. Joseph McClay; c., Anna J., and Marion A.
   v. Nora S., b. Feb. 4, 1880.
   vi. Winnie F., b. May 23, 1883.

21 THOMAS PEACH,[4] (Jacob,[3] Joshua,[2] Jacob[1]) b. May 18, 1829. Lived some years on the north side of Jefferson Hill, where Robert Carruth now lives. Was influential in building the "Swamp Road" in 1860. He enlisted at Wells River for three yrs., May 10, 1871, in Co. C., 3d Vt. Mustered into U. S. service July 17, 1871. Dis. at Finley hospital, Washington, Nov. 8, 1862. He kept a diary during his service, and contributed a series of valuable letters to the Vt. Journal; 1865-69 in trade at the Centre in what had been the "old Gibson store"; farming and other business in Iowa and in Springfield, Mo., 1869-1900. In the latter year he returned to Newbury and bought the homestead, on Jefferson Hill. He contributed much to the press. He m. in Humboldt, Iowa, March 30, 1875, Mary Florence Carey (b. Feb. 6, 1857, in Wisconsin).
   Children, the three oldest born in Ocheyedan, Osceola Co., Iowa.
   i. Alice May, b. Feb. 1, 1876.
   ii. Arabella P., b. Oct. 19, 1879.
   iii. Henrietta H., b. April 10, 1883.
   iv. Emily B., b. Humboldt, Ia., July 12, 1887.

22 JOHN,[4] (John,[3] Joshua,[2] Jacob[1]) b. Jan. 30, 1822. Farmer on Jefferson Hill till 1869, when he rem. to Wells River and engaged in business. Was Auctioneer, Deputy Sheriff and Sheriff. Prominent in town and county business: Postmaster, Director in Newbury National Bank, Director and President of Wells River Savings Bank, Town Representative, 1870-71, 1884, Senator, 1886. Mr. Bailey has had an unusual experience as sheriff. His first exploit was the capture of Levi Fickett, who forged an indorsement on a thousand dollar draft. He was taken in Boston, but the requisition papers were defective, and Mr. B. had to make two trips to Vermont to have them made right. He held the man, however. Later, he was sent to Rome, N. Y., for two men, whom he secured, after a legal fight. On the morning of July 6, 1875, a telegram was received at Wells River, stating that the Barre bank had been robbed, four men entering the house of Mr. King the cashier, and forced him to open the bank, and that two suspicious men had crossed Piermont bridge. Mr. Bailey at once took a train for Plymouth, and at Rumney two men came on board. One of them, finding that he was watched, jumped from the train. Mr. Bailey had the train stopped, and after three hours' search found the man and took him to Barre. The other man, George E. Miles, escaped from the train. The third man, Joe Kingsland, alias Joe Tyson, was arrested by Mr. B. on the 27th of August, after a search of 23 days, but, as he was wanted to serve a term of eight years at Sing Sing prison, he could not be brought to Vermont. On the 5th of September Mr. B. arrested Miles in New York City, and after a two weeks' legal fight, brought him to Vermont, where he served out a fourteen years' sentence in states prison. The fourth man was not taken, although Mr. B. spent several thousand dollars in search for him, but the banks declined to furnish more funds in the search. This exploit gave him a great reputation for daring and skill. Mr. Bailey has rendered most efficient service in securing the publication of this history of Newbury. He m. Oct. 21, 1847, Isabel, dau. of Dea. George Nelson, (b. Ryegate, Feb. 18, 1826.)
   Children, all b. in Newbury:
   i. Ellen M., b. Oct. 7, 1848; m. June 22, 1887, Newton H. Field, (b. Athens,

Vt., Aug. 12, 1851); c., (1), Roscoe, b. May 2, 1888; d. from burns accidentally received, June 19, 1890. (2), Isabel Clara, b. June 20, 1892.

ii. Albert H., b. Apr. 26, 1850; res. Wells River; R. R. employee; postmaster four years, and in town business; m. March 8, 1876. Ardella, dau. of John Buchanan, (b. Groton, June 17, 1856); c., Sophia Isabel, b. Jan. 7, 1877, d. y. (2). Fred J., b. July 19, 1878. Student in Middlebury College, class of 1901. (3) Edward T., b. April 6, 1880. Enlisted for the war in Cuba, served at Chickamaugna, now with U. S. army at Manila. (4) John, b. Aug. 5, 1882; d, Sept. 3, 1885. (5) George N., b. Oct. 26, 1886. (6) Margaret, b. Aug. 15. 1889; d. Oct. 1, 1890. (7) Nellie Mary, b. June 13, 1892. (8) Leslie, b. March 15, 1894. (9) Jacob, b May 15, 1895.

iii. Margaret J., b. July 7, 1852; m. Apr. 9, 1879, E. D. Carpenter, (b. Brookfield, Sept. 4. 1849); res., Wells River.

iv. Lizzie B., b. Aug. 18. 1855; m. Jan. 1, 1874, Oscar Warden. (b. March 15, 1845; furniture dealer); c., (1) Florence C., b. Dec. 13, 1877. (2) Harold N., b. May 13. 1884. (3) Lizziebell, b. July 23, 1898.

v. Nelson H., b. Oct. 4, 1863. Teller in Newbury National Bank; became cashier upon the death of Mr. George Leslie; m. Oct. 24, 1895, M. Louise Whitney; c., Dumont, b. Sept. 28, 1896.

vi. Clara B., b. Oct. 28, 1865; m. Oct. 20, 1892, Simeon E. Clark, q. v.

16 BENJAMIN F.,[3] (Joshua,[2] Jacob[1]) b. March, 1800. Carpenter in Newbury; rem. 1836 to Massena, N. Y., where he lived ten years, then he returned to Newbury. He was also a hunter and with a rifle which he made killed over 300 deer. He m. Emeline Smith, (b. 1811; d. 1893.) He d. Nov. 3, 1855.

Children:

i. Edson Carolus, b. 1831; d. May 7, 1853.

23 ii. Edwin Frank, b. Jan. 5, 1832.

iii. Charles Allen, b. 1834. Rem. to the state of Washington. Farmer. M. a Miss Parker. One son.

iv. Alice A., b. 1836; m. Chester Fisk of Lisbon, N. H.; res. Seattle, Washington. No c. living.

v. W. S., b. 1838; merchant at Lancaster, N. H.; m. a Miss Griffin, who d. Nov. 1879. 2 c.: (1) Harry B., res. Lancaster. One son. (2) Nina, m. Fielding Smith, postmaster at Lancaster.

23 EDWIN F.,[4] (Benj. F.,[3] Joshua,[2] Jacob[1]) b. Jan. 5, 1832; carpenter; m. Oct. 16, 1855, May M., dau. of Joseph Hutchins Bailey, (28), (b. Oct. 16, 1836; d. June 14, 1883).

Children:

i. Emma J., b. Sept. 12, 1856; m. F. W. Streeter of Lancaster, N. H. C., (1) Mary Glenn, b. Jan 23, 1885. (2) Katherine, b. June 11, 1899.

ii. Alice W., b. Oct. 4, 1858.

iii. Edson C. b. Sept. 3, 1862. In clothing business at Littleton, N. H.

iv. Lula E., b. Sept. 5, 1869.

v. Ray Clifton, b. July 9, 1871; m. July, 1898, Nella Perkins of Danville, Vt. C., Clifton, b. March 14, 1899.

vi. Nora Blanche, b. July 9, 1873; m. Ernest Hallett of Maine.

vii. Frank L., b. July 6, 1875.

F. W. Streeter, R. C. and F. S. Bailey are in business at Lancaster, N. H., under the name of Bailey & Co.

3 JACOB,[2] (Jacob[1]) b. Oct. 3, 1755, Hampstead, N. H. Served in the Revolutionary war. Quartermaster in Col. Bedel's regiment, served 138 days. Also served in several alarms; was aid to his father, and his widow received a pension of $600 per annum. Lived on the Ox-bow until about 1805, when he settled on a farm near the Centre, south of Daniel Taisey's; buildings all gone. He also lived in Haverhill; d. Newbury, June 28. 1837. He m. 1st, about 1776, Ruth, dau., of Col Timothy Bedel; d. in Salem, N. H., 1779, while visiting there. He m., 2d, October, 1782 May, dau. of Ezekiel and Ruth (Hutchins) Ladd, (b. Haverhill Feb. 14, 1766; d. March 1, 1855).

Children:

24 i. Abner, (by 1st marriage), b. April 30, 1778; d. May 9, 1852.

ii. Timothy B., (by 2d marriage), b. June 30, 1784; m. June 30, 1808, Phebe Woodward; res. Rutland. He d. Jan. 22, 1858.
25 iii. Ezekiel L., b. June 12, 1786; d. Dec. 10, 1863.
iv. Jacob Noyes, b. June 18, 1788; lived in Rutland; d. July 15, 1876; m., 1st, Lucy Young. 2d, Nov. 4, 1842, Polly Thrall; d. Nov. 12, 1877.
v. Ruth L., b. April 28, 1790; m. Jeremiah Nourse, q. v.: d. Dec. 19, 1862.
vi. Moody B., b. Dec. 15, 1792; lived in St. Lawrence County, N. Y. He m. Jan. 17, 1829, Mrs. Fanny Day, (b. Jan. 23, 1796; d. Feb. 9, 1871). He d. Dec. 18, 1866.
vii. William Wallace, b. Oct. 29, 1794; d. Jan. 12, 1854.
viii. Mary B., b. Oct. 20, 1796; m., 1st, Oct. 4, 1831, David Runnels of Warner, N. H., who d. Dec. 31, 1838; m., 2d, Sept. 24, 1839, Col. Moody Chamberlain. She d. July 8, 1884.
ix. Abigail L., b. Jan. 10, 1798; m. Charles George, q. v.; d. March 21, 1886.
x. Aaron K., b. Feb. 3, 1801; d. Feb. 24, 1817.
xi. Deborah C., b. June 2, 1803; m. Jeremiah Boynton, q. v.; d. Nov. 28, 1863.
26 xii. Joseph Hutchins, b. Jan. 28, 1809; d. June 5, 1890.

24 **Abner,**[2] (Jacob,[2] Jacob[1]) b. April 30, 1778. While yet young he purchased a farm on Kent's meadow which was, formerly, that of Levi Sylvester, to which he added from time to time. He began life a poor boy, but by careful management accumulated what was then considered a handsome property. He m. 1st, Aug. 9, 1801, Polly Barker, who d. Oct. 27, 1803, leaving one son: 2d, (published in Haverhill, Feb. 22, 1808) Lucinda, dan. of Maj. Nathaniel Merrill, (b. Jan. 20, 1787; d. Nov. 15, 1809); no c. 3d, Feb. 28, 1811, Betsey, dan. Col. Aaron Hibbard, a niece of 2d wife, (b. Oct. 11, 1790; d. Nov. 17, 1857); member of 1st Ch.; d. May 9, 1852.
Children:
27 i. Moody B., b. Oct. 19, 1803.
28 ii. Nathaniel M., b. June 7, 1812.
iii. Azro, b. June 30, 1814.
iv. Lucinda, b. Dec. 4, 1816; d Sept. 3, 1828.
30 v. Albert, b. March 21, 1818; d. Nov. 9, 1879.
31 vi. Edwin, b. July 16, 1820; d. Oct. 11, 1888.
32 vii. Nelson, b. Jan. 6, 1822; d. July 19, 1881.
33 viii. Milo, b. Feb. 4, 1824.
ix. Ruth, b. Nov. 17, 1825; d. July 9, 1897.
x. Martha, b. July 20, 1827; d. Aug. 30, 1828.
xi. Allen, b. May 29, 1829. Farmer in Haverhill afterwards in trade there with his brother Milo; m. Pheobe Clark of Groton, Vt.; d. June 18, 1875; no c.
xii. George, b. Feb. 28, 1831. Farmer with his brother Nelson. Served in 12th Vt. (see war record); d. Nov. 9, 1892.
xiii. Lucinda, b. Feb. 5, 1833; m. John B. Buxton, q. v.; d. Sept. 9, 1892.
xiv. Mary S., b. Sept. 10, 1836; m. Nov. 16, 1860. Rev. Charles C. Wallace. Mr. Wallace was a Presbyterian clergyman of considerable note who filled several important pulpits, and among other publications, was the author of "History of Presbyterianism in New England". After his death Mrs. Wallace returned to Newbury, where she res. One dau., Grace.

25 **Ezekiel Ladd.**[3] (Jacob,[2] Jacob[1]) b. June 12, 1786; m. Elethear Ruggles of Rutland; d. Dec. 10, 1863.
Children:
i. Thomas R.
ii. Mary L.
iii. Franklin L. Res. Boston. In genealogical work.
iv. Eleanor.
F. L. Bailey has rendered valuable assistance in the preparation of these Bailey family records. He published in 1896, an account of the Ruggles and kindred families.

26 **Joseph Hutchins**[3], (Jacob[2], Jacob[1]) b. Newbury, Jan. 28, 1809. Farmer at the Center. He was the youngest and last survivor of the grandchildren of Gen. Jacob Bayley. Member of the Methodist church about 60 years.

Vt., Aug. 12, 1851); c., (1), Roscoe, b. May 2, 1888; d. from burns accidentally received, June 19, 1890. (2), Isabel Clara, b. June 20, 1892.
ii. Albert H., b. Apr. 26, 1850; res. Wells River; R. R. employee; postmaster four years, and in town business; m. March 8, 1876. Ardella, dau. of John Buchanan, (b. Groton, June 17, 1856); c., Sophia Isabel, b. Jan. 7, 1877, d. y. (2). Fred J., b. July 19, 1878. Student in Middlebury College, class of 1901. (3) Edward T., b. April 6, 1880. Enlisted for the war in Cuba, served at Chickamaugua, now with U. S. army at Manila. (4) John, b. Aug. 5, 1882; d, Sept. 3, 1885. (5) George N., b. Oct. 26, 1886. (6) Margaret, b. Aug. 15. 1889; d. Oct. 1, 1890. (7) Nellie Mary, b. June 13, 1892. (8) Leslie, b. March 15, 1894. (9) Jacob, b May 15, 1895.
iii. Margaret J., b. July 7. 1852; m. Apr. 9, 1879, E. D. Carpenter, (b. Brookfield, Sept. 4, 1849); res., Wells River.
iv. Lizzie B. b. Aug. 18. 1855; m. Jan. 1, 1874, Oscar Warden. (b. March 15, 1845; furniture dealer); c., (1) Florence C., b. Dec. 13, 1877. (2) Harold N., b. May 13. 1884. (3) Lizziebell, b. July 23, 1898.
v.   Nelson H., b. Oct. 4, 1863. Teller in Newbury National Bank; became cashier upon the death of Mr. George Leslie; m. Oct. 24, 1895, M. Louise Whitney; c., Dumont, b. Sept. 28, 1896.
vi. Clara B., b, Oct. 28, 1865; m. Oct. 20, 1892, Simeon E. Clark, q. v.

16 BENJAMIN F.,[3] (Joshua,[2] Jacob[1]) b. March, 1800. Carpenter in Newbury; rem. 1836 to Massena, N. Y., where he lived ten years, then he returned to Newbury. He was also a hunter and with a rifle which he made killed over 300 deer. He m. Emeline Smith, (b. 1811; d. 1893.) He d. Nov. 3, 1855.
    Children:
    i.   Edson Carolus, b. 1831; d. May 7, 1853.
23 ii. Edwin Frank, b. Jan. 5, 1832.
    iii. Charles Allen, b. 1834. Rem. to the state of Washington. Farmer. M. a Miss Parker. One son.
    iv. Alice A., b. 1836; m. Chester Fisk of Lisbon, N. H.; res. Seattle, Washington. No c. living.
    v.   W. S., b. 1838; merchant at Lancaster, N. H.; m. a Miss Griffin, who d. Nov. 1879. 2 c.: (1) Harry B., res. Lancaster. One son. (2) Nina, m. Fielding Smith, postmaster at Lancaster.

23 EDWIN F.,[4] (Benj. F.,[3] Joshua,[2] Jacob[1]) b. Jan. 5, 1832; carpenter; m. Oct. 16. 1855, May M., dau. of Joseph Hutchins Bailey, (28), (b. Oct. 16, 1836; d. June 14, 1883).
    Children:
    i.   Emma J., b. Sept. 12, 1856; m. F. W. Streeter of Lancaster, N. H. C., (1) Mary Glenn, b. Jan 23, 1885. (2) Katherine, b. June 11, 1899.
    ii. Alice W., b. Oct. 4, 1858.
    iii. Edson C. b. Sept. 3, 1862. In clothing business at Littleton, N. H.
    iv. Lula E., b. Sept. 5. 1869.
    v.   Ray Clifton, b. July 9, 1871; m. July, 1898, Nella Perkins of Danville, Vt. C., Clifton, b. March 14. 1899.
    vi. Nora Blanche. b. July 9. 1873; m. Ernest Hallett of Maine.
    vii. Frank L., b. July 6. 1875.
         F. W. Streeter, R. C. and F. S. Bailey are in business at Lancaster, N. H., under the name of Bailey & Co.

3   JACOB,[2] (Jacob[1]) b. Oct.3, 1755, Hampstead, N. H. Served in the Revolutionary war. Quartermaster in Col. Bedel's regiment, served 138 days. Also served in several alarms; was aid to his father, and his widow received a pension of $600 per annum. Lived on the Ox-bow until about 1805, when he settled on a farm near the Centre, south of Daniel Taisey's; buildings all gone. He also lived in Haverhill; d. Newbury, June 28. 1837. He m. 1st, about 1776, Ruth, dau., of Col Timothy Bedel; d. in Salem, N. H., 1779, while visiting there. He m., 2d, October, 1782 May, dau. of Ezekiel and Ruth (Hutchins) Ladd, (b. Haverhill Feb. 14, 1766; d. March 1, 1855).
    Children:
24 i.   Abner, (by 1st marriage), b. April 30, 1778; d. May 9, 1852.

   ii. Timothy B., (by 2d marriage), b. June 30, 1784; m. June 30, 1808, Phebe
        Woodward; res. Rutland. He d. Jan. 22, 1858.
25 iii. Ezekiel L., b. June 12, 1786; d. Dec. 10, 1863.
   iv. Jacob Noyes, b. June 18, 1788; lived in Rutland; d. July 15, 1876; m., 1st,
        Lucy Young 2d, Nov. 4, 1842, Polly Thrall; d. Nov. 12, 1877.
    v. Ruth L., b. April 28, 1790; m. Jeremiah Nourse, q. v.; d. Dec. 19, 1862.
   vi. Moody B., b. Dec. 15. 1792; lived in St. Lawrence County, N. Y. He m.
        Jan. 17, 1829, Mrs. Fanny Day, (b. Jan. 23, 1796; d. Feb. 9, 1871). He
        d. Dec. 18, 1866.
  vii. William Wallace, b. Oct 29, 1794; d. Jan. 12, 1854.
 viii. Mary B., b. Oct 20, 1796; m., 1st. Oct. 4, 1831, David Runnels of Warner,
        N. H., who d. Dec. 31, 1838; m., 2d, Sept. 24, 1839, Col. Moody
        Chamberlain. She d. July 8, 1884.
   ix. Abigail L., b. Jan. 10. 1798; m. Charles George, q. v.; d. March 21, 1886.
    x. Aaron K., b. Feb. 3, 1801; d. Feb. 24, 1817.
   xi. Deborah C., b. June 2, 1803; m. Jeremiah Boynton, q. v.; d. Nov. 28, 1863.
26 xii. Joseph Hutchins, b. Jan. 28, 1809; d. June 5, 1890.

24 ABNER,[3] (Jacob,[2] Jacob[1]) b. April 30, 1778. While yet young he purchased a
     farm on Kent's meadow which was, formerly, that of Levi Sylvester, to
     which he added from time to time. He began life a poor boy, but by
     careful management accumulated what was then considered a handsome
     property. He m. 1st, Aug. 9, 1801, Polly Barker, who d. Oct. 27, 1803,
     leaving one son; 2d, (published in Haverhill, Feb. 22, 1808) Lucinda, dau.
     of Maj. Nathaniel Merrill, (b. Jan. 20, 1787; d. Nov. 15. 1809); no c. 3d,
     Feb. 28, 1811, Betsey, dau. Col. Aaron Hibbard, a niece of 2d wife, (b.
     Oct. 11, 1790; d. Nov. 17, 1857) ; member of 1st Ch.; d. May 9, 1852.
     Children:
27   i. Moody B., b. Oct. 19, 1803.
28   ii. Nathaniel M., b. June 7, 1812.
29 iii. Azro, b. June 30, 1814.
   iv. Lucinda, b Dec. 4, 1816; d Sept. 3, 1828.
30   v. Albert, b. March 21, 1818; d. Nov. 9. 1879.
31   vi. Edwin, b. July 16, 1820; d. Oct. 11, 1888.
32 vii. Nelson, b. Jan. 6, 1822; d. July 19, 1881.
33 viii. Milo, b. Feb. 4, 1824.
   ix. Ruth, b. Nov. 17, 1825; d. July 9, 1897.
    x. Martha, b. July 20, 1827; d. Aug. 20, 1828.
   xi. Allen. b. May 29, 1829. Farmer in Haverhill afterwards in trade there
        with his brother Milo; m. Pheobe Clark of Groton, Vt.; d. June 18, 1875;
        no c.
  xii. George, b. Feb. 28, 1831. Farmer with his brother Nelson. Served in 12th
        Vt. (see war record) ; d. Nov. 9, 1892.
  xiii. Lucinda, b. Feb. 5, 1833; m. John B. Buxton, q. v.; d. Sept. 9, 1892.
  xiv. Mary S., b. Sept. 10, 1836; m. Nov. 16, 1860. Rev. Charles C. Wallace. Mr.
        Wallace was a Presbyterian clergyman of considerable note who filled
        several important pulpits, and among other publications, was the author
        of "History of Presbyterianism in New England". After his death Mrs.
        Wallace returned to Newbury, where she res. One dau., Grace.

25 EZEKIEL LADD,[3] (Jacob,[2] Jacob[1]) b. June 12, 1786; m. Elethear Ruggles of
     Rutland; d. Dec. 10, 1863.
     Children:
    i. Thomas R.
   ii. Mary L.
  iii. Franklin L. Res. Boston. In genealogical work.
   iv. Eleanor.
     F. L. Bailey has rendered valuable assistance in the preparation of these
     Bailey family records. He published in 1896, an account of the Ruggles and
     kindred families.

26 JOSEPH HUTCHINS[3], (Jacob[2], Jacob[1]) b. Newbury, Jan. 28, 1809. Farmer at
     the Center. He was the youngest and last survivor of the grandchildren
     of Gen. Jacob Bayley. Member of the Methodist church about 60 years.

He m., 1st, July 9, 1833, Mary, dau. of Joseph Sawyer, (b. Feb. 14, 1809; d. June 27, 1850). 2d. June 10. 1851, Judith A., dau. Hale Grow, (b. Corinth, Sept. 7, 1816). He d. June 5, 1890. Four c. by 1st m.; two by 2d.

  i. Mary Melissa, b. Oct. 16. 1835; m. E F. Bailey, (Benjamin,[3] Joshua,[2] Jacob[1]) q. v.; d. June 14, 1883.
 ii. Joseph Runnels, b. March 13, 1839; d. Oct. 5, 1854.
iii. Milo Chamberlain, b. Dec. 12, 1841. Served in the Union Army, Oct. 4, 1862, to July 14, 1863, in Co. H, 12th Vt., and in 3d Vt. Battery Sept. 1, 1864, till the end of the war, June 15, 1865. Farmer in Newbury. He m. March 19, 1867, Helen M., dau. of John Hazeltine; d. Oct 7, 1900.
 iv. Jacob Emery, b. April 23, 1845. Res. Newbury. Unm. Carpenter.
  v. Hale Grow, b. Dec. 10, 1852; farmer on homestead.
 vi. Charles Alonzo, b. Dec. 1, 1856. At home and at school till 1881; clerk in Deming's store at Wells River one year; bookkeeper in National Bank of Newbury, 1882-3; bookkeeper and teller in Lancaster National Bank 1883 to Feb. 15, 1890; cashier of Stoneham, Mass., National Bank from organization, March 1, 1890, till date; director in same; trustee of Stoneham Five Cents Savings Bank, which has deposits of about $800,000.

27 MOODY BEDEL,[4] (Abner,[3] Jacob,[2] Jacob[1]) b. Oct. 19, 1803; m. Lydia Vance. He rem. to Marengo, McHenry Co., Ill, where he d. subsequently to 1884.
   Children:
    i. Abner H., b. May 27, 1839.
   ii. Elizabeth A., b. Aug. 23, 1841.
  iii. Alice J., b. Aug. 21, 1843.
   iv. Orrin B., b. Feb. 17, 1845.
    v. Lucinda S., b. May 3, 1851.
   vi. Kate R., June 16, 1853.
  vii. Nellie C., b. Sept. 16, 1855.

28 NATHANIEL M.,[4] (Abner,[3] Jacob,[2] Jacob[1]) b. June 7, 1812; m. June 10, 1880, Phebe (Clark), widow of his brother Allen. No c. Nathaniel and Albert Bayley were in trade at East Topsham many years; then a short time in Haverhill, where he res. till death, and represented that town in the legislature of 1857; d. Nov. 24, 1892.

29 AZRO,[4] (Abner,[3] Jacob,[2] Jacob[1]) b. June 30, 1814; m. Feb. 22, 1843, Hannah, dau. of Sherburne Lang of Bath, where he lived until 1867, when he rem. to Haverhill. Farmer on Ladd Street; d. Haverhill, July 10, 1884.
   Children:
    i. Henry S., of Haverhill; b, in Newbury.
   ii. Emery A.. of Newry, Me.
  iii. Clara Nelson, of Chelsea, Mass.
   iv. Edwin, now in Montana.
    v. Charles, of Lawrence, Mass.
   vi. Hazen H.. in Texas.
  vii. Herbert, in Montana.
 viii. Mary, (Mrs. Alonzo Prescott), of Helena, Montana.

30 ALBERT,[4] (Abner,[3] Jacob,[2] Jacob[1]) b. March 21, 1818. In business with his brother, Nathaniel, in Topsham and Haverhill, then at the latter place alone, afterward removing to Bradford, where he became the first president of the Bradford Savings Bank & Trust Co. Town Representative from Haverhill, 1862. He m. May 8, 1848, Harriet A. Blake of Topsham. He d. Nov. 5, 1879.
   Children:
    i. Nelson Albert.
   ii. Isabelle, m. Phinehas Chamberlin, a lawyer of Bradford, (b. Bath, March 7, 1855; d. Minneapolis, Minn.. August, 1887).

31 EDWIN[4], (Abner,[3] Jacob,[2] Jacob[1]) b. July 16, 1820. Clerk in a store in Corinth, and afterwards in the store of John Pratt at Post Mills, Vt. Clerk in a store in Boston, 1842 to 1847, then in partnership with John A. Park at Gardiner, Me. After some years he bought out his partner and continued in business alone till 1861, when he removed to Jamaica Plain, Mass. In Newbury, 1867, till death. He m. Oct. 23, 1861, Vesta (Capen), widow

of Peter Grant of Gardiner, Me., dau. of Aaron and Izannah (White) Capen of Dorchester, Mass., a descendant of Bernard Capen who came from England to America, 1662, and on her mother's side from Peregrine White, who was born on the "Mayflower" in Cape Cod harbor, Nov. 20, 1620. He d. Oct.11, 1888.

Children:

   i. Edwin Allen, b. July 30, 1862, Jamaica Plain, Mass. Fitted for college at Newbury and St. Johnsbury Academy. Graduated Dartmouth College, 1885. Business and teaching, 1885-87. Graduated Boston University Law School, 1891. Admitted to the bar in Suffolk County, 1891, and located in Boston. Formed a law partnership with John H. Colby, 1892. He m. at Newbury, June 15, 1892, Lucia A., dau. E. V. Watkins, M. D. Res. Lexington, Mass. C., Marian Vesta, b. Lexington, Jan. 9. 1895.

  ii. Wallace, b. March 22, 1864; d. Aug. 25, 1864.

32 NELSON,[4] (Abner,[3] Jacob,[2] Jacob[1]) b. Jan. 6, 1822; m. Oct. 29, 1861, Eliza A., dau. of Gilman Barnett; d. July 19, 1881. Farmer on homestead with his brother George.

Children:

   i. Martha Frances, b. Aug. 29, 1862; m. June 12, 1894, Frederic Hodgdon of Rumford Point, Me., merchant.

  ii. Abner, b. Sept. 30, 1864. Merchant at Lancaster, N. H., with his brother Louis, since April, 1892. They have been twice burned out, and are now located in a fine brick block built by themselves in 1899, on corner of Main and Middle streets.

 iii. Louis Gilman, b. Sept. 18, 1866; m. June 24, 1896, Clara W. Jacobs of L. Res. Lancaster, N. H.

 iv. William Nelson, b. June 17, 1870; d. Jan. 17, 1890.

  v. Florence V., b. March 30, 1872; d. Sept. 26, 1888.

 vi. Helen M., b. Feb. 8, 1875; d. Apr. 15, 1877.

 vii. Mabel Louise, b. June 28, 1878; d. Oct. 21, 1888.

viii. Albert Edward, b. May 18, 1880; d. Apr. 3, 1882.

33 MILO,[4] (Abner,[3] Jacob,[2] Jacob[1]) b. Feb. 4, 1824; m. Ellen, dau. Samuel Page. Merchant at Haverhill Corner many years and res. there.

Children:

   i. Anna Gertrude.

  ii. Maud Edith, m. Ned Barber of Haverhill.

4 JAMES,[2] (Jacob[1]) b. Oct. 1, 1757; d. April 19, 1784. "Killed by an accident," his grave stone says. Old people used to say that he came to his death by foul means. Served in the revolutionary war, and was taken prisoner on the evening of June 15, 1782 by the party which had just failed in their attempt to capture his father. He was returning from the sawmill, bareheaded and barefooted, and was carried to Canada in that condition and held a prisoner for several months. He m. Sarah, dau. Capt. John G. Bayley, (b. Nov. 25, 1765). After his death she m. Otho Stevens, q. v. C., Lydia, who m. a Mr. Cunningham of Bradford and went West. 2d, James A., b. Jan. 23, 1784; m. Mary Christie, who d. Dec. 16, 1854. He d. Dec. 14, 1866.

Children:

   i. Abigail L., b. Dec. 14, 1809; m. Oct. 22, 1838, Joseph Chamberlin, (Joseph,[3] Joseph,[2] Richard[1]) q. v.

  ii. Mary Ann, b. July 4, 1812; m., March 1, 1854, James Gage; d. July 28, 1896.

 iii. Sophronia, b. May 18, 1815; m. Feb. 4, 1848, Charles J. Scott; d. Feb. 20, 1888.

 iv. Thomas C., b. Nov. 11, 1817; d. Nov. 27, 1842.

  v. Josiah L., b. Aug. 15, 1820; d. Aug. 21, 1839.

 vi. Richard, b. Feb. 8, 1824. Res. Lancaster, N. H.

 vii. Harriet, b. May 15, 1829; m.   Cyrus son of James Gage. He d. at Sherbrooke, P. Q., Jan. 28, 1899. She d. at Sherbrooke, Oct. 17, 1898; buried at Newbury.

5 COL. JOHN BAYLEY,[3] (John,[2] Jacob[1]) b. Newbury, May 20, 1765; m. May 5, 1785, Betsey, dau. of Capt. John G. Bayley, q. v., (b. Jan. 29, 1770; d. Dec. 24, 1788); one c., Prudence, b. Apr. 28, 1786; m. Dea. John Buxton, q. v.; m. 2d, Nov. 19, 1789, Hannah, dau. of Ezekiel and Ruth (Hutchins)

Ladd; (b. Haverhill, May 13, 1772) ; served a short time in guarding and scouting, near the end of the revolutionary war; Lieut.-Col. in the war of 1812; Colonel in the militia; lived some years at West Newbury on the "Atwood place"; returned to the Ox-bow, and lived in a two-story house opposite the cemetery, where he d. July 26, 1839. His family was very prominent in the Meth. ch.

Children by 2d marriage:

ii. Betsey, b. Oct. 30, 1790; m. Dr. Samuel Putnam, q. v.
34 iii. George W., b. June 15, 1792.
35 iv. Jeffrey A., b. Feb. 21, 1794.
v. Hannah, b June 10, 1796; m. Dr. John Stevens, q. v.
vi. Lucia, b. June 8, 1798; m. Tappan Stevens, q. v.
vii. Adaline, b. Apr. 25, 1800 ; d. Apr. 20, 1803.
36 viii. John H., b. Feb. 25, 1802.
ix. Adaline, b. July 10, 1804; m. Dec. 11, 1828, Moses Rogers, q. v.
x. Jane, b. Oct. 15, 1806; m. Arnold Johnson of Barnet.
xi. Mary, b. Dec. 24, 1808; m. Thomas Thornton.

34 GEORGE WASHINGTON,[3] (John,[2] Jacob[1]) b. June 15, 1792; m. May 25, 1820, at Rutland, Lucia M. Reed. Res. Saratoga, N. Y., where their three c. were b. Removed to Baton Rouge, La., 1830. Carpenter. His wife returning from a visit to New York, with her youngest child and sister was ship wrecked. She and her sister were drowned, but the child was picked up on the beach and saved.

35 JEFFREY AMHERST,[3] (John,[2] Jacob[1]) b. Feb. 22, 1794. Served in the war of 1812. Colonel in militia. Lived in Newbury, then in Stanstead, P. Q., (1830-34) and Newbury. where Rev. G. N. Bryant now lives. Wheelwright. He m. Dec. 2, 1819, Melissa, dau. of Col. Simeon Stevens, q. v., (b. Oct. 3, 1798; d. Sept. 9, 1885 at Evanston, Ill., buried in Newbury). He d. Oct. 12, 1858.

Children:

i. Hannah Stevens, b Sept. 6, 1820; m. Oct. 26, 1842, John Alonzo, son of John and Hannah (Putnam) Pearsons, (b. Bradford, Sept. 8, 1818; rem. to Evanston, Ill., and built in 1853, the first house in that place. Mr. and Mrs. Pearsons have been intimately connected with the development and growth of Northwestern University from its beginning, and their house has been the home of many students who were preparing for the ministry. C., (1) Henry Alonzo, b Aug. 14, 1843; enlisted in the 8th Ill. Cav.; pro. to Lieut.; served four years, 1861-65; m. Jan. 3, 1867, Catharine J. West; one son, Henry Putnam, b. Jan. 15, 1873. (2) Lucy Isabella, b. Mar. 9, 1848; m. Rev. Wilbur F. Mappin; c., Alice and Lillian M. (3) Charles Edward, b. May 6; d. Oct. 15, 1862. (4) Helen M., b. Dec. 4, 1865; m. July 8, 1890, Rev. Harvey R. Calkins; d. Mar. 27, 1893.
ii. Betsey, b. Dec. 2, 1822; d. Dec. 11, same year.
iii. Marian Wallace. b. Oct. 12, 1824; m. Jan. 2, 1843. Rev. Zadoc Seymour Haynes (b Guilford, Vt., May 15, 1816. In Methodist Episcopal ministry, 1842 till death. At Newbury, 1865-7. Pastor of Methodist church, 1868-71). C., (1) Emery J., b. Cabot, Feb. 6, 1846. Graduated Wesleyan University, 1867. Pastor of several prominent Methodist and Baptist churches. Now engaged in literary work. He m. 1st, May 6, 1869, Jennie Crowell of Norwich, Conn , who d. April 26, 1873; 2d, Grace Farley of Poughkeepsie, N. Y. 3 c. (2) Carlos J., b. June, 1849. (3) Albert, b. March 9, 1855. (4) Hattie, b. April, 1857. Graduated Wesleyan University.
iv. Sarah,b . March 25, 1826; m. Dec. 13, 1848, Daniel Wooster Stevens.
v. Melissa, b. April 4, 1828; d. Oct. 16, 1887; m. July 22, 1850, Rev. Joseph Elijah King. q. v.
vi. William Little Stevens, b. March 5, 1830; teacher; m. 1st, Aug. 15, 1854, Maria Louise, dau. of David Goodall of Bath; 2d, Ellen Hewes; d.
vii. Harriet Amelia, b. July 3, 1833; m. Nov. 1868, George Shuttleworth; d. Oct. 14, 1898.
viii. Ellen Augusta, b. Aug. 22, 1836; m. Oct. 15, 1857, George Batchelder.
ix. Charles Francis, b. Sept. 12, 1839; soldier in the civil war; d. Sept. 19, 1874, unm.

x. Sophia Louise, b. Oct. 14, 1843; m. Jan. 31, 1867, Ezekiel T. Johnson of Buffalo, N. Y.; d. B. May 17, 1870.

36 JOHN H.,[3] (John.[2] Jacob[1]) b. Feb. 26, 1802; m. Feb. 27, 1823, Harriet, dau. of Samuel Rogers, and removed to Buffalo, N. Y., where she is living (1901) at the age of 97.

Children:
i. John, d. y.
ii. Charles, lives in Canada.
iii. Elizabeth, m. a Mr. Savage; res. Penn Yan, N. Y. C. living, (1) John of Illinois. (2) Helen, a teacher of Brooklyn, N. Y.

6 ISAAC,[2] (Jacob[1]) b. June 29, 1767. Farmer on the Ox-bow, built the house in which his grandson, Henry W. Bailey, now lives. Was justice of the peace many years, and generally known as "Esq. Isaac." Town clerk 19 years. County clerk, 1801-12. Representative, 1805, 1815, 1825. Member of a council of censors; m. March 25, 1788, Betsey, dau. of Col. Thomas Johnson, (b. Feb. 28, 1770; d. March 13, 1844). He d. August 30, 1850.

Children:
i. Amelia, b. Aug. 5, 1788; m. Sept. 26, 1810, Col. William Barron of Bradford; d. April 6, 1816. C., (1) Elizabeth, m. Joseph M. Bean of Lyme, N. H. (2) Mary, m. Silas Burbank of Montpelier.
ii. Betsey L., b. Jan. 26, 1790; m. Simeon Stevens, q. v.
iii. Clarissa, b. Feb. 4, 1792; m. John Chamberlain, q. v.; d. Dec. 27, 1819.
37 iv. Thomas J., b. Nov. 30, 1793; d. 1868.
38 v. Isaac A., b. Oct. 17, 1795.
39 vi. Richard W., b. Nov. 20, 1797; d. July 31, 1848.
vii. Abigail J., b. Dec. 20, 1799; d. Sept. 5, 1830.
viii. Nancy D., b. Dec. 6, 1801; d. Aug. 8, 1810.
40 ix. Harry C., b. Feb. 10, 1804.
x. Susan W., b. Aug. 30, 1806; d. July 24, 1810.
xi. Horatio N., b. Oct. 1, 1808; d. Aug. 5, 1810.
xii. Susan, b. July 25, 1810; d. Nov. 2, 1815.
xiii. Nancy, b. Dec. 29, 1812; d. Nov. 12, 1834.

37 THOMAS J.,[3] (Isaac.[2] Jacob[1]) b. Nov. 30, 1793; merchant at Boston; m. 1st, July, 1819, Eliza Handley, (b. Acton, Mass., 1791; d. 1854); 2nd, Sophia Williams, (d. 1859); 3d, Augusta Foster, (who m. 2d, Prof. Stems of Harvard College; d. 1873). He d. 1869.

Children:
i. William B., b. 1819; d. 1894.
ii. Elizabeth, b. 1821; m. George Bemis of Boston; d. 1859.
iii. Amelia, b. 1823; d. 1837.
41 iv. Thomas, b. 1827.
v. Horace, b. 1829; enlisted in 22d Mass.; d. in Boston, from wounds received at the battle of the Wilderness, 1864.
vi. Henrietta, m. Charles M. White, who d. 1889; res. Winthrop, Mass.
vii. Mary E., m. George E. Carbee of Newbury; res. Burlington.
viii. Charles H., emigrated to the island of Ceylon in 1857 and d. from sunstroke.

38 ISAAC ALPHA,[3] (Isaac,[2] Jacob[1]) b. Oct. 17, 1795; m. Feb. 2, 1826, Ruth. dau. Raymond Chamberlin, (d. April 7, 1854); farmer on homestead; d. July 7, 1880.

Children:
i. Jacob, b. Dec. 24, 1826; d. Feb. 10, 1827.
ii. Harvey W., b June 7, 1828; m. Nov. 20, 1856, Hannah Jane Bailey, who d. Nov. 2, 1863. He d. Jan. 15, 1901, at Chattanooga, Tenn. C., (1) Gertrude M., b. June 16, 1858. (2) Frederick, b. July 7, 1859.
iii. Amelia, b. July 12, 1833; d. June 6, 1896.
iv. Martha H., b. July 8, 1835; d. July 19, 1838.
v. Henry Ward, b. Feb. 10, 1839; farmer on homestead, also musician. See p. 345 and war record; m. Jan. 26, 1865, Julia Ellen, dau. of Jacob G. and Abigail (Hazen) Dutton of Hartford, Vt. C., (1) Agnes Ellen, b. Dec. 3, 1865. (2) Frank Dutton, b. Dec. 15, 1867. (3) William Henry, b. Aug. 4, 1871.

39 RICHARD W.,[3] (Isaac,[2] Jacob[1]) b. Nov. 20, 1797; merchant in Boston; m. Martha Bates; d. Troy, N. Y., July 31, 1848.
   Children:
   i. Henry, disappeared and never heard from.
   ii. James, merchant in Boston; d. there leaving a widow and children.
   iii. Ellen, m. Dec. 2, 1847, Joseph C. Bayley; three sons.
   iv. George, m.
   v. Martha, unm.

40 HARRY CROSWELL,[3] (Isaac,[2] Jacob[1]) b. Feb. 10, 1804; m. 1st, May 26, 1828, Lucy Ann, dau. of Capt. Uriah Ward of Haverhill, (b. Aug. 10, 1808; d. March 22, 1841); 2d, Nov. 18, 1841, Maria, dau. of Joseph Herbert of Haverhill, who d. Oct. 27, 1858; 3d, 1860, Sarah, dau. of Calvin Jewett, (b. St. Johnsbury, Sept. 30, 1815). Farmer on the Ox-bow; lived where Mrs. E. E. Miller now lives; a quiet, industrious, unassuming man, and a faithful member of the Cong. ch., from March 6, 1842, till death, Aug. 5, 1879.
   Children, three by 1st and three by 2nd marriage:
   i. Harriet Elizabeth, b. 1830; m. Nov. 25, 1852, Ezra B. Chamberlain, q. v.
   ii. Sarah Ward, b. April 9, 1834; d. 1856.
   iii. Mary Belle, b. Feb. 2, 1839; d. 1841.
   iv. Harriet, b. 1843; d. 1859.
   v. Susan M., b. 1845; m. George Carbee; d. 1878.
   vi. Charles H., b. 1847.

41 THOMAS,[4] (Thomas J.,[3] Isaac,[2] Jacob[1]) b. Boston, Apr. 10, 1827. Educated at the Boston Latin School. Organized and drilled the 116th Ill. Vols. in the civil war, and was appointed by President Lincoln colonel of the 9th regiment U. S. colored troops, and participated in some of the battles before Richmond. After the close of the war he was ordered to service on the Rio Grande and was not mustered out till 1867. Now Notary Public at St. Louis, Mo.; m. 1864, Lizzie Thomas of Belleville, Ill., who d. 1869.
   Children:
   i. Clara, d. Decatur, Ill., Sept. 10, 1880.
   ii. Mary Isabelle, d. Belleville, Ill., Jan. 4, 1884.

BAYLEY.

ENOCH, son of Joshua Bayley, and brother of Gen. Jacob Bayley, was born in Newbury, Mass., Sept. 20, 1719. He graduated at Harvard College, and entered the ministry, and, according to generally accepted accounts, became a chaplain to the Massachusetts troops in the old French war, and d. at Crown Point in 1757. He m. Priscilla Frye, and their children were Frye, who settled in this town, Sarah, Elizabeth and Enoch. Sarah m. Farnum Hall of Methuen, Mass. Elizabeth m. George Smith, a Scotchman, and settled at Nassau, New Providence. Enoch was a shipmaster and lived in Baltimore. He m. Dorothea Gardner, a German woman. Frye, the oldest of the family, b. Newbury, Mass., Jan. 1, 1749, O. S. He was induced by his uncle, Col. (afterwards General) Jacob Bayley, to come to Newbury at the age of fourteen, and was made a grantee of the town. He settled on a farm which included the two northerly rights on Cow meadow. He built a log house at the foot of the hill, at the north end of the meadow, and in 1775 dug the cellar and began the house in which J. G. Learned, the present owner of the farm now lives. The frame was not raised till two years later, and the house was not completed till after the war. In March, 1776, he was one of the four men employed by Col. Thomas Johnson to go with him, and mark out a road for the passage of troops to St. Johns. In the spring he joined the army in Canada as an ensign. A fragment of his diary, kept during the retreat, is elsewhere given. In October, 1777, he commanded a company which went from Newbury to Saratoga, which rendered valuable service, and was present at the surrender of Burgoyne. In December, 1777, he was sent to Canada by order of Maj. General Gates, with a flag, to escort a British officer; Nehemiah Lovewell of Newbury, and John Powell of Strafford, were the others of the party. They were overtaken by a severe storm, their

provisions were exhausted, and they came near starving. On arriving in
Canada their flag was disregarded, and they were thrown into prison
where he remained a year, returning to Boston by way of Halifax, after
being exchanged, Oct. 8, 1778. He was captain of a company attached to
Col. Peter Olcott's regiment, in guarding and scouting till May, 1781.
Captain also of a company under Col. Robert Johnston, from that date
till the end of the war, in similar duty. He was often dispatched by Gen.
Bayley on important service. After the war he settled on his farm, and
was engaged in a great amount of town and county business, and
was colonel in the militia. He also accumulated an extensive library, for
those days, and many of the books are still preserved in this town. Being
appointed sheriff of the county, he rem. to Chelsea, where he spent his last
years, receiving in old age a pension of $250 per annum. In his prime he
was one of the most prominent men in the county; his acquaintance was
very extensive; and the services rendered, and hardships undergone by him
in the service of the country were excelled by very few in the Coös region.
Yet, from the fact that he is mentioned only once, casually, by Rev. Grant
Powers, his memory has been neglected, and his services are forgotten.
He was very hospitable and many noted men gathered under his roof.
The members of this family were buried in the garden of the house in
which Mr. Learned now lives, but when the farm was sold in 1863, their
remains were removed to the cemetery at the Ox-bow. He m., 1st,
Deborah, dau. of Daniel Tillotson, q. v., (b. 1748; d. Jan. 30, 1772.) Her
funeral sermon, by Rev. Peter Powers, was printed, and is supposed to be
the first publication in this town. He m. 2d, Mary Porter, (b. 1753; d.
Jan. 15, 1807). She was a member of the Congregational church. He m.
3d, Mrs. Eddy of Chelsea. He d. Jan. 11, 1827; buried at Newbury.
Children, one by 1st and twelve by 2d marriage:
  i. Abigail, b. March 25, 1770; m. Daniel Tillotson of Orford; d. September,
      1848. Their son, B. F. Tillotson was prominent in Orford.
 ii. Deborah, b. Nov. 24, 1773; d. Sept. 10, 1777.
iii. Anne, b. Sept. 14, 1775; d. July 19, 1776. (See diary.)
 iv. Mary, b. Nov. 7, 1777; d. Nov. 18, 1778.
  v. Enoch, b. Sept. 20, 1779. Thrown from a horse and killed, Aug. 16, 1792.
 vi. Sarah, b. Aug. 19, 1781; d. Aug. 23, 1863.
vii. Lavinia, b. Nov. 24, 1783; d. June 18, 1817.
viii. Frye, b. March 21, 1786. Farmer on homestead. Was a man of great
      intelligence. Many of the incidents related in the earlier part of this
      volume came through him. He d. June 30, 1837.
 ix. Gardner, b. Feb. 3, 1789. Settled on the eastern shore of Maryland and m.
      in Baltimore, Elizabeth Howard, by whom he had one son, James, who d.
      y., and m. 2d, a Mrs. Goldsboro. Res. where he d. about 1850, at
      Cambridge, Md.
  x. Hannah, b. March 5, 1791. She lived on the homestead with her sister
      after the death of their brother Frye, until her death, the last of the
      family here. She d. Oct. 18, 1863.
 xi. Elizabeth, b. June, 1793; d. June 26, 1812.
xii. John Morris, b. Oct. 13, 1795. Grad. at Harvard College. Settled in
      Baltimore where he was a lawyer; m. Elizabeth Evans; d. 1823. Three c.
xiii. Enoch, b. Jan. 29, 1800. Episcopal clergyman in Maryland, where he m.
      Gertrude Travers. Three c. Died in Vienna, Dorchester county.

BAYLEY.

JOHN G. This family, having a common ancestor with that of General Jacob
    Bayley is related to it in many ways. The early ancestry is the same.
    John[1] the emigrant; John[2] (1615-1691); Joseph,[3] (brother of Isaac, the
    grandfather of Gen. Jacob Bayley), was killed by the Indians in 1723, near
    Portland, Me.; m. 1st, a Miss Putnam of Danvers and 2d, "Widow Sarah
    Giddings." By the latter he had several sons, one of whom had several sons, one
    of whom, known as John Gideon Bayley,[5] was somewhat prominent in his
    time. He m. in 1764 Abigail, dau. of Col. Moses and Abigail (Bayley)
    Little, a niece of Gen. Jacob Bayley. The marriage was opposed by her
    parents and they came to Newbury, and settled on Musquash meadow, on

part of what is now F. E. Kimball's farm. Some time subsequent to the revolution they removed to West Newbury and settled where William Carleton now lives, where he d. in the winter of 1816-17. Abigail Bayley Little was b. Apr. 2, 1749. She was a woman of remarkable strength of character, and showed great bravery during many emergencies of the revolutionary war. She d. Sept. 23, 1838, having, says Mrs. J. D. Martin, 250 descendants at the time of her death. Capt. John G. Bayley commanded a company in Col. Peter Olcott's regiment, from April, 1777, to May, 1779. This company only served during several alarms in guarding and scouting, few of the men serving more than two months. He commanded a company in 1780, and seems to have had the general oversight of affairs in the abscences of Gen. Bayley, and was several times sent by him as bearer of important messages. He represented the town (says Deming's catalogue) in the convention at Cornish, 1778, Town Representative 1781, 1785, also delegate to the convention which met at Windsor June 4, 1777. (See Town Officers). On account of his opposition to Rev. Peter Powers during the last years of his ministry, he is not mentioned by Rev. Grant Powers.

Children:
i.   Sarah. b. Nov. 25, 1765; m. 1st, James, son of Gen. Jacob Bayley, q. v. 2d, Otho Stevens, q. v.
1 ii.   James, b. Aug. 1767.
   iii. Elizabeth, b. Jan. 29, 1770; d. December, 1788.
2 iv.   Moses L., b. 1772.
    v.   Abigail L., b. June 23, 1774; m. 1st, Phinehas Stone, 1 dau., and 2d, Hon. F. A. Summer of Claremont, N. H. Six c. One of their sons graduated at Harvard, 1823, and was a physician; d. Feb. 23, 1850.
   vi.   Anna, b. May 12, 1776; m. Isaac Duffs. She has many notable descendants in Maine.
   vii. John, b. July 17, 1778. Rem. to Ohio.
   viii. Prudence, b. Nov. 18, 1780; m. Zebedee Briggs, a tailor of Wells River. Eight c. No record.
   ix.   Daniel, b. Sept. 27, 1782; m. Nov. 13, 1804, Hannah Hibbard. Soldier in the war of 1812. and d. at New Orleans near its close. Thirteen c.
3 x.   Josiah L., b. May 28, 1786.
   xi.   William W., b. May 12, 1788. Served in war of 1812. Settled in Maine.
   xii. Elizabeth M., b. Nov. 26, 1789; m. Simon Blake, who succeeded his father-in-law on the homestead at West Newbury. He built a tannery there, which he conducted successfully several years. He was a very active business man. He d. October, 1838. Their c. were Royal, Betsey, who m. a Mr. Gould, and Oscar, who became a merchant at Chicago.
   xiii. Mary F., b. Jan. 28, 1793; m. 1st, Ebenezer S. McIllvaine, 2d, Charles K. Merrill.

1 JAMES,[2] (JOHN G.[1]) b. Newbury, Mass., Aug. 17, 1767. Farmer in this town; m. 1st, Sarah Stevens; 2d a Mrs. Heath. He d. 1847.
Children:
i.   Anna, m. Reuben Batchelder of Bradford; d. Burlington. One son, Carlos.
ii.   Betsey.
iii. Tristram, b. May 1, 1805; m. Eunice, dau. John Strong of Orford, N. H. Physician and farmer at Adrian, Mich.; d. July 1, 1863. Ten c.
iv.   Robert, lived in Boston.
v.   Jackson, lived in Boston.
vi.   Henry, in Newbury.

2 MOSES LITTLE, b. 1772; m. Elizabeth Dennis of Marblehead, Mass., sister of the wife of Rasmus Jonson.
Children:
i.   Michael, b. Feb. 5, 1792. Soldier for 32 years in the regular army. Was in the war of 1812, and the Seminole war. He spent his last years with his sister Alice; d. Nov. 7, 1862.
ii.   Laura M., b. Oct. 17, 1794; m. Dec. 4, 1817, Enoch P. Chase, nine c.
iii. Elizabeth, b. Sept. 23, 1796; m. Isaac Wilkins.
iv.   Erasmus J., b July 15, 1798.
v.   John D., b. Oct. 10, 1802.

vi. Sarah M., d. y.
vii. Alice J., b. March 28, 1811. She never m. and lived in the house built by Rasmus Jonson, where she d. suddenly, December, 1874.
viii. Sarah M., b. Feb. 20, 1813; m. Wyatt Osgood of Amesbury, Mass.

3 JOSIAH LITTLE,[2] (John G.[1]) b. May 28, 1786; m. Anna, dau. Dea. William Carter. He d. Feb.6, 1835. She m. 2d, John Peach, Sr., and d. Aug. 1877, aged 83.
Children:
  i. Mary Ann, b. July 29, 1812 m. Burke Tyler, of Keene, N. H.
  ii. William H., b. July 13, 1813. Lived in Waterford.
  iii. John G., b. April 23, 1815. Lived in New York.
  iv. Betsey M, b. Dec. 29, 1816; m. John Peach, Jr., q. v.
  v. Fred, b. May 22, 1818. Lived in West Virginia. Served in the Union army.
  vii. George, b. Feb. 11, 1821; d. un-m. July. 1877.
  viii. Jasper, b. Dec. 5, 1823; d. July, 1854, leaving one son, William H. Bailey of Whitefield.

BAILEY.

This family was descended from James Bailey, who came to Rowley, Mass., about 1640, and d. 1677.
II. JOHN, of Rowley, (1642-1790) m. Mary Mighill. He perished in the expedition to Canada.
III. JAMES, of Bradford, Mass., (1680-1769) m. Hannah Wood.
IV. STEPHEN, of Bradford, (1715-   ) m. 2d Judith Varnum. (A Stephen Bailey, who d. March 3, 1777, in his 65th year, is buried at the Ox-bow, near the c. of Charles Bayley).
V. CHARLES, b. Bradford, Mass., Aug. 27, 1744. He came to Newbury as early as 1774, as he is mentioned in Dr. Samuel White's account book at that time, and rem. to Hardwick about 1790. He was a potter by trade, and had a shop where he made earthern ware, which was at the brick yard on the Ox-bow. He also owned land on Musquash meadow. He served in the revolutionary war. His wife was Abigail Safford of Harvard, Mass., whom he m. in 1767. She d. at Hardwick, Feb. 15, 1828. They were members of the church and were well esteemed in town. He d. at Hardwick, May 15, 1835.
Children:
  i. Charles, b. Brookfield, Mass., Nov. 24, 1768. He settled on land which afterward became the farm of Capt. James Wallace, but rem. to Hardwick about 1797. He d. at Hardwick, Aug. 31, 1839.
  ii. Kiah, b. Newbury, Mass., March 11, 1770. Graduated at Dartmouth College, 1793, and was a Congregational minister from 1797 to 1829. Lecturer and writer. Settled finally in Hardwick, where he d. Aug. 17, 1857, and his wife, March 18, 1846. His younger days were spent here. Kiah Bailey and Jonathan Powers were the first students who went to college from this town.
  iii. Enoch, b. Oct. 1, 1771. Farmer in Hardwick, and after 1839, in Delevan, Wis., where he d. April 8, 1866. Twice married. Thirteen c.
  iv. William, b. Haverhill, Jan. 13, 1773; d. Newbury, Aug. 24, 1774.
  v. Whitefield, b. Newbury, Dec. 8, 1775; m., 1st Aug. 30, 1799. Sally, dau. of Webster Bailey, q. v. She d. May 15, 1828. He m. 2d, Fanny Graves. He d. at Hardwick, March 8, 1847.
  vi. William, b. March 11, 1777; d. Aug. 1, 1779.
  vii. Martha, b. Feb. 29, 1780; m. Dr. Huntington of Greensboro; d. Sept. 13, 1850.
  viii. Abigail, b. March 2, 1782; m. John Cobb, and lived in Brookfield and Peacham. He d. Sept. 19, 1855.
  ix. Ward, b. April 27, 1784; rem. to Hardwick and was a farmer there; m. Judith Hall; d. March 8, 1847. Seven c.
  x. Calvin Porter, b. June 11, 1792; rem. to Perry, N. Y.; d. Sept. 8, 1860.

JAMES BAILEY, brother of Stephen, the father of Charles Bailey, was one of the first settlers of Haverhill, and a prominent man, living on what was afterward called the Dow farm, and now the Keyes farm. He seems to have lived in Newbury at one time, and with his wife and one or two sons, was a member of the 1st ch. He was b. at or near Newbury, Mass., Feb. 11, 1721-22, served in the French war. Was a ship carpenter, and was employed in building boats while in service. He was taken prisoner on Lake George, and carried to France where he was confined 19 mos. in Denan Castle. He came to Haverhill before 1770, and later bought land in Peacham, where he died about 1807. A small copy of Ralph Erskine's Gospel Sonnets, printed in Edinburgh, nearly 200 years ago and carried by him through the French war, and his imprisonment in France, to the end of his life, is now owned by his descendant, Mrs. Elkins of North Troy. He was twice married, 1st to Rachel Berry, and 2d to Mary Kincaid; by the first he had seven children, and by the latter three. His sons were, James, b. 1750, member of 1st ch. in Newbury, became a Baptist minister; Joshua, Abigail, Benjamin, b. May 25, 1760, m. Polly McCawber, and settled in Groton; Luther, who m. Anna Kincaid, and settled in Peacham; and Charles, and five daughters. James, Benjamin and Luther served in the revolutionary war and were carried to Canada. Anna, dau. of Benjamin Bailey, m. John Renfrew of Newbury. Other descendants of James Bailey have lived in Newbury, and the Kincaid family into which James and Luther married is the same to which the wives of Col. John Smith, Joseph Smith and Moses Clark, Sr., belonged.

BAYLEY.

Still another Bayley family lived in Newbury, and their ancestry is understood to be, Stephen, brother of Gen. Jacob Bayley, m. Hannah Kelley of Newbury, Mass., where they lived and died. They had nine children, of whom Enoch, b. April 26, 1741, m. Esther Sawyer of Amesbury, Mass.; rem. to Berlin, but returned to Newbury, Mass., and d. there. They had nine c.

ENOCH, b. Feb. 26, 1772. He m., about 1797, Elizabeth, dau. of Stephen and Sarah (Bailey) Morse, b. Oct. 25, 1777. They came the next year to Newbury, and settled in the extreme southwest part of the town, where he built a log house and later a frame one, burned long ago. He d. Sept. 16, 1819, and is buried in the cemetery near there. His widow m. Simon Ward of Haverhill.

Children, all b. here:

i. Enoch, b. Dec. 11, 1798 or 9, settled in Hyde Park.
ii. Stephen, b. Dec. 9, 1800; m. Hannah Dustin. Went west.
iii. Richard, b. April 14; d. May 12, 1804.
iv. Joshua, b. Feb. 24, 1806. Went, about 1820, to Ashford, Conn. Teacher and farmer. He m. Andalusia Merrick. They settled finally in Coventry, Conn., and there died Feb. 14, 1892. C., (1) Norman Brigham, b. Mansfield, Conn., Sept. 17, 1847. Graduated at the medical department of Yale College 187 . House physician one year at Conn. State Hospital. In practice at Brewster, N. Y., eight years; Haverstraw, N. Y., since 1880. He m. Jan. 10, 1872, Etta Hermion of Preakness, N. Y. No c living; two d. y. (2) Marion Julia, b. Nov. 6, 1848; m. 1875, John Cooley of Coventry, Conn.
v. James Spencer, b. Feb. 18, 1809; m. Betsey, dau. of Mark Banfield. Rem. about 1840 to Michigan. Three c.
vi. Clarissa, b. Feb. 9, 1811; d. un-m. in Lowell, Mass., about 1870.
vii. Betsey, or Elizabeth, b. April 29, 1817; m., 2d, as 2d wife, John Dowse, She d. in Newbury, March 30, 1898.

*THE WEBSTER BAILEY FAMILY.

Webster Bailey's first American ancestor was Richard Bailey, sometimes called Richard of Rowley. As nearly as can be ascertained, he came from Yorkshire, England, between 1630 and 1635. Another authority says that "Richard Bailey came with Richard Dummer in the ship Bevis, 150 tons, Robert Batten, Captain, in April, 1638, when he was fifteen years

---

*By Horace W. Bailey.
NOTE.—For births and deaths see genealogical table on p. 458.

old." The exact date of his death is not known. The records in the office of the Clerk of Courts at Salem, Mass., contain a copy of his will, dated "Rowley 15 of the last month, 1647." In the Salem Court files, Book 1, leaf 98, is found a record of his estate inventoried after his death, dated "6th mon: 23: 1648." So that his death must have occurred between the two last mentioned dates. The records shows him to be a man of comfortable means for those days, the footing of the inventory being "106 L. 08 s. 10 d." His wife was Ednah Holstead by whom he had one child, viz:

II. JOSEPH, who settled in the north part of Rowley, now incorporated as Groveland, Mass. He is now mentioned as he was in his own time, as "Deacon Joseph," having had long church relations, being one of the 18 original members of Congregational church at Bradford, Mass., organized in 1682. He d. Oct. 11, 1712. He was the father of eight c., the fifth being Joseph, Jr.

III. JOSEPH, JR., was b. in 1683, Feb. 13, at Bradford, Mass., (now Groveland), and settled in West Newbury, Mass., on the border of Bradford near his father. He m. Feb. 14, 1710, or 11, Abigail Webster of Bradford, Mass., a dau. of Nathan Webster. Joseph, Jr., d. April 4, 1755. He was the father of seven c., the third being Ezekiel.

IV. EZEKIEL was b. at West Newbury, Mass., in July, 1717; m. Sarah Green of East Haverhill, Mass., June 17, 1746; settled on the home farm where he d. Feb. 6, 1813, aged 96 years. His wife d. at the age of 95 years. They lived as husband and wife, 67 years. He was the father of eight c., the second being Webster.

V. WEBSTER was b. at West Newbury, Mass., Aug. 23, 1747. He m. Mary (or, as she was frequently called, Molly) Noyes, August 25, 1772. A brief sketch of the Noyes family contains a very interesting coincidence, viz: 1639, In Rev. James Noyes and Nicholas, his brother, came from Wiltshire, England, to America, first to Ipswich and then settled in Newbury, Mass. The generations of these two brothers are:

1. Rev. James Noyes	1. Nicholas Noyes
2. William Noyes	2. James Noyes
3. John Noyes	3. Ephraim Noyes
4. William Noyes	4. Prudence Noyes who m. Gen.
5. Mary Noyes who m. Webster Bailey	Jacob Bayley

From Richard of Rowley and John of Salisbury descend the two principal Bailey families in Newbury. As far as can be ascertained, there is no relationship known to exist between Richard and John. It is safe to say that the first representatives of these two families in Vermont came to Newbury. The first forty years of Webster's life were spent in W. Newbury, Mass., where seven of his eleven c. were b. But little is known of his life prior to his coming to Newbury. Judging from a lease published by the West Newbury, Mass., Messenger of May 19, 1888, under the title of "An Old Document," which lease comprises farm and stock from Enoch Plummer to Webster Bailey, dated Dec. 18, 1778, it is probable that Webster Bailey was a farmer prior to his advent in Newbury and well founded tradition says that he was also engaged in the butchering business in his Massachusetts home. It is also presumptive that he served an apprenticeship in the tanning, as well as the boot and shoe business before coming to Vermont. The exact date of Webster Bailey's arrival in Newbury cannot be determined. Alfred Poor, in his Researches in the Merrimack Valley published in 1858, from which many facts of the earlier generations are gleaned, says (page 140) "That Webster resided at West Newbury, Mass., until after March, 1787, and removed his family to Vermont." The first mention of Webster Bailey's name in our land records is found in book 2 at page 211 where the record of a purchase of seven acres of land is made from William Kincade, described as being between Col. Jacob Kent's and Col. Wallace's land, the purchase money being "seventy bushels of wheat." The date of the purchase being Dec. 20, 1788. Then follows the record (in book 2) of various purchases of contiguous lands. These premises which became the Webster Bailey homestead are situated on the river road about one mile and a half south of Newbury village and are now owned and occupied by James A. Johnson. In book 2, page 403, of land records, is found a record of the purchase of a pew (No. 28) in the meeting-house from Frye Bailey for which 10 pounds lawful money was paid, dated Feb. 26, 1794. Webster Bailey united with the Congregational church, Nov. 6, 1791, under the pastorate of Rev. Nathaniel Lambert who came from the same neighborhood in Massachusetts. On August 10, 1811, he was chosen clerk of the church. Molly, wife of Webster, united with the church September, 1813. Webster Bailey was probably a man in comfortable circumstances for those times for he immediately built a tannery and established a wholesale boot and shoe manufacturing business, supplying dealers, neighborhoods and large families in all the new settlements for miles around, employing from 20 to 30 apprentices and journeymen. This was probably the first establishment of its kind in Vermont. The first mention of Webster Bailey's name in the book of "Town Proceedings" is in the record of a town-meeting held on the second Tuesday of March, 1789, at which meeting Gen. Jacob Bayley was moderator and Col. Jacob Kent was clerk. The record reads "10thly, Voted Webster Bailey Leather Sealer." On April 10, 1816, (see Real Estate Records, book 7, page 408) Betsey Lovewell, widow of Nehemiah Lovewell, deeded the "Lovewell Tavern Stand," which included a large tract of land, afterwards sometimes called "The Seminary Farm" to William Bailey. To this place, William Bailey moved with his father and mother, Webster and Molly where they lived until 1830 when Webster d. February 7th and his wife September 30th of the same year. From his advent in Newbury until his removal to Newbury village, Webster Bailey was an important factor in the business affairs of the town. Webster Bailey and wife were genial, lively people with a well appointed house; a happy home noted for real hospitality.

LYDIA, 1st c. of Webster, m. Jesse White Dec. 4, 1800, and moved to Topsham which town has been and is the ancestral home of a large and thrifty family. (See White family).

WILLIAM, 2nd c. of Webster, un-m., was the business center of the Webster Bailey family in this town. He, with his brothers, Ezekiel and Parker, were the successors of Webster Bailey, continuing the shoe and leather business, until about 1827. While he owned the "Betsey Lovewell Stand," 1825-30, he carried on a large general store business at that place, having as partner, Deacon John Buxton. For a time afterwards, he was in the mercantile business at North Haverhill, N. H., with Russell Hurd as partner. However, his life was practically spent in this town. On January 26, 1833, (See Land Records, Book 10, pp. 448), he sold the Betsey Lovewell property to Simeon Stevens and Timothy Morse for $4,500, they conveying it to the Methodist Conference Trustees for the establishment of Newbury Seminary. The "Betsey Lovewell Stand" being converted into the "Seminary Boarding House," its present use, after being remodeled, being a hotel kept by George A. Sawyer. "Uncle Bill," as he was usually called in later years, was a genial, whole-souled man, a large dealer in live stock, raising and buying for the markets. Some of his quaint stories and cute sayings are quoted to this day. On November 20, 1831, he united with the Congregational church and for a long series of years was its collector. He d. at an advanced age, a much respected man.

EZEKIEL, 3d c. of Webster, came to this town with his parents when about ten years old. During his minority and until about 25 years of age, he worked at home as apprentice, journeyman and partner, mastering all the details of tanning and turning leather into boots and shoes. On Sept. 8, 1803, he m. Lucy Bayley, a dau. of Ephraim and Lucy (Hodges) Bayley and a granddaughter of Gen. Jacob Bayley. He moved immediately to Hardwick, where he purchased several tracts of land. In 1808, he bought a tract of three acres of Abel Curtis, on the Hazen road, on which he built a tannery and shoe shop, the first of its kind in that section. In 1813, he sold out to David Tuttle. In 1815, he moved to Orfordville, N. H., built a tannery and continued in the boot and shoe business; also carrying on farming on a large scale. He was appointed postmaster by Andrew Jackson which office he held for many years. He was a Justice of the Peace, also village librarian, keeping both the library and the postoffice in his dwelling house. He was in every sense of the word a man of affairs, prosperous in his business undertakings. Desiring to spend his declining years in this town, he sold his large holdings at Orfordville and moved back to Newbury in 1853. He met with an accident soon after his return, breaking his hip, necessitating the use of crutches the balance of his life. He. d (as also did his brother William) in the house where A. Greer now lives. His widow spent the balance of her years with her nephew, Ephraim B. Strong, at Orford where she died March 1, 1870, aged 87 years, 6 months, 16 days, and was buried by the side of her husband at Newbury. They never had children. "Uncle Zeke" was a strong man physically, blunt of speech, out-spoken in his opinions, with a large streak of brusque humor in his make-up.

SALLY, 4th c. of Webster Bailey, m., August 30, 1799, Whitefield Bailey, who was a descendant of James Bailey, a brother of Richard of Rowley; the generations of Whitefield being: James,[1] John,[2] James,[3] Stephen,[4] Charles,[5] Whitefield.[6] Whitefield Bailey is also a descendant of John of Salisbury as follows: John[1] of Salisbury, John, Jr.,[2] Sarah,[3] who married a Cheney, Elenor Cheney,[4] who married a Safford, Daniel Safford,[5] Abigail Safford,[6] who married Charles Bailey, Whitefield Bailey.[7] Therefore, it is evident that the descendants of Sally have a threefold portion of Bailey blood in their veins. Whitefield Bailey was born at Newbury, Dec. 8, 1775. They settled in Hardwick, where they lived and died. The Whitefield Bailey homestead remained in the family for over a hundred years. Sally's descendants were more numerous and perhaps more widely scattered than any other of Webster's children, many of them are now living in Caledonia County. Wherever located this family has been leaders in affairs, well-to-do, and noted for their integrity. Whitefield Bailey d. March 14, 1847. Both are buried in the Sanborn graveyard at Hardwick. None of their descendants ever lived in this town.

MARY, 5th c. of Webster, m. Samuel Hibbard, (see Hibbard family). They lived in Canada, Hardwick, North Haverhill, N. H. In this town from 1833-9 on the river road at the place now owned by Carlos E. Brock; then back to North Haverhill where the remainder of their days were spent. Uncle Sam Hibbard was a prominent figure in his time and was as well known in Newbury as in Haverhill. He was b. Oct. 28, 1778, d. June 10, 1852. Mary d. Oct. 30, 1878 at the great age of 95 years and 17 days, living to a greater age than any other of the c. of Webster Bailey. They were both buried in the Horse Meadow burying ground at North Haverhill. Five of their seven c. grew to maturity: (3) Ezekiel Bailey Hibbard, b. Dec. 12, 1810 at Hardwick. (4) Thomas William Bailey Hibbard, b. Feb. 8, 1814 at Hardwick; m. Betsey Jane Burnham Feb. 9, 1839; lived in Ashland, Ohio; salesman in New York City; d. at Haverhill, N. H., May 25, 1887. (5) Parker Bailey Hibbard, b. April 4, 1817 at Hardwick; m. Priscilla Eastman Dec. 12, 1842, went west and d. probably in 1851, date unknown. (6) William Bailey Hibbard, b. March 28, 1820; m. Elizabeth, dau. of Col. Moody Chamberlin, of this town, July 11, 1850; m., 2nd time, Susan Graham Ford. He d. at Chicago, Sept. 2, 1899. (7) Mary Hibbard, b. March 22, 1829, at North Haverhill; m. March 14, 1850, Langdon Bailey, who d. at Woodsville, N. H., June, 1898. (3) Ezekiel Bailey Hibbard, m. Esther Johnston, dau. of Col. Robert Johnston, Dec. 26, 1839. He was merchant, mechanic and farmer, lived at North Haverhill, spent several years in the south, but finally settled on the home place of Col. Robert Johnston where his declining years were spent and where he d. Nov. 27, 1892. Mr. Hibbard was a much esteemed citizen of this town. C., a, Robert J., b. at North Haverhill, Aug. 14, 1841; m. Hattie E. Hunt, July 20, 1865. (No c). b, George, d. in infancy.

BETSEY, 6th c. of Webster, m. Rev. John Dutton, (March 19, 1819), a Congregational minister who was b. at Hartford, Vt., Nov. 29, 1776, graduated at Dartmouth College, class of 1801, preached in Maine, and at Pomfret, and Topsham, Vt., moved to North Haverhill where he d. May 18, 1848. Both he and his wife are buried in the Horse Meadow burying ground. They were the parents of one child who grew to maturity, Dorcas, who m. Charles West. Betsey's posterity live at or near Royalton.

TEMPY or TEMPERANCE, 7th child of Webster, was the only one of eleven c. who did not live to maturity. (See genealogical table). She was the last c. b. at West Newbury, Mass., and the only one buried there.

TEMPY, 8th c. of Webster, un-m., always lived at the homestead, was said to be of a very lovable disposition. She was the first of the family b. in Vermont.

PARKER WEBSTER, 9th c. of Webster, was b. at the old homestead in this town, spent his early years as an apprentice in tanning and shoe-making, and at the age of 25, m. Eliza, (pub. Nov. 27, 1817), (b. May 14, 1800), 2d c. of Captain Uriah Ward of Haverhill, N. H. Uriah Ward was the fourth son in the sixth generation from William Ward who came from England in 1639, born in Worcester, Mass., Feb. 2, 1774. He was captain of Artillery in the northern frontier war of 1812. He was widely and well known in this town from the fact of his being a hatter by trade. He lived near the bridge at "Oliverian" village in Haverhill. He was twice married. He d. in March, 1845. Lucy Ann, his sixth c., was the wife of the late Harry C. Bailey, the mother of Elizabeth, wife of Ezra B. Chamberlin. Immediately after his marriage, Parker W. assumed the leadership at the Bailey homestead (his parents and brother William having moved to the village) and continued the tanning and boot and shoe business in partnership with his brother William until the business was discontinued sometime about 1827. In 1828, Parker W. moved to Waits River in Topsham where he built mills on Waits River which were ruined by the great freshet of 1829, causing his financial ruin and necessitating his giving up his business enterprise, adding to this misfortune bodily accident which confined him many months. Parker's course was fraught with hardships never known to his older brothers. He lived for a time in Stanstead, Canada, Orfordville, and Wentworth, N. H., and returned to Newbury in 1851, where he lived in the Greer house with his two brothers, all well advanced in years. Parker W. Bailey and wife united with the Congregational ch. Nov. 20, 1831. Mr. and Mrs. Bailey were devoted to each other, to their family and church, a model couple, great readers of current affairs and devoted Bible students. Their very last years were lovingly ministered to in the home of their son William U. When Parker W. d. in 1881, they had lived happily as man and wife 64 years. Eliza, his wife d. Oct. 1, 1883.

HANNAH, 10th c. of Webster, and PHOEBE, 11th c. both un-m., always lived at the old homestead. Phoebe was a prominent society woman in her day. Hannah united with the Congregational church Nov, 12, 1812; Phoebe July 24, 1819.

HENRY WEBSTER BAILEY, the oldest son of Parker W. Bailey was b. at the old homestead January 18, 1819. As a boy, he took to mercantile life, serving for a time as clerk in Portland, Maine. Afterwards, serving the customary apprenticeship as country store clerk with Nathan Blake, Senior, at East Corinth. He was afterwards employed by John Merrill at East Corinth, East Orange and Piermont Crossing. On May 15, 1849, he m. Harriet, dau. of John Merrill, who now survives him. Mr. Bailey d. childless. Judge Bailey, as he was usually called in his last years, was a prominent man in this section of the state. For 25 years after returning to Newbury, he was the popular foreman in the large Keyes mercantile establishment. He was town clerk thirty years from 1856, town treasurer from 1865 to 1876, Judge of Probate for the Bradford District, 1868 to 1876, and Newbury's member to the General Assembly, 1859 to 1860, and Justice of the Peace for many years. He was a man trustworthy in all the numerous places he occupied. He d. at his home in Newbury village, March 5, 1897.

WILLIAM URIAH, 2nd son of Parker W., was b. Sept. 25, 1820, at the old homestead where his boyhood days were spent. He also lived for a while during his minority with his Uncle William. On December 24, 1844, he m. Abigail Harriman Eaton, (b. Aug. 22, 1824), the eldest of the seven

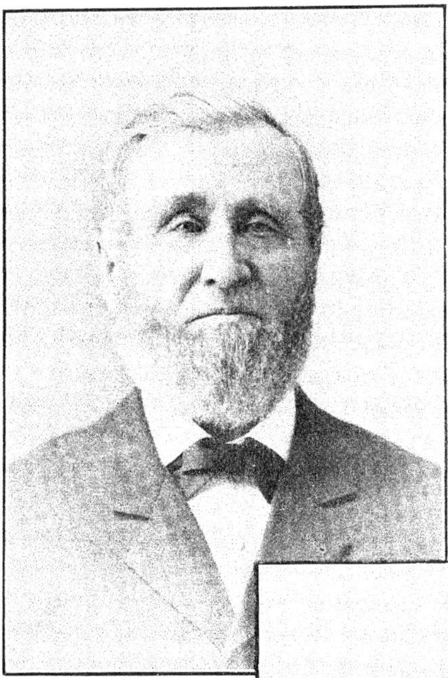

HON. HENRY W. BAILEY.

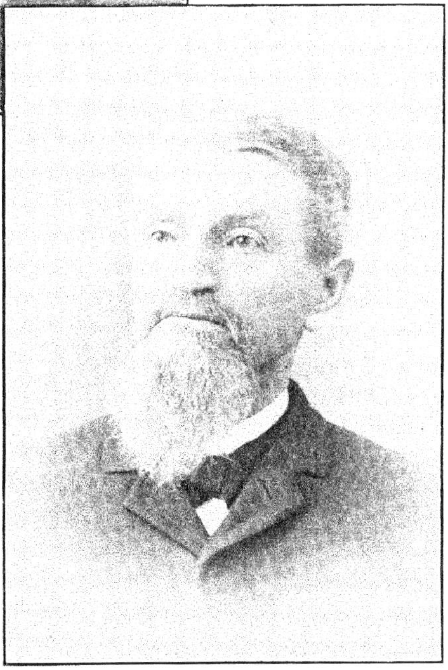

DEA. DANIEL P. KIMBALL.

children of Jesse and Elanor P. Eaton of Wentworth, N. H. They lived at Wentworth, N. H., until May, 1851, when they moved to Newbury, having purchased of Hiram Smith the "Sam White" farm so called, which place has been and now is the William Bailey homestead, being the first farm north of the old Webster Bailey homestead. William U. has been a hard working farmer all his life, holding but few public places, attending to his own affairs. His wife d. Nov. 25, 1880. William U. Bailey and Mary Hibbard Bailey of Woodsville, N. H., are the only surviving grandchildren of Webster Bailey.

HORACE WARD, 3d c. of Parker W., b. Nov. 13, 1822; d. (by drowning in a tan vat) June 2, 1824.

William Bailey's children:
i. Ellen Eliza, b. at Wentworth, N. H., Dec. 26, 1845; m., March 20, 1867, Remembrance Sawyer Chamberlin, a farmer living at Newbury Center. They have one c., William Clark, b. July 28, 1876.
ii. Henry John, b. Wentworth, N. H., April 1, 1850; d. (drowning in Connecticut river) July 7, 1862.
iii. Horace Ward, b. Newbury Jan. 16, 1852, was a State Senator in 1894, was a trustee of the Bradford Savings Bank for ten years, was appointed by Gov. Woodbury in 1894 a Commissioner in the State department of Fisheries and Game which position he held for six years, being also a trustee of the Citizens' Savings Bank and Trust Co. at St. Johnsbury and is the Orange county member of the Republican State committee; was a teacher in the village schools in 1878-1879, and is a member of the Vt. Historical Society.*

WARREN WARD, 4th c. of William U., b. Newbury Dec. 5, 1859. His minority was spent on the home farm with common school advantages. He m. Delia Hatch of Groton.

Their children are:
i. Albert, b. at Groton April 5, 1879. He was a graduate of the International Business College at Manchester, N. H., his diploma bearing date of January 12, 1898; d. at Newbury Feb. 9, 1898.
ii. Abigail Martha, b. Groton, Oct. 3, 1880.
iii. Warren, b. Groton, April 15, 1884.
iv. Horace, b. Newbury, July 14, 1886.
v. Clara, b. Newbury, April 28, 1889.
Warren's home, with the exception of a few years spent in Groton, has been at the home farm where he now resides and where, in addition to his farming, he has carried on a small but profitable lumber business.

JESSE PARKER, 5th c. of William U., b. at Newbury July 20, 1866, d. at Passumpsic, Vt., Jan. 29, 1899. At the age of 16 years, Jesse m. Clara Hatch of Groton, left the homestead and began life's battle. For nearly ten years he was the trusted foreman (although only a boy) of Hon. L. D. Hazen's lumber establishments at Groton and Miles Pond. On Jan. 1, 1898, he began mercantile life at Passumpsic, Vt. with Henry E. Wilson under the firm of J. P. Bailey & Co. in which business he was engaged at the time of his death. By his first wife who d. August, 1886, he had one son, Jesse Parker, Jr., b. at Groton June 7, 1883. On May 5, 1893, Jesse P., m. for his second wife Mary Jennings by whom he had one son, Clarence, b. at Groton Feb. 5, 1895.

In politics, this family of Baileys were whigs, then Republicans, with, (in the earlier generations) very strong Abolition tendencies, being leaders and holding offices under the political party of their choice. William and Ezekiel Bailey were Royal Arch Masons, very prominent in early masonic circles. In religion this family are Congregationalists, and in the earlier generations strong sectarians. Webster Bailey's house was the home of visiting clergyman and delegates.

The war record of this family is meagre. In the ten generations in America of

---

*Besides the pamphlets mentioned in the Bibliography of Newbury, Mr. Bailey published in April, 1901: "A Souvenir of the Seminary Memorial Window, including a History of Methodism in Newbury and of Old Newbury Seminary." Illustrated p. p. 100, Republican Press, St. Johnsbury.—Ed

which Webster is in the fifth, so far as the writer is able to learn, no Bailey in the regular line of descent has ever borne arms regularly enlisted by the U. S. Government. Of Webster Bailey's posterity, there were four war volunteers, two in the war of the rebellion, Carlos and Thomas White of Topsham, and two in the war with Spain, Asher White of Topsham and Paul Burdick of Lake Geneva, Wisconsin.

Webster Bailey's family have been and are tillers of the soil. However, in the third and fourth generations there is a large percentage of literary attainments, college graduates, teachers, authors and writers.

The generations to Webster Bailey are as follows: Richard 1, Joseph 2, Joseph, Jr. 3, Ezekiel 4, Webster 5.

Webster, m. Mary (or Molly) Noyes, Aug. 25, 1772. CHILDREN.	6 Gen. Living	6 Gen. Dead	7 Gen. Living	7 Gen. Dead	8 Gen. Living	8 Gen. Dead	9 Gen. Living	9 Gen. Dead	10 Gen. Living	10 Gen. Dead	Total Living	Total Dead	Total Descendants	Born, M. D. Y.	Died. M. D. Y.	Age. Y. M. D.
Lydia, 1,	1		5	10	5	34	7	9			53	18	71	5—19—1774	2— 1—1833	58— 8—12
*William, 2,	1											1	1	4—15—1776	12—22—1866	90— 8— 7
†Ezekiel W., 3,	1											1	1	9—14—1778	8—18—1862	83—11— 4
Sally, 4,	1		9	7	11	26	5	16			49	26	75	4—19—1781	5—15—1828	47— 0—26
Mary, 5,	1	1	6	6	6	4	5	2	1		13	19	32	10—13—1783	10—30—1878	95— 0—17
Betsey, 6,	1		1	3	3	7	1				10	6	16	11—28—1785	1—19—1842	56— 1—21
‡Tempy, 7,	1											1	1	3—31—1787	12—27—1787	0— 8—26
*Tempy, 8,	1											1	1	12— 1—1789	5—11—1839	49— 5—10
Parker W., 9,	1		1	2	3	2	7	1			11	6	17	1—25—1792	7—12—1881	89— 5—17
*Hannah, 10,	1											1	1	3—23—1794	3—20—1874	79—11—27
*Phebe, 11,	1											1	1	10—14—1797	1—20—1872	74— 3— 6
Total,	11		2	23	29	27	78	19	27	1	136	81	217			

*Unmarried.
†Married Lucy, a granddaughter of Gen. Jacob Bayley; no children.
‡Died in infancy.

Summary: 11 children in the 6th generation, 25 grandchildren in the 7th generation, 56 great-grandchildren in the 8th generation, 97 great-great-grandchildren in 9th generation, and 28 great-great-great grandchildren in the 10th generation: total, 217.

136 living, 81 dead. Average age of the eleven children including the infant Tempy, 66 years, 3 months, 5 days. Average not including the infant Tempy, 73 years, 1 month, 15 days.

Dec. 1, 1899.

BALDWIN.

I. JONATHAN, came from Westminster, West Parish. He m., 1st, Sally Crawford of Westminster. 2d, Hannah Tabor of Topsham. He d. in Topsham. Children, (dates of birth from Topsham records):
   i. Sally, b. Feb. 3, 1795; m. Leverett Page of Groton.
   ii. Ezra, b. Dec. 2, 1796; m. a Miss Peck; farmer in Topsham.
   iii. Hannah, b. April 2, 1803; m. John Bullard of Topsham.
   iv. Fanny, b. Feb. 2, 1805; m. Enoch Page of Groton.
   v. Levi, b. June 5, 1807; m. Ruth White; settled in New York state.
   vi. Jonathan, b. June 25, 1809; m. Elvira Hibbard; settled in New York.
1 vii. Erastus, b. Nov. 6, 1811.
   viii. Leverett, b. Feb. 19, 1814; settled in Biddeford, Me.
   ix. Lydia, b. Jan. 14, 1818; m. John Romney of New York.

1 ERASTUS, b. Nov. 6, 1811, came to Wells River, 1836, and carried on the harness-making business. He also owned the farm which is now that of C. W. Eastman, and was interested in other enterprises. Member of Congregational church. He m., Nov. 13, 1831, Louisa Richardson, (b. Topsham, Sept. 6, 1812). He d. July 16, 1889.
Children:
   i. Addison Ring, b. Topsham, 1832; educated at Newbury Seminary and Norwich University. Went to South Royalton, thence to Ogdensburg, N. Y., and settled finally in Charlotte, N. Y. In produce and shipping business; Episcopalian; m. Carrie Wheeler of Greece, N. Y.; d. at Charlotte July 12, 1896. C., Charles A., Frank E., Alvi T., Carolyn L. and Daisy M.
   ii. Alvi Twing, b. Topsham, 1835; educated at Newbury Seminary and St. Johnsbury Academy. Clerk in Wells River Bank, then bought the William

ALVI T. BALDWIN.

ERASTUS BALDWIN.

Webster store, which he sold to F. Deming. In wholesale boot and shoe business at St. Johnsbury with Mr. Burpee. Returned to Wells River, and was in partnership with his brother, Erastus, in the wholesale boot and shoe business, which they closed out. Then in lumber firm of Henry, Joy & Baldwin, of Zealand, N. H., selling his interest to J. E. Henry. Next he bought the Groton Pond property, which he conducted for some time and sold. Member of Wells River Congregational church, and leader of the choir for many years. He m., March 6, 1861, Mary S. Butler of Haverhill, who d. July 7, 1870, aged 30. He d. Dec. 3, 1884. C., (1) Ralph, d. Dec. 25, 1884, aged 21 years, 4 months. (2) Mary B., d. at four weeks of age. (3) Hammon T., d. at 14 years of age.

iii. Erastus, b. Newbury, August 31, 1841. In wholesale boot and shoe business with his brother. Dealer in carriages, harnesses, etc. President of Wells River Savings Bank from its formation till 1900. Director in National Bank. Proprietor of Baldwin's mineral spring. In 1892 he presented the village library association with a library building in memory of Alvi T. and Ralph Baldwin. Trustee of Tenney Memorial Library. Member of the staff of Gov. Josiah Grout, 1896, with rank of colonel. He m. Jan. 6, 1863, Ellen, dau. of William B. Abbott. Res. Wells River. C, (1) Hammon T., b. Dec. 18, 1863, who owns the Edward Hale farm on Upper Meadow, now called Baldwin's Valley Farm. Town representative, 1900. He m. Nov. 3, 1886, Hattie Cobb of Hardwick. C., a, Bernice E., b. May 29, 1890.

BANFIELD.

GEORGE, came here, it is believed, during the revolutionary war, from Newburyport, Mass. He served during several campaigns, and in old deeds is called a boat-builder. He m. Anna Sanborn, dau. of one of the first settlers of Orange, Vt. At one time he lived at Wells River, but much of his life resided in Topsham. The name is often spelled Banfill. He d. in Newbury, July, 1838, aged 92; his wife a few years later, aged 84. They are buried at the Lime Kiln, in the "Nourse burying ground."
Children:
i. Anna, m. a Mr. Sawyer of Topsham.
ii. Mark, m. Mary Banfield of Newburyport. They lived in Corinth. James Boyce of West Newbury m. their dau. Miriam.
iii. Hannah, m. John Batten of Topsham.
iv. Samuel, m. Sarah Eastman of Topsham. They d. in Nashua, N. H.
v. Betsey, m. Ephraim Bagley of Topsham.
|vi. Benjamin, unknown.
vii. John, lived in Newbury.
viii. Reuben, m. Miss Gates in Whitefield, and had two daus. who m. John and Peter Goddard of Bethlehem, N. H.
ix. George, lived in North Haverhill but d. and buried at Wells River.
x. Abigail, m. Moses Rowell of Bath. Moses Clark of Newbury m. their dau. Martha P.
xi. Mary, m. Caleb Rowell of Walden.

BANNISTER.

WILLIAM BOSTWICK, b. Brookfield, Mass., Nov. 8, 1773. He first came to Newbury in 1796, while a student at Dartmouth College, being recommended by President Wheelock as a proper person to teach a select school. He was a young man of winsome personality, a fine musician, and very social. After graduating, in 1797, he returned and read law with Hon. Daniel Farrand, teaching meanwhile for three years. In practice here 1800-07. He was not eminent at the bar, but his skilful management of several land cases brought him a good practice and laid, it is said, the foundation of a considerable fortune. He occupied, and, it is understood, built, the house under the great elm, south of the Ox-bow cemetery. He became a merchant at Newburyport, accumulated a large estate, and at his death divided $40,000 among several benevolent and missionary societies. Member of the Mass. State Senate, and one of the founders of the American Board of Commissioners for Foreign Missions. Trustee for 16 years of Amherst College. He m. 1st, Jan. 1, 1801, Susan Upham of Brookfield, his native town, who d. after he went from Newbury and 2d, Mary Brown of Newburyport, by whom he had two daus., one of whom d. y., and the other m. Dr. Ebenezer Hale. His 3d wife, whom he m. in 1841, was Zilpha P., dau. of Joel Grant of Norfolk, Conn. She was one of the most distinguished teachers of her time, at Ipswich, Mass., and was associated with Mary Lyon in the establishment of Mt. Holyoke Female Seminary. He d. Newburyport, July 1, 1853.

BARNETT.

There were several Barnett families in Newbury before 1800, whose names have come down to us, but their relation to each other, or their connection, if any, with the present family of that name is not known. Benjamin Barnet served in Capt. James Hawes Co. (N. H.) 1777. Benjamin and John Barnet in Capt. Runals's Co., John also in Capt. Simeon Stevens Co., 1777, one year, Samuel and John were in Capt. John G. Bayley's Co., 1779, guarding and scouting, the former 2 mos., 7 days, and the latter one mo., Benjamin Barnate, (probably Barnet) in same Co. one mo., Hugh Barnett also served in a New Hampshire regiment, Samuel, who was one of Washington's guards came here before 1770, as his wife is mentioned as Mrs. Samuel Barnet in that year. He rem. to Bolton about 1785, and cleared a farm. In 1814, he with other old men, formed a company called the Silver Grays which marched all night to Burlington where they took a sloop for Plattsburgh and were present at the battle. Four weeks later he d. in his 68th year. Andrew Barnett and James also lived here, the former is mentioned in a deed as from Connecticut. Some of this family rem. to Cabot. Samuel Barnet and Samuel Barnet, Jr., signed the N. Y. petition of 1770, and Samuel Barnet is given as head of a family in the census of 1771. Mary, w. of Hugh Barnet received a divorce from him and m. Sept. 28, 1786, Ashbell Shepard. Job Barnet and Sarah Briant were m. Aug. 17, 1787. James Blair and Molly Barnet were m. Oct. 4, 1787. The births of the following children of Job and Sarah Barnet are recorded. (1) Ann, b. June 7, 1788. (2) John, b. May 17; d. June, 1789. (3) Job, b. May 16, 1791. Samuel Barnet was one of a committee of seven chosen by the town June 3, 1783, to prevent the tories from returning to Newbury.

The present family of the name are from the Scotch-Irish colony of Londonderry, N. H., and are supposed to be descendants of John Barnett who d., aged 86, at Londonderry, Oct. 8, 1740. He served in the defence of Londonderry, Ireland, 1689.

Robert, James and David Barnett were brothers; James and David went to Topsham before 1800, where the former had nine c. b. to him between 1800 and 1811, as appears by the records of that town About 1820, he rem. to Barnet, and later, to western New York.

DAVID BARNETT is said to have opened the first store in Topsham, and built, about 1800, a large, two-story, square-roofed house, still standing near the Newbury line on Currier hill. He was a member of the first Masonic Lodge in Newbury. He m. May 8, 1800, Betsey Tenney, who d. April 7, 1813, leaving two daus., Wealthy and Betsey, and a son, John. He m. 2d, Feb. 17, 1814, Eliza Patterson, and a few years later rem. from Topsham.

ROBERT BARNETT, b. Londonderry, N. H., Sept. 14, 1772; m. Dec. 24, 1801, Betsey Varnum of Dracut, Mass., b. Jan. 8' 1777. They lived in Goffstown, N. H., till about 1808, when they rem. to Topsham, and about 1812, to Newbury, and carried on the Tenney farm. Later they lived where Charles Greenleaf now lives, and after that rem. to the Centre, where she d. Nov. 5, 1845, and he d. Nov. 22, 1847.

Children, the 1st five b. in Goffstown. N. H.:

i. Eliza, b. April 28, 1802; m. July 21, 1835, Phillips Greenleaf of Bradford as 2d wife; d. May, 1883.

1 ii. Gilman, b. Sept. 9, 1803; d. Oct. 5, 1888.

iii. Clarissa, b. April 11, 1805; m. Charles Bryant of Sherbrooke, P. Q., and d. there.
iv. Persis, b. Feb. 15, 1807; m. May 9, 1850, Ephraim Bagley of Topsham. Member of Congregational church sixty-four years; d. May 7, 1892.
v. Hannah, b. April 3, 1808; m. Sept 20, 1832, Samuel H. Rowe of Stanstead, P. Q.
2 vi. Obadiah C., b. Topsham, July 9, 1811, q. v.
vii. Anna, b. Newbury, Sept. 22, 1814; m. April 4, 1867, Capt. Ezekiel Johnson of Bradford, who d. Oct. 9, 1880. She d. January, 1899, at Worcester, Mass.
viii. Frye Bayley, b. Newbury, March 11, 1819; d. Methuen, Mass., 1859, leaving a son and a dau.

1 GILMAN, b. Sept. 9, 1809. Lived at the Centre; his farm is now owned by John Buchanan. Rem. to the village 1863. He m. Apr. 28, 1831, Mary, dau. Dea. William Burroughs, (b. Nov. 21, 1807; d. Jan. 14, 1877). He d. Oct. 4, 1888. Member of 1st ch., sixty years and his wife fifty years.
Children:
i. Mary E., b. Apr. 14, 1835; m. John Kendrick, q. v.
ii. Emmeline B., b. May 29, 1837; m. Jan. 7, 1874, Orrin Green Page (b. Tilton, N. H., May 7, 1827; d. Newbury, Aug. 26, 1895); sailor seven years. Res. Newbury, after 1888. Ch., William Orrin, b. Jan. 7, 1876.
iii. William, b. April 21, 1839; m. Sept. 10, 1863, Lydia J. Paul. Farmer. Rem. to Groton and went into the carriage making business where he d. Sept. 20, 1876. C., (1) Alice A., b. Newbury, Aug. 25, 1863. (2) Lulu, b. Groton, June 1, 1870. Two d. in infancy.
iv. Eliza A., b. June 5, 1841; m. Nelson Bailey, q. v.
v. Harriet, b. June 24, 1843; m. July 20, 1861, David H. Blood of Bradford (b. Dec. 24, 1835; d. June 24, 1894). She d. Dec. 4, 1899. C., (1) Minnie L., b. April 12, 1862; m. Dec. 24, 1891, Frank Howard. (2) Mary L., b. Feb. 10, 1865. (3) Elijah, b. Sept. 30, 1867; merchant at Lancaster. (4) Edward S., b. Oct. 16, 1874; m. June 21, 1900, Dora Johnston of Newbury. (5) Sarah A., b. Nov. 21, 1876; m. Roger C. Eastman Sept. 14, 1898.
vi. Amanda D., b. Dec. 14, 1845.
vii. Clara A., b. July 4, 1850; m. Everett Stevens of Haverhill; d. Piermont, Sept. 27, 1899. One c.

2 OBADIAH CARLETON, b. Topsham, July 7, 1811. Bought in 1840, the farm of James Abbott. on which he spent the rest of his life excepting one year. He m., 1st, Dec. 23, 1841, Elizabeth, dau. of Jacob Bayley, (b. Feb. 1, 1817; d. Aug. 22, 1856). He m., 2d, May 5, 1859, Ruth, widow of Oliver Elkins, and dau. of John Wells, (b. Marshfield, April 25, 1824). Member of Congregational church sixty-five years. He d. May 6, 1894.
Children, three by 1st m., and one by 2nd:
i. George B., b. May 1, 1844. Enlisted at Bradford, September, 1862, in Co. H, 12th Vt. Mustered into United States service, Oct. 4, 1862. Mustered out July 14, 1863. Re-enlisted Aug. 12, 1864, Vt. Vet. Battery Lt. Art. Mustered out June 16, 1865. Cabinet maker. Res. Newbury since 1890. He m. in Newbury Dec. 7, 1887, Rose E. Bancroft, (b. in Michigan, great granddaughter of John Wells of Newbury) C., (1) Harry Carleton, b. Oct. 28, 1888, Somerville, Mass. (2) Florence E., b. Aug. 1, 1890, Newbury.
ii. Persis A., b. March 23, 1846. Res. Lowell, Mass.
iii. Sarah M., b. July 9, 1848; m., March, 1875, Mark Sherman. Res. Lowell, Mass.
iv. Robert E., b. July 30, 1860; m., Nov. 19, 1890, Mima W., dau. of Daniel Eastman. C., (1) Carleton Eastman, b. June 8, 1898. (2) George Frye, b. July 8, 1900. Robert Barnett and his wife with nearly all of their descendants were members of the Congregational church.

BARKER.

Alexander Barker, James Latto, William Chalmers and Alexander Laing with their families left Leven, Scotland, in March, 1834, on the ship "Cyrus of Dundee." They sailed around the north of Scotland, after being delayed by storms at the mouth of the Moray Frith. After a rough voyage of 12 weeks, in which they saw no sail, they reached the mouth of the St.

Lawrence, where they were detained a week by floating ice, and finally reached Montreal. They came by steamboat and canal to Burlington, thence, by teams to Newbury, where all their families settled. They were hospitably entertained by Capt. Samuel Gibson, and others of their countrymen, till they could make homes for themselves and clear land. Nearly all of their company have passed away, and the few survivors have collected such memorials as remain. All were Presbyterians.

ALEXANDER BARKER, b. in Fifeshire, Scotland, settled at West Newbury, 1834. He m. Grace Lockhart, the daughter of an officer on Lord Nelson's flagship at the battle of Trafalgar, (b. Scotland, 1786; d. Newbury March 1, 1846); he d. at Ryegate Nov. 28, 1859. Buried at West Newbury.

Children, all b. in Scotland:

i. Isabella, b. March 9, 1804; m. William Chalmers, q. v.; d. Feb. 8, 1883.

ii. Janet, b. 1806; m. in Scotland, 1831, James Latto; they settled in Groton; d. 1861; he d. 1878. C., (1) David, in Wisconsin. (2) Grace, m. Charles Lamphear of South Ryegate and d. there. (3) Isabella m. Daniel Taisey; d. Newbury, 1872. (4) Janet, m. James Manson of South Ryegate. (5) Alexander, un-m.; d. Ryegate. (6) John C., d. at Boston.

iii. Grace, b. about 1808; m., about 1836, Joseph Holmes of Newbury; d. about 1898; he d. about 1847. C., (1) John, m. Harriet George of Bradford; res. Fairlee. (2) Grace E., m. Ruel Mack of Orford, N. H. (3) Sarah M., m. Eben Osgood of Lawrence, Mass. (4) Laura, m. William Noyes; res. Springfield, Mass.

iv. Elsie, b. about 1811; m., about 1838, Alexander Allison; lived in Newbury village; removed to Dodgeville, Wis., and d. there. Three c., two living in Wisconsin.

v. Alexander, b. about 1818; m., about 1838, Betsey Messer; d. about 1894; she d. about 1898 at Cornish, N. H. (1) Alexander, res. Windsor. (2) Mary, m. John Smith of Andover, Mass.; d. about 1880. (3) Grace, d. at Andover, about 1880. (4) William, res. and d. at Andover. (5) Julia, res. Windsor.

vi. George, b. about 1820; m., about 1847, Eliza Hendry; he d. about 1881; she res. Hartford, Conn. Five c., two live in Brandon.

vii. John Calvin, b. 1822, came to America with his parents. They lived at first in a small house that stood between Jonas Tucker's and Dudley Carleton's. He was recommended by Esq. Tucker to Col. A. B. W. Tenney, and set out on foot and alone for the latter's house. He was small of his age, and the Colonel looked at him and said, "Is this the little boy who has come to live with me?" John was a little alarmed, but spoke up manfully, "Weel sir, if ye dinna like me, ye need na keep me?" The colonel was pleased with the answer and rejoined, "No backing out, my lad!" He lived there till he was of age; was brought up as one of the family, sent to school, and trained to correct habits, taken regularly to church, and taught all the details of management of one of the largest farms in the county. When of age, with a thorough business training, he went to Hartford, Conn., and engaged in the lumber business, and dealt largely in produce. When the famous Charter Oak fell, in 1856, its wood was saved, and worked into many souvenirs in Mr. Barker's mill. He retired from business many years ago, and res. at 205 Wethersfield Avenue, where he has an estate of 25 acres. He has generously remembered the Tenney Memorial Library. He m. Jeannie W., dau. of Thomas Hendry, who came from Glasgow, Scotland, to Newbury, and removed to Forestdale, Conn., where he d. 1868. C., (1) John Tenney, dentist at Wallingford, Conn., m. Zuilee Hubbard of Fulton, N. Y. C., John Eric. (2) William Hendry, mechanical draftsman and patent lawyer, in the office of Col. Burdett of Hartford; m. Emily Woods. (3) Grace Maria, m. Dr. Frank Louis Waite of Hartford. Dr. Waite is an occulist and aurist, associated with Dr. Samuel B. St. John.

BARTLETT.

The Bartlett family is nearly extinct in Newbury, but their memorial is here preserved.

I. RICHARD of England and Newbury, Mass.

II. RICHARD, b. 1621.

III. RICHARD, b. 1649; d. 1724.

IV. DANIEL, b. 1682; d. 1756.

V. DANIEL, b. 1706; d. 1786.

VI. DANIEL, b. June 28, 1744; d. 1818; m., 1st, Priscilla, dau. of Roger and Mary (Hale) Merrill. 2nd, Hannah Martin, sister of Peter Martin of Andover, Mass., and this town. By his first wife he had several children, among whom was James, owner of Bartlett's wharf, and other real estate in Boston, and Dea. Daniel Bartlett. The latter b. in Newbury, Mass., rem. to Bath, N. H., where he m., and where his c. were b. Later he came to Newbury, about 1835, and lived at the village where Alfred Corliss now lives. He was a blacksmith, his shop being opposite his house at the foot of the hill, the road around by the Ox-bow schoolhouse, until the railroad was built, went down the hill opposite that house. C., *a*, Hannah, m. Ezra Sanborn of Bath. *b*, Daniel, m. a Mrs. Thayer, and lived in Boston. *c*, Mary Ann, who m., Nov. 6, 1839, Elijah Cleveland of Coventry, long clerk of the Passumpsic railroad corporation. Daniel Bartlett and wife were admitted to the Congregational church, Jan. 3, 1836. The church records give his death as August, 1853.

NATHAN M., son of Daniel and Hannah (Martin) Bartlett, b. Methuen, Mass., Aug. 3, 1803; m. in Litchfield, N. H., in 1831, Fanny Jones, (b. in Litchfield, July 6, 1811; d. Grinnell, Iowa, Jan. 4, 1899). They lived some years in Hooksett, N. H., and came to Newbury in 1851 or 1852, and bought of William Burroughs the present town farm, and also owned the farm which is now that of John S. Burroughs, and other lands. They were members of the Methodist church, and Mr. Bartlett was quite a wealthy man for those days. He sold his farm to Porter Watson in 1865, and in the fall, rem. to Iowa. He d. at Mantour, Iowa, Nov. 27, 1876.
Children were b. in Newbury:

i. Lydia, res. in Cambridge, Mass.; dressmaker.

ii. Julia A., m. Abram Mitchell of Hooksett. N. H., and d. in Newbury.

iii. Daniel S., served nine months in Co. H., 12th Vt., 1862-1863. He m. April 30, 1859, Hannah S., dau. of Ross Ford. They rem. to Iowa where she d. and he m., 2d, Kate, dau. of John Wallace of Newbury. Res., Grinnell, Iowa.

iv. John M., served with his brother in Co. H., 12th Vt. He m. Emily, dau. of Alonzo Fleming, and went to Iowa, and lives in Mantour.

v. Mary Vashti, m. Jan. 1, 1862, Ansel B. Gage, who was from Burke, and served in the army with her brothers. Res., Grinnell, Iowa. One son.

HOSEA, b. Newbury, July 23, 1795. Farmer, and long sexton at Ox-bow cemetery; m. Dec. 20, 1819, Betsey Muliken (b. Plymouth, N. H., April 21, 1798). He d. January, 1868. Not related to the preceding family.
Children:

i. Nancy, b. Aug. 27, 1820; m. Jan. 20, 1850, Luther Battles.

ii. Harriet J., b. August 6, 1822; m. March 29, 1854, Anthony B. Emery.

iii. Jarvis, b. Nov. 16, 1824; d. Sept. 7, 1826.

iv. John G., b. March 16, 1826; m. Oct. 28, 1849, Lydia A. Emery.

v. Charlotte A., b. March 15, 1828; m. March 19, 1854, Horace V. Barton.

vi. Jarvis, b. Dec. 12, 1831; d. in St. Johnsbury.

vii. Charles P., b. April 16, 1834. Res. Wells River. Served in the Union army; m. Sarah, dau. Samuel Boyce.

BATES.

SAMUEL LYSANDER, son of Samuel and Lucina (Crane) Bates, was b. in Brookfield, Nov. 11, 1831. Preparatory studies for college were at Northfield and Barre Academies under C. C. Webster and J. S. Spaulding, LL. D.; graduated from the University of Vt., July, 1857; teacher of languages in Brandon Seminary, 1857-8; principal of Underhill Academy, 1858-61; graduated from Andover Theological Seminary, July, 1863; ordained and installed, Underhill, March 24, 1864; superintendent of schools there 1865-67; dismissed November, 1871; installed Newbury, Jan. 16, 1872; dismissed February, 1890; supplied Congregational churches in Brookfield, Manchester and Benson, 1890-93; pastor Congregational church, Winooski, 1893-7; resigned Winooski on account of ill health; supply of vacant churches since 1898. Publications, (see Bibliography of Newbury); secretary of the Congregational convention of Vermont since 1888; resided in Burlington since 1890; m. Sept. 27, 1871, Marion Elizabeth, dau. of Morrill J. and Jerusha (Russell) Walker, b. in Norwich, Jan. 29, 1843; educated at Thetford Academy, Thetford, under Gilbert Hood, and North Granville, N. Y. Female Seminary and Glenwood Female Seminary, West Brattleboro, under Hiram Orcutt, LL. D.; graduated from Glenwood in 1861; teacher in Chelsea Academy and other schools.

Children:
i.   Mary Russell, b. Newbury, Sept. 9, 1872; prepared for college in Newbury under Edwin A. Bayley and Lucia A. Watkins, and Burlington High School under S. W. Landon; graduated from the University of Vermont, 1894; principal of Shelburne High School, 1895-98; assistant librarian and cataloguer, Billings Library, University of Vermont, 1898 to date.
ii. Samuel Walker, b. in Newbury, Sept. 9, 1880; d. Burlington, April 27, 1891.

BERRY.

Hon. Joseph, his ancestry or birthplace are unknown. Town representative from Guildhall in 1816, and was State's Attorney for Essex county for nine years, and chief judge of the county court in 1822, 1823, and a member of the Governor's Council from 1822 to 1825. He came to Newbury about 1830; his admission to the Congregational church was by letter from the church in Guildhall, Nov. 20, 1831. In the church records his age is given as 42. Register of Probate for Bradford District, 1840, and clerk of Orange County court, 1850-1852. Judge Berry built and occupied the house called the "Henry Keyes house," and an advertisement in the Democratic Republican in 1833 shows that he kept a bookstore. He was one of the prominent men of the state; was widely known. The legal papers drawn up by him are models of clearness in style, and his handwriting is a marvel of beauty and legibility. He did much for the schools in his time and with David Johnson became financially responsible for the young ladies' school established here in 1830. He m., about 1814, Betsey, dau. of Otho Stevens, (b. Feb. 16, 1789; d. March 9, 1850). In 1853 he rem. to Maquoketa, Iowa, where he died some years later.

Children:
i.   Betsey, m. Rev. E. E. Adams. He was a sailor's missionary during several years in Europe, and seamen's chaplain at Havre, France. During a visit to this country she d. at a hotel in New York city, Dec. 4, 1846, aged 31. Buried in Newbury.
ii. Caroline, m. Hiram Tracy of Wells River and d. there.
iii. Lucia, m., Jan. 20, 1846, Dr. J. G. Dearborn; rem. to Iowa, 1853, and d. there of cholera in the next year.
iv. William, went south and d. in Georgia in 1854.

BIGELOW.

I.   John, (1641-1703) of Watertown, Mass., m. Mary Warren.

II. Joshua, m. Elizabeth Flagg.

III. Eleazer, b. 1705, m. Mary Fiske, or Fife, and had five c., of whom Mary, m. Dr. Gideon Smith of Newbury; Joshua was the father of Mrs. Jeremiah Ingalls; and Jabez, who m. Deborah Knowlton.

IV. Jabez, son of Jabez and Deborah (Knowlton) Bigelow, b. Westminster, Mass., March 6, 1724; m. Betsey, dau. Ebenezer McIntosh, (b. Boston, Dec. 12, 1768; d. Ryegate, Oct. 10, 1848). He came to Newbury about 1785, and about 1795, rem. to Ryegate where he was farmer and shoemaker, major in the militia. He d. Dec. 31, 1851. Buried at Wells River.

Children:
i. Elizabeth McIntosh, b. July 12, 1788, m. Daniel Darling; d. 1863.
ii. Jabez, b. Nov. 25, 1789; farmer in Ryegate; m. Eleanor, dau. of Abial Chamberlain, (b. March 1, 1787; d. Hartford, Conn., Dec. 28, 1863). He d. Nov. 13, 1850.
iii. Roxalana, b. Oct. 15, 1794; m. John Sly; d. Dec. 20, 1863.
iv. Sirena, b. Ryegate Dec. 19, 1796; m. James Bayley of Newbury; d. Dec. 10, 1868, in St. Lawrence County, New York.
v. Cynthia, b. March 4, 1799; m. Robert G. Nelson; d. April 9, 1883.
vi. Laura, b. April 13, 1802; unm.; d. Jan. 13, 1872.
1 vii. John, b. Dec. 28, 1803.
viii. Mary, b. March 20, 1807; d. April 1, 1811.
ix. Anna, b. July 24, 1809; d. Oct. 1, 1811.

1 JOHN, b. Ryegate, Dec. 28, 1803; farmer and in other business, a prominent man in Ryegate; member of Wells River Congregational church; m. Dec. 26, 1836, Mary Catherine, dau. of Dea. Daniel Thompson, (b. Corinth, May 21, 1821; res. St. Paul, Minn.) He d. at Ryegate, April 12, 1891.
Children, all b. in Ryegate:
i. Emily Adelaide, b. Sept. 10, 1838; d. Aug. 19, 1839.
ii. Alexander Thompson, b. April 5, 1841; res. St. Paul, Minn.; physician; m. Nov. 26, 1883, Edna A. Kelley.
iii. Sarah Arabella, b. Sept. 6, 1843; m., Aug. 11, 1870, Prof. Horace Goodhue, of Carleton College, Northfield, Minn.
iv. William Ladd, b. Aug. 31, 1846; d. Feb. 22, 1860.
v. Francis Hallan, b. Jan. 16, 1850; m., May 26, 1880, Adeline H. Kent; res. Ryegate, till April, 1896, when they moved to Wells River, where he d. Feb. 18, 1898.

·

BLAIR.

MRS. ELIZA (FARNUM), widow of Hon. Walter Blair, came here from Plymouth, N. H., in 1851, and bought the house in which Mrs. Nelson Bailey now lives. She was the dau. of Haines and Betsey (Whitehouse) Farnum, b. Pembroke, N. H., Nov. 25, 1809; m. as 2d wife to Mr. Blair in 1835; d. Newbury, 1881.
Children, all b. in Plymouth:
i. Sarah Eliza, b. March 23, 1837; graduated Newbury Seminary, 1858; teacher in district schools and for twelve years 1st assistant at Concord, N. H., High School; m. Moses C. Dole, Campton Village, N. H.
ii. Frances Maria, b. April 25, 1839; graduated Newbury Seminary, 1860; teacher; preceptress of Macedon, N. Y., Academy; m. Jan. 25, 1864, Capt. Harris B. Mitchell; d. Newbury, December, 1896. C., Harry W., b. Newbury, 1867; graduated at the medical college, Burlington. Now assistant superintendent at Danvers Asylum, Mass.
iii. Millie M., b. Jan. 24, 1841; graduated Newbury Seminary, 1862; teacher in district schools, and at Wheaton Seminary, Norton, Mass.; m. Jan. 14, 1866, Dr. E. Mellen Wight, and has since lived in Chattanooga, Tenn. Dr. Wight d. 1880. C., living: (1) Mellen B., b. 1873; in business at Chattanooga. (2) Walter B., b. 1875; in business at Chattanooga.
iv. Flora Adelaide, b. Sept. 9, 1846; graduated Newbury Seminary, 1867; m. at Chattanooga, Tenn., April 7, 1870, to Charles H. Peabody, who d. Oct. 31, 1900. No c.
v. Arthur W., b. May 22, 1848; fitted for college at Newbury Seminary; graduated Dartmouth, 1872-5; taught in Middleboro, Mass., High School; Northfield Graded School; Washington Co. and Montpelier High School; studied 1½ years at Hartford Theological Seminary; studied medicine and graduated from the medical department of Vermont University; practiced at Orford, N. H., five years, where he was superintendent of schools one year, and president of White Mountain Medical Society one year. Rem. to Dorchester, Mass., 1886, and has since been in practice there. Surgeon-in-chief of Commercial Travelers Eastern Accident Association; member of Massachusetts Medical Society, and New Hampshire Medical Society; m. July 25, 1877, Ellen S. Chamberlin of St. Johnsbury. C., (1) Walter, b. Montpelier, Aug. 12, 1878; fitted for

college at Boston Latin School; graduated Dartmouth, 1900. (2) Hugh, b. Orford, N. H., Aug. 31, 1882; fitted for college at Boston Latin School; now in Dartmouth College, class of 1904.

BLISS.

This family name has long been extinct in Newbury, but a memorial of them is here preserved through the kindness of Mr. S. E. Bliss of Chicago. The Bliss family of Newbury has the same ancestry as those of Bradford and Haverhill, but were not nearly connected with them. The ancestry is as follows:

I. Thomas, of Belstone, Devonshire, Eng.

II. Thomas, (1580–1640) of England, Braintree, Mass., and Hartford, Conn.

III. John, (1640-1702) of Hartford and Longmeadow.

IV. Nathaniel, (1671-1751) of Springfield, Mass., and Lebanon, Conn.

V. Henry, (1701-1761) of Lebanon, Conn.

VI. Peletiah, (1725-1808) of Lebanon and Bolton, Conn., m. Hepzibah Goodwin.

VII. Peletiah, b. April 3, 1749. He came to Newbury before 1770, and settled at the Ox-bow. Minuteman in 1775. He served in the revolutionary war as private in Capt. Simeon Stevens' Co. of Olcott regiment, 1779–81. In same, under Col. Bedel, May 4, Nov. 10, 1778, 127 d. In Capt. John G. Bayley's Co., rangers, April 1777-1779. In Capt. Frye Bayley's Co., guarding and scouting, 1781, till the end of the war. After the war he rem. to Bradford, and represented that town in the General Assembly, 1787. In 1791, he was living at West Newbury, where he was a blacksmith, and had a shop near the present Rogers Hill schoolhouse. Later, one of his sons had a shop near the sawmill, where J. C. Johnston now lives. Notice of administration was given upon his estate, Jan. 17, 1798. William Wallace, Isaac Bayley and Asa Tenney were commissioners and Thomas Johnson and Ruth Bliss, administrators. He appears to have been a man of substance and good standing in town. He was m. by Rev. Peter Powers, Aug. 22, 1772, to Ruth, dau. of George Lowell, and sister of the 1st wife of Col. Thomas Johnson. He d. 1797 or 1798.

Children:
i. Betty, b. Aug. 2, 1775; d. July 28, 1791.
ii. Polly, b. Jan. 13, 1777; m. Jonathan Ring of Corinth.
iii. Davenport, b. Dec. 27, 1779; Blacksmith and wheelwright of Newbury and Haverhill. He m. Oct. 13, 1800, Ruth, dau. of Thos. Hibbard, (b. May 3, 1781; d. June 5, 1857). He died at Concord. Vt., Nov. 23, 1856. C., (1) Peletiah. b. June 24, 1801; blacksmith; d. at 24. (2) Betsey, b. Aug. 4, 1803; d. Dec. 27, 1860; m. Bailey White, q. v. (3) Mary, b. Oct. 17, 1810; m. Harry Smith of Canton, N. Y. (4) Hannah, b. April 18, 1813; m. John R. Stevens of Haverhill. (5) William, b. April 1, 1817. (6) Alden E., b. Sept. 7, 1821; hardware dealer in Lowell, Mass. (7) Lucy A., b. May 2, 1824; m. Thaddeus B. Dowse of Concord; d. 1899.
iv. Ruth, b. Aug 31, 1782; m. John Brown of Williston.
v. Hannah, b. Sept. 6, 1784; d. Sept. 13, same year.
vi. Henry, b. Newbury, Nov. 5, 1785; lived in Essex, but rem. to Hartford, Licking County, Ohio; m. Dec. 6. 1810, Sybil F. Butler. He had seven c., of whom Samuel B., b. Essex, June 8, 1816; m. Jan. 28, 1841, Sally C. Cadwell, of Salisbury; d. Underhill, May 1, 1895, and had c., (1) George H., b. March 23, 1844; teacher and bookkeeper of Burlington and Chicago. (2) Samuel Eugene. b. Jan. 31, 1846; hardware and commission merchant at Chicago. (3) Edmund A., b. Aug. 18, 1848; farmer in Jericho. (4) Sybil F., b. April 30, 1850; m. Geo. L. Wells of Chicago.
vii. Peletiah, b. March 12, 1787; lived in Essex; d. Sept. 20, 1870. Eight children.
viii. John, b. 1795; d. Monkton, 1807.
ix. Hannah, m. Samuel Smith of Essex and rem. to Iowa.

BOLTON.

I. WILLIAM, of Reading, Mass., m. Jan. 5, 1720, Elizabeth White of Andover; d. Sept. 10, 1725. A genealogy of their descendants was prepared and published by Charles K. Bolton.

II. WILLIAM, b. Reading, Oct. 25, 1721. Rem. to Shirley, Mass., where he d. April 30, 1804; m. Mary, dau. of Benjamin Nurse. Ten c.

III. WILLIAM, b. Reading, Jan. 21, 1744; m. at Reading, March 28, 1765, Mrs. Abigail Sheldon; d. May 7, 1780. Revolutionary soldier.

IV. JOHN, b. Shirley, Mass., Oct. 24, 1774. Rem. to Danville where he built a sawmill and a fulling mill, at Greenbank's Hollow; m. 1st, 1798, Betsey Tilton, b. June 30, 1783; 2d, Sept. 6, 1806, Cynthia Chamberlin, (b. Dec. 30, 1782); 3d, March 4, 1830, Abigail Wesson, (b. Jan. 26, 1790). He d. March 28, 1843. Of the c. of John and Betsey Bolton:

1 i. William, lived in Newbury.
2 ii. Luther C., lived in Newbury.

1 WILLIAM b. Loudon, N. H., May 8, 1799. Rem. with his parents to Danville while a child, and there learned the trade of coloring and cloth dressing; m. 1st, June 18, 1818, Alma Hooker of Danville. They lived one year in Barnet, and in 1820, came to Newbury and settled at "Brock's Falls," since called Boltonville, where he was a miller; postmaster at Boltonville, 1831; was an anti-mason, whig and republican; retired from active business in 1854. His wife d. Feb. 9, 1840, and he m. 2d, Jan. 1, 1846, Lydia (Aldrich) widow of Josiah W. Rogers, (b. April 29, 1804; d. Jan. 7, 1892). He d. Oct. 27, 1883.
   Children, all b. in Newbury, (Boltonville) except the eldest:
   i. Mary, b. Danville, June 7, 1819; m. Hector M. Page; res. New York City; d. Jan. 15, 1889.
   ii. John, b. July 30, 1820; m. Matilda Reed and went to Wisconsin; res. Big Springs, Wis.
   iii. Alden, b. Jan. 11, 1822; m. Aug. 27, 1849, Sarah Cole; rem. to Malabar, Fla.; in hotel and orange grove business; one son, Charles, unm; d. at Malabar, Jan. 27, 1891.
   iv. Harriet, b. Nov. 23, 1823; m. A. J. Bailey, q. v.; d. May 1, 1851.
   v. Cynthia, b. March 3, 1826; m. Amplias Chamberlin and lives at Kilbourne City, Wis.
   vi. Carlos Edson, b. April 3, 1847. Enlisted June, 1862, into Co. C, 9th Vt., and was considered the youngest private soldier Vt. sent into the civil war. He was one of the first to enter Richmond, April 3, 1865; afterward employed in the Boston post office; went to California, 1876, then to Idaho, and was postmaster at Bolton, a place named for him; res. since 1898, Gibbonsville, Idaho; m. Oct. 26, 1869, Augusta H. Somes of Charlestown, Mass., who d. Jan. 28, 1895. C., Frederica Gladys, b. Bolton, Idaho.
   vii. Arabelle F., b. Jan. 15, 1849; m. April 26, 1870, Nathaniel Robinson, (b. of Scotch parents at Rockport, Ireland, April 26, 1849; came to America when a child, and has been engaged in various business; res. Boltonville). C., adopted, Florence Shaw, b. Benton, N. H., Nov. 4, 1882.

2 LUTHER CHAMBERLIN, b. Danville, Feb. 19, 1801; m. 1st, Julia, dau. Thomas Hooker and 2d, Elizabeth Emerson Page of New Sharon, Me.; d. Oct. 25, 1873.
   Children:
3 i. Charles Sargent, b. Sept. 4, 1822.
   ii. Plynn, b. Barnet, Sept. 16, 1824. Twice m. Four c.
   iii. Lucy, b. Newbury, Sept. 6, 1826; m. Dec. 21, 1846, James Whittemore of Leicester, Mass. Five c.
   iv. Nathan P., b. Newbury, June 16, 1830; m. March 31, 1858, Agnes N. Paddleford of North Monroe, N. H., where he res. Five c.
   v. Milo, b. Newbury, Aug. 2, 1832; m. 1st, Sept. 10, 1856, Ann J. Woodward; 2d, March 27, 1864, Mary A. Loring; res. Leicester, Mass. Eight c.

3 CHARLES SARGENT, b. Sept. 4, 1822; m. June, 1846, Lydia Norris, of Glenns
      Falls, N. Y. Lived in Greenbank's Hollow, Danville, and Passumpsic.
      Came to Boltonville, 1870, to carry on the carding and cloth dressing
      business, which his mother received by the will of John Bolton, and in
      which he was succeeded by his son, Francis; d. Jan. 11, 1901.
   Children:
   i.   Julia A., b. April 26, 1847; m. April 18, 1876, Ira W. Cunningham of
        Lyndonville.
   ii. Lucy L., b. July 18, 1848; m. Aug. 10, 1874, Bina L. Hastings of St.
        Johnsbury.
   iii. Martha Y., b. Dec. 23, 1853; m. Apr. 3, 1876, Edwin Sly of Boltonville.
   iv. Francis Charles, b. April 8, 1857; m. Nov. 16, 1881, Kate L. Bullard of
        Lyndonville. One dau. Jessie, b. April 7, 1882.

BONE.

DAVID, b. in Scotland, 1804; m. Margaret, dau. William and Margaret
      (Winnie) Buchanan, (b. in Scotland, 1802).   They came to America,
      October, 1835, and, 1838, settled in what is now the village of South
      Ryegate. He. d. Jan. 17, 1846. She d. March 4, 1953.   *
   Children:
   i.   William.
   ii. David.
   iii. Margaret.
   iv. Jean.
   v.   Mary.
   vi. James Beattie.

WILLIAM, b. Glasgow. Scotland, May 6, 1834. Rem. to Newbury April 1, 1865,
      and bought of Plato Eames the large farm which he still owns, on the
      north side of the river, between Boltonville and Wells River. Member,
      since 1849, of the Ref. Pres. (Covenanter) ch., Ryegate; m. 1st, Dec. 5,
      1866, Jane, dau. Archibald Ritchie; she d. Jan. 28, 1875; m. 2d, in
      Ryegate, March 16, 1877, Ellen, dau. Dea John Smith, (Dea. Smith was b.
      at Amenia, N Y., May 23, 1800; d. Newbury, March 20, 1894).
   Five children, besides three who d. in infancy.
   i.   William, b. June 4, 1868; res. South Berwick, Me.. blacksmith and
        machinist; m. Aug. 8, 1899, Mabel Louis Davis.
   ii. Archie Ritchie, b. Nov. 22, 1871; farmer in Barnet; m. Dec. 1, 1899, Edith
        Plummer.
   iii. Herman David, b. March 14, 1878, now in Vermont University, Burlington.
   iv. John Smith, b. Dec. 1, 1879; at home.
   v.   Ellen Jane, b. Aug. 26, 1884. At school.

BOWEN.

WILLIAM BOWEN, one of the first settlers of Grafton, N. H., came there from
      Connecticut when the country was a wilderness, guided by spotted trees.
      After clearing some land, and building a log house he went back after his
      wife, who came on horseback, bringing her linen wheel on the horse behind
      her. They reared a large family. He served in the revolutionary war, and
      d. in Grafton, aged 94
His son. Beneiah Bowen, a captain in the militia, b. Grafton, March 29, 1785,
      came to live with his son in Piermont in 1857, and in 1870, to the home of
      his grandson, A. A. Bowen in Newbury, and d. Sept. 23, 1877.

AUGUSTUS B., son of the latter, b. Grafton, Sept. 7, 1813; m. Oct. 9, 1842, Sybil
      V. Bliffin of Freetown. Mass.   Helped build the old B. C. & M. R. R.;
      settled on a farm in Piermont, and d. there March 19, 1860.

ALBERT A., son of Augustus, b. Grafton, N. H., Aug. 3, 1843. Came with his
      parents to Piermont in 1857: enlisted in 1862 in Co. B, 15th N. H., and
      was mustered out with the regiment in 1863; came to Newbury in March,
      1875, to the farm formerly owned by Thomas Abbott, and later by Charles
      Leet; m. July 3, 1865, Rachael A., dau. John Dean of Haverhill.

Three children, all b. in Piermont:

i. John A., b. June 29, 1866. Res. Newbury; m. Jan. 15, 1890, Augusta Newbauer, (b. Nuremburg. Germany, dau. John Newbauer, a pencil maker); d. Aug. 2, 1900. C., (1) Ina H., b. Newbury, Dec. 31, 1891. (2) Arthur, b. Newbury, Aug. 25, 1893. (3) Marion, b. Haverhill, July 7, 1895. (4) Bertram K., b. Haverhill, May 25, 1897.

ii. Nellie M., b. Dec. 20, 1868; m. W. H. Kendrick, q. v.

iii. Charles B., b. March 15, 1871. Became blind at the age of seven, in consequence of having a knife thrown at him while at school, by a playmate, in sport. The sight of one eye was destroyed, and that of the other was soon lost. At the age of eleven he was admitted to the Perkins Institution for the blind at South Boston and graduated there at the age of nineteen. There he learned music and the trade of tuning pianos, and is now tuner in the factory of George P. Bent, Chicago. Like many other blind men, he has developed considerable skill in the management of horses and the estimation of their value. He m. in Chicago, Feb. 15, 1900, Anna W. James, her mother being Rachel Lother, formerly of Newbury.

BOYCE.

This family originally came from Newburyport. Mass. Capt. William Boyce, the first of whom there is record, met his death by falling from a load of hay, while coming up from the meadow, on the farm now owned by W. W. Brock.

CAPT. WILLIAM and Sarah Anderson were m. about 1760.

Children:

i. Hugh, b. Aug. 19, 1764.
ii. Joseph, b. May 17, 1766.
1 iii. James, b. March 22, 1768; d. May 13, 1849.
iv. Sarah, b. Sept. 14, 1770; m. Capt. Gideon Tewksbury; d. Dec. 26, 1854.
v. Robert, b. 1772. Studied medicine and settled in Chautauqua County, N.Y.; d. about 1852.
vi. William, b. Nov. 20, 1774.
vii. Labella, b. June 29, 1777.
viii. Margaret, b. Dec. 2, 1779; d. Feb. 27, 1841.
2 ix. Samuel, b. Oct. 10, 1782; d. Sept. 14, 1863.
x. John, b. Oct. 16, 1786; d. in Kansas.

1 JAMES,[2] (William[1]) b. New Boston, N. H., March 22, 1768. When seventeen years of age he came to Newbury, in 1785, and found a desirable location, on an elevated, hard-wood, south-east slope, in what is now Topsham. This farm is now owned by Alexander Eastman. After two years he returned home with such a favorable report that his parents persuaded him, as he was young, to let them have his place. They came north the next year with several of their children. James settled at West Newbury, south of the Daniel Eastman farm, near Wright's Mountain. In 1842, he rem. to Guildhall, where he d. May 13, 1849. He was m. three times: 1st, Abigail, dau. of John Haseltine; 2d, Miriam Titcomb, who d. Aug. 29, 1820; 3d, in 1823, Miriam, dau. Mark Banfield.

Children, all b. in Newbury:

i. John Haseltine, b. 1793.
ii. William Anderson, b. 1795. Lived at West Newbury, till 1835, when he rem. to Albany; m. 1st, Martha, dau. David Haseltine, who d. July 25, 1834; 2d, Sept. 7, 1835, Judith, dau. Robinson Brock. He d. Dec. 20, 1854; buried at West Newbury.
iii. Sarah. m. Alva Eastman. C., living, Mrs. David Moore of Barre; Mrs. Bisnette of Bellows Falls.
3 iv. Richard T., b. June 24, 1808; d. about 1896.
v. James Madison, b. 1809; d. Sept. 14, 1833.
vi. Elizabeth H., b. September, 1811; m. Sept. 22, 1835, Joshua Glover; one dau. survives, Mrs. Johannett of Burlington; d. December, 1849.
vii. Abigail H., b. May 3, 1815; d. July 24, 1860.
viii. John H., b. April 9, 1824. Was prominent in Guildhall; d. Jan. 20, 1874.
4 ix. George S., b. Aug 11, 1827; d. Feb. 4, 1899.
5 x. Nathaniel S., b. May 24, 1829.

6   xi. Miriam T., b. May 20, 1832.

4 GEORGE SULLIVAN,[3] (James,[2] William[1]) b. Aug. 11, 1827; m. 1854, Fannie S.,
        dau. Joshua B. and Sallie (Schofl) Lamkin; d. Feb. 4, 1899.
    Children:
    i.   Guy L., b. 1856. In the boot and shoe business at Boston, with his uncle,
         Guy Lamkin, from March, 1873, and after 1885, in the shoe trade with
         his brother, John, having branches in other cities; m. March 13, 1884, Ida
         Florence Baker of Lincoln, Mass.; d. Feb. 4, 1899. Two c.
    ii. John W., b. May 20, 1862. In business with his brother, then retired to a
         farm in Guildhall; m. July 4, 1825, Ella M. Hunter of Somerville, Mass.
    iii. Sadie, b. Dec. 25, 1870; m. May 31, 1894, Henry S. Smith of Lancaster,
         N. H.

5 NATHANIEL S.,[3] (James,[2] William[1]) b. May 24, 1829. Fitted for college at
        Guildhall and Newbury; graduated Michigan University, 1854; studied
        medicine with Dr. J. D. Folsom of Guildhall; in practice Guildhall,
        Colebrook, N. H., and North Stratford; three years in Boston City
        Dispensary; Guildhall since 1861; m. July 11, 1878, Mary B., dau.
        Ebenezer Abbott of Newbury. C., Helen M., a teacher; and Angie C., who
        d. in her third year.

6 MIRIAM T.,[3] (James,[2] William[1]) b. May 20, 1832; teacher; m. 1856, M. A. W.
        Grow, who d. 1886. She d. March 22, 1879.
    Children:
    i.   Emma, a teacher; m. A. A. Potter of Stark, N. H.; d. about 1887.
    ii. Sherlie, m. Rev. Elwin L. Houseman, of Lebanon, N. H., a graduate of
         Harvard University; chaplain of 5th Mass. in Spanish-American war.
         Two c.
    iii. Walter A., res. in Massachusetts. Two c.
    iv. Alystyne, res. Providence, R. I. Jeweler.
    v.   Eliza A., b. Feb. 10, 1840; m. Julius T. Grow, a wood engraver, but now a
         paper box manufacturer, Lebanon, N. H. C., (1) Eugene, b. October,
         1874; graduated Dartmouth, 1894; medical college, 1897; post graduate
         Cornell University; surgeon in the navy; medical officer on the "Dixie"
         1898.

3 RICHARD TITCOMB,[3] (James,[2] William[1]) b. June 24, 1808. Farmer, also hunter
        and fishermen; rem. 1843 to Guildhall; in 1864 to Granby; lived some
        years with his dau., Mary A., in Stark, N. H.; served in the Union army,
        1861-65; was in the battle of Gettysburg, in Col. Proctor's regiment; m.
        at Topsham, Dec. 2, 1830, Joanna Banfield, (b. Corinth, Oct. 1, 1808, d.
        Aug. 2, 1865), a woman of noble christian character. He d. Oct. 5, 1896.
    Eleven children; the first seven b. in Newbury; the rest in Guildhall:
    i.   Allen R., b. June 30, 1832; farmer and teacher; lived in Guildhall, Granby
         and West Burke; representative from Granby, 1861; assistant judge of
         Essex County court, 1882-84; gave up farming because of failing health;
         in insurance and other business at West Burke several years; res. in Barre
         till Jan. 20, 1899; m. 1st, June 20, 1860, Sarah D. House of Lowell, Mass.,
         2d, Helen M. Howard of Barre. Three c. survive him; (1) Alma. (2)
         James W. (3) Alfred A.
    ii. Caroline, b. Dec. 3, 1833; d. June 23, 1834.
    iii. Elizabeth A., b. March 25, 1835; m. 1st, April 16, 1857, Abel Carpenter of
         Granby, who d. 1860; 2d, 1864, Charles Damon of Victory who is dead;
         now res. Barre. One dau. Mrs. Lillian A. Mills.
    iv. Mary A., b. Sept. 16, 1836; m. Jan. 2, 1864, Nehemiah Cole of Stark, N.
         H.; d. there Aug. 16, 1893.
    v.   James M., b. May 9, 1838; enlisted May, 1862, in 10th Vermont regiment;
         d. at Culpepper, Va., Oct. 6, 1863.
7   vi. William A., b. Dec. 3, 1839.
8   vii. Osman B.. b. Nov, 24, 1841; d. June 1, 1895.
    viii. John Wesley, b. Guildhall, Sept. 10, 1843; a young man of fine talent;
         enlisted 1861 in Co. K., 8th Vermont; d. in serviee at Brattleboro, Feb.
         28, 1862.
    ix. Martha J., b. Oct. 28, 1845; teacher; m. July 23, 1870, Charles E. White of
         Deerfield, N. H.; res. Barre. C., (1) Carrie M. (2) Mary E. (3) Elizabeth
         G. (4) Fred L. (5) Priscilla G.

    x. Caroline A., b. Aug. 16, 1847; teacher; d. Aug. 17, 1869.

    vi. George P., b. July 12, 1849; educated Montpelier seminary; clothing merchant, Barre; steward in Meth. ch.; m. Dec. 10, 1874, Cora A. Hutchinson. No c.

7 WILLIAM A.,[4] (Richard T.,[3] James,[2] William[1]) b. Newbury, Dec. 3, 1839. Educated at Barre Academy; principal for two years of Cabot High School; studied law and admitted to Washington Co. bar, 1869; in practice at Barre; judge of the city court Dec. 1, 1898-Dec. 1, 1890, and has been town representative and held other offices; is also a director and vice president in the Barre Savings Bank and Trust Co.; member of Meth. ch.; delegate, 1888 to General Conference; superintendent of Sunday School about twenty years; is an active citizen of Barre; has never m.

8 OSMAN C. B.,[4] (Richard T.,[3] James,[2] William[1]) b. Newbury, Nov. 24, 1841. Educated at Barre Academy; read law with his brother; graduated at Albany, N. Y., Law School 1871; in practice at Guildhall and editor there one year of the Essex County Herald; rem. to Barre 1874, and partner with his brother till death; states attorney, Essex County, 1872; state senator from Washington County, 1892; m. 1st, June, 11, 1871, Amelia A. French of Northumberland who d. September, 1877, leaving one child, Edith A. 2d, Jan. 15, 1881, Louisa L. Dodge of Barre; in failing health 1894; d. suddenly while in his garden, June 1, 1895.

2 SAMUEL,[2] (William[1]) b. Oct. 10, 1782. Farmer near Boltonville; m. Cynthia, dau. Horace Stebbins (b. April 12, 1797; d. Jan. 12, 1884). He d. Sept. 14, 1862.

    Children, (not in regular order. Information received by W. N. Gilfilan).

    i. Henry. Farmer on the "Avery Place" some years; m. June 14, 1864, Harriet N., dau. George W. Avery, (b. May 20, 1830; d. Jan. 26, 1890). He d. March 31, 1897, aged 77.

    ii. George, res. White River Junction.

    iii. James M., in employ of the Passumpsic railroad for about 40 years, as conductor, etc., now yardmaster at St. Johnsbury; m. 1st, Jan. 1, 1867, Harriet, dau. William Gardner, who d. June 27, 1877; m. 2d, Dec. 24, 1878, Augusta P. Towne.

    iv. Samuel, res. Newbury.

9   v. Alonzo.

    vi. Adeline, m. John Roberts of Groton.

    vii. Caroline, m. Thomas Quimby.

    viii. Sarah, m. Charles Bartlett.

9 ALONZO. Farmer on homestead; m. Dec. 24, 1872, Abbie M., dau. William Gardner.

    Children:

    i. Harry, d. Feb. 23, 1878, in his third year.

    ii. Hugh G., b. July 25, 1877.

    iii. Myrtilla, b. Aug. 14, 1878.

    iv. Martena, b. Aug. 14, 1878.

    v. Bertie, b. Sept. 9, 1881.

    vi. Bertha, b. Sept. 9, 1881.

    vii. Agnes, b. July 25, 1883.

BOYNTON.

DAVID S., of Richard and Rebecca (Abbott) Boynton, b. March 7, 1776; m. June 1, 1804, Lydia, dau. of Peter, and sister of Jeremiah Nourse; lived in Newbury and Rockingham; d. December, 1813.

    Children:

1   i. Jeremiah, b. Sept. 29, 1805.

    ii. Elvira, b. Dec. 4, 1806; m. Sept. 1, 1829, Daniel B. Lake.

    iii. Clarissa, b. June 28, 1808; m. June, 1836, Freeman Lake.

    iv. David, b. Feb. 28, 1810; m. Lydia Roberts; lived some years where Orrin W. Brock now does, but rem. to the north part of the state.

1 JEREMIAH, b. Newbury, Sept. 29, 1805; was brought up by his uncle, Mr. Nourse; farmer and stone cutter; lived some years where Daniel Taisey

now does, then on one of the farms now owned by the Chalmers brothers m. 1st, Sept. 26, 1831, Deborah C., dau. of Capt. Jacob Bayley (b. June 2, 1803; d. Nov. 28, 1863); she was an invalid all her married life. (See p. 238). 2d, June, 1865, Mrs. Jane (Renfrew) Haseltine. Members of 1st ch. He was a man of phenomenal industry, who never accepted office of any kind, or any position of public trust, but whose opinions and advice were held in great regard. His excellent Christian character led the church to desire him for a deacon, but he declined, on the ground that he was not good enough to be one. He told the minister that he had a bad temper, and often said things which a deacon ought not to say. He said that the Sunday before a neighbor's cow got into his corn while he was gone to meeting and was there all day, and his neighbor knew it. "I drove the cow home," said he, "and I was mad, and told John Messer that he was worse than a heathen. Do you think that a man who would talk like that is good enough for a deacon?" His first wife was bed-ridden for thirty-two years. After her death he spent a year in the west. He d. March 1, 1876.

BRICKETT.

This family was from Haverhill, Mass. The Bricketts were among the earlier settlers there and the family was prominent during several generations.

ABRAHAM and Sarah (Kelley) his wife, came here before 1790, and settled at West Newbury, on the farm now called the "Robinson Brock place." Admitted to 1st ch., Sept. 14, 1794.

Children:
1 i. John, b. March 19, 1790. Town record.
   ii. Eunice, b. March 15, 1792. Town record.
   iii. Samuel, b. July 7, 1793. Town record.
   iv. Abraham A., baptized June 7, 1795. Church record.
   v. Sally, baptized Dec. 31, 1797. Church record.
   vi. Abraham, baptized August 31, 1800. Church record.
   vii. Edmund, date of birth unknown.
       Abraham rem. to the north part of this state. Edmund, after some years went to Maine. Dr. George C. Brickett, b. Newbury, long in practice at China, Me., and Augusta, now retired, at the latter place, is his son.

1 JOHN, b. March 19, 1790. Farmer on the homestead, and manufacturer of pearlash which he transported to Boston by teams. He was a man of excellent reputation; m. Eunice, dau. Tarrant Putnam.

Children:
2 i. Harry, b. Feb. 1, 1818.
   ii. Eunice, b. 1820, d. y.
   iii. Sarah Ann, b. 1822; m. John Underwood of Bradford; d. Feb. 6, 1871. Two c.
   iv. Eunice Jane, b. 1826; d. 1845.

2 HARRY, b. Newbury, Feb. 1, 1818. Fitted for college at Bradford and Haverhill academies; graduated Dartmouth College, 1840; taught Melville Academy at Jaffrey, N. H., two years; principal of Francestown Academy, 1844-51; of Brown Latin School, Newburyport, Mass., 1851-53; of Merrimack Normal Institute, Reed's Ferry, 1853-56, preaching a part of the time; pastor of Congregational churches, Hillsborough Bridge, 1857-65; at Geneseo, Ill., 1865-72; East Lake George, N. Y., 1872-76; Hillsborough Bridge, 1876-82; Thetford, 1882-90; retired at Hooksett, Mass., 1890 till death, Dec. 17, 1891; delivered many lectures, published sermons and addresses, also a history of Hillsborough, published 1886; m. Aug. 18, 1846, Eliza Cutter of Jaffrey, N. H.

Children:
   i. Joseph C., dea.
   ii. Ellen J., (Mrs. Prescott of Hooksett, N. H.); graduate Oberlin College, 1875.
   iii. Harry L., b. Sept. 14. 1852; Congregational minister; graduate Oberlin College, 1875; Andover Theological Seminary, 1882.

BROCK.

I. Dea. Thomas, b. about 1745. Little is known of his early history. He is said to have come to America as an indentured servant, under another name, but when his term of service had expired, he resumed his own name. He was probably from Scotland, but is not known to have been in any way connected with the Brock families of Ryegate and Barnet. It is not known when he first came to Newbury, but the Haverhill town records give the publication of marriage between Thomas Brock of Newbury and Judith Abbott of Haverhill on Sept. 19, 1772. He served in the revolutionary war; was corporal in Capt. Frye Bayley's company which went to Saratoga Sept. 23-Oct. 27, 1777; private in Capt. John G. Bayley's company, guarding and scouting 29 days, in 1777-78; in Capt. Samuel Young's company, Bedel's regiment, Jan. 29-April 1, 1779; in Capt. Frye Bayley's company, guarding and scouting 11 days, in 1781-82. He settled on Hall's meadow, building in 1800 the house owned by his grandson, W. W. Brock. He probably joined the 1st ch. before the existing records begin and as he is spoken of in the records as Dea. Thomas Brock, he must have been chosen a deacon before 1784; m. as before stated, Judith, dau. James Abbott, then of Haverhill, afterward of Newbury, (b. Jan. 19, 1753; d. Dec. 30, 1806). The first house which he built stood a little north of the one built in 1800; d. June 10, 1811.

Children:
   i. Mary, b. Dec. 28, 1773; m. Samuel Tucker, q. v.; d. Jan. 10, 1840.
   ii. Sarah, b. and d. Jan. 24, 1775.
2 iii. Thomas Robinson, b. Dec. 5, 1775; d. Jan. 19, 1839.
   iv. Sarah, b. Sept. 27, 1777; m. Samuel White, q. v.; d. Aug. 2, 1841.
3   v. Benjamin, b. June 15, 1779; d. June 8, 1841.
4 vi. Samuel, b. Dec. 18, 1780.
5 vii. James, b. Feb. 23, 1782; d. July 23, 1857.
6 viii. Judith, b. Aug. 6, 1783; d. Jan. 26, 1797.
7 ix. Jacob, b. Nov. 1, 1784; d. Feb. 17, 1868.
   x. Susan, b. Dec. 24, 1785; m. John Brown; rem. to Dalton, N. H.
  xi. Olive, b. April 3, 1787; d. Sept. 4, 1789.
8 xii. Moses, b. Jan. 17, 1789; d. Oct. 2, 1874.
9 xiii. William, b. Sept. 14, 1790; d. Oct. 2, 1857.
10 xiv. Olive, b. Oct. 13, 1792; m. John Wyatt of Castleton.
  xv. Ethan S., b. March 11, 1794; m. Mary Doyle; lived in the Brock neighborhood till 1867, then at West Newbury; d. Nov. 15, 1870. No c.

2 Thomas Robinson,[2] (Thomas[1]) generally called Robinson Brock, b. Dec. 5, 1775. He settled first where C. E. Brock now owns, near the Brock schoolhouse, where some of his c. were b. That farmhouse is believed to be about 100 years old. No one can tell who built it. This farm was deeded, in 1822, to Ethan S. Brock, who, in 1867, sold it to the present owner. He afterward lived at West Newbury, his farm lying west of that now owned by Fred Sawyer. It was a fine farm, but the buildings are nearly all gone, and only the cellar and foundation walls mark where they stood. Later he lived where Joseph Sawyer now does; m. in 1803, Rebecca, dau. Reuben Abbott of Concord. N. H., and granddaughter of Reuben Abbott, also of Concord, brother of James who settled in this town; (b. May, 13, 1781; d. Oct. 3, 1872). He d. Jan. 19, 1839.

Children:
   i. Charles, b. April 24, 1804; m. Dec. 15, 1830, Elvila, dau. Samuel Smith, who d. Dec. 29, 1863; lived on the Jacob Brock place, where Davis Cheney lately lived; d. May 22, 1863. No c.
   ii. Rebecca, b. May 10, 1835; m. Ebenezer Abbott, q. v.; 2d, Gilman Brown; d. Nov. 18, 1897.
  iii. Robinson, b. Oct 18, 1806; rem. to Springfield.
  iv. Judith, b. Feb. 23, 1808; m. 1st, Sept. 7, 1835, William A. Boyce of Albany who d. and she m. 2d. John Atwood, q. v.; d. Jan. 26. 1897.
   v. Zerviah, b. Nov. 6, 1809; m. R. C. Sawyer, q. v.; d. June 2, 1888.
  vi. Reuben Chandler, b. Apr. 15, 1813; m. 1st, July 3, 1839, Eliza Sweet, who d. 1840; 2d, Caroline Sweet, rem. to New York state, then to Davenport, Iowa, where he d.

vii. Mary F., b. Oct. 17, 1815; m, Adams Wilson, q. v.; d. March 13, 1842.
viii. William, b. Sept. 27, 1817; m. Mary J., dau. Abner Chamberlin. C., (1)
      Amelia May, of Milwaukee, Wis.; (2) son, d. in infancy; d. July 27, 1852.
ix.   George A., b. July 14, 1822.

3 BENJAMIN,[2] (Thomas[1]) b. June 15, 1779. Settled first where his brother Moses
      long lived, but later bought the farm which was first owned by Stevens
      McConnell, adjoining the Bradford line, on the river road, to which much
      has been added, and which is now owned by his grandson, James A. Brock,
      and is one of the largest in town. About 1835, he divided the farm
      between his sons, Horatio and Thomas; m. 1st, 1806, Margaret, dau.
      Samuel Gibson, (b. Jan. 14, 1784; d. Aug. 27, 1815); five c. 2d, Jan. 22,
      1817, Ruth Chadwick, widow of Tarrant Putnam Jr., who d. May 12,
      1838, aged 52 years, 8 months, 1 day; one c. 3d, Martha C. Johnson who
      survived him. He d. June 9, 1841.
   Children:
11   i.   Horatio, b. Aug. 5, 1807; d. March 8, 1863.
      ii. Betsey, b. May 1; d. May 4, 1810.
      iii. Thomas, b. May 28, 1811; m. 1839, Abby C., dau. Hanes Johnson of
           Newbury. C., (1) Albert H., b. January, 1840; d. y.; (2) James M., b.
           June, 1841; d. August, 1842. He d. March 6, 1842.
      iv. Jane, b April 3; d. April 8, 1814.
      v.   James, b. Aug. 3, 1815; d. at Nashua, N. H., 1845; unm.
      vi. Sophronia Chloe, b. Jan. 9, 1818; m. Sept. 7, 1835, Thomas M. Stevens of
           Piermont; d Piermont, N. H., March 22, 1863. C., (1) Helen Adela, b.
           April 18, 1836; m. Jan. 21, 1858, John Bixby of Piermont; one son,
           Edward. (2) De Sevigna, b. Sept. 28, 1837; m. July 6, 1856, Abigail
           Stevens of Piermont; drowned in Connecticut river Aug. 4, 1861. Two c.
           (3) Sophia Ruth, b. Nov. 14, 1839; m. Dec. 3, 1858, Abel M. Bowen of
           Piermont. Three c., now living in Hillsboro, N. H. (4) Benjamin LeRoy,
           b. Nov. 23, 1841; d. Newark, N. J., Sept. 5, 1880. (5) Eugene, b. Dec. 19,
           1843; m. Oct. 13, 1868, Emma J. Brooks of Providence, R. I., where they
           now reside. One dau., Maud Sophronia.

11 HORATIO, COL.,[3] (Benjamin,[2] Thomas[1]) b, Aug. 5, 1807; m. March 24, 1835,
      Miranda Lovewell of Corinth, moving the next day into the brick house,
      built the year before, and still the home of the family. He was prominent
      in the old militia, and was promoted, step by step to the rank of colonel;
      state senator, 1860-61. Mrs. Brock d. Sept. 6, 1894. He d. March 8,1863.
   Children:
      i.   Benjamin Harrison, b. June 12, 1836; d. Aug. 4, 1838.
      ii. Hartwell Lovewell, b. March 5, 1837; d. Sept. 18, 1859.
      iii. Adeline Prichard, b. Oct. 8, 1839. At the homestead.
      iv. Thomas Allen, b. Sept. 4, 1841. Served in the war of the rebellion in the
           1st Vermont, three months, and as lieutenant in 12th Vermont, 9 months.
           He m. Dec. 30, 1867, Ellen E. Witt of Bradford; res. Omaha, Neb. C., (1)
           Frederic Harrison, b. Sept. 17, 1868; d. Feb. 8, 1878 at Mattoon, Ill. (2)
           Flora Isabel, (twin to Frederic).
      v.   Alma Gibson, b. Dec. 20, 1843; m. May 21, 1873, Loami F. Hale of
           Bradford. No c.
      vi. James Albert, b. Aug. 15, 1846. Farmer on homestead.
      vii. Harriet Ellen, b. Aug. 14, 1849. At the homestead.

4 SAMUEL, b. Dec. 18,1780. He is said to have been a sailor, and being dissatisfied
      with the settlement of his father's estate, went away, and his after history
      is unknown. The Abbott register says that he m. Nancy Field in 1806.

5 JAMES, DEA., b. Feb. 23, 1782; lived on the homestead; m. 1812, Chloe Buck of
      Bath, who d. Feb. 15, 1879; was a deacon in the 1st ch. and at his death
      bequeathed $500 as the foundation for a fund with which to purchase a
      parsonage; d. July 23, 1857. No c.

6 JUDITH, b. Aug. 6, 1783; d. Jan. 26, 1797. (The Abbott register says 1802).
      She was long remembered in Newbury. The editor well recollects hearing
      his grandfather, John Wells, ask one of his music-loving associates, "Can
      you sing Judith Brock?" "No." was the reply. "I can sing Polly Gould,
      but I can't sing Judith Brock." This enigmatical reply deserves

WILLIAM W. BROCK.

COL. HORATIO BROCK.

elucidation. A hymn of eighteen stanzas was composed and sung at her funeral, in the old meeting-house. This extraordinary production begins;—

> "Death loud alarms, we feel the shock,
> Louder than thunder's roar,
> With grief we learn that Judith Brock,
> Is known on earth no more."

It goes on to describe the youth and attractions of Judith, her long and painful illness, the scenes of her death and the grief of her friends, ending with solemn admonition. This dirge was sung to a tune composed by Mr. Ingalls, who may have written the words. This tune, called "Lamentation," and the words, may be found on p.p. 169, 170, of the "Christian Harmony." It was a fugue, with many repetitions, and the rendering thereof must have required at least half an hour. Such was the taste of our ancestors. The composition was intricate and when well rendered was considered very fine, and seventy years ago it was thought quite a feat for a company of singers to sing it through without a mistake. One, somewhat like it, was sung at the funeral of Polly Gould.

7 JACOB,[2] (Thomas[1]) b. Nov. 1, 1785. In his younger days he was a raftsman, but settled and spent most of his life in this town, owning several farms in succession; owned the farm and built the house where the late Davis Cheney lived and d. where his son, C. E. Brock now owns in the Brock neighborhood. (See Thomas Robinson Brock). He joined the Congregational church May 7, 1819, and was among those set off to form the Topsham church in 1829; he was m. four times; 1st in Haverhill, Jan. 22, 1807, to Abigail Sanders, who d. April 27, 1830; 2d, in Topsham, Oct. 13, 1830, Mrs. Betsey Sinclair, who d. July 16, 1849, in her 49th year; 3d, in Dracut, Mass., March 16, 1850, Abigail Eastman; 4th, Jan. 16, 1856, Mehetabel Kimball Tice, who d. Jan. 3, 1870.

Children, twelve by 1st, and three by 2d m.:

i. Edna, b. June 20, 1807; d. Aug. 10, 1829.
ii. Adeline, b. Jan. 2, 1809; d. Oct. 3, 1829.
iii. Jacob, b. July 5, 1810; m, in Hartford, Conn., lived there some years, then went south and settled in Jacksonville, Fla., owning steamboats; was captain of a boat and carried the mail during the civil war; was captured while trying to run the blockade and taken to New York. After the war he returned to Jacksonville, and his former business, also owned and conducted a hotel till death; d. 1876. Five c., all settled in Florida.
iv. Samuel, b. April 8, 1812; d. July 20, 1822.
v. Alden, b. Jan. 3, 1814. He lived many years on what was called the Israel Putnam place in Topsham, but about 1875, rem. to Yreka. Sisco Co., Cal., where he is a mine-owner; served in the Union army during the civil war; m. March 17, 1843, Agnes, dau. of John Somers of Barnet, who d. in 1888. C., (1) Louisa, d. 1864. (2) Reuben, served in the army, killed at Fredericksburg. (3) Claudius, in Montana some years; m. Cora Butterfield, who d. 1875, leaving two c.; 2d, Mrs. Mary Somers, four c.; res. Ryegate. (4) Isabel, lives in Ryegate. (5) Milo, m. Leonora Mills; d. in Topsham.
vi. Ethan S., b. Jan. 4, 1816. Farmer of Topsham and Piermont; m. Aug. 22, 1839, Mary Jane, dau. Duncan McKeith (b. Topsham, Jan. 31, 1818; d. Piermont, 1893). He d. March, 1889. No c.
vii. Harriet, b. Jan. 25, 1818.
viii. Abigail, b. Aug. 19, 1819; d. Apr. 15, 1834.
ix. Moses, b. May 12, 1821; d. July 18, 1823.
x. Louisa, b. Sept. 1, 1823; d, Feb 21, 1851.
xi. Moses, b. June 30, 1825; d. July 8, 1826.
xii. James, b. Oct. 27, 1828; d. Sept. 13, 1852.
xiii. Edward A., b. July 18, 1832; served in the Union army, was in seventeen battles unharmed; m. Sarah Carpenter; d. of fever in hospital in Virginia, Oct. 14, 1864. C., (1) Cora, m. E. A. Fairbanks; res. Claremont, N. H. (2) Harry A., lives in Orange; is m. (3) Cyrus C., adopted by Charles Dickey; lives at East Corinth.
xiv. Clarissa Jane, b. March 28, 1834; m. at Concord, N. H., Charles Brooks; d. July 14, 1860. Two c., both b, New Haven, Conn. (1) Charles, b. Sept. 8, 1857; res. Manchester, N. H. (2) Frank, b. Aug. 12, 1859.

xv. Carlos E., b. June 14, 1839; farmer, on the "John Kent farm;" m. March 20, 1861, Mary J., dau. Ephraim Bailey. C., (1) Everett C., b. Haverhill, March 18, 1862; res. Barre; express business; m. Jan. 24, 1888, Ella J. Woodward. C., a, Gerald W., b. Sept. 11, 1894; b, Dean Merlyn, b. April 30, 1899. (2) Gertrude M., b. March 1, 1869; m. Nov. 26, 1896, Ralph E. Bailey; res. Springfield. C., a, Carl L.; b, Lyle N. (3) Bessie, b. May 1, 1873. (4) Ernest F., b. Sept. 17, 1878; on the old farm in the Brock neighborhood; m. May 12, 1898, Olive, dau. A. J. Knight. C., Erle F., b. Feb. 6, 1899.

8   MOSES, b. Jan. 17, 1789; settled first in company with his brother William on Lot 49, which they bought of Josiah Little, Oct. 5, 1813, clearing a part of it, and building a house and barn about 90 rods south of Round pond. March 5, 1816, they bought Lot 68 of Benjamin Brock, who had bought the lot Dec. 24, 1808, of Josiah Little, and had cleared the eastern half, and built a barn and a house. The latter is the one in which John B. Brock now res. The brothers permanently settled there, moving the house which had been built near Round pond to its present site, and is the house in which the present Moses Brock, and his son, Moses L., now res. Benjamin rem. to South Newbury. The brothers dissolved partnership in 1822, Moses conveying the north half of Lot 68, with the buildings erected by Benjamin, and the south half of Lot 49 to William. In 1859, William's son, William Wallace, sold his half of Lot 68 to Thomas Flanders, who April 6, 1875, sold to Moses Brock Jr., who then held it all. Jan. 14, 1886 Moses Jr., conveyed the south half of Lot 68 with barn, but no house to his son, John B. Brock. Moses was a farmer and carpenter, took an active part in military affairs, was a musician in the cavalry, and taught singing schools. In politics a whig and republican, joined the 1st ch. May 4, 1819 and was made a deacon in the West Newbury church at its organization, and at his death bequeathed $500 as a fund for its support. He m. (Topsham records) March 19, 1815, Lydia Nourse, who d. Sept. 26, 1872. He d. Oct. 2, 1874.
    Children:
12 i.   John, b. July 15, 1816; d. Oct. 10, 1849.
    ii. Orrin, b. June 10, 1818; d. Apr. 23, 1823.
    iii. Sarah b. March 14; d. March 25, 1820.
    iv. Christine, b. July 30, d. Nov. 11, 1821.
    v.   Mindwell, b. Aug. 19, 1822; m. John N. Town of Corinth; d. there November, 1874. C., a. Mary E., who m. George Jackman, and lives on her father s homestead; b, Vioella, c, Herbert, d, Lydia, who are dead, and e, Ida B., who makes her home in the family of James A. Brock of South Newbury.
    vi. Thomas, b. May 1, 1825; d. July 6, 1826.
13 vii. Moses, b. July 17, 1826.

12 JOHN N., b. July 15, 1816; farmer and captain in the militia; his farm was that which is now S. F. Putnam's; m. July 22, 1843, Lucinda, dau. of David McAllister, (b. Oct. 10, 1849; d. June 15, 1871). He d. Oct. 10, 1849.
    Chiidren:
    i.   Elizabeth L., b. July 23, 1844; m. 1st, George Jewell; 2d, James H. Minard.
    ii. Ellen J., b. Oct. 5, 1846; m. M. B. Abbott, q. v.
    iii. John N., b. Jan. 30, 1849; in a store in Boston five years; partner with H. K. Wilson at West Newbury, 1875-79; in business at Bradford till death, Aug. 27, 1881; m. Aug. 25, 1875, Hattie, dau. William C. Carleton.

13 MOSES, b. July 17, 1826; farmer on homestead, and carpenter, erecting many barns and other buildings at West Newbury, and the Free Christian church at Newbury Village; m. March 30, 1853, Abigail, dau. John Bayley (b. May 20, 1830). Mr. and Mrs. Brock, with most of their children and several of their grandchildren, are members of the Free Christian church at Newbury village.
    Children:
    i.   Orrin W., b. Dec. 20, 1854; farmer on the David McAllister place and at one time lieutenant in the militia; secretary of the State Association of the Free Christian church; m. May 17, 1878, T. Alpha Spaulding of Lowell, Mass. C., a, Benjamin, b. Feb. 21, 1879; b, Albert, b. July 1, 1880; c, Eva Rose, b. March 1, 1890.

ii. John B., b. Nov. 25, 1856; farmer on part of homestead; m. Sept. 20, 1878, Mary E., dau. P. C. Tewksbury. No c.

iii. Martha M., b. Feb. 15, 1859; m. May 12, 1884, William Henry Tewksbury, q. v.

iv. Moses L., b. Nov. 16, 1860; farmer on homestead with his father; mechanic and in other business; member of state militia since 1882; served with the Vermont regiment of reserve in the Spanish-American war at Chickamaugua, Tenn., as 1st Lieutenant, Co. G, 1st Reg. Inf. U. S. Vols.; mustered into U. S. service May 16; discharged Nov. 28, 1898; upon reorganization of militia, was elected captain of Co, G, 1st Reg. Inf. Vt. Nat. Guards, Oct. 2, 1899; m. Dec. 25, 1894, A. Louise Page of Haverhill. C., *a*, Unola Frances, b. Dec. 1, 1895; *b*, Gwendolin Enrita, b. Dec. 11, 1900.

v. W. Malcolm, b. Aug. 25, 1863; res. Wells River; tinsmith and plumber; m. Oct. 2, 1893, Rose Stearns of South Newbury. C., *a*, Harold W., b. June 27, 1894.

vi. Minnie B., b. Dec. 16, 1869.

9 WILLIAM, b. Sept. 14, 1790; settled on part of the farm now owned by Moses Brock and his sons, at West Newbury, where he d. His home is now occupied by John B. Brock; m. Nov. 1, 1818, Ann, dau. Col. William Wallace, (b. April 29, 1794; d. Freeport, Ill., April 26, 1876; buried in Newbury). He d. Oct. 2, 1851.
Children, all b. in Newbury; three d. y.:

14 i. William Wallace, b. June 7, 1819.

ii. Flora A., b. Nov. 6, 1820; m. July 13, 1852, N. K. Robbins; d. New York City, Jan. 14, 1894. Four c., three of whom are dead.

iii. Benjamin, b. March 4, 1827; m. Jan. 13, 1853, Alma Bliss of Wolcott and after two or three years went west, and settled at Manson, Iowa. Three c.

iv. Elvira, b. Jan. 1, 1834; m. Martin Emmert of Freeport, Ill.; rem. later to Beloit, Kansas. Pive c.

v. Robert G., b. Feb. 5, 1832; m. March 15, 1865, Frances, dau. William Doe; went west, and settled finally at Cedar Rapids, Iowa. One son.

vi. Henry C., b. Jan. 10, 1847; m. and lived in the west; killed Oct. 17, 1895, while leaving a train at McAllister, I. T., and buried there.

14 WILLIAM WALLACE, b. June 7, 1819; settled on his father's farm, but in 1858, rem. to the Brock homestead at South Newbury, the buildings being thoroughly repaired and improved; town representative, 1865, (see town officers); m. March 11, 1847, Sophia E., dau. Joseph and Sallie (Robie) Taplin, who were from Corinth but lived in Fairfield, where she was b. April 11, 1824, d. Aug. 20, 1900.
Children, all b. in Newbury:

i. B. Frank, b. July 22, 1848; in Manchester Locomotive Works from December, 1868-83; in Aurora, Ill., in machine shop, one and one-half years; went to Washington Territory and engaged in lumbering on the Columbia river. The business was then conducted in a primitive way, the logs being drawn on skid-roads with oxen. He has opened up a large tract of country, and built a railroad extending among the hills. The logs are now handled by steam engines, and a village has sprung up around his camp, with a post office called Eufaula. He m. 1885, Selena McAdam of Stella, Washington. Eight c.

ii. William W., b. Nov. 11, 1849; res. Newbury, except two years in the west; bought, 1885, the Caleb Stevens farm at South Newbury; m. Jan. 18, 1882, Orinda J., dau. W. H. Nelson of Haverhill. One son, Frank Nelson, b. Haverhill, Dec. 6, 1882.

iii. Eugene, b. May 8, 1853; started for California, May 8, 1874, where he worked one season in lumbering for the Towle brothers; in Washington Territory with his brother a few years; then in farming; has twice represented his district in the state legislature; m. Nov. 30, 1881, Anna McAdam of Stella, Wash. Three c.

iv. Clarence T., b. Aug. 29, 1857. March 11, 1878, he left home for Washington Territory; with his brothers nearly a year; at Cedar Rapids, Iowa, with his uncle Robert G., nearly three years; since in Washington; m. Apr. 17, 1885, Maggie McAdam of Stella, Wash. Three c.

v.   Clara Belle, b. March 19, 1865; has remained at home; m. Oct. 12, 1898, Frederic G. Cline from Massena, N. Y., station agent at South Newbury.

10   OLIVE, b. Oct. 13, 1792; m. June 6, 1816, John Wyatt of Richmond; later they rem. to Castleton and of their c. John, b. Dec. 31, 1818 is dead; lived in Castleton; James, b. Feb. 8, 1828, is quite prominent in Astoria, Oregon; a dau., Julia P., b. May 7, 1822; m. 1842, D. H. Hawkins of Castleton. They lived in Brooklyn, N. Y., where she was prominent in Plymouth church, a deaconess, and lost her life from fever contracted in doing mission work.   There were other c.

*BROCK.

ROBERT and ANDREW, sons of Robert and Jean (Miller) Brock, were among the first settlers of Ryegate.   Andrew, b. Kilpatrck Parish, Renfrewshire, Scotland, 1749, came to New York in 1772, and to Ryegate, 1774; built the first house at Boltonville, and lived there a part of the time, purchasing the mills in 1787, and the place from that time till about 1820, was called "Brock's Falls"; deacon in the Associate Pres. ch., at Ryegate Corner, 1779, till death, June 12, 1817; was one of the most prominent men in Ryegate; m. Mary, dau. Archibald Taylor (b. Scotland, March 4, 1764; d. Ryegate, March, 1858).
  Children:
i.   Jean, b. Sept. 29, 1783; m. William Dean of Dalton, N. H.
ii.   Mary, b. July 26, 1785; m. William Grant of Ryegate and Newbury; d. Newbury, May 12, 1865.
iii. Robert, b. May 30, 1787; m. Sabra Strong; d. 1835.
iv.   Nancy, b. April 6, 1789; was a noted nurse; m. Oct. 1, 1838, Sabin Johnson of Bath; d. about 1870.
v.   Margaret, b. Oct. 17, 1791; d. June 17, 1794, the first burial in the old church yard at Ryegate Corner.
vi.   Andrew. b. Jan. 27, 1794.
vii. Archibald, b. March 19, 1796; d. July 19. 1796.
viii. Elizabeth, b. June 16, 1797; m. 1st, Joel Nutter of Newbury in 1818, who d. about 1829; m. 2d, April 3, 1834, William Wright of Ryegate.   Five c. Andrew, oldest son of Joel and Elizabeth Nutter, b. May 11, 1819; was a farmer in Newbury, and sexton of the Ox-bow cemetery some years; m. May 8, 1860, Mrs. Martha B. Cooledge, dau. of John Bayley. He d. 1895. No c.
ix.   William, b. June 30, 1800.   He was known far and wide for his marvelous skill upon the violin; m. Tryphena Clement of Barnet; d. in the west.
x.   Margaret, b. Sept. 4, 1802; d. March 4, 1805.
1 xi.   Walter Miller, b. Sept. 14, 1804; d. Jan. 28, 1889.
xii. James, b. June 9, 1806.

1 WALTER MILLER, b. Sept. 14, 1804; farmer in Barnet and Newbury; m. Dec. 20, 1832, Mary, dau. Caleb Wilson and granddaughter of Dea. Thomas McKeith (b. Topsham. Oct. 10, 1814; d. Newbury, April 8, 1896). He d. Newbury, Jan. 28, 1889.
  Children:
i.   Son, b. and d. in Barnet.
ii.   Mary Jane, b. Oct. 26, 1842; m. April 21, 1886, David Peach of Newbury; d. July 30, 1895.
iii. Sarah.
iv.   Susan, m. Rev. Benjamin Cross of the Baptist Board of Missions.   They went to India as missionaries about 1873, and remained there several years, where their children were born.   Mr. Cross is now preaching in Massachusetts.

BROCK.

JAMES, of Barnet, m. Mary, dau. of Job Abbott, and their son, Alexander Harvey

---

*Prepared by Edward Miller, Esq.

Brock, (b. Barnet, Jan. 7, 1811; d. Ryegate, May 3, 1890) m. Janet, dau.
Robert Gibson. Of their five c. two have lived in Newbury.

i. Robert G., b. Ryegate, June 11, 1843; served in the Union army; res. Wells
River; carpenter and manufacturer of watering tubs, etc.; m. 1st, Oct. 2,
1867, Martha Helen, dau. George and Helen (Goodwin) Rhodes, who d.
Sept. 2, 1872. Two c., (1) Flora Emily, b. Sept. 28, 1868; at home. (2)
Alice Jennett, b. Nov. 13, 1871; m. J. H. Morrill of Ashland, N. H.; studied
some years at the Boston Conservatory of Music. He m. 2d, Nov. 2, 1875,
Addie Dorrilla Jay, who d. Nov. 19, 1883. C., (3) Fred Harvey, b. April 3,
1880. (4) Herbert Jay, b. Nov. 6, 1883.

ii. David, b. March 5, 1847; carpenter at Wells River; m. May 2, 1871, Emily
Annette Rhodes, sister of the first wife of Robert G. Brock. C., Cora Annette,
b. Ryegate, Nov. 13, 1872; graduate of Middlebury College; preceptress
of Lyndon Academy for several years. (2) George Harvey, b. March 24,
1878.

BROWN.

ABRAHAM, b. Strafford, Aug. 29, 1793; m. Feb. 1, 1813, Polly, dau. Jotham
Tuttle, (b. Andover, Mass., May 6, 1796; d. Jan. 11, 1879). They came
to Newbury in 1824; carried on the place which had been Rev. Mr.
Lambert's two years, then rem. to Leighton hill, where they cleared the
farm which is now owned by John Reid, where they built a house and barn.
They were members of the Meth. ch. About 1863, they sold their farm
and rem. from Newbury. He d. Lebanon, N. H., May 12, 1870.
Children:

i. Mary A., b. Sept. 7, 1822; m. Albert G. Page, q. v.
ii. Nathaniel, b. Oct. 23, 1824; d. Oct. 21, 1826.
iii. Lorenza, b. Dec. 7, 1827; m. Sept. 29, 1852, Philetus Bliss, (b. Compton,
Conn., 1818; served three years in Co. C., 3d Vt. in the civil war).
iv. Moses T., b. Oct. 31, 1829; m. 1st, Sept. 3, 1853, Lavinia V. Crown, who d.
July 15, 1857; 2d, May 1, 1859, Lizzie Hazeltine, who d. Feb. 24, 1880;
3d, September, 1883, Helen Merritt.
v. John L. T., b. May 8, 1832; m. 1st, Dec. 6, 1855, Mary J. Page, 2d, Aug.
21, 1878, Annie Belle Weston.
1 vi. Wells B., b. March 31, 1835.
vii. Harvey B., b. April 19, 1837; d. March 4, 1841.

1 WELLS B., b. Newbury, March 31, 1835; m. May 25, 1857, Sarah Jane, dau.
Thomas Smith of Newbury, (b. Sept. 15, 1837). Res. Vergennes.
Children:

i. Harrie W., b. Feb. 9, 1860; d. July 20, 1878.
ii. Frank B., b. Sept. 25, 1863; d. June 4, 1873.
iii. Jennie A., b. Oct. 28, 1865.
iv. Carrie D., b. May 21, 1868; m. Silas Page.
v. John L. T., b. Sept. 26, 1875; d. April 25, 1877.

BROWN.

DR. IRA, son of Josiah and Susannah (Wilmarth) Brown, b. Kirby, Sept. 20,
1818. (Descended from William and Mary (Murdock) Brown, who came
from England to Plymouth, Mass., before 1656; rem. to Seekouk, R. I.).
Studied medicine with his brother, Dr. Abel Brown of Burke, who d.
lately, aged 92; graduated, Castleton Medical School, 1845; in practice
Northumberland, three years; Burke, 1849-64; Wells River, 1864-81; in
broken health at Lyndon two years; rem. to Minneapolis, Minn.; in
practice forty-two years, till within two weeks of death; m. June 6, 1848,
Emily, dau. Rev. John Clark, Congregational minister at Burke; she d.
Wells River, 1877. He d. Jan. 6, 1887.
Children, all b. at Burke, but lived at Wells River:

i. Edward J., b. Jan. 14, 1851; graduate Kimball Union Academy, 1870,
Dartmouth College, 1874, Dartmouth Medical College, 1879; in practice
at Littleton, N. H., 1879-80; Haverhill, 1880-82; Minneapolis, 1882 to
date; m. April 23, 1890, K. Mary Fullerton. Five c.

ii. Abby Ann, b. Nov. 23, 1852; educated at St. Johnsbury Academy and Mt.
Holyoke Seminary; m. Henry K. White of Newbury, son of Ebenezer T.
White; res. Washington, D. C.; one dau.
iii. Esther Myanda, b. Dec. 19, 1855; educated St. Johnsbury Academy and
Norwich, Conn., Free Academy; res. Escondido, Cal.
iv. John Clark, b. April 4, 1859; studied Philadelphia College of Pharmacy;
druggist in Washington, D. C., about fourteen years; graduate 1900, at
National Medical College; in study in New York City, intending to locate
with his brother at Minneapolis.

BUCK.

CAPT. WILLIAM, of Connecticut ancestry, was a native of, and farmer in
Waterford. Of his c., William H., b. in Waterford, 1847; educated at
McIndoe Falls Academy and a graduate of Randolph Normal School;
teacher and clerk; came to Wells River, 1876, as principal of the village
school; entered the druggist business, 1881, which he has since conducted
in that place; superintendent of schools five years; Mason and Odd Fellow
and has been representative in both grand bodies; m. Aug. 27, 1876, Mary,
dau. Gawn and Sarah J. Dunlap, a teacher, who d. March 17, 1890,
leaving an infant son, Malcolm Fletcher.

BUELL.

WILLIAM, came from England to Dorchester, Mass., about 1630, and in 1635,
became one of the original proprietors of Windsor, Conn. From him he
descended many notable men and women. From him in the sixth
generation was;—
ASHBEL, b. Litchfield, Conn., Jan. 12, 1765. It has been claimed that he was a
revolutionary soldier, but there is no record of his service, and his
grandson, the late Ashbel C. Buell, had never heard of his being such. He
moved his family to Newbury with an ox team in the winter of 1796, and
settled on what was then called the Charles Bayley farm, on the hill
southwest of Wells River. This he sold in 1801, to James Wallace, from
Scotland, and, in 1802 bought the John Brown place, now called the "old
Buell place" at West Newbury. He m. Nov. 1, 1787, Huldah Webster of
Litchfield, (b. Feb. 22, 1767; d. Oct. 10, 1856). He d. Nov. 3, 1853;
buried at West Newbury. They had six c., the two younger b. in Newbury
the elder ones in Litchfield.
i. Ward, b. Sept. 4, 1788; m. Dec. 5, 1811, Theodotia, dau. David Ladd of
Haverhill, (b. Feb. 15, 1786; d. April 1, 1852). He d. Newbury, March 6,
1874. They had six c., who are all dead, or rem. from here.
ii. Candace, b. April 1, 1791; m. 1st, Jan. 18, 1821, John E. Tuxbury; 2d, Dec.
9, 1836, Capt. Elijah Rowe of Bradford, (b. Nottingham, N. H., March 9,
1769; d. Bradford, Jan. 26, 1858). She d. Bradford, Oct. 19, 1870.
iii. Loveman, b. April 22, 1794; m. Hannah Willey; d. Charlestown, Mass.,
Aug. 25, 1852. Three c.
iv. Elnathan, b. Jan. 4, 1797; d. Bradford, Penn., April 20, 1887.
v. Ashbel, b. July 23, 1799; settled on the homestead, but rem. later to
"Goshen"; m. Jan. 20, 1822, Sarah Cochran, (b. Londonderry, N. H., April
11, 1784; d. March 30, 1861). He d. Oct. 12, 1884. C., (1) Mary H., b.
April 18, 1823; res. Newbury. (2) William, b. June 11, 1825; d. March
25, 1865. (3) Ashbel C., b. Sept. 3, 1827; farmer and cooper; prepared,
some years before his death, a careful record of the Buell and Cochrane
families of Newbury and Bradford; m. in Brownington, March 31, 1867,
Sabrina L. Burroughs (b. Coventry, Oct. 26, 1822). He d. July 2, 1899.
vi. Albert, b. May 20, 1803; m. August, 1829, Martha, dau. Philip Tuxbury,
who d. Sept. 22, 1843; d. Feb. 1, 1891. C., (1) William H., b. Jan. 24,
1830; m. 1855, Hannah Wallace of Haverhill; four c. (2) Hannah L., b.
Oct. 13, 1837; m. 1862, Amos L. Bowen; rem. to Canada.

BUCHANAN.

MATTHEW ROBEN came to this country from Scotland in 1801, with the

Wallaces, Robert Fulton, the Allens, Andrew Buchanan and Jean Arbuckle. He had two sons and two daughters.

i. Walter, the elder, lived in Ryegate and d. there.
ii. John, went to New York and d.; both of them old men.
iii. Jean, b. Scotland Yocker, 1785; m. Andrew Buchanan, q. v.; d. Jan. 18, 1863, aged 77 years, 8 months. Eleven c.
iv. Isabel, m. William Gray of Ryegate and also had eleven c.

ANDREW BUCHANAN, b. Barritan, Scotland, 1770; m. Jean, dau. Matthew Roben; d. Nov. 19, 1839, aged 67 years, 8 months, 8 days). Farmer in Ryegate.

Children:
i. Moses, at the age of twenty-one, came to Wells River and worked for Timothy Shedd one year, 1830, then went into company with Samuel Hutchins, the firm name being Hutchins, Buchanan & Co.; d. July 1, 1859, aged fifty-four.
ii. Andrew, went into business in Philadelphia, where he continued for about twenty years; d. June 25, 1863, aged 54 years, 4 months.
iii. James, came to Wells River, 1834, and went into company with Hutchins, Buchanan & Co., and continued in that company until 1851, when he bought out Mr. Hutchins and William G. Buchanan bought out Moses; then the firm name was J. & W. G. Buchanan, which continued until 1867, when Col. James Buchanan d. He m. 1st, Sarah Jane, dau. Charles Hale, (d. March 27, 1843); 2d, a Mrs. Mansfield. His title of Colonel came from his connection with the old militia; town representative, 1845-46; d. June 24, 1867.
iv. Willliam G., b. Jan. 21, 1828, being the surviving partner of the firm, settled the estate. He came to Wells River in 1848; clerk for Hutchins, Buchanan & Co., until he bought into the firm with his brother James; m. Oct. 11, 1854, Helen, dau. Ira White; res. at Wells River; d. June 14, 1855, aged 26 years. One c., Kate, who m. F. L. Mace.
v. Matthew, d. July 19, 1854.
vi. John, d. July 3, 1897, aged 82 years.
vii. Walter R., b. Feb. 26, 1824; d. Oct. 30, 1873.
viii. Jean, living in Kentucky.
ix. Lillian, m. S. A. Moore, q. v.
x. Isabella, m. Robert Nelson, q. v.
xi. Margaret, b. May 21, 1821; m. Archibald Bachop; is dead.

BUCHANAN.

WALTER, b. Baldornoc Parish, near Glasgow, Scotland, Feb. 28, 1789; farmer in Scotland; Presbyterian; m. in Glasgow, Dec. 7, 1825, by Rev. Michael Willies, Mary Buchanan, (b. Stirling, Scotland, Nov. 13, 1802; d. Newbury, March 26, 1876). The Buchanans rented the same farm for 400 years, but the rent being raised, they resolved to emigrate. They came to Canada in 1832; lived in Montreal four years; in Broome one year; in Craftsbury one year; in Barnet two years and in Ryegate five, coming to Newbury in 1847; d. April 14, 1870.

Children:
i. John, b. Scotland, Nov. 12, 1826.
ii. William, b. Scotland, Nov. 29, 1828; d. March 13, 1830.
iii. Walter, b. Glasgow, Scotland, June 25, 1831.
iv. William, b. Broome, P. Q., April 5, 1834.
v. Mary, b. Craftsbury, Dec. 31, 1836; d. Dec. 31, 1853.
vi. Jane, b. Aug. 19, 1839; m. D. J. Walker, see below.
4 vii. George W., b. Ryegate, Nov. 1, 1841.
viii. Isabella. b. Ryegate, Nov. 23, 1843; m. George A. Johnson, q. v.
6 ix. Robert, b. Ryegate, Feb. 18, 1846.

1 JOHN, b. Glasgow, Scotland, Nov. 12, 1826; farmer at Centre; m. April 8, 1858, Ellen D., dau. Richard Patterson.

Children:
i. Richard, b. June 4, 1859; carpenter.
ii. Frank J., b. Nov. 25, 1860; farmer.

2 WALTER, b. Glasgow, Scotland, June 25, 1831; res. Newbury till 1881, when he
   rem. to Antrim, N. H.; farmer; m. Nov. 30, 1858, Susan D., dau. Jonas
   Tuttle, (b. Antrim, N. H., Dec. 19, 1839; d. there Dec. 10, 1894).
   Children:
   i. Mary Eva, b. Feb. 27, 1860; m. Edson S. Corliss, q. v.
   ii. E. Elmer, b. March 28, 1861; res. Henniker, N. H.; m. 1st, Nov. 4, 1885,
       Mary A. C. Jameson of Antrim, who d. Feb. 19, 1893; 2d, Nov. 24, 1894,
       Mary M. Davis, who d. June 17, 1897. C., (1) Nanabell, b. Oct. 13, 1886.
       (2) Eva E., b. Dec. 11, 1887; d. Aug. 23, 1897. (3) Amanda M., b. Feb. 9,
       9, 1893; d. Sept. 3, 1897.
   iii. Henry F., b. Jan. 20, 1863; res. Peterboro, N. H.; superintendent Cotton
        Bleachery some years; farmer; m. Annie J. Blair, May 2, 1888. C., Waldo
        K., b. July 30, 1891; d. same day.
   iv. Ansel E., b. Jan. 19, 1866; res. Winchester, N. H., farmer; m. Oct. 1, 1890,
       Mabel Cochrane of Antrim. C., (1) Arthur P., b. May 10, 1892. (2)
       Agnes M., b. Oct. 13, 1893. (3) Clarence B., b. Sept. 30, 1898.
   v. Elsie, b. Aug. 28, 1867; d. Sept. 18, 1885, at Antrim.
   vi. Olive P., b. May 15, 1870; m. Nov. 25, 1891, Herman W. Matthews; res.
       Peterboro, N. H. C., Ellen R., b. March 1, 1895.
   vii. Susie L., b. April 13, 1873; m. Sept. 13, 1892, John M. Dodge; res.
        Arlington, Mass. C., (1) Ethel B., b. March 9, 1893. (2) Warren C., b.
        April 14, 1897.
   viii. Stella M., b. Nov. 29, 1875; d. March 9, 1876.
   ix. Nellie L., b. May 5. 1877; m. Nov. 11, 1896, William C. White; res.
       Arlington, Mass. C., (1) Chauncey W., b. Feb. 7, 1897. (2) Isabelle
       Beatrice, b. Sept. 19, 1898.

3 WILLIAM, b. Broome, P. Q., April 5, 1834; res. Boston, 1859-82; Antrim, N. H.,
   1882-93; Rockingham till death; represented Antrim in legislature,
   1889-90; held many town and society offices; m. March 12, 1857, Mary
   E., dau. Jonas Tuttle, (b. Jan 22, 1838). He d. Rockingham, May 18, 1897.
   Children:
   i. Charles H., b. April 11, 1862; m. Oct. 21, 1883, Eliza J. Godfrey. C., Helen
       and Edith.
   ii. Vienna H., b. Sept. 23, 1864; d. Sept. 20, 1865.
   iii. George T., b. May 18, 1867.
   iv. William M., b. Aug. 27, 1875.

4 JANE, b. Aug. 18, 1839; m. Oct. 3, 1867, D. G. Walker.
   Children:
   i. Walter B., b. Feb. 24, 1869.
   ii. Robert W., b. Aug. 24, 1871.

5 GEORGE T., b. Nov. 1, 1841; served in Union army in a Massachusetts regiment;
   m. 1870, Annie Moody; d. at Soldiers' Home, Augusta, Me., Nov. 18, 1872.

6 ROBERT, b. Feb. 18, 1846; m. Annie Moody, widow of his brother, George T.
   Res. Boston.
   Children:
   i. George W., b. Feb. 6, 1874.

BURBANK.

This family, long extinct here, was once very prominent. John Burbank came
from England in 1640, settled in Haverhill, Mass., rem. to Suffield, Conn.,
in 1674, and bought land. He had two sons, John and Ebenezer. The
latter had a son, named also Ebenezer, a revolutionary soldier. Ebenezer,
son of the latter, was an early settler of Wells River, where four sons and
four daughters were b. to him:—Lester, Ebenezer, Alanson S., and a fourth
who d. in infancy; Harriet S., Sophronia, Eunice and one who d. y. They
returned to Suffield about 1828, as Ebenezer, and Sarah, his wife, were
dismissed to the church at Enfield Centre in that year. W. E. Burbank of
Suffield, is a son of Lester, and res. on the estate which has been in the
family since 1674. Sophronia, sister of Ebenezer, m. Simon Douglass, q. v.

GEORGE A., and HON. PETER, long prominent at Wells River, were cousins of Ebenezer. The former was a merchant, and m. Polly Maxwell, Dec. 27, 1815.

GUSTAVUS, their son, was adopted by Hon. Peter Burbank, and lived with him at the "Hermitage." After the latter's death, he went into the stage business a few years, then read law with George B. Chandler, was admitted to the bar, and after three years was made clerk of Caledonia County Courts. Cashier of Danville bank some years, then in banking business at Kenosha, Wis., Winona, Minneapolis, and Hastings, Minn. In 1875, he went into private banking in Chicago, with an individual capital of $90,000. In 1889, he joined with three others, all from Caledonia County, in establishing the Market Street bank, at San Francisco, and d. since 1897, leaving several c.

PETER, was one of the most remarkable men who ever lived in Newbury. He has been dead so long, that few remember him personally, and little but tradition remains of him. In addition to the account given of him elsewhere, by Mr. Leslie, some particulars are worth preserving. He was influential in securing the charter of Wells River bank, and was its first president. It was through his adroitness that the bank was located at Wells River, instead of at Newbury Street. The business men of the latter place were confident of having it placed there, and Mr. Burbank assumed an air of indifference as to its location. But before the time came for the decision, he had, by great energy, and rapid driving, secured proxies in favor of Wells River, which he produced at the meeting, to the consternation of the "Street" men, some of whom refused all business dealings with the institution, or to take its bills for several years. Mr. Burbank contemptuously referred to Newbury Village as "good for nothing but to raise white beans in," and the name of "Beanfield" clung to the place for many a year. Many anecdotes have been told of his peculiarities, his absent-mindedness, his fits of parsimony, and seasons of unbounded generosity. He was very eccentric, and those who estimated the man by his outward appearance, were often bewildered by the sudden transformations in his manner. He delighted in a long coat which came nearly to the ground, a ruffled shirt, stained with tobacco juice, and a broad-brimmed Quaker hat. In this garb, with a boot on one foot and a shoe on the other, he would come to court followed by a crowd of men and boys, whom he entertained by telling stories, by quirks and gibes, keeping them in a roar of laughter. Those who judged him from his manner alone in these moments, rated his abilities but meanly, and were astonished when he shook off the clown and resumed the gentleman. In society where he desired to please, no man could be more brilliant or more entertaining. At the bar he was almost irresistible, and some of the most eminent lawyers of his time were chagrined at the ease with which he would "walk off with the jury." He had an intuitive perception of the weak point in his opponent's case, and directed all his attention to it. He was so successful at the bar that at his death he had amassed a fortune estimated at $30,000. His handwriting is a marvel of illegibility. The letters look as if they were made with the end of a poker. He was once asked why he wrote such a wretched hand and replied, gravely: "If I write better, people will find out how I spell!" He once indorsed a man's note, which, in the end, he was obliged to pay. Contemplating the recovered document he was heard to remark: "People say they can't read my writing, but they can read it well enough on the back of another man's note!" Judge Leslie says in "Bench and Bar of Orleans County" of him: "His style of oratory was not scholarly or grammatical, but his arguments to court and jurors were full of strong common sense logic, going right to the point. He was a very rapid speaker when he became excited. He was of the Gov. Mattocks school of oratory, and was the peer of such men as Mattocks, Collamer, Marsh, Fletcher, Bell, and other members of the bar of Vermont in his day." When he found himself seized by an incurable disease he retired to the "Hermitage" to die. His death was hastened, it is said, by his persistence in sitting by an open window, in a strong draft of air. He was buried in the old cemetery at Wells River, a long procession accompanying his remains, by way of Newbury Village to the burial ground. His epitaph reads:

Hon. Peter Burbank,
Counsellor at Law,
Obit. Jan. 16, 1836,
Aged 55 years.

ANDREW JACKSON, son of Gustavus A. Burbank and Mary, sister of the late E. C. Stocker, was b. at "The Hermitage," July 25, 1833. He was adopted by Hon. Peter Burbank and was one of the three residuary legatees named in the latter's will, but never received anything from the estate. Educated at the academies at Danville and St. Johnsbury and at Newbury Seminary. Machinist in the Amoskeag Locomotive Works at Manchester and had the charge of setting up the machinery for the Jackson Manufacturing Co. at Nashua. Located in Minnesota in 1855, and lost all he invested there by the panic of 1857. In lumber business at Hannibal and at St. Joseph, Mo. but at the outbreak of the civil war, holding Union sentiments, he had to leave the place. Returned to Newbury and was in business a short time, but went to Pittsburgh, Pa., and was employed in the office of the Collector of Internal Revenue. He was soon afterward appointed United States Inspector and Gauger of distilled spirits and coal oil for the 22d District of Pennsylvania. This office was abolished at the close of the war, when he engaged in steam-boating on the Ohio, Missouri and Mississippi rivers, as first clerk and quarter owner of a boat. Then in the oil and real estate business at Pittsburgh where he has represented his ward as Councellor. In Masonry has reached the 32d degree and has been connected with other fraternal and temperance orders. Mr. Burbank has contributed many volumes to the Tenney Memorial Library; m. 1st, Haverhill, N. H., Aug. 26, 1862, Mrs. Esther Eaton, who d. Nov. 28, 1886; 2d, April 29, 1891, at Sharpsburg, Pa., Mrs. Sarah M. Gercke.
    Children, all by 1st marriage:
    i.   Andrew C.
    ii. Mary E.
    iii. Cora E.

*BURNHAM.

DENISON R., b. Rumney, N. H., Jan. 2, 1799; m. in Rumney June 21, 1824, Abigail Hopkinson Carlton, (b. Goffstown, N. H., Jan. 18, 1803; d. Plymouth, N. H., Sept. 26, 1864). They moved to Groton in 1824, where he was a merchant and came to Newbury, 1830, where he was in business till 1841, (see p. 276) when here m. to Plymouth, and kept the Pemigewasset House until it was burned in 1862. He built the house in which Mrs. C. C. Wallace lives.
    Children:
    i.   Thomas J., b. Groton, June 29; d. November, 1829.
    ii. Garaphelia M., b. Newbury, Sept. 13. 1831; m. at Plymouth, March 30, 1854, Joseph F. Merrill, and rem. to Ottumwa, Iowa, where they still live.
    iii. Desevignia S., b. Newbury, April 25. 1834; m. December, 1858, Lura E. Marston, who d. February, 1893; d. August, 1893.
    iv. Sarah Aspasiah, b. Newbury, Dec. 3, 1838: m. Jan. 1, 1863, Charles B. Pope, who d. Aug. 31, 1885. Lived in Chicago.
    v.   Abby F., b. Newbury, Jan. 18, 1841; m. May 2 1867, Charles H. Greenleaf of the Hotel Brunswick, Boston; and the Profile House.

BURROUGHS.

THOMAS and WILLIAM, brothers, came from Marblehead, Mass., before 1790.

---

*NOTE. On page 275 it is stated that Timothy Morse, Seth Greenleaf and W. W. Simpson married sisters, who were daughters of Cotton Haines of Rumney. This not correct. W. W. Simpson, Seth Greenleaf, Robert Morse and Capt. Moses Sinclair m. sisters of Denison Burnham. Information by Rev. J. L. Merrill.

I. THOMAS, b. March 17, 1767; · m. 1st, May 29, 1791, Amy, dau. John and Elizabeth (Conant) Peach of Marblehead, (b. Jan 25, 1768; d. Sept. 23, 1828); 2d, Feb. 15, 1830, Persis (Goodall), widow of Ebenezer Ruggles, who d. May 2, 1854. He d. June 16, 1852.
Children:
  i. John, b. Dec. 13, 1791; d. Dec. 20, 1791.
  ii. Amy, b. June 29, 1793; d. April 2, 1840.
  iii. John, b. Feb. 16, 1795; d. March 29, 1795.
  iv. Rebecca, b. March 10, 1796; m. July 27, 1815, Guy C. Taplin; d. Jan. 9, 1858.
  v. Eliza, b. April 24, 1798; m. Dec. 21, 1821, Philarmon Ruggles, q. v.; d. Dec. 21, 1862.
  vi. Sally, b. May 10, 1800; m. Aug. 30, 1821, William Bagley of Corinth; d. Jan. 31, 1843.
  vii. Thomas, b. Sept. 5, 1802; m. Nov. 29, 1829, Louisa Ruggles, dau. Ebenezer, (b. April 30, 1805; d. March 31, 1882); d. Feb. 14, 1870. C., (1) Allen, b. May 18, 1831; railroad engineer; m. 1st, Nov. 16, 1856, Mary A. Crane of Greensboro, (b. 1834; d. Jan. 19, 1878); 2d, Dec. 25, 1883, Catherine Ward of Swanton; d. St. Johnsbury, Oct. 9, 1894. (2) Harriet, b. Sept. 5, 1834; m. Feb. 22, 1859, John P. Eaton of Wentworth, N. H.; d. Oct. 10, 1900. (3) Augusta, b. March 1, 1837; m. March 17, 1870, Samuel Eastman 2d, q. v. (4) Laura C., b. Sept. 26, 1842; m. 1st, Sept. 3, 1861, Alvin McKinstry, q. v.; one dau.; m. 2d, Dec. 18, 1867, Cornelius L. Babcock of Rutland, b. Poultney, March 4, 1833; res. Woburn, Mass.; insurance agent. C., *a*, Helen, b. Fairhaven, Jan. 29, 1870; m. Samuel W. Merrill of Woburn; *b*, Mary, b. Rutland, March 27, 1873; m. Nathaniel Currier of Reading, Mass.
  viii. Nancy, b. Aug. 5, 1805; m. a Mr. Crockett; d. Nov. 26, 1859.
  ix. Mary Ann, b. Sept. 13, 1808; m. as 2d wife, Philaman Ruggles; d. June 27, 1864.
  x. Allen D., b. Feb. 14, 1811; d. Aug. 24, 1828.

II. WILLIAM, b. Marblehead, Mass., Feb. 24, 1777; farmer and carpenter; built the house called the Spear Johnston house, where A. B. Chamberlin now lives. About 1810, he rem. to the farm still owned by his descendants, south of the present town farm, where he built house, barns and sawmill; chosen deacon in 1st ch., September, 1812; m. March 28, 1799, Elizabeth (Betsey) dau. William Peach, (b. July, 1781; d. July 25, 1856). He d. June 12, 1835.
Children:
  i. Betsey, b. April 1, 1800; m. Perley Ruggles, q. v.
  ii. Anna, b. July 27, 1802; m. Samuel Martin, q. v.
  iii. William, b. May 16, 1805; carpenter and bridge builder for the Passumpsic railroad; m. Jan. 17, 1833, Anna, dau. Jacob Kent, (b. Aug. 10, 1805; d. Nov. 1, 1866). He lived for some years on what is now the town farm, and built the older part of the house; d. Feb. 7, 1861. No c.
  iv. Mary, b. Nov. 21, 1807; m. Gilman Barnett, q. v.
  v. George, b. May 9, 1812; d. April 13, 1887.
  vi. Martha, b. Dec. 16, 1817; d. Jan. 31, 1818.
  vii. Samuel E., b. July 16, 1820; d. April, 1821.

GEORGE, b. May 9, 1812; settled on his father's farm; chosen deacon in 1st ch. in 1871; m. Feb. 9, 1843, Mary D., dau. John Sawyer of Bradford, (b. Feb. 27, 1817; d. June 21, 1897). He d. April 13, 1887.
Children:
  i. Frances, b. July 27, 1844; m. March 5, 1891, Horace Everett McDuffee of Bradford.
  ii. William Henry, b. Nov. 4, 1846; m. May 30, 1877, Mary Lavender; res. Somerville, Mass. C., (1) Carl E., b. May 11, 1878, Blue Hill, Maine. (2) Ethel, b. Feb. 7, 1885, Somerville, Mass.
  iii. John Sawyer, b. Nov. 30, 1848; farmer in Newbury; m. Feb. 21, 1878, Hattie E., dau. Robert Laing. C., (1) Ralph, b. Aug. 28, 1881. (2) Ray, b. Dec. 17, 1882; (3) Elsie, b. March 1, 1885.
  iv. Martha, b. May 28, 1854; d. April 2, 1898.
  v. George Edward, b. Jan. 11, 1858; d. Nov. 2, 1890; unm.
  vi. Mary Elizabeth, b. Sept. 10, 1861; m. Frank P. Leighton, q. v.
Nearly all the members of these Burroughs families belonged to the 1st ch.

BURTON.

[I. ISRAEL, of Voluntown, R. I.; m. June 23, 1748, Silena Herrick of Preston. Ten c.

II. JACOB, b. 1761-2, Rev. Sol.; m. Katura Palmer, and rem. to Washington. Six c.

III. STEPHEN, b. probably in Stonington, Conn., Sept. 23, 1796; m. Dec. 12, 1821, Judith Noyes Peaslee; lived in Washington till 1864, then in Newbury with their youngest son, A. H. Burton, where she d. Jan. 3, 1865. He d. at the home of his eldest dau., Mrs. Marcia B. Emory, Woodsville, Sept. 13, 1896, aged 90. Both buried in Newbury. Eight c., of whom Horatio Nelson and Alexander Hamilton lived in Newbury.

i. Horatio Nelson, b. Washington, Dec, 17, 1826; on farm till 1844; went to Beloit, Wis., with his brother James, and rem. one year; fitted for college at Kimball Union Academy; graduated Dartmouth College 1853, teaching in the meanwhile; two years at the Theological Seminary at East Windsor Hill, Conn.; graduated Andover Theological Seminary, 1856; supplied South Congregational church, St. Johnsbury, 1857, a few months, then came to Newbury; ordained pastor of 1st ch., Dec. 31, 1857; dismissed, 1869; was Superintendent of schools two years and was often called upon to deliver addresses upon public occasions, both in and out of Newbury; pastor of Pres. ch., Sandusky, Ohio, 1869-75; Plymouth Cong. ch., 1876-79 Kalamazoo, Mich.; then four months in Europe; Cong. ch., Sycamore, Ill., 1880-83; farming in Jackson County, Mo., two years; then with improved health, pastor of Cong. ch., Union City, Mich., April, 1885-January, 1888; in East Burke, 1888-August, 1890; rem. to Minneapolis, Minn., in broken health. D. D. from Dartmouth College, 1875; published occasional sermons and addresses, and was a man of great intellectual force; m. May 18, 1858, Amelia, dau. Charles C. and Florilla (White) Newell of East Burke; d. March 5, 1893; buried in Lakewood cemetery, Minneapolis. C., (1) son, d. in infancy. (2) Charlotte Elizabeth, b. April 10, 1860; two years at Oberlin College; res. Minneapolis. (3) Stephen E., b. Nov. 8, 1862; two years at Oberlin College; two years at Chicago Theological Seminary; in business at Minneapolis. since 1867; m. Dec. 31, 1895, Mary E. Lee of Minneapolis. C., Horatio Lee, b. July 14, 1898. (4) Charles Newell, b. March 20, 1866; graduated Michigan University, medical department, 1889; in practice East Burke. one year; in Minneapolis five years; now at Elmore, Minn.; m. Dec. 24, 1894, Gertrude G. Bell of Minneapolis. C., a, Hervey N., b. March 24, 1884; b, Marion G., b. Dec. 16, 1898.

ii. Alexander Hamilton, came to Newbury about 1862; farmer on Ox-bow; superintendent of schools; in trade at Woodsville; farmer in Bath; m. Oct. 7, 1863, Ella A., dau. John G. White; d. Woodsville.

BUTLER.

The residence of Rev. James Davie Butler in Newbury was brief, as he was pastor of the Wells River Congregational church only three years, but he is too well known to allow his sojourn here to pass without notice. He was b. in Rutland, March 15, 1815; graduated Middlebury, 1836, Andover Theological Seminary, 1840; in Europe 1842-43, as a student and traveler; professor in Norwich University, 1845-47; pastor at Wells River, 1847-49; professor of Greek in Wabash College, four years, and in the University of Wisconsin, nine years. The years 1867-68 were spent in travel in Europe and Asia; 1869-70 in exploration in California and Oregon; in 1890, he traveled in Asia, exploring China and Japan, and ended by visiting the North Cape. Dr. Butler has been a voluminous writer, his best known works being "Prehistoric Wisconsin," and "Words Used Once for All by Shakespeare". He delivered before the Vermont legislature, while living at Wells River an address upon the "Battle of Bennington" elsewhere referred to. He also delivered the historical address at the centennial of Rutland in 1870; res. since 1858, Madison, Wis., where he is vice president of the State Historical Society, and, in his 85th year, 1899, chaplain of the Minnesota senate. Dr. Butler has interested himself in this history of Newbury, and some of the historical data in the early part of this volume, were collected by him. His handwriting at 85 has a boldness and vigor, which might be envied by young men; m. 1845, Anna, dau. Joshua Bates, president of Middlebury College. Two of their c., who were b. at Wells River, d. y.

BUTTERFIELD.

JONATHAN, is understood to have come here from near Dunstable, N. H., and was b. about 1713. He is said to have held a commission of Captain under the crown, and was always known by his military title. He served in the French and Indian war as a scout, under Putnam, and was a member of Rogers' expedition. He came to Newbury before 1768, and in 1773, signed the New York petition. He built a grist-mill at South Newbury, on same privilege where Mr. Runnels' mill is now, but on the other side of the brook, also a sawmill, and the place was called "Butterfields Mills," for some years and is so mentioned in old deeds. In 1785, he rem. to Topsham and settled. He served in the revolutionary war, in several "alarms." He d. at Topsham, May 17, 1804, aged 91. Samuel and Welbe were his sons and there may have been other children.

SAMUEL, b. Dunstable, Mass., April 17, 1765; served in the revolution in several "alarms." In 1785, he rem. to Topsham, settling at "Butterfields Corner"; town representative, etc.; m. a Miss Leach; d. Topsham, Aug. 15, 1835.

Children:

i. Samuel, b. Oct. 28, 1792.
ii. Jonathan, b. May 27, 1794.
iii. Prudence, b. Feb. 4, 1796; m. Benjamin Scribner.
iv. Ira, b. Dec. 16, 1798.
v. Welbe, b. Aug. 15, 1800; m. Eliza, dau. of Dudley Brown, and granddaughter of Dudley Carleton of Newbury. She d. Dec. 9, 1884, aged 83 years, 9 months, 24 days. C., (1) Eliza, d. y. (2) Ira A. (3) Welbe J., merchant at Dover, N. H., and captain in a New Hampshire regiment in the civil war. (4) Eliza, who m. Eri Chamberlin of Ryegate. (5) Dudley, d. y. (6) Susanna. (7) Diodama, m. James W. George of Newbury. (8) Prudence. (9) Charles.
vi. James, b. April 26, 1802.
vii. Mannessah, b. May 15, 1804.
viii. Polly, b. June 12, 1806; m. Nathan Parker.
ix. Henry, b. July 24, 1808. Lived in Topsham; major in the militia.
x. Laura, b. Oct. 9, 1809.

Many of the descendants of Jonathan Butterfield and his son Samuel intermarried with Newbury families.

BUXTON.

This family is of English origin. Daniel Buxton of Barre, Mass., m. in 1772, Lucy Allen, and d. at the age of 56. His widow m. 2d. in 1790, Joseph Bacon, and d. in her 97th year. The c. of Daniel and Lucy Buxton were: John; Daniel, who settled in Jericho; Anna, who m. in 1798, Manassah Osgood, and lived in Westford, and another dau., who m. a Mr. Bullard, settled in Shrewsbury, Mass. One of her sons was a missionary in Burmah, India.

JOHN, b. Barre, Mass., Nov. 5, 1779. He came here before 1804, and built about 1822, the large house at the south end of the village, still called by his name. He was a harness maker, his shop being that owned by the late E. C. Stocker, which in his time stood a little farther south. Mr. Stocker was his partner during the last years of his active life. He was also in mercantile and other business with William Bailey, in what is now the Sawyer House. He joined the Cong. ch. July 24, 1819, and was chosen a deacon in 1819. He m. 1st, Sept. 24, 1804, Prudence, dau. Col. John Bayley. Her mother was a dau. of Capt. John G. Bayley. She was b. April 18, 1786, and d. Dec. 18, 1811, at Newburyport, Mass., while on a visit there.

Children:

     i. Betsey, b. June 20, 1805; d. Oct. 14, 1825.

1 ii. John B., b. May 4, 1807, q. v.

   iii. Emeline, b. March 17, 1809; m. July 24, 1834, Wright Saunders, of Macon, Ga., and d. at Macon, Nov. 6, 1834.

   iv. Lucy Ann, b. April 6, 1811; d. June 10, 1834. Dea. Buxton m. 2d, 1814, Lavinia, dau. Joseph Ladd of Haverhill, (b. Sept. 18, 1787; d. Sept. 6, 1855).

    v. Prudence, b. Feb. 26, 1815; d. April 11, 1816.

   vi. Harriet, m. Aug. 10, 1841, Daniel P. Bassett of Albany, N. Y.; d. at Providence, R. I., March 1, 1895. C., (1) Frederic, an Episcopal clergyman, and D. D. Rector of the Church of the Redeemer at Providence. (2) Harriet. (3) Daniel. (4) Nellie. (5) Leonora. (6) Lillian.

  vii. Charlotte A., m. Sept. 1, 1842, Rev. Emery M. Porter, then of Litchfield, Conn.; d. Newbury, Aug. 31, 1844. One son, Rev. Emery H. Porter, Rector of Emanuel ch., Newport, R. I.

 viii. Mary F., m. in 1850, Addison W. Eastman, of Warren, N. H.; d. Feb. 8, 1886.

   ix. Sarah Louise, m. Dec. 8, 1842, William D. Atwood, q. v., and had three c. (1) Mary Louise, who m. Rev. D. C. Bixby of Warren, N. H., and d. Oct 9, 1875, leaving three c., *a*, Ella M., who m. April 4, 1899, Rev. G. H. Credeford of Wells River; *b*, Charlotte B., and *c*, Francis L. (2) John B., who d. Aug. 18, 1867. (3) Henry B., d. July 2, 1865. Mrs. Atwood studied medicine in Boston and Philadelphia; graduated at Boston Female College, Feb. 28, 1872; practiced in Watertown, Mass., fifteen years; in Wilbraham, Mass., while educating her grandchildren, three years; returned to Newbury, 1889.

    x. Lavinia, b. 1825; m. Simeon Shephardson; d. May 6, 1872, in Chester, Pa. Two sons, Franklin P., an engineer on the Southern Pacific Railroad, and Edward E., a grocer in Boston.

   xi. Henry Martyn, b. Aug. 5, 1827; farmer of Newbury and Fairlee; later in insurance business in Boston; m. May 15, 1849, Sarah Jane, dau. Enoch Wiggin; d. Bradford, Dec. 17, 1897. C., all b. in Newbury: (1) Charles Henry, b. May 23, 1851; salesman; res. Bradford. (2) Lillian, b. April 19, 1859; m. Frederick Lawrence Brainerd of Boston, (b. St. Albans). C., *a*, Lillian S.; *b*, Helen Katherine. (3) Luella Ladd, b. Jan. 29, 1863; m. William S. Wells of Boston, (b. Deerfield, Mass).

1 John, b. May 4, 1807; in trade at Topsham; studied law with Philip H. Tabor; went to New York City and engaged in furniture, paints and varnishes; m. 1st, Azubah, dau. James Heath; 2d, Myra Blake of Topsham; d. April 28, 1855.

    Children, two by 1st, and one by 2d marriage:

2   i. John Bayley, b. April 4, 1831.

   ii. James Heath, became an officer in the navy.

   iii. William Blake, thrown from a carriage in Topsham and killed, Aug. 19, 1867, aged 17.

2 John Bayley, b. April 4, 1831; res. New York City and Newbury; dealer in furniture and real estate; m. Sept. 14, 1852, Lucinda, dau. Abner Bailey, (b. Feb. 5, 1833; d. Sept. 9, 1892). He d. Newbury, Aug. 16, 1877.

    Children, the four eldest b. Morrisana, N. Y.

    i. Jonn Francis, b. Nov. 24, 1855; dentist at Paola, Kansas; m. at Paola, May 6, 1891, Bertha McLaughlin.

   ii. Carrie, b. June 27, 1858; m. March 14, 1878, Charles H. Deming, q. v.

   iii. Mary Belle, b. Nov. 15, 1859; d. Oct. 31, 1885.

   iv. Clarence Bayley, b. Jan. 19, 1867; in grocery business at Lowell, Mass., where he d. 1890.

    v. Ralph Hibbard, b. Newbury, March 11, 1872; cashier of bank, Blue Mound, Kansas; m. there Jan. 1, 1901.

CARBEE.

JOEL, a revolutionary soldier, came to Newbury before 1790, and in 1795, bought of James Andrew, lot No. 156 where he cleared a farm. This farm was the one where George Chalmers, and after him, Jefferson Hall, long lived. He was a very powerful man, large, muscular and fine looking, physical characteristics inherited by all his sons, and many of his grandsons, who are all remarkably tall, large men. He never received a pension, but his widow obtained one; m. Louis Downer, who d. April 11, 1844, aged 83. He d. Feb. 19, 1834, in his 71st year. In "Massachusetts Men in the Revolution" the following record of service is given. "Carbee, Joel of Dedham, Priv. Capt. Abel Richards Co., Col. McIntosh's reg. March 23-Apr. 6, 1778, at Roxbury and Boston." "Carby, Joel, of Dedham, served 5 mo. 25 d., 1780; also enlisted for 3 yrs. March 29, 1781 and served till the end of the war." These are believed to be one and the same person, with Joel Carbee of Dedham and Newbury.

Children. all b. in Newbury:

1   i.   John H., b. June 1, 1791, q. v.
     ii.   Moses P., b. May 18, 1793. He was a farmer in Bath; m. 1822, Marcia Kasson of Topsham. who d. June 4, 1863. He d. June 19, 1869. Seven c.
     iii.   Joel, b. April 24, 1795; lived in Ryegate and m. there Aug. 24, 1823, (Ryegate record says Aug. 26, 1824) Dorcas Johnson, who d. Jan. 23, 1874. He d. April 18, 1865. Nine c.
     iv.   William, b. Nov. 3, 1798; lived in Bath; m. Feb. 1, 1827, Euseba Smith. She d. June 10, 1887. He d. July 9, 1876. Eight c.
     v.   Andrew, b. Aug. 16, 1802. Settled in Canada, where he m. Martha Powers; d. 1855. They had four c. She d. and he had four more by a second m.
     vi.   Thomas Henry, b. Dec. 23, 1804. He lived in Newbury. but later in Bath; m. Dec. 10, 1829, Olive L., dau. John Robinson. She d. Newbury, Jan 7, 1881. He d. Lancaster, N. H., Nov. 2, 1874. Nine c., of whom Moses Dyer, b. Newbury, May 13, 1847, was a physician; graduated at the Medical College at Burlington; in practice at Haverhill, in partnership with Dr. Samuel P. Carbee, and then alone, till his sudden death from diphtheria, Oct. 23, 1889; m. Haverhill, Oct. 23, 1879, Mary Dexter.
     vii.   Sarah, b. July 15, 1807; m. March 5. 1829, Stephen D. Leighton of Bath, where he d. Sept. 4, 1870; d. Haverhill, Feb. 5, 1885. Twelve c.

1   JOHN H., b. Newbury, June 1, 1791; rem. to Bath after marriage, and settled on the farm now owned and occupied by his son, Henry C. Carbee; town representative from Bath eight or ten years, holding other offices. In his younger days he was a river man piloting boats down the river, returning with flat-boats laden with merchandise, which he poled up the stream; m. March 4, 1819, Anna, dau. Samuel Powers, (b. Newbury, Feb. 14, 1797; d. Bath, Dec. 20, 1884) ; d. Bath, June 25, 1877.

Children:

     i.   Lois, b. Newbury, Oct. 24, 1819, m. March 15, 1848, Moses Kelsey of Derby. One c.
     ii.   Sarah, b. April 5, 1821 ; d. Aug. 1, 1823.
     iii.   John Powers, b. May 3, 1823; rem. to Springville, Iowa, where he m. June 12, 1853, Sarah G. Hampton, who is living; d. Springville, Oct. 20, 1893. Six c.
     iv.   William Peach, b. Apr. 20, 1825; served in the Union army and was killed at the battle of Champion Hill. Miss., May 16, 1863; m. Oct. 6, 1851, Harriet Smith of Haverhill, who d. at Springville, Iowa, Nov. 30, 1879. Three c., living in Iowa.
     v.   Sarah, b. April 22. 1827 ; m. Nov. 18, 1851, Daniel Quimby, who d. March 21, 1862; d. April 25, 1882. Two c.
     vi.   Henry C., b. Aug. 31, 1829; farmer in Bath; town representative, 1897-8; m. April 21, 1858, Phidelia E. Clark. Six c., of whom only the eldest, Jennie, and the youngest, Ellen, survive.
     vii.   Milo, b. Dec. 4, 1831; res. East Boston, Mass; m. Sarah E. Leavitt of Exeter, N. H., who d. Jan, 17, 1891. Three c., one living.
     viii.   Mary P., b. Dec. 23, 1833; m. March 17, 1858, John Morrill of Derby, who d. Nov. 20, 1873; d. Jan. 16, 1898. One dau. lives in Chelsea, Mass.
     ix.   Samuel Powers, b. June 14, 1836; teaching and in the next two years

studied medicine with Dr. Dixi Crosby; enlisted as a private in Co. D, 12th
N. H., and later was appointed assistant surgeon of the regiment, which
position he held till the close of the war. He was in several battles, and
was the first surgeon of the Union army to enter Richmond after its
surrender; graduated Dartmouth Medical College 1865; physician at
Haverhill Corner till death, having a very extensive practice on both sides
of the river; town representative two years, and was surgeon-general on
the staff of Governor Busiel; m. Sept. 30, 1885, Della, dau. Lyman Buck
of Haverhill: d. Haverhill, Jan 31, 1900.

x. Ann P., b. March 6, 1840; m. Oct. 15, 1861, Edward H. Johnson
Littleton.

CHALMERS.

WILLIAM and GEORGE were two of the four sons of George and Christian
(Wilson) Chalmers. One of their two sisters m. Alexander Blackie and
came to America, but returned to Scotland. This family were Scotch
Presbyterians, and connected with that of Rev. Dr. Thomas Chalmers.
The father of William and George, a devout man, often conducted the
services at the kirk in the absence of the minister, and delivered the sermon.
These two brothers settled in Newbury, and reared large families.

I. WILLIAM, b. Church Calder, Fife, Scotland, March 10, 1801; m. in 1822, Isabella,
dau. Alexander and Grace (Lockhart) Barker, (b. Mathel, Fife, Scotland,
March 8. 1804; d. Newbury, Feb. 8, 1883). William, with his wife and
five c., and Alexander Barker and family, came to America in the ship
"Cyrus of Glasgow," 1834. They came via Montreal to Burlington, thence
to Newbury in June and three years later settled on what was then called
the Benjamin Leet place, where William and Henry, their sons now live
and there spent the remainder of their industrious lives. He was a linen
dresser and spinner. He started a mill for the manufacture of thread and
cordage at Corinth, in company with Dr. Hinckley of that place, and
conducted the business many years. The machinery for the mill was
imported by Mr. Chalmers from Scotland, and was detained ten years in
transit, on account of difficulties in relation to the tariff; d. Oct. 7, 1865.
Children:

i. Grace, b. Church Calder, Scotland, Jan. 9, 1824; m. March 18, 1847,
George D. Roberts. They lived on and owned the farm long known as the
Jeremiah Boynton place, now part of the Chalmers farm. They rem. to
Wisconsin in 1853, where he was a farmer and butcher, holding public
office. She d. Fox Lake, Wis., Jan. 6, 1860. C., (1) Isabella. (2) Anna.
(3) William. The former spent several years of her girlhood in Newbury.

ii. George, b. Church Calder, Scotland, March 10, 1826; carpenter and builder,
working in Boston; went to California 1850, during the gold excitement;
carpenters were so scarce that he received ten dollars per day; later he
owned and operated a ferry. In 1854, he went into partnership with his
brother Alexander, in cattle-raising, buying a tract of land ten miles square
rearing thousands of cattle, and cultivating land on a large scale. He also
designed and built many buildings; m. about 1854, a Miss Smith, who
survived him with one dau.; d. San Juan, Cal., in the fall of 1898.

iii. Christian R., b. Scotland Feb. 6, 1828; m. about 1848, Dennis Crowley,
who d. about 1870. C., (1) John. (2) Ella. (3) Isabelle. (4) Mary; all
d. She m. 2d, John Forsyth, who was killed by falling from a building in
Lowell, 1877; 3d, William Rand, who d. 1893; lives in Lowell, Mass.

iv. Alexander, b. Scotland, Feb. 26, 1830; carpenter and builder; went to
California in 1853, and into partnership with his brother George which
they dissolved in 1870. He erected a mill for getting out and finishing
lumber, and as contractor and builder. President and director of a bank
at Watsonville. Cal. His wife was from New York. They have five c.

v. William, b. Church Calder, Scotland, March 8, 1832; farmer on the
homestead; in the lumber business with his brother Robert several years,
and now with his brother Henry; owns the mill and several farms; has
never m.

vi. Robert M., b. Newbury, June 22, 1834, on the farm where Hale G. Bailey
now lives; carpenter and architect; began as a builder with hish rother,

Alexander, at the age of fifteen, building two houses in Fairlee. In 1852, they built the house on the homestead, and after that one for O. B. Rogers, now owned and occupied by George B. Barnett. He had the entire charge of a sawmill in Lawrence, Mass., before he was twenty. In 1854, William and Robert went to Jackson, Miss., where they designed and erected the buildings on a plantation, and a church. Returning to Newbury they engaged in the lumber business, erecting a sawmill, putting in the first circular saw in town, and in the raising of fine horses. In 1872, they dissolved partnership: Robert went to California, and in 1874, was in business as an architect and builder at Lowell, Mass., designing and erecting several blocks and residences. From 1879 till death, on the homestead, in business, and drafting plans and preparing specifications for public and private buildings. As a worker in wood he had few equals. Published one or two pamphlets, giving his views upon scientific subjects. He never m; d. at the homestead Feb. 4, 1892.

vii. John, b. April 12, 1837; carpenter and builder; built several houses in Newbury; in 1864, John and James Chalmers had charge of a gang of men erecting a hospital at Washington, D. C. They also built houses in Springfield and Lowell, Mass., and business blocks and the high school building in the latter place; in 1879, he returned to Newbury, broken in health and mind; m. Miss Ella Blood of Lowell, who survived him but a few months; d. on the homestead in December, 1881. No c.

viii. Isabella, b. May 15, 1840. She possessed much of the ingenuity of the family, but was attacked by consumption and d. y., Feb. 28, 1869.

ix. James, b. June 12, 1842; carpenter with his brother John in many places, and for himself in Springfield. He inherited the mechanical skill of the family, but d. before he could display his ability; d. Feb. 27, 1866.

x. Albert B., b. Oct. 12, 1845. Like his brothers he was skillful with hand and pen, and excelled in the training of horses; carpenter in Lowell with his brother John, but his mind became clouded, and his last years were spent in the Insane Asylum at Brattleboro, where he d. in the fall of 1884.

ix. Henry K., b. March 9, 1848; carpenter and farmer on the homestead, with his brother William; he prepared an account of the family which is here somewhat condensed.

II. GEORGE, b. at Church Calder, Fifeshire, Scotland, September, 1803; m. Nov. 3, 1821, Euphemia, dau. James and Annie (Eddy) Fairfull, (b. Feb. 23, 1805, in Dumbarton Castle, her father being a soldier of the garrison; d. July 31, 1895). He was a weaver and they lived in Kinross, Auchtermuchty, and Cupar, coming to America in 1838; settled on a farm lying between the present residence of William and Henry Chalmers, and Hall's pond, and now owned by them; became a molder and worked some years for Horace Strickland, in Bradford; later he bought the "old Carbee place" and lived there till death, Jan. 8, 1875.

Children:

i. Ann, b. Aug. 25, 1822; d. in Scotland.

. Christian, b. July 27, 1824; m. P. C. Tewksbury, q. v.

iii. Janet, b. Dec. 28, 1827; d. in Scotland.

iv. Elizabeth, b. June 22, 1829; d. in Scotland.

v. George, b. Dec. 27, 1832; d. in Scotland.

vi. George, b. June, 1835; served in the Union army. (See record). Farmer and carpenter; m. July 1, 1858, Isabel P., dau. James Ross; d. Oct. 15, 1865. One son, Edmund E., b. Newbury, July 22, 1861; fitted for college in Boston; graduated Dartmouth College, 1887; now in successful practice of law at Blackfoot, Idaho; m. 1889, Rosabel Watson of Leverett, Mass. C., a, Maurine; b, George W.; c, James Ross.

vii. Margaret, b. May 3, 1837; m. T. Jefferson Hall and lived on the homestead; d. Sept. 14, 1890.

3 viii. William W., b. Newbury, May 2, 1839.

ix. Mary L., b. Dec. 12, 1842; m. Andrew Aitkin, q. v.; d. July 7, 1867.

x. Johny Robinson, b. Aug. 3, 1845; fitted for college at Kimball Union Academy; in Dartmouth College, 1870-71; graduated at Bangor Theological Seminary, 1874; ordained pastor of Congregational ch. at Wilton, Me., July 7, 1874; dismissed Sept. 14, 1875; acting pastor, Pavillion ch., Biddeford, Me., September, 1875 to June, 1876; Fairhaven,

1876-77; Albert Lea, Minn., 1878-9; Sioux City, Iowa, 1879-82; Norwood, N. Y., 1883-85; without charge at St. Johnsbury till death; July 12, 1885; m. April 11, 1871, Ella, dau. William Ward of Rutland. Two c. After his death she m. Alexander Dunnett, lawyer of St. Johnsbury.
   xi. James H., b. Jan. 20, 1848; studied for the ministry with Rev. W. S. Palmer and was a student at Bangor Theological Seminary, when his health failed; d. Aug. 26, 1873.

3 WILLIAM WALLACE, b. Newbury, May 2, 1839; served in Co. D, 15th Vt; mustered in Oct. 22, 1862; mustered out Aug. 5, 1863; m. Nov. 28, 1861, Almira A., dau. Isaac Olmsted, who d. July 14, 1893; m. 2d, Nov. 20, 1894, Laura J. Mills of Topsham. Blacksmith at Topsham, where he d. Jan. 6, 1897.
   Children, twelve by 1st, and two by 2d:
4   i. William Herbert, b. May 28, 1862.
5   ii. Ella M., b. May 15, 1864.
6 iii. Clara B., b. Oct. 4, 1865.
7 iv. Martha A., b. May 2, 1868.
8   v. Mary E., b. May 2, 1868.
9 vi. H. Wallace, b. Jan. 18, 1871.
10 vii. Lizzie E., b. May 25, 1873.
11 viii. Anna A., b. July 23, 1876.
   ix. Florence E., b. July 2, 1880.
   x. John A., b. July 8, 1882.
   xi. George I., b. Nov. 22, 1884.
   xii. Nancy J., b. Nov. 8, 1886.
  xiii. Robert M., b. Sept. 6, 1895.
  xiv. Eri McKinley, b. July 8, 1897.

4 WILLIAM H., m. July 31, 1883, Minnie J. Buxton of Brookfield.
   Children, all b. West Topsham:
   . Fannie A., b. March 2, 1884.
   ii. James R., b. Sept. 7, 1885.
  iii. Mary P., b. Sept. 30, 1886.
   iv. Benjamin, b. March 17, 1889.
   v. Rebecca R., b. Aug. 15, 1891.
   vi. Ella M., b. June 7, 1893.
  vii. Carl A., b. Sept. 12, 1894.
  viii. Carrie A., b. Sept. 12, 1894.
   ix. Margaret Hall, b. Oct. 17, 1896.
   x. Dorothy Fairfull. b. Jan. 7, 1898.
   xi. Ruth W., b. March 3, 1899.

5 ELLA M., m. Feb. 22, 1883, George H. Pillsbury of Topsham.
   Children:
   i. Charles J., b. Dec. 6, 1883.
   ii. Wilson William, b. Aug. 9, 1885.
  iii. Ralph E., b. May 23, 1887.
   iv. G. Waldo, b. Feb. 27, 1889.

6 CLARA B., m. Dr. E. J. L. Robinson of Denver, Colorado, Feb. 15, 1893.

7 MARTHA A., m. Newton Hall of Groton, Feb. 22, 1893.
   Children:
   i. Mary E., b. Sept. 27, 1895.

8 MARY E., m. Aug. 30, 1888, Eugene Charles Wilson of Pueblo, Colorado.
   Children:
   i. Martha May, b. June 19, 1890.
   ii. Joe Ketchel, b. Sept. 5, 1891.
  iii. Clara Margaret, b. July 11, 1893; d. Oct. 17, 1894.
   iv. Clara, d. Oct. 17, 1894 in Seattle, Wash.

9 H. WALLACE, m. Anna Colby of Corinth, October, 1892.
   Children:
   i. Anna Belle, b. Aug. 15, 1893.
   ii. Clifford Wallace, b. Aug. 30, 1895.

10 LIZZIE E., m. Dec. 31, 1893, Herbert L. Avery of Campton, N. H.
Children:
  i. Zilpha, b. October, 1896.
  ii. Frank L. H., b. December, 1898.

11 ANNA A., m. Dec. 30, 1893, Fenton Miles of Topsham.
Children:
  i. Beatrice Florence, b. June 7, 1898.

CARLETON.

The Carletons in America are descended from an English family of the name, whose seat for about seven hundred years was called Carleton Hall, near Corrinth, in the county of Cumberland. Branches of this family settled in Lincolnshire, and from these came the Carletons of London and Surrey. Edward, son of Erastus Carleton, a mercer of London, was one of the company of Rev. Ezekiel Rogers, who came to America in 1639, and settled in Rowley, Mass., where he d. in 1678. His wife was named Eleanor.

II. LIEUT. JOHN CARLETON, son of the emigrant, m. Hannah Jewett, and d. in Bradford, Mass., Jan. 22, 1668. They had four sons.

III. EDWARD, b. March 22, 1664; m. Elizabeth Kimball; d. at Bradford, Mass., 1711. They had six sons and three daughters.

IV. BENJAMIN, b. 1693; m. Elizabeth Dolton; d. 1772.

V. DUDLEY, b. Jan. 5, 1722; m. Abigail Wilson, (b. Nov. 25, 1725; d. Oct. 23, 1799.) They lived in Haverhill, Mass. He d. Sept. 15, 1801. The Newbury families are reckoned from him in these annals.
Children. (From the Family Bible of Dudley Carleton[1]).
  i. Rebecca, b. May 26, 1746.
  ii. Dudley, b. May 16, 1748, q. v.
  iii. Abigail, b. March 30, 1750; m. Col. Thos. Johnson, q. v.
  iv. David, b. Dec. 7, 1751.
  v. Hannah, b. Jan. 7, 1754; m. Col. William Wallace, q. v.
  vi. Michael, b. May 23, 1757.
  vii. Moses, b. Feb. 17, 1759.
  viii. Marah, b. Sept. 17, 1760.
  ix. Edward, b. July 2, 1762.
  x. William, b. June 1, 1764; d. May 19, 1794.
  xi. Ebenezer, b. April 4, 1766.
  xii. Phebe, b. March 4, 1768.

I. DUDLEY,[2] (Dudley,[1]) b. May 16, 1748; he m. in Boxford, Mass., Feb. 10, 1776, Mehetabel Barker of Andover, Mass., and settled in Newbury, on land owned by his father, the same year, his home being at the foot of the hill, on the road that runs through the Ox-bow. The first mention of him on record here, is May 28, 1776, when the town voted "to lay a rode to the river, nigh the potash, or through Dudley Carleton's land." His skill as a cabinet-maker is attested by the fact that articles of furniture, made by him 120 years ago, have been in constant use and are still in good condition. He made clocks, cider mills, etc., and was one of the committee to build the "old meeting house," in 1787. Served during the revolutionary war in several alarms, and in Capt. Frye Bayley's Co. which went to Saratoga. Justice of the Peace after 1786. Admitted to 1st church, May, 1813, and his wife in July, 1816. Captain in the militia and held town offices. Bought in 1798, parts of lots 121 and 122 at West Newbury, on which he settled, and on which George W. Carleton now lives. The house which he built is still standing, and used as an out-building by the present owner. He d. there April 21, 1835, and his wife, Nov. 13, 1842, aged 90.
Children, all b. in Newbury.
  i. Mehetabel, b. Nov. 2, 1776; m. Col. John Kimball, q. v.
  ii. Moses, b. and d. 1778.
  iii. Rebecca, b. Nov. 1, 1779; m. John Calvin Johnson; d. 1850.

    iv. Susanna, b. Sept. 6, 1781; m. 1st, Dudley Brown of Topsham. 2d, Blanchard Chamberlain, q. v.

    v. Abigail, b. July 9, 1783; d. May 21, 1785.

    vi. Sally, b. Jan. 24, 1785; m. July 22, 1802, Joseph Spencer, Indian Stream, N. Y.

2 vii. Dudley, b. Sept. 11, 1787, q. v.

  viii. Abigail b. July 12, 1789; d. May 8, 1802.

3 ix. John B., b. Sept. 19, 1791,

    x. Michael, b. Nov. 4, 1793; rem. to Haverhill; m. Oct. 10, 1816, Betsey, dau. of Daniel Putnam; both d. 1875–76.

    xi. Hannah, b. Mar. 18, 1798; d. May 25, 1838; un-m.

2 DUDLEY,[3] (Dudley,[2] Dudley,[1]) b. Sept. 11, 1787; m. June 26, 1814, Sarah Rogers, dau. Dea. William Carter, (b. May 15, 1796; d. June 15, 1871). Lived at West Newbury, on part of homestead. Members of Methodist church for many years, devout people, industrious and frugal. He d. April 11, 1879.

There were no deaths in this family till the youngest son had reached his fifty-sixth year.

Children:

4   i. William C., b. March 31, 1815.

   ii. Sally Spencer, b. Sept. 11, 1816; m. 1st, L. D. Prescott. 2d, Israel Prescott, q. v.; d. July 3, 1893.

  iii. Polly Ann Woodman, b. Feb. 6, 1818; m. Oliver B. Rogers, q. v.; d. Dec. 24, 1900.

5 iv. Dudley B., b. June 10, 1820.

6   v. George, W. K., b. Oct. 15, 1822.

   vi. Betsey P., b. April 22, 1824; m. L. L. Tucker, q. v.

7 vii. Laura Bell, b. Feb. 17, 1827; m. Jan. 14, 1849, Horace Sanborn, of Tilton, N. H.

8 viii. John N., b. Oct. 23, 1829.

   ix. Luthera M., b. April 4, 1831; m. Oct. 18, 1854, Kimball K. Wilson, (b. Oct. 15, 1822; d. June 29, 1893). No c.

9   x. Henry K. W., b. Nov. 29, 1837.

3 JOHN BARKER,[3] (Dudley[2], Dudley,[1]) b. Sept. 19, 1791. Farmer on homestead at West Newbury. (See Town Officers). Member of Methodist church. He m. May 26, 1814. Betsey, dau. Israel Putnam, (b. July 15, 1789; d. Dec. 5, 1849). He m. 2d, October, 1850, Mrs. Elizabeth (Powers) Tyler (b. St. Stephen, N. B., Aug. 12, 1805; d. June 8, 1878). A man of worth and intelligence. He d. April 7, 1873.

Child, by 1st marriage:

    i. Horatio Nelson, b. May 15, 1815. Merchant at West Newbury, with H. K. Wilson many years. He m. March 17, 1842, Sarah J., dau. of Joseph Prescott, (b. October, 1828; d. Dec. 24, 1882). He d. Nov. 17, 1895. No c.

4 WILLIAM CARTER,[3] (Dudley.[2] Dudley,[1]) b. March 31, 1815. Farmer at West Newbury, where George Putnam lives, till 1866 when he bought the "Old Town Farm," now called "Maplewood Farm," to which large additions have been made. He m. Jan. 29, 1840, Sarah Luthera, dau. of Dr. Caleb Stevens, of Enosburg, Vt., (b. Jan. 4, 1819; d. Aug. 29, 1891).

Children:

    i. Dudley, b. Aug. 13, 1845. Farmer on "Maplewood Farm." Has held town offices; m. Oct. 5, 1869, Martha, dau. Solomon Jewell. C., (1) William Everett, b. Dec. 17, 1870; d September, 1875. (2) Arthur A., b. Oct. 26, 1873; m. Aug. 18, 1897, Sarah E., dau. of John Norcross of Bradford, (b. Feb. 5, 1873). C., a, Harold Arthur, b. Sept. 9, 1898. b, Marion Estelle, b. Aug. 31, 1900. (3) Luthera M., b. Dec. 3, 1880. Teacher. Four generations of this family are now living in the same house.

   ii. Hattie, b. June 25, 1850; m. Aug. 25, 1875, John N. Brock, who d. Aug. 27, 1881.

5 DUDLEY B.,[3] (Dudley,[2] Dudley,[1]) b. June 10, 1820. Went to California in 1849. In boot and shoe business at Davenport, Iowa, many years. Res. Des Moines, Iowa. He m. Jan. 21, 1844, Ruth D. Huckins, (b. May 10, 1819; d. Sept. 11, 1891).

CARLETON HALL, CUMBERLAND, ENGLAND.

BIRTHPLACE OF ROBERT FULTON IN SCOTLAND.

Children:
i. Carlotta D., b. 1844; m. Warren Huckins. Res. Appleton, Wis.
ii. Frank P., b. 1857. Res. Des Moines, Iowa.
iii. Harriet P., b. 1859; m. Robert Willerton, Rock Island, Ill.

6 GEORGE WASHINGTON KIMBALL,[3] (Dudley,[2] Dudley,[1]) b. Oct. 15, 1822; farmer on the old Carleton homestead at West Newbury; m. April 7, 1847, Deborah Huckins, (b. Strafford, N. H., Aug. 20, 1822.)
Children:
i. Luella C., b. Feb. 19, 1850; m. Dec. 25, 1873, Edward C. Burbeck of Haverhill, (b. Hanover, July 18, 1846. Graduated Dartmouth College, 1871. Principal of high schools at East Arlington and Winchendon, Mass., Nashua, N. H., and Danvers, Mass.; d. Denver, Col., March 27, 1897: buried Bradford). C., (1) Herbert T. Johnson of Bradford. (2) Edward, now in Dartmouth College.
ii. Ida M., b. Jan. 15, 1856; m. April 7, 1875, Arthur F. Johnson of Bradford. C., Haynes E., George C., Edith B., Arthur F.
iii. George Warren, b. April 25, 1864; farmer at West Newbury on the old Thos. Eastman farm; m. April 17, 1889, Abbie, dau. Charles Leet, (d. November, 1889). One c., Harvey W., b. Nov. 12, 1889; m. 2d, Feb. 10, 1892, Alice, dau. of Hiram Kimball of Bradford. C., a, Mary Louise, b. Feb. 6, 1896; d. July 3, 1896. b, Esther Martha, b. Oct. 11, 1898. c., Ruby Alice, b. Nov. 3, 1899.
iv. Carrie Campbell, b. Jan. 24, 1862; m. Geo. W. Putnam, q. v.

7 LAURA BELL,[3] (Dudley,[2] Dudley,[1]) b. Feb. 17, 1827; m. Jan. 14, 1849, Horace Sanborn, of Lowell, Mass., now of Tilton, N. H.
Children:
i. Luthera Wilson, b. Sept. 24, 1857; m. Dr. Edward Abbott of Tilton, (dea.) Two c.
ii. Carlotta, b. Dec. 28, 1859. Teacher at Tilton.
iii. H. Herbert, b. July 19, 1861; d. 1882.

8 JOHN N.,[3] (Dudley,[2] Dudley,[1]) b. Oct. 23, 1829. Fitted for college at Newbury Seminary. In Wesleyan University one year. Went to Chattanooga, Tenn., 1852, or 1853, as clerk, then telegraph operator, at Wilmington, N. C., in the last named occupation, then in Augusta, Ga., sending the first message from Augusta to Washington, D. C. Located at Mountville, Ga., in the carriage making business till the war broke out. Teacher, 1861–62. Then three months in the Confederate Army, as distributor of clothing to the troops. Teacher, 1862–63. Then in the Georgia state cavalry. Was in Atlanta till the city was taken. Teacher at Mountville, 1865, and 1875–76. Member of school board 25 years. Justice of the Peace, 20 years. Representative in the Georgia legislature, 1888–89. Prominent in the Methodist church and in Masonry. He m. Dec. 31, 1857, Angelet M. Evans. He d. at Mountville, Ga., April 6, 1898.
Children:
i. Olin, b. Feb. 14, 1859. In milling and ginning business at Mountville. He m. April 6, 1893, Ada M. Strosin. Two c., Ruby and Sarah.

9 HENRY K. W., (Dudley,[2] Dudley,[1]) b. Nov. 29, 1837; m. 1st Jan. 27, 1858, Lizzie M. Winship; 2d, Carrie Usher; d. Groton, July 10, 1894.
Children, two by 1st, and one by 2d:
i. Fred Elmer, b. Bradford, Nov. 23, 1859. Res. Boston, Mass. Machinist. He m. Clara Champney. C., (1) Edith Norma, b. June 16, 1887. (2) Elmer Champany, b. June 16, 1892. (3) Dudley Barker, b. May 1, 1889.
ii. Leonora M., b April 21, 1864.
iii. Harry, b. July 27, 1884; res. Bradford.

CARTER.

One of the families which has disappeared from Newbury, is the Carter family. During the first sixty years of the ninteenth century they were numerous and influential, substantial farmers, around West Newbury, people of decided convictions, always to be counted on the side of good order, men and women of much more than average intelligence. The daughters m.

into other families, their neighbors, and reared sons and daughters, who possess many of the Carter traits. As no attempt was made in the life-times of the older ones to collect the records of these families, only scanty memorials can be gathered now. Several families bearing this name settled in the southwest part of Newbury, and the vicinity in Bradford, Topsham and Corinth, between 1775 and 1815. They originated near Hampton, N. H. Of these, the following were c. of the same father. ·

I. DEA. WILLIAM, was a native of Kingston, N. H., and came to Topsham very soon after the close of the revolutionary war, and was the third settler in that town, residing there a few years. During this time he cleared a field, and sowed wheat, covering it with a hoe. From this he harvested a crop of eighty bushels. He carried his grain to South Newbury to mill, on horseback, guided by marked trees. He next moved to the place now owned by N. W. Cunningham in the west part of Newbury, moving later about a quarter of a mile across the line into Bradford, where he remained until his death. He was a deacon in the Christian church at Goshen. He m. 1st, at South Hampton, N. H., Jan. 29, 1788, Anna, dau. Hilton Woodman, (b. 1767; d. Dec. 18, 1797) ; 2d, Polly or Mary Hale, who d. Jan. 21, 1850, aged 83. They are buried in the Rogers hill cemetery. He d. Sept. 21, 1837, in his 73d year.
    Children, five by 1st and two by 2d marriage:
2   i.   Levi, b. Nov. 9, 1788; d. March 9, 1873.
     ii.   Anna, b. May 24, 1790; m. Josiah L. Bailey, q. v.
     iii.   Hannah, b. March 23, 1792; m. Ayer White.
     iv.   David, b. May 22, 1794; m. Mary Wiggin.
     v.   Sarah Rogers, b. May 15, 1796; m. Dudley Carleton, q. v.
     vi.   Mary, b. Feb. 9, 1799; m. Enoch Wiggin; d. Jan. 9, 1833. .
3   vii.   William H., b. May 28, 1801 ; d. Dec. 10, 1886.

II. NOAH, m. Abigail, dau. John Johnson.
    Children:
     i.   Betsey, m. Bethuel Welton and their dau. m. James Stevens.
     ii.   Dolly, m. Frank Martin and d. in Bradford.
     iii.   Sally, m. Rufus Taplin.
     iv.   Anne, m. Nov. 10, 1806, Silas Aldrich and rem. to Compton, P. Q., where both d. Several c.

III. JOHN.
    Children:
     i.   Eunice, m. Richard Miller and d. in Topsham, leaving a son John, who has since d. leaving several children.
     ii.   Benjamin, settled and d. in Piermont.
     iii.   Eliza, m. Ware McConnell, who lived at West Newbury. He served in the war of 1812; was badly wounded in the face and mouth; d. June 28, 1853. She d. Jan. 23, 1861.
     iv.   Laura Maud, who moved to the north part of the state.

IV. MOSES, m. Sally Rowe.
    Children:
     i.   Lentura.
     ii.   Cynthia.
     iii.   Moses.
     iv.   A dau., who m. a Mr. Merrill and lived in Landaff, N. H.

2   LEVI,[2] (William[1]) b. Topsham, Nov. 9, 1787; m. Dec. 8, 1808, Martha Wiggin, who d. Jan. 2, 1865, aged 76 years, ten months; farmer, near "Goshen," and held various town offices; d. March 9, 1873.
    Children:
     i.   Laura J., b. Nov. 24, 1811 ; m. Jan. 14, 1836, William McDuffee, who d. July 12, 1865; d. Jan. 14, 1888. C., (1) Louise, m. Clement S. Worthen, of Enfield, N. H. (2) George, m. 1st, Sadie Getchell; 2d, Jennie Woodman and lives in Topsham. (3) Etta S., m. Nathaniel Cunningham, who is engaged with his son in the drug business at Bradford, and owns the farm first settled in Newbury, by Dea. William Carter.
     ii.   William Tarleton, b. April 23, 1815; farmer at West Newbury; m. Oct. 4, 1855, Submit Waterman; rem. to St. Johnsbury in old age and d. there,

Nov. 15, 1894. C., (1) Fred A., in business at St. Johnsbury; m. Jennie, dau. C. C. Doty of Bradford. (2) William H., res. St. Johnsbury; m. Minnie Bisnet.
iii. Hannah W., b. June 13, 1818; m. March 1, 1855, Thomas Heath of Newbury; farmer on the Joseph Kent farm; d. November, 1874. C., (1) John T., on the homestead. (2) Mary Ella, m. Charles C. Day of Winchendon, Mass. (3) Levi L., m. Nellie Robie; lives in Concord, N. H. (4) Henry W., m. Laura Houghton; lives also in Concord.
iv. Martha W., b. Nov. 7, 1821; m. Feb. 14, 1844, Moses S. Rowe of Bradford, (b. Sept. 5, 1811; d. March 2, 1901; blacksmith); d. November, 1874. C., (1) Lizzie A., m. John Norcross of Bradford. (2) Leroy L., and (3) Thomas H., associated in business in Boston. (4) Moses E., in Chicago.
v. Mary W., b. April 19, 1827; m. July 6, 1854, Nicholas Greenleaf; d. May 11, 1882. C., Viola C., m. Elroy Davis of Bradford.

3 WILLIAM H.,[2] (William)[1] b. Newbury, May 28, 1801; educated at Bradford Academy; studied medicine with Dr. Petrie of Topsham and Dr. Jewett of Newbury and attended lectures at Dartmouth Medical College; in practice at West Newbury, where he built the house opposite the parsonage, 1827-1853; in Bradford, 1853, until he retired from practice, in all, over fifty years. He was considered especially skillful in fevers, and was a man of great intelligence and esteemed for his kindliness and worth, and for the extent and variety of topics upon which he could converse. Town Representative, 1842,. He was a member of the Congregational ch. fifty-seven years; was the originator of a compound called "Carter's Pulmonary Balsam"; m. Nov. 25, 1824, Hannah, dau. David Eastman of Topsham, (b. 1799; d. Oct. 13, 1881). He d. Bradford, Dec. 10, 1886.
Children:
i. Susan E., m. Dr. A. A. Doty, (b. Elmore, March 15, 1828; d. Bradford, Feb. 17, 1882). She d.Bradford, Sept. 18, 1874.
ii. Jennie A., m. Dr. Eugene L. Boothby of Fairlee.

CARTER.

JAMES, son of John, is understood to have been a native of Kingston, N. H., and came to Newbury about 1808, and settled on the highest cultivated land in town, on the hill formerly called "Carter's mountain," but now sometimes called "Tucker's mountain," from John Tucker and John W. Tucker, his son, who afterward owned a part of the Carter farm. He was a man of affairs, often being selectman, lister, etc. He built about 1810, a two story house, still standing on the mountain. He was known as "Mountain Carter," and was a man of great size, and his wife, who was his cousin, was also very large, both weighing, it is said 700 lbs. Later he rem. to East Topsham, where he built the two story house, which stands on the corner of the road which comes over the hills from the Lime kiln, in which he kept tavern, and where he d. April 4, 1852, aged 68 years, 6 mos., and his wife Oct. 23, 1859, aged 77 years, 1 mo. He m. a Miss Edmunds.
Children:
1 i. Mary Jane.
ii. Mehetable, who d. at six years of age.
iii. James, who was not a year old when he d.

1 MARY JANE, b. Salisbury, Mass., July 4, 1867; m. in Newbury, March 28, 1823, Jacob B. Stevens, (b. Corinth, Feb. 8, 1797; d. Topsham, Sept. 29, 1874); farmer of Newbury and Corinth, where she d. Feb. 19, 1852.
Children, all b. in Newbury, but the last:
i. Roxanna, b. July 22, 1824; d. Aug. 14, 1826.
ii. James C., b. June 20, 1827; m. Topsham, May 17, 1853; d. Nov. 11, 1889.
iii. Mehetable C., b. Nov. 19, 1828; m. Feb. 10, 1848, J. P. Tabor; res. Topsham where he d. 1899.
iv. Mary Ann, b. May 19, 1830; d. Sept. 19, 1875.
v. Hannah E., b. March 26, 1832; m. Sept. 20, 1853; d. Corinth, Dec. 6, 1887.
vi. Curtis S., b. Corinth, April 25, 1835; d. Oct. 21, 1888.

32

MARY, sister of James Carter, b. Aug. 13, 1787; m. Moses Currier, q. v.; d. May 24, 1875.

There was also another Carter, believed to be Samuel, who lived on Carter's Mountain, and afterward joined the Shakers and with his wife, became members of the Community at Enfield, N. H.   Mention is also asked for Simon Carter of Topsham, whose connection with the other Carters is unknown.   The mention of his death in Topsham town records says that he was son of Samuel and Abigail Carter.   He lived on the homestead, near the Newbury line, and was noted for his skill in mathematics, being often appealed to for the solution of hard problems.   He was also a musician.   He m. Lorenza Cross.   They had one dau., Belinda, who survived her mother, but d. in her 15th year, June 5, 1850.   Her father never recovered the shock which her death caused him, but became somewhat eccentric and lived alone, on his large farm.   He sometimes made his appearance at the village in a vehicle which the boys styled "Uncle Simon's whirligig."   He kept a drum suspended over the head of his bed, and said that if he was ill he would beat upon it, and the first person who came should receive a dollar.   One night he beat upon it, and a little boy, the first comer, received a dollar.   He d. Jan. 24, 1868, aged 70 years. All the above mentioned Carter families are understood to have a common ancestry and originated near Kingston and Hampton, N. H.   There was an Edmund Carter, who lived in Bradford and Newbury, and who m. February, 1814, Fanny, sister of Robert McAllister. Sr.   Their son, Ira, a native of Newbury, was a student at Newbury Biblical Institute and a member of Vermont Conference some years.   Now retired, at Wahpeton, N. D.

CHADWICK.

JOHN of New Bedford, Mass., was 1st Lieutenant in Capt. Nathan Peters' Co. in the 3d regiment of foot, commanded by Col. Ebenezer Larned in the armies of the United Colonies.

Children:
i.   John, m. Mary Stevens and lived in Bradford, in the Goshen neighborhood. Their c. were, (1) Nicholas, who became a minister and lived in Maine. (2) James Madison. (3) Mary Jane, (Mrs. Severance, now living in Bradford). (4) John. (5) Thomas, who m. Chloe, dau. of Ebenezer Abbott. (6) Benjamin, now living in Georgia.

JAMES M., b. May 13, 1809; was a merchant here, coming from Haverhill.   He was in partnership with Timothy Morse and others, and for several years carried on a branch store at South Newbury, in the house A. B. Rogers now lives in.   Later he removed to the Street, and was in business with the Morses, and afterwards alone, till a year or two before his death. Town representative, 1854.   He m. 1st, May 9, 1836, Harriott. dau. of Col. Moody Chamberlain, (b. July 19, 1816; d. May 1, 1840).   2d, Jan. 17, 1850, Charlotte, dau. of Maj. Isaac Pearson, of Haverhill, (b there March 26, 1819; d. East Saginaw, Michigan, April 28, 1895.   Buried at Newbury).   He d. June 7, 1873.

Children, one by 1st, and three by 2d, two of whom are living.
i.   Ellen F., b. Jan. 11, 1839; d. Feb. 24, 1841.
ii.   Harriott Frances, m. Farnham C. Stone of Saginaw, Mich.
iii.   Elizabeth, m. Thomas A. Harvey, of Saginaw.

CHAMBERLAIN.

If the Bayleys were numerous in Newbury, the Chamberlains were also many, and there went a saying that "you couldn't turn up a stone in the pasture, without finding a Bayley or a Chamberlain under it!"   The pioneers of the Chamberlain families were: Thomas, who came in March, 1762; Richard who came in June of the same year; and Moses, whose oldest son came as early as 1770.   The two last are understood to have been brothers.   The descendants of Thomas usually spell their name with an a, in the final syllable, those of Richard without it, etc., and those of Moses either way. Such records of the descendants of Thomas, Richard and Moses, as can be gathered, are given in the order of the advent to Newbury of the pioneers. The Thomas Chamberlain family is understood to be descended from Thomas Chamberlain of Dunstable, N. H., 1714, but there is some uncertainty about the intermediate generations.

THOMAS, b. Dunstable, now Nashua, N. H., Aug. 10, 1735; served in the old French war. in Capt. Joseph Blanchard's company; came first to Coös in 1760, as chain-bearer for this same Joseph Blanchard, when he fixed the boundaries of the towns along the river; in the next summer he came again, hunting, with Abiel Chamberlin, son of Richard; in the early spring of 1762, he came to Newbury, in the interest of Blanchard, and settled on Musquash Meadow, near the river, but afterward built a house whose site is marked by a depression in the ground, in the newer part of the cemetery on the Ox-bow; he held town offices, and was Justice of the Peace under the crown and held the office for several years; served in the revolutionary war in local service, but near its close was involved with those who carried on a correspondence with Canada; in 1780, he took up land in what is now Topsham, with his sons, Jacob and Blanchard, and cleared the first land in that town, on the farm which he continued to occupy till his death, on Chamberlain Hill, now generally known as Currier Hill. His house was burned about 1854, with the other farm buildings. Esquire Chamberlain, as he was generally called, was a man of very high standing in the community, in Newbury and afterward in Topsham; was admitted to the 1st ch., Jan. 22, 1792, and his wife about the same time. The late Ezekiel White of Topsham, who d. 1900, remembered him well, and was present at his funeral. His first wife d. about 1784, and was buried in a small, unfenced burying place, on the John Renfrew farm, in Newbury, adjoining the Topsham line. There are about twenty-five unmarked graves and she is the only occupant whose name is known. It is believed that no one has been buried there for more than a hundred years. He m. 2d, Margaret Spear of Newbury. She d. June 4, 1835, in her 90th year. He d. March 22, 1818, and is buried on Currier Hill.

> "Beneath this stone I turn to dust
> But I hereafter shall arise
> When He in whom I put my trust
> Shall call me upward to the skies."

Children, two by 1st, (whose names are known) and two by 2d marriage:
    i. Jacob Bayley, b. Newbury, May, 1763, the first male child. He settled in Canada, revisited Topsham about 1835.
1 ii. Blanchard, b. Newbury, 1769; d. Sept. 24, 1843.
   iii. Susan, b. Oct. 19, 1787; d. May 28, 1811.
   iv. Thomas, baptized Aug. 29, 1794; drifted away and was never heard from; his widow was buried at East Corinth; d. July 16, 1862, aged 67.

1 BLANCHARD, b. Newbury, 1769; farmer on homestead in Topsham, captain in the militia and prominent in the town. In person a small man, very lively and hospitable; had a large farm, with a great housefull of c.; m. 1st, Feb. 19, 1789, Betsey Leach, who d. Sept. 15. 1818, in her 49th year; 2d, Jan. 2, 1822, Susanna, widow of Dudley Brown and dau. Dudley Carleton of Newbury; d. Nov. 8, 1861 in her 81st year. He d. Sept. 24, 1843.
Children, eight by 1st, and three by 2d marriage:
    i. Betsey, b. December, 1789; never m.; lived on homestead; d. Nov. 27, 1863.
   ii. Sally, m. Ephraim Jones; d. Dover, N. H.
  iii. Dr. Thomas, physician at Burlington; d. there.
  iv. Rebecca, b. February,.1804; d. Dec. 25, 1874; lived on homestead; un-m.
   v. Blanchard, settled and d. in Canada. Two sons, Norman and Blanchard.
  vi. Jacob B., d. at five years.
 vii. Polly, d. at about twenty-six.
2 viii. James, b. 1800; d. March 4, 1874.
  ix. Morrison, d. about eighteen.
   x. Jacob B., b. about 1807; d. Aug. 24, 1880; never m.
  xi. Susannah, b. July 20, 1820; m. William Hunter, q. v.; d. Aug. 17, 1898.

xii. Mehetable, b. Sept. 11, 1822; m. Reuben George, q. v.; d. Jan. 7, 1889.
xiii. John D., b. May 21, 1824; d. May 31, 1844.
Capt. Blanchard Chamberlain, with his two wives and six c., are buried on Currier Hill.

2 JAMES, b. 1800; farmer on homestead; town representative. 1850; captain in militia, etc.; m. Hannah Knight, who d. July 31, 1872. He d. March 4, 1874; buried East Corinth.
Children:
i. Thomas Knight, b. 1833.
ii. James Hale. b. Sept. 22, 1834; at the age of eighteen, he went to sea on the ship "New World," trading between New York and Liverpool, commanded by Capt. Hale Knight of Corinth; made captain of the same ship, 1859, and in 1861, master of ship "Liverpool" running between New York and London. In those days packet ships brought to America all the emigrants they could accommodate. In 1867, he was sent by his employers, to reside in London, and superintend their fleet of packet ships, holding that position eleven years; res. 1878-83, East Corinth; town representative, 1882; in 1883, appointed surveyor of ships, at New York, for the Bureau Veritas, International Register of Shipping, whose head office is in Paris. This position he still holds; member, since 1883, of the Marine Society of the City of New York (a charitable institution founded 1769) and has been its treasurer since 1890; m. 1st, September, 1862, Addie E. Smart, who d. April, 1871; three sons, two living; m. 2d, October, 1873, Hannah K. Smart, who d. November, 1886; 3d, 1894, Dora E. Möller. Two c., son and dau.

CHAMBERLIN.

The second family by this name was the third family of pioneers to settle in Newbury, and their advent is thus described by Rev. Clark Perry: "In June, 1762, came up Richard Chamberlin, from Hinsdale, with a family of thirteen c. Seven only of these came with their parents, the rest afterwards. Richard and family landed about noon at the Old Ferry. Before night a hut of posts, bark, etc., was erected, in which they lived three months. He settled near what is called Chamberlin's Ferry on Musquash Meadow. The cellar where the house stood may now, (1831), be seen near Josiah Little's barn, not far from the river. This fruitful vine has still many flourishing branches among us." Joseph, his son, had been here before, and perhaps others of them.

I. The researches of Joseph Edgar Chamberlin embodied in a pamphlet published by him in 1894, show that Richard Chamberlin is first mentioned as in Braintree, Mass., in 1637, whence he rem. to Sudbury and d. before April 15, 1673. He left sons, Benjamin and Joseph and several daughters.

II. JOSEPH, b. Roxbury, baptized June 4, 1655; m. at Sudbury Aug. 26. 1682, Hannah Gilbert; soldier in the Narragansett war. With his brother Benjamin he rem. to Oxford in 1713, where he d. Aug. 8, 1721.

III. NATHANIEL, b. Sudbury, Mass., at the present village of Wayland, 1689; rem. to Oxford, 1713; m. Elizabeth Hunkins; both were members of the church in Oxford; rem. to Hatfield about 1722; soldier in Father Rasle's war. Taken prisoner. After his return from captivity he rem. to Northfield, Mass. Soldier in the Crown Point expedition, 1755. In Col. William's regiment 1759. He d. Nov. 7, 1780, and the church record of Northfield says, "He left a good name behind him."

Children:
1 i. Richard, b. July 9, 1714.
ii. *Moses, b. March 30, 1716.
iii. Nathaniel, b. Jan. 3, 1718; d. Aug. 22, 1745.
iv. Elizabeth, b. Aug. 30, 1719.

---

*See Moses Chamberlain family.

    v. Sarah, b. May 31, 1721, at Oxford.
    vi. Mary, b. July 13, 1727, at Northfield.

1 RICHARD, b. Oxford, Mass., July 9, 1714. Rem. to Northfield. Was in Capt. Phinehas Stevens' Co. of 60 men at Charlestown, N. H., during the siege in 1747. In Capt. Selah Barnard's Co., Col. Wm. William's regiment for the invasion of Canada from March 13 to Dec. 13, 1758, with his son, Abial. Came to Newbury in June, 1762, (See early chapters of this volume), where he settled on Musquash Meadow, and kept the ferry. Was in a company of minute men in 1775. He seems to have been a man of substance and held in esteem, and in the town and church records is always spoken of as Mr. Chamberlin. He was, probably, a member of the 1st ch., as there is record of several church meetings being held at his house. He held various minor offices, and appears to have been a substantial citizen, and the oldest man in the settlement. His gravestone, which may be found in the cemetery at the Ox-bow, a few feet from the monument to Col. Thomas Johnson, says that he d. 16 - - ber, 1784. Traditions, handed down through various branches of the Chamberlin families, assert that Richard, and Moses the pioneer of the third Chamberlin family to settle here, were brothers, and m. sisters, daus. of Remembrance Wright of Northampton. (See Moses Chamberlain family). His wife's name was Abigail, and the date of her death unknown. She survived her husband several years, as she is mentioned, as late as 1795, in Dr. Samuel White's account book, as "Widow Richard Chamberlin." She was one of the earliest members of the Congregational church.

    Children.
    i. Abigail, b. Aug. 28, 1736. Nothing further is known of her.
2 ii. Joseph, b. March 18, 1738; d. Sept. 5, 1815.
3 iii. Abiel, b. Nov. 22, 1739; d. May 14, 1787.
4 iv. Uriah, b. Feb. 24, 1742.
5 v. Er, b. June 24, 1744; d. about 1830.
6 vi. Nathaniel, b. May 5, 1746; d. 1802.
7 vii. Benjamin, b. Dec. 15, 1747; d. June 11, 1832.
    viii. Rebecca, b. March 13, 1749; m. John Foreman, q. v.
    ix. Louisa, b. Dec. 25, 1751; m. Jacob Page, q. v.
8 x. Silas, b. Jan. 19, 1754.
9 xi. Richard, baptized Nov. 2, 1755.
    xii. Martha, b. April 16, 1758; m. probably, William Taplin.
    xiii. Eri, baptized Feb. 22, 1761; drowned July 3, 1773. His gravestone may still be seen in good preservation, near his father's.

2 JOSEPH,[2] (Richard[1]) b. Northfield, Mass., March 18, 1738; soldier in the French and Indian war under Capt. John Catlin, 1757-58; in Coös in 1760; came to Newbury, 1762; grantee of the town; ensign, 1775, in Capt. Thomas Johnson's company of Minute Men; second Lieutenant, 1777-79 in Capt. Frye Bayley's company, guarding and scouting; was with that company at Pawlet, Aug. 16-Oct. 1, 1777; 1779-81, 1st Lieutenant in Capt. Simeon Stevens' company, Olcott's regiment; private in Capt. Frye Bayley's company "in sundry alarms" to the end of the war; carpenter and some time blacksmith; built the large house at the top of the hill south of Montebello; m. Ruth, dau. William Preston of Chester, N. H., (b. 1745; d. Oct. 16, 1831. (Church record). He d. Sept. 6, 1815. Joseph Chamberlin appears to have been a very prominent man in town, and held many positions of trust.

    Children:
10 i. Raymond, b. Aug. 19, 1769; d. Feb. 7, 1849.
    ii. Abigail, b. Dec. 25, 1775; m. Isaac Waldron, q. v.; d. Oct. 3, 1860.
11 iii. Joseph, b. Sept. 8, 1777; d. Nov. 9, 1845.
    iv. Ruth, b. May 30, 1779; m. John Witherspoon, q. v.; d. June 29, 1854.
12 v. Erastus, b. Sept. 27, 1782; d. July, 1348.
    vi. John, b. Sept. 10, 1874; m. Ruby Wright; lived at White River Junction.
    vii. Mary, b. Sept. 7, 1786; m. April 15, 1823, George W. Wheeler of Littleton; d. Littleton, N. H., Oct. 8, 1865. Three c.

    viii. Silas, b. Jan. 9, 1789; lived in the Brock neighborhood; went west; m. Susan C., dau. Josiah Eastman, who d. Nov. 21, 1860, aged 73.

    ix. Hannah, b. March 9, 1791; m. March 24, 1829, Elijah Blaisdell of Boscawen, N. H.

10 RAYMOND,[3] (Joseph,[2] Jacob[1]) b. Aug. 19, 1769; farmer; lived a little east of L. W. McAllister's, no trace of buildings remain, also a little north of Frank Leighton's; m. 1st, Sarah Hibbard, who d. 1811; 2d, Clarissa Whitmore. He d. Feb. 7, 1849.

    Children:

    i. Betsey, b. Sept. 10, 1790; m. Francis G. McAllister, q. v.; d. May 26, 1877.

    ii. Rhoda, d. at sixteen years of age.

    iii. Charlotte, b. June 6, 1799; d. May 3, 1865.

    iv. William, m. Betsey Cameron of New York state; both dead. C., (1) Henry, who d. in Texas. (2) Amelia, m. George Burrage of Boston, where she d. 1899, and two others.

    v. Ruth, b. 1802; m. Isaac A. Bayley, q. v.; d. April 7, 1854.

11 JOSEPH,[3] (Joseph,[2] Richard[1]) b. Sept. 8, 1777; farmer; settled in 1801, on land bought of Matthew Gibson, where R. S. Chamberlin now lives, where he built a log house and, a few years later, a house which stood a little north of the present one. This, built on the hillside, had a brick basement in front, in which were the living rooms, opening into the cellar behind. Such houses were once very common, but few are left. The lower rooms were damp and unhealthy. This house, after being long unoccupied, was taken down in 1875. Farmer, also blacksmith and shoemaker; m. 1st, Sept. 17, 1801, Nancy, dau. Archibald McAllister, (b. New Boston, N. H., Sept. 16, 1776; d. Dec. 7, 1838); 2d, Feb. 9, 1841, Mrs. Fanny Goss, sister of 1st wife. Joseph and both of his wives were members of 1st ch. He d. Nov. 9, 1845.

13   i. Preston, b. Oct. 2, 1802; d. Feb. 20, 1859.

14   ii. Abner, b. Aug. 11, 1804; d. Oct. 4, 1884.

15   iii. Clark, b. July 24, 1806; d. July 18, 1874.

    iv. Joseph, b. July 16, 1808; lived where Joseph Fuller does; m. Oct. 22, 1838, Abigail L., dau. James A. Bayley; went west; d. Nov. 20, 1880.

    v. Eliza J., b. Sept. 8, 1810; m. Luther Chapin; d. July 13, 1845.

16   vi. Nancy, b. Jan. 4, 1813.

    vii. Mary Ann, b. April 13, 1815; m. 1st in Wisconsin, a Mr. Rublee; 2d, a Mr. Hartshorne.

    viii. Sophronia, b. May 2, 1818; m. Amos Eastman; d. March 19, 1880.

    ix. Amplias, b. May 1, 1821; m. Cynthia Bolton; settled at Kilbourne City, Wisconsin.

13 PRESTON,[4] (Joseph,[3] Joseph,[2] Richard,[1]) b. Oct. 2, 1802. Graduated Middlebury College and Burlington Medical College. Is believed to have settled first in Canaan, N. H., but rem. to Herkimer Co., N. Y., where he practiced medicine till his death, Feb. 20, 1859. He m. Laura, dau. Dr. Richard Huntley of Topsham.

    Children, nine, of whom seven are living:

    i. Milo. res. Waltham, Mass.; machinist.

    ii. George H., res. Rock Falls, Wis.; merchant.

    iii. Henry P., res. Chicago; bookkeeper.

    iv. Joseph A., res. Springfield, Mass., with Smith & Wesson, pistol manufacturers.

    vi. Hiram H., res. Eau Claire, Wis.; farmer.

    vii. Clarence A., res. Eau Claire, Wis.; lumber business.

    viii. Daughter, res. Waltham, Mass.

14 ABNER,[4] (Joseph,[3] Joseph,[2] Richard,[1]) b. Aug. 11, 1804. Lived on the homestead, next where Frank Putnam now does, then on the farm which E. E. Putnam owns and occupies, where he built the present house. Captain in the militia, and held town offices. In 1857, he rem. to Spring Prairie with his wife and younger child; in 1867, to Burlington, Wis. In 1878, returned to Vermont. He m. Dec. 1, 1825, Mary, dau. Capt. David Haseltine, (b. May 1, 1808; d. Burlington, Wis., Nov. 19, 1877). He d. at Bradford, Oct. 4, 1884.

Children:
i.   Martha Ann, b. May 8, 1827; m. June 2, 1847, Simeon Avery. They rem. to Minnesota, where she d. May 20, 1875. Three c.
ii. Mary Jane, b. June 23, 1829; m. 1st, Aug. 22, 1849, William Brock, 2d, (who d. July 27, 1852); 2d, June 1, 1867, Hiram W. Kimball of Bradford. C., Alice, m. G. W. Carleton, of West Newbury.
iii. Everett, b May 5; d. Dec. 20, 1831.
17 iv. Preston Samuel, b. Nov. 28, 1832.
18 v.   Adeline, b. March 8, 1835.
19 vi. George Campbell, b. Feb. 24, 1837; d. Nov. 8, 1896.
20 vii. Everett, b. May 8, 1839; d. Feb. 19, 1875.
   viii. Helen Sophronia, b. July 3, 1842; m., Aug. 31, 1865, John R. Drake of Milwaukee, Wis., where she resides.
   ix. Julia E., b. June 8, 1845; m , Dec. 5, 1871, Harvey W. Drake, of Milwaukee.
21 x.   Joseph E., b. Aug. 6, 1851.

17 PRESTON SAMUEL,[5] (Abner,[4] Joseph,[3] Joseph,[2] Richard[1]) b. at Newbury Centre, November 28, 1832; m. Hannah S. Corliss of Bradford, Jan. 17, 1857, and since that time has resided in Bradford; enlisted under the first call for volunteers, in the civil war, in 1861, and went out with the First Vermont Volunteer regiment; mustered out at the expiration of his term, he re-entered the service as captain of Company H. (the Bradford Guards) Twelfth Vermont Volunteers. He has held several town offices in Bradford and represented that town in the Vermont legislature of 1890. Three c., Mrs. Annie F. Spaulding, Mrs. Mary H. Grant and Edith J. Chamberlin.

18 ADALINE[5], (Abner,[4] Joseph,[3] Joseph,[2] Richard,[1]) b. March 8, 1835; m., Oct. 21, 1856, to Charles E. Benton, (son of Samuel Slade, and Esther (Prouty) Benton, b. Waterford, Dec. 11, 1825. Rem. from Newbury to Guildhall, 1860. Representative from Guildhall, 1866, 1867. Senator from Essex County, 1874, 1875. Appointed clerk of Essex County Court, 1865. Elected Judge of Probate, 1888, holding both positions at time of death, June 10, 1892.)
    Children.
i.   Charles Abner, b. Newbury, Aug. 12, 1857; d. Guildhall, Aug. 20, 1877.
ii. Everett Chamberlin, b. Guildhall, Sept. 25, 1862. Educated at Colebrook and Lancaster Academies. Appointed, 1874, page of the Vermont senate; 1876, clerk to the Secretary of State. Went to Boston, 1882, entering the insurance office of John C. Paige & Co., of which concern he is now a member. Has held important positions on the Republican state and congressional committees. Appointed, 1893, aid-de-camp to Gov. Greenhalge, with the title of colonel. Member, 1896, of the executive council of Gov. Wolcott, but declined re-election the next year, on account of the pressure of business. Member of several clubs and societies, including the Vermont Association, and the Ancient and Honorable Artillery. Res. Waverly, Belmont, Mass., but has a summer home at Guildhall, where he has erected a beautiful building for a Masonic Hall and Public Library. He m. Jan. 24, 1885, Willera Rogers. Six c., five living. Jay R., Charles E., Blanche A., Dorothy D., Hannah S.
iii. Jay Bayard, b. April 10, 1870. Entered Dartmouth College from St. Johnsbury Academy in 1886, after one year's interim as librarian of the Young Men s Institute, New York City. Graduated from college in 1870, having been one of the editors of the Dartmouth, president of the Handel Society, and assistant librarian. Chosen member of the Phi Beta Kappa Society. Received degree of A. M. 1893. Went to Boston 1890. Reporter on the Evening Transcript. In 1894 became assistant managing editor of the Journal. Returned 1897 to the Transcript of which he is city editor. Member of several clubs, including the Papyrus and Dartmouth, is Boston correspondent of the New York Dramatic Mirror, and press representative of the Boston Museum, Hollis street, and Colonial Theaters. Not married, res. with his mother, Winchester, Mass.

19 GEORGE CAMPBELL,[5] (Abner,[4] Joseph,[3] Joseph,[2] Richard[1]) b. at Newbury Centre, Feb. 24, 1837. He learned the printer's trade when young, at Windsor, and New Haven, Conn. Afterward he came to Bradford, where for

several years he published the Orange County ˙Telegraph. Selling out in 1863, he enlisted as a private in the Ninth Vermont Volunteers. He served until December, 1865, when he was mustered out as first lieutenant. He went west early in 1866, with health shattered by long service in a malarious district of North Carolina, and located in Southwestern Minnesota. He founded the town of Jackson in that state, building, with a friend, the first house in that place, which he lived to see grow to a town of 2,000 people. He started a newspaper in Jackson under circumstances of great difficulty; the material was hauled fifty miles by team, and when the press and type arrived in this manner, he found that the paper was left behind. The team which he sent for this was caught in a blizzard. He published this paper, the Jackson Republic, many years; during this time he served as Sergeant-at-Arms of the Minnesota Senate for one session, was a member of the Minnesota House of Representatives during two sessions, and was for six years a member of the Minnesota State Board of Equalization. He became interested in a daily paper at St. James, in the same state, until failing eyesight compelled him to give up all newspaper work. He sold out his interests and returned to Jackson, where he became totally blind in 1884. He built a residence at Jackson, but in 1893 came back to Vermont, where he lived, mostly with his brother, Captain P. S. Chamberlin and d. at Bradford, Nov. 8, 1896. He was never m.

20 EVERETT,[5] (Abner,[4] Joseph,[3] Joseph,[2] Richard,[1]) was b. at Newbury Center, May 8, 1839. He attended Newbury Seminary, and very early in life adopted the occupation of a teacher. In the exercise of this calling he went in 1857 to Elkhorn, Wisconsin. In 1862, he returned to Vermont to enlist in Company H, 12th Vermont Volunteers, of which company he became orderly sergeant. When his term of service with his regiment had expired, he went to Milwaukee, Wisconsin, where he went out as captain of Co. I, 39th Wisconsin Volunteers. Leaving the service in 1864, he became city editor of the Milwaukee Sentinel, and from that time forward followed the career of a journalist and writer. In 1868, he went to Chicago to join the staff of the Evening Post of that city, on which journal he gained a wide reputation through the wit and pungency of his paragraph writing, and the excellence of his critical judgment, especially in music. He afterward joined the staff of the Chicago Tribune as an editorial writer, and afterward that of the Chicago Times. In 1873 he was compelled by delicate health to relinquish all editorial work. He went to California, Colorado and Florida in quest of health, and d. at Jacksonville, Florida, Feb. 19, 1875, of consumption. He was the author of three books, "Chicago and the Great Conflagration," (with Elias Colbert), a history of the Chicago fire of 1871, published in 1872; "The Struggle of '72," an account of the political campaign in which Grant was elected president over Greeley; and "Chicago and Her Suburbs," (1873), a work of reference on Chicago and the surrounding towns. Everett Chamberlin was m. to Anna E. Martin, at Big Bend, Wisconsin, Oct. 10, 1866. Of their c. there now survives Miss Minnie E. Chamberlin and Mrs. Julia Robertson, both res. in Wisconsin.

21 JOSEPH EDGAR,[5] (Abner,[4] Joseph,[3] Joseph,[2] Richard,[1]) was b. at West Newbury, August 6, 1851. He rem. with his parents to Wisconsin in 1857. Educated in the common schools, he went to Chicago in December, 1868, and went to work on the Evening Post, newspaper of that city. Here he served until after the great Chicago fire of 1871, when he was for a brief time city editor of the Daily Journal of Indianapolis, Ind. Returning to Chicago, he served in various editorial capacities on the Chicago Times until December, 1880, when broken down in health by over-work, he resigned the managing editorship of that paper to return to the East. He was, from 1881 to 1884, editor of papers in Newport, R. I., and Fall River, Mass.; in 1884 he went to Boston and was editor of the Evening Record and Daily Advertiser of that city, until 1887, when he went to the Boston Transcript. In 1890 he became one of the editorial staff of the Youth's Companion, with which paper, as well as with the Boston Transcript, he is still connected. In 1898 he went to the Spanish war as correspondent of the New York Evening Post and Youth's Companion,

and went through the Santiago campaign. He is the author of three books, "The Listener in the Town," "The Listener in the Country," (Boston, 1896,) and "John Brown," a biography, (Boston, 1899.) The two former books are made up out of the "Listener" series of essays in the Boston Transcript, which Mr. Chamberlin founded in 1887 and still (1900) writes. He is a member of the St. Botolph Club and Authors' Club of Boston. He was m. at Chicago, June 26, 1873, to Ida Elizabeth Atwood.

Children:

i. Mrs. Helen Dodd. One c., David Haseltine, b. Wrentham, Mass., May 2, 1900. Rem. to Topsham, 1901.
ii. Elizabeth.
iii. Raymond.
iv. Mary Eleanor.

15 CLARK,[4] (Joseph,[3] Joseph,[2] Richard,[1]) b. July 24, 1806; farmer on his father's homestead; m. Jan. 30, 1834, Amanda, dau. Joseph Sawyer, (b. March 13, 1807; d. Nov. 13, 1868). He d. July 17, 1874. Members of the Meth. ch.

Children:

i. Joseph Allen, b. Aug. 26, 1835; served in 1862-3, nine months in Co. H, 12th Vt; rem. 1867 to Wisconsin, later to Texas; farmer in Newbury; m. April 30, 1857, Lucia A., dau. Ross Ford, (b. July 20, 1838). He d. Denison, Texas, Dec. 24, 1881. C., (1) Mary Emma, b. Oct. 10, 1858; d. Burlington, Wis., Feb. 3, 1870. (2) Carrie Amanda, b. Nov. 13, 1861; m. in Denison, Texas, Jan. 1, 1879, William H. Taylor, who d. in Bozeman, Montana, June 24, 1883.
ii. Remembrance Sawyer, b. Oct. 24, 1840; farmer on homestead; m. March 20, 1867, Ellen E., dau. William U. Bailey. C., William Clark, b. July 28, 1876.
iii. Charles Franklin, b. Feb. 5, 1850; d. April 11, 1852.

16 NANCY,[4] (Joseph,[3] Joseph,[2] Richard,[1]) b. Jan. 4, 1813; m. Jan. 7, 1841, James Caldwell of Topsham, (b. Ryegate, Dec. 10, 1808; farmer in Topsham where his c. were b.)

Children:

i. Joseph C., b. Dec. 3, 1842; physician at Buckfield, Maine; twice m. Three c.
ii. Eliza, b. March 20, 1845; m. James Lang of Topsham. Six c.
iii. James R., b. Sept. 3, 1846; farmer in Topsham; m. 1st, Jan. 15, 1878, Ella Vance, who d. July 15, 1893. C., (1) Rosamond N. (2) Nathan R. (3) Joseph C. He m. 2d, Nov. 14, 1890. Mrs. Martha Jones.
iv. Martin, b. April 22, 1848; graduated from Rush's Medical School, Chicago, and d. while in practice at Hershaw, Ill. Left a wife and c.
v. John Preston, d. in infancy.
vi. Eber C., b. Dec. 12, 1853; d. Dec. 9, 1876.

12 ERASTUS,[3] (Joseph,[2] Richard,[1]) b. Sept. 27, 1782; lived many years on the homestead, but rem. to Canada, then to Livingston County, New York. He m. September, 1805, Betsey Goodall, (b. Pomfret, Conn., November, 1783; d. Sept. 15, 1863). He d. York, New York, Jan. 11, 1848. After his death his wife returned to the old home in Newbury in 1856.

Children:

i. Finette, b. May 17, 1806; m. James B. Johnston, q. v.; d. Nov. 20, 1897.
ii. Richard, rem. to Jackson, Mich.; farmer; he survived wife and child; dead some years.
iii. Harriet, m. William Osborn, of Troy, N. Y.; d. in Chicago about 1890, leaving two sons.
iv. Henry, lawyer; m. Amanda Lyon, eight c., two living; d. in Westchester County, N. Y.
v. Erastus, d. Brooklyn, N. Y., left a dau., Mrs. Tyler, who d. in Toronto, Canada.
vi. George, d. in Canada, un-m., at 21.
vii. Elizabeth C., b. 1821; m. in Canada, April, 1842, David Owen. Still living in Bath, Me. Res. Alabama, New York City and Maine. Five c. One son in St. Louis, one in Bangor, Me., and a dau. in Bath. One dau., Elizabeth, was b. in Newbury, 1856.

viii. Mary, d. Canada, in 1839, aged 18.
ix. Samuel Alden, drowned in the Hudson at Albany, N. Y., at the age of 12, while returning from school at Canandaigua, N. Y.

3 ABIEL,[2] (Richard[1]) b. Nov. 22, 1739; served in the old French war with his father in Col. William William's regiment; served in the revolutionary war; was in Capt. Thomas Johnson's company of minute men, 1775; in winter of 1775-6 was one of the men who went with Capt. Johnson to mark out a road from Newbury to St. Johns. On reaching the latter place, he went on, says Johnson, and joined the army at Quebec. In Capt. John G. Bayley's company, guarding and scouting, and in other service. He is called "Lieutenant" on his gravestone. Grantee of Newbury and settled on upper meadow, near the river; m. March 27, 1769, Elinor, dau. Elihu Johnson, who after his death m. Ezra Gates and d. Sept. 24, 1822, aged 69. He d. May 14, 1787.
   Children:
22 i. Martin, b. Jan. 12, 1770; d. Aug, 24, 1820, q. v.
23 ii. Charles. b. Jan. 9, 1772; d. Dec. 5, 1834, q. v.
    iii. Eunice. b. Jan. 14, 1774.
24 iv. Phineas, b. Dec. 7, 1779; d. Feb. 14, 1859.
25 v. Seth, b. March 8, 1781; d. Bath, Oct. 24, 1843, q. v.
    vi. Zibbie, b. Oct. 15, 1784.
    vii. Elinor, b. March 1, 1787; m. Jabez Bigelow of Ryegate.

22 MARTIN,[3] (Abiel,[2] Richard,[1]) b. Jan. 12, 1771; m. Feb. 15, 1792; Mary, dau. Joshua Ricker, (b. Aug. 3, 1772; d. 1862). Rem. to Bath. He was drowned in Connecticut river, Aug. 24, 1820.
   Children:
    i. Abiel, b. April 1, 1794; d. June 21, 1797.
    ii. Eunice, b. Jan. 14, 1796; m. Joshua Hunt of Bath.
    iii. Matilda, b. March 25, 1798; m. Jan. 9, 1827, Samuel Thompson; d. Nov. 23, 1827.
    iv. Joshua R., b. March 8, 1802; m. Sophia Smith; settled in Jay; d. July 23, 1874.
    v. John D., b. June 23, 1806; d. July 23, 1814.
    vi. Charles, b. Feb. 6, 1809; m. July 15, 1838, Rosan Hoskins; d. Aug. 17, 1878. Mrs. Arthur W. Blair of Dorchester, Mass., and Miss Emma Chamberlin of St. Johnsbury are the only ones living of their seven daus.
    vii. Mary Ann, b. Aug. 27, 1811; d. Nov. 2, 1813.
    viii. Walter P., b. Nov. 15, 1814; m. Sophia Utley; lived in Hartford, Conn.; d. May, 1890.

23 CHARLES,[3] (Abiel,[2] Richard,[1]) b. Jan. 7, 1772; farmer on his father's homestead on upper meadow; m. Mrs. Rachel Varnum McDole, who d. April 13, 1840, aged 74. He d. Dec. 5, 1834.
   Children:
26 i. Abiel, b. May 5, 1800.
    ii. Betsey V., b. Jan. 8, 1803; d. Sept. 11, 1872.
27 iii. Diodama, (twin to Betsey), m. William Scales; d. June 1, 1875.
    iv. Clarissa, b. Nov. 2, 1804; d. Oct. 1, 1864.
    v. Sally, b. March 3, 1808; d. Feb. 13, 1892.
    vi. John Varnum, b. May 19, 1810; m. July 29, 1838, Sarah L., dau. of Barnard Brickett, who d. January, 1895. He d. December, 1839. One son, John.

26 ABIAL,[4] (Charles,[3] Abiel,[2] Richard[1]) b. May 5, 1800; farmer on upper meadow. His buildings were far out on the meadow, and were burned a few years ago; m. 1st, March 17, 1823, Eunice P., dau. Hezekiah Weatherbee, (b. Grafton, Vt., Jan. 27, 1805; d. Sept. 6, 1852); m. 2d, Emmeline, widow of Samuel Eastman and dau. Jacob and Hannah Bayley, (b. June 30, 1802; d. Jan. 30, 1869). He d. Feb. 5, 1882.
   Children, all by 1st marriage:
    i. Lucy, m. Daniel F. Wood of Boston. No c.
    ii. Rachel, m. Dec. 22, 1857, Dan Y. Bailey, q. v.
    iii. Charles, m. Ruth Eastman of Haverhill.
28 iv. John V., b. 1832; d. January, 1891, q. v.
    v. Elizabeth, never m.

    vi. Sarah, m. William Rockwood.
    vii. Clara.
    viii. Abigail.

28 JOHN V.,[5] (Abial,[4] Charles,[3] Abial,[2] Richard,[1]) b. Newbury, 1832; left Newbury when a young man; entered railroad business; was senior partner of Chamberlin, Gibbs & Co., railroad contractors and bridge builders; among other large undertakings they built the Maysville and Lexington Railroad in Kentucky; did all the lumber work on the Cincinnati Southern Railroad, and the great inclined plane for elevating street cars at Cincinnati. He m. 1st, July 27, 1852, Louisa A., dau. Alanson Work of Hartford, Conn., and sister of the composer, Henry C. Work, author of "Marching through Georgia" and many other well known pieces. She was b. Middletown, Conn., and d. at Delhi, O., Sept. 6, 1877. He m. 2d, Sept. 6, 1883, Mrs. C. H. Fishback who d. Hickerson, Tenn., 1888. He d. at Hickerson, January, 1891.
    Children, four by 1st, and one by 2d marriage:
    i. Frederick A., b. Lebanon, N. H., Jan. 21, 1855; m. at Delhi, O., 1876, Hattie Baker. Three c.
    ii. E. Helen, b. Bath, N. H., March 20, 1856; m. at Delhi, O., 1879, George S. Mayhew of Cincinnati, O.; res. at Minneapolis Minn., where she d. March, 1889. Four c.
26 iii. Edwin A., b. Lebanon, N. H., Sept. 11, 1859, q. v.
    iv. Charles, b. 1862; d. at 12 days.
    v. John V., b. Delhi, O., Dec. 12, 1884.

29 EDWIN A.,[6] (John V.,[5] Abiel,[4] Charles,[3] Abiel,[2] Richard[1]) b. Lebanon, N. H., Sept. 11, 1859; graduated Cincinnati Law School, May 14, 1879; on survey of Texas Pacific railroad, 1880; in business till 1887, when he spent two years in exploring the continent of South America, ascended the Amazon to its source and crossed the Andes; has crossed the Atlantic fifteen times and the Pacific once, as United States Sea Post official; res. Trenton, N. J.; m. at South Williamport, Penn., Dec. 31, 1883, Eva Rupert, dau. Hon. Daniel Steck of Lycoming County, Penn.
    Children:
    i. Helen, b. Oct. 4, 1884.
    ii. Edwin A., b. May 31, 1886.

27 DIODAMA,[4] (Charles,[3] Abiel[2], Richard,[1]) b. Jan. 8, 1803; m. 1840, William Scales, (b. Lisbon, N. H., Aug. 7, 1812; d. June 13, 1885). She d. Sept. 11, 1872.
    Children:
    i. Raebel C., b. Feb. 13, 1841.
    ii. Sarah C., b Jan. 13, 1844; m. March 5, 1868, Henry K. Heath, q. v.
    iii. Charles C., b. Nov. 23, 1847; farmer on upper meadow, living in the house built by his grandfather.

24 PHINEAS,[3] (Abial,[2] Richard,[1]) b. Newbury, Dec. 6, 1778; settling with his brothers, Seth and Martin, on adjoining farms in Bath. Farmer. He m. Betsey Downs, (b. Aug. 20, 1783; d. Sept. 7, 1861). He d. Bath, April 14, 1859.
    Children:
    i. Eleanor, b. April 21, 1803.
    ii. Abigail, b. May 11, 1805.
    iii. Sibyl, b. April 6, 1807.
    iv. Abial, b. June 12, 1809.
    v. Sybil, b. July 16, 1811.
    vi. Mary Ann, b. July 16, 1813; m. Wm. B. Abbott, q. v.
    vii. Isaac, b. June 1, 1815; m. Jane Lang. 7 c.
    viii. George, b. June 24, 1817.
    ix. Betsey, b. Feb. 10, 1819.

25 SETH,[3] (Abiel,[2] Richard,[1]) b. Newbury, March 8, 1781; m. Sarah Harris; d. Bath, Oct. 24, 1843.
    Children:
    i. James, b. Newbury, Dec. 3, 1808; m. Elizabeth Whiting; d. Bath, Feb. 27, 1889.

    ii. Julia Ann, b. Bath, Jan. 12, 1813.
   iii. Phineas, b. Oct. 15, 1810; m. Susan Powers.
   iv. Jane E., b. Nov. 15, 1817.
    v. Mary, b. Jan. 1, 1819.
   vi. Martin P., b. April 5, 1822.
  vii. Seth J., b. Troy, July 25, 1834.
 viii. Roxana, b. Canada, Feb. 13, 1818.

4 URIAH,[2] (Richard,[1]) b. Feb. 24, 1742. Very little is known about him. His
"pitch" was Lot 9, on Musquash Meadow. He served during a large
part of the revolutionary war, and is said to have settled in the northeast
part of Ryegate, at least to have lived there several years, after 1785.
Of the family very little is known. He is given as head of a family in the
census of 1771, and the church records mention the baptism of a son,
James, Feb. 20, 1785. The Ephraim Bayley family records say that Jacob,
son of Ephraim, m. Hannah, dau. Uriah and Rachel (Colby) Chamberlin.
Some of the numerous Chamberlin families in the northern part of the
state are probably descended from him.

5 ER,[2] (Richard)[1] b. June 24, 1744; came to Newbury in the fall of 1762, he, with
others, making their way by spotted trees; served in the revolutionary
war, in local service. About 1770, he moved to Wells River, and was the
first settler there, where he built a sawmill, a grist-mill, and a blacksmith
shop. He began to keep a ferry across Connecticut river about 1778, and
kept it till the bridge was built in 1803. Of this he was one of the
incorporators. He bought, of the widow of Governor Wentworth, her
share in the "Governor's Farm." His first house stood a little above the
mouth of Wells River, and, later, built one which seems to have stood
about where Mr. Deming's now does, and which, later, was occupied by
Josiah Marsh, and by John L. Woods. About 1808, he rem. to Ryegate,
and bought a farm in the east part of the town, where he lived till his
death; m. twice; was head of a family in 1771; his second wife was a
Wright. He d. about 1830, and with his second wife, is buried in the
"Whitelaw cemetery," Ryegate. The names of his c. are not all known.
    Children, nine by each marriage:
    Nicholas, m. Widow Sarah Gates, March 15, 1791.
    Stephen, m. Prudence Poor from Massachusetts; d. in Ryegate, aged about
      eighty. She d. in Iowa.
    Eri.
    Sophila, never m.
    Elsie, m. Peter Gilchrist, a Scotchman of Ryegate. Both lived to old age.
      John Gilchrist of Leighton Hill is their son.
    Dudley.
30   Hardy, b. March 23, 1777; d. May 26, 1850.
    Adolphus or Rodolphus, lived in Newbury; m. Betsey Grant, 1794.
    Phila.
    Electa.
    Fanny, baptized Nov. 12, 1786. (Church record).
    Reuben, m. Martha Sanborn of Lyman; lived in Barnet many years where
      she d. He d. in Ryegate in his ninety-first year. Solomon Chamberlin, a
      well known citizen of Ryegate, is their son.

30 HARDY,[3] (Er,[2] Richard,[1]) b. March 23, 1777. Farmer. Kept the toll bridge at
Wells River for many years. He m. Nov. 9, 1800, Lucretia, dau. John
Clark, who d. April 26, 1842, aged 68 years. He d. while asleep in the
afternoon, May 26, 1850, and his daughters, Melinda and Sarah, kept
the toll bridge till the former d.
    Children:
    i. John Clark, b. Aug. 23, 1801.
   ii. Lowell, b. April 10, 1803; d. Feb. 9, 1805.
   iii. Melinda, b. Feb. 24, 1805; d. Aug. 27, 1868.
   iv. Friend, b. Jan. 21, 1807; farmer of Newbury; d. at Woodsville, Dec. 23,
      1883. His wife, Hannah Woods, d. Dec. 30, 1868, aged 60 years, 5
      months. C., Lucretia S., b. 1845; m. April 19, 1866, Alvah C. Haynes of
      Rumney, N. H. Res. Lancaster, N. H. Seven c., three living.

    v. Mahala, b. Jan. 10, 1809; m. William Pool. He lived at Charlestown, Mass. Was city treasurer many yaers.
    vi. Sarah. b. March 14, 1813.
    vii. Lowell W., b. Jan. 15, 1818; lived at Windsor Locks, Conn.; d. many years ago. One son, John, living there.

6 NATHANIEL,[2] (Richard,[1]) b. May 5, 1746. Very little can be learned about him or his descendants. He settled on the farm now known as the Col. Tenney farm, on the upper meadow, and may have built the present house. The buildings stood on the "old road," and were moved to their present location about 1800. Revolutionary soldier. Owned land in Grafton County, and probably rem. there. Administrators of Nathaniel Chamberlin's estate were appointed in 1802. He is believed to have had several c. One dau. is known, Elizabeth, b. 1794, m. a Mr. Johnson, an Englishman, and rem. to Canada in 1824, where he d. leaving several c. She returned to Newbury, and educated her c. In 1852 she went south to live with them, and d. at Belleville, Ala., June 21, 1859. One son, William, became a teacher, then a merchant, and is now retired at Pensacola, Fla. One dau., Sophia, m. Dr. S. S. Forbes of Pensacola.

7 BENJAMIN,[2] (Richard[1]) b. Northfield, Mass., Dec. 15, 1747; came to Newbury with his parents; farmer on Musquash meadow and carpenter (see chapter on bridges); served a short time in the revolutionary war; after 1800, he moved to the farm still called the "Ben Chamberlin place," on what was once called "the back road," southwest of Wells River.; m. the Widow Eaton, who had three daughters by her former marriage, one of whom m. Horace Stebbins, another m. as 2d wife, John Johnson, and a third m. a Mr. Webb. Her name was Hannah. She d. May 10, 1833, in her 85th year. He d. June 11, 1832, or 1833; buried at the Ox-bow. The account of this family is but fragmentary at the best, and is made from such records as remain, and the recollections of older people.
    Children:
    i. Polly, b. Nov. 8, 1774; m. Willoughby Corliss, of Corinth, q. v; d. April 30, 1841.
    ii. Mindwell, b. Dec. 20, 1781; never m.; d. Dec. 21, 1847.
    iii. Sarah (or Sabra) b. 1783; m. Thomas Eames of Northumberland, N. H., but when a widow returned to Newbury; d. Jan. 10, 1851.
31 iv. Benjamin, b. October, 1784; d. Dec. 3, 1872.
    v. Wright, lived in Corinth.
    vi. Amity, b. March 2, 1788; m. William Page, q. v.; d. Oct. 19, 1860.
32 vii. Tural Tufts.
    viii. Abigail, m. Joseph Kimball Page of Ryegate.

31 BENJAMIN,[3] (Benjamin,[2] Richard,[1]) b. October, 1784; farmer on homestead; m. Sally, dau. Thomas Kasson, (b. February, 1787; d. April 15, 1868). He d. Dec. 3, 1872; buried at Boltonville.
    Children:
    i. Julia Ann, b. 1808; m. Dec. 4, 1828, Ezra W. Smith of Bath, who d. May 10, 1875. She d. Aug. 26, 1889.
    ii. Chester, lived in Monroe, N. H.; m. a Miss Johnson of Ryegate.
33 iii. Warren K. b. May 6, 1815.
    iv. Wright, m. 1st, Abigail Taylor.

33 WARREN K,[1] (Benjamin,[3] Benjamin,[2] Richard,[1]) b. May 6, 1815; farmer in Newbury; m. Dec. 26, 1847, Statira F., dau. of David Edwards; d. at Bethlehem, N. H., at the home of his daughter, July 30, 1894.
    Children:
    i. Helen M., m. Geo. Hutchins.
    ii. Mary Ann, d. Sept. 20, 1869.
    iii. William H., m. Alice Kinney; d. June 12, 1889.
    iv. George A., m. Hattie Weare.
    v. Flora J., m. Frank W. George.
    vi. Velma J., m. W. D. Leighton, was divorced from him, and became a trained nurse at the Mary Fletcher Hospital, Burlington.

vii. Herbert D.
viii. Hermon D., m. Nellie Gilchrist.

32 TURAL TUFTS,[3] (Benjamin,[2] Richard,[1]) b. 1794; farmer near the homestead; m.
March 14, 1816, Betsey Martha, dau. Thomas Kasson, who d. Nov. 24,
1889, aged 80 yrs. 9 mos. 13 days. He d. in 1870.
Children:
34   Helen S., m. Charles Rumsey of Woodsville.
        Alvin, m. Jan. 16, 1863, Louisa Webber, dau. Charles Webber.   Several c.
35   Alfred.
        Ann, m. George Hayward.
        Alden.
        Alonzo Gale, b. March 18, 1832; lived in Boston; d. Newbury, 1892.
        Frank, m. Sophronia Frost of Groton; served in the army; d. in the civil
        war.
36   Azro B.

34 HELEN L.,[4] (Tural T.,[3] Benjamin,[2] Richard,[1]) b. Aug. 12, 1827; m. July 26,
1852, Charles E. Rumsey, (b. Dec. 22, 1834). Res. Wells River.
Children:
i. Addie J., b. Nov. 18, 1854; m. Warren S. Davis of Montpelier.
ii. Genevieve E., b. Sept. 18, 1857.
iii. Franklin, b. Aug. 5, 1859.
iv. Maude, b. May 18, 1866.

35 ALFRED,[4] (Tural T.,[3] Benjamin,[2] Richard[1]) b. March 19, 1821; farmer on upper
meadow; m. March 17, 1850, Lucy Adeline Hayward, who d. Oct. 10,
1896.
Children:
i. Harriet, N., b. Aug. 13, 1851; m. Nov. 18, 1877, David Harlow.
ii. Eva, b. Nov. 15, 1853; m. April 1, 1882, Nathaniel Eastman.
iii. Lucy A., b. Sept. 16, 1855; m. June 24, 1880, Hiram Merrill.
iv. Emma V., b. Feb. 24, 1860; m. Jan. 11, 1901, Albert Hood.
v. Jessie F., b. Oct. 16, 1861; m. October, 1891, Guy Roby.
vi. Clara F., b. Oct. 26, 1864; m. June, 1893, Clarence H. McAllister.
vii. Mary Lizzie, b. July 20, 1868.

36 AZRO B.,[4] (T. Tufts.[3] Benjamin,[2] Richard,[1]) b. Newbury, Oct. 6, 1829. Res.
Newbury till 1867, then in Boston. being part of the time on the police
force. Return to Newbury, 1877; farmer at Newbury village. He m. 1st,
1853, Jennette Dick, dau. Marvin Kasson, who d. in Boston, July 1, 1871.
One son. He m. 2d, July 4, 1877, Elvira Stone of Salem. He d. Feb. 10,
1901.
Children:
i. Henry, b. 1854. Res. at Northumberland, N. H.
ii. Louis F., b. Aug. 17, 1878, now at Norwich University.
iii. Rosamond Jeanette, b. May 5, 1883.

8   SILAS,[2] (Richard[1]) b. Jan. 19, 1754. Of him all that is known is that he was one
of the three young men who started for Cambridge, Mass., in the night
that the news of the battle of Lexington reached Newbury, and served in
the battle of Bunker Hill. He also served during most of the war. His
after history connot be traced. He later settled at Wells River, where he
built in 1792, the "old parsonage" now Dr. Munsell's house.

9   RICHARD,[2] (Richard[1]). Of him nothing whatever is known, save the date of his
baptism, Nov. 2, 1755, his record of service in the revolutionary war, and
the fact stated by Mr. Perry, that at a training held at Col. Robert
Johnston's he shot a man who tried to take a gun away from him, and
was branded "M." on the forehead.

CHAMBERLAIN.

The third family bearing this name, was that of Dea. Moses Chamberlain, who
is believed to have been a brother of Richard Chamberlin. This seems as
certain as anything can be which depends on family traditions, in lack of
written statements to that effect. He was, then, the 2d son and child of
Nathaniel and Elizabeth (Hunkins) Chamberlain, b. at Oxford, Mass.,

March 30, 1716. His after history for more than thirty years is unknown, but in 1748, he bought land in Litchfield, Conn., and is described in the deed as of Litchfield, and his name is on the book of the Congregational ch. at South Farms, in 1787. The older records have been destroyed. He m. Jemima, dau. Remembrance Wright, who is believed to have been a sister of the wife of Richard. This Remembrance Wright was the son of that Capt. Benjamin Wright, who is mentioned on page 8 of this volume, as visiting the Coös county in 1725. This was not his first visit, as he was here as early as 1708, at the head of a scout and later. In the spring of 1709, the governor of Massachusetts, issuing an order for scouting parties to hold themselves in readiness to invade Canada, Captain Wright sent to him the following letter:
"May it please your excellency :—

Northampton, Sept. 19, 1709.

With submission and under correction I offer my services to ye Excellency, if that in wisdom you send forces to Canada from our posts by land that, 'Here am I, send me.' This year I have done service, and hope I may again, not that I would trouble your Excellency, but am willing to go. Not else, but in Duty I subscribe myself:

Ye Excellencys most Humble sevt,

BENJAMIN WRIGHT."

His grandfather, Dea. Samuel Wright, was one of the prominent men of Northampton, and his father, Sergeant Samuel Wright, was killed by the Indians while guarding Northfield, Mass., in 1675. The name "Wright" has been borne by several members of both Chamberlain families, while "Remembrance" is a common name among the Chamberlain, Johnson and Sawyer families, who have a common ancestor in Remembrance Wright. This family came here as early as 1772, as on Nov. 20 of that year, Remembrance Chamberlain received from Jacob Bayley, a deed of Lot No. 2 in Sleeper's Meadow, with the house lot belonging to it, one 50 acre, and two 100 acre lots. The names of Asher and Moses Chamberlain are on the roll of minute-men in 1775, and in Capt. John G. Bayley's company, guarding and scouting. Remembrance and Moses were in Capt. Steven's company, serving nineteen days between May, 1779, and May, 1881. Remembrance was 2d Lieutenant in Capt. Frye Bayley's company, guarding and scouting, and Moses a private in the same company in 1781-2. Moses' name is in Capt. Samuel Young's company of Haverhill, in Bedel's regiment from December, 1777, to March, 1778, also in a "Company raised for the Defense of the Frontier." He was 2d Lieutenant from June 1, 1778, for 138 days, and 1st Lieutenant from Dec. 1, 1778, 121 days. In Capt. Simeon Steven's company "for the Defense of the Frontier" Asher Chamberlain served in 1778 and 1779. Moses was Sergeant Major in Young's company of Bedel's regiment from Feb. 12, to March 31, 1778, "a Company raised for the Expedition against Canada." It is understood that both Dea. Moses and his son Moses served in the war, but which of the foregoing records of service was that of the father, and which of the son, cannot now be distinguished. Moses and his wife were members of the Congregational ch, but his title of Deacon was held by him before he came here. He d. June 25, 1796. His gravestone states that he was b. Litchfield, Conn., 1715, but Litchfield was not settled till 1724. She d. July 30, 1801. Her mother's name was Elizabeth.

Children :

. Susanna, b. Winchester, N. H., Aug. 29, 1740; m. 1st, as second wife, a Mr. Shepard, whose sons, Aaron, Ashbel and Horace, settled here, but rem. to Greensboro. 2d, Nov. 25, 1784, Capt. Ephraim Stevens, of Newbury, and 3d, October, 1789, James Corliss, then of Haverhill, but later of Greensboro, where she d. Oct. 4, 1840, aged 100 years, 25 days. Buried in the Lincoln graveyard at Greensboro.

ii. Azubah, b. Nov. 2, 1741; m. a Mr. Muncy of Litchfield, Conn., where she d. Her husband settled in Orwell, and was the man who gave the woman a dollar, about which Rev. Silas McKeen wrote a tract, entitled "The Worth of a Dollar."

iii. Jemima, b. Aug. 25, 1743; m. Johnson of Connecticut. Revolutionary soldier.

  iv. Lydia, b. Jan. 30, 1746; m., as 2d wife, Capt. Robert Hunkins, q. v., of Newbury and Bradford; d. January, 1831.
1 v. Remembrance, b. Dec. 19, 1747; d. Jan. 10, 1813.
  vi. Moses, b. Litchfield, Dec. 10, 1794; revolutionary soldier; m. Abigail, sister of Col. Simeon Stevens; settled in Bradford, and town clerk there, 1794–97. He sold his farm to his nephew, Moses Chamberlain, and rem. to Pennsylvania.
2 vii. Asher, b. Litchfield, April 14, 1751.
  viii. Wright, b. Litchfield, June 14, 1757; m. in Connecticut, and lived next to his father's; rem. later to Pennsylvania. He is said to have been m. four times and had 21 c.

1 COL. REMEMBRANCE,[2] (Moses,[1]) b. Dec. 19, 1747. He owned the farm long known as the Chamberlain Farm, north of Bedel's bridge, where he kept tavern many years. This farm remained in the family for three generations. He served in the revolutionary war in several campaigns, and was made 1st Lieutenant by Gov. Chittenden. The original commission is owned by a descendant. He was made, successively, Captain, Major, and Colonel in the militia. In town he was prominent, holding offices, and was a substantial citizen. He and his wife were, probably, members of the church, joining it before the present records began. He was very particular to keep the Sabbath, and brought up his family in strict Puritan principles. He was a kind and generous man. He m. Elizabeth Elliott, widow of Haynes Johnson, q. v., and dau. of Edmund and Mehetable (Worthen) Elliott, descendants of Amesbury, (Mass.,) families. After the death of Mr. Johnson she returned to Chester, for fear of the Indians and tories, but came back to Newbury bringing her three c. with her on the horse, fording streams and sometimes compelled to lodge in the woods. She was b. at Chester, 1751; d. Feb. 8, 1829.
  Children, all b. here.
3 i. Moses, b. Nov. 25, 1777; d. November, 1854.
  ii. Azubah, b. Nov. 6, 1779; m. Joseph Sawyer, q. v.
  iii. Elizabeth, b. Dec. 19, 1781; m. Joseph Kent, q. v.
  iv. Mehetable, b. Dec. 3, 1783, m. 1st, (Pub. in Haverhill, May 1, 1806,) Green Saunders. He lived at West Newbury on the farm where the late John Wilson lived, building that house. She m. 2d, as second wife, Oct. 6, 1831, Israel Willard, of Bradford; d. March 13, 1849.
  v. Rembrance, b. July 12, 1785; d. Sept. 4, 1789.
4 vi. Moody, b. Sept. 12, 1787; d. July 12, 1863.
  vii. Remembrance, b. Dec. 2, 1789. Graduated at Middlebury College, 1814; became a Presbyterian minister in Georgia. He rode to Georgia on horseback, afterward returning to Newbury, and going back to Georgia, using the same horse for each trip. He was a tall, slender man, and always rode standing in the stirrups, with one hand resting on the saddle. At the time of his visit here, the feeling against slavery was intense, and because he held slaves, it was not thought best to permit him to preach in the church, so services at which he presided were held elsewhere. He m. Mrs. Mehetable Peoples, of Shady Side, Jasper County, Ga. He d. in Decatur County, March 4, 1855. Two sons, Elliott and Benjamin.
  viii. Olive, b. Feb. 4, 1792; m. Ephraim B. Stevens, q. v.

3 MOSES,[3] (Remembrance,[2] Moses[1]) b. Newbury, Nov. 25, 1777; farmer at Bradford, on the upper plain, where he bought out his uncle Moses; m. 1st Martha, dau. Cephas and Martha Child of Woodstock, Conn., and West Fairlee. She d. 1839, and he m. 2d, Mrs. Jemima Peckett. He d. November, 1854, and she m. 3d, a Mr. Morris of Bradford.
  Children, all by 1st marriage:
5 i. John Elliott, b. Nov. 4, 1806; d. Oct. 7, 1886.
  ii. Cephas Child, b. Jan. 21, 1809; m. June 3, 1835; lived in Boston; d. there Feb. 1, 1876.
  iii. Martha E., b. April 10, 1811; m. John Y. Cross of Bradford.
  iv. Mary C., b. Aug. 9, 1813; m. Benjamin Chamberlain of Bradford.
  v. Moses Remembrance, b. April 20, 1816; farmer on homestead at Bradford; m. Sept. 24, 1840, Ruby S. Johnson. Five c.
  vi. Elizabeth A., b. Aug. 1, 1818; d. y.

JOHN ELLIOTT CHAMBERLAIN.

vii. Benjamin F., b. Dec. 21, 1821; d. un-m.
viii. Elizabeth E., b. Aug. 16, 1823; m. Jaret M. Haseltine of Newbury. Lived at Janesville, Wis., where he was at one time city treasurer.
ix. Amanda N., b. May 21, 1826; m. Henry E. Sawyer; rem. to Chicago.
x. Azubah A., b. Sept. 2, 1831; m. Lutha S. Grover; lived at White River Junction.

5 JOHN ELLIOTT,[4] (Moses,[3] Remembrance,[2] Moses[1]) b. Bradford, Nov. 4, 1806; farmer at South Newbury; member of Constitutional Convention, 1843; held most of the town offices; railroad contractor, and with Robert Morse built the White Mountain railroad from Woodsville to Littleton, and later, with Joseph A. Dodge, built the Boston, Concord and Montreal railroad extension from Littleton to Fabyan House; was also interested in other enterprises; m. March, 1831, Laura, dau. Israel Willard of Bradford, (b. Feb. 5, 1807; d. May 16, 1864). He d. Oct. 7, 1886.
Children;
6 i. George Willard, b. March 15, 1832.
7 ii. Horace Elliott, b. Nov. 30, 1834.
8 iii. Remembrance Wright, b. March 21, 1836.
iv. Leona Eveline, b. April 9, 1842; m. Nov. 9, 1865, John W. Currier of Newbury, now of North Troy. She d. April 27, 1896. One c., d. y.
v. Ella Amanda, b. Aug. 1, 1845; m. Sept., 1867 George B. Harriman of Bradford and settled there. One c., d. y. She d. June 25, 1901.
vi. Charles Wesley, b. Nov. 4, 1849; lives on homestead.

6 GEORGE WILLARD,[5] (John E.,[4] Moses,[3] Remembrance,[2] Moses[1]) b. March 15, 1832; in Boston, 1853-58, in produce commission business; in Kansas, 1858-62; farming, trade and hotel business; farmer on homestead, town and other business, 1862, till death; m. 1873, Mrs. Eliza (Woolley) Harriron, who d. 1876. One c., d. at birth. He d. April 3, 1897.

7 HORACE ELLIOTT, (brother of preceding) b. Nov. 30, 1834. Began railroad service as agent of the White Mountain railroad at Littleton, N. H., April, 1856; in 1859, was made General Freight and Ticket Agent, in addition to the local agency. When the White Mountain railroad came under the management of the Boston, Concord and Montreal railroad, he remained its agent till 1864; station agent of the Rutland and Burlington railroad at Burlington one year; General Freight Agent of that railroad, 1865, to January, 1871, when he became General Superintendent of the Concord railroad, holding that office nearly twenty years. When the Concord railroad and the Boston, Concord, and Montreal railroad were consolidated he was General Traffic Manager two years; a year later became Superintendent of the Concord Division of the Boston and Maine railroad, retiring therefrom after eight years service; m. March 3, 1880, Nellie Mary Putnam of Laconia; res. Concord, N. H.

8 REMEMBRANCE WRIGHT, b. March 21, 1836; served in Co. D, 1st Vt., three mos. men, 1861; 1st Lieutenant, Co. H, 12th Vt., 1862-3; in business Newbury Village; postmaster, 1885-91; farmer on homestead; m. March 13, 1862, Helen F. Corliss of Bradford.
Children:
i. George Elliott, b. Feb. 12, 1869; graduated Dartmouth Medical College, 1896; interne one year, in Mary Hitchcock Hospital; studied in New York; began practice at Lawrence, Mass; became acting assistant surgeon. U. S. A., 2d Division, 7th Army Corps at Havanna, Cuba; now in service in the Philippine Islands.
ii. Laura Helen, b. Jan. 7, 1877.

4 COL. MOODY,[3] (Remembrance,[2] Moses[1]) b. Sept. 12, 1787; farmer on homestead and inn-keeper; colonel in the militia; town representative 1838, 1851; member of Constitutional Convention, 1828; m. 1st, Mary, dau. Cephas and Martha Child of Woodstock, Conn., and Fairlee. She d. Aug. 8, 1838. He m. 2d, Sept. 24, 1839, Mrs. Mary B. Runnels, dau. Capt. Jacob Bayley. (b. Oct. 20, 1796; d. July 8, 1884).
Children, all by 1st marriage:
9 i. Remembrance Johnson, b. Nov. 16, 1814.
ii. Harriott, b. July 19, 1816; m. James M. Chadwick, q. v.; d. May 1, 1840.

33

iii. Moody, b. Nov. 28, 1818; lived in Mobile and Montgomery, Ala. He was
      lame and did not enter the Confederate service. When Sherman's army
      approached Montgomery he was chosen by the citizens to carry a flag of
      truce, with the surrender of the city; d. un-m. at Cairo, Ill., Jan.1, 1866.
iv.   Ezra Bartlett, b. May 9, 1821, d. y.
v.   Elizabeth Elliott, b. March 9. 1823; m. July 11, 1850, William B. Hibbard;
      settled at Elkhart, N. Y.; afterward at Chicago, where she d. March 30,
      1871. C., (1) Elizabeth, m. Walter J. Baxter; res. Clinton, Iowa. (2)
      Mary E., m. 1st, Franklyn W. Hall, 2d, Horace B. Childs. (3) Frances
      C., m. Charles A. Hoffman; res. Clinton, Iowa. One c., a, Maude S.
10 vi. Ezra B., b. June 14, 1825.
vii. Emeline Buxton. b. Feb. 4, 1828; m. Nov. 25, 1852, Harry Fox of Westfield,
      Mass., son of Hiram Fox and grandson of John Fox of Springfield, Mass.;
      settled in Chicago. He d. Sept. 4, 1883. She d. May 28, 1900. C., (1)
      Harry C., d. y. (2) Harriott A., res. Chicago Miss Fox collected all the
      records of this Chamberlain family, excepting those of the families of Asher
      and John E. Chamberlain. (3) Alice E., d. y. (4) Frederick H., res.
      Chicago. (5) Harry, d. y.
viii. Mary Child, b. Sept. 21, 1830; d. Chicago, Feb. 9, 1899.

9 REMEMBRANCE JOHNSON,[4] (Moody,[3] Remembrance,[2] Moses[1]) b. Nov. 16, 1814;
   farmer where C. C. Doe now owns; bought the old homestead where he
   lived. The house was burned, March 6, 1876. He m. Oct. 8, 1838, Olive,
   dau. David Haseltine, (b. Sept. 25, 1810; d. Dec. 9, 1881), He d. suddenly
   March 13, 1876.
   Children:
i.   Charles, b. July 14, 1840, d. y.
ii. Wright, b. Aug. 27, 1843; farmer on homestead; rem. to Davenport, Iowa;
     m. Nov. 25, 1868, Abbie F. Smith of Corinth. One dau. living.
iii. Francis, b. Feb. 4, 1845; served in the union army, afterwards four years in
     the regular army; d.
iv. Charles, b. Jan. 13, 1849; m. March 19, 1873, Lucy Smith of Corinth; res.
     Chicago. Two c.

10 EZRA BARTLETT, (brother of preceding) b. June 14, 1825; farmer at South
   Newbury, on homestead, which he sold and rem. to Newbury Village; in
   hotel and other business; m. Nov. 25, 1852, Elizabeth, dau. Harry C.
   Bailey.
   Children:
i.   Sarah Belle, b. Jan. 16, 1858; d. 1860.
ii. Harry Bailey, b. Nov. 1, 1862; salesman at Bradford; member of Co. G, V.
     N. G. of which he was captain two years; appointed upon the staff of Gov.
     Woodbury, 1894-96, with rank of Colonel; mustered into U. S. Army as
     Reg. Q. M. Sergeant; commissioned captain. and Assistant Q. M., July 16,
     1898; commissioned captain in regular army, Feb 1901; m April 6, 1892,
     Kathlyn, dau. General Gilmore of Fairlee. One c., Dorothy, b. Aug. 4, 1896.
iii. Martha Page, b. Nov. 24, 1866; graduated St. Johnsbury Academy; m.
     May 19, 1896, George C., son of Albert L. Fabyan. He was a salesman,
     who became manager of the clothing and furnishing house of Browning,
     King & Co., Minneapolis, where he d. suddenly, April 18, 1900; buried at
     Newbury. C., (1) Margaret, b. Feb. 11, 1897. (2) George Chase, b. Dec.
     29, 1900.

2 ASHER,[2] (Moses[1]) b. Litchfield, Conn., Apr. 14, 1751; settled in Bradford on the
   upper plain; town representative from Bradford, 1790; member of the
   church in Newbury, from which, in 1793. he was dismissed with bis wife to
   Thetford church; he afterward rem. to Peacham, and later to Troy, where
   he d.; revolutionary soldier; m. Olive Russell. and is understood to have
   had two sons, Wright and John. He had other c. of whom nothing is
   preserved, except the name of one, Susannah, bapt. by Rev. N. Lambert,
   (church record) May 26, 1792.
i.   Wright, settled in Stanstead, P. Q.; was twice m., and was said to have
     had twelve c., by 1st marriage, ten of whom lived to be men and women,
     of whom four are living.
11 ii. John, b. Bradford, Dec. 17, 1787.

11 JOHN[3] (Asher,[2] Moses[1]) b. Bradford, Dec. 17, 1787; studied law, and was in

practice here, according to "Walton's Register," from 1818 to 1822; later he rem. to Stanstead, P. Q.; m. March 7, 1813, Clarissa, dau. Isaac Bayley, (b. Feb. 4, 1792; d. Dec. 27, 1819); d. there, Nov. 24, 1847.

Children:

i. Clarissa, b. Aug. 26, 1813; m. (published in Haverhill, July 10, 1834), Samuel, son of Capt. Uriah Ward; d. about 1878, at Chicago, leaving two sons.

ii. John Russell, b. Sept 27, 1815; d. 1877 in Lyndonville, N. Y., leaving a wife and three daus., who are still living.

12 iii. Horatio Nelson, b. Newbury, Oct. 10, 1818; d. April 21, 1875.

12 HORATIO NELSON, b. Newbury, Oct. 10, 1818, in the house now Mrs. E. E. Miller's, formerly that of Harry C. Bailey; civil engineer; he laid out the Connecticut and Passumpsic Rivers railroad from Wells River to Newport, and the Massawippi Valley railroad. from Newport to Sherbrooke; he also laid out the village of Lyndonville, and his services were in constant demand, he being esteemed competent and faithful in his profession; m. while living in Canada, Jan. 15, 1844, Lemira Sophia, dau. Harmon Titus; res. Newbury, after 1846; d. April 21, 1875.

Children:

i. Sarah Amanda, b. St. Johns, P. Q., Dec. 25, 1844; m. Jan. 31, 1866, James Burrell Lawrie, son Andrew and Margaret (Burrell) Lawrie; (b. Dunfermline. Scotland, Sept. 27, 1828; came to America, 1848; in business in Boston till marriage; farmer on the Ox-bow). C., (1) Maggie. b. Aug. 14, 1867; graduated at Abbott Academy, Andover, Mass.; m. Sept. 16, 1896, Harry W. Hibbard, now merchant at Woodsville. (2) James Nelson, b. Sept. 22, 1882; d. Sept. 20, 1885.

ii. Clara Rebecca, b. Newbury, (W. R.) April 29, 1849; m. Sept. 20, 1877, Dr. George H. Atkinson, q. v.

iii. Albert Mott, b. March 7, 1851; res. Des Moines, Iowa; m. there, Ella Hastings. C., (1) Nelson, b. Des Moines, January, 1887.

iv. Louis Henry, b. March 15, 1861; d. June 8, 1864.

*CAMPBELL.

REV. GEORGE W., son of Alexander and Ruth (Johnson) Campbell, b. Lebanon, N. H., 1794; graduated Union College 1820; Union Theological Seminary 1823; ordained Nov. 17, 1824; pastor 1st Ch. Newbury; installed Jan. 27, 1836; discharged July 9, 1850. He was regarded as a superior preacher. His sermons were models of clearness and precision. Several of his sermons and addresses were printed. In the ministry till 1866; d. Bradford, Mass., Feb. 2. 1869. He m. Feb. 2, 1830, Serena J. William, of Kennebunk, Me. They had five dau., two of whom at least, d. un-m., and another m. Mr. George Peabody Russell, nephew and namesake of George Peabody, the banker and philanthropist, and res. at the Isle of Wight, England. Another dau. d. in Europe.

CHAPMAN.

Jonah and Molly (Blaisdell) Chapman were among the first settlers in the Grow neighborhood. where they built first a log house, and then a framed one still standing, but now unoccupied, and believed to be over 100 years old.

JONAH CHAPMAN. d. July 13, 1831, in his 83d year, and his wife Nov. 20, 1820, aged 68. The records of the 1st Ch. give the following baptism of their c.: Oct. 29, 1791, Polly, Esther, Lydia. Nathaniel, Blaisdell, Samuel and Abigail; March 18, 1793, John; Sept. 21, 1796, Stephen and Josiah.

JOHN CHAPMAN, b. May 13, 1792; was a harness maker at East Corinth, and began there, while, yet a young man, the construction of a house which he intended should be the finest in Orange County. It was modelled, it is said, after a mansion which he had seen in Philadelphia. It contained over 100,000 brick, and large quantities of hewn stone, many of which were

---

*Received too late for insertion in the proper place.

brought from the "Catamount," in Haverhill. Upon this house he spent
the savings of a life time, in all over $15,000 and old age found the
mansion still unfinished, only one or two rooms being habitable. John
Chapman's last years were spent with his brother in Fairlee, and the
house, sold for a small fraction of its cost, was finished, and made into a
hotel called the "Saginaw House," which, some 25 years after the
builder left it, was burned June 12, 1899.   The memorial library, now
being erected by the Blake family, stands on the site of "Chapman's
Folly," much of the material being used in its construction. John
Chapman never m.

STEPHEN, b. Oct. 22, 1793 ; settled in Fairlee, where he was town representative.
He m. a Miss Ordway, sister of Mrs. John Fulton ; no c.

BLAISDELL, who m. Lizzie Dickey, and is a well-known farmer in the Grow
neighborhood, and Wilson Chapman, of East Corinth, who m. a dau. of
William Grant, are sons of Samuel Chapman.   The loss of early records has
prevented a more complete account of the Chapman family.

CHENEY.

James Davis, and Harrison, sons of Ezekiel and Betsey (Atwood) Cheney, came
here while young from Hampstead, N. H., and settled as farmers in this
town.

I. JAMES DAVIS, b. April 14, 1821 ; lived with Samuel Eastman many years ;
later owned the farm in the Doe neighborhood called the "Jacob Brock
place." He m. 1st, Lois, dau. James McKindley, who d. Nov. 20, 1869,
aged 41. 2d, Miss Hodges. He d. March 13, 1896.
Children :
i. John, who d. at the age of 13.

II. HARRISON, b. June 18, 1822 ; farmer at West Newbury, where Harry B. Hoyt
lives ; m. 1st, Sarah Ann Dearborn, who d. leaving one dau., who d. at the
age of 7 ; m. 2d, 1868, Mary, dau. John Allen.   He was a member of the
Methodist church and a worthy man. He d. Nov. 27, 1894.

CLARK.

JOHN, is said to have come from England to America, and to Newbury from
Bridgewater, N. H., with his wife and four c.   There were others who
never lived here. He d. February, 1804, and his wife in July of the same
year.
Children :
1   i. Timothy, b. 1766 ; d. 1855.
2 ii. Moses P., b. 1777 ; d. 1856.
3 iii. Choate.
iv. Lucretia, m. Hardy Chamberlin, q. v.

1 Timothy, b. 1766. He lived in the family of Gen. Jacob Bayley, from the time he
was ten years old, till he was twenty-one, when he received a deed to a lot
of land, on which he settled, but the title proving defective, he was obliged
to give it up. It is the farm now owned by R. S. Chamberlain, near the
Centre. Later he lived about a half mile east of the town farm. Buildings
all gone ; m. 1st, Betsey Ladd of Haverhill. She d. Aug. 3, 1822, aged 53.
(Dates of birth from town record) ; m. 2d, Mrs. Martha A. Whitman
Gerould, and had one son. He d. 1855.
Children, eleven by 1st, and one by 2nd marriage :
i. David, b. Jan. 17, 1789 ; raftsman, lost his life on the river.
ii. Susannah, b. Oct. 16, 1791 ; m. James Chamberlin of Wells River.
iii. Polly, b. Aug. 9, 1793 ; d. Jan. 15, 1875.
iv. Lucretia, b. Aug. 10, 1795 ; m. John Messer.
v. Hannah, b. Feb. 9, 1798 ; m. Aug. 8, 1818, Zenas Holmes of Lebanon, N. H.
vi. Betsey, b. Nov. 9, 1800 ; m. Moses Goodwin, q. v.
vii. Timothy, b. July 20, 1803.
viii. Sally, b. Jan. 20, 1806.

ix. Lavinia, b. June 6, 1808.
4 x. Hiram, b. April 11, 1811, q. v.
xi. Lucy, b. May 4, 1813; m. Isaac Bedel of Bath, who was killed while working on the White Mountain railroad.
5 xii. Edward J. L , b. Aug. 28, 1825, q. v.

5 EDWARD J. L., b. Aug. 28, 1825; served during the rebellion in Co. B, 16th N. H.; enlisted Sept. 2, 1862; mustered out Aug. 13, 1863; farmer; m. 1st, Lucinda Pixley, who d. Sept. 21, 1856, aged twenty-seven; m. 2d, Lavinia McLean, who d. Nov. 12, 1872; m. 3d, July 15, 1873, Harriet S., dau. of John Corliss.
Children, all b. in Newbury, three by first and two by second marriage:
i. William, b. March 14, 1846. Served in the Union army and d. 1863, aged 17.
ii. Isaac, b. Jan. 11, 1849. Served in the army, enlisting in December, 1863, in his 15th year. Photographer several years at Worcester, Mass. Rem. to West Newbury, farmer, twice m.
iii. Lucy L., b. Nov. 21, 1853; m. Frederic Siebert of New Haven, Conn. C., (adopted), Florence G., also the youngest child of her deceased sister, Nellie.
iv. Harry A., b. March 2, 1859; m. Nellie, dau. of John Evans.
v. Nellie R., b. June 18, 1861; m. at Thetford, Dec. 22, 1888, Charles Turcott; d. Thetford, June 22, 1892. C., (1) Ethel Lucy, b. Nov. 22, 1889. (2) Margaret Ellen, b. Sept. 18, 1871, both in Thetford.

3 CHOATE, 3d son of John, b. Aug. 5, 1771; m. 1st, Hannah Willis of Norwich, who d. Jan. 17, 1807; m. 2d a Mrs. Kenniston, and 3d, Nov. 4, 1819, Susan Cochrane of Bradford, (b. May 12, 1782; d. Oct. 18, 1862). He lived many years where his grandson, Joel C. Temple, now lives. He d. Sept. 11, 1847.
Children, by first marriage:
6 i. Moses. b. Oct. 8, 1796.
ii. Mary (Polly), b. Nov. 9, 1798; m. Rev. John Hatch of Groton.
iii. Hannah, b. July 10, 1804. Her mother d. when she was three years old, and she was brought up by Mr. and Mrs. Rasmus Jonson. She m. Joel Temple; d. January 21, 1851.

6 MOSES, b. Oct. 8, 1796; m. Anna Kincaid of Peacham, (b. Oct. 17, 1797; d. Jan. 6, 1883). He d. Feb. 5, 1876.
Children:
i. Isaac, b. Feb. 19, 1819; d. March, 1843; m. Ann Chapman of Haverhill, who after his death m. Charles Bailey.
7 ii. Moses, b. May 7, 1821.
iii. Susan, b. Jan. 28, 1825; m. Simeon F. Ellenwood of Charlestown, N. H. He is not living. She res. Charlestown.
iv. Mary, b. Oct. 8, 1827; m. Thos. Britton of Boston, Mass.
v. Elizabeth, b. July 12, 1831; m. J. M. Goodwin. q. v.
vi. Nancy, b. March 19, 1835; m. William Morrill of Ryegate and d. there.
vii. Martha, b. Oct. 5, 1837; m. Hiram Ellenwood of Charlestown, N. H.
viii. Fred Ezra, b. Nov. 8, 1842. Served three months in Co. D, 1st Vt., 1861. In 2d Co. Sharpshooters Dec. 31, 1861, to Dec. 4, 1862. 1st Vt. Battery, Dec. 3, 1863. Transferred to 2d Vt. Battery, Feb. 13, 1865. Res. St. Johnsbury. Merchant. He m. 1st. June 14, 1865, Sarah E. Page of Ryegate. She d. July 20, 1894. He m. 2d, May 28, 1895, Mrs. Eva E. Moore. C., (by 1st marriage), (1) Fred D., b. Feb. 21, 1868. (2) Charles E., b. July 22, 1872. (3) Mabel, b. Jan. 18, 1879; d. in infancy.

7 MOSES, Jr., b. May 7, 1821; res. Newbury; m. Feb. 29, 1848, Martha P., dau. of Moses and Abigail (Banfield) Rowell, (b. Bath, Dec. 26, 1827).
Children:
i. Charles Britton, b. May 23, 1849; d. May 26, 1871.
ii. Henry K., b. July 24, 1851; res. Walla Walla, Washington. Farmer.
iii. George B., b. Oct. 17, 1853; res. Walla Walla.
iv. Clarence H., b. June 22, 1855; studied medicine with Dr. Watkins; grad. Dartmouth Medical College, 1878. Employed in hospital at Montreal, attending lectures. In practice at Haverhill 1879. Went to Colorado; d. March 14, 1882, of consumption at home.

    v. Annie, b. Oct. 11, 1857; teacher; m. Nov. 27, 1883, Ned G. English, now merchant at Lisbon. N. H. C., Harold, b. June 16, 1887.
    vi. Willard Parker, b. Oct. 11, 1859; res. Walla Walla, Washington; farmer; m. Gertrude Lyle. C., Harvey E., b. June 10, 1894.
    vii. Ezra, b. Aug. 27, 1861; res. Seattle, Washington; hotel clerk.
    viii. Simeon Ellenwood, b. Feb. 27, 1863. Clerk for F. Deming at Wells River. Admitted partner under the firm name of Deming & Clark, 1899. He m. Oct. 20, 1892, Clara, dau. John Bailey. C., Wendell Bailey, b. Nov. 7, 1899.
    ix. Mary A., b. Nov. 15, 1867; m. Oct. 12, 1898, Harvey Lee, of Lisbon.
    x. Mattie, b. March 21, 1870; d. Feb. 21, 1872.
    xi. Harvey A., b. May 19, 1872; res. Bellows Falls; hotel clerk. He m. Oct. 19, 1895, Alice M. Farr.

2 MOSES P.,[2] (John,[1]) b. 1777. Came to Newbury with his parents, was never at college, but obtained some education, and taught extensively, being known as "Master Clark." He studied theology with Rev. Ethan Smith of Haverhill. He was ordained to the Congregational ministry, and preached in Wolcott for some time, and at intervals in other places. He organized the first Sunday School in Orange County. Town Clerk. He m. 1st, June 3, 1802, Lydia Haseltine, of Haverhill, who d. April 18, 1826. He m. 2d, Nov. 26, 1828, Betsey Stevens. He d. Sept. 12, 1856, while riding in his wagon near Friend Chamberlin's, living at that time in what was called the Powers neighborhood.
  Children, the last two by 2d marriage:
    i. Nehemiah Lovewell, b. May 25, 1803; m. Oct. 11, 1825, Sarah, dau. of Robert McAllister. Lived at Manchester, N. H., and d. there.
    ii. Abigail Boyce, b. Aug. 11, 1805; m. March 7, 1826, Erastus Hunt of Danville, who d. May 26, 1829. She lived in Newbury, but d. at Manchester, N. H., Jan. 26, 1876.
    iii. Betsey Lovewell, b. April 26, 1808; d. Aug. 12, 1854.
    iv. Mary Taplin. b. Jan. 20, 1811; d. April, 1811.
    v. Susanna Sinclair, b. March 6, 1812; m. Jan. 11, 1837, Archibald McAllister, q. v.; d. Jan. 31, 1876.
    vi. Mary Tenney, b. May 21, 1814; d. June 14, 1822.
    vii. Moses Ben Porter, b. Feb. 14, 1819; d. April 20, 1823.
    viii. Jonathan Stevens, b. Dec. 3, 1829.
    ix. Moses Hobart, b. Oct. 14, 1831. Res. in Wolcott.

4 HIRAM, b. Newbury, Aug. 4, 1811; farmer of Newbury and Topsham after 1856; peddler for many years; in younger days was a river man. He m. 1st, June 27, 1831, Affa, dau. of Ebenezer Temple, who d. Jan. 10, 1855; m. 2d, Barbara Batchelder, who d. June 15, 1890; 3d, Mrs. Chamberlin. He d. at Monroe, N. H., Feb. 12, 1897.
  Children:
    i. Alvira, (dead.)
    ii. Lorenzo, (dead.)
    iii. Betsey, (Mrs. R. C. Blodgett of Monroe, N. H.)
    iv. Jane W., (Mrs. Ora Kittredge of Walden.)
    v. Joel T., b. 1838; m. June 16, 1870, Clara Dickey of Topsham and has one dau., Hattie. Res. Manchester, N. H.

*CLARK.

Jonas, b. Dummerston, 1781. He was of English descent. His father, a wealthy citizen of Dummerston, represented that town in the legislature which met at Newbury in 1801. Jonas, Jr., came to Topsham, among the first settlers, but soon rem. to a farm in Newbury, adjoining Topsham line near Currier hill, which, in those early days, was a hamlet of a few houses, with a store and a tavern. He was a man of prominence in town affairs, and long Justice of the Peace, was known as Esq. Clark. He m. Betsey Florida, who d. Dec. 30, 1851, aged 69 years. He d. Dec. 22, 1866.

*By Miss Carrie Clark.

Children:
i. Infant.
ii. Eliza, m. Michael Stevens of Corinth, and their c. were, (1) Helen. (2) Augusta. (3) Daniel, (deacon). (4) Jonas and (5) Edson, who had the home farm, and have dealt in fine stock. (6) Oscar, a dentist at Bradford.
iii. Jonas W., educated at Peacham Academy; m. Sarah A. Corliss and settled at East Corinth; was a business man, holding many public offices. Two c., Byron, who d. in infancy, and George M., in early manhood.
iv. John F., attended Bradford Academy; m. Abigail, dau. of Robert Fulton, and settled on what was before called the Andross place, in the southwest part of the town. but near the end of his life rem. to an adjoining farm. Mrs. Clark d. April 16, 1900. C., (1) Carrie A., fitted for college at Peacham Academy, and attended Oberlin College. Engaged in teaching, literary work, and the sale of subscription books. (2) Robert Jonas, educated at Newbury Seminary and Peacham Academy. In business at East Corinth. He m, Lizzie, dau. of Rev. E. W. Hatch. C., Marguerite Frances.
v. Catherine, m. Feb. 13, 1845, Orrin Heath. They settled on her father's farm, where he d. July 24, 1888, aged 72 years, 3 months, 18 days, and she d. May 26, 1889, aged 77 years, 5 months, Three sons, (1) Hannibal H., and (2) Thomas B., own the John F. Clark place, and (3) Joel Clark Heath owned the home farm. These brothers own several hundred acres of land and are successful farmers. None of them are m.
vi. Joel, settled in Chelsea, and d. May 11, 1858, aged 42 years, 3 months.
vii. Caroline, d. May 11, 1844, aged 23 years, 11 months.

> "Adieu, dear Caroline, Adieu,
> Till the last trumpet sound;
> We hope to mingle joys with you,
> And stand on holy ground."
> EPITAPH.

COBLEIGH.

EDWIN REUBEN, b. St. Johnsbury, Dec. 25, 1830. Two years at Wesleyan University, and began the practice of law in St. Johnsbury. He m. July 4, 1852, Jane, dau. of George W. Leslie, of Newbury. He d. at St. Johnsbury, Sept. 9, 1857.
Children:
i. Herbert Eugene, b. St. Johnsbury, July 20, 1854. Was employed by the Keyes family for about 30 years. Res. Newbury; m. May 24, 1881, Rhuamah B., dau. of Alvah C. James. He d. Feb. 12, 1901.
Children:
i. Alvah Edwin, b. Feb 19, 1890.
ii. George Leslie, b. Oct. 4, 1897.

COBURN.

ASA, b. 1755. Came to Newbury after the revolutionary war, in which he served. His wife, Charlotte Page, was b. Nov. 30, 1760; d. May 28, 1852. He was known as Captain Coburn, and carried on Josiah Little's farm many years. He d. Dec. 2, 1841.

ASA, JR., b. Pelham, N. H., March 2, 1787, Farmer of Newbury. He m. 1st, Nov. 11, 1809, Sally Page, (b. Nov. 3, 1790; d. Thetford, Nov. 21, 1827). m. 2d, June 22, 1831, Hannah Taylor, (b. May 14, 1798; d. March 12, 1871). He d. Nov. 4, 1853.
Children, eight by 1st and four by 2d marriage.
i. Esther b. Aug. 4, 1810; m. March 6, 1833. John R. Dowse, q. v.; d. June 30, 1878.
ii. Charlotte, b. Feb. 7, 1813; m. March, 1833, James Webster, q. v.; d. April, 1900.
iii. Almira, b. Dec. 15, 1814; m. Cyril Emerson of Thetford, June, 1858.
iv. Harriet, b. Jan. 28, 1816; d. December, 1828.
v. Calvin P., b. May 6, 1818; m. May, 1853, Rachel Farrand. Farmer of Newbury. Rem. to Maine.

vi. George M., b. Feb. 14, 1820; m. September. 1858, Joanna Coburn; d. March 1, 1864.
vii. Sarah Ann, b. Feb. 6, 1822; m. May 26, 1843, Joseph L. Clark, (b. Topsham Feb. 24, 1817; d. Hyde Park, Mass., April 20, 1900). She d. Aug. 23, 1886. C., Arthur and M. Bell. both b. in Newbury.
viii. Daniel N., b. June 24, 1824; d. April 5, 1843.
ix. Charles T., b. May 8, 1832.
x. Manly, b. Aug. 26, 1833; m. November, 1834, Abigail Hadley. Res. Fitchburg, Mass. Cabinet maker. She d. April 25, 1882.
xi. Frances, b. Dec. 5, 1835; m. Jan. 1858, Harvey H. Caldwell, of Thetford.
xii. Emmeline, b. Newbury, Feb. 15, 1838; d. Oct. 2, 1853.

*COCHRANE.

John Cochrane and Lilly Kilgore, his wife, were b. and bred in the parish of Glendorment, in the north of Ireland, where they were members of the Presbyterian church. They came to America in 1718, and settled in Brunswick, Maine, upon the present site of Bowdoin College. They left that place for fear of the Indians, and settled among their countrymen in Londonderry, N. H. Of their 13 c , Samuel was the youngest, b. Londonderry, October, 1729; m. in Nottingham, N. H., Feb. 12, 1767, Agnes McCrillis.
Children, all b. in Londonderry.
i. Margaret, b. June 28, 1768; m. Samuel Cochrane of Londonderry; d. Nov. 26, 1853.
ii. Mary Ann, b. Nov. 26, 1769; m. Hugh Wilson of Windham.
1 iii. John, b. June 12, 1761.
iv. Isaac, b. May 9, 1773; d. 1792.
v. Elizabeth, b. March 6, 1775; m. Samuel Wilson of Londonderry.
vi. Andrew, b. Nov. 22, 1776. Settled in Albany, N. Y.
2 vii. William, b. Sept. 29, 1778.
viii. Agnes. b. June 2, 1780; un-m. ; d. 1839.
ix. Susanna, b. May 12, 1782; m. Choate Clark of Newbury; d. Oct. 18, 1862.
x. Sarah, b. April 11, 1784; m. Ashbell Buell of Newbury; d. March 30, 1861.

1 John, b. Londonderry, N. H., June 12, 1771; m. Feb. 14, 1799, Agnes Wilson, (b. Londonderry, June 1, 1771; d. Newbury, March 22, 1847.) They came to Bradford in 1802, and to Newbury, 1812, settling on the northern slope of Wright's Mountain. He d. at Craftsbury, March 1, 1857. Buried in Bradford.
Children:
i. Isaac, b. Londonderry, Oct. 21, 1799; m. Oct. 30, 1824, Anna McKeen; d. Newport, Oct. 8, 1884. Six c.
ii. James W., b. Londonderry, Feb. 26, 1801; m. at Newbury, Dec. 2, 1824, Permelia Moore. Lived at Alexandria, N. Y. Five c.
iii. Samuel, b. Bradford, Dec. 13, 1802; d. 1804.
iv. Nancy, b. June 12, 1804; m. June 29, 1834, John Wilson of Bradford; d. Bradford; d. June 10, 1885. C., (1) Mary W., b. July 2, 1835. (2) Byron B., b. Nov. 18, 1836. Killed in the civil war. (3) Persis A., b. June 17, 1838; m. Bailey Avery of Newbury. (4) John D., b. May 6, 1842, in Minnesota. (5) Boyd H., b. Sept. 24, 1849. Farmer on homestead.
v. William K., b. Bradford, April 10, 1806; m. Nov. 15, 1831, Lydia Swasey of Salem, Mass.; d. Manchester, N. H. C , (1) Ellen, b. Newbury, Nov. 17, 1832. (2) William Henry, b. Chelmsford, Mass., Dec. 29, 1837. Served in the Union army. Prominent in political circles of New Hampshire. Pension Commissioner for New Hampshire and Vermont several years. Res. Nashua, N. H.
vi. Eleanor H., b. Bradford, Jan. 11, 1808; m. 1st, as third wife, Feb. 24, 1846, Simeon Avery, q. v. 2d, Josiah Knight and rem. to Charles City, Iowa. After the death of Mr. Knight, she returned to Newbury, where she still lives, the oldest person in town.
vii. Louisa J., b. May 23, 1810; d. Sept. 30, 1811.

*From manuscript prepared by A. C. Buell.

viii. John H. McC., b. Newbury, Oct. 8, 1808; settled in Craftsbury; d. Aug. 18, 1885.

ix. Andrew J., b. Newbury, Dec. 22, 1814; m. Olive Stewart; d. Penville, Mo.

2 WILLIAM, b. Sept. 29, 1778; m. in Londonderry, June, 1807, Elizabeth Wilson. They came to Bradford, 1808; to Newbury, 1813, and, in 1823, rem. to Saranac, N. Y., where he d. May 8, 1851. She d. Nov. 18, 1842.

Children:
i. Almanda B., b. Dec. 10, 1807; d. Sept. 11, 1811.
ii. Eliza Jean, b. Bradford; d. y.
iii. Samuel W., b. Bradford, June 30, 1812; d. Feb. 11, 1847.
iv. Elizabeth H., b. Newbury, Dec. 8, 1814.
v. Ira A., b. Newbury, Jan. 25, 1817.
vi. Stephen C., b. Newbury, Nov. 20, 1818.
vii. Anna H., b. Newbury, March 19, 1821.
viii. Roxanna S., b. Saranac, Nov. 11, 1824.
ix. Hepzibah R., b. Saranac, April 19, 1827.
x. Edith P., b. Saranac, July 18; d. Aug. 15, 1829.

COLBURN.

ELLIS, a native of Shrewsbury, m. Lucy, dau. of Hezekiah Wetherbee, her mother being a sister of Joshua Hale. He came to Newbury from Plymouth in March, 1843, and bought the farm of Josiah Quint near Boltonville, and d. there Dec. 12, 1855. His wife was b. in Grafton, Dec. 12, 1897, and d. at Walpole, Mass., Feb. 1, 1879. Their farm was sold to Leander Quint about 1863.

Children:
i. Elizabeth, b. Shrewsbury, Aug. 7, 1822; m. Granville C. Meader of Ryegate, who d. May 20, 1900, aged 78. They lived in Newbury a few years. C., (1) Julius, b. Ryegate, July 15, 1847; d. April, 1850. (2) Charlotte C., b. May 9, 1849; d. Jan. 4, 1851. (3) Lewis H., b. Ryegate, April 27, 1851. Graduated Dartmouth College, 1878. Principal of Academy Avenue Grammar School, Providence, R. I. He m. Mary G. Divall of Warren, R. I. Four c. (4) Percy, b. Newbury, April 7, 1853; res. Montgomery, Ala.; m. Jennie Stevens of Eugene, Ind.; bridge builder. (5) Lucy H., b. Newbury, April 1, 1855; m. 1st, Edgar P. McAllister. 2d, William B. McMurray, and lives in Montgomery, Ala. Is now a widow. One dau. Edna. (6) Lois E., b. Sept. 29, 1857; d. May 7, 1859. (7) Granville E., b. Dec. 16, 1859. (8) Lois E., b. May 7, 1861; d. May 22, 1863.
ii. Charlotte b. Dec. 21, 1823. Studied with Prof. and Mrs. Robert Wright of Boston and attended the normal school at West Newton, Mass., but d. Nov. 17, 1848, before graduating. Buried in Newbury.
iii. Julius, b. June 1, 1825; d. Dec. 21, 1832.
iv. Emily, b. May 21, 1827; graduated Newbury Seminary; teacher; m. Jan. 3, 1860, Rev. Samuel L. Eastman, q. v.; d. Erie, Mich , Aug. 5, 1862.
v. Dwight, b. Jan. 22, 1829; d. July 9, 1832.
vi. Everett, b. Nov. 26, 1830; went to Kansas, 1856; served during the war from Aug. 1862, in Co. G., 11th Kansas; deacon in the Baptist church at Manhattan, and the last of the original members. He m. June 22, 1865, Eliza A. Parish, who d. 1884, leaving one son, Edgar B. He d. at Manhattan, Kan., Sept. 10, 1874.
vii. Hepzibah A., b. Nov. 16, 1832; m. March 28, 1857, William Southard Johnson of Bath. C., (1) Martha C., b. Bath, May 21, 1858; m. 1st, G. F. Wilson, who d. in 1888, leaving one dau., Mary A., b. July 14, 1878, who m. October, 1899, Arthur W. Crosby of Manchester, N. H. (2) Willard J., b. July 13, 1859; res. Wells River. (3) Mary C., b. Newbury, Sept. 3, 1861; m. Dec. 31, 1887, Arthur J. Nutting of Manchester, N. H. C., Genevieve, b. Jan. 18, 1889.
viii. Cynthia, b. Oct. 23, 1834; teacher in Kansas before the civil war and later in Newbury; res. South Ryegate.
ix. Edgar, b. March 9, 1836; d. Nov. 8, 1866, at Soldiers' Home, Boston, from disease contracted in the army.

x. Ellen A., b. March 17, 1839; res. South Ryegate.
xi. May C., b. June 21, 1841; res. Boston, Mass.

CORLISS.

I. All the Corliss families in this region, and many bearing other names are descended from George Corliss, who is first mentioned in Haverhill, Mass., as having married Joanna Davis, Oct. 26, 1645. the second marriage in that town. The line of ancestry is from the "Corliss Genealogy."

II. JOHN, b. March 4, 1648; m. Mary Wilford; farmer and soldier in Queen Anne's war; d. Feb. 16, 1698.

III. JOHN, b. 1668; m. Ruth Haynes of Haverhill, Mass., where they lived. He d. 1766.

IV. TIMOTHY, b. 1717; farmer of Haverhill, Mass., and Norwich, Conn.; m. Ann Willoughby of the latter place and had sons, Timothy, Samuel and Bliss, who were ancestors of nearly all the large Corliss families of Corinth and Topsham, in which the Christian names of Willoughby, Samuel, Timothy, Jonathan and Bliss continually recur. He d. 1760.

V. SAMUEL, b. 1748; m. Sept. 8, 1774, Hannah Silver of Haverhill, Mass., (b. 1750; d. 1843). Farmer of Haverhill, Mass., and Corinth.
     They had several children:
1   Willoughby, b. Nov. 8, 1775; d. Jan. 25, 1830.
     Daniel, b. April 5, 1777.
2   Jonathan, b. June 6, 1782.
     And other sons and daughters.

1   WILLOUGHBY, b. Nov. 8, 1775; m. Martha, dau. Benjamin Chamberlin of Newbury, (b. Nov. 8, 1774). Inn keeper at East Corinth, at the "Old Parade Ground." He d. Jan. 25, 1830.
     They had seven children:
     i. David, b. March 21, 1799; d. Aug. 1, 1821.
     ii. Hiram, b. Oct. 19, 1800; d. Nov. 27, 1823.
     iii. Hannah, d. y.
     iv. Samuel, b. April 7. 1805; d. Nov. 18, 1872.
     v. Bryan, b. Aug. 17, 1807; d. Nov. 30, 1870.
     vi. Polly, b. March 24, 1816; m. Guy Corliss of Newbury.
     vii. John B., b. Jan. 18, 1819; d. Aug. 19, 1857.

2   JONATHAN, b. June 6, 1782; m. Dec. 25, 1803, Polly Taplin. Thirteen c., most of whom settled in Bradford, Corinth, Topsham and Newbury. Their fourth son and child, Guy C., was b. April 14, 1811.

    GUY C., b. April 14, 1811; m. Dec. 11, 1836, Polly, dau. of Willoughby Corliss, (b. Mar. 24, 1816.) They came to Newbury in 1839, and settled on the "Tarrant Putnam place," living in their house 53 years. spending but one night of all that time from under their own roof. He d. May 7, 1892. She d. May 14, 1901.
     Children:
     i. Eliza Marilla, b June 22, 1839; teacher; d. Sept. 28, 1881.
     ii. Hiram, b. Jan. 13, 1841; d. April 7, 1842.
     iii. Emily M., b. Nov. 17, 1842; d. Dec. 11, 1862.
     iv. Charles J., b. Nov. 13, 1844; farmer on homestead, and cattle buyer.
     v. Jane H., b. June 28, 1849; res. Newbury.
     vi. Helen S., b. June 15, 1852; d. Nov. 18, 1872.
     vii. Evelyn, b. Oct. 9, 1859; d. Dec. 17, 1881.

CORLISS.

A second Corliss family is descended from George (i.) through John (ii.) John (iii.) and Jonathan, (iv.) brother of Timothy, b. Feb. 25, 1730; m. March, 1749, Lydia Emerson, (b. April 13, 1731; d. May 16, 1799). Farmer of Haverhill, Mass., and Salem, N. H. .Revolutionary soldier. He d. 1776.
     Children:
1   Samuel, b. July 27, 1752, q. v.

2   Emerson, b. March 27, 1758, q. v.
     And perhaps others.

1 SAMUEL,[1] b. Haverhill, Mass., July 27, 1752. Served in the revolutionary war. Lived in Salem, N. H., and Rockingham. Came to Newbury about 1817, but d. in Marshfield. His wife is understood to have been Jane Jennison.
     Children:
3   i.   Thomas, b. October, 1783, q. v.
    ii. Silas, lived some years in Newbury, but rem. to Watertown, N. Y.
4 iii. John, b. Sept. 18, 1787, q. v.
    iv. David, lived some years in Newbury, but rem. to Alstead, N. H.
     v. Polly, d. un-m.
    vi. Abigail, m. Solomon Jewell, q. v.
   vii. Nancy, d. un-m.

2 EMERSON, son of Jonathan and Lydia (Emerson) Corliss, and brother of Samuel, b. Haverhill, Mass., March 27, 1758. Served in the battle of Bunker Hill, the expedition to Canada, the battles of Trenton, Princeton and Bennington, and was captain of a company of reserves in the war of 1812. Settled in Bradford, where he d. December, 1843. He m. Mehetabel Mitchell of Haverhill, Mass., and they had sons, Jonathan, Jacob and George. Mrs. R. W. Chamberlain of Newbury, and Mrs. P. S. Chamberlin of Bradford are daughters of George Corliss.

3 THOMAS,[2] (Samuel,[1]) b. Rockingham, October, 1783; came to Newbury about 1817; lived in a log house where Isaac Clark's house now is, and later, built a large house with a brick basement, which stood a little south of Frank Putnam's house in the "Brock neighborhood." This house was taken down in 1882. He served in the war of 1812, in Capt. Rogers' Co., of Fifield's Regiment, detached militia. He m. in Bradford, Feb. 11, 1811, Charlotte, dau. Dr. Frederick Aubrey, (b. Germany, June 17, 1775; d. Newbury, April 7, 1868). He d. at Newbury March 14, 1857.
     Children:
5   i.   Thomas, b. Nov. 20, 1811.
    ii. Louisa C., b. April 2, 1813.
   iii. Frederic, b. May 13, 1815; d. Aug. 12, 1818.
    iv. Atalanta, b. Aug. 28, 1817; d. Oct. 1, 1837.
     v. Philaura B., b. Aug. 30, 1818; m. 1st, John Smith, 2nd, Daniel Lord, and 3d, H. N. Stebbins; d. May 21, 1896.
6   vi. Rinaldo, b. May 2, 1819.
7 vii. Samuel, b. Dec. 15, 1822.
  viii. Albert, b. May 1, 1823.
    ix. Lucetta, b. Aug.4,1829; m. Philip Wright.
     x. Ariel, b. Jan. 4, 1832.
    xi. Florilla, b. March 21, 1834; m. 1st, Nov. 30, 1853, John C. Wright of Topsham; m. 2d, Alvah C. Wright; m. 3d, William J. Rodgers of Shasta, Cal.

4 JOHN,[2] (Samuel,[1]) b. Rockingham, Sept. 18, 1787; came to Newbury about 1808, with his brothers, Silas and David; began to clear his farm about 1810, and built the house where his dau., Mrs. Clark, lives, in 1815 or 1816; served two months and 22 days in Rogers' Co., Fifield's Regiment, war of 1812; discharged for sickness; drew a pension of $8 per month; member of the "Christian" church, Bradford. He m. 1st, April 11, 1812, Mary, dau. of Josiah Eastman, of Bradford, (b. July 25, 1790; d. July 21, 1829); m 2d, Judith Eastman, sister of above, (b. Dec. 8, 1799; d. July 16, 1872). He d. March 9, 1875.
     Children:
    i.   Susan, b. Oct. 31, 1814; m. David Eastman, q. v.
8   ii. Nathan E., b. March 31 1817.
   iii. Mary H , b. Feb. 3, 1831; m. April 18, 1854, Ezra B. Knapp, of Haverhill, (b. Haverhill, Feb. 11, 1827; d. Marysville, Cal., Oct. 6, 1888). She rem. to California in 1882, and d. at Gold River, Cal., Dec. 2, 1898. C., (1) John C., b. Haverhill, March 31, 1855. Went to California, 1876. Twice m. Res. Blue Canyon, Cal. Railroad engineer. (2) James, b. Newbury, Feb. 6, 1858; d. Haverhill, Nov. 3, 1859. (3) James B., b. Haverhill, Sept.

29, 1859; in California since 1880; m. Jan. 21, 1888, Rosa M. Browne.
One c. Res. Blue Canyon, Cal. Telegraph operator and station agent.
(4) E. Elmer, b. Haverhill, March 31, 1861; d. Blue Canyon, Cal., Dec. 4,
1881, un-m. (5) Fanny E., b. Haverhill, Jan. 27, 1863; teacher; m. at
San Francisco, Cal., March 24, 1883, Frank C. Hood, M. D., a native of
Newbury or Topsham. Two c.
iv. Harriet Sarah, b. July 16, 1835; m. as third wife, July 15, 1873, Edward
J. L. Clark. Lives on homestead.

5 THOMAS,[3] (Thomas,[2] Samuel,[1]) b. Newbury, Nov. 20, 1811; carpenter and
lumber man; owned and carried on a saw mill near Hall's Pond; m. Dec.
6, 1849, Martha D., dau. William Lindsey, (b. March 15, 1825). He d.
Oct. 29, 1897.
Children:
i. Elizabeth B., b. Feb. 10, 1853; m. Washington Patterson, q. v.
ii. Freeman L., b. May 28, 1858; carpenter and builder, Grand Forks, N. D.;
m. Jan. 19, 1898, Libbie Brown of East Grand Forks.
iii. William L., b. Oct. 11, 1862; carpenter in Michigan, Dakota and
Washington; res. Newbury; un-m.

6 RINALDO,[3] (Thomas,[2] Samuel,[1]) b. May 2, 1819; farmer of Newbury and
Piermont; m. Jan. 11, 1849, Helen M., dau. of Jonathan Martin of
Bradford, b. April 5, 1833. He d. Piermont, April 20, 1894.
Children:
i. Jonathan M., b. Oct. 16, 1849; m. 1891, Boston, Mass., May Ramsdell.
ii. Thomas A., b. Nov. 22, 1853; d. June 19, 1854.
iii. Edson S., b. March 16, 1856; m. Oct. 6, 1877, Eva, dau. Walter Buchanan;
res. Rutland. C. (1) George B., b. Newbury, April 12, 1878. (2) Charles
F., b. Piermont, March 13, 1880.
iv. Hiram, b. Nov. 28, 1860; d. April 21, 1864.
v. Silas N., b. April 25, 1868; m. 1888, Agnes M. Campbell of Piermont,
where they res.

7 SAMUEL,[3] (Thomas,[2] Samuel,[1]) b. Dec. 15, 1822; m. 1st, Aug. 16, 1862, Mrs.
Mary Otis, dau. Samuel Rollins, (b. Dec. 13, 1824; d. Sept. 15, 1881);
m. 2d, Mrs. Mitchell, 1888. He d. May 26, 1892.
Children:
i. Nelson, b Sept. 24, 1863; d. May 27, 1864.
ii. Herbert, b. May 16, 1865; d. Aug. 31, 1884.
iii. George Edward, b. Sept. 22, 1866.

8 NATHAN E.,[3] (John,[2] Samuel,[1]) b. March 31, 1817; farmer on south part of
homestead till 1888. Lived in Newbury all his life, except in 1846, at
Windsor Locks, Conn. He m. Jan. 2, 1840, Sarah J., dau. Daniel and
Sarah Sargent, (b. Haverhill, April 9, 1823; d. June 28, 1888). He d.
April 6, 1899. Members of Cong. Ch.
Children:
i. Julia A., b. July 28, 1842; m. Nelson B. Tewksbury, q. v.
ii. Daniel S., b. July 25, 1849; studied medicine with Dr. Doty at Bradford;
attended lectures at Dartmouth Medical College, and Ann Arbor, Mich.,
and graduated Dartmouth, 187—; in practice Orford and Wentworth, N.
H., and at Springfield, 1877, till death; he m. May 15, 1878, Elvira, dau.
Isaac Eastman; d. Feb. 13, 1879. No c.
iii. Everett F., b. Sept. 25, 1857; farmer; teacher day and singing schools,
winters, till 1884; from March, 1884, to October, 1887, attendant at
Massachusetts Hospital, Taunton, Mass.; in charge of supply department,
state institutions, Howard, R. I.; pharmacist at same, 1887 to date;
musician; Free Mason. He m. Boston, Sept. 9, 1890, Frances F. Sanborn.
No c.

CORLISS.

Another related family is descended through Timothy Corliss, son of John, and
grandson of the emigrant, who m. 1726, Sarah Hutchins of Haverhill,
Mass., and settled in Weare, N. H., where he d. 1775, leaving a son
Jeremiah, b. at Weare in 1734, whose sons, Jeremiah, Peletiah, and David

emigrated to Bradford in 1800. David, the youngest, rem. to Topsham, and d. there. He m. Abigail Taplin and had two sons.
  i. William S., b. 1815.
  ii. George W., b. 1820, m. Catherine, dau. of Duncan McKeith.

GEORGE W., b. 1820; m. Catherine, dau. of Duncan McKeith. Lived many years on what is called the "Old Chapman place." Of their children, George and Charles are farmers in the southwest part of the town. Both are un-m. Duncan McKeith Corliss lived in Piermont, where his 1st. wife died. He m. 2d. Jane, dau. of Edward Miller of Ryegate, where both died.

CORRUTH.

JAMES, came from Kilmalcolm, Scotland, to Ryegate in 1794, at the age of 24.

WILLIAM, his son, b. Ryegate, March 19, 1806; m. Oct. 25, 1838, Rebecca Brown, (b. Barnet, April 1, 1807). Settled in Groton, where the c. were all born; came to Newbury in March, 1855. He d. Aug. 9, 1877. She d. Jan. 22, 1892.
  Children:
  i. Robert Brown, b. Aug. 11, 1839; enlisted May 22, 1861; mustered into service July 16, 1861, in Co. C, 3d Vt.; fifer; re-enlisted Dec. 23, 1863; mustered out, July 11, 1865; farmer in the Lime-kiln neighborhood; has also taught singing schools; un-m.
  ii. Martha, b. May 20, 1841; m. Albert H. Langmaid.
  iii. Rebecca, b. May 27, 1843; m. Samuel Tuttle.

CROSBY.

DR. ALBERT, b. Gilmanton, N. H., April 23, 1828, son of Dr. Dixi Crosby; graduated at Dartmouth College, 1848; studied law; graduated Dartmouth Medical College, 1860; in practice at Wells River, 1860–62; surgeon of the 13th N. H., in the civil war; assistant to his brother, Dr. Thomas Crosby in Columbia hospital at Washington, D. C., and afterward of the military hospital at Concord, N. H. He m. at Wells River, Nov. 20, 1860, Rebecca, dau. of Moody Moore and granddaughter of Dr. Isaac Moore, of Bath.
  One child:
  i. Jennie L., b. at Wells River, Oct. 3, 1861.

CURRIER.

MOSES, b. Kingston, N. H., June 1, 1784; m. Aug. 13, 1805, Mary Carter, sister of James, commonly called "Mountain Carter," (b. Kingston, N. H., Aug. 13, 1787; d. May 24, 1875). They settled on Carter's Mountain, later known as Tucker's Mountain, but after some years rem. to Topsham, giving the name to the locality known as Currier Hill, where they spent the rest of their lives and are buried. Moses Currier was a farmer and shoemaker. He d. at Topsham, June 22, 1845.
  Children:
1 i. Thomas J., b. May 10, 1806.
  ii. Bagley C., b. Sept. 25, 1808; tanner and shoemaker; d. Nov. 3, 1875.
  iii. Frederick P., b. April 10, 1812.
  iv. Parmelia H., (twin to Frederick P.,) d. April 10, 1894.
  v. Emeline B., b. June 5, 1814; tailoress; m. a Mr. Smith; d. April 20, 1891.
  vi. Mary Jane, b. July 4, 1816; tailoress; d. April 28, 1889.
  vii. Elizabeth P., b. April 2, 1820; m. Hiram Abbott, (b. Aug. 8, 1805; d. Jan. 20, 1890). She d. Jan. 25, 1896.
  viii. Moses, b. June 1, 1822; farmer and carpenter; m. Mahala O. Doe; d. July 31, 1883.
  ix. Harriet E., b. April 10, 1825; d. July 17, 1828.
  x. Richard B., b. July 4, 1827; carpenter; d. July 21, 1894.
  xi. James C., b. May 2, 1830; carpenter, farmer and banking business.

1 THOMAS J., b. May 10, 1806; farmer; d. Feb. 8, 1869.
   Children:
2   i. James E., b. Topsham, Mar. 10, 1829.
2 JAMES E., b. Topsham, March 10, 1829. His farm was formerly that of James
      McKindley, who built the home, now remodelled, in which Mr. Currier
      lives. He m. Oct. 3, 1854, Pluma, dau. of James McKindley, (b. Sept. 20,
      1832). Carpenter, farming and other business.
   Children:
      i. Frank P., b. Feb. 26, 1856.
     ii. Lois A., b. Sept. 14, 1858; m. Samuel A. Tucker, q. v.
    iii. Charles A., b. May 21, 1860; d. Oct. 4, 1865.
     iv. Roy E., b. Aug. 10, 1864.
      v. John D., b. July 4, 1866.
     vi. Mary J., b. Aug. 13, 1868.
    vii. Addie B., b. April 4, 1871.

CUSHING.

Mathew and Resia (Woodruff) Cushing of Burke reared a large family, of
   whom two sons were, for a time, residents of Newbury.

I. HAYNES P., b. Burke, June 30, 1816; educated at Newbury Seminary; entered
   the ministry of the Methodist church, 1842; was one of the original
   members of the Vermont Conference, with which he was connected 46
   years, making 48 years in the ministry, during 20 of which he was
   a presiding elder; pastor at Newbury 1850–51; placed upon the
   superannuated list, 1870, after which he res. in Burke, preaching where
   needed; twice m.; d. Burke, 1890. One son and one dau. survived him.

II. CHARLES WESLEY, b. Burke, June 6, 1824; entered Newbury Seminary 1845;
    pupil and teacher till 1855, when he became principal, holding the office
    three years; in the ministry 1858–64; principal of Lassell Seminary,
    Auburndale, Mass., 1864–1874; pastor at Cleveland, O., four years;
    two years in Italy, engaged in Educational Missionary work; in the
    ministry, New York and Pennsylvania, 1879–87; presiding elder, Niagara
    District, Genesee Conference, New York; in 1898, after 50 years in the
    ministry, he took superannuary relation and now preaches only
    occasionally. While pastor at Troy, N. Y., about 1862, he was
    principal of New Hampshire Conference seminary, going to Tilton once a
    month, between Sundays for a week; has delivered many lectures and
    addresses, and contributed much to the press; m. at Plainfield, N. H.,
    Aug. 14, 1850, Thirza Johnson, dau Bradbury and Calista (Stevens)
    Dyer, (b. Plainfield, Nov. 11, 1827). While at Newbury, their last eight
    years were lived in the house now R. W. Chamberlain's. Six c., of whom
    Clara, graduate Lassell Seminary, and Carlos were b. in Newbury.

DR. ALVIN M. CUSHING, homeopathic physician at Bradford, 1856–66, was a
   brother of the foregoing; he m. Miss Hannah E. Pearsons, sister of
   Daniel K. and John A. Pearsons, (b. Burke, Sept. 28, 1829).

DAILY.

This name is often spelled Daly and Dailey. David Daily, a revolutionary soldier
   who served at Bunker Hill, came from Connecticut to Westminster, Vt.,
   and later to Lisbon, N. H., where he m., it is believed, a Miss Badger, and
   d. there. Their c. were: Gideon, Benjamin, David, John, Philena,
   Samantha, Nancy and Martha, and a younger dau. Philena m. a
   Mr. Sargent, and lived in Brattleboro, Vt.; Samantha m. a Mr. Wheeler
   of Danville, Vt.; Nancy m. a Mr. Streeter, and lived in Lisbon They had
   16 c., who lived to maturity. Martha became Mrs. Whiting of Lisbon, N.
   H., and the younger dau. m. a Mr. Verbeck and went to Ohio.

DAVID, b. probably in Lisbon, about 1780, rem. to Barnet, and came to Newbury
   about 1824; lived some years at the village, then settled where Charles B.
   Rollins now lives. He volunteered in the war of 1812, was called out

but once, and was never in any battle. He m. 1st, Melinda Bemis, of Brattleboro, who d. in Lisbon. He m. 2d, in Bradford, Sept. 25, 1811, Fanny Green, who d. Oct. 19, 1870, aged 86 years, 5 months. They were members of the Meth. Ch.

Children, one by first marriage.

i. Melinda B., m. Matthew Temple.

ii. Philena S., m. Andrew Grant, (q. v.) No c. She d. 1888.

iii. Alden, went to California, 1849, by the overland route. He was in mining at first, but afterward went on a ranch and engaged in stock-raising. About 1859 he sold the ranch and was not heard from for six or seven years, when a report came that he had died in Mexico. This was all that his friends ever knew.

iv. Sarah Jane, m. Albert Henderson, q. v.

1   v. Walter.

2   vi. John S., b. July 14, 1822,

    vii. Finett, d. July 21, 1849.

1 WALTER, m. 1st, Mary Priest, of Whitefield. from whom he was divorced. He lived some years in Newbury, his house being a little north of his father's on the other side of the road. He afterwards lived in Topsham. and m. 2d, Susan Cutting, of Thetford, who d. in Topsham, Sept. 13, 1875, aged 44. He d. in Thetford, Jan. 5, 1890, aged 71.

Children, three by first m.

i. Vespucius, b. Whitefield, N. H., June, 1844; enlisted in Topsham, Sept. 9, 1862; in the 10th Vt., and was transferred to the 3d Vt. District, June 19, 1865. Is m. to Sarah L. Doty and lives in East Haverhill. C., James H., m. Vivia Elliott of Haverhill. Two daughters.

ii. Sarah Jane. b. Whitefield, Feb. 27, 1846, was brought up by her uncle and aunt, Mr. and Mrs. Andrew Grant, and lived with them until their death. Is now living in Haverhill.

iii. Etta, m. a Mr. Clapp, who d in the west. She res. in Boston.

By 2d m. he had seven children, none of whom ever lived here.

2 JOHN S., b. Barnet, July 14, 1822, came to Newbury with his parents, lived here till 21; worked in Massachusetts five years; then drove an eight-horse team from the end of the railroad in Franklin, N. H., to Derby Line for several years; in California two years; express messenger between Littleton and Boston for some time; returned to Newbury to care for his parents; in 1871, rem. to Richford, and was in trade till 1897; represented Richford in the legislature 1886–87, besides holding other offices. He m. at Peacham, Aug. 30, 1858, Mahala D., dau. of James and Diodama (Arms) Gibson of St. Armand, P. Q. He d. March, 1900. No c.

DAVIS.

ANSEL T., b. Tilton, N. H., March 7, 1847; rem. with parents to Plymouth, N. H , and lived there till 1876; came to Wells River in that year, Mr. Davis buying out the interest of C. D. Penniman in the hardware business. Mr. Penniman began trade in the Bachop block in 1865; in 1869, Adna F. Mullikin bought a half interest in the business, the firm being known as C. D. Penniman & Co. In 1871 the present building on the corner of Main and Cross streets was built. Mullikin & Davis were in partnership 1876-'99· In the latter year Mr. Davis bought his partner out, the former going into business at Woodsville. He m. 1876, Ella C. Mullikin of Rumney.

Children:

i. Bertha May, b. Feb. 13, 1880; has been a student in the art department of Smith College.

ii. Maude, b. July 22, 1886.

DEAN.

REV. ARTEMAS, pastor of the 1st Ch. from 1851 to 1857, was in the sixth generation from Walter Dean, who emigrated from Chard, near Taunton, Eng., in 1637, and was one of the two first settlers of Taunton, Mass. His son, Ebenezer, and grandson, Joshua, were soldiers in the Indian wars.

Joseph, son of Joshua, was a revolutionary soldier, and captain of a company called out to support the court in Shay's rebellion.

REV. ARTEMAS, senior, was b. in Taunton; graduated at Union College, 1803, and was long pastor of the Bethlehem Pres. Ch., at Cornwall-on-the-Hudson. He d. in 1859, aged 76 years.

ARTEMAS, his son, b. Cornwall, Feb. 9, 1824; graduated Amherst College, 1842; one year in Auburn (N. Y.) Theological Seminary; teaching three years; graduated Andover Theological Seminary, 1848; ordained pastor of the 1st Ch., Johnson, 1848; pastor of the 1st Ch. in Newbury from July 9, 1851, to March 31, 1857. He was a very earnest and faithful preacher, and greatly beloved. His dismissal was demanded by his sudden breaking down in health. He has since filled several pastorates, and in April, 1900, was dismissed from the charge of the Reformed church at Fort Lee, N. J. Received the degree of M. A. from Vermont University, 1853, and that of D. D., from Hampden Sidney (Va.) College in 1890. He m. February, 1849, Emma Carleton of Chelsea.
Children;
    i.   Charles Edward, b. Johnson, 1849; d. High Bridge, N. J., 1880.
    ii. Henry Cutler, b. Newbury, April 24, 1852; now in business in London, England.
    iii. Samuel Halsey, b. Newbury, July 18. 1853; studied two years in Vermont University; two years in the Normal School at Westfield, Mass.; three years in Lawrence Scientific School, Cambridge, Mass., from which he graduated; superintendent of schools at Mt. Carmel, Pa.
    iv. Susan, b. Newbury, Aug. 24, 1856; studied at Lawrence Academy, Mass., d. 1886.
    v.   Albert C., b. Schenectady, N. Y., 1857; res. Oakland, Cal.
    vi. Sara Elizabeth. b. Greenfield, Mass., 1864; educated at Westfield Normal School; teacher in New York City.

DEMING.

I.   JOHN, came from England about 1632, and settled in Wethersfield, Conn. He m. in 1637, Hannah, dau. of Richard Treat.

II. EBENEZER, d. May 2, 1705. The name of his wife was Sarah.

III. JOSIAH, b. about 1688; m. Prudence, dau. of Capt. James Steele.

IV. ELISHA, m. Elizabeth Williams.

V.   BENJAMIN. baptized Sept. 24, 1758; revolutionary soldier; m. Laura Hopkins; settled in Danville, where he d. in 1846.

VI. BENJAMIN F., b. Bennington, May 12, 1790; m. June 6, 1816, Eunice Clark. He d. at Saratoga, N. Y., May 12, 1834. He was a prominent business man of Danville, and member of Congress, at the time of his death. After his death she m. 2d, Oct. 1, 1837, Ira Brainerd, and d. at Danville, June, 1870.
Children:
       i.   Harriet, b. June 3, 1817, at Lyndon, now living in Colorado.
1   ii. Henry Hopkins, b. Danville, Nov. 3, 1819, q. v.
2   iii. Franklin, b. Sept. 11, 1828, q. v.
       iv. William Wirt, b. Apr. 1, 1832, d. at Savanna, Ill., March 7, 1894.

1   HENRY HOPKINS, b. Danville, Nov. 3, 1819. In business at St. Johnsbury some years. Came to Newbury in 1862, and was a merchant here. He bought out C. M. Morse, and carried on business in that building till it was burned, Aug. 1876. In 1877 he erected the building now occupied by James B. Hale as a general store. Removed to Montpelier, 1882. Deacon in the 1st Ch. He m. Dec. 27, 1843, Laura Davis, daughter of Joshua T. and Mary (Tuthill) Vail.
Children:
       i.   CHARLES HENRY, b. Danville, March 27, 1851; in business with his father in Newbury, then in Lowell, Mass. Rem. to Montpelier, junior partner in the firm of Brooks & Deming, hardware dealers. He m. March 14,

1878, Carrie, dau. of John B. Buxton. C., (1) Mary Vail, b. Lowell' Mass., Sept. 22, 1885. (2) Laura Ruth, b. Lowell, Apr. 22,, 1889. (3) Ben. F., b. Montpelier, Oct. 1, 1894.

  ii. Benjamin Franklin, b. St. Johnsbury, Sept. 4, 1827; d. Newbury, Oct. 15, 1876.

2 FRANKLIN, b. in Danville, Sept. 11, 1824; m. in 1854 to Catherine C. Bingham, dau. of Maj. Francis Bingham, of St. Johnsbury; has two dau., Katie B., who m. Henry H. Lee, M. D.; and Alice, who m. John J. Peach, (Mrs. Lee has 3 c.; Mrs. Peach has 2 c.) Mr. Deming came to Wells River in 1857, succeeded A. T. Baldwin in the mercantile business and is now in the same business. He was for several years half owner of the paper mill at Wells River; President of the National Bank of Newbury; represented the town of Newbury in the legislature in 1888 and 1889; has been deacon in Con. ch. at Wells River for the past six years.

DOE.

JACOB, probably of English extraction, was b. 1734; d. in the Continental army March 9, 1776. He m. Sept. 4, 1759, Sarah Neally, who was b. Sept. 11, 1744, and d. about 1841, in her 96th or 97th year. She m. 2d, John Philbrick, by whom she had a son, John; 3d, a Mr. Morrill and 4th, a Mr. Robinson.

  Children:
1 i. William, b. Nov. 11, 1760; d. Newbury, Jan. 21, 1828.
2 ii. John, b. Nov. 15, 1762.
  iii. Sarah, m. a Mr. Harris.
  iv. May, m. Mathew Ramsey.
  v. Jacob, m. Sarah Janes.
  vi. Jeremiah, captain in war of 1812; m. — Morris.

1 WILLIAM,[2] (Jacob,[1]) b. Deerfield, Nov. 11, 1760. The name of William Doe appears in Capt. Daniel Moore's Co. of Stark's regiment from April 23d to Sept. 9th, 1775, receiving £5 2s. 10d., and his travel was 70 miles. This company served at Bunker Hill. His name also appears as a fifer in Capt. James Steven's Co. from July 27, 1777, to Jan. 9, 1778. Steven's Co. was attached to Senter's regiment for the defense of Rhode Island. Somewhere about 1780 Jacob Doe removed with his family to Rumney, N. H., and pitched land in the neighborhood of "Doetown Hill." William Doe came with his family to South Newbury in the fall or winter of 1789-'90, where they lived in a small red house, which stood on a knoll at the junction of the Topsham and river roads, on land purchased in May, 1792, of John Mills, containing about five acres, and now owned by Azro B. Rogers. He was a blacksmith and worked in a brick shop that stood just across the road from his house. In person he was tall and slight, his wife, on the contrary, being large and stout. She was Joanna Hall, of Candia, N. H., b, Jan. 24, 1764, and was married to William Doe May 30, 1781, whom she survived nearly 12 years, living with her son Henry, in the house now owned by Edwin Davenport, built by John Mills, and afterwards called the "old Porter place." She d. July 20, 1840, and is buried with her husband at the Ox-bow. He d. Jan. 21, 1828.

  Children, the three eldest b. in Deerfield, the rest at N.
3 i. Henry, b. Sept. 24, 1782; d. May 6, 1867.
4 ii. Jacob, b. Dec. 17, 1785.
  iii. Reuben, b. Sept 30, 1788; d. Aug. 28, 1789, at Rumney.
  iv. Betsey, b. June 29, 1790; m. Mr. Mills. A daughter married Joshua Hall of Peacham.
5 v. William, b. Nov. 7, 1792; d. 1876.
6 vi. John, b. May 7, 1795; d. Feb. 17, 1866.
7 vii. Bradley, b. May 22, 1797; d. March, 1828.
8 viii. Noah, b. Sept. 3, 1799.
  ix. Anna, b. Oct. 24, 1801; m. Benjamin Atwood, q. v.; d. Jan. 6, 1847.
9 x. Thomas J., b. Sept. 26, 1803; d. Nov. 21, 1878,

2 JOHN,[2] (Jacob,[1]) m. Mary Sanborn. They had three sons and eight daughters. Several of them married and settled in Hardwick. Two of the daughters

34

married men by name of Bronson of that town. Louisa m. Oct. 22, 1826, Luman Bronson, and is still living, (1899) in her 98th year. Mahala m. Timothy G. Bronson.

3 HENRY,[3] (William,[2] Jacob,[1]) b. Deerfield, N. H., Sept. 24, 1782; lived many years in the Porter house at South Newbury; m. about 1805, Jane, dau. of David McKeen, and sister of Rev. Silas McKeen, D. D., b. Corinth, Feb. 28, 1786. He d. May 6, 1867, at Corinth.
Children, all b. Newbury, except the last, who was b. in Corinth:
  i. Annie, b. Nov. 30, 1807; m.——Towle; res. California.
  ii. Madison, b. April 3, 1809; lived in Corinth; blacksmith; d. 1898.
  iii. Jane, b. Feb. 2, 1811; m. William Dera.
  iv. Emaline, b. Feb. 10, 1813.
  v. Henry, b. Aug. 9, 1814.
  vi. John, b. Nov. 29, 1815.
  vii. Mary, b. May 7, 1818; m. June 1, 1844, Hon. John A. Tenney of Corinth; d. May 5, 1847.
  viii. Lydia, b. Nov. 2, 1820.
  ix. Harriet, b. Dec. 3, 1822; m.——Tenfant; d. 1898, leaving a dau., Hattie.
  x. William, b. Corinth, March 11, 1828; res. Brooklyn, N. Y.

4 JACOB,[3] (William,[2] Jacob,[1]) b. Dec. 17, 1785; m. in Newbury, Lydia Harding, of Corinth. This family was quite migratory, living in Newbury, Swanton, Fairfield, Highgate. and, after 1844, in Lowell, Mass.
Children:
  i. Liberty, who m. a Fleming, and lives at Compton, P. Q.
10 ii. Franklin B.
  iii. Richard.
  iv. Hulda, m. a Mr. Reynolds of Lowell, Mass.

5 WILLIAM,[3] (William,[2] Jacob,[1]) b. Newbury, Nov. 7, 1792; lived for some years before his death in the house at South Newbury, where the post office now is, and kept the office a long time. He m. 1833, Mrs. Phebe Brown of Haverhill. He d. 1876.
Children:
  i. Abby Ann, b. Oct. 7, 1834; m. as 2d wife Stillman Jenne, q. v.; d. April 21, 1891. One dau. m. a Mr. Chamberlain of Bradford.
  ii. Josephine, m. John Hardy of Bradford. One son, Frank E., a farmer of Bradford. Four c.
  iii. Frances, m. Robert G. Brock, q. v.; res. Cedar Rapids, Iowa.
  iv. Helen, b. Sept. 9, 1839; d. March 9, 1842.

6 JOHN,[3] (William,[2] Jacob,[1]) b. May 7, 1795; m. March 15, 1820, Lydia Ordway. They rem. to a farm in the west part of Newbury, near the Topsham line, that locality being long called the Doe neighborhood. He d. Feb. 17, 1866.
Children:
  i. Hilas, b. April 17, 1821; m. 1st, April 8, 1847, Annie Chapman of Corinth by whom he had a son, Alvah H., b. April 5, 1848; d. in infancy; m. 2d, July 8, 1851, Elizabeth Cates of Maine, who had one c., Charles Alphonso, b. Nov. 23, 1854; m. 3d, Philena C. Grant of Maine.
  ii. Jefferson, b. Aug. 16, 1823; m. Emily, dau. of Thomas Kasson; d. July 20, 1865. C., Mary E., b. April 4, 1858.
11 iii. Richard, b. May 17, 1826.
  iv. Alleana, b. April, 1829; m. 1st, Dec. 25, 1856, George Rowe; lived in Corinth. No c. She m. 2d, Oct. 20, 1861, George Thompson. Res. Galesburg, Illinois. C., (1) Rose Isabella, b. July 25, 1862. (2) George O., b. April 3, 1865.
  v. Mahala, b. Nov. 24, 1831; m. 1st, March 28, 1850, Moses Currier, and after his death, m. his brother, Fred Currier, and res. in Michigan.
  vi. George L. B., b. Sept. 4, 1837; d. April 12, 1861.
  vii. Annette, b. April 14, 1841; m May 30, 1861, Alonzo Grant. One son, George R., b. May 2, 1865. Farmer of Bradford.

7 BRADLEY,[1] (William,[2] Jacob,[3]) b. May 29, 1797. Lived in the old house, now part of the Doe homestead at South Newbury. He m. Oct. 13, 1825, Eliza, dau. of Levi Rogers, (who after his death m. John Atwood); d. March, 1828.

Orlando W. Doe

8 NOAH,[3] (William,[2] Jacob,[1]) b. Sept. 3, 1799. He m. 1st, April 19, 1827, Fanny
   Bailey of Piermont; 2d a Miss McKinley. He lived several years at South
   Newbury, but later removed to a farm at South Ryegate; d.

   Children, 3 by 1st marriage, 1 by 2d.
   i. Marion, m. a Mr. Buell and went to Chicago.
   ii. Bradley., b. March 13, 1828. Became a sailor, and was lost in the Philip-
       pines.
   iii. Elizabeth, never m; met her death in a railroad accident.
12 iv. James M., b. Ryegate, March 20, 1837.

9 THOMAS JEFFERSON. b. Sept. 26, 1803; lived at South Newbury in a small
   one-story house which stood on the Topsham road, just west of the
   Porter house. His last years were spent on the Doe homestead.
   Blacksmith and machinist, and at various times associated with his
   father and his brothers, Noah and William, in the manufacture of plows
   and cultivators. He m. Dec. 13, 1828, Lydia Cilley, of Piermont. She d.
   Nov. 11, 1879. He d. Nov. 21, 1878.

   Children:
13 i.   Freeman J., b. June 16, 1829.
   ii. Jane S., b. March 14, 1831; m. Edwin R. Davenport; d. March 14, 1888.
14 iii. Nelson R., b. Feb. 16, 1836.
   iv. Edson. b. 1840; wheelwright and painter, has taken out several valuable
        patents; res. on the homestead; m. December, 1879, Esther, dau. of
        Cyrus Howland. C., Harry Freeman, b. May 14, 1884, now at Norwich
        University.
   v.   Orlando W., b. Sept. 29, 1843; went to Boston at ten years of age; fitted
        for college at Boston Latin School; graduated Harvard University, 1865;
        Studied at Harvard Medical School. Was a physician of note in Boston,
        and on the staff of the City Hospital; d. un-m. Dec. 10, 1890.

10 FRANKLIN B., b. Highgate. Dec. 5, 1827. Fitted for college at Lowell, Mass.;
   graduated Amherst College, 1851; Bangor Theological Seminary, 1854;
   ordained Oct. 19, 1854, over 1st Ch. at Lancaster, Mass., Appleton, Wis.,
   1st Ch., 1858–68; superintendent American Home Missionary Society,
   for Wisconsin, 1868-83; superintendent Missouri, Arkansas and
   Indiana Territory, 1883; financial agent of Ripon College, 1899. He m.
   1854, Mary A. Beecroft of Bangor, Me., who d. April, 1900. He d.
   Ashland, Wis., May 23, 1901. Five c.

11 RICHARD,[4] (John,[3] William,[2] Jacob,[1]) m. Oct. 27, 1853, Jane H., dau. of John
   Wallace. They lived in the back part of the town till 1877, when he
   bought the south farm on the Ox-bow. which was once Gen. Jacob Bayley's farm, and later owned by the Littles. He owns more Newbury land
   than any other man, and has filled many town offices.

   Children:
   i. Lucia, b. Sept. 25, 1854. Teacher. She m. June 8, 1881 C. Francis
       Darling of Boston. Res. till 1890, Cambridge, Mass. Returned to New-
       bury, buying the house long owned and occupied by Hon. Edward Hale.
       Four children, all b. Cambridge. Mass. (1) Richard F., b. Sept. 10, 1882,
       now in Vt. University. (2) Mary Louise. b. June 24, 1884. (3) Jeannie
       Wallace, b. Feb. 21, 1886. (4) Lucia, b. Apr. 24, 1889.

12 JAMES M., b. Ryegate, March 20, 1837. Farmer of Ryegate. He m. Nov. 1,
   1865 Isabel McLam; d. Jan., 1901.

   Children all b. in Ryegate.
   i.   Frederic J., b. July 19, 1867; m. Sept. 16, 1892 Etta M. Aldrich. Res.
        Ryegate. C., (1) Elmer F., b. May 25, 1893. (2) Max E., b. Aug. 13,
        1896. (3) Pearle E., b. May 9, 1899.
   ii. Isadore A., b. June 13, 1869; m. April 24, 1894 Burton A. Hatt. C., (1)
        Mildred A., b. Ryegate Sept. 24, 1897.
   iii. John Luther, b. Aug. 16, 1871; d. Nov. 14, 1874.
   iv. Marion L., b. July 16, 1874; m. Feb. 28, 1900, Robert J. Miller of Ryegate.
   v.   George Albion, b. Aug. 15.1876; m. March 8, 1899, Abigail Armstrong.
        Res. (1901) Newbury. Manager of creamery.

13 FREEMAN J., b. June 16, 1829. Went to Boston in 1847, and into the produce
    commission business in Faneuil Hall market. In 1850 he became a member
    of the firm of Chamberlin, Kimball & Doe. In 1868, Mr. Kimball died and
    the firm name was changed to Goss, Doe & Chapin, and later to Goss, Doe
    & Co. In 1899 Mr. Goss died, and a new firm was established, Doe, Sulli-
    van & Co., Charles C. Doe being admitted. Mr. Doe was the first presi-
    dent of the Boston Produce Exchange, in 1877, and connected with a num-
    ber of public institutions. He gave the bell to the South Newbury school-
    house in 1865, and, with his brother, Dr. Doe, the one to the Methodist
    church in 1887. He m, Oct. 14, 1852, Mary Jane Cutler of Boston. C.,
    (1) Ellen Louise, b. Feb. 22, 1856. (2) Mary Frances, b. July 14, 1860.
    (3) Charles C., b. Sept. 15, 1864; graduate of Chauncey Hall School, 1882,
    and the Mass. Institute of Technology, 1886. Farmer in Newbury several
    years, till 1899, and still owns a large farm. He m. Jan. 15, 1889, Ruth
    M. Conant of Louisville, Ky. C., (a) Freeman Conant, b. Jan. 5, 1890.
    (b) Orlando Cutler, b. Aug. 9, 1892. (c) Janet and Whitney Goldsmith, b.
    Aug. 11, 1895. The latter d. Aug. 1, 1896.

14 NELSON R., b. Feb. 16, 1836. Went to Boston when a young man, and now
    lives in New York. where he is manager of the Porter Bros. Co. Fruit Com-
    mission house. He m. Sept. 26, 1860, Ellen Aurelia Chamberlain of Brad-
    ford C., (1) Fred Everett, b. Sept. 29, 1863. Merchant at Bradford. He
    m. April 10, 1888, Sadie Louise Haskins. C., (a) Nelson L., b. Nov. 23,
    1889. (b) Franklin William, b. Jan. 30, 1892. (2) Lorison Wesley, b.
    July 10, 1865. Merchant with his brother at Bradford. He married June
    1, 1887, Euphemia Annie, dau. of Thomas Wright.

*DAVENPORT.

In the first volume of town proceedings is the following record of the children
    of Amos Davenport:
  i. Phinehas, b. July 3, 1788.
  ii. Lucinda, b. May 3, 1789.
  iii. Lydia, b. Jan. 14, 1792.
  iv. Eli, b. March 3, 1795.
1 v. Amos, b. June 14, 1798.
  vi. Davis L., b. Sept. 14, 1800.
  vii. Ruth, b. May 14, 1805.

1 AMOS, m. a Miss Sinclair, of Scotch ancestry, who. d. in Lowell, Mass., about
    1880; c., five daus., one son; the latter, Edwin R., b. Newbury, Dec. 27,
    1820. Left home while a young man, and was for many years engaged in
    the hotel business in various parts of the country. About 1863 he returned
    to this town and remodelled the old "Porter house," at South Newbury,
    which he still owns. He m. Nov. 21, 1848, Jane S., dau. of Thomas J.
    Doe (b. March 14, 1831; d. March 14, 1888).
  Children:
  i. Roy, b. July 9, 1850; is dead.
  ii. Nelson, b. 1855; d. in infancy.
  iii. William, b. 1858; d. in infancy.
  iv. Lillian J., b. June 13, 1860; m. Aug. 17, 1882, Jerome F. Hale, of Bradford.
    Mr. Hale has been the successful landlord of several hotels, and for the
    past seven years of " Hale's Tavern " at Wells River. C. (1) Adine, b.
    Dec. 25, 1883. (2) Cedric, b. Aug. 22, 1889; d. in infancy. (3) Kathleen,
    b. Nov. 9, 1894; d. in infancy.
  v. William, b. July 28, 1867; studied law with Orrin Gambell of Bradford, and
    opened a law office at Holyoke, Mass., where he d. 1895.

DOUGLASS.

SAMUEL, a revolutionary soldier from Conn.; d. and bur. at Littleton, N. H. He
    had three sons, Samuel, Simon and John. The latter settled at Littleton.

*Not received in time for insertion in its proper place.

Freeman J Doe

Simon was one of the earlier residents of Wells River, was a boat builder and river man. He built the house in which Henry W. Adams lives. He m. June 22, 1811, Euphemia Burbank. They removed to Suffield, Conn., in 1820, and d. there. Of their five children Samuel and Barton M. were b. in Wells River.

Samuel, b. Jan. 3. 1812. He removed to Enfield, Conn., with his father's family in 1820. Was in boating business, a member of a firm which did an extensive business between Hartford and Springfield. He was the last of the "old river pilots." Later in life he was an extensive farmer at Suffield, and a director in both Suffield and Thompsonville banks. Member Cong. ch. about forty years. He m. 1st Emeline Bronson, who d. soon after. 2nd, 1847, Caroline Abbe He d. Suffield, Conn., June, 1900. Two children, George A. of Suffield and Mrs. L. A. Upson of Thompsonville.

Barton M., b. Wells River, March 13, 1818. In boating business until the railroad was built, then engaged in boat building, constructing steam and other boats. Went to South America in 1874, for a transportation company, thoroughly explored the Magdalena river, and crossed the border on horseback. Owner of ferry between Windsor Locks and Warehouse Point for 30 years; d. Windsor Locks, Conn., Sept. 6, 1887. Four sons.

DOW.

Rev. John G., b. Gilmanton, N. H., June 15, 1785. Farmer and captain in militia. Entered the Methodist ministry in 1822; joined Vermont Conference, 1844; was 36 years in the effective ministry, and 12 years presiding elder; pastor of the Methodist church, Newbury 1837-38, and again in 1854. It was through his energy and influence that the parsonage was built, in 1838. He was long a trustee of Newbury Seminary, and its general agent, 1840–43. In old age he returned to Newbury and built the house south of the "Sawyer House." Elder Dow was one of the prominent ministers of his church and time. His education was very limited, but he possessed strong power of application; he was a natural orator, a very earnest and effective speaker. He m. Betsey Lance, (b. Chester, N. H., 1796; rem. with her parents to Cabot, 1804; d. at Worcester, Mass., 1860). He d. suddenly May 18, 1858, while on a visit to his daughter at Chelsea, Mass. Buried at Mount Auburn.

Children:

i. Sarah, b. Walden, 1814; m. April, 1844, Albert H. Danforth of Montpelier; res. in Barnard; d. Claremont, N. H., 1897.

ii. Betsey, b. Cabot, 1818; teacher and preceptress, Newbury Seminary, 1837-38; m. 1844, Rev. J. H. Twombly, (b. Rochester, N. H.; graduated Wesleyan University, 1843; teacher and clergyman; president of the University of Wisconsin some years; member, two years, of the Board of Overseers, Harvard University.) Mrs. Twombly rendered most valuable assistance in the preparation of earlier parts of the chapter upon Newbury Seminary. She d. Newtonville, Mass., Feb. 3, 1900.

iii. Lorenzo, b. Cabot, 1821; m. 1844, Mary Mills; d. Iowa City, Iowa, 1868.

iv. Frances Ann, b. Dover, N. H., 1835; m. 1860, Lorin F. Kittler; d. Chicago, 1887.

*DOWSE.

This name is variously spelled Dowse, Dows and Douse.

I. Lawrence Dows, b. about 1613, in Broughton, Hants, England. Came to Boston before 1642. Settled in Charlestown about 1649; d. March 14, 1692.

II. Samuel, (1642-1735), of Charlestown, Mass.

III. Ebenezer, (1693-1777), of Billerica, Mass.

*Ancestry from "The Dowse family."

IV. JOHN, (1717-1790), of Roxbury, Mass.

V. JOHN, (1752-   ). of Dorchester, Mass., m. Harriet Morton; revolutionary
    soldier; ship carpenter.

VI. JOHN,'(1783-1855).carpenter; soldier in war of 1812; m. 1st, Harriet Hibbard
    of Norwich; 2d, Eliza, dau. Enoch Bayley, (b. Newbury; d. April, 1898).

VII. JOHN REDING, b. April 6, 1810; farmer; m. 1st, March 6, 1833, Esther, dau.
    of Asa Coburn, (b. Aug. 4, 1810; d. June 10, 1878). 2d, ————————
    He d. April 5, 1886.

    Children:
    i.   Henry, b. Dec. 31, 1834; silversmith in Massachusetts; served in the Union
         army; mustered into Co. H, 12th Vt., Oct. 4, 1862; promoted Corporal;
         mustered out July 4, 1863; employed by Connecticut River R. R.,
         1864-75; farmer of Newbury and Landaff. He m. Dec. 10, 1868, Harriet,
         dau. of Uzzel Clough, (b. Bath, April 30, 1837). He d. at Landaff, N. H.,
         Dec. 24, 1897. No c.
    ii. Harriet, b. May 29, 1836; d. February, 1892.
    iii. Charlotte, b. July 8, 1837; d. July 22. 1838.
    iv. Almira, b. Dec. 8, 1838; d. Dec. 26, 1862.
    v.   Mary, b. Aug. 24, 1840; d. Nov. 10, 1862.
    vi. John E., b. Aug. 24, 1842; m. March 8, 1869, Janet, dau. of Gilbert
         Cowdry, (b. Jan. 29, 1837). No c. living. She d.————————
    vii. Joseph E., b. Aug. 24. 1842; d. July 6, 1846.
    viii. Asa, b. April 2, 1845; enlisted Dec. 8, 1863; private in Co. G. 4th Vt.
         Wounded May 8. Discharged 1864. Farmer and harness maker. Res.
         Warren, N. H., since 1887. He m. March 13, 1873, Cynthia Bishop, b.
         Jan. 28, 1846. C., (1) Fred V., b. April 21, 1874. (2) J. Leonard, b. May
         31, 1876; d. Oct. 19. 1882. (3) Abbie M., b. July 7, 1878; m. in Canada.
         (4) Edward H., b. Oct. 9, 1880. (5) Jennie R., b. March 19, 1883. (6)
         Ellen S., b. Jan. 2, 1885.
    ix. Ellen F., b. Sept. 6, 1846; d. Dec. 2, 1862.
    x.   Martha, b. Feb. 20, 1848; d. Feb. 12, 1901.
    xi. Harlan P., b. Sept. 2, 1850; m. Oct. 8, 1873, Anna Brooks of Haverhill;
         farm laborer. C., (1) Nathan W., b Dec. 25, 1875. (2) Harvey R., b.
         Feb. 4, 1878. (3) Mary E., b. March 4, 1882. (4) Walter J., b. May 25,
         1884. (5) Herbert D., b. Sept. 19. 1886.
    xii. Newton, b. Nov. 19, 1852; d. Dec. 23, 1862.

DUNBAR.

JOHN C., b. Danville, May 16, 1788; lived in Peacham, Lowell, Mass., Newbury
    and Littleton, N. H.; m. Feb. 10, 1811, Sally, dau. Seth Ford; d.
    February, 1870. Of their eight c., (all now dead) the youngest was:

HENRY E., b. Peacham, Oct. 13, 1827; res. Newbury from about 1845 to 1867;
    enlisted June 1, 1861, in Co. C, 3d Vt., as a corporal; was in several severe
    battles; was discharged for disability May 24, 1862; enlisted for harbor
    defense at Boston, but as men were wanted, he went to the front, and
    served till the end of the war; carpenter; steward in the Methodist church
    here, and later at Malden, Mass., in the Central Methodist church; rem.
    to Reading. Mass., and later to Malden, where he d. He m. Jan. 1, 1851,
    Mary R., dau. Charles George.

    Children:
    i.   Mary Ella, b. Newbury, Oct. 25, 1851; m. at Reading, Mass., July, 1874,
         John H. Webb of Malden. Three c., of whom Harry L., of Malden, is the
         survivor.
    ii. Lizzie Emma, b. Newbury, Jan. 23, 1856; m. Reading, Mass., June 3, 1874,
         Franklin I. Welch of Malden. Two c., one, Edwin A., living.
    iii. William Albert, 'b. Boston, Mass., March 18, 1864; m. in Pasadena, Cal.,
         Minnie M. Canfield of Ohio; res. Lynn, Mass. Two c., one, Ramona,
         living.

EASTMAN.

There are three families by the name of Eastman in Newbury and vicinity, which have the same emigrant ancestor, but whose connection with each other is not clearly understood by many of the name. By the courtesy of Mr. Guy S. Rix of Concord, N. H., the line of ancestry of each of these is here given.

I. ROGER, b. in Wales, who came to Salisbury, Mass., before 1640; m. Sarah (Smith?) and d. 1694.

II. JOHN, b. Salisbury, Mass., Jan. 9, 1640; m. Oct. 27, 1665, Mary, dau. William Boynton; d. March 25, 1720. Eight c.

III. ROGER, b. Feb. 26, 1682; m. Hannah Kimball; lived in Amesbury, but rem. to Connecticut; d. about 1743.

IV. ROGER, b. Amesbury, Mass., April 11, 1711; settled in Newton, N. H.
   Children:
   i. Thomas, b. 1741.
   ii. Samuel, b. Oct. 3, 1746.
   iii. Ichabod, b. March 17, 1749.
   iv. Nicholas, b. June 16, 1751.
   v. Isaac, b. Oct. 30, 1754. See third Eastman family.

V. THOMAS, b. Salisbury, Mass., or Newton, N. H., 1741; m. 1767, Sarah Jane Sargent, who d. Newbury, March 25, 1831, in her 90th year. He d. Newbury, Oct. 11, 1828. ·Both buried in the old cemetery on Rogers' hill. Thomas Eastman was one of the first settlers of Weare, N. H., about 1767. He served three months, eight days, in Capt. Ezra Currier's Co. of Drake's regiment, which marched to reinforce the army at Saratoga in 1777, and, perhaps, in other service. His religious views were those of Friends or Quakers.

   Children:
   i. Roger, b. Jan. 2, 1769; clerk in a store in Weare several years; d. un-m. in 1790.
   ii. David, m. Susan Ordway, and settled in Topsham, and had three sons and five daus.
   iii. Isaac, b. April 13, 1775; m. Nov. 21, 1796, Mehetabel George and settled in Wendell, (now Sunapee) N. H., about 1795. She was b. April 13, 1773; d. about 1813. He m. 2d, Mary Conant. He d. June 16, 1856.
1 iv. Daniel, b. Feb. 25, 1777.

1 DANIEL, b. Feb. 25, 1777. He m. March 6, 1797, Mina Worthley, (b. Feb. 15, 1775) He was a man of middle size and height in his prime, but afterwards grew very corpulent and weighed about 400 pounds when he died. She d. June 14, 1852. They started for Newbury the day they were married, his father driving a four-ox team with their goods, Daniel driving cattle and sheep, and his wife on horseback. They settled at West Newbury, where Warren Carleton now lives, his farm including also a large part of what is now that of W. C. and D. Carleton. They carried on a large farming business, also a cider mill and distillery. He d. March 22, 1840. Mr. David Eastman gives some particulars regarding his father and grandfather which give some idea of what farming was in the earlier part of the 19th century. "Thomas Eastman, like most farmers in those days, went barefooted in summer. Thomas and Daniel Eastman had a large farm, raising about 150 tons of hay, 100 bu. of corn, 300 bu. of grain, 1200 bu. of apples, most of which were made into cider. They owned a distillery, making 25 or 30 barrels of cider brandy, and potato whiskey, at 35 cts. per gallon. They raised about ½ acre of flax each year, which the girls of the family made into cloth. From 1800, to 1825, oxen were worth $40 to $60 per pair, cows $8 to $14. Butter brought from 8 to 12 cts. and 125 lbs. was thought a good annual yield for a cow. The staple product of the farm was wheat, usually worth $1.50 per bu. Labor by the month was $8 to $10: in haying a man received one dollar for mowing two acres."
   Children all b. in N.

    i. Mary, b. Nov. 6, 1798; d. Sept. 30, 1804.
2 ii. Roger, b. Aug. 16, 1800; d. May 25, 1883.
3 iii. Samuel, b. March 11, 1803; d. May 6, 1885.
   iv. Mary, b. March 23, 1805; d. Aug. 23, 1821.
    v. Fanny, b. Apr. 16, 1807; m. Sept. 2, 1834 Thomas Eastman of Sunapee, N.
       H.; d. April 7, 1859. 2 c.
   vi. Sarah Ann, b. Sept. 24, 1809; d. Jan. 7, 1869 (?).
  vii. Louisa, b. Dec. 10, 1811; m. Jan. 25, 1836, Isaac Eastman of Sunapee, N. H.
       d. Aug. 15, 1875.
4 viii. David, b. Apr. 2, 1814, q. v.
   ix. Daniel, b. Feb. 23, 1816. Farmer on homestead; m. July 18, 1821 Laura A.
       dau. of Enoch Wiggin, q. v. One c. which lived but a short time. He d.
       Dec. 2, 1856.
    x. Susan, b. March 9, 1819; d. Nov. 9, 1820.

2 ROGER,[3] (Daniel,[2] Thomas[1]) b. Aug. 16, 1800. Was employed on the river in
    rafting and boating. Later, farmer and mechanic. Lived at West
    Newbury; m. 1st. Feb. 1, 1826, Mary, dau. of Samuel Tucker, (b. July 1,
    1797; d. March 8, 1864) 2d, Betsey (Jewell) widow of Daniel Lindsey, (b.
    Aug. 28, 1800; d. June 19, 1868) 3d, Dec. 17, 1868, Lucy Ruggles, who d.
    Oct. 1883.
    Children:
5 i. Daniel, b. Jan. 30, 1827.
  ii. Samuel A., b. April 30, 1828. Farmer in Newbury. Served in the Union
      army in the Civil war. m. 1st, Emily Ladd, from whom he was divorced.
      2d, March 17, 1870, Augusta, dau. of Thomas Burroughs. (b. March 1,
      1837; d. Aug. 3, 1891). No children. He owned and occupied for several
      years the farm on the river road now owned by C. C. Doe, where he d. Jan.
      7, 1890.
 iii. Mary, b. Jan. 15, 1830; d. Dec. 12, 1832.
  iv. Judith T., b. Sept. 14, 1831; d. Nov. 22, 1833.
   v. Duncan M., b. May 22, 1836; m. Feb. 16, 1865 Lizzie L. Tebbetts. Two c.
      in Claremont, N. H.

3 SAMUEL,[3] (Daniel,[2] Thomas[1]) b. March 11, 1803. In company with Nicholas
    White, in 1833, they contracted to build the Union Meeting House. He was
    a farmer some years on the farm where George C. Tyler lately lived, which,
    with Mr. White, he cleared, and erected the buildings. He went, in 1841,
    into the mercantile business at West Newbury, and carried on a large
    trade for some years and built the store where John B. C. Tyler now trades.
    He also built a starch factory in 1847, at the falls near the Union Meeting
    House, which he conducted two years. He became embarrassed in business
    and failed. Later he went into the business again with the same result.
—— He carried on the town farm several years. Captain in the old militia
    three years, and usually known by his military title. He m. Sept 12, 1826,
    Judith, dau. of Samuel Tucker. (b. Aug. 5, 1803; d. July 6, 1887) He d.
    May 6, 1885. C., Mary, b. Feb. 18; d. March 3, 1828.

4 DAVID,[3])Daniel,[2] Thomas[1]) b. April 2, 1814. Farmer on homestead where
    Warren Carleton now lives; also a blacksmith. He sold that farm when
    advanced in years, and has since lived near the Union Meeting House. He
    m. Nov. 10, 1835, Susan, dau. of John Corliss. He is the last survivor of
    the children of Daniel Eastman. Mr. and Mrs. Eastman have lived
    together longer than any other couple in town. Mr. Eastman has
    communicated many facts for this volume. C., Susan, b. Jan. 12, 1837;
    m. Jan. 12, 1864, Lowell F. Greenleaf. She d. May 31, 1888. No c.

5 DANIEL,[4] (Roger,[3] Daniel,[2] Thomas,[1]) b. Jan. 30, 1827; m. in Newbury, Aug.
    29, 1854, Sophronia Ann Chase, (b. Bradford, Nov. 9, 1833). Carpenter
    and builder. Res. West Newbury, in the house which Dr. Carter built,
    1854-66; Barnet, 1866-72; Bradford till his death, March 28, 1887.
    Children, the first six, b. in Newbury:
   i. Celia Celeste, m. August, 1872, Ellis Norcross of Bradford.
  ii. Roger Carroll, farmer in Bradford, (Goshen). He m. Sept. 14, 1898, Sarah,
      dau. of David Blood.
 iii. Emma V., graduated Johnson Normal School, 1884; teacher.

    iv. Daniel J., res. Worcester, Mass. He m. at Worcester, August 10, 1888, Marion Emily Stone.
    v. Horace Tucker, graduated at Vermont University, 1891, with degree of C. E. He m. June 18, 1894, at Springfield, Cora Lowell.
    vi. Sophronia, d. Sept. 20, 1883.
    vii. Mima Worthley, b. Barnet; m. Robert E. Barnett, q. v.
    viii. Fannie b. Barnet; graduated at Vermont Universisy, 1896, with degree of A. B.; teacher; now (1899) principal of Randolph Academy.
    ix. Mary Abigail, b. Bradford, June 17, 1874; graduated at Randolph Normal School, 1895; teacher.

*EASTMAN.

Isacc Eastman, the son of Roger and brother of Thomas of Newbury, b. Newton, N. H., Oct. 30, 1754; m. Hannah George, b. March 3, 1759. She came to Newbury with her son, Samuel, and d. June 16, 1838. Buried in Topsham, west of the Lime-Kiln. He d. suddenly at Newton July 8, 1792.
    Children:
      i. Roger, b. July 13, 1776; settled in Lisbon, N. H., (Sugar Hill).
1   ii. Timothy, b. Aug. 16, 1778; settled in Walden.
      iii. Thomas, b. Feb. 11, 1779; settled in Dennysville, Me.
      iv. Betsey, b. July 2, 1783; m. Richard Currier.
      v. William, b. April 1, 1785; settled in Newburyport; lost at sea.
2   vi. Samuel, b. Sept. 19, 1787; settled in Newbury.
      vii. Nicholas, b. Sept. 8, 1789; settled in Landaff, N. H.
      viii. Isaac, b. April 22, 1792; settled in Chichester, N. H.; came to Topsham, 1838.

1 Timothy,[2] (Isaac[1]) b. Newton, N. H., Aug. 16, 1778. Settled in Walden, Vt., where he had four c., Olive, Hannah, (3) Thomas and Isaac.

2 Samuel, b. Newton, N. H., Sept. 19, 1787; m. Nancy, dau. of Bernard Eastman, of Kingston, N. H., b. July 30, 1788, and lived on the homestead till 1826, when they came to Newbury, and settled at the Lime Kiln, where C. B. Fisk now lives. She d. Aug. 4, 1855. He m. 2d, Emeline, dau. of Jacob Bayley, (b. June 30, 1802; d. Jan. 30, 1869), who after his death m. Abial Chamberlin.
Nine children, the seven oldest b. in Newton, the two youngest in Newbury.
4   i. Bernard, b. March 19, 1809; d. Nov. 18, 1889.
5   ii. Isaac, b. Jan. 11, 1812.
      iii. Sarah Ann, b. Feb. 5, 1814; m. Archibald Mills, of Topsham; d. 1896, at Chelsea.
      iv. Harriet, b. March 3, 1816; m. Nelson Whitcher of Groton.
      v. Emily, b. May 6,1818; m. William Randall of Topsham. Rem. to Loveland, Col., and there d., aged about 76.
      vi. Betsey, b. May 30 1821; d. Aug. 25, 1846.
      vii. Alvira b. Oct. 20, 1823; m 1st Wyatt Perkins, a Methodist minister. He enlisted in the Civil war and d. in hospital, leaving a son and daughter, who m. aud are all dead. She m. 2d, a Mr. Whitehead and 3d, a Mr. Hume.
      viii. Samuel, b. Sept. 11, 1827; d. Aug., 1829.
6   ix. Samuel L., b. Feb. 11, 1830.

3 Thomas,[3] (Timothy,[2] Isaac,[1]) b. in Walden in 1800, m. Sylvia Burbank of that town in 1822.
    Children:
      i. Loren.
      ii. Martha; m. Mr. Young; d. in Iowa in 1866.
      iii. John, d. in Cabot, 1870.
      iv. Curtis, served in the Union army and was severely wounded.

---

*For ancestry see the preceding family.

v. Horace, served in the army, wounded in the Wilderness. Lived several
years in Newbury. He m. Sophronia, dau. of Isaac Eastman, q. v;
d. Groton, Vt., 1876.

vi. Merrill, served in the army, was sent home ill and d. in nine days, in the
winter of 1863.

vii. Gideon, served in the army, d. 1862, near Washington, D. C.

7 viii. Dennison H.

ix. Ann.

x. Lettie.

xi. Carlie, (Mrs. Colburne) d. Nashua, N. H., 1891.

xii. Eliza, (Mrs. Martin) d. Calais, Vt., 1880.

4 BERNARD,[2] (Samuel,[1]) b. Newton, N. H., March 19, 1809. Came to Newbury
with his parents. Settled in Topsham where Henry B. White now lives.
He m. Nov. 25, 1831, Hannah J., dau. of Charles Weed, (b. Topsham, Aug.
10, 1810; d. Sept. 4, 1897.) He d. Nov. 18, 1889.
Children:

. Abigail W., b. Oct., 1832; d. June 16, 1838.

ii. Jane, b. Sept. 16, 1834; d. Oct. 14, 1856.

iii. Allen F., b. Aug. 2. 1836; m. Dec. 26' 1861, Lois D. White, dau. of Ezekiel
White, who d. Aug. 13, 1899. He d. Blue Earth, Minn., Jan. 17, 1894.
Four children.

iv. Charles W., b. March 31, 1838; m. Emma Gray. Two children. Res.
Bethlehem, N. H.

v. Abbie A., b. Dec. 2, 1839; m. Nov. 29, 1863, Horace White. Five c.

vi. Infant, b. Nov. 4; d. Nov. 25, 1841.

vii. Seth N., b. Aug. 4. 1843; physician at Groton; served in the Union army,
and was a prisoner at Andersonville and elsewhere.

viii. Harriet G., b. March 26, 1847; m. July 4, 1865, Henry B. White; d.
March 4, 1897. Five c.

ix. Ruth, b. Aug. 12, 1849; d. Aug. 19, 1853.

5 ISAAC,[3] Samuel,[2] Isaac.[1]) b. Newton, Jan. 11, 1812; rem. to Newbury, 1825,
and settled at the Lime Kiln, where his son, James W., now lives. In
1887, he rem. to South Ryegate. His farm was one of the largest in that
part of the town. He also conducted the burning of lime, which had
been carried on upon that farm by former owners; m. Jan. 1, 1835,
Sophronia B., dau. Oliver Smith, b. Gifford, N. H., Jan. 10, 1817. He d.
Jan. 5, 1898.

Children, all b. in Newbury.

i. Emily R., b. Oct. 25, 1835; m. Feb. 2, 1857, Oliver S. Davis of Sonora, Cal.,
Her son, Oliver D. Eastman, b. in Sonora, Cal., July 8, 1858, is a
physician at Woodsville, N. H. He m. Dec. 14, 1882, Addie Davis, and
has c.: (1) D. K., b. Jan. 8, 1884. (2) Ollie N., b. Aug. 13, 1885. (3)
Burns R., b. Aug. 22, 1887. (4) Abel E., b. May 15, 1890, (dead). (5)
Milo D., b. Feb. 22, 1895.

ii. Newel B., b. Oct. 24, 1837; d. Lundy, Cal., May 21, 1883.

8 iii. Alexander W., b. Feb. 17, 1842, q. v.

iv. Sophronia J., b. June 10, 1844; m. in Topsham, Jan. 30, 1867, Horace D.
Eastman of Cabot; farmer of Newbury and Groton; served in the Union
army; d. Groton, July 24, 1876. C., Addie J., b. Newbury, April 26, 1868;
d. May 30, 1893. Buried at the town house.

v. Elvira P., b. Jan. 13, 1849; m. 1st, May 15, 1878. Daniel S. Corliss. M. D.,
who d. at Springfield, Vt., Feb. 13, 1879; m. 2d, May 4, 1882, Elliott E.
Johnson of Bradford, who d. May 6, 1895. She d. at Bradford, Dec. 25,
1895. C., Louise M. Johnson, b. Dec. 6, 1885.

vi. Bell, b. Nov. 11, 1851; m. Boston, Sept. 10, 1881, Edward M. Carter, of
Wilmington, Mass. C., Ethelyn E., b. Oct. 3, 1882.

vii. Daughter, b. July 19; d. July 21, 1855.

viii. Evelyn R., b. Jan. 27, 1857; m. Sept. 20, 1881, Sumner E. Darling, M. D.
C., Sumner E., b. Hardwick, Nov. 12, 1886.

ix. James W., b. March 16, 1860; farmer on homestead; m. in Ryegate, June 4,
1884, Maryett S. Clark. C., Isaac W., b. April 12, 1885. (2) Margaret
E., b. Nov. 10, 1887. (3) James W., b. Aug. 22, 1893. (4) Infant son, b.
March 6, 1896; d. March 18, 1896.

6 SAMUEL L.,[3] (Samuel,[2] Isaac,[1]) b. Newbury, Feb. 11, 1830; fitted for college at

Newbury Seminary; graduated Northwestern University, 1857; teacher; while in charge of an academy at Wabash, Ind., he m. Jan. 3, 1860, Emily, dau. of Ellis Colburn of Newbury. She d. Erie, Mich., Aug. 5, 1862. He m. 2d, April 10, 1867, Emilie Batchelder of Montpelier. He joined the Vermont conference of the Methodist church, 1866. In 1871, Mr. and Mrs. Eastman took charge of the Newbury Seminary property and opened a school which they conducted till 1887. In 1889, he went west, joined the Iowa conference, and was in the ministry till a short time before his death. Mrs. Eastman d. at Buffalo Center, Iowa, March 22, 1895. He d. Kansas City, Mo., March 10, 1899.

Children, one by first, and one by second marriage:
i.   Ellen C., b. Toledo, O., Jan. 21, 1861; d. Newbury, March 31, 1863.
ii. Ada, m. W. A. Settle of Kansas City.

7 Dennison H., b. Woodbury, Vt., 1844; m. 1868 Anna Whitcher of Groton, Vt. They settled on the "Oliver Smith place,' in the lime-kiln neighborhood, near the Topsham line. She d. in Boston in 1890. C., (1) Hattie B., (Mrs. Lord, of Orange.) (2) Nathan T.)3) Albert E. He m. 2d, 1891, Leila Currier of Topsham. 1 c., Harold D., b. 1895.

8 Alexander W,[4] (Isaac,[3] Samuel,[2] Isaac,[1]) b. Feb. 17, 1842; farmer of Topsham; m. Feb. 14, 1864, Lucy A. Caldwell.

Children, all b. in Topsham:
i.   David C., b. Aug. 6, 1865; m. Jan. 1, 1891, Grace A. Grimes of Indianapolis, Ind. C., Harold W., b. Sept. 13, 1895.
ii.   Isaac N., b. July 25, 1866; physician at Woodsville; ed. at College of Physicians and Surgeons, Baltimore; graduated at Kentucky Medical College, 1893. He m. Nov. 28, 1895, Fannie M., dau. of David C. White. She d. April 19, 1899.
iii. May N., b. Nov. 30, 1867; m. June 30, 1896, B. Frank Ricker of Groton. C., Nelson C., b. May 16, 1899.
iv.   Jennie L., b. April 11, 1871; m. July 4, 1894, John N. Crown of Groton, who d. Sept. 23, 1899.
v.   Infant, b. March 12, d. July 6, 1879.
vi.   Alexander W., b. May 31, 1883.
vii. Anna B., b. Oct. 17, 1884.
viii. Alice M., b. May 20, 1886.

EASTMAN.

I.   Roger, b. Wales, 1611. Sailed from Southampton, Eng., 1638, and settled in Salisbury, Mass., 1640. He m. in 1639 Sarah Smith.

II. Thomas, 4th son of Roger, b. 1646; m. 1679 Deborah Corliss, dau. of George Corliss, a sister of the nurse of Hannah Dustin during her captivity. Thomas was killed by the Indians, as was also his dau. Sarah, at the time Hannah Dustin was captured.

III. Jonathan, only son of Thomas, b. 1680; m. Hannah Greene, who was captured by the Indians Feb. 8, 1704, taken to Canada, and rescued a year later by Jonathan. The late Eber Eastman of Haverhill, N. H., published some years ago, a narative of her captivity.

IV. William, b. Oct. 3, 1715; m. 2d, 1748, Rebecca Jewett.

V.   Obadiah, b. Hampstead, N. H., Jan. 26, 1749. He m. Feb. 8, 1774 Elizabeth Searle of Hollis. They settled in Bath, where he built the first mill. Late in life they removed to North Littleton, where she d. Jan. 30, 1830, and he d. Nov. 13, 1831. He served in the Revolutionary war. They were the parents of eight children, of whom Seaborn was the 6th. He was b. in Bath, Aug. 27, 1787. He m. Ruth, dau. of Nathaniel and Esther (Clark) Rix, b. Landaff, Aug. 8, 1791. She d. in Newbury, Jan. 19, 1838. Her father was b. in Boscawen, N. H., in April 1753. Rem. to Landaff while yet a young man, and served four different terms in Col. Bedel's regiment in the Revolutionary war. He d. in North Littleton, 1828, Seaborn Eastman was a brick maker and mason, and was reputed to build the best fire-place of any man in this part of the country. He came to Newbury in 1828, and lived at South Newbury till a short time before his death. He d. in Brad ord, Feb. 13, 1862.

Children:

i. George Rix. b. Bath, Nov. 19, 1812. Brickmaker at South Newbury, at first for Benjamin Atwood, and then on his own account, his father working with him. He m. Hannah, dau. of David Young of Landaff, who d. Nov. 1884. He d. at Newbury, Nov. 4, 1889. C., (1) Ruth Rix. b. Feb. 14' 1840. She graduated at Newbury Seminary. Teacher. She m. Feb. 12, 1868 James Smith, a farmer of Danbury, N. H.; d. at Manchester, N. H., Nov. 1, 1891. Two daughters, Emma and Estella. (2) Jane. b. 1842. A brilliant scholar; d. Feb. 1859. (3) George, b. May, 1848; d. Feb. 1850.

ii. Esther Rix, b. Bath, Jan. 20, 1815; m. David Greene, a printer of Concord. She d. at Concord, N. H., Jan. 24, 1876.

iii. Lucretia Hutchinson, b. Bath, Sept. 21, 1817. She m. Ezekiel R. James, for forty years superintendent of the eastern division of the Boston water works; d. in Boston, July 11, 1875.

iv. William, b. Bath, Oct. 21, 1820. He learned the trades of brick maker and mason of his father, worked in Boston some years. He became a master mason and had charge of some fine buildings. Among them were the hotel at Claremont; the public school house, and one of the paper mills at Bellows Falls; the depot at White River Junction, and buildings in Cambridge and Boston. With L. L. Tucker he built the schoolhouse at Wells River of brick made by his brother George, and had entire charge of the construction of St. Johnsbury Athenæum. He m. March 20, 1853, Mary E., dau. of Daniel Farr ot Bradford. He d. at Bradford, May 31, 1892.

v· Searle, b. Bath, Jan. 25, 1823; m. Mary Ann Lother of Newbury. He d. at Boston, Aug. 30, 1854.

vi. Jason, b. Bath, Jan. 20, 1826; d. Newbury, Oct. 1, 1851.

vii. Charles Wesley, b. Newbury, Nov. 22, 1830. Lived with John B. Carleton of West Newbury from the age of seven till he was twenty-one. He went to New York, then to Georgia, where he worked in an iron mill. Returned to Newbury 1853, and m. July 4, 1855, Elizabeth C., dau. of James Abbott of South Newbury. Farmer .with his father-in-law till 1869, when he bought the Baldwin place at Wells River. Trustee of Wells River village 1892-'99. Steward in M. E. church at Woodsville. C., (I) Clara, b. June 7, 1856. Graduate of Montebello Ladies' Institute, 1877, Teacher. In 1881 and '82, teacher in the Avery Normal Institute at Charleston, S. C. She m. June 20, 1888, S. I. Smith of Lyndonville, Vt. One son, Wendell P., b. Sept. 17, 1892. (2) William, b. Sept. 10, 1858. Farmer with his father. (3) Helen, b. March 22. 1863. Teacher of drawing and painting several years until her health failed.

EDWARDS.

DAVID, b. at Gilmanton, N. H., Aug. 2, 1796; m. in Gilmanton, Feb. 21, 1819, Alcemena Frishee, (b. Fryeburg, Me; d. Newbury, Sept. 3, 1875). They came to Newbury with their c. March 6, 1843, and lived on Wallace hill. He d. at Newbury, Oct. 13, 1883. On July 4, 1849, John and James, their sons, bought wild land adjoining Harriman's pond, which they cleared and erected the buildings now occupied by Sidney Temple, and where their parents d.

Children:

i. Eliza, b. Gilmanton, Dec. 20, 1819; m. July 7, 1844, Park, son of George Avery. q. v.

ii. James. b. Gilmanton, Feb. 17, 1822; farmer with his brother, John; m. Oct. 25, 1854, Jane W., dau. of Geo. Avery. He d. Oct. 31, 1893.

iii. John, b. Gilmanton, Jan. 31, 1824, q. v.

iv. Statirah F., b. Gilmanton, July 9, 1827; m. Dec. 30, 1847, Warren K. Chamberlin.

v. Alcemena F., b. Gilmanton, May 23, 1830; m. in Cincinnati, O., July 4, 1857, Joseph F. Bell.

vi. Almira A., b. Bristol, N. H., April 10, 1834; m. April 13, 1854, William W. Brownhill.

JOHN, b. Jan. 31, 1824; m. July 20, 1848, Margaret, dau. of George W. Avery.
Children, all b. in Newbury:
i.   Lewis H., b. Nov. 30, 1848; d. June 24, 1900.
ii. Belle H., b. May 22, 1850; m. at Wakefield, Mass., July 18, 1874, Henry
     Kimball; d. Newbury, Dec. 10, 1896.
iii. Jennie W., b, May 8, 1854.
iv. F. Eugene, b. Feb. 29, 1856; m. at Haverhill, Mass., May 26, 1890, Etta
     L. Emerson.
v.   George G., b. May 8, 1864.
vi. Nellie M., b. July 22, 1866.

EMERSON.

JOHN, came from Haverhill, Mass., and settled in the Grow neighborhood, east
of the Metcalf place, on the road that runs past the burying ground. The
buildings are all gone, no trace of them is left. The maiden name of his
wife was Abigail Duty. He d. Feb. 18, 1861, aged 84 years, 8 days.
They had 12 children of whom:
i.   John, m. Ruth Taplin, and lived in Newbury next to John Wilson's, which
     is in Bradford. He d. at about 90. Three c. One dead. Annie and John
     Plummer live on the farm.
ii. Charles, bought the Moody Grow farm and lived there nearly all the rest of
     his life. He m. Sept. 7, 1828, Dorothea, dau. of Rev. Isaac Hall, a
     Christian Baptist minister. C., 11, of whom, Julia, m. Abner Flanders.
     Olive, d. un-m. Nancy, m. Samuel Stevens, probably of Corinth. May, m.
     a Mr. Rowe, of Corinth. Martha, m. James McKinley. Lucy, m. a Mr.
     Parker of Boston, and d. there. Ida, d. in Boston. Harriet, m. and lives
     in Lancaster, N. H. Horace, is a section master near Lyndonville. Isaiah
     lives in New Hampshire. Charles is a farmer in Lancaster, N. H.
iii. Ephraim, m. Betsey Hall, lived near East Corinth, where his son, Arthur
     D., now lives. He d. April 4, 1868, aged 58 years.
iv. Mary, m. Jesse Hall. C., Mahala, who m. and d. in Haverhill, Mass., and
     Oscar, who lives in Newbury.
v.   Relief, m. Samuel Grow, q. v.
vi. Daniel, m. and reared a large family. His son, Daniel, lives on the
     "Mountain Carter place."

ENGLISH.

JOHN, b. Lyme, N. H. Sept. 1. 1809. He was the son of Andrew and Mary
(Godell) English, and grandson of James English, a Revolutionary soldier,
and an early settler of Lyme. Learned the printer's trade at Haverhill,
joined the M. E. church, 1832; attended Newbury Seminary; admitted to
N. H. Methodist Episcopal conference 1838; ordained deacon 1840, and
elder at Newbury in 1842. In the active ministry about 30 years. Came
to Newbury to live, 1866, purchasing what had been called the Hemenway
house, on the west side of the common. He m. June 10, 1843, Ellen M.
Drake, of Windsor, Vt., a descendant of George Drake of Westerly, R. I.,
and of Benjamin Drake, a revolutionary soldier, and early settler of
Windsor. She removed 1896, to Claremont, N. H. He d. of heart disease
in J. B. Hale's store, Newbury, March 26, 1884. Buried Brownsville, Vt.
Children:
i.   Grace, b. Deering, N. H., Oct. 31, 1851. Educated at Newbury and Tilton
     Seminaries; m. May 15, 1872, Albert Hale. Two children. Res.
     Claremont, N. H.
ii. William F., b. Tuftonboro, N. H., Feb. 6, 1863. Reared in Newbury; united
     with 1st Cong. Ch., 1875. Graduated Newbury Seminary, 1878,
     Dartmouth College, 1882, Hartford Theo. Sem., 1885. Pastor of Cong.
     Ch. at Essex Junction, 1885-'87. Ordained, July 2, 1885. Missionary of
     the A. B. C. F. M., at Sivas, Turkey, 1887-'92. Pastor of 1st Cong. Ch.,
     East Windsor, Conn., since 1892. Published, 1895, "Evolution and the
     Immanent God.". He m. May 19, 1889, Janet S. McCrone of Hartford,
     Conn. Five children.

FARNHAM.

EVELYN H., b. in Hardwick, was son of Aaron Farnham, of Killingsworth, Conn., and his wife, Florilla, dau. of Rev. Cyprian Strong of Farmington, Conn. He m. in 1824, Martha, dau. of John Ellsworth of Windsor, Conn., a lineal descendant of Rev. Timothy Edwards, of East Windsor, Conn., her mother being also dau. of Rev. Cyprian Strong of Farmington. The family came to Newbury in 1848 and have since owned and occupied the same house, one of the oldest in town. Mr. Farnham d. 1889, and she d. 1892.

Eight children:

i.   Martha E., m. S. N. Plumer of Boston.
ii. Flora S., d. 1889.
iii. Julia M., of Newbury.
iv. Evelyn H., cabinet maker of Newbury, and with his sister, occupies the homestead; served as sergeant in Co. C, 3d Vt., from July 16, 1861, to Nov. 4, 1862. He m. Mrs. Rachel Mains of New York, who d. 1892.
v.   William D., d. 1854.
vi. Amelia A., d. in infancy.
vii. Frederick E., private in Co. C, 3d Vt.; mustered into service, July 16, 1861; d. in hospital April 10, 1862.
viii. Frank E., private in 3d Vt. Battery; mustered into service Sept. 3, 1864; mustered out June 15, 1865; res. Florence, Mass. He m. Emma Hazen of Hartford, who d. 1897. A son of his was with the 2d Mass., during the siege of Santiago, Cuba, 1898, and d. of typhoid fever at Montauk Point, N. Y.

FARRAND.

NATHANIEL FARRAND, of French extraction was living in Milford, Conn. in 1645. In the fourth generation from him was Rev. Daniel Farrand, whose biography fills several pages of Sprague's "Annals of the American Pulpit." He was minister at Canaan, Conn., 1752, till death in 1803. His oldest son, Daniel, b. about 1760, graduated at Yale College, 178-; studied law with Judge Jacobs. Came to Newbury about 1787, taught school and opened a law office. He lived where the late Harry C. Bailey so long lived. His office was a small building which stood in front of the house, and was afterwards Benjamin Porter's law office, and later, was used for a young ladies' school. It is now the kitchen part of Silas Leighton's house. Esq. Farrand was one of the most prominent men in the town and state, an eminent lawyer, a man of wide reading and mental culture. He held many town offices and was member from Newbury in the Constitutional convention at Bennington in 1791. Register of probate, 1788-'90, town representative in 1792, '93, '94, '95, '96, '97, '98, in the latter year being speaker of the House, the only speaker Newbury has ever furnished. Removed to Bellows Falls 1800, and to Burlington in 1804, where he built in 1809 the house now owned and occupied by Hon. George G. Benedict, editor of the Free Press. He was chosen assistant judge of the supreme court in 1813. In politics Judge Farrand was a federalist, and when the war of 1812 broke out he opposed it with remarkable force. "He presided at a public meeting held in Williston, which denounced the administration, and passed a series of resolutions in which the graphic language and stubborn intellect of Daniel Farrand are plainly seen." Although a Unitarian, he seems to have been a strong supporter of the 1st church while in Newbury. He was a member of the corporation of Vt. University after 1798. Mr. Farrand was married at Haverhill, May 1, 1794, to Mary, dau. of Col. Asa Asa Porter, b. Aug. 23, 1773 and d. March 24, 1812. He d. at Burlington, Oct. 13, 1825. They had nine daughters, all handsome and accomplished women.

i. Eliza Crocker, b. Newbury, Sept. 11, 1795; m. Dr. A. L. Porter of Dover, N. H., and removed to Detroit, Mich., where she d. in March, 1875
ii. Mary Porter, b. Newbury, Dec. 11, 1796; m. N. P. Rogers, (b. Plymouth, N. H., June 3, 1794; d. Concord, N. H., Oct. 16, 1846. Graduated at Dartmouth College, 1814. Lawyer, teacher and editor. One of the earliest

and most prominent abolitionists). She d. 1890. They had eight children and some of their descendants are notable people.

iii. Lucia Ann, b. Newbury, July 29, 1798; m. Geo. A. Kent, Esq., of Concord, N. H. He was long cashier of the "Old Concord Bank." She d. in Feb., 1838.

iv. Frances Jacobs, b. Newbury, Sept. 6, 1800; m. 1st, Rev. Mr. Murdock and 2d, John Richardson, Esq., lawyer of Durham, N. H. She d. 1880.

v. Caroline Thompson, b. Bellows Falls, Apr. 8, 1802; d. un-m., 1871. Teacher.

vi. Charlotte Parmalee, b. Feb. 3, 1804; m., as 2d wife, Dr. Stephen C. Henry, a noted physician and surgeon of Detroit. She d. Jan. 25, 1884. One son, D. Farrand Henry, b. May 27, 1833. Graduate of Sheffield Scientific School and Yale College. Connected with U. S. Lake Survey 17 years. Engineer of Detroit water works, designing and constructing the present water works at Detroit. Chief engineer and promoter Lake St. Clair and Lake Erie ship canal

vii. Arabella Marie, b. Burlington, Aug. 23, 1806; m. Mr. Geo. Willson, instructor at Canandaigua Academy, and author of "Willson's Arithmetic," "Willson's Readers," etc. She was a lady of rare talent, and authoress of "Lives of the Three Mrs. Judsons," "History of the 126th N.Y.Regiment in the Civil War," etc. She also contributed to the press a great number of articles and poems, one of the best known of which is, "An appeal for pewer air. To the sextant of the Old Brick Meetin' House." She d. at Canandaigua, N. Y., March 13, 1884.

viii. Martha Olcott, b. Burlington, Sept. 6, 1808; d. 1878.

ix. Ellen, b. Burlington, Feb. 7, 1812; m. Nathaniel E. Russell, founder of the Green River Cutlery Works, Greenfield, Mass.

FARWELL.

AUGUSTUS STARR, son of Jonathan and Susan Farwell,b. Rumney, N. H., 1821; came to Wells River, Dec. 6, 1848, and has been in business there since; 1848–1872, as merchant, postmaster, etc., agent of the Vermont and Canada Telegraph Co., and its successor, the Western Union Co., 1853–1890; express agent since 1858. While in trade he sold the first gallon of kerosene oil in this town, the price being $1.50 per gallon. Since 1848, Mr. Farwell, has employed from one to three young men, many of whom are now in business for themselves. He established and for some years maintained a select school in the Eames building, which he owned at the time. In politics a democrat. Member of the Episcopal church at Woodsville. He m. 1845, Susannah G. Norris, of Pittsfield, N. H., who d. 1883.

Children:

i. Julia Hutchins, b. Newbury; graduated Mt. Holyoke Seminary. After a few unimportant engagements she was appointed First Assistant at St. Mary's School, Garden City, L. I., was connected with the school four years in that capacity, and five as principal. Resigned the position to study in Germany. Senior at Barnard College, 1897–1898. Received in June, 1899, the degree of A. B., from Mt. Holyoke, in recognition of her work at other colleges, and in the same month the degree of Master of Arts from Columbia College.

FISK.

Pierce's Genealogy of the Fisk and Fiske families traces their ancestry back to the 14th century. In the 14th generation from the first known ancestor was Saul Bartlett Fisk, b. Rhode Island, Feb. 12, 1780; d. Rochester, N. Y., July 8, 1840; mill wright; he m. Vianna Estes, by whom he had two sons, Ebenezer and James. The latter, b. Providence, R. I., Jan. 6, 1812; m. in 1832, Laura B. Ryan. They had two c., one of whom James, Jr., b. Bennington, April 1, 1835, became a stock operator in New York, and was noted for his daring and unscrupulous operations. He was one of the kings of Wall street for a brief time, and possessed powerful qualities of good and evil. On Jan. 6, 1872, he was assassinated in the Grand Central

Hotel in New York City by Edward S. Stokes. His sister, Minnie G., m, Col. Hooker of Brattleboro.

EBENEZER FISK, elder brother of James, (senior), b. Canterbury, N. H., Jan. 6, 1786. He was brought to Newbury the year of his birth, and served in the war of 1812, being wounded at the battle of Plattsburg, for which he drew a pension till his death. He m. April 4, 1806, Sally Hood of Topsham. He d. Newbury, Oct. 22, 1858.
Three of their sons were:
  i. Alvin, b. Topsham, Jan. 6, 1807; drowned in the river at Orford, while working there June 19, 1828.
1 ii. Curtis, (twin brother of Alvin).
  iii. Aaron S., b. Groton, March 28, 1808. Served in the Union army during the civil war and d.

1 iv. CURTIS, son of Ebenezer, b. Newbury, Jan. 6, 1807; m. 1826, Sarah, dau. of Dr. Jonathan Cowdry, who was surgeon on the frigate Philadelphia, when she ran upon the rocks, Oct. 31, 1801, in the Tripolitan war, when all the crew were made prisoners. (She was b. in Tunbridge, July 31, 1808; d. Newbury. July 16, 1875). He d. March 28, 1880.
Children, all b. in Newbury:
  i. Lucinda, b. Nov. 19, 1827; d. Nov. 22, 1845.
  ii. Nancy B., b. Sept. 24. 1830; d. July 4, 1880, Lyndon.
  iii. Jane M., b. July 30, 1832; m. April 19, 1855, William Bowditch of Randolph; res. Lyndon.
  iv. Alvin F., b. Aug. 18, 1834; d. March 28, 1838.
2 v. Curtis B., b. Aug. 28, 1836, q. v.
  vi. Sarah A., b. April 7, 1838; m. Jan. 9, 1862, Charles Colley of Lyndon.
  vii. George R., b. April 11, 1839; d. Oct. 11, 1840.
  viii. Sophronia E., b. April 7, 1841; d. May 11, 1870.
  ix. Isaac E., b. Feb. 20; d. June 15, 1844.
  x. Ada L., b. Jan. 6, 1847; d. Jan. 16, 1857.

2 CURTIS BARTLETT FISK, b. Aug. 28, 1836; m. Jan. 9, 1862, Margaret Buchanan of Ryegate; carpenter for some years; 1872-76, in employ of the Sturtevant Manufacturing Co., Lebanon, and while there studied medicine with Dr. James A. Davis; res. Newbury; carpenter and farmer.
Children, all b. in Newbury:
  i. Alonzo Bole, b. March 10, 1864; farmer; m. Abbie Minard of Groton. C., (1) Fanny E., b. Oct. 23, 1893. (2) James C., b. Oct. 19, 1896.
  ii. David B., b. Dec. 31, 1869; m. Dec. 27, 1893, Clara F. Gibson of Ryegate; farmer. C., Hugh Gibson, b. April 17, 1895.
  iii. Eunice Annette, b. June 8, 1878.

¡FLEMING.

ALONZO, b. Ascot, P. Q., July 26, 1806. Came to Newbury, 1831. Carpenter and farmer. Was entirely self taught, yet accounted a skillful workman, and, although he erected many large buildings in this and other towns, was never known to make a plan of any kind. He owned and operated many years a saw mill on Hall's Brook, below the Center, which was washed away in the freshet of June 5, 1878. He m. June 2, 1826, Naomi Erwin, who d. June 19, 1881. He d. Oct. 26, 1896.
Children:
  i. Ephraim, b. Canada, Feb. 12, 1829. Carpenter and farmer. Enlisted for three years in Co. A, 10th N. H. Taken prisoner and confined 18 months at Andersonville, where he was a personal witness of some of the most fearful scenes which took place there. Exchanged, 1864. Discharged, Jan. 13, 1865; m. Dec. 6, 1849, Lydia E., dau. of John Messer, (b. Dec. 23. 1833; d. June 24, 1900.) He d. July 30, 1896. Four children living.
  ii. Lucinda, m. Wm. K. Putnam, q. v.
  iii. Freeman, died in the army, was a teamster; m. Janet Cowdry. No children living.
  iv. Mary Ann, m. Wm. Goodwin; d. June 3, 1901.

v. Lydia, m. 1st, Horace N. Abbott, 2d, John Hutchinson; d. in the West.
vi. Emily, m. John Bartlett, and lives in California.
vii. Henry E. Served in the army. (See record.) m. and d. in Mass.
viii. Alice, m. B. Frank Greenough of Bradford; d. 1883 in Cal. Buried in Bradford.
ix. Belle, m. 1870, Frank M. Jones.

FORD.

PAUL, came here before 1780, and began to clear land on what has long been known as the "Old McIndoe place," at West Newbury, and built the house still standing on that farm. He served several short enlistments in the revolutionary war. The town record of him is brief: "Paul Ford and Elinor Kelley were m. May 10, 1781. Moses Morrison, the adopted son of Paul Ford and his wife, was b. Dec. 26, 1788. Paul Ford departed this life April 30, 1809." This Moses Morrison is understood to have become a doctor, and succeeded Mr. Ford on that farm, but, later, rem. to Bath.

SETH, b. Cornwall. Conn., March 7, 1757; m. Mary Andross, (b. Northfield, Mass., July 17, 1757). Settled as early as 1776 in Piermont, N. H. A year or two later he rem. to Bradford, and finally to Fairfax where he d. He was one of the men who went from Piermont to bring in the people at Strafford and Randolph, at the time Royalton was burned. Later, in 1781, he served seven days in Capt. Robert Hunkins Co., in the "Peacham Alarm." He also served 11 months in Capt. Ezekiel Ladd's Co. of Bedel's regiment.
Children:
i. Seth, b. Piermont, April 22, 1776; settled in Campton, N. H.
ii. Polly, b. Bradford, Jan 27, 1778: d. Sept. 27, 1779.
iii. Betsey, b. Bradford, Feb. 12, 1780; settled in Enosburg.
iv. Nabby, b. Bradford, March, 18, 1782; settled in Enosburg.
v. Polly, b. Piermont, Sept. 17, 1784.
vi. Sally, b. Piermont, Jan. 21, 1787; m. John C. Dunbar, q. v.
vii. Zebina, b. Piermont, Dec. 4, 1788; settled finally in Illinois.
viii. Lucy, B. Piermont, June 30, 1791; m. Eben Burbank and settled at Lowell, Mass.
1 ix. Ross C., b. Fairfax, June 7, 1793, q. v.
x. Hollis, b. Fairfax, Aug. 4, 1795.
xi. Alanson, b. March 13, 1798.
xii. Almira, b. Fairfax, June 1, 1801; deceased.

1 Ross C., b. Fairfax, June 7, 1793. He was a "Plattsburg volunteer" in the war of 1812. His wife, Hannah, dau. of Reuben Leighton, was b. March 7, 1796, and d. in Lowell, Mass., February, 1879. They were members of the Methodist church, Mr. Ford being class leader nearly fifty years. Farmer. He d. Barnet, May 5, 1874.
Children:
i. Hazen, b. April 26, 1815; farmer of Newbury and Barnet; m. 1st, March 25, 1841, Christian, dau. of William Wallace, (b. April 29, 1817; d.) Five c., all d. young. He m. 2d, Eliza Paddleford of Monroe, N. H., by whom he had one dau., Nellie E., (Mrs. J. C. McClay of St. Johnsbury). He d. Dec. 6, 1894.
ii. Ross, b. Jan. 11, 1817; farmer and blacksmith; m. Feb. 1, 1841, Deborah Noyes of Tunbridge, now living in Groton. He d. June 1, 1885. Three c., d. in infancy.
iii. Seth, b. Aug. 29. 1818, now retired from business in Barnet; farmer in that town, horse dealer, and ran a stage line 28 consecutive years in the White Mountains. He m. Amanda Paddleford. C., (1) Frank M., a farmer in northern Texas. (2) Patience M., (Mrs. M. E. McClary).
iv. Dan Young, b. Newbury, Sept. 13, 1820. Farmer on river road; m. 1st, Sept. 17, 1838, Charlotte A. Woodbury, who d. Feb. 14, 1870. One dau., Angeline, m. B. P. Wheeler, q. v.; 2d, Sept. 22, 1870, Ava B. Morgan of Lyndon. One dau., May Belle, b. May 1, 1874. Music teacher and organist at the Cong. Ch. Graduate of New England Conservatory of Music, Boston, June, 1900.

35

    v.   Emily S., b. Dec. 18, 1822; m. James Y. Prescott, q. v. d. Dec. 4, 1889.
   vi. Jane S., b. April 3, 1825; m. Austin Paddleford of Monroe, N. H.; d. Jan.,
        1864.
  vii. Mary S., b. March 26, 1828; m. a Mr. Sherman; d. at Lowell, Mass.,'Aug. 7,
        1854.
 viii. Eliza W., b. Sept. 26, 1832. Res. Montour, Iowa; m. Edward Taplin.
   ix. Hannah H., b. May 3, 1835; m. Daniel Bartlett; d. Jan. 11, 1887, at Ord,
        Neb.
    x. Lucia A., b. July 26, 1837. Res. Dennison, Texas; m. 1st, Joseph Allen
        Chamberlin, q. v., 2d, a Mr. Levy.
   xi. Helen H., b. June 22, 1842; m. Nov. 18, 1857 Henry M. Niles. Res. Monroe,
        Wis.

FOREMAN-FARMAN.

ROBERT FOREMAN came from London, England, to Maryland, in 1674. He
settled near Bodkin Bay, fourteen miles north of Annapolis, and became a
planter. He was succeeded on the same estate by his son, William, and
later by his grandson, Joseph, the latter born Oct. 17, 1699. The records
of the wills of these three, and those of the widows of William and Joseph,
are still to be found in Annapolis.

  I. JOHN FOREMAN, was the sixth child and fifth son of Joseph, b. September 16,
1739. In the year 1756, he entered the British army as a volunteer, "for
the war," then being waged by the English against the French colonists in
North America. He went from Maryland to New York, thence up the
Hudson, and through the wilderness, by the way of the Mokawk, Oneida
Lake and Oswego river, to Oswego, and in the last year of the war, 1760,
down the St. Lawrence to Montreal, and later to Three Rivers. In 1763,
having been retained in the service nearly three years after he was entitled
to his discharge, he, with two other volunteers, left the army at Three
Rivers, "without leave," and made their way through forests to the
colony of New Hampshire. They were lost and wandered in the wilderness
six months, subsisting by hunting and such fruits and roots as they could
obtain. At one time they came so near starvation that they sat down on
a log to cast lots to determine which of the three famishing men should be
food for the others. While thus occupied, a moose and two calves came in
sight. They secured the mother and one calf, and were thus relieved from
their desperate situation. They remained at this place a number of days
to recover their strength, and dry their meat. They had with them a
small amount of silver money. This, in their weak condition, had become
a burden and was buried. Some time afterwards they came to the
Connecticut river, or one of its tributaries, which they followed
down-stream for many days, finally coming to an open place covered with
grass, where a horse was feeding. This gave the name to "Horse
Meadow" in Haverhill. Supposing the horse had strayed they shot it for
food. Starting again on their journey, the next morning, they soon
discovered smoke on the Ox-bow at Newbury. They had met an Indian a
few days before, the only human being they had seen since leaving the
vicinity of Three Rivers, and fearing they were near an Indian village, one
of the men cautiously crossed the river to reconnoiter. He soon returned
accompanied by white settlers to the relief and great joy of his comrades.
The owner demanded payment for his horse, and the men gave one or
more of their guns in settlement of his claim, but the settlers, on learning
the facts, raised by subscription a sum to satisfy him, and returned the
guns. The gun of John Foreman is said to have been carried by Silas
Chamberlin, one of his brothers in-law, at the battle of Bunker Hill.
John Foreman served in the Revolutionary War in Capt. Barron's Co. of
Bedel's regiment, and was also employed, on account of his knowledge of
the French language, in special service in Canada, particularly to visit the
settlements along the St. Francis and the St. Lawrence, with a scouting
party in 1779 and 1780. He m. in 1764, Rebecca, dau. of Richard
Chamberlin, (b. March 13, 1749, in Northfield, Mass). He remained in
Newbury until 1771, when he settled in Bath, N. H., on what is known as
the William Abbott farm, at the mouth of the Ammonoosuc, opposite the

Scientific Publishing & Engraving Co. New York.

E. E. Farman.

present village of Woodsville, where he resided till his death in 1792. His widow, Rebecca, who landed with her father at Newbury in 1762, was only fifteen years old at the time of her marriage. In 1801, she went with her son, John, to Augusta, Oneida Co., N. Y., and as late as 1820–21 was a vigorous lady, living with her son, Moody, in the adjoining town of Vernon, where she d. soon afterwards. At the time of the death of John Foreman, Sr., the family name was changed to Farman, for what reason is unknown. Some of the sons who had previously held town offices under the name of Foreman, afterwards held, in the same town, the same positions under the name of Farman.

Children:

i. Roswell, b. in Newbury, March 20, 1765; m. 1st, Ruth Turner; 2d, Abiah, dau. of Capt. Jeremiah Hutchins of Bath; 3d, Polly Wheeler; d. in New Haven, Oswego Co., N. Y., Oct. 17, 1839.

ii. Joab, b. in Newbury, May 22, 1766; removed to Paris, N. Y., 1797, to Ellisburg, N. Y., 1808, where he d. Oct. 11, 1864, in his 99th year; m. 1st, May 26, 1791, in Bath, N. H., Rebecca Powers, b. Sept. 22, 1771; d. July 6, 1806, in Paris, N. Y.; 2d, Abigail Whitney, Aug. 22, 1807; b. April 10, 1774, in Ridgefield, Conn.; d. June 20, 1856, in Ellisburg, N. Y.

iii. John, b. in Newbury in 1768; m. Esther Goodwin of Haverhill, N. H., in 1799 (probably dau. Simeon Goodwin); she was born Aug. 15, 1777; d. May 15, 1872, at Ellington, N. Y.; d. in Oppenheim, N. Y., Feb. 15, 1812, while on his way from Albany to his home in Augusta, N. Y.

iv. William, d. in childhood.

v. Benjamin, b. in Bath, N. H., Dec. 25, 1773; m. 1st, Keziah Powers, 1795, b. 1777; died in Bath, Aug., 1822; 2d, Mrs. Lois Stebbins, widow Capt. Benj. Stebbins of Westfield, Vt., in 1836; d. Sept. 25, 1858, in Lowell, Vt., and buried in adjoining town of Troy. (Said in notice of his death to have been the first male child born in Bath that lived to manhood).

vi. Moody, b. in Bath, N. H., in 1775; m. Hannah McEuen, 1809, of Oneida Valley, N. Y.; d. in Rochester, N. Y., Sept. 27, 1825.

vii. Simpson, b. in Bath, N. H., May 31, 1776; m. 1st, Hannah Ward, b. 1780; d. 1832; 2d, Rachel Hosolton ; d. in Poke Co., Wis., Sept. 23, 1863.

viii. Samuel, b. in Bath, N. H., Sept. 5, 1777; m., in Bath, N. H., Polly Psalter, b. Oct. 13, 1785; d. in Ellisburg, N. Y., Nov. 1, 1870; d. in Ellisburg, N. Y., Dec. 20, 1849.

ix. Wealthy, m. John Henry Hunt; lived in Bath, N. H.

x. Harvey, b. in Bath, 1784; removed from Bath to Westfield, 1820; d. in Troy, Vt., May 20, 1844; buried in adjoining town of Westfield.

The daughter and eight of the nine sons of these hardy pioneers of Newbury left children, and six of the sons large families. Their descendants are numerous, scattered in most of the northern and western states. Benjamin and Harvey settled in Orleans Co., Vt. The other sons, some in 1797, and the others a few years later, removed to the State of New York. Roswell went first, in 1803, to Oneida County, and in 1806 to Oswego County, N. Y., being attracted to the latter place by the accounts given him by his father of his long sojourn as a soldier at Oswego. His oldest son, Zadok, m. Marthy Dix, b. in Wethersfield, Conn., Dec. 12, 1796. She was a descendant on the paternal side of Leonard Dix, one of the original settlers of that town, and on her maternal of Thomas Wells, also a settler of Wethersfield (1635), and the first Colonial Treasurer of Connecticut, and afterwards Secretary, Deputy Governor and Governor of that colony, and twenty-four years one of the judges of the General Court and the writer and one of the enactors, in 1642, of the severe criminal statutes that have given rise to the tradition of the existence of a criminal code commonly called the "Blue Laws."

ELBERT ELI FARMAN, traveler and diplomatist, was the third son and the fifth child of Zadok and Martha Dix Farman. He was b. in New Haven, N. Y., April 23, 1831; fitted for college at Genesee Wesleyan Seminary; was two years at Genesee College, but graduated at Amherst College 1855, from which he received the degree of A. M., in 1858, and in 1882 that of L.L. D. He took an active part in the Fremont campaign of 1856, delivering over fifty addresses. Studied law at Warsaw, N. Y., and was admitted to the bar in 1858, and settled at Warsaw, which has since been his permanent residence. Was also, for several years, editor of the Western New Yorker, attending at the same time to a very large practice. From 1865 to 1867 he traveled and studied in Europe. District Attorney for Wyoming County, N. Y., 1868–76. He was appointed by President Grant, in 1876, diplomatic agent, and consul general at Cairo, Egypt, holding this position till 1881, when he was appointed by President Garfield, on the last day of his public service, July 1, 1881, as one of the judges of the mixed tribunals of Egypt. This is a court composed of representatives of the various powers, who try all cases in which foreigners are interested. In January, 1883, he was designated by President Arthur, a member of the International Commission to determine the amounts to be paid as damages caused by the riots, burning and pillage of Alexandria in 1882. These scenes and the bombardment and burning of the city he witnessed. When Gen. Grant visited Egypt, Mr. Farman presented him to the Khedive, and accompanied him in his voyage up the Nile. It is to his personal efforts and his friendly relations to the Khedive, that New York city is indebted for the obelisk in Central Park. He also made, while in Egypt, extensive collections of antiquities, which he has since classfied, and are now on exhibition in the Metropolitan Museum in Central Park. Mr. Farman has been an indefatigable traveler, has crossed the Atlantic many times, has visited nearly every country in Europe and Asia, has explored Yucatan, Central and South America. At the time this work goes to press he has just returnd to America from a long residence in France, where he and Mrs. Farman have educated their children. Their home is in Warsaw, N. Y., where he is a member, and for 35 years a trustee of the Congregational church. Judge Farman has several times visited Newbury, and has taken a deep interest in this history, to whose success he has contributed in many ways. He was one of the first to urge its undertaking upon the editor, and, at the earnest solicitation of the latter, has caused a steel portrait of himself to be placed in this volume.

FOSTER.

REUBEN, was a prominent man, and an early settler, came here before the revolutionary war in which he served. In 1777, he with Gen. Bayley, represented Newbury in the first Windsor Convention, and the next year was chosen, with Col. Kent, to the second convention held at that place. He was, evidently, a man of affairs. The family has long been extinct here, but a record of the children of Reuben Foster, and Hannah Bayley, his wife, is from the town records, and inserted for the information of any member of the Foster family who may be in search for data.

Children:
i. Edward, b. May 14, 1768.
ii. Lydia, b. Sept. 21, 1770.
iii. Cyrus, b. July 10, 1772.
iv. Mary, b. June 19, 1774; d. Aug. 11, 1776.
v. Ebenezer, b. June 25, 1776.
vi. Nathaniel, b. May 25, 1778.
vii. Dorcas, b. Jan. 4, 1782.

FOWLER.

This family was prominent in the early years, but disappeared before the 19th century came in. Mr. F. L. Bailey says that the wives of Col. Joshua Bayley and his brother, Capt. Ephraim Bayley, were sisters, and daughters of Dea. Abner Fowler of Pembroke, N. H. This being the case, there are many descendants of the Fowlers living here now, and a few scanty details are here preserved, as there is no mention of the Newbury family in the "Book of the Fowlers." The family came early. Jacob Fowler was here in 1764, and in the town records is called "Captain" Fowler, by which it is presumed that he was an officer in the old French war. In 1769 he was a selectman.

JACOB and his wife were members of the Congregational church, and the record reads: "Jan. 23, 1785. At five o'clock this morning, Lieut. Jacob Fowler, a member of this church, deceased." The N. Y. petition, 1773, is signed by Abner, Peter, Jonathan, Abner, Jr., and Joseph Fowler. In 1771, Jacob, Jonathan, Abner and Abner, Jr., are given as heads of families. All these, with Jacob, Jr., and Jacob 3d, were in Revolutionary service. The name once must have been as common as that of Bayley or Chamberlain, but it has long disappeared from the town.

FULLER.

REV. STEPHEN FULLER, b. Mansfield. Conn., Dec. 3, 1756; grad. Dartmouth College 1786; ordained pastor of Cong. ch., Vershire, Sept. 3, 1788, and d. in office April 2, 1816. Published a volume of sermons. His salary never exceeded $400, on which he and his wife reared and educated a large family, sending five sons through college. He m., Sept., 1788, Phebe, dau. of Moses Thurston.
    Children:
    i. Henry, Presbyterian minister and D D. at Huntington, Long Island; three children.
    ii. Sewall, farmer, of Bradford; six c.
    iii. Stephen, physician, at Northampton, Mass.; four c.
    iv. David, lawyer, in Ohio; four c.
1   v. Edwin, farmer, in Bradford and Fairlee.
    vi. Edward C., minister at Brooklyn, N. Y.
    vii. Joseph. minister, d. in Vershire.
    viii. Lucy. d. un-m.
    ix. Lydia, d. y.
    x. Phebe. b. Dec. 18, 1794; m. June 4, 1816, Rev. Silas McKeen of Bradford, d. Nov. 30, 1820.

1 EDWIN. farmer, of Fairlee and Bradford; he m. Wealthy. dau. of Moody Clark of Bradford, who d. in Fairlee, April 30, 1854; d. Bradford, Nov. 4, 1887.
    Children:
    i. Susan Clark, m. 1st, John Thompson (q. v.); 2d, Isaac Olmsted (q. v.); 3d, —— Jones, and is a widow, living at South Newbury.
2 ii. Joseph H., b. Feb. 21, 1832.
    iii. Edward P., d. at two years of age.
    iv. Edward P., m. Carrie Bacon of Conn.; lived in Mount Vernon, N. Y.; d. Nov. 25, 1896.
    v. H. Maria, m. Joseph M. Warden of Bradford.
    vi. Dan Blodget; served in the civil war in the 10th Vt. ; mustered into U. S. service Sept. 1, 1862; was in nine battles and was mortally wounded at the battle of Winchester and died on the field, Sept. 19, 1864.
3 vii. Albert C., b. July 4, 1844.

2 JOSEPH, b. Fairlee, Feb. 21, 1832; farmer in Newbury, near Round Pond; served in Co. C, 9th Vt.; mustered in Jan. 6, 1864; mustered out May 13, 1865. He m. Jan. 8, 1861, Sarah J., dau. Jacob Bayley. (b. Dec. 4, 1833).
    Children:
    i. Lizzie J., b. April 23, 1862; m. June 28, 1900. Edgar L. Smith of Lowell, Mass. He d. Oct. 4, 1900, aged 38.
    ii. Henry E., b. March 25, 1864; farmer; m. Nov. 11, 1896, Emily Nichols. C., Harold E., b. Oct. 28, 1897.
    iii. Dan B., b. Oct. 31, 1867; farmer; m. Jan. 30, 1901, Ellen Nichols.
    iv. Mary E., b. Dec. 12, 1870.

3 ALBERT C., b. Fairlee, July 4, 1844; served in the civil war in Co. D, 8th Vt.; enlisted, Jan. 1, 1864; mustered out June 28, 1865; farmer of Fairlee and Newbury. He m. 1st, March 23, 1867, Nancy J., dau. of Benjamin Stebbins, of Groton. She d. at Bradford, Nov. 28, 1884. He m. 2d, in Newbury, April 8, 1886, Sarah L., dau. of Archibald McAllister.
    Children, one by 1st and one by 2d marriage:
    i. Mary Blanche, b. Fairlee, July 17, 1870; m. Feb. 13, 1892, Fred C. Renfrew, who d. Dec. 23, 1892.
    ii. Grace E., b. Fairlee, March 11, 1890.

FULTON.

ROBERT and JAMES, twin sons of Archibald and Mary (Young) Fulton, were born July 6, 1783, at a farm known as "Leechland," in the parish of Elderslie, Scotland, nine miles from Glasgow. This parish was the birthplace of Sir William Wallace. Margaret, their sister, b. 1786, m. John Craig of Paisley, and their son, Archibald Craig, originated in 1868 the Caledonia Engine Works at Paisley. This establishment has constantly increased in business, and now ranks among the principal industrial concerns of Great Britain. Archibald Craig d. in 1894, leaving a large fortune to his son, Archibald Fulton Craig. Robert Fulton came to America in 1801, on the ship "Commerce," the voyage occupying three months. He came at once to Newbury, with others of his countrymen, and settled on the "Jacob Brock place," near the Topsham line, later removing to the farm now owned by Mrs. V. N. Daniels. At the Freemen's Meeting in 1835, at which he was First Constable, there was a very hotly contested election, and when there was no choice at the ninth ballot, Mr. Fulton took up the ballot box and marched out of the house, expressing his opinion of the proceedings in vigorous Scotch. As there was no one who had authority to receive the votes, Newbury was unrepresented in the General Assembly of that year. He m. 1st, 1805, Jane Park of Ryegate, who came from Scotland with her brother, Archibald, in 1794. She d. 1816, aged 30. 2d, Feb. 15, 1820, Abigail. dau. Col. John Smith (b. Feb. 21, 1783; d. May 14, 1873). He d. June 27, 1852; buried on Currier Hill, Topsham.

Children, four by first m., two by second m. :
    i.   Jane, b. Dec. 27, 1807; m. Thomas J. Smith, q. v.; d.
    ii.   Eliza, b. April 7, 1810; m. Ralph Kendrick.
1 iii. John, b. May 16, 1812.
2 iv. George, b. Nov. 21, 1814.
    v.   Abigail, m. John Clark, q. v.
3 vi. Robert R., b. May 20, 1824.

1 JOHN,[2] (Robert,[1]) b. May 16, 1812; farmer, where his son, Dexter S., now lives; m. 1836, Sophia F. Ordway of Corinth. He d. July 19, 1872. She d. April 20, 1879, aged 64
    Children:
    i.   John F., b. Sept. 11, 1837; farmer and carpenter, and in other business; res. Lakeport. N. H.; m. Emma G., dau. William Grant, of East Corinth. C., Florence E., b. July 24, 1880.
    ii.   Asa C., b. Jan. 9, 1840; farmer in Bradford; m. Cynthia Farnham of Hartland. C., (1) Mary. (2) Edward. (3) Lambert.
4 iii. Dexter S., b. June 15, 1842.
    iv. Robert, b. Oct. 23, 1844; farmer in Bradford; m. Lucy, dau. Adams Wilson. C., (1) Aulie. (2) Mabel. (3) Frank. (4) Fay. (5) Jay.
    v.   Stephen C., b. Feb. 3, 1847; m. 1893, Jennie Currier; res. Lakeport, N. H.
    vi. Henry K., b. July 20, 1854; m. Blanche Grow of Claremont, N. H. Several c. Res. Barre.

2 GEORGE.[2] (Robert,[1]) b. Nov. 21, 1814; m. Susan, dau. Ebenezer Kendrick, (b. June 9, 1817; d. April 21, 1873). He d. April 21, 1879.
    Children:
    i.   Francis R.
    ii.   Almira, who m. Wm. Young of Patterson, N. J., and is the only one living of the family.
    iii. George.

3 ROBERT REED,[2] (Robert,[1]) b. May 20, 1824. Educated at Thetford and Corinth Academies. Was prominent in town affairs, and town representative in 1867–68. Rem. to East Corinth, 1870, and was a merchant there, and town representative in 1888. Postmaster many years. Republican in politics, and member of the Cong. ch. at East Corinth. He m. Nov. 28, 1861, Ann, dau. James Halley of Newbury. No c. He d. Jan. 18, 1893.

4 DEXTER SMITH, b. June 15, 1842. Educated at Newbury Seminary and Barre Academy; went to Iowa in 1873, and was for some time with Col. Oscar

ROBERT REED FULTON.

DEXTER SMITH FULTON.

C. Hale, formerly of Wells River, at Keokuk, where he succeeded in placing large amounts of money for people in Vermont and New Hampshire in county, city and town bonds; returned to Newbury and resides on the homestead near the s. w. corner of the town; director and vice-president of Wells River Savings Bank; has been in town business, and was, in 1901, elected a school director; in 1896 he was chosen a presidential elector on the Democratic ticket, but declined to serve, not being in sympathy with the free silver movement; in 1900, with his son, he visited the Paris Exposition and other places of interest in Europe, spending some time in London and Scotland, where they were successful in locating relatives in Glasgow and Paisley. He m., 1875, Eva C. Gilman of Corinth (b. in Hardwick). C., Harley D., b. July 10, 1883.

FURY.

THOMAS, b. Dublin, Ireland, Dec. 25, 1819. Came to America 1835, and helped build the Boston and Lowell railroad from Boston to Nashua, the Concord railroad, and the Boston, Concord and Montreal, from Concord to Littleton. Came to Newbury 1856, and was employed much in laying foundation walls and stoning wells. He m. Katherine Cunningham, (b. Ireland, 1825; d. Newbury Aug. 27, 1861). He d. Feb. 22, 1891.

Children:
i. Mary A., b. Plymouth, N. H., April 10, 1853; m. Dec. 23, 1871, W. H. Martin: res. Davenport, Iowa. Three c.
ii. John, b. Haverhill, Aug. 27, 1855; in the west.
iii. Ellen, b. Newbury, March 10, 1858; m. June 24, 1878, John S. Demerritt, (b. Randolph, Aug. 26, 1848; d. Franklin, Mass., Aug. 27, 1891). C., (1) Nellie M., b. Franklin. Mass., June 1, 1879. (2) Katherine E., b. Newbury, Aug. 8, 1881. (3) James J., b. Newbury, Aug. 14, 1885.
iv. James P., b. July 4, 1860; res. Laconia, N. H.

GAMSBY.

HARVEY D., son of Victory Gamsby, and grandson of George Gamsby, a revolutionary soldier, b. Stratford. N. H., 1837; came to Newbury, 1860; enlisted 1861 at Stratford, N. H., in 2d U. S. Sharpshooters; was wounded at the battle of Fredericksburg in 1862; discharged from Annapolis (Md.) hospital, for disability, 1862; enlisted 2d, 1862, in 15th Vt., for nine months; enlisted, 3d, 1864, for one year, in the 42d Wisconsin; mustered out June 29, 1865; m. Nov. 25, 1868, Ellen F. Leet.

Children:
i. Albert E., b. March 20, 1870; an engineer on Boston & Maine railroad.
ii. Bertha M., b. Oct. 20, 1874; m. Arthur D. Runnels.

GARDNER.

HUGH was an early and prominent citizen of Ryegate, and an elder in the Pres. ch. He m. Mary Nelson and reared a large family. Two of his sons lived in Newbury, of whose families the following was prepared by the late Edward Miller, Esq., of Ryegate.

1 WILLIAM, b. Ryegate, Aug. 9 1803; m. April 15, 1829, Eliza, dau. Enoch Nelson (b. Newbury, April 22, 1812). They lived at the upper end of "Scotch Hollow." He d. Oct. 15, 1879.

Children all born in Newbury, except the second and third:
i. Hugh N., b. Aug. 22, 1831; m. 1st, Sept. 11, 1859, Mary A. Elkins of Chelsea; four c.; 2d, Aug. 29, 1870, Clarissa Emery of Groton; one c., Timothy, b. January 9, 1872; was brought up by Andrew Grant; res. Newbury.
ii. Horatio W. H., b. July 27, 1833; served in the Union army; m. Sept. 10, 1854, Mrs. Wheaton, dau. of Michael Cross of Newbury; six c.
iii. Mary H., b. Oct. 7, 1835; m. Dec. 19, 1834, Alexander Gibson, Jr.; rem. to Iowa; ten c.

   iv. John R., b. Feb. 17, 1838; m. Hannah Peach.
    v. George N., b. May 22, 1840; served in Co. C, 3d Vt.; killed at the battle of
       Spottsylvania, May 12, 1864.
   vi. Lydia N., b. Sept. 26, 1842; m. Aug. 6, 1865, Mark Page, Jr., of Ryegate.
  vii. Nancy Jane, b. May 18, 1845; d. July 23, 1860.
 viii. Abbie Ellen, b. Aug. 10, 1847; m. —— Nelson in Iowa; is dead.
   ix. Jane G.. b. Feb. 22, 1850; m. ——.
    x. Rebecca, b. Aug. 24, 1852; d. 1875.
   xi. Lizzie Bell, b. Nov. 22, 1855; m. Allen Felch; d.; six c.

2 HUGH, b. Ryegate, May 18, 1812; farmer at Boltonville; m. Sept. 27, 1832,
      Nancy, dau. James Henderson, (b. May 25, 1815). He d. May 1, 1869.
     Children:
    i. Mary Jane, b. Jan. 14, 1834; d. Oct. 22, 1849.
   ii. Hannah. b. Jan. 2, 1836; d. Oct. 25, 1859.
  iii. Isabel, b. Dec. 23, 1837; m. David B. Reid, q. v.
  iv. Elizabeth H., b. Nov. 19, 1840; d. Aug. 9, 1862.
   v. Harriet, b. Aug. 28, 1843; m. Jan. 1, 1867, James M. Boyce; d. St.
      Johnsbury, June 27, 1887.
3 vi. James H., b. April 6, 1849.
  vii. Charles H., b. March 11, 1849; d. Jan. 1, 1850.
 viii. Abbie M., b. March 29, 1852; m. Dec. 24, 1872, Alonzo Boyce.

3 JAMES H., b. April 6, 1849; farmer on the homestead at Boltonville; m. Oct. 26,
      1870, Martha W., dau. Royal H. Abbott.
     Children:
    i. Herbert M., b. June 8, 1871; merchant at Barton; m. Carrie Whitney.
      One c.
   ii. Emogene, b. Jan. 20, 1873; m. George A. Kelley, manager of Marshfield
      creamery; four c.
  iii. Lizzie, b. Oct. 26, 1875; m. William Reid; d. Sept. 22, 1896. One c.
  iv. Ethel. b. Sept. 7, 1880.
   v. Birdella, b. March 19, 1887.
  vi. Lawrence, b. Dec. 25, 1890.

GARLAND.

JOHN PARKER. b. Topsham, March 6, 1825. His father, Amos Garland, b. in
    Sept., 1795, was the fifth child of Amos, son of John Garland of
    Hampstead, N. H. His mother, Betsey Parker, b. March 18, 1797, was
    a daughter of Daniel Parker, who was a lad of twelve at the burning of
    Charlestown, in 1775, and served in the revolutionary war while very
    young. Amos Garland moved from Salisbury to Topsham in 1819. The
    father, son and grandson were blacksmiths, who began to learn the trade
    in childhood. John P. Garland m. in 1849, while at work in Billerica.
    He worked at Concord, then at Meredith, and at the latter place was
    badly injured by the giving way of the floor of the town hall, when
    several were killed. He lived in Stowe, then in Montpelier, doing carriage
    ironing. His wife died in 1858, leaving one son. George D., now of
    Chicago. He m., 2d, in May, 1861, Eliza N., dau. of Hale Grow. He came
    to Newbury 1863, buying the shop of H. N. Burnham, which was a brick
    building, back of M. A. Gale's house, and afterwards built a shop on Pine
    street. His wife d. in Jan., 1890. Of their five children, only one, Alfred
    C., survived infancy. He m., 3d, Aug. 1892, Emilie, dau. of Moses Knight.
    Member of Charity Masonic lodge of Bradford. He was a good musician
    and had belonged to several bands; d. Newbury, Aug. 1896.

GEORGE.

STEPHEN, of English descent, was b. June 8, 1793; settled first in Bradford, but
    about 1827 came to Newbury and settled on Leighton hill, at the corner
    of the road near the schoolhouse; m. in Bradford, March 10, 1822, Lydia,
    dau. of Reuben Leighton, (b. May 3, 1794; d. March 9, 1883). They were
    members of the Methodist church, as were most of their children, and

MOSES L. BROCK,
1ST LIEUT., 1ST REGT. INFANTRY, VT. VOLS.,
SPANISH-AMERICAN WAR.

many of their grandchildren. As nearly as can be ascertained he was born in Keene, N. H. He d. Oct. 2, 1867.

Children:

1 i. Reuben L., b. Bradford, Feb. 4, 1823; d. Aug. 26, 1886, q. v.
   ii. Samuel L., b. Bradford, July 30, 1824.
   iii. Gideon, b. Bradford, May 7, 1826.
   iv. Stephen L., b. Newbury, April 16, 1828.
2 v. John S., b. Newbury, Aug. 29, 1830, q. v.
3 vi. James W., b. Newbury, May 13, 1832, q. v.
   vii. Alphonso W., b. Newbury, Feb. 4, 1836.

1 REUBEN L., b. Bradford, Feb. 4, 1823; farmer; he cleared most of the farm which his son, John F., now owns, and erected the buildings. He m. in Topsham, Feb. 12, 1850. Mehetabel, dau. of Blanchard and Susanna (Carleton) Chamberlain, (b. Sept. 11, 1822; d. Jan. 7, 1889). They were members of the Methodist church, in which he was a steward and class-leader for many years. He d. Aug. 26, 1886.

Children, all b. in Newbury:

   i. Charles N., b. April 19, 1851; m. Eliza Burrell of Winthrop, Mass. C., (1) Willard. (2) Clifford.
   ii. W. Scott, b. July 14, 1853; m. Nettie Morse of Newton Center, Mass.; stone cutter; now in California in orange business.
   iii. R. Dexter, b. May 13, 1855; now in the west.
   iv. John F., b. May 12, 1858; farmer on homestead; m. Sept. 24, 1883, Charlien F., dau. Benjamin Wheeler. C., (1) Roscoe M., b. Dec. 7, 1885. (2) D. Albertis b. Dec. 13, 1888.
   v. Eri C., b. July 25, 1860; res. Plymouth, N. H.; plumber; m. Nov. 29, 1887, Lilla, dau. of Samuel M. Rollins. One c., Hattie M., b. Plymouth, June 5, 1889.

2 JOHN S., son of Stephen, b. Aug. 29, 1830; lived when a boy six years in the family of Edward Hale; went to Boston at the age of 18; returned 1853; farmer on Upper Meadow ; carried on the town farm, as overseer, for several years; steward in the M. E. church ; he m., in Haverhill, Jan. 24, 1854, Mary Jane, dau. of George and Mary (Lake) Woodward (b. Springfield, Vt., Oct. 7, 1833 ; d. July 20, 1897).

Children:

   i. Frank W., b. Oct. 4, 1859; m. Feb. 17, 1880, Flora J., dau. of Warren K. Chamberlain; farmer on homestead.
   ii. William J., b. Nov. 14, 1872; m. —— Mary, dau. of William Allen ; one c.

3 JAMES W., b. Newbury, May 13, 1832; farmer on Leighton hill; steward in Meth. ch.; he m. in Topsham, March 9, 1856, Diadama, dau. of Welbe Butterfield, (b. Topsham, Oct. 18, 1836) ; d. Newbury, Aug. 1, 1892.

Children:

   i. Stephen W., b. Nov. 15, 1856; farmer and stonecutter; res. in Newbury and Dover, N. H.; now in Montpelier; m. Aug. 20, 1885, Eliza, dau. of J. Welbe Butterfield of Topsham and Dover, N. H.; c. all b. in Dover; (1) Laura A., b. Sept. 16, 1887; (2) Diodama, b. July 13, 1889; (3) Florence, b. Feb. 6, 1891; d. Aug. 23, 1892; (4) Prudence, b. Nov. 10, 1895.
   ii. James Herbert, b. Sept. 20, 1858; lives in California; he m. in San Francisco, Cal., Feb. 22, 1888, Hannah Cousins; c (1) Adah Ruby.
   iii. Ira W., b. Jan. 12, 1862; farmer on homestead; un-m.; d. Oct. 18, 1894.
   iv. Eliza J., b. Aug. 1, 1863; res. Newbury.
   v. Ruby D., b. Aug. 3, 1870; teacher; m. Feb. 28, 1898, Homer A. Barrows; lives in Underhill, Vt.; c. William L., b. Troy, Vt., Feb. 6, 1899.
   vi. Laura, b. March 11, 1872; d. Jan. 13, 1884.

GEORGE.

JOHN, of Hopkinton, N. H., came to Topsham with his wife and 15 children, and cleared a farm on George hill, where were born to them two children more. Fifteen of these children lived till the youngest was 40 years old.

Their oldest son, James, m. Lydia Jones, and settled in Warner, but rem. to Topsham.

Children:

1 i. Charles, b. Nov. 30, 1796.

    ii. Judith, m. George Divoll.
    iii. Lydia, d. Jan. 4, 1888.
    iv. Sally.
2   v. James, b. Jan. 26, 1804, q. v.
    vi. Martha, m. Thomas Mellen, Jr., q. v.
    vii. Joanna, m. John S. Cook.
    viii. Eliza.

1 CHARLES,[3] (James,[2] John,[1]) b. South Hampton, N. H., Nov. 30, 1796; lived in Corinth, but came to Newbury, about 1820; m. 1st, Fidelia Blanchard, who d. about a year later. One c., Hiram, d. y. He m. 2d, Jan. 1, 1823, Abigail, dau. Capt. Jacob Bayley, (b. Jan. 10, 1798; d. March 21, 1886). He d. Aug. 24, 1851.
    Children:
    i. Fidelia, b. Corinth, Dec. 6, 1823; m. Samuel M. Rollins, q. v.; d. March 20, 1850.
    ii. Sophila, b. Jan. 24, 1824; d. Dec. 26, 1841.
    iii. James L., b. Feb. 26, 1828; res. Newbury; served three years in the civil war; m. 1st, Mary Randall; m. 2d, Sophronia Kasson.
    iv. Mary E., b. Dec. 13, 1831; m. Henry E. Dunbar, q. v.
    v. Edmond Harriman, b. Dec. 29, 1834; served in the Union army, (see record); res. Newbury; house painter; m. Nov. 29, 1876, Jane E. Ham of Bath, (b. 1857). C., (1) Lula May, b. July 14, 1878; d. Dec. 25, 1895. (2) Leona, b. Sept. 11, 1880. (3) Emma Sophila, b. Aug. 23, 1882. (4) Russell Lowell, b. June 21, 1889. (5) Forrest Wesley, b. April 15, 1898.
    vi. Abigail, b. Aug. 4, 1836; d. Aug. 7, 1854.

2 JAMES,[3] (James,[2] John,[1]) b. Jan. 26, 1804; m. May 22, 1828, Maria, dau. of Jeremiah Nourse, (b. Feb. 25, 1809; d. June 15, 1890); farmer in Topsham and Newbury; d. Nov. 7, 1882.
    Children:
3   i. Ann Maria, b. May 16, 1829; m. Rev. G. N. Bryant.
4   ii. Charles H., b. Feb. 15, 1831.
5   iii. Ruth N., b. April 24, 1834; m. B. B. Clifford.
6   iv. Jeremiah N., b. Oct. 5, 1837.
    v. Osman C. B., b. Sept. 26, 1840; served in the Union army and died in service Dec. 2, 1863. (see war record).
7   vi. James Herbert, b. Oct. 28, 1843.
8   vii. Emma S., b. April 3, 1848.

3 ANN MARIA, dau. of James George, b. May 26, 1829; m. May 16, 1851, Rev. Geo. N. Bryant. Mr. Bryant was b. in New Boston, N. H., May 21, 1824; son of Asa Bryant, a soldier in the war of 1812, and a near relative of William Cullen Bryant, the poet and journalist. Of the seven children of Asa, two sons made their way to the ministry; James C., the elder, was pastor of the 1st Cong. ch. at Littleton, Mass., but died a missionary of the American Board to South Africa, at the age of 38, in 1850. George N. entered Newbury Seminary in 1844, taught school winters, worked for his board while at school and on farms summers, studied for the ministry, being one of the last surviving pupils of the Newbury Biblical Institute; entered the N. H. Conference 1849, his first appointment being at Stark and Milan. He was 41 years in the ministry, a faithful pastor and diligent student. Superintendent of schools at Lancaster, Littleton and Lisbon. Retired from active ministry, 1891, and settled in Newbury. Mrs. Bryant was his pupil while teaching in the "Nourse neighborhood." He d. May 9, 1901. C., Arthur Peyton, b. May 7, 1868; res. Middletown, Ct.; in work connected with the Department of Agriculture, Washington; he m. April 4, 1893, Fannie W. Burr, b. April 27, 1874.

4 CHARLES HARVEY, b. Feb. 15, 1831; served in the Union army (see record); m. Oct. 15, 1856, Ellen M., dau. of John Peach; rem. west about 1870; res. River Falls, Wis. C., (1) Nellie E, b. ————; m. Dr. Elbridge A. Toby, formerly in practice at Warren, N. H., but now at River Falls; four c. are living. (2) Arabella, b. 1869; d. young. (3) Eva B., b. Dec. 13, 1870; m. Charles Ritchie; two c.; res. in Dakota. (4) Bessie L., b. April 13, 1873; m. Geo. McLean; res. Dakota.

5 Ruth N., b. Feb. 15, 1831; m. April 30, 1856, B. B. Clifford, who d. August, 1873. C., (1) George B., b. March 10, 1858; m. May 23, 1888, Minnie E. Cooley. Two c. Res. Grand Forks, N. D. (2) Charles H., b. July 18, 1860; drowned in North Dakota, Aug. 4, 1883. (3) Joseph E, b. July 2, 1862; m. May 14, 1890, Anna H. Parsons. Three c. Res. Grand Forks, N. D. (4) Frederic W., b. Nov. 13, 1867; m. Nov. 24, 1898, Grace Parsons; res. Minneapolis, Minn. (5) Alvin P., b. Sept. 4, 1871; m. June 15, 1897, Katherine Stewart; res. Grand Forks, N. D.

6 Jeremiah Nourse, b. Oct. 5, 1837; first telegraph operator at Newbury; served in the Union army, (see record); m. August, 1869, Olivia E. Glazier; d. Dec. 24, 1887. C., Frank L., b. Aug. 18, 1870; m. Sept. 12, 1893, Nettie Legg. Two c. Res. Boston.

7 James Herbert, b. Oct. 28, 1843. A musician from his cradle; studied telegraphy, but enlisted while stationed at Greenfield, Mass., as drum major in the 10th Vt., in 1861; promoted band leader and served till the end of the war; served apprenticeship in a piano factory, Boston; res. since 1871, Norwich, Conn.; leader of church choirs, concerts; teacher the past ten years of vocal music in the public schools of Norwich, and in the Y. M. C. A. of that city. Is prominent in Grand Army matters. He m. Sept. 8, 1870, Mary A. Mason. C., (1) Mabel D., b. Dec. 16, 1872; d. Jan. 1, 1875. (2) Herbert M., b. Sept. 24, 1876. (3) Marian L., d. at three years old. (4) James E., d. at two years old.

8 Emma Sophia, b. April 3, 1848; teacher one year at Drew Female Seminary; m. May 10, 1871, Robert W. C. Farnsworth, b. Haverhill, N. H.. Feb.20, 1844; he enlisted in the 10th Vt., 1862; after two years of hard service was transferred and made captain in a colored regiment; severely wounded in hip and arm; dis. March, 1865; fitted for college at Newbury Seminary; grad. Wesleyan University, 1871; professor of Latin at Fort Edward Institute one year; in Boston Theo. Sem. one year; in the M. E. ministry in New England seven or eight years. Went to Southern California; pastor three years at Pasadena; presiding elder four years; dean of the Theo. Sem. connected with Leland Stanford University one term, where he d. of pneumonia, Jan. 3, 1888. He was a man of very high standing in the Methodist church. C., (1) Ruth W., b. Aug. 20, 1872; m. Nov. 8, 1893. Elmer E. Hall. (2) Edith E., b, July 5, 1877. Mrs. Farnsworth m. 2d, Nov. 12, 1896, Prof. G. Wharton James; res. Pasadena, Cal.

GEORGE.

Stephen, and his wife, Sarah Towle, came from Kingston, N. H., about 1795, and made a pitch near what is now called Bradford Center. After two or three years they rem. to the southwest corner of Newbury and took up land, on which he built a house 20x24, with timber which he hewed, framed and raised in one day. The boards for covering the building he dragged upon the ground from South Newbury through the woods with an ox team. He d. Aug. 27, 1853, aged 81 years, 7 months, 10 days, and his wife, April 2, 1865, aged 93 years, 6 months, 26 days.
Children:
. Electa, b. Feb. 12; d. May 12, 1797.
ii. Jeremy, b. Oct. 16, 1799; settled on Indian Stream, N. H., and d. there, leaving four c.
1 iii. Nicholas, b. Oct. 11, 1801; m. Laura Farr, who d. July 14, 1860, aged 59. He d. June 3, 1891.
iv. Stephen, b. Nov. 8, 1804; d. Jan. 20, 1829.
v. Charles G., b. June 11, 1811; went west; is believed to be dead.
vi. Sargent T., b. Sept. 3, 1813; lives in Bradford.

1 Nicholas and Laura (Farr) had children:
i. Augustus, d. in infancy.
ii. Relectas. m. Joseph F. Laird.
iii. Roswell F., m. Avarissa Simpson; res. in East Corinth; served in the Union army from 1863 to the end of the war. C., (1) Lestina E., m. Dr. R. C. Jenne. (2) Harriet A. (3) Charles F. (4) Roswell E. (5) Laura A. (6) John H. (7) Jennie B.

GILMORE.

WILLIAM GILMORE, b. Fifeshire, Scotland, 1799; m. Ann, dau. Wm. Halley, (q. v.)
b. Scotland, 1801; d. Illinois, August, 1877. They came from Scotland to
Ryegate, 1830 or '31, to Topsham in 1833, to Newbury, 1838, and lived
where William Allen has long lived. In 1860, they rem. to Illinois, where
some of the children had already gone. He d. near Rockford, Ill., June,
1871.
Children:

i. Ann, b. Scotland, 1823; m. Feb. 25, 1845, David Webster, q. v.
ii. John, b. Scotland, 1824; m. Jan. 4, 1854, Margaret, dau. Richard
Patterson; res. in Illinois.
iii. William, b. Scotland, 1826; m. 1857, Jane Mack; d. near Rockford, Ill.,
1891. Five c.
iv. Elizabeth, b. Scotland, 1828; m. 1860, Charles Bates, who d. 1888; res.
Cass County, Neb. One son.
v. Mary J., b. Ryegate, 1832; m. Oct. 15, 1855, Nathan Marston; res. Black
Hawk, Iowa.
vi. James, b. Topsham, 1834; m. 1869, Elizabeth Mills; res. Rockford, Ill.
vii. Robert, b. Topsham, 1838; rem. from Illinois to Iowa, 1869; res. Cherokee
County, Iowa.
viii. Margaret, b. Newbury, 1840; m. 1869, Edward Mascrip; res. Sioux Falls,
S. D.
ix. Janette, b. Newbury, 1842; m. 1879, George Clark; res. Cherokee, Iowa.
x. Jane, b. Newbury, 1845; m. 1877, James Patterson; res. Cherokee, Iowa.

GIBSON.

MATTHEW, son of Samuel Gibson of Merrimack, N. H., came to Newbury from
Francestown, N. H., before 1780. His wife was Betsey McClary, of
Litchfield, N. H. Settled on the farm where Albert Fuller now lives, and
rem. to Great Valley, N. Y., about 1823. She returned to Newbury and d.
March 21, 1830.
Children:

i. David, m. Jean, dau. of Archibald and Maria (McKeen) McAllister; rem. to
Grand Isle, and d. at Great Valley, N. Y.
ii. Mary, m. Zaccheus Dustin. His farm was that now owned by Hale G.
Bailey, and old people still call it the " old Dustin place." The building
stood up the "lane" toward R. S. Chamberlain's. Six children b. between
1808 and 1818; rem. to Chazy, N. Y.
iii. Margaret, b. Jan. 14, 1784; m. Benjamin Brock, Dec. 29, 1806, q. v.; d.
Aug. 27, 1815.
iv. Matthew, b.　　　　 ; rem. to Michigan.
v. Lowell, b.　　　　 ; rem. to Great Valley, N. Y., and d. there.
vi. Rebecca, b. May 23, 1770; m. Ebenezer Temple, q v.
vii. Rachel, m. William Gibson of Hillsborough, N. H., Jan. 6, 1807.
viii. Samuel was born in 1778 ; captain in the militia; built the house at the
Center where John Wood lived many years and kept tavern there; m. 1st,
Jan. 17, 1804, Betsey, dau. of Thos. Mellen ; d. Aug. 25, 1830, (church
record). C., (1) Samuel, m. Catherine Crawford, June 15, 1837; built the
house where Hale G. Bailey now lives. (2) Jane, m. 1829, Seth Austin,
a lawyer of Topsham and Bradford, (b. Suffield, Conn., September,
1797; d. Bradford, March 1, 1855); three c. (3) Ann, b. June 12, 1805;
m. Capt. James Wallace as 1st wife; d. March 28, 1836. (4) Alexander,
b. ——— ; m. and went west. (5) Adaline, b. ———. (6) John, b.——
——; un-m.; d. (7) Louisa, b. ———; m. —— Austin. (8) Archibald,
b. ———; un-m.; d. (9) Betsey, b. —— ——; d. at 22. He m. 2d,
Rebecca Waddell; 3d, Mrs. Betsey Eastman of Landaff. He d. July 17,
1862, in the house now owned by Miss Julia Goddard at Newbury
village.
ix. Thomas, d. un-m. at Great Valley, N. Y.
x. Betsey, m. a Mr. Farrington of Great Valley, N. Y.

* GIBSON.

Hugh Gardner, son of Alexander and Jean (Gardner) Gibson; b. Ryegate, May 29, 1815; farmer near Ryegate Corner till 1881, when he bought the Capt. John Miller farm in Newbury; the buildings, which are in South Ryegate village, are on the Newbury side of the line. The house and barns were burned in the spring of 1895, at a loss of about $6,000, and he had a new set of buildings nearly completed at the time of his death. He m. April 4, 1839, Abigail, dau. William Nelson 2d; six c., four living. Mr. Nelson was a prominent man in Ryegate and a member of the Ref. Pres. ch. about 67 years. He d. Jan. 14, 1896.

GODDARD.

Nathan, b. Shrewsbury, Mass., Aug. 4, 1746; grad. Harvard College, 1770; came to Newbury not far from 1783; was a member and clerk of the church, and seems to have occasionally preached, as there are accounts preserved of sums "paid Mr. Goddard for supplying the pulpit at sundry times." He was Register of Probate in 1786, '87; whether he ever practiced law here or not is uncertain, but there are legal papers extant drawn up by him. He seems to have lived near where Mr. James Lawrie now does, and was very highly esteemed. He left Newbury before 1792. Mr. Goddard m. Dec. 15, 1772, Martha Nichols (b. Oct. 31, 1746; d. Gerry, Mass., 1814); d. Framingham, Mass., July 24, 1795.
Children:
i. Nichols, b. Shrewsbury, Mass., Oct. 4, 1773; d. Rutland, Vt., Sept. 29, 1823; he m. Charity, dau. of Job White of Northampton, Mass.
ii. Grace, b. April 12, 1775; m. Ephraim Drury.
iii. Nathan, b. Dec. 15, 1777; m. Prudence Hemenway; 2d, Polly Bacon; d. Framingham, Mass., July 4, 1832.

Rev. Edward N. Goddard, an Episcopal clergyman of Windsor, Vt., is a gr. gr. son of Nathan Goddard of Newbury.

GOODWIN.

Simeon, John and Samuel were brothers. Simeon was private in Capt. Jacob Bayley's Co., which marched to Oswego from Albany in 1759. He was also adjutant in Col. Israel Morey's regiment from Sept. 25 to Oct. 26, 1777, and was especially recommended for fidelity and bravery. He was a grantee of Newbury, and came here as early as 1763. He rem. about 1802 to Marietta, O., where he d.
Children:
i. Jonathan.
ii. Nathaniel.
iii. Simeon.
iv. Asa.
v. Mary, m. her cousin, Willoughby Goodwin.
vi. Harriet, m. John Merrill.

Jonathan's name is given as head of a family in the New York census of 1771, and he signed the New York petition of 1773. He served one month, 29 days, in Capt. John G. Bayley's Co., guarding and scouting in the revolutionary war and perhaps in other service. He settled on Hall's Meadow, Lot 9, his house standing a little below the South Newbury schoolhouse on the other side of the road. This land he bought of Thomas Shirley of Chester, N. H., in 1768. The deed was not acknowledged, but the title was comfirmed by a special act of the General Assembly in 1785. Jonathan Goodwin d. Oct. 28, 1811, aged 71, and Elizabeth, his wife, d. Oct. 8, 1813, aged 73.
Among their children were:
i. Phebe, b. in Newbury, 1780, and d. June, 1881, at the home of Dea. George

---

* By the late Edward Miller.

Burroughs, in her 101st year, preserving her mental and physical faculties to the end.

ii. Elizabeth, m. Philip Tewksbury, and d. Oct. 3, 1841.
And perhaps Isaac, b. Newbury, 1783; m. Jemima Ford.

NATHANIEL, according to town record, m. March 27, 1789, Elizabeth Marsh, and had, at least, the following c.:
  i. Martha, b. Nov. 8, 1787.
  ii. Moses, b. June 28, 1789.
  iii. Nathaniel, b. June 8, 1791.
  iv. Aaron, b. Feb. 2, 1794. The youngest son of Aaron, J. W. Goodwin, was long editor of the Sedalia, Mo., Bazoo.

SIMEON, m., and had four daus., Susan, Margaret, Sarah and Roxanna.

ASA, rem. to Marietta, O., thence to St. Louis where he d. He had eight c.

JOHN, the second of the three brothers, was also a grantee of Newbury and a signer of the New York petition of 1773. He served one month in Capt. John G. Bayley's Co., guarding and scouting, also 40 days of similar service in Capt. Simeon Stevens' Co.
Children:
  i. Moses, q. v.
  ii. Willoughby, who m. April 10, 1781, his cousin, Mary Goodwin.
  iii. Daniel, lived in Cambridge.
  iv. James, lived in Grafton.
  v. Judith, m. John Thomas.
  And another m. ———— Dunbar.

SAMUEL lived in Newbury at one time.

1 MOSES.[2] (John,[1]) lived in Newbury, Ryegate and Haverhill; m. Tryphena, dau. James Ladd of Haverhill.
Children (order of birth not known):
2   Wells, b. Nov. 9, 1784; d. Dec. 11, 1894.
3   Moses, b. Feb. 14, 1798; d. March 28, 1865.
  Timothy.
  George.
  Hannah; m. Geo. Chapman of Haverhill.
  Abigail; m. ——— Fisher of N. Haverhill.
  Dau., m. ——— Kelsea.
  Dau., m. 1811, Daniel Heath of Piermont.

WELLS,[3] (Moses,[2] John,[1]), born on the Gray farm in Ryegate, Nov. 9, 1894. He enlisted Feb. 14, 1813, for 18 months, in the 11th U. S. infantry, commanded by Col. Moody Bedel of Haverhill. He served in the battles of Chippewa and Prescott, and was wounded in the leg at the battle of Lundy's Lane, July 25, 1814. In 1818 he received a pension of $4 per month, dating back to his discharge from the army. This was increased to $8 in 1852, and later to $12. He was m. in Haverhill, by Rev. Grant Powers, Oct. 3, 1819, to Lydia, dau. of Daniel and Martha (Merrill) Heath (b. New Salem, N. H., Nov. 8, 1794; d. Newbury, Dec. 27, 1887), their married life being 68 years, 1 month, 19 days. They lived in Ryegate till 1847, where he was farmer and shoemaker; since in Newbury, excepting a few years in Corinth and Haverhill. He voted at every presidential election, from that of James Monroe, in 1816, to that of Grover Cleveland, in 1892. He drew pay and pension for military service rendered the United States nearly 82 years, and was the last enlisted soldier of the war of 1812 in Vermont. His last years were spent with his daughter, Mrs. Leavitt, his mind having given way before his death, Dec. 11, 1894, aged 100 years, 2 months, 2 days.
Children, all born in Ryegate:
4   i. John Merrill, b. July 17, 1820.
  ii. Helen, b. Oct. 19, 1821; m. George Rhodes of Ryegate; d. Dec. 30, 1891.
  iii. Jane, b. June 18, 1823; d. Dec. 1, 1834.
  iv. Austin, b. May 22, 1825; d. Dec. 18, 1854.
  v. Timothy, b. Sept. 24, 1827; was last heard of in New York.
  vi. Lavinia, b. April 5, 1829; d. Dec. 18, 1854.

5 vii. William, b. April 16, 1831.
  viii. Daniel W., b. Dec. 1, 1832; d. May 25, 1856.
  ix. Annette, b. Feb. 7, 1834.
   x. Jane, b. Oct. 30, 1835; m. J. C. Leavitt, q. v.
  xi. Edwin, b. July 7, 1838; d. March 12, 1839.
  xii. Elizabeth, b. July 7, 1841; m. Orvin C. Temple, q. v.

4 JOHN MERRILL, b. July 17, 1820; served in the Mexican war; enlisted at Manchester, N. H., in April, 1847, in Co. C, 9th U. S. Infantry; transferred to Co. H. They arrived at Vera Cruz in June, marched to Pueblo under Gen. Pierce, joining Gen. Winfield Scott's army there and had a few skirmishes before reaching the city of Mexico. The first great battle was that of Cantreras, a volcanic mountain, Aug. 19 and 20, 1847. The Mexicans were defeated, and driven to Churubusco, which surrendered. After an armistice which lasted about two weeks, the battle of Malino del Rey was fought on the 8th of September. The American army was driven back twice, but at the third charge they drove the Mexicans before them. Mr. Goodwin was twice promoted for good conduct, first made a Corporal, then Sergeant, and during the last part of the war was acting Orderly Sergeant. Discharged at Newport, R. I., Aug. 23, 1848. Farmer in Newbury and near-by towns. He m. March 28, 1849, dau. of Moses Clark. She d. June 11, 1898. He res. with his son in Piermont.
Children:
  i. John Merrill, b. Boston, Mass., July 9, 1857; m. Sept. 17, 1884, Cora Ada, dau. of Horace N. Abbott,' b. Jan. 3, 1864; res. Piermont; in creamery. C., (1) Lois M., b. Nov. 7, 1886. (2) Horace M., b. May 3, 1888.

5 WILLIAM,[2] (Wells,[1]) b. April 16, 1831; m. Mary Ann, dau. of Alonzo Fleming, who d. June, 1901.
Children:
  i. Elizabeth, b. 1856; m. 1878, James Ryle; res. Chicopee, Mass.
  ii. Charles, b. Jan. 18, 1888.
  iii. Herbert, b. Nov. 24, 1871.
  iv. Blanche, b. Oct. 30, 1878.

MOSES,[3] (Moses,[2] John,[1]) b. —— Feb. 14, 1798; lived in Ryegate, and for some years in Newbury, in what is now called Montebello House, then in South Newbury; he m. Feb. 13, 1823, Elizabeth, dau. of Timothy Clark (b. Nov. 9, 1800); d. Lisbon, N. H., March 28, 1865.
Children:
  i. Charles, b. Ryegate, March 22, 1827; served in the Civil war in Co. A, 20th Mass. Vols.; killed in the first day's battle of the Wilderness, May 5, 1864: he m. June 8, 1853, Christina Schaffer. C., (a) Ellen, (b) Frank, (c) William.
  ii. Elizabeth Ann, b. Ryegate, Aug. 24, 1829; m. Sept. 5, 1850, Charles Page, of Lisbon, N. H.; res. Waterford, N. Y. C., Nellie, Frank and William.
  iii. Frank F., b. Newbury, July 23, 1834; res. St. Johnsbury.
  iv. Henry S., b. Newbury, July 23, 1836; d. St. Johnsbury, Feb. 26, 1894; machinist 24 years in Fairbanks' scale manufactory, St. Johnsbury, and member for many years of the M. E. church choir. He m. Sept. 24, 1861 Carrie A. Aldrich, (b. Littleton, N. H., Sept. 12, 1841.) C., Karl H., b. Lisbon, N. H., May 19, 1864; res. Chicago; Mabel E., b. St. Johnsbury, Aug. 28, 1870; music teacher; member of the Cecilian quartette of St. Johnsbury; teacher in conservatory of music connected with Knox college, Galesburg, Ill., and one year in the Chicago Conservatory of Music; res. Chicago.
  v. William H., b. Newbury, Oct. 25, 1840; enlisted April 20, 1861, in Co. G, 2d N. H. Vols., for three months; mustered out July 20, 1861; enlisted 2d, Aug. 5, 1861, in Co. H, 3d N. H., for three years; wounded at the battle of James Island, June 16, 1862; discharged for wounds, Sept. 11, 1862. He m. 1st, Nov. 1, 1866, Eva M. Dexter; 2d. Sept. 20, 1876, Mary B., dau. of John G. White. C., Muriel E., b. June 17, 1887.
  vi. Ellen A., b. Newbury, April 16, 1843; d. Nov., 1887.

GOULD.

STEVENS, b. Feb. 1, 1769; m. Sept. 14, 1798, Lydia Titcomb (b. Dec. 20, 1778; d. Feb. 10, 1871); d. Jan. 26, 1839. They had eight children, of whom Allen is the only one on record as having remained in Newbury.

ALLEN, b. Thetford, Aug. 10, 1812; d. Newbury, Oct. 10, 1865. Resided in Newbury many years: station agent 1858 till death. He m. 1st, Jan. 10, 1843, Harriet Newell Keyes (b. Cambridge, Feb. 17, 1815; d. Nov. 8, 1856); 2d, Nov. 22, 1858, Adeline A. Hurlburtt.
Four children, all by 1st m. and all born in Newbury:
  i. Charles Stevens, b. Oct. 23, 1844; res. Kansas City, Mo.; he m. April 4, 1872, C. Irene Bangs.
 ii. Mary Louise, b. July 27, 1846; res. Kansas City.
iii. Emma Newell, b. June 10, 1849; res. Detroit, Mich.; she m. Jan. 30, 1872, George A. Ellis.
 iv. William Allen, b. Sept. 22, 1851; res. Kansas City; he m. Dec. 12, 1883, Della C. Early.

GRANT.

WILLIAM was b. at Burrahan Mills, Scotland, 1774; came to America about 1800, and was m. to Mary, dau. of Dea. Andrew Brock, Feb. 9, 1804, the first marriage solemnized in America by Rev. David Sutherland. They lived some years in Cambridge, N. Y., but returned to Ryegate. William Grant was of a roving nature, and late in life went to California, remaining some time. He d. Nov. 8, 1860. His wife, b. July 26, 1785, d. at the home of her son, Andrew, May 12, 1865. Both buried at Ryegate Corner.
  Children:
1   i. Jane, b. Aug. 2, 1804; d. June 7, 1889.
2 ii. William, b. 1806; d. Nov. 17, 1873.
3 iii. Andrew, b. May 14, 1808; d. March 10, 1889.
   iv. Mary, b. May 12, 1800; m. George R. Leslie, q. v.; d. Jan. 30, 1895.
    v. Nancy, b. Oct. 18, 1812; m. a Mr. Matthews; settled at Akron, O.; dead many years.
   vi. Alexander, b. Nov. 8, 1814.
  vii. Janet, b. Aug. 22, 1819.

1 JANE, b. Charlestown, N. H., Aug. 2, 1804; m. April 26, 1829, Robert Hall, Jr., farmer, of Ryegate, who d. April 17, 1868; d. Ryegate June 7, 1889.
  Children:
   i. Albert.
  ii. T. Jefferson, m. Margaret, dau. George Chalmers; lived on her father's farm many years; then on the Upper Meadow; now in Topsham. She d. Sept. 14, 1890. C., George C., Louis (dead).
 iii. Lucinda.
  iv. Alexander.
   v. Edward.

2 WILLIAM, b. Charlestown, N. Y.; farmer in Newbury; lived where John Allison now lives; rem. to East Corinth, 1845, where he carried on the carriage making business; m. March 17, 1831, Finett, dau. of Stephen P. Nelson, who d. July 14, 1877, aged 66. He d. East Corinth, Nov. 17, 1873.
  Children:
   i. Oscar F., b. Newbury, Dec. 30, 1832; was employed many years in one of the large flouring mills at Akron, O.; m. at Middleburg, O., Jan. 5, 1859, Anna E. Potter; d. St. Louis, Mo., Feb. 13, 1896.
  ii. James W., b. Newbury, March 14, 1834; res. Rome, Ga.; he has been employed by E. & T. Fairbanks & Co. for more than 40 years; m. 1st, Jan. 15, 1859, Ada J. Powers of Barnet, who d. Nov. 19, 1860; m. 2d, Diodama N. Smalley of Troy.
 iii. Amanda M., b. Newbury, Oct. 30, 1835; m. Sept. 27, 1876, Wilson Chapman of Corinth.
  iv. George A., b. Newbury, Aug. 25, 1837; m. Dec. 29, 1859, at St. Johnsbury, Hannah Walter, who d. March 17, 1885.

v. Alonzo B., b. Newbury, May 27, 1840; m. June 12, 1861, Annette S. Doe.
vi. Edwin R., b. Newbury, Sept. 15, 1842; m. July 14, 1868, Ella Vansickle of Akron, O.
vii. Augusta A., b. Corinth, Aug. 10, 1847; d. Dec. 1, 1862.
viii. Emma G., b. Corinth, Nov. 17, 1850; m. Oct. 30, 1879, J. Frank Fulton, q. v.

3 ANDREW, b. Newbury or Ryegate, May 14, 1808; was "bound out" to James Wallace, and later was a porter at Mount Holyoke Female Seminary when that institution first opened, under Mary Lyon; farmer and carpenter; lived about 40 years where Philip Webber now lives; was a member of the Methodist church about 50 years, and a most worthy man. "I have never known a better man than Andrew Grant." In person he was said to bear a considerable resemblance to Sir Walter Scott. He m. Philena, dau. of David Daily, (d. May, 1888). No c.

GREIG.

ROBERT and CHRISTIAN (Wallace) of Fifeshire, Scotland, had among their children James, Robert and May. Robert, May (who m. Alexander Laing) and Robert, son of James, came to America and settled in Newbury, and of these two Roberts, and their descendants, is the following account:

ROBERT, b. Weymes, Fifeshire, Scotland, Sept. 1, 1795; farmer. He m. Nov. 12, 1824, Euphemia Mackie of Markinch, Fifeshire. They came to America and Newbury in 1850 and settled on Leighton Hill, west of the Laing place; Presbyterians. He d. Dec. 2, 1858, and she d. in Brattleboro, June 30, 1878.
Children:
i. Nancy, b. Aug. 14, 1825; m. March 16, 1858, Thomas Wright (b. Grism, Norfolk, England, Aug. 10, 1812; d. Bradford, April 29, 1892). They lived in "Goshen," just over the Bradford line. C., (1) Robert A., b. May 7, 1859; d. Nov. 22, 1897. (2) Euphemia A., b. May 13, 1861; m. June 1, 1887, Louison W. Doe of Bradford; merchant. (3) Emma A., b. March 5, 1863; d. Aug. 21, 1883. (4) Julia E., b. Oct. 8, 1865; m. 1st, May 10, 1883, Stephen P. Scales, who d. July 23, 1898; two c.; 2d, April 3, 1901, Seneca Dickey of Bradford.
ii. Robert, b. May 11, 1828; d. Nov., 1845.
iii. Andrew R., b. July 5, 1834; in foundry at Bradford 1851–'59; in California 1859–'61. During the civil war was employed making gun machinery; in business till 1884; res. Brattleboro. He m. Nov. 14, 1861, Clara Powers; one dau., Jessie L. He d. Brattleboro, Nov. 7, 1900.
iv. James W., b. March 20, 1843. Lived on his father's farm during his father's long illness, attending school a very little. Began to teach in Newbury before he was 18; taught some years; student at Newbury seminary and teacher of penmanship, having taken a course in Eastman's Business college. Studied medicine with Dr. Watson ot Newbury and Dr. Flanders of E. Corinth; attended a course of lectures at Burlington and graduated at Dartmouth Medical college 1866; in practice at E. Corinth one year; Ryegate, 1867–'75, where he was four years superintendent of schools; in practice and druggist at Brattleboro, 1875–'84; took a post graduate course in medicine at New York; in practice at Brattleboro since. He m. April 30, 1867, Lutheria H. Cochran of Ryegate. C., (1) Emma J., b. Ryegate, Nov. 14, 1868; teacher of vocal music in the public schools of Brattleboro and member of church choirs twelve years. (2) Lewis A., b. Ryegate, Dec. 2, 1870; junior partner of the firm of Morris & Greig, Brattleboro; m. Oct. 21, 1896, Eleanor Burke of Brooklyn, N. Y. (3) Maddie A., b. Ryegate, Aug. 22, 1872; teacher in Springfield, Mass. (4) Robert C., b. Brattleboro, Feb. 24, 1877; clerk.

ROBERT, son of James and Elizabeth Greig, b. Weymess, Fifeshire, Scotland, Aug. 27, 1815; m. Auchtermuchty, Scotland, Feb. 6, 1840, to Helen, dau. Thomas and Janet Arthur, (b. Dunshalt, Scotland, Nov. 14, 1816); linen weaver and station agent; came to America and Newbury in 1855, being two months and ten days on the voyage from Scotland to New York;

settled on a farm between the Center and the Lime-kiln. He was a machinist seven years in the scale works at St. Johnsbury. He. d. May 29, 1879, and she d. May 2, 1881.

Children:

i. James, b. Jan. 22, 1841, Drumsholt, Scotland; enlisted July 16, 1861, Co. C, 3d Vt.; killed at the battle of Cedar Creek, Oct. 19, 1864.

ii. Thomas, b. Auchtermuchty, Scotland, Feb. 22, 1843; enlisted in Co. H, 12th Vt.; mustered in Oct. 4, 1862; mustered out July 14, 1863; in 2d Vt. Battery, Jan. 13, 1864; d. April 11, 1864, in service, at Port Hudson, La.

iii. Janet, b. Feb. 28, 1845; m. Feb. 4, 1873, William, son of John Laing, formerly of Newbury, at Otisville, Mich. Five c.

iv. Robert, b. Feb. 10. 1848; d. March 20, 1852.

v. Lizzie, b. Dec. 9, 1851; res. Flint, Mich.

vi. Ellen, b. June 17, 1854; d. Newbury, May 4, 1875.

vii. Agnes, b. Aug. 6, 1858, Newbury; d. Feb. 17, 1877.

viii. Christena, (adopted) b. June 27, 1865.

*GROW.

I. JOHN, came from Wales, and settled in Ipswich, Mass., in 1664. He m. in 1669, and had one dau. and six sons.

II. THOMAS, b. 1684, m. and rem. to Andover, Mass.; had five sons, and in 1730, rem. to Pomfret, Conn., with his family.

III. JOSEPH, his 3d son, was m. in Connecticut, in 1747, to Abigail Dana and had 13 c.

JOSEPH and ABIGAIL (Dana) Grow were residents of Pomfret, Conn., until about the end of the revolutionary war, when they rem. to Hartland. They had eight c., who survived infancy; Joseph and John, who settled in Hartland; Ambrose, who m. a Miss Parsons of Springfield, Mass., and rem. to New York, where he d. in 1845, aged 89; Tirzah, who m. a Mr. Royce, and settled in Western New York; (1) Samuel, who m. Damaris Powers; Polly, who m. Stephen Powers, and Anna, who m. Samuel Powers, two brothers and their sister, children of Rev. Peter Powers. Abigail, wife of Joseph Grow, died in Newbury, April 2, 1808.

1 SAMUEL, b. Pomfret, Conn., Jan. 19, 1755; m. 1785, in Haverhill, Damaris Powers, (b. Newent, Conn., Jan. 8, 1761; d. Aug. 22, 1836). They lived in Hartland till 1794, when they came to Newbury, and settled on Lot No. 23, in the southwest part of the town, their house being the first framed house in that locality, their lot being the site granted to the first settled minister of the town, and still owned by his descendants. They were members of the 1st church. He d. May 18, 1842.

Children all born in Hartland except the last:

2   i. Hale, b. Aug. 8, 1786; d. March 8, 1865.
3   ii. Moody, b. Nov. 1, 1787; d. April 10, 1871.
4   iii. Charles, b. May 12, 1790; d. June 16, 1886.
    iv. Eliza, b. June 17, 1794; m. Jesse Putnam, q. v.; d. July 23, 1872.
5   v. Samuel, b. Oct. 20, 1799; d. Nov. 28, 1883.

2 HALE, b. Aug. 8, 1786; d. March 8, 1865; farmer in Newbury, Corinth and Topsham; he m. —— ——, Judith, dau. of Nathaniel Dustin. She was in the fourth generation from Hannah Dustin, "who killed the Indians;" (b. Atkinson, N. H., April 15, 1789; d. Newbury, March 29, 1886).

Children:

i. Eliza Nancy, b. Newbury, April 8, 1810; m. Jan. 31, 1828, Amos White of Topsham; d. Nov. 20, 1829.

ii. Clarissa Parsons, b. Corinth, Dec. 27, 1813; d. July 12, 1821.

iii. Judith Ann, b. Corinth, Sept. 7, 1816; m. June 10, 1851, Joseph H. Bailey, q. v.

iv. Samuel Hale, b. Corinth, Oct. 29, 1819; d. July 22, 1821.

v. Alonzo Dustin, b. Topsham, May 10, 1822; m. June 16, 1870, Adaliza Smith. Res. Newbury, with his sister, Mrs. Bailey.

---

*By Mrs. H. L. Tower.

vi. Clara Demaris, b. July 26, 1825; m. 1st, Dec. 15, 1861, Harmon D. Eastman; 2d, Nov. 19, 1871, Abram A. Chase of Stoneham, Mass.

vii. Harriet Atwood, b. Topsham, March 30, 1827; m. June 4, 1857, Abram A. Chase; d. Stoneham, Mass., Feb. 28, 1868.

viii. Eliza Nancy, b. Topsham, Nov. 15, 1831; m. as 2d wife, May 7, 1861, John P. Garland of Topsham and Newbury, q. v.; d. Newbury, Jan. 31, 1899.

ix. Electa Dustin, b. Topsham, July 13, 1834; m. June 14, 1870, Rev. C. D. R. Meacham, now pastor of the Baptist church at Passumpsic.

3 MOODY, s. of Samuel, b. Nov. 1st, 1787; m. 1st, Clarissa Parsons of Springfield, Mass., (b July 9, 1790; d. Dec. 17, 1813). They had one son, Daniel Putnam, b. Feb. 27, 1813; m., about 1837, Comfort Highlands of Bradford, and lived in West Newbury, then in Maidstone, till 1848; in Bradford till 1850, when he removed to Prairie du Sac, Wis., where she died Feb. 22, 1892, and he died Sept. 29, 1896. They had four children, of whom George was b. in Newbury, Aug. 24, 1841, and d. near Seattle, Wash., in 1896; and Martha E., Mary and Charles, b. elsewhere, and settled in the west. He m. 2d, Hannah Parker of Newbury and lived about 20 years in a house north of his father's, not now standing. He rem. to Bradford, and in 1867 to Prairie du Sac, Wis., where she d. Oct., 1867, and he d. April 10, 1871.

Children of Moody and Hannah Grow (2d w.):

i. Eliza Ann, b. Nov. 22, 1815; m. Thomas Highlands of Bradford, where they lived until about 1865, when they removed to Wisconsin, and later to Sac City, Iowa; two sons, John M. and Walter T.

ii. Jesse Putnam, b. Aug. 15, 1817 ; d. Feb. 25, 1819.

iii. Damaris, b. July 12, d. July 20, 1819.

iv. Hale P., b. March 3, 1823; m. 1850, Julia A. Davis, of Bradford, where they lived until 1871, when they removed to Stoneham, Mass., where she d. in May, 1876, and he d. Feb. 14, 1892, at Prairie du Sac, Wis. One dau., now Mrs. Davis of Brighton, Mass.

v. Olive, b. Feb. 22, 1825; d. Aug. 1, 1826.

vi. Olive R., b. Jan. 26, 1827; d. June 14, 1832.

vii. John G., b. Feb. 24, 1829; d. Aug. 28, 1875, in Iowa.

viii. Hannah R., b. Sept. 1, 1832; m. Holmes Drew of Prairie du Sac, Wis.; no children.

ix. Carlos M., b. Oct. 26, 1834; m. 1860, Harriet M. Getchell of Bradford, and rem. 1867 to Prairie du Sac, Wis., where he d. March 9, 1885. No children.

4 CHARLES, son of Samuel, b. May 12, 1790. He m. July 4, 1816, Lydia Sawyer. He lived on the opposite side of the road from his father's house, but removed to Topsham about 1828 and in 1865 to Bradford; d. June 16, 1886; his wife d. in Neponset, Ill., Jan. 9, 1876.

Children; the three younger were born in Topsham :

i. Hale, b. March 27, 1817; d. Feb. 12, 1821.

ii. Moody, b. 1818; m. Agnes Craig of Topsham, and lived there until 1850, when he removed to Neponset, Ill. Four children.

iii. John, b. 1820; d. 1822.

iv. Ann M., born Aug. 17, 1822; d. Haverhill, Mass., Nov. 13, 1867.

v. John Hale, b. Jan. 5, 1825; m. 1852, Amanda Johnson of Bradford, where they lived a short time and where he was associated with A. C. Brown in the publication of the "Northern Inquirer." They removed to Topsham, where Mrs. Grow d. in 1856, leaving a son, Warren. He m. 2d, 1860, Angie Ropes of Topsham and rem. to Neponset, Ill., where he d. in 1876, leaving four children.

vi. Mary S., b. June 6, 1826; m. Nov. 25, 1847, William Merrill of Haverhill, Mass. They rem. to Illinois, and later to Fayette, Iowa, where he d. January, 1879. Six c.

vii. Mahala O., b. October, 1827; m. Percy M. Batchelder; d. Haverhill, Mass., December, 1851.

viii. Nancy, b. Oct. 11, 1829; d. 1846.

ix. Lucinda S., (twin to above), m. Gilbert A. Sargent of Haverhill, Mass.

x. Charles, b. July 16, 1835.

5 SAMUEL, son of Samuel, b. Newbury, Oct. 20, 1799; lived on his father's farm; was called Esq. Grow; held many town offices and was town representative 1847–48. He m. Relief, dau. of John Emerson, (b. Jan. 14, 1804; d. March 10, 1859). He d. Nov. 28, 1883.
Children:
 i. Samuel Hale, b. Feb. 6, 1830; m. Susan J., dau. of Peletiah Corliss, who d. Oct. 2, 1896.
 ii. Melissa Diantha, b. May 11, 1838; m. Sept. 15. 1863, Francis M. Corliss, (b. Haverhill, Mass., September 17, 1839). They own and occupy the "old Grow place" which was her grandfather's, and have one son, Irving L., b. July 26, 1867.

*HALE.

There have always been Hales in Newbury, and there have been four different families having a common emigrant ancestor, but whose connection with each other is very slight. They are presented in the order of their coming to this town.

I. THOMAS, b. Watton, Hertfordshire, Eng., June, 1606, (another account has it, King's Walden, Hertfordshire, May 15, 1606). He came to Newbury, Mass., about 1635; was a glover; d. Nov. 9, 1682, (by another record, Dec. 21, 1682). His wife, Tamosin, d. Jan. 30, 1683. Four c.

II. THOMAS, b. England, Nov. 18, 1633; came to New England with his parents; res. Newbury, Mass.; m. May 26, 1657, Mary, dau. Richard Hutchinson, of Salem; d. Oct. 22, 1688. She m. 2d, William Watson, of Boxford; d. Dec. 8, 1715.

III. SAMUEL, b. June 6, 1674; m. Nov. 3, 1698, Martha Palmer; res. Bradford, Mass.; d. Dec. 13, 1745. She d. June 14, 1723.

IV. JONATHAN, b. Jan. 9, 1701-02; m. Nov. 10, 1729, Susannah Tuttle of Ipswich, N. H., and rem. to Sutton, Mass., about 1747; d. before 1777.
Children:
 i. Dr. John, (1731–1791), physician at Hollis, N. H.; surgeon in the Old French war and in the Revolutionary war.
 ii. Abigail, (1733–1821), m. Col. William Prescott of Pepperell, Mass., commander of the Massachusetts troops at Bunker Hill. The historian Prescott was their grandson.
 iii. Dr. Samuel, b. Bradford, Mass.; came to this town before 1770, and was in practice here for several years; rem. to Orford, N. H.; lived at the Ox-bow; m. Mindwell, dau. Daniel Tillotson.
 iv. Jonathan, b. Bradford, Mass.; lived in Sutton, Mass., Concord and Haverhill, N. H., and this town; member of Congregational church; served in the Revolutionary war, and was a prominent man; maker of wool cards; rem. to Benton, N. H.; d. 1837.
 v. Martha, m. Rev. Peter Powers, q. v.

HALE.

The second Hale family to come here is descended from Thomas, the emigrant, through I Thomas, II Thomas.

III. THOMAS, b. Feb. 11, 1658-59; m. May 16, 1682, Sarah, daughter Ezekiel Northend. He was a magistrate and a man of distinction in Newbury, Mass. He was a man of immense size, weighing nearly 500 pounds.

IV. MOSES, b. Newbury, Mass., 1702, or 1703; m. Dec. 4, 1727, Elizabeth, dau. Jethro Wheeler; lived in Rowley, Mass.; rem. to Rindge, N. H., about 1740; d. June 19, 1762; she d. Jan. 9, 1780.

V. COL. ENOCH, b. Rowley, Mass., Nov. 28, 1733; res. (1760-1784) Rindge, N. H., then at Walpole, and at Grafton. He was one of the prominent men in N. H. in his day. Served in the old French war; was at the

---

*Early dates from "Descendants of Thomas Hale," and other sources.

massacre of Fort William Henry; colonel in the revolutionary war; built the first bridge over the Connecticut river in 1785. He m. in Rindge, N. H., Dec. 22, 1763, Abigail, dau. Jonathan Stanley; d. Grafton, April 7, 1813. Seven children, of whom we have occasion to mention only two—Lucy and Joshua.

1 Lucy, m. Hezekiah Weatherbee of Grafton, and of their eleven children, (1) Lucy m. Ellis Colburne of Newbury; (2) Azubah, m. Dr. Eli Perry of Ryegate, and (3) Eunice, m. Abial Chamberlin.

2 Joshua, b. Rindge, Aug. 24, 1764; served in the revolutionary war at the age of 16; was in Col. Nichols' regiment at West Point. Res. Walpole, N. H., 1785–94; Rindge, 1794–98. Came to Wells River about 1804 (see Chapter XXIV); was very prominent in town and military affairs and in the 1st church at Newbury. In his latter years he became very fleshy, weighing nearly 400 pounds. He m. April 23, 1787, Sarah, dau. Capt. Solomon Cutler of Rindge, half sister of Mrs. Col. Tenney (b. Bedford, Mass., Oct. 7, 1767). He d. July 22, 1825, from the effects of the heat on returning from church at Horse Meadow. She d. June 10, 1853; buried at Wells River.

Children:
3   i. Charles, b. Oct. 30, 1788; d. May 21, 1862.
  ii. Sally, b. June 9, 1796; m. Thomas Barstow of Piermont; both dead. Nine c.

3 Charles,[2] (Joshua,[1]) b. Rindge, N. H., Oct. 30, 1788; res. Wells River; was Justice of the Peace for 30 years, and served as captain of militia in the war of 1812; held many positions of trust; was director in the bank 11 years, and one of the prominent men of the town and county. He m. Dec. 30, 1813, Mary Ann, dau. Stephen Reed, (q. v.) Rem. to Concord, N. H., about 1860, where he d. May 21, 1862. She d. Dec. 14, 1854. Buried at Wells River.

Children:
  i. Thomas A., b. Nov. 18, 1814; d. Jan. 26, 1815.
4   ii. Oscar C., b. July 26, 1816; d. May 30, 1880.
  iii. Sarah Jane, b. Feb. 11, 1819; m. Col. James Buchanan, q. v.; d. March 21, 1843.
  iv. Charles Albert, b. Nov. 27, 1821; d. June 17, 1847.
  v. John Reed, b. June 23, 1824; d. July 3, 1826.
  vi. Mary Ann, b. Oct. 23, 1826; d. Jan. 24, 1857.
  vii. Horace Reed, b. Feb. 3, 1828; m. Feb. 14, 1855, Julia H. Hutchins; d. March 16, 1859.
5 viii. Martha Ann, b. Feb. 8, 1831.
  ix. William Henry, b. July 30, 1853; d. July 12, 1858.

4 Oscar Cutler,[3] (Charles,[2] Joshua,[1]) b. Newbury, July 26, 1816; educated at Kimball Union Academy; in trade at Wells River six years; cashier of Wells River Bank, 1841-58, (chapter XLI.); Aid, 1843, to Gov. Mattocks, with rank of Colonel; Town Representative, 1852-53; rem. 1858 to Keokuk, Iowa, and engaged in banking business; cashier of the Keokuk branch of the Iowa State Bank from 1862, and of its successor, the State National Bank, till his death; city treasurer, and a trustee of Grinnell College. He m. June 26, 1844, Susan D. Rix, sister of Mrs. Abel Underwood. She res. at Keokuk, Iowa. He d. May 30, 1880. No c.

5 Martha Ann, b. Feb. 8, 1831; m. Sept. 1, 1856, George W. Hoyt; d. March 14, 1870.
Children:
  i. Kate, b. March 4, 1857.
6   ii. Charles Hale, b. March 8, 1859.

6 Charles Hale Hoyt,[4] (Martha Ann [Hale,][3] Charles,[2] Joshua,[1]) b. Concord, N. H., March 8, 1859; began his career as a writer for the Boston Post, where his papers began to attract attention. He was the author of several of the most brilliant, popular and successful plays ever produced in this country, which brought him both fame and fortune. The first of these was "Gifford's Luck," followed by "A Bunch of Keys." Then came "A Parlor Match." Then there were "A Rag Baby," "A Tin Soldier," "A

Hole in the Ground," "A Brass Monkey," "A Midnight Bell," "A Texas Steer," and "A Trip to Chinatown." which had a run of 656 performances at Hoyt's Theater, the largest consecutive run on record in New York City. After this were "A Temperance Town," for which certain persons at Wells River are said to have sat for their portraits, "A Milk White Flag," a satire upon the Vt. Militia system, "A Black Sheep," "A Contented Woman," "A Stranger in New York," "A Day and Night," and "A Dog in the Manger." He was also connected with several theatres as manager or proprietor. He owned an estate at Charlestown, N. H., and was for several years a member of the New Hampshire legislature. He m. 1st, Flora Walsh, an actress, who d. 1893. 2d, 1894, Caroline Scales, known to the stage as Caroline Miskel, who d. October, 1898. He never recovered from the loss of the latter, and remained in broken mental and physical health till he d. at Charlestown Nov. 20, 1900. No c.

HALE.

A third Hale family was that of Benjamin, in the sixth generation from the emigrant, his ancestors for five generations bearing the name of Thomas Hale.

VI. BENJAMIN, b. Plaistow, N. H., April 30, 1735; served in the Revolutionary war; m. Dec. 6, 1762, Lydia, dau. Nicholas White (q. v.). He d. Dec. 4, 1781, and a few years later the widow came here to live with her brother, Dr. Samuel White, till her death, Nov. 14, 1791.
Children:
   i. Joshua came to Newbury at the age of 25 ; rem. to Corinth; d. un-m.
   ii. Nicholas came here at the age of 22, and four years later rem. to Corinth, where he d., 1847, in his 81st year.
   iii. Lydia G., m. James Meserve of Corinth.
   iv. Mary, d. 1803; un-m.
1 v. Thomas, b. Jan. 23, 1773.
   vi. Col. Ebenezer, merchant and shipowner at Newburyport; colonel in the war of 1812; his dau., Lucy B., m. Hon. Benjamin Hale ; d. Aug. 19, 1848.
   vii. Hannah, m. Joseph Knight of Corinth; d. 1839; 12 c. They have many well known descendants.
   viii. Benjamin, d. y.

1 THOMAS, b. Jan. 23, 1773. He lived for some years in Newbury, on the Upper Meadow, owning what is now Baldwin's meadow farm, and built the house which was burned, 1898. He m. 1797, Alice, dau. Josiah Little, q. v. She d. July 27, 1819, and he m. 2d, Sept. 27, 1822, her sister, Mary. She d. Jan. 26, 1871. He d. Aug. 14, 1836.
Eleven children all b. Newburyport, some of whom lived here, and all were well-known here:
2 i. Rev. Benjamin, D. D., b. Nov. 30, 1797.
   ii. Moses L., b. 1797; was in the insurance business in Boston; d 1874.
   iii. Thomas. b. 1800; was in the insurance business in New York; d. 1854.
   iv. Sarah, b. 1802; d. un-m. 1834.
   v. Josiah L., b. 1803; was in the insurance business in New York City, where he was very prominent.
   vi. Edward, b. Nov. 8, 1805; merchant some years at Saco, Me.; came to Newbury about 1832, and lived on the Upper Meadow, the farm which had been his father's. He was a large land owner. a wealthy and benevolent man. Rem. to Newbury village 1864, to the house where Mr. Darling now lives. He was lame all his life. The Hale family was very prominent in society, and in the Congregational church. He m. Jan. 30, 1837, Mrs. Elizabeth (Wigglesworth) Brown. She d. May 19, 1884. He d. Oct. 3, 1886. Buried at Newburyport. No c.
   vii. Mary, b. 1807; d. 1859.
   viii. Ebenezer, b. 1809; graduated Dartmouth Medical College, 1829; in practice here a year or two; in practice and in the insurance business at Newburyport and Boston. He m. June 13, 1844, Sarah W., dau. William B. Bannister, (q. v.), who. d. Feb. 29, 1880. He d. 1847.

Edward Hale

ix. Alice L., b. 1811; m. Rev. John C. March of Newburyport; d. 1889.

x. Joshua, b. Dec. 14, 1812; was in the insurance business many years; sea captain 15 years; vice president of the Union Marine Insurance Co., and in other business; res. after 1846, Newburyport. He m. in Newbury, Jan. 4, 1844, Sophia C., dau. Col. A. B. W. Tenney, (b. Newbury, April 4, 1824; d. Jan. 19, 1901). He d. C., Alice Little, b. Newburyport, Mass., Aug. 27, 1845; m. 1st, May 9, 1866, Cyrus K. Hale, a graduate of Hobart College and Harvard Law School. He was in the insurance business. He d. June 5, 1874. C., *a*, Cyrus K., b. Jan. 24, 1867; *b*, Joshua, b. May 8, 1869; *c*, Josiah L., b. Nov. 24, 1870; *d*, Benjamin, b. May 6, 1873. She m. 2d, Nov. 5, 1885, Charles H. Atkinson, q. v.

xi. James W., b. 1827; d. 1832.

2 REV. BENJAMIN, D. D., b. Nov. 30, 1797; graduated Bowdoin College, 1818; professor in Dartmouth College, 1827-35; president of Geneva, now Hobart College, 1836-58; m. Mary, dau. of Hon. Cyrus King, of Saco, Me., who d. Jan. 22, 1867. He d. Newburyport, July 15, 1863.

Of their children, one lived here, viz:

3 i. Benjamin, b. Oct. 31, 1827.

3 BENJAMIN.[3] (Benjamin,[2] Thomas,[1]) b. Oct. 31, 1827; graduated Hobart College, 1848. He lived many years in Newbury, on the farm now that of Richard Doe, at the Ox-bow. That house was built by his grandfather, Josiah Little, in 1820. Mr. Hale was prominent in society, and had a large library. He neither held nor desired office, but was a valued citizen. Removed to Newburyport, of which he was mayor a year or two. He furnished extracts from the Litttle papers for this volume. He m. Oct. 29, 1855, Lucy B., dau. Col. Ebenezer Hale.

One child:

i. James W., b. June 12, 1858; graduated Dartmouth College, 1881.

HALE.

The fourth family by this name is descended from Thomas, the emigrant, in this wise:

I. THOMAS, of Walton, England, the ancestor of the family in America came here with his wife, Thomasin, about 1637, and settled in Newbury, Mass. He was the son of Thomas and Joan Hale, of the parish of Walton, Hertfordshire, England. His baptism is recorded in Parish church of Walton, on the 15th of June, 1606, as son of Thomas and Joan Hale.

II. THOMAS,[2] (Thomas,[1]) b. in England, 1633; came with his father and mother to America probably in 1637; lived in Newbury, Mass.; m. at Salem, May 26, 1657, Mary, dau. of Richard and Alice (Bosworth) Hutchinson. Nine c., of whom Joseph, b. Feb. 20, 1670, was third son and eighth child.

III. JOSEPH.[3] (Thomas,[2] Thomas,[1]) of Newbury, Mass., b. at Newbury, Feb. 20, 1670; m. November 1693, Mary, dau. of William and Sarah Watson of Boxford; m. 2d, Jourma Dodge. Joseph Hale was called Captain and a man of substance and local standing. He had seven children by his first wife and also seven by second wife. Abner was the fourth son by his first wife.

IV. Abner,[4] (Joseph,[3] Thomas[2], Thomas[1],) b. in Boxford, Aug. 2, 1700; m. 1st, Sept. 5, 1734, Ruth Perkins; m. 2d, Nov. 28, 1738, R. Smith. By that marriage, Jacob was 2d son. He m. 3d, Eunice Kimball. He was father of 11 children by this marriage.

V. JACOB, (Abner,[4] Joseph,[3] Thomas,[2] Thomas,[1]) of Boxford and Winchendon, b. in Boxford, Dec. 8, 1744, m. in Boxford, Dec. 7, 1767, Ruth Towne; rem. to Winchendon, 1770; was a soldier in Revolutionary war; marched to Lexington alone as far as Cambridge; again in battle of Bennington, 1777. He had eleven children; Joseph, seventh son.

VI. JOSEPH,[6] (Jacob,[5] Abner,[4] Joseph,[3] Thomas,[2] Thomas,[1]) of Winchendon, Mass., and Waterford; b. in Winchendon, Feb. 21, 1787; m. Mary Hall; rem. to Waterford, afterward to Whitefield, N. H., where he died. He was father of eight children; John was fourth son.

John, b. in Waterford, Aug. 25, 1817, clerk, merchant and traveling salesman; m. Laura (Burns) Hutchins. Her lineage is of the Scottish family of Burnes. About the time which brought William of Orange and Mary to the throne, more than one hundred families of Scotch Presbyterians settled in Londonderry, Ireland, then under Protestant rule. Among them were the Burns family, who came early in the seventeenth century, with others, and founded Londonderry, N. H. The town of New Boston became the home of John Burns, of which he was one of the first settlers, and here was born John Burns, his son, known later as Major John Burns, who was born in 1755, and died in Whitefield, N. H., May 6, 1852. He married Susan (Smith) McMaster, widow of William McMaster, and dau. of Deacon John Smith, son of Deacon Thomas Smith, the first settler in New Boston. John Burnes, Sr., was active in service in the Colonial wars, and also, at the age of 50 years, he enlisted on the first call for troops in the same company with his son, John Burns, Jr., aged 20, in Col. John Stark's Regiment, and both did valiant fighting at the battle of Bunker Hill. Major John Burns was in service and marched to Canada at the invasion of Quebec. He was also at Bennington under General Stark, and in the war of 1812. He was remarkable for mental and physical vigor, and celebrated his 90th birthday by walking upon Mt. Washington and returning to Fabyans the same day. In 1802 he built the first house in Whitefield and moved there with his family (the first settlers), with his son, David Burns, who was born in New Boston, July 31st, 1782, died in Whitefield, N. H., April 30th, 1864. David Burns married Susannah Knight, daughter of Thomas Knight of Worcester, Mass., and early settlers of Bethlehem, N. H. They were a family of local standing and highly esteemed. David Burns had much influence in the community in which he lived. The Burns homestead still stands, facing the highway, between Littleton and one-half mile from Whitefield village, the highway first built by Major John Burns, and near the beautiful sheet of water bearing the name of Burns Pond. David and Susannah (Knight) Burns had nine children, of whom Laura Burns, born September 23d, 1828, is the youngest and only living one. Laura Burns married, 1st, Jeremiah Hutchins, who started for California among the gold-seekers of 1849, and died before reaching there, leaving one son, Nathaniel, now living in Newbury. She m., 2d, John Hale. John Burns, oldest son of David, born August 19, 1808, lived at the Burns homestead during his life. He died Sept. 20th, 1890. Calvin W. Burns, second son of David and Susannah Burns, born in Whitefield, March, 4th, 1811, died in Lancaster, N. H., April 20th, 1897.

Children :

1   ii.   Susie, b. Oct. 8, 1853.
2   i.   James B., b. Haverhill, N. H., July 13, 1855.

1   Susie, b. Oct. 8, 1853; m. July 9, 1879, James F. McElroy, a graduate of Dart‧mouth College, and for some years principal of the Michigan School for the Blind. He is widely known as the inventor and patentee of steam and electric car heating apparatus; res., Albany, N. Y.

Children :

i.   John Hale, b. May 1, 1880; now in Dartmouth College.
ii.   Edith, b. 1883.
iii.   Alice, b. 1885.

2   James B., b. in Haverhill, N. H. His parents moved to Littleton, 1858, and from there to Newbury, February, 1867. In 1871, he commenced work in F. & H. T. Keyes' store as clerk, remaining with that firm until August, 1882, when he purchased the store of H. H. Deming, where he is now in trade. Became a trustee of Bradford Savings Bank and Trust Co., and its president. Upon the failure of the bank in 1898, he was appointed receiver and has been since engaged in liquidating the assets of that institution. He m. Dec. 7, 1880, Carrie M., dau. Daniel P. Kimball.

Children.

i.   Mary K., b. Dec. 27, 1885.
ii.   Harold B., b. Oct. 23, 1890.

HALLEY.

JOHN and WILLIAM were brothers in Markinch, Fifeshire, Scotland, and both had children who came to Newbury.

JOHN, b. Sept. 10, 1769; m. Elizabeth Henderson (b. Aug. 1776; d. March 9, 1850); d. July 4, 1854. Of their seven children, John and James came here.

1 JOHN, b. Aug. 3, 1808, who was lame, was a schoolmaster and lived on Rogers hill at West Newbury. He was a fine teacher, but unduly severe. His wife died of ship fever on the voyage to America; he d. Aug. 4, 1852.
Children:
5 i. John.
ii. Mary Ann and, iii., Lizzie were teachers, who went west and became the first and second wives of Samuel Newton.
6 iv. William.

2 DAVID, b. Dec. 25, 1815, m. April 20, 1841, Isabella, dau. David Webster (b. Leslie, Scotland, 1817). They settled in "Scotch Hollow" on the farm where William Halley had lived, and on which they remained until 1866, when they removed to Winnebago county, Ill., where Mr. Halley died May 2, 1886.
Children, all born in Newbury and m. in Ill.:
i. William, b. June 29, 1843.
ii. Marian, b. Aug. 11, 1844; m. a Mr. Faulkner of Iowa.
iii. David, b. Oct. 17, 1847.
iv. Robert, b. Sept. 11, 1851.
v. Agnes, b. April 27, 1856; m. John P. McNeilage; d. Owen, Ill.
vi. Edwin R., b. Oct. 29, 1860.

3 JAMES, b. in Markinch, May 13, 1817, came to America in 1842 and lived at West Newbury and the Centre until 1895, when he removed to South Ryegate; shoemaker and farmer; elder in Presbyterian church, South Ryegate. He revisited Scotland in 1868. He m. 1st, in Scotland, Euphemia Skinner, who d. in Newbury, Oct. 7, 1847, aged 28; 2d, May 22, 1848, Janet, dau. John Waddell, who d. in Newbury, July 9, 1877, aged 68 y., 11 mo., 6 d.; 3d, Jan. 21, 1879, Mary Lumsden.
Children:
i. John, b. Scotland, March 2, 1838; went west when a young man and became a steamboat captain; d. Milwaukee, Wis., Feb. 25, 1897. One son.
ii. Margaret, b. Dec. 28, 1839; d. Jan. 22, 1840.
iii. Elizabeth, b. Jan. 23, 1842; m. Dr. Erdix T. Smith of Corinth.
iv. Ann, b. Feb. 19, 1844; m. R. R. Fulton, q. v.
v. Euphemia, b. Nov. 4, 1849; m James R. Laing, son of John, who became a lawyer, and died in Michigan.
vi. Jean, b. June 3, 1851; m. Charles Gould of Malden, Mass.

WILLIAM, brother of John, Sr., had three children who came to Newbury: William, Ann, who m. William Gilmore (q. v.), and David, the latter being a half brother to the other two.

4 WILLIAM settled in "Scotch Hollow" and built a stone house where Allen Tewksbury's house now stands. He went west.

5 JOHN lived many years with Jeremiah Boynton; served three years in the 4th Vermont during the civil war, and m. Evaline, dau. of Daniel Richardson (b. in Embden, Me.) and d. in Iowa, where they removed, about 1866, leaving a daughter, Mabel, who was brought up by Mr. and Mrs. Peach.

6 WILLIAM m. March 24, 1870, Agnes Arthur of Ryegate and lived a few years at the Centre, where Allen Tewksbury lives, but rem. in 1874 to Mass.

HASELTINE.

This name is variously spelled, but the pioneer of this family, John, of Hampstead and Newbury, followed an early spelling, which is as above.
This John was, without doubt, a descendant of John Haseltine, who came from England, with his brother, Robert, to Rowley, Mass., where Robert died,

and John bought in Haverhill. He was made freeman May 13, 1640. He m. Joan Auter of Biddeford, Devonshire. Eng., who d. July 17, 1698. He d. in Haverhill, Dec. 23, 1690. Their children were Samuel, Mary, John and Nathaniel.

In 1690, John Haseltine, Jr., had a garrison house in Haverhill, with seven men under his command. In the list of polls and ratable estate in the west parish of Haverhill in 1745 are the names of Philip, Samuel, Joseph, Jeremiah, James, Nathaniel and John Haseltine. Hampstead, N. H., was made up of two segments, one from Haverhill, the other from Amesbury, cut from those towns by the state line in 1741, and some of the Haseltine families were included in that town.

JOHN, of Newbury, served in the old French and Indian war, and probably passed through the Coös County, as he was one of the very first settlers here. Having a wife and children, he would hardly have come so far into the wilderness on the mere hazard of finding a suitable place to settle in. He came in the summer of 1762 and remained some time at the Ox-bow, but later, settled on Kent's meadow, just above Bedell's bridge. In his old age he lived with his son, David, at West Newbury, and probably died there, and is supposed to be buried in the old burying ground near the Rogers hill schoolhouse. In September, 1788, he filed a certificate with the town clerk stating that he was a member of the Baptist church in Bradford, thus claiming exemption from minister's rate in Newbury. Jan. 23, 1797, "Widow Sarah Haseltine," filed a similar certificate, so it is probable that he died not long before the latter date. He served one month in Capt. John G. Bayley's Co., guarding and scouting 1781, and also in other service. His record has been confounded with that of John Hazelton of Haverhill.

JOHN and SARAH (Beadle) HASELTINE had a large family, but the names of several of their children are not known. There is said to have been a John, who settled in Canada. The following can be given:
i.   Sarah, b. 1756; m. Dea. Thomas McKeith, q. v. d. Jan. 12, 1825.
1 ii. David, b. April 17, 1759; d. Feb. 26, 1824.
iii. Betsey, b. Newbury, May 4, 1763; m. Nehemiah Lovewell, q. v.; d. Nov. 19, 1850.
iv. Martha.
v.   Abigail, m. James Boyce, q. v.

1 DAVID[2], (John,[1]) b. probably in Hampstead, N. H., April 17, 1759; came to Newbury with his parents in 1762; served one month, twenty-nine days, in Capt. John G. Bayley's Co., guarding and scouting; was also in Capt. Frye Bayley's Co., which went to Saratoga in 1777; also in Capt. Simeon Stevens' Co. of Bedell's Regiment, from May 9, 1778, 10 months, 22 days. He settled at West Newbury, on the farm still called the "Old Haseltine place," where he built the large, square-roofed house, at the top of the hill, in which Joseph Hutton lives, that road being then the main thoroughfare from Concord and Haverhill, N. H., to Montpelier and Burlington. Captain in the militia, etc. He m. at Landaff, N. H., Dec. 9, 1786, Anna, sister of Dea. William Carter, (b. Sept. 9, 1765; d. Dec. 26, 1821). He d. Feb. 26, 1824. Both buried at Roger Hill. The Haseltine family was very prominent at West Newbury, David was a large farmer and quite a wealthy man for those times.
     Children.
2 i.   David, b. Dec. 2, 1787; d. Feb. 1, 1860.
ii. John, b. Dec. 31, 1789; d. June 3, 1817.
iii. Samuel, b. May 3, 1792. He was a remarkable young man, possessing much literary, musical and mechanical ability. Taught school in Newbury, Bradford and in New York. He prepared a pamphlet which was published after his death. entitled "The Religious Experience of Samuel Haseltine, with Fragments of the Exercises of his Mind, to which is prefixed a Sketch of his Life, with an Elegy on the Death of his Brother." A few copies of this little work are extant, and are highly valued by their owners. He d. April 10, 1819. Buried in Rogers Hill cemetery.
iv. Anna, b. March 21, 1794; m. William Wilson of Bradford.

v. Martha, b. Nov. 30, 1796; m. William Boyce, q. v.; d. July 25, 1834.
vi. Elijah, b. Feb. 1, 1797; settled on part of the homestead, which is now the farm of Harry B. Hoyt. He was quite a character, and possessed some literary ability. On the back of his grave stone are some curious verses which were written by him near the end of his life, when somewhat deranged. He m. Elizabeth, dau. Col. John Smith, (b. Aug. 31, 1802; d. March 4, 1861). He d. Aug. 8, 1852.
vii. Sally, b. March 30. 1801.
viii. Levi, b. Oct. 19. 1803.
3 ix. Ebenezer, b. March 10, 1806.
x. May, b. May 1, 1808; m. Abner Chamberlin; d. Nov. 19, 1877.

2 DAVID,[3] (David.[2] John,[1]) b. Dec. 2, 1787; farmer on homestead: served in the war of 1812. He m. Feb., 1810, Olive Chamberlain (d. Sept. 30, 1863). He d. Feb. 1, 1860.
Children:
i. Olive Ann, b. Sept. 25, 1810; m. Johnson Chamberlain, q. v.; d. Dec. 9, 1881.
ii. George W., b. Feb. 18, 1812; m. 1837, Hannah Balch; res. Boston. He d. Aug. 27, 1864.
iii. Harriet, b. July 27. 1815; m. E. R. Aldrich of Bradford.
4 iv. John, b. Oct. 30. 1817; d. Jan. 4, 1863, q. v.
v. Hector D., b. Jan. 24, 1827; farming and insurance business; m. Nov. 20, 1860, Lucy, dau. of Hiram Smith. He d. Oct. 28, 1895. No c.
vi. Wright C., b. March 10, 1830; d. July 19, 1854.

3 EBENEZER,[3] (David.[2] John[1].) b. March 10, 1806; m. Margaret Wilson of Bradford. They rem. to Taunton, Mass., where both d. and are buried.
Children.
i. William H., killed at the battle of Fredericksburg, Va., May 3, 1863; was a member of Co. B, 7th Mass.
ii. Eben, res. Taunton, Mass.; d. and buried there.
iii. Hiram, served in the Union army; sergeant of color guard; wounded at the battle of Fair Oaks; lived in Wheeling, West Virginia; d. there and buried with his wife at Woburn, Mass. One son, Charles F., res. Boston.
iv. Charles E., res. in Middleboro, Mass.; buried in Taunton.
v. Martha, the youngest child, only dau. and last of the family, has been a teacher for thirty-seven years at Taunton, Mass.

4 JOHN,[4] (David.[3] David,[2] John,[1]) b. Oct. 30, 1817; farmer on Rogers Hill. He m. 1st, May 6, 1845, Mary C., dau. of Enoch Wiggin, who d. May 29, 1855; m. 2d, Oct. 23, 1856, Jane, dau. of James Renfrew. He d. Jan. 4, 1863.
Children:
i. Helen M., m. Milo C. Bailey.
ii. George Enoch, went to Chicago 1871, and has been in business there since. He m. and has two daus., Mabel and Blanche.
iii. Hattie E., b. 1853; m. 1869, Samuel Fisk of Fall River, Mass; d. Newbury, Sept. 14, 1876. C., (1) Carrie, b. Newbury, 1870. (2) Mamie, b. Newbury, October, 1871. (3) Annie, b. Fall River.

HATCH.

I. JACOB, b. Kennebunk, Me., 1765; m. —— Maxwell; res. Groton, where he d. July 16, 1824; farmer.

II. JACOB, b. Groton, 1795; res. Groton; m. Sally Morrison (b. May, 1797; d. Dec. 9, 1875); d. Sept. 4, 1873.

III. GEORGE, b. Groton, April 1, 1820; shoemaker; also kept a small store at Wells River; m. Dec. 8, 1847, Hannah Vance (b. Groton, Aug. 9, 1824; d. Newbury, Sept. 20, 1872); d. Sept. 20, 1872.
Four children:
1 i. Oscar Cutler, b. Newbury (W. R.), Nov. 11, 1848, q. v.
ii. Fred B.
iii. Martha J.
iv. Amelia B.

1 OSCAR CUTLER, b. Nov. 11, 1848; clerk for two years with Deming & Baldwin, at Wells River; four years as general clerk in the bank; cashier Orange Co. Bank two years; cashier of Littleton (N. H.) National Bank, 1872–1888; president of same. 1888, till date; director and treasurer of Littleton Savings Bank, 1874, till date; member of Littleton Board of Education, 1885–'87; pres. Littleton Mus. Assn., 1891–'93; is prominent in political circles in N. H.; member of the staff of governor. He m. Jan. 4, 1871, Flora Louise, dau. of Henry W. Adams of Wells River.

Children:
  i. Leslie A., b. Jan. 17, 1875; in Dartmouth College, 1894–5–6; clerk; res. Boston, Mass.
  ii. Henry O., b. May 11, 1877; m. May 26, 1897, May Belle Keith; clerk in Littleton Nat. Bank.
  iii. George A., b. May 12, 1882; d. Nov. 30, 1883.
  iv. Marguerite Elizabeth, b. Dec. 19, 1885.
  v. Oscar C., b. May 10, 1890.

HAZEN.

I. EDWARD, of England, and Rowley. Mass., where he d. 1683, was the ancestor of all the Hazen families that ever lived here. His son, Richard, of Haverhill, Mass., was father of Moses, whose sons, John and Moses, were once prominent in Newbury and Haverhill. Capt. John Hazen is often mentioned in the early chapters of this history. He d. in Haverhill, before the revolutionary war, and is understood to be buried at the Ox-bow. He had only one dau., who m. Maj. Nathaniel Merrill, q. v. John Hazen was b. Aug. 11, 1731, and is believed to have died in 1774.

His brother, Gen. Moses Hazen, b. June 1, 1733; served with his brother, John, in the old French war, and was a distinguished officer in the revolution. He cut the military road from Peacham to Hazen's Notch, still called the Hazen road. He d. at Troy, N. Y., Feb. 4, 1803.

ASA, of Hartford, in the fifth generation from the emigrant, was father of Austin Hazen, who had a remarkable family of 11 c., of whom,
  i. Allen, who has recently died, was 27 years a missionary in India. He lived in Newbury a number of years, as did his children.
  ii. William S., has been pastor of the 1st ch. at Northfield, since 1863.
  iii. Azel W., pastor of the 1st ch. at Middletown, Conn., since 1869.
And the others were well-known.

THOMAS, brother of Asa, had ten c., of whom Lucius was the ninth. He was b. in Hartford, February, 1801; m. April 11, 1826, Hannah B. Downer; came to Newbury in 1857, where he bought the farm now owned by Frank E. Kimball, paying $25,000. During the war, the Hazens were said to own the largest flock of sheep in the state. He d. at Newbury, Aug. 27, 1862. His sons sold the farm in 1867, and rem. to Barnet, thence to St. Johnsbury. They were very prominent and active here, both in business and in the 1st ch.

Children:
  i. Lucius Downer, b. Hartford, Jan. 19, 1834, now living in St. Johnsbury, and postmaster there. Has been member of House of Representatives twice, and of the Senate in 1894–96. Delegate-at-large to the Republican National Convention in 1892. He m. in Newbury, June 12, 1861, Orinda G. Kimball. C., (1) Lucius K., b. Newbury, July 31, 1863; m. Laura K. Nelson; (2) Charles D., grad. Dartmouth College; is at the head of history department at Smith College; m. June, 1901, Sarah S. Duryea of New York; (3) Mary L., m. Dr. N. H. Houghton of Boston; three c.; (4) Margaret E., m. W. W. Bradley, of Minneapolis, Minn; one c.
  ii. Louis Tracy, b. July 11, 1836; farmer in Newbury; rem. to Barnet, then to St. Johnsbury; farmer in Whitefield, N. H., and member of the New Hampshire legislature. Now res. in Melrose, Mass. He m. E. Frances, dau. Frank P. Johnson. C., (1) Frank Johnson, b. Newbury, May 24, 1866; grad. Dartmouth College; now in business in Montana. (2) Maria Frances, b. Barnet, Jan. 18, 1868; m. William D. Woolson of Springfield; she was a student at Smith College, but did not graduate. (3) John Downer, b.

Barnet, June 15, 1870; music teacher at Tarrytown, N. Y. (4) Louis Tracy, d. in infancy. (5) Grace Stevens, b. Whitefield, N. H., Nov.5, 1875; music teacher at Melrose, Mass.

iii. Hannah Maria, b. July 31.1841; m.in Newbury, March 20,1866, Dr. Henry C. Newell of St. Johnsbury. C., (1) Margaret Farrington, m. W. H. Heywood, of Holyoke, Mass., assistant treasurer of the American Writing Paper Co.; (2) Selim, in Customs dept., St. Albans; (3) Downer H., in Yale University.

HEATH.

SYLVANUS, one of the first settlers of this town, came here from Sandwich, Mass., in 1762, and settled at the north end of Upper Meadow, where he is supposed to have built the house in which Mr. McAllister lives. He did local service in the revolutionary war, held town offices, and was one of the committee that built the second meeting house in 1762. He was m. at Mooretown, (Bradford), by Rev. Peter Powers, Sept. 24, 1769, to Azubah Sawyer. He d. Feb. 26, 1787, leaving his wife with nine children, and another was born after his death. She reared this large family, surviving her husband 47 years, dying July 26, 1834, aged 81.

Children, (dates of birth taken from town records).
i. Polly. b. Dec. 24, 1769; m. Joseph Ricker, q. v.; d. Bath, N. H., Jan. 21, 1821.
ii. Prudence, b. Nov. 17, 1771; m. Hugh Johnson of Ryegate.
1 iii. Joseph, b. Aug. 19, 1773.
iv. Nathan, b. July 16, 1775; settled and d. in Bath, Several c.
v. Simon, b. June 27, 1777.
vi. James, b. April 14, 1779. He m. and d. y., leaving a dau., Azubah, b. May 21, 1809, who m. John Buxton, Jr.
vii. Isaac, b. Nov. 7, 1783; settled on the homestead, m. Anna Cutler, sister of Mrs. Joshua Hale. He d. Aug. 27, 1825, and she m. 2d, King Heaton of Thetford. No c.
viii. Azubah, b. Nov. 7, 1783; d. y.
ix. Abigail. b. Oct. 27, 1785; d. y.
x. Anna, b. Sept. 5, 1787; d. y.

1 JOSEPH, b. Aug. 19, 1773; m. Mary Kimball; settled in Bath, where both died not many years later.
Children:
2 i. Amos K., b. Newbury, Sept. 30, 1799.
ii. Everett, lived and died on the homestead; m. Louisa Meader. C., (1) Henry, now in Australia, if living; (2) Maria S., m. Abner Webber; d. 1888, in Warren, N. H.

2 AMOS K., b. Newbury, Sept. 30, 1799; lived in Bath, Newbury, and Canada till he m., 1827, Lutheria Childs of Bath. About 1830 he moved to where C. B. Rollins lives; then resided near the town house, but later settled at the Ox-bow; they were members of the Cong. ch. He d. Jan. 20, 1891; she d. March 5, 1889.
Children:
i. Dudley C., b. 1830; res. Newbury; un-m.; with Henry K. owns and occupies the farm which was the homestead of Col. Thomas Johnson on the Ox-bow.
ii. Mary, b. 1832; d. un.m., Sept., 1888.
iii. Abner T., b. 1835; res. Newbury, but now in Fairlee; m. April 5, 1870, Susan Page.
iv. Sophia T., b. 1837; m. 1860, Henry Sargent of West Wilton, N. H.
v. Everett, b. 1840; served through the civil war in 3d Vt.; m. 1st, 1872, Luella Guild. C., (1) William. He m. 2d, 1884, Lena George. C. (2) Frank, d. y. (3) Lulu, b. June 9, 1888.
vi. William W., b. 1842; served in the war, in 4th Vt. Killed at the Wilderness May 5, 1864.
vii. Henry K., b. 1845; farmer with his brother on the Ox-bow; m. March 5, 1868, Sarah C., dau. William Scales. C., (1) Nellie, b. Jan. 22, 1870. (2) Lizzie, b. Sept. 4, 1871; m. Feb. 10, 1897, Charles H. Dodge. One dau.

viii. Willard C., b. 1846; res. Barnet; m. 1873, Imogen Guild.
  ix. Edward H., b. 1849; res. Barnet; section master on railroad; un-m

HEATH.

JOHN W., b. 1777; d. Oct. 30, 1851. Emma, his wife, b. March 24, 1781; d
    July 9, 1831.
Nine children, of whom Thomas, b. probably in Bradford, Sept. 3, 1810, bought
    the Joseph Kent farm, where his son, John T., now lives, in 1854. He m.
    March 1, 1855, Hannah W., dau. Levi Carter (b. June 13, 1818; d.   ).
    He d. Jan. 23, 1881.
  Children:
  i.   Mary Ella, b. Jan. 22, 1856; m. Dec. 24, 1877, Charles C. Day, (only son of
       Joseph W. Day, who bought the farm south of the town house in 1863,
       where he d. July, 1866). Res. at Winchendon, Mass., where he is a harness
       maker. One c., d. aged 11 months, 15 days.
  ii. John T., b. March 29, 1858; farmer on homestead; un-m.
  iii. Levi, b. Nov. 28, 1860; m. Nov. 12, 1885. Nellie Roby. Two c.
  iv. Henry W., b. July 4, 1863; m. July 6, 1886, Laura C. Houghton. Three c.

*HENDERSON.

JAMES, b. Balfroune, Scotland, 1749, was one of the earliest settlers of Ryegate
    (see p. 65), and built most of the first buildings in that town and Barnet,
    and the first mills and dwellings at Boltonville. He settled near the head
    of Ticklenaked pond. The old homestead is now occupied by W. J.
    Henderson, Esq., having been in the family more than one hundred years.
    He m. Jan. 9, 1777, Agnes Syms, the first marriage in Ryegate. He d.
    Aug. 12, 1834, aged 85 years; she d. Dec. 20, 1819, aged 60 years.
  Children:
    i.   Jean, b. Oct. 20, 1777; m., 1801, William Nelson of Ryegate d. Oct., 1816.
1   ii. Alexander, b. Nov. 22, 1779; d. Jan. 12, 1883.
    iii. William H., b. April 3, 1782; m. Sarah Learned.
2   iv. James, b. April 22, 1785; d. June 12, 1859.
    v.   John, b. Sept. 18, 1789; un-m.
    vi. Nancy, b. Nov. 3, 1793; m. Benj. Folger.

1   ALEXANDER[2], (James,[1]) lived near South Ryegate; the farm is now owned by D.
    B. Fisk, but was in the Henderson family over 80 years. He m.
    Abigail, dau. of Gen. James Whitelaw, and granddaughter of Col. Robert
    Johnston of Newbury, b. May 23, 1783. She was well educated for those
    times, and after her marriage, taught a young ladies' school in her own
    honse.† This was one of the earliest schools of the kind in Vermont.
    "One of her pupils named Slafter, painted her portrait, which shows great
    strength and calmness. She was a lady of the old school." He died Jan.
    12, 1883. She died April 13, 1861. Both buried at South Ryegate. Of
    their c., John, Robert, Abigail and Jennett never married. but lived
    together on the homestead. John was long in mercantile life. Robert
    was noted for his skill upon the violin, for which he composed pieces of
    merit.
JAMES, the eldest son, m. Mrs. John Foster, gr-dau. of Col. William Wallace of
    Newbury. C., (1) M. W. of Portland, Ore., president of Willamet Iron
    Works; (2) Eustis, d. in Washington.
ALEXANDER, b. May 20, 1818; lived in Newbury, South Hadley and Lowell,
    Mass.; m. Oct. 5, 1841, Sarah J., dau. David Dailey of Newbury. He d.
    Lowell, May 7, 1861. C., (a) Whitelaw W., d. Newbury, July 22, 1849;
    (b) Allen W., d. Lowell, May 31, 1868; (c) Edride L., d. Sept. 22, 1863;

---

* Prepard by W. N. Gilfillan.

†Her advertisement appears several times in Spooner's Journal for 1813, by which she
undertakes to teach 15 or 20 pupils at $15 per quarter.   ED.

HAINES JOHNSON.

DEA. GEORGE SWASEY.

(*d*) Alden W., b. July 19, 1854; music teacher at Lowell; his mother lives with him.

2 JAMES,[2] (James,[1]) settled at Boltonville, where James Gardner now lives. A man named Mulvaire had made a small clearing there, and is said to have used a thorn tree for a harrow. When about 21 he m. Elizabeth Todd (b. Glasgow, Scotland, 1789). Her father, an Englishman, was a cotton manufacturer on the Clyde and m. Jane Scott; ten c. He took his sons into partnership and became wealthy. Elizabeth had been engaged to a young man who died in the East Indies and was sent to America with an agent of her father for the benefit of her health. They came to Ryegate Oct. 26, 1805, in the second wheeled carriage which came into that town. At the house of Gen. Whitelaw she met James Henderson, whom she married before the expiration of the year at the end of which time she was expected to return to Scotland. She was reared in a home of wealth, but adapted herself to pioneer life and became a notable housekeeper, and kind to the poor. In person she was very small. After a few years James Henderson erected the house and barns where Edwin Henderson now lives. She d. Oct. 21, 1846, aged 58. He d. June 12, 1859, aged 74. They were members of the Presbyterian church.

Children:
  i. Son, d. in infancy.
 ii. Susan, b July 27, 1808; m. 1846, Moses Gilfillan of Barnet. They lived near McIndoes 34 years, then at West Barnet, where she still lives, and recalls with wonderful exactness the events and people of an earlier day. He d. 1882.
iii. Henrietta; studied with Rev. James Milligan, the noted Covenanting minister of Ryegate; teacher; d. 1886, aged 73.
 iv. Jane, b. 1812; d. June 13, 1844.
  v. Agnes, b. May 25, 1815; m. Sept. 27, 1832, Hugh Gardner (q. v.). Has been blind for many years; she has given many particulars for this volume; res. at D. B. Reid's. Died July 28, 1901.
 vi. James; res. at South Ryegate in the house now owned by John Whitehill; carpenter; he m. Mrs. Hannah Pollard, dau. William Lindsey of Newbury; d. July 24, 1872, aged 55.
vii. Arthur (named for her aunt); m. William Forsyth and lived on the farm now owned by D. Ritchie. She d. April 3, 1842, aged 22 years. They had two c. One died in infancy. The other, Nelson, was a soldier in the Civil war; m. Lizzie Abbott, who has been dead several years. They had two daughters, both of whom are married.
3 viii. David T., b. Feb. 25, 1832.
4 ix. Charles, b. May 23, 1824.
  x. Eliza; m. Austin Sly, a carpenter and clothier at Boltonville; both d. C., (1) Charles, a carpenter. (2) Jane; m. E. Colby. (3) Stephen; was a carpenter, and for some time in trade at South Ryegate with J. B. Darling; d. Sept. 24, 1878, aged 27. (4) Alma, m. James B. Darling, a merchant at Barre; two c.
 xi. Abigail; m. Robert Bailey of Newbury; d. Aug. 7, 1857, aged 29.
xii. Barzilla; carpenter, and in stage business in Cal., where he m. Jannett Monteith; d. Nov. 16, 1868, aged 38.
xiii. Mary, d. Sept. 3, 1835, aged 3.
xiv. Alma; teacher; educated at Newbury Seminary; she taught in Newbury and in Kansas, where she m. Neil Wilkie, one of the pioneers of Douglas, me c a and banker; state senator two years; in farming and grain business.

3 DAVID TODD,[3] (James,[2] James,[1]), b. Feb. 25, 1822; carpenter; ran the carding mill at Boltonville for a time; lived many years on Jefferson Hill; rem. 1875 to the homestead. He m. April 24, 1844, Mary, daughter Jacob Bayley, (b. Jan. 15, 1820); he d. July 23, 1893.
Children:
  i. Luella and Edwin (ii.) res. on the homestead.
iii. Bailey J., d. March 5, 1873, aged 23.
 iv. Henrietta, d. Feb. 12, 1871, aged 18.

v. S. Elizabeth; m. March 14, 1877, W. N. Gilfillan; res. Ryegate, on the
Walter Buchanan farm. C., (1) Irving H., b. Sept. 24, 1878. (2) Bailey
H., d. Jan. 16, 1895, in his 14th year.

vi. Thomas Elmer; has been in Pray's carpet store, Boston, but in the
spring of 1901 became a member of the firm of Stearns & Henderson, on
Portland street, Boston; he m. June 27, 1900, Eva C. Gery of Worcester,
Mass.

4 CHARLES T.,[3] (James,[2] James.[1]) b. May 23, 1824; lived in Newbury; m. June
21, 1852, Marion T., dau. Joshua Bailey (b. Dec. 8, 1820; d. July 11,
1898); he d. May 4, 1880.
Children:
i. Eva, b. Dec. 14, 1853; m. March 25, 1879, Alexander Greer, b. Shipton,
P. Q., April 29, 1849 (son of Alexander, b. England, and Mary [Hall], b.
Barnet); res. Newbury: owns the "Colonel Stevens farm" on Kent's
meadow; is also a dealer in live stock. C., (1) Charles H., b. April 18,
1882. (2) Earl B., b. May 15, 1884.

HIBBARD.

THOMAS, said to have been born in England, came to Haverhill and settled and
lived in Newbury between 1770 and the war. In June, 1775, he was
appointed adjutant in Bedell's regiment and accompanied it through the
march to Canada, and did not return until January, 1776. In the same
month was appointed adjutant in another regiment commanded by Col.
Bedell, which went into Canada and was gone more than a year. In the
summer of 1777 he was again in service and present at the surrender of
Burgoyne. Later he was adjutant of a regiment which guarded the
frontier until the end of the war. In all he saw about three years and a
half of service. He was a schoolmaster, and wrote a minute but beautiful
hand, and his writing may be found upon many old deeds. He taught
school in Newbury, Haverhill and Bath, and in 1800 went to Cambridge,
N. Y., to open an academy, where he died suddenly July 1 of that year.
He m. Feb. 22, 1772, Lucy, dau. Levi Sylvester (b. 1751), who married as
2d husband, Jan. 10, 1801, Mark Sanborn of Bath, who d. July 26, 1821.
The children of Thomas and Ruth Hibbard were:
i. Mary, b. Oct. 7, 1774; m. a Mr. Rider of Haverhill.
ii. Lucy, b. Feb. 26, 1776; m. Joseph Wood, and was living in Burke in 1837.
iii. Samuel, b. Oct. 28, 1779.
iv. Ruth, b. May 3, 1781; m. Davenport Bliss of Haverhill.
v. Lydia, b. Sept. 11, 1783; d. 1784.
vi. Elihu, b. May 22, 1784; lived in Haverhill, 1837.
vii. Simeon, b. March 12, 1788; d. 1797.

SAMUEL, m. Mary, dau. of Webster Bailey, and an account of their descendants
will be found among the annals of that family. Robert J. Hibbard is
probably the only descendant of Thomas remaining in Newbury.

*HIBBARD.

I. Robert, b. Salisbury, Eng., 1612; was in Salem, Mass., 1639, and m., probably
in England, to Joanna ———. They settled in that part of Salem now
called Beverly. He d. May 7, 1684, and his wife before 1796. They had
ten children. Their youngest child, Samuel, b. April 4, 1658, died before
1702. He m. Nov. 16, 1679, Mary Band of Haverhill, Mass., who is supposed to have removed to Connecticut with her son, Jonathan, the
youngest of six children.

JONATHAN, b. May 24, 1689. In 1718 he lived in Coventry, Conn. The name
of his wife was Anna, and they had six children. He died in Dudley,
Mass., 1753.

---

*From the pension application of Mrs. Lucy Hibbard-Sanborn, 1837, now in possession
of the N. H. Historical Society.

SETH, b. April 16, 1724. He m. March 19, 1749, Eunice, dau. of Captain Penuel and Dorothy (Dwight) Child. They settled in Woodstock, Conn. He d. Oct. 25, 1761.
They had six children:
i. Lois, b. July 18, 1750, m. 1st, a Mr. Bullard, and, 2d, Daniel Morse.
ii. Sibyl, b. Dec. 5, 1753, m. Dec. 24, 1776, Amasa Buck. They settled in Bath in 1786 on the farm now owned by Timothy Buck.
iii. Zerviah, b. April 10, 1755; m. Abner Fisher of Francestown, N. H.
iv. Timothy, b. Feb. 20, 1757; m. Sarah Chamberlain of Woodstock, Conn., and settled in Bath.
v. Elihu, b. Jan. 14, 1759; settled in St. Mary's, Ga.
vi. Aaron, b. Jan. 17, 1761.

AARON, b. Jan. 17, 1761; served in the Revolutionary war as fifer in Capt. Childs' Co., Col. Bradly's regiment from April 8, 1777, to April 18, 1780. Was also in the "Rhode Island Expedition" ten or twelve days. He was in a company of Canfield's Regiment stationed at West Point for three months in 1781. He was in the battles of Germantown and Monmouth and at Valley Forge. He used to relate incidents of terrible suffering among the soldiers at Valley Forge, and of the sympathy he received because he was young and small, and how often the good dames gave him bread and butter and hominy because of his boyish appearance. He settled in Bath, N. H., in 1784, on the farm now owned by Charles Hibbard. He was a surveyor and much of the land in Bath and vicinity was surveyed by him. Colonel for many years of the 32 Reg. N. H. State Militia. Col. Hibbard m. Oct. 14, 1789, Sarah, dau. Major Nathaniel Merrill, (b. probably in Newbury, May 5, 1772; d. Feb. 24, 1842). He d. Feb. 12, 1835.
Children:
i. Betsey, b. Oct. 11, 1790; m. Abner Bayley of Newbury; d. Nov. 17, 1857.
ii. John, b. Sept. 4, 1792; lived in Bath; m. Abigail Child; d. April 22, 1883.
iii. George, b. June 16, 1794; lived in Piermont; m. Myra, dau. Nathaniel S. Runnels. Their dau. m. Dea. John Sawyer of Bradford. He d. Dec. 5, 1863.
iv. Lina, b. June 11, 1796; m. 1st, William Nelson; m. 2d, William Scott; lived in Newbury.
v. William, b. April 22, 1798; m. Seraphina Learned of Littleton; lived in Littleton, and in Glover; d. Dec. 23, 1868.
vi. Moses, b. May 10, 1800; physician in Lisbon, N. H., and Townshend; m. Jane, dau. Rev. David Sutherland; d. Townshend, Vt., Sept. 29, 1863.
vii. Lucius, b. May 10, 1802; m. 1st, Fanny Harvey of Utica, N. Y.; m. 2d, Mary A. Burnett; lived in Marengo, O.; d. July 24, 1865.
viii. Nancy, b. June 27, 1804; m. Daniel S. Smith of Bristol, N. H.; d. Sept. 13, 1857.
ix. Arthur, b. June 30; d. Oct. 29, 1806.
x. Horatio, b. Oct. 9, 1807; m. Joanna M. Moulton; lived in Newbury, Lyman and Lisbon; d. Dec. 18, 1868.
xi. Mary, b. Sept. 14, 1809; m. David Sutherland, Jr., of Bath; d. July 10, 1836.
1 xii. Aaron H., b. Nov. 29, 1811; d. Dec. 10, 1870.
xiii. Frederick, b. May 8, 1814; lived in Bath and in Hartland; m. 1st, Rebecca Clough of Bath; m. 2d, Eliza A. Keith; d. Dec. 2, 1877.
xiv. Nathaniel C., b. May 12, 1817; m. Ruth F. Baldwin of Connecticut; lived in Talahassee, Fla. Mr. Baldwin was editor of "The Floridian." Both Mr. and Mrs. Hibbard d. of yellow fever less than six months after marriage.

1 AARON HAZEN, b. Nov. 29, 1811; farmer in Bath; m. Maria, dau. Sherburne Lang; d. Dec. 10, 1870. After his death his wife made her home in Newbury with her c. till her d. Apr. 10, 1892.
Childr^en:
i. Mary, b. Nov. 16, 1839; d. Aug. 16, 1883.
ii. Louise, b. July 4, 1842; teacher in New England, later in California; now in Bradford.
iii. Ella M., b. Oct. 13, 1845; m. Wm. H. Atkinson of Newbury.
iv. Belle, b, May 4, 1848; teacher in Bath and this town; d. here Apr. 6, 1893. A memorial window was placed in the 1st ch. by her pupils.

37

v. Sherburne Lang, b. Dec. 5, 1849; res. Dixon, Kansas; surveyor; m. 1st, Helen, dau. Dea. J. P. Kimball, of Haverhill; 2d, Jennie Dixon, in Kansas.
vi. Harry Wade, b. Nov. 4, 1853; clerk several years for James B. Hale; merchant at South Ryegate till burned out Oct. 13, 1898; now merchant at Woodsville. He m. Sept. 16, 1896, Margaret, dau. James B. Lawrie.

HOISINGTON.

IN the Ox-bow cemetery lies buried in an unknown grave, Maj. Joab Hoisington, one of many non-resident soldiers who died here during the Revolutionary war. The following acccount of him was written for this volume by A. J. Hoisington of Great Bend, Kansas, who is preparing a history of his family :

JOAB HOISINGTON,[4] (John,[3] John,[2] John,[1] the English emigrant to Connecticut), b. Southington, Conn., Sept. 19, 1736. He m. there Jan. 14, 1759, Mary, dau. Ephraim Boardman. Their children were: Isaac, Bliss, Ozias, Verlina, Cynthia, Lavinia, Mary, Barzava and Joab, Jr. In 1763 he and two other men selected the present site of Windsor for a town, and he moved there in 1764 and was prominent in the affairs of the settlement. In 1771 he sold out and bought 1,000 acres of land where Woodstock now is, built a log house, and moved therein April 4, 1772. From that log house has grown the town of Woodstock, of which he was the first town clerk, held other civil offices, and was delegate to the first Vermont convention in 1774. He took naturally to military affairs and was captain of the first militia company in Woodstock. He was an active and zealous patriot, donating largely his time and means to raising men for military purposes at the opening of the Revolutionary war. On Nov. 21, 1775, he was elected Colonel of the "Upper" Vermont regiment, and confirmed Jan. 4, 1776. He devoted all his time to the duties of his command, and was exceedingly active in the field until his appointment as Major of the "Vermont Rangers," July 24, 1776, a regiment which he was to recruit and organize. This he did in a few short weeks, and in September took post at Newbury, "that he might be able to watch the movements of the Indians and Tories and guard the northern frontier from their incursions." The following months were spent in scouting the frontier through Vermont and New Hampshire. The last of December he journeyed to Fishkill, N. Y., where the New York Committee of Safety was in session, to obtain settlement for his regiment, his men being in sore need of food and clothing. His mission was successful. He made the journey on horseback, stopping one night with his family at Woodstock on his return. Rejoining his command, he was, later, stricken with small-pox, and died Feb. 28, 1777, near the camp, and was buried in the cemetery at the Ox-bow. His sons, Isaac, Bliss and Verlina, were with him in the camp at the time of his death.

HOLMES.

HON. LEMUEL HOLMES, b. about 1737; served in the French and Indian war. In the war of independence he was lieutenant in a company of Rangers from Jan. 1, 1776, and was for bravery promoted to be captain by special order of General Washington, Sept. 1, 1776. He was captured at Fort Washington, Nov. 16 in the same year, and kept prisoner till Sept. 20, 1778. After his release he was detained five weeks in New York. In 1780 he petitioned Congress for relief on account of his sufferings and obtained from that body a grant of £80. He settled in Surry, N. H., where he was deacon in the Congregational church and town clerk. Town representative for Gilsum and Surry several years between 1764 and 1786, 1790-1792. Councillor, 1790–94; Judge of the Court of Common Pleas for Cheshire County until 1808, when he became incapacitated by reaching the age of 70 years. Some years later, about 1814, he came to Newbury to live with his son, Asa, who carried on the farm now owned by F. E. Kimball, where he closed his long, eventful and useful life, Nov. 2, 1822, aged 85. He was buried at the Ox-bow, where his gravestone may still be seen. He was very prominent in New Hampshire in his day. Abigail, his wife, d. May 15, 1817, aged 75. Seventy years ago the name was very common in Newbury, but has long been extinct. The Cong. ch. records give the names of the following, and about all that is now known of them here.

William, Edmund Eliza, and Ruth Holmes, admitted July 19, 1819. Edmund was dis. to Dalton, N. H., church, April, 1830; Eliza, (Mrs. Fogg) to ch. in Alexandria, N. H., Sept. 30, 1831. Dea. Lemuel Holmes, ad. May 6, 1821.

Rev. William E. Holmes, son of Asa and Joanna Holmes, b. Burke, March 23, 1805, came here with his parents; educated for the ministry; minister in northern Vermont, New York and Pennsylvania; d. Newton, Pa., May 5, 1867.

*HOWLAND.

CYRUS, b. Lisbon, N. H., Dec. 25, 1816; captain in the 32d Regiment of the old N. H. Militia, 1839-43; m. in Lisbon, Sept. 13, 1840, Evelina Bishop, (b. Lisbon, April 17, 1824; d. Newbury, Oct. 12, 1898). They came to Newbury about 1845. He was foreman for Hon. Benjamin Hale many years. He d. Newbury Feb. 23, 1892.

Children, the three eldest b. in Lisbon:

i. Duaine, b. Nov. 22, 1841; d. Oct. 12, 1850.
ii. Levi Parker, b. July 2, 1843; served in the Union army, has not been heard from since July, 1864.
iii. Lucy Bishop, b. Feb. 25, 1845; m. in Lynn, Mass., to James Parker Mudge; 3 c.
iv. Elizabeth Hale, b. March 10, 1847; d. Sept. 6, 1848.
v. Mary Elizabeth, b. Feb. 14, 1849; m. Frank Benton of Wells River; 2 c.
vi. Edward Hale, b. Newbury Dec. 13, 1851; m. Nellie Dutton of Brandon; 2 c.
vii. Moses Hale, b. Nov. 19, 1854. In California some years. He m. in Newbury April 15, 1899, Ellen S. Barber, b. London, Eng., 1869.
viii. Esther B., b. Aug. 23, 1856; m. Edson Doe, q. v.
ix. Hiram Bishop, b. June 20, 1858; m. Bertha Somers of Jefferson, N. H.; 1 c.
x. Cyrus Guy, b. April 29, 1860; farmer, owning and occupying the William Peach farm. He m. Dec. 20, 1892, Elvira L., dau. of Samuel Rollins, (b. March 18, 1870). C., Edna May, b. Oct. 22, 1897.
xi. Scott Morris, b. Sept. 25, 1862; d. March 22, 1863.
xii. Josiah Hale, b. Dec. 4, 1863; m. Zaidee Bernard, of Concord, N. H.; res. Concord; brass founder.
xiii. Evalina Grace, b. Sept. 19, 1866.

†HOYT.

REV. BENJAMIN RAY, b. Jan. 6, 1789, at New Braintree, Mass.; removed with his parents to Craftsbury, 1795; m. Dec. 1, 1812, Lucinda Freeman, of Barnard. Ordained deacon in the M. E. ch., 1811; elder, 1815; presiding elder, 20 years. His early advantages were very small, but by application he became proficient in both Hebrew and Greek languages. Came to Newbury, 1838, and bought the house in which Rev. Mr. Temple lives; rem. to Claremont, N. H., about 1844.

Several children, of whom:

i. Benjamin Thomas, b. Boston, Oct. 18, 1820; grad. Wesleyan University, 1846; teacher; pres. Indiana Female College, 1856–58; prof. of Latin at Asbury University, Greencastle, Ind., 1858 till death. He m. Emeline Lewis of Boston.
ii. Francis Southack, b. Lyndon, Nov. 5, 1822. Fitted for college at Newbury Seminary; grad. Wesleyan University, 1844; principal Newbury Seminary, 1847. From 1850 to 1861 principal of Oregon Institute, which, in 1856, developed into Willamette University. In 1861 he became a member of the faculty of Ohio Wesleyan University. In 1872 he became editor of the

*By Mrs. E. Doe.

†In part from "Hoyt Family."

Western Christian Advocate, holding the position 12 years. Presiding Elder in the Northern Ohio Conference, 1884–96; is now connected with Baldwin University at Berea, O. He m. Dec. 24, 1848, Phebe M. Dyar of Phillips, Me., who was, 1847-48, preceptress of Newbury Seminary. Six children, all living in 1898.

iii. Albert H., b. Dec. 6, 1826; fitted for college at Newbury Seminary; graduated Wesleyan University, 1850; lawyer at Portsmouth, N. H.; was colonel in the army during the civil war. He has been engaged in literary work, and was editor, 1868-70, of the New England Historical and Genealogical Register.

HUNTER.

ARCHIBALD, b. in Scotland; m. in Scotland, June 11, 1812, Ann Stevenson. She was taken sick on the passage to America, and d. at Montreal in 1819. Mr. Hunter settled on the east side of Jefferson hill, where Andrew Arthur now lives. He d. Newbury, Jan. 5, 1857, aged 84.

Children, all b. in Scotland:

i. Eliza, b. June 12, 1813.

ii. Thomas, b. May 8, 1815; lived on the homestead, which he sold in 1876, and bought a farm in the place where he died. He m. May 22, 1838, Sally, dau. of Nathan Avery, b. Aug. 12, 1815; d. May 10, 1865. He d. Ellington, Conn., 1876. C., (1) Archibald, b. July 15, 1841; d. June 28, 1872. (2) Nathan A., b. May 6, 1843; served in the civil war nine months; in Co. D, 15th Vt.; res. Wells River; mechanic. He m. Clarissa Tuttle, who d. 1878. One son, William A. (3) William J., b. Nov. 2, 1845; d. Blackfoot, Idaho, Dec. 29, 1892. (4) Mary Eliza, b. Oct. 20, 1852; m. 1st, May 2, 1872, Frederic Claffee, who d. 1884; m. 2d. Dec. 2, 1890, Wilbur F. Chapman of Ellington, Conn. (5) Henrietta Ella, b. March 26, 1859; m. Nov. 3, 1877, J. Henry White, Clinton, Mass.

iii. William, b. February, 1817; was long a blacksmith and mill owner at East Topsham. He m. Jan. 8, 1845, Susannah, dau. of Blanchard Chamberlain, (b. Topsham, July 20, 1820; d. Newbury, Aug. 17, 1898). He d. August, 1900. C., (1) Archibald B., b. Nov. 8, 1845; d. March 6, 1871. (2) William C., b. June 15, 1847; d. Sept. 8, 1847. (3) Ann E., b. June 26, 1848; m. Geo. B. Palmer, Aug. 24, 1872; d. Dover, N. H., Nov. 11, 1895. (4) Betsey J., b. Nov. 23, 1849; d. April 17, 1864. (5) William T., b. Oct. 23, 1851; m. March 29, 1877, Betsey Philbrick. (6) John C., b. Sept. 8, 1853; d. Feb. 24, 1855. (7) Elizabeth C., b. July 14, 1855; photographer at Newbury; m. Sept. 1, 1886, Alfred Corliss, a carpenter and painter of Newbury. C., Roy C., b. Aug. 11, 1889. (8) James Hale, b. July 14, 1857; m. Jan. 14, 1888, Mary E. Corliss, who d. at Denver, Col., May 11, 1896.

INGALLS.

JEREMIAH,[6] eldest son of Abijah,[5] and Eliza (Hutchinson) in the sixth generation from Edmund[1] (Henry,[2] Henry,[3] Francis,[4]), was born at Andover, Mass., March 1, 1764. He was a cooper by trade and a singing master by profession. He was mainly self-taught, possessed a sweet and powerful tenor voice and great aptness in teaching vocal music, as it was taught in those days. His skill as a composer was in demand to furnish music for public occasions, to which he often added hymns and songs of his own composition. He composed the music for the "Election Ode" and "Election Hymn," which were sung at the meeting of the General Assembly in 1801, when the election sermon was preached in the old meeting house. He is also said to have been the author of the music to the "Ode on Science," a production once very famous. In 1805 he gathered these compositions into a volume of two hundred pages, entitled "The Christian Harmony," which was printed by Henry Ranlet, at Exeter, N. H. These tunes are of unequal merit. Some of them were in their time very popular at camp meetings and other religious gatherings. Several of his tunes are still sung, of which "Northfield" is immortal. "New Jerusalem," "Exhortation," "Iowa," "Kentucky," and a few others, still find a place in modern collections, while later composers have not scrupled to appropriate his finest strains to their own use. Concerning the production of "Northfield," the following anecdote is preserved: Returning from fishing one rainy day, he laid down before the fire to get dry, and impatient at the slow progress of dinner began to sing a parody to a well-known hymn:

> " How long, my people, Oh ! how long
> Shall dinner hour delay ?
> Fly swifter round, ye idle maids,
> And bring a dish of tea."

"Why, Jerry," said his wife, "that's a grand tune." "So it is," replied the man of song; "I'll write it down." And dinner waited the completion of "Northfield."

Mr. Ingalls came to Newbury about 1787, and m. April 29, 1791, Mary (Polly) Bigelow, dau. of Joshua and Majora (Knowlton) Bigelow, and adopted dau. of Dr. Gideon and Mary (Bigelow) Smith of Newbury. She was b. March 16, 1768.

Mr. Ingalls was chosen by the town to lead the singing on the Sabbath, in 1791, and was also a deacon in the 1st church from from 1803 to 1810. He succeeded to the farm of Dr. Smith after the death of the latter in 1799 and built at the top of the hill, south from the Upper Meadow, in 1800, a large house, which was taken down in 1886, in which he kept tavern several years. He was rather unfortunate in business, and about 1810 sold his farm and removed to Hancock. Mr. Ingalls has been pronounced by eminent musical authority as one of the best musicians of his age. His children were proficient in music and were people of standing wherever they went. He d. ——— April 6, 1838, and his wife d. ——— April 14, 1848.

* Children all born in Newbury but the last:

i. Smith, b. Feb. 10, 1792; settled in Berea, Ohio; had a son, who was a physician, and a daughter.

ii. Jeremiah, b. Feb. 3, 1794; d. Feb. 24, 1794.

iii. Joshua, b. Jan. 13, 1795; removed to Ohio in 1840, and thence to Wisconsin, where he died, leaving four children.

iv. Jeremiah, b. Dec. 17, 1796; went west; lived near Cleveland, Ohio, and died Feb. 2, 1858.

v. Polly, b. March 30, 1798; m. Page Chaplin. Twelve children of whom nine lived to maturity. Her husband d. while the children were young. She d. in Rochester, Jan. 1, 1875. Daniel C. Clafflin, a prominent merchant in Boston, senior partner of the firm of Clafflin, Young & Stanley, 77 Bedford street, who d. February, 1901, were their son.

vi. Moses, b. Feb. 15, 1800; settled in Hancock; shoemaker; inn-keeper, and town representative; rem. to Bethel; m. Eliza Alden; d. at Bethel, June 1885. They had a son and daughter.

vii. Betsey, b. March 9, 1802; many years a teacher; went to Berea, O., about 1840; m. Daniel Clafflin; d. at Berea, O., about 1880.

viii. John, b. April 22, 1804; settled in Cornwall; rem. to Peoria, Ill., about 1835, and to Indianola, Iowa; was a Free Soiler; m. Susan Foster; d. at Indianola, Iowa, Aug. 9, 1887. They had four sons and four daughters.

ix. Myra, b. Jan. 1, 1806; m. Josiah McWain; lived in Salisbury and Ripton, but rem. to Rochester some time before her death, Aug. 5, 1886. They had three sons who served in the Union army, and three daughters.

x. Isaac, b. June 7, 1809; d. Nov. 10, 1812.

xi. Hannah, b. Aug. 2, 1811; m. March 7, 1830, Holland W. Everts of Salisbury, where she d. Sept. 4, 1886. Two sons and two daughters.

Copies of the Christian Harmony, very much dilapidated, are owned by Joseph C. Johnston and by Mrs. E. J. L. Clark. A perfect copy is owned by Charles Graves of Littleton, N. H.

The following critical paper upon Mr. Ingalls' production was prepared by Rev. S. L. Bates of Burlington:

Newbury has one distinction which few if any other towns can claim. It was for many years the home of Jeremiah Ingalls, who was a composer and compiler of sacred music of no mean ability. On "Ingalls Hill," so named from his family, he revelled in the art of music, and prepared the singing book, "Christian Harmony," which was truly a unique production. This book, though limited in its sale and use, served important ends without any apparent design on the part of its author. It contributed indirectly to the peaceful issue of a long continued controversy over singing in public worship, and gave to the public a style of music, at that time needed by the New England churches. For a large part of the eighteenth century many churches had been rent asunder and whole communities set ablaze by heated discussions on the subject of singing in the worship of God. Conscientious Christian people not a few, considered it a positive sin to sing by rule or even to attempt any adequate expression of the words employed in song. Naturally the singing in the churches became distracting and subversive of spiritual religion, and at last provoked measures for reform in its character. Hence the protracted controversy which extended through so many years and ended only as a better style of singing prevailed. One of the important means by which the reform in singing in worship in those days was rendered permanent and peace restored in the churches was the publication of numerous collections of church music. In the space of about 30 years beginning with 1770, the average issue of tune books was at least one for each year. Mr. Ingalls' book did not appear until 1805, but much of the music of his own composition, which it contained, had found its way into collections previously made by others, and had taken part in elevating the public taste and meeting the public want. For this reason it cannot be known how far the Christian Harmony of itself, added to the permanency of the great reform. That it did much in this respect is evident from the fact that many of Mr. Ingalls' choicest compositions have been in constant use in the churches to the present day. The tunes Northfield, Delay, Unity, Jerusalem, and others of like character, are standing proofs of its influence upon the musical taste of Mr. Ingalls' time. Some of the tunes are of such rare excellence that they have been appropriated by other composers and with slight alterations, sent forth as their own. By many it is believed that this is the case with the tune, "New Jerusalem," and the tunes commonly sung to the hymns, "A charge to keep I have," and "The day is past and gone." Every lover of sacred music uses these tunes with reverent affection and delight. That Mr. Ingalls' book is open to serious criticism no one can deny. Many of its so called hymns are mere snatches of rhyme on local incidents and themes. Instead of using the grand hymns which, even in his day, were the possession of the churches, he seems to have entertained himself by depicting in verse the character and death of some personal friends, and thus composing tunes for his weak productions. The acrostic on the name of Judith Brock is one instance of this freak, and others are lines on the death of Judith Brock and Polly Gould, each numbering eighteen stanzas, with accompanying tunes. Evidently these persons were very excellent young women, but it is absurd to suppose that any one should receive a spiritual uplift by rehearsing in song the harrowing incidents of their sickness and death. Such machine work in a singing book naturally rendered much of its music weak and evanescent. It seems, however, that Mr. Ingalls had no thought of the needs of the churches in preparing his work, but rather designed it as a sort of musical treasury for his townspeople. That it was such is beyond question. What one old lady said to her pastor on her death bed, was probably true of many people, "I have had no end of comfort," said she, "in repeating the hymns and singing the tunes in Mr. Ingalls' singing book." "Christian Harmony" never had a wide circulation and never came into competition with other musical works. Still it did unquestionably exert a positive influence in the New England congregations, and the name of its author will be spoken with reverent gratitude, by the generations to come, because of the spiritual vitality of many of his tunes.

JAMES.

JABEZ AND LEVI, brothers; came here about 1813, and settled in the Lime Kiln neighborhood, near Topsham line. Jabez d. Nov. 4, 1855, aged 76.

S$_o$me of his children were:

i. William, m. Apr. 9, 1840, Charlotte, dau. Thomas Corliss, of Newbury, and rem. to Granby.
ii. Elsie, b. Apr. 3, 1807; d Jan. 26, 1887; never m., but lived with her brother, ·Levi, on the homestead.
iii. Mary Ann, m. Roswell Leighton; d. March 24, 1887.
iv. Levi, never m.; lived on the homestead and was quite wealthy, but was defrauded of all his property, and, broken in mind and body, was taken to the town farm where he d. Oct. 4, 1875.

LEVI, m. 1st, Rhuamah, dau. Elder Daniel Batchelder, of Corinth, who d. Oct. 27, 1827, aged 34; 2d, Serena, sister of his 1st wife.

Children:
i. Alvah C., b. Dec. 1817, d. Apr. 11, 1898.
ii. Daniel B., m. Ann George, of Topsham; rem. to Sycamore, Ill., where he became a lawyer, city judge and postmaster.
iii. Ransom, d. in Union army; and others whose names are not given.

1 ALVAH C., b. Dec. 1817; farmer on Jefferson Hill; m. March 27, 1845, Nancy W. Peach; d. Apr. 11, 1898.

Children:
i. Althea M., b. July 27, 1847; d. Sept. 27, 1882.
ii. Adelaide b. Sept. 6, 1850; res. with her mother.
iii. Rhuamah B., b. May 29, 1856; m. H. E. Cobleigh; q. v.

JENNE.

STILLMAN, seventh child of James and Betsey (Carey) Jenne, b. in Derby, Feb. 21, 1820; m. July 4, 1841, Miranda Jane, dau. of Asa and Sarah (Burns) King, b. April 28, 1820, in Whitefield, N. H. Mrs. Jenne d. in Whitefield, N. H., July 20, 1870. He m. the second time Abbie A., dau. of William and Phebe Doe. Mr. Jenne enlisted in the 6th Vt. Regt., in 1861. In 1862, he was detailed to take charge of the supply train, a duty which he performed until the close of the war. He was some years engaged in mechanical business at South Newbury. He afterwards bought the Ebenezer Abbott farm on Rogers hill, where he d. suddenly July 11, 1892. His wife d. April 12, 1891.

Children, five by 1st, and one by 2d marriage:
i. Sarah E., b. in Whitefield, N. H., May 15, 1842; m. Andrew J. Knight of South Newbury, May 16, 1859. They have seven c.
ii. Roswell C., b. in Whitefield, N. H., June 9, 1844; m. Lestina E., dau. of Roswell George of East Corinth, 1869. He enlisted in the 6th Vt. Regt., October, 1861; served three years, was wounded once in the arm. He re-enlisted in 1864 in the 17th Vt. Regt., and was severely wounded in April, 1865, by a shell; he lost a leg and was otherwise badly hurt. He afterwards studied medicine and settled in East Corinth, where he practiced for several years, but about six years before his death his health failed, he sold out his practice and moved to Lowell, Mass. He d. in East Corinth, April 15, 1894, of heart disease contracted in the war.
iii. William S., b. in Derby. Nov. 25, 1845; m. Nettie, dau. of Thomas L. Tucker, Feb. 18, 1874; she d. Aug. 8, 1874. In October, 1878, he was m. to Emma Hoagland of New York City. She d. at Peacham, in September, 1879. He m. April 18, 1881, Ida May, dau. of John Young, of South Troy, where they now reside. He enlisted with his brother in the same regiment, 6th Vt. Regt., being a little less than 16 years old. In 1863, he was wounded by a minie ball which entered his right lung, where it remained nine days. Before the wound was fully healed he re-enlisted; he next lost a finger in the battle of the Wilderness, and at the close of the war was honorably discharged. A few years later he studied for the ministry and entered the Methodist Episcopal church.
iv. Viola M., b. Sept. 6, 1847; m. October, 1866, Charles M. Andross. They have one child, Ella J., the wife of Oscar Course of Vershire.
v. Cora S., b. in Newbury, Jan. 20, 1861; m. March 20, 1880, Fred W. Stevenson, of Barnet. They had two c., Harry M., and M. Genevieve.

vi. Mary Louise, b. June 20, 1876; m. William Chamberlain of Bradford.
They have two c., Anna and Frances L.

JEWELL.

SOLOMON, came to Newbury from Rockingham about 1790; bought one of the
"Porter lots" of Mills Olcott; cleared a farm, where he died. He m.
Abigail, dau. of Samuel Corliss.
Children:
1   i. Solomon, b. Sept. 1, 1798; d. June 9, 1868.
    ii. Elizabeth, b. Aug. 28, 1800; m. 1st, March 26, 1834, Daniel Lindsey; 2d,
Wright Chamberlin; 3d, Roger Eastman. She d. June 19, 1868.
    iii. Fanny, b. July 26, 1802; m. Dec. 18, 1826, Enoch Bagley of Topsham.
    iv. Hiram, b. Sept. 11, 1805.
2   v. David, b. Sept. 27, 1807; d. Jan. 4, 1892.
    vi. Charlotte, b. Aug. 27, 1810; m. Jan. 1,1835, William Sanborn of Topsham;
d. March 23, 1884.
    vii. Lydia, b. Sept. 12, 1812.
    viii. Jane, b. March 25, 1814; m. George R. Sly of Ryegate, Nov. 21, 1839.

1 SOLOMON, b. Sept. 1, 1798; m. April, 1835, Anna, dau. of John Peach (b.
Feb. 9, 1807; d. Oct. 12, 1859); farmer on homestead; d. June 9, 1868.
Children :
    i. Mary, b. Jan. 29, 1836.
    ii. Nancy, died in infancy, March 17, 1838.
    iii. Nancy, b. Feb. 12, 1839; m. Leonard W. McAllister; q. v.
    iv. George, b. April 10, 1840; farmer on the homestead, where W. H.
Tewksbury now lives; m. April 8, 1869, Elizabeth L., dau. of John N.
Brock; he d. June 25, 1882. C., (1) Lillian C., b. Feb. 19, 1870; m.
Horace Washburn; c., (a) Mildred E., (b) Arlene E., b. Aug. 30, 1899.
(2) Ellen L., b. Sept. 4, 1875; d. July 31, 1884. (3) Mina L., b. Oct. 19,
1877; m. Sept. 29, 1897, Harry B. Hoyt. (4) Addie V., b. Dec. 10, 1879,
teacher; grad. N. H. Normal School, 1898.
    v. Martha A., b. Dec. 24, 1849; m. Dudley Carleton; q. v.

2 DAVID, b. Sept. 27, 1807; lived near Jefferson Hill; m. Christian, daughter of
John Peach; he d. Jan. 4, 1892.
Children:
    i. Amy, m. Robert Arthur of South Ryegate.
    ii. Abbie, m. May 2, 1868, Charles Leet. C., (1) Abbie; m. G. Warren
Carleton; d. Nov. 22, 1889. (2) Edgar B. of Keene, N. H.

JEWETT.

I. EDWARD, b. about 1580, at Bradford, Yorkshire, Eng.; m. Oct. 1, 1604, Mary
Taylor of Bradford. He d. 1616. Three sons, William, Maxmilian and
Joseph. The two latter, with about twenty other Puritans and their
families, sailed from Hull, Eng., and landed in Boston, Dec. 1, 1638. In
the following year they founded Rowley, Mass.

II. JOSEPH, b. Bradford, Eng., 1609; m. 1st, Mary Mollinson. Settled in Rowley,
Mass., where he was a prominent and wealthy citizen. He d. 1661.
Nine c.

III. NEHEMIAH, b. Rowley, Mass., 1643; m. Exercise Pierce of Lynn; d. Jan. 1,
1720. Ten c.

IV. BENJAMIN, b. Ipswich, Mass., probably 1691; m. Dec. 12, 1714, Reform
Trescott of Milton; d. Jan. 22, 1716. One c.

V. BENJAMIN, b. Ipswich, 1716; m. Hannah Butler; settled finally at Windham,
Conn. He d. Sept. 19, 1801. Ten c.

DANIEL, b. Manchester, Mass., Feb. 24, 1744; blacksmith; m. 1769, Zilpha
Hibbard of Windham, Conn., and rem. to Canterbury, Conn. In 1774, he
moved to Putney; served through the revolutionary war; town
representative 16 or 17 years; d. March 30, 1829. His wife d. 11 days
earlier.

Ten children, of whom the following lived in Newbury:

1 ii. Luther, b. Canterbury, Conn., Dec. 24, 1772.
2 vii. Calvin, b. Putney, Sept. 16, 1782.

1 LUTHER, b. Canterbury, Conn., Dec. 24, 1772; grad. Dartmouth College, 1795; studied medicine and began practice at Putney. He m. Feb. 7, 1799, Betsey Adams of New Ipswich, N. H. She died in April, 1816. Removed to St. Johnsbury, 1800, and practiced medicine. Elected Representative to Congress in 1815. He m., 2d, Nancy Chamberlain; licensed to preach May 27, 1818; rem. to Newbury, 1821; ordained and installed as pastor of 1st Congregational church, Feb. 28, 1881. He lived in the house under the great elm south of the Ox-bow cemetery. Resigned and rem. to St. Johnsbury, 1825, but was not dismissed till February, 1828; published 1828-32, "The Farmers' Herald" at St. Johnsbury. William T. Porter of Newbury was associated with him one year. He d. March 8, 1860, leaving ten children, of whom Ephraim (b. 1811, d. 1865) and Samuel (b. 1819, d. 1879) were merchants at St. Johnsbury.

MIRA, sixth child of Rev. Luther Jewett, b. St. Johnsbury, Nov. 1, 1809, m. there, Aug. 12, 1829, Dr. Nicholas, son of Bancroft Abbott of Newbury. Dr. Abbott practiced at Blue Hill, Me., till 1834; Troy, O., till 1871; res. in Lafayette, Ind., till his death, Sept. 29, 1871; she d. Fremont, Neb., April 23, 1890.

Children:
i. Luther J., b. Blue Hill, Me., Sept. 19, 1831; physician, and in 1895, became Superintendent of Nebraska Hospital for the Insane at Lincoln; m. Sept. 12, 1854, Clara Culbertson of Troy, Ohio.
ii. Ephraim A., b. Blue Hill, Me., June 9, 1833; m. 1870, Mary J. Dorsey of Virginia; res. San Jose, Cal.; in fruit culture.
iii. Jane F., b. Troy, O., Jan. 27, 1841; m. there Dec. 24, 1857, Dr. M. L. Harter of Troy. He was in practice at Troy with Dr. N. Abbott till 1871, when he moved to St. Louis, Mo., and died there Nov. 1, 1882. She m. 2d, Oct. 12, 1875, Rev. Samuel Dimock. They rem. to Denver, Col., where he d. April 19, 1898. Two children by first marriage.

2 DR. CALVIN, second son and seventh child, of Daniel Jewett, b. Putney, Sept. 16, 1782. In practice at St. Johnsbury till about 1822, when he came to Newbury, and was in practice here till March, 1828, when he rem. to Rumney, N. H., and a few years later to St. Johnsbury. He lived in the house in which Mr. Lawrie now lives; seems to have had a large practice, and usually had students studying medicine with him. He m. 1st, May 17, 1807, Sally Parker of Putney, who d. at St. Johnsbury, Jan. 12, 1837; m. 2d, July 16, 1837, Mrs. Matilda Hopkins, who d. April 1, 1874. He d. Dec. 11, 1853.

Eleven children, all by 1st marriage, and all born at St. Johnsbury, except Fayette:

3 i. Milo P., b. April 27, 1808; d. June 9, 1882.
ii. Emeline C., b. Aug. 20, 1809; m. Dea. Freeman Keyes of Newbury; d. June 20, 1878.
iii. Darwin E., b. April 6, 1811; lived in Massachusetts; m. Dec. 22, 1837, Caroline M. Redding; d. March 30, 1886. Five c.
iv. Amelia R , b. Jan. 1; d. April 27, 1813.
v. Roswell P., b. and d. Aug. 22, 1814.
vi. Sarah Amelia, b. Sept. 30, 1815; m. Sept. 23, 1859, Harry C. Bailey of Newbury.
vii. Jarvis, b. Oct. 21, 1817; m. Kate M. Beattie, of Ryegate; d. June 14, 1860, at San Francisco, Cal. One c.
viii. Harriet N., b. Jan. 1, 1820; m. April 16, 1839, Ephraim Wilcox, who d. June 29, 1871. C., of whom, (1) Edwin A., b. Zanesville, O., Feb. 2, 1840; clerk for several years in F. & H. T. Keyes' store; served in the army. (See record).
ix. Henry C., b. Feb. 14; d. Sept. 18, 1822.
4 x. Fayette, b. Aug. 15, 1824; d. June, 1862.
xi. Ellen A., b. April 11, 1832; has never m.; lived in Newbury a good deal, and was organist at the 1st ch., in the '60s.

3 Milo Parker, b. St. Johnsbury, April 27, 1808; graduated Dartmouth College,
    1828; Andover Theological Seminary, 1833; Professor of Rhetoric and
    Political Economy, Marietta College, 1833-38; founded 1839, Judson
    Female Academy, Marion, Ala., and was its principal 17 years. In 1855,
    he established a seminary for girls at Poughkeepsie, N. Y. He suggested
    to Matthew Vassar the plan of an endowed institution for the higher
    education of young women, and when Vassar College was founded he was
    its first president, (1862-64). In literary work till he d. at Milwaukee,
    June 9, 1882. He m. Sept. 13, 1838, Jane A., dau. Moor Russell of
    Plymouth, N. H. No c. Professor Jewett spent much time in Newbury
    and is well and pleasantly remembered. He traveled extensively in Europe
    and Asia. Received the degree of LL. D. from Rochester University,
    1861.

4 Fayette C., b. Newbury, Aug. 15, 1824; grad. University of Vermont, 1848;
    studied medicine and began practice at Nashua, N. H. He m. 1st, Susan
    A. Clark of St Johnsbury, Nov. 25, 1850. She d. Oct. 6, 1853. He m. 2d,
    at St. Johnsbury, Feb. 16, 1853, Mary Ann Brackett. They sailed from
    Boston March 14, 1853, for Turkey, to engage in work as a medical mis-
    sionary, under the auspices of the American Board. He was first stationed
    at Tocat, but in 1855 removed to Sivas, and in 1858 to Yozgat, going where
    the work and the mission families seemed most to demand the services of
    a physician. These necessities often called him to very arduous labors and
    much exposure. He was ordained an evangelist at Constantinople, May
    28, 1857. Returned to America, 1860, on account of his health, and com-
    menced practice at Waltham, Mass. In the spring of 1862, with his
    family, he again set out for his missionary field, leaving Boston May 31,
    1862, reaching Liverpool June 12th, where he died suddenly, June 18,
    1862.
    Children:
    i. Mary Amelia, b. Marsovan, Asia Minor, July 16 ; d. July 25, 1854.
    ii. Henry Martyn, b. Tocat, Asia Minor, July 8, 1855. Spent his boyhood at
        Newbury in Dea. Freeman Keyes' family; appointed U. S. Consul at Sivas,
        Turkey, holding that position several years.
    iii. Herbert, twin brother of Henry M.; d. in Tocat.
    iv. Milo Augustus, b. Sivas, Oct. 27. 1857. Spent much of his boyhood in
        Newbury; physician at Danvers (Mass.) Lunatic Hospital several years.
        Appointed by President Harrison, 1891, to succeed his brother as Consul
        at Sivas, which office he still holds. During the Armenian massacres he
        rendered invaluable service in the protection of the American schools and
        missionaries. He is the author of several medical and scientific works. He
        m. at Constantinople, Sept. 17, 1897, Mrs. Fanny (Powers) Dudley,
        formerly of Newbury. As this record goes to press, Dr. and Mrs. Jewett
        are in America on leave of absence.

JOHNSON.

I. William, b. Kent, England, in the reign of James 1st. Admitted freeman of
    Massachusetts Colony, March 4, 1634-5. Received with wife, Elizabeth,
    into Charlestown church, Feb. 13, 1635. He d. Dec. 6, 1677, and his wife,
    1685. Eight children.

II. Joseph, of Haverhill, Mass., (1636-1714), m. Hannah Tenney. Eleven c.

III. Dea. Thomas, (1670-1741), m. Elizabeth Paige, who d. at Hampstead, N. H.,
    June 12, 1752. Ten c.

IV. John, b. Nov. 15, 1711; m. 1st, Nov. 25, 1731, Sarah Haynes; m. 2d, Sarah,
    Morse. He was one of the first settlers of Hampstead, N. H. He d. April
    1, 1762.
    Children, ten by 1st, and seven by 2d marriage:
    i. Jesse, b. Oct. 20, 1732, O. S.; grantee of Newbury. In an old deed is

* In 1860 Dr. Jewett and wife brought to America a little Armenian girl, known here as
Deruhe Jewett, who lived in the family of Dea. Keyes a number of years. She became proficient
in music and taught successfully. She died young and was buried at St. Johnsbury.

mentioned as a "stationer" of Hampstead.

   ii. Sarah, b. July 9, 1734; d. y.

   iii. Miriam, b. March, 1736; m. 1st, ——— Mudgett; m. 2d, Capt. William Marshall. She has descendants near Cambridge.

   iv. Caleb, b. Feb. 3, 1738-9. Colonel in the revolutionary war; grantee of Newbury.

   v. Moses, b. April 13, 1740.

1 vi. Thomas, (Colonel), b. March 21, 1741-2; q. v.

   vii. Ruth, b. Feb. 3, 1743-4; d. in infancy.

   viii. Elizabeth, b. March 6, 1744-5; d. y.

   ix. John, b. Feb. 9, 1746-7; d. Aug. 18, 1757.

2 x. Haynes, b. Aug. 28, 1749; q. v.

   xi. Sarah, b. Oct. 29, 1751; m. July 29, 1773, Jacob Page; q. v.; d. Sept. 17, 1791.

   xii. Ruth, b. April 23, 1754; m. a Mr. Hoag. She was living at Charlestown, in 1808.

   xiii. Elizabeth, (twin to Ruth).

   xiv. Peter, b. June 7, 1756; m. Isabel Simpson, who d. Feb. 7, 1837; served in the revolutionary war; wounded at Bunker Hill; they lived in Newbury, Peacham and Haverhill. He d. Aug. 29, 1806. Buried at Horse Meadow. Among their c. were, (1) Caleb, d. 1806. (2) Thomas S., who went to Ohio about 1800. (3) John S., b. Haverhill, April 5, 1783; m. February, 1810, Lydia, dau. of Benjamin Ricker; d. Ryegate, 1851. The late Moses D. Johnson of Barnet was their son.

  xv. Judith, b. April 4, 1758; m. Nov. 15, 1776, Jesse Prescott of Deerfield, N. H.; d. April 25, 1844. Descendants by the names of Prescott, Libbey and others, have lived in Bath, Newbury, Bradford and Piermont.

  xvi. John, b. Feb. 9, 1760.

The descent of Johnson families of Newbury is reckoned from John Johnson of Hampstead.

1 THOMAS,[2] (John,[1]) b. Haverhill, Mass., March 22, 1742, O. S. Came to Haverhill of which he was a grantee, 1762, but settled in Newbury, on the Ox-bow. Built his first house in 1766, and the house now owned by the Heaths, in 1775. Innkeeper, farmer and merchant, his store being now a corn barn, owned by J. R. Weed Captain in the militia, and of a company of minute men organized in May, 1775, and reorganized in October. Captain of an independent company which marched to Ticonderoga in 1777, in which campaign he acted as aid to General Lincoln. Placed in charge of prisoners after the surrender. Captured Feb. 18, 1781, in Peacham, taken to Canada. Returned in October. (See chapters on the Revolutionary war). After the war, he became owner of great tracts of land in Newbury and elsewhere. Represented Newbury in the Convention at Cornish, 1778. Town Representative, 1786, '87, '88, '89, '90, '95, '97, 1800, '01· His journal, while a captive in Canada, is now owned by the sons of A. G. Johnson. Admitted to 1st ch., September, 1812. He m. 1st, Feb. 12, 1765, at Newburyport, Mass., Elizabeth, dau. of George Lowell, (b. June 30, 1741; d. Sept. 19, 1772). He m. 2d, Nov. 26, 1772, Abigail, dau. of Joseph Merrill, and widow of a Mr. Pool, (b.——— ———; d. Dec. 2, 1774). He m. 3d, Feb. 17, 1775, Abigail, dau. of Dudley Carleton, (b. March 30, 1750; d. March 23, 1833). He d. Newbury, Jan. 4, 1819. His funeral sermon was preached by Rev. David Sutherland of Bath. Col. Johnson d. in the house which he built in 1800, where his son, Hanes, lived after him, and where his grandson, Dea. Sidney Johnson, now resides. In 1830, a brick tomb about four feet in height, covered by a single massive stone, was built over his grave and those of his wives, which remained until the present fine monument was erected by the bequest of his grandson, Hiram Johnson, in 1869.

   Children, five by first wife, one by second wife, and eight by third wife, fourteen in all:

3 i. John, b. April 2, 1766; d. May 9, 1847.

4 ii. Moses, b. Feb. 29, 1768; d. May 17, 1840.

   iii. Jessie, twin to Moses, died on day of birth.

   iv. Betsey, b. Feb. 28, 1770; m. Isaac Bagley; q. v.

   v. Lowell, b. Aug. 7, d. Aug. 17, 1772.

vi.   Abigail, b. Nov. 18, 1773; d. May 22, 1796.
vii. Hanes, b. July 29, 1776; d. Dec. 18, 1783.
5 viii. David, b. Sept. 13, 1778; d. May 17, 1865.
ix.   Hannah, b. Sept. 8, 1781; d. April 9, 1782.
x.   Hannah, b. Dec. 20, d. Dec. 28, 1783.
6 xi. Hannah, b. Aug. 4, 1785; m. David Sloan, Esq., of Haverhill; d. May 30, 1861.
7 xii. Hanes, b. Nov. 9, 1787; d. July 3, 1878.
xiii. Thomas, b. Oct. 26, 1790; d. July 7, 1792.
8 xiv. Sally, b. March 9, 1792; m. Charles Story, Esq.; d. Jan. 27, 1859.

3 JOHN, (Thomas,[2] John,[1]) b. April 2, 1766; farmer on the Ox-bow, where he lived in a large house, built about 1785 and taken down 1891, which stood a short distance south of Dea. Sidney Johnson's. About 1820 he removed to wild land on the old road from West Newbury to South Newbury, where he cleared a farm and erected the buildings lately occupied by his grandson, Charles Edward Johnson. That locality was formerly known as Stagsboro. He m. Polly, dau. of ——— Pool. She fell into the river while washing yarn and was drowned, June 23, 1798. He m. 2d, Nov. 2, 1803, Abiah Eaton, who d. April 18, 1849.   He d. May 9, 1847.
    Children, six by first and six by second marriage:
    i.   John, b. Jan. 24, 1790; d. same day.
    ii.   John, b. April 29, 1791; m. Charity Parkhurst; d. Stanstead, P. Q., July 10, 1820.
    iii. Polly Pool, b. Jan. 29, 1793; m. March 19, 1812, Robert Rogers (q. v.); d. Stillwater, N. Y., April 4, 1817.
    iv.   Schuyler, b. Aug. 26, 1794; m. Jan. 10, 1819, Abigail Wood; d.
    v.   Moses, b. June 7, 1796; m. Dec. 15, 1819, Abigail J. Carleton; d.
    vi.   Nabby, b. Feb. 25, 1798; m. Oct. 7, 1816, Noah Carter.
9 vii. William, b. Jan. 9, 1804; m. Elizabeth Kent; d.
    viii. Elizabeth L., b. May 13, 1805; m. Peabody W. Ladd; q. v.; d. May 8, 1880.
    ix.   Miriam, b. Feb. 21, 1807; m. George Ropes; q. v.
    x.   Catherine, b. Nov. 12, 1808; m. July 21, 1832, Horace Whitcomb of Lancaster, N. H., and d. there.
10 xi.   Henry E., b Sept. 29, 1810; d. Aug. 4, 1890.
11 xii. Charles Story, b. Nov. 18, 1812; d. April 17, 1892.

4 MOSES,[3] (Thomas,[2] John,[1]) b. Feb. 29, 1768; m. 1st, Sept. 11, 1790, Phebe, dau. of Gen. Moses Dow of Haverhill (b. Feb. 17, 1772; d. Aug. 16, 1830); 2d, Dec., 1830, Betsey Pierson of Haverhill, who died in Boscawen, N. H.; farmer and innkeeper on the Ox-bow; d. May 17, 1840.
    Children:
    i.   Cynthia, b. March 20, d. April 9, 1791.
    ii.   Phebe, b. Feb. 9, 1793; d. Jan. 8, 1794.
    iii. Moses, b. Dec. 5, 1799; d. Dec. 20, 1812.
12 iv.   Frank P., b. May 19, 1805; q. v.
    v.   Hiram, b. Oct. 16, 1807; m. Sarah Kimball; in the grocery business on Long Wharf, Boston, where he made a large fortune, which was swept away in the panic of 1837. In the varnish and furniture business in New York city and later in St. Louis, where he became very wealthy. He died in St. Louis, Dec. 10, 1866, and she at same place, July 3, 1875, and both were buried at the Ox-bow.
    vi.   Moses, b. March 28, 1815; grad. Dartmouth College, 1834; read law with Doe & Kimball of Waterford, Vt., and at Troy, N. Y., with L. J. Lansing. In practice New York city, 1841-47; Cincinnati, 1847-49; Boston, 1853. He m. 1st, Sarah A., dau. of Angell Austin, of Hanover, N. H., and 2d, Adaline Dean Peabody of Chichester, N. H. No children. He d. March 31, 1872.
    vii. Nancy, b. and d. Aug. 28, 1818.

5 DAVID,[3] (Thomas,[2] John,[1]), b. Sept. 13, 1778; farmer and merchant; settled for a few years and began to clear a farm at the head of the pond, south of Ryegate Corner, but returned to Newbury and built, 1833 or '34, the brick building now occupied as a dwelling by Mr. Southworth, in which he

carried on the mercantile business. He owned several farms and much other land, was very precise and methodical in business matters, wrote a clear and elegant hand, and was an excellent accountant. He was postmaster from 1800 to 1812 and town clerk in 1837 and 1838, and from 1840 to 1856. He accumulated what was in his time considered a good property and gathered a valuable library. His acquaintance was very large and his correspondence extensive. His minute information upon a great variety of subjects made his society valued by men of very different tastes. He did much for the cause of education in Newbury, and several times became responsible for the financial support of select schools. In politics he was a Federalist, then a Whig, and later a Republican. He was a regular attendant at the First church, of which he was a liberal supporter. Of his Meteorological Journal, use is made elsewhere in this volume. More is due to David Johnson than to any other man for the preservation of the early annals of the town. He copied and arranged his father's correspondence, and at considerable expense obtained copies of valuable papers at Albany and Washington. It was at his instigation and by his assistance that Rev. Clark Perry prepared his historical discourse in 1831, and he furnished much of the material used by Rev. Grant Powers in his "Historical Sketches of the Coös Country," but was very much displeased with the manner in which Mr. Powers suppressed mention of all the prominent men at Coös who had opposed the course taken by Rev. Peter Powers during the last years of the Revolutionary war. The editor of this volume returns thanks in behalf of himself and the readers of this history to the present custodians of the Johnson papers for the free and unlimited use which he has been allowed to make of them. He lived in the house, built in 1807, now the residence of his grand-daughter, Mrs. Wheeler. He m. 1st, May 25, 1812, Lucy, dau. of John Town of Boxford, Mass., (b. Oct. 31, 1785; d. April 29, 1820); 2d, Feb. 9, 1831, Eliza S., dau. of William and Susanna Smith of Franklin, N. H., (b. —— July 21, 1796; d. Sept. 23, 1883). He d. May 17, 1865.

Children (one by first and four by second marriage) :

13 i. Alexander G., b. Feb. 14, 1813; d. Feb. 7, 1879, q. v.
14 ii. Harriet, b. July 29, 1814; d. Oct. 30, 1865, q. v.; m. Isaac Hale.
15 iii. Edward Carleton, b. Sept. 30, 1816.
16 iv. Nancy Cummings, b. Sept. 25, 1818; d. Dec. 15, 1892.

6 HANNAH,[3] (Thomas,[2] John,[1]) m. Nov. 21, 1811, David, son of David Sloan, a farmer of Pelham, Mass., and Elizabeth Scott, his wife. He was b. in Pelham, Jan. 9, 1780. He was one of five sons, one of whom was a farmer, one a doctor, and three were lawyers. He fitted for college at Leicester Academy, and graduated at Dartmouth in 1806. He first came to Haverhill as preceptor of the academy, but returned to Hanover to study law. After being admitted to the bar he opened an office in Haverhill and continued in practice until his death. He was known as Squire Sloan; his practice was extensive; he was well-known throughout the state; was a trustee of the academy and held many offices and positions of trust. "He was," says Mr. Livermore, "genial, social, and a very good story teller." He lived in the house on the east side of the common, at the Corner, in which his daughter now resides, which was built more than a century ago, by Alden Sprague, a noted lawyer in his time. Hannah had attended school at Bradford (Mass.) Academy, going and returning all the distance on horseback. She was a very beautiful young lady, with a fine figure, and the charm of her character and disposition brought her a wide circle of friends, and she was one of the leading spirits in the church and society of Haverhill Corner, in her day. He d. in Haverhill, N. H., June 7, 1860. She d. May 30, 1881.

Children, all educated at Haverhill and Meriden academies:

i. Thomas Carleton, m. Mrs. Mary Grant of Montreal, where he resided some years. Later he removed to New York and engaged in the furniture business. His latter years were spent in Haverhill. His c. were John David, Scott, and William Henry. The first of these was educated at Haverhill and Cambridge, Mass.; became Assistant Engineer in the United States Navy. Res. Dubuque, Iowa; Supervising Inspector of steam vessels of that district. Two c., dau. and son. Scott, 2d son of Thomas C.,

b. in Montreal, educated at Haverhill and Montpelier; in business some
years in Boston; studied law; admitted to the bar in 1885; in partnership
1885-91 with E. W. Smith of Wells River with an office at Woodsville.
He has no partner now. He m. Miss A. E. Nelson of Haverhill. William
Henry, 3d son of Thomas C.; educated at Haverhill and New York
City; is connected with a wholesale furniture business. One dau.

ii. Jonathan, d. y.
iii. David Scott, educated at Haverhill, Meriden and Exeter Academies.
Graduated at Dartmouth College 1836; studied law, but engaged as
teacher in a select school. Received degree of A. M. from Hobart College,
in which he was offered a tutorship. In August, 1841, he started to
visit an uncle at Ravenna, Ohio, taking passage in the steamer, Erie,
which took fire and was burned. It is supposed that Mr. Sloan jumped
into the water and was drowned. His body was recovered.
iv. Charles Story, educated at Haverhill Academy. A genial, energetic man;
many years in the furniture business in New York. During the Civil war
he went south and died.
v. William, educated at Haverhill and Meriden Academies; graduated
Dartmouth College, 1841. Studied law with Judge Wilcox at Orford, N.
H.; in practice at Woodstock and Chicago, Ill. The Illinois & Wisconsin
railroad (now the Chicago & Northwestern) will ever stand as a
monument to his indomitable energy. He died at Chicago in his prime.
vi. Edward, fitted for college at Haverhill and Meriden; entered Dartmouth,
but did not complete the course; teacher, and at the time of his death
editor of "The Abstract," at Woodstock, Ill.
vii. Henry, d. y.
viii. Henry S., educated at Haverhill; merchant in New York; then in the real
estate business in Chicago. He m. Frances Bentley of Woodstock, Ill.;
two daus.
ix. Elizabeth Abby, res. Haverhill, in the old home of her parents.

7 HANES,[3] (Thomas,[2] John,[1]) b. Nov. 9, 1787; m. March 14, 1813, Phebe, dau.
John Hazeltine, Jr., and granddaughter of Gen. Moses Dow of Haverhill,
(b. 1789; d. April 10, 1881). Farmer on the Ox-bow. Admitted to 1st
ch. May 4, 1829. Captain in the militia, and was generally known by his
military title. He d. July 3, 1878.
Children:
i. Thomas, b. March 27, 1814. Res. on the homestead, excepting a short
time in Minnesota. He m. June 24, 1857, at Hastings, Minn., Mrs. Ann
Austin, who d. in Newbury, Dec. 10, 1891. He d. May 2, 1901.
ii. Leonard, b. Aug. 19, 1815; in dry goods business; d. Oakland, Cal., Aug.
14, 1858.
iii. Alfred, b. April 17, 1817; m. Feb. 6, 1845, Frances Edson; d. at Boston,
Mass., Oct. 14, 1882; 10 c.
iv. Abigail Carleton, b. Sept. 29, 1818; m. 1st, March 14, 1839, Thomas
Brock, who d. March, 1842; m. 2d, October, 1845, George Severance.
She d. Nov. 27, 1861.
v. Mehitabel Hazeltine, b. June 12, 1820; m. Dec. 25, 1845, John Nelson
Dewey; res. Des Moines, Iowa.
vi. Amelia Bailey, b. March 22, 1822; d. April 16, 1842.
vii. John, b. Dec. 1, 1823; m. June 26, 1853, Elizabeth F. Stickney; d. Boston,
Mass., May 17, 1861.
viii. Mary Elizabeth, b. Oct. 9, 1825; m. Dec. 19, 1855, Albion P. Maxwell.
ix. Edwin Haines, b. Aug. 15, 1827; m. Mary Jane Galloway; d. July 11, 1881.
x. Perry, b. May 28, 1829; m. Feb. 22, 1860, Sarah H. Daggett; res. Oakland,
Cal.
xi. Richard Baxter, b. April 17, 1831; d. Feb. 16, 1834.
xii. Charlotte Foxcroft, b. June 29, 1833; m. Sept. 4, 1853, David Russell.
xiii. Eliza Smith, b. May 22, 1835; m. Oct. 19, 1858, Newell Z. Tabor; res.
Woburn, Mass.
xiv. Baxter, b. June 7, 1837; d. March 30, 1841.
17 xv. Sidney, b. Aug. 15, 1840.
xvi. Emma Grant, b. March 31, 1843; m. Dec. 25, 1863, N. W. Johnson; res.
Des Moines, Iowa.

8 SALLY,[3] (Thomas,[2] John,[1]), b. March 9, 1792. She was m. Aug. 20, 1812, to

Charles Story, Esq., son of Alexander and Sally (Myers) Story, both of whom were born in England. Alexander Story was a sea captain and owner of his vessel, who retired from the sea and bought the farm in Orford, N. H., now owned by Mr. Houghton of Boston, upon which he spent the rest of his life. Charles Story was born in Salem, Mass., Dec. 30, 1788; studied law with J. Y. Vail of Montpelier; admitted to the bar, 1819; in practice in Barnet ten years, and in Coventry twenty years, representing both towns in the legislature. In politics he was a strong Whig. Came to Newbury in 1849 and practiced until his sudden death, April 9, 1851. She d. Jan. 27, 1859.

Children:
i. Abby Maria, b. Cambridgeport, Mass., Sept. 11, 1814; d. Newbury, April 15, 1897.
ii. Dolly, b. Barnet; d. young.
iii. Sally J., b. Barnet; m. 1st, Sept. 10, 1850, to John Ellis Tenney (b. Corinth, April 22, 1824; d. Concord, N. H., April 6, 1858). She m. 2d, C. Myric Holden of Worcester, Mass. C., (1) son, died before he was two days old; (2) Charles Ellis, b. May, 1855; d. March 3, 1856.

9 WILLIAM,[4] (John,[3] Thomas,[2] John,[1]) b. Jan. 9, 1804. Lived on the homestead at the Ox-bow, but rem. to Vernon County, Wis., and d. there. He m. Nov. 15, 1827, Elizabeth, dau. Joseph Kent. b. March 15, 1804. C., three d. in Newbury, the others went west: (1) Lucy Town, b. Aug. 26, 1828. (2) Jesse, b. May 23, 1830. (3) John, b. April 29, 1833. (4) Elizabeth, b. May 6, 1835. (5) Henry, b. Feb. 28, 1838; d. Jan. 8, 1842. (6) Moody K., b. Jan. 20, 1840; d. Jan. 6, 1842. (7) Henry, b. Feb. 22, 1842; d. Sept. 13, 1843. (8) Mary Ellen, b. Sept. 24, 1857.

10 HENRY EATON,[4] (John,[3] Thomas,[2] John,[1]) b. Sept. 10, 1810; farmer, and life-long resident of Newbury, except one year, when in charge of a plantation at Norfolk, Va. He m. June, 1844, Ruth, dau. of Noyes Bayley, (b. Feb. 20, 1819; d. March 26, 1879). He d. Aug. 3, 1890.

Children:
i. Miriam, b. March 14, 1846; d. May 19, 1867.
ii. Sarah E., b. Oct. 4, 1848; d. July 23, 1863.
iii. Kate H., b. Dec. 24, 1849; res. Newbury.
iv. Henry H., b. Aug. 4, 1854; engineer some years in Danvers (Mass.) Lunatic Hospital; went to Hartford, where he rose to be superintendent of the Electric Light Co. of that city. He m. in Danvers, November, 1879, Emma Wyatt, and d. at Hartford, Conn., Nov. 15, 1890. He left two sons, Henry Wyatt and Herbert.
v. Jennie, b. Nov. 5, 1855; d. Aug. 29, 1879.
vi. George Dan, b. July 21, 1859. He went to Hartford in 1882, where he become manager of the Electric Light Co., and upon the death of his brother, became superintendent. He m. March, 1885, Kate Bolyn, of Hartford. He d. Hartford, Conn., Sept. 18, 1894. One dau., Ruth Bailey Johnson.

11 CHARLES STORY,[4] (John,[3] Thomas,[2] John,[1]), b. Nov. 18, 1812. Farmer on the homestead at West Newbury. He m. 1st, Sally A., dau. of Asa Aldrich (b. April 25, 1818; d. Feb. 12, 1860); m. 2d, Jan. 1, 1865, Betsey King Folsom, who d. Dec. 23, 1890. He d. April 18, 1872.

Children:
i. George A., b. Dec. 25, 1841. Served in Co. D, 1st Vermont Regiment of three months' men, and was in the first battle of the war, Big Bethel, June 10, 1861. He was employed for several years as a guide at the White Mountains. In 1876 he removed to a farm which he bought in Piermont. He m. 1st, May 3, 1863, Sarah J., dau. of William Chamberlain of Bradford, who died April 25, 1868; m. 2d, Feb. 16, 1871, Isabel, dau. of Walter Buchanan of Newbury. C., (1) Mabel, J., b. Feb. 25, 1873; teacher. (2) Lizzie Aldrich, b. March 26, 1874; d. May 30, 1891. (3) Charles Walter, b. Feb. 16, 1876. (4) John Buchanan, b. March 20, 1880. (5) Ellen R., b. June 5, 1883.
ii. Charles Edward, b. Oct. 25, 1847. Farmer on the homestead. He m., July 4, 1883, Annie, dau. of George King. C., (1) Julia May, b. April 22, 1892. (2) Lizzie, b. June 17, 1894.

iii.   Albion Ernest, b. March 1, 1870; in creamery business.

12 FRANK PHELPS,[4] (Moses,[3] Thos.[2], John,[1]) b. May 19, 1805; m. Sept. 9, 1828,
      Eleanor Ford, dau. of Otho Stevens, (b. March 18, 1806; d. Whitefield, N.
      H., May 2, 1892). He d. Aug. 26, 1842.
      Children:
      i.   Josephine, b. April 26. 1829; m. Nov. 6, 1849, Royal Beal of Orfordville, N.
           H. C., (1) Abby Ellen, b. Aug. 11, 1850; m. H. E. Morey of Malden,
           Mass. (2) Georgiana, b. June 2, 1856; m. Abram Washburn of Lexington,
           Mass. (3) Frank J., b. Nov. 11, 1860; m. Elizabeth L. Avery. (4) Rufus
           C., b. March 2, 1863; d. Feb. 7, 1876. (5) Fenner L. R., b. March 29,
           1867; m. Alfaretta L. McClellan of Nova Scotia.
      ii. Matilda, b. March 29. 1831; m. John D. Martin; q. v.
      iii. Ellen Frances, b. April 25, 1838; m. Oct. 6, 1863, L. Tracy Hazen; q. v.

13 ALEXANDER GEORGE,[4] (David,[3] Thomas,[2] John,[1]), b. Feb. 13, 1813. Fitted for
      college at Kimball Union Academy; graduated at Dartmouth College,
      1837. Law student in office of Henry Z. Hayner, Troy, N. Y., 1837–40;
      at Albany, 1840–41; admitted to the bar in the latter year. In practice
      as partner with Mr. Hayner, 1841–48. Deputy superintendent of common
      schools of the State of New York, Feb. 1, 1848, to Dec. 8, 1849. From
      Dec. 31, 1851, to May 1, 1852, Deputy Secretary State of New York.
      Editor of the Troy Daily Post, 1852–54, the paper having been conducted
      by himself and Mr. Enoch Davis since 1850, the name being afterwards
      changed to that of the Troy Daily Traveller. Deputy Secretary of State
      again, 1854–55. In practice of law until 1862. Editor. 1861, of the
      Troy Daily Arena. From 1862 to 1865, partly in practice and connected
      with the Troy Daily Whig, of which he was editor, 1868 to April 18, 1878.
      From 1869 until 1873 he was professor of rhetoric and English literature
      in the Rensselaer Polytechnical Institute at Troy. He prepared, in 1869,
      the school laws of New York, in one large octavo volume, with practical
      comments and instructions for school officers. This code of laws stands
      today as he drew them. In addition to these services he served a term in
      the Board of Supervisors of Rensselaer County; was for a time deputy
      collector of the port of Troy, and in 1865 and 1867 was engaged in the
      Department of Instruction at Albany. Mr. Johnson was also editor of a
      paper very influential in the New York politics of the time, from 1845, one
      one or two years, the Albany Freeholder, the organ of the Anti-Renters, a
      party almost forgotten. He became editor at the instance of Thurlow
      Weed, in place of Thomas A. Dwyer, an Irishman, who had fled from
      England on a charge of being engaged in the Chartist riots. He also
      furnished nearly all the editorials of the Family Journal during the years
      1859–60. Mr. Johnson was an able and successful editor, and intimately
      acquainted with the men and measures of his time. In politics he was a
      Whig and later a Republican, but too independent in his views and policy
      to be a politician. His favorite study was history, in the knowledge of
      which he had few equals, and it is to be regretted that he did not live to
      prepare his projected history of Newbury. He was a fine classical scholar.
      He wrote entire all of Madame Willard's History of the United States,
      from 1860 to 1875, and much of the earlier part of it. When he first
      settled in the practice of law he had an opportunity of engaging in
      partnership with William H. Seward before the latter became famous. He
      died after an illness of nearly a year at Brunswick, Rensselaer county,
      New York, Feb. 7, 1879. Mr. Johnson married at Windsor, September 2,
      1846, Charlotte P., dau. of Allen Wardner, sister of the wife of Hon.
      William M. Evarts. She res. at Watertown, Conn.
      Children:
      i.   Helen Minerva, b. Albany, N. Y., July 27, 1848; educated partly at the
           Convent Sacred Heart, Montreal; teacher 18 years, at St. Agnes School,
           at Albany, N. Y., under Bishop Doane; d. Watertown, Conn., March 29,
           1889.
      ii. George Carleton, b. Bethlehem, N. Y., now a part of Albany, June, 1, 1851;
           began as clerk for J. M. Warren & Co., Troy, N. Y.; traveled six years for
           Lamson & Goodnow of Shelburne Falls, Mass; now head clerk (Actuary
           Department) ot the Pennsylvania Mutual Life Insurance Co., Philadelphia.

ALEXANDER G. JOHNSON.

iii. Lucy Town, b. Troy, N. Y., Jan. 21, 1853; m. Oct. 22, 1879, Alfred H. Scovill of Watertown, Conn. Five c.

iv. Jane Root, b. Troy, N. Y., Sept. 1, 1855; lives with her mother at Watertown, Conn.

v. Martha Wardner, b. Troy, July 31, 1857; m. June 22, 1880, Allen G. Lamson; d. Brooklyn, N Y., May 31, 1883; buried at Troy. She left two c., Charlotte Wardner and Guy Carleton, who live with their grandmother at Watertown.

vi. Anna Charlotte, b. Troy, July 13, 1859; d. Aug. 13, 1864, at Troy.

vii. Thomas Harrington, b. Troy, June 28, 1862; d. Aug. 9, 1864, at Troy.

viii. Allen Wardner, b. Troy, Dec. 13, 1866; graduated Yale College, 1887; studied law and is now with Howlands & Murray, 35 Wall St., New York City.

14 HARRIET,[3] (David,[2] Thomas,[1]) b. July 29, 1814; m. (by Rev. Geo. W. Campbell) Sept. 25, 1838, Isaac, son of Isaac and Ruth (Jewett) Hale, of Newbury, Mass., b. there Sept. 26, 1807. He d. July 15, 1890, from injuries received by falling from a ladder. Res. Providence, R. I., where all their children were born. She d. Oct. 30, 1865.

Children:

i. Alice, b. Jan. 19, 1840; m. July 26, 1860, at Providence, R. I., to Nathaniel P., son of Nathaniel P., and Matilda (Crawford) Hill, b. Montgomery, N. Y. Mr. Hill graduated at Brown University, 1859. Teacher, then professor of chemistry at Brown for several years. In 1864, he rem. to Black Hawk, Colorado, to become manager of the Boston and Nevada smelting works. These works were afterwards rem. to Denver, where he still resides. United States Senator, 1879–85, and was the leading advocate of bimetalism. C., (1) Nathaniel P., b. March 29, 1862. (2) Isabel, b. April 10, 1864. (3) Gertrude, b. Jan. 29, 1869.

ii. Maria, b. Aug. 19, 1842; m. Oct. 13, 1863, to Rev. Adoniram Judson Gordon, son of John C. and Sally (Robinson) Gordon, b. New Hampton, N. H., April 19, 1836. Graduated Brown University, 1860, Newton Theological Seminary, 1863. Pastor of Jamaica Plain (Mass.) Baptist church, July, 1863. Pastor of Clarendon St. Baptist church, Boston, December, 1869, till death, Feb. 2, 1895. He was one of the most prominent and beloved ministers of Boston. Author of many valuable spiritual books, also compiler of a hymn book in use in many churches. He composed several well-known hymns and tunes. He d. from typhoid pneumonia, the result of a chill. y C., (1) Harriet Hale, b. Oct. 25, 1865. (2) Ernest Barron, b. March 2, 1867. (3) Elsie, b. Dec. 19, 1868. (4) Arthur Hale, b. March 2, 1872. (5) Helen Maria, b. Jan. 13, 1874. (6) Theodore L., b. April 28, 1886.

iii. Harriet, b. May 18, 1844; m. in Boston, June 6, 1872, to Timothy Underwood Roworth, b. probably in Elmira, N. Y., March, 1833; merchant at Central City, Col., where he d. July 17, 1872, as the result of a fall. Mrs. Roworth res. in Providence, R. I.

iv. Wendell Phillips, b. Sept. 26, 1846; m. in Providence, R. I., Oct. 16, 1872, Elizabeth, dau. of James and Martha (Hill) Guy, b. Norwich, Conn., March 16, 1849. Her parents were from Nailsworth, Eng. Mr. Hale is a grain dealer at Providence. He has been a generous giver to the Tenney Memorial Library. C., (1) Carleton, b. Aug. 6, 1873. (2) Elizabeth G., b. Oct 8, 1874. (3) Gordon D., b. Dec. 22, 1877. (4) Martha J., b. Aug. 18, 1883.

v. Thomas Johnson, b. May 9, 1849; d. July 26, 1854.

vi. Arthur Towne, b. June 12, 1852; d. Feb. 21, 1859.

vii. Jesse D., b. Dec. 9, 1855; m. at Denver, Col., March 18, 1885, Grace A., dau. of Frederic J., and Mary J. Butler, b. Buffalo, N. Y., Sept. 27, 1860. C., Philip Jewett and Alice, (twins) b. Feb. 4, 1886.

15 EDWARD CARLETON,[3] (David,[2] Thomas,[1]) b. Sept. 30, 1816. Graduated Dartmouth College 1840; read law with Lucius Peck of Montpelier 1841-43; rem. to New York 1845 and became a merchant. He travelled extensively and was a fine public speaker. He m. Aug. 31, 1847, Delia Maria Smith of Hamilton, N. Y.; d. Dec. 29, 1878; bur. in Greenwood Cemetery, N. Y. She d. July 7, 1881.

One child:

i. Louisa F., m. 1st, April 9, 1868, James Underhill, a lawyer of New York City. who was of an old Knickerbocker family. He d. August, 1878. C., James Underhill, b. Apr. 9, 1871. She m. 2d, Dec. 23, 1880, John H. Wheeler. Mr. Wheeler's father was a Congregational clergyman, his grandfather and great grandfather were lawyers and judges. He graduated from Harvard University, at the age of 19, with highest honors; held a scholarship for one year at Johns Hopkins University, and one for three years while he studied in Europe. Received the degree of Ph. D., from the University of Bonn, Germany. Was instructor in Latin and Greek at Harvard University, then taught at Radcliffe, then called Harvard Annex. Professor of Latin one year at Bowdoin College. Professor of Greek at the University of Virginia until three months before his death, Oct. 10, 1887. Buried at the Ox-bow. C., Frances Parkinson Wheeler, b. July 21, 1885. Mrs. Wheeler res. on the homestead.

16 NANCY CUMMINGS,[4] (David,[3] Thomas,[2] John,[1]) b. Sept. 25, 1818. She was a fine scholar, and her father purchased for her the first or second piano brought into this town. She became a cripple in early life, a sore which developed upon her right foot rendered its amputation necessary. She was one of the first to use the artificial limbs invented by Palmer. The first one Palmer made was for himself, the second was for her. She became a teacher, and was preceptress of the Newbury High School in 1844. Nancy Johnson, whom Allibone's Dictionary of Authors calls Anna C. Johnson, was, probably, the most unusual literary personage whom Newbury has produced. Her first contributions to the press were some stories for children, and her first book, "Letters from a Sick Room," was published by the Massachusetts Sunday School Society. The following account of her life was written for our use by Mrs. A. G. Johnson, of Watertown, Conn., who probably knows her history better than anyone else now living:

' My acquaintance with Nancy did not commence until the early '40s, although I had known her brother, George, since I was six years old. A large part of her youth was spent in a sick room. Her brother, George, assisted her much in her studies and reading. I do not know of her attending school anywhere, excepting one year in Greenfield, Mass., a boarding school kept by a Mr. Jones. This must have been in the '30s. In 1847, she spent some months with us at Troy, and left us to travel with Miss Catherine Beecher, in the west that same year. They visited all the chief towns and cities, west and south, and I think they established schools in various places. I don't remember how long she was engaged with Miss Beecher, I think that the summers of '49, '50, and '51 were spent at Saratoga. She felt that she received some benefit from the waters. Even there I think that she wrote letters for some papers. From that time till '54, she remained with us and in New York. In 1854, she went to visit *Mrs. Asher Wright, who was missionary at the Seneca Mission. Here she gathered materials for her book about the Indians. I think "The Iroquois" was considered as good as anything she wrote. It was translated into the French language while she was in Paris. She wrote for the New York Times, of which Henry J. Raymond was editor and proprietor. You will notice that "Myrtle Wreath" is dedicated to him. She was in his family a good deal before going to Europe, and was with them the first of her life there. They sailed from New York, March 21, 1857, and she spent the next winter with them at Hiedelberg, Germany. She traveled all over Germany, living among the peasantry,

---

*NOTE.—Mrs. Wright's maiden name was Laura Maria Sheldon. She was born July 10, 1809, at St. Johnsbury, made her home in Newbury at different times; was admitted to the 1st ch. March 9, 1828; taught school here several terms, and was m. at Barnet, Jan. 21, 1833, by Rev. Clark Perry, to Rev. Asher Wright, missionary to the Indians on the Cattarangus reservation, where she remained 53 years, dying there Jan. 21, 1886. Mr. Wright d. 1875. She revisited Newbury in 1838, and brought with her a little Indian girl, named Austria Two Guns, who was brought up in the family of Henry Keyes. There are several yet living who will remember her. She returned to her own people in later years, and m. one of her race, William Tallchief.   ED.

and learning their language, manners and custom, gathering material for her "Peasant Life in Germany." She went all over Switzerland in the same way; climbed mountains, rode donkeys, and did all sorts of venturesome things. "Cottages of the Alps," was written at that time. She went to Paris in 1858, was there through all of our civil war. She would go out into the country every little while, gathering what she could for another book about the French, the same as of Germany and Switzerland. About this time her mind first began to break down, and what she wrote about France was never published. In 1863, Henry Ward Beecher went to see her, and engaged her to write for the "Independent." She also wrote for the "Congregationalist," "The Sacramento Union," some Chicago paper, and several others. She wrote for the press long before she went abroad, earning her means to go in that way. Her correspondence and authorship of "Minnie Myrtle" made her quite famous among the literary circles of New York. The winter before she left she was quite gay, and became acquainted with all the gentlemen and ladies of note there. Paris was her headquarters for a long time. In 1869, she, with two lady friends, (Americans), traveled all over Spain, went to Madrid, Grenada, Seville, Tangier, Barcelona, Marseilles, Nimes, Malaga, Nice, and so on. There seems no end to her journeys. Some of her letters from Spain are very interesting, and a few were published in the Troy Whig. In 1871, she spent some time in Venice. I think she must have been there at least two years. She was in Naples and Florence. I know she went to Rome, but I find nothing written from there. I think it was there that her mind began to break down a second time. Previous to that I saw nothing in her writings which would indicate that anything was the matter. How she ever accomplished what she did, I cannot imagine. Especially when it is considered that she was more or less of an invalid all the time, suffering privations, and more or less anxiety about receiving any remittances. I do not wonder her poor head and nerves became unstrung; perhaps, she, herself, was to blame. She was too anxious to be independent, and make herself famous, an immense amount of energy and pride. Her intellect we cannot dispute; it was something wonderful. But it was a great mistake for her to be left so alone. She needed, (like all geniuses), a kind, honest, practical friend to stand by her, and take care of her. She was easily imposed upon, and loved flattery. In person she was quite attractive, and fine looking, without being really handsome. I do not recall the precise date of her return to Newbury. My husband went down to New York to meet her. Even then she seemed perfectly sane upon all general subjects. I never saw her again."

Thus far the narrative of Mrs. Johnson, which needs little addition. To the present generation her name is almost unknown, but, fifty years ago, she was considered as one of the brilliant women of America. But she produced nothing that survived her own generation. Some of her books passed through several editions; her correspondence was very extensive; she was intimately acquainted with many of the prominent literary men and women of her own country and of Europe. She returned to Newbury and passed the remainder of her life among the scenes of her childhood. Her intellectual powers gradually gave way, but there were times when she was roused, and her conversation attained somewhat of its former brilliancy. She was admitted to the 1st ch., Sept. 4, 1842. She d. at the house of Miss Elizabeth Sloan, at Haverhill, Dec. 15, 1892, and is buried at the Ox-bow.

17 SIDNEY,[4] (Hanes,[3] Thomas,[2] John,[1]) b. Aug. 15, 1840; farmer on homestead; chosen deacon in 1st ch. 1883; m. Nov. 16, 1870, Mary Elizabeth Ford of Lowell, Mass.

Children:

i. Leonard, b. Nov. 26, 1871; educated at Phillips Exeter Academy and Dartmouth Medical College; physician at Franconia, N. H. He m. July 9, 1896, Mabel, dau. of Robert G. Laing.

ii. Erwin Arthur, b. Feb. 26, 1873; educated at Newbury; graduated Boston Dental College, June 1897; in practice in Boston.

iii. Louise Carleton, b. March 21, 1882.

iv. Hanes Holden, b. Jan. 13, 1884.

JOHNSON.

HAYNES, son of John, and brother of Col. Thomas, b. Aug. 28, 1784. He was one of the grantees of Newbury; lived some years on Hall's Meadow, his house being near the river on the J. J. Smith farm; m. Elizabeth Elliott, who went back to Chester, N. H., after his death, for fear of the Indians and Tories. She was a daughter of Edward and Mehitabel (Worthen) Elliott of Chester. She returned to Newbury and m., 2d, Col. Remembrance Chamberlin, q. v. Haynes d. at Concord, N. H., Sept. 2, 1775.

Children, by first marriage, all born in Newbury:
1   i.   Jonathan, b. ——; d. Jan. 19, 1812.
     ii. Jesse, b. March 27, 1773; d. July 18, 1830.
     iii. Haynes, b. Aug. 13, 1775; d. Nov. 1, 1863.
These three Johnson brothers married three daughters of Capt. Ezekiel Sawyer of Bradford. Jesse and Haynes settled there, and for their families see McKeen's History of Bradford.

1 " CAPT. JONATHAN JOHNSON," says our town record, "departed this life sorely lamented by his friends and connections, Jan. 19, 1812." He settled on Hall's Meadow, where J. J. Smith now lives. His wife was Hannah Sawyer, b. March 26, 1779. They had only one child:
2   i.   Haynes, b. Sept. 23, 1800.

2 HAYNES,[4] (Jonathan,[3] Haynes,[2] John,[1]) b. Sept. 23, 1800; d. Apr. 8, 1856; graduated Dartmouth College, 1822; farming and teaching till 1830, when he studied divinity with Rev. S. Chamberlin, and was ordained a deacon in the M. E. ch., 1833; elder, 1836, and was an able and successful minister for about 25 years. In his time the term of service was very short, and the work laborious. He served 16 appointments, being stationed at Newbury in 1847, and in 1856 till death. He m. June 10, 1842, Hannah, dau. of Col. Simeon Stevens, (b. Apr. 29, 1805;) d.

Children:
     i.   Jonathan, b. Newbury, March 15, 1824; d. Jeffersonville, Ind., Aug. 15, 1896; fitted for college at Newbury Seminary; graduated Wesleyan University, 1849; teacher of Latin and Mathematics at Newbury Seminary, 1854; teacher in other academies and colleges in New Hampshire and Vermont; also in Wesleyan Female College in Cincinnati; teacher at Jeffersonville, Ind., and in the druggist business till death. Civil Engineer; surveyed the Vermont Central railroad from Windsor to White River Junction; held various city offices. He m. March 27, 1849, Anna McCracken; no c.
     ii. Simeon Stevens, b. Athens, July 27, 1836; fitted at Newbury Seminary for Yale College, but his father's death prevented his entering. Rem. to Jeffersonville, Ind., 1856; clerk in his brother's drug store and studying law till 1861, when admitted to the bar; in practice since, besides being City Attorney and Councillor; is also Grand Master of the Indiana State Lodge of Free Masons. He m. June 24, 1874, at Dedham, Mass., Ellen S., dau. of Jerome B. Bailey, (b. Fairlee, Aug. 2, 1841; d. Jeffersonville, Ind., Aug. 26, 1892). C., Martha H., m. Captain S. C. Baird of the United States Army; Frank H., killed by falling from a railroad bridge in 1897, and Hannah S.

JOHNSON.

ALEXANDER, son of Thomas and Elizabeth Johnson, was b. in Bath. N. H., in 1805. He was twice m., first to Hannah Walker of Lyman, N. H., and second to Margaret Shaw of McIndoes Falls, where he engaged in the manufacture of lumber, in the firm of Kimball, Gilchrist & Co., until 1856. In 1857, he rem. to Barnet and engaged in farming for three or four years. He next located on a farm in Fairlee, where he remained six years. About 1866 he rem. to this town, where he remained until his death, in 1884, aged 79 years. Mrs. Johnson died in 1885, aged sixty-nine years.

Alexander Johnson was a Republican and represented the town of Barnet in 1856 and 1857 and was selectman a number of years.

Children:

i. Janet S.
ii. Daniel S., res. Littleton since 1888; m. Abbie L. Kimball of Bradford. C., (1) Walter E., in the employ of the American Express Co., on the Boston & Maine R. R. (2) Florence L. Mrs. Johnson d. in July, 1884.
iii. Elizabeth C.
iv. James A., a farmer in this town; his farm being the original homestead of Webster Bailey.
v. Frank R., a millwright.

JOHNSTON.

Col. Charles of Haverhill and his brother, Col. Robert, of Newbury, were among the most prominent men in Coös in their day. They were of Scotch descent and are understood to have come to Hampstead, and thence to Coös, Haverhill, Mass., being their native place. Their parents were Michael and Mary (Hancock) Johnston. Rev. Grant Powers says that Michael, their brother, was one of the men sent up by Bayley and Hazen in 1761, with cattle to be wintered here, and that, on their return he was drowned at the upper end of Olcot's Falls. A family record gives his name as John. The three brothers served in the Old French war. Michael was a private in the 7th Co. of Blanchard's Reg., enlisted for service against the French Forts. Served from April 28 till October, 1755. In the 2d Regiment (Col. Peter Gilman's) Charles and Robert were privates in the 4th Co., of which Jacob Bayley was a lieutenant, from Sept. 22, 1755, until the end of the campaign. Michael and Robert were privates in the 11th Co. of Meserve's Regiment in the Crown Point expedition of 1756, and served seven months. They served also in the same regiment the next year from March 8th. Michael was also private in Capt. John Hazen's Co. of Goff's Regiment from March 5, 1760, to the end of the war in November. Charles was quartermaster in the same regiment. In the Revolutionary war he was Lieutenant Colonel of Hobart's Regiment, in Stark's Brigade, and distinguished himself at the battle of Bennington. He was Judge of Probate for Grafton County 26 years. County Treasurer many years. He was b. at Haverhill, Mass., May 29, 1737, and d. at Haverhill, N. H., March 5, 1813.

Col. Robert, b. Sept. 3, 1738, at Haverhill, Mass. He built the first two story house in town in which he kept tavern. This building, which is now a barn at the south end of Newbury village, stood a little above Mr. Laing's house, and was surrounded by a stockade during the revolutionary war. He is mentioned as keeping tavern in 1769. Later, (a family tradition says in 1775), he built the house, now very much altered, where Robert J. Hibbard now lives. The first spirits sold at his bar were brought up from Concord in square kegs on horseback, says Rev. Clark Perry. Besides his service with his brother in the Old French war, before mentioned, he served twenty days in Capt. Thomas Johnson's Co. of minute men in 1775. He also served as minute man in Peter Olcot's Regiment in 1776. Capt. Thomas Johnson's Co., guarding and scouting, 57 days. In Oct. 1778, he was commissioned Lieut-Col. of the 4th Regiment, and is later spoken of as Colonel. He was also recruiting officer, and his house was the rendezvous several times for troops. Col. Frye Bayley's diary for 1776 states that the training field was behind Col. Johnston's house, and from that place the company under Col. Bayley started for Saratoga. He was chosen constable in 1769, and was one of the representatives from Newbury to the Constitutional Convention at Windsor, June 4, 1777. He seems to have declined to serve as Assistant Judge for Orange County in 1781, being elected Sheriff of the County. In 1787, he was chosen one of a committee of five to build the meeting house. In 1788, he was one of a committee to purchase a parsonage. Some years before his death he relinquished his fine farm to his sons, Charles and Robert and rem. to the farm long owned by the late John E. Chamberlain. Col Robert Johnston was one of those who opposed the course taken by Rev. Peter Powers in the last year of his ministry, and when the Rev. Grant Powers prepared his historical sketches he avenged his uncle by entirely neglecting him, with others. He d. Feb. 29, 1824. Col. Robert Johnston was four times married; 1st to Abigail Hadlock (Hadley), who d. May 25, 1771; 2d, Abigail Way, who d. July 25, 1772; 3d, Jane, (Jean) Bell, d. in 1780; 4th, Hepzibah (Tyler), widow of *James Bell; b. Dec. 5, 1754 at Pembroke, N. H.; d. July 8, 1846. He had sixteen c., six by the 1st, one by 2d, two by 3d, and seven by 4th. Their records differ in the following list; the records in brackets are those given by Mrs. Jennie Goodwin of Minneapolis from a family Bible.

Children:
- i. Abigail, b. April 25, 1760; m. Gen. James Whitelaw of Ryegate; d. July 11, 1790.
- ii. Sally, [Sarah] b. April [May] 3, 1762; m. John Scott, q. v.; d. July 25, 1835, [1836].
- iii. Ruth, b. April 8, 1764; m. William Tice of Barnet; d. May 22, 1844. She had daus., who m. Noyes and Joshua Bayley, q. v.
- 1 iv. James, b. May 31, 1766; d. July 28, 1849.
- v. John, b. May 13, (3) 1768; rem. to Greensboro and settled there; d. October, 1831.
- vi. Mary, b. March 31, 1770; d. Jan. 28, 1859, [July 27, 1860].
- vii. Cyrus, b. July 22, 1772; rem. to Berlin, and d. there July 24, 1860.
- viii. Elizabeth, b. Sept. 24, 1773; m.——— Andrews; d. March 19, 1833.
- 2 ix. Robert, b. July 4, 1776; d. July 11, 1849.
- x. Jane, b. May 6, 1781; teacher and author of some children's books and tracts; d. March 10, 1853, at Danville.
- xi. Hannah, b. March 28, 1783; m. 1st, Feb. 25, 1803, William Bell; m. 2d, April 11, 1816, Barnard Brickett; d. July 11, 1846, Groton.
- xii. Nancy, b. March 26, 1785; m. Jonas Tucker, q. v.; d. Nov. 30, 1830.
- xiii. Charles, b. Oct. 13, 1787; major in the militia; town representative, 1822, 1826; one of the first settlers of Beloit, Wis. Un-m. He d. Aug. 20, 1838.
- xiv. Lydia, b. Oct. 16, 1789; un-m.; d. Aug. 29, 1803.
- 3 xv. Abigail, b. Jan. 29, 1792.
- xvi. Myra A., b. April 22, 1793; teacher; un-m.; d. at Danville, May 23, 1865.

1 JAMES,[1] (Robert,[2]) b. May 31, 1766; m. 1790, Nancy, dau. of Joshua and Elizabeth Foster, (b. Aug. 26, 1760; d. May 17, 1835.) James Johnston lived in the old house long unoccupied, opposite that of Joseph C. Johnston. He owned and conducted several mills at the falls near his house. He d. July 28, 1844.
Children:
- 4 i. John F., b. Sept. 28, 1790; d. Jan. 16, 1870.
- ii. Betsey C., b. Aug. 8, 1792; m. March 3, 1822, Daniel Woods of Corinth; d. Sept. 21, 1876.
- iii. Fanny M., b. Nov. 30, 1794; un-m.; d. Jan. 4, 1869.
- 5 iv. James B., b. June 14, 1798; d. June 14, 1864.
- v. Robert, b. April 19, 1800; d. same day.
- vi. Abigail, b. June 15, 1802; d. Feb. 6, 1842.

2 ROBERT,[2] (Robert,[1]) b. July 4, 1776; d. July 11, 1849; lived on the homestead; farmer; m. Dec. 12, 1805, Betsey, dau. James Spear; d. Feb. 19, 1860.
Children:
- i. James Spear, b. Oct. 15, 1806; d. July 28, 1872; m. Nov. 29, 1829, to Susan, dau. Joseph Smith, (b. Jan. 17, 1808; d. Feb. 19, 1860); no c.; farmer; lived where Mrs. A. B. Chamberlain does.
- ii. Eliza; d.
- iii. Laura, b. Feb. 15, 1812; d. March 3, 1888; m. March 5, 1835, to Horatio N. Burnham; (d. Aug. 7, 1865.)

---

*James Bell of Lyme, N. H., was accidentally killed in 1775, leaving a son, James, then two years old. His widow m. 2d, Col. Robert Johnston. The boy, James, lived with them till of age; rem. to Hardwick, 1800, and m. Lucy Dean, 1801. He became involved in a law suit, but, being too poor to employ a lawyer, he defended his case, won it, and became eminent at the bar. Rem. to Walden, 1804, where his son, Hon. James D. Bell, lived, and d. April 17, 1852.

iv. Esther, b. Aug. 28, 1815; d. Sept. 3, 1870; m. Ezekiel Hibbard; (see Webster Bailey family).
v. Robert.
vi. Jane, b. Feb. 28, 1820; d. Mar. 22, 1863; m. Dec. 12, 1840, Jacob Shepard, (b. 1816; d. Nov. 26, 1884).

3 ABIGAIL TYLER, b. Jan. 29, 1792; m. 1817, Salma Davis of Danville; d. Sept. 21, 1850.
Children:
i. Charles Johnston, b. Danville, March 17, 1823; m. Dec. 6, 1849, Sallie C. Sias at Danville; d. Sept. 21, 1850. Two daus., the 2d, Lizzie Paddock Davis, b. Chicago, Ill., Aug. 8, 1862; m. Nov. 20, 1889, John L. Bacon, lawyer at Randolph, and now state treasurer, b. June 18, 1862.

4 JOHN F.,[3] (James,[2] Robert,[1]) b. Sept. 28, 1790; m. 1st, Jan. 6, 1827, Dorcas, dau. Peter Martin, (b. Nov. 19, 1795; d. Nov. 1, 1847); 2d, Sept. 1849, Abby W. Jones, (b. July 2, 1806, d. Aug. 12, 1898, in Groton); d. Jan. 16, 1820.
Children:
i. William W., b. Aug. 11, 1829; m. Feb. 10, 1831, Mary Bowles; d. Nov. 23, 1887, at Washington, D. C.; bur. in Newbury.
ii. Hannah, b. June 16, 1832; d. Nov. 8, 1847.
iii. Joseph C., b. Oct. 22, 1836. Farmer on homestead. Served in Co. H., 12th Vt., as sergeant from Oct. 1862 till mustered out July 14, 1863; m. Apr. 12, 1865, Rosa Barnes. C., (adopted) Dora, b. Sept. 9, 1872; m. June 21, 1900, Edward H. Blood of Bradford. C., Doris Harriet, b. June 6, 1901.

5 JAMES B.,[3] (James,[2] Robert[1]) b. June 14, 1798. Farmer in Newbury; m. Feb. 26, 1826, Finette, dau. of Erastus Chamberlain; (b. May 17, 1806; d. Nov. 20, 1897, Washington, D. C.). He d. June 14, 1864.
Children:
i. Elizabeth C., b. April 12, 1827; d. Oct. 8, 1839.
ii. Robert, b. Oct. 8, 1828; d. Sept. 20, 1835.
iii. Charles, b. May 29, 1830; d. June 1, 1830.
iv. Sarah Finette, b. Jan. 15, 1832; d. Aug. 2, 1858.
v. Harriet Frances, b. Oct. 2, 1836; d. March 21, 1857.
vi George C., b. Feb. 28, 1840. Res. Washington, D. C. Served three years in Co. A., 3d N. H., in the rebellion; m. June 26. 1869, at Jersey City, N. J., Elizabeth Kelley. C., (1) Ella E., b. Jersey City, May, 1870; d. May 25, 1891. (2) Gertrude M., b. Jersey City, March 28, 1876.
vii. Erastus C., b. June 22, 1842. Served in Co. C., 3d Vt. and in Co. G., 9th Vt. in the rebellion. He m. 1st, Aug. 10, 1869, Lexington, Va., Annie M., dau. of Dea. Joseph Filer of Dixmont, Me. She d. Washington, D. C., Nov. 21, 1892. He m. 2d. Sept. 1, 1897, Josephine A. Cox, dau. of Geo. W. Mooney of Holderness, N. H. C., Birdie Finette, b. Madison, N. H., on Sept. 10, 1870; d. Washington, D. C., July 31, 1879.
viii. Ella E., b. March 11, 1847; music teacher; res. Washington, D. C.

JONSON.

RASMUS OR ERASMUS, a native of Sweden, and an officer who saw considerable service in the Swedish army, came here soon after our war for independence. It is said that he left the army "without leave," and came to this country in company with Bent Holm Green who, about 1808, rem. to Topsham, where he d. April 7, 1847, aged 84. He m. Judith Randall, who d. May 31, 1854, aged 86. Their descendants are numerous in Topsham and Groton. Rasmus Jonson bought what had been "General Bayley's malt-house," or distillery, the premises now called the "old tannery." at the village. where he made whiskey for many years, that business then being considered perfectly reputable. He was known as "Stiller" (distiller) Jonson. He built the house where Mrs. Lupien has lived for some years. In 1811, he was admitted "to occasional communion" in the 1st ch., he being a member of a church in Sweden. In 1829 he gave the land on which the Methodist church was built in that year. He m. Alice Dennis of Marblehead, Mass. She d. No c., but they "brought up" Hannah Clark, who m. Joel Temple. He d. "in hope of a

' blessed immortality." The sword of Rasmus Jonson is now owned by Joel C. Temple, and his Swedish Bible by Dr. Watkins' family.

KASSON.

JOHN, from Hartford, Conn., rem. to Topsham before 1795, and began to clear land in the northwest part of that town on what is still called the "old Kasson place." His wife was Betsy Cheney.
  Children:
1   i. Thomas, b. about 1778; d. 1853.
2   ii. Marvin, b. 1784; d. June 18, 1881.
   iii. Sally, b. Feb. 1787; m. Benjamin Chamberlin; d. Apr. 15, 1868.
   iv. Lucia, b. 1795; m. John Wallace; d. Oct. 19, 1888.
    v. Betsey M., b. Feb. 21, 1809; d. Nov. 24, 1889.
   vi. Marcia, m. 1827, Moses Carbee.

1 THOMAS,[2] (John,[1]) b. in Connecticut about 1778; m. Clarissa Hutchins of Corinth; lived in Topsham; d. 1853.
    .Childr[e]n :
    i. Sarah, m. R. E. Robie.
   ii. Diana, m. Orange Butler.
3 iii. Thomas, b. July 4, 1825; q. v.
   iv. Charles, d. at 26.
    v. Marvin, d. at 24.
   vi. Emily, m. Jefferson Doe.
  vii. Hartwell, d. un-m.

3 THOMAS,[3] (Thomas,[2] John,[1]) b. July 4, 1825; m. Naomi Whitcher; b. Feb. 3, 1833. They lived on the homestead in Topsham five years after marriage; came to Newbury about 1860, and bought the farm of John Weed, which had been that of A. W. Nourse.
  Children:
    i. Carrie, (adopted), b. Lancaster, Aug. 28, 1869; graduated St. Johnsbury Academy; m. Ambrose Mitchell of Hull, Mass.

2 MARVIN,[2] (John[1],) b. Pomfret, Conn., 1784; m. March, 1830, Elizabeth, dau. of Capt. John Dick; lived in Newbury, Dalton, Bath and Newbury; d. June 18, 1881.
  Children:
    i. Wm. Wallace, b. June 4, 1831; served in the Union army; res. Somerville, Mass.
   ii. Janette D., b. May 11, 1834; m. Azro B. Chamberlin, as 1st wife; d. July 1, 1871.
   iii. Sophronia B., b. March 28, 1837; m. James L. George, as 2d wife.
   iv. Harry B., b. June 11, 1839; served in the Union army; taken prisoner and died at Andersonville, Ga., after 18 months imprisonment.
    v. Lucia W., b. June 28, 1841; m. Lyman Buck of Haverhill.
   vi. Mary Lucinda, b. Sept. 11, 1844; m. Samuel Colby of Dorchester, Mass.
  vii. Marcia C., b. Aug. 20, 1846.
 viii. Gilbert, b. July 10, 1848; d. March, 1855.
   ix. Alden C., b. 1850; d. March, 1855.

KELLEY.

BENJAMIN, came to Newbury about 1807. from Goffstown, N. H., and m. Phœbe Green, then 18 years of age. He d. 1834, aged 66, and his wife, in 1873, aged 84.
  Thirteen children, of whom four d. in infancy:
    i. Alice, d. at the age of 26.
   ii. William, m. Polly Stebbins, and d. 1853, aged 49. He left a dau. who d. at five years of age.
   iii. Alden S., who went to Wisconsin and there d. at the age of 66.
1 iv. Asa T.

v. Loren F., served in the 6th Vermont, and was killed at Port Hudson, June 14, 1863.

vi. Thomas Freeland, served in Co. K, 3d Vt., as a 2d enlistment. In the battle of the Wilderness he was lost, and compelled to remain almost without food for ten days, and saw other hard service, in consequence of which he became totally deaf. He m. in 1869. His wife d. Oct. 30, 1892, aged 44. He d. in 1894, aged 68. Their only child, a son, d. Oct. 10, 1891, aged 21.

1 ASA TENNEY, son of Benjamin; laborer; m. Lavinia Randall. He d. at Brattleboro, Sept. 12, 1900, aged 82.

Children:

i. Andrew Grant, b. Sept. 24, 1853; res. Newbury.
ii. Anna, b. July 29, 1855; m. Willard Bailey, of Newport, N. H.
iii. Levi R., b. March 21, 1858; carpenter; m. 1889, Mrs. Lydia Silver of Haverhill.
iv. Virgil W., b. Oct. 28, 1860; is m. and has one c., Emma H., b. June 11, 1893.
v. Hattie E., m. Charles W. Hutton, of Piermont. Four c.
vi. Mayo C., b. March 11, 1866; res. Bethel.
vii. Phebe J., b. April 27, 1869; d. June 4, 1892.

KENDRICK.

I. JOHN, b. in England, 1604; was the ancestor of nearly all the Kendricks in America.

II. JOHN, b. in England, 1622; probably came over with Rev. Dr. Mather in the ship "James," in 1635. He m. in 1650, Ann, sister of Robert Smith, who came with him from England. He was admitted to the 1st ch. in Boston, 1638; they had seven c.; he d. Aug. 29, 1686.

III. ELIJAH, b. Oct. 19, 1645; m. Hannah, dau. of John Jackson; (b. 1647, d. 1728); d. Dec. 24, 1680.

IV. EBENEZER, b. Dec. 12, 1680; m. Hannah———; two c.

V. NATHANIEL, b. June 29, 1713; m. Judah———; lived in Coventry, Conn; but in 1777, with his son, Ebenezer, and grandson, Ariel, he rem. to Hanover, where he was killed by a falling tree the next year; eight c.

VI. EBENEZER, b. 1741; m. Anna, dau. of Richard and Alice Davenport, of Coventry, Conn.; d. Aug. 11, 1786.

Children:

i. Thomas, b. 1745.
ii. John, b. March 6, 1769; lived in Vershire, Lyme and Piermont; d. Jan. 1, 1860.
iii. Ariel, b. 1772, at Coventry, Conn.; Baptist minister at Hanover and Cornish, N. H., and Woodstock. He published in 1847 "Sketches of the Life and Times of Elder Ariel Hendrick," which is of much historical value, and went through several editions.
iv. Anna, m. ——— Norris.
v. Clark, b. Oct. 6, 1775; Baptist minister at Poultney, till death. Rev. James R. Kendrick, (1821-89) acting President of Vassar College at the time of his death, and Rev. Ashael Kendrick, D. D., LL. D., Greek Professor in Madison University, and afterward in the University of Rochester, and a member of the committee on the authorized version of the New Testament, were sons of Rev. Clark Kendrick.
vi. Eliza.
vii. Richard, b. Hanover, March 30, 1780; farmer at Plainfield; d. Feb. 4, 1863.
viii. Ebenezer, b. Hanover, Feb. 18, 1785.

8 EBENEZER, b. Hanover, Feb. 18, 1785; farmer at Lyme, Thetford, Piermont and Newbury. Came to this town and lived near where Charles Corliss now does at West Newbury; rem. to Piermont; returned to Newbury, 1865 and bought the Peter Martin farm. He m. at Lyme, Feb. 24, 1810, Susanna, dau. of Abraham Pushee, (b. Jan. 24, 1789; d. Feb. 13, 1867); member of a Cong. ch. more than 70 years; d. in Newbury, Sept. 9, 1881.

Children:
i. Ralph, b. Lyme, April 24, 1811; m. Eliza, dau. Robert Fulton; (b. Apr. 6, 1810; d. 1899); served in the Union army as wagoner in the Vermont Regiment; d. Nov. 28, 1864, in a hospital in Virginia and buried there; three c.
1 ii. Anna, b. Sept. 1, 1812; m. Jesse Jones; (b. Dec. 1795; d. June 10, 1872).
iii. Susan, b. June 9, 1817; m. George Fulton; d. Apr. 21, 1873.
iv. Jane, b. Jan. 24, 1820; d. March 6, 1826.
v. Lewis, b. July 7,.1814; d. Aug. 5, 1815.
vi. John, b. Nov. 18, 1822.
vii. George, b. Nov. 29, 1827; m. 1st, Philena Woodward; 2d, Nellie Talfero; two c.

1 ANNA,[2] (Ebenezer,[1]) b. Sept. 1, 1812; m. Jesse Jones, (b. December, 1795; d. June 10, 1872). He lived in the south many years, but returned to Newbury before the war.
Children:
i. Sarah C., m. R. W. Borden.
ii. George W.
iii. Susan P., m. R. C. Borden.
iv. Frank M., b. 1850; m. 1871, Belle, dau. Alonzo Fleming; lived in Newbury and Lyme; d. Dec. 28, 1893. Four c.

JOHN,[2] (Ebenezer,[1]) b. Thetford, Nov. 18, 1822; came to Newbury about 1848; farmer; has also been in the lumber business, owning mills in this town and elsewhere. He m. 1st, Nov. 18, 1851, Sophia, dau. Samuel Martin, (b. Oct. 20, 1827; d. Jan. 31, 1868). 2d, Jan. 17, 1870, Mary E., dau. Gilman Barnett, (b. April 14, 1835; d. Sept. 19, 1899).
Children.
i. Albert N., b. Feb. 9, 1853; farmer in Newbury; m. Nov. 16, 1881, Emma Pierce.
ii. Henry E., b. Aug. 5; d. Dec. 13, 1855.
iii. Flora A., b. Sept. 26, 1856; d. Tilton, N. H., June 13, 1871.
iv. William H., b. Aug. 10, 1862; m. Oct. 24, 1887, Nellie, dau. Albert A. Bowen, (b. Dec. 20, 1868). Farmer. C., (1) Annabelle, b. Norwich, Nov. 17, 1888. (2) Vernon, b. Newbury, Nov. 21, 1890.
v. Arthur E., b. Oct. 1, 1876; m. Sept. 25, 1899, Robina Ada, dau. Robert Benzie. C., John Robert, b. Aug. 8, 1900.

*KENT.

I. THOMAS, b. in England; emigrated with his wife to Gloucester, Mass., prior to 1643, and settled in what is now the town of Essex, where he d. May 1, 1656, and his widow d. at Gloucester, Mass., Oct. 16, 1671. Their sons were, Thomas, Samuel and Josiah.

II. THOMAS, b. probably in England; m. Joan, dau. of Thomas Penny, March 28, 1658-9, and d. Aug. 14, 1691-6. Six c., of whom Josiah was the eldest.

III. JOSIAH, b. March 31, 1660; m. April 17, 1689, Mary Lufkin; d. May 14, 1725. They had five c., of whom a dau., Abigail, b. July 9, 1697, is understood to have been the one who m. March 21, 1723, Otho Stevens. They were the ancestors of the Stevens families in this part of the country.

IV. JOHN, b. March 29, 1700; m. Jan. 10, 1723, Mary, dau. of James Godfrey, (b. June 17, 1703. He d. 1780. They had ten c., seven were sons, all whose names began with the letter J. Of these, Jacob settled in this town, and descendants of Job Kent have lived here.

V. †JACOB, pioneer of Newbury and soldier in the French and Indian and Revolutionary wars, was b. at Chebacco, since called Essex, Mass., June

*By Henry O. Kent.
†Ancestry from Kent Genealogies.

COL. H. O. KENT.

CHARLES B. LESLIE.

12, 1726. During his long and useful life, he was closely identified with the military, civic, religious and social life of the community and region, and his descendants have been and are among the best known and best esteemed citizens of the Connecticut valley. It has always been understood that his introduction to the Lower Cohos came through his service in the Old French war. In 1760 a regiment was raised in New Hampshire under command of Colonel John Goffe of Bedford, for service in that campaign, under General Jeffrey Amherst. Jacob Bailey, a well-known Newbury pioneer, was Lieutenant Colonel, and one of the companies was officered by John Hazen as captain. Jacob Kent and Timothy Bedel, Lieutenants, Asahel Harriman, Ensign. At the close of this campaign, Bailey, Hazen, Bedel and Kent came through the woods from Canada, striking the great intervals at the Lower Cohos. So well satisfied were they with the location and the fertility of the soil, that they returned in 1761 to aid the settlement. Bailey and Kent of Newbury on the west side of the river and Hazen and Bedel of Haverhill on the eastern side. Kent made several trips between Newbury and Plaistow, N. H., his old home, bringing on his family in 1763.

Commission of Jacob Kent in this Campaign.

PROVINCE OF NEW HAMPSHIRE.	BENNING WENTWORTH, ESQ., Captain, General and Governor in Chief, in and over His Majesty's Province of New Hampshire in New England, etc.

[L. S.]

To MR. JACOB KENT, Gentleman, Greeting:

By Virtue of the Power and Authority, in and by His Majesty's Royal Commission to Me granted, to be Captain, General, etc., over this, His Majesty's Province of New Hampshire aforesaid, I do (by these presents) reposing especial trust and confidence in your loyalty, courage and good conduct, constitute and appoint you the said Jacob Kent, to be First Lieutenant of a company whereof John Hazen, Esq., is Captain, in a regiment of Foot, raised in this province, whereof John Goffe, Esq., is Colonel, being part of the forces demanded by His Majesty from his several colonies and provinces in New England, etc., to act in conjunction with His Majesty's regular forces in an expedition intended for the reduction of the whole country of Canada to His obedience, of all of which forces His Excellency Jeffrey Amherst, Esq., is His Majesty's commission, appointed Captain, General and Commander in Chief.

You are therefore carefully and diligently to discharge the duty of a First Lieutenant, in leading, ordering and exercising said company in arms, both inferior officers and soldiers, and to keep them in good order and discipline; hereby commanding them to obey you as their First Lieutenant, and yourself to observe and follow such orders and instructions, as you shall from time to time receive from Me or the Commander in Chief for the time being, or other, your superior officers for His Majesty's service, according to Military Rules and Discipline of War, pursuant to the trust reposed in you.

Given under my hand and seal at arms, at Portsmouth, the fifth day of March in the thirty-third year of the reign of His Majesty, King George the Second, A. D. 1760.

B. WENTWORTH.

BY HIS EXCELLENCY'S COMMAND,
THEODORE ATKINSON, Secretary.

September 6, 1764, in the fourth year of the reign of King George the Third, a similar commission was granted by the same authority to Captain Jacob Kent, "to be Captain of an Independent Company of Militia, which company is to consist of all the inhabitants by law obliged to attend military duty in the towns of Haverhill and Newbury in this province, respectively."

This company expanded into a regiment which had existence from about

1775, to the time when the militia of the state ceased to perform active duty about 1845. Jacob Kent was the first Colonel of this regiment and commanded it at Saratoga, at Burgoyne's surrender, Oct. 17, 1777, as appears by his diary kept during the campaign, and official documents. It was commended in due time by his oldest son, Jacob Kent, and later by his son, Colonel Jacob Kent, who was the last of the family to reside on the family homestead, and who d. in 1886.

This farm, about two miles below the village, extended back from the Connecticut across the plain and over the crest of the ridge to the west. It was divided by Colonel Jacob, the pioneer, among his three sons, Jacob, (the site of the present homestead), John, (next north, who sold his portion and moved to Parker Hill, Lyman, N. H.,) and Joseph, (north of John, and the place now owned by John Heath).

A topographical plan of the original farm, then comprising 550 acres, by curious coincidence being the same area as "Kent Island," a homestead of the family at old Newbury, near the mouth of the Merrimack, plain and clear as copper plate, bearing date September, 1791, made by Gen. James Whitelaw, the surveyor of Ryegate, is in the possession of Colonel Henry O. Kent of Lancaster, as is the sword, a blade bearing the etched date 1555, carried in all the wars, and the white whalebone patriarchal staff, carried in old age and civic life by his pioneer ancestor.

The Newbury Kents were of the older branch, and sprang from Gloucester, Mass., or Cape Ann, Cephas Kent, of the Vermont Committee of Safety, and contemporary of Ethan Allen and Seth Warner, was of the same stock, as was the distinguished Chancellor James Kent of New York, Governor Edward Kent of Maine, and Moody Kent of Concord, all deceased. The family has a long and honorable record of military and civic service. Colonel Kent was Justice of the Peace at sundry times, was Clerk of the Proprietors' Meeting at Plaistow, N. H., in 1762, and Town Clerk, 1764 to 1799, inclusive, and Selectman, 1762-6-7, '84-6 and 9, in all, six years. He represented the town in the State Legislature, 1788-89-91, was Judge of Probate from 1786 to 1794, inclusive, was County Clerk and Assistant Judge of the Common Pleas and Commissioner to receive the estates of those who had joined the enemy during the Revolutionary period. He was an original member of the Congregational Church. Parish Clerk for many years, and one of its Deacons as long as he lived.

In 1894, the Original Desk, made by Colonel Kent from pine boards hewn out by him, and used by him so many years, was discovered. and purchased by the sons of Richard Peabody Kent, of Lancaster, N. H., who presented it with a silver plate properly inscribed, attached thereto, to the town. After a lapse of so many years it is again in the Town Clerk's office, a receptacle of town papers.

*Col. Jacob Kent m. 1st, Dec. 26, 1752, Abigail, dau. Joseph and Abigail (Webster) Bailey. She d. July 4, 1756, leaving one daughter, Abigail, who m. Thomas Little, of Atkinson, N. H. He m. 2d at Plaistow, N. H., June 16, 1762, Mary, dau. Nicholas White, q. v., (b. Aug. 14, 1736; d. June 17, 1834, aged 98). It was from her unimpaired memory in 1831 that Rev. Clark Perry derived many of the details of the early history of this town, which he used in preparing his historical discourse. Col. Kent d. Dec. 13, 1812.

Children, b. in Newbury:
1 i. Jacob, b. Oct. 17, 1764; d. Feb. 23, 1852.
2 ii. Mary, b. Jan. 13, 1766; d. Oct. 29, 1835.
   iii. Elizabeth. b. Oct. 21, 1767; m. Jacob Dunbar; lived in Littleton, N. H., but d. in Newbury, July 26, 1823.
3 iv. John, b. March 14, 1772; d. July 4, 1842.
4 v. Joseph, b. Dec. 29, 1773; d. July 20, 1859.

1 JACOB, b. Oct. 17, 1764; served a short term of guarding and scouting in the Revolutionary war; settled on the south of three farms into which his

*In another portion of this volume will be found extracts from Col. Kent's diary, and other papers.

father's estate was divided, which Robert Meserve now owns. Colonel in the militia, and prominent in town affairs. He m. at Hampstead, Feb. 6, 1794, Martha Noyes, (b. Aug. 9, 1766; d. March 17, 1854). He d. Feb. 23, 1852.

Childr^{e}n:
  i. John, b. Dec. 26, 1795; d. in Connecticut, Feb. 13, 1862.
  ii. Clark, b. Feb. 25, 1795; farmer on homestead; Captain in the militia; never m. He was a man of sterling qualities; d. Jan. 13, 1884.
5 iii. Jacob, b. Apr. 26, 1800; d. March 13, 1886.
  iv. Relief, b. Dec. 12, 1802; never m; lived on the old homestead; d. Nov. 1, 1880.
  v. Anna, b. Aug. 10, 1805; m. Williams Burroughs; d. Nov. 1, 1866.

2 MARY, b. Jan. 13, 1766; m. Dec. 28, 1789, Dr. Arad Stebbins of Bradford; (b. Oct. 21, 1759; d. Apr. 30, 1828). She d. Oct. 29, 1835.
Children:
  i. Polly, b. Oct. 17, 1790; d. Apr. 23, 1791.
  ii. Mary, b. Jan. 18, 1792; m Alfred Corliss of Bradford; d. July 23, 1839.
  iii. Sophia, b. Feb. 9, 1794; d. un-m.
  iv. Lucy, b. Jan. 3, 1796; m. March 24, 1833, Theodore Dame; d. in Newbury.
  v. Betsey, b. Sept. 12, 1797; d. Oct. 5, 1863; m. Nicholas W. Ayer of Bradford.
  vi. Matilda, b. Sept. 19, 1797.
  vii. Louisa, b. June 3, 1801, d. Nov. 5, 1835; m. a Mr. Moulton.
  viii. Arad, b. Jan. 11, 1803; d. Jan. 1862.
  ix. Harriet, b. March 10, 1806; m. a Mr. Ward of Plymouth, N. H.

3 JOHN, b. March 14, 1772; farmer on the middle one of the three farms into which the original estate was divided, now owned by C. E. Brock. He rem. to Lyman, N. H., Oct., 1804 and 1811. He m. Nov., 1804, Tabitha, dau. Richard and Tabitha Peabody of Littleton, N. H. She d. Apr. 30, 1836; he d. July 4, 1842.
Children, the four last b in Lyman:
6 i. Richard P., b. Dec. 21, 1805; d. March 30, 1885.
7 ii. John C., b. Apr. 19, 1808; d. Jan. 2, 1878.
  iii. Harriet, b. Oct. 21, 1811; m. Rinaldo Moulton, q. v.; d. Apr. 14, 1879.
  iv. Adriel, b. Aug. 29, 1813; m. Candace Mason, who d. at Alton, Ill., Oct. 21, 1859. He d. Burlington, Kansas Oct. 24, 1861.
  v. Lucia, b. Oct. 15, 1815; d. July 16, 1826.
8 vi. Nelson, b. Dec. 30, 1818; d. Lancaster, Feb. 1, 1899.

4 JOSEPH, b. Dec. 29, 1773; farmer, where John T. Heath now lives; m. April 3, 1800, Elizabeth, dau. Remembrance Chamberlain, (b. Dec. 19, 1781; d. Feb. 26, 1837). He d. July 20, 1859.

Childr^{e}n:
  i. Mary, b. Nov. 25, 1800; m. Jehial Downer, and was the last of Kent family in Newbury; d. May 28, 1889. No c.
9 ii. Arad S., b. March 27, 1802; d. Feb. 1. 1871.
  iii. Eliza, b. March 15, 1804; m. William Johnson, q. v.
  iv. Remembrance C., b. June 11, 1806; d. in Texas.
  v. Lucinda, b. Aug. 22, 1808; d. Dec. 17, 1876.
  vi. Moody, b. Sept. 13, 1812; d. Oct. 8, 1838.
  vii. Martha, b. Jan. 20, 1815; d. Sept. 17, 1857.
  ix. Joseph, b. June 22, 1815; served in the Union army; came home and d. Jan. 8, 1865.
  x. George W., b. March 23, 1821. He lived in the house under the great elm at the Ox-bow, and was sexton of the cemetery. He m. Nov. 30, 1854, Anna E. Tyrrell of Berlin. She d. April 16, 1867. He d. July 4, 1887. Three c., who went west.
  xi. Marion W., b. Nov. 8, 1825; m. a Mr. Farmer of Chicago. Two daus.

5 *COLONEL JACOB, third in lineal descent of the name and title, was b. on the homestead April 23, 1800, and there passed from life March 13, 1886. His long life was eventful and for many years he was a prominent figure in the public affairs of Vermont. Possessed of great courtesy, dignity and

*By Henry O. Kent.

integrity he had many friends in all walks of life. His earlier years were spent in Newbury and for nearly 20 years he was landlord of the popular Coösuck Hotel at Wells River. From there he went to Chicago in the early fifties, being connected with many enterprises in the development of that city, returning to Newbury on the death of his sister, Anna, 1866, whose property he inherited. On the decease of his elder brother, Captain Clark Kent, in 1884, he came into possession of the home farm, where he lived during his declining years, preserving great mental and physical vigor to the last. He was United States Deputy Marshal, taking the census of Orange County in 1830, 1840 and 1850, and was United States Marshal for the District of Vermont, during the administration of President Pierce. He was Sheriff of the county in 1841, 1842, 1843 and 1844. Was for years an active trustee of Norwich University to which institution he introduced as a cadet his young kinsman, Henry O. Kent, of Lancaster. His tastes inclined him to a military life, and he was a superb horseman. He passed through all the grades, from private to Colonel of the local Militia Regiment, that his father and grandfather, (who led it to Saratoga in 1777) commanded before him. Until a late year he preserved its colors, now unfortunately lost. Later in life he accompanied the Illinois Volunteer Regiment, of which his young kinsman, Loren Kent, (afterwards Brigadier General, and who died of yellow fever, as collector of the Port of Galveston, Texas), was colonel, being present at the battle of Shiloh or Pittsburg Landing. He was a faithful Mason, having been made in 1826, and bringing down the gavel as Master of the Newbury Lodge, to close its work in 1834, consequent upon the Morgan excitement. He was much interested in the Royal Arch degrees, frequently walking from preference, when much above 80, to the meeting at Bradford. He was contemporary with Alden Partridge and Truman B. Ransom of Norwich University, and like them was a stout believer in physical exercise and pedestrianism. His obsequies were attended by the Masonic fraternity of the region, and he is interred in the original lot of this ancient family in the old cemetery at the Ox-bow. His love for Newbury was deep and abiding, and his ability and worth become more apparent as the years go by.

6 RICHARD PEABODY, b. Newbury, Dec. 21, 1805; settled at Lancaster, N. H., where he was a merchant nearly 60 years. He m. at Littleton, N. H., June 5, 1832, Emily Mann Oakes, (b. Barnet, May 31, 1814; d. July 30, 1888). He d. March 30, 1885.
   Children:
10   i.   Henry O., b. Feb. 7, 1834.
     ii. Edward R., b. Feb. 1, 1840; m. Jan. 16, 1862, Adeline D. Burton of Guildhall; six c.; res. Lancaster; merchant.
     iii. Charles N., b. May 14, 1843; m. June 2, 1868, Julia A. Draper; seven c.; res. Merrick, Long Island, N. Y.

7 JOHN CHILDS, b. Newbury, April 19, 1808; lived in Lyman, Barnet and Monroe. He m. Dec. 20, 1837, Jannette S. Shaw, who d. at Clinton, Mass., May 6, 1897. Of their children the oldest son was killed at the battle of Gettysburg. He m. Angie Day of Littleton. Lucia, the oldest dau., and Emily J., who m. Daniel Maynard, live at Clinton, Mass. The second dau., Adaline, m. Frederic W. Wheeler, and d. in Bolton, Mass., 1898, leaving two sons and a dau. The youngest son, John W., m. Flora Dutton of North Monroe and lives in Muskegon Mich.; d. Jan. 2, 1878.

8 NELSON, b. Dec. 30, 1818; came to Lancaster as clerk for his brother, Richard Peabody, afterwards his partner, and head of other firms. He m. July 16, 1850, Debby Ann Spaulding.
   Children:
   i.   Sarah E., b. Aug. 13, 1852; m. Charles L. Griswold. One c., Anna.
   ii. George Nelson, b. July 15, 1857; m. Dora La Rue of Burlington, Kansas. She d. He m. 2d, Sept. 25, 1889, Mary N. Rice. One c., Harold Weeks, b. Sept. 30, 1890.

9 ARAD STEBBINS, b. March 27, 1802; farmer on the John Kent farm. He m. in

Boston, Mass., May 3, 1828. Mary Ann Griffin, (b. Gloucester, Mass., Dec. 19, 1806; d. Jan 2, 1885). He d. Feb. 1, 1871.

Children:
   i. George F., b. June 4, 1829; d. Nov. 7, 1849.
  ii. Mary Ann, b. Aug. 28, 1830; d. Aug. 31, 1849.
 iii. Harriott, b. Apr. 1833; m. W. K. Wallace, q. v.
 iv. Joseph F., b. March 13, 1836; d. April 4, 1837.
  v. Joseph F., b. Feb. 13, 1845; res. Derby. Two c.
 vi. William H., b. March 16, 1848; res. Piermont; m. June 13, 1878, Eda E., dau. Col. Isaiah and Elizabeth Emerson. She d. Jan. 23, 1896. C., Elizabeth B., b. July 23, 1884.

7 HENRY OAKES, b. Feb. 7, 1834; fitted for college at Lancaster Academy; graduated Norwich University, 1854; studied law and admitted to the bar, 1858; editor and business manager of the Coös Republican, 1858–70; clerk of the New Hampshire House of Representatives, 1855–59; commissioner, 1858, on the part of New Hampshire, "to ascertain, survey and mark" the boundary line between that state and Maine. In 1860, alternate delegate-at-large to the convention at Chicago which nominated Abraham Lincoln to the presidency. When the rebellion broke out in 1861, he was put in charge of recruiting, and commissioned Assistant Adjutant General of the state, with rank of Colonel. Commissioned Colonel of the 17th N. H., 1862. Town Representative from Lancaster, 1862, '68, '69, '83. Presidential elector on the Republican ticket, 1864. Member of the bank commission, 1866–68. In 1872, he engaged in the liberal movement which resulted in the nomination of Horace Greeley for the presidency. Three times candidate for Congress. President of the Democratic state convention, 1877 and 1884. In the latter year, State Senator, and delegate-at-large to the Democratic National Convention at Chicago, seconding the nomination of Mr. Cleveland. Naval officer for the port of Boston, 1886–90. Candidate for Governor, 1894 and 1896. Governor of the Society of Colonial Wars in New Hampshire, and member of the Society of the Sons of the American Revolution. Senior of the board of trustees of Norwich University from which he received the degree of A. M. in 1863, and LL. D., in 1895. At the laying of the corner stone of Dewey hall, in October, 1899, he delivered the address of welcome to Admiral Dewey. President of the Lancaster Trust Co. since 1891, and senior warden of St. Paul's Episcopal church. He m. Jan. 11, 1859, Berenice A. Rowell; res. Lancaster, N. H., at "Indian Brook." C., Henry Percy, and Berenice Emily, both of Lancaster. Col. Kent has taken a deep interest in this history of Newbury; was one of the first to urge the present editor to undertake the work; and has prepared copious extracts from the papers of the first Colonel Kent for this volume. Col. Kent was offered the portfolio of Assistant Secretary of War under the second Cleveland administration. He is a 33 degree mason.

Job, brother of Col. Jacob Kent, lived in Hampstead, N. H. His son, James, m. Apr. 4, 1792, Tamar Mills and lived here a few years, then rem. to Piermont, where many decendants now live; ten c., of whom Miriam, the oldest was b. here. James, son of James, lived in Piermont; his house was burned Apr. 3, 1832, and three daus. were burned to death. The following is from the first volume of Newbury records:—

"Jacob Kent Richard, the son of Bradley Richards and Judith Kent, his wife, was b. Oct. 8, 1784. Betsey Richards, their dau., b. Oct. 18, 1786. Joseph, their son, b. Jan. 21, 1789, at St. Johnsborough." This is the 1st recorded birth in St. Johnsbury.

KEYES.

The original spelling of the name appears to have been Keies, and the first mention of the family is the marriage of Solomon Keies and Frances Grant at Newbury, Mass., Oct. 2, 1653. In 1664 and 1665, Solomon and Joseph Keies took up land in Chelmsford; the house built by Solomon about 1675, is still standing in that part of Chelmsford now called Westford. Solomon and Joseph are believed to have been brothers. An old town book of Chelmsford has the following: "Sargent Solomon Keys dyed March 28, 1702." Frances, his wife d. 1708. Eleven c. of whom the 5th and 1st son was:

II. SOLOMON, b. June 24, 1665; was twice m., his first wife's name being Mary and the second, Priscilla.

III. SOLOMON, third son of Solomon and Mary, b. May 11, 1701; was in Capt. Lovewell's Co. in the fight at Fryeburgh, Me., April 18, 1725. He received three bullet wounds and was believed to be dying. He rolled himself down the beach, and into a canoe, to prevent his body from being mangled by the Indians. The canoe was blown across the pond, and he escaped. He rem. to Warren, Mass., served in the Old French War, and was killed at Lake George, Sept. 8, 1755. His oldest son was wounded in the same battle, and d. at Fort Edward, Oct. 1, 1755. Solomon Keyes m. Sarah ————. Eight c.

IV. DANFORTH, b. Warren, Mass., 1740; soldier in the Old French war; was in the same battle in which his father was killed, but escaped unharmed. Served through the war, and saw the surrender of Montreal. He also served in the Revolutionary war, in the battles of Lexington and Bunker Hill. During the whole war he was at home but twice. The town of Hardwick was granted to Danforth Keyes and associates. He m. Dec. 6, 1764, Sarah Cutler of Warren, Mass., (b. April 2, 1745; d. Aug. 19, 1831). Eight c., several of whom settled in Vermont. Their third son and fourth c. was:

V. THOMAS, b. Warren, Mass., Nov. 3, 1774; settled in Vershire, about 1800, where he was a farmer. He m. in Chelsea, Margaretta McArthur, (b. Thornton, N. H.; d. Newbury, Aug. 15, 1853). He d. Vershire, March 26, 1850. Thomas Keyes was State Senator for some years.
   Children:
1   i. Freeman, b. Oct. 3, 1807; d. June 10, 1871.
2 ii. Henry, b. Jan. 3, 1810; d. Sept. 24, 1870.
  iii. Sally, b. July 5, 1812; d. July 13, 1812.
3 iv. Horace T., b. Nov. 14, 1813; d. Jan. 4, 1883.
    v. Harriet N., b. May 4, 1816; d. March 10, 1832.
   vi. John D. W., b. Jan. 19, 1823; d. Feb. 22, 1848.

1 FREEMAN, b. Vershire, Oct. 3, 1807; merchant at Newbury village, in partnership with his brothers, Henry and Horace T., and with his son, Thomas C., (see pages 277, 278). In addition to their mercantile business, they were interested in a great variety of enterprises, both in and out of Newbury, and later in life, in western land. He m. Nov. 1, 1831, Emeline C., dau. Dr. Calvin and Sallie (Parker) Jewett of St. Johnsbury. They united with the 1st ch. Nov. 20, 1831, of which he was chosen a deacon in 1853; superintendent of Sunday school about 25 years, and a constant and generous giver to all the benevolent and religious enterprises of his day, and active in the temperance reform. He was also greatly interested in all those benevolent societies which aim to provide homes for friendless children. In politics, Whig, and later, Republican. He d. Chicago, Ill., June 10, 1871, while on a business trip. She d. June 20, 1878.
   Children:
    i. Edward P., b. Feb. 1, 1836; clerk in the store; was also at one time in business in Boston; member of Co. H, 12th Vt., in the Civil war. He m. Nov. 3, 1863, Anna, dau. Joshua T. Atkinson, q. v., (b. Nov. 26, 1836; d. April 15, 1900). He d. Aug. 28, 1881. No c.
   ii. Charles, b. March 28, 1839; d. Jan. 21, 1840.
  iii. Harriet, E., b. Sept. 14, 1841; res. Newbury, occupies the house built by her father in 1833, and interests herself in the benevolent enterprises which employed so much of her father's time and care.
   iv. Thomas C., b. Jan. 1, 1844; educated at Newbury Seminary and the Commercial and Collegiate Institute of New Haven, Conn.; has been in mercantile business in Newbury since 1864; postmaster, 10 years; town representative, 1886. He m. at Chicago, Ill., Nov. 24, 1881, Martha P., dau. John and Elizabeth (Hosmer) Morse of St. Johnsbury.

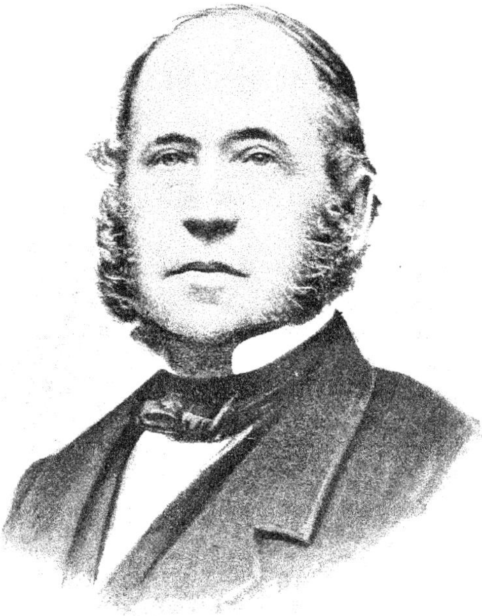

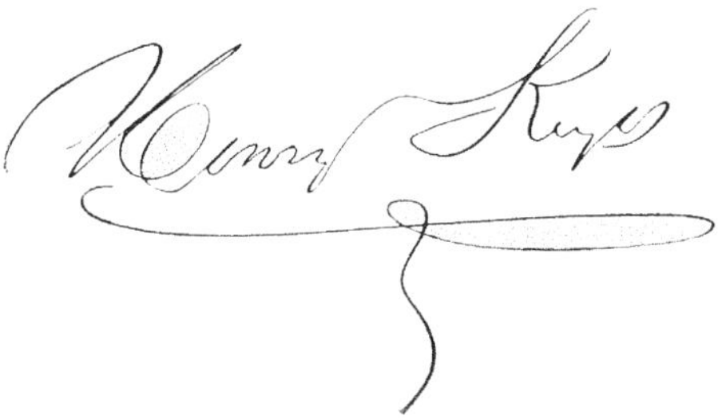

To Mr. Keyes more, perhaps, in some respects, than to any other person, the completeness of this history of Newbury is due, as he has spared no pains to secure for the editor everything written or printed which he could obtain relating to its history. As he is the present owner of large quantities of the Johnson papers, his aid has been invaluable.

   v. Ellen M., b. April 13, 1846; d. Aug. 27, 1847.

   vi. John F., b. May 14, 1849; d. Jan. 10, 1851.

   vii. Emeline A., b. May 27, 1851; m. June 23, 1875, Mahew P. Aiken of Milwaukee, Wis.; d. suddenly Aug. 3, 1886, at the old homestead, while on a visit. C., all b. in Milwaukee: (1) Helen Rocelia, (2) Gertrude Emeline, both b. Sept. 11, 1877. (3) Margaret Harriet, b. Sept. 21, 1885.

2 HENRY, b. Jan. 3, 1810; came to Newbury in 1825, and was in the mercantile business till 1854, the firm name being F. & H. Keyes. He was one of the original proprietors of the Connecticut and Passumpsic Rivers R. R.; was one of the first directors. In 1854 he succeeded Gov. Erastus Fairbanks as President of the road, and devoted all his energies to pushing the enterprise through to a connection with the Grand Trunk R. R. in Canada. This seemed a hopeless undertaking, and for a long time shares sold as low as $5.00 each. But Mr. Keyes had faith in the road, and under his management the stock rose to par. The road was opened to Barton in 1857, to Newport in 1863, to Derby in 1867, and to Lennoxville in 1870. He was also one of the proprietors and a director in the Mt. Washington R. R. He was also interested in the Atchison, Topeka and Santa Fe R. R., in which he was a large stockholder, and became its president in 1869. Under his administration about 160 miles were completed. He was, also, interested in the United States Hotel in Boston, and in several stage and steamboat lines. President of the Vermont State Agricultural Society. He was a practical farmer, owning and conducting the great "Dow farm" in Haverhill. Town representative in 1855; state senator in 1847-48; candidate for Governor, 1856, '57 and '58. Delegate to several successive National Conventions of the Democratic party, and chairman of the Vermont delegation at the Baltimore convention which nominated Stephen A. Douglass for President in 1860. Member, and for some years chairman of the First Congregational Society. He lived in the house south of the 1st ch. As a business man he had few equals. "The entire detail, however minute, or apparently unimportant, in matters of business, was ever in his mind, and never forgotten, and all so regulated by system that he always seemed to have time for everything. He could attend to the wants of a child, or the demands of a railroad with like facility, promptitude and good nature, and the little courtesies which other men so absorbed would forget, never escaped him." His honesty and intregrity were never questioned; he was scrupulous in the smallest details of business; he never forgot a promise, even to a child. Mr. Keyes was offered the presidency of one of the largest railroads in Massachusetts, but this he declined, as it would necessitate his living in Boston, and he always wanted Newbury for his home. He m. 1st, May 2, 1838, Sarah A. Pierce of Stanstead, P. Q., who d. Dec. 8, 1853; no c.; 2d, May 6, 1856, Emma F. Pierce, sister of 1st wife; she res. in Boston. He d. Sept. 24, 1870, after an illness of ten days.

Children:

   i. Isabella F., b. June 21, 1859, at Newbury; res. Boston with her mother.

   ii. Henry W., b. May 23, 1862, at Newbury; graduated from Harvard University, 1887; res. on the farm in Haverhill, formerly owned by his father. The farm is one of the largest in the state and well-known for its fine stock. Represented Haverhill in the Legislature, 1889 to 1893: president Woodsville National Bank; director Connecticut & Passumpsic railroad; vice president Nashua River Paper Co., and has other large business interests.

   iii. Martha G., b. April 26, 1864, at Newbury; m. at Boston, Nov. 16, 1892, to Ezra Henry Baker; d. June 16, 1896.

   iv. George T., b. Sept. 7, 1867, at Newbury; graduated Harvard University, 1889, and after studying law at Harvard Law School, entered the paper business and at present is president and treasurer of the Nashua River Paper Co., of Pepperell, Mass.

v. Charles W., b. Jan. 16, 1871, at Newton, Mass.; graduated from Harvard
   University 1893, and at once became identified with the Nashua River
   Paper Co., of which he is secretary; res. at Pepperell, Mass.
3 HORACE T., b. Nov. 14, 1813; in business at Vershire; came to Newbury, 1854;
   was partner in the firm till 1872; m. 1st, May 17, 1842, Sarah, dau. of
   Peter Powers of Vershire. She d. April 9, 1852. He m. 2d, May 18, 1863,
   Lucy E. Rhodes of St. Johnsbury. He d. Jan. 4, 1883. C., John L., b.
   Sept. 5, 1866; in business in the west.

*KIMBALL.

I. RICHARD, the ancestor of most of the Kimballs in this country, came with his
   family in the ship Elizabeth, leaving Ipswich, Suffolk, England, Apr. 10,
   1634; settled in Watertown, Mass., but rem. to Ipswich, where he d.
   June 22, 1675, aged 80 years.

II. BENJAMIN, b. Ipswich. 1637; lived many years in Bradford, Mass.; m. in
   Salisbury, Apr. 1661, Mercy, dau. Robert and Ann Haseltine. He d. June
   11, 1695.

III. EBENEZER, b. Bradford, Mass., June 20, 1684; m. Ruth Eaton; d. Jan. 23, 1715.

IV. ABRAHAM, b. Jan. 3, 1713-14; lived in Bradford and Haverhill, Mass.; m. as
   2d wife, Apr. 36, 1747, Mary Pike.

V. AMOS, b. Bradford, Mass., Aug. 31, 1750; res. there till about 1772, when he
   became one of the first settlers of Barnet, but rem. to Haverhill, some
   time later. The family record gives his son. John, as b. in Haverhill, June 4,
   1775; but in the muster roll of Capt. Thomas Johnson's Co. of Minute
   Men, Aug. 1775, Amos is credited to Barnet. He also saw other service.
   Colonel in the militia. He m. Feb. 20, 1774, Abigail Corliss of Bradford,
   Mass., who d. Oct. 11, 1803. He d. Sept. 20, 1820; 13 c., of whom the
   eldest was John.

JOHN,[2] (Amos,[1]) b. Haverhill, Jan. 4, 1775; farmer on Horse Meadow; Colonel
   in the militia; town representative from Haverhill, 1813-14; deacon in
   ch. at Horse Meadow; rem. to Newbury with his son, Dudley C., in 1866.
   He m. Mehitable, dau. of Dudley Carleton, (b. Newbury, Nov. 2, 1776; d.
   Nov. 11, 1839). He d. in Newbury, May 4, 1869, in his 95th year. Buried
   at Horse Meadow.
   Children:
   i. John, b. Sept. 30, 1796; graduated Dartmouth College 1822; lawyer at
      Claremont, N. H., and Putney.
   ii. Dudley C., b. 1800; d. Sept. 11, 1887.
   iii. Benjamin F., b. 1810; lived some years in Newbury with his brother.
   iv. Isaac B., b. 1818; lived in St. Johnsbury and Concord. N. H.
   v. Harriet C.

1 DUDLEY CARLETON,[3] (John,[2] Amos,[1]) b. Haverhill, 1800;ʼ armer on Horse
   Meadow till 1866, when he came to Newbury with his son Daniel P., and
   bought the Hazen farm on Musquash Meadow; Town Representative
   from Haverhill, 1851; deacon in Cong. ch. at Wells River. He m. Aug. 27,
   1823, Sally, dau. Daniel Putnam of Newbury, (b. March 17, 1800; d. Dec.
   8, 1866). He d. Sept. 11, 1887. Buried at Horse Meadow.
   Children:
2 i. Daniel P., b. July, 1824; d. Oct. 14, 1895.
   ii. Joseph Porter, farmer on the homestead at Horse Meadow. (His name as
       deacon in the ch. at Wells River was accidentally omitted in the list of
       deacons of that church given the editor of this volume).
   iii. Mehitabel, m. Lyman Southard, of North Haverhill.

2 DANIEL PUTNAM,[4] (Dudley C.,[3] John,[2] Amos,[1]) b. Haverhill, N. H., July, 1824;
   farmer on Horse Meadow till 1866, when he rem. to Newbury; Town
   Representative, 1880; deacon in 1st ch., 1883, till death; he held nearly
   every town office. He m. 1856, Melissa A., dau. Phineas D. Keyes, b.

*Early dates from "Kimball family."

Putney, January, 1835. He d. Oct. 14, 1895.
Children:
i. Carrie M., b. May 18, 1858; m. James B. Hale.
ii. Frank E., b. January, 1861; farmer on the homestead, which is one of the largest farms in the state, also deals extensively in western horses; Town Representative, 1898. He m. 1887, Emma Clark, of Janesville, Wis.

KING.

REV. JOSEPH ELIJAH, son of Rev. Elijah King, b. Laurens, Otsego County, N. Y., Nov. 30, 1823; graduated Wesleyan University, 1847; came to Newbury in the same year as teacher in Newbury Seminary; principal, 1848-1853, (See chapter XXIX); principal of Fort Plain (N. Y.) Institute, 1853-54; became principal of Fort Edward Institute, 1854, which position he still holds. He is widely known as teacher, preacher and lecturer. Trustee for 51 years of Wesleyan University. Visited Europe 1867 and 1889. Received degree of D. D., from Union College, 1862. He m. in Newbury, July 22. 1850, Melissa, dau. J. Amherst Bayley (b. April 4, 1828; d. Oct. 16, 1887.)
Children:
i.   Mary Ellen, b. Newbury, July 20, 1852; m. Dec. 12, 1872, Dr. Marvin Van Denbury; d. Feb. 14, 1879; 2c.
ii. Charles J., b. Dec. 27, 1855; d. March 25, 1858.
iii. Alice Eliza, b. Fort Edward, Sept. 10, 1859; m. July 2, 1881, William McGilton. He was for several years vice principal of Fort Edward Institute, but is now professor of Chemistry at Middlebury College.
iv. Helen Melissa, b. April 2, 1863; m. Dec. 2, 1871, James E. Cheeseman. Two c., both b. at Cleveland, Ohio.

KING.

GEORGE W., b. Bristol, Eng., June 18, 1833. He enlisted in the British army when 13 years of age as a drummer boy, and served three years. In 1849, he enlisted as a soldier, serving nine years and six months. He saw service and hard fighting in the Crimean war, after which, his regiment being ordered to Quebec, he and Owen O'Malley deserted, and both settled in Newbury. He came here in April, 1859, and m. Nov. 8. of that year, Elizabeth Ann Bowen, b. Grafton, N. H., March 15, 1837. He d. Newbury, Aug. 19, 1895.
Children:
i.   Annie E., b. Jan. 7, 1861; m. Edward C. Johnson, q. v.
ii. George H., b. Dec. 2, 1862; m. Jan. 27, 1887, Jennie T., dau. of L. D. Leighton. C.. (1) Charles R., b. March 20, 1887. (2) Georgia L., b. Oct. 24, 1897.
iii. Mary Jane, b. March 17, 1864; m. June 16, 1885, George H. Page of Topsham.
iv. Charles R., b. June 21, 1869; d. March 7, 1887.

KNIGHT.

DR. JONATHAN, ot Westmoreland, N. H., b. Jan. 21, 1761; m. as 2d wife, Betsey, dau. of John Dudley, of Acton, Mass., and his wife, Sybil Russell, of Groton, Mass., b. Acton, Oct. 31, 1763; d. Piermont, N. H., April 30, 1866, aged 102 years and 6 months, in full possession of her faculties. She is remembered by many people in this town, as giving interesting details of the battles of Lexington and Bunker Hill, which fell under her observation, after she had passed her century. He d. Dec. 15, 1836. Among their c. were Josiah, who m. as 2d wife Mrs. Elinor (Cochrane), widow of Simeon Avery. who is still living here; Dr. Jonathan Knight of Piermont; Curtis of Piermont and South Bend, Ind., and Prentiss of Newbury. The latter b. Westmoreland, N. H., Jan. 21, 1797; rem. to Haverhill and about 1830 to Newbury, where he built the brick house north ot the old Newbury House, and was postmaster there many years in the old stage days when mail would arrive in the night, and the stage driver waited while the mail for Newbury was taken from the bag. Secretary of the trustees of Newbury Seminary, 1844–68. Prominent in the Methodist church and in the Masonic Lodge. Lived some years where J. C Leavitt now does. He was a tailor by trade. He m. Jan 2, 1822, Melinda Gould, (b. Hanover, N. H., Nov. 7, 1800; d. Bradford, Dec. 5, 1872). She was dau. of Ralph Wait Gould, (b. Hollis, N. H., June 19, 1767; d. Hanover, Oct. 20, 1825.) and Annie Smith, his wife. His father, James Gould, (b. Groton, Mass., Feb. 22, 1743; d. Oct. 11, 1822), m. Mary Lovejoy of Hollis. The father of James Gould was killed in the massacre at Fort William Henry, July 22, 1758. Other c. of Ralph W. Gould were Mrs. Bacon, who lived many years in Bradford, and Mrs. Simeon Stafford, whose husband was long toll keeper at Haverhill bridge. The rest settled in New York. Prentiss d. at Medina, N. Y., March 25, 1874.

Children, of Prentiss Knight:
i. Prentiss Dudley, b. Westmoreland, N. H., Sept. 5, 1822; d. Medina, N. Y., Dec. 14, 1897.
ii. Harriet Melinda, b. Haverhill, Oct. 5, 1827; m. Nelson B. Stevens, q. v.; d. Sept. 28, 1870.
iii. Charles Henry, b. March 29, 1832; d. July 31, 1833.
iv. Martha Ann, b. Jan. 16, 1838; m. 1st, April 21, 1858, Henry C. Mahurin of Lemington; m. 2d, July 26, 1875, Horace B. Morse of Newbury; res. in Boston.
v. Emmeline Louisa, b. Newbury, Jan. 31, 1840; d. April 28, 1842.
vi. Josiah Adelbert, b. Newbury, May 2, 1845; res. Dunkirk, N. Y.; machinist.

KNIGHT.

BENJAMIN, b. in Landaff, N. H., April, 1796; m. Elvira P. Morton of Concord, Jan. 13, 1831. In 1849 he located in South Newbury, where he purchased the wool carding and cloth dressing mill which he operated about two years, when he converted it into a sawmill and mackerel-kit factory. He d. Nov. 10, 1858, aged 62 years. His wife lived with her son until her death, Feb. 17, 1897, in her 92d year.

Children:
i. Almeda, b. Jan. 13, 1832, d. y.
ii. Vienna, b. Jan. 10, 1834, d. y.
iii. Andrew J., b. Aug. 27, 1836.

ANDREW J., m. Sarah E., dau. of Stillman and Jane (King) Jenne, May 16, 1859, and succeeded to his father's business in manufacturing lumber, etc., is also engaged in mill-wright work and is agent for the "Eureka" turbine water wheel.

Children:
i. Lelah C., b. July 16, 1860; m. Freeman W. Cilley of Barre, April 12, 1887. One c., (1) Andrew F., b. Dec. 9, 1888; d. Oct. 26, 1891.
ii. M. Clarence. b. Sept. 24, 1861; in business at Newbury village; m. Clara A., dau. of William H. Silsby, Dec. 26, 1887. C., (1) Horace B., b. Sept. 9, 1889. (2) William A., b. June 16, 1891. (3) Harvey S., b. Jan. 17, 1897.
iii. Arthur B., b. Nov. 19, 1868; m. Sept. 12, 1894, Eva M. Nims of Manlius, N. Y., where he still res. One c., Arthur B., Jr., b. June 26, 1895.
iv. Leon E., b. Sept. 16, 1876; m. Aug. 24, 1897, Dora M. Orser; res. in Elkton, Colorado. One c., b. Feb. 2, 1899.
v. Carrie L., b. Dec. 17, 1877; m. Francis D. Hathaway, April 12, 1898. One c., Sarah M., b. March 26, 1899.
vi. Olive, b. Nov. 17, 1879; m. Ernest T. Brock, May 12, 1898. One c., Earl E., b. Feb. 6, 1899.
vii. Edith M., b. Nov. 23, 1883; res. with her parents.

LADD.

I. DANIEL, of England and Haverhill, Mass.; emigrated 1634; d. 1693.

II. SAMUEL, (1649-1699) m. Martha, dau. of George Corliss; lived in Haverhill, and was killed there by the Indians, Feb. 22, 1699.

PEABODY WEBSTER LADD.

EBENEZER CARLETON STOCKER.

III. DANIEL, b. Nov. 19, 1676; m. Susanna Hartshorn; taken by the Indians, 1698, and retained all his life the marks of tortures inflicted by them, so that he was called "the marked man." He d. June 15, 1751.

IV. DANIEL, b. November, 1710; m. Mehitabel Roberts. Twelve c., of whom, Ezekiel. Daniel, Samuel, John, David, James and Jonathan settled in Haverhill, N. H., and gave the name to Ladd street. They have long been gone from Haverhill, and all of their lineage.

V. EZEKIEL, b. April 10, 1738; m. Ruth Hutchins; was one of the prominent men in Grafton County in his time; d. July 12, 1818.

Eight children, three of whom—:

1 ii. Joseph, b. Dec. 15, 1764; d. Dec. 21, 1836.

iii. Molly, b. Feb. 14, 1766; m. Capt. Jacob Bayley of Newbury, as 2d wife; d. March 1, 1855.

v. Hannah, b. May 13, 1772; m. Col. John Bayley of Newbury, as 2d wife.

1 JOSEPH, b. Dec. 15, 1764; merchant at Haverhill; m. Sarah Ring of Newburyport; d. Dec. 21, 1836. She d. March 8, 1851, in Newbury.

Thirteen children, of whom the following lived in Newbury:

i. Lavinia, b. Sept. 14, 1787; m. Dea. John Buxton; d. Sept. 6, 1855.

v. Persis, b. Jan. 11, 1793; m. Dea. Daniel Thompson; d. April 1, 1879.

x. Louisa, b. Aug. 4, 1803; m. Warren Ives of Topsham and Newbury; d. February, 1871.

2 xi. Peabody W., b. Aug. 15, 1805.

2 PEABODY WEBSTER, b. Haverhill, Aug. 15, 1805; came to Newbury, 1826; blacksmith; then in tin and hardware business till old age. He built, 1828, the house where H. A. Webb now lives. In that year a boy named Alvi T. Twing, b. in Topsham, Feb. 9, 1812, was apprenticed to him, and joined the 1st Ch., May 2, 1828. Finding him anxious to obtain an education, Mr. Ladd cancelled his indentures, and helped him through college. He entered the Episcopal ministry, where he became very prominent and became Superintendent of Missions, receiving the degrees of D. D., and L L. D. Mr. Ladd m. Aug. 30, 1827, Elizabeth, dau. of John Johnson. He joined the 1st Ch., May 2, and his wife July 6, 1828. He was chorister in the "old meeting house" many years. Superintendent of Sunday School 15 years. Justice of the Peace, and Associate Justice of the County Court. He d. June 30, 1891. She d. May 8, 1880.

Children:

3 i. John Johnson, b. May 11, 1828; d Jan. 27, 1889.

ii. Mary Elizabeth, b. Dec. 21, 1830; m. Sept. 27, 1855, David Child of Montreal, who d. Newbury, Dec. 22, 1863. Mrs. Child res. in Newbury, spending one year in Europe; d. Jan. 20, 1894. C., Charles E., b. Montreal, Oct. 22, 1856; was reared in Newbury; res. Northampton, Mass., since 1873; has been in the cotton manufacturing business about 20 years. Treasurer of the Hampton Co., of Easthampton, and connected with the West Boylston Manufacturing Co. He m. Dec. 23, 1885, Annie, dau. Geo. A. Hill, of San Francisco, Cal.

iii. Ezra, b. Oct. 24, 1832; d. Oct. 29, 1856.

iv. Hallan, b. Aug. 17, 1834; d. Feb. 4, 1842.

v. Harriet, b. July 3, 1842; d. June 19, 1861.

3 JOHN JOHNSON, b. May 11, 1828; fitted for college at St. Johnsbury Academy; graduated Dartmouth College, 1852; taught in Vermont; in Beverly, Mass.; Master of Providence High School several years; Principal of Warren Academy, Woburn, Mass. During the Civil war he was a paymaster in the army, after which he was for several years Principal of Littleton (N. H.) High School Teacher under Dr. Sears, agent for the Peabody fund, where he was 10 years, with headquarters at Staunton, West Va. In 1881 he bought a plantation at Lyndhurst, Va. Rem. 1884, to Brockville, Ont. He m. 1st, Dec. 1, 1853, Sophia Williams, dau. Tappan Stevens, who d. at Lyndhurst, Va., January, 1882. He m. 2d, 1884, Caroline Lathrop, niece of Dr. Spalding of Haverhill. He d. Brockville, Ont., Jan. 27, 1889.

Children:

i. Jennie S., b. Feb. 9, 1857.

ii. William S., b. May 8, 1862; res. Brockville, Ont.

LAING.

ALEXANDER, son of Robert and Margaret (Barrick) Laing; b. Nov. 20, 1792, in Fifeshire, Scotland. He m. June 9, 1817, Mary, dau. of Robert and Christian (Wallace) Grieg, (b. Scotland, July 2, 1792; d. in Newbury, Jan. 1, 1862). Mr. Laing was a weaver in Scotland. They left Scotland in March, 1834, reached Montreal in May, and came to Newbury via Burlington. Settled first where Daniel Taisey now lives, but later bought a farm on Leighton hill. Presbyterians. Their descendants usually spell the name Lang. He d. in Newbury, Dec. 6, 1871.

Children, all b. in Scotland but the last:
i. Christian, b. Jan. 7, 1818; m. March 3, 1847, Edward Mulliken; d. March 25, 1896, Medina, Mich.
ii. Margaret, b. Jan. 6. 1819; m. Sept. 7, 1841, Ransom Young of Medford, Mass.; d. Oct. 18, 1842, Newbury.
iii. Helen, b. May 24, 1821; m. Dec. 9, 1847, Andrew Govan; d. Apr. 16, 1895, Metamara, Mich.
1 iv. Robert G., b. Nov. 22, 1823.
v. May, b. Nov. 11, 1825; d. Dec. 29, 1826.
vi. Margary, b. Nov. 3, 1827; d. April 28, 1854.
vii. Alexander, b. Apr. 1, 1830; m. Oct. 8, 1855, Eliza Bowley; rem. to Washington.
viii. Elizabeth, b. May 3, 1833; m. March 11, 1855, Geo. Downing; d. Jan. 21, 1860.
ix. Mary Ann, b. Newbury; m. March 27, 1855, George Leighton; d. June 21, 1859. Barnet.

1 ROBERT GREIG, b. Nov. 22. 1823; m. June 19, 1855, Sarah Elizabeth, dau. of J. B. W. Tewksbury, (b. Jan. 21. 1836); farmer on Leighton hill; rem. to the village, 1892.

Children:
i. Harriet Ella, b. March 18, 1856; m Feb. 21, 1878, John S. Burroughs, q. v.
ii. Alexander Nelson, b. Aug. 26, 1860; m. June 30, 1883, Sadie L. Derby of Bradford. C., (1) Ethel May, b. Apr. 14, 1888. (2) Robert Greig, b. Aug. 4, 1891. (3) Daughter, b. Aug. 20, d. Sept. 1892. (4) Sadie Josephine, b. Dec. 26, 1897; d. Jan. 28, 1899.
iii. Mabel M., b. Dec. 19, 1871; m. July 9, 1896, Dr. Hiram L. Johnson.

*LANG.

SHERBURNE, b. Feb. 25, 1782, Monroe, N. H.; farmer of Bath; m. 1815, Mehitabel, dau. of Joshua Ricker, (b. Bath, April 5, 1797; d. December, 1867). He d. 1857.

Children:
i. Mary, b. Dec. 13, 1816; m. Rev. Edward Cleveland, at one time pastor of the Cong. Ch. in Bath, and author of the History of Shipton, P. Q. She d. Burlington, Kansas, Oct. 24, 1887.
ii. Maria (twin to above), m. A. Hazen Hibbard of Bath; d. Newbury, April 6, 1892.
iii. Louisa, b. Sept. 23, 1818; m. Dea. George Swasey, q. v.; d. Newbury, Dec. 25, 1881.
iv. Hannah, b. Oct. 31, 1820; m. Azro Bailey, of Newbury, Bath and Haverhill; d. Aug. 14, 1889.
v. Susan, b. Jan. 25, 1823; m. Henry Wade, of Memphis; d. Memphis, Tenn., July 4, 1895.
vi. Henry S., b. April 11, 1825; res. in Bath; m. 1st, Martha Lang; m. 2d, Martha J. Hibbard, both of Bath.
vii. John H., b. May 15, 1827; m. 1st, Luella Weeks of Bath; m. 2d, Orinda Cole; d. Monroe, N. H., June 30, 1898.
viii. David R., b. May 6, 1829; m. Josephine Smith of Bath; d. Orford, N. H.,

*By Caroline H. Lang.

Aug. 30, 1875.

  ix. Melissa R., b. April 2, 1831; m. Ezra B. Gale of Bath; d. Sept. 7, 1883.
   x. Caroline B., b. Aug. 5, 1833; m. Dr. William Child of Bath; d. May 10, 1867.
1 xi. James, b. Oct. 5, 1835.
  xii. Luvia L., b. Dec. 12, 1837; m. Dr. William Child of Bath, as 2d wife; d. New Hampton, N. H., Nov. 29, 1886.
 xiii. William H., b. Sept. 11, 1840; res. Bath; m. 1st, Ellen Titus of Lyman; m. 2d, Emily A. Titus.

1 JAMES, b. Oct. 5, 1835; farmer; came to Newbury, 1862, buying the farm on the Ox-bow, which was owned successively by Maj. Nathaniel Merrill, Moses Swasey, and his son, George Swasey. He m. Sept. 28, 1859, Ellen dau. of Ezra Parker.
    Children:
    i. Frederick Burleigh, b. Bath, N. H., Nov. 5, 1860; educated at Montebello Institute and a law school; read law with Hon. C. B. Leslie of Wells River; in practice at Minneapolis, Minn., 13 years; now at Woodsville, N. H.
   ii. Ellen Wade, b. Littleton, N. H.; educated at Montebello Institute and Haverhill Academy; res. at the homestead.
  iii. James Sherburne, b. Newbury, Jan. 25, 1869; educated at New Hampton Commercial College and at St. Johnsbury Academy and at the University of Minnesota, receiving degree of B. M. E., 1896, and B. E. E., 1897.
  iv. Caroline Hannah, b. Newbury, Sept. 15 1871; graduated St. Johnsbury Academy, 1892; Woman's College, Baltimore, Md., one year, class of '99; teacher in Newbury Graded School; m. June 27, 1900, Prof. Gay W. Felton, (b. at St. Albans; graduated Vermont University, 1892; teacher; principal of Newbury High School, 1898–1900; Bradford Academy, 1900–01; appointed by the United States government, teacher in the Philippine Islands, June, 1901). C., James Lang, b. June 25, 1901.

LEAVITT.

JAMES, b. Washington, Vt., June 18, 1800; m. 1827, Affa, dau. James and Polly Atwood of Hampstead, N. H., (b. Apr. 3, 1791; d. Apr. 25, 1871). Came to Newbury, 1832, and was a farmer on Leighton hill, where he d. June 28, 1879.
    Children, all b. in Tunbridge:
    i. Eliza Jane, b. 1829. She became blind, or nearly so, while a young woman, and was called "Blind Jane;" d. Freemont, N. H., Dec. 15, 1891.
   ii. Hester Ann, b. 1830; m. Phineas Bede of Freemont, N. H.; d. 1876; 1 son, Charles.
  iii. James Carlos. b. June 12, 1832; farmer and mechanic; m. May 1, 1853, Jane, dau. Wells Goodwin. C., (1) Frank, b. Feb. 18, 1854; twice m.; res. Malden, Mass.; several c. (2) Fred, b. June 20, 1858; salesman; res. Malden, Mass.; m. Dec. 22, 1881, Lizzie Frazer, (b. Black Rock, N. S.) ; c., Lottie (b. Wellington, Mass., Oct., 1886). (3) Kate, b. March 14, 1860; m., 1st, Harlan W. Brock; 2d, F. A. Rice; res. Malden, Mass.

LEARNED.

FRANKLIN, b. Weathersfield, Aug. 1, 1814; m. 1840, Philinda Leet; came to Newbury from Orford, N. H., in 1862, and bought the farm known as the Col. Frye Bayley farm, where he lived till 1886, when he went to live at Wells River village, where his wife d. June 28, 1884, aged 66; in the lumber and meat business with his son, Daniel W., and were part owners of the paper mill at Wells River; d. Newbury.
    Children:
    i. Daniel W., b. Jan. 11, 1841; in business with his father, and engaged in many other affairs; was partner in the Ryegate Granite Works Co., and president of it at the time of his death, March 26, 1890. He m., 1869,

Cora A. Page of Ryegate, and their c. were, Frederic H.·an'd George H.
ii. Julia Ann, b. Oct. 11, 1842; d. Aug. 13, 1848.
iii. James G., b.·June 24, 1849; worked 'for his brother, Daniel, till his death;
since farmer, owning Col. Frye Bayley 'farm. He m. Mary A. Page of
Ryegate. C.,· Franklin F. and Harley·L.

LEET.

BENJAMIN, settled and cleared the present home farm of Wm. and Henry
Chalmers. He was b. Oct. 15, 1785. He m. Eunice B. Russell, (b. Oct. 3,
1787; d. Oct. 28, 1860). Their children were: sons, Benjamin, Charles,
Lemuel, and George; daus., Louisa, (b. Apr. 30, 1809; d. Apr. 10, 1890).
' Philinda, who m. Frank Learned; Susan, who m.·Charles Webber; Sarah,
'who never m.; and Eunice, who m. Adams Wilson of Bradford. Benjamin
was long a baggagemaster on the Connecticut River R. R.; George went to
California in 1850; Charles and Lemuel remained in Newbury. He d. Sept.
1, 1848.

1 CHARLES, b. 1813; m. 1848, Mary Jackman in Boscawen, N. H.; she d. March,
1866. They had 11 c.
Caroline, Fidelia and Louise are m. and live in New York state.
Mary, m. Charles Merrill, and d. in Wa$_{rre}$n, N. H.; Elvira, m: Milo Aiken of
Wentworth, N. H., where she d.; Ida, m. W. F. Colton of Warren, N. H.,
and d. at Kensington, Conn.
Charles served in the Civil War; m. Abbie, dau. of David Jewell, and lives at
Haverhill; two c., Abbie, who m. Warren Carleton, d. ·in 1889; Edgar
B., res. in Keene, N. H.
Henry, youngest son of Charles, Sr., b. Sept. 19, 1845; enlisted Dec. 8, 1863,
with his brother, Charles, in the 1st Vt. cavalry, was in 28 battles and
skirmishes, and once wounded, He was a farm laborer and sheep shearer;
settled in Topsham in 1872, where he has held public offices, and
commander for four years of Ransom Post, G. A. R.   He m. 1st, Sept. 30,
1868, Caroline, dau. Calvin Mills, who d. Nov. 28, 1878; m. 2d, Feb. 25,
1879, Mary O. Lambert.
Children, two by 1st, b. in Newbury, and 5 by 2d, b. in Topsham:
i. Frank H., b. March 16, 1870; d. July 11, 1896.
ii. Cora E., b. Dec. 1, 1871.
iii. Gertrude L., b. Feb. 20, 1880.
iv. Felette F. G., b. June 6, 1883.
v. Carrie M. O., b. Aug. 28, 1888.
vi. Helena G., b. Oct. 19, 1890.
vii. Christie L., b. Aug. 11, 1892.

2 LEMUEL, b. Jan. 5, 1824; farmer at West Newbury. He m. Mary Ann Gage,
who d. July 16, 1877, aged 49 years 8 months. He d. July 31, 1892.
They had several c. of whom we have no record.

LEIGHTON.

This name is sometimes spelled Laton, Layton and Laiton.

REUBEN, b. Dover, N. H., 1770; came to Newbury about 1800, and lived two
years on the Ben Porter place at South Newbury. He bought wild land
on Leighton hill, then a wilderness and began to clear a farm where the
late Barsabas Dinsmore long lived. He and his wife were early members
of the M. E. ch. and aided greatly in its usefulness and growth in that part
of the town. He d. June 28, 1842, aged 72, and his wife, Mary; Feb. 21,
1862, aged 92 years, 5 months. Their c. were Reuben, (q. v.) Samuel and
Silas, who settled in York state; Jacob, who settled on Waits River
in Bradford; Jonathan, who went to Massachusetts; Stephen, who settled
in Bath; Hannah, who m. Ross Ford; Sarah, who m. Stephen Bennett;
and Mary, who d. y.

REUBEN, Jr., b. about 1791; m. Mary Sargent of Strafford, who d. Sept. 29,
1878, aged 84. 'He d. 'Feb. 25, 1843, aged 52.

Children:
1 i. Lorenzo Dow, b. March 26, 1815; d. Apr. 19, 1872.
2 ii. Roswell, b. Oct. 22, 1818; d. March 15, 1897, q. v.
    iii. Susan, b. ————; m. William Wallace, jr., q. v.
    iv. Mary Ann, b. ————; m. John Wallace.
    v. Charles, b. Oct. 27, 1827; m. Aug. 29, 1851, Jane, dau. Justin Lindsey; d. Oct. 29, 1858.
3 vi. John Lovejoy.

1 LORENZO DOW, b. March 26, 1815; farmer. He m. Dec. 3, 1857, Salina R., dau. Hardy Lindsey, (b. Whitefield, N. H., Jan. 4, 1840; d. Deerfield, N. H., July 22, 1888. She m. as 2d husband, Nov. 26, 1884, Martin W. Childs of Deerfield). He d. Apr. 19, 1872.
Children:
    i. Harry Bailey, b. Oct. 1, 1858; res. Milford, N. H.
    ii. Ida May, b. May 18, 1860; m. Oct. 27, 1891, Charles A. Childs of Deerfield, N. H. C., Martin L., b. Manchester, N. H., June 15, 1897.
    iii. George Watkins, b. Dec. 7, 1861; res. Minneapolis, Minn.
    iv. Herbert C., b. Dec. 27, 1863; m. Jan. 5, 1893, Emma L. Brown of Bradford.
    v. William Dow, b. May 6, 1865; m. June 19, 1889, Velma Chamberlin. C., Harold, b. Sept. 19, 1893.
    vi. Jennie Inez, b. March 19, 1867; m. Geo. H. King, q. v.
    vii. Katie Belle, b. Dec. 20, 1869: adopted by Alfred Chase of Stoneham; m. June 17, 1891, John Wilson Crowley of Stoneham, but b. in Newbury.
    viii. John Wesley, b. Jan. 27, 1872; some time manager of the creamery at West Newbury, He m. May 10, 1899, Katharine Adams of Bradford.

2 ROSWELL, son of Reuben, b. Oct. 22, 1818; m. Feb. 28, 1849, Mary Ann, dau. Levi James, who d. March 24, 1889. He d. March 15, 1897.
Children:
    i. Henry E., b. April 15, 1850.
    ii. Silas M., b. Sept. 12, 1851; farmer on Ox-bow; m. 1st, June 20, 1888, Harriet, dau. Charles and Sarah Boyce Bartlett, who d. June 5, 1893, aged 34; 2d, Oct. 16, 1895, Alice Jenne, (b. Oct. 14, 1862; d. June 21, 1898).
    iii. Frank P., b. Sept. 25, 1853: farmer on homestead; m. October, 1888, Mary E., dau. of Dea. George Burroughs. C., (1) Mary Frances, b. Feb. 13, 1890. (2) Agnes Amy, b. May 30, 1892. (3) Margaret Helen, b. July 13, 1894. (4) George, b. Aug. 19, 1896. (5) Martha Emma, b. July 4, 1901.
    iv. Milo, b. Oct. 3, 1855; d. Oct. 17, 1892.
    v. Mary Etta, b. Sept. 14, 1858; m. Sept. 18, 1888, Frank P. Downs of Groton. C., Katie May, b. July 17, 1890; Carrie, b. Nov. 29, 1893.

3 JOHN LOVEJOY, farmer in Newbury on Wallace Hill; m. Aug. 8, 1849, Mary Jane, dau. Hardy Lindsey.
One child:
    i. Charles Wesley, b. July 5, 1853; farmer, his farm adjoining his father's; steward in Methodist church, and superintendent of its Sunday school. He m. Nov. 27, 1878, Ermina Holt of Derby. Drowned, Jan. 21, 1895, while gathering ice in Harriman's Pond. So far as is known, no other person was ever drowned in any of the ponds in this town.

LESLIE.

This family is of Scotch descent, tracing its ancestry back for centuries.

ALEXANDER, of Londonderry, N. H., m. Lucy Warriner. They had two sons who settled at Wells River, and were prominent there.
Children:
1 i. John W., b. Aug. 18, 1791; d. Feb. 1, 1868.
2 ii. George R., b. November, 1798; d. May 10, 1865.

1 JOHN WARRINER, b. Aug. 18, 1791; fuller and cloth dresser at Wells River; m. 1818, Lucia, dau. Dr. Thomas Brigham of Norwich and granddaughter of Paul Brigham, a Revolutionary soldier, who was lieutenant governor of this state for 22 years, (b. March 8, 1796; d. May 1, 1873).

Children:

3 i. Charles Brigham, b. Nov. 5, 1819; d. Aug. 2, 1901.
    ii. Elizabeth B., b. Oct. 19, 1822; m. Aug. 31, 1843, Judge Julius A. Hayden, then a resident of St. Louis; d. She d. at Memphis, Tenn., March 5, 1845.
    iii. Lucia A., res. Wells River.

2 GEORGE REID, b. Londonderry, N. H.; came to Wells River, 1820, and carried on the business of finishing and dressing of woolen cloth. He lived where his dau., Mrs. Graves, now does. He m. Aug. 2, 1831, Mary, dau. William Grant, a woman of rare excellence, (b. Ryegate, May 12, 1810; d. Jan. 30, 1895). He d. May 10, 1865.

4 i. George, b. Apr. 24, 1834; d. Nov. 21, 1893.
    ii. Kate, m. Sept. 25. 1867, J. L. Whitcomb, of Savannah, Ga.
    iii. Harry A., res. Boston, Mass.; salesman; m. Feb. 8, 1872, Clara Perry, of Gardiner, Me. C., (1) Marion Grant. (2) Harry M.
    iv. Mary Elizabeth, d. Aug. 12, 1849.
    v. Ella J., m. Dec. 5, 1883, Edgar C. Graves of Wells River. C., (1) Arthur L. (2) Katherine J.

3 CHARLES BRIGHAM, b. Newbury, Nov. 5, 1819; was a river man for one or two seasons; attended Bradford Academy; read law with Elijah Farr, and was admitted to the bar June, 1843; in Mr. Farr's office one year; in practice at East Corinth, June to November, 1844; in partnership at Wells River with Mr. Farr, till the latter's death, July, 1845; in partnership with Asa M. Dickey, 1852–56; R. H. Heath, ——; D. A. Rogers, 1860–81, and since the latter's death, with A. H. Carpenter and W. D. Laird. Postmaster at Wells River during two terms; register of probate for Bradford district. 1850–52; Judge of Probate, 1853, '54, '58; U. S. commissioner of the Circuit Court for the district of Vermont from 1859. His practice has been in Vermont and in Grafton and Coös Counties. N. H. His reputation was that of a well read lawyer, who thoroughly prepared his cases, and was always honorable and fair toward his opponents at the bar. In his latter years his growing infirmity of deafness restricted his practice to his desk work, but, as he often said, he had always found enough to do. He had been for several years the senior member of the bar of Orange County." Judge Leslie spent his entire life at Wells River, he had known all its business and professional men, and he was interested in preserving the history and traditions of his native town. He was one of the first to suggest to the editor of this volume the preparation of the work, and has aided him in every possible way. He prepared, while in feeble and failing health, from time to time, as his strength permitted, the chapter upon Wells River, in which he has preserved much which had otherwise passed into oblivion. He contributed to the press occasionally, and prepared several of the biographies in "Bench and Bar of Orleans County." In politics he was a democrat, but not an active politician. He had long been a member of the Congregational church. Mr. Leslie m. Jan. 16, 1845, Harriet Heaton, dau. of Smith and Rhoda (Heaton) Skinner. Judge Leslie d. Aug. 2, 1901. He was one of the last of a race of lawyers, who came into practice in the earlier days; he had known all the legal giants of two states; he was familiar with the details of a thousand cases famous in their time. "He was esteemed an excellent lawyer by the members of his profession, as well as by the business public; in his d. the Vermont bar has lost one of its ablest and wisest members; the Cong. Ch. an earnest member, and the town of Newbury an honest citizen."

Children:
  i. Julius Hayden, res. Wells River with his father.
  ii. Elizabeth B., res. with her parents.
  iii. Charles E., fitted for college at St. Johnsbury Academy; graduated; admitted Dartmouth College, 1877; read law with Leslie & Rogers; to the bar, 1879; in practice at Hillsboro, N. D., where he has an extensive practice, and has held many positions of trust. Is m.; three c.

4 GEORGE, was for a short time in the Barre Bank, but became cashier, Jan. 1, 1858, of the Wells River Bank, and continued in the position after it became a National Bank, till his death, Nov. 21, 1893, filling this responsible place, and other positions of trust, to the entire satisfaction of all with whom he had any business. He was long the treasurer of the town, the village, and the Congregational society, and was the friend of every one. He was a large man, in frame and in heart.

Mr. Leslie was probably known to more people than any other business man in the Connecticut valley. The confidence which every one had in his perfect honesty and sound judgment brought people to the bank; they liked to do business with him. He loved to assist hard working people in the investment of their small savings. "In private life he was always willing to do more than his share for any worthy cause, and his death brought sadness to hundreds of homes." He m. May 25, 1859, Anna D. Smith, of Thetford.

Children:
i. Margaret, (Mrs. F. M. Kendall of Montpelier).
ii. Roscoe, now in business at Fargo, North Dakota.

*LESLIE.

GEORGE W., b. in Claremont, N. H., April 29, 1804; m. Dec. 18, 1828, Mehitabel Williams of Plainfield, N. H., and they immediately settled in Newbury, their first house being located on the present road-bed of the Passumpsic railroad near where the station now stands, the possibility of such an institution in that locality being then an entirely unthought-of thing. Eight c. were b. to them, but three d. in infancy. The survivors are Mrs. Jane L. Cobleigh, who res. at Newbury, Mrs. Mary P. Wells and Emma L. Freeman, both of Montpelier, Mrs. Helen L. Worthen, who res. at the old homestead and George W. Leslie of Montpelier. Squire Leslie, as he was familiarly called, was identified with the organization of Newbury Seminary and gave liberally to the institution in its infancy, and probably no other resident of the town has been more pleasantly remembered by the thousands of students of this grand old seminary. During his long residence in town he was an active, honorable and highly respected citizen. He d. Sept. 21, 1885, aged 81 years. His wife survived him five years when she too was called home, March 13, 1890.

LINDSEY.

SAMUEL, whose mother's maiden name is said to have been Austin, and whose wife was a Silver, came to Newbury about 1800, and settled on a farm, now a pasture, lying between the Chalmers farm and Hall's Pond. "Mrs. Mehitabel Lindsey d. Jan. 19, 1823." Church record.

Children:
i. Samuel, served in the war of 1812; d. soon after 1820.
ii. Mehitabel, m. March 26, 1801, Sargent Rowe of Topsham and Derby.
iii. Daniel, m. in Canada, Roxanna Bates, and lived in Newbury, where she d., and he m. Betsey Jewell. C., (1) Alonzo. (2) Mary, who m. Harvey Tracy. (3) Vernon. (4) Melissa Fanny. (5) Christian, who m. Freeman Cunningham.
1 iv. William, b. October, 1799; d. September 28, 1867.
v. John, m. 1st, Pluma Ball in Canada and lived in Derby. He m. 2d, the widow of Charles George, but they separated ten days later. He d.———— C., (1) Marshall. (2) Diana, m. Timothy Holt. (3) John. (4) Harriet, m. Sanford Hinman. (5) Richmond.
2 vi. Justin, b. Feb. 15, 1803; d. Apr. 10, 1894.
3 vii. Hardy.
viii. Hannah, d. un-m.
ix. Mary, m. Sept. 19, 1811, Thomas Henry.

1 WILLIAM,[2] (Samuel,[1]) b. October, 1799; m. 1st, March 22, 1822, Betsey, dau. Samuel Meservey, (b. Marblehead, Mass., November, 1796; d. Aug. 11, 1844). He m. 2d, Jan. 24, 1847, Ann, dau. Edward Rollins, (b. Aug. 1, 1814; d. Jan. 21, 1885.) He d. September 28, 1867.

*By Mrs. Helen Worthen

Children, six by 1st and five by 2d marriage:

4   i.   John, b. March 18, 1823; d. Dec. 19, 1890.
    ii.   Martha D., b. March 15, 1825; m. Thos. Corliss, q. v.
    iii.   Hannah, b. Aug. 17, 1826; m. 1st, 1851, Thos. F. Pollard of Brookfied; music teacher; m. 2d, Dec. 13, 1863, James Henderson, who d.; m. 3d, 1877, Charles E. Lamphere, of Ryegate. She d. March 4, 1895. No c. by either m.
    iv.   Mary Ann, d. y.
    v.   Nancy, d. y.
    vi.   Freeman, b. Oct. 31, 1832; served in the Civil war in a N. H. Regiment. He m. Helen Hall. Res. Lancaster, N. H. Two daus.
    vii.   Ellen, b. 1848; d. December, 1873.
    viii.   Harriet, m. November, 1872, Fred A. Wilkins, of Tilton, N. H. Two daus., one living.
    ix.   William, d. California, September, 1881.
    x.   Henry, b. April 1, 1853; m. Sept. 28, 1882, Susan Martin, (b. Sept. 30, 1862). C., (1) Norma M., b. Ryegate, Dec. 31, 1883. (2) Charles H., b May 16, 1886; d. Sept. 20, 1886. (3) Ned B., b. June 28, 1893.
    xi.   Mary Ann, m. March, 1874, William Terry, q. v.

2 JUSTIN,[2] (Samuel,[1]) b. Feb. 15, 1803; carpenter and farmer; m. June 4, 1826; Amy Meservey, who d. Nov. 2, 1886. He d. at Canaan, April 10, 1894, buried in Newbury.

Children:
    i.   William Wallace, b. 1827; hotel keeper at West Stewartstown. N. H., many years. From 1891 till death, proprietor of the Stetson House at Norton, where he d. April 11, 1898. He m. 1st, March 1, 1851, Mary, dau. Capt. Isaac Abbott of Littleton, who d. Jan. 20, 1887. He m. 2d, Nellie Perry. No c.
    ii.   Jane, m. 1st, Aug. 27, 1851, Charles Leighton, who d. Oct. 29, 1858; m. 2d, Lafayette Bass of Piermont, who d. Nov. 18, 1887. She d. Nov. 12, 1886, aged 54. C., Justin L., merchant at Lancaster, N. H. William, res. at Lancaster; Jennie; all m.
    iii.   Susan T., m. March 27, 1857, Van Ness Bass, (b. Bath, N. H., July 14, 1830; printer and publisher of White Mt. Banner, at Littleton, 1855-59; publisher of the Grafton County Democrat, at Plymouth, 1879-84; connected several years with Plymouth Record, and now with the Woodsville News.)
    iv.   Emily, m. Thomas Westgate.

3 HARDY,[2] (Samuel,[1]) farmer in Newbury and elsewhere; m. 1st, Oct. 27, 1825, Letitia Gerould; m. 2d, Betsey Johnson.

Children:
    i.   Mary Jane, m. John Leighton.
    ii.   Sarah, m. Richard Watson.
    iii.   Pluma, m. —— —— Muzzey.
    iv.   Horace.
    v.   Harriet.
    vi.   Henry, m. Nancy Bailey.
    vii.   Salina, m. L. D. Leighton.

4 JOHN,[3] (William,[2] Samuel,[1]) b. March 18, 1823; in hotel and stage business; began to drive stage between Littleton and Fabyan House, about 1843; then driver on various routes, for five years; became proprietor of the Granite House, Littleton, 1849; of the old Coös House, Lancaster, 1851; became one of the proprietors of the Crawford House, 1855, and later, of the American House at Lancaster; in 1858, he built the old Lancaster House, which was burned in 1877; proprietor, some years, of the Eagle Hotel at Concord, N. H.; from 1868 to 1870, he was associated with S. S. Thompson of Lyndon, in building the railroad between Whitefield and Groveton, N. H. In 1870-72, he was in company with Whitman Thompson in the Glen House stage business; in 1873, he went into the Fabyan House, as senior member of the firm of Lindsey & French, proprietors. He greatly enlarged that vast hotel, but lost much money in the enterprise. Proprietor of the Ocean House, Old Orchard Beach, 1879-81, and the Preble House at Portland; was also associated with his

son, Ned A., in the proprietorship of the Lake Auburn Mineral Spring House. Me.; he was also, for two winters, landlord of the Uplands Hotel, Eastman, Ga.; in 1882, with his son, Ned A., he built the Lancaster House, where he d. Dec. 19, 1890. He m. Oct. 10, 1848, Susan, dau. of Capt. Isaac Abbott, of Littleton, (b. Sept. 20, 1826; d. June 9, 1891.)
Children:
i. Ned A., b. March 14, 1855; was associated with his father in various enterprises; m. Carrie Allen; d. Feb. 5, 1891.
ii. B. Abbott, b. Jan. 29, 1857; physician in New York City, where he d. Nov. 13, 1898. He m. Ida Parker. Two c.
iii. Charles Isaac, b. March 14, 1858; twice m.; three c.; res. in Boston; is one of the proprietors of the Parker House.
iv. Susie Larrabee, b. Nov. 9, 1860; m. Loren B. Whipple, proprietor of the Lancaster House, Lancaster, N. H. Six c.

LITTLE.

I. GEORGE, came from London, Eng., in 1640, and settled at Newbury, Mass., where he d. in 1693, or the following year. His first wife was Alice Poor, who d. Dec. 1, 1680, aged 62.

II. MOSES, their fourth c. and third son, b. March 11, 1657. He m. Lydia Coffin. She survived him and m. 2d, John Pike. He d. March 8, 1691.

III. MOSES, youngest son, b. Feb. 6, 1691. He m. Feb. 12, 1716, Sarah Jaques; they lived in Newbury, Mass., where she d. in 1763. He d. Oct. 17, 1780.

IV. MOSES, their fourth c. and third son, b. May 8, 1724; m. June 5, 1743, Abigail, dau. of Joshua Bayley, and twin sister of Judith, who m. his brother, Stephen. They were sisters of Gen. Jacob Bayley. It is not known that any descendants of Stephen Little ever settled in this town. Abigail (Bayley) Little d. Feb. 6, 1815. Moses Little commanded the men from Newbury, Mass., who went to the siege of Louisburg in 1758. He was Colonel of a regiment at Bunker Hill and of another at the battle of Long Island. In 1777 he left the army on account of ill health. In 1781 he received an attack of paralysis which destroyed his power of speech. Col. Little was one of the largest land owners in New England. He was surveyor of the King's land and acquired large domains in Maine and New Hampshire. He made a large purchase of land in the town of Apthorp, N. H., which was divided into Littleton and Dalton, the former being named for him. He also became the owner of a large part of what is now Androscoggin County, Maine. By his influence with Governor Wentworth, he greatly aided Bayley and Hazen in their efforts to obtain the charters of Newbury and Haverhill, and was a grantee of this town, his right, and one purchased by him of Peter Page, and that of his brother, Stephen, now being part of the Baldwin farm on the upper meadow. It is not believed that he ever made his residence in Newbury, but he spent much time here, and from here directed his land operations in the north country. On the earlier land records of Newbury, his name appears more frequently as grantee of land than any other. He was b. and d. in "Old Newbury," Mass. Moses and Abigail Little had three c., and descendants of three of them, Josiah, Abigail and Elizabeth, have lived in this town. The latter m. as 2d husband, William Wigglesworth, and their son, Samuel, was father of Mrs. Edward Hale. Abigail, b. Apr. 2, 1749; m. Capt. John G. Bayley, q. v. Moses Little d. May 27, 1798.

V. JOSIAH, b. Feb. 16, 1747. He m. March 23, 1770, Sarah, dau. of Edward Tappan. Her mother was another sister of Gen. Jacob Bayley. He lived in Newburyport and was a wealthy land owner in Maine, New Hampshire and Vermont. His wife was b. May 27, 1748, and d. Oct. 11, 1823. He d. Dec. 26, 1830.
Children:
i. Michael, b. March 14, 1771; lived in Maine; graduated at Dartmouth College, 1792; d. March 16, 1830.
ii. Edward, b. March 12, 1773; graduated Dartmouth College, 1792; lived in this town some years; succeeded Col. Wallace in the ownership of the

Spring Hotel, which he enlarged in 1810. He lost most of his property by a fire in Newburyport in 1811, but became wealthy by inheritance, and removed to Maine. He built and endowed the Edward Little High School at Auburn. He d. Sept. 21, 1849.

iii. Alice, b. Feb. 1, 1775; m. as 1st wife, Thomas Hale, q. v. She d. July 27, 1819.

iv. Anna, b. Nov. 29, 1783; m. William Atkinson; d. Nov. 13, 1866, q. v.

v. Josiah, b. Jan. 13, 1791; graduated Bowdoin College, 1811; m. Jan. 24, 1814, Sophronia Balch. He owned the farm on Musquash meadow which is now that of F. E. Kimball, and spent much time in Newbury. Mr. Little founded the Public Library of Newburyport, and was a wealthy and benevolent man. He was interested in this town and it was quite common for him to select steady young men from Newbury to go to Newburyport and work for him. He d. Feb. 5, 1860.

LOCKHEAD.

Mention is asked for this family, but little is really known about them. John Lockhead came from Scotland to Ryegate, then bought the farm where Mrs. V. N. Daniels now lives. He was quite prominent in certain ways, as he was a skillful musician, had a very sweet voice and was thought to excel all others in rendering the songs of Burns. He belonged to several musical associations and was an active Mason. The c. were John, jr, and two daus., who were all teachers, intelligent people, and fine singers. About 1855, Mrs. Lockhead d., and the family went west. It is understood that none of the c. were m. and are all d.

LOVEWELL.

I. JOHN, an ensign in Cromwell's army in 1653; settled on Salmon Brook, in what is now Nashua, N. H., where he d. about 1754, at the remarkable age of 120.
   Children, or some of them:
1 i. John, b. Oct. 14, 1691.
   ii. Zacheus, b. May 14, 1713; Colonel in the Old French war. (Appleton's American Biography says that he was b. in Dunstable, July 22, 1701; served in the Old French war, succeeding Joseph Blanchard as Colonel of the New Hampshire regiment of volunteers in April, 1758, and was ordered to join Prideaux at Niagara, July 29, 1759).
   iii. Jonathan; preacher and judge; d. 1792.
   iv. Hannah, m. Josiah Farwell, who was killed at Pequaket, (Fryeburg).

1 JOHN, b. Oct. 14, 1691; captain in the Indian wars; was in command of a company of 34 men in May, 1725, who on their way to destroy the Indian villages on the Upper Saco, were attacked by the Indians at Fryeburg, Me. In the famous fight which followed Capt. Lovewell and nineteen others perished. He m. Hannah ————
   Children:
   i. John, b. June 30, 1718; d. July 2, 1763. Four c.
   ii. Hannah, b. July 24, 1721.
2 iii. Nehemiah, b. Jan. 9, 1726.

2 NEHEMIAH, b. Jan. 9, 1726. He commanded a company in Col. John Goffe's regiment under Gen. Amherst in the French war, 1758. Came to Newbury before 1771, and served in the Revolutionary war. Rem. to Corinth, where he d. He m. Rachel Farwell, Nov. 24, 1748, (another record says Nov. 24, 1745).
   Children, several of whom settled in Corinth:
   i. Catherine, b. June 17, 1749; m. Major John Taplin.
   ii. Susannah, b. July 22, 1750; d. y.
   iii. Hannah, b. July 22, 1750; d. y.
3 iv. Nehemiah, b. July 1, 1752; d. July 14, 1801.
   v. Betsey, b. June 25, 1754; m. Mansfield Taplin.
   vi. Henry, b. Jan. 9, 1757; Revolutionary soldier.
   vii. Zachens, b. Nov. 8, 1758; Revolutionary soldier.

4 viii. Jonathan, b. Nov. 7, 1760; d. Jan. 1, 1817.
  ix. Robert, b. Oct. 1, 1762.
   x. Vodica, b. April 18, 1764; m. John Lovewell.
  xi. John, b. March 18, 1766.
 xii. Joseph, b. Jan. 6, 1768.
xiii. Rachel, b. June 8, 1770; m. Samuel Hilliard.

3 NEHEMIAH, b. July 1, 1752; came to Newbury with his parents; was one of three young men who started at once for the seat of war when the news of the battle of Lexington reached Newbury, and served at Bunker Hill in Walker's Co. of Reed's regiment. In November, 1775, he marched to Boston as sergeant in a company of 16 or 18 men, who assisted in fortifying Dorchester Heights. In March, 1777, he was commissioned Lieutenant in Burton's Co. of Herrick's regiment of rangers, which marched to Manchester and Bennington, and joined the army under Stark, but was ordered to scout and range the woods near Lake George, rejoined Stark, and was in the battles near Saratoga. Served eight months. In 1778, appointed a corporal in Bedel's regiment, and was sent to Canada with Capt. Frye Bayley and John Powell of Strafford, to escort some officers. They were thrown into prison and held a year, when they were exchanged. In 1780, he was employed by Gen. Bayley to range the woods near Lake Champlain, and discovered the force which was on its way to attack Royalton. In 1781, he was commissioned a captain by Gov. Chittenden, and served in the regiment of which Samuel Fletcher was Lieutenant Colonel. He m. Aug. 8, 1781, by Rev. John Richards, of Piermont, Betsey, dau. John Haseltine, the first white child b. in this town, (b. May 4, 1763; d. Nov. 19, 1850). No c. Capt. Lovewell built, about 1785, the oldest part of the present Sawyer House, where he kept tavern till his death, (buried at the Ox-bow) July 14, 1801, and which his widow kept after him till she sold the premises to William Bailey and Dea. John Buxton in 1825.

4 JONATHAN, b. Nov. 7, 1760; farmer of Corinth; m. Sophia Taplin; d. Jan. 1, 1817.
  Children:
   i. Susan, b. 1802; d. July 21, 1818.
  ii. Hartwell, b. Sept. 3, 1804; spent the later years of his life with his sister, Mrs. Brock, where he d. un-m , May 17, 1879.
 iii. Harriet, b. March 20, 1807; m. Horatio N. Taplin of Montpelier.
 iv. Meranda, b. Jan. 20, 1809; m. Col. Horatio Brock of Newbury.

LUMSDEN.

JAMES, b. in Scotland, and a linen weaver there; m. Margaret Gourly, and their c. were, George, Agnes, called Nancy, James, Margaret and David. They came from Star-Markinch in Fifeshire, whence several of our Scotch families came. James came with his son, George, about 1830, and two years later sent for his family. With them came one or two families named Melville, who settled on farms which are now pastures, in the extreme northwest part of the town, and who lived there till about 1860. James Lumsden, after living a few years on the farm west of the town house, lived near where Mr. Gamsby does now, and near Jefferson Hill, but spent his last years with his dau., Mrs. Ritchie, where he d. May 24, 1854, aged 73, and is buried on Jefferson Hill. His wife and son, David, are buried at the Ox-bow. He was a man of extensive information, and the family were all Presbyterians.
  Children:
1   i. George, d. Jan. 4, 1863.
  ii. Agnes, m. as 2d wife, Archibald Ritchie, Oct. 17, 1849.
 iii. James.
 iv. Margaret, m. Oct. 22, 1815, Walter Buchanan, of Ryegate; d. Jan. 28, 1886. Eight c., of whom Margaret m. Curtis B. Fisk of Newbury.
  v. David, d. y.

1 GEORGE, b. April, 1811; came to America with his father; settled on Jefferson

Hill; went to California in 1849; served three months in Co. K, 3d Vt., in 1862; m. Mary Buchanan of Ryegate, (b. April 15, 1810; d. Oct. 24, 1898). He d. Jan. 4, 1863.
Children:
i. Jennet.
ii. Mary, m. James Halley, as 3d wife.
iii. Margaret, m. N. H. Ricker.
iv. David, farmer at the Lime Kiln.
v. Nelson, d. March 30, 1879, aged 28 years.
vi. Lillian J., d. March 7, 1881, aged 33 years.

MARCY.

JULIUS GARDNER, son of Jacob G. and Charlotte (Wheeler) Marcy, b. Windsor, April 10, 1856; came to Haverhill, 1857; began to learn the wheel-wright trade at 19; came to Newbury, 1878, and has carried on the carriage repairing and painting business; he worked 2½ years in the Farnham shop; then over the Stocker shop, purchasing the Ladd shop, 1890. He m. 1st, May 5, 1879, Emma J. Harris, of Warren, N. H., who d. 1882. He m. 2d, Nov, 29, 1882, Nellie E. Philbrick, of Topsham. They have one dau., Edith May, b. March 9, 1885.

MARTIN.

I. SAMUEL, came to America in 1635; was a ship carpenter of Gloucester, Mass. Is believed to have returned to England.

II. SOLOMON, was at Gloucester, 1635; came in the "James" from London, at the age of 16; m. March 21, 1643, Mary Pindar; came to Andover, Mass., 1651. C., Samuel and Mary.

III. SAMUEL, b. 1645; m. 1676, Abigail Norton, and had four sons.

IV. JOHN, b. 1685; m. Hannah ————; d. 1754.

V. SAMUEL, m. Elizabeth Osgood, and of their eleven c., Peter settled in Newbury, and Hannah m. Daniel Bartlett, q. v.

PETER, b. Andover, Mass., Feb. 22, 1759; Revolutionary soldier; served eight months, at the beginning of the war; was at Bunker Hill, and at the surrender of Burgoyne; enlisted 1777 for three years in Capt. Benj. Varnum's Co., and discharged March, 1780, at Morristown, N. J.; was at Valley Forge, and at West Point; re-enlisted, and was at Yorktown, Va., and saw the surrender of Cornwallis; in Washington's body guard at one time. He m. March 7, 1786, at Andover, Mass., Hannah Dean, (b. Nov. 3, 1764). Came to Newbury, and settled where A. A. Bowen now lives, where his first recorded purchase of land was in 1806, and where he d. June 23, 1820, having cleared the farm on both sides of the road. In person he was tall and muscular; a merry man, who made many rhymes, some of which are still remembered. Mrs. Martin d. March 15, 1840, (Church Record). Buried at the Ox-bow.
Children:
1   i. Peter, b. March 25, 1787; d. Dec. 24, 1864.
   ii. Hannah, b. Aug. 17, 1789; m. Asher Hunkins of Bradford; d. Aug. 30, 1872.
   iii. Elizabeth Wyman, b. June 29, 1791; m. James Abbott; d. Dec. 2, 1863.
   iv. Dorcas, b. Nov. 19, 1795; m. John F. Johnson; d. Nov. 1, 1847.
   v. Clarissa, b. Feb. 27, 1798; d. 1800.
2   vi. Samuel, b. April 2, 1800; d. Aug. 13, 1866.

1   PETER, b. Andover, Mass., March 25, 1787; m. Catherine, dau. Dea. Thomas McKeith, q. v., of Topsham, (b. April 5, 1788). Settled on his father's farm, where he d. Dec. 24, 1864, and she d. at Piermont, April 24, 1871.
Children:
i. Charles, b. May 8, 1823; d. Concord, N. H., Nov. 27, 1869.
3   ii. John D., b. Dec. 24, 1829.

iii. Sarah, b. July 18, 1825; m. January, 1851, Calvin P. Clark of Bradford, where she d. Jan. 25, 1863.

2 SAMUEL, b. Claremont, N. H., April 2, 1800; m. Dec. 28, 1826, Anna, dau. of Dea. William Burroughs, (b. July 27, 1802; d. June 10, 1867). Lived where John Kendrick now does, where he d. Aug. 13, 1866. Peter and Samuel Martin were substantial citizens.

Children:
i. Sophia, b. Oct. 20, 1827; m. John Kendrick, q. v.
ii. Henry, b. Nov. 6, 1829; m. May 18, 1853, Martha A. Hoyt of St. Johnsbury; rem. to Iowa. Eight c.

3 JOHN D., b. Dec. 24, 1829; farmer on homestead till 1865, when he rem. to Piermont, where he is a deacon in the Cong. Ch., and has been town representative; m. Feb. 10, 1853, Matilda, dau. Frank P. Johnson. One c., Katherine Anna, b. Nov. 16, 1853; m. Oct. 16, 1876, Frank W. Blaisdell of Geneseo, N. Y., where he d. Feb. 19, 1880. She is a teacher of drawing and painting in Boston, has studied in Paris.

Nearly all the children and grandchildren of Peter Martin, Sr., were members of the 1st Ch., and several were fine singers.

McALLISTER.

This family originated in Argyleshire, Scotland, where the name is common in many parishes at the present day. In the Scotch colony in the north of Ireland were many of the name, and from thence came John McAllister, and settled in New Boston, N. H., in 1748, but rem. to Francestown, where he d., leaving three sons, Archibald, Angus and Daniel. Angus settled in Fryeburg, Me., and reared a large family, and Daniel rem. to New Brunswick.   ·

ARCHIBALD, b. in Ireland; m. Maria McKeen; lived in New Boston, Francestown and Antrim; served in the Revolutionary war, in Capt. Wm. Boyce's Co., of Col. Kelley's regiment, in the Rhode Island expedition, 1778, and, perhaps in other service. His c. were, John, who never m.; Betsey, who m. Prescott Varnum, of Dracut, Mass.; Robert, of Newbury; Jane, who m. David Gibson, of Newbury; Jean, who m. James McClary; Polly, who m. Samuel Dow; Hannah, who m. James McPherson; Nancy, who was the first wife of Joseph Chamberlin of Newbury; Samuel; Sarah, who m. a Mr. Dutton; Fanny, who m. 1st, Edmund Carter, 2d, Ziba Goss, and 3d, Joseph Chamberlin as 2d wife; and Naomi, who m. Daniel Moore.

ROBERT, b. New Boston, N. H., Aug. 26, 1772; m. Sarah Stewart of Amherst, (b. Aug. 11, 1773; d. Oct. 17, 1843); lived in New Boston, Francestown and Antrim; came to Newbury in the winter of 1806, and settled where his grandson, Leonard W. McAllister, now lives; farmer and carpenter; teaching day and singing schools for twenty winters; he was precentor for many years in the Presbyterian church at Topsham, of which he was a member, but was ex-communicated in 1842, for having taken Freeman's oath, and voting at a presidential election, after which he joined the 1st Ch. at Newbury; d. March 7, 1861.

Children:
i. Reuben, b. New Boston; never lived here.
ii. William, b. New Boston, Feb. 10, 1795; m. Jane Delano of Acworth; cabinet maker; served in the war of 1812; rem. to New York in 1823 or '24; d. Norway, N. Y., 1846. No c.
1 iii. Francis Green, b. Francestown, Jan. 23, 1797; d. Feb. 27, 1882.
2 iv. Jonathan, b. Francestown, April 26, 1799; d. Aug. 10, 1861.
3 v. David, b. Antrim, Sept. 11, 1801; d. Sept. 27, 1879.
vi. Sarah, b. Antrim, Oct. 8, 1803; m. Nehemiah L. Clark, q. v.
vii. Mary, b. Newbury, Feb. 16, 1808; m. Archibald Dow of Hillsborough, N. H.
viii. Harriet, b. Newbury, Feb. 9, 1811; m. J. B. W. Tewksbury, q. v.
4 ix. Archibald, b. May 15, 1813; d. Nov. 20, 1898.

40

1 FRANCIS GREEN, b. Francestown, N. H., Jan. 23, 1797; farmer and carpenter. His farm is now owned by Dan B. Fuller. He m. Dec. 30, 1819, Betsey, dau. of Raymond Chamberlin, (b. Sept. 10, 1790; d. May 26, 1877). He d. while on a visit at Manchester, N. H., Feb. 27, 1882.
Children:
  i. Sarah Elizabeth, b. Dec. 11, 1821; m. Jan. 15, 1852, William Bailey of Manchester, N. H. One dau., Harriet, who m. Frank W. Patten.
  ii. Laura H., b. Sept. 16, 1823; m. Dec. 5, 1844, Benjamin Waldron, q. v.
  iii. Mary Helen, b. June 19, 1825; m. Jan. 1, 1850, David Willey of Manchester, N. H. They rem. to Iowa, thence to South Dakota. One son, Frank, now of Grand Rapids, Mich.
  iv. Harriet S., b. May 15, 1829; m. Nov. 29, 1850, Joseph Newhall, as 1st wife; d. Feb. 28, 1851.
  v. Lucy A., b. June 6, 1827.
  vi. Nancy C., b. Aug. 20, 1832; m. Nov. 17, 1853, Joseph Newhall, as 2d wife; d. Aug. 26, 1873. C., (1) Hattie, d. (2) Mattie J., who m. Frank P. Gurney, and lives in Brookhaven, Miss. (3) George, d. (4) Bessie, d. Joseph Newhall, d. March 10, 1871, and, with both his wives and three c., is buried at Clinton, Mass.

2 JONATHAN,[2] (Robert,[1]) b. Francestown, April 26, 1799; m. in Haverhill, Nov. 20, 1823, Charity Scott Chapman, (b. Haverhill, Nov. 22, 1799; d. Keeseville, N. Y., Aug. 12, 1882). He d. Willsborough, N. Y., Aug. 10, 1861.
Children:
  i. Eliza Jane, b. Newbury, Sept. 15, 1825; m. Hiram Palmer of Willsborough, N. Y.
5 ii. Edwin, b. Jay, N. Y., Jan. 2, 1828.
  iii. George, b. Aug. 2, 1830; d. July 26, 1832.
  iv. Mary Ann, b. Ausable, N. Y., Dec. 27, 1832; m., May, 1851, Joel Caswell, (b. Haverhill, Feb. 2, 1825; d. Morrisonville, N. Y., April 4, 1895; carpenter). She d. Morrisonville, N. Y., Feb. 4, 1897. One son, Alfred, a contractor and builder at Plattsburg, N. Y.
  v. Ora Pierce, b. Jay, N. Y., July 20, 1836; d. Lewis, N. Y., Aug. 5, 1853.

3 DAVID,[2] (Robert.[1]) b. Antrim, N. H., Sept. 11, 1801; farmer in the southwest part of the town, later in the Brock neighborhood. He was, like his brothers, a fine singer, He m. Feb. 1, 1822, Elizabeth, dau. of Samuel Tucker, (b. March 30, 1801; d. Oct. 12, 1878). He d. Newbury, Sept. 27, 1879. Buried at the Ox-bow.
Children:
  i. Lucinda T., b. Feb. 18, 1823; m. 1st, John N. Brock; m. 2d, Samuel T. Putnam; d. June 15, 1871.
  ii. Robert, b. Aug. 30, 1874; lived in Newbury; d. in New Hampshire, 1898; had several c. No record.
6 iii. Samuel, b. April 6, 1826; d. Dec. 21, 1872.
7 iv. John R., b. Nov. 30, 1827,
  v. William E., b. May 28, 1836; entered the Methodist ministry, 1858; was seven years in the itineracy. His advantages were very limited, but he was useful. He d. May 1, 1865. C., (1) Olin E., d. May, 1865. (2) Carrie E., d. August, 1860. (3) Ellen M., d. September, 1866.

4 ARCHIBALD,[2] (Robert,[1]) b. Newbury, May 15, 1813; farmer on homestead, and later on the farm cleared by Matthew Gibson; deacon in West Newbury church 30 years; Justice of the Peace. He was a fine singer, and taught singing school a little. He m. 1st, at Greensboro, Jan. 11, 1837, Susannah S., dau. of Rev. Moses P. Clark, (b. March 6, 1812; d. Jan. 31, 1876). He m. 2d, October, 1877, Anna, dau. of P. C. Tuxbury. He d. Nov. 20, 1898.
Children:
  i. Leonard W., b. Sept. 30, 1841; enlisted in Co. H, 12th Vt., Aug. 16, 1862; discharged July 14, 1863; has held town offices. He m. Oct. 12, 1863, Nancy J., dau. of Solomon Jewell. C., (1) Emma E., b. May 24, 1865; d. March 16, 1874. (2) Martha J., b. Nov. 25, 1868; m. Nov. 28, 1888, E. E. Putnam. (3) George L., b. Dec. 17, 1874. (4) Susie E., b. Sept. 3, 1879; teacher; graduated New Hampshire Normal School, 1901.
  ii. Sarah L., b. Aug. 21, 1845; m. April, 1886, Albert L. Fuller, q. v.

5 EDWIN,[3] (Jonathan,[2] Robert,[1]) b. Jay, N. Y., Jan. 2, 1828; m. Louisa
    Boardman of Willsborough, N. Y., 1848; res. Manchester. C., William
    Charles; Warren, d.; Mary, d.; Frederick, d.; Abbie, d.; Arch A.; Ella S.,
    d.; Arthur W., and Bertha.
  i. William Charles, b. Lewis, N. Y., June 19, 1849; fitted for college at
    Keeseville academy; graduated Madison (now Colgate) University;
    pastor of Baptist church, Mariah, N. Y., 1873-76; West Plattsburgh, five
    years; First Baptist church, Manchester, N. H., 1887-99; now pastor
    since May, 1899, of Baptist church in Randolph, Mass.; A. M. from
    Madison University, 1883, D. D. from Olivet College, 1895. Dr.
    McAllister has been very successful in the ministry, and under his several
    pastorates new churches have been built, and a large increase in
    membership of each. He m. Nov. 20, 1873, Angela M. Brownson of
    Elizabethtown, N. Y. C., (1) Lillian A., b. Oct. 28, 1874; graduated
    Vassar College, 1896; teacher of French in Gloucester (Mass.) high school.
    (2) Ralph W., b. Sept. 15, 1877; senior at Harvard University. (3) Grace
    E., b. Jan. 26, 1886.

6 SAMUEL F.,[3] (David,[2] Robert,[1]) b. April 6, 1826; m. March 27, 1851, Jennette
    Randall, (b. Feb. 17, 1828; d. March 9, 1898). They settled in the
    northeast part of Topsham, on the Samuel Stevens place, but in 1871
    bought the Edward Hale farm on Upper Meadow, where he lived till he d.
    Dec. 21, 1872.
  Children:
  i. Ada A., b. May 3, 1852; d. Feb. 28, 1873.
  ii. John D., b. March 17, 1854; res. South Ryegate; m. Jan. 4, 1876, Lydia A.
    Batchelder of Topsham. C., (1) Samuel F., b. Oct. 8, 1876. (2) Lyman
    C., b. June 11, 1884; d. May 11, 1886. (3) John A., b. March 7, 1889.
  iii. Frank S., b. Jan. 27, 1856.
  iv. Clarence H., b. Feb. 12, 1858; farmer on Upper Meadow; m. June 21,
    1893, Clara F. Chamberlin. C., Carlos A., b. Jan. 13, 1897.
  v. Ambrose E., b. April 7, 1862; farmer on Upper Meadow; m. April 20,
    1887, Mary J., dau. of Robert Lackie. C. (1) Ada J., b. Feb. 2, 1888. (2)
    Roland L., b. Feb. 7, 1890. (3) Lilla M., b. Dec. 8, 1891. (4) Robert A.,
    b. March 28, 1894. (5) Mary A., b. May 8, 1899.
  vi. Lizzie B., b. Dec. 5, 1863; m. July 23, 1889, Lincoln A. Somers, of Barnet;
    res. Boston. C., Ernest R., b. March 15, 1896.
  vii. Carrie J., b. Aug. 11, 1865; m. March 12, 1889, Norman F. Garland of
    Barnstead, N. H.; res., Roxbury, Mass. C., (1) Earl N., b. Oct. 11, 1890.
    (2) Clarence H., b. April 19, 1892. (3) Elwin L., b. Jan. 22, 1896.
  viii. Cora E., b. May 16, 1867.
  ix. Mary M., b. Sept. 20, 1870.

7 JOHN RENFREW, b. Nov. 30, 1827; farmer and carpenter; lived some years
    where Thomas Kasson now lives at the Lime Kiln; res. South Ryegate,
    m. Nov. 28, 1850, Nancy Melissa Page, (b. April 11, 1832).
  Children:
  i. Ella Melissa, b. Clinton, Mass., June 22, 1851; m. Dec. 9, 1869, A. J.
    Whitcher, q. y.
  ii. Edgar Page, b. Newbury, Feb. 8, 1857; m. Nov. 27, 1878, Lucy H. Meader;
    d. Jan 26, 1883.
  iii. Wilbur Albert, b. Newbury, July 5, 1860; m. Nov. 28, 1883, Nettie M.
    Carpenter; d. St. Johnsbury, Jan. 11, 1897.
  iv. Edna Betsey, b. Newbury, June 23, 1863; m. Dec. 27, 1883, William H.
    Goodfellow.
  v. William Olin, b. Newbury, Feb. 26, 1866; teller in Merchants National
    Bank, Manchester, N. H.
  vi. Hattie Maria, b. Newbury, April 2, 1868.
  vii. Lora Belle, b. Ryegate, Jan. 8, 1876; m. Jan. 2, 1900, Rev. W. I. Todd,
    formerly of Groton.

McINDOE.

I. JOHN, b. in Scotland; came from the parish of Claren. with his wife, whose
    maiden name was Janet Lowrie, and sons, John, Robert and James.

His wife, and son, John, d. in Philadelphia, and he m. there Mrs. Agnes Furguson. They came to Barnet in 1784, and settled at the head of what has since been called McIndoes Falls, where he cleared a farm, and built a framed house and barn. He was a very hard-working man, but became almost helpless from rheumatism in old age. He d. in 1806, and his son, Robert d. in 1805. His wife d. in 1819, at the home of her son, Alexander Furguson, in Lyman, N. H.

II. JAMES, b. in Scotland 1782, was, after the death of his father, the only male in this part of the country bearing the name of McIndoe. Lived on the homestead till 1822, when he rem. to this town and bought of Dea. John Buxton, the "Paul Ford farm" at West Newbury, where he d. Oct. 28, 1844. He m. November. 1810, Abigail, dau. John and Elizabeth (Rich) Baker, (b. Thetford, April 17, 1792; d. May 15, 1852). Richard Wallace, who swam Lake Champlain in November, 1777, m. her mother's sister, Elizabeth Rich. From the age of 4 to 14 she lived in the family of John Way of Barnet.
        Children:
1   i.   John B. W., b. Jan. 11, 1812; d. June, 1870.
    ii.   Robert, b. Barnet, Dec. 25, 1813; learned the cabinet trade with Michael Carleton of Haverhill, and there made the organ which was formerly in the Union Meeting House. He rem. to Nashville, Tenn., and became a manufacturer of pianos. He d. un-m. Feb. 10, 1839.
   iii.   Eliza, b. Barnet, Jan. 21, 1816; m. March 4, 1838, Calvin S. Waterman of Fairlee, who d. June 6, 1854. She d. Dec. 31, 1880. C., four sons, two daus., all dead, except James E. Waterman, of South Framingham, Mass., and Ellen M. Yerrington of Cambridge, Mass., a music teacher.
2   iv.   Lyman J., b. Jan. 17, 1819.
    v.   Lavinia Sophia, b. Barnet, July 8, 1821; teacher; m. June, 1841; d. April 3, 1846. C., (1) George Robert, d. y. (2) Mary Sophia, graduated Newbury Seminary, 1868; m. March 30, 1871, Albert H. Young, of Foster, R. I.; d. Aug. 3, 1895. Three c.
   vi.   David, b. Newbury, April 26, 1824; educated Newbury Seminary and Biblical Institute; teacher; licensed to preach, 1849; joined the New Hampshire Methodist Episcopal Conference, May, 1857; preacher in that conference and in Wisconsin, 1854–63; returned to Vermont and was connected with the "Vermont Journal" and "Aurora of the Valley," residing in Newbury till 1868. He m. Dec. 31, 1850, Harriet S. Youngman, No c. He d. Windsor, Feb. 4, 1879.
3 vii.   George, b. March 4, 1828.
   viii. Laura Ann, b. Dec. 17, 1831; d. June 21, 1889.

1 JOHN BAKER WAY, b. Barnet, Jan. 11, 1812; farmer on the homestead at West Newbury, also purchasing the Boyce farm. He was a very hard-working man. He m. June 10, 1852, Frances Jane, dau. Hugh and Jane Somers, of Barnet. He d. June, 1870. She res. in Belleview, Fla.
        Children, all b. Newbury.
    i.   Charlotte Lavinia, b. June 1, 1853; graduated at Montpelier Methodist Seminary; teacher in California 12 years; joined the Salvation Army, and is a very successful worker on the Pacific coast, Colorado, Wyoming and New Mexico.
    ii.   Emily Jane, b. June 1, 1855; compositor in the Vermont Journal office, Windsor, and a leading member of the church and Christian Endeavor Society.
   iii.   John Franklin, b. Feb. 11, 1860; went to Florida and d. Feb. 19, 1885.
    iv.   Mary Abbie, b. Oct. 27, 1862; m. Frank M. Ramsdell, of Barnet, Oct. 8, 1881; rem. to Florida, and d. Dec. 5, 1888. C., Augusta, b. Feb. 16, 1888.

2 LYMAN JAMES, b. Barnet, Jan. 17, 1819; learned the printer's trade in the office of the Democratic Republican at Haverhill; worked at the trade till 1844, when he opened a printing office at Newbury, where he printed many Sunday School books for Rev. Orange Scott. Began March 3, 1848, the

publication of the "Aurora of the Valley," issuing it for two years in quarto form, as a semi-monthly, then changing it to a weekly. Mr. McIndoe prospered, and in 1856 he purchased a paper at Bradford, which he published as the "Orange County Journal." In 1857, he bought the entire establishment of the "Vermont Journal" at Windsor, and devoted to it the best years of his life. The "Aurora" was continued for several years as a separate paper, being printed at the Vermont Journal office. In 1863, he became proprietor of the "Vermont Chronicle," which he published in connection with the Vermont Journal till death, Dec. 24, 1873. He m. 1st, Feb. 24, 1846, Lucia Kent Porter, of East Lyman, N. H., who d. Feb. 8, 1854, leaving one son. He m. 2d, Abbie Blake Locke of East Lyman.

    Children, one by 1st marriage, and four by 2d:

    i. Robert Harrison, b. Newbury, March 22, 1849; d. San Francisco, Cal., June 24, 1893.

    ii. Lucia Abbie, b. Newbury, Aug. 24, 1859.

4 iii. Clara Alice, b. Aug. 24, 1859.

    iv. Abbie, b. Windsor, Feb. 2; d. March 17, 1868.

    v. Florinda, b. Windsor, July 9, 1869; m. Oct. 8, 1893, Ernest I. Morgan, an attorney of Worcester, Mass.

3 GEORGE, b. Newbury, March 4, 1828; educated at Newbury Seminary; was traveling agent for the "Aurora of the Valley," and other papers in Vermont and Massachusetts, also agent for the sale of mowing machines. He m. March 16, 1870, Cedelia B. Griswold; bought the homestead at West Newbury; rem. March, 1880, to the Waterman place in Fairlee, where he has since res.

    Children, the four eldest b. Newbury:

    i. George James, b. July 17, 1871; fitted for college at Thetford Academy; graduated Dartmouth College, 1895; Thayer School of Civil Engineering, 1896; is with the Hastings Pavement Co., New York City. He m. Jan. 26, 1899, Arlina M. Simonds of Thetford.

    ii. Eliza Ardella, b. April 13, 1875; m. Oct. 18, 1892, W. H. Tarbox, of Keene, N. H.; a jeweler; res. in California till 1896; since then in Vermont. C., (1) Herbert, b. Santa Rosa, Cal., Dec. 25, 1893. (2) Cedelia T., b. Santa Barbara, Cal., May 25, 1896.

    iii. David Hiram, b. March 5, 1875; farmer in Fairlee; m. Dec. 9, 1896, M. Ada Kelley. C., Florence Ada, b. April 10, 1898.

    iv. Ada Lavinia, b. March 3, 1878; teacher; graduated Thetford Academy, 1896.

    v. Lyman H., b. April 25, 1880; d. June 7, 1881.

    vi. John G., b. Jan. 5, 1886.

    vii. Mary Alice, b. Dec. 9, 1888.

4 CLARA ALICE[2], (Lyman J.,[1]) b. Newbury, Aug. 24, 1859; m. Dec. 31, 1878, Col. Marsh O. Perkins of Windsor, who became editor of the Vermont Journal, a position which he still retains.

    Children:

    i. Locke McIndoe, b. Nov. 20, 1879.

    ii. Gail Giddings, b. Aug. 4, 1882.

    iii. Margaret Eloise, b. Sept. 9, 1889.

    iv. Marion Florinda, b. Sept. 9, 1889.

    v. Herbert Marsh, b. Jan. 19, 1891.

    vi. Katherine Lucie, b. May 24, 1898.

McKEITH.

THOMAS, b. Erskine, Scotland, Oct. 14, 1756. He came to Ryegate in 1775, and served several terms in the Revolutionary war. Later he rem. to Currier hill in Topsham, about 1783. That part of Topsham was then claimed by Newbury. He was an elder in Rev. David Goodwillie's church in Ryegate, and was generally called Dea. McKeith. He was a man of great worth of character. He m. in 1778, Sarah, dau. of John Haseltine,

of Newbury, (b. Haverhill, Mass., Oct. 19, 1757; d. Topsham, Jan. 12, 1825). He d. in Topsham, May 17, 1823.
Children:
i. Pearl or Margaret, b. Ryegate, Nov. 30, 1779; m. in Newbury, May 8, 1800, Joseph Rogers, and settled in Topsham.
ii. Sarah, b. Ryegate, Sept. 6, 1781; d. Topsham, June 13, 1810.
iii. Mary, b. Topsham, (the first c. born there), Oct. 1, 1783; m. April 24, 1800, Caleb Wilson.
iv. Betsey, b. Topsham, April 16, 1786; m. Moses Wallace, q. v.
v. Catherine, b. Topsham, April 5, 1788; m. Peter Martin, q. v.; d. Piermont April 24, 1871.
1 vi. Duncan, b. March 9, 1790; d. Aug. 29, 1864.
vii. Thomas. b. June 21, 1795; d. at Peacham, May 31, 1827.
viii. John, b. Dec. 28, 1797; d. July 31, 1817.

6 DUNCAN, b. Topsham, March 9, 1790; farmer on the homestead. until his 2d marriage, when he rem. to his wife's farm at the Ox-bow. He was a very genial man. with an inexhaustible fund of Scotch stories. He m. 1st, Nov. 12, 1812, Mary Page, who d. in. Topsham, Oct. 1, 1847, aged 63. He m. 2d,   Elinor S., widow of Frank P. Johnson. He d. Newbury, Aug. 29, 1864; buried in Topsham.
Children, all by 1st marriage, in Topsham:
i. Sarah G., b. May 26, 1812; d. Feb. 9, 1816.
ii. Clarissa, b. March 10, 1815; m. April 2, 1835, Bagley Currier; d. March 31, 1883, at Northampton, Mass.
iii. Mary J., b. Jan. 31, 1817; m. Aug. 22, 1839, Ethan S. Brock; d. Piermont, Aug. 21, 1893.
iv. Harriet O., b. April 22, 1819; d. May 12, 1820.
v. Catherine, b. Feb. 16, 1822; m. George W. Corliss; d. Newbury, March 2, 1858.

McKINSTRY.

DR. NATHAN was a son of William McKinstry, who was b. in Carrickfergus, Ireland, of Scotch parentage, in 1772. He came to Southbridge, Mass., 1740 or '41· and m. in 1751, Mary Morse. Nathan was the youngest of their 13 c. He studied medicine, and settled in Newbury, not far from 1796, his office being in the southwest front room of the Col. Johnson house at the Ox-bow. He was thoroughly equipped for his profession, as it was in those days, had a very large practice, and usually had several students studying with him. He was well read, a brilliant talker, and of a genial, kindly temper. Dr. McKinstry never m., and d. Feb. 6, 1815, aged 43. Upon his gravestone at the Ox-bow are these lines:

> In-urned beneath lies no poor worthless quack,
> But the dear ashes of good Dr. Mc,—
> Whose talents, honors, virtues, could not save
> His generous bosom from an early grave."

This epitaph is said to have been written by Dr. McNab.

*McKINSTRY.

PAUL, b. at Bethel, 1807, rem. to Newbury, 1854, buying the house now owned by G. B. Barnett. He came here to educate his family of seven c. at the Seminary, remaining until his youngest dau., Ellen M., graduated in the class of 186–. Rem. to Northfield, 1866, to Winnebago City, Minn.,1869, d. at the last named place in 1890, aged 83 years. Harriet, his wife, b. Royalton and d. at Winnebago City, Minn., as the result of a mistep, breaking a limb. She was called "mother" by the city and was honored

---

*By A. P. McKinstry.

at her burial by the hanging of crape, and the closing of every business house in the city. She was mistress of her own house, walking over two miles making sick calls on the day that closed her active life, aged 87 years.

Children, all b. in Bethel:

i. Alvin L., 1835; enlisted in 12th Vermont Volunteer Infantry, serving the full time of enlistment. He m. Laura Burroughs of Newbury; d. at Rochester, Minn., in 1867 and was buried at Newbury. He had one dau., Harriet L., living in Boston. Mass.

ii. Clara L., m. Alonzo P. Hatch of the New Hampshire M. E. Conference, later being transferred to the Rock River, Illinois, Conference, and now living at Oregon, Ill. Her husband d. Sept. 1899. Six c., living, George, Harriet, Winnifred, Florence, Alice and Paul.

iii. Alice, m. Josiah F. Winship of Ipswich, N. H.; rem. to Winnebago City, Minn., 1866; d. in 1870. Two c., twins, Fred W., and Pauline A.

iv. Henry, b. 1841; enlisted in the 12th Vermont Volunteer Infantry, serving the full time of enlistment. He m. Alice D. Packer; moved to Syracuse, N. Y., 1868; to Winnebago City, Minn, 1872, and remaining 24 years, and now lives at Worcester, Mass. Two c., Helen May, and Arthur Packer.

v. Azro P., b. July 30, 1844; attended school at Newbury from 1855 to 1860, then apprenticed himself to E. C. Stocker to serve three years at the harness trade for the sum of $30, $40 and $50 for each year. In 1862 he received permission from Mr. Stocker to enlist in Co. G., (Capt. Damon), 10th Vermont Volunteer Infantry—agreeing, if alive at the end of the war, to return and fill out his contract. He was discharged at Burlington, July 1, 1865, returning as agreed upon to Mr. Stocker's shop and remaining until 1867. He m. Lauribel, dau. Oliver B. Rogers, Jan. 4, 1867; went into the harness business in Northfield for two years; rem. to a farm in Bradford in 1868; to Minnesota in 1870, engaging in general farming and dairying. He represented Minnesota at the New Orleans Centennial Exposition, winning the Grand Sweepstakes prize on butter for his state. Also at the World's Fair at Chicago, again bringing the dairy interests of the state into special prominence, and at this writing is employed by "The National Dairy Union" in its fight against "Oleomargarine colored in semblance of butter." He has four c., Harry C., Ned G., Florence L., Mabel H. Mr. McKinstry was killed Sept. 12, 1900, by being thrown from a sulky plow.

vi. Ellen M., graduated at Newbury Seminary in the class of 186—; m. as 2d wife, Josiah F. Winship of Winnebago City, Minn., 1872, and has one son living, Louis C.

vii. Laura, d. 1855.

McLEOD.

ALEXANDER, of Glasgow, Scotland; m. about 1830, Marian Pendre. They had six sons, James, William. Robert, Alexander, John and Magnus.

ROBERT, b. in Glasgow, Oct. 8, 1831; came to America in 1849 and worked at his trade, which was that of a machinist, in New York city. Went to Australia, 1852, and was m. at Balarat, Australia, 1854, to Margaret, dau. of Andrew Wylie. She was b. in Paisley, Scotland, Feb. 14, 1832; came to America in 1851, lived with her brother, Andrew, in Danville a few years, when these with their sister, Jessie, (now Mrs. Cole), went to Australia. The McLeods returned to America in 1857, and settled on the Robert Renfrew farm, now owned by Henry Whitcher. No one lives there now. They rem. to Burlington, Kan., in the early '80s· She d. Denver, Col., June 1, 1901.

Children:

i. Marian Pendre, b. Balarat, Aus., May 23, 1855. Came to Newbury with her parents and went after 1880 to Leadville, Col., to teach, but returned east and taught some years in Bradford and Woodsville. She m. in Newbury, Oct. 1893, Wm. Harvey Gray, a native of Ryegate; res. Burlington, Kan. C., (1) Matthew R., b. Dec. 9, 1892. (2) Harvey D., b. June 13, 1898.

ii. Lillian B., b. on board the ship "Morning Star," while coming round Cape

Horn, March 12, 1857. Teacher; m. 1885, Cyrus Snow, res. Texas. C.,
Wylie M., Walter D., Marian G., Annie J., Robert S., and Helen C.
iii. Robert Douglass, b. Newbury, Oct. 9, 1858; graduated at University of
Michigan, 1888; lawyer in Leadville, Col., and City Attorney. He m. Jan.
1900, Helen T. Stebbins of Leadville.
iv. Andrew A., b. Newbury, Jan. 12, 1861; d. 1863.
v. Flora E., b. Newbury, Dec. 14, 1863. Teacher; m. 1896, Manfred Frazer of
Leadville, Col. One c., Margaret.
vi. Annie N., b. Newbury, Dec. 26, 1866. Music teacher in Burlington, Kan.
vii. John W., b. Sept. 2, 1869; d. in infancy.
viii. William N., b. Oct. 29, 1872; res. Chilicothe, Mo.

McNAB.

DR. JOHN, b. Glenarchay, Scotland, Jan. 24, 1784. His parents came to
Thornton, N. H., and thence to Barnet while he was still a child. He
graduated at Dartmouth Medical College, 1824, and came to Wells River
to practice before 1831, where he remained (there and at Barnet), where he
practiced till 1845, when he rem. to Woodsville. He was a skillful
physician, somewhat brusque in manner, and daring in operation. His
practice was extensive. His left arm was amputated because of a cancer
humor contracted in performing an operation. He was also a prominent
Mason. He d. Haverhill, (Woodsville), 1879, aged 94. He made a trip to
Boston, unattended, about ten days before he d. Four c. survived him:
Capt. John McNab, formerly of the U. S. Army; Mrs. J. G. Cheney, of
Woodsville; Mrs. Calvin Dewey, of McIndoes, and Mrs. N. M. Loomis, of
Charlestown, Mass.

MEADER.

SAMUEL came from Barrington, N. H. His mother's maiden name was Hill,
that of his wife was Ayer. The c. of Samuel were, Samuel, Daniel, Stephen
and one who m. a Lackie.

DANIEL was b. Oct. 21, 1782. He studied law, was admitted to the bar, and
practiced in small cases, during most of his life, also was a farmer, and
held various town offices. He lived many years on the farm of the late
James Ross, building that house. Several of his c. are buried on that farm.
Later, he rem. to "Meader hill," near the town house. He was a very
large man, with a slow, peculiar utterance. He m. 1st, April 25, 1803,
Nancy, dau. Nathan Avery, (b. March 17, 1788; d. Feb. 23, 1861). He
m. 2d at 82 years of age, Mrs. Sarah (Burns) King. He d. in Newbury,
March 19, 1872.
Children:
i. Ann, (Nancy), b. Oct. 8, 1803; m. 1825, James R. Brown of Peacham; d. in
Illinois, July 4, 1839.
ii. Eliza, b. May 31, 1805; d. Oct. 7, 1828.
iii. Mary, b. May 4, 1807; d. Sept. 22, 1825.
iv. Ruth Hill, b. May 31, 1809; m. Jan. 1, 1833, William Brownhill, an
Englishman; d. Oak Grove, Ill., July 31, 1840. Four c.
v. Ensebia, b. June 3, 1811; d. Jan. 2, 1826.
vi. John Ayers, b. June 30, 1813; carpenter and farmer; he lived at Newbury
village most of his active life, and built a number of houses. He m. Dec. 7,
1843, Ann M., dau. Capt. Wm. Page, (b. Ryegate, March 22, 1816; d. at
the home of her adopted dau., Mrs. Paul Smith, at Monroe, N. H., Sept.
15, 1898). He d. March 6, 1897.
vii. Sarah A., b. April 21, 1815; m. Oct. 21, 1856, George A.   d.
viii. Nathan A., b. March 20, 1817; m. 1st, Oct. 16, 1836, Mary Ann Lamphere,
of Lyme, N. H. She d. at Claremont, and he m. 2d, 1854, Eliza, dau. of
Zadoc Sturdevant. Lives in Chester. Two c. by 1st m. lived in Newbury:
Martha, now Mrs. Smith, of Monroe, and Charles C., who lived with his

grandfather, served three years, 1861-64, in the 3d Vt., and went west after the war. He m. a Miss Harper.

ix. William Henry, b. May 1, 1819; farmer and carpenter. He served in the Union army; went west after the war, and is understood to have d. many years ago. He m. Jan. 8, 1840, Susan, dau. of Nathaniel McConnell, who d. March 19, 1863. C., (1) Mary, d. (2) Harriet. d. (3) Horace, who served in Co. D, 8th Vt., and dropped dead at New Orleans, March 25, 1863. (4) Frank, d. (5) Maria.

x. James, b. Feb. 24, 1821; d. Aug. 19, 1822.

xi. James Madison, b. Mar. 1823. He m. 1st in Bradford, 1844, Emily, dau. of ————Chapman of Haverhill, who d. in Claremont, N. H., March 22, 1850; 2d, in Bradford, Dec. 31, 1853, Olive Philbrick; no c. He was a private in Co. J., 1st Mich. Regiment of Engineers and Mechanics during the Civil War; d. at the Soldiers' Home, Michigan, Feb. 17, 1899.

xii. Robert F., b. April, 1825; d. June 17, 1848.

xiii. Mary Eliza, b. Nov. 29, 1826; d. Dec. 9, 1842.

xiv. Charles C., b. Oct. 31, 1830; served in the army during the Civil War.

MELLEN.

THOMAS, b. 1756, in Londonderry, N. H.; served in the "Lexington Alarm;" served also in the battle of Bunker Hill, being stationed at a very dangerous part of the rail fence. He also served in other campaigns, and in the battle of Bennington. His father, Charles Mellen, rem. with his family from Londonderry to Francestown, about 1772, with sons, Thomas, Robert and Charles, and two daus. He was somewhat prominent there for several years before his death which was in 1779. Thomas came to Newbury soon after the war, and lived at the Ox-bow for some time, but later cleared the farm where J. C. Leavitt now lives, near the town house, building that house, which is the oldest in that part of the town. Afterwards he lived where the road to Jefferson hill branches from the Lime-kiln road. His latest years were spent with his son, Robert, who lived where John Buchanan now does, and where he d. in his 97th year, the last survivor of the Revolutionary war, who had been a resident of this town. Few of the revolutionary soldiers who were buried in Newbury saw more service than Thomas Mellen, and the fact that he was one of the last survivors of the battle of Bennington, and retained a vivid recollection of that event to the end of his life, renders his narrative, given elsewhere in this volume, a pleasant memory. He was a very hard working man; in person he was below the medium height, very erect and active, and when past 80, still sang well, with a fine tenor voice. When he was 81, he made a sleigh with his own hands, in which, the next winter, he traveled to New Boston. N. H., alone, and from there with a nephew, to Boston, visiting the battlefield of Bunker Hill and the (then) unfinished monument. At the time when his narrative was taken down by Professor Butler, Mr. Mellen lived by himself in a small building of only one room, which was on the back side of what is now Mr. Buchanan's house, taking his meals with the family. The late Edward Miller of Ryegate, then a young man, taught school in "Scotch Hollow," boarding at Robert Mellen's. He said that the old veteran was a man of large information, who narrated, with clearness and precision, the events of his long and useful life. It was Mr. Miller's great regret, to the end of his own life, that he had not realized the value which would have accrued by the transmission in writing of these reminiscences. Thomas Mellen was admitted to the Cong. Ch., May 5, 1844. He m. about 1778, Janet McCollom, who d. Sept. 10, 1835, aged 75. He d. Jan. 21, 1853, and was buried at the Ox-bow. Many remember him as the only Revolutionary soldier they ever saw.

Children:
1 i. Esther, b. Jan. 14, 1780; d. April 14, 1867.
   ii. Betsey, m. Samuel Gibson, q. v.
   iii. Charles, b. Nov. 8, 1784. d. y.
2 iv. John, b. Dec. 19, 1786; d. July 17, 1881.
3 v. James, b. April 24, 1792.
   vi. Thomas, b. Oct. 5, 1794.
4 vii. Archibald, b. Jan. 31, 1797; d. Jan. 22, 1889.
5 viii. Robert, b. June 15, 1799.
   ix. Mary, b. July 31, 1803; d. April 4, 1830.

1 ESTHER, b. Jan. 14, 1780; m. in 1806 or 1807, Daniel Thomas Gregg. She was
   one of the earliest pupils at Haverhill Academy, boarding in the family of
   Col. Charles Johnston She d. April 14, 1867.
   Children:
   i. Jane Elizabeth, b. March 31, 1808; d. July 26, 1883.
   ii. Rowena, b. June 17, 1811; m. 1870, William Beard; d. Aug. 14, 1879.
   iii. John Harrison, b. Sept. 21, 1813; d. Feb. 5, 1895.
   iv. Maria Louisa, b. Nov. 25, 1815; m. in Boston, 1842, Thomas B. Delano,
        who d. May, 1880. She d. Aug. 5, 1884.
   v. Ann B., b. Oct. 13, 1818; d. Dec. 1, 1834.
   vi. Charlotte, b. June 26, 1821; teacher in the west. 1847-1884. The last 24
        years she had a school for young ladies in Chicago. She has furnished
        most of the Mellen family records.
   vii. Esther M., b. April 30, 1824; d. May 24, 1843.

2 JOHN, son of Thomas, b. Dec. 19, 1786. He went to Boston while young and
   learned the trade of cabinet maker. In the same business at Philadelphia.
   Joined a Militia Co., called the Philadelphia Blues, and served in the war
   of 1812 as fifer of that company. Soon after the war he went to Toronto,
   Canada, and worked as a builder. He m. 1831, the dau. of a friend from
   New York, a Mr. Hawley, who had taken up a large tract of land there.
   Later he returned to this country and settled at Oscoga, Mich.
   Children, all b. in Branford, Ontario:
   i. Nancy, b. 1836; now Mrs. Charles H. Tanner, of Aberdeen, Washington.
       Three sons, Eugene, Harold and Charles, the two latter in the lumber
       business in northern Michigan.
   ii. Thomas J., b. 1838; res. Massy Station on Georgian Bay. Served in the
        Civil war; was at Missionary Ridge; is m. and has five c., Edward, Walter,
        John, Florence and Mamie.
   iii Harriet, b. 1840; now Mrs. Samuel L. Bayley, of Wyoming, Ont.; has 12 c.
        One son, Thomas, in Vancouver, B. C., and John, private secretary to his
        uncle John at Duluth; three c. at home and seven other daus. m.
   iv. Sarah M., b. 1847; now Mrs. C. A. Fridlander, of Black River, Mich. One
        son, Charles M.   Mr. Fridlander served in the Union army from the fall
        of 1861 to the end of the war.
   v. John, b. 1849; res. Duluth, Minn. He is managing partner in the firm of
       Alger, Smith & Co., probably the largest lumbering concern in the country,
       operating in Michigan, Ontario and Minnesota.

3 JAMES, b. April 24, 1792; built the second house north of the town house. He
   m. Lucy Webber, June 2, 1819. He d. in Edgartown, Mass.
   Seven c., three are living, b. in Newbury:
   i. Augusta, b. 1824, now a widow; m. James Fisk; has one dau., who is m.
       and has three c.; res. Edgartown, Mass.
   ii. Mary, also a widow; m. Frank Brow; has three sons and two daus.
   iii. Amos, m. a Miss Ripley of Edgartown; both are d.; left two sons.
   iv. Helen, m. a Mr. Presby of Taunton; both d.; left two daus.
   v. Thomas, was master of a vessel during the Civil war; taken prisoner by a
       privateer and confined in Libby prison. When liberated he was a mere
       skeleton, and so broken that he has never been able to take care of himself.
       Is an inmate of the Sailor's Snug Harbor at Chelsea, Mass.

4 ARCHIBALD, b. Newbury, Jan. 31, 1797. He was for some years a teacher, then
   merchant, but in the latter years of his long life was trial justice at
   Edgartown. He was m. to Sarah——— Dec. 15, 1825, by Rev. Mr.

Thaxter, who had been a chaplain in the Revolutionary war, and lived to offer prayer at the laying of the corner stone of Bunker Hill monument. She was b. Oct. 22, 1801; d. Nov. 5, 1852. He d. at Edgartown, Mass., Jan. 22, 1889.

Children:

i. Susan M., b. Sept. 30, 1826; m. June 13, 1853, George Mayhew, (b. Nov. 23, 1822; d. Dec. 1, 1861); two c., son and dau.

ii. Thomas, b. Sept. 7, 1827; d. March 7, 1830.

iii. Archibald, b. June 25, 1830. He became a sailor, and while still young, was first mate on a whaling voyage. In 1858, he sailed from New Bedford as master of the brig "Junior," and d. before the end of the voyage, 1858. He was a very promising young man.

iv. Jane, b. May 5, 1832.

v. Thomas, b. Oct. 8, 1834, sailor. He was m. Aug. 22, 1862, to Katherine J. Courtney; ten weeks later he sailed as master of the ship, Levi Starbuck, of New Bedford. On the fifth day out they encountered the Confederate steamer, Alabama, Nov. 2, 1862, and after a chase of eight hours they were obliged to surrender. The officers were taken on board the Alabama and put in irons; their ship after being plundered was burned. After 18 days of suffering they were landed at Fort de France, Island of Martinique, whence he received free passage to St. Thomas. From there he worked his passage to New York on an English brig, having been absent two months. Eight months later he sailed again and continued in the business till 1889, having followed the sea for forty-three years. He has a son and a dau.

5 ROBERT, b. June 15, 1799; farmer in Newbury; m. a dau. of John George of Topsham, who d. at Sparta, Wis. He d.

Children:

i. Martha, a teacher; m. a Mr. Newberry; res. at Sparta, Wis., and d. before her mother.

ii. Eliza Jane, m. James Divoll of Topsham, and went to California.

MERRILL.

So many families in this vicinity are of Merrill ancestry, that the following account of early members of the family, prepared by Rev. J. L. Merrill, will be of interest:

I. NATHANIEL, with his brother John, emigrated from England as early as 1633. He first settled in Ipswich, Mass., but rem. to Newbury, in that state, in 1634, or the following year. He m., probably in England, Susanna Willerton. She d., the widow Jordan, Jan. 12, 1672. He was of Huguenot descent, and the original spelling of the name was Merle. As his ancestors fled from France because of their fidelity to the reformed faith, they naturally cast in their lot with the Puritans of England. This family in France are still Huguenots, the most distinguished member of recent years being Merle D'Aubigne, the historian. As the patronymic Merle means blackbird, the earliest generations of the family in that country, used a seal on which is displayed three blackbirds. He d. March 16, 1654–55.

II. NATHANIEL, 3d c. of the emigrant, b. 1638; m. Joan Kinney; was left by will, heir to the farm of his father.

III. NATHANIEL, his oldest son, rem. to Haverhill, Mass.

IV. JOSEPH, b. Haverhill, July 3, 1709; m. Sept. 23, 1731, Ruth Corliss, a descendant of that George Corliss, ancestor of so many families in this valley.

Children:

i. Joseph, d. y.

ii. Mehetabel, d. un-m.

iii. Joseph, lived in Bethel, Me.

iv. Benjamin.

v. Elizabeth.
vi. Ruth, b. March 15, 1743; m. Jesse Wilson of Pelham. Their son, Nathaniel Wilson, came to Haverhill, N. H., in 1801.
vii. John, m. Ruth Cleveland and lived in Bath, N. H.
viii. Abigail, m. 1st, a Mr. Poole, who was drowned in the Connecticut river at the Narrows, after which she m. as 2d wife, March 26, 1772, Col. Thomas Johnson, and d. Dec. 2, 1774.
1 ix. Nathaniel, b. March 2, 1747.

1 NATHANIEL, son of Joseph and Ruth (Corliss) Merrill, b. March 2, 1747; m. Sarah, dau. Col. John Hazen, (published June 22, 1771, "Nathaniel Merrill of Bath and Sarah Hazen." Haverhill town records), b. 1754; d. Feb. 7, 1819. He was first in Bath about 1770, then in Newbury, of which he was a grantee, his farm being that one long owned by Capt. Moses Swasey, and later by his son, Dea. George Swasey, and now for many years, by James Lang. His house was near the east end of the Ox-bow, near the river. He rem. He rem. to Haverhill, and in old age to Piermont, dying in the house built by Capt. Uriah Stone on Moose Meadow, May 3, 1825, and is buried in the old burial ground on the river road, in that town. He was in Capt. Thos. Johnson's Co. of Minute Men, 1775. First Lieutenant in Capt. John G. Bayley's Co. Guarding and scouting, April, 1777, to May, 1779, one month, 14 days. First Lieutenant in Capt. Frye Bayley's Co., which marched to Saratoga, Sept. 23 to Oct. 27, 1777. He was also Major in the militia, and a very active and busy man of strong common sense, an invaluable man in a new community. He was noted for his strong voice, a peculiarity inherited by many of his descendants. Major Merrill and Capt. Joshua Hale could converse when a mile apart with perfect ease. He was collector of taxes in Newbury in 1776, and his name is on the muster roll as of this town in 1778. Town representative from Haverhill, 1794, '95· '96 and 1806.
Children, births of the first 8 from Haverhill town records. Deaths in part from the Hibbard family Bible.
i. Sarah, b. May 5, 1772; m. Col. Aaron Hibbard of Bath, q. v.; d. Feb. 24, 1842.
ii. Elizabeth, b. Newbury, March 3, 1774; m. Capt. Moses Swasey of Newbury, q. v.; d. Feb. 4, 1855.
iii. Abigail, b. Jan. 29, 1776; d. April 2, 1778.
iv. Mary (Polly), b. March 16, 1778; m. Nathaniel Runnels of Piermont; d. Oct. 7, 1838.
v. Anna (Nancy), b. Feb. 7, 1780; m. Obadiah Swasey of Haverhill; d. Dec. 6, 1850.
vi. Abigail, b. June 16, 1782; d. April 2, 1818.
vii. Charlotte, b. July 15, 1784; m. Isaac Pearsons of Haverhill; d. Aug. 19, 1817.
viii. Lucinda, b. Jan. 20, 1787; m. Abner Bayley of Newbury; d. Dec. 15, 1809.
ix. Ruth, b. 1789; m. James Morse of Corinth; d. September, 1854.
x. Hannah, b. 1789, (twin to Ruth), m. Gov. John Page of Haverhill, and had nine c. She d. Feb. 13, 1855.
xi. Mehetabel, b. 1792; m. Thomas Morse; d. March 22, 1812.
xii. Nathaniel, b. 1795; d. April 29, 1817.
xiii. Louisa, b. 1797; m. Samuel Page of Haverhill; d. Dec. 23, 1821.
Another Merrill family has the same emigrant ancestor—Nathaniel of England and Newbury, Mass.

I. NATHANIEL.

II. ABEL, b. 1643-4.

III. ABEL, b. 1671; m. Sarah Hazzleton.

IV. ABEL, b. 1697, settled in Atkinson, N. H., where his son John became one of the earliest deacons of the Cong. Ch. Two sons of Abel Merrill, Stevens and Joshua, settled in Warren, N. H., and three of his grandsons followed their uncles to Warren. Nathaniel and Samuel, sons of Rev. Nathaniel Merrill of Boscawen, and Abel, son of Dea. John Merrill of Atkinson. Abel m. Tamar, dau. of Benjamin Kimball, a Captain in

REV. JOHN L. MERRILL.

DEA. FREEMAN KEYES.

the Continental army. Thirteen c. were b. to them in Warren. Joshua, son ot Dea. John Merrill of Atkinson, emigrated to Corinth. He m. Dorcas Richardson of Lyndeborough, N. H., and to them were b. 16 c. Benjamin and John, eldest sons, respectively, of Abel and Joshua, were both merchants, the first in Haverhill, N. H., and the second in Corinth. Harriet, dau. of John Merrill of Corinth, m. Hon. Henry W. Bailey of Newbury. Benjamin Merrill of Haverhill was succeeded in his business at the Corner by his eldest son, Dea. Abel Kimball Merrill; for the family of the latter, see later. George Alfred Merrill, at one time superintendent of the Passumpsic R. R., and afterward of the Rutland R. R., was a great grandson of Stevens Merrill, son of Abel, who settled in Warren. Still another numerous race claims descent from the same emigrant. Roger Merrill, a cousin of the first Abel, spoken of in this paragraph, descended from Nathaniel through his son Abel, and grandson Abel, was b. March 10, 1713, and m. Mary, dau. of Ezekiel Hale. He was a deacon in the Cong. Ch., West Newbury, Mass. His dau., Hannah, b. July 7, 1733, m. Ebenezer White, (q. v.), an early settler of this town. Dea. Abel Merrill of Haverhill, a prominent business man of that town, was twice m., his wives being sisters, daus. of John Leverett of Windsor and descendants of Gov. John Leverett of Massachusetts.
Children:
i. John Leverett, b. Haverhill, May 29, 1833; graduated Dartmouth College, 1856; Princeton Theological Seminary, 1859; ordained and installed pastor of a Presbyterian church, at Chanceford, Penn., Oct. 31, 1860; dismissed November, 1865; principal of the combined high schools of Lancaster, Penn., till April, 1866; pastor of the Cong. Ch. at Acworth, N. H., 1866-1870; Marlborough, N. H., 1871-1887; Rindge, N. H., 1887-1891; Newbury, Aug. 2, 1891, to Aug. 2, 1901; published in 1869, a History of Acworth, N. H. Mr. Merrill has also rendered most valuable assistance in the preparation of this history. He m. Sept. 11, 1860, Mary L., dau. of John A. and Nancy (Clarkson) Murphy of Chanceford, Penn. At the end of ten years of most faithful service, Mr. Merrill resigned the pastorate here, to the great regret of the entire community. Advancing years and failing health compelled the change. He was the first president of the trustees of Tenney Memorial Library, and had freely given to it the fruits of his ripe experience. The editor of this volume desires to express, in behalf of himself and the town, his sense of obligation to him for his wise assistance and patient suggestion, in his work. He was succeeded, as president of the library trustees, by T. C. Keyes. Res. at Fitchburg, Mass. C., (1) Mary L., b. June 18, 1862; teacher. (2) Annie C., b. Dec. 27, 1867; d. July 8, 1868. (3) Charles C., b. March 3, 1872; graduated Dartmouth College, 189-; Yale Theological Seminary, 189-; ordained pastor of Cong. Ch., Steubenville, O., 189-.
ii. Benjamin, b. March 25, 1836; graduated Dartmouth College, (scientific department), 1858; Princeton Theological Seminary, 1864; ordained by Carlisle Presbytery, June 7, 1864: pastor, Barton, Md., 1864-66; Pembroke, N. H., 1866-70; Ausable Forks, N. Y., 1870-83; Swanzey, N. H., Oct. 1882, till d., Nov. 16, 1888. Survived by wife and a son.
iii. Charles H., b. 1845; graduated Dartmouth College, and Andover Theological Seminary; pastor at Monkato, Minn.; West Brattleboro, 14 years, now secretary of the Vermont Domestic Missionary Society. He m. Laura B., dau. of Daniel Merrill of Haverhill, and Washington, D. C.; res. St. Johnsbury. He received the degree of D. D. from Dartmouth College, 1901.

MESERVE or MESERVEY.

SAMUEL, of Marblehead, Mass., m. Dec. 8, 1768, Elizabeth Bowden. He d. leaving one son, Samuel, and his widow, m. 2d, William Peach, Sr., of Marblehead and Newbury. Their son, Samuel, m. Feb. 13, 1791, Ann, dau. of Nathaniel and Anna (Larkin) Pearce, (baptized Dec. 9, 1770), his wife and the wife of William Peach, Jr., being sisters. They came to

Newbury about 1800. He was killed in a sawmill, and she d. Jan. 15, 1854, aged 84. Buried at the town house.
Children:
i. Nancy, m. Edward Rollins, q. v.; d. Aug. 14, 1869.
ii. Samuel, drowned in Connecticut river in 1823.
iii. Betsey, m. William Lindsey; d. Aug. 12, 1844, aged 43.
1 iv. Jonas, b. Aug. 4, 1799; d. April 7, 1869.
v. Amy, b. 1802; m. Justin Lindsey; d. Oct. 31, 1887, aged 84.
2 vi. William, b. 1803; d. Nov. 20, 1851.

1 JONAS, b. Aug. 4, 1799; farmer in Newbury; deacon in 1st Ch., 1853, till death; m. in Haverhill, Jan. 19, 1825, Jane Chapman, (b. Feb. 29, 1804; d. March 9, 1865). He d. April 7, 1869.
Children:
i. Elizabeth, b. Haverhill, June 24, 1826; m. Aug. 28, 1848, Joseph Slocomb, who d. Sept. 11, 1880. C., (1) Clara J., b. April 6, 1850. (2) Louis A., b. April 24, 1853. (3) Elmer E., b. June 8, 1861.
ii. Grant Powers, b. June 29, 1829; m. 1st, May 28, 1854, Emily Martin, who d. Jan. 8, 1886, aged 54 years, 8 months. He m. 2d, Addie Hook, who d. Jan. 3, 1898. He d. March 14, 1897, at Penacook, N. H., where he had res. some years.
iii. George P., b. May 31, 1831; carpenter; deacon in 1st Ch., Easthampton, till death. He m. May 28, 1854, Laura Martin, sister to the 1st wife of his brother, Grant, b. Dec. 7, 1832. He d. Easthampton, Mass., April 25, 1895. C., (1) Henry S., b. 1855. (2) Clara A. (3) Addie, b. January, 1860; d. Jan. 1, 1861.
iv. Henry J., b. Aug. 31, 1833; farmer in Newbury; m. July, 12, 1865, Mary A. Cummings, of Plymouth, N. H., (b. Plymouth, April 14, 1843). He d. Oct. 15, 1892. C., (1) Jennie May, b. Aug. 16, 1867; d. July 23, 1881. (2) William H., b. Feb. 9, 1870; station agent at Haverhill, now at Penacook, N. H.; m. April 12, 1891, —————— Barber. (3) George D., b. May 8, 1872.
v. William B., b. Oct. 9, 1835; d. Oct. 21, 1855.
vi. Nancy J., b. Jan. 15, 1838; m. Feb. 1, 1866, James Pride. C., Lillie Estelle, b. Dec. 23, 1866; d. June 12, 1887.
vii. Joseph Gibbs, b. April 6, 1840; m. Aug. 5, 1867, Kate J. Pray; res. in Maine. No c.

2 WILLIAM, b. 1803; farmer. He m. Susan C., dau. of Samuel Thompson, (b. Feb. 1813; d. Oct. 2, 1871). He d. Nov. 20, 1851.
Children:
i. Lois A., d. Dec. 21, 1846, aged 12 years, 8 months.
ii. Amos, a young man highly esteemed. He enlisted in Co. C., 3d Vt. Volunteers, for three years, and was killed in a skirmish at Lewinsville, Va., Sept. 11, 1861. His remains were brought home and buried at the town house cemetery, and he was the only soldier from Newbury killed in battle whose remains were brought back.
iii. Robert M., b. in Newbury, Jan. 16, 1839. Served in the Civil war in Co. D., 1st Vt., for three months, and as Sergeant in Co. H., 12th Vt., for nine months. He had charge of the Freeman Keyes farm in Newbury, and later the Henry Keyes farm in Haverhill, many years. He now owns and res. upon the farm which was for 112 years owned by Col. Jacob Kent, his son and grandsons. He m. 1st, March 19, 1872, Margaret G., dau. of Andrew and Christian G. Dunnett, who d. June 3, 1890, aged 39. (1) William Andrew, b. May 7, 1873; educated at Dartmouth College; now in the west. (2) Nettie May, who d. March 9, 1879, aged 2 years, 2 months. (3) Frank Robert, b. June 21, 1880. (4) Milo Alexander, b. Sept. 6, 1884; m. 2d, Eva Preston, dau. of Stephen and Ella Farrar, who d. Nov. 24, 1894, aged 27 years, 5 months.
iv. William A., marble worker, learning his trade of Mr. Jenkins of Bradford; rem. to New York state, and d. at Bath, N. Y., in September, 1892; was m.
v. Mary Jane, teacher; d. in Haverhill, March 6, 1880, aged 35 years.
vi. Wallace L., res. in Lakeville, N. Y.

METCALF.

EPHRAIM, b. in England, in the year 1770; emigrated to America some twenty years later, and settled on a farm in Newbury, near the northwest corner of Bradford, and was one of the first settlers in that region, clearing the land and building the buildings on the farm that still bears his name. His wife, Martha, d. in 1845, and he d. in 1858, leaving two sons, John and Burgess. Burgess continued on the homestead and m. Lucy Hall of Newbury, in 1819. They had three c., Ephraim, Olive and Isaac, the two latter dying young, while Ephraim continued on the farm with his parents. Mrs. Metcalf d. in 1860, and Burgess in 1880. Ephraim B. Metcalf m. Sophronia Avery of Topsham in 1854. Their c. were, Isaac J., C. H., Lucy, Fannie, John, Mary and Sarah. All died young except Isaac J., and Sarah, who m. James Clark of Bradford, while Isaac J. continues on the old farm with his mother.

MILLS.

This family originated in Argyleshire, Scotland, and were of the Scotch colony which came from the north of Ireland about 1725, and settled in Londonderry, N. H. With them came the McDuffies, McKeens, McGregors, McAllisters, and other well-known families. John and Robert Mills, brothers, came about 1720, or the next year. John settled in Haverhill, Mass., but after a few years rem. to Coleraine, in that state, where he was killed by the Indians. Robert settled in Chester, N. H. He was m. before coming to America. John, son of Robert, m. Susan Ferrin of Chester. Their c. were, John, Thomas, James and Mary. The last named John served in the French and Indian war, came early to Coös, and was a grantee of Haverhill, but settled in Newbury, his farm being that now owned by W. W. Brock, Jr. His wife was a daughter of Archibald McDuffie. He built not far from 1780, the house now known as the Davenport house at South Newbury. This house has been greatly altered, and was, back in the early '60s, a square-roofed house of large size. John Mills and his son, John, served as scouts in Capt John G. Bayley's Co. in the Revolutionary war, one month, each. John Mills (whether father or son is unknown) served as a corporal in Capt. Ezekiel Ladd's Co. of Bedel's regiment, from April 6, 1778, 11 months, 25 days. John Mills, Sr., was a carpenter, mechanical ingenuity being hereditary in that family. The date of his death is unknown. He was a member of the Presbyterian church at Chester; as witness, this certificate in the town records:

"Chester, Nov. 25, 1787. This may certify whom it may concern, that John Mills, son of Deacon John Mills, was in full communion in the Presbyterian church of Chester, and was brought up a Presbyterian. Witness my hand. Matthew Forsyth, Ruling Elder."

Both father and son were held in respect and filled many public offices. One of them was of the committee which built the "Old Meeting House" in 1788. The names of all the c. of John Mills, Sr., are not known, but the following marriages recorded on our town records are believed to be of his family: "Josiah Pratt and Mary Mills, Oct. 13, 1785. James Kent and Tamar Mills, Jan. 31, 1793. James Caruth and Molly Mills, Oct. 20, 1800. Archibald McDuffie Mills and Anna Aikin, Dec. 4, 1800. Samuel Hall and Sally Mills, Dec. 28, 1800." Another dau. m. John Orr of Ryegate. John Mills, Jr., was admitted to the church, Dec. 2, 1791, and his wife, May 5, 1793, and the following baptism of c. are reported: Nathan, May 5, 1793; Susanne, Sept. 25, 1796; Betsey, April 29, 1798; Mindwell, Sept. 8, 1799. He is said to have become one of the first settlers of Derby, but seems to have returned here, as the following inscriptions in the cemetery at the Ox-bow seem to indicate. "John Mills, d. March 21, 1833, aged 78. Elizabeth, his first wife, d. June 5, 1796, in her 44th year. Susanna, second wife, d. March 6, 1843, aged 84." Archibald McDuffie Mills settled on the homestead, where most of his c. were b., but later, exchanged his farm with Ben Porter for wild land in Topsham, whence he rem. He built the house called the John Johnson

house, just below the Bradford line, before he went to Topsham, and lived
there some years. He was b. Sept. 13, 1775, and his wife, Anna Aikin,
was b. April 16, 1780.

Children of Archibald and Anna Mills.   (Dates of their births from Topsham
      town records).

.   William, b. Nov. 7, 1802; m. Aug. 27, 1829, Esther, dau. of Adam Dickey.
ii.   Jacob, b. March 30, 1805; m. Jan. 22, 1829, Marion Dickey.
iii.   Archibald, b. March 4, 1807; m. Jan. 8, 1832, Sarah Ann, dau. of Samuel
      Eastman; d. 1894.
iv.   Calvin, b. June 26, 1809; m. Mary Forsyth; d. March 22, 1891.
v.   Caroline, b. June 9, 1813; m. a Mr. Dickey.
vi.   Horace, b. Nov. 30, 1815; m. Jane Batchelder.
vii.   Joseph, b. March 6, 1817; m. 2d, Nancy Felch.
yiii.   John, b. March 5, 1820; d. y.
ix.   Hiram, b. March 1824; m. Jane Forsyth.

The Mills brothers were all carpenters of rare skill and they probably erected
      more buildings in this vicinity than any equal number of men. This
      family has always been prominent in Topsham.

MINARD.

JOHN H., son of Amos and Betsey (Hopkins) Minard, b. Tunbridge, May 25,
      1817; lived in Duxbury, Waterbury and Bradford, coming to West
      Newbury in 1877. He m. in Duxbury, Feb. 26, 1843, Roxalana, dau. of
      Amos and Mary (Fuller) Moore, (b. Andover, N. H., March 10, 1826; d.
      Jan. 14, 1900).
   Children:
i.   Edwin Abbey, b. Duxbury, Apr. 7, 1844; d. 1859.
ii.   James H., b. Duxbury, Sept. 3, 1848. Was in the west several years. Came
      to Newbury, 1879 and m. Dec. 27, 1887, Mrs. Elizabeth (Brock) Jewell.
      He has a collection of rare books.
iii.   Susan E., b. Duxbury, Dec. 22, 1850; d. y.
iv.   Edwin Asa, b. Waterbury, June 16, 1862; laborer; res. West Newbury; m.
      Feb. 25, 1891, Jennie Godfrey. C., (1) Alice, b. May 21, 1892. (2) Jessie
      J., b. May 15, 1894.
v.   Jesse, b. May 15, 1885; d. 1891.

MOORE.

SAMUEL A., b. in Dorset, N. H., Jan. 29, 1810; was in the lumber business at
      McIndoes for 30 years before 1873. He operated mills at McIndoes, and
      before the days of railroads was largely occupied in taking large quantities
      of lumber down the Connecticut river in rafts. He lived in Wells River
      after 1873, then rem. to St. Johnsbury, but returned to Wells River to
      engage in the lumber business again. He m. Jan. 29, 1846.
   Children:
i.   John A., b. Jan. 13, 1847; d. Feb. 18, 1898. He was in the clothing business
      in St. Johnsbury, where he was succeeded by his son.
ii.   Lillias B., m. Dr. James R. Nelson.
iii.   Jane, m. Charles P. Joy.

MORSE.

TIMOTHY, son of Stephen and Sally (Ray) Morse, b. Haverhill, N. H., April 27,
      1803. He came to Newbury about 1824, and was one of the most active
      business men in this region for about thirty-five years. He was in trade
      with several men, and erected a large building where J. B. Hale's store
      now stands, in which he kept store. Mr. Stevens was his partner some
      years, D. N. Burnham for some time before and after 1834, and James M.
      Chadwick. He owned the large farm which is now that of F. E. Kimball,
      and built the house which was burned in 1898, also built, among others,
      the brick house where the Leslie family have long lived, the one in which
      S. L. Swasey lives, and the one now owned and occupied by C. F. Darling,

in which he d. He also owned other houses and farms, dealing, later in life, largely in western lands. Mr. Morse was prominent in the Meth. Ch., was one of the first trustees of Newbury Seminary, and treasurer from 1833 to 1845. He was, probably, more influential than any other man in securing the establishment of the institution here, and had the oversight of the erection of the building. It is probable also that had Mr. Morse been living here in 1866, and in the full enjoyment of his health and energies, Newbury Seminary would not have been moved away. He gave largely of his money and time, and helped carry the institution through more than one financial strait. He m. Jan. 27, 1822, Parmelia, dau. of Colton Haines, of Rumney, and granddaughter of Rev. Cotton Haines. She d. Sept. 9, 1863. He d. Sept. 7, 1862.

Children:
   i. Martha H., b. Oct. 2, 1824; m. Aug. 8, 1841, Rev. Clark T. Hinman. (see Newbury Seminary chapter), who d. at Troy, N. Y., Oct. 21, 1854. She d. February, 1858. One son and two daus., now in the west.
1 ii. Horace B., b. Aug. 13, 1826.
  iii. Carlos M., b. Jan. 19, 1829; res. Plymouth, N. H. Succeeded his father in trade after 1862, rem. to Plymouth, and for many years was proprietor of the Pemmigewassett House; now retired. He m. April 19, 1853, Sarah R., dau. of Emory Gale of Wells River. Of their c. a son is living and dau. d.
  iv. Sarah K., b. Feb. 15, 1832; m. George E. Scott of Chicago. C., one son and two daus. are living. She d. May 28, 1888.
  v. Elizabeth N., b. May 2, 1834; m. May 5, 1853, Anson M. Stevens. C., two sons who are d.; 2 daus. living. She d. Aberdeen, Mass., July 14, 1901.
  vi. Helen M., b. Aug. 29, 1837; m. George L. Seaver of Boston; two c., both d. She d. April 1895.
  vii. Henry C., b. June 8, 1846. In business in Jersey City, N. J., some years; m. Sept. 9, 1865, Laura J., dau. of David Felker of Newbury, who d. March 20, 1894; buried at Wells River. He d. in Jersey City, N. J., March 16, 1894. C., two sons; one m. Elsie, dau. of David R. Allison of Wells River.

1 HORACE B., b. Aug. 13, 1826. In business with his father, and later was postmaster till about 1871. He afterward was in business in Boston. He m. 1st, Sept. 27, 1851, Elizabeth, dau. of William Page, (b. Aug. 8, 1825; d. Jan. 20, 1868). He m. 2d, Feb. 19, 1871, Sarah E. Page, sister of 1st wife, (b. Oct. 29, 1823; d. Lowell, Mass., Oct. 13, 1878). He m. 3d, July 26, 1875, Mrs. Martha A. (Knight) Mahurin. He d. Boston, Mass., Jan. 13, 1894.

Children, by 1st marriage, b. in Newbury:
  i. Edwin T., b. Nov. 25, 1856; studied medicine at Rochester, N. Y., four years; in the druggist business in Boston till 1885, when he was appointed an officer in the medical department of the United States Navy, and ordered for duty on board the United States Steamer Essex, which was going to China via Europe. Remained in China and Japan waters till May, 1889, when he was at home two months. Three years on board the training ship Portsmouth, crusing during the summer in European waters and spending the winter in the West Indies. One year, from July 1st, 1892, on board the receiving ship, Wabash, at the Boston navy yard. Since that time assistant medical officer at the navy yard, Boston. He m. June 3, 1879, Minnie E., dau. of Hon. Frank Smith of Lancaster, N. H. C., Frank S., b. Boston, April 4, 1880.
  ii. William H., b. Dec. 2, 1859; d. at sea on board the steamer, Grace M. Parker, June 9, 1879, and buried at sea.

MOULTON.

HARRIET, dau. of John Kent, b. Lyman, N. H., Oct. 11, 1811; m. Rinaldo Moulton of Lyman. They later rem. to Haverhill where Mr. Moulton d. in 1849, leaving six c. After his death the oldest son, William O., and 2d dau., Harriet F., came to live with Clark and Relief Kent in Newbury. William enlisted in Co. H., 12th Vt., and d. in hospital, April 7, 1863, and buried at the Ox-bow. Harriet, m. Henry Dame of Orford, N. H.; they lived in the house now owned by Dr. Hatch, in Newbury, some years before Mr.

Dame's death in 1879. Mrs. Dame with her son, Arthur K., and William
M., are now living in Fremont, Neb. Lucia Moulton, the eldest dau., m. in
St. Johnsbury, where the family then lived, Elmer C. Bacon, formerly of
Haverhill; their home was in Cleveland, Ohio, where she d. in 1891, leaving
three c. Emily Oakes and Hurd Rinaldo Moulton, d. in Monroe, N. H.,
and are buried in Newbury. Mrs. Harriet (Kent) Moulton d. in Muskegon,
Mich., in 1895 and is buried in Newbury. Her son, Charles Carroll, now
lives in Anderson, Indiana.

MUNSELL.

WILLIAM HENRY, son of John and Eliza C. (Wingate) Munsell, b. Swanton, Dec.
9, 1843; served in the Civil war, in Co. L, 1st Vt. Cavalry, from Sept. 29,
1862, till mustered out, May 17, 1865; studied dentistry with Dr. L.
Gilman of Swanton, and opened an office in that place in 1871. In
practice there till April, 1880, when he came to Wells River and has
continued in practice here till the present time. He m. June 14, 1870,
Antha Myra Warren, of St. Albans.
  Children:
  i.   Ella E., b. Swanton, May 17, 1872.
  ii. Lottie, b. Swanton, July 8, 1874; graduated 1898 at Ripon (Wis.) College;
       teacher in the grammar school at Wells River; now in Wisconsin.
  iii. Hattie C., b Swanton, Jan. 8, 1877; graduated 1894 at the conservatory of
       music connected with Ripon College; music teacher. She m. July 20, 1898,
       J. Edwin Worthen, of Bradford, clerk for Clark & Gage, Bradford. C.,
       Harold M., b. Newbury, June 7, 1899.
  iv. John Wingate. b. Swanton, June 26, 1879.
  v.   William Warren, b. Newbury, Jan. 21, 1883; d. Sept. 18, 1885.
  vi. Antha Warren, b. Newbury, July 22, 1884.
  vii. William Henry, b. Newbury, Feb. 2, 1891.

*NELSON.

WILLIAM, Sr., b. Erskine parish, Scotland, 1712, and his wife, Jean Stuart, were
among the first settlers of Ryegate. They came with their three c.,
William, Robert and Mary, landing in Portland. Maine, and reached
Ryegate, Oct. 9, 1774. They settled about a mile east of the Corner,
where four c. were b. to them They lived to be very old, and accumulated
a large property for those times. Of their c.: William and Robert settled
in that part of Lyman, now called Monroe, and reared large families.
Their· sister, Mary, m. Hugh Gardner Esq., of Ryegate, and were
ancestors of the Gardner families of Ryegate and Newbury. His farm was
the one now owned by John W. Nelson. John, son of William, b. Ryegate,
Feb. 5, 1776; d. 1865; was a very prominent man in that town,
representative, etc. Most of his c. went west. but his son. John F., lived
and d. in Ryegate, a good farmer and citizen. Sophia, dau. of John Nelson,
b. April 15, 1830; m. Dec. 24, 1856, Rev. James M. Beattie, who was
pastor, for nearly 38 years. of the Covenanter church. Their living c. are
Dr. Beattie of Littleton, N. H., Mary and Wilson of South Ryegate.

JAMES, son of William, Sr., b. 1778; town representative from Ryegate, several
years. He m. 1808, Agnes Gibson, who d. 1838, aged 51. She was from
Scotland. He d. 1840.
  Children, all b. in Ryegate:
  i.   William Gibson, b. March 27, 1809; educated at Peacham Academy, and
       studied medicine under Prof. R. D. Mussey, of Hanover; was then in the
       Marine Hospital at Chelsea, Mass.; physician in Barnet several years,
       then in Cambridge, N. Y., where he became noted. He m. Eliza Mary,
       dau. of Rev. Alexander Bullions, D. D., of Cambridge, N. Y. He d. suddenly
       Feb. 7, 1852. Their c. were: (1) Alexander B., and (2) William H., d. in

*By Robert Nelson.

the Union army, in Virginia. (3) Mary E., of Cambridge. N. Y. (4) Seraph, d. 1899, at Cambridge. (5) James Robert who studied medicine in New York, and was in practice several years at Wells River, then at St. Johnsbury, and is a resident of Flushing, N. Y. He m. Lillias A., dau. of Samuel A. Moore, of Wells River, and has a son and a dau.

ii. Jean S., b. Aug. 28, 1810; m. 1834, Nathaniel Batchelder of Barnet, and had seven c. Both are d. at 89 and 82 years.

iii. Margaret, b. April 28, 1812; m. about 1832, William S. Holt. He was a blacksmith at Wells River, owning the brick shop, where he made axes and other edge tools. He built and occupied the house where H. T. Baldwin now lives. About 1848, they rem. to Iowa, where both d. Of their eight c., two or three are living.

iv. John, b. April 26, 1814; major in the militia; res. in Ryegate; d. Nov. 27, 1838.

v. Mary, b. May 21, 1816; d. Wells River, Nov. 13, 1893.

vi. Elizabeth, b. May 19, 1818; d. Nov. 15, 1838.

vii. Robert, b. Feb. 24, 1820; farmer in Ryegate till March, 1890, when he retired from business and rem. to Wells River; town representative from Ryegate, 1862–63; justice 30 years. He m. Dec. 20, 1849, Isabel R., dau. of Andrew Buchanan, (b. Ryegate, May 21, 1819.) He d. Oct. 25, 1900. C., (1) Robert B., b. May 15, 1851: res. Wells River. (2) Ibbie Jean, m. Archibald A. Miller, of Ryegate, a farmer on the "Old Warden Place," or "Longmeadow Farm." Two c., son and dau. (3) Martha A., m. O. H. Renfrew of Ryegate. Two c., son and dau. Robert Nelson and wife celebrated their golden wedding in Ryegate, Dec. 20, 1899.

viii. James, b. July 12, 1821; farmer in Ryegate; town representative, etc. He m. Dec. 23, 1852, Mary L. Gray. He d. 1891. Four c.

ix. Peter, b. June 27, 1823; d. May, 1839.

THOMAS, son of William, Sr., b. 1780; was a farmer in Ryegate and town representative. One of his sons, Major Thomas Nelson, was an officer in the Union army.

William Nelson, the emigrant, was half brother of James Nelson, the two being ancestors of nearly all the Nelson families in this vicinity.

NELSON.

ROBERT, son of George and Margaret (Gardner) b. Ryegate, Sept. 4, 1824; attended Peacham Academy and Newbury Seminary, and taught eight terms of school. In 1849, he went to California, via Cape Horn, time 130 days. Returned 1853 via Panama, in one month. He m. April 5, 1855, Judith, dau. of John and Judith (Brock) Darling, (b. Jan. 16, 1825). Lived where E. E. Putnam lives, at West Newbury, then bought the Col. Thos. Johnson farm on the Ox-bow, living there four years. He bought, in 1869, the John Randall farm on Jefferson Hill, which was once that of Merrill Bayley. He d. Newbury, Feb. 22, 1895.

Children:

i. George Darling, b. Ryegate, May 1, 1856; res. Davenport, Iowa. He m. Dec. 3, 1879. Clara Matilda Karl, (b. Jan. 2, 1866; d. Sept. 9, 1894). C., (1) George William, b. Nov. 3, 1880 (2) Robert John, b. Nov. 6, 1881; d. Nov. 27, 1881. (3) John Andrew, b. Nov. 27, 1882; d. May 18, 1883. (4) Judith M., b. May 21, 1886. (5) Robert H., b. June 18, 1887. (6) James D., b. July 4, 1888; d. Aug. 7, 1890.

ii. Hannah F., b. Newbury, Aug. 21, 1858; m. Sept. 8, 1887, Owen E. Kingsbury, b. Sept. 23, 1851. C., Bertha A., b. Jan. 2, 1891.

iii. John, b. Newbury, Aug. 9, 1860; m. June 7, 1895, Mamie Louise Smith.

iv. Jennie Richardson, b. Newbury, Nov. 15, 1865; m. Jan. 27, 1886, Albert Wright, and lives on the homestead. C., Ben Harrison, b. Oct. 6, 1888.

NELSON.

WILLIAM, came from Bothwell, Scotland, in 1836, and bought the farm called "The Hermitage," where Hon. Peter Burbank had lately d., and which before was called "The Scott place," near South Ryegate. He was called "Scotch Nelson," and "Scotch Willie," to distinguish him from the other

William Nelsons in this vicinity. Mr. Nelson was a good farmer, who made the barren knolls blossom like the rose. He m. Mary, dau. of William Buchanan, of Ryegate. They were members of the Covenanter church at Ryegate Corner, and never failed to be in their places, rain or shine on the Sabbath.

Children:

i. Margaret B., b. July 29, 1836; m. Robert James Nelson, and rem. to Iowa. Three c.
ii. Isabel A., b. 1838; graduated Newbury Seminary, 1865; m. Alexander Davidson; d. in Ryegate, 1879, on the Whitelaw farm. Four c.
iii. Agnes C., b. July 26, 1846; m. Oct. 25, 1876, Henry E. Whitehill, and lived on her father's farm. She d. Feb. 19, 1885. Five c.
iv. Annie, d. of diphtheria while attending Newbury Seminary.
v. Son, who d. at 18 years of age.

NELSON.

Enoch and Stephen, brothers, came here not far from 1804, from Salisbury, N. H., and settled south of Boltonville. They have long been dead, and none of their name live here now. The following records were prepared by Edward Miller, and corrected by Mrs. Agnes Gardner, both now deceased. Enoch Nelson settled on what is now called the "John Miller place," below Boltonville, and built the large house still standing there. He m. 1st, a Miss Pike; m. 2d, Lydia (Alexander), widow of James Taylor; m. 3d, Mrs. Wheeler. He d. Jan. 29, 1863.

Children:

i. Polly, b. Jan. 22, 1807; m. Mason Randall; d. March 26, 1875.
ii. Hannah, m. Paul Wheeler.
iii. Sarah, m. Dennis Wheeler.
iv. Eliza, b. April 22, 1812; m. William Gardner, q. v.
v. Lydia, m. Dec. 26, 1839, Jacob F. Page of Groton.
vi. Rebecca, d. un-m. May 1, 1842.
vii. Abigail, m. March 8, 1838, Lewis Page of Groton.
viii. Alice, or Elsie, m. Reuben Pike.
ix. Nancy, b. June 26, 1821; m. John Miller and settled on her father's farm; d. Jan. 21, 1866. Mr. Miller was b. in Ryegate, April 7, 1814, and d. at Woodsville, a few years ago. 12 c.

Stephen, was a large farmer and a substantial citizen. He owned four or five hundred acres of land on "Nelson Hill," one mile south of Boltonville. The buildings are all gone, and most of the farm is pasture now. He m. Rachel, dau. Ezra Gates.

Children:

i. Betsey, m. Timothy Hinman, and rem. to Derby.
ii. Major, m. Mehetable Deming of Bath.
iii. Stephen, m. 1st, Emerenza Allis; m. 2d, Sally Johnson.
iv. Finette, m. William Grant, Jr.
v. Oswell, went west.
vi. Rachel.
vii. John, d. y.
viii. Effie, m. Franklin Learned.
ix. Robert, went west.
x. Charles, m. Caroline Wesson, of Corinth.
xi. Marion.
xii. Mary, m. a Mr. Williams.

NILES.

Nathaniel, b. Orford, N. H., Nov. 30, 1793; m. about 1817, Silence Sawyer, who d. in Newbury, Nov. 23, 1854, aged 57. They came to West Newbury 1823, and bought the farm where Charles Corliss now lives. Their house was burned, and he built the present house. He was a very industrious man, a soldier in the war of 1812. member of the Cong. Ch., nearly 60 years, and long superintendent of the Sunday school at West Newbury. He sold his farm about 1863, lived in Orford some years, then with his dau. in Maidstone, till death, Dec. 28, 1885. Buried at West Newbury.

Children:

i. John Sawyer, b. Orford, April 25, 1820; went to Wisconsin in 1849; was a traveling salesman, and later a farmer, holding many public offices; member of the Disciples Ch. He m. 1854, Sarah H. Carpenter. He d. Monroe, Wis., Sept. 13, 1896. C., Rev. C. F. Niles, of Menominee, and T. W. Niles of Monroe.

ii. George A., b. Newbury, 1825; carpenter in Boston; killed by falling from the roof of a house, Jan. 14, 1863; buried at West Newbury. He left a wife and dau.

iii. Tabitha Maria, became a dressmaker in Boston; m. a Mr. Lemont, and rem. to Wisconsin, where she d., leaving a daughter.

iv. Nathaniel Lewis, went west and lives in Iowa where he has two sons who are educated men.

v. Harriet Buxton, m. J. H. Benton, then of Bradford, afterward of Maidstone, and now of Lancaster, N. H. C., (1) Samuel, b. Bradford, Jan. 10, 1858; farmer in Guildhall. (2) Hattie M., b. Bradford, Feb. 3, 1859; m. George Balch of Lunenburg. (3) Benjamin B., b. Bradford, June 24, 1863; res. Lancaster. N. H. (4) Joseph, b. Maidstone, Dec. 7, 1866; res. Concord, N. H. (5) Caroline E., b. June 7, 1870; res. Portland, Me. (6) Hugh H., b. Jan. 19, 1872; graduate Boston University; lawyer. (7) John E., b. May 14, 1875; graduated Boston University; lawyer. (8) Mary E., b. Sept. 3, 1878. J. H. Benton, Jr., a well-known lawyer of Boston, is half-brother of these.

vi. Henry Wallace, m. 1st, Helen, dau. Ross Ford; went west, and lives in Wisconsin. Four c. One dead.

vii. Edwin Carter, enlisted in Co. H, 11th N. H., in the Civil war, and d. while serving as a nurse in a hospital at Newport News, March 16, 1863, aged 24. Buried at West Newbury.

viii. Adeline Silence, m. Luther Gage of Orford, N. H., and d. about 1883, leaving five c.

NOURSE.

PETER, lived in Danvers, Mass., and m. Lydia Low. Rem. to Rockingham where both d. at nearly 100 years of age. They had 11 c. of whom 10 lived until the youngest was 60 years old. Of their c., Lydia m. David Boynton, (q. v.)

JEREMIAH, b. probably in Danvers, Nov. 26, 1777; m. Dec. 25, 1806, Ruth, dau. of Jacob Bayley, (b. Apr. 28, 1790; d. Dec., 1862). They settled in Newbury where he owned a farm of about 500 acres at the Lime-Kiln, living where Horace Brown now does. Rem. to Bradford about 1850, where both d. He d. Jan. 21, 1857.

Children:

i. Maria, b. Feb. 25, 1809; m. James George, q. v.

ii. Sophila, b. June 14, 1811; m. March 4, 1830, Dr. Israel Huntley of Topsham; two c.; d. Sept. 26, 1841.

iii. Ruth, b. Sept. 4, 1813; m. Aug., 1836, Rev. James H. Patterson; d. Dec. 31, 1836.

iv. Alonzo, b. May 20, 1816; d. March 31, 1817.

v. Alonzo W., b. March 23, 1818; m. March 18, 1841, Isabel Renfrew; three c.; d. He lived where Mr. Kasson now does.

vi. William Harvey, b. July 4, 1821; m. May 22, 1844, Lydia Renfrew, dau. of Robert Renfrew; rem. to Bradford; 3 c.; all d. y.; d.

Jeremiah Nourse was a fine man and a sterling citizen, whose opinions were held in high esteem. He was not a professor of religion, but was a serious thoughtful man. The following anecdote is worthy of preservation. "Many years ago he, with others, was on his way to Salem, Mass., with wheat, and the party stopped for the night at a tavern, and in the course of the evening the conversation turned upon religious subjects, the topic of discussion being the relative value of religious denominations. Mr

Nourse listened to the conversation without taking part in it, when one of the company turned to him and asked, 'Mr. Nourse, what do you think of these things?' He replied. 'Sir, when we come to Salem they will not ask us 'Did you come by the turnpike?' or 'Did you come by the river road?' or 'Did you come over the hill?' but they will ask us 'Is your wheat good?' It is not our profession but our character which will entitle us to acceptance or rejection in the great day.' " The part of the town now known as the "Lime-Klin" was long known as the "Nourse neighborhood."

*OLMSTED.

JAMES, with nephews, Richard and John, and niece, Rebecca, came from London in the ship, "Lion," to Cambridge, Mass., in 1632   John had no c., and it it believed that all of the name in this country are descended from Richard or James. The Newbury branch can trace its connection back to Jabez Olmsted, who was b. about 60 years after the coming of Richard and John. Thomas' Olmsted Genealogy says that John, son of Richard, had ten c., but does not give the name of the 10th, who may have been Jabez. Richard, the emigrant, settled in Hartford. Conn., in 1636, but rem. in 1650 to Norwalk, where the name is still common.

I. JABEZ, of Deerfield, Mass., b. about 1690, appears as a scout in Capt. Benjamin Wright's expedition (Chapter II. this volume) up the Connecticut and White rivers in May, 1709. He was one of ten men who passed down "French or Onion river," went out upon Lake Champlain, where they routed a party of Indians and killed four of them. For this exploit each man of the company was granted £6 by the General Court of that year. He settled in Brookfield, and several purchases of land are recorded by him in what is now Ware. He was a prominent citizen, owning a large farm and mills, captain in the militia, and of the 10th Co. in Capt. Samuel Willard's regiment (4th Mass.) in the expedition against Louisburg in 1745. He m. 1712, Thankful, dau. Thomas Barnes of Brookfield, (b. Marlborough, May 1, 1695, who d. after January, 1736). He m. a 2d wife and d. in 1752 or 1753. Eleven c., of whom Israel, third c. and second son, was b. in Brookfield, Mass.

II. ISRAEL, b. March 24, 1716. In business with his father; soldier in the Old French war; sergeant of a company which marched in 1757, for the relief of Fort William Henry, and probably saw other service. Settled in Hardwick, but rem. to Lyman, (now Monroe), N. H , about 1771, to take charge of the lands of Col. John Hurd of Haverhill. No trace of him is found after 1789, except a tradition that he d. at about 90, not far from 1806. He m. 1st, May 12, 1737, Sarah, dau. Joseph Bannister, who d., and he m 2d, Anna Safford. Seven c. by 1st m. and four by 2d, of whom, Timothy, b. 1744, m. Susan Killam, and settled in Monroe, N. H.; d. 1812. John lived in Hanover, N. H., Joseph, who lived in Newbury, and Sarah m. Daniel Hall of Burke.

III. JOSEPH, b. Brookfield, Mass., 1745; lived in Brookfield, and marched from there in Capt. John Wolcott's company in the "Lexington alarm." Served 8 months in Capt. John Cowles' Co. of Woodbridge's regiment, being stationed at Cambridge. This regiment served at Bunker Hill. He is supposed to have re-enlisted at the expiration of his term, about Jan. 1, 1776, as he was in service in August of that year, at Ticonderoga and Fort Edward, as a corporal in Hamilton's Co. of Brewer's regiment. In Feb., 1777, he was at Brookfield as a member of the 1st Co. of "Matross" (artillery), at which time he enlisted for three years in Capt. Noah Nichol's Co. of Gen. Knox's artillery, in which he was commissioned 2d Lieut., June 11, 1778, having before that date served 16⅔ months in the army. In Jan. and in Feb., 1779, he was in command at Brookfield of a company of volunteers guarding military stores. Soon after this he resigned from the service. He rem. to Hartland; in 1792 to Lyman, N. H., and came to this town about 1780. He was a carpenter and was employed on the "old

---

*From a manuscript prepared by Anson Titus of Somerville, Mass.

court house" in 1801, as appears by Col. Johnson's account. He is said to have used the "square rule" in framing the timber. the first time it was used here. He m. June 11, 1774, Sarah Wood. He d. in 1804, at the house of Joseph Prescott; buried in Rogers Hill cemetery. His descendants were usually connected with the M. E. church.

Children:
   i. Sarah, b. Brookfield, Mass., March 16, 1775; m. Ebin Hidden; 11 c.
   ii. Sophia, b. Oct. 4, 1776; m. ——Irwin.
   iii. Simeon, b. Oct. 31, 1778, m. Susan Ladd; res. Haverhill where the births of 7 c. are recorded. He was b. in Hartland.
   iv. Serepta, b. Jan. 3, 1780; m. Joseph Prescott, q. v.
   v. Joseph, b. Feb. 28, 1783; m. 1822, Betsey Noyes.
1 vi. John, b. Sept. 30, 1785.
   vii. Mary, m. Charles Harding of Haverhill; two daus.

1 JOHN, b. Hartland, Sept. 30, 1785; rem. to Haverhill, where he was a carpenter and built the house near the cemetery, long occupied by Rev. Grant Powers; rem. to Methuen, Mass. In October, 1818, he enlisted at Boston, in Co. E, 6th U. S. Infantry, under Capt. W. S. Foster. After a brief service at Plattsburg the company was sent to St. Louis, thence to the Missouri river, where he d. at Fort Martin, after 10 months army life, Aug. 30, 1819. He m. Feb. 9, 1806, in Salem, N. H., Sarah Ayer.

Children:
2 i. Isaac H., b. Jan. 27, 1808; d. Aug. 30. 1878.
   ii. Lois Ann, b. Oct. 2, 1809; m. Feb. 10, 1842, Rev. James Madison Eaton; d. Williamsburg, Mass., Oct. 2. 1899.
   iii. Adeline Melissa, b. Aug. 29, 1814; m. May 3, 1837, Charles Gordon of Hampstead, N. H.; d. Worcester, Mass , Jan. 2, 1892.

2 ISAAC HOWE, b. Haverhill, N. H., Jan. 27, 1808; worked in Boston and vicinity a few years; learned the chair making trade of Charles Harding of Haverhill; came to Newbury in 1828–9, and made chairs in the shop of Israel Prescott. In the same business in the Nourse neighborhood 1830–33; from 1833 to 1840, on the Westgate place; rem. to South Newbury, 1840, where he built a chair factory and continued in business till death, Aug. 30, 1878. He m. 1st, May 27, 1830, Eliza, dau. Joseph Prescott, (b. Oct. 24, 1812; d. Oct. 20, 1840). Five c. He m. 2d, April 29, 1841, Mary, dau. John Atwood She d. Nov. 10, 1842. One c. He m. 3d, June 7, 1843, at Irasburg, Sarah Ann Allyn. She d. April 3, 1861. aged 48 years, 6 months. Four c. He m. 4th, Oct. 5, 1863, Mrs. Susan C. (Fuller) widow of John Thompson, now (Mrs. Jones). Res. at South Newbury.

Children:
   i. Sophila A., b. Sept. 28, 1831; m. George G. Dimick of Chicago; d. 1875.
   ii. Infant, b. March 8; d. March 19, 1834.
   iii. George Stowers, b. Aug. 21, 1835; d. March 7, 1842.
   iv. Mary H., b. Nov. 9, 1837; m. July, 1863, Elijah Cook; lived in Newbury, but rem. to Meriden, N. H., where she d. Five c. Four living.
   v. Infant, b. Oct. 12, 1840; d. aged one month.
   vi. Almira Atwood, b. Oct. 20, 1842; m. William W. Chalmers, q. v.; d. July 14, 1893.
   vii. Laura Eliza, b. May 20, 1844; d. March 8. 1862.
3 viii. Perley Ayer, b. July 22. 1848; d. Aug. 10, 1896.
4 ix. Abner Allyn, b. June 15, 1850.
   x. Frank E., b. May 11, 1856; d. March 25, 1861.

3 PERLEY AYER, b. July 22, 1848. Fitted for college at Newbury and Montpelier Seminaries; graduated Vermont University 1877; teaching and other business in Colorado, 1878-82; took post graduate course at Northwestern University; returned to Newbury and was in business with his brother. Railway mail clerk for some time after 1887, receiving 98½ per cent at the civil service examination. Member of the Methodist church, and connected with the Sunday School at West Newbury. He was a fine scholar, of quiet retiring manners; loved the society of books and had his life been spared might have produced something well worth doing. In Aug., 1896 he went to New York to work for the National Democratic committee. He was taken ill and d. at the city hospital Aug. 10, 1896; buried at West New-

bury. A memorial service was held in the church the following Sunday. He never m.

4 ABNER ALLYN, b. June 15, 1850; in partnership with his father, 1872-78. Built in 1879, part of the present factory building for the manufacture of chairs, and for other mechanical purposes, the premises being also used during the season by the Orange Co. Canning Co. Town representative 1890-92, serving four years, where he introduced and conducted the bill incorporating Wells River Savings Bank. Appointed by Hon. J. Sterling Morton, Sec. of Agriculture, State statistician, holding the office several years. Nominated, 1878, for Lieutenant Governor upon the Democratic ticket. Member of the Democratic State committee, 1892 to '96· Candidate for presidential elector, 1896. Member of the M. E. church; and steward 15 years. He m. 1st, May 27, 1880, Jennie M., dau. John Thompson, her mother being the 4th wife of I. H. Olmsted. She d. Dec. 25, 1889; no c.; m. 2d, Aug. 11, 1896, Laura R., dau. E. C. Stocker.
  Children:
  i. Howard Stocker, b. Aug. 6, 1898.
  ii. Gordon Clement, b. Oct. 27, 1900; d. June 15, 1901.

PAGE.

JOSIAH and JACOB were brothers, who came from the vicinity of Haverhill, Mass., to Newbury before the Revolutionary War in which both served.

JOSIAH, b. Haverhill, Mass., or Plaistow, N. H., 1748; m. Lydia Pettee of South Berwick, Me.; rem. to Ryegate in 1782, where he was town clerk and representative.
  Children:
  i. Jonathan, b. Feb. 22, 1770, Haverhill, Mass.
  ii. Mary, b. March 14, 1772, Haverhill, Mass.
  iii. Abigail, b. July 18, 1774, Newbury.
  iv. Joseph Kimball, b. Aug. 16, 1776, Newbury.
  v. John, b. Aug. 25, 1778, Newbury; d. Sept. 1, 1779.
  vi. Sarah, b. Sept. 18, 1780, Newbury.
  vii. John, b. Aug. 11, 1782, Ryegate.
  viii. Phebe, b. Nov. 23, 1786, Ryegate.
1 ix. William, b. Aug. 20, 1790, Ryegate.

JACOB, b. 1750; came to Newbury about 1771; served in the Revolutionary war; taken prisoner with Col. Thomas Johnson in Peacham and carried to Quebec, but returned in the same year. He m. 1st, July 29, 1773, Sally, sister of Col. Thomas Johnson, (b. Oct. 29, 1751; d. Sept. 17, 1791). He m. 2d, 1792, Louisa, dau. of Richard Chamberlin. Lived on the Ox-bow, but rem. to Ryegate, 1793, and settled on a farm at the head of the pond below Ryegate Corner. He d. 1831.
  Children, b. Newbury:
  i. Eunice, b. Jan. 26, 1775; m. Jonathan Fowler.
  ii. Sarah, b. Oct. 17, 1776; d. Oct. 16, 1778.
  iii. Sarah, b. April 24, 1778; m. Rufus Hosmer.
  iv. Jacob, b. 1781; m. Judith Carter.
  v. Ruth, b. May 4, 1783; m. Samuel Whittaker. Mrs. Bailey White is their dau.
  vi. Abigail, b. Aug. 5, 1785; m. Stephen Smith of Danville.
  vii. John, b. April 30, 1787; m. Sarah Heath of Danville.
  viii. Hannah, b. July 15, 1789, Haverhill; m. Daniel Lang of Bath.
  ix. Polly, b. Nov. 26, 1792.
  x. Betsey, b. Jan. 27, 1795, Ryegate.

1 WILLIAM[2] (Josiah[1]), b. Ryegate, Aug. 20, 1790. Lived in Ryegate and Newbury, He m. Sept. 16, 1812, Emily, dau. of Benjamin Chamberlin, (b. Newbury, March 2, 1788; d. Oct. 19, 1860). Their son says (1899) that when his parents were m. his father came on horseback from Ryegate to Newbury, took his bride on the horse behind him and went to General Whitelaw's in Ryegate, where they were m. Captain in the militia. He d. in Lebanon, Oct. 16, 1883.
  Their c., were all b. in Ryegate :
2 i. Albert G., b. Feb. 26, 1813, q. v.

    ii. Ben P., b. Sept. 25; d. Dec. 12, 1814.
    iii. Ann Maria, b. March 22, 1816; m. Dec. 7, 1843, John A. Meader; d. Monroe, N. H., Sept. 15, 1898; q. v.
    iv. Jane T., b. Sept, 25, 1818; m. Oct. 31, 1843, Theodore Andrews; d. Groton, Mass., Feb. 13, 1893.
    v. Amaret J., b. Jan. 20, 1821; m. Oct. 17, 1843, at Bradford, Thaddeus Clark; d. Washington, D. C., Sept. 26, 1890.
    vi. Sarah E., b. Oct. 29, 1823; m. Feb. 19, 1871, Horace B. Morse, as 2d wife; d. Jan. 20, 1868. She d. Lowell, Mass., Aug. 13, 1878.
    vii. Elizabeth, b. Aug. 8, 1825; m. Sept. 27, 1851, Horace B. Morse, as 1st wife; she d. Jan. 20, 1868; q. v.

2 ALBERT G.,[3] (William,[2] Josiah[1]), b. Ryegate, Feb. 26, 1813; m. Apr. 14, 1844, Mary Ann, dau. of Absalom Brown, (b. September 7, 1822); farmer in Newbury; res. (1899), Woburn, Mass.
    Children:
    i. Sarah M., b. Newbury, March 10, 1845; m. at Lebanon, N. H., June 5, 1871, Charles E. Davis; res. Newtonville, Mass.; two c.
    ii. Adna A., b. Lowell, Mass., 1846; m. 1st, Thetford, 1871, Ella M. Newcomb, who d. 1875. He m., 2d, at Lyndeboro, N. H., Carrie Blanchard; res. Woburn, Mass.; B. & M. R. R. employee.
    iii. Frank M., b. Aug. 23, 1848; m. Jan. 17, 1882, at Charlestown, Mass., to Elizabeth Heaton of Boston; res. Woburn.
    iv. Dan Carlos, b. Oct. 24, 1851; m. at Gorham, N. H., March 1, 1875, Nancy McKnight of Sawyerville, P. Q.; res. Woburn, Mass.; R. R. employee.
    v. Henry Ovando, b. Nov. 1, 1853; res. Manchester, N. H.; un-m.

PARKER.

JONATHAN, moved from Rumney, N. H., to Boltonville—Newbury, with his wife and two c., Eliza Ann and E. George, March 20, 1832, and bought the farm now owned and occupied by the widow of the late Stephen Putnam, and lived on said farm, until his death. Mr. Parker was a man of decided character, a wise adviser, and safe councilor; his judgment was sought for by his neighbors, as he was a man of rare ability. Prior to this he was deputy sheriff for many years of Grafton County, N. H., and was one of the leading men in the town of Plymouth in his earlier days. Jonathan Parker was b. Oct. 11th, 1777, at Plymouth, N. H; d. Sept. 17, 1851, at Boltonville. Susan Parker, his wife, b. May 14, 1801, at Plymouth, N. H.; d. March 15, 1877, with her son, E. G. Parker, at Woodsville, N. H.
    Children:
    i. Eliza A., b. April 14, 1826, Rumney, N. H.; m. George W. Miller, of Lowell, Mass.
1   ii. E. George, b. Nov. 30, 1827, at Rumney, N. H.; m. Matilda P. Cook of Lyme, N. H.
    iii. Maria E., b. May 6, 1833, at Newbury; m. John H. Wills of Farmington, Maine.
    iv. Charlotte, b. April 20, 1835, Newbury; m. Augusta Wills, Vienna, Me.; d. May 6th, 1871.
    v. Martha H., b. March 30, 1837, at Newbury; m. Joel P. Felker, Wells River; d. Sept. 10, 1855.

1 ENOCH GEORGE, b. Rumney, N. H., Nov. 27, 1827; came to Newbury with his parents; was in business at Woodsville and Wells River; proprietor of the Parker House at Woodsville some years; director in Woodsville National Bank, and prominent in Odd Fellowship and Masonry, also held town offices. He was superintendent of the Wells River Sunday school for several years. He d. June 20, 1901, leaving a widow and one son, Dr. George Parker, of Concord, N. H.

PATTERSON.

RICHARD, b. Markinch, Fife, Scotland, Jan. 3, 1809. He had very limited advantages, his only schoolmaster being one John Anderson, who had been a soldier in the British army during the American war, and lost his right arm at the battle of Bunker Hill. He was a weaver by trade, and m.

March, 1829, Janette Donaldson, (b. Jan. 23, 1810; d. Jan. 20, 1882). In company with his wife's brother, George Donaldson, he started for America Sept. 20, 1832, and after a voyage of nine weeks reached Montreal, and later Ryegate, on foot from Burlington. In 1834, he bought 80 acres of wild land of Samuel Gibson, on which he built a log house, Donaldson, whom he afterwards bought out, settling near him. He spent the rest of his life here, re-visiting Scotland in 1868. A natural turn for mathematics led him to study surveying, in which he became proficient; he knew more about the boundaries of land in this vicinity than any other man, and his knowledge made him a valuable witness in cases involving the title to land in this and other towns. He studied law with Elijah Farr, and although never admitted to the bar, practiced considerably, and was much resorted to for legal advice. Member of the Constitutional Convention of 1870. He also accumulated a valuable library, and with the contents he was thoroughly familiar; in politics he was a Democrat of the ante-bellum school. Mrs. Patterson was one of the last of the fine old Scotch ladies of an earlier generation than any who remain. He d. Newbury, June 6, 1895.
    Children:
    i.   Margaret, b. Aug. 30. 1830; m. John Gilmore, (q. v.)
    ii. Richard N., b. May 8, 1834; d. April 15, 1860.
    iii. Ellen D., b. March 11, 1839; m. John Buchanan, (q. v.)
    iv. Washington, b. Feb. 22, 1841. Read law with Leslie & Rogers, Wells River, and with Dickey & Worthen, at Bradford; admitted to the bar, Jan. 1867, and practiced law in Tama and Benton Counties, Iowa, for four years; returned to Newbury, 1871, and has not been in active practice for some years. Has written much for the press; farmer on homestead. He m. June 14, 1876, Lizzie B., dau. of Thomas Corliss. C., (1) Richard T., b. Dec. 14, 1879; now in Vermont University. (2) Roscoe F., b. Apr. 22, 1881, now in Vermont University. (3) Victor, b. July 11, 1893.

PEACH.

    The following paper, prepared with great care and patient research for this volume, by Rev. R. W. Peach, has sufficient historical and local interest to justify its insertion without abridgement.   EDITOR.

    THE REV. ROBERT WESTLY PEACH, was b. at Oak Hill, near O'Fallon, Ill., Nov. 27, 1863; being the oldest child of Samuel W., (now of Port Townsend, Wash, title abstractor), and Anna R. (Wiggins); grandson of William and Elizabeth (Grotts); great grandson of the William who moved from Newbury to Illinois. Cadet, West Point, 1883–85; graduate, Reformed Episcopal Theological Seminary, Philadelphia, '90; ordained Presbyter, June, '90; m. to Harriet Elizabeth, only dau. of the Rev. Joshua L. Burrows, Ph. D., Oswego, N. Y., Sept. 24, 1890; pastor, Trinity Reformed Episcopal church, Ashtabula, Ohio, '90–'93; acting pastor, First Reformed Episcopal church, Boston, Mass., '93–'94; pastor, First Presbyterian church, Quincy, Mass., '94–1900: pastor, Second Presbyterian church, Camden, N. J. 1900——; moderator, Presbytery of Boston. South Ryegate, October, '98; commissioner, Presbyterian General Assembly, Minneapolis, May, '99; moderator, Presbytery of West Jersey, April, 1901; declined call to Reformed Episcopal church of the Reconciliation, Brooklyn, N. Y., just before entering Presbyterian church ; resumed academic studies in Boston University; Ph. B., '96; student in graduate school, '96 —— ; they have four c., Ruth E., Anna H., Eggleston Westly and Dorothy S. Mr. Peach has visited Newbury several times.

THE ANCESTRY OF THE PEACH FAMILY.

    The name Peach, originally Peche, is Norman-French, and the family in England dates back to the time of William the Conqueror. The Peaches of Newbury are descended from John Peach, Jr., one of the early settlers of Marblehead, Mass. John Peach, Sr., one of the founders of that town, had no family.

He was a near relative, probably first cousin, of John, Jr. The two men are named together in Seventeenth Century documents over forty times. Including these instances, I have found the name of John, Sr., one hundred times, and that of John, Jr., over eighty times. in contemporary records of Salem and Marblehead. Besides these, there are over thirty cases in which the distinction of senior or junior is omitted, part of them referring to one and part to the other. Both men lived to the age, approximately, of fourscore years; and it came to be a saying in Marblehead, which passed without question in depositions, "the two Peaches " The first mention of Marblehead in the records of Salem, as Roads, in his history of the former town, has noted, concerned John Peach and another man. This minute is found on page 8 of the "Salem Towne Booke" (of Grants of Land), in the office of the clerk of that city. Its quaint spelling entitles it to reproduction:

"By the towne repsentative, viz the 13 men deputed, the 28th of the first moneth, 1636.

"John Peach, [Sr.?] ffysherman and Nicholus mariott, having fenced about five acres of ground on marble neck (though contrarie to the order of the towne) yet Its agreed that they may for psent improve the said place for building or planting, pvided alwayes that the ppriety thereof be reserved for the right of the towne of Salem, to dispose of in pcess of tyme to them or any other ffyshermen, or others as shalbe thought most meet, yet soe as that they may haue reasonable consideracon for any chardge they shalbe at."

Jany. 1, 1637, Salem assessed £8 upon twenty-four inhabitants of Marblehead, of whom John Peach (Sr.?) named the sixth named.

Again, nearly fifty years afterwards, John Peach (probably Sr.) made a most interesting deposition, which is preserved in the Essex County Court papers, xliv. 30:

"The testimony of John Peach Aged 80 yeare or therabout.

"This deponent testefieth that John Bennett deceased came with him into New England in the same ship in the year 1630: and his [Bennett's] wife some years after came into New England," etc.

John, Sr., probably did not know his exact age, for in 1669 it was given as "above 50," and in 1672 as 60. He was elected a selectman of Marblehead the year that town was separated from Salem, 1649, and nine or more other years. He was frequently an appraiser of estates, court constable, etc. In 1672 he was one of a committee of four to assign seats in the new "Lentoo" to the meeting-house. He d. Aug. 20, 1684, having lived in Marblehead probably fifty-four years. Peach's Point took its name from him. In his will, which is on file in the Essex County Probate office, he bequeaths property to relatives in Simsborough, England, Barbados Island and Marblehead. and calls William Peach, son of John, Jr., his "cousin," a term used rather indefinitely in those days.

Having differentiated "the two Peaches," we may now trace the line of descent of the Newbury branch of the family, which begins in America with

I. JOHN, Jr., and ALICE (————————) PEACH. John, Jr., was b., it would appear from various depositions, between April 26 and July 22, 1613. Pope's "Pioneers of Massachusetts," p. 349, says that John, Sr., and John, Jr., had lived in Marblehead 41 and 33 years, respectively, Jan. 25, 1672. Therefore, in 1638 or 1639, John, Jr., came to Marblehead. His wife, Alice, is named in different documents dating from 1644 onward. She was one year younger than he. They were m before 1640, for their eldest dau. was a widow in 1660. They had three daus.: Hannah, first the wife of John Bradstreet, then of William Waters; Mary, who m. William Woods, and Elizabeth, who m. John Legg. Their only son was William. John, Jr., lived in Marblehead for about fifty-four years. In 1656, '59, '60, '61, '62 and '71 he was a selectman,or "towne's man," and was often besides appointed on responsible committees, to "lay out" land that was to be divided, "view ffences," guard the rights of the commoners to pasturage of their cattle, etc. On the latter committee he was elected as late as April 11, 1692. He was often a witness to wills and deeds. In 1674–5, when disputed rights in the commons were settled by the General Court, out of 116 commoners who subscribed agreement, his rights to five cows' commonage were exceeded only by Moses Maverick (nine), and equalled beside only by Samuel Cheever, the minister, (five). He was admitted a freeman, May 16, 1683. His lands are frequently referred to as boundaries. Within a fortnight before making his will, he deeded his share (of six or eight acres) of the "Coye-pond" lands to his daughter, Elizabeth Legg, and his portion of "the Humphrey farme" to his dau., Mary Woods. He also gave land to the heirs of his daughter, Hannah Waters, during his lifetime. The date of his death is not known, but the earliest date in the settlement of his estate is Nov. 28, 1693. His will is on file in the Essex County Probate office. His remaining estate was inventoried at £389, and consisted of two dwelling-houses with adjoining lands, and four several lots, two of ten each, one of five and one of four (?) acres, household goods, and "six cattle." His real estate was to be a life tenure of his "dear and beloved wife, Alice Peach," and after her of his "onely sonne William Peach," and after him of his "present wife Emme," and then to be divided between John and Thomas, sons of William and Emme. William, their youngest son, was left out.

II. WILLIAM and EMME (DEVEREUX) PEACH. William, only son of John, Jr., and Alice, was b. April 8, 1652. His wife, Emme, dau. of John Devereux, (said to have been a lineal descendant of Sir Walter Devereux, one of the knights of William the Conqueror,—a Peche was another of his knights), was b. in 1657 or 1658. They were m. before 1680. William was several times chosen on important town committees. Emme united with the 1st Ch. of Marblehead, April 29, 1687, and on June 19, following, had their c., John, Thomas, William and Hannah. baptized. Hannah m. first John Calley, and after his death one Waters. She alone survived her mother, who d. in April, 1737, in her eightieth year. William's tombstone recorded his death June 16, 1715, aged 63 years, 2 months, 8 days. The wills of both husband and wife are preserved in the Essex office. Each of their three sons had a son William; John and Thomas, in fact, had two, the first one in each case having doubtless d. in infancy. The surviving William of Thomas was b. too late to have been number four of our line, who must have been either John's surviving son or William's son of that name.

III. JOHN and SARAH (STACEY) PEACH. John was b. about 1680 and m. Sarah Stacey of Salem, Nov. 30, (or Dec 30), 1700. They had five c., of whom the surviving William was baptized as an infant, Feb. 24, 1712.

Or,

III. WILLIAM and SARAH (ELKINS) PEACH. William was b. in 1683, and m. Sarah Elkins of Lynn, Jan. 4, 1711. They had six c., of whom William was b. Feb. 13, 1712, (?) and baptized March 28, 1714.

IV. WILLIAM, JR., and AMY (TREFRY) PEACH. William was b. in 1711 or 1712, and m. Amy Trefry, Sept. 12, 1734. Their c., according to the baptismal records of the 1st Ch. of Marblehead, were John, Amy, Agnes, Sarah, Mary, William, Hannah and Elizabeth. Note that only two of the eight c. were sons. It is a tradition amongst us that we are descended from two brothers who came from England; in truth, 'twas their great grandfather who came from England. William was a carter, and his business descended to John, his first-born son. He held several offices by election at town meetings, "hayward," constable, sealer of leather, "hogg reave," juror, etc. He d. before Feb. 5, 1771.

Of the other Williams contemporary with the carter, and his first cousins, one was a fisherman, who d. before Sept. 7, 1773. Which one of the Williams had a negro servant, Cesar, who was publicly whipped for stealing, in 1769, and which William was one of ten heads of families, out of 712 in Marblehead, who, in 1770, obstinately refused to sign an agreement against trade with Great Britain, and particularly against the use of India tea, is not known.

We come now to the William who settled in Newbury:

1 WILLIAM and ELIZABETH (BOWDEN) PEACH. William, son of William and Amy (Trefry), was b. in 1748 and baptized May 7, 1749. He m. Elizabeth, widow of Samuel Messervy, (and mother of the Samuel Messervy who

settled in Newbury), Aug. 2, 1772. Her maiden name was Bowden. They had eight c. baptized in the 1st Ch. of Marblehead, of whom the first and fifth were named Elizabeth and the second and third William—the first of each name having evidently d. in infancy. The others were John, Thomas, Amy Trefry and Twisden Bowden, Sarah, their ninth c. was b. June 12, 1790. In Marblehead, William followed the craft of "house-wright," "joyner" and "cabinet-maker;" after his removal to Vermont he was designated as "yeoman."

William Peach was a Revolutionary soldier. From July 15, 1775, to Jan. 1, 1777, he belonged to the Sea Coast Defence service, in the company at the fort in Marblehead commanded successively by Captains Wm. Hooper and Edw. Fettyplace. (See archives in the State House, Boston.) This company was called to Bunker Hill, but not in time to engage in the battle. William's name is found in certain memoranda of the same company, dated Feb. 18, Aug. 26 and Dec. 31, 1777, indicating his continuous service throughout that year also. He was a matross (cannoneer). In August, 1778, a Marblehead company to which he belonged marched to Rhode Island and joined the army under Gen. Sullivan. Here he served two months, when the siege of Newport was abandoned; to this, William Hooper made affidavit Nov. 21, 1833. Wm. Peach was one of the soldiers engaged in transporting bread in small boats for the army at Tiverton, who were fired upon by the British, and some of the bullets were found lodged in the bread; an experience of which his son John testified having heard him often tell. Aug. 22, 1834, Joseph Berry wrote from Newbury to the Commissioner of Pensions at Washington, urging the claim of William Peach in these words: "The old man and his wife are both infirm and helpless as infants, and his mental capacity is even more impaired than his bodily faculties, and he has been endeavoring for I believe near fifteen years to establish what he thought to be a just claim to a pension." Sept. 3, 1834, the claim was allowed, based on seventeen months and fifteen days of service, and he received $204.16 back pay, and $58.33 yearly for the remaining five years of his long life. He should have been credited with at least thirty-one and one-half months; and it was his own recollection that he continued to serve at the Marblehead fort until the close of the war.

In 1788 and before, William was a member of the fire company of the engine, "Friendship." Just before his removal from Marblehead, occurred an interesting episode connected with his craft. On April 6, 1789, he was one of nine men who bought a lot from Knott Martin, Jr., upon which to erect a meeting-house. August 5 of the same year Dr. Hopkins. (author of the "Hopkinsian theology"), preached the dedicatory sermon from Haggai ii: 9. Nov. 8 of the same year their house was shut, "Moses Bradford, an illiterate man," having preached the last sermon. March 29, 1790, the nine men resold the property to Knott Martin, Jr., for his personal use. It was used from time to time for Methodist and Baptist services, and eventually turned around and converted into a double dwelling-house, now numbers 9 and 11 Watson street.

William's name is on the Assessors' lists of Marblehead from 1769 to 1790. Sept. 7 of the latter year, two months before removing to Vermont, he sold the northeast end of his former "mansion-house" to John Seawood, and the other end to Joseph Brown, Oct. 19, 1796. Two years later Joseph Brown, who was a black man and a Revolutionary patriot, bought the Seawood half from Mary, widow of John. "Black Joe" and "Aunt 'Crease," his wife, are historic names in Marblehead. Their adopted daughter inherited the estate, and sold it in 1867 to Henry Berry, whose widow still owns it. The house is most picturesquely hidden away behind the trees on the hill back of the junction of Beacon and Norman streets, and is reached by a narrow, winding, rock-walled lane.

William's life in Newbury is touched upon by the author of this history, in the proper place. The present contributor may add a word concerning William's older and only brother, John, who was baptized May 16, 1736, m. Elizabeth Conant, Jan. 6, 1761, (?) and d. in the house which he had built at "the ferry," (now the Curtis house), June 21, 1792. His widow lived until May 27, 1816. John and Elizabeth had thirteen c. spared to grow up, six sons and seven daus. At least two of the daus. m. in Newbury,

Amy to Thomas Burroughs, 1794, or before, and Sarah to Nicholas White, Oct. 25, 1803. With the exception of a French family who assumed the name, all of the Peaches now living in Marblehead are descended from two of the six sons, John and Lot, and nearly all from Lot. The last son of Thomas, another of the six, was Benjamin F., Sr., who d. Oct. 4, 1899, at the age of 82 years, 11 months and 4 days; he was the father of Maj.-Gen. Benj. F. Peach, Jr., of Lynn. Four of Lot's c. are living: Mary (Merritt), aged 80, (1899), Stephen B., Eben and Ruth. The next to youngest of the six sons of John and Elizabeth, Ebenezer W., moved to Mt. Desert Island, Me., where his descendants now live. Of William's four sons two abode in Newbury and two emigrated.

William Peach was in Newbury as early as 1788. Tradition says that he came here as chain-bearer with a party of surveyors. June 9, 1790, he bought of John C. Foster a farm of 128 acres for £60, ten acres was cleared, on which was a house. The deed is dated at Marblehead, June 9, 1790. To this purchase he added much out-lying land and became a large land owner. This farm remained in the family till 1865, when it was sold to Ezra B. Willoughby. At his death in 1893 it was bought by F. G. Howland, who now lives on it.

They came to Newbury in 1790, he on foot and his wife on horseback, bringing her son, Twisden, two years old, with them in her arms. He used a willow staff and his wife a willow riding whip. When they arrived at their destination they stuck both staff and whip into the ground where they took root, and still stand, on each side of the road that turns off to Wallace hill, a few rods below Mr. Howland's house. The one which carries the guide board was the whip and the other the cane. The girth of the latter is about twelve feet. These trees are mentioned in a survey of a road in 1810. In his old age William Peach drew a pension. He d. on that place, Aug. 3, 1837, aged 91, his wife having d. Jan. 20, of the same year, aged 91, their married life being 66 years, 5 months, 18 days. Their first dwelling was a log house which stood on the south side of the road, and the first framed house, built 1805, was taken down in 1872.

Children:
i. Elizabeth, d. in infancy.
ii. William, d. in infancy.
2 iii. William, b. May 3, 1776; d. Dec. 11, 1822.
3 iv. John, b. Aug. 20, 1779; d. July 1, 1867.
v. Betsey, (Elizabeth), b. July 1781; m. Dea. Wm. Burroughs; q. v.; d.
4 vi. Thomas, b. Jan. 9, 1784: d. Feb. 8, 1882; q. v.
vii. Amy Trefry, b. Jan. 10, 1786; d. Nov. 24, 1871; she never m.
5 viii. Twisden Bowden, b. May, 1788; d. Feb. 24, 1855; q v.
ix. Sarah, (Sally), b. June 12, 1790; m. Jacob Bayley of Jefferson Hill; d. Feb. 8, 1870; q. v.

2 *WILLIAM,[2] (William,[1]), was b. in Marblehead May 3, and baptised June 15, 1777; went back to his birthplace for a wife, marrying Sarah Pearce, Jan. 22. 1800. In 1815, they left Newbury, stopping first near Marietta, Ohio; then, in 1818, removing in flat boats down the Ohio river to its mouth, and "cordelling" up the Mississippi to Kaskaskia. They settled in "Horse Prairie" near Red Bud, Randolph County, Illinois, where William d. Dec. 11, 1822. Their c. were b. in Newbury with the exception of the last two. They were: William, b. Oct. 20, 1800; Mary, Feb. 4, 1803; Sarah, Dec. 27, 1804; Lois, Jan. 23, 1807; Thomas, Jan. 23, 1809; Nathaniel, Jan. 27, 1811; Samuel, June 17, 1813; John, Nov. 6, 1818; and Eliza Ann, Oct. 17, 1820. Thomas and Nathaniel d. in childhood and the others have all followed, the last surviving one having been John, who d. at Lebanon, Ill., March 31, 1895, shortly after celebrating his golden wedding.——Many of William's grandchildren are living in Illinois and

---

*William Peach lived in a house which stood on the east side of the road, about half way between W. M. Rollins' and J. C. Temple's. It has been gone 70 years, or more.
                                                                            J. J. PEACH.

further West. The c. of his oldest son, William, (the one who visited Newbury in 1858), who was thrice m., and d. March 17, 1875, are: William, b. Oct. 25, 1826, now living near Greenville, Illinois; Lois, [Ehly], Jan. 24, 1829, O'Fallon, Ill., widow; Rebecca [Swift], Feb. 20, 1831, widow of the Rev. John Swift, Baptist; lives with (her youngest son, Fuller, who is also a Baptist minister and lecturer, Madison, Ind.);—the foregoing three by his first marriage to Priscilla Simmons, Dec. 18, 1825, (she d. Aug. 20, 1835); by his 2d wife, Elizabeth (Grotts), Gregory, wedded May 21, 1837, the following: Elizabeth [Elliott], b. Apr. 24, 1838; d. Dec., 1891; Samuel, May 19, 1840, Port Townsend Wash.; John, Feb. 9, 1842, O'Fallon, Ill.; Eliza Ann [Morey], Oct. 9, 1847, Mountain View, Mo.————William's grandchildren by his son Samuel, (b. June 17, 1813; d. Dec. 17, 1888, at Waterloo, Ill.,) were: William H. (b. Aug. 20, 1845; d. Apr., 1878); Malinda [Daws], O'Fallon, Ill.; Mary [Moore], St, Louis, Mo.; Josie [Forester], Tonamack, Ill.; Maggie [Evans], O'Fallon, Ill.——William's grandchildren by his son John, (Nov 6, 1818; d. March 31, 1895), are: James S., (April 10, 1845), Lebanon, Ill.; William Preston, (Feb. 26, 1848), Rogers, Ark.; Emma [Ducket], (May 29, 1850), Bogard, Mo.; Edward, (Sept. 3, 1854), Lebanon, Ill.; Cyrus, (March 19, 1857), St. Louis, Mo. Two sisters, Clara and Mary Etta, d. un-m. The widowed mother, whose maiden name was Mary Brickey. survives at Lebanon. Ill.*

3 *JOHN,[2] (William,[1]) b. Marblehead, 1779; came to Newbury with his parents. In 1801, he, with Joshua and Noyes Bayley, began settlement on Jefferson Hill, his farm being that owned by his son, A. M. Peach. He m 1st, 1803, Jane Smith, of Scotch descent. who d. Feb. 6, 1831. He m. 2d, Anna, (Nancy), widow of Josiah L. Bayley, who d. Oct. 15, 1877. He d. July 1, 1867.

6   Children, all by 1st marriage:
   i. James, b. Feb. 8, 1804; d. April 7, 1802.
   ii. Anna, b. Feb. 9, 1807; m. Solomon Jewell, q. v.; d. Oct. 12, 1859.
   iii. Jane, b. 1808; m. Aaron Morse. They lived near where Mrs. James now does, and had six c.
   iv. John, b. April 17, 1812; farmer in Newbury, but rem. to Dakota in old age. He m. Betsey, dau. Josiah L. Bailey. Both d. in the west. C., two d. y. Ellen, m. Charles H. George.
   v. Christian, b. 1814; m. David Jewell.
   vi. Mary, b. 1816; m. John Thomas, q. v.; d. March 25, 1857.
   vii. Amy, b. Aug. 30, 1818; never m.; d. April 20, 1901.
   viii. Alexander M., b. Jan. 18, 1822; farmer on homestead. He was a justice of the peace and grand juror. He m. Phebe Hadley, who d. Oct. 5, 1888. Several c., only one, Martha, survived infancy. She fell down stairs and was killed, Feb. 6, 1866, in her 9th year. Mr. Peach was found dead in his house, where he lived alone, June 29, 1901.
   ix. Nancy W., b. April 12, 1824; m. Alvah C. James.

4 THOMAS,[2] (William,[1]) was a remarkable man. He was b. Jan. 9, and baptised Jan. 11, 1784, in Marblehead. He became a physician, and was a surgeon in the war of 1812, on the staff of Col. Fifield of the Vermont militia, serving from Sept. 18, to Dec. 12, inclusive, of that year. He afterwards made his home in Boscawen, N. H., where he m. Sukey Gerrish, Feb. 2, 1815. She was said to have been a lineal descendant, in the twelfth generation, of John Rogers, who was martyred at Smithfield, England. They had four c: Henry Gerrish, (Dec. 5, 1816—Sept. 6, 1858), Mary Gerrish, (Nov. 13, 1818—Nov. 8, 1837), Susann, (March 2, 1826—), and Elizabeth, (June 3, 1828—Nov. 7, 1892). Henry moved to Indiana in 1855, and his parents followed in April, 1858, only a few months before the son's death. The mother d. Dec. 6, 1871. But Dr. Thomas on April 23, of the next year, being then past eighty-eight years old, was granted a pension of eight dollars monthly, which he drew for almost ten years, until his death, at West Creek, Lake County, Ind., Feb. 8, 1882, at the extraordinary age of over ninety-eight years.——The son, Henry, m. Esther E. Coffin of

*The record of this family was supplied by the editor.

Boscawen, April 16, 1840, and they had one son, George Henry, b. June 10, 1841, now living near Toledo, Ohio. Esther d. Oct. 28, 1843, and Henry m. Betsey C. Watson, Sept. 5, 1844, the issue being one son, Abiel Plumer, now living in Nebraska, and three daus.——Susann, m. E. N. Morey, 1846, and lives at Lowell, Lake County, Ind. Her eldest son, Thomas Peach Morey, m. her cousin William Peach's youngest dau., Eliza Ann, Oct. 17, 1871; they live at Mountain View, Mo. Susann had also two daus., and a younger son.——Elizabeth became the second wife of her cousin William Peach's oldest son, William, of Greenville, Ill., March 12, 1866, and their only c., Carrie, m. Emslie Peach of O'Fallon, Ill., the son of John, her father's half brother—a notable series of intermarriages of kinsfolk, but in no case of first cousins.

5 *Twisden Bowden, b. Marblehead, Mass., May, 1788; settled in Newbury, and later on the homestead. but d. while on a visit at Farmsville, Mass., Feb. 27, 1855. Buried in Newbury. He m. Dec. 31, 1811, Mary, dau. of Col. John Smith, (b. Jan. 1, 1788; d. Jan. 15, 1849).
Children:
i.   William S., b. Sept. 20, 1815; m. Lucia Brewster, of Burlington; d. Dec. 11, 1881. Two c., George, killed by the Indians while in the army, and Hattie, who m. a Mr. Drew.
ii. Elizabeth, b. Jan. 30, 1818; m. Sylvester Lee, and lived in Milbury, Mass., but d. in a hospital in Philadelphia, while being treated for cancer. One son, Charles, lived in Newbury in boyhood; served in a Rhode Island regiment in the rebellion; taken prisoner while carrying dispatches, and confined at Andersonville, where he suffered greatly. He m. and went west after the war.
iii. Jonathan J.,[3] (Twisden,[2] William,[1]) b. April 27, 1820; he m. 1st, Phebe, dau. Daniel Richardson, of Embden, Maine; farmer on homestead, which he sold in April, (1865); served nine months, (1862, 1863), in Co. 11, 12th Vt.; went west after the war, and lived in Kansas. During a long period of hard times they became dissatisfied with the country, and wishing to return to Vermont, but being without funds, Mr. Peach built a covered vehicle containing a stove and bedding, in which he and his wife and the latter's niece returned to Vermont. They left Phillips County, Kansas, about Nov. 10, 1883, went to Lincoln, Neb., crossed the Missouri at Nebraska City, through the southern tier of counties in Iowa, to Princeton, Ill., where he bought a sled, and put his wagon on it, and went through northern Ohio, northern Pennsylvania, to North Adams, Mass., and Newbury. They were on the road 74 days, with the same pair of horses, reaching Newbury the last of March. Mrs. Peach d. April 16, 1891, and he m. 2d, October, 1892, Mrs. Jones. Rem. to North Haverhill, 1898.
iv. Sarah Jenness, b. Sept. 9, 1822; m. 1st Ammaziah Holbrook, and went west where he d. at Red Wing, Minn. After some years she m. 2d, John S. Butterworth of Philadelphia, where they lived. In 1890 they came to West Newbury and opened a store where John Tyler now trades, where she d. May 15, 1891, and he returned to Philadelphia, and soon after d. there.
v.   Mary Ann, b. March 20, 1826; d. Sept. 23, 1828.
vi. Charles S., b. May 10, 1828; went to Massachusetts about 1848, and worked in a machine shop, which was burned soon after he learned the trade; began work as "spare hand" in the Dwight Mfg. Co. at Chicopee, a cotton mill, at 61 cents per day, and remained there 17 years, 7 months; at the close of that time he received a salary of $1600 per annum. This time included the period of the Civil war. At one time the cotton mills were closed, and he entered the United States Armory at Springfield, Mass., where his experience as a machinist came into use. Maj. A. B. Dyar was then superintendent of the armory. After a time Mr. Peach was appointed by Col. Thornton, the head of the ordnance department, as inspector of guns, etc., made at public armories, retaining the position till the war closed. Leaving the Dwight Co., he became superintendent of the

Freeman Mfg. Co.'s three cotton mills at North Adams, where he still resides. His salary was $2000 per annum. He held the position thirteen years and three months, when he resigned on account of his health. Assessor of North Adams seven years. Registrar one year. Member of Lafayette Lodge of Free Masons. and of the Berkshire Club, and a director of the board of trade. He m. Sept. 23, 1873, Hannah M., dau. of John W. and Emily A. Haynes, of Rowe, Mass. C., Clara Belle, b. Oct. 7, 1875, and Charles Henry, b. June 25, 1877. Mrs. Peach is a sister of Prof. Haynes, the distinguished Asiatic explorer.

   vii.   Mary Ann, b. Nov. 26, 1830; m. 1851, Henry F. Livesey of Milbury, Mass., where he d. Jan. 14, 1881, aged 50. C., (1) Frederick, m. Agnes Smith; d. Spencer, Mass. (2) Charles, m. 1st, Lilla Sly of Newbury; 2d, Lizzie Foss. (3) Nellie, d. at two months old. (4) Clara, m. James Morse of Hopkinton, Mass.; res. Worcester. (5) John, m. Mary Allen; lives in Spencer, Mass. (6) Samuel, in Illinois.

   viii.   Samuel Smith, b. June 15, 1835; m. May 7, 1867, Sophia A., dau. David Felker. Clerk some years for C. M. Morse, then for H. H. Deming at the village, then for Franklin Deming at Wells River. In 1871 he went into partnership with Ferdinand Sherwin as general merchants, later he has conducted business for himself in the Baldwin block, employing two or three clerks. In 1901 he sold out to Ora Bishop and others.

6 JAMES,[3] (John,[2] William,[1]) b. Feb. 8, 1804; the 1st c. b. on Jefferson Hill, where he was a farmer near his father, but afterward bought where Mr. Randall lately lived, whose house was burned in June, 1900. He m. March 28, 1828, Agnes Gardner, (b. Ryegate, June 1, 1799). He d. Apr. 7, 1872; she d. Nov. 25, 1883.

   Children:

   i.   John, b. March 28, 1829, went to California and d.

   ii.   Mary Jane, b. Apr. 9, 1830; m. ————————. Their dau., Belle, m. 1st, Valentine Weed, and 2d, William Whitehill.

   ii.   Hugh G., b. Dec. 29, 1831; m. a Miss Hadley, sister of Mrs. A. M. Peach. Farmer on the "David Jewell place;" 7 c.

   iv.   William, b. Oct. 15, 1833; went to Oregon where he m.

   v.   George N., b. March 20, 1835; enlisted in the 3d Vermont; re-enlisted and was killed at Petersburg. Va., near the end of the war.

   vi.   Thomas, b. Aug. 15, 1837; went to Oregon. He m. in Newbury in 1872, Augusta, dau. Hiram and Augusta (Martin) Nutt. They went to Oregon where he d. leaving c.

   vii.   David, b. March 30, 1839; farmer in Newbury; went to Oregon. He m. Apr. 21, 1866, Mary Jane, dau. W. M. Brock, (b. Oct. 6, 1842; d. July 30, 1895). (On page 478 the date of their m. is incorrectly given as 1886).

   viii.   Hannah, b. Jan. 10, 1842; m. 1st, J. Gardner; m. 2d, William Corey, both d. Res. Newbury Center. Her c. living are Mrs. Brown and Mrs. Herbert Waldron and a younger dau.

PORTER.

SAMUEL and his wife came from the west of England in 1622, and settled at Plymouth, Mass. In the sixth generation from the emigrant was Col. Asa Porter, b. probably at Boxford, Mass., May 24, 1742, graduated at Harvard College in 1762, and became a merchant at Newburyport. He came to Haverhill before 1771, and settled on Horse Meadow, where he built the large, old-fashioned house on the Southard place, which was his farm. He was a man of great influence, and a large land owner, at one time, it is said, owning over 100,000 acres. He was a prominent tory during the Revolutionary war, and for his losses and sufferings, received from the crown, a grant of the township of Broome, in the Province of Quebec. He owned a great part of Topsham, and large tracts of land in Newbury, which still go by the name of the "Porter lots." He was Lieutenant Colonel in the colonial militia, and held many positions of trust. In his religious views he was an Episcopalian. He d. Dec. 28, 1818, and his wife, Mehitabel Crocker, Feb. 7, 1821, aged 80. They are buried at Horse Meadow.

Arthur Livermore thus speaks of Colonel Porter: "Col. Porter's manner and mode of life were such as become a gentleman, and his discriminating hospitalities were generous and extensive. He invested very advantageously in lands in Canada, as well as nearer home, but did not live long enough to realize the magnificent estate which they would, in a few more years, have become. It might not be easy to find his equal among his numerous descendants, but they have been, to an extraordinary degree, bright, gay, graceful and winning. Col. Porter was tall and spare in his figure. He was largely conversant with men, and a great many of his pithy sayings were currently repeated seventy years ago."

Col. Porter employed a great many men, some of whom were colored, on his farm. He had a balcony built upon the roof of his house, whence he could, with a glass, survey his fields, and see if the men worked steadily. Children:

    i.   John, lawyer, settled finally in Broome, P. Q.
1   ii.   Benjamin, lawyer of Newbury.
   iii.   Mary, m. Hon. Daniel Farrand, of Newbury.
   iv.   Elizabeth, m. Hon. Thomas W. Thompson.
    v.   Sarah, m. Hon. Mills Olcott of Hanover. Of her daus, one m. W. H. Duncan of Hanover, another m. Joseph Bell, a noted lawyer of Haverhill and Boston, and a third became the wife of Rufus Choate, the great advocate. Moses Porter, the youngest of the family, d. in Haverhill.

1   BENJAMIN, was b. at Newburyport, July 13, 1771, and was m. Oct. 11, 1800, to Martha, dau. of Col. Peter Olcott, of Norwich. He was admitted to the bar, and succeeded to Mr. Farrand's practice, when the latter left Newbury in 1800, and lived in the same house, where Mrs. Miller now lives, at the Ox-bow. Some years before his death, he rem. to South Newbury, to the house which was built by John Mills, and is now very much altered, called the Davenport house. He was widely known as a lawyer and man of business, and was considered by Daniel Webster, who knew him well, as the most attractive social companion he had ever known. Benjamin Porter was town representative in 1811, 1812 and 1816. He introduced the grass generally called "witch grass," into this part of the country, in the idea that it would be of great benefit to farmers. It was formerly called "Porter grass." He visited Saratoga for his health, in the summer of 1818, and d. at the house of his brother-in-law, Mills Olcott, at Hanover, Aug. 2d, of that year, and is buried there. Mrs. Porter rem. to Hanover in 1821, and d. there May 4, 1825. She was a member of the 1st church. Children:

    i.   Timothy Olcott, b. Feb. 23, 1802, graduated at Dartmouth College, 1822; was some years in the south, returned and graduated at the medical college at Hanover, in 1829. He practiced medicine a while, then engaged in literary pursuits, and was for some years a professor in Coudert's French Academy, New York. In 1839, Dr. Porter and N. P. Willis started a weekly journal, called "The Corsair," which had for its contributors, some of the best writers of that day. In literary work until death, Jan. 6, 1852.
   ii.   Benjamin, b. Jan. 31, 1804; m. Rebecca Seton Maitland, a ward of Bishop Hobart. In business at Mobile, Ala., then associated with his brothers in literary work. He d. Dec. 11, 1840.
   iii.   Mehetabel, b. Dec. 28, 1805; m. a Mr. Paine, was living at Washington, D. C., in 1894.
   iv.   Martha, b. Dec. 5, 1807.
    v.   William Trotter, b. Dec. 21, 1809; learned the printer's trade at Andover, Mass.; connected with the Farmers' Herald at St. Johnsbury one year; went to New York city in 1831, and worked with Horace Greeley in John T. West's printing office. Mr. Porter and James How started a weekly sporting paper called the "Spirit of the Times" in Dec. 1831, Mr. Greeley being their foreman for a short time. This paper soon reached a very large circulation, it was carefully edited and was considered an authority upon sports of the turf. In 1845, he published a collection of sketches entitled "The Big Bear of Arkansas," which had a large sale. In 1839 Mr. Porter began the publication of the American Turf Register, an illustrated magazine. He also contributed largely to the Tribune and the magazines

of the day, and was engaged in active literary work. He was greatly esteemed and one of the best known men of his time in New York. He d. after some months of failing health, July 19, 1857. His life was written by Francis Brinley, and published by the Appletons in 1860.

vi. Sarah Olcott, b. Nov. 16, 1811; m. Francis Brinley, a well known literary character of New York.

vii. George, b. Nov. 27, 1813; graduated at Dartmouth College 1831; studied law in New York and practiced there. Went to New Orleans in 1842, and became associate editor of the "Picayune." He had a perfect knowledge of the Spanish language; went to Mexico as reporter during the Mexican war. He d. at the St. Charles Hotel, May 24, 1849. His death was greatly lamented.

viii. Francis, b. 1816; in a counting house in New York, 1835-37; in Mississippi, 1837-39; in New York with his four brothers, 1841-45; went to New Orleans and was associated with his brother, George, on the Picayune, succeeding him as associate editor. Visited Europe, 1854; d. in New Orleans of consumption, Feb. 28, 1855.

These brothers, excepting the youngest, were remarkable for their large size, being each of them over six feet four inches in height, and large in proportion.

POWERS.

WALTER was the emigrant ancestor of this family. He was b. in Devonshire, Eng., in 1640; came to Massachusetts, while young, and m. Tryal, dau. of Dea. Ralph Shepherd, of London, Eng., and Malden, Mass. He settled in Nashobah, now Littleton, Mass. They had seven sons and two daus. Of these, Daniel, b. 1669, m. Elizabeth Bates, and their c. were seven sons and three daus. Of these Peter, b. Littleton, 1707, m. Anna Keyes of Chelmsford, and settled in West Dunstable, now Hollis. Captain in the militia, and of an exploring company to the Coös country in 1754, and of the Hollis company in the Crown Point Expedition in 1755. He d. in Hollis, Aug. 5, 1757, (History of Hollis says Aug. 27), and his wife, Sept. 21, 1798, aged 90. Their c. were Peter, Stephen, Anna, Whitcomb, Phebe, Alice, Levi, Nahum, Francis, Fanny, Philip, Sampson and Farma. Stephen, Whitcomb and Levi were in the Old French war; Stephen, Francis, Nahum and Sampson served in the Revolution. Sampson, who m. Elizabeth Abbott, was the father of Rev. Grant Powers, author of "Historical Sketches of the Coös Country." Peter, the oldest son, b. Nov. 28, 1728, in Dunstable, fitted for college with Rev. Daniel Emerson of Hollis, and graduated at Harvard College in 1754, in the same class with John Hancock, John Adams and Governor Wentworth being in the class below him. He declined a call to the church at New Ipswich, N. H., and was settled over the church at Newent, now Lisbon, Conn., 1756-64; came to Newbury, in May, 1764; received a call from the town, Jan. 27, 1765, which he accepted Feb. 10, following. Installed pastor of the "Church of Christ at Newbury and Haverhill," at Hollis, Feb. 27, 1765, and moved his family to Newbury the following April. For further account of his ministry in Newbury see, in this volume, "First Congregational Church" and "Bibliography of Newbury," also see "Historical Sketches of the Coös Country," by Rev. Grant Powers. He rem. to Haverhill in 1781, closed his ministry there in 1783, and after preaching for some time in Cornish, N. H., rem. to Deer Island, Me., and was the first minister there, dying of a cancer, May 13, 1800, in his 72d year, and the 56th of his ministry. He revisited Newbury in 1788 and in 1796. Mr. Powers preached the Election Sermon before the General Assembly at Windsor. in 1778. The Assembly appointed a committee to receive any contributions for the preacher which might be given, and obtained £10 which was paid him. In person, Mr. Powers was above the middle height, strong and athletic. He was a ready speaker, possessing a strong voice, and a very distinct utterance. His dress on the Sabbath was a Kerseymere coat with breeches and stockings, a three cornered hat, a fleece-like wig, a white band, and white silk gloves. Mr. Powers m.

probably in 1756, Martha, dau. of Jonathan Hale of Sutton, Mass., (See Hale Family). She d. Jan. 22, 1802, while on a visit to her c. in Newbury, being found dead upon her knees after returning from church on the Sabbath, and was buried at the Ox-bow. The figure of Rev. Peter Powers stands out from the obscurity of the early days, as does that of no other man. He seems to have been an able and faithful minister of the gospel, widely known and beloved, and won the affectionate regard of the people. He was the man for the time and place, and filled, admirably, every position to which he was called. His labors were arduous, and he must have possessed a constitution of iron to have accomplished all he did. His parish at first included all the settlements from Hanover to Lancaster; he was often called to go on long and lonely journeys through the wilderness to solemnize marriages, bury the dead, and break the bread of life to the people, and he did not shrink from any labor however great. Very little of his actual work has come down to us; a few printed sermons, which are earnest and devout, and letters, hardly more in number, concise, practical, and to the point. In his views he was very decided, and for those times, very liberal. His letter of acceptance to the church at Deer Isle, copied from the records of that town, has been much admired:

"To the Church of Christ on Deer Island. Dearly beloved in our Lord Jesus Christ. You having invited and called upon me to take the paternal oversight of you in the Lord, and it appearing to be of God, after mature deliberation and prayer, I now publicly return my answer in the affirmative. I ask a daily interest in your prayers for the gracious fulfilment of that great promise, 'Lo, I am with you alway, even to the end of the world.' Amen.' To the inhabitants and good people who have concurred with the church in the call and liberally offered for my support, I thankfully accept it, and promise through the grace of God to serve you all, the poor as well as the rich, according to my ability. You will, I trust, strive together with me in your prayers for me, that I may be enabled to be faithful unto the death, and present you and your dear children faultless before the presence of our Lord Jesus Christ, at his coming, with unspeakable joy. Finally, brethren, be perfect, be of good comfort, be of one mind, live in peace, and the God of love and peace shall be with you. So prays your pastor elect.   PETER POWERS."

He is buried at Deer Isle, and his epitaph reads thus:

"REV. PETER POWERS.

Born at Dunstable, N. H., Nov. 28, 1728,
Died May 13, 1800, after a successful
Ministry of about fifty-five years.
The joys of faith triumphant rise,
And wing the soul above the skies."

Their c. were as follows, the dates of birth as given by Mrs. Farr:

    i.   Peter, b. Oct. 9, 1757; d. at New York in the Continental army, Sept. 3, 1776, and buried there.
    ii. Martha, b. May 24, 1759; d. Haverhill, Oct. 16, 1782.
    iii. Damaris, b. Jan. 8, 1761; m. Samuel Grow, q. v.
1 iv. Stephen, b. July 15, 1762.
2 v.   Jonathan, b. March 17, 1764.
3 vi. Samuel, b. Jan. 31, 1766.
    vii. John, b. Dec. 13, 1767; d. Apr. 18, 1778.
    viii. Prescott, b. Jan. 8, 1770; settled in Maine.
    ix. Hale, b. Dec. 22, 1771; settled in Maine.
4 x.   Moody, b. Nov. 9, 1773.
    xi. Anna, b. June 27, 1775; d. June 4, 1777.
    xii. Peter, b. Aug. 4, 1777; settled in Maine; d. 1870.
    xiii. Anna, b. July 25, 1779; d. in Maine.

In the Hale genealogy, Samuel is given as 5th and Jonathan as 6th, the latter b. in Newbury. Chipman's "Dartmouth Alumni" gives Jonathan as b. here.

1 STEPHEN, b. Newent, Conn., July 15, 1762; served in Capt. Frye Bayley's Co., guarding and scouting, 1 month, 20 days, in 1781; m. Feb. 12, 1786, Mary (Polly) Grow, b. Pomfret, Conn. They settled at West Newbury,

and cleared a farm where George Page now lives. He d. March 22, 1843;
she d. Apr. 1, 1843; buried at West Newbury.
Children:
i. Peter, b. Apr. 17, 1787; m. Ruth. dau. Josiah Rogers. Lived in Corinth
and had c.; Alden, who served in the navy; Peter, Nelson, Grenville, d. y.;
Abigail, m. Col. Sanborn of Bunker Hill, Iowa; Luthera, who. m. Joel
Derby of Vershire; Grenville of Corinth, and Sarah, twin sister of Alden,
who m. Horace T. Keyes of Vershire and Newbury. He d. June 25, 1857.
ii. Martha, d. in infancy.
iii. Martha, b. May 23, 1790; m. John Bailey; q. v.
iv. Anna, b. May 12, 1792; m. Thomas Abbott; q. v.
v. Jonathan, b. March 8, 1792; m. Harriet Corliss, March 21, 1822; d. July 1,
1873, at West Burke.
vi. Polly, b. Dec. 5, 1795; d. Oct. 12, 1823.
vii. Abigail, b. Sept. 7, 1797; m. Thomas Abbott as 2d wife.
viii. Stephen, b. July 16, 1799; m. Mary Stevens of Piermont; b. Sept. 14, 1802.
C., b. Newbury. (1) Joseph, b. Aug. 24, 1823; m. Sarah Downing; d. 1866.
(2) Mary, b. Jan. 16, 1825; m. Jonathan Merrill. (3) Betsey, b. Nov. 23,
1826; m. Daniel Cleveland. (4) John, b. Nov. 27, 1828; m. Ann Moore.
(5) Isaac, b. Dec. 23, 1830; m. Mary Baldwin; d. March, 1875. (6) Love,
b. Jan. 19, 1833; m. John Aiken. (7) Anne, b. Nov. 19, 1835; m. William
Harding. (8) Harriet, b. Jan. 25, 1837; m. W. E. Hill; d. Dec. 12, 1872.
He d. in New York, Dec. 12, 1869.
ix. John, b. July 30 1802; d. July 13, 1803.
x. Betsey, b. June 6, 1804; m. John Powers.
xi. Electa D., b. Dec. 13, 1806; m. Jonathan Powers.

2 JONATHAN, b. March 17, 1764; (Chipman's Dartmouth Alumni gives Newbury
as his birthplace). Served 15 days in Capt. Frye Bayley's Co., guarding
and scouting in 1781. Taught the first school in Ryegate; graduated at
Dartmouth College 1793; pastor of Cong. Ch. at Penobscot, Me., 1796,
till death, 1808. Twice m.; 1st to a sister of the wife of Rev. Nathaniel
Lambert of Newbury.

3 SAMUEL, b. Newbury, Jan. 31, 1766; (another record makes him b. in Hollis,
1764). Farmer; lived a little north of the schoolhouse in the Powers
(now Rollins) neighborhood. His father intended him for the ministry,
but he thought his brother Jonathan was better fitted for the calling and
gave place to him. He was a member of the Cong. Ch. more than 75
years, and greatly respected, holding many town offices. He was a very
good scholar, and a practical surveyor. For the last ten years of his life
he was blind. He m., 1st, Feb. 14, 1788, Anna Grow, who d. June 16,
1789; one c.; 2d, March 13, 1795, Sarah Ford, who d. Sept. 1799, in her
28th year; two c.; 3d. March 23, 1802, Mary, dau. Ebenezer White, (b.
March 23, 1761; d. Feb. 16, 1849). He d. Jan. 21, 1857; buried at
Boltonville.
Children:
i. John, b. Jan. 26, 1789. Lived near his father's; m. Nov. 27, 1826, his
double cousin, Betsey, dau. Stephen Powers, (b. June 16, 1804; d. Dec. 25,
1877). C., (1) John, b. July 5, 1827; d. Jan. 1, 1885. (2) Anna S., b. Nov.
11, 1840; d. Jan. 28, 1881.
5 ii. Moody, b. Dec. 5, 1795; d. July 1, 1869.
iii. Anna, b. Feb. 14, 1797; m. John H. Carbee of Newbury and Bath.

4 MOODY, b. Nov. 9, 1773; physician at Deer Isle, Me., excepting one year at St.
Stephen, N. B. He m. Elizabeth Eaton. Nine c., of whom Elizabeth E., b.
St. Stephen, N. B., Aug. 12, 1805, m. in Boston, David Tyler; res. Deer
Isle until his death. when she came to Newbury, and m. Oct. 1850, John B.
Carleton, as 2d wife. She d. June 8, 1878. Mr. Powers d. Nov. 30, 1853.
Children by 1st marriage:
i. George P. Tyler, b. Deer Isle, Sept. 16, 1833; farmer at West Newbury. He
lost his right arm by falling from a load of wood while descending Sawyer
Hill, Jan. 9, 1880, getting caught under the sled. Thrown from his wagon
in "Goshen," Dec. 30, 1899, and d. same day. He m. Dec. 31, 1862, Eliza
H., dau. Thomas Smith, who d. May 12, 1899. C., (1) Clarice L., b. Dec.
4, 1864. (2) John B. C., b. Feb. 22, 1869, merchant at West Newbury;

m. Nov. 1893, Abbie E. Parker of Wentworth, N. H. C., *a.*, Russell Parker, b. July 13, 1896. *b.*, Margaret, and *c.*, Lawrence Gordon, (twins), b. May 7, 1898. (3) Bessie C., b. Sept. 2, 1872; teacher. (4) George L., b. May 24, 1884.
  ii. Hannah H., b. Nov. 23, 1839; m. Joseph Sawyer; q. v.

5 MOODY, (Deacon), b. Dec. 5, 1795; m. June 17, 1819, Anna, dau. of Col. Joshua Bayley; (b. Jan. 17, 1795; d. March, 1858). Dea. Powers lived where Mrs. H. T. Swan now lives, and rem. to Iowa about 1863. Deacon in Wells River church; d. July 1, 1869, Marshalltown, Iowa.
  Children:
  i. Prescott, b Feb. 10, 1821; d. June 11, 1881. at Keneesaw, Neb.
  ii. Hale, b. Aug. 18, 1823; m. Mary Bailey of Lyman; d. May 15, 1872, at Franconia, N. H.; one son.
  iii. Joshua, b. June 4, 1826; served in the Union army and d. Nov. 20, 1862, in service at Georgetown, D. C.
  iv. Ephraim, b. May 9, 1828; m. Janette Whitehill; 3 c.; d. Jan. 26, 1898, Keneesaw, Neb.
  v. Moody, b. Aug. 31, 1830; m. Juliette Whitehill; 2 c.; d. Oct. 31, 1864, Newbury.
  vi. Charles J., b. March 12, 1833; 2 c.
  vii. Sarah F., b. Jan. 3, 1836; m. J. H. Roberts. Marshalltown, Iowa.

6 JONATHAN, b. Deer Isle, Nov. 12, 1808. Sailor and captain of a coasting vessel many years. He m. Jan. 21, 1837, Electa, dau. of Stephen Powers, and settled on the latter's farm. They rem. to Bradford, where she d. Nov. 9, 1888. He d. Bradford, Jan. 28, 1882.
  Children:
  i. Elizabeth, b. Jan. 3, 1838; m. March 6, 1861, George W. Farr of Bradford; architect and builder; rem. to Kansas City, 1885. Mrs. Farr has rendered valuable aid in collecting these records of the Powers family.
  ii. John Hale, b. Nov. 1, 1840; enlisted 1861, 1st Vt. Cavalry; surgeon's clerk and assistant; was under fire. in 43 battles; graduated Wesleyan University. 1869; in business and studying law at Cincinnati, where he d. suddenly, Sept. 26, 1877. He m. Nov. 8, 1870, Josephine Haggatt of Sidney, O., and had c., Josephine P., b. Dec. 25, 1873, and H. Hale, b. Nov. 7, 1885, now at Wesleyan University.
  iii. Martha B., b. Jan. 3, 1845; graduated Vermont Conference Seminary, 1872; one year teacher in Grammar school, Union City, Ind.; preceptress of Bradford Academy, 1874-86; preceptress of Indian mission school, supported by the government at Pawhuska, Indian Territory. 1889-90; teacher in a mission school among the Digger Indians at Ukiah, Cal., where there had never been a school or missionary before, 1891-94. She m. April 15, 1893, James E. Glazier of Ukiah, Cal.

POWERS.

MATTHIAS, b. Tramore Bay, Waterford County, Ireland, March 31, 1820; m. in Ireland, Aug. 12, 1844, Johannah O'Brien, b. Kilcomera, Waterford County, Aug. 14, 1824. She d. Littleton. Dec. 13, 1900. He came to America in 1847, landing in Boston, barefoot and penniless. He earned money and sent for his wife and child. In 1848, he worked on the Connecticut River Railway at Westminster, and later helped build the White Mountain R. R. from Woodsville to Littleton. Came to Newbury in 1858, and bought the William Meader place. Rem. 1865 to Corinth, where he worked in the copper mines. In 1870 he bought a farm near South Littleton, N. H., on which he lived till death, Dec. 13, 1898, having acquired a comfortable estate.
  Children, who survived infancy:
  i. Mary, b. Ireland, Aug. 12, 1845; m. March 10, 1869, George M. Stowell of Springfield, Mass; d. Springfield, Mass., Oct. 13, 1871. One dau., Mary P., b. August, 1871; m. a Mr. Morris of Philadelphia.
  ii. Fanny R., b. Bath, N. H., Jan. 11, 1852; attendant in lunatic hospital, Northampton, Mass.; m. June 21, 1876, Charles H. Dudley, from

Winthrop, Me. They were connected with the State Alms house at Tewksbury, Mass., several years, and then entered the Danvers Lunatic hospital, where she attained the position of matron, and superintendent of nurses, and principal of school for nurses. Mr. Dudley d. Aug. 19, 1896, and she resigned her position. She m. 2d at Constantinople, Turkey, Sept. 17, 1897, Hon. Milo A. Jewett, consul at Sivas, Asiatic Turkey; res. Sivas. One son, Charles H. Dudley, b. Oct. 9, 1877, now in Dartmouth College.

iii. Thomas C., b. Littleton, Oct. 19, 1853; attendant from 1874, and afterwards steward at Northampton Lunatic hospital. He m. May 19, 1878, Hattie A. Aldrich of Cuttingsville. He d. Northampton, Mass., Feb. 12, 1893. Three c., Katie Alice, Fanny D. and Thomas C., all residents of Northampton.

iv. Margaret, b. Littleton, June 7, 1855, d. Littleton, Oct. 17, 1874.

v. Maurice, b. Newbury, March 14, 1860; d. Cornith, May 2, 1865.

vi. Alice, b. Newbury, Feb. 8, 1862; teacher for 20 years; now, 1901, with her sister at Sivas, Turkey.

vii. Matthew, b. Newbury, Aug. 16, 1863; two years in Dartmouth College, teacher; m. Kate Foshey; now farmer on homestead.

PRESCOTT.

I. JAMES, ancestor of many families in Newbury, emigrated from Dryby, Lincolnshire, England, in 1665, and settled in Hampton, N. H. In 1694, he became a grantee of the town of Kingston to which place he rem. in 1725, and where he d., Nov. 25, 1728, aged about 85. He was a member of the church at Hampton, and afterwards at Kingston, about fifty years. He m. in 1668, Mary, dau. of Nathaniel and Grace Boulter, (b. Exeter, May 15, 1648; d. at Kingston, Oct. 4, 1735). "The Prescott Memorial," published in 1870, by Dr. William Prescott of Concord, N. H., has furnished most of the records of this family. They had nine c., of whom Dea. James was b. Sept 1, 1671; farmer of Hampton; m. March 1, 1695, Maria, dau. of William Marston, Jr., (b. May 16, 1672). Their c. were eight, of whom the 2d,

II. SAMUEL, b. March 14, 1697, farmer of Hampton Falls, of which he was town clerk. He m. Dec. 17, 1717, Mary Sanborn. They were parents of six sons, five of whom served in the Old French war and the Revolution. She d. June 12, 1759. The date of his death is not known.

III. JEREMIAH, eldest son of Samuel, b. Sept. 29, 1718; m. 1st, Jan. 15, 1741, Mary Hayes; settled in Epping. Served in Capt. Folsom's Co., of Blanchard's regiment in the expedition against the French fort at Niagara, in 1755. In 1756, he served in Capt. Doe's Co. of Merserve's regiment in the expedition against Crown Point. He d. 1780.
Their c. were nine:

IV. COL. JEREMIAH, the eldest, b Dec. 22, 1741. Lieut. in Capt. Sanborn's Co. in Col. Evan's regiment, 1777; captain in Col. Stickney's regiment; settled in Epsom, where he was a farmer, and colonel in the militia. He m. Jan., 1764, Jane Sherburne, (b. Oct., 1745; d. Sept., 1828). William Prescott, brother of Col. Jeremiah, settled in Vershire. Col. Jeremiah, d. Apr. 25, 1817.
The c. of Col. Prescott were as follows:

i. John, (1764-1857), of Epsom and Bristol, N. H.

ii. Jeremiah, (1767-1817), of Epsom, N. H., and Vershire; lived in Newbury in 1801.

iii. Huldah, (1770-1815); m. Daniel Kimball of Pembroke, N. H., and Bradford.

iv. Samuel, (1773——); settled in Vershire.

v. Sarah, b. 1776; m. Stephen Maltby; settled in Vershire.

1 vi. Joseph, (1779-1866).

vii. Sherburne, b. Sept. 29, 1782; settled in Vershire; m. 1st, 1805, Betsey Rand, who d. leaving six c., of whom Mary, b. July 16, 1814, m. Thomas L. Tucker of Newbury, and Irene C., b. Feb. 15, 1818; m. Feb. 15, 1843, Samuel Alden Tucker; d. Feb. 15, 1888.

1 JOSEPH, b. Epsom, July 21, 1879; m. Jan. 1801, Sarepta, dau. of Joseph and
   Sarah Olmsted of Bradford, (b. Jan., 1781; d. Feb. 15, 1850); settled at
   West Newbury about 1800 on the farm still called the "old Prescott place"
   where N. C. Randall now lives, building a log house and later a framed
   one. They were members of the first Methodist class formed in this town,
   in 1801, and among the earliest members of the M. E. church, in which he
   was a class leader for many years. He d. Oct., 1866.
   Children:
   i.   Israel, b. Apr. 4, 1803; m. 1st, March 8, 1826, Betsey E. Putnam of Bradford,
        (b. Feb. 22, 1802; d. Boston, March 8, 1850). One son, Wm. P., b.
        Newbury, Jan. 21, 1824; res. Boston; connected with Boston Theatre; has
        two c.; Lizzie, m. ——————————, and William. He m. 2d, Sept. 15,
        1850, Sally, widow of his brother, Lorenzo.
   ii. Mary, b. Apr. 25, 1805; m. Ephraim, son of Col. Joshua Bailey; q. v.
   iii. Sophia, b. Sept. 5, 1809; m. Sept., 1829, William Heath.
   iv. Eliza, b. Oct. 25, 1812; m. Isaac Olmsted; q. v.
   v.   Jane S., b. June 14, 1814; m. Feb. 15, 1838, Lowell G., son of Nathan
        Taplin of Corinth; rem. to Oskosh, Wis., in 1848 and died there. C., (1)
        Osman Baker, b. Newbury, Dec. 19, 1840; studied medicine; enlisted Apr.
        21, 1861, in Co. E., 2d Wisconsin for three months; re-enlisted June 11, for
        three years; was in the first and second battles of Bull Run, Gainesville and
        South Mountain; was mortally wounded at Antietam, Sept. 17, 1862,
        and d. at Keedysville, Md., Sept. 24, and buried there. (2) Carrie S., b.
        Corinth, July 1, 1843; m. Chas. A. Johnson of Oshkosh; d. St. Luke's
        Hospital, Chicago, April 13, 1898. (3) Sarah A. C., b. in Boston, Dec. 19,
        1851; d. June 8, 1852.
   vi. Amanda, b. Nov. 10, 1816; m. Jan. 10, 1837, David G. Bickford, who d. at
        Corinth, Jan. 20, 1843, leaving a son, Israel P., b. Newbury, March 28,
        1838; res. Concord, N. H.
   vii. Lorenzo Dow, b. Aug. 7, 1818; m. Dec. 15, 1843, Sally, dau. of Dudley
        Carleton, (b. Sept. 11, 1816; d. July 3, 1893). One son, Lorenzo D., b.
        Oct., 1847; d. May 4, 1898, while staying over night at a hotel in
        Newport, Vt.; un-m.
   viii. James Young, b. Dec. 21, 1820; m. Oct. 5, 1843, Emily, dau. of R. C. Ford.
        Sold the old farm in 1871 and rem. to Lowell, Mass., where he d. Apr. 21,
        1884; she d. Dec. 3, 1889. C., (1) Adda E., b. Jan. 22, 1845; d. Sept. 29,
        1864. (2) Arabella A., b. July 7, 1848. Teacher in the Bartlett Grammar
        School, Lowell, having risen from the middle grade to the highest, also in
        the model and practice school connected with the state normal school. (3)
        Frank P., b. Feb. 8, 1853; res. Boston; un-m. (4) Frederick M., b. Oct.
        17, 1855; jeweler at Lowell; 1899 chosen private secretary to the Mayor
        of Lowell.
   ix. Sarah Jane, b. Oct. 1828; m. March, 1842, Horatio N. Carleton; q. v.

PROUTY.

SAMUEL, of Spencer, Mass., m. Miriam Stevens, of Shrewsbury, and had four c.,
   of whom Samuel, b. May 10, 1780, m. Mary, dau. of Elijah and Mary
   (Stevens) King. They rem. to Barnet, where others of the Stevens family
   resided, but settled in Charlestown, N. H. Of their six c., Elijah King
   was b. in Charlestown, N. H., 1801; teacher of vocal and
   instrumental music, from about 1825, till death, and composer of many
   church tunes and secular pieces; teacher of vocal music at Newbury
   Seminary, 1851, and lived here several years, teaching music. After some
   years' absence he returned to Newbury about 1856, where he exercised his
   profession, and was much engaged in holding musical conventions. He
   possessed a clear and strong tenor voice, and was considered an authority
   upon all musical subjects. He was chorister at the Cong. Ch. many years.
   He m. 1st, Cynthia ——————, who d. in Waterford. He m. 2d, 1838,
   Mary Ann Converse, of Lyme, N. H. He d. Newbury, Sept. 26, 1869.
   Children, three by 1st, and two by 2d marriage:
   i.   Beriah Loomis, b. Oct. 14, 1831; res. Lynn, Mass.
   ii. Chloe Emeline, b. Dec. 22, 1833; m. Charles F. Johnson of Lyme, N. H.;
        res. Minneapolis, Minn.

iii. Elijah King, b. March, 1836; served in the Union army; was officer in a colored regiment. He d. in Birmingham, Ala., about 1888.
iv. Mary Jane, b. 1842; d. Wilson, N. C., 1859.
v. Edith Josephine, b. July 30, 1855; m. A. J. Holbrook; res. London, Eng.

PUTNAM.

·I. John, b. about 1580, of England and Salem, Mass.; d. at Salem Village, now Danvers, Dec. 30, 1662. He came from Buckinghamshire, Eng., in 1634, with three sons.

II. Nathaniel, b. in England 1617 or 1621; m. Elizabeth Hutchinson, by whom he had seven c. He had a considerable landed estate, much of which remains in the family. He d. Danvers, July 23, 1700. He had two sons, John and Benjamin; one of the Newbury Putnam families is descended from John, and the other from Benjamin.

III. John, b. Danvers, March 26, 1657; m. Hannah Cutter; d. September, 1722. They had 15 c.

IV. Amos, b. Danvers, Jan. 27, 1697; d. 1774.

V. Dea. Daniel, b. Danvers; m. Elizabeth Putnam; lieutenant in Capt. Samuel Flint's Co., which marched to Lexington, April 19, 1775.

VI.˙ Daniel, b. Danvers, Oct. 3, 1762; came to West Newbury before 1796, and built a log house on the farm where the late Joel Putnam lived; later he built a two-story house which, with the barns, was burned, August 5, 1882. He m. Sarah Porter, of Danvers, who d. Feb. 13, 1834. He d. Dec. 19, 1802, Newbury: They were buried in a small, disused yard on their own farm.
Children:
i. Betsey, b. Jan. 22,·1791; d. Aug. 27, 1791.
ii. Daniel, b. Jan. 9, 1792; went west.
iii. Betsey, b. May 12, 1794; m. Oct. 10, 1816, Michael Carleton, of Haverhill; d.
1 iv. Joel, b. Newbury, July 28, 1796; d. June 5, 1860.
v. Sally A., b. March 17, 1800; m. Aug. 27, 1823, Dudley C. Kimball, q. v.

1 Joel,[2] (Daniel,[1]) b. Newbury, July 28, 1796; m. March 7, 1821, Mindwell, dau. Samuel Tucker, (b. July 7, 1799; d. Sept. 5, 1853); farmer on homestead; d. June 5, 1860.
Children:
i. Joel P., b. Dec. 2, 1823; farmer on homestead; m. Feb. 13, 1872, Lydia M. Gove; d. March 22, 1899.
ii. Samuel T., b. March 11, 1825; m. Nov. 3, 1858, Lucinda, dau. of David McAllister, and widow of John N. Brock, (b. Feb. 18, 1823; d. June 15, 1871); farmer, on the farm before owned by John N. Brock. He d. Nov. 16, 1895. One son, Samuel Frank, b. Aug. 25, 1860; farmer on homestead; m. June 15, 1885, Alice Josephine, dau. of John Crawford, b. Jan. 1, 1865. C., a, John Harrington, b. Jan. 15, 1886. b, Ned Franklin, b. Dec. 12, 1889. c, infant, b. April 7; d. April 10, 1891. d, Tressie Lucinda, b. April 17, 1894. e, Marjorie Josephine, b. Nov. 15, 1898.
iii. Mindwell, b. Feb. 17, 1827; d. April 6, 1866.
iv. Mary, b. Nov. 28, 1829; d. May 11, 1878.
v. William K., b. June 1, 1833; farmer; m. Sept. 5, 1860. Lucinda R., dau. Alonzo Fleming. C., (1) George W., b. Jan. 22, 1862; farmer in Newbury; m. July 2, 1890, Carrie, dau. G. W. K. Carleton. C., a, George William, b. May 31, 1896. (2) Edward E., b. Aug. 1, 1863; farmer at West Newbury; m. November 28, 1888, Mattie J., dau. L. W. McAllister. (3) Hattie, b. November 20, 1872; m. Jonas Tucker.
vi. Sarah, b. Jan. 15, 1836; d. y.

PUTNAM.

This family is also descended from John Putnam, who came to Salem in 1634, through

II.   NATHANIEL, b. 1621; d. Feb. 23, 1700.   He had two sons, John and Benjamin.

III. BENJAMIN, b. 1664; had seven sons.

IV.   ISRAEL, b. 1699.

V.   *TARRANT, b. about 1732.   The history of Danvers, Mass., mentions a Tarrant Putnam whom it calls "Ensign Tarrant Putnam," and gives the date of his birth as 1733.   He was clerk of the 1st church in Danvers, in 1775, and may be the Tarrant Putnam who came here about ten years later.   The latter was a man of very high standing, wrote an excellent hand, and seems to have been familiar with the details of business.   Tarrant and Daniel Putnam came to Newbury about the same time and settled in what is now called West Newbury.   Daniel Putnam m. Sarah Porter.   Tarrant Putnam m. 1st, Hannah Porter and 2d Eunice Porter, but it is not known that there was any connection between the three.   It used to be said in early days that one-third of the people in Danvers were Putnams, and another third were Porters.

Tarrant Putnam, b. Danvers, Mass., 1732; m. Hannah Porter, July 1, 1756.   They were the parents of 5 c.   She d. and he m. 2d about 1775, Eunice Porter.   They came to Newbury about 1790, and settled where the late Guy Corliss long lived.   They were members of the 1st church, and in 1801, the town voted that "Rev. Mr. Lambert should preach at the house of Mr. Tarrant Putnam in the back part of the town on the fourth Sabbath of each month."   He d. 1819, as Asa Tenney, Isaac Bayley and David Wilson were appointed commissioners on his estate, Apr. 17th in that year.

Children:

1   i.   Eleazer P., b. Dec. 7, 1758.
2   ii.   Israel, b. Nov. 22, 1760; d. March 13, 1849.
   iii. Asa, b. Dec. 28, 1765; rem. to Brookfield, N. Y., and d. about 1840.
   iv.   Abigail, b. July 13, 1768; m. and d. in Danvers.
   v.   Polly, b. Apr. 28, 1771; m. Wyman Smith.   (He was a stone cutter and made gravestones, many of which are still in the older cemeteries about here.   The births of 9 c. between Apr. 18, 1794, and Apr. 5, 1811, are recorded in Newbury.   He appears to have rem. to Piermont, where he d. Oct., 1852).   George Jenkins of Bradford is a grandson.
   vi.   Sarah, b. 1777; m. Josiah Moore of West Fairlee.
   vii. Daniel, d. y.
   viii. Tarrant, m. Nov. 10, 1805, Ruth Chadwick.   He d. leaving two c., who rem. to New York., and she m. 2d Jan. 21, 1817, Benjamin Brock, q. v.
   ix.   Elizabeth, b. 1788; m. John Brickett; q. v.
   x.   Eunice, d. y.
   xi.   Ruth, d. y.
   xii. Elisha, b. 1794; m. and went west.

1   ELEAZER PORTER, commonly called Porter Putnam, b. Dec. 7, 1758; served in the Revolutionary War with his brother, Israel, for two years. after which he m and rem. to Maine, and in 1786, came to Newbury where his brother Israel had settled and where their father and the rest of the family followed them.   Later he rem. to Topsham, then to Corinth.

Children:

   i.   Samuel, b. Salem, Mass., 1782; studied medicine with Dr. Richard Huntley of Topsham and settled in Burke, in 1804, as the 1st physician in that town.   In 1808 he came to Bradford and lived in "Goshen."   In 1816, he moved to Newbury to the "John Atwood place;" d. of consumption, July 17, 1817, and buried in Rogers Hill cemetery.   He m. March 11, 1812, Betsey, dau. Col. John Bayley.   C., a dau. who d. y. and a son, Samuel

---

*Mrs. Tower collected the records of the Grow and Tarrant Putnam families for this volume.

who m. Lydia, dau. Abner Bayley; reared a large family; d. Chicago, 1857.

ii. Benjamin, b. Bakerstown, Me., Sept. 1, 1788; ordained an evangelist in the Free Will Baptist church at Strafford, Feb. 6, 1809, and preached in the Christian denomination some years in Bradford, and Topsham; ordained to the Baptist ministry, Aug. 21, 1820, and was settled in Bethel. In 1834 he was pastor of the First Baptist church at Springfield, Mass., and later, settled in Billerica, Mass., where he d. In 1821, he published a small volume of his religious experiences. He had several c. of whom Harriet L., m. a Mr. Packer of Brooklyn, N. Y., where they founded a school which afterwards became widely known as the "Packer Institute." Maria, m. Rev. Mr. Bellamy, and their son, Edward, a journalist, was the author of "Looking Backward." Julia, the other dau., m a Rev. Mr. Savage, and went to India as a missionary, and d. there. leaving a dau. still in India.

iii. Israel, became a physician and settled in Boston; several c.

iv. Smith, m. a Mrs. Ormsbee of Fairlee and rem. to Elmore. A dau., Maria L., m. Asa T. Shaw, of Bradford; 6 c.

v. Sally, m. Paschal Raymond. Mrs. John B. Wilson is their dau.

vi. Louisa, m. a Mr. Scott of Randolph and Dorchester, Mass.

2 ISRAEL, b. Nov. 22, 1760; served in the Revolutionary War with his elder brother; came to Newbury about 1784, and m. March 17, 1788, Susanna Heath. In that year they rem. to Topsham, and settled in the east part of the town, on what is sometimes called the "Alden Brock place." The buildings are all gone. In 1838, he rem. to Bradford, where he d. March 13, 1849, and she d. Jan. 16, 1847; both buried at West Newbury.

Children:

i. Betsey, b. July 15, 1789; m. John B. Carleton, q. v; d. Dec. 5, 1849.

3 ii. Jesse, b. Dec 21, 1790; d. March 3, 1868.

iii. Susan, b. Feb. 27, 1794; m. Luke Cross, and rem. to Fonda, N. Y.; d. 1856.

3 JESSE, b. Dec. 21, 1790; farmer and schoolmaster; m. April 18, 1816, Eliza, dau. Samuel Grow, (d. July 23, 1872). Farmer with his father in Topsham till 1838. when he rem. to Bradford, and in 1867 to Rutland where he d. March 3, 1868.

Children:

i. Eliza S , b. March 31, 1817; teacher nearly 40 years; d. Hyde Park, Mass., Jan. 24, 1873.

ii. Israel C , b. April 15, 1821; d. Sept. 19, 1823.

iii. Samuel G., b. Newbury, Nov. 27, 1822; m. March 12, 1863, Priscilla C. Pattee of Milton, and lived in Rutland. where he d. Dec. 25, 1888. C., (1) Henry C., b. Nov. 13, 1865; now of Seattle, Washington. (2) John A., b. Feb. 9, 1869. now of Troy, N. Y.; m. Ernestine Ploss.

iv. Harris A., b. March 23, 1825; d. Aug. 26, 1826.

4 v. Harriet L., b. July 2, 1827.

vi. Jesse D., b. Nov. 29, 1829; d. Jan. 1, 1832.

vii. Sophia Relief, b. Sept. 26, 1831; d. Hyde Park, Mass., May 21, 1894.

4 HARRIET L., b. July 2. 1827; m. in Somerville. Mass., March 30, 1853. Charles B. Tower; res. Somerville, Attleboro and, after 1870, Hyde Park, Mass. where he d. June 11, 1891. She res. at Hyde Park.

Children:

i. Charles P., b. Boston, Feb. 6, 1854; res. New York City; editor of "The Paper Mill," a weekly publication devoted to the paper trade. He m. 1st, May 7, 1879, Martha A. Weeks of Rutland; m. 2d, Sept. 17, 1894, Dorothy Frances Gray of New York.

ii. Harriet, b. Attleboro, April 25, 1856; teacher about 14 years, one term in Newbury; d. April 28, 1890.

iii. Harry E., b. July 7, 1858, Somerville; res. Jersey City; employed on daily papers in New York. He m. June 25, 1889, Margaret A. Cook; 2 c.

iv. Samuel F., b. Feb 24, 1861, at Boston; graduated Dartmouth College, 1884; junior master, since 1888, of the English High School. Boston.

v. Jessie B., b. Dec. 13; d. Dec. 16, 1867.

vi. Walter S., b. Dec. 23, 1870; d. May 18, 1892.

QUIMBY.

REV. SILAS, b. Deering, N. H., May 19, 1811. Pastor of the M. E. church in Newbury, April 1858—April 1860, and resided here till May 1863. He m. June 9. 1834, Penelope C. Fifield of Unity, N. H. C., Julia, (Mrs. Dr. Butler of Strafford, N. H.); d. 1861. Silas E., (q. v.). Alice, a graduate of Newbury Seminary, 1863, now Mrs. George Nichols of Claremont, N. H., and Moses F., who d. 1834. He d. Unity, N. H., Jan. 25, 1883.

SILAS E., b. Haverhill, N. H., Oct. 19, 1837; graduated Weselyan University, 1859. Teacher in Newbury Seminary Aug., 1859 to May, 1863, and from May, 1864 to July, 1867; principal Feb., 1866, to July, 1867. Principal of New Hampshire Conference Seminary, Tilton, N. H., March 1878, till June, 1885. Member of New Hampshire Conference since 1863 and in the pastorate when not teaching. He m. in Newbury, July 10, 1862, Anna W., dau. of Rev. Orange Scott, (b. Lowell, Mass., May 10, 1840; d. Salem, N. H., March 8, 1901).
Children:
i. Clarence E., b. Newbury, May 4, 1863; educated at Tilton Seminary; now member of the firm of Lord Bros., opticians, Tilton.
ii. Carl N., b. Newbury, Nov. 27, 1866; graduated Wesleyan University, 1890. Optician, 373 Washington, St., Boston.
iii. Mabel, b. Plymouth, N. H., Feb. 6, 1870. (Mrs. Horatio Moore of Wilkesbarre, Penn).
iv. Ernest S., b. Exeter, N. H., July 15, 1872; graduated Wesleyan University, 1896.
v. Alice Lency, b. Tilton, N. H., Sept. 21, 1877; d. Aug. 30, 1878, buried in Newbury.

*RANDALL.

(I.) LEMUEL, (II.) ISAAC, and (III.) MASON, brothers, came from England about 1795, and settled in Newbury.

I. LEMUEL, m. Betsey Hood, of Topsham, about 1808, and settled in the Lime Kiln neighborhood. He d. Aug. 17, 1846, aged 82. His wife d. Oct. 2, 1864, aged 87.
Children:
i. Daniel, b. Nov. 3, 1809; m. Eliza Hood of Topsham, March 16, 1838, and lived in Topsham. C., (1) Mary J., b. Oct. 6, 1841; d. July 22, 1863. (2) George, b. Nov. 15, 1845. (3) Adaline, b. Dec. 15, 1848. Daniel Randall d. May 19, 1866; his wife, April 5, 1883.
ii. William, b. 1812; m. Emily Eastman of Newbury. Sept. 16, 1840; lived in Topsham. He d. Jan. 26, 1855; his wife, Feb. 24, 1892. C., (1) Luella, b. Aug. 22, 1841; m. David Lang; d. April 8, 1860. (2) Horace, b. Jan. 18, 1844. (3) Emma J., b. July 2, 1848. (4) Charles N., b. Oct. 2, 1851.
iii. John, b. July 9, 1814; d. un-m. Oct. 17, 1889.
iv. Mary A., b. April 5, 1819; m. May 30, 1838, Henry Johnson, and settled in Monroe, N. H.

II. ISAAC, never m.; lived in Newbury.

III. MASON, m. Hannah Brown, of Londonderry, Eng., about 1797, and settled on Jefferson Hill. He was killed in 1810, by a tree falling on him while chopping wood. His wife d. July 18, 1839.
Children:
1 i. William, b. April 18, 1799; d. April 18, 1867.
2 ii. John, b. May 29, 1801; d. Aug. 18, 1874.
iii. Olive, b. about 1803; m. about 1823, Andrew Smith, of Bath; d. about 1848. C., John, Eliza J., Mary A., Olive, Martha, Lucy, James, Havillah and Luella.
iv. Betsey, b. about 1805; m. about 1825, Chester Spooner of Haverhill; d. about 1848. Six c.
3 v. Mason, b. July 12, 1807; d. Oct. 11, 1876.
vi. Samuel, b. about 1810; m. about 1829 Jane Chase of Groton, and settled there; d. 1869. C., Hannah, Frank, Nancy, Lizzie.

*By M. H. Randall.

1 WILLIAM,[2] (Mason,[1]) b. April 18, 1799; m. Sept. 15, 1817, Mary Gates of Ryegate, and settled on the farm where the Quint family now live. He was engaged in stock dealing several years. Mrs. Randall d. about 1853, and he m. 2d, Helen McClary, of Ryegate, in 1856.

Children, eight by 1st marriage, three by 2d:

i. William M., b. Sept. 18, 1818; m. Wealthy Eastman, of Topsham; lived on Jefferson Hill; rem. to Topsham, thence to La Crosse, Wis., where he d. Oct. 28, 1873. Eight c.
ii. Jonathan W., b. Aug. 27, 1820; carpenter; lived in Groton and Ryegate. He m. 1st, January, 1846, Alma Emerson, of Ryegate. She d. 1855. He m. 2d, 1856, Elizabeth Orr, of Groton. C., (1) Wallace, b. March 19, 1857; d. Jan. 19, 1864. (2) Charles, b. July 17, 1863; d. in infancy. (3) Sydney G., b. Nov. 9, 1865; d. Aug. 9, 1887.
iii. Susan P., b. Sept. 28, 1822; m. 1852, Thomas Young. He was a clerk in Boston.
iv. Robert B., b. Nov. 20, 1824; m. 1854. Nancy Hill; lived in Lowell, Mass; merchant. He d. 1882. One c., George M., b. June, 1857.
v. Mary J., b. July 9, 1827; m. 1850, John R. Wilson; lived in Boston.
vi. Charles W., b. Feb. 6, 1830; went to California, 1852, and d. 1854.
vii. Moses H., b. Aug. 31, 1832; m. April 9, 1833, Ann C. Forsyth, of Topsham; lived in Boston, then on the homestead. C., (1) Lillian V., b. Jan. 11, 1862. (2) Alma J., b. Oct. 17, 1871; m. March 6, 1894, Clarence E. Miller, of Ryegate.
viii. Orintha M., b. Nov. 5, 1836; m. Cushing Fearing, of Boston; truckman; was also a musician and band leader.

2 JOHN,[2] (Mason,[1]) b. May 29, 1801; m. about 1827, Eliza J. Gardner, and settled first on the farm where the late Duncan Ritchie long lived, then on Jefferson Hill, where Albert Wright lives. ' Farmer and drover. He d. Aug. 18, 1874; she d. Apr. 13, 1881.

Children:

i. Jennet G., b. Feb. 17, 1828; m. Samuel McAllister.
ii. John N., b. Oct. 8, 1829; m. about 1872, Mrs. Griggs of Derby; went to San Joaquin county, Cal.; farmer and miner; d. 1886.
iii. Isabel M., b. Dec. 19, 1830; m. about 1860, George A. Bang of Boston, a machinist.
iv. Hugh G., b. June 1, 1832; farmer, also drover, doing a very large business; was prominent in town affairs. Rem. to Geneseo, Ill., where he was a drover; m. Apr. 30, 1856, Eliza J., dau. Robert Renfrew. C., Milo, b. 1861; d. 1889. He d. 1888.
v. George N., b. Aug. 14, 1834; went to California and was a miner; has been there four times; settled on the James Peach farm on Jefferson Hill, where his home was burned, May 28, 1900. He m. 1st, Dec. 10, 1860, Martha W. Hancock of Haverhill, who d. Feb. 26, 1887. He m. 2d, Nancy B. Gardner. C., by 1st wife. (1) Mary, b. Nov. 19, 1867; d. Jan. 11, 1868. (2) Henry, b. Apr. 1, 1869. He bought a large farm in Monroe, N. H., but rem. to California, and is a large owner of real estate. He m. Aug. 17, 1892, Agnes G. Hotchkiss of South Ryegate. C., a., J. Hancock, b. Dec. 4, 1893. b., Reginald H., b. Oct. 6, 1898. (3) Lizzie, b. Sept. 2, 1872; m. Robert Darling of South Ryegate; lives in Shermantown, Cal. (4) Hannah A., b. June 18, 1891.
vi. Orrin B., b. June 25, 1836; went to Stockton, Cal., about 1855. Farmer; d. un-m., 1864.
vii. Martin V., b. Nov. 7, 1838; went to Columbia, Cal., at the age of 17. Mining and teaming; d. un-m., 1877.
viii. Nicholas W., b. March 15, 1840; went to Modesto, Cal., in 1858. Farmer; m. about 1867, Mary Myers of Stockton. C., Mary, b. 1879.
ix. Martha B., b. July 22, 1843.
x. Mary, (twin to Martha), m. July, 1866, Noah Grover of Boston; d. June 28, 1869.
xi. Helen A., b. June 6, 1845; d. 1849.
xii. Edward M., b. Aug. 15, 1848; d. 1855.
xiii. Jackson M., b. June 26, 1851; m. March 3, 1884, Jane B. Annis of Groton. Lived in Missouri some time, but returned to Newbury. She d. Sept. 21, 1885.

3 MASON, b. July 12, 1807; m. Mary, (Polly), dau. Enoch Nelson, (b. Jan. 22, 1807; d. March 26, 1875). Settled where his son Henry F. lives, and d. Oct. 11, 1876.
  Children:
  i. Rebecca N., b. Jan. 27, 1830; m. Oct. 22, 1850, David B. Ingalls, a machinist, of Windsor. They went to California, but settled finally in Clinton, Mass., where he is a dentist, and has held responsible positions in town and state.
  ii. Mary A., b. Aug. 14, 1831; m. March 9, 1854; lived in Worcester, Mass., where he was steward at the asylum a few years; farmer at Spring Green, Wis., five years, then lived in Newfield, N. J. She d.——
  iii. Eliza G., b. Dec. 5 1832; went to Madison, Wis., about 1853, and was a teacher in the high school about 8 years, then teacher in Alabama, one year, then went to Washington, D. C., where she taught and founded a school. After teaching there about 11 years she d., Dec. 6, 1874. After her death the building where she had taught was remodelled, and named "The Randall School" in her honor.
  iv. Almira P., b. July 13, 1834; m. Azro B. Rogers, q. v.
  v. Sophia T., b. Jan. 28, 1836. Teacher two years at Sauk City, Wis.; m. Feb. 24, 1863, Union Durant of Wells River, long the landlord of the Coosuck House; now res. in Manchester, N. H.
  vi. Newell C., b. Nov. 23, 1837; went to California 1857, mining there, and was four years in Oregon. Returned, 1868; in Missouri for a time. He m. May 24, 1871, Lucinda C., dau. Thomas L. Tucker and settled on the "Prescott place" at West Newbury. C., Maurice H., b. July 6, 1872. Farmer with his father; has been school director. He m. Oct. 1899, Jessie Guthrie of Barnet.
  vii. Luthera C., b. July 2, 1839; d. Oct. 24, 1868.
  viii. Hiram N., b. April 3, 1842; in California and Oregon three years. He m. Oct 24, 1868, Rosalia L. Tabor of Wells River. Rem. to Clinton County, Iowa, then to Shelbina, Mo. Farmer, d. May 13, 1877. C., (1) Edward P., b. June 13, 1869; d. Feb. 9, 1875. (2) Alfred A., b. and died, Dec. 25, 1870. (3) Hattie A., b. March 2, 1871; m. Aug. 8, 1889, G. A. Holt; 4 c.
  ix. Oscar H., b. May 10, 1844; in California and Oregon, 1862-68, farming and mining. He m. Aug. 24, 1871, Martha B. Randall of Newbury. Settled in Shelby county, Mo.; farmer and stock raiser. C., (1) Orrin H., b. June 24, d. Nov. 17, 1872. (2) Birdella A., b. June 18, d. Sept. 8, 1874. (3) Anna E., b. Aug. 8, 1875; m. Oct. 16, 1895, Joseph Mahaffey; two c. (4) Mary E., b. May 27, 1877; d. Apr. 26, 1878. (5) Vertie C., b. Sept. 17, 1878. (6) Myrtle B., b. Feb. 19, 1881.
  x. Henry F., b. June 9, 1846; in Iowa a year or two; farmer on the homestead. He m. Dec. 31, 1871, Clara R., dau. Samuel A. Tucker. C., (1) Herbert T., b. Feb. 9, 1873; m. Dec. 19, 1900, Hattie F. Morrison of Ryegate, res. Wolcott. (2) Emma T., b. Sept. 30, 1874; d. May 23, 1891. (3) H. Greely, b. Apr. 18, 1884.
  xi. Alice W., b. March 10, 1848.

REED.

The father of Stephen Reed, of Scotch descent, came to Londonderry, N. H. Stephen m. Jane, dau. of John and Mary (Barnet) Cochrane. He d. at Wells River, May 15, 1815, aged 52. She d. there Dec. 21, 1851, aged 88.
  Children:
  i. Susan, m. Timothy Shedd; d. March 19, 1853, aged 48 years, 11 months, 5 days.
  ii. John, m. Caroline Gaylord.
  iii. Mary Ann, m. Charles Hale; d. Dec. 14, 1854.
  iv. Polly, m. Emory Gale; d. Jan. 22, 1879, aged 87.
  v. Samuel, m. Mary Gillett.
  vi. Stephen, m. Cynthia Gillett Simpson; d. Kappa, Ill., Feb. 7, 1869.
  vii. James, d. 1826.
  viii. Eliza, m. Ira White; d. March 14, 1869, aged 64.
  ix. Sally, d. 1825.

REID.

WILLIAM and Jane ——————, his wife. came from Scotland, in 1832, and after being in Lowell, Mass., came to Newbury in 1843, and settled on Leighton Hill, where both d.
Children:
  i. William; m. Aug. 11, 1846, Janette Allison. He d. Lawrence, Mass., leaving a son, Robert, who lives in Medford, Mass., and a dau., Margaret, who lives in Lawrence.
1 ii. Margaret, b. 1811; d. March 22, 1864.
2 iii. John, b. Aug. 22, 1828.
3 iv. David, b. 1831.
  v. Janett, m. Mr. Campbell; one dau. living.

1 MARGARET, b. June, 1811; m. in Scotland, Edward Stewart. They came to America in 1836. He d. July 12, 1846, aged 31. She d. in New York City, March 22, 1864, aged 52. They are buried at the Ox-bow with their three daus, who d. of consumption.
Children:
  i. Margaret. b. 1835; d. Newbury, Sept. 11, 1868.
 ii. Jane, b. March, 1839; d. Aug. 24, 1863.
iii. Janet, d. New York City.

2 JOHN, b. Bannockburn, Scotland, Aug. 23, 1828; came to America. 1832, and to Newbury, 1843; farmer on Leighton Hill. His house was burned March 13, 1901. He m. Feb. 25, 1858, Jane, dau. William Wallace, (b. 1829; d. Jan. 17, 1895.)
Children:
  i. Edward S., b. April 19, 1862; d. May 1, 1882.
 ii. William W., b. March 25, 1868; m. 1st, June 22, 1895, Lizzie, dau. of James Gardner. She d. Sept. 23, 1896. C. He m. 2d, Lillian, dau. of Henry T. Swan; 2 c.

3 DAVID B., b. Bannockburn, Scotland, 1831; came to Lowell, Mass., with his parents, 1832, and to Newbury, 1843. In 1850, he went to Boston, and worked, sometimes as a sailor, and part of the time in Newbury. In 1860, he went to New Jersey as a track layer on a railroad, and there enlisted in the U. S. Navy, and was sent to the receiving ship, North Carolina, then transferred to the torpedo boat, Canoe, and went up the James river, and was in the "Casco," at the surrender of Richmond. This boat going out of commission at Washington, he was sent to Boston navy yard, and served as guard on the ship Ohio, then transferred to the ram Dictator, then to the Bainbridge, and later to the monitor Monadnock, which was ordered to San Francisco, and was the first monitor to take a long sea voyage, in company with the Vanderbilt, Tuscarora and Powhatan. They left the navy yard at Philadelphia May 2, 1865, and were absent three years. During this time, Mr. Reid kept a careful diary, recording with minuteness his observations of the countries and cities which he visited. and, incidentally, much of the war between Spain and Chili. They touched at the principal ports on the eastern coast, and entered the straits of Magellan Feb. 3, 1866, reaching the harbor of Valparaiso, March 1, and on the 31st witnessed the bombardment of the city, and the withdrawal of the Spanish fleet, which they followed to the harbor of Callao, Peru, and there saw the bombardment of Callao, May 2d, and the repulse of the Spaniards. They left the harbor of Callao, took coal at San Diego, and, after encountering a severe gale which lasted 72 hours, the Monadnock reached San Francisco on the 22d of June. Mr. Reid remained on the Pacific coast, being stationed on different ships, till February, 1868, when they were sent home to New York. Mr. Reid returned to Newbury in 1868, bought the farm south of the cemetery. near Boltonville, intending, as he said, "to plow the land instead of the sea for the rest of his life." He m. Feb. 9, 1869, Isabel M., dau. of Hugh Gardner.
Children:
  i. Arthur W., b. Jan. 9, 1870; m. March 22, 1899, Mrs. Sarah (Lane), widow of F. A. Tucker; rem. to Piermont, and is a merchant there.
 ii. Charles, b. June 15, 1875.

RENFREW.

JAMES, b. Paisley, Scotland, 1755, where he was a weaver. Came to America, 1804, and bought a farm lying partly in Ryegate, and partly in Groton, the house being in the latter town, where he d. 1818. He m. Jan., 1783, Margaret Smith, b. Paisley, Scotland, 1761; d. in Groton, 1857, aged 96.
    Children:
1   i.   James, b. Feb., 1784; d. Sept. 30, 1870.
2   ii. John, b. Feb. 14, 1788; d. July 6, 1876.
    iii. Margaret, b. 1790; m. Archibald Park: lived in Ryegate; 12 c.; d.
    iv. William, b. 1792; m. June 1, 1815, Jean Esden. They lived in Ryegate and had 7 c.
    v.   Andrew, b. 1794; m. Elizabeth, dau. of James Nelson; (b. Sept. 19, 1797); lived in Groton.
3   vi. Robert, b. 1800.
    vii. Matthew, b. 1802; m. Sally Roberts of Groton.

1 JAMES,[2] (James[1],) b. Feb., 1784, Paisley, Scotland. Came to America, 1803; farmer. Rem. to Newbury, 1825, and lived where Charles Thompson now does, and m. Jean, dau. James Nelson, (b. Ryegate, Feb. 3, 1790; d. Newbury, April 2, 1880). He d. Sept. 30, 1870, and buried in West Newbury.
    Children:
4   i.   James, b. Ryegate, Feb. 26, 1810.
    ii.   Eliza, b. Groton, Nov. 12, 1811; m. Geo. Whitcher of Groton; 3 c.
5   iii. George, b. Groton, Oct. 6, 1813.
    iv.   Margaret, b. Groton, Dec. 11, 1816; never m.
    v.   William, b. 1818; d. in infancy.
    vi.   William, b. Nov. 9, 1820; d. Sept. 14, 1854.
    vii. Jane, b. Sept. 28, 1822; m. 1st, Oct. 23, 1856, John Hazeltine; q. v.; m. 2d, 1865, Jeremiah Boynton.
    viii. Robert, b. Oct. 12, 1824; m. Vilinda Collier of Hardwick, who d. June 6, 1884; lived in Newbury until 1871, when he rem. to Bradford; no c.
    ix.   Alexander N., b. Newbury, Jan. 5, 1837; m. Sarah Gove of Holland. Res. Newbury, till 1864, when he rem. to Fairlee. C., Olin and Carlos, the latter d. at two years of age.

2 JOHN,[2] (James,[1]) b. Paisley, Scotland, Feb. 14, 1788; came to America in 1803, to Newbury, 1821; rem. to Topsham, 1864, where he d. July 6, 1876. His farm is now owned by Lovina Renfrew. He m. 1st, Anna, dau. of Benjamin Bayley, of Peacham, who d. April 20, 1838; m. 2d, May 12, 1842, Mrs. Jane (Craig) Caldwell; 3d, June 29, 1859, Mrs. Euphemia Greig.
    Children, all b. in Groton:
    i.   Archibald, b. February, 1812; m. Asenath Corliss of Topsham; Calvinistic Baptist minister; rem. to Remington, Ind., where he and his wife d., leaving one son, Alvah, now in Mississippi.
    ii. Anna, b. March 10, 1813; m. Horace Divoll, who d. Feb. 17, 1882. She d. March 31, 1890. No c.
6   iii. John, b. Sept. 20, 1814.
7   iv. Andrew, b. Dec. 18, 1815.
    v.   Isabel, m. A. W. Nourse.
    vi. Angeline, b. May 1, 1820; m. John Weed, q. v.

3 ROBERT,[2] (James,[1]) b. Paisley, Scotland, 1800; came to America with his father; m. April 1, 1824, Lois Roberts, and came to Newbury at once and lived on a farm now owned by Henry Whitcher, where he d. and she d. in Bradford.
    Children, all b. Newbury:
    i.   Lydia, b. Feb. 14, 1825; m. Harvey Nourse, who d. Aug. 18, 1893.
    ii. Sylvester, b. Sept. 16, 1826; rem. to Illinois, and later to Hastings, Neb., where he d. 1888. Seven c.
    iii. Thomas, b. Sept. 17, 1828; rem. to Bradford; m. Lizzie Cate. C., Harry and Carlos.
    iv. Lois Ann, b. Dec. 11, 1830; m. Aug. 29, 1854, Harvey J. Allbee; res. Newbury, Haverhill and Nashua, where he d. Aug. 4, 1896. One c., Clara, m. A. K. Woodbury; res. Nashua.

ANDREW RENFREW.

HENRY WHITCHER.

RICHARD PATTERSON.

LEVI LIVERMORE TUCKER.

v. Eliza Jane, b. May 4, 1833; m. April 10, 1856, Hugh G. Randall. One c., Milo. All d.
vi. Mira J., b. Sept. 25, 1840; m. Reuben Bisbee.

JAMES,[3] (James,[2] James,[1]) b. Ryegate, Feb. 26, 1810; m. April 5, 1838, Sarah Waldron, (d. May 15, 1884); lived in Newbury, Groton and Topsham; bought the old homestead, 1864; d. Aug. 18, 1873.
Children:
i. Horace, b. May 31, 1840; served three years in the Union army, Mass. Regiment; m. 1st, Olive, dau. of Smith Corliss, of Topsham, who d. Nov. 11, 1865. One son, Fred, m. Feb. 13, 1892, Blanche May, dau. of Albert Fuller; d. Dec. 23, 1892. He m. 2d, Emma Smalley of Bradford. Rem. to Bradford, 1882.
ii. George, b. Aug. 8, 1842; enlisted in the Civil war and was killed in battle.
iii. Nancy Jane, b. April 23, 1848; m. as 3d wife, Samuel Fisk of Fall River, Mass. One c.
iv. Abbie Eliza, b. March 11, 1850; m. John Patten of Manchester, N. H. Two c.

5 GEORGE,[3] (James,[2] James,[1]) b. Groton, Oct. 6, 1813; m. June 25, 1840, Eliza, dau. of Amos Noyes, (b. Ryegate, Jan. 22, 1819). Lived in Newbury, Hartford and Littleton. Teacher, farmer and railroad employee. He d. Dec. 24, 1898. His farm was owned later by Milo C. Bailey.
Children:
i. Clara, b. Newbury, Jan. 30, 1846; m. May 17, 1894, in Springfield, Mass., George N. Merrill of Jackson, N. H.
ii. Ellen, b. Topsham, July 14, 1848; m. July 21, 1875, Rev. C. C. Lovejoy; Res. Morris, Ill. No c.
iii. William R., b. Hardwick, Aug. 19, 1850; m. April 2, 1881, at Suncook, N. H., Jennie Moore; res. Springfield, Mass. C., (1) Clara Belle, b. Chester, Mass., Nov. 7, 1886. (2) Bernice, b. Springfield, Mass., December, 1893.

6 JOHN[3], (John,[2] James,[1]) b. Sept. 30, 1814; rem. to Peacham, 1864; m. 1st, Mary A. Hodgson, who d. May 10, 1846, aged 26. John and Andrew, brothers, m. sisters. They lived in the same neighborhood. Their wives d. within 36 hours of each other, and were buried in the same grave, in the cemetery on the Orrin Heath place. He m. 2d, April 28, 1853, Maria, dau. John and Margaret (Hoyt) Harvey. He d. May 17, 1875. Buried in Newbury.
Children:
i. Mary A., b. Newbury, 1857; d. 1863.
ii. John, b. Newbury, 1864; m. 1886, Luella Barnard, of Lunenburg. C., Earl R., Florence, Marion, Mabel.
iii. Irving, b. Peacham, 1868; m. 1893, Hattie, dau. Henry G. Rollins, of Newbury. John and Irving Renfrew res. at Littleton, N. H., where they are engaged in the clothing business under the firm name of Renfrew Brothers, and have a flourishing trade.

7 ANDREW,[3] (John,[2] James,[1]) b. Groton, Dec. 18, 1815. Farmer, schoolmaster, surveyor. Town representative in 1857–58. Lived in the southwest part of the town until 1897, when he rem. to the Ox-bow. He held nearly all the town offices at one time and another. He m. 1st, Feb. 4, 1842, Chastina Hodgson of Groton, (b. July, 1818; d. May 12, 1846). He m. 2d, May 25, 1848, Lavinia, dau. Hiram Whitcher. He d. Apr. 3, 1896.
Children, one by 1st m., and four by 2d:
i. Charles H., b. Apr. 12, 1846. Left Newbury 1869; res. Urbana, Ill. Teacher in public schools. Six c., Belle, Frank, Marie, Adelia, Clara, Carlos.
ii. Eva, b. March 30, 1849; m. Jan. 26, 1878, S. H. Jones of Weathersfield. C., Ella F., b. Nov. 15, 1887. Kenneth, b. April 1889.
iii. Ella, b. Jan. 7, 1853; m. Jan. 1, 1884, Hugh Gilchrist; res. Great Falls, Montana. C., Walter, b. Nov. 6, 1884. Percy, b. Nov. 1887. Raleigh, b. Jan. 8, 1893.
iv. Oscar A., b. Dec. 31, 1856; m. Jan. 31, 1880, Kate H. Goodall of Topsham. C., Margie M., b. Oct. 25, 1886. Beth L., b. June 16, 18 .
v. Ludell N., b. March 15, 1865; res. Newbury and Norwood, Mass.

The Renfrews have been, one and all, substantial citizens, noted for their intelligence and worth; men always ready and willing to give well-considered reasons for whatever faith, political or religious, that they held. Only one family bearing the name, is left here, and their disappearance is a public loss.

RICKER.

MATURIN and GEORGE came from England about 1670, and were both killed by the Indians June 4, 1706. Joseph, son of Maturin, m. Elizabeth Garland of Berwick, Me. Joshua, his son, b. Berwick, April 9, 1737, O. S. He m. June 28, 1756. Betsey Drew, (b. Oct. 28, 1740, O. S.; d. Nov. 12, 1811). Came to Newbury before 1765; were members of 1st Ch. in Newbury; lived awhile on Musquash Meadow, and perhaps on the Ox-bow. Rem. to Bath, N. H , and he d. March 5, 1818. They are buried on the Carbee place.

Children:
  i. Elizabeth. b. July 27, 1757; m. James Hamilton; d. May, 1803.
  ii. John, b. May 23, 1759.
  iii. Abigail. b. Feb. 25, 1762; m. M. W. Downes.
1 iv. Joseph, b. Feb. 23, 1765; d. Jan. 21, 1851.
  v. Benjamin, b. April 23, 1766; m. Ruth, dau. Ebenezer White, q. v.
  vi. Joshua, b. May 11, 1768; d. Nov. 27. 1769.
2 vii. Joshua, b. May 6, 1770; d. May 27, 1813.
  viii. Polly, or Mary, b. Aug. 3, 1772; m. 1st, Martin Chamberlin, q. v.; m. 2d, Ezekiel Manchester; d. 1863.
  ix. Andrew, b. Jan. 27; d. Sept. 27, 1775.
  x. Nahum, b. Jan. 25, 1777; m. Oct. 13, 1800, Lucretia Spear; d. Oct. 27, 1827.
  xi. Mehetabel, b. March 5, 1780; m. Parker Dodge.
  xii. Ebenezer, b. Jan. 23, 1782; m. 1st, Jan. 11, 1804, Betsey Hurd; m. 2d, Oct. 29, 1819, Polly Lang.

1 JOSEPH, son of Joshua, b. Bath, Feb. 13, 1765; m. 1st, Newbury, Oct. 27, 1792, Polly, dau. Sylvanus Heath, (b. Newbury, Dec. 25, 1769; killed by a team in Bath, Jan. 21, 1821). He m. 2d, Peacham, March 27, 1821, ———— ————; d. Lowell, Mass., May 26, 1868. He owned in 1797, Lots 1, 2 and 3, Upper Meadow, and rem. later to the Ox-bow, and after some years to Groton. He d. Groton, Jan. 21, 1851.
Children, 13 by 1st marriage, 6 by 2d, all b. in Newbury, except
  i. Venus, b. Aug. 20, 1793; d. 1795.
  ii. Abigail, b. March 9, 1795; m. April 6, 1814, Capt. Andrew McClary; d. Peacham, June 4, 1868. Eight c.
  iii. Eunice, b. Dec. 22, 1797; d. Groton, Nov. 28, 1815.
  iv. Azubah, b. Sept. 19, 1799; d. Groton. May 6, 1806.
  v. Simon, b. Oct. 5, 1801; m. Judith Hosmer; m. 2d, Mary Carter; d. Groton, Oct. 30, 1873.
  vi. Amaziah, b. July 14, 1803; d. about 1815. (See Bibliography of Newbury).
  vii. Joseph. b. Feb. 12, 1805; m. April 7, 1830, Meribah Morrison; d. Groton, Feb. 28, 1770. Nine c.
  viii. Benjamin, b. Nov. 15, 1806; d. Peoria, Ill., Nov. 5, 1843. Two c.
  ix. Orson, b. Nov. 18, 1807; m. Dec. 6, 1829, Lydia Taisey; d. Groton, Dec. 10, 1887. Thirteen c.
  x. Mary, b. April 19, 1809; d. Groton, March 1, 1814.
  xi. Andrew, b. Feb. 10, 1810; m. Groton, Dec. 5, 1833, Ruth Bennett; d. Forest Mills, Iowa, March 2, 1895. Two c.
  xii. Betsey, b. June 8, 1812; d. Groton, May 6, 1820.
  xiii. Azubah, b. Dec. 22, 1814; d. Ryegate, Jan. 13, 1884; un-m.
  xiv. Electa, b. Dec. 19, 1821; d. Aug. 7, 1824.
  xv. Louisa, b. July 2, 1823; d. Barton, Feb. 15, 1890.
  xvi. Almira C., b. Dec. 1. 1827.
  xvii. Allen G , b. June 4, 1829; served in Civil war; d. Baton Rouge, La.
  xviii. Chester, b. Jan. 12; d. June 12. 1830.
  xix. Edwin, b. March 7, 1832; d. March 11, 1834.

2 JOSHUA, son of Joshua, b. Newbury, May 6, 1770; m. Abigail, dau. Abiel
Chamberlin, (b. Newbury, Jan. 14, 1774). Lived on Ingalls hill some
years; later, rem. to the vicinity of Toronto, Canada. He d. May 27,
1813.
Children:
i.   Betsey, m. a Mr. Goddard; lived in the north part of this state, later in
Illinois.
ii. Louisa, m. a Mr. Eaton; lived in Canada, later in Indiana.
iii. Lois, m. a Mr. Sims; lived in Canada.
iv. Hannah.
v.   Melissa, twin to Hannah. They m. brothers named Wright; settled in
Toronto.
vi. David, settled in Canada, about 1840.
vii. Nathaniel, never m.
viii. Mehetabel, m. Sherburne Lang of Bath, q. v.

RITCHIE.

ARCHIBALD, came from Kilmarcome, Scotland, in 1844. His wife, Elizabeth
Leitch, d. on the voyage. They had five c. One dau., Jean, m. William
Bone of Newbury, and d. in 1876. Mr. Ritchie bought the John Miller
farm near South Ryegate, where he lived until his death in 1885. He was
a Covenanter, and many times walked from South Ryegate to the Walter
Harvey meeting house in Barnet to hear what was to him sound
doctrine. He m. 2d, Agnes Lumsden, whose father lived in Scotch hollow,
but who d. at the house of his daughter, Mrs. Ritchie.

DUNCAN, who owned the John Randall farm near Boltonville, and was also b.
in Scotland, is a son of Archibald. He m. April 1, 1852, Ann, 2d dau. of
Andrew Wylie. They had four c: Elizabeth, b. 1854; Free, b. 1856;
Archibald, 1859; Lilla, 1861. Elizabeth, Archibald and Lilla d. all three
of diphtheria, in one week, in 1869, leaving Free, who grew up to
manhood, and was one of the finest young men whom this town has ever
produced. He went to New York City in April, 1883, and d. suddenly
there of Bright's disease in the following July. Mr. Ritchie has been for
more than fifty years a member of the Reformed Presbyterian, commonly
known as the Covenanter church at Ryegate Corner, of which he was long
the session clerk. He d. suddenly, June 20, 1900.

ROBINSON.

JOHN, b. Tolland, Conn., May 18, 1771. He m. Esther White; settled first in
Weathersfield, but came to Newbury before 1834 and settled on a farm
now owned by H. G. Rollins. He was a farmer and carpenter, also taught
singing schools. He had a brother, Benjamin, and two sisters, Ruth and
Lois, who lived in Barton and Brownington. The sisters never m. He d.
Apr. 30, 1852.
John and Esther Robinson had 8 children:
i.   John, m. Ruth Smith; res. Bath; afterwards rem. to Barton, where he
reared a large family.
1 ii.   Harvey J., b. June 21, 1798.
iii. Lois, m. Moses Dyer, and res. at Canton, Conn.
iv.   Thankful, m. Sept. 23, 1824, Holland DeWitt, who d. while she was yet
young, and she lived with her sister at Canton, Conn.
v.   Lavania, m. Dec. 10, 1829, Thomas Henry Carbee, q. v.
vi.   Naomi, never m.; lived in Newbury.
vii. Esther, m. March 5, 1837, Benjamin Blodgett. Two sons, Edwin, a
conductor for many years on the Passumpsic railroad, and Clark Perry,
a resident of Newbury, who has two sons.

1 HARVEY JOHNSON, b. Wethersfield, June 21, 1798. Carpenter. He was a fine
singer, as were all his family. He m. March 7, 1839, Sarah A., dau. of

Samuel White, (b. Nov. 13, 1811; d. Portland, Me., Oct. 30, 1898). He
d. Newbury, Jan. 1, 1863.

Children:
i. Olive W., b. April 2, 1840: m. April 18, 1871, Henry M. Parker of Putney;
   rem. to Portland, Me., 1873. C., (1) Laura Ellen, b. Newbury, March 24,
   1873. (2) Marion Kimball, b. Newbury, Sept. 13, 1875. (3) William
   Harvey, b. Portland, Me., Jan 12, 1877.
ii. Ellen S., b. June 27, 1842; m. February, 1879, N. C. Munson, a contractor
    on the Montpelier and Wells River R. R., who d. Sept. 16, 1894, leaving a
    daughter, Ada Robinson, b. Portland, Me., Feb. 9, 1881.
iii. Harvey E , b. Nov. 24, 1843; d. Dec. 10, 1844.
iv. Julia Kingsbury, b. Dec. 5, 1844; m. April 20, 1887, Capt. Pliny Crowell,
    who is now deceased.
v. Emma C., b. Oct. 12, 1846; m. Nov. 29, 1871, Samuel R. McCaw, of Port
   Perry, Ont. C., Henry Robinson, b. Newbury. Jan. 21, 1877.
vi. Emery Curtis, b. Oct. 28, 1848; m. Dec. 29, 1882, Alice Coffin of Portland,
    Me.; res. Deering, Me. C., (1) Agnes Almena. b. Portland, Me., March
    18, 1886. (2) James Albert, b. Deering, Me., Jan 12, 1892.
vii. Albert Drake, b. Sept. 16, 1850; res. Porland, Me.
viii. Sophia Hale, b. July 29, 1852; res. Portland, Me.

*ROGERS.

This family claim descent from Rev. John Rogers, the martyr. His widow and
children rem. to Wales, from whence, a century later, Stephen Rogers, a
descendant came, who settled in Newburyport, Mass., from whence his father
to Hampton, N. H. A descendant of his, bearing the same name. m. Mary
Nichols from England, whose father was high sheriff of Massachusetts
colony. This Stephen d. y.,leaving two c., son and dau , the latter m., it is
understood, a Mr. Morrill. The son, Josiah, was the pioneer of the family
in Newbury. He was b. about 1747, and m. Hannah Woodman of
Hampton; her sister m. Dea. Wm. Carter. They were daus. of Hilton
Woodman, b. 1712, a descendant in the 4th generation of Edward
Woodman, who came over in 1635. According to family tradition Josiah
Rogers came here about 1774, but the first recorded mention of him here is
in 1785. He settled on what has been since called "Rogers Hill," where he
cleared a fine farm with the aid of his sons. His mother came with them,
and despite her dislike of the wilderness, lived to the remarkable age of 99
years, 8 months, having survived her husband nearly 80 years, dying in
1816. Josiah Rogers d. Nov. 26, 1828, in his 81st year. On his tombstone
in the old burial ground on Rogers Hill he is styled "Lieutenant Josiah
Rogers."

Children, most of whom came with their parents:
i. Stephen, b. Feb. 5. 1771; lived in Topsham; m. a Miss Carter; d. Newbury,
   Oct. 7, 1857. They had several c. One dau. m. Peter Grattan. of Bath.
   N. H. Another m. Stark Huntley and had a son, and a dau. who m. A. T.
   Clarke of Bradford, and has a dau., Maude H.
ii. Moses, tanner and currier; rem. to Kingston, Ont., and m. a dau. of Col.
    O'Neil of the British army. Both d. y., leaving one son, who, in 1876,
    lived at Norwalk. O., having a son and dau.
1 iii. Levi, b. Oct. 12, 1776; d. Sept. 22, 1839.
2 iv. Samuel, d. Sept. 8, 1857.
v. Lydia, m. John True, a plow-maker, and d. at North Haverhill.
vi. Hannah, m. Oliver Barrett, Jr., of Windsor, and d. at Zanesville, O., about
    1858. The names of five sons were John, Oliver, William, George and
    Charles.
vii. Mary, m. James Smith, q. v.
viii. Ruth, m. 1st a Mr. Ferrin, a schoolmaster, who came here with the Rogers
     family to teach the children. They had two sons, called "Eben and Aaron. She
     m. 2d, Peter Powers, of Corinth, a son of Stephen Powers, of Newbury.
     Four c. She d. at the age of 98, at the home of her son, Granville Powers.
3 ix. Josiah, d.

*Communicated by Byron O. Rogers, Mrs. A. P. Webster, Mrs. N. Robinson and others.

x. Nancy, m. 1st Bliss Corliss, of Corinth; m. 2d ———— Eastman. Four c. One dau. m. Day Osgood. No. c. Another, Alma, m. a Mr. Craig, and had a son, Charles, of Bradford, who m. May Wright, and has one dau.

xi. Robert, m. March 19, 1812, Mary, (called Kate in Rogers record), dau. John Johnson; res. in New York state, where he was a merchant, then built a stone house on the boundary line at Stanstead, P. Q. He went south, and no more is known of him.

1 LEVI,[2] (Josiah,[1]) b. Hampton Beach, Oct. 12, 1776; m. April 24, 1800, Betsey, dau. Uriah Stone of Piermont, who was a soldier in the Old French war and in the revolution. (She d. Jan. 29, 1856). Lived in Topsham a few years, but returned to Rogers Hill about 1807, where he built the house owned now by James Johnston. He was prominent in town affairs. Representative, 1821. He was active in the militia, and captain of a company of detached militia in Fifield's regiment, in the war of 1812, and was afterwards colonel in the militia. He d. suddenly Sept. 22, 1839.
Children, two d. in infancy:

4 iii. Moses, b. March 2, 1803; d. Aug. 27, 1864.

iv. Eliza, b. Newbury, May 4, 1807; m. 1st, Bradley Doe; m. 2d, John Atwood; d. Oct. 16, 1853. (See Atwood family).

v. Hannah H., b. Jan. 1, 1812; d. September, 1849.

5 vi. Levi, b. July 10, 1814; d. Oct. 3, 1852.

vii. Henry Edwin, b. March 6, 1819; d. in infancy.

6 viii. Angelina P., b. May 13, 1820; d. Dec. 11, 1900.

ix. Betsey M., b. March 14, 1822; went to Richmond, Ind., as a teacher in May, 1848, and m. March 3, 1850, William G. Scott. She d. Nov. 16, 1862. He d. November, 1877. C., (1) Charles Edwin, b. May 9, 1852; m. Feb. 20, 1870, Eleanor R. Mitchell; d. Freeport, Ill., Sept. 8, 1894. (2) Clara Rogers, b. June 3, 1856; d. Dec. 25, 1876. (3) Helen Logan, b. Nov. 16, 1876, John B. Dougan of Richmond.

x. Amanda, b. Nov. 19, 1826; d. in infancy.

7 xi. Bradley Doe, b. Aug. 6, 1828; d. June 20, 1900.

2 SAMUEL, b. Hampton, N. H., (according to town record) Feb. 5, 1773; farmer on homestead, where he kept tavern for a time, and was prominent in town affairs, and belonged to the Whig party. He m. 1799, Ruth, dau. Daniel Stevens of Haverhill. (See Stevens family). He d. Sept. 8, 1857. She d. Jan. 10, 1864.
Children:

8 i. Josiah W., d. Feb. 17, 1846.

ii. George, m. Eliza Blake; had sons, Samuel and George. He d. in Boston, and has no descendants living.

iii. Harriet, m. John Bailey, of Newbury, q. v.; and rem. to Buffalo, N. Y., and lived to be 98 years of age, d. in summer of 1901.

iv. Samuel Frank, lived at West Topsham, owning a carding and cloth dressing mill. He m. Augusta Sawyer. C., (1) Ellen, m. Arad Corliss. Four c. (2) Augusta, m. a Mr. Place. No c. (3) Frank, merchant at East Corinth till burned out. He m. 1st, a lady from Chateaugay, N. Y. C., Ernest S., and Hattie R., of Milton; 2d, Clara Austin, of Milton. He d. a few years ago.

9 v. Nancy, b. Dec. 12, 1807; d. Sept. 11, 1850.

10 vi. Oliver B.

vii. Horace G., m. Lucy Clapp; lived in Milton, Mass.; d. 1869. C., (1) Horace C., m. and d. No c. (2) Lucy, m. Henry C. Rogers; lives at Quincy, Mass. C., Minnie and Molly. (3) Charles H., m. Florence Merry; lives in Buffalo, N. Y. C., Florence.

viii. Lucia, m. Michael Carleton of Haverhill; d. 1843. One c., Louise, who m., and d. without c.

11 ix. Azro B., b. March 28, 1823.

JOSIAH,[2] (Josiah,[1]) m. Catherine Barrett of Windsor.
Children:

i. William B., res. in Philadelphia, where he was the publisher of a weekly literary paper. Rem. to Bristol, Pa., where he engaged in the raising of sage, and became the largest producer of it in the world. He spent much time and research in tracing the various branches of the Rogers family and

left a record of it which was nearly complete. He m. Rebecca Wright; 5
c.; d. Apr. 2, 1883.
  ii. Catherine, m. Abel Walker of Canton, N. Y.
  iii. Oliver Barrett, res. Canandaigua, N. Y.; rem. to California; twice m.; d.
about 1873; 6 c.
  iv. Josiah F., physician; d. about 1855; no c.
  v. Robert, lived in St. Charles, Ill.; 2 c.
  vi. Eleutheria, m. Oliver Grow of Lorraine, N. Y.; 4 c.
  vii. Christina, m. Hiram Walker; lives near Manistee, Mich.; 3 c.
  viii. Eliza, m. a Mr. Spaulding; lives near Topeka, Kan.; 1 son.
  ix. Emily, never m.
  x. George W., physician at Mazalton, Mexico; is m; no c.

4 Moses,[3] (Levi,[2] Josiah,[1]) b. Topsham, May 2, 1803; m. *Dec. 12, 1829, Adeline,
dau. Col. John Bailey. Lived at West Newbury; rem. to Guildhall, then to
Northumberland, N. H., where he d. Aug. 27, 1864.
  Children:
  i. Robert B., b. June 8, 1831; d. y.
  ii. Adeline B., b. Newbury, June 19, 1834; m. Richmond, Ind., Sept. 10, 1857,
Timothy Allen; res. at Columbus, Ohio. C., (1) Lemuel E., b. Richmond,
Ind , July 1, 1858; res. Canton, Ohio. (2) Helen M., b. Columbus,
Ohio, Aug. 28. 1860; d. Dec. 15, 1876. (3) Mary B., b. Feb. 16, 1863;
res. Columbus, Ohio. (4) Bradley R., b. Oct. 12. 1865; res. in St. Louis;
d. May 8, 1897; 1 c. (5) Estelle E., b June 12, 1867; res. Columbus,
Ohio. (6) William A., b. Feb. 12. 1871; d. Feb. 18, 1874. (7) Elizabeth,
b. June 8, 1870; res. Hartford, Wis. (8) Walter A., b. Jan. 18, 1872; res.
Columbus, Ohio. Angeline W., b. Nov. 12, 1874; d. May 13, 1896.
  iii. Estelle L., b. May 21, 1837; m. Sept. 22, 1857, Horace T. Adams at
Guildhall. She res. in Hartford, Wis.
  iv. Helen Maria, b. Guildhall, Dec. 1, 1841; m. in Buffalo, N. Y., Dwight
Jackson of Hartford, Wis., where she d. Sept. 2, 1889.
  v. John Bailey, b. March 24. 1847; m. Emma L. Wheelock of Hartford, Wis.,
where he d. May 6, 1877.

5 Levi,[3] (Levi,[2] Josiah,[1]) b. Newbury, July 10, 1814. [This branch of the family
and some others spell the name Rodgers.] He m. at Haverhill, Dec. 8,
1841, Mehetable. dau. Michael Carleton. Rem. to Guildhall where he d.
Oct. 3, 1852. She returned to Haverhill and d. June 15, 1896.
  Children:
  i. Levi, b. Guildhall. May 9, 1843; fitted for college at Kimball Union
Academy. Graduated Dartmouth College 1866; Andover Theological
Seminary, 1871. Pastor Cong. Ch. at Claremont, N. H., 1871–80; 1st ch.
Georgetown, Mass., 1880–89; Cong. Ch. North Greenwich, Conn., 1890.
He m. 1st. Aug. 6, 1866, Mrs. Ella S. Dimmick of Quechee; she d. Oct. 1,
1883; 2d, July 5, 1894, Jessie C. Gilmore.
  ii. Harriet C., b. March 9, 1845; res. Haverhill.
  iii. Michael C., b. March 7, 1847. Fitted for college at Kimball Union
Academy; graduated Dartmouth College, 1871; in business at Bridgeport,
Conn. He m. July 25, 1872, Laura J. Chamberlain of McIndoes Falls. C.,
Bradley C., b. Apr. 14, 1874; graduated Dartmouth College, 1898, and
took a post-graduate course.
  iv. Betsey M., b. May 7, 1840; d. Nov. 5, 1867.

6 Angelina Putnam,[3] (Levi,[2] Josiah,[1]) b. Newbury, May 13, 1820; m. Oct. 6,
1844, in the Union Meeting House. Samuel Cummings Webster, a merchant
of Plymouth, N. H., where she lived till her death, Dec. 11, 1900. He d.
Jan. 23 1883. In 1894, Mrs. Webster and her brother, Bradley D. Rogers,
presented a bell to the Union Meeting House in memory of their parents.
  Children:
  i. Winnifred A., b. Apr. 19, 1851; res. Plymouth.
  ii. Margaret C., b. July 28, 1858; m. Dec. 3, 1879, James H. Stone of Detroit,
Mich. C., (1) Samuel W., b. Oct. 24, 1881. (2) Lucile H., b. Feb. 19,
1883. (3) James B., b. March 11, 1884.

*The town and Bailey family records give the date Dec. 11, 1828.

7 BRADLEY DOE,[3] (Levi,[2] Josiah,[1]) b. Aug. 6, 1828. He went to Buffalo, N. Y., in
1851, and engaged in the wholesale provision trade, in which he was very
successful, and from which he retired leaving it to his sons. He m. April,
1855, Mary Louise Williams, of Buffalo. Mr. Rogers d. June 20, 1900.
Children, all b. in Buffalo:

i. Mary Louise, b. April 6, 1856; d. May 2, 1871.
ii. Emily Williams, b. May 13, 1857; m. May 16, 1878, David Clark Ralph, of
Boston. C., (1) Edmund Bradley, b. Feb. 20, 1879. (2) Roger, b. May
21, 1880.
iii. George Bradley, b. Feb. 1, 1859; d. in infancy.
iv. Charles Otis b. July 3, 1860; in the provision business at Buffalo; m. Aug.
29, 1882, Mary Lampp.
v. Frank Albert, b. Apr. 17, 1862; in the provision business at Buffalo. He m.
Apr. 23, 1884, Ella McNeal of Buffalo. C., (1) Bradley Albert, b. Dec.,
1885. (2) Edith, b. Jan. 8, 1888.
vi. Clara Winifred, b. June 12, 1866; d. in infancy.
vii. Harry Edwin, b. Aug. 8, 1867; in the provision business at Buffalo; m.
March 20, 1890, Rebecca Hodge of San Monica, Cal.
viii. Anna Lois, b. March 30, 1869; m. June 11, 1889, Matthew Baines of
Buffalo.
ix. William Brayton, b. March 4, 1872; d. in infancy.

8 JOSIAH W.,[3] (Samuel.[2] Josiah,[1]) farmer, and major in the militia. Lived in West
Newbury till 1831, when he settled a half mile west from Hall's Pond, and
built in that year the house known later as the Myron Abbott house,
which was burned Jan. 17, 1900. In 1841, he built a house, and, later,
barns on the highest point on the road between the town farm and
Newbury village where he d. Feb. 16, 1846. These buildings are also
gone. He m. March 7, 1822, Lydia S., dau. of Richard and Anna
(Maynard) Aldrich. After his death she m. Jan. 1, 1846, William Bolton,
(q. v.), and d. Jan. 7, 1892.
Children:

i. Edwin Aldrich, b. Oct. 20, 1824. Fitted for college at Newbury Seminary;
one year at Wesleyan University, but graduated at Harvard. Studied
law with Judge Underwood; admitted to the bar, Jan. 20, 1854. Went to
California in that year and settled at Sonora, Tanhumine county, in the
practice of law, in which he was very successful. He m. Dec. 24, 1864,
Henrietta G. Morrow of Jamaica Plain., Mass.; d. Feb. 2, 1900; no c. He
d. at St. Luke's Hospital, San Francisco, June 20, 1898.
ii. George Edson, b. Feb 19, 1826; d. Oct. 23, 1846.
iii. Russell Kimball, b. Oct. 19, 1827; lawyer. Went to California, 1852; m.
1856, Clara Walbridge of Peacham. A son and two daus. survived their
father. He d. Oct. 30, 1886.
iv. Frank S., b. Aug. 14, 1830. Went to California, 1855; m. at San Francisco,
1858, Mary Byrne; rem. to Nicasio. Marin county; 2 sons and 3 daus.
v. Henry W., b. Aug. 28, 1832; d. Jan. 26, 1853.
vi. Nelson Josiah, b. Nov. 5, 1834. Went to Boston, 1851, and to California,
1854; returned to Vermont , 1862. Served during the Civil War in Co. H,
12th Vermont; m. in Boston. Oct. 3, 1865, Clara Hunkins, (b. in
Haverhill, N. H.); rem. to San Francisco, 1856, where his wife d. June 6,
1875, aged 36. Two c., Elva W., d. in her 21st year, and Clarence J., who
d. in his 18th. He m. 2d, June 3, 1883, D. Augusta Peer, a native of
Whichchurch, Ont. She d. Aug. 26, 1890. Two c., Annie Grace, and
Roswell.
vii. Eliza Lawrence, b. Sept. 13, 1836. Went to California with her brother,
Edwin, in 1854, and m. in 1855, Dr. Mark T. Dodge. a native of New
York City. He d. 1866, leaving two c. Mrs. Dodge resides in Stockton,
Cal.
viii. Lydia Annette, b. Sept. 26, 1839; m. Aug. 10, 1862, J. Frances Jenness, a
native of Beverly, Mass., a member of the 40th Massachusetts in the Civil
War. Rem. to San Francisco, 1872, and later to Southern California,
where he d. April 1, 1886. C., Herbert H., and Ina P., b. in Boston; Maud
P., b. and d. in California. Mrs. Jenness and children now live in San
Francisco.
ix. Emily Stevens, b. Jan. 2, 1842; m. March 15, 1866, Nathaniel Frances
Fletcher of Wrentham, Mass.; res. in Boston; no c.

680   HISTORY OF NEWBURY, VERMONT.

9 NANCY,³ (Samuel,² Josiah,¹) b. Dec. 12, 1807; m. Feb. 27, 1827, Ezekiel
    Johnson, (b. Sept. 26, 1803; d. Oct. 9, 1880). They settled in Bath, but
    rem. to Bradford about 1840. She d. Sept. 11, 1850.
  Children:
    i. Mary E., b. Jan. 19, 1828; m. Dec. 25, 1849, Roswell Farnham, of
       Bradford, lawyer; colonel of the 12th Vt., in the Civil War, and governor
       of Vermont, 1880–82. C., (1) Charles C., a lawyer of Buffalo, N. Y. He
       m. Grace Hall. Two c. (2) Florence, m. Edward C. Osgood, of Bellows
       Falls. One dau. (3) William H., res. Buffalo, N. Y. Two c.
   ii. Ruth Ann, b. Jan. 26, 1839; m. B. B. Chadwick; d. 1897.
  iii. Nancy J., b. April 19, 1835; m. John H. Ruckel, of Buffalo. Five c.
   iv. Harriet B., b. Dec. 19, 1837; m. Mortimer Bradley, of Buffalo. Both d.; 2 c.
    v. Ezekiel T., b. May 1, 1839; served in the 10th Vt. in the Civil War; res. in
       Bradford, Penn., where he is in the oil business. He m. Sophia Louise,
       dau. J. Amherst Bayley, who d. at Buffalo, May 17. 1870.
   vi. William Henry, b. March 7, 1840; res. in Buffalo. Thrice m., 1st, Virginia
       Hartley; m. 2d, Mary Adelia Lord; 3d, Mary Hill. C., by 1st m.,
       Evedena, m. Benjamin Love, of Buffalo; by 2d m., Harry, who is m.; by
       3d m., several c., one of whom, Roswell, graduated at Harvard University.

10 OLIVER B.,³ (Samuel,² Josiah,¹) b. March 29, 1812; farmer on the homestead,
    after spending six years in Boston. He m. March 21, 1838, Polly Ann
    Woodman, dau. Dudley Carleton, (b. Feb. 6, 1818; d. Dec. 24, 1900).
    They were members of the Methodist church more than 60 years, of which
    he was a steward, and most liberal supporter, in that part of the
    town. Steward of Newbury Seminary, 1850–52, keeping the boarding
    house, and built, 1853, the house which Geo. B. Barnett owns and
    occupies. He built, 1838, the farmhouse in which his son lives, and in
    which no one died till 1894. In politics, Whig and Republican, holding
    town offices. He d. Aug. 1, 1900.
  Children:
    i. Lucia B., b. June 15, 1843; res. with her parents; teacher; d. Aug. 17, 1894.
   ii. Lauribel, b. Jan. 4, 1848; m. Azro P. McKinistry.
  iii. Byron O, b. Jan. 10, 1856; farmer on homestead, has held town offices, and
       is a trustee of the Tenney Memorial Library. He m. May 24, 1898, Ella
       May, dau. of B. Frank, and Alice A. (Bixby) Williams, (b. May 24, 1880).
       C., Hope, b. Jan. 9, 1900.
  This last mentioned family is the last of the name on Rogers Hill.

11 AZRO BUCK,³ (Samuel,² Josiah,¹) b. March 22. 1823. Farmer on Rogers Hill;
    was also engaged in the sale of patent rights and farm machinery. He was
    a large producer of maple sugar and was, for a time, in the orange
    business in Florida. His fine set of farm buildings on Rogers Hill was
    burned March 14, 1889. Res. South Newbury. He m. 1st, Sophronia
    Wilson, who d. 1852; 2d, March 2, 1859, Almira P., dau. Mason Randall.
  Children, one by 1st m., and four by 2d:
    i. George H., res. Somerville, Mass.; 3 c.
   ii. Hattie Francena, b. Nov. 17, 1861; d. Apr. 19, 1871.
  iii. Mary Alice, b. July 9, 1865; m. Dec. 6, 1893, John Gardner Shepard, (b.
       Plainfield, Conn., Aug. 3, 1864). Is manager of Haverhill creamery. C.,
       (1) Azro Rogers, b. Dec. 7, 1897. (2) Almira L., b. July 28, 1900.
   iv. Harry Azro, b. Jan. 16, 1870; d. Jan. 31, 1889.
    v. Charles Arthur, b. Oct. 17, 1873; drowned in Connecticut River, June 1,
       1892.
  Azro B. Rogers, and his nephew, Byron O. Rogers, are the last male descendants
    of Josiah, the pioneer, in Vermont, bearing the name of Rogers.

ROGERS.

DANIEL ALLEN, b. East Columbia, N. H., Sept. 11, 1828. He was son of Daniel
    and Phebe (Tibbitts) Rogers, his grandfathers being Enoch Rogers and
    Richard Tibbits. He was educated at Farmington, Me., studied law with
    Lyman T. Flint of Colebrook, N. H ; admitted to Coös County bar, May,
    1854. In practice at Colebrook, N. H., six years, St. Johnsbury one year,
    Wells River 20 years. He was auditor, referee, and master in chancery in

Vermont and New Hampshire. Town representative, 1872-73. State's attorney for Orange County. (See also Judge Leslie's chapter upon Wells River). He m. Nov. 29, 1855, Sarah Amanda Cooper of Beloit, Wis. He d. July 11, 1881. Mrs. Rogers res. in Beloit.
Children:
  i. Edwin Louis.
  ii. Charles Herbert.
  iii. Phebe Amanda.
  iv. Sarah Helen.

ROLLINS.

EDWARD, b. Wolfboro, N. H., Aug. 1, 1788 came to this town about 1810; settled on a farm in the Wallace district, where his son, Samuel M., afterwards long lived. In 1831 he removed to the farm where his son Henry G.. still lives. Served in war of 1812. He m. Nancy P., dau. of Samuel Meserve, who d. Aug. 14, 1869. He d. Newbury, Oct. 16, 1864.
Children:
  i. Ann, b. Aug. 1, 1814; m. William Lindsey.
  ii. Edward, b. 1816.
  iii. Betsey, b. 1817.
1 iv. Samuel M., b. Oct. 22, 1819; d. Oct. 3, 1893.
  v. Marion W., b. December, 1821.
  vi. Mary J., b. Jan. 31, 1824; m. 1st, George Otis; m. 2d, Samuel Corliss; d. Sept. 15, 1881.
  vii. William W., b. March 5, 1827; conductor on B. C. & M. R. R. many years; m. in Barnet, May 30, 1852, Olive S. Thayer; d. Dec. 4, 1873.
  viii. Jonas M., b. March 14, 1830; res. Danvers, Mass.; served in union army; wounded at Antietam.
2 ix. Henry G., b. July 7, 1832.
  x. Justin L., b. May 14, 1834; served in an Ohio regiment during the Civil War; was in 19 battles; unharmed.

1 SAMUEL M., b. Oct. 22, 1819; farmer; m. 1st, Nov. 3, 1844, Fidelia, dau. Charles George, who d. March 20, 1850, leaving one son. He m. 2d, August, 1852, Martha Smith, who d. April 7, 1856, leaving two sons. He m. 3d, Oct. 28, 1857, Samantha, dau. of Jacob Sulham. He d. Oct. 3, 1893.
Five children by 3d marriage, eight in all:
  i. George F., b. July 3, 1849; d. 1879.
  ii. Charles B., b. March 12, 1854; m. 1877, Martha Stearns of Bradford. C., (1) Martha, m. Winthrop Southworth. (2) Goldie.
  iii. William M., b. March 26, 1856; m. May 5, 1880, Bertha, dau. Robert Wallace; farmer on the William Wallace farm. C., (1) daughter, b. Feb. 8; d. March 10, 1883. (2) Leonard, b. May 8, 1889. (3) William, b. Jan. 14, 1895.
  iv. Fidelia G., b. April 18, 1858; d. November, 1876.
  v. Lilla M., b. April 9, 1866; m. Nov. 29, 1887, Eri C. George.
  vi. Edwin L., b. March 21, 1868; m. and res in Morristown, N. J
  vii. Elvira L., b. March 18, 1870; m. Guy C. Howland.
  viii. Robert J., b. July 1, 1876.

2 HENRY G., b. Newbury, 1832; was five years in lumber business with his brother, Samuel, at Wells River; served in the union army nine months in the 12th Vt.; farmer, building his present house on what was known as the "Robinson place," 1885. He m. Dec. 2, 1857, Harriet, dau. of John Waddell.
Children:
  i. Mary E., b. March 2, 1859; m. Sept. 24, 1889, W. A. Cable, of Concord, N. H., who d. at Woodsville. C., Wendell R., b. Concord. N. H., Nov. 1, 1890.
  ii. Julia E., b. Oct. 10, 1860; m. Feb. 2, 1887, H. G. Darling of South Ryegate. C., Gladys R., b. Ryegate, Sept. 9, 1888.
  iii. Clara Anna, b. Oct. 1, 1862; m. Feb. 28, 1886, C. A. Sinclair. C., Arthur R., b. Montpelier, Sept. 16, 1890.

iv. Robert W., b. April 12, 1864; m. Jan. 22, 1888, Adelia Boyce of Hartford, Conn. C, Robert W., b. Hartford, Jan 30, 1890.
v. Edward H., b. July 21, 1867; m. Dec. 30, 1891, Anzanette M. Darling of Barnet. C., (1) Walter S., b. Elizabeth, N. J., Sept. 28, 1892. (2) Henry B., b Palmer. Mass., May 5, 1896.
vi. Hattie J., b. Jan. 30, 1869; m. June 11, 1891, Irving C. Renfrew of Littleton, N. H. C.. (1) Phyllis E., b. Littleton, April 26, 1872. (2) Marguerite E., and (3) Percy L., b. Littleton, Nov. 5, 1894.
vii. L. Josephine, b. Apr. 16, 1872.

*ROPES.

In the year 1637, George Ropes and Mary, his wife, constituting the first generation of the American branch of the family, came from England and settled in Salem, Mass. They were the parents of nine c., from whom have sprung, so far as is known, all in America bearing the name of Ropes. From John Ropes, the fifth of these c., came the Ropes family of Newbury, Hardy Ropes of the fifth generation being the immediate ancestor of the family.

Hardy Ropes was b. Jan. 17, 1763. He m. Aug. 28, 1786, Hannah, dau. of Joseph and Hepsibah Elson. He was a mariner in the merchant service, and lost several vessels in the war with France, which constituted a part of the "French Spoliation Claims" so long before Congress. His health failing, about 1800, he bought a farm in Orford N. H., where he spent the most part of a long life. By his wife, Hannah Elson, he had eleven c., constituting the sixth generation of the family. George, the eighth of these c., was b. at Orford, Nov. 29, 1800. He learned the cabinet maker's trade and settled in Newbury. In 1826, he m. Miriam, a dau. of John Johnson, and granddaughter of Colonel Thomas Johnson, the pioneer settler in Newbury. She was b. Feb. 21, 1807; d. May 15, 1844. They were the parents of eight c., who compose the seventh generation of the family. In 1849, Mr. Ropes moved to Passumpsic, a village in Barnet, and in 1851 to St. Johnsbury, where he d. Aug. 29, 1869.

Their children were:

i. Hannah Elson, b. in Newbury, Jan. 13, 1827. She received her education in the schools of the town and at Newbury Seminary, and was a teacher in the common schools of Newbury and elsewhere. She m. George P. Cummings, a civil engineer, Oct. 20, 1851. They moved to Marquette, Mich., in 1857, where Mrs. Cummings d. Sept. 27, 1892. A son, Charles, is the only c. of this marriage. He is a graduate of Amherst College, and follows the profession of his father.
ii. Miriam Johnson, b. Newbury, Aug. 26, 1829. She is a graduate of Newbury Seminary, and has spent the greater part of her life as a teacher in the schools of Vermont, New Hampshire and Michigan. She is now living in Ishpeming, Mich.
iii. George, Jr., b. in Newbury, March 12, 1829. He spent his earlier days in attending school and at farm labor. He was employed at Passumpsic in building the bridges on the extension of the railway to St. Johnsbury, in the early fifties, and afterwards learned the carpenter's trade. In 1854 he began the study of architecture in Boston, opened an office in that city and practiced his profession there until 1877. He was the architect of many fine and important buildings, among them the new Massachusetts State Prison, the Reformatory Prison for women at South Framingham, the Girls' High and Normal School, Boston, and other public buildings in the city and throughout the state. He rem. to Kansas in 1877, opened an office in Kansas City, Mo., and afterwards in Topeka, where he was employed as architect and superintendent of construction of the new State Capitol. He was the architect of several other public buildings and of many private residences in Kansas and Missouri. His last professional work was in connection with the construction of the Planters' Hotel, St. Louis, Mo. He is now residing in Detroit, Mich. June 17. 1860, he m. Sophia A. Taft, b. in Boston, Jan. 8, 1835; d. in St. Louis, Dec. 12,

*By Arthur Ropes. Esq., Montpelier.

1900. The c. of this marriage are Arthur Judson, who d. in infancy; Ella Elson, a graduate of Kansas State University, latterly a teacher in the schools of St. Louis, dying in that city Jan. 4, 1901; Alice Hayward, a graduate of Kansas State University, and a teacher of music; George Hardy, a graduate of the Institute of Technology, Boston, and now an architect in Detroit, Mich. In 1875, the centennial of the building of Col. Thomas Johnson's house was observed at the Ox-bow, at which the following poem, written by Mrs. Ropes, was read by her daughter, Alice:

> For centuries had the cloud capped hills
>   In silence watched this spot,
> In silence had the green banks there
>   The river's kisses shyly caught,
> When with his gun, his axe and spade,
> One came, and here his homestead made,
>   One hundred years ago.
>
> The pine tree pointing to the skies
>   The neighboring oak caressed of yore,
> The soft wind whispered thro' the trees
>   Answered the murmurs on the shore.
> In quiet else the Ox-bow slept,
> Or converse with the bright heavens kept,
>   One hundred years ago.
>
> The red man, wolf and catamount
>   Stalked lordly masters of the soil,
> The earth still wore its virgin dress,
>   Ere married to the hand of toil.
> Then all was changed, the forests rang
> With blows of axe, with hammer's clang,
>   One hundred years ago.
>
> And now we celebrate the day
>   When bravery and faith in God
> Conquered the wild and tangled wood,
>   And plowed the meadow, turned the sod,
> And under Heaven's protecting dome
> Made here a dwelling place, a home,
>   One hundred years ago.

iv.   Julia, b. Dec. 25, 1833; d. March 2, 1835.
v.   Julius, b. Newbury, Apr. 22, 1835. After leaving school at St. Johnsbury Academy, he worked at the carpenter's trade. He went to Marquette in the early sixties and learned there the druggist business. He became an expert analytical chemist, the rich mineral resources of the region affording a wide field for the practice of this profession. He devoted much time to explorations for mineral wealth. He discovered silver in the country about Ishpeming and became the president of the Ropes Gold and Silver Mining Company, organized for the development of the deposits of these metals. Mr. Ropes is an ardent explorer and an apt student of the face of nature. His explorations have extended to the mineral regions of the Pacific slope and the southern states. He m. Oct. 12, 1867, Eunice Louisa Rouse, at Marquette, Mich. Their c. are Leverett Smith, a mining engineer in the South; Eunice Luella, Ursula Elson, and Julius Bigelow.
vi.   Arthur, b. in Newbury, May 5, 1837. Educated at St. Johnsbury Academy, entered Dartmouth College in the class of 1864, withdrawing at the end of Freshman year to become principal of St. Johnsbury High School. He had previously been a teacher in the public schools and for a short time assistant teacher in St. Johnsbury Academy. He was for several years teller in Passumpsic Bank at St. Johnsbury, and Jan. 1, 1864, was chosen cashier of Northfield Bank, an office from which he retired in 1868 by reason of impaired health. He subsequently engaged in manufacturing at Waterbury and Montpelier. In Jan., 1880, he entered the office of the Vermont Watchman, at Montpelier, and was editor of that paper till 1885. In 1886 he began the publication of the Rural Vermonter at Montpelier, and in 1888 became associated with others in Montpelier and Washington county in the purchase of the Vermont Watchman and in the printing business connected with the paper, in which the Vermonter was merged. Mr. Ropes was made editor of the Watchman and business manager of the association. In 1897 he became sole proprietor of the Watchman

establishment. In connection with the Watchman he publishes and edits the Montpelier Daily Journal. He m. June 28, 1864, Mary J., dau. of G. W. Hutchins, of Waterbury. They have two daus., Charlotte, and Laura Livingston.

vii. Leverett, b. March 24, 1839; d. March 12, 1842.
viii. Ellen, b. Newbury, March 27, 1841. From her earlier years her home was with her sister Hannah. She received her later education in the public schools at Marquette, Mich., and was afterwards teacher there. She m. Aug. 12. 1868, Charles L. Sheldon of Ishpeming, Mich., and in the latter part of 1899, they moved to Seattle, Wash. They have two c., Elsie Miriam, the wife of L. T. Turner. Esq., a lawyer of Seattle, Wash., and George Ropes, a mining engineer.

ROSS.

JAMES, son of John and Helen (Black) Ross, was b. in Kinglassie, Fifeshire, Scotland, Sept. 14, 1814. and was m. 1837, to Jean, dau. of John and Isabella (Russell) Kennaird, b. Jan. 12, 1813. He was by trade a tanner and currier. In 1846, with two children, they sailed from Liverpool to Quebec, being seven weeks on the voyage. They came to Newbury via Burlington, and he worked several years at his trade in Woburn, Mass. In 1851 he bought the farm on which he lived 41 years. He d. Feb. 7, 1893. Mr. Ross was remarkable for the extent and variety of his information.

Children:
i. Isabella, b. Scotland. May 28,1838; m. July 1, 1858, George Chalmers, q. v.
ii. Ellen, b. Scotland, Feb. 19, 1840; m. Feb. 18, 1879, William Scott of Barton. One dau., Ellen Ross Scott, b. March 13, 1881.
iii. Eliza, b. Newbury, June 20, 1852.

RUGGLES.

I. THOMAS, b. Sudbury, Suffolk. Eng., 1584; m. Nasing, Essex, England, 1620, Mary Curtis; came to Massachusetts in 1632; settled at Roxbury, 1637, where he d. in 1644, and his wife Feb. 14, 1674.

II. JOHN (1624–1658) of Roxbury, m. Abigail Croft.

III. JOHN (1653–1694) of Roxbury, m. Martha Devotion.

IV. EDWARD (1691–1765) of Roxbury and Cambridge, m. Hannah Croft.

V. EDWARD (1724–1797) of Pomfret, Conn., and Montague, Mass., m. Ann Sumner.

VI. SAMUEL, (1752-1778) of Pomfret and Killingly, Conn. This ancestry is from "The Ruggles Family," prepared 1896 by F. L. Bailey of Boston.

VII. EBENEZER, b. Pomfret, Conn., Dec. 17, 1773; m. at Walpole, N. H., Persis Goodall, who after his death, m. 2d, Thomas Burroughs, q. v. She d. May 16, 1854. Members of 1st Ch. Ebenezer Ruggles came to Newbury in 1802. Lived opposite Richard Doe's at the Ox-bow. He d. Newbury, June 22, 1823.
Children:
1 i. Perley, b. March 27, 1796; d. June 7, 1824.
2 ii. Philarmon, b. Apr. 30, 1798; d. Apr. 15, 1876.
iii. Electa, b. Walpole, N. H., July 16, 1800; m. Dec. 13, 1816, Thomas Downer; rem. to Bellows Falls; d. March 21, 1868.
iv. Lucy, b. Newbury, April 30, 1803; m. Roger Eastman, q. v.
v. Louisa, b. April 10, 1805; m. Thomas Burroughs, Jr., q. v.
vi. Persis, b. March 9, 1808; m. Thomas Church; d. 1888.
vii. Phebe, b. Dec. 5, 1811; d. Aug. 24, 1862.
viii. Mary Ann, b. March 5, 1814; un-m.; d. Oct. 24, 1831.
ix. Ebenezer W., b. Nov. 10, 1818; m. Eliza Taylor; d. Feb. 10,1881, Neponset, Mass.

1 PERLEY, b. Pomfret, Conn., March 27, 1796; m. Dec. 2, 1821, Betsey, dau.
Dea. William Burroughs, (b. April 1, 1800; d. Aug. 3, 1868). He was
drowned at Millen Falls, Mass., June 7, 1824, while rafting.
Two children who grew to maturity:
  i. Henry Edwin, b. Nov. 27, 1822; fitted for college at Newbury Seminary;
graduated Dartmouth College, 1845; Union Theological Seminary, 1848;
teacher of classics at Lyndon Academy one year; Hoosac Falls (N. Y.)
Academy, two years; city missionary, New York City; pastor of a church
in St. Louis, and of a Cong. Ch. at Eaton Vill., N. Y., until his health
failed; returned to Newbury and d. greatly lamented at the home of his
grandfather, Dec. 24, 1856. He m. Dec. 31, 1853, at Eaton, N. Y., Julia R.
Pierce. They had a son, William B., and a daughter.
  ii. Harriet Elizabeth, b. Dec. 29, 1824, after her father's death, at the house of
her grandfather; educated at Newbury Seminary; teacher with her
brother at Lyndon Academy, and at Hoosac Falls, N. Y.; teacher, 1847-52,
in Adelphi College, Booneville, Mo.; teacher, 1854, of drawing and
painting in a seminary at Arrow Rock, Mo.; assistant principal, 1856–59,
of Saline County Institute, Mo. She was m. Sept. 7, 1859, to Rev.
Chauncey L. Loomis, (b. Booneville, Mo., 1819; graduated Western
Reserve College, 1846; Union Theological Seminary, 1856; studied
medicine in New York). They sailed for the island of Corisco, West Africa,
a few degrees south of the equator, where they established a mission under
the auspices of the Presbyterian Board, until she was stricken with African
fever, and d. Aug. 20, 1861. One c., Henry Lester Loomis, b. and d. at
Corisco. Mr. Loomis returned to America, and after a few years sent to
Africa for his wife's remains, which were interred at the Ox-bow, Jan. 11,
1865. Mr. Loomis practised medicine many years, and d. at Middletown,
Conn., Jan. 13, 1894. Upon the memorial stone to Mrs. Loomis is carved
a picture of the mission village, from a drawing made by her.

2 PHILARMON. b. April 30, 1798, at Pomfret, Conn.; m. 1st, Dec. 27, 1821. Eliza,
dau. of Thomas Burroughs, (b. April 24, 1798; d. Dec. 21, 1862); m. 2d,
Mary Ann Burroughs, sister of his first wife, (b. Sept. 13, 1808; d. June
27, 1874). He rem. to Dalton, N. H., in 1823, and later to Milton, Mass.,
where he d. April 15, 1876.
Children:
  i. Eliza N., b. Aug. 20, 1822; d. Sept. 29, 1863.
  ii. Amanda R., b. Nov. 14, 1826; d. Dec. 14, 1888.
  iii. Mary A., b. Sept. 4, 1830; d. May 16, 1858.
  iv. Thomas Edwin, b. May 19, 1838; graduated Yale College, 1859· res.
Milton, Mass.; m. Sept. 13, 1866, Harriet W. Murray. Seven c.

RUNNELS.

HORACE HERRICK son of Jonathan C. and Mary (Dimond) Runnels, b. Deering,
N. H, Jan. 16, 1834; m. at Henniker, N. H., Mary Carter, (b. at Deering,
N. H., March 13, 1836); miller at Deering and Lancaster, N. H.; came to
South Newbury, 1881, and bought the grist mill there, dealing also in feed
and groceries. He is a steward in the Methodist church.
Children:
  i. Nettie Elma, b. Deering, Sept. 2, 1866; graduated at Salem, Mass., Normal
School, 1892; teacher at Everett, Mass.
  ii. Arthur Dalton, b. Deering, June 15, 1868; clerk, and later, in business with
his father. He m. in Newbury, Nov. 7, 1894, Bertha May Gamsby. C.,
Lester Carter, b. Newbury, Oct. 31, 1896.

RUSSELL.

THOMAS K., came to Wells River before 1818, from Claremont, N. H., and lived
in a house which stood where the residence of the late Hon. C. B. Leslie
now stands. Later he rem. to a house on the north side of the river, a
little way above the dam, near the present residence of Robert G. Brock.
There was a sawmill on that dam, of which Mr. Russell had charge. He
afterwards rem. to Cabot. His wife, as remembered by Mr. Leslie, was a

very fine woman. Their sons were Willis, Willard, William and Oramel. These sons were all paper makers, and worked in the paper mill at Wells River, in their early days. Willie and Oramel went into the hotel business, and kept two hotels in Quebec. The latter never m. Willard and William continued in the paper business, one at Bellows Falls and the other at Franklin, N. H. These brothers were all strong, sensible men who made a good record of themselves. William m. Almira Heath, and their c. were William A., Henry O. and George W , who were in the paper business in Lawrence, and Mrs. C. H. Sawyer of Bellows Falls. He d. at Bellows Falls, Dec. 18, 1892, aged 87 years.

WILLIAM A. was b. at Wells River, April 22, 1831. His parents rem. to Franklin, N. H., where he went to school, and learned the paper trade. In his father's mill 1848–51. In partnership with his father at Lawrence, Mass., then in business alone. In 1861, he owned several mills and was one of the foremost paper manufacturers in the country. He was the first to manufacture, with success, paper from wood pulp, and, in 1869, established a mill of that kind at Franklin, N. H. In the same year he built a paper mill at Bellows Falls, and, later, purchased the entire water power there, built a new dam, and enlarged the canal. That place has been mainly built up through his enterprise. He was also interested in several mills in Maine. and at St. Anthony's Falls, Minn. In 1897, Mr. Russell became the president of the International Paper Company, which was composed of the owners of about 20 of the largest mills in the country. In 1898, he resigned this office, and retired from active business. He was elected an alderman in the city of Lawrence, 1867. Member of the legislature, 1868, and in the same year, delegate to the National Republican Convention at Cincinnati Member of Congress from the 7th Mass. district, 1878, 1880 and 1882, declining re-election in 1884. He served on several important committees He m. Feb. 1, 1859, Elizabeth H., dau. of Wm. A. Hall, of Bradford, Mass. They had three daus. She d. in 1866, and he m. in 1872, her sister, Frances S., and their c. were two sons and one dau. He d. at his home, 39 Beacon street, Boston, Jan. 13, 1899.

RUSSELL.

FRED CUTLER, b. Feb. 23, 1866, at Lovell, Maine. Educated in the public schools of Lovell; prepared for college at Bridgeton Academy, North Bridgeton, Me.; was graduated from Bowdoin College, class of 1889 with the degree of A. B. In 1892, received the degree of A. M.. Bowdoin. Was principal of Warren High School, Warren, Me., 1889–90; 1890–91, principal of Pembroke, Me.. High School; and 1891–93, superintendent of schools at Rockland, Me. Studied medicine at Maine Medical School and Dartmouth Medical College, receiving the degree of M. D., in 1894 from the latter institution. Commenced the practice of his profession at Newbury, Jan., 1895, also practicing in Haverhill, N. H., in 1896–97; m. Dec. 16, 1891, Carrie A. Farrington of Lovell, Me. C., John Farrington, b. Newbury, July 21, 1899.

SAWYER.

CAPT. EZEKIEL. b. Rowley, Mass., May 9, 1743; settled in Bradford, on the farm owned and occupied by his grandson, the late John H. Sawyer, on the river road. He d. Jan. 13, 1817, and his wife. Mary Payson, d. July 6 1819. They had 11 c., of whom Joseph, their 3d son and 6th child, b. March 28, 1777, settled in West Newbury, where his granddaughter, Mrs. Hazeltine, now lives. He was a prominent man in his day, and major in the old militia. He m. Dec. 28, 1801, Azubah, dau. of Col. Remembrance Chamberlain, (b. Nov. 6, 1779; d. March 31, 1830). He d. Sept. 22, 1818 Children:

1   i.   Remembrance C., b. March, 1803; d. Aug. 19, 1862.
     ii. Elizabeth, b. Jan. 10, 1805; m. April 7, 1828, Hiram Smith, q. v.; d. April 16, 1879.
     iii. Amanda, b. 1807; m. Jan. 11, 1834, Clark Chamberlin, q. v.; d. Nov. 13, 1868.

iv. Mary Payson, b. Feb. 14, 1809; m. July 9, 1833, Joseph Hutchins Bailey, q. v.; d. June 27, 1850.
2 v. Ezekiel, b. 1811; d. Feb. 9, 1863.
3 vi. Jonathan J., d. May 3. 1865.
vii. Hannah J., m. May 27, 1839, Enoch Wiggin, q. v.; d.
4 viii. Joseph, d. Sept. 14, 1881.

1 ·REMEMBRANCE CHAMBERLAIN, b. March, 1803; farmer at West Newbury, on the farm now that of F. W. Sawyer. He m. Aug. 29, 1832, Zerviah, dau. of Thos. R. Brock, (b. Nov. 6, 1809; d. June, 1888). He d.
Children:
. Azubah, b. May 7, 1833; d. Feb. 25, 1842.
ii. Joseph, b. Aug. 5, 1835; farmer and in hotel business at Wentworth, N. H., and elsewhere; m. Dec. 31, 1862, Hannah H., dau. of Daniel Tyler of Deer Isle, Maine. C., (1) Remembrance C., b. Sept. 30, 1863; proprietor during several seasons of the Summit House on Moosilauke. (2) Frederic W., b. Feb. 21, 1870; m. April 14, 1891, Ida M. Black of Memarancook, N. B. C., a, John B., b. June 2, 1895; b, Hilda M., b. Feb. 17, 1901.

2 EZEKIEL, b. 1811. Farmer and hotel keeper. In 1838, he went into the Wells River House with Col. Jacob Kent. In 1842 they dissolved partnership, and Matthew Chaplain became his partner. In 1850, he sold out to Mr. Chaplain, and went into the stage business with V. A. Newell and L. L. Farr. He drove stage from Wells River to Canada Line till the railroad was opened to St. Johnsbury. From 1854 to 1856, he kept the Newbury House, and from 1856 to 1861, the Eagle Hotel at Concord, N. H. Returned to Newbury and spent his last days in the house at the village now owned by Miss Goddard. His farm at West Newbury was bought of Daniel Eastman, the large two-story house was built in 1840 by Daniel Eastman, Sr., and burned in 1885. He m. 1838, Eliza. dau. of Silas and Phebe Howe, (b. Hancock, N. H., 1811). Her sister, Lorinda, m. about 1840, Matthew Chaplain. One dau., m. L. Bart Cross of Montpelier, and another, Louise, m. and lives in Union City, Mich. Ezekiel Sawyer d. Feb. 9, 1863. She d. Sept. 1, 1878.
Children:
5 i. George A., b. March 7, 1840.
ii. Susan, b. at Wells River, 1840; m. Feb. 14, 1865, Joseph Sawyer, of Bradford, and rem. to Chicago, where she d., leaving two c., (1) Ruth, b. 1867; d. Newbury, Jan. 9, 1874. (2) Frank, now in Texas.

3 JONATHAN J., b. 1813. Hotel keeper at Danvers, Lawrence and Lowell, Mass. He m. 1845, Prudence Brock of Barnet. She d. Lowell, 1864. He d. Newbury, May 3, 1865.
Children:
i. Addie, lived in Newbury, but went with her brother to Portland, Oregon, where she m. and has recently d., leaving five c.
ii. Frank, lives in Oregon.

4 JOSEPH, b. 1819; went to California, 1849, and later to Oregon, and carried on a ranch. He m. in Oregon, Sarah K., dau. John Wallace, of Newbury. Returned to Newbury, 1881, and d. suddenly, Sept. 13, of that year.

5 GEORGE A., b. at the Wells River House, March 7, 1840; kept the Newbury House, 1867–70; farmer at West Newbury, 1870–82; in the latter year he bought of A. L. Woods the house now owned by George B. Barnett, in which he kept hotel five years. In his present location which was formerly the Lovewell Tavern and later the Seminary Boarding House to the present time. He m. Dec. 1, 1864, Sophia Belle, dau. Jacob and Jane (Johnston) Shepard.
Children:
i. Ida Belle, b. Oct. 13, 1865; m. 1885, Maurice A. Gale, hotel keeper in Newbury seven years, now proprietor of the Winona House, Fairlee. C., (1) William M., b. Oct. 31, 1886. (2) Florence Burnham, b. Oct. 2, 1888.
ii. Louis, b. West Newbury; d. at 7 years of age.
iii. Jennie Lona, b. 1872; m. 1892, Arthur S. Cheever, now of St. Johnsbury

C., (1) Floyd, b. 1893, and (2) Glenn Arthur, b. 1894.
iv.   Sue S., b. 1876; teacher, and now postmistress at Newbury.
v.   George Alfred, b. 1880.

SCALES.

STEPHEN PALMER, b. Lebanon, N. H., Aug. 23, 1804. Came to West Newbury
in 1849, from Hanover, N. H. He m. Feb., 1828, Sarah Noyes, (b. Warren,
N. H., Apr. 25, 1801; d. June 28, 1873). He d. in Newbury, March 18.
1877.
Children:
i.   Leroy H., b. Apr. 20, 1829; m. 1st, Nov. 26, 1854, Abby Howard of Rose,
Wayne county, N. Y., who d. Aug. 7, 1884. C., (1) Sarah J., b. Newbury,
Nov. 3, 1856; d. Rose, N. Y., Feb 24, 1861. (2) Hattie B., b. March 5,
1858; d. May 1, 1874. (3) Stephen P., b. Jan. 3, 1861; m. May 10, 1883,
Julia, dau. Thomas Wright; 2 c; d. July 23, 1898. (4) Nellie C., b. March
24, 1863; m. Oct. 18, 1883, James Mills; 1 c. (5) Clara B., b. June 17,
1869; m. Oct. 18, 1893, George W. Dow. (6) Jennie. b. Sept. 29, 1870.
Leroy H., m. 2d, Jan. 27, 1887, Chloe, dau. of Ebenezer Abbott and widow
of Thomas Chadwick.
ii.   Ellen P., b. May 17, 1834; m. 1st, while living in Springfield, Ill , a Mr.
Smith, a lawyer, who d. there; m. 2d, Horace McDuffie of Bradford. One
dau., Mabel. b. 1870. Graduated Wellesley College; studied in Europe
with Miss Strickland; now private secretary to Mrs. Mary E. Hunt,
Dorchester, Mass. She d. July 4, 1899.
iii.   Marion B., b. May 15, 1838.

SCOTT.

JOHN, b. Woodside, near Glasgow, Scotland, in 1751. He came here during
the Revolutionary War, lived in the family of Gen. Bayley, and after
spending a few years in Ryegate, settled near the northwest corner of the
town on the "glebe." He cleared that farm, and built a sawmill on the
stream which is named for him, Scott's brook. This farm, after his death,
became the property of Hon. Peter Burbank, and was called by him "The
Hermitage." Mr. Burbank d. there. John Scott m. about 1784, Sarah,
dau. of Col. Robert Johnston. (b. April 3, 1762; d. July 25, 1836). He d.
Newbury, June 29, 1828. They had thirteen c., of whom three d. y., and
all the older ones went west to Ohio and Illinois, and of them no account
can be given. Charles J., and Cyrus Johnston Sidney Scott. remained in
Newbury, living at Wells River, and were engaged in the lumber business,
bought and cleared large tracts of land, owned sawmills. and brought the
first steam sawmill to Newbury. They had two sisters, Mary and Sally,
who d. un-m, Mary, June 18, 1872, aged 77, and Sally, in 1885, aged 86.

CHARLES JOHNSTON, b. Oct. 12, 1802; d. at Wells River, Aug. 2. 1879, and has
one son, Sidney W., living in Worcester, Mass. He m. 1st, Sarah Clark of
Landaff; m. 2d. Feb. 4, 1848, Sophronia L., dau. of James Bailey, (b. May
18, 1815; d. Feb. 20, 1888).

CYRUS J. S., b. about 1806; in business with his brother, and was, at one time,
quite wealthy. He m. Dec. 15, 1840, Susan M., dau. of Timothy Shedd,
(b. Dec. 30, 1831; d. Jan. 21, 1881). He d. April 30, 1886.
Children:
i.   Cyrus W., d. 1885.
ii.   Susan E., res. Woodsville, N. H.; m. 1st. Mr. Moore. C., Arthur C. and
Kathleen, (Mrs. Partridge of Reading, Mass.) She m. 2d. John P. Colby,
son of Hon. Stoddard B. Colby of Montpelier.

SCOTT.

REV. ORANGE, son of Samuel and Lucy (Whitney) Scott, b. Bradford, Feb. 13,
1800. Attended school thirteen months in all. Licensed to preach 1821;
joined M. E. Conference 1822; stationed at Charlestown, Mass., and
Lancaster, N. H. Presiding elder, 1829; delegate to general conference,

1831. Became an advocate of the abolition of slavery, 1833, and being delegate to the general conference of that year, he introduced resolutions against slavery and for so doing was refused re-appointment as presiding elder. Became traveling agent of the American Anti-slavery Society, 1837. In the conference of that year he was attacked in an address by Bishop Hedding, but in spite of opposition and censure he persitesd in preaching and lecturing in behalf of the slave. In 1841, he, with others, withdrew from the Methodist Episcopal church, and organized the Wesleyan Methodist church. of which he was made the first president. Became editor of the "True Wesleyan," and was manager of the Book Concern. Mr. Scott came to Newbury in 1840, to educate his eldest c. and lived at first in the house where the late Dea. George Swasey lived. Later he built that (then a one story house) in which D. Y Ford now lives. He was appointed agent for Newbury Seminary. and while residing here, employed himself in lecturing. correspondence and editorial work. In 1845 he traveled through the west, attending conferences, as agent of the Book Concern. He returned to Newbury in broken health, and in 1846, rem to Newark, N. J.. where he d. after a lingering illness, July 31, 1847; buried in Springfield, Mass. His biography by Rev. L. C. Mattock was published in 1851. His family returned to Newbury and lived until 1865, in the house in which Mrs. Mary S. Wallace lives. Elder Scott m. 1st, at Lyndon, May 7. 1826, Amy Fletcher, who d. at Springfield. Mass., April 4, 1835; m. 2d. Oct. 6, 1835, Eliza, dau. of Samuel and Eliza (Ward) Dearborn of Plymouth, N. H , (b. March 22, 1803; d. Dec. 31, 1898).

Children:
i. Laura, m. E. C. Stocker, q.v.; d. in Newbury, 1856.
ii. Amy, b. Lowell Mass., June 21, 1837; m. Feb. 23, 1860, Rev. James Noyes of the New Hampshire Conference; d. Lancaster, N. H., Dec. 4, 1875.
iii. Anna, b. Lowell, Mass., May 10, 1840; m. July 10, 1862, Rev. Silas E. Quimby principal of Newbury Seminary, 1866-67; now in the ministry; q.v. She d. Salem, N H.. March 8, 1901.
iv. Orange W., b. Newbury, Oct. 15, 1842. Fitted for college at Newbury Seminary, entering. one year in advance, Wesleyan University, which he left in his junior year. Received degree A M., 1889. Entered Maine M. E. Conference 1867, and was pastor at York and South Berwick; N H. Conference. 1870, and held pastorates at Haverhill, Mass., New Market, Dover, Concord; transferred to Wyoming conference 1879. pastor Kingston, N. Y., Pittston, Penn., Binghamton. N. Y.; N. E. Conference 1885. Principal of Greenwich, R. I., Academy. In ministry at Newport, R. I., Rockville, Norwich and Willimantic, Conn.; Brockton and Chicopee, Mass. He has held various positions upon educational boards and has also been one of the officers of the Epworth League. In addition has been a constant contributor to the secular and religious press He m. July 16, 1867, Lucy A. Jameson of Irasburg. a graduate of, and teacher in Newbury seminary. She has published eight books; editor of the "Children's Friend," and contributor to the Youth's Companion and other literature. C., Everett, Arthur, Alec, Gertrude and Florence.

SHEDD.

ABEL, b. in that part of Groton, Mass., now called Pepperell, March 9, 1743; was son of Jonathan and Sarah (Barron) Shedd. He m. Ruth Haskell, and d. Sept. 21 1819.
They had seven children, of whom,
i. Josiah, b. Rindge, N. H., Nov. 1, 1781; m. Lydia Chamberlain. and settled in Peacham, where he d. Sept. 4, 1851.
1 ii. Timothy, b. Rindge, 1783.

1 TIMOTHY, b. Rindge. 1783; was in business at Wells River. (See Judge Leslie's account of Wells River for a more particular notice of him). He built and occupied, among others, the large house now owned by Mrs. Slack. He m. 1st, Susan, dau. of Stephen Reed, (q. v.), who d. March 19, 1853. aged

48 years, 11 months, 5 days. He m. 2d, widow of Dr. Dean of Bath mentioned on pages 157 and 305. He d. Wells River, Dec. 7, 1855.
Children:
i.   Charles Henry, b. April 16, 1810; d. Nov. 5, 1830.
ii. Jane Eliza, b. May 14, 1812; m. Sept. 20, 1831, Hiram Tracy; d. Feb. 9, 1851.
iii: William A., b. Aug. 17, 1814; d. Aug. 14, 1816.
iv. William Reed, b. Aug. 23, 1816; went on a voyage to Labrador while a young man; in business with his father at Wells River and connected with other business interests; was director in the bank from 1853, till his death, and president in 1871; director of the state prison five years; town representative in 1863. 1864; state senator, 1872.   Mr. Shedd lived in this town all his life, residing about twenty years at Newbury Village, in the house next north of the Cong. vestry.   He m. May 28, 1850, Charlotte, dau. of Peter Butler of Oxford, Mass., (b. April 18, 1824; d. April 12, 1885).   He d. April 4, 1896.   One dau., Ruth Annie, b. Feb. 10, 1854; d. April 12, 1885.   They were all members of the Cong. ch.
v.   Ruth Annie, b. Feb. 10, 1827; d. June 25, 1846.

SHELDON.

JESSE, came to Wells River from Massachusetts, and has since been engaged in the jewelry business, succeeding Harry Holton, who had carried on that indispensible branch of mechanics at Wells River for 20 years or more.   He is also a watch inspector for the B. & M. R. R.   He m. June 1, 1892, Hattie J., dau. Samuel and Julia A. E. (Chamberlin) Smith of Bath; no c.

SHEPARD.

ASHBELL, AARON and HORACE, with their sister, Susan, came here from Connecticut about 1784. Their stepmother was Susanna. dau. Dea. Moses Chamberlain. Aaron and Ashbell Shepard were somewhat prominent here. Aaron was a surveyor, and laid out, in 1785, the road from South Newbury, through West Newbury to Topsham line   He laid out others of the earliest roads.   In 1789, Aaron and Ashbell Shepard, each having a wife and one child, began the first settlement in Greensboro, where they were joined in the next year by their brother, Horace, and sister, Susan. The latter m Col. Levi Stevens of Newbury and Hardwick.   She d. Sept. 26. 1802.   Ashbell Shepard m. in Newbury, Sept. 28, 1786, Mrs. Mary Barnett. and they were admitted to the Cong. Ch., May 25, 1788.   He d. in Greensboro, June 4, 1808.   She d. June 9. 1809   Several c.   These three brothers reared large families.   A record of their descendants was prepared in 1874 by Chester Brown of Hardwick.

SHURTLEFF.

WILLIAM S., b. Newbury, Feb. 17, 1830.   His mother was somewhat of an invalid, and found the sulphur springs beneficial; the family spent considerable time here, and in one of these visits this son was born.   He afterward attended Newbury Seminary with his brother, Roswell F. Shurtleff, now a noted artist; graduated at Yale College and Harvard Law School, and was admitted to the bar in 1857.   When the war broke out he enlisted as a private in the 47th Mass., and in a few months rose to be colonel of that regiment.   Judge of Probate and Insolvency for Hampden County, Mass., from 1863 till death.   Only one or two of his decisions were ever reversed by the Supreme Court.   He delivered the ode at the 250th anniversary of the founding of Springfield; the oration at the dedication of the soldiers' monument, and the address at the opening of the Fitchburg public library, and several times visited Europe   Judge Shurtleff was fond of Newbury. and made himself better acquainted with its history and topography than most of its permanent inhabitants.   He m. in 1857, Miss Clara Dwight, and of their two daus., one survived him. He d. Longmeadow, Mass., Jan. 14, 1896.

SIAS.

REV. SOLOMON, son of Benjamin and Abigail Sias, b. Loudon, N. H., Feb. 25, 1781; rem. with his parents to Danville, in 1792. Entered the Methodist itineracy 1805, as a member of the N. E. Conference. Appointed 1811, in charge of the New Hampshire district, which embraced northeastern Vermont, all New Hampshire, north of Charlestown on the west, to Rochester and a few towns in Maine on the east. He rode about 3000 miles per annum in years of great scarcity and for his first years services received $19.75, his traveling expenses in the same time amounting to $18.71. In the third year his compensation had increased to $40.18, and he had left after expenses, $18.24. In 1824 he became publisher of Zion's Herald, which was begun Jan 9, 1823, with a small list of subscribers, and was financially embarrassed. During the three years in which he published the paper, he paid all its debts, placed it on a firm financial basis with a list of 6000 subscribers. He closed his connection with the Herald Sept. 30, 1827. He retired from the active ministry on account of ill health in 1828 and returned to Danville. Came to Newbury 1838 and built the house where the late Gilman Barnett lived and where his dau., Mrs. Page, now resides. Elder Sias had much to do with the location of Newbury Seminary here, and was a trustee for some years. He was a prominent mason, and when the anti-masonic controversy broke out he refused to join the popular clamor by denouncing the order, and came near being expelled from the conference. He yielded so far, however, for the sake of peace, as to withdraw from active participation with masonry, at least for a time. Mr. Sias' connection with Zion's Herald deserves a further word. The paper would have died had it not been for his energetic business management of its affairs; he placed it upon firm financial ground, and under him it took the position, which it has continued to hold, as the organ of the Methodist church in New England. This statement rests upon the best authority. Yet his services are so far forgotten that in the number of that paper which closed the 75th year of its publication with an historical review, his name was not even mentioned. He. m. 1825, Mrs. Amelia Hewes of Boston, Mass., dau. of Benjamin and Amelia Rogers, (b. Apr. 11, 1789; d. Oct. 19, 1856). He d. in Newbury, Feb. 12, 1853.
Children:
i. Amelia, b. Boston. July 19, 1827: m. in Newbury, Apr. 13, 1853, Azro B. Mathewson. who d. July 18, 1881, leaving two c., Charles F., a lawyer in New York city, and Lillian, who resides with her mother in Malden. Mass.
ii. Solomon, b. Danville, June 13, 1829. Educated Newbury Seminary and Wesleyan University. Professor of Natural Science, Fort Edward Institute 1854–59. Principal of Schoharie Academy, N. Y., since 1874. He m. July 2, 1857, Angelina S. Baker of Youngstown, N. Y.

SLY.

STEPHEN, of Ryegate, m. 1802, Elizabeth, dau. of William Abbott of Haverhill, and granddaughter of James Abbott of Newbury. They had 14 c., of whom Israel, b. 1808, d. 1889, was a blacksmith at Boltonville nearly all his active life. He m. 1838, Martha Page of Ryegate. Nine c.
Children:
i. William Henry, b. Jan. 20, 1840; m. May 6, 1866, Mary Parker; d. May 11, 1891. Four c., of whom Fred and M. Adella survived him.
ii. Charles C., b. April 3, 1841; d. Aug. 1, 1843.
iii. Ellen M., b. Nov. 14, 1843; m. Sept. 4, 1872, C. P. 'Smith; res. Alstead, N. H.
iv. Emily J., b. Sept. 18, 1845; m. Feb. 28, 1865, Henry K. Worthley; d. March 21, 1884. C., Elmer G.
v. Mary Eveline, b. Feb. 1, 1848; went to India as a missionary under the Presbyterian board in September, 1871; m. in Mynpoorie, India, April 2, 1872, Rev. James J. Lucas; returned to America, 1880; went back in 1882; returned a second time in 1892, and resided in Worcester, Ohio, until September, 1897, when she went back to India. Five c. living; Frances H., a teacher and graduate of Wellesley College. Katharine S.,

m. H. H. Johnson of Cleveland. Ohio. William P. and Edmund, who are
in college at Worcester, Ohio and Eva C., who is with her in India.
vi. Edwin, b. Feb. 19, 1850; blacksmith at Boltonville; m. April 5, 1876,
Martha, dau. of Charles S. Bolton. C , living, Bertha E., and Harley E.
vii. Frank E., b. March 3, 1852; m. May 13, 1880. Emma Joseph. C., Lewis
B., Clara B., Frank and Vernie.
viii. Augustus B., b. Dec. 20, 1854; m. July 3, 1890, Myra Oliver. C., Walter J.
ix   Lilla V., b. July 6, 1860; m. C. P. Livesey; was killed by a kick from a
horse at Farmsville, Mass , Nov. 5, 1891.

SMITH.

DR. GIDEON, the first physician, and one of the first settlers of Newbury, came
here before June, 1764. from Westminster, Mass., and was in practice here
many years. He seems to have been a man of good education, and his
standing in town is attested by the frequency with which his name is
mentioned in the early records, and by his being chosen to represent the
town in the convention at Cornish in 1778. He m April 11. 1761. Mary,
dau. of Joshua Bigelow, (b. Sept. 13, 1730). Her brother, Jabez Bigelow,
was father of Maj Jabez Bigelow, who settled in Ryegate. Dr. Smith
lived for some years near the subsequent site of the "old meeting house,"
but later. bought the south farm on the Upper Meadow. His house stood
on the top of the high hill, behind Ingalls hill, on the old road, and the
cellar may still be seen He served in the Revolutionary War. They had
no c., but adopted Mary, dau. of Mrs. Smith's brother. Joshua Bigelow,
(b. March 16, 1768; d Rochester. April 18, 1848). She m April 29, 1791,
Jeremiah Ingalls, q. v. Mr and Mrs. Smith were among the earliest
members of the Cong Ch., in which he was very prominent. By his will
he bequeathed to the church a sum of money with which, by his request,
the first silver articles of the communion service were purchased in 1810.
He d. April 22, 1799, and his wife rem. to Rochester in 1812.

SMITH.

COL. JOHN, b. Hampstead, N. H., Feb. 13, 1758; served under the name of John
Vance in Reed's Co. of Stark's regiment, which was engaged in the battle
of Bunker Hill. He enlisted May 4, and was discharged Aug. 1. 1775. He
did later service in New Hampshire regiments, and after he came to
Newbury. which was before 1779, as his name is found in an old account
book of that year, in January He began to clear land and built a log
house on what is now called the "Guy Corliss Place," but. about 1790,
settled where his grandson, the present John Smith, has always lived. He
kept tavern there for some years after, and perhaps before, 1802. His
tavern sign is preserved at the homestead. When the war of 1812 came
on he was a major in the militia, and served at the time of the invasion
of Lake Champlain.   Afterwards he was colonel in the militia. His sword
is owned by J J. Smith. Late in life he built the house in which his
descendants the Tyler sisters, live, south of the Union Meeting House.
For the latter he gave the site, and gave the land for the cemetery. Col.
Smith was prominent in his day, a man of pronounced opinions, and
accumulated a comfortable property. He m. at Haverhill, by Rev. Peter
Powers, April 6, 1780. Sarah Kincaid, (b. Windham, N, H., Dec. 2 1761;
d. Jan. 23, 1854). Their married life lasted 71 years 6 months. 27 days.
He d. Oct. 28, 1851. Col. Smith was a democrat of the Jeffersonian school,
and for more than a century his family has been prominent in town affairs.

1   Children:
i. James, b Feb. 10, 1781; d. Dec. 9, 1866.
ii. Abigail, b Feb. 21, 1783; m. 1st, Dec. 26, 1802, Thomas Jenness of
Topsham; m. 2d. Robert Fulton of Newbury. She d. at Corinth May
14. 1873.
iii. Samuel, b. Sept. 8, 1785. He m. Nov. 27, 1808, Ruth Ladd of Haverhill.
He d. Cambridge, N. Y., Oct. 21, 1813. They had several c., of whom (1)
Samuel, b. 1814; m. Mehetabel, dau Thos. Henry. He d. Dec 12, 1878.
A dau., Sally. lived in Newbury, and d. at the home of her grandson,
Charles B. Rollins, Nov. 8, 1890.

iv. Mary, b. Jan. 1, 1788; m. Twisden B. Peach; d. Jan. 15, 1849.
v. Sarah, b. April 25, 1790; m. Sept. 16, 1813, Jonathan Jenness of Topsham, (b. Deerfield, N. H., March 30, 1780; rem. to Topsham, 1807; town representative, 15 years; state senator, 2 years; presidential elector on the Van Buren ticket, 1836; farmer and inn-keeper; d. Nov. 2, 1846).
vi. Nancy, b. Jan. 17. 1792; m. Dec. 26, 1815, Jonathan Mitchell, who d. May 27, 1849. She d. May 11. 1849.
2 vii. Joseph. b. Aug. 12, 1794; d. May 19, 1870.
viii. Ruth J., b. Sept. 25, 1795; m. 1st, Oct. 2, 1817, John Jenness, who d. in Topsham; m. 2d, Dec. 18, 1827, Thomas Richardson, She d. in Minnesota, Aug. 29, 1862.
ix. John. b. Sept. 16, 1798; began to clear the farm which is now that of J. E. Currier, but went into the stage and hotel business as driver and proprietor of stage lines and hotels. He long kept the Oxford House at Fryeburg, Me., which was burned, 1887. (See New England Magazine, September, 1893). He d. at Fryeburg, June 4, 1889. Buried at West Newbury.
3 x. Charles J., b. July 15, 1800; d. Aug. 30, 1854.
xi. Elizabeth, b Aug. 31, 1802; m. Elijah Hazeltine; d. March 4, 1861.
4 xii. Thomas J., b. July 16, 1804; d. March 24, 1890.

1 JAMES,[2] (John,[1]) b. Feb. 10, 1781; farmer; cooper and basket maker at West Newbury; m. May 27, 1803, Polly (Mary), dau. of Josiah Rogers; d. Dec. 9, 1866. This was a very unfortunate family. One son, Charles, died in the Insane Asylum at Brattleboro. John obtained some education, m. and became a Methodist minister, but d. insane. Truman was partially demented and a wanderer; was found dead Oct. 5, 1860, in a pasture at the town farm in his 58th year. James M., known as "King Smith," was an idiot who d. on the town farm in Jan. 5, 1874. Lydia, who was a cripple, and Maria, a most worthy woman, lived by themselves, in the house which had been their grandfather's, until they became too feeble to live alone, when they deeded their property to the town and d. at the town farm, within a few hours of each other, Feb. 8 and 9, 1891, and were buried in the same grave. Descendants of John and of another sister, who are of sound mind, are understood to be living near Windsor.

2 JOSEPH,[2] (John,[1]) b. Aug. 12, 1794; lived in the west part of the town a few years, then in Topsham till 1837; returned to Newbury and bought the John Atwood place on Hall's Meadow, on which he built a brick house, which, with its extensive outbuildings, was burned Oct. 8, 1888. Rebuilt, 1889. Joseph Smith was a very quiet, unassuming man, of excellent judgment and his views carried great weight. He was a selectman for many years. He m. 1820, his cousin, Polly Kincaid, of Peacham, who d. March 27, 1870, and he followed her May 20, of the same year.
Children, all b. in Topsham, but the 1st:
i. John, b. Newbury, March 8, 1882; settled in Iowa; d. in the Union army, April 5, 1864.
ii. Mary Ann, b. July 9, 1826; m. Henry V. Stanley of Boston.
iii. Sarah, b. July 19, 1828; m Wesley Miner of Lyman, N. H.
iv. Asa Burton, b. Sept. 13, 1831; lived in Newbury or Bradford nearly all his life; d. March 7, 1901.
v. Jane, b. Oct. 2, 1834; d. Nov. 13, 1893.
5 vi. Jonathan J., b. Dec. 15, 1836.

3 CHARLES JOHNSTON,[2] (John,[1]) b. July 15, 1800. Farmer on the homestead and captain in the militia. He also had his share in town affairs. He m. May 1, 1828, Jane, dau. of James Wallace, (b. Apr. 18, 1803; d. June 30, 1890). They were members of the Cong. ch. He d. Aug. 30, 1854.
Children:
i. John, b. June 11, 1829; d. Jan. 11, 1830.
ii. Infant, b. Jan. 12, d. Jan 13, 1831.
iii. John, b. June 21, 1832; farmer on homestead. Has also been a large buyer of bark and lumber throughout northern Vermont and New Hampshire, and has dealt extensively in cattle, fertilizers and farm machinery. He m. Apr. 4, 1891, Abby H. Stuart of Barnet.
iv. William. b. Aug. 7, 1834; d. May 26, 1838.
v. James W., b. May 15, 1837; d. March 17, 1842.

4 THOMAS JENNESS, b. July 16, 1804; farmer and shoemaker at West Newbury;
    m. about 1836, Jane, dau. Robert Fulton, (b. Dec. 27, 1807; d. Nov. 14,
    1843). He d. March 24, 1890.
    Children:
    i.   Sarah Jane, b. Sept. 15, 1837; m. May 25, 1857, Wells B. Brown, who d.
         June 3, 1901.
    ii. Robert F., b. Aug. 16, 1839; enlisted December, 1861, in Co. D, 8th Vt.;
         discharged Oct. 17, 1862, and d. Nov. 17, in New York City, on his way
         home.
    iii. Eliza H., b. Sept. 20, 1841; m. George C. Tyler, (see Powers family); d.
         May 12, 1899.

5 JONATHAN JENNESS,[3] (Joseph,[2] John,[1]) b. Topsham, Dec. 15, 1836; farmer on
    Hall's Meadow, succeeding his father, also owns much out-lying land. He
    m. Feb. 13, 1870, Sophronia E. Stearns of Bradford, who d. April 20, 1893;
    Children:
    i.   Mary Elizabeth, b. Aug. 22, 1870; graduate of Randolph Normal School.
         teacher.
    ii. Joseph, b. July 20, 1872.
    iii. Fanny, b. Oct. 30, 1873.
    iv. Minnie, b. May 16, 1875.
    v.   Vodia, b. May 26, 1877; d. Sept. 21, 1879.
    vi. Jane, b. Jan. 21, 1879; d. April 17, 1895.
    vii. John Bliss, b. Feb. 25, 1881.

SMITH.

DANIEL and JOSEPH, came from Deerfield, Mass., about 1787. Daniel was a
    distiller and made potato whiskey in a building which stood nearly
    opposite where Joseph P. Bailey now lives, on the road from the village to
    West Newbury. He had no family. Joseph m. Lucy Spurr, and they,
    soon after coming here, opened a tavern in the house in which E. H.
    Farnham now lives, which they carried on till Mr. Smith's death in 1815.
    He was the third postmaster, succeeding David Johnson in 1812. After
    his death Mrs. Smith m. March 26, 1818, Col. Simeon Stevens as 2d wife.
    She d. April 12, 1850.
    Children:
    i.   Hiram, b. May, 1800; d. Aug. 1801.
    ii. Emily b. Nov. 11, 1801; m. Dec. 7, 1823, Thos. J. Stevens; d. May 1, 1871;
         q. v.
    iii. Hiram, b. Dec. 5, 1803. Farmer at West Newbury where his dau. now lives.
         Many years a member of the Methodist church. He m. April 7, 1828,
         Elizabeth, dau Joseph Sawyer, (b. Jan. 10, 1805; d. Apr. 16, 1879). C.,
         Lucy A., m. Nov. 20, 1860, Hector D. Haseltine, who d. Oct. 28, 1895.
         He d. Dec. 31, 1882.
    iv. Susan, b. Jan. 18, 1808; m. Nov. 9, 1829, James Spear Johnston; d. Feb.
         19, 1860.

SMITH.

JAMES, of Windham, Conn., son of Stephen and Mary (Preston) Smith, b. Jan. 6,
    1744.
    Children:
    i.   Alitheah, b. April 5, 1767, m. Thomas Ruggles, whose dau., Alitheah, m.
         Ezekiel L. Bayley of Newbury and Rutland, (p. 443, in which her name is
         not correctly spelled).
    ii. Stephen, b. Oct. 19, 1768.
    iii. Polly, b. Jan. 9, 1771.
    iv. Olive, b. Nov. 22, 1772.
1   v.   Lois, b. Nov. 3, 1774.
2   vi. Nathaniel, b. Jan. 9, 1778; d. March 1, 1824.

1 LOIS, b. Nov. 3, 1774; m. Nov. 27, 1794, Clark Elliott, and came to Newbury a
    few years later. They had eight c., the youngest of whom, Henry, b.
    Newbury, September, 1812, obtained some education, entered the

Methodist ministry while still very young and was one year on a circuit in New Hampshire. In 1833 or '34· he went to Ohio, and joined the Erie Conference, and was in the itinerant ministry there till 1855. He m. August, 1836, Lucy Ann Taft, of Braceville, O. In 1855, they rem. to Minnesota, and settled in Glencoe, being the first Methodist minister to settle west of what were known as the "great woods." With the aid of his sons he cleared a farm and erected buildings from which they were driven by the Indians in August, 1862, during the "Minnesota Massacre," and their buildings and crops were destroyed. He d. 1891.

Children:
i. Wilbur Fisk, d. in the Union army in the 9th Minnesota.
ii. Robert N., a prominent citizen of Norwood, Minn., b. July 19, 1840; d. June 4, 1900.
iii. Auren Clark.
iv. Clara Jane.

2 NATHANIEL, b. Jan. 9, .1778; farmer in Newbury; m. Experience Goodall, (b. Walpole, N. H., May 5, 1776; d. Dec. 14, 1860). He d. March 1, 1824. She lived in a small house north of the great elm south of the Ox-bow cemetery, and was called "Aunt Speedy Smith."

Children:
i. Maria, b. November, 1808; d. Oct. 11, 1860.
ii. Harriett, m. Thomas Bartlett of Lyndon.
iii. Louisa, m. Nov. 2· 1852, George A. Bingham, a lawyer of Lyndon and Littleton, N. H. She d. at Concord, April 25, 1856.
iv. Laura C., b. March 13, 1817; m. Raymond C. Witherspoon; d. New York City; buried at Newbury.
Three other c.

SMITH.

EDGAR W., son of Elijah W., and Dolly (Higgins) Smith, b. Randolph, July 3, 1845; was educated in the common schools, and in New Hampton (N. H.) Literary Institution; began the study of law in 1868, with Philander Perrin of Randolph, and continued studies with George W. Hendee of Morrisville, N. L. Boyden of Randolph and Abel Underwood of Wells River; admitted to the bar at Chelsea, Jan. 1, 1872, in which year he began practice at Wells River; formed a partnership with Scott Sloan, Sept. 1, 1884, having an office at Woodsville; in 1899, they dissolved partnership, and Mr. Smith has taken his son, Raymond U., into the business with him, having also an office at Woodsville. He received the honorary degree of A. M., from Norwich University in 1874, and has published papers upon legal subjects, and the Proceedings of the Grafton and Coös Bar Association. State's attorney, 1884–86; town representative 1882-83; member of Vermont and New Hampshire Bar Associations and that of the Grafton and Coös Bar; res. Wells River; is leader of the choir in the Congregational church, in which Mrs. Smith is organist. He m. Aug. 17, 1869, Emma M. Gates of Morrisville.

Children:
i. Percy G., graduated Norwich University; civil engineer at Worcester, Mass.
ii. Raymond U., b. Newbury; graduated Norwich, 1894; in partnership with his father, under the firm name of Smith & Smith, since May 1, 1899.

STEBBINS.

HORACE, b. Newbury, 1773; was a blacksmith, and built the house in which W. H. Atkinson lives, his shop being near that place. He m Hannah ——————, (b. Newbury, 1774; d. July 21, 1847). He d. Jan. 31, 1842.

Children, all b. here:
i. Gustavus, b. April 7, 1795.
ii. Cynthia, b. April 12, 1797; m. Samuel Boyce, q. v.; d. Jan. 12, 1884.
iii. Mindwell, b. June 10, 1799.
iv. Benjamin, b. Oct. 24, 1801.
1 v. John, b. Jan. 30, 1804.
vi. Horace, b. March 14, 1807.

vii.   Chastine, b. Dec. 3, 1809.
viii. Amity, b. Aug. 6, 1811.
ix.   Hannah. b. Feb. 26, 1813.
2   x. Horatio N., b. June 2, 1816; d. Nov. 20, 1863.

1 JOHN,[2] (Horace,[1]) b. May 30, 1804; lived in Newbury; m. Oct. 9, 1825, Caroline Bartlett.
   Children:
3   i.   John.
    ii.   Mary, m. Sylvester McKellup. C., Ella, Ellen, Kate, Charlotte.
4   iii. Schuyler.
    iv.   Milo, d.
    v.   Amanda, m. Everett Martin, and is d. C., Carrie and Stephen.
    vi.   George, served and d. in the Union Army during the Rebellion.
5   vii. Edward.
    viii. Alice, d. y.

2 HORATIO NELSON,[2] (Horace,[1]) b. June 2, 1816; lived south of Boltonville; m. Margaret, dau. Capt. John Miller of Ryegate, (b. April 18, 1811; d. March 16, 1861). They had several sons, all but one of whom are d. He m. 2d, Jan. 30, 1862, Mrs. Philaura B. (Corliss) Lord, who d. May 21, 1896. He enlisted Sept. 22, 1862, in Co. C, 3d Vt., and d. Nov. 20, 1863.

3 JOHN,[3] (John,[2] Horace,[1]) lived and d. in Newbury; was long employed on the Passumpsic R. R.; m. Betsey Manning. No record received.
   Children:
    i.   Ella.
    ii.   Ellen, m. Elmer Wallace.
    iii. Kate.
    iv.   Charlotte.

4 SCHUYLER C.,[3] (John,[2] Horace,[1]) Res. Newbury. Served in Co. H, 12th Vt., in the Civil War. Farmer, and sexton of Ox-bow cemetery. He m. June 27, 1856, Joanna Tuma.
   Children:
    i.   Frances, b. Sept. 5, 1858; m. 1st, Dec. 31, 1894, George A. Mitchell of Philadelphia, who d. 1895; 2d, Robert A. Crunden of London, Eng. C. Schuyler William, b. Nov. 6, 1900.
    ii.   Harry, b. Aug. 29, 1861; m. Effie Perkins of Haverhill. C., Clarence, b. April 14, 1892.
    iii. Alice, b. Feb. 25, 1863; m. May 1, 1888, Van H. Dodge of Whitefield, N. H., C., Frank Schuyler, b. Jan. 5, 1889.

5 EDWARD HALE,[3] (John,[2] Horace,[1]) b. Jan. 27, 1843; res. Newbury; teamster. He m. in Ryegate, July 14, 1865, Martha Ann Spaulding, (b. Bethel, Jan. 27, 1843).
   Children:
    i.   Caroline Alice, b. Jan. 9, 1868; d. Jan. 4, 1881.
    ii.   Ida May. b. Dec. 22, 1869; m. March 14, 1890, Fred S. Barrie.
    iii. Martha Ann, b. May 5, 1872; m. Oct. 27, 1892. John E. Avery.
    iv.   Minnie Estelle, b. May 30, 1874; m. Oct. 9, 1892, Charles W. Hartwell of Newbury.
    v.   Edward Richard, b. June 7, 1876; m. Jan. 29, 1896, Lucy Benton.
    vi.   Lena Isabelle, b. Oct. 23, 1879.
    vii. Frederick Bernard, b. Aug. 4, 1881; d. Oct. 24, 1882.
    viii. Herbert James, b. March 5, 1883.
    ix.   Jesse Albert, b. March 25, 1886.

STEVENS.

OTHO and SIMEON, brothers, came from Wales about 1710-15 to Plymouth, Mass. Simeon is believed to have settled on Hudson river, and to have many descendants. Otho settled in Hampstead, N. H., and was a farmer, constable, etc. He there m. a woman of one-fourth Indian blood named Susan Kent. (The Kent record states that Abigail, dau. of Josiah Kent, and aunt of the 1st Col. Jacob Kent of Newbury, b. July 9, 1697; m.

March 21, 1723, Otho Stevens). Their c. were, Samuel, Levi, Otho, Archaleus, Simeon, Josiah, Daniel, Susan and Abigail. Archaleus and Josiah settled in Enfield, N. H., and d. there Simeon in Newbury, and Daniel in Haverhill. Otho, Ephraim, Simeon Daniel and Samuel Stevens were in Capt. Jacob Bayley's Co. in Goff's Regiment of Amherst's expedition in 1759. The following extract from Capt. Bayley's journal will preserve the name of one of them. They were at Oswego. "Friday, Sept. 21, 1759. Cool morning, but pleasant. About 2 o'clock in the afternoon dies Otho Stevens of a long and tedious illness of 22 days, much lamented by his relations and friends, he being a loving brother and a faithful friend. He was sensible to the last breath he drew, and sensible of his approaching near another world, which did not, in the least ruffle his spirits. But he seemed to have his hope firmly placed in God."

SIMEON, b. 1736, served with several brothers in the Old French war, and was one of the first settlers of this town, coming here in the spring of 1762. He was a grantee of both Newbury and Haverhill, by which it is certain that he stood high in the estimation of Bayley and Hazen. He settled on Kent's Meadow, where he built the large house now standing, owned by Mr. Greer. He was lieutenant in the 1st company of minutemen organized here, who were in service 20 days. Captain also of a company in Bedel's regiment "Raised for the Defense of the Frontier," from April 1, 1778, to Nov. 30, 1779. Served also, several short terms in various alarms. He m. 1st in 1752, Sarah Hadley, who d. 1779; m. 2d, Mrs. Susanna Shepard, dau. of Dea. Moses Chamberlain, who, after his death, m. James Corliss of Greensboro, and lived to be over 100 years old. Capt. Simeon Stevens d. July 6, 1788, aged 52. On his gravestone his name is spelled Stephens, and he sometimes wrote it that way.
  Children of Capt. Simeon and Sarah Stevens, all b. here:
    i. Abigail, b. Oct. 8, 1763; d. April 22, 1839.
1 ii. Otho, b. July 5, 1765; d. Aug. 26, 1821.
2 iii. Simeon, b. May 15, 1767; d. May 8, 1858.
    iv. Sarah, b. Sept. 2, 1768; d. Jan. 15, 1813, or Jan. 13, 1806.
    v. Levi, b. Jan. 22, 1770; m. Susan Shepard; rem. to Greensboro and d. there colonel in the militia.
3 vi. Judith, b. Oct. 26, 1771; d. Dec. 28, 1855.
    vii. Ruth, b. May 26, 1773; m. a Mr. Ingalls; d. Jan 28, 1820, (another record says 1836).
4 viii. Samuel, b. May 11, 1775; d. April 22. 1838, q. v.
    ix. Moses, b. May 31, 1776; d. March 25, 1778.
    Two younger who d. in infancy.

1 OTHO,[1] (Simeon,[2]) b. July 15, 1765; lived in Newbury, Chelsea, Northumberland, Maidstone, but d. in Waterford, Aug. 26, 1821. He m. Sarah, dau. of Capt. John G. Bayley, and widow of James, son of Gen. Jacob Bayley, (b. Nov. 3, 1765; d. June 1, 1840).
  Children:
    i. Abigail, b. Newbury, March 25, 1787; m. Thomas Tillotson of Orford. Five c.
    ii. Betsey B., b. Newbury, Feb. 16, 1789; m. Hon. Joseph Berry, q. v.; d. March 9, 1850.
    iii. John G. B., b. May 4, 1791; m. Sophia Sawyer of Waterford; d. Franconia, N. H. 11 c.
    iv. Otho, b. 1793, d. .
    v. Tabitha, b. April 9, 1794; m. William, brother of Hon. Joseph Berry, and had a son, William. Mr. Berry d. in Kansas, and she m. 2d, Nathan Carter of Littleton, N. H. Two c.
    vi. Otho, b. Dec. 20, 1797; m. Mary Gordon of Bath; lived in Waterford.
    vii. Simeon, b. Dec. 30, 1799; m. Zeora Bennet, and lived in Waterford. Several c.
    viii. Moses, b. and d. April 11, 1802.
    ix. Thomas J., b. March 15, 1803; m. Maria Stoddard of Waterford, where he lived and d.
    x. Eleanor F., b. March 18, 1806; m. 1st, Frank P. Johnson, q. v.; m. 2d, Duncan McKeith, q. v., both of Newbury.

2 SIMEON,[2] (Simeon,[1]) b. May 15, 1767; farmer on the homestead; colonel in the
      militia; prominent in town affairs, and in the Methodist church of which
      he was an early member. He m. 1st, Hannah, dau. Ephraim Bayley, (b.
      1772; d. April 21, 1817); m. 2d, March 26, 1818, Mrs. Lucy Smith, (d.
      April 12, 1850). He d. May 15, 1858.
   Children, all b. in Newbury:
5   i.   Simeon, b. March 24, 1789; d. March 22, 1862.
6   ii. Ephraim B., b. April 13, 1790; d. June 22, 1867.
7   iii. John, b. Oct. 10, 1793; d. May 3, 1860.
8   iv. Tappan, b. April 11, 1795; d. Dec. 18, 1878.
    v.   William T., b. Jan. 10, 1797; rem. about 1820 to Cincinnati, O., and d.
         there.
    vi. Melissa, b. Oct. 3, 1798; m. J. Amherst Bayley, q. v.; d. Dec. 9, 1885.
9   vii. Thomas J., b. May 3, 1801; d. 1860.
    viii. Hannah, b. April 29, 1805; m. Rev. Haynes Johnson, q. v.
    ix. Amanda, b. March 11, 1808; d. y.
    x.   Nelson, b. July 31, 1812; d. y.

3 JUDITH,[2] (Simeon,[1]) b. Oct. 26, 1771; m. March 23, 1800, George Washington,
      son of Capt. Uriah Stone of Piermont. They lived on his father's farm,
      now called the "Old Hibbard place," in Piermont, and had several c. She
      d. Dec. 28, 1865. One dau. m. Col. Levi Rogers of Newbury. q v. Another
      was named Malvina, whose feet when an infant were placed against some
      damp plastering in her father's house, and the impression of the little feet
      remained there until the house was repaired, about thirty years ago. She
      m. Rev. William Arthur, and their son, Chester A., became the 18th
      president of the United States.

4 SAMUEL,[2] (Simeon,[1]) b. May 11, 1775; m. at Hardwick, 1797, Puah Mellen, (b.
      March 4, 1774; d. Nov. 1, 1845); rem. to Hardwick, 1798, where he built
      the first saw and grist mills at Stevens Village, now East Hardwick. He
      d. April 22, 1838. They had 11 c., of whom, Simeon Hadley Stevens, the
      youngest, b. March 19, 1811, was a graduate of Vermont University, and
      studied at Bangor Theological Seminary, but failing in health, settled on a
      farm. He afterwards was principal of Lamoille County Grammar School
      at Johnson, where he d. April 30, 1842. He m. Augusta Young. One son.

5 SIMEON,[3] (Simeon,[2] Simeon,[1]) b. March 24, 1789; m. Feb. 19, 1817, Betsey,
      dau. of Isaac Bayley, (b. Jan. 26, 1790; d.); lived in Newbury, near the
      Ox-bow cemetery; town representative, 1817, '19, '36, '37, '43. He d.
      March 22, 1862. Merchant and farmer.
   Children:
    i.   William Barron, b. Dec. 21, 1816.
    ii. Harry Bayley, b. Aug. 22, 1818; m. Mary, dau. of Jacob Leighton of
         Newbury; res. Bradford; was long in the stage business as driver and
         proprietor.
    iii. Anson Morrill, b. Rumney, N. H , where his parents kept tavern, Oct. 19,
         1830. In partnership with C. M. Morse, two years; hotel and stage
         business. He m. Elizabeth, dau. Timothy Morse.
    iv. Martha Jane, b. Feb. 22, 1835; m. James Carter Stevens of Corinth. No c.

6 EPHRAIM BAYLEY,[3] (Simeon,[2] Simeon,[1]) b. April 13, 1790; lived in Newbury;
      farmer and mechanic; was many years steward of the seminary, and
      known to all the students as "Father Stevens." The last years of his life
      were spent in the large house at the north end of the common, formerly
      known as the "Yellow Boarding House." He m. Feb 21, 1816, Olive,
      dau. of Remembrance Chamberlain, (b. Feb. 4, 1792; d. March 17, 1876).
      He d. June 22, 1867. Ephraim Stevens and his family were very prominent
      in the Methodist church.
   Children:
    i.   Simeon, b. July 28, 1811; lived in St. Louis, Mo., where he m. Nov. 1, 1837,
         Clara Hidden, (b. Sept. 8, 1810; d. ————————). He d. July 12, 1849.
         C., (1) George W., b. July 22, 1838; d. April 21, 1842. (2) Martha O., b.
         Dec. 11, 1839; d. July 9, 1841. (3) Charles W., b. Nov. 16, 1841; d.
         March 22, 1843. (4) Edwin T., b. Dec. 6, 1843; d. Aug. 11, 1844. (5)
         Ella M., b. May 31, 1845; d. Aug. 25, 1847. (6) Alice C., b. Sept. 25,
         1847; d. Nov. 26, 1848.

JOHN ELLIOTT STEVENS.

ii. Amanda, b. March 6, 1814; m. May 25, 1846, Rev. Warren Weymouth. He is still living, and in the ministry. She d. June 29, 1848. C., (1) Amanda Olive, b. June 4. 1848; m. March 17, 1869, George A. Pearson; res. Newburyport, Mass. C., *a*, Charles W., b Jan. 8, 1871; d.; *b*, Hattie O., b. Jan. 30, 1872; *c*, Helen F., b. Dec. 13. 1880.

iii. George N., b. Oct. 18, 1816; res. St. Louis, Mo.; m. April 14, 1842. Martha A. F. Hidden d. Jan. 25, 1885. C., (1) Clara L., b. April 15, 1842; m. Dr. C. M. Wright of Cincinnati, O.; d. Sept. 21, 1865. (2) Martha O., b. May 25, 1845; d. Nov. 27, 1848. (3) Charles H., b. Aug. 2, 1847; res. St. Louis, Mo.; m. June 26, 1876, Jennie O'Mara, who d. Feb. 16, 1897. C., *a*, Martha R. A., b. Nov. 3, 1886. (4) Olive B., b. Sept. 15, 1849; d. Nov. 6, 1850. (5) Abbie Elliott, b. Oct. 4, 1851; d. July 30, 1854.

iv. Charles E., b. Jan. 1, 1822; went to California; m. June 13, 1877, Clara L. Mason; d. Dec. 30, 1896. No c. Mrs. Stevens res. at San Jose, Cal.

v. John Eliot, b. July 27, 1831; educated at Newbury Seminary; entered the Methodist Book Concern in New York City, as a clerk, while a young man, was connected with it till death, and had charge of one of its departments. His acquaintance was wide and he was influential in many ways. He m. in Newbury, Sept. 5, 1867, Harriet E. Foster, and d. at his home in Elizabeth, N. J., March 16, 1895. C., (1) Arthur F., b. Nov. 1, 1869; m. Sept. 10, 1895, Carolyn Hartley, (b. Nov. 10, 1869). (2) Clara, b. March 26, 1874.

7 JOHN,[3] (Simeon,[2] Simeon,[1]) b. Oct. 10, 1793; m. 1st, Feb. 21, 1816, Hannah, dau. of Col. John Bayley, (b. June 10, 1796; d. Dec. 20, 1847); m. 2d, Lucinda, widow of Alden Sprague. Studied medicine with Dr. McKinstry and practiced in Newbury about thirty years. He long led the choir in the Methodist church. He d. May 3, 1860.

Children:
i. Infant, b. and d. Jan. 17, 1817.
ii. Charles E., b. May 18, 1818; d. 1819.
iii. Helen M., b. March 18, 1820; m. 1st, Sept. 5, 1837, Wm. G. Turner of Winchester, N. H.; m. 2d, Feb. 28, 1849, Rev. Thomas Carlton of the Methodist Book Concern, N. Y.; 4 c., 3 now living; d. Nov. 16, 1884.
iv. Emily S., b. June 18, 1822; d. June 15, 1865.
v. John. b. Aug. 24, 1824; d. Dec. 30, same year.
vi. Harriet H., b. Sept. 2. 1826; m. Nov. 20, 1849. Charles E. Dennison of Woodstock, and Peoria, Ill.; (educated at Norwich University, civil engineer. Captain in regular army; served in the U. S. Infantry and killed at the battle of Stone River). She d. Sept. 21, 1852; one dau. living.
vii. Hannah B., b. May 18, 1829; m. May 18, 1848, William A. Wells of Franconia, now living in Mooers, N. Y.; one son living.
viii. Mary Jane, b. Dec. 16, 1831; m. 1st, March 29, 1854, Charles E. Denison, as 2d wife; m. 2d, Franklin Farrington of Brandon, where she res. Two sons. Charles lives in Boston; John, d. 1890.
ix. John E., b. Feb. 13, 1836; d. Feb. 18, 1864.
x. Lucy Ann, b. June 8, 1838; m. Dec. 22, 1864, Daniel Denham of New York; res. Elizabeth, N. J.

8 TAPPAN,[3] (Simeon.[2] Simeon,[1]) b. Apr. 11, 1795. Proprietor of the Spring Hotel for many years; sheriff, 1829; associate judge several years, member of the Constitutional Convention of 1836. He m. May 6. 1819, Lucia K., dau. of Col. John Bayley, (b. June 8, 1798; d. Aug. 28, 1864). He d. Dec. 18, 1878.

Children:
i. Infant, b. and d. June 11, 1821.
ii. Elizabeth, d. y.
iii. Sophia. b. Sept. 28, 1862; d. y.
iv. Lucia M. B., b. Jan. .10, 1826. Teacher of music at Newbury Seminary several years. She m. July 25, 1849, Daniel Peaslee. who d. March 4, 1854, leaving one son. Edward Stevens, b. Sept. 7, 1850. He m. and went into business in Chicago, where he d. 1901, leaving one son.
v. Sophia W., b. Apr. 8, 1828; m. John J. Ladd, q. v.; d. Jan. 1882.

9 THOMAS JEFFERSON,[3] (Simeon,[2] Simeon,[1]) b. May 3. 1801; farmer on homestead. He m. Dec. 24, 1821, Emily, dau. Joseph Smith, (b. Nov. 11,

1801; d. May 1, 1871). One son, Nelson Burnham, b. Feb. 3, 1828; d. in Boston, Mass., 1881. Student at Newbury Seminary; clerk in the store of Morse and Stevens in 1842, and in a store till 1857, when he entered the hotel business. Proprietor of the "Spring Hotel" and the "Newbury House," also was owner of stage lines in the White Mountains. Proprietor of the "Stevens House" at Rutland, the "Trotter House" at Bradford, the "Marlboro Hotel," and the "Washington House" at Boston, and the "Ross House" at Cambridgeport, Mass. In the hotel business till 1880. At the time of his death he was in the livery stable business in Boston. He m. Dec. 23, 1847, Harriet, dau. of Prentiss Knight, who d. Sept. 28, 1870. Thomas Jefferson d. March 22, 1872.

Children:
i. Charles Nelson, b. Newbury, Apr. 2, 1849. Received his education in Newbury and graduated at the Hahneman Medical College; now in practice at Somersworth, N. H. He m., 1889, Helen B. Potter. One c., Margaret M., b. Dover, N. H., 1891.
ii. Emma Frances, b. Newbury, Sept. 6. 1854; d. 1860.
iii. Frank S., b. Newbury, Apr. 16, 1857; educated in Newbury and Bradford; m. 1881, Hattie Chandler of Boston. C., Emma Pearl, b. Boston, 1884.
iv. Emma A., b. Newbury, May 10, 1863; educated in Boston and Somerville; d. in Boston, 1883.
v. Harry E., b. Rutland. 1869; educated in Boston; m. in 1898
Nelson B. Stevens m. 2d, Semantha M. Balch of Rutland; no c.

*STEVENS.

DANIEL, son of Otho the emigrant, and brother of Simeon of Newbury, b. Hampstead, N. H., 1740; m. about 1762, Hannah Hill of Hampstead. They rem. to Haverhill, N. H., in March, 1773. In 1805, they rem. to Enosburg, where Daniel d. 1810, and his wife d. in 1828.
They had five c., b. in Hampstead—Hannah, Daniel, Eliphalet, Betsey and Otho, and eight in Haverhill, Archelaus, Abigail, Lydia, Caleb, Ruth, Charles and Johnson, (twins), and Polly:
i. Hannah, m. John Lawrence of Haverhill and had 14 c.
ii. Eliphalet, m. Betsey Bedel of Bath; lived in Corinth and had 12 c., five of whom were by a second wife, Dolly Flanders.
iii. Betsey, m. Reuben Page, and lived in Corinth, just across the Newbury line. They are buried in the cemetery near D. S. Fulton's.
iv. Otho, m. Elizabeth Hastings; lived in Bradford where 10 c. were b. to them. They rem. to Berkshire and d.
v. Abigail. d. in childhood at Haverhill.
vi. Lydia, m. James Woodward of Bradford; 14 c
vii. Caleb, a physician; m. Sarah Austin of Enosburg, and settled there. C., Rosina, Elvira, Caleb A., and Sarah Luthera, who m. Wm. C. Carleton of Newbury.
viii. Ruth, m. Samuel Rogers of Newbury, q. v.
ix. Charles, m. Miranda Fuller of Hardwick and lived in Enosburg.
x. Johnson, m. Saga House; lived at Enosburg; 6 c.
xi. Polly, m. George Woodworth and lived at Berkshire, Bakersfield, Fairfield and Sheldon, Saratoga. N. Y., and Northampton, Mass. Three c. of whom Laura R., m. Charles Fairbanks of St. Johnsbury and Nice, France.

STEVENS.

CALEB, son of Caleb of Haverhill; m. Jan. 27, 1819, Mary Matthews, and lived at South Newbury, where he built in 1854, the house where W. W. Brock, Jr., now lives. Farmer and auctioneer; d. Feb., 1868, aged 77 years; she d.
Children:
i. George Shubael Blanding, b. 1820; res. in Newbury and Bradford. Taught singing school and was in various other business; d. 1900.
ii. William Barron, b. Apr. 9, 1822; clerk for F. & H. Keyes, having for some time the charge of the store in "Goshen." In 1851, with his brother Charles, he opened a store in Bradford, in which he carried on the mercantile

---

*Partly from a record prepared by Albert G. Stevens.

business till his death, as the head of a firm with several partners. These brothers were also engaged in other transactions, owning several mills and dealing largely in farm produce. He m. Sept. 17, 1856, Harriet, dau. of Austin Ladd of Haverhill. Mr. Stevens. d. March 2, 1893. C., (1) Helen Luella, d. in infancy. (2) Carrie B., res. Bradford. (3) Anna E., m. A. W. Porter of Brooklyn, N. Y. C., William S., b. Oct. 20, 1887. (4) Mary L., m. Oliver S. Baker of Bradford. C., Katharine S., b. June 4, 1889.

iii. Charles S., b. 1824; in partnership with his brother 1851 till death, November, 1872. He m 1st, 1856, Harriet Brown of Boston. Two c., both d. He m. 2d, Martha Brown of Canada. One c.

STEVENS.

WILLIAM B., b. Topsham, April 4, 1809. He was a carpenter and cooper by trade when young. He m. Hannah, dau. of Stephen Chase, and moved to the Lime-kiln neighborhood in Newbury. They were members of the Methodist church. Mrs. Stevens d. January, 1849, aged 38 He m. 2d, in Barnet, Mary Etta Chamberlin. He lived some years in Topsham, but returned to Newbury, and bought a small place outside of the village He m. 3d, the widow of William Brown, and sister of James Aytoun. These and Mrs. Aytoun were English people. William Brown froze to death, Dec. 24, 1860, on the stone bridge south of Hale Bailey's. She d. July, 1894, and he was cared for by his dau., Mary. He d. Dec. 2, 1897.

Children:
i.   Sarah A., now Mrs. Vermouth of Bradford.
ii.   Samuel C., served in a Vermont regiment during the Civil War. He m. 1st, Etta Ring of Topsham; m. 2d, Mrs. Randall of Groton.
iii. Mary C., res. in Newbury; un-m.
iv.   Daniel J., served in the Union army; d. in service, 1861.
v.   Hannah Jane, now Mrs. Hannaford of Bradford.
vi.   Alversa, d. y.
vii. Alex T., res. Topsham.
viii. John C., res. Providence, R. I.
ix.   Ellen J., now Mrs. Granger of Walden.
x.   William S., d. un-m. 1889.

STOCKER.

EBENEZER, m. Sarah Carleton of Bath.
Children:
i.   Mary S., b. 1814; m. Samuel Wilson of West Newbury, (b. 1803; d. 1874); d. 1880.
ii.   Abigail Newell, m. 1st, George W. Boynton; m. 2d, Theodore C. Elliott, both of Georgetown, Mass.
iii. Rebecca, m. William Kendall of Georgetown.
iv.   Ebenezer Carleton, b. Bath, N. H., April 19, 1821. He came to Newbury as apprentice to Dea. John Buxton in the harness business, afterwards entering into partnership with him, and, later, conducted the same business until his death; town representative, 1874, and held other offices; member of the Methodist church from 1843 till death; steward, 30 years; class leader, 26 years, and Sunday school superintendent about 20 years. He m. 1st. in Lowell, Mass., Jan. 16, 1851, Laura, dau. of Rev. Orange Scott, who d. 1856; m. 2d, December, 1856, Mary M. Parker, (b. Jan. 4, 1832; d. April 23, 1881); m. 3d, Nov. 25, 1890, Annette Carleton of Haverhill. He d. Newbury, Feb. 3, 1892. C., both by 2d m., (1) Laura Rebecca, b. Oct. 3, 1857; m. Abner Allyn Olmsted, q. v. (2) Harriet Newell, b. Dec. 25, 1859; m. March 8, 1898, James H. Fuller of Georgetown, Mass.

SULHAM.

JACOB, son of William and Betsey (Bryant) Sulham, b. Woodstock, N. H., May 24, 1804; rem. to Danville while young, and came to Boltonville in 1830, and was a shoemaker on the upper floor of the gristmill. After some years he bought a farm and also worked as a mason. He was a fine tenor

singer, and a skillful performer upon the violin. He m. 1st, Dec. 23, 1832,
Betsey Selingham of Woodstock. She d. March 1, 1873, in her 67th year.
He m. 2d, February, 1877, Mrs. Ann (Smith) Niles of Haverhill, who d.
September, 1895. He d. Nov. 28, 1896, aged 91 years, six months..
Children :
i. Semantha L., b. Jan. 27. 1834; m. Samuel M. Rollins, q. v.
ii. Jacob B., b. Oct. 29, 1835; res. in Massachusetts.
iii. William B., b. Nov. 27. 1837; d. July 7, 1846.
iv. Mary E., b. Feb. 10, 1840; m. William Cunningham; d. May 22, 1868.
v. Abbie C., b. Sept. 18, 1842; d. April 4, 1846.
vi. Martha C., (twin to above), d. March 25, 1846.
vii. Leander Q., b. Dec. 27, 1845; res. Massachusetts.
viii. Emily C., b Dec. 17, 1850; m. Dec. 17, 1874, Horace E. Brown, farmer on
the "Old Nourse place."
ix. Olive V., b. May 19, 1863; m. Aug. 10, 1883, Oliver E. Barber; d. Aug. 27,
1885.

SUTHERLAND.

No man, not a resident of Newbury, ever held here, during such a long period of
years, the influence and acquaintance of Rev. David Sutherland of Bath. At
the request of many of the older people in town, who wish to preserve some
memorial here of this remarkable man, the following account is prepared,
to accompany his portrait, presented by John Smith of West Newbury.
He was a native of Edinburgh, Scotland, and educated at a theological
seminary there. He came to Barnet in 1803, and in January, 1804, began
his labors in Bath, where he was pastor of the Congregational church till
1843, but continued in the ministry until near his death. At the time of
his settlement in Bath, that town had rather a hard name, b·t a great
change followed his coming, which was due says President Dwight, to the
example and faithful preaching of Mr. Sutherland. He was, probably, the
most noted minister who ever lived in this vicinity, and he was well
known, not only here, but throughout New England and the Middle
States, often preaching in the most noted churches of New York and
Philadelphia. He was called upon to deliver addresses upon public
occasions, several of which were in this town. A number of these were
printed, as were also several funeral discourses. He delivered a remarkable
sermon at the execution of Josiah Burnham at Haverhill, in 1806, before
an assembly of 10 000 people. He was moderator of the Congregational
church at Newbury at several periods when it had no settled minister, and
often preached in the Union Meeting house at West Newbury. In 1805,
he organized a Sunday school in Bath which is believed to have been the
first of the kind in the United States His personal appearance was
attractive, and in speaking he posse-sed a graceful delivery. earnest,
animated and impressive. He seldom used any notes to aid his discourse;
was able to adapt himself to every occasion, and having stored his
memory with many facts and anecdotes he employed them freely. and with
great effect in his sermons. He contributed to the press a great number of
papers. many of them upon subjects of local history. His last appearance
in public was on the evening of Jan 23, 1854, when he delivered an
historical discourse upon the fiftieth anniversary of his coming to Bath.
After his death this was published, with an appendix prepared by Rev.
Thomas Boutelle, and is one of the most valuable productions upon local
history we have. One sentence must be quoted here : After speaking of his
inadequate salary he says, "Were it not for handsome ·presents I
occasionally received, and some property by my most beloved wife, I
must have been reduced to absolute poverty. But now that I am very
aged. having entered my seventy-seventh year, to my Lord and Master,
when he may ask me, 'Lacked ye anything? I can truly answer, Nothing.'"
Mr. Sutherland spoke with a broad Scotch accent. In his old age he was
known as "Father Sutherland," and is often spoken of as "Priest
Sutherland." This latter adjective was formerly applied occasionally to
some Protestant minister of eminent ability, whose long and effective
service in one place gave him a sort of intellectual dictatorship. Rev. Silas

REV. DAVID SUTHERLAND
OF BATH.

REV. WILLIAM WYLIE.

McKeen of Bradford and Rev. James Milligan of Ryegate were also known by this title. In these days few ministers remain long enough, anywhere, to acquire any lasting influence. Rev. David Sutherland, b. Edinburgh, Scotland, June 19, 1777; m. in Leith, Scotland, April 29, 1803, Anna Waters. b. Dec. 22, 1774, who d. Path, Feb. 3, 1852. He d. while visiting in Bethlehem, N. H., July 25, 1855.
Children, all b. in Bath:
i. Jane E., b. Oct. 1, 1805; m. Sept. 20, 1827, Dr. Moses Hibbard of Lisbon, N. H., and Townshend, Vt., where he d. Sept. 29, 1863. and she spent the rest of her life with her sister, Mrs. Prichard. She d. Bradford, Nov. 27, 1881.
ii. David. b. Dec. 9, 1807; m. 1st, Sept. 16. 1830, Mary Hibbard, who d. July 10, 1838; m. 2d, June 17, 1841, Maria W. Bartlett. They rem. to Danville, thence to Iowa. He d. Grinnell, Iowa, April 12, 1890. She d. Dec. 15, 1893.
iii. William W., b. Dec. 20, 1809; d. Framingham, Mass., Nov. 22, 1828.
iv. John B., b. Feb. 3, 1812; farmer of Bath, excepting two years in Barnet and four in Wentworth; m. Jan. 27, 1846, Mehetable Lang of Bath, who now lives with her daughter, Mrs. Clough, at North Haverhill, and is the only one left of the original family. He d. Feb. 4, 1879.
v. Ann M., b. Oct. 1. 1813; m. Oct 4. 1843, Frederic Morrison of Bath, a glove maker. They rem. to Grinnell, Iowa, where he d. Aug. 11, 1876. She d. Jan. 10, 1899.
vi. James, b. Nov 26, 1816; d. Jan. 19, 1818.
vii. Mary P., b. Jan. 10, 1820; m. as 2d wife, Feb. 7, 1854, Dea. Geo. W. Prichard of Bradford, who d. Aug. 8, 1867. She d. Bradford, Feb. 8, 1879.

SWASEY.

Moses, b. about 1735; lived in Haverhill, Mass.; m. 1st, Eunice Merchant, Sept. 25. 1755, who d. Sept. 16, 1760; m. 2d, Mehitable Page. July 20, 1761, who d. Feb. 17. 1825. He d. March 2, 1800. Three c. by 1st and nine by 2d marriage. Of the latter, two sons, Moses and Obadiah, came to Newbury.

Moses, Jr., b. Haverhill, Mass., Aug. 5, 1768. He came to this town about 1790, and was a mechanic. Later he bought the farm of his father-in-law, Major Merrill, now owned by James Lang. He built, in 1797, the quaint looking house in which his dau., Mehitable, lived until her death in 1896. He was captain of a troop of cavalry in the old militia. He m. March 10. 1793. Elizabeth, dau. of Major Nathaniel Merrill, (b. March 3, 1774; d. Feb. 4, 1855). He d Newbury, Aug. 1, 1823.
Children:
i. Polly. b. Dec. 10, 1793; m. Aug. 12, 1819, John Melindy of Cincinnati, O., who d. in 1869. at Cedar Rapids, Iowa. She d. Feb. 15. 1821.
ii. Hazen. b. Nov. 21 1795; went to Cincinnati in 1817, and became a merchant. He m. Sophia Allen, and they had several c., who d. y. He d. Aug 19, 1830.
iii. Eliza, b. March 5, 1798; m. March 25, 1823, as 2d wife, Samuel Page of Haverhill; d. March 27, 1876. Of their c., William H., is a merchant at Haverhill; Elizabeth, m. Jonathan S. Nichols of Haverhill; Samuel, also of Haverhill; Harriet, m. Simeon C. Senter of Thetford; Josephine, rem. to Kansas: Hannah. m. a Mr. Bowen; Ellen, m. Milo Bailey; Mary, res. in Haverhill; Emily, m. Rev. C. N. Flanders, and Moses S., is in business in Boston.
iv. Harriet, b. May 22, 1801; m. March 21, 1836, Levi P. Parks of Barnet, who d. Feb. 4. 1856, leaving a son, Levi P., Jr., whose widow and five c. live at Lamoille. Ill. She d. Aug. 9, 1868.
v. Infant son, b. April 14; d. May 2, 1802.
vi. Lucinda, b. July 11, 1804; m. Jan. 10, 1828, Ira Butterfield of Cincinnati, O.; d. Sept. 28, 1845. They had one dau., Lucinda, who m. Henry Jenkins of Ludlow, Kentucky.
vii. Sally, b June 29, 1806; d. Oct. 12, 1866.
viii. Mehitabel, b. Oct. 7, 1809; d. July 13. 1896. These two last sisters never married. and lived their entire lives in the house in which they were born.

ix. Moses, b. Feb. 23, 1812; went to Cincinnati, O., in 1838, and became a merchant. He m. Mrs. Maria Ruth (Park) Martin. He d. Nov. 1, 1874. C., Julia, William, Edward, George, Ella.
x. Charlotte, b. June 3, 1814; m. Joseph Atkinson, q. v.; d. Sept. 9, 1850.
xi. George, b. Aug. 3, 1818; farmer on the Ox-bow, till 1867, when his health failed and he rem. to the village. He dealt in agricultural implements, bringing the first mowing machine into Newbury in 1854. Later he was for 14 years agent for the Vt. Mutual Fire Insurance Co. Deacon in 1st Ch. He m. 1st, Dec. 25, 1844, Louisa R., dau. of Sherburne Lang (q. v.) of Bath, (b. Sept. 23, 1818; d. Dec. 25, 1881). He m. 2d, Jan. 18, 1883, Mrs. Mary B. (Parker) Holt, who d. March 23, 1900. Dea. Swasey was still active in body, and intellectually acute at 82, and has rendered valuable service in the preparation of this history. He d. Jan. 11, 1901. C., (1) Elizabeth, b. Sept. 30, 1845; m. Jan. 16, 1873, Joseph Poor, a merchant of Haverhill. One dau., Mary Louise, b. Feb. 23, 1874; m. Sept. 30, 1897, Dr. Henry C. Stearns of Haverhill. (2) Sherburne Lang, b. March 3, 1850; jeweler; in the jewelry business in Boston two years; in Newbury, 1875 to 1897, also carried on a druggist business for 14 years. He m. Nov. 14, 1877, Leona A., dau. of Jacob Worthen. One son, Roland G., b. Nov. 18, 1880.

OBADIAH, son of Moses of Haverhill, Mass., b. March 20, 1775. He came to Newbury soon after his brother, Moses, and lived in a house which stood where that of S. C. Stebbins now stands. He rem. to Haverhill after some years and carried on a saw mill, also owned the farm on the Little Ox-bow, where his son, N. M. Swasey lived after him. and which was before the Revolutionary War the farm of Col. John Hazen. He m. ——
———, Nancy, dau. of Maj. Nathaniel Merrill, (b. Feb. 7, 1780; d. Dec. 7, 1850); both buried at Horse Meadow. He d. Haverhill, N. H., July 21, 1836.
They had 13 c. of whom the first two or three were b. in Newbury, the rest Haverhill:
i. Benjamin M., b. May 13, 1800; d. Jan. 31, 1877; never m.
ii. Mary Ann, b. Jan. 7, 1802; m. John L. Wood; d. June 29, 1874.
iii. Samuel, b. Feb. 22, 1804; graduated Dartmouth College. 1828; lawyer; d. June 20, 1887, at Belvidere, Ill.
iv. Nancy. b. Apr. 27, 1805; m. Dr. Henry B. Leonard of North Haverhill; d. Aug. 3, 1867.
v. John H., b. Nov. 27, 1808; d. 1890.
vi. Hannah, b. Nov. 30, 1810; d. Aug. 28, 1827.
vii. Louisa, b. March 13, 1813; m. E. S. Elkins of Kenosha, Wis.; d. Nov. 2, 1876.
viii. Nathaniel M., b. June 4, 1815; m. Mary M., dau. of Dr. Angier; farmer on the Little Ox-bow, Haverhill; d. Montpelier, June 4, 1893.
ix. Jane, b. Oct. 20, 1817; res. Chicago.
x. Franklin. b. Dec. 18, 1819; d. Feb. 3, 1821.
xi. Sarah L., b. Sept. 20, 1823; m. Joel M. Angier; res. Chicago.
xii. Hetty or Mehetable, b. Aug. 6, 1824; m. Henry K. Elkins, (b. in Peacham, Nov. 2, 1818); res. Chicago.
xiii. Franklin, b. May 31, 1827; d. March 30, 1828.

SYLVESTER.

This family has long passed away from Newbury, but the family was quite prominent once. The following is from a record prepared by A. H. Silvester of Worcester, Mass.

I. PETER, the emigrant, settled in Weymouth. Mass., 1630; m. Naomi Torrey; d. in Scituate, 1663.

II. ISRAEL, their 5th son, b. 1651, had 11 c., of whom

III. PETER, b. Scituate, Apr. 15. 1687; m. Marie Torrey, in 1712. They rem. to Leicester, Mass., 1730-35, where he d. early in 1745. They had seven c., of whom Levi was an early settler of Newbury, and Hannah m. Samuel Tucker, father of the Samuel who settled in Newbury.

IV. LEVI, b. Jan. 12, 1723; m. Dec. 5, 1745, Ruth Merritt. He must have come to
Newbury very early, as at the March meeting in 1765, he was elected a
surveyor of highways. He settled on Kent's meadow, on the farm now
owned by Mr. Kimball, and appears to have been a man of good standing,
whose name recurs frequently in our early records. He served in the
Revolutionary War, in local service, with his son, Levi, and the latter was
in other service, in Bedel's regiment. During the last years of the war the
son was implicated in the dealings which certain parties carried on with
Canada, and acted as a messenger between the disaffected in Coös and the
British in Canada. He was one of the party which captured Col. Thomas
Johnson, and of that which attempted the capture of Gen. Jacob Bayley.
When and where Levi Sylvester d. is unknown.
The names of the following c. are known :
  i. Levi, before mentioned, served 11 months, 22 days in a New Hampshire
     regiment and afterward gave the authorities considerable trouble. He
     seems to have been a man of good standing in town long after the war.
     Nothing is known of his family, but he was believed by the late Dea.
     Swasey to have rem. to New York state.
 ii. Ruth, m. 1st, Thomas Hibbard, q. v.; m. 2d, Mark Sanborn of Haverhill.
iii. Daughter, who m. a Bailey.
 iv. Peter, m. a Miss Ryder, and settled in Waterford, where he d. 1810. Most
     of his c. settled in that vicinity where many descendants remain. The
     following record of the children of Peter is given space here by request
     for preservation. (1) Abigail, m. John Keach. (2) Peter, m. Patience
     Goodell; settled in Waterford; 7 c. (3) Mary, m. Ephraim Harrington.
     (4) Betsey, m. Moody Beard. (5) Levi, b. Dec. 23, 1795; m. Tryphosa
     Harrington of Waterford; 7 c., of whom Charles A., b. Waterford, Aug.
     21, 1828, was in the meat and grocery business at St. Johnsbury,
     1871–95; res. at St. Johnsbury. (6) Abner, m. Thirza Park; settled in
     Coventry. (7) Ruth, m. Andrew Martin. (8) Anna, m. Moses Stone. (9)
     John, m. Abigail Bugbee; settled in Albany. (10) Lydia, m. Hibbard
     Quimby.

TAPLIN.

According to information and records, John Taplin was b. in Charlestown,
Mass., in 1727, date uncertain, but baptized Oct. 27, 1727. His father's
name is given as Mansfield Tapley. John was an officer in the Old French
war. The Massachusetts records show that he was a captain from March
28, 1755, to Dec. 27, of that year; captain in Col. Jonathan Bayley's
regiment, Nov. 29, 1755, to March 14, 1756. In August, 1756, he was at
Fort William Henry, and a pay-roll, dated there, states that he was from
Southborough, Mass. In 1758 and '59, he was again in service, this time
it is said, with the rank of colonel. He was a grantee of Haverhill, his
name appearing upon its charter as John Taplin, Esq. In two deeds of
land in Haverhill, one in August and the other in November, 1764,
recorded at Exeter, to John Taplin of Haverhill, he is spoken of as of that
town. He came to Newbury very soon after that date as he was
moderator of town meeting March 12, 1765, again in 1768 and 1769. He
held offices under the crown; was commissioned March 17, 1770, and
again 1772. Judge of the Inferior Court of Common Pleas, Commissioner
to administer oaths of office, and Justice of the Peace. His house stood, it
would seem, not far from the Tenney Library building. He was a grantee
of Corinth, and was, it is believed, the only one of the grantees of that
town who settled there. He was an early settler, locating on Taplin hill,
but later, settled at the present village of East Corinth. July 17, 1775, he
wrote to the New York Provincial Congress, "The country seems to be
very well united and firm in the cause of liberty, and will, I make no doubt,
cheerfully join in whatever measures and directions the honorable Congress
may point out." Thompson in his History of Montpelier says of Col.
Taplin, "Declining to take up arms against the King, who had honored
him, he retired into Canada during the Revolutionary War." He certainly
returned to Corinth before the end of the war, whence he kept up a
correspondence with Canada, as Col. Thomas Johnson expressly states

45

that Col. Taplin came to Newbury in June, 1782, to warn him that Gen. Bayley was in danger. Col. Taplin m. Hepzibah Brigham, (b. 1731; d. Dec. 27, 1815), and from them are descended many of the most noted families in Vermont. He d. Nov. 9, 1803

The children of Col. John and Hepzibah Taplin were ten. Some of them were born in Newbury, but most of them settled in Corinth.

1   i.   John, b. July 17, 1748.
     ii. Johnson, m. Miriam Haselton.
     iii. Brigham, m. Polly Haselton.
     iv. Elisha.
     v.   Mansfield, m. Betsey Lovewell.
     vi. William, m. Martha Chamberlin; settled in Corinth.   Ten c.
     vii. Nathan, m. Elizabeth Taylor.
     viii. Polly, m. Robert Lovewell.
     ix. Hepzibah, m. Zacheus Lovewell.
     x.   Gouldsburn, b. Newbury, 1776; m. Susan Page; d. Nov. 16, 1862.

1 JOHN, son of Col. John Taplin, b. Marlboro, July 14, 1748; served at the age of 12, in the Old French war with his father; came to Newbury with his father; rem. to Corinth; in 1770, '72 and '74, he was sheriff under New York, and served in the Revolutionary War. He became prominent in public affairs and was widely known. The record of his military service is in guarding and scouting in Capt. John G. Bayley's Co. and in Capt. Simeon Stevens' Co   John m. 1st, Catherine, dau. Col. Nehemiah Lovewell, (b. July 10, 1748; d. July 16, 1794). He m. 2d, Lydia Gove, (b Nov. 12, 1763; d. Feb. 11, 1849). In 1787, he rem. to Berlin, and d. at Montpelier. November, 1835.

Children, twelve by 1st and nine by 2d marriage:
     i.   Katy, b. Dec. 30, 1770; d. July 15, 1794.
     ii.   Augustus, b. June 30, 1773.
     iii. Susan, b. April 8, 1775.
     iv.   John, b. July 31, 1777.
     v.   Henry, b. March 27, 1780; d. Sept. 6, 1843.
     vi.   Robert, b. Apr. 24. 1782; d. Apr. 3, 1848.
     vii. Ira, b. June 14, 1784; d Jan. 24, 1846.
     viii. Hannah, b. March 21, 1786; d. Feb. 19, 1815.
     ix.   Walton, b. May 14, 1788.
     x.   Chittenden, b. June 14, 1789; d. Jan. 10, 1791.
     xi.   Thomas, b. Apr. 30, 1792; d. Jan. 11, 1864.
     xii. William, b. June 15, 1794; d. 1834.
     xiii. Ebezener, b. March 2, 1796; d. Aug. 19, 1835.
     xiv. Hazen, b. Apr. 5, 1797; d. June 9, 1840.
     xv.   Edward L , b. May 5, 1798; d. Dec. 6, 1880.
     xvi. Harriet, b. Sept. 2, 1799; d. March 12, 1840.
     xvii. Horatio N., b. Apr. 15, 1801; d. Oct. 23, 1883.
     xviii. Sidney Smith, b. Feb. 5, 1803; d. July 8, 1833.
     xix. Guy C., b. Apr. 29, 1804; d. Dec. 1, 1846.
     xx.   John A., b. Oct. 4, 1805; d. Feb. 28, 1886.
     xxi. Susan, b. May 30, 1807.

TAISEY.

DANIEL, son of James and Ruth (Darling) Taisey, b. Groton, Aug. 16, 1831. His father d. in 1841. Daniel, after working for various farmers, went to Lowell, Mass, in 1848, and worked till 1850. He then started for California on foot and alone, was joined by his cousin, Cyrus Taisey. They went via Chagres, going up the river on a barge propelled by Indians with poles. Thence they crossed the isthmus on foot 28 miles to Panama, where, 19 days later, they left on a schooner for San Francisco. After leaving Acapulco. they were becalmed three weeks, then were driven out of their course 1000 miles by a storm, and finally reached San Francisco four days after their provisions were exhausted. Cyrus Taisey was killed at Mormon Island, and Daniel worked in the mines at what is now Placerville till March, 1853, when he shipped on the brig Katherine Brown for Australia. The brig was dismasted in a storm, and made the port of Honolulu, where it was repaired. Their voyage to Melbourne was interrupted by a severe storm of three days and nights, which drove them out of their course, so they made the port of Sydney instead, costing $100 to go from there to Melbourne. They had to change American gold for English money, and were forced to accept 40 per cent discount. Worked eight months at Bendigo, now called Sandhurst, paying seven dollars and a half a month for license to dig. Then, with a party, he went to a place called the Ovens, now called Beechwood, in Sidney colony, 280 miles on foot, through the forest, where he worked till his return to California, being away from America 26 months. Worked at Placerville till the spring of 1856, when he started for home via the Nicaraugua route, but that being the time of Walker's filibustering expedition they had to cross the isthmus to Aspinwall, whence, after 18 days, he sailed for New York, and reached home, May 20, 1857. Blacksmith, farmer and lumbering. Enlisted at East Topsham, Sept. 5, 1862. Corporal in Co. D, 15th Vt. In the Gettysburg campaign. Discharged Aug. 5, 1863. Farmer in Newbury since 1870. He m. 1st, Jan 1, 1857, Isabel J., dau. of James Latto, who d. in Newbury, Sept. 23, 1872; m. 2d, Dec. 24, 1872, Mary Belle, dau. John Laing.

Children, five by 1st marriage, six by 2d:
i. David, b. Dec. 25, 1857; d. Sept. 16, 1884.
ii. Frank, b. Oct. 14, 1860.
iii. Alick, b. June 19, 1865.
iv. Seth P., b. Nov. 23, 1867.
v. Dan, b. Sept. 23; d. Dec. 1872.
vi. Willie D.. b. Sept. 7, 1875; d. Jan. 24, 1882.
vii. Katie Belle, b April 20, 1878; m. Frank Chandler.
viii. Jessie May, b. Oct. 6, 1881.
ix. Annie L., b. Sept. 19 1883.
x. Mary F., b. June 22, 1885.
xi. Willie J., b. Sept. 16, 1890.

TEMPLE.

I. RICHARD, the earliest known ancestor of the Temple family was b. about 1668, and was killed by the Indians at Saco, Me.

II. EBENEZER, b. May 7, 1716.

III. BENJAMIN, b. July 23, 1746.

EBENEZER, son of Benjamin, b. Milford, N. H., March 4, 1770. Came to Newbury from Hillsboro, N. H., before 1798. His sister, Lucy, m. Feb. 17, 1803, Jonathan Johnson of Ryegate. Ebenezer m. April 11, 1799, Rebecca, dau. Matthew Gibson, (b. May 23, 1770; d. March 7, 1857). They settled about 1800 on wild land on Wallace hill. The buildings are gone, except the barn frame and the farm is a pasture. He d. March 21, 1858.

Children:
i. Sally, b. April 25, 1800; m. Benjamin Ordway of Hillsboro, N. H.
1 ii. Joel, b. July 27, 1801; d. June 27, 1871.
iii. Affa, b. June 12, 1803; m. Hiram Clark, q. v.; d. Jan. 10, 1855.
iv. Christian, b. June 19, 1805; m. Amasa Kasson.
2 v. Matthew, b. Sept. 8, 1807; d. July 15, 1890.
vi. Mark, b. June 22, 1809; d.
3 vii. Luke, b. Sept. 6, 1811.
viii. Betsey, b Feb. 21, 1815; m. Robert Dick of Bath; d. April, 1874.
ix. John, b. March 10, 1817; d. Bethel, Me., 1879.
x. Rebecca, b. March 21, 1820; m. Nov. 24, 1846, Truman Crosby of Bethel, Me.; d. Dec. 27, 1847.
xi. Abigail, b. Oct. 19, 1822; m. Zadoc Farmer of Nashua, N. H.; d. Sept., 1874.
xii. Rachel, b. Feb. 21, 1824; d. Sept. 14, 1859.

1 JOEL, b. July 27, 1801; m. July 10. 1834, Hannah, dau. Choate Clark, (b. July 10, 1804; d. Jan. 21, 1851). He d. June 27, 1871.
Children:
  i. Joel C., b. April 11, 1835. Farmer and schoolmaster; has taught 27 terms of winter school; un-m.
  ii. Ann W., b. Nov. 18, 1837; m. Nov. 27, 1880, Amos Elliott of Lisbon, and d. there Nov. 23, 1882
  iii. Orvin C., b. May 5, 1841; enlisted July 1861, Co. G, 3d Vermont; discharged Jan. 22, 1864. Painter; lived in Newbury and Haverhill. He m. April 9, 1863, Elizabeth, dau. of Wells Goodwin, (b. Oct. 1841). He d. Dec. 11, 1887. C., (1) Flora, b. July 5, 1864; m. Dec. 25, 1893, J. F. Willey of Thornton, N. H.; res. Manchester, N. H. (2) Jesse, b. June 6, 1866; clerk in Passumpsic railroad-office, Lyndonville; d. Oct. 30, 1885. (3) Maude, b. July 14, 1868; m. Oct. 16, 1888, John W. Belcher of Chicopee Falls, Mass.; 1 c.; d. Nov., 1892. (4) Claude, (twin to Maude); m. Oct., 1892, Agnes Leroy of Winchester, Mass. C., Horace Austin and Gladys Maude.

MATTHEW, b. Sept. 8, 1807. Lumberman and raftsman in younger days; farmer and mechanic. He m. March 31, 1836, Malinda B., dau. David Daily, (b. Oct. 29, 1807; d. Jan. 31, 1870). He d. July 15, 1890.
Children:
  i. Mary H., m. Sept. 7, 1865, at Lowell, Mass., Edwin Tuttle of Newbury; d. June 26, 1882. One dau., Lulu R., who m June 29, 1890, Melvin G. Morse. Two c., May G., and Arthur M.
  ii. William, m. in St. Johnsbury, Sept. 30. 1868, to Jennie Degoosh, who d. Aug. 19, 1870. He d. Sept. 22, 1872. One son, Frank A., who m. Nov. 16, 1898, Annie, dau. John Norcross of Bradford.
  iii. Ellen, d. March 13, 1874, aged 33 years.
  iv. Sarah, at homestead.
  v. Carrie, at homestead.
  vi. Matthew G., carpenter, lives on homestead.

3 LUKE, b. Sept. 6, 1811. Farmer; m. Dec. 7, 1844, Mary Ann, dau. George Avery, (b. Dec. 30, 1817).
Children:
  i. George W. B., b. Newbury, April 23, 1845; m. June, 1883; d. June 1, 1888. C., (1) Mrs. Clarence Spooner of Haverhill. (2) Wm. H., drowned in Connecticut River, 1897.
  ii. Ebenezer, b Jan. 19, 1848; d. at Lunenburg.
  iii. Rebecca, b. Lunenburg; d. at five years of age.
  iv. Sidney, b. Feb. 17, 1854; m. Annie Conley. Farmer on homestead. Bought 1899. the Edwards farm on which he now lives.
  v. Julia E., b. July 30, 1857; d. 1893.
  vi. Vashti A., b. Nov. 7, 1860.

4 JULIA E., m. S. W. Durand, Piermont.
Children:
  i. Nellie E., m. 1896, Charles B. Cochran of Piermont, and d. Aug. 8, 1898, leaving one c., Gertrude J., b. May 12, 1898; d. Feb. 1, 1899.
  ii. Mamie M., m. Henry Jacobs of Bradford; 1 c., Fred E., b. Feb. 17, 1898.
  iii. Maude V.

*TENNEY.

I. THOMAS, from Yorkshire, Eng., came to Salem, Mass., in December, 1638, settled the next April in Rowley, where he spent most of his life, but d. in Bradford, Mass., Feb. 20, 1699–1700. He m. Ann ————, who d. in September, 1657. They had four sons and three daus.

II. JOHN, b. Dec. 14, 1640; lived in Bradford, Mass., where he m. Feb. 26, 1663, Mercy Parrot of Rowley, who d. Nov. 27, 1667, leaving a dau. and a son. He d. April 13, 1722.

---

*From "The Tenney Family" and later information.

III.   SAMUEL, b. Nov. 20, 1667; lived in Bradford, Mass.; was a deacon in the
church. and member of the colonial assembly. He m. as 2d wife, Dec. 18,
1690, Sarah, dau. of Capt. Joseph Boynton, who d. Oct. 29, 1745. He d.
Feb. 3, 1747–8.

IV.   JONATHAN, fourth son of Samuel, b. Dec. 8, 1703; lived in Bradford, Mass.,
where he was a farmer, and deacon in the church. He was twice m., 1st,
to Rebecca. dau. of Daniel Hardy, by whom he had two sons and three
daus. He d. Feb. 24, 1786.

V.   JONATHAN, b. Bradford, Mass., July 25, 1736. (by town record) or Aug. 5,
1737, (Family Bible); captain in the militia; lived in Salem, N. H., but
after 1782, rem. to Corinth. He m. Oct. 1, 1755, Mehitabel Peaslee, who
d. Sept. 16, 1809. He d. in Corinth, Jan. 12, 1806.
Children:
    i. Susannah, b. Nov. 30, 1756.
1 ii. Asa, b. Jan. 6, 1759; d. May 25, 1831.
  iii. Mehitable, b. Dec. 6, 1761; d. Jan. 3, 1781.
  iv. Joshua, b. March 31, 1764; physician at Corinth; m. Susanna Allen; d.
     Corinth, Feb. 10, 1844. Among their c. were: Rev. Erdix Tenney, who
     was father of Miss Mary E. Tenney, principal of Montebello Ladies'
     Institute. Another was Judge John A. Tenney, who m. for his two wives,
     Mary Doe and Lydia McKeen Doe, daus. of Henry Doe, of Newbury.
  v. Abigail P., b. Sept. 16, 1766; m. March 15. 1798, Ebenezer White of
     Newbury and Corinth.
2 vi. Jonathan, b. Aug. 16, 1769, q. v.
  vii. Eliphalet, b. July 31, 1771; lived in Corinth.
  viii. Joanna, b. April 21, 1776; d. Jan. 10, 1781.
  ix. Betty. b. Nov. 6, 1782; m. May 8, 1800, David Barnett of Topsham, q. v.;
     d. April 27, 1813.

1   ASA,[2] (Jonathan.[1]) b. Salem, N. H., Jan. 6. 1759; farmer in Newbury. His home
stood a little in front of the present residence of Ezra B. Chamberlain. He
held many public offices, and was high sheriff in 1795. He was an active,
public spirited man, holding a prominent position in town. He m. Salem,
N. H., Feb. 20, 1791, Mary, dau. William White, brother of Ebenezer,
Noah, Joseph and Dr. Samuel White of Newbury. Her mother was Mary,
dau. Rev. Abner Bayley of Salem, N. H., brother of Gen. Jacob Bayley, (b.
Plaistow, N. H., Jan. 6, 1768; d. April 6, 1825). Asa Tenney d. suddenly,
May 25, 1831.
Children:
3 i. Abner B. W.. b. June 10, 1795; d. Sept. 17, 1873.
  ii. Mary, b. Dec. 14, 1802; m. Asa P. Tenney, q. v.

2   JONATHAN,[2] (Jonathan,[1]) b. Salem, N. H., Aug. 16, 1769; farmer in Corinth,
but came to Newbury, and bought the farm where his nephew, Col.
Tenney long lived, on the Upper Meadow. He m. April 14, 1795, Anna,
dau. of Ephraim Bayley. who d. the widow of John Ellis, at Chenango, N.
Y., Aug. 8, 1832. He d. Newbury, March 19, 1813; buried at the Ox-bow.
Children, ten. of whom two are of interest to Newbury people:
4 i. Jonathan, b. Aug. 18, 1796; d. June 18, 1865.
5 ii. Asa P., b. Feb. 4, 1821; d. March 1, 1867.

3   ABNER BAYLEY WHITE,[3] (Asa,[2] Jonathan,[1]) b. June 10, 1795; fitted for college
at Bradford, Mass., Academy; entered Dartmouth College in 1814, but
left after two years because of failing health. He bought the farm on
Upper Meadow which was, formerly, Uriah Chamberlin's, and later, that
of Jonathan Tenney. He was interested in the militia and rose to be
captain in 1821 of a company of cavalry, major in 1823, and colonel in
1825 of the 1st regiment, 1st brigade and 4th division of the state militia.
This office he held till 1827. and was, thereafter. always known by his
military title. He was one of the most extensive farmers in town, and had
other large interests. Town representative. 1832, '33, '34, '39, '40, '41,
'49, '50, '56; state senator, 1836, '38; sheriff, 1834; presidential elector
on the Harrison ticket, 1840; director in the old Wells River bank, from
1843; president, 1843–48, and director in the National bank from its

commencement, and president, 1872, till death. He m. June 14, 1818, Sophia Cutler, a native of Rindge, N. H. They were admitted to the 1st Ch , May 6, 1829, became members of the Wells River church in 1842, in which he was elected a deacon in 1863, holding the office the rest of his life. Their home was a hospitable one, and was, says J. C. Barker, while he was an inmate of it, the meeting place of music-loving people in this region, where they rehearsed, under the leadership of E. K. Prouty and others, the best music accessible at that time   Col. Tenney was a genial man, abounding in anecdotes and pithy sayings. He was kind to the poor and knew how to stand between a poor man and a hard creditor. A certain poor man had incurred the enmity of a rich but grasping merchant by making good at law the title to his own farm, to which the rich man had set up a claim. A year or two later the former met with misfortune, and his note, for a sum very large for him, fell into the hands of his rich enemy. The times were very hard, and the creditor demanded immediate payment, the note being on demand. The poor man appealed to Colonel Tenney for aid, having sought in vain for help elsewhere. Mr. Tenney told him that he was, himself, much embarrassed, and could not help him directly, but would see what could be done. He called upon the creditor, and brought the conversation around to the unfortunate debtor. The creditor produced the note, and exulted over the ruin to which he had brought his late opponent. Col. Tenney looked at the note, and merely remarking, "I guess you can hold him," changed the conversation. While the creditor's attention was called to something else, Mr. Tenney wrote his name on the back of the note, and laid it down and his action was not seen. Soon after, this note, with others, was placed in the hands of a lawyer, with instructions to proceed upon them. The latter seeing Col. Tenney's signature, asked the creditor if he had notified the endorser. The creditor, who was taken by surprise, was furious, but helpless, as he could not proceed against the poor man without notifying Tenney, a proceeding he did not venture upon, so the debtor remained in safety until able to pay the debt. Mr. and Mrs. Tenney's married life lasted 55 years. She d. Aug. 7, 1873, and he followed her on the 13th of the next month:

Children:
i.   Asa, b. March 31, 1819; d. July 29, 1829.
ii. Mary, b. April 2, 1821; d. Feb. 11, 1858.
iii. Sophia C., b. April 4, 1824; m. Joshua Hale, q. v.; d. Jan. 19, 1901.
iv. Hepzibah Ann, b. Oct. 12, 1826; m. Jan. 29, 1851. James D. White of Haverhill, Mass.; d. Feb. 14, 1893. C., (1) Elizabeth P., b. July 27, 1856; m. March 25, 1885, Nathaniel Stevens of North Andover, Mass. (2) Sophia T., b. March 31, 1889; d. July 22, 1861. (3) Abner Tenney, b. July 29, 1862; educated at Institute of Technology, Boston; res. Manville, R. I.
v.   Asa A., b. Sept. 29, 1829; d. Dec. 23, 1851.
vi. Martha Jane, b. July 23, 1832; res. Haverhill, Mass. In addition to many other services for the public, she compiled and published in 1891, "The Tenney Family" which contains the annals of 4044 descendants of Thomas Tenney. In 1896, she erected the Tenney Memorial Library building for the use of the citizens of this town. Miss Tenney has taken a deep interest in this history of Newbury and has aided the editor in every way which she could devise. She needs no enconium from the editor's hand.

4   JONATHAN,[3] (Jonathan,[2] Jonathan,[1]) b. Corinth, Aug. 18, 1796; farmer in Corinth and Newbury; m. Nov. 21, 1816, Lydia Owen Crane, (b. Bradford, Dec. 8, 1795; d. West Concord, N. H., aged 103). He d. Boscawen, N. H., June 19, 1865.
     Children, all lived in Newbury in youth:
i.   Jonathan, b. Corinth, Sept. 14, 1817; graduated at Dartmouth College, 1843; taught school in Newbury several winters before his graduation, where he is well remembered as a model teacher; principal of Newbury High School, 1844, '45; Pembroke Academy, five years; master of South Grammar School at Lawrence, Mass.; principal of Pittsfield High School, 1850-53; editor in Manchester; secretary of the state board of education; originated the New Hampshire state teachers association, 1854; editor of New Hampshire Journal of Education; principal of Elmwood Institute

nine years, and from 1869 to 1874, principal of Oswego Free Academy; appointed, 1874, Deputy Superintendent of Public Instruction for the state of New York; he rem. to Albany; author of "New England in Albany," "History of Albany City and County," and author and editor of a great number of other works; he also lectured much; was a member of many learned societies, and was licensed to preach by the Susquehanna Association. He was twice m., and was survived by four of his eight c. He d. at Albany, N. Y., Feb. 24, 1888.

ii. Daniel C., b. Corinth, Nov. 9, 1819; farmer and mechanic; was twice m., and had two c.; d. West Concord, N. H.

iii. Asa P., b. Bradford, Dec. 14, 1821; lived at Wentworth, N. H.; m. Louisa F. Gove; d. Dec. 15 1885. Three c.

iv. John E., b. April 22, 1824; m. Sept. 10. 1850, Sarah J., dau. of Charles Story of Newbury. He d. Concord, N. H., April 6, 1858.

Five others d. y.

5 ASA P.,[3] (Jonathan,[2] Jonathan,[1]) b. Corinth, Feb. 4, 1801; pastor for 35 years of Congregational church at West Concord, N. H; m. May 22, 1829, Marv, dau. of Asa Tenney of Newbury, (b. Newbury, Dec. 14, 1802; d. Concord, N. H., Nov. 17, 1869). He d. March 1, 1867.

Children:

i. Mary, b. Groton, N. H., Aug. 21, 1831; m. Aug. 25, 1857, to W. M. Hatch; lawyer at Bloomington. Ill., now res. at Colorado Springs, Col. Mrs. Hatch has been of much assistance to the editor of this volume.

ii. Dr. Asa P., b. Concord, N. H , Sept. 21, 1833. In charge many years of the insane asylum at Topeka, Kan. Now in practice at Kansas City. He m. his cousin, Minerva Tenney. Two c. living.

iii. Edward Payson, b. Concord, N. H., Sept. 29, 1835; pastor of several churches, among others the Congregational church at Orford, where he now res., engaged in literary work. Twice m. and has two c.

iv. Helen A., b. Sept. 9, 1837; d. Sept. 29, 1854.

v. Abner B., b. Aug. 28, 1841; d. April 3, 1862.

vi. Elizabeth M., b. Aug. 11, 1843; d. March 17, 1863.

TERRY.

WILLIAM, son of Armigal and Sarah Terry, b. Lewes, County Sussex, England, June 25, 1848. Landed in Portland. Me., in Jan., 1867, after a voyage of 23 days, penniless and without friends in America. Worked one year at Melburne, P. Q., for $3.00 per month. Came to Newbury in 1868, worked three years for R. G. Lang, going to school winters; drove a peddlar's cart for L. K. Quimby & Co., of Lyndon, 7 years, then in the same line for himself until that business became no longer profitable. In trade with others under the firm name of Terry, George and Gay, later Terry and George, general merchants, at South Ryegate, about nine years until now, residing on a small place he bought of John A. Miller on the Newbury side of the line. His mother for whom he sent in 1872, d. at the home built of her own savings from her work in service, in April, 1893, in her 60th year. He also sent for his two brothers and one sister, who lived in Newbury. Thomas lived here three years or more, and d. March, 1873. George went to Chicago and became a baker. Lizzie is m. and lives at South Duxbury, Mass.; 3 c. William Terry m. March, 1874, Mary A., dau. of William Lindsey.

Children:

i. Alice L., b. Nov. 29, 1874, (Mrs. Whitcher); m. Oct. 13, 1898, A. C. Moore, of Woodsville. N. H.

ii. William Wallace, b. July 9, 1877; m. Sept. 21, 1899, Delia, dau. of Austin Hatch of Groton; res. Hartford. Conn.

iii. Burnest Lewes, b. Aug. 23, 1879; m. July 19, 1899, Mabel Nelson of Ryegate.

iv. Mertie Estel, b. Jan. 2, 1882; d. July 17, 1883.

v. Adna M., b. March 1, 1885.

TEWKSBURY or TUXBURY.

PHILIP, Jacob and Thomas were brothers. Philip and Jacob lived in Newbury and Thomas settled and d. in Maine. They had two sisters, one m. Elijah Rowe, and settled in Washington, Vt. The other m. a Mr. Colby of Canaan, N. H. Philip, b. 1768; m. Elizabeth, dau. Jonathan Goodwin, (b. 1773; d. Oct. 3, 1841). They lived at South Newbury on her father's farm, but rem. three years before he d. to South Ryegate. Philip d. Sept. 24, 1813.

Children:
   i.   Hannah, d. July 23, 1836, aged 41.
1 ii. Jeremiah B. W., b. July 16, 1800; d. Nov. 21, 1866.
  iii. Mary, m. William Webber, q. v.; d. Jan. 18, 1849.
  iv. Eliza, m. William Hills.
   v. Martha. m. Albert Buell; d. Sept, 22, 1843.
  vi. Almira, d. Oct. 10, 1845, aged 35.
2 vii. Philip Currier, b. March 1, 1815; d. Feb. 18, 1899.

1 JEREMIAH B. W., b. July 16, 1800. His father lived on the farm of his wife's father, Jonathan Goodwin on Hall's Meadow, but after the death of the latter in 1811, his widow exchanged that farm for one lying between S. W. Tewksbury's and S. S. Tucker's, to which the widow of Philip Tewksbury rem. after the death of her husband in 1813. Jeremiah settled where his son Stratton lives, and built that house in 1832, where he d. Nov. 21, 1866. He m. Aug. 13, 1833, Harriet, dau. of Robert McAllister, b. Feb. 9, 1811.

Children:
   i.   Amplias, b. Nov. 18, d. Nov. 26, 1834.
  ii. Sarah, b. Feb. 21, 1836; m. R. G. Lang, q. v.
  iii. William Allen, b. Nov. 18, 1837. Fitted for college at Newbury Seminary, and Barre Academy. Graduated Middlebury College, 1865. Read law with Dickey and Worthen of Bradford, and C. W. Clarke of Chelsea. Admitted to the bar, Jan., 1867; in practice at Belle Plain, and, later, at Vinton, Iowa, till his death, Jan. 7, 1884. He m. Nov., 1868, Lizzie Douglas. who d. May 6, 1882. C., (1) Allen D., b. July 28, 1869; engineer in Texas. (2) Fred, b. Sept. 28, 1871; dentist at South Ryegate. (3) Jerry, b. July 22, 1876.
  iv. Harriet Luella, b. July 12. 1840; m. Dec. 29, 1869, her cousin, Otis Hills of Waterloo, P. Q. He d. there Oct. 13, 1898; no c. She d. Newbury, Aug. 28, 1899.
   v. Nelson Bailey, b. April 4, 1842. Served in Co. H, 12th Vermont, nine months in the Civil War; farmer. Began trade at the Centre in 1870, building a store and dwelling the next year. Postmaster there since the office was established in 1871. He m. May 24, 1864, Julia E., dau. of Nathan E. Corliss. (d. July, 1891). One son, Algernon B., b. July, 1869, m. Aug 7. 1895, Mabel Hackett of Haverhill.
  vi. Stratton Westgate, b. Aug. 30, 1844; farmer on homestead. He m. Sept., 1881, Eliza Bailey of Waterloo, P. Q. C., (1) Luella, b. March 30, 1884. (2) Julia, b. April 14, 1893.
  vii. d. in infancy.
  viii. d. in infancy.

PHILIP C., b. March 1, 1815; farmer; m. Nov. 3, 1847, Christian, dau. George Chalmers, (b. Scotland, July 27. 1824). He d. Feb. 18, 1899.
Children:
   i.   Elizabeth E., b. Aug. 28, 1848; m. March 20, 1872, James Miller of Ryegate, (b. June 10, 1831; d. Feb. 13, 1890). After his death she rem. to Newbury. C., (1) Clarence E., b. Jan. 10, 1873; m. March 6, 1894, Alma J., dau. Moses Randall; 2 c. (2) John H., b. Feb. 23, 1879. (3) James C., b. Feb. 8, 1881. (4) George H., b. June 1, 1882. (5) Christina J., b. Nov. 14, 1886; d. Sept., 1887.
  ii. George P., b. Jan. 8, 1850; res. Virginia City, Nev.; carpenter; un-m.
  iii. Twins, b. May 22, 1851; d. y.
  iv. Anna, b. March 11, 1853; m. Dea. Archibald McAllister, q. v.
   v. Mary, b. July 31, 1857; m. John B. Brock, q. v.
  vi. Henry W., b. Sept. 27, 1860; m. April 12, 1884, Martha B. Brock. C., (1)

Raymond C., b. Dec. 21, 1884. (2) Francis V., b. June 29, 1886. (3) Christian Bell, b. Dec. 28, 1889. (4) Henry W., b Feb. 1, 1893. (5) Abbie M., b. July 24, 1895. (6) Minnie L., b. Sept. 22, 1897. (7) Martha E., b. July 14, 1899.

vii. Allen G., b. June 12, 1867; farmer on homestead; m. June 25, 1896, Susie E., dau. of Charles H. Thompson. C., (1) Susie Pearl, b. Nov. 29, 1897. (2) Elsie E., b. Sept. 15, 1900.

THOMAS.

JOHN, son of Abraham and Rebecca (Barker) Thomas from Andover, Mass., b. Bath, N. H., 1817; m. Jan. 11, 1843, Mary, dau. of John Peach; d. May 2, 1849. After the death of John Thomas, his widow with her two children, rem. to West Newbury, where she d. March 22, 1857. The c. were Peach and Lydia. The latter, who lived with her aunt Amy, m. C. A. Newman of Lunenburg; res. Austin, Minn. Three sons and two daus.

PEACH, m. July 15, 1868, Mary Jane, dau. of Alden Tucker; res. Newbury and South Ryegate.
Children:
  i. John, b. Feb. 28, 1872; graduated March 25, 1897, from the American Veterinary College, New York City; veterinary surgeon at Wells River; m. Oct. 25, 1898, Annie Grant of Barre, a native of Scotland.
 ii. Horace T., b. Aug. 9, 1874; graduated in a chemical engineers' course at State Agricultural College, Lansing, Mich., 1901.
iii. Jessie Irena, b. Nov. 18, 1877; d. July 20, 1879.
 iv. Son, b. April 28; d. May 20, 1881.
  v. Daughter, (twin to above), d. May 14, 1881.
 vi. Charles P., b. Oct. 5, 1886; at home.

THOMPSON.

ALEXANDER, b. Perth, Scotland, 1761; settled in Antrim, N. H., and m. Elizabeth Nutt. He d. 1827. She d. May 27, 1840, aged 78. They had eight c., of whom Alexander, the 2d, and Daniel, the 5th, lived in Newbury.

ALEXANDER, b. 1792; m. Matilda Richardson; lived in the west part of the town, near Topsham line. They had several c., of whom no record is available.

DANIEL, b. Antrim, N H., Feb. 9, 1794; m. Sept. 3, 1818, Persis Matilda, dau. Joseph Ladd of Haverhill, (b. Jan. 11, 1793). They settled in Corinth, but came to Newbury, 1822, where he was a blacksmith, and lived in the house opposite the one in which the late P. W. Ladd so long lived. He rem. to Topsham, 1831, to Francestown, N. H., 1834, where he was a deacon in the Congregational church. They rem. to West Newbury, Mass., but passed their last years in Lancaster, N. H., where he d. December, 1878. She d. April 1, 1879.
Children:
1   i. Alexander, b. July 11, 1819; d. Sept. 9, 1882.
   ii. Mary Charlotte, b. Corinth, May 21, 1821; m. Hon. John Bigelow, q. v.
2 iii. William Ladd, b. June 6, 1823; d. Sept. 30, 1894.
   iv. John Buxton, b. Dec. 14, 1824; res. Boston, Mass.
    v. Sarah Arabella, b. Dec. 19, 1826; d. Newburyport, Mass., September, 1872.
   vi. Daniel, b. Oct. 25, 1828; d. June 26, 1895, at St. Johnsbury, where he owned and operated a machine shop.
  vii. Warren Ives, b. May, 1830; d. October, 1831.
 viii. Warren, b. Topsham, Jan. 5, 1832; d. Augusta, Me., Sept. 28, 1867.
   ix. Augusta Lavinia, b. April 24, 1834; res. Lynn, Mass.
    x. Persis Serena, b. Francestown, N. H., February, 1838; d. there July 4, 1872.

1 ALEXANDER,[3] (Daniel,[2] Alexander,[1]) b. Corinth, July 11, 1819; m. 1st, Anna Reid Tyler, who d.; m. 2d, Ellen Armington, who d.; m. 3d, Dec. 25, 1866,

Alice Twitchell. He d. Lancaster, N. H., Sept. 3, 1882.
Children, one by 2d marriage, and five by 3d:
  i.   Ellen A., b. Aug. 10, 1865.
  ii. Mary, b. May 1, 1868.
  iii. Mabel Chase, b. Aug. 7, 1872.
  iv. Grace, b. April 21, 1876.
  v.   Agnes Sarah, b. March 23, 1878.
  vi. Persis Alexandrina, b. April 19, 1881.

2 WILLIAM LADD, b. Newbury, June 26, 1823. He obtained his education by hard
     labor. Studied medicine, attended Dartmouth Medical College and
     Hahnemann College, Philadelphia. Began practice.1857, at Newburyport,
     Mass., but rem. to Dover, N. H., where he remained 9 years. In Augusta,
     Me., 1866, till death, Sept. 30, 1894. He was a prominent physician
     there, and twice president of the Maine Homeopathic Society ȳand a
     beloved member of the Cong. church. Buried in Dover, N. H. He m. 1st,
     Susan Emeline Cummins, (b. Boxford, Mass., Jan. 15, 1830; d.
     Georgetown, Mass , Dec. 25, 1858); m. 2d, Sarah Bickford Varney.
   Children, three by 1st marriage; eight by the 2d, of whom three are living:
  i.   William Sylvester, b. Newburyport, April 10, 1853; physician, in practice at
        Augusta, succeeding his father.
  ii.   George Ladd, (Col.), b. Newburyport, April 15, 1855; res. Brunswick, Me.
  iii. Charles Cummins, b. Dover, Jan. 7, 1857; d. there March 29, 1862.
  vii. Daniel V., b. May 10, 1867.
  viii. Frederick L., b. April 12, 1869.
  x.   Mary E., b. July 14, 1874.

TUCKER.

  I.   ROBERT, was in Weymouth, Mass., as early as 1635, rem. to Gloucester, where
       he was recorder, but returned to Weymouth, whence he went to Milton, of
       which he was the first town clerk. Town representative, and member of
       the 1st ch. in Milton. He m. Elizabeth Allen.

  II. BENJAMIN, (1646—Feb. 27, 1713-14), 3d son and 9th c. of Robert; m. Ann,
       dau. Edward and Mary (Eliot) Payson. The latter was sister of the
       Rev. John Eliot. the Apostle to the Indians. In 1684 he and others
       purchased of the Indians the township now called Spencer, Mass.

  III. BENJAMIN, (March 8, 1670-1728); m. as 2d wife, Elizabeth Williams of
       Roxbury.

  IV. SAMUEL, b. July 5, 1696; m. June 19, 1740, Hannah, dau. Peter and Sarah
       Sylvester, (b. April 2, 1716, at Scituate, Mass). She was sister of Levi
       Sylvester. one of the first settlers of Newbury, q. v. They lived in Leicester,
       but rem. to Spencer about 1752.

  V.   SAMUEL, b. Leicester, Mass., Jan. 8, 1749, m. 1768, Elizabeth Livermore of
       Lincoln, a descendant of John Livermore of England and Watertown,
       Mass. Lived in Oxford and Spencer; came to Newbury about 1787, and
       bought several lots and parts of lots. about 500 acres, between the main
       road at West Newbury and Hall's Pond. His house stood where E. E.
       Putnam's now stands, which was taken down by Robert Nelson, and
       the present house built from its material. It was a large square roofed
       house. They were admitted to the 1st ch. by letter, July 1, 1803. He d.
       June 10, 1813, and his wife in 1826.
     Children:
  i.   Anna, b. Oxford, June 28, 1769; m. Dr. Samuel White, q. v.; d. March 26,
        1845.
1 ii.   Samuel, b. Oxford, Oct. 26, 1770; d. April 14 1825.
2 iii. Jonas, b. Spencer, May 24, 1775; d. March 23, 1855.
  iv.   Betsey, d. when about 20 years of age.
  v.   Elijah, b. Spencer, 1781. Very deaf from childhood ; lived with his brother,
        David. He was remarkably tall, being 6 ft. 7 in. in height; un-m. He
        d. in Kansas, 1858.
  vi.   Lucinda, d. Aug. 4, 1821.
3 vii. Levi Livermore, d. 1815.
  viii. David, b. Newbury, June 2, 1791; d. Nov. 3, 1869.

The Tuckers were substantial men, and of marked individuality. In person they were above the usual size, and it used to be said, sixty years ago, that "ninety lineal feet of Tuckers go into the Union Meeting House every Sunday."

1 SAMUEL,[2] (Samuel,[1]) b. Oxford, Mass., Oct 26, 1770. He m. Aug. 30, 1796, Mary, dau. Thomas Brock, (b. Dec. 28, 1773; d. Jan. 10, 1840). Settled where his son Thomas lived after him; built that house in 1807. Members of the 1st ch. He d. April 14, 1825, from injuries received by a log falling upon him at his mill on Hall's Pond. They are both buried in a small disused grave yard on the "Putnam place."
Children:
   i. Mary, b. July 1, 1797; m. Roger Eastman, q. v.
   ii. Mindwell, b. July 9, 1799; m. Joel Putnam, q. v.
   iii. Elizabeth, b. March 30, 1801; m. David McAllister, q. v.
   iv. Judith, b. Aug. 5, 1803; m. Samuel Eastman, q. v.
   v. Sarah, b. Nov. 8, 1805; m. Harvey Westgate, q. v.
   vi. Jonas L., b. Dec. 5, 1807; d. April, 1809.
4 vii. Samuel A , b. Feb. 4, 1810.
5 viii. Thomas L., b. Aug. 7, 1814.

2 JONAS,[2] (Samuel,[1]) b Spencer, Mass., May 24, 1775; m. 1st, Nov. 23, 1809, Nancy, dau. Col. Robert Johnston, (b. May 26, 1785; d. Nov. 30, 1830); m. 2d, in 1840, Mrs. Abigail Morse of Ryegate, (b. Oct. 15. 1789; d. Dec. 14, 1881). Settled where his grandson, Jonas Tucker now lives, and built that house about 1812. Member of the 1st ch. with most of his c. Was known as Esquire Tucker, being Justice of the Peace 28 years. (See town officers). Farmer and mason. He was one of the substantial men in that part of the town. He d. March 23, 1856. An account book in which he noted many interesting matters has been of much service in the preparation of this work.
Children:
   i. Hepzi Eliza, b. July 4, 1811; m. Oct. 13, 1844, Wm. R. Austin, q. v.; d. April 3, 1890.
6 ii. Myra Jane, b Nov. 12, 1812; d. Jan. 28, 1845.
7 iii. Levi Livermore, b. Nov. 17, 1814; d. Jan. 22, 1883.
   iv. Abi Johnston, b. Dec 24, 1816; m. July 18, 1853, William T. Bailey, q. v.; d. May 4, 1893.
8 ⁻ v. Lucinda Ann, b. Nov. 10, 1818; d. March, 1900.
9 ♂ vi. Nancy Johnston, b. Nov. 27, 1821; d. Feb. 4, 1896.
10 ♀ vii. Lydia Johnston, b. June 14, 1824.
11 viii. Mary White, b. May 8, 1826.
   ix. Hannah Bell, b. July 26, 1828. Teacher and contributor to various periodicals; m. July 19, 1857, Willis Palmer; d. Apr. 18, 1863. C., Mary Bell, b. July 13, 1858; d. March 21, 1872.

3 DAVID,[2] (Samuel,[1]) b. Newbury, June 2, 1791; m. 1st, Nov. 1, 1824, Lydia Barker, (b. Bradford, April 7, 1795; d. Maidstone, Dec. 28, 1842); m. 2d, Mrs. Eunice Perkins. who d. Eureka, Kan., Feb. 20. 1863. Rem. to Maidstone about 1838, to St. Johnsbury, about 1845, to Beloit, Wis., 1846, to Kansas, 1857. He d. Eureka, Kan., Nov. 3, 1869.
Children. all b. Newbury:
   i. George Livermore, b. Sept. 19, 1825. Graduated Beloit College, 1853; Union Theological Seminary, 1856; ordained Congregational minister, April 2, 1856; pastor Madison Street church, New York City, 1856–57. Was obliged to suspend preaching one year because of a throat trouble. Fox Lake, Wis., Cong. ch., 1857–60; Trempleau, Wis., 1860–65; Brighton, Ill., Pres. ch., 1865–68; Quindora, Kan., since. Farming and real estate, occasionally preaching. He m. June 26, 1858, Isabella Randall; no c.
   ii. Elizabeth L., b. May 5, 1830; teacher many years; res. Eureka, Kan.
4 iii. Edwin, b. Dec. 23, 1835.

4 SAMUEL ALDEN,[3] (Samuel.[2] Samuel,[1]) b. Feb. 10, 1810; farmer on homestead; rem. to Jefferson Hill, 1861; m. Feb. 15, 1843, Irene, dau. of Sherburne

716 HISTORY OF NEWBURY, VERMONT.

Prescott of Vershire, (b. Feb. 15, 1818; d. Feb. 15, 1888). He d. March 8, 1886.
Children:
i. Horace, b. Dec. 9, 1843; d. April 1, 1863.
ii. Mary Jane, b. April 10, 1846; m. Peach Thomas, q. v.
iii. Clara R., b. Oct. 4, 1848; m. Henry Randall, q. v.
iv. Emma, b. March 28, 1852; m. Nov. 17, 1892, Pringle Gibson of Ryegate.
v. Freeman P., b. July 4, 1854; attendant at Insane Asylum, Concord, N. H.; miller and postmaster at Boltonville, till death, April 4, 1895; m. Sadie Lane, who, after his death, m. Arthur Reid. C., Leon L., b. July 22, 1892.
vi. Samuel A., b. March 4, 1858; m. Nov. 17, 1892, Lois. dau. James E. Currier; farmer; miller at Boltonville since his brother's death. C., (1) Emma C., b. Feb. 20, 1896. (2) Clara L., b. Aug. 21, 1898.

5 THOMAS LIVERMORE,³ (Samuel,² Samuel,¹) b. Aug. 7, 1814. Farmer on homestead and lumberman. Teacher of vocal and instrumental music. Taught singing school for more than thirty years. Fifer at fourteen in the old militia, drum major at thirty. Drummer in Co. D. 1st Vermont regiment in the Civil War. Led the choir in the Union Meeting House many years. He m. June 18, 1839, Mary, dau. Sherburne Prescott of Vershire, b. July 16, 1814. He d. Nov. 19, 1887.
Children:
i. Sherburne S., b. May 13, 1840; farmer on homestead; m. Nov. 28, 1872, Hattie J., dau. Amos Cutting of Lyme, (b. Sept. 26, 1849). C., (1) Nettie E., b. June 24, 1875; teacher. (2) Sherburne S., b. June 14, 1881.
ii. Lucinda, b. Jan. 9, 1844; m. Newell C. Randall, q. v.
iii. Annette J., b. April 8, 1849; m. Feb. 18, 1874. Rev. Wm. S. Jenne of New York; d. Corinth, Aug. 8, 1874.
iv. Franklin H., b. May 5, 1854; d. Jan. 19, 1855.

6 MYRA JANE,³ (Jonas,² Samuel,¹) b. Nov. 12, 1812; m. Nov. 12, 1835, Jonathan J. Peck of Groton, (b. Montpelier, Aug. 29, 1808; d. Barre, June 1, 1884). She d. Groton, Jan. 28, 1845.
Children:
i. Jonas Oramel, b. Groton, Sept. 4, 1836; stage driver four years between Groton and Wells River; fitted for college at Newbury Seminary; graduated Amherst College, 1862; entered New Hampshire Conference, 1860; pastor of prominent churches in Lowell, Worcester, Springfield, Chicago, Brooklyn, Baltimore and New Haven; prominent in the lecture field; published sermons and essays; appointed, 1888, missionary secretary of the Methodist church, and held the position till death; received degree of D. D. from Wesleyan University. He m. 1862, Susan Robinson of Amherst, Mass, who d. January, 1888. He d. Brooklyn, N. Y., May 17, 1894. C., (1) George C., b. September, 1865; graduated Yale University; now in the ministry and has published sermons. (2) Carl R., b. February, 1871; graduated Yale University; res. New York City.
ii. Abbie J., b. Feb. 12, 1838; m. 1862. Dr. J. L. Perkins of St. Johnsbury; associated with Miss Frances Willard in temperance work as lecturer; secretary of Vt W. C. T. U. Two c., Isabel and Karl.
iii. Eugene C., b. May 29, 1841; served in 3d Vt. Regiment in Civil War; studied medicine at Burlington Medical College and Bellevue Hospital; physician at Walpole, Mass.

3 LEVI LIVERMORE,³ (Jonas,² Samuel,¹) b. Nov. 17, 1814; farmer on homestead and mason; built many fine brick buildings in this state and elsewhere. He was a man of sterling worth, of fine literary taste, kindly and generous. Town representative, 1878, (see town officers). He m. Dec. 11, 1851, Betsey P., dau. of Dudley Carleton, b. April 22, 1824. He d. Jan. 22, 1883.
Children:
1 Levi L., b. Dec. 10, 1853 graduated at Troy Business College, New York, in 1876; teacher in Schofield's Business College, Providence, R. I.. 1880–82; Miller's Business College, Newark, N. J., 1883–98; principal Wood's Business College, 1898, and also engaged in real estate business; 1901, superintendent commercial department of Mount Union College, Alliance,

Ohio. He m. May 7, 1877, Nettie L., dau. of Rev. George Bryant of Lisbon, N. H. C., (1) Lulu N., b. Newbury, March 3, 1878; d. Newark, N. J., May 13, 1885. (2) Aurora Mildred, b. Providence, R. I., April 17, 1882; d. Sept. 22, 1882. (3) Mildred Livermore, b. Newbury, Aug. 19, 1883. (4) Marjorie Hope, b. Newark, N. J., July 15, 1886; d. April 11, 1894. (5) Livermore Bryant, b. Feb. 15, 1888; d. Jan. 19, 1889. (6) Bryant Carleton, b. Aug. 26, 1890. (7) Joyce Johnston, b. Jan. 13, 1892. (8) Lee Parker, b. Oct. 11, 1896.

  ii. Katharine, b. July 24, 1858; m. June 30, 1897, F. P. Wells, q. v.

  iii. Jonas, b. May 8, 1860; farmer on homestead; m. Aug. 2, 1898, Hattie, dau. of William Putnam. C., Eva Lucinda, b. Feb. 25, 1900.

8 LUCINDA ANN,[3] (Jonas,[2] Samuel,[1]) b. Nov. 10, 1818; m. May 3, 1838, Aaron Vance, of Groton, (b. Groton, Oct. 14, 1812); rem. to Barnet, 1840; Ryegate, 1848; Minnesota, 1866; res. Houston, Minn. She d. March, 1900. Mr. and Mrs. Vance were not separated more than one month, altogether, in the 61 years of their married life.

  Children:

  i. George L., b. Groton, March 16, 1839; m. April 29, 1868, Betty K. Fowler of New York, (d. Nov. 6, 1872); m. 2d, July 19, 1876, Jennie Lewis; clerk in Treasury Department, Washington, 1864–72; in Europe and Asia, 1894; res. Joliet, Ill.; furniture dealer, and vice president of Mill County National Bank; lay preacher and in charge of several missions in and near Joliet. Three c. His son, George A., is cashier of Mill County National Bank. Two daus., Grace and Beulah.

  ii. David E, b. Barnet, Jan. 6, 1841; served in Co. G, 9th Vt. Regiment, from June 13, 1862, till June 13, 1865; went to Minnesota, 1866; teaching and studying law; admitted to the bar, 1879; lawyer at Winona, Minn. He m. Nov. 20, 1879, Alice I. Maybury. Four c.

  iii. William A., b. April 5, 1843; farmer at Houston, Minn.; m. 1st, March 13, 1872, Mary Gray, who d. November, 1872; m. 2d, Jan. 12, 1875, Abigail, dau. of Robert Sims of Ryegate. Three daus.

  iv. Albert N., b. June 9, 1845; res. Decorah, Iowa; grocer; m. May 12, 1874, Ida Dunbar. Three c.

  v. Nancy J., b. Barnet, Aug. 13, 1847; m. Oct. 2, 1871, D. C. Dyar; res. Houston, Minn. She is now blind. Six c

  vi. Nicholas W., b. Ryegate, Oct. 31, 1849; in banking business, Wolsey, South Dakota, 1888–96; res. Winona, Minn., 1896–98; in business with his brother, Albert, at Decorah, Iowa. He m. Libbie Burns of Caledonia, Minn., Aug. 14, 1879. Two daus.

  vii. Abigail, b. Ryegate, Nov. 23, 1851; m. October, 1893, Calvin C. Vance; res. Money Creek, Minn.

  viii. Aaron E., b. Ryegate, April 2, 1854; res. Joliet, Ill; m. March, 1879, Clara Birdsell. Three c.

9 NANCY JOHNSTON,[3] (Jonas,[2] Samuel,[1]) b. Nov. 27, 1821; m. Dec. 4, 1845, Albert G Newcomb of Fairlee, who d. 1900. She d. Feb. 4, 1896.

  Children:

  i. Lelia Annette, b. July 22, 1848; d. July 9, 1854.

  ii. Lester A., b. Sept. 13, 1855.

10 LYDIA JOHNSTON,[3] (Jonas,[2] Samuel,[1]) b. June 14, 1824; m. Robert Bradford Sargent of Orford, Jan. 1, 1851, (b. Jan. 28, 1826; d. July 9, 1892).

  Children:

  i. Delia Jane, b. Dec. 10, 1852; d. Aug. 17, 1876.

  ii. Lucius Hancock, b. Aug. 7, 1854; m. Ella Spaulding of Rumney, N. H.; 1 c.

  iii. Annette, b. May 23, 1858; d. Jan. 12. 1862.

11 MARY WHITE,[3] (Jonas,[2] Samuel,[1]) b. May 8, 1826; m. Jan. 6, 1848, John Bailey Sargent, (b. June 30, 1819).

  Children:

  i. Willis Bailey, b. Feb. 17, 1850.

  ii. Harvey Adrian, b. April 28, 1852.

  iii. Clara Bell, b. July 6, 1862.

  iv. Charles Johnston, b. Jan. 10, 1864.

  v. Hannah May, b. Dec. 1, 1865.

  vi. Frank Herbert, b. Jan. 8, 1870.

12 EDWIN,[3] (David,[2] Samuel,[1]) b. Newbury, Dec. 23, 1835; rem. to Kansas with his father; farmer, and in banking business; president of Eureka Bank, Eureka, Kan.; member of House of Representatives, Kansas, 1867-68; senator, 1869, '70, '89, '90; president of the Board of Regents of the state Normal School; trustee of Washburn College. He m. Aug. 15, 1863, Amelia Willis.
  Children:
  i.   David H., b. Feb. 13, 1865; graduated Washburn College.
  ii. Albert, b. Feb. 25, 1867; graduated Washburn College.
  iii. Mabel, b. March 25, 1872; m. 1897, a Mr. Finney.
  iv. George, b. Aug. 9, 1874.
  v.   Mary, b. Sept. 27, 1878.
  vi. Nettie, b. Aug. 27, 1880.
  vii. Florence, b. Dec. 8, 1883.

TUTTLE.

SAMUEL, son of Samuel and Betsey (Baker) Tuttle, of Acton, Mass., came to Antrim, N. H., from Temple, in 1816. He m. September, 1806, Mary Wright, of Concord, Mass. They had 16 children, of whom Jonas M., b. Acton, Mass., Dec. 31, 1807; m. Feb. 20, 1834, Mary. dau. of Samuel and Mary (Park) Dinsmore, (b. Sept. 22, 1810; d. Aug. 30, 1884). Rem. to Newbury, 1840; in railroad business; was in Kentucky when the Civil War broke out, and served 13 months in the 9th Kentucky cavalry; discharged Sept. 20, 1862. He d. Dec 2, 1883.
  Children:
  i.   Edwin, b. Antrim, N. H., Oct. 3, 1834; served three years in the 10th Vt. in the Civil War; was wounded three times in one day, and never fully recovered; res. in Newbury and Boston. He m. 1st, March 12, 1857, Ruth, dau. Hiram Whitcher, (b. Sept. 4, 1834; d. March 26, 1861). He m. 2d, Mary, dau. Matthew Temple, (d. 1882). He m. 3d, Alice Guild, who d. a few months after his own death. He d. Sept. 12, 1892. One dau., Lulu, by 2d m., lives in Boston.
  ii. Mary E., b. Antrim, N. H , Jan. 22, 1838; m. William Buchanan, q. v.
  iii. Susan D., b. Antrim, N. H., Dec. 19, 1839; m. Walter Buchanan, q. v.
  iv. Samuel, b. Newbury, Oct. 26, 1841; m. May 26, 1866, Rebecca Corruth; farmer on homestead; served three years in the Civil War in the 3d Vt.; wounded in the right shoulder in the battle of the Wilderness. He has communicated some interesting reminiscences of army life, which want of space compels us to omit. C., (1) Emma E., b. Dec 25, 1867; d. Dec. 18, 1871. (2) Ida Mae, b. Feb. 14, 1873; d. Aug. 3, 1873. (3) Robert I., b. Ryegate, Oct. 27, 1875. (4) Clara B., b. Newbury, March 4, 1878; graduated New Hampshire Normal School, 1900. (5) Burton H., b. Oct. 8, 1886. (6) George S., b. Feb. 21, 1887.
  v.   Clarissa, b. Aug. 19, 1844; m Nathan Hunter, q. v.; d. 1878.
  vi. Silas M., b. Jan. 16, 1851; m. May 19, 1875, Ella M. Maloon of Haverhill; res. Grinnell, Iowa, West Newbury, and Lowell, Mass ; harness maker. One c., L. Edna.

TUTTLE.

JOTHAM, one of the earliest settlers of Weare, N. H., m. Mary Worthley, and rem. to Goffstown. Timothy, their 3d son, b. July 20, 1764; m. 1st, Mary Ann, (b. Jan. 17, 1767; d. Feb. 4, 1821); m. 2d, Rachel,———————
(d. Sept. 3,1848). Rem. to Tunbridge, and d. there Feb. 22, 1851.
  Of their eight children, four came to Newbury:
  i.   Polly, b May 6, 1796; m. Absalom Brown.
  ii. Moses, b. July 7. 1798; m. Deborah Bennett; he came to Newbury and bought the Atwood sawmill; built in 1841, the house where H. H. Runnells lives; d. June 29, 1867.
  iv. Eli, b. April 10, 1802; lived on Leighton Hill one year; returned to Tunbridge; d. Sept. 30, 1883.
  vii. Elias S., b. April 10, 1802; m. Lois, dau. of Joshua and Lois King, (b. March 15,1804; d. Jan. 3,1877). Came to South Newbury in the fall after

the great fire of June 12, 1851; rebuilt the R. R. Aldrich house; farming and lumber business; d. Sept. 20, 1883. C., (1) infant son, b. and d. Dec. 12, 1834. (2) Elias J., b. Aug. 26, 1836; enlisted Dec. 26, 1861, Co. D, 12th Vt., ; served two years and enlisted for three more; mustered out June 28, 1865; farmer and mill owner. He m. 1st, Feb. 13, 1859, Mary Ann, dau. Abel Sargent, (b. July 21, 1838; d. Jan. 17, 1883). He m. 2d, May 16, 1886, Randilla F. Wheeler (Brown), (b. May 16, 1836; d. Aug. 7, 1888). He m. 3d. June 18, 1890, Dora D. Webster, (b. August 13,1865). No c. (3) Mary Ann, (b. April 28, 1840); m. as 2d wife, Oct. 20, 1861, Owen F. O'Malley, (b. Ireland, 1834; soldier in the British army; served in the Crimean War; was in the battles of Balaklava, Inkermann, and the taking of Sevastopol. His regiment was ordered to Quebec, whence he and George King deserted, and both settled in Newbury, where Mr. King d. in 1896. Enlisted Dec. 26, 1861, Co. D, 8th Vt ; re-enlisted, Jan. 5, 1864; mustered out July 17, 1865). Several c. He d. Newbury. She m. 2d, ——— Jones. (4) George L., b. Aug. 8, 1844. (army record, same as that of his brother, E. J.); m. 1st, dau. of Moses King, who d. Nov. 19, 1870; m. 2d, July 26, 1873, Helen L. (Clough) Bedell.

THRALL.

REV. SAMUEL ROWLEY, b. West Rutland, Jan. 16, 1811; graduated Middlebury College, 1835; in Andover Theological Seminary two years and a Congregational minister, 1839; pastor of Wells River church, 1839–47; after his dismission there he filled several pastorates. He m. Oct. 12, 1842, Miriam Hunt Bowman of Lexington, who d. Nov. 22, 1886. Eight c. Three sons became Congregational ministers, Rev. J. B. Thrall of Albany, N. Y., Rev. George S. Thrall, who d. 1886, and Rev. William H. Thrall, Home Missionary superintendent for South Dakota. Their sister m. Rev. A. W. Jenney, and they were missionaries in Turkey, several years. They returned to America and settled at Boscobel, Wis., where Rev. S. R. Thrall d. Feb. 27, 1894.

UNDERWOOD.

JOHN, b. Westford, Mass., Oct. 28, 1755; settled in Bradford in 1784; m. Mary Fassett, (b. Westford, June 15, 1759; d. Bradford, Oct. 21, 1821). He d. in Bradford Nov. 19, 1837.

Ten c., the first three b. in Westford, the rest in Bradford:
i. John, b. July 10, 1779; farmer in Bradford; d. Oct. 22, 1851.
ii. Benjamin, b. Feb. 3, 1782; farmer in Bradford; d. Aug. 25, 1863.
iii. Silas, b. Dec. 7, 1783; farmer in Hardwick; d. April 24, 1859. Hon. Levi Underwood of Burlington was his son.
iv. Mary, b. Nov. 2, 1785; m. Sans Niles of Fairlee; d Aug. 23, 1860.
v. Russell, b. April 9, 1787; carpenter of Lyman, N. H., and St. Johnsbury; d. Dec. 23, 1871.
vi. Levi, b. March 7, 1789; farmer; d. in St. Johnsbury, Feb. 19, 1872.
vii. Timothy, b. May 21, 1791; clothier; d. at Hardwick, Dec. 25, 1870.
viii. Reuben, b. May 24, 1793; farmer in Craftsbury; d. Jan. 31, 1876.
ix. Joseph, b. Oct. 2, 1796; Cong. minister; d. July 27, 1876.
x. Abel, b April 6, 1799.

ABEL, b. April 6, 1799. Fitted for college at Thetford Academy; graduated Dartmouth College, 1824. Studied law with Gen. Fletcher of Lyndon; admitted to the bar, April, 1827; in practice at Wells River, 1828 till death. (See Judge Leslie's chapter on Wells River). State's Attorney, 1839–41; United State's District Attorney, 1848–52; Judge of Circuit Court, 1854–57. During the construction of the Vermont Central R. R. he was in company with Judge Adams of Grand Isle and Judge Curtis of Westfield, a commissioner for the settlement of land damages, attending that enterprise. Director and president of the bank at Wells River. Town representative, 1861–62. He m. July 12, 1827, Emily, dau. of Elisha and

Elizabeth (Flynn) Rix, (b. Royalton, Jan. 16, 1805; d. Oct. 15, 1861). They were members of the Cong. ch. at Wells River. He d. April 20, 1879. Children:

i. Elizabeth, b. March 31, 1830; m. July 24, 1856, B. B. Clark of St. Johnsbury. C., (1) Carrie E., b. Apr. 11, 1857. (2) Emily L., b. Aug. 27, 1858. (3) Susan E., b. July 24, 1860. (4) Alice G., b. Sept. 12, 1863. (5) George B., b. Jan. 24, 1866; d. April 13, 1872.

ii. George Rix, b. April 15, 1832. Went south and engaged in business, and d. at Gainsville, Ala., Oct. 10, 1856; buried at Wells River.

iii. Emma R. Ellis, b. Feb. 13, 1835; d. May 15, 1839.

iv. Ellen M., b. May 18, 1840; m. 1st, July 14, 1858, Wm. Roscoe Dean, who d. Aug. 13, 1861. She m. 2d, April 10, 1872, Horace D. Hickok, a dentist at Wells River and Malone, N. Y., where they reside. C., (1) Alice, b. Sept. 20, 1860; d. July 2, 1861. (2) Harry Abel, b. Dec. 16, 1867; d. Sept. 23, 1874. (3) Nellie H., b. June 17, 1877; d. Nov. 16, 1887.

v. Susan A., b. Sept. 2. 1842; m. 1st, Jan. 25, 1859, George A. Damon, who was an officer in the Union army. She d. Nov. 3. 1895. C., (1) Emily J., b. Oct. 31, 1861; m. June 7, 1882, George P. Arthur, b. Scotland. At one time cashier Bradford Bank; res. Montpelier. C., a, Leslie P., b. March 17, 1883; d. Dec. 24, 1889. b, Malcolm Underwood, b. Jan. 22, 1886. (2) Ellen D., b. Oct. 16, 1864; m. 2d, March 7, 1876, to John P. Flanders, who d. Jan. 7, 1894.

WADDELL.

JOHN, b. 1732, in Erskine, Scotland; m. 1761, Rebecca Allison, b. 1738. William, grandfather of John, was one of those who were persecuted for their faith in the reign of Charles II, and had many adventures in escaping from the King's troops. James, son of William, was father of John, who came to Ryegate in 1774, and was one of the first settlers of that town. Owing to the Revolutionary War, he was unable to bring his family over till 1784. He d. in Barnet in 1822, aged 90 years, and his wife in 1795, aged 56 years. Of their seven c., John Jr., b. July 1767, m. Severance Patton of Candia, N. H., about 1796, and settled on Jefferson Hill in 1815. Children, all b. in Barnet:

i. Betsey.

ii. John.

iii. Jane, who lived on Jefferson Hill, and d. there Aug. 13, 1896, aged 92 years, 6 months.

iv. Rebecca, who m. Samuel Gibson, q. v.

v. William, who settled in Bath.

vi. Robert, never m.; settled on the old farm on Jefferson Hill where he d. Dec. 18, 1880, aged 79 years.

vii. Jennett, m. James Halley.

viii. James, a mechanic, lived in Groton; d. July 18, 1846.*

JOHN, son of John the emigrant, b. Barnet Dec. 14, 1797. He came with his parents to Jefferson Hill in 1815. He m. Feb. 12, 1832, in Hardwick, Mrs. Mary Wheeler, b. Glastonbury, Conn., dau of John Strong. She d. at Providence, R. I., Nov. 2, 1880. John Waddell settled in Boltonville in 1832, and opened a shop where he made and repaired furniture. He d. in Newbury, Feb. 26, 1860. Children:

i. Mary Elvira, b. May 20, 1833; m. J. Henry Wilbur of Providence, R. I., where she still lives.

ii. Harriet Jane, b. Jan. 13, 1836; m. Henry G. Rollins, q. v.

iii. John S., b. Dec. 17, 1838; d. Providence, R. I., May 8. 1881.

iv. Julia A., b. Nov. 16, 1839; d. Providence, July 8, 1865.

v. Lucy Josephine, b. Jan. 3, 1846; m. J. Frank Brown of Providence, R. I.

*The above particulars were from Edward Miller.

WALDRON.

Isaac, b. Warner, N. H., January, 1778; came to Newbury, 1800, and resided here until death, Oct. 30, 1853. He m. June 20, 1802, Abigail, dau. of Joseph Chamberlin, (d. Oct. 3, 1860).
Children:
  i. John, b. Oct. 27, 1802.
  ii. Isaac, b. Jan. 22, 1804.
  iii. Hannah, b. July 30, 1807.
  iv. Sarah, b. March 1, 1813; m. April 5, 1838, James Renfrew, Jr.
  v. Nancy, b. July 16, 1814.
1 vi. Benjamin, b. Dec. 22, 1816.

1. Benjamin, b. Dec. 22, 1816; farmer in Newbury; served in the Union Army; enlisted Nov. 28, 1861; mustered in Feb. 18, 1862, into Co. C, 8th Vt., for three years; went to Louisiana with Butler, and was in several battles near Port Hudson; re-enlisted, Jan. 4, 1864; was with Sheridan in the Valley; in the battles of Winchester, Fisher's Hill and Cedar Creek; taken prisoner, Oct. 19, 1864; confined in Libby Prison and at Salisbury, N. C.; exchanged April, 1865, and d. three days later at Annapolis, Md. He m. 1844, Laura H., dau. of F. G. McAllister.
Children:
  i. John Mervin, b. March 7, 1845; enlisted Dec. 3, 1861, in Co. C, 8th Vt.; mustered in Feb. 18, 1862; went to Louisiana with Butler's expedition, and was in several battles near Port Hudson; wounded at Port Hudson; went to New York on detached duty with prisoners; re-enlisted Jan. 4, 1864; was with Sheridan in the Valley; in battles of Winchester, Fisher's Hill and Cedar Creek; wounded at the last battle, Oct. 19, 1864, in the right lung; in hospital at Brattleboro till Jan. 1, 1865; in service till discharged June 28, 1865; farmer and carpenter. He m. Feb. 23, 1870, Lucy Ann, dau. of Richard Patterson. C., (1) Richard Herbert, b. March 25, 1871; m. June 22, 1898, Addie H. Corey, (b. Feb. 5, 1878). (2) Maggie, b. April 12; d. Aug. 25, 1873. (3) Francis M., b. Aug. 17, 1874. (4) Jennie, b. Sept. 22, 1876; m. April 30, 1898, Henry G. Hatch of Groton, (b. Jan. 25, 1872). (5) George A., b. Aug. 13, 1878. (6) Laura, b. Oct. 11, 1881. (7) Edith A., b. Nov. 18, 1886.
  ii. Helen Elizabeth, b. Nov. 21, 1876; m. Oct. 7, 1869, Samuel H. Patten; res. Woburn, Mass. C., (1) Bessie B., b. July, 1870; d. (2) Lewis, b. June 15, 1872. (3) Mabel E., b. Sept. 8, 1874. (4) Joseph F., b. Sept. 3, 1874. (5) Charlotte H., b. March 29; d. September, 1880.
  iii. Abigail N., b. July 12, 1848; m. Jan. 1, 1868, Austin G. French of Bedford, N. H.; lived in Newbury; rem. 1872, to Woburn, Mass. C., (1) George F., b. Newbury, Sept. 2, 1868; m. Margaret A. Hall; d. April 5, 1899. C., Hazel and Ruth H. (2) Walter M., b. Nov. 29, 1872; m. Eva M. Wilson of Roxbury, Mass. (3) Frank W., b. June 29, 1876.
  iv. Harriet S., b. Sept. 29, 1849; m. Edward H. Patten of Bedford, N. H.; res. Woburn, Mass. C., (1) Laura B., b. July 16, 1874; d. Aug. 8, 1878. (2) Lucia K., b. March 17, 1876.
  v. Benjamin F., b. May 22, 1855; res. Woburn, Mass.; m. Nov. 9, 1881, Gertrude M. Richardson of Woburn. C., (1) Wilbur R., b. July 21, 1882, (2) Raymond E., b. June 16, 1893. (3) Marion F., b. Nov. 10; d. Dec. 8, 1898.
  vi. Laura Belle, b. Aug. 24, 1862; m. Feb. 7, 1881, John B. Thompson; res. East Corinth. C., (1) Hattie B., b. Sept. 13, 1881. (2) Amanda, b. Jan. 6, 1883. (3) Helen G., b. Aug. 29, 1884. (4) John F., b. Feb. 6, 1886. (5) Lucia L., b. March 9, 1899.

WALLACE.

Col. William was b. near Glasgow in Scotland, and came to Newbury, says Mr. Perry, in 1775. He was bred to mercantile pursuits in Glasgow, and began business at once in Newbury, in a building which stood near the present residence of Henry W. Bailey at the Ox-bow. This building he moved, about 1779, to the present site of the library. He enlarged it, and kept store there, until he erected the house which afterward became the Spring Hotel, when he rem. the earlier building to the other side of the street, where it still stands, the back part of the old Newbury House. "It was." says Mr. Perry, "for a series of years, the principal store for trading, for all the northern towns of Vermont, and did a vast amount of business. And from all that appears, had he been less generous and kindhearted to his debtors, and more careful and exact in the management of his business, he might have died in the possession of vast wealth. His business was extensive, and his influence great, for a number of years, but he lived to see his riches take to themselves wings, and flee away." He was sheriff of the county, and colonel in the militia. He was clerk to General Bayley, during a part. at least, of the war, and many of the latter's military papers are in his handwriting, which was as clear and plain as type. Col. Wallace was frequently dispatched by Bayley on important missions, and himself served as a private in Capt. Frye Bayley's Co., which went to Saratoga in 1777. Col. Wallace m. Hannah, dau. of Dudley Carleton of Haverhill, Mass. (b. Jan. 7, 1754; d. Oct. 5, 1831). He d. in a house which stood where the railroad depot is now, but the date, and the place of his burial in the Ox-bow cemetery are unknown.

Several children, the names of all are not known:

 i. Dudley Carleton, became a physician.
1 ii. John, a lawyer; d. July 1826.
2 iii. Moses, farmer and merchant.
 iv. Ann, b. April 29, 1794, d. April 26, 1876; m. William Brock, q. v.

1 JOHN,[2] (William,[1]) b. Newbury, Feb. 10, 1790; graduated Dartmouth College, 1808; principal of New Salem (Mass.) Academy, 1808-11, studying law meantime. Admitted to the bar in August, 1811, and opened an office in Newbury where he practiced till death in 1826. He was more fond of literature than of the law, and contributed to the public press of his day. He also had an office in Haverhill for some time. Two of his public addresses were printed. (See Bibliography of Newbury). Mr. Wallace never married.

2 MOSES, son of Col. William Wallace, b. Newbury, about 1783; was a farmer and business man in this town, but rem. about 1808 to West Topsham, where he kept store many years. In the war of 1812 he was an officer in the Topsham militia, which were called out by the Burlington alarm. They marched as far as Bolton, where they were met by the news of the victory of Plattsburg, and returned home. He m. Betsey, dau. of Dea. Thomas McKeith, (b. Topsham, April 16, 1786; d.)

Children, (dates of birth, except the first, from Topsham records):

3 i. Victor M., b. Newbury, Aug. 22, 1807.
 ii. Sally McKeith, b. Oct. 12, 1809.
 iii. Caroline J., b. June 20, 1813.
4 iv. Andrew J., b. April 12, 1815.
 vi. Hannah, b. Feb. 14, 1817.
 vii. John, b. Feb. 10, 1819.

3 VICTOR M.,[3] (Moses,[2] William,[1]) b. Newbury, Aug. 22, 1807. A man of remarkable ingenuity; made several improvements upon the clarionet while still very young. In 1835 he rem. to St. Louis, Mo , where he opened a shop in which he made and repaired guns and pistols. In that year he perfected the model and obtained the patent of the first breech-loading pistol. In 1841 he m. Isabel Roy, (b. Scotland, 1819; d. Keleo, Washington, Jan. 13, 1899). In May, 1847, with three other families, they started for Oregon in wagons drawn by oxen, and reached Oregon City about Dec. 10, where he made the dies with which the first gold pieces were struck at the Oregon mint. He made the first threshing machine used in Oregon and the first printing press. When the gold excitement broke out in California, he started for the mines, and was with the first party of 60 men, who opened the way from the Williamette to the Sacramento river. In 1850, he rem. to Washington Territory, and took up land, on which he spent the rest of his life. He held various county offices, and help build the first schoolhouse in what is now the state of Washington. He d. Keleo, Wash., Sept. 5, 1895.

4 ANDREW J.,[3] (Moses,[2] William,[1]), b. Topsham, April 12, 1815; hotel keeper at West Topsham; m. 1st, June 19, 1842, Caroline, dau. of Jonathan Jenness. Four c. He m. 2d, Kate, dau. John Wallace of Newbury, (b. June 9, 1837; d. Sept. 10, 1886). C. He d. March 9, 1888.

WALLACE.

JAMES, came from Scotland the place from which he emigrated being Kinsland, near Glasgow. With his wife, Christian (Hoag), and three sons he settled in that part of Newbury called Wallace Hill, southwest from Wells River, in 1801. The family came to New York and thence to Hartford, proceeding up the Connecticut River in a flat boat run by Joseph Chamberlin. There were forty persons in the party and their boat was tied to an elm tree which is still standing at the foot of Ingalls Hill. James Wallace was a relative of Col. William Wallace and was induced, it is said, by the latter to settle here. Robert Fulton,. Andrew Buchanan and others were of the same party of emigrants. James Wallace bought a farm which was cleared by Charles Bayley and sold to Ashbell Buell in 1796. His house, demolished some years ago, was south of the one built by his son, James, where the McGinnis family has long lived. He d. Feb. 28, 1814, in his 47th year, (cem. record), and his wife Dec. 29, 1845, (ch. record). Their three sons, William, James and John, were b. in Scotland, and a daughter, Jane, was b. in Newbury.

Children:

1 i. William, b. 1793; d. Jan. 5, 1877.
2 ii. James, b. July 28, 1794; d. Sept., 1883.
3 iii. John, b. 1797; d. Aug. 12, 1861.
    iv. Jane, b. Newbury, April 18, 1803; m. Capt. Charles Smith, q. v.; d. June 30, 1890.

1 WILLIAM, b. Scotland, 1793, came to America with his parents in 1801; lived eleven years in the family of Gen. James Whitelaw in Ryegate, whose dau., Marion, he m. Aug. 18, 1814. In 1818, he came to Newbury and bought the William Peach farm, as it was then called, on which he lived till his death. He was a very kindly, hospitable man, and was called "Uncle Will Wallace," and his wife was called "Aunt Will." She inherited many of the traits which distinguished her father. After the death of William Wallace the farm became that of his son Robert, who had always lived at home. The present house, erected in 1892, is the eighth dwelling house which has been built on that farm. William d. Jan. 5, 1877, aged 84. Mrs. Wallace was b. Jan. 31, 1787; d. Jan. 5, 1866.

Their children were:

i. James, b. Ryegate, May 15, 1815; d. 1850.
ii. Christian, b. Ryegate, April 29, 1817; m. March 25, 1841, Hazen Ford, and d. a few years later.
iii. William, b. Newbury, March 27, 1819; lived in Newbury most of his life; was a peddler, etc. He m. July 2, 1843, Susan, dau. Reuben Leighton. He d. in Cambridge, Mass., Jan. 19, 1894. C., (1) Ellen, m. Barron Sulham. (2) Georgiana, m. Jan. 1, 1868, Hugh Cameron. (3) Kirk, d. un-m. (4) Gertrude, m. Frank Sawvin.
iv. John, b. July 29, 1821; farmer, owning in succession several farms in this town. Rem. to Green Mountain, Iowa, 1868. Farmer there till 1874, when he went into the livery business at Grinnell, Iowa. Returned to Newbury to spend the later years of his life in 1897. He m. March 3, 1845, Mary Ann, dau. of Reuben Leighton. C., all b. in Newbury. (1) William Robert, b. April 4, 1847; res. Marshalltown, Iowa. (2) Elmer, b. July 20, 1848; railroad conductor; res. Newport; m. Ellen Stebbins. (3) Adeline, b. Sept. 3, 1850; m. William Crawford. (4) Frank, b. March 30, 1853; m. E. L. Bernard. (5) Kate, b. Sept. 24, 1856; m. Daniel Bartlett as 2d wife.
v. Robert, b. Oct. 27, 1822; farmer on the homestead; a very quiet, industrious, kindly man; m. Olivia, dau. ot Daniel Richardson; d. 1893. C., Bertha, b. April 2, 1862; m. W. M. Rollins.
vi. Jane, b. 1829; m. Feb. 25, 1858, John Reid, q. v.; d. Jan. 17, 1895.

2 JAMES, b. Glasgow, Scotland, July 28, 1794; farmer on the homestead, until past middle life, when he rem. to the village; captain in the militia, and generally known by his military title. In 1847, when the smallpox broke out in this town, and it was almost impossible to secure anyone to take care of the sick, James Wallace laid aside his affairs, and took care of several of these until they recovered. For this he refused to receive any compensation, saying that it was a man's duty to assist the distressed. For this act a vote of thanks was passed by the town, in March meeting, 1848. He m. 1st, March 15, 1827, Ann, dau. of Samuel Gibson, (b. June 12, 1805; d. March 28, 1836). He m. 2d. January, 1837, at Barre, Mrs. Rebekah Lawson, who d. 1860. He m. 3d, March 1, 1865, at Barnet, Mrs. Matilda Towle, who d. at St. Johnsbury, 1897. He d. Newbury Sept. 1, 1883.

Children, both by 1st marriage:
i. Louisa G., b. Sept. 26, 1829; m. Jan. 2, 1848, George W. Avery, 2d. She is now a widow living in Wisconsin. Two daus., both married. One has four children.
ii. William K., b. Oct. 9, 1833; learned the trade of watchmaker and jeweler, and carried on the business in Newbury from 1855 till 1872, except that he served in the Union army, nine months as a private in Co. H, 12th Vt. Manufacturer of jewelry in Boston, 1872-74. In the watch and jewelry business at Woodsville, May, 1875 to 1889. During this time he dealt much in horses. In 1889, he bought a farm in Haverhill, near Woodsville, called Wallace Hill horse farm. He m. Jan. 20, 1859, Harriott C., dau. of Arad S. Kent.

3 JOHN WALLACE, son of James Wallace, was b. in Scotland in 1797. He m. Dec. 7, 1822, Lucia Kasson of Topsham and they lived on the same farm, in the house which they built, until their decease. These farm buildings were burned Feb. 25, 1894. He d. Aug. 12, 1861, aged 64 years. She d. Oct. 19, 1888, aged 93 years 4 months. They had ten c.

Children:
i. Mary A., m. William S. Magoon, Sept. 26, 1854; d. May 22, 1876, leaving one son, Frank P. Magoon, who is in the office of the Adams Express Company in Boston and resides in Somerville, Mass. He m. Frances Snow, and they have three c., Gladys, William L., and Frances Louise.
ii. Erastus H., m. Myra Chamberlain. C., (1) George Franklin, m. Lula Bell of Minnesota; he d. July 15, 1899 in Newbury, aged 42 years 22 days. (2) Ida, d. in 1895. (3) Eddie d. in infancy.
iii. Jane H.. m. Richard Doe, q. v.
iv. Anna H., m. Sept. 26, 1854, Frank H. Pecker. She d. July 7, 1863, aged 36 years. He d. Jan. 10, 1862. C., (1) Hattie Louise, d. June 1. 1873, aged 17 years. (2) Lizzie A., d. July 16, 1863, aged 5 years. (3) Katherine Wallace, b. Aug. 10, 1861, at Rutland. She m. Colonel Frank West Rollins of Concord, N. H. They have one son. Col. Rollins is a member of the banking house of E. H. Rollins & Sons of Boston, Mass., and was elected governor of New Hampshire in 1898.
v. Lucia K., m. Samuel Danforth, who d. October, 1873. Two c. (1) John W., d. Sept. 15, 1882. (2) Frank P., m. Ina Wheaton of West Concord, and lives in Newbury.
vi. Kate N., m. Andrew Jackson Wallace of West Topsham. She d. Sept. 10, 1886, aged 53 years. He d. March 9, 1888. aged 73 years. Two c. (1) John L., now of Barre. (2) Seth E., now of Brockton, Mass.
vii. Sarah K., m. in Oregon, Joseph Sawyer, both returning to Newbury, in 1881. He d. at the Wallace homestead Sept. 13, of that year, aged 62 years.
viii. James, now resides on a farm between Wallace Hill, where his grandfather, James Wallace, settled, and the old homestead, the John Wallace farm, called the "Old Avery place." He served in the Civil War, in Co. H, 12th Vt., from Oct. 4, 1862, till March 13, 1863.
ix. Lizzie C., m. William S. Magoon, and lived in Keene, N. H., where she d. Aug. 14, 1891, aged 48. W. S. Magoon d. in Newbury, Nov. 18, 1894, aged 51 years.
x. Charles S., was a soldier in the Civil War. He d. Jan. 22, 1884, aged 38 years.

WATKINS.

DR. EUSTACE VIRGIL, b. Stockbridge, May 11, 1823; educated at Royalton and Charleston Academies; studied medicine with Drs. Crosby and Peaslee, and graduated at Dartmouth Medical College, 1850; came to Newbury in that year, and was in practice here till near his death. He was esteemed skillful in his profession, and was frequently called to consult with leading physicians in Northern New England. His practice was not confined to this vicinity, but he was often called to distant places to render service both as physician and surgeon. His health failed some years before his death, and he spent some time in London, under the care of eminent physicians. Member of the Congregational church and of several medical associations. He m. April 14, 1851, Emily, dau. Dr. Ira and Sophia (Hazen) Tenney, of Hartford. He d. Newbury, Dec. 18, 1888.

Children:
i. George Tenney, b. Oct. 12, 1855; d. Oct. 19, 1860.
ii. Emily Sophia, b. April 30, 1858; m. Oct. 9, 1888, Albert W. Silsby; res. Newbury. C., Emily Tenney, b. Northampton, Mass., March 28, 1890.
iii. Lucia Anna, b. Jan. 21, 1864; m. June 15, 1892, Edwin A. Bayley, q. v.
iv. Harris Ralph, b. March 8, 1866; graduated at Dartmouth College, 1888, and at Burlington Medical College; in practice at Burlington where he is city physician; member of the medical staff of Mary Fletcher Hospital, and one of the faculty of the medical department of Vermont University. He m. Sept. 26, 1894, Nellie Elizabeth Chapman of Hartford, N. Y. C., Eustace Virgil, b. Burlington, Feb. 28, 1901.

WATSON.

DR. HENRY L. and PORTER B., brothers, lived here in the '60s. (The following dates are from Coffin's History of Boscawen and Salisbury).

HENRY L., b. Salisbury, N. H , Feb. 10, 1811; educated at Salisbury and Philips Academies; graduated Vt. Medical College, 1848; in practice, Guildhall, 1849, where he was state senator, till he came here, about 1860. and was in practice here till 1867. when he rem. to Littleton, N. H. He m. 1st, June 4, 1840, *Roxanna, dau. Jesse Hughes of Maidstone, who d. 1850. He m. 2d, Mary J. Hardy. She d. August, 1884. He d. Jan. 22, 1894. Two c., Henry Porter and Ellen. The former, b. Guildhall, Jan. 18, 1844; graduated Dartmouth Medical College, 1867; in practice several years at Haverhill, but now at Manchester, N. H. He has traveled extensively.

PORTER B., b. Corinth, during a short residence of his father's family there; came to Newbury 1865, from Salisbury, N. H., and bought the Nathan Bartlett farm; rem. to Littleton, N. H., 1869. He m. Luvia E. Ladd of Lunenburg. He d. Littleton, 1894. Several c., of whom Irving Allison, the eldest, b. Sept. 6, 1849; educated in Newbury; studied medicine with his uncle, and graduated at Vermont University, (medical department), 1871; in practice, Northumberland, N. H., 1871-81, when he was appointed secretary of the State Board of Health, which important position he still holds; res. at Concord. He m. 1872, Laura A. Farr of Littleton. Dr. Watson has written much upon medical subjects.

*NOTE. John Hugh, grandfather of Mrs. Watson, was b. in Musselburgh, Scotland, 1737; was empressed on board a British man-of-war at the age of 16. From this he escaped, and went to Hampstead, N. H., where he m. Anna Harriman. He came to Haverhill in 1762, his being the seventh family to settle in Coos. He was a grantee of Newbury and rem. here, bought a farm on the Ox-bow, which he sold, receiving his pay in Continental money, which became worthless before he could purchase other land with it. He settled in Maidstone, in 1781, where he d. Sept. 27, 1814, his wife having died the year before. They had eight c., and among their descendants are many prominent people, especially in Western New York and Cleveland and Chicago. The name is usually spelled Hughes.

*WEBBER.

I. EDWARD, of Ipswich, Mass., who m. Patience Hobbs, in 1703.

II. WILLIAM, b. Ipswich, April 22, 1711; settled Methuen, Mass., ; m. 1st, Mary Wells of Ipswich, who d. 1753; m. 2d, 1754, Lucy Kimball of Wenham. Twelve c.

III. ANDREW, b. Feb. 18, 1763, at Methuen; m. Nov. 29, 1784, Lucy Cross of Methuen, and they rem. to the vicinity of Bath, N. H. He was a stone mason. His wife d. in Bath, June 11, 1828. He m. 2d, Mrs. Mary Kincaid. He lived in Bath, Benton, Lyman and Landaff. He d. May 10, 1845, and was buried in Bath.
   Children:
   i. Joseph.
1 ii. Andrew, b. July 27, 1794.
2 iii. William, b. about September, 1797.
   iv. Lucy, b, Feb. 3, 1799; m. Jan. 16, 1822, Sylvester Gordon of Landaff, N. H., who d. Oct. 16, 1873. She d. at North Haverhill, Jan. 19, 1890. Their daus., Martha and Lucy A., were the 1st and 2d wives of Caleb Wells of North Haverhill.
   v. Nathaniel Peabody, b. March 3, 1801 ; m. Mary, sister of Sylvester Gordon, and lived in Landaff, where she d. 1862, and he rem. to Manchester, Iowa, and d. Aug. 16, 1878.
   vi. John Cross, b. Aug. 20, 1803; preacher and farmer; d. Sanbornton, N. H., March, 1868. Eight c.
   vii. Horace, b. Lyman, April 19, 1807; Free Will Baptist minister in Benton, Haverhill, and Ossipee, where he d. Dec. 30, 1889. He m. Relief Tyler of Benton, N. H.; five c.

1 ANDREW J., b. July 27, 1794; m. Oct. 31, 1816, Sophia Wilkins, (b. Sept. 18, 1794; d. Jan. 3, 1840). They lived in Newbury till 1828, when they settled in Monterey, Schuyler County, N. Y., where he d. June 17, 1847. She d. Jan. 3, 1840.
   Twelve children, the five eldest born Newbury:
   i. Lorenzo, b. Newbury, Sept. 12, 1817; settled with his parents; rem. to Elmira, N. Y., where he d. Nov. 15, 1884; representative in the New York Assembly, 1864-65. He m. Feb. 27, 1840, Jane A. Welch. Three c.
   ii. Azro Buck, b. Newbury, Aug. 29, 1819; m. 1842, Hannah Lockwood, of Monterey; d. Aug. 11, 1883, and she d. Dec. 13, 1883.
   iii. Samuel Wilkins, b. Newbury, May 25, 1823; settled in Monterey, but rem. 1855, to Ionia County, Mich., where he is a farmer and banker. He m. June 27, 1846, Maryette Bowen, who d. April 8, 1859; m. 2d, June 8, 1860, Harriet Bowen. Five c. Res. Lyons, Mich.
   iv. George W., b. Newbury, Nov. 25, 1825; engaged in lumbering in Manistee County, Mich., 1852-58; rem. to Ionia, Mich , where he was in banking business and president of the 2d National Bank; was also in lumber business with his brother, A. J. Webber, in Mecosta County; twice mayor of Ionia, and member of the 47th Congress from the 5th district of Michigan. Three times m. Two c.
   v. Oscar, b. Newbury, June 25, 1827; merchant at Ionia, Mich., and in banking business at Stanton, Mich.
   vi. Andrew Jackson, b. Monterey, Jan. 7, 1831; in lumber and banking business with his brother, George W. Webber.
   These brothers had five sisters, all b. in Monterey, N. Y,

2 WILLIAM, b. about 1797; m. Mary, dau. John Tewksbury, q. v. They settled on the farm where the late William Wallace, and his son, Robert, long lived, and built the old house, now deserted of all its former inmates. She d. Jan. 17, 1846, and he m. 2d, Mrs. Louisa Heath, and d. July 23, 1870.
   Children, all b. in Newbury:
3 i. Charles, b. Oct. 26, 1816; d, October 1, 1899.
   ii. Harriet, b. Oct. 9, 1817; m. Rodolphus Frizzle. (He was a student at

---

*In part from a pamphlet prepared by Lorenzo Webber, Portland, Michigan.

Newbury Seminary, and worked his way partly through college, and preached somewhat as a Methodist itinerant. He lost his mind, wandered off in the woods and was never found). Five c., of whom Charles H., lives in Lunenburg.

iii. Ellen, b. Jan. 27, 1820; m. Thomas Frizzle; d. Woodsville, N. H., Sept., 1892. One son.

iv. Eliza, b. April 11, 1821; m. Grove A. Frizzle. He fell in C. E. Brock's barn, and was killed, 1890. She d. March 28, 1872.

v. William, b. Dec. 14, 1823; m. Hannah Larkin; d. Lynn, Mass., long ago.

vi. Philip, b. April 7, 1825; d. Dec. 18, 1853.

vii. Mary Ann, b. April 21, 1831; m. Feb. 10, 1849, Alfred P. Webber; d. Omaha, Neb., Aug. 13, 1874. Two c.

viii. Andrew J., b. Sept. 22, 1834; has been employed in railroad construction; m. Sept. 20, 1851, Sybil Gordon, who d. Newbury, Nov. 16, 1875. He rem. to Rockland County, N. Y., and m. again. One c.

ix. Martha, b. Sept. 31, 1836; m. Sept. 9, 1858, Winthrop Cline, an engineer on the Passumpsic railroad, who d. Oct. 23, 1890. One c living.

x. Abner, b. May 21, 1838; section foreman on the Passumpsic railroad many years, but bought a farm near Concord, N. H., where he d. August, 1901. He m. November, 1858, Maria Heath, who d. Sept. 21, 1887. C., Henry, Frank and Ernest.

3 CHARLES, b. Oct. 26, 1816; stone mason; m. 1835, Susan, dau. Benjamin Leet, who d. June 1886. He d. October, 1899.

Children, who survived infancy:

i. Russell, b. Nov. 24, 1838; res. Groton.

ii. Elizabeth M., b. Jan. 20, 1841; res. Thetford.

iii. Louisa, b. Aug. 4, 1842; res. St. Albans; m. Alvin Chamberlin.

iv. Mary E., b. Dec. 6, 1843; res. Woodsville, N. H.

4 v. Phillip, b. Aug. 11, 1845.

vi. George, b. Feb. 20, 1847; res. in Groton.

vii. William, b. Oct. 11, 1850; d. Thetford, 1874.

viii. Charles, b. 1856; d. in the west, Sept. 2, 1894.

4 PHILLIP, b. Aug. 11, 1845; served in the Civil War; farmer on the "Andrew Grant place." He m. Sept. 26, 1868, Mary A. Scruton.

Children:

i. Andrew J., b. Sept. 13, 1869.

ii. Clara B., b. April 28, 1871; m. Fred D. White.

iii. Lillian E., b. May 17, 1873; m. Oct. 4, 1899, Herbert A. Wheeler.

iv. Grace, b. July 28, 1878.

v. Martena, b. Oct. 15, 1881.

vi. Etta M., b. May 29, 1884.

vii. Herman J., b. Oct. 24, 1886.

viii. Perley P., b. Dec. 30, 1891.

WEBSTER.

Of this family we should know little or nothing except for some facts gathered by David Johnson, and transmitted by him to Rev. Grant Powers. They are, in substance: That, in the fall of 1777, Richard Wallace of Thetford, and Ephraim Webster of Newbury, swam across Lake Champlain, between Fort Ticonderoga and Mount Independence, bearing dispatches from General Lincoln to the commanding officer on the east side of the lake. The water was cold, the distance they had to make, about two miles. It was in the night, and the men came near perishing, but gained the shore, and delivered their dispatches. Mr. Johnson further says that Webster was residing among the Oneida Indians, who made him their chief, the last he knew of him. Our early records make mention of Asa, Lemuel, Samuel, Ephraim and Ephraim, Jr. Ephraim was here very early, as he is mentioned in 1773. He appears to have owned land on Musquash Meadow, and "Ephraim Webster's north bound" is frequently mentioned in old records. Mr. Johnson says that he came from New Chester, (now Hill), N. H., and in 1787, Ephraim Webster of New Chester sells land on Musquash Meadow, by which we may infer that he returned to that place. In the Ox-bow cemetery one of the oldest stones marks the grave of

"Phebe, wife of Ephraim Webster, who d. May 21, 1775, in her 41st year."
It was probably the son, Ephraim, who swam the lake, and afterward
joined the Indians. Stearns' History of Rindge, N. H., mentions one
Ebenezer Webster, b. Newbury, 1773, who afterward lived in Rindge, but
d. in Piermont in 1850.

WEBSTER.

PETER, b. in Salem, N. H.; m. Mary Webster, (b. July, 1774; d. May 26, 1861).
Settled in the Lime Kiln neighborhood, and their c. were b. there. He d.
Newbury, Jan. 25, 1835.
Children:
    i. Hannah W.
1 ii. James R.
   iii. Peter, m. Mehetabel Perry.
   iv. Stephen, lived in Ryegate; m. Cynthia Sly.
    v. Mary, m. ———— Randall.
   vi. Anna, m. Josiah Dow; lived in Newbury. One son, Henry G., lives here.
  vii. Benjamin, m. Anna Woods.
 viii. Wealthy, m. Stillman Stevens.

1 JAMES R., m. 1833, Charlotte, dau. of Asa Coburn, Jr., (b. Feb. 7, 1810; d.
Thetford, April 20, 1900). He d. May 5, 1871.
Children:
    i. Harriet, b. Jan. 1, 1836; d. Aug. 24, 1841.
   ii. Sarah, b. June 3, 1838; m. John Forsythe; d. Mechanics Falls, Me., May
26, 1870.
   iii. Albert, b. Aug. 2, 1844; d. July 30, 1852.
   iv. Emery, b. Sept. 7, 1847; mustered into 17th Vt. Vols. Dec. 31, 1863; d. in
hospital at Washington, Feb. 15, 1864.
    v. Charlotte, b. March 11, 1849; m. Sept. 16, 1871, J. G. Lord of Thetford.
Three c.
   vi. Anna M., b. Dec. 11, 1851; m. Sept. 15, 1897, C. N. Balch of North
Thetford.
  vii. Mary Addie, b May 4, 1854; m. March 4, 1874, Frank Stevens of Thetford.
Three c.
 viii. Hattie, b. April 10, 1858; m. Sept. 13, 1876, Charles Emerson of Thetford.
Two c.

WEBSTER.

DAVID, b. Leslie, Fifeshire, Scotland, 1771; he and his sons left Scotland May,
1834, were shipwrecked at the mouth of the Saint Lawrence, May 14,
and reached Newbury about the middle of June with their families. He d.
Nekimi, Wis., 1866. His farm is now J. M. Waldron's.
His sons were:
1 i. David, b. Leslie, 1796; d. Elo, Wis., August, 1879.
2 ii. Robert, b. Leslie, 1798; d. Oskosb, Wis., October, 1884.

1 DAVID. m. Agnes Shairp, (b. Leslie, Scotland; d. Newbury, Feb. 24, 1855, aged
68. Her sister, Margaret, d. in Newbury, March 11. 1858, aged 75).
This David was an iron molder and worked at Brandon some years. His
farm is now M. B. Abbott's. Later he lived where Mrs. B. P. Wheeler does.
Children:
    i. Marion, d. Newbury, June 20. 1834, one week after their arrival here.
   ii. Isabella, b. Leslie, 1817; m. David Halley, q. v.
3 iii. David, b. Leslie, 1820.
4 iv. William, b. Nov. 9, 1823.

2 ROBERT, m. Margaret Weird, (b. Scotland, 1800; d. Oshkosh, Wis., 1870). He
lived where Phillip Webber does.
Children:
    i. Margaret, b. Leslie, 1822; m. W. Mackey; d. Nekimi, Wis.
   ii. David, b. 1824.
   iii. John, b. 1826.
   iv. Isabella, (Mrs. Cross), b. 1828.

3 DAVID, son of David, Jr., m. Feb. 25, 1845, Ann Gilmore of Newbury, and had a son, David. In the summer of 1859, the four David Websters, father, son, grandson and great grandson hoed corn together in the same field. This family were Scotch Presbyterians. David Webster, Sr., was a very shrewd man. There was a piece of ground in this town whose ownership was disputed. A man obtained leave of one of the claimants to sow the land, which he did, to oats. Another man got leave from the other claimant to sow their newly cleared land, which he did, harrowing up the oats and sowing wheat. When the grain was ripe the men quarrelled, but were persuaded to leave the matter to David Webster. The old Scotchman heard the evidence and decided that in his view neither man had any "superior" right to the land, but that each had a right to what grain grew from his seed, he therefore decreed that the men should thresh out the grain, which Andrew Grant and William Wallace should measure into a box, and that one man should sit on one side and pick out all his oats, and that the other should sit on the other side and pick out all his wheat. This unique decision caused so much amusement that the litigants settled the matter peaceably.

4 WILLIAM, b. Leslie, Scotland, Nov. 9, 1823; m. Oct. 3, 1855, in Newbury, Judith A., dau. of John Wells; studied medicine with Dr. Poole of Bradford, and attended lectures at Dartmouth Medical College; rem. to Harmony, Vernon County, Wis., 1857; farming and in practice till death. He d. Harmony, Wis., Oct. 9, 1882. Of their five c., a son, William, and a dau., Agnes, survive. Mrs. Webster res. at La Crosse, Wis.

WEED.

CHARLES, b. Amesbury, Mass., Oct. 5, 1750. Revolutionary soldier; wounded severely at Bunker Hill and was always lame. Came to Topsham 1809, where he was farmer and blacksmith. He d. April 5, 1832, buried in a small cemetery near the road from the Lime-kiln to Topsham. Among his c., were Joseph, who d. Feb. 20, 1856, aged 80 years, 7 months. He m. Miriam Currier, who d. April 23, 1846, in her 75th year. Charles Weed, Jr., b. in Amesbury, Mass., come to Topsham in 1812 and settled where he d. Oct. 21, 1854. His wife, Abigail Colby, was b. in Amesbury and d. in Topsham, Feb. 8, 1867, at 82.

Their children were 8, the two eldest b. in Amesbury, the rest in Topsham:
  i. Hannah, b. Aug. 10, 1810; m. Bernard Eastman q. v.; d. Sept. 4, 1897.
  ii. Abigail, b. Aug. 20, 1812; m. Aug. 21, 1855, Robert Dickson; d. Oct. 27, 1887.
  iii. John, b. Aug. 21, 1814, q. v.
  iv. Harriet, b. Dec., 1816; m. Hon. Wm. T. George.
  v. Julia, b. Sept., 1818; m. Henry Whitcher, q. v.
  vi. Sarah, b. Nov., 1821; m. June 21, 1863, Hon. Peter Buchanan, who d. Mar. 8, 1886.
  vii. Volentine, b. July, 1823; m. Belle Peach; d. May 12, 1885, q. v.
  viii. Elizabeth, b. Aug., 1825; m. Warren C. Meserve.

JOHN, b. Aug. 21, 1814; lived at the Lime-kiln, 1848-60, when he rem. to the Ox-bow. He m. Dec. 25, 1845, Angeline, dau John Renfrew, (b. May 1, 1820; d. June 9, 1888). He d. June 9, 1897. Their son, John Renfrew, b. Newbury, Nov. 28, 1854; farmer on the Ox-bow, (see town officers). He m. in Lowell, Mass., Oct. 29, 1890, Della B. Orser, (b. Oct. 4, 1860).

WELLS.

I. WILLIAM, son of Rev. Wm. Wells, b. at Norwich, Eng., Feb. 10, 1604; came to Massachusetts, 1638, and in 1640, was one of the first settlers of Southold, Long Island; lawyer and recorder; deputy to the General Court at New Haven, 1657–61; member of the Council of Gov. Nichols of New York; high sheriff of Long Island; d. Nov. 13, 1671, and his wife, Mary, dau. of Rev. John Youngs, 1709. "William Wells of Southold and His Descendants," was published in 1878 by Rev. Charles Wells Hayes, D. D., then of Portland, Me.

II. JOSHUA, of Southold, (1664-1744), m. Hannah Tuthill.

III. JOSHUA, of Southold, (1691-1761), m. 1713, Mary, granddaughter of Elder William Brewster of the Mayflower.

IV. JOSHUA, of Southold, (1716- ——), m. Mary Reeve.

V. DEA. SELAH, b. Southold, April 1, 1750; m. at Aquebogue, N. Y., Mehitabel Tuthill, (b. April, 1753; d. Newbury, May 6, 1838). They rem. to Amenia, Dutchess County, N. Y., 1780, to Marshfield, 1798, and about 1836, came to live with their son, John, on Ingalls hill, Newbury, where she d., and he d. March 3, 1842, where his grandson, David T. Wells, long lived. He was the first deacon of the Congregational church, at Marshfield.

Seven children, of whom the following settled in Vermont:

   i. Joseph, b. Southold, Aug. 14, 1776; d. in Burlington. Jan., 1861.
1 ii. Ebenezer, b. July 8, 1779; lived in Marshfield, Peacham and Newbury, but d. in Michigan, Jan. 19, 1855.
2 iii. John, b. Feb. 9, 1890; d. June 4, 1862.

1 EBENEŻER, m. Susanna Spencer of Marshfield, and their c. were: Electa, m. B. F. Tilton of Danville; Tabitha, m. Rev. Joseph Morton of Michigan; Dea. Gideon S., d. in Michigan; George G., b. March 20, 1816, lives in St. Johnsbury; Charles K., lived in Burke, but d. in rebel prison at Andersonville, and Marvin Henry, who lived some years in Newbury, b. May 18, 1814. He m. Aug. 8, 1839, Harriet Bingham, (b. 1816; d. Newbury, May 4, 1849). C., (1) Charles, A., b. Newbury. June 6, 1841; served in Co. A, 4th Michigan Infantry; wounded at the battle of Malvern Hills, and d. in hospital July 7, 1862. (2) Roxanna, b. March 15; d. April 1, 1843. (3) John Milton, b. Newbury, April 13, 1844; served from September, 1863. to May 8, 1865, in Co. M, Michigan Eng. and Mech. Regiment. He m. Lucinda Adelaide, granddaughter of John Wells of Newbury. Three c. (4) Edwin Allen, b. Oct. 21, 1847; d. July 10, 1850. M. H. Wells m. 2d, March 26, 1850, Mrs. Phoebe Philbrick, who d. Aug. 13, 1856. He moved to Michigan in that year, and d. at Union City, Jan. 2, 1900.

2 JOHN, b. Amenia. N. Y., Feb. 9, 1790; m. Marshfield, Sept. 12, 1812, Betsev Willis, (b. Windsor, April 6, 1789; d. Oct. 5, 1878.) He served a few days as a "Plattsburg Volunteer," in the war of 1812; rem. to Bradford, 1825; to Ingalls hill, 1834, and to the center of the town, 1842. He d. June 4, 1862.

Children. all b. in Marshfield except the last:

   i. Lucinda W., b. April 30, 1814; m. Dec. 5, 1833, William, son of John Moore of Bradford; rem. to Michigan, 1843; d. Union, Mich., Dec. 20, 1894. Of their c., these were b. in Vermont: (1) Harriet, b. Bradford, Sept. 11, 1835; m. Cornelius Bancroft of Michigan. Their dau., Rose E., m. George B. Barnett of Newbury, q. v., and her sister, Amelia S., has been a teacher here. (2) William Henry, b. Newbury, Jan. 26, 1842; served two and one-half years in Co. I, 9th Michigan Cavalry. Res. Elk Rapids, Mich.
   ii. Jonathan, b. May 22, 1815; d. March 2, 1822.
3 iii. David Tuthill, b. Jan. 18, 1817.
  iv. Charlotte S., b. Feb. 12, 1819; d. June 7, 1884.
   v. Hiram T., b. July 28, 1822; farmer and stone cutter; m. Nov. 30, 1854, Mary, dau. of Aaron Currier of Plymouth, N. H, where she d. Dec. 18, 1871. He d. Nov. 11, 1857. One son, Hiram F., b. Plymouth, July 8, 1857; m. Linnie A. Hunt, and lives at Plymouth; glove manufacturer and farmer.
  vi. Ruth P., b. April 25, 1824; m. Feb. 14, 1850, Oliver B. Elkins of Penacook, N. H., who d. Nov. 30, 1851; m. 2d, O. C. Barnett, q. v.
 vii. Judith A., b. Feb. 21, 1829; m. Dr. William Webster, q. v.
viii. Catherine S., b. Bradford, June 12, 1830; d. Sept. 23, 1831.

3 DAVID TUTHILL, b. Marshfield, Jan. 18, 1817; came to Newbury, 1834; in Illnois, 1838, '39; farmer and stone cutter; bought in 1841, the farm on which he afterwards lived; member of Congregational church 67 years, and chosen deacon in 1853, holding the office 46 years. He m. at Brighton, Me., Sept. 14, 1846. Maria, dau. Dudley and Abigail (Pickering) Palmer, (b. Brighton, May 14, 1813; d. June 15, 1897). He d. May 6, 1899.

Children:
i. Maria Elizabeth, b. Nov. 6; d. Dec. 21, 1847.
ii. Frederic Palmer, b. Nov. 14, 1850; farmer on homestead; m. June 30, 1897, Katharine, dau. L. L. Tucker, C., Mary Elizabeth, b. Oct. 2, 1898.

WESTGATE.

HARVEY and ISAAC STRATTON, brothers, came to Newbury from Cornish, N. H., and settled where the late Milo C. Bailey lived, building that house. Later, Harvey bought the farm next south of N. C. Randall's, and lived there until a few years before his death, March 12, 1878. That house was burned March 2, 1877. Mr. Westgate was a lover of trees, and set out the trees around the Milo Bailey house and the double row of maples, now grown large, along the road between his house and S. W. Tewksbury's. He m. Sarah, dau. Samuel Tucker, (b. Nov. 8, 1805; d. April 1, 1891). One son, Thomas W., who m. Emily, dau. of Justin Lindsey; no c. He d. Aug. 26, 1876, aged 39.

ISAAC STRATTON, b. April 9, 1803, he settled finally where George C. Tyler has lately lived, a farm cleared and buildings erected by Samuel Eastman and Nicholas White. He m. Mrs. Sarah (Kempton) Keyes, (b. Nov. 3, 1800; d. March 3, 1873). She became blind some years before her death and they were cared for by her son, William Keyes, and wife, who lived on their farm. He d. Sept. 10, 1869. Mrs. Keyes, whose maiden name was Pushee, m. 1st, a Mr Cutting, and their dau., Hattie P., m. Sherburne S. Tucker. After the death of Mr. Keyes, Jan. 21, 1876, she m. 3d, a Mr. Kent of Orford.

WHEELER.

NATHANIEL, understood to have been b. in England, Feb. 5, 1765, came when a child with his parents to Canada where he m., his wife being Olive ———— a native of Ireland, (b. Aug. 10, 1770).
The following list of their children is given here for preservation. Nearly all lived and died in Canada:
i. Eben, b. June 1, 1791.
ii. Lucy, b. March 18, 1793.
1 iii. Jabez, b. Jan. 30, 1796.
iv. Malinda, b. April 13, 1798.
v. Lucinda, b. Nov., 1800.
vi. John, b. March 25, 1805.
vii. Ira, b. April 20, 1807.
viii. Lavinia, b. Nov. 20, 1810.
ix. Phias, b. Jan. 24, 1813.

1 JABEZ, b. Capleton, P. Q , Jan. 30, 1796. He m. March 1, 1818, Lois Canfield, (b. Charleston, Feb. 14, 1796; d. Newbury, July 4, 1882). Miller and wheelwright. Was in the mill at Rock Island, P. Q., 20 years, when people would come twenty miles to mill with a huge grist, staying over night with the miller. They rem. to Manchester, N. H., and in old age to Newbury, where two of their sons had settled. He d. in Newbury, April 27, 1887.
Children:
2 i. Benjamin P., b. Dec. 8, 1818; d. July 2, 1893.
ii. Asenath C., b. July 2, 1820; d. May 8, 1843.
iii. Alonzo. b. Aug. 23, 1822; d. Dec. 14, 1897.
iv. Randall, b. July 4, 1824; d. Aug. 23 1849.
v. Lois L., b. Nov. 26, 1826; d. March 18, 1851.
vi. Mortimer, b. March 17, 1833; lived some years at South Newbury; mechanic.
vii. Lucy Ann, b. April 15, 1835; d. Oct. 12, 1879.
viii. Homer, b. May 4, 1838.
Four who d. in childhood.

2 BENJAMIN P., b. Brownington, Dec. 8, 1818; wheelwright by trade, but farmer by choice. Settled on Leighton Hill, in April, 1861. He taught singing school at different times. Was one year in California. Member and class

leader of the Methodist church. He m. 1st, Amy Burroughs of Stanstead, P. Q., who d. two years later; m. 2d, Sept. 17, 1847, Esther Sly of Ryegate, from whom he was divorced. One c., Estella, who m. Charles Reed of Auburn, N. H., and d. Nov. 2, 1888. Three c., Benjamin, Ira and Mabel, the last d. Oct., 1898; m. 3d, Angeline, dau. Dan G., and Charlotte (Woodbury) Ford. He d. Newbury, July 2, 1893.

Children, by 3d marriage:

3 i.   Osgood P., b. Sept. 21, 1858.
   ii. Willimina, b. Aug. 21, 1862; d. Sept. 29, 1890.
   iii. Charlien W., b. March 28, 1867; m. John F. George, q. v.

3 OSGOOD P., b. Sept. 4, 1858; m. June, 1880, Eliza S., dau. Azro J. Bailey; res. Lancaster, N. H. Salesman for Grand Union Tea Co.

Children:

   i.   Beatrice H., b. May 26, 1881.
   ii. Charlotte A., b. Oct. 13, 1882.
   iii. Infant, b. May 24, d. July 5, 1884.
   iv. B. Clinton, b. July 30, 1885.
   v.   Errol, b. Dec. 25, 1887.
   vi. J. Elwyn, b. April 20, 1892.

WHEELOCK.

PETER, b. Lancaster, Mass., 1766; d. Newbury, Sept. 9, 1851.

PETER, Jr., b. Royalton, Oct. 10, 1802; came to Newbury in 1833, and kept the Spring Hotel 1833-36; was also steward at the seminary, and kept the boarding house; in the hardware business in the "old depot building," and bought the "Old Bliss house" at the south end, next to the "Buxton house." He afterward became traveling agent for the Fairbanks Scale company, and, in 1853, rem. to Milwaukee, to which place his wife's father and brother had rem. He m. a dau. of Prof. Amasa Buck of Bath, (b. Lyman, N. H., March 18, 1811; d. Sioux Falls, South Dakota, May 30, 1886). He d. Sioux Falls, April 8, 1880.

Children:

   i.   Martha R., b. Rochester, Oct. 6, 1830; graduated Newbury Seminary, (Institute), November, 1851; music teacher. She m. Wm. S. Trowbridge, a civil engineer of Milwaukee.
   ii. Arthur Buck, b. Royalton, April 19, 1832; served three months in Co. A, 1st Wisconsin, 1861; mustered out August, 1861; re-enlisted, Sept. 17, 1861; 2d lieutenant, 7th Wisconsin Light Artillery; was in the Mississippi campaign; taken prisoner, Aug. 21, 1864; Ex. Oct. 27, 1864; pro. captain, April 18, 1865; mustered out July 20, 1865; service four years, 5 months; city justice of Sioux Falls, South Dakota.
   iii. Mary Elizabeth, b. Newbury, Nov. 29, 1834; d. Milwaukee, Jan. 13, 1865.
   iv. Sarah Frances, b. Newbury, May 11, 1839; m. Henry E. Southwell of Chicago.
   v.   William Henry, b. Newbury, Dec. 11, 1841. While the family lived in Milwaukee he, then a school boy, went out to walk one evening, and was never seen or heard of afterwards.

*WHITTIER—WHITCHER.

I THOMAS, b. Millchill, Wiltshire, Eng , 1622; came to America in the ship, Confidence, which sailed from Northampton, April 24, 1638. They settled first in Salisbury, Mass., afterwards lived a short time in Newbury, where he m. 1646, Widow Ruth Green, a sister of Henry Rolfe, with whom he had come from England. About ten years later he rem. to Haverhill, where he lived on what has since been called the Whittier homestead, until his death, Nov. 28, 1696. In 1688, he built the large two-story house still standing, and used for memorials, relics, etc., by the John G. Whittier

* Ancestry by W. F. Whitcher, Esq., Woodsville.

Memorial Society. In was in this house that the poet was born, and it was this house which was the scene of his immortal New England epic, "Snow Bound." The fact that the name, Whittier, was originally pronounced as of two syllables, Whit-tier, (Whitcher or Whicher) fully accounts for the corruption of the spelling on the part of some of the descendants of Thomas Whittier.

II.   THOMAS and Ruth had 10 c., of whom Nathaniel, b. Aug. 11, 1658, m. Aug. 26, 1685, Mary, dau. of William Osgood of Salisbury. They had a son and a daughter.

III. REUBEN, their one son, b. May 17, 1686; m. Dec. 19, 1708, Deborah Pillsbury of Newbury, and lived in Salisbury where their seven c. were b.

IV.   RICHARD, 4th son, b. 1717; was twice m.; his first wife d. in Stratham, April 10, 1750. He m. 2d, Mary Chase by whom he had:

V.   *PERLEY FOXWELL WHITCHER (Whittier), b. Berwick, Me., March, 1757, (or 1758); m. Ruth Hill of Kittery, Me., (b. 1760), in 1779. He was, while in Maine, a buyer of pine lumber, for one Paul Lord, a ship contractor. For this buying of lumber and' delivering a it, he received one dollar a day, boarding himself. In March, 1800, he came to Vermont with his family, consisting of a wife and eight c., and settled in Ryegate, on the farm now owned by Lester Low. Their team was six cows shod like oxen, drawing the family and furniture; they were seven days on the road, bringing $800 in silver. In Ryegate he engaged in lumbering, and in clearing land for the Scotch settlers, receiving from $2.50 to $4.00 per acre, for this work. In 1815, he sold in Ryegate and bought a farm in Groton, where he remained until his death. He was a very active man, being also a great reader, especially of the Bible, and having a very retentive memory. it was said by Rev. William Gibson of Ryegate that if the Scriptures were struck out of existence, Foxwell Whitcher, and one more like him, could reproduce the whole. He d. June 6, 1842. The c. of Perley F., and Ruth Whitcher were, Richard, Reuben, John, Perley F., Hiram, Joseph, Lucinda, Lavinia, who m. James Allen, Abner, and Ruth, who d. at the age of 17, at the home of her aunt, Mrs. John Hall. The two youngest were b. in Ryegate, the others in Maine.

HIRAM, son of Perley F., b. in South Berwick, Me., Dec. 15, 1790; came to Ryegate in 1800; in 1817, he settled on the southeast corner lot in Groton, and m. April 1, 1818, Margaret, dau. of James and Elizabeth (Miller) Nelson, (b. Dec. 26, 1794; d. Oct. 14, 1880). He afterwards bought 100 acres in the northeast corner of Topsham, and 200 of lease land in the northwest corner of Newbury. In March, 1838, he sold his farm and bought the Robert Johnston farm, where his son, Henry, now lives. He was a hard working man, a Bible scholar, and constant at church. His mother being of the Quaker persuasion, he was taught that taking Freeman's oath was of doubtful legality. He took the oath for the first time, and voted in September, 1840, and never afterwards. In 1828 or '29, he and his wife united with the Methodist church in Groton, being the first members of the church in that town, under the charge of Revs. Paul C. Richmond and W. Peck. A class of about 14 was formed which included Mrs. Burnham, mother of Rev. Benjamin Burnham, Mrs. Hall, Job Welton and wife, and Miss Polly Low. Hiram Whitcher d. Aug. 17, 1852.
Children, all born in Groton, except the last:

1   i.   Henry, b. May 2, 1819.
2   ii. Abner, b. Oct. 9, 1820; d. Sept. 16, 1893.
    iii. Alexander N., b. February, 1822; d. November, 1827.
    iv. Eliza Jane, b. March, 1825; d. September, 1830.
    v.   Almira, b. Dec. 14, 1827; d. March 8, 1848.
    vi. Lavinia, b. Nov. 3, 1830; m. Andrew Renfrew, q. v.
    vii. Naomi, b. Feb. 3, 1833; m. Thomas Kasson of Topsham and Newbury.
    viii. Ruth, b. Sept. 4, 1834; m. March 12, 1857, Edwin Tuttle; d. Boston, Mass., March 26, 1861.

_____

*By Henry Whitcher.

ix. Julia, b. March 14, 1837; m. Nov. 3, 1861, N. H. Richardson of Topsham; res. Lancaster, N. H.

x. Lois Jane, b. 1840; m. Henry C. Richardson; d. Lancaster, N. H., Sept. 6, 1867.

1 HENRY, b. Groton, May 2, 1819; received a common school education, as such was in his younger days, with one term at Newbury Seminary, the winter of 1838. The same year he rem. with his parents to the farm on which he still resides, teaching school winters, and working on the farm summers. To this farm he has added greatly by purchase has always been one of the most progressive farmers in town, and in the breeding of fine blood stock and the introduction of farm machinery and appliances, has been one of the foremost. Mr. Whitcher has rendered valuable aid in the preparation of that portion of this history which relates to the section of the town in which he res. He m. Jan. 19, 1844, Julia, dau. of Charles and Abigail (Colby) Weed of Topsham.

Children:

i. Infant son, b. and d. July 17, 1846.

ii. Abner John, b. June 28, 1847; farmer on homestead; member of school board, etc. He m. Dec. 9, 1869, Ella M., dau. of John R. McAllister. C., (1) Fred J., b. June 29, 1870; res. Auburn, Me. (2) Frank E., b. May 6, 1872. (3) Edna Maud, b. Jan. 18, 1881. (4) Perley H., b. April 5, 1889.

2 ABNER, son of Hiram, b. Oct. 9, 1820. Went to California in July, 1850, and remained about eleven years, being most of the time engaged in mining, on the north fork of American river at a place called Beal's bar. High sheriff for three years of Sacramento County, living at Folsom. Returned from California in 1861, and went into business in Boston as a dealer in country produce, for about three years having a stall in Quincy Market. In 1864, he returned to Newbury, and in 1866 bought the home farm on which he afterwards lived. He m. 1st, Jan. 12, 1854, Mary Jane Thorne of Boston, who went out to him from Boston in a clipper ship around Cape Horn, the voyage lasting nine months, being twice wrecked. She d. Jan. 26, 1862, aged 36 years. One dau., Mary Louise b. in California, Feb. 26, 1860; graduated Tilden Female Seminary, now librarian of San Francisco Public Library. He m. 2d, April 19, 1866, Grace Crawford, b. Erskine Parish, Renfrewshire, Scotland, March 1, 1831, came to America in 1853. Abner Whitcher d. Sept. 16. 1893. C., (1) Florence Isabella, b. Feb. 23, 1867; d. Oct. 22, 1869. (2) James Roger, b. Oct. 3, 1869; farmer on the homestead; selectman 1901. A twin brother d. at birth. (4) Eliza Jane, b. April 23, 1872; d Oct. 6, 1892. Twins, b. and d. Oct. 10, 1875. Infant, b. and d., 1877.

(The following record is inserted here for the sake of its preservation).

SUSANNA, dau. Richard Whitcher, brother of Hiram; m. Joseph Hill.

Children, all of whom but one settled in Sanford. Me:

i. Polly, m. Col. Ebenezer Norwell; 10 c. of whom Eben S., of Salmon Falls, N. H., Mrs. Theodate S. Haines, and her sister, Anna, of Somersworth, N. H., and Mrs. Phebe, widow of Capt. Nicholas Varnia of Newburyport, Mass., are living.

ii. Ruth, m. Nathaniel Chadburn; 11 c. living; four of their sons were in the banking business; two at Columbus, Wis., one at Minneapolis and one at Blue Earth City, Minn.

iii. Joseph, m. Olivia Beal. Mrs. Frances Pease of Newburyport is living.

iv. Abner, m. Mercy Norwell; 7 c., 2 living.

v. John, m. Lydia Butler; 4 c., all d.

vi. Reuben W., was a physician at Montpelier where he practiced till 75 years of age; m. Lydia Hill of Groton; 3 c., of whom Emma A., of Barton is living.

vii. Theodate, m. Ichabod Frost; 7 c., 2 living.

WHITE.

IRA, b. Swansey, N. H., March 22, 1789. In 1801, he went to Surry, N. H., to live with Hon. Lemuel Holmes, and in 1810, went to Bellows Falls to learn the paper business. He came first to Wells River, when there were

but seven houses in the place. In 1814, he took a load of naval officers from Bellows Falls to Vergennes, who took part in the battle of Lake Champlain. After 1816, he resided in Wells River, permanently, where he built the house still called by his name. (See further, Judge Leslie's paper upon Wells River). He m. 1823, Eliza, dau. of Stephen Reed. She d. March 21, 1869. He d. Newbury, Nov. 17, 1886, in his 98th year.
Children:
  i. Henry K., b. 1825. In the paper business at Wells River, but rem. to Toronto, Ont., where he d., leaving a wife and dau.
 ii. *Helen, b. 1830; m. Wm. G. Buchanan, q. v.
iii. Sarah, b. 1838; m. George H. Fay, a jeweler of Boston; d. Nov. 10, 1884.

WHITE.

  I. WILLIAM, b. in England, 1610; came to Ipswich, Mass., 1635, and in 1640, with eleven others, made the first settlement in Haverhill, Mass., where he d. Sept. 28, 1690. He m. Mary ——, who d. Feb. 22, 1681.

 II. JOHN, b. March 8, 1639-40; m. in Salem, Nov. 25, 1662, Hannah, dau. of Edward French; one son. He d. Jan. 1, 1668-9.

III. JOHN, b. March 8, 1663-4; m. Oct. 24, 1687, Lydia, dau. of Hon. John Gilman of Exeter. They had 14 c., of whom Nicholas was the ancestor of the Whites in Newbury, and his sister, Abigail, who m. Moses Hazen, was the ancestress of hundreds of people in this town and Haverhill. This John White represented Haverhill in the General Court many years, and was a captain in the Indian wars. He d. Nov. 20, 1727.

IV. NICHOLAS, b. Dec. 4, 1698. He m. 1st, Nov. 6, 1722, Hannah Ayer, who d. Jan. 25, 1732, having had five c., and m. 2d, Mary Calfe or Calef of Ipswich, by whom he had 10 c. He d. Plaistow, N. H., April 7, 1782. For the sake of convenience the descent of the Newbury Whites will be reckoned back only to Nicholas, seven of whose c. settled in Newbury and there are descendants of others.
    Children, five by 1st m., ten by 2d m:
      i. Mary, b. and d. April, 1725.
     ii. Hannah, b. Sept. 8, 1726; d. Aug., 1803.
1   iii. Noah, b. Feb. 15, 1788.
     iv. Abigail, b. March 29, 1730; m. John Cogswell, Jr.
2   v. Ebenezer, b. Dec. 2, 1731; d. July 24, 1807.
3   vi. Joseph, b. Dec. 14, 1734.
    vii. Mary, b. Aug. 14, 1736; m. Col. Jacob Kent, q. v.; d. June 17, 1834.
   viii. Lydia, b. July 2, 1738; m. Dea. Benjamin Hale, q. v.; d. Nov. 14, 1791.
4   ix. William, b. March 19, 1740.
      x. John, b. March 21, 1742; d. Oct. 29, 1808.
     xi. Sarah, b. Aug. 17, 1744; d. June 10, 1745.
    xii. Elizabeth, b. May 31. 1746; m. Timothy Ayer, of Haverhill, Mass.
   xiii. Martha, b. Aug. 9, 1748; m. James Dodge of Haverhill, Mass.
5 xiv. Samuel, b. Nov. 6, 1750; d. Jan. 25, 1848.
     xv. Abigail, b. May 14, 1757; m. James Davis of Haverhill, Mass.

1 NOAH,[2] (Nicholas,[1]) b. Feb. 18, 1728; m. Sept. 18,. 1751, Sarah Sweet. They came to Newbury in the fall of 1763, bringing their infant, Sarah, in their arms, camping out at night without shelter. They rem. to Bradford a few years later where he became a Judge of Orange County Court.
    Their c. were, (from Bradford town records):
      i. Nathaniel, b. April 10, 1752.
     ii. James, b. May 26, 1754.
    iii. Abigail, b. Aug. 18, 1756.
     iv. Nicholas, b. May 2, 1759; m. Deborah Ford.
      v. Sarah, b. Sept. 5, 1761; m. Dea. Reuben Martin of Bradford; d. June 7, 1840.

*NOTE. On page 481, the record of William G. Buchanan is made to read that he d. June 14, 1855. It should have read Kate m. F. L. Moore and d. June 14, 1885. Mr. Buchanan is still living at Wells River.

vi. Anna, b. in Newbury, Oct. 30, 1764; d. Feb. 24, 1788.
vii. John, b. in Newbury, Jan. 1, 1768.
viii. Hannah, b. Dec. 30, 1772.
ix. William, b. May 1, 1777.

2 EBENEZER,[2] (Nicholas,[1]) b. Plaistow, Dec. 2, 1731; m. 1st, April 14, 1757, Hannah Merrill, (b. July 7, 1733; d. Nov. 11, 1767); m. 2d, Ruth Emerson, (b. Sept. 23, 1746; d. Oct. 10, 1815). Came to Newbury, 1763; farmer and shoemaker; settled on Hall's meadow and later where Wm. U. Bailey has long lived. Town representative 1785, (see town officers). In their old age they went to Topsham to live with their son, Moses H., where they d. and are buried on Currier Hill. Served 23 days guarding and scouting in Capt. John G. Bayley's Co., 1779, and perhaps in other alarms. He d. July 24, 1807.
Children:
i. Hannah, b. Aug. 28, 1758; d. Jan. 1, 1778.
ii. Roger Merrill, b. Nov. 26, 1759; d. Dec. 12, 1776, at Albany, N. Y., in the Continental army, from the accidental discharge of a musket.
iii. Mary, b. March 23, 1761; m. Samuel Powers, q. v.; d. Feb. 16, 1849.
iv. Lydia, b. Jan. 1, 1763; m. Bancroft Abbott, q. v.; d. June 25, 1853.
v. Nicholas, b. in Newbury, Feb. 11, 1765; m. at Hampstead, N. H., Nov. 14, 1793, Sally Kent.
vi. Elizabeth, b. Nov. 21, d. Dec. 17, 1766.
vii, Ebenezer, b. Nov. 8, 1767; m. Abigail, dau. Jonathan Tenney; lived in Corinth; two sons; d. June 11, 1820.
viii. Timothy, b. Jan. 29, 1769.
6 ix. Jesse, b. Feb. 4, 1771; d. May 12, 1851.
x. Ruth, b. Nov. 20, 1772; m. a Mr. Sawyer, it is thought.
7 xi. Samuel, b. Dec. 12, 1774; d. Sept. 15, 1846.
xii. Roger M., b. May 27, 1777; d. Aug. 24, 1779.
xiii. Hannah, b. June 30, 1779; m. Abner Bayley, son of Ephraim, q. v.
xiv. Ayer, b. Feb. 26, 1781; m. Hannah, dau. Dea. William Carter, (b. March 23, 1792). C., Ayer and Spencer, perhaps others.
xv. Gilman, b. June 21, 1783. He had a son, Rev. John White.
xvi. Abigail, b. June 2, 1785; m. Dec. 27, 1804, Edmund Brown of Topsham.
xvii. Dea. Moses Hazen, b. Nov. 14, 1787; m. July 11, 1816, Mary Dickey; lived in Topsham; d. April 24, 1857. C., (1) Mary J., b. Aug. 22, 1820. (2) Elizabeth, b. June 5, 1822; d. May 6, 1823. (3) Julia K., b. Nov. 29, 1824; res. Lowell, Mass. (4) Moses B., b. Dec. 30, 1826.
xviii. Noah, b. May 13, 1792.

3 JOSEPH,[2] (Nicholas,[1]) b. Dec. 11, 1734. Came to Newbury in 1763, and settled on Kent's meadow. Served with his son, Joseph, in several short campaigns of the Revolution, but they turned tories and both were of the party which tried to capture Gen. Jacob Bayley, June 15, 1782. Later, Joseph, Jr., was taken prisoner and carried to Canada on the charge of having betrayed certain plans. The father entreated Gen. Bayley to use his influence to have his son exchanged, but he refused, saying that those who had done all they could to ruin others, had no right to beg them for help when their own turn came. Joseph, Jr., was forbidden to return to Newbury, and the family soon after the war rem. to Canada.

4 WILLIAM,[2] (Nicholas,[1]) b. March 27, 1740; m. Mary, dau. of Rev. Abner and Elizabeth (Baldwin) Bayley of Salem, N. H. He lived in Plaistow, N. H., but was in Newbury a good deal, and owned much land here. In his will dated Jan. 7, 1775, on record here, he gives ⅜ of his land in this town to his son, Abner Bayley White, ⅔ to his daughter, Mary White, and ⅜ to his son, Nicholas White. He d.
Their c. were:
i. Abner Bayley.
ii. Mary, b. Jan. 4, 1768; m. Asa Tenney of Newbury, q. v.; d. April, 1823.
8 iii. Nicholas, b. 1770: d. Dec. 23, 1831.

5 DR. SAMUEL,[2] (Nicholas,[1]) b. Plaistow, N. H., Nov. 6, 1750. He came here first in 1763, but returned to Plaistow, and afterward studied medicine with Dr. Brickett of Haverhill, Mass. He located permanently in Newbury in 1773, and was, for many years, the principal physician in this part of the

country. His practice extended all through the settlements on the river, his account books showing visits to Guildhall and Northumberland. He had the confidence of people, and was esteemed very skillful. Many of his journeys were on foot, and, in the winter, on snow shoes. He was surgeon to the troops stationed in Coös, and accompanied the soldiers who went to Saratoga. He reached Bennington the day after the battle, and helped care for the wounded. Two account books kept by him are now owned by Mrs. Z. A. Richardson at St. Johnsbury, and are in a beautiful handwriting, each entry being clear and exact, and the ink as fresh as if just written. These accounts begin in 1773 and end in 1790. For an ordinary visit the charge was one shilling here in Newbury; to Haverhill, from two to six shillings; to Bath the charge was from three to seven shillings; a visit to Capt. Ward Bayley at Upper Coös, April 5, 1782, is charged at forty shillings. Medicine was always extra. In these books about one hundred and fifty remedial agents are mentioned. Physic stands first, some sort being used over fifteen hundred times. Bleeding was common. Surgical operations were few, scarcely a dozen are mentioned in these volumes, and these were simple fractures of arms or legs. Dr. White lived, at first at Col. Kent's, or with one of his brothers; later, about 1785, probably, he built the large house now owned by C. C. Doe, that being his farm. In 1806, he rem. to Jefferson Hill, and lived in a house which stood a little north of the schoolhouse. Later, he lived a few years at West Newbury, but returned to Jefferson Hill, where he spent his last days. In person Dr. White was tall and large in frame, capable of great endurance, and of strong constitution as his great age testified. He was fond of anecdote, and abounded in wit and humor. He used to say that he was "apt to have poor luck with his patients in their last illness." He was generous to a fault, somewhat slack in business, and would take notes from people whose financial ability he knew nothing about. For some years he drank heavily, but afterwards discontinued the use of spirits. Late in life he made a profession of religion, and was admitted to the Congregational church at a special service held at his house Sept. 19, 1844. The date of his death is often given as Feb. 20, 1847, but is, as previously stated, Jan. 25, 1848, in his 98th year, as attested by his grave stone and by the church and town records. Many articles owned by Dr. White are carefully preserved in this town. He m. March 26, 1793, Anna, dau. of Samuel Tucker, (b. Oxford, Mass., June 28, 1769; d. Newbury, March 26, 1845). They had a large family of children, none of whom ever married, and the family is now extinct. Dr. White and his wife and nine children are buried in the cemetery on Jefferson hill under a long row of white grave stones. Three others are buried elsewhere.

Children, (those buried on Jefferson hill):
  i. William, b. March 26, 1794; served two months, 18 days, in Capt. Levi Rogers Co. of Fifield's regiment in the war of 1812; farmer on Jefferson hill; d. June 1, 1878.
 ii. Samuel, b. Oct. 24, 1795; d. June 28, 1833.
iii. John, b. July 15, 1797; d. April 13, 1839.
 iv. Eliza, b. 1799; d. June 17, 1827.
  v. Mary, b. 1800; d. Nov. 26, 1823.
 vi. Nicholas, b. 1804; in business with Samuel Eastman, for some years. They were the contractors who built the Union Meeting House. He d. June 27, 1846.
vii. Nancy, b. 1809; d. Dec. 22, 1823.
viii. Elijah, b. Aug. 29, 1815; d. Jan. 23, 1864.
 ix. Lucinda, b. Aug. 29, 1815; d. April 5, 1887.
"The last of the Dr. White family," says her gravestone.

6 JESSE,[3] (Ebenezer,[2] Nicholas,[1]) b. Newbury, Feb. 4, 1771; settled in Topsham about 1795, clearing the farm afterward owned by his son, Amos; m. Dec. 4, 1800, Lydia, dau. of Webster Bailey, (b. May 19, 1774; d. Feb. 1, 1833). He d. Topsham, May 12, 1851.
Children:
10   i. Amos, b. Oct. 2, 1801; d. May 1, 1868.
    ii. Jesse, b. Jan. 28, 1803; d. Feb. 23, 1886.
   iii. Son, b. June 28, 1804; lived 12 hours.
11 iv. Ezekiel, b. Oct. 1, 1808; d. July 30, 1899.
     v. Phebe, b. June 3, 1811; m. Gilman Brown; d. March 26, 1876.

7 SAMUEL,[3] (Ebenezer,[2] Nicholas,[1]) b. Newbury, Dec. 12, 1774; farmer; lived some years at West Newbury; then on the farm now owned by Wm. U. Bailey; m. Sept. 18, 1806, Sarah, dau. of Thomas Brock, (b. Sept. 27, 1777; d. Aug. 2, 1841). He d. Sept. 15, 1846.
  Children:
9 i. Bailey, b. Nov. 30, 1807; d. Feb. 9, 1892.
  ii. Olive, b. Nov. 3, 1809; d. Sept. 9, 1822.
  iii. Sarah Almena, b. Nov. 13, 1811; m. Harvey Robinson, q. v.; d. Oct. 30, 1898.
  iv. Samuel Leonard, b. Oct. 10, 1813; d. Jan. 12, 1821.
  v. Abia, b. April 13, 1815; m. Charles Severance of Windsor; lived also in Burlington and Montpelier, where she d., leaving a son and a dau.
  vi. George W., b. April 20, 1822; res. Ryegate; m. Lois Carbee.

8 NICHOLAS,[3] (William,[2] Nicholas,[1]) b. Plaistow, 1770; m. March 22, 1799, Eunice, dau. of William and Rachel (Tewksbury) Johnson, who d. in Bradford, March, 1856, aged 80. He d. Ryegate, December, 1831.
  Children:
  i. Mary, b. March 4, 1800; m. 1st, Mr. Hoyt; m. 2d, Mr. Morse.
  ii. Nancy, b. Nov. 28, 1801.
  iii. Moses W., b. Aug. 1, 1803.
12 iv. William J., b. Dec. 25, 1804.
  v. Abigail, b. April 20, 1806.
  vi. Asa.
  vii. Jane.
  viii. Abner B., b. Feb. 1, 1812; lived at Wells River. Mrs. White is still living.

9 BAILEY.[4] (Samuel,[3] Ebenezer,[2] Nicholas,[1]) b. Newbury, Nov. 30, 1807. Most of his life was spent in this town, but not many years in one place. He built the house where John Buchanan lives, and that of Orrin W. Brock. Farmer. He m. 1st, in Danvers, Mass., 1831, Rebecca Mayhew, who d. the same year. He m. 2d, Dec. 5, 1833, Almira, dau. of John Atwood, who d. April 7, 1839, aged 33. He m. 3d, 1840, Betsey, dau. of Davenport Bliss, (b. Aug. 4, 1803; d. Dec. 27, 1860). He m. 4th, in Ryegate, April 16, 1862, Mrs. Emeline Scott, (b. Oct. 14, 1812. She was a daughter of Samuel Whitaker, and granddaughter of Jacob Page of Newbury.) He d. Feb. 9, 1892.
  Children, two by 2d marriage, and one by 3d:
  i. Mary Ann, b. July 31, 1833; m. and d., leaving three children.
  ii. Almira, d. 1839.
  iii. Charles, b. March 22, 1841; res. Hudson, N. H.

10 AMOS,[4] (Jesse,[3] Ebenezer,[2] Nicholas,[1]) b. Oct. 2, 1801; farmer in Topsham; m. Jan. 31, 1828, Eliza N., dau. of Hale Grow, (b. April 8, 1810; d. Nov. 20, 1829). He m. 2d, March 15, 1832, Melissa M., dau. of Samuel Greenleaf of Bradford, who d. Nov. 30, 1880. He d. May 1, 1868.
  Children, one by 1st and four by 2d marriage, all b. in Topsham:
  i. Amos G., b. Nov. 10, 1829; d. Nov. 26, 1846.
  ii. Lydia Eliza, b. Jan. 15, 1834; teacher and authoress. (See Bibliography of Newbury).
  iii. Hannah G., b. Sept. 25, 1836; m. James L. Woodward of Chicago.
  iv. Carlos, b. June 9, 1842; graduated Dartmouth College, 1868. In newspaper business in California. The last years of his life were spent in Great Britain. He d. at Cardiff, Wales, Jan. 20, 1901.
  v. Noel Byron, b. Nov. 10, 1844; two years in Dartmouth College; farming and literary work in Wisconsin; m. Mary E. Penney; three c.

11 EZEKIEL,[4] (Jesse,[3] Ebenezer,[2] Nicholas,[1]) b. Topsham, Oct. 1, 1808; farmer of Topsham; captain in the militia; member of Cong. Ch. about 65 years. He m. Feb. 14, 1832, Laura, dau. of John K. Dustin, b. Sept. 15, 1813. Their married life was 67 years, 5 months, 17 days. Mr. and Mrs. White gave many interesting particulars for this volume. He d. July 31, 1899.
  Children:
  i. Horace, b. Feb. 14, 1833; m. Dec. 4, 1863, Abbie A., dau. Bernard Eastman, (b. Dec. 2, 1839). Six c. Res. at West Topsham.
  ii. Sally, b. Sept. 4, 1834; d. April, 1843.
  iii. Laura, b. July 24, 1836; d. March 26, 1861.

iv. Thomas H., b. Feb. 15, 1838; served in the Union army; m. 1867, Winnie
Clabank. One c. Res. California.
v. Lois D., b. Aug. 12, 1839; m. December, 1862, Allen F. Eastman, son of
Bernard, q. v.; d. Aug. 13, 1899.
vi. Henry B., b. Nov. 1, 1844; m. July 4, 1865, Hattie G., dau. of Bernard
Eastman, (b. March 26, 1847; d. March 4, 1897). Six c. Res. Topsham.
vii. George, b. Feb. 9, 1848; m. June 18, 1875, Amanda E. Taplin, (b. Aug. 7,
1845). Three c.
viii. Hattie B., b. Nov. 21, 1851; d. June 4, 1863.
ix. Fred H., b. July 30, 1856; m. October, 1889, Sarah A. McLam; res. Ryegate.

12 WILLIAM JOHNSON,[4] (Nicholas,[3] William,[2] Nicholas,[1]) b. Dec. 25, 1804; m. Sept.
8, 1834, Abigail, dau. of Robert and Mehetabel (Barron) Whitelaw, (b.
Ryegate, June 11, 1811; d. St. Johnsbury, July 5, 1895). He d. Sept. 4,
1887.
Children:
i. Susan J., b. Nov. 9, 1837; m. Z. A. Richardson of St. Johnsbury.
ii. Sophia H., b. May 20, 1844; m. Henry W. Hill.

WHITE.

JOHN GILMAN, youngest son of Jacob March and Fanny (Cook) White, b.
Lebanon, N. H., Oct. 20, 1810; rem. in 1814, with his parents, to "Briar
Hill," in Haverhill; educated in the district school and Bradford Academy;
became a teacher. He m. March 1, 1837, Susan, dau. John and Clarissa
Sanborn of North Haverhill. Farmer on homestead, but rem. to Bath,
and to Wells River about 1851, and engaged in the meat and provision
business, and the purchase and sale of cattle and produce in Boston. He
lived some ten years in what was then called the Abbott house, built by
Charles Brigham, which then stood on Main street, but which, removed,
is the residence of Hon. John Bailey. He lived, later, in the "old McLaren
house," which, much altered, was that of the late Hon. C. B. Leslie. He
was Justice of the Peace, and held other offices. He d. April 30, 1890.
Mrs. White d. Sept. 30, 1882.
Children, all b. in Haverhill:
i. Ella A., b. Jan. 18, 1838; m. Oct. 7, 1863, Alexander H. Burton, then of
Newbury, and brother of Rev. H. N. Burton, D. D. (Mr. Burton owned
the John Johnson farm on the Ox-bow a few years, but later was a
merchant at Woodsville, and after some time bought the Moses Abbott
farm in Bath. He d. Aug. 30, 1898).
ii. Clara A., b. March 23, 1840; m. Dec. 24, 1863, Moody C. Marston; res. in
Bath.
iii. Melissa W., b. Jan. 14, 1842; m. Dec. 7, 1869, B. Morrill Blake; res.
Woodsville.
iv. Harriet F., b. Feb. 6, 1845; m. July 16, 1867, George F. Smith; res.
Woodsville.
v. Mary Bell, b. May 19, 1847; m. Sept. 20, 1876, William B. Goodwin, q. v.

WHITELAW.

GEN. JAMES, although never a resident of Newbury, was so intimately connected
with the earlier events of its history as to merit the special notice which is
desired to be given him in its annals. He was b. Feb. 11, 1748, in a house
which stood till 1896, in the parish of Old Monkland, Lanarkshire,
Scotland. He came to America in 1773, as agent for the Scot's American
Co., as related in Chapter XI. In 1790, he was appointed surveyor-general
of Vermont. In 1796, he prepared the first map of the state, several
editions of which, enlarged and improved, were printed. He was widely
known and respected, not only in Vermont, but in other states, and his
letters are those of a man of good education, even mental balance, and
kindness of heart, as well as of large executive ability. In 1801, the New
Hampshire legislature voted that General Whitelaw, and two other
gentlemen in Vermont, should be the committee to survey and locate the
fourth New Hampshire turnpike. Local jealousies, political and personal

740   HISTORY OF NEWBURY, VERMONT.

hostilities, were so strong in that state at the time as to prevent the choice of any three men in that state for the purpose, while all could agree to leave the matter in the hands of Gen. Whitelaw of Ryegate, Gen. Elias Stevens of Royalton, and Major Micah Barron of Bradford. He settled on the farm still called the "Whitelaw place," between Ryegate Corner and Wells River; the kitchen part of the house, built, says Mr. Edward Miller, in 1775, is the oldest building in that town. He m. 1st, March 5, 1778, Abigail, dau. of Col. Robert Johnston of Newbury, (b. April 25, 1760; d. July 11, 1790); m. 2d, Susannah Rogers; m. 3d, Janet (Brock), widow of Col. Alexander Harvey of Barnet. General Whitelaw d. April 29, 1829. He has been well called "The Father of Ryegate." The best account of him was prepared by Rev. Thomas Goodwillie, and published in the St. Johnsbury Caledonian, Nov. 18, 1864.

Children, all by 1st marriage:
i.   Robert, b. Nov. 26, 1778; was a prominent citizen of Ryegate and Caledonia County; m. 1803, Mehetabel, dau. Col. John Barron, of Bradford. Eight c.
ii. William, b. July 14, 1781; lived in Ryegate and was prominent there; m. Helen, dau. Col. Harvey of Barnet.
iii. Abigail, b. May 23, 1783; m. Alexander Henderson. (See Henderson family).
iv. Marion, b. Jan. 31, 1787; m. William Wallace of Newbury.

General Whitelaw and his 3d wife brought up a young girl, Marion, dau. of George and Mary (Smith) Ronalds, b. Ryegate, March 18, 1803. She m. a Mr. Reid, and rem. to Ohio. Their eldest son, b. near Xenia, in 1837, was named James Whitelaw Reid. In after life he dropped the first name. Whitelaw Reid is a man of national fame. The journal of General Whitelaw containing the narrative of his travels in behalf of the Scot's American Co., and of the settlement of Ryegate is owned by the Vt. Historical Society. The spy-glass which he used in surveying is in the museum at St. Johnsbury.

WHITMAN.

A volume of 1246 pages entitled "John Whitman of Weymouth" contains the records of more than 15,200 persons, who are descended from this emigrant who came from England prior to 1638, and settled in Weymouth, Mass., where he d. Nov. 13, 1692. One family of his descendants has lived in Newbury, whose ancestry is as follows:

I.   JOHN, the emigrant.
II.   THOMAS, of Bridgewater, Mass., (1629—1712).
III. NICHOLAS, of Bridgewater, (1675—1746).
IV.   JOHN, of Bridgewater, (1704—1792).
V.   SAMUEL, of Bridgewater and Cummington, Mass., (1730—1824).
VI.   DAVID, b. Bridgewater, Feb. 22, 1762. He served several years in the Revolutionary War, after which he settled in Lyme, N. H. He m. about 1790, Abigail Howard. It is related of him that after living in Lyme for some years, he determined to return to his native town to visit his father; money for the journey being lacking, he took a bag of flour on his shoulder and started for Massachusetts, paying for his lodging each night in flour. Member of the Baptist church in Lyme. He d. Orford, N. H., Oct. 24, 1846. Of their eight c.
VII. DAVID, b. Lyme, March 11, 1798. He came to Newbury with seven of his eight children in 1854, and settled near Hall's Pond, where J. J. Peach had made a clearing and built a house; the farm is now owned by his son, Levi. He was a member and deacon of the Free Will Baptist church in Lyme, N. H., and a man of singularly quiet, industrious life. He was nearly blind. He m. Feb. 7, 1833, Rebecca G., dau. of Caleb and ———(Storrs)

Freeman, who d. July 2, 1887. Member of the M. E. church. He d. in Newbury, Aug. 12, 1874.
Children:
i. Caleb Freeman, b. April 29, 1834; farmer at Orford; m. March 26, 1861, Mary W. Norris; four daus.; all m.
ii. John H., b. March 25, 1835; m. Sept. 4, 1858, Harriet E. Warren of Lyme, who d.; res. Manchester; bobbin maker; one dau.
iii. Shepard B., b. March 10, 1838. Enlisted for three years in Co. E., 2d Vt. sharpshooters; was in nine battles; wounded at the battle of Antietam, Sept. 16, 1862; discharged 1863. He m. Aug. 10, 1863, Elvira S. Davis, adopted dau. of John Wood of Newbury, who d. Jan. 12, 1899; rem., 1866, to Fond du Lac, Wis., and in 1877, to Hastings, Adams Co., Neb. Farmer; five c.; three living.
iv. Monroe D., b. Oct. 8, 1839. Enlisted, Aug., 1862, in Co. H, 12th Vt.; served nine months; went west in 1866. He m. Oct. 8, 1867, Anna Bryant; res. Steele Centre, Minn. Farmer. Seven c.; one son is a Baptist minister.
v. Levi, b. Feb. 8, 1842. Farmer on homestead, and proprietor of boats on Hall's Pond. He m. 1st, Aug. 16, 1873, Ann H., dau. of Joseph Martin, a native of Bradford, (b. in Maine, June 5, 1840; d. April 2, 1890.) He m. 2d, Dec. 24, 1890, Ella F. Martin, a sister of his first wife. Four c. by 1st m., four by 2d. (1) David, b. Oct. 28, 1874; d. March, 1875. (2) Dora, twin to above, m. Feb. 28, 1901, Daniel Mace. (3) Eugene, b. May 13, 1876. (4) Fanny R., b. March 18, 1879; m. June 5, 1901, Fred R. Campbell of Lakeport, N. H. (5) Hester A., b. Dec. 26, 1892. (6) Horace N., b. June 12, 1895. (7) Ruth E., b. March 23, 1898. (8) Elfreda Josephine, b. May 15, 1901.
vi. Harriet M., b. May 8, 1844; d. Aug. 29, 1866.
vii. Nelson S., b. Aug. 23, 1846; studied medicine; druggist at Nashua, N. H. Has held various public offices and was representative in the New Hampshire legislature. He m. Feb. 8, 1874, Nettie A. Quimby.
viii. Lucy A., b. Aug. 25, 1849; teacher; m. Sept. 15, 1880, Nathaniel A. Pike of Haverhill. C., Harriet E., b. July 30, 1881.

WIGGIN.

BROADSTREET, b. Exeter, N. H.; m. Margaret Tarleton of Newmarket, N. H.; lived in Washington, Bradford and Corinth.
Children:
i. Martha, b. Newmarket, N. H. Feb. 15, 1787; m. Levi Carter, q. v.; d. Newbury, Jan. 2, 1865.
ii. Mary, b. Newmarket, N. H., July, 1792; m. David Carter; d. Newbury, Nov. 13, 1866.
iii. Hannah, m. Thomas Lowell of Piermont.
iv. John Tarleton, b. May 26, 1796; m. 1820, Nancy Plummer, (b. Washington, Nov. 4, 1803; d. Jan. 21, 1844). He d. Aug. 18, 1887. Nine c.
1 v. Enoch, b. Bradford, Feb. 6, 1799; d. March 10, 1865.
vi. Stillman T., b. 1801; m. Susan Merrill of Washington; d. Vershire, 1850. Two c.

1 ENOCH, b. Bradford, Feb. 6, 1799; farmer and cattle dealer; m. 1st, 1818, Mary, dau. of Dea. William Carter, (b. Bradford, Feb. 9, 1799; d. Newbury, Jan. 9, 1833). He d. Newbury, March 10, 1865.
Children:
i. Laura Ann, b. Bradford, July 18, 1821; m. 1st, Oct. 5, 1840, Daniel Eastman; m. 2d, April 5, 1858, George L. Butler, of Bradford.
ii. Mary Carter, b. Bradford, Dec. 7, 1823; m. John Haseltine, q. v.; d. May 29, 1855.
iii. Charles Enoch, b. Newbury, 1827; d. 1828.
iv. Sarah Jane, b. Bradford, March 23, 1829; m. Henry M. Buxton, q. v.

WILLOUGHBY.

JOSIAH, b. Feb. 23, 1780. His wife, Betsey Manson, (b. Plymouth, N. H., Sept. 9, 1781; d. Newbury, July 28, 1872.) Their son, Ezra Bartlett, b. Haverhill, April 6, 1816; m. April 24, 1851, Vilera S., dau. of John and

Lydia (Gould) Jeffers, (b. Haverhill, Sept. 10, 1817). The latter, when a young girl, went to Lowell, Mass., to work in a factory. and in the year 1838. she started the first cotton loom in what is now the city of Manchester, N. H. They came to Newbury in April, 1865, having bought the farm which had been that of William Peach, his son, and grandson, where she d. May 18, 1890, and he d. April 20, 1892. They were devout members of the Methodist church. Their only c., Mary E., b. Haverhill, Aug. 16. 1853; d. Newbury, April 25, 1865. Josiah Willoughby d. Haverhill, March 2, 1850.

WILSON.

JOHN, and two brothers came from England; the two brothers settled in the western part of this state, but, later, went west and died, and have many descendants. John settled in Corinth, and d. there. He m. Carrie Underhill, who d. at Chelsea. They had 12 c., of whom Samuel, b. 1803; lived at West Newbury and in "Goshen." He m. Mary, sister of E. C. Stocker, (b. 1814; d. 1880). He d. 1874. Thomas, son of John, b. about 1792; m. Betsey Barker; lived in Bradford, but came to West Newbury and settled where his son John long lived. That old house was built by Green Saunders. He d. March 12, 1859, aged 66. She d. Sept. 27, 1861, aged, 72.
Children, besides a son who died young:
1   i.   Hazen K., b. Jan. 12, 1825; d. July 5, 1892.
   ii.   John B., b. Sept. 12, 1828; farmer on homestead; m. Henrietta, dau. Paschal and Sally (Putnam) Raymond, b. April 7 1827. (Her parents formerly lived where Joseph Sawyer does). He d. Feb 28, 1897.
   iii. Betsey Ann, b. 1836; m. E. J. Cauley; d. March 11, 1877.

1ᴈHAZEN KIMBALL, b. Jan. 12, 1825; merchant at West Newbury, (page 279). In 1883, he went to Florida, but settled at Spring City, Tenn., where he d. July 5. 1892. Buried at West Newbury. He m. Harriet Merrill, (b. Oct. 5, 1833; d. at Spring City, Dec. 27, 1898).
Children:
   i.   Alice Jane, b. Dec. 20, 1856; d. Sept. 7, 1871.
   ii. George W., b. July 11, 1858; m. Lizzie, dau. Isaac Pike; d. in Florida, Dec. 28, 1884. Two c.
   iii. Thomas Franklin, b. Oct. 28. 1859; d. Sept. 29, 1873.
   iv. Jasper Hazen. b. April 23, 1864. He m. Lilla. dau. Archibald Bachop, who d. in Tennessee, leaving children. Jeweler at Rockwood, Tenn., of which place he is mayor in 1901.
   v.   Edward E., b. Dec. 9, 1865; d. March 8, 1881.

WITHERSPOON.

I. JOHN, came from the north of Ireland and settled in Chester, N. H., about 1741.

II. DAVID, m. Agnes Linn. He was an officer in the Revolutionary War. His son John lived in Newbury, and d. Jan. 26, 1839. He m. March 26, 1801, Ruth, dau. Raymond Chamberlin. (b. May 30, 1779; d. June 29, 1854). They had several children, of whom were:
   i.   Joseph, b. 1805; m. Lucy ————; d. Aug. 13, 1837.
   ii. Mary, b. 1809; d June 14, 1824.
   iii. Samuel P.
   iv. William, b. 1813; went to Rochester, N. Y., in 1841, and was in the grocery business many years with his brother Samuel P. Became blind in 1880. He m. a sister of E. R. Davenport. He d. Feb. 3, 1897. Four c. living in 1897.
   v.   Raymond C., b. July 7, 1816; lived many years at South Newbury, where A. B. Rogers lives; m. Feb. 20, 1840, Laura, dau. Nathaniel Smith, (b. March 23, 1817; d. 1900). He d. Dec. 1, 1889. Two daus., Adelaide and Hattie, were teachers, and m. Stuart and W. D. McDougal, and live in Brooklyn, N. Y.

WORTHEN.

JACOB, son of Samuel and Susan (Owen) Worthen, grandson of Jacob Worthen, one of the first settlers of Barre, was b. in that place, Sept. 7, 1823; d. Newbury, March 9, 1890. His great grandfather, Sylvanus Owen, was a Revolutionary soldier. Jacob was a farmer for many years. He rem. to Newbury from McIndoes Falls in 1874, and was in the meat business some years. He m. Sept. 15, 1850, Irene Richardson of Topsham.
Children ·
i. Leona A., b. Jan. 23, 1854; m. S. L. Swasey, q. v.
ii. Wilbert H., b. Oct. 27, 1861. In livery business; m. May 23, 1883, Jennie D. Cheever of Walden. C., Raymond A., b. Newbury, Aug. 21, 1889.

WYLIE.

ANDREW, b. in Stirlingshire, Scotland, in 1804; came to Newbury and settled on Jefferson Hill. He was a man of stalwart frame, and father of stalwart sons and daughters. He was a member of the Presbyterian church, as were all his children. He m. Lillias, dau. of William Buchanan of Ryegate. Both are now dead. Seven children. Andrew, the oldest, b. in Scotland, 1829; came to America with his grandfather Buchanan; went back to Scotland in 1846, and returned a few years later; in 1853, he with his sisters, Jessie and Margaret, went to Australia. Their voyage in a sailing vessel from Boston to Melbourne occupied five months and eleven days. He engaged in the lumber business, in which he was very successful. Returned to Newbury in 1869, and settled on the home farm, with his sister Jean, and is an elder in the Presbyterian church. Margaret, the eldest daughter, m. in Australia, Robert McLeod, q. v. Jessie. m. there Mr. Cole, and now resides in Newbury. William, the 3d son, b. in Scotland; educated at Newbury Seminary, and Kimball Union Academy, at Meriden, N. H.; graduated at the Reformed Presbyterian Theological Seminary, at Philadelphia, in 1871; licensed to preach, 1872; pastor of the 1st Reformed Presbyterian church in New York City, 1872–85; in Paris, Ontario, Presbyterian church, 1885–94; pastor of 2d Reformed Presbyterian church, Philadelphia, 1895–99; preached in Newbury and Ryegate, summer and fall of 1899; then pastor of the 1st Presbyterian church at Quincy, Ill. He has one son, now a junior at Yale University.

INDEX

TO THE

HISTORICAL EVENTS OF THIS VOLUME.

PLACES MENTIONED IN THE HISTORICAL EVENTS OF THIS VOLUME.

INDEX

TO

PEOPLE MENTIONED IN THE HISTORICAL EVENTS OF THIS
VOLUME.

INDEX

TO

BIOGRAPHICAL SKETCHES AND FAMILY RECORDS.

INDEX

TO

ILLUSTRATIONS IN THIS VOLUME.

NOTE.—While it might have been desirable to give a complete personal index to the soldiers' record, the lists of town and state officers, the miscellaneous papers, and the genealogical portion, the editor could not command the necessary time, while the additional pages would add materially to the size of a volume already large enough.

Page 705 Sylvester

It is an error to say ?
Ruth married Thomas
Hibbard. It was Lu-
-cinda did. See Hibbard
page 576. That has been
-entirely(?) documented.
For that matter see
the fox- note on page
576. The asterisk, how-
ever, should apply to
the previous Hibbard
.....

In a volume conta
from a number of cause
are here given.

On page 16, and la
according to Judge Ald
in the latter part of this

On page 71. For
On page 92. For
On page 186. For
On page 189. For
On page 216. For
On page 265. For
On page 275. Last
On page 319, line 7
On page 326. For
On page 277. For
Main street.

On page 421. For
On page 425. For
On page 443. Nat
Nathaniel M., but he
Sept. 12. and for one d
read Alitheah.

On page 444. For
(29) read. iii. Clara,
record of Albert Bayle
For Isabelle, read Isa
John A. Park read John A. Parks.

On page 445, in Milo Bayley (33) read. Child. i. Anna Gertrude, b. June 21,
1858; d. Aug. 24, 1884. ii. Mary Louise, b. June 8, 1863; d. Sept. 30, 1863. iii.
Maud, b. Sept. 14, 1865. iv. Edith Isabel, b. Sept. 3, 1870; m. Aug. 11, 1892, Ned
T. Barker.

On page 468. Bone. For 1953 read 1853.

On page 470. Boyce, Allen R. For "res. in Barre till Jan. 20, 1899," read, "till
d. Jan. 20, etc."

On page 474. Brock, Benjamin. For Samuel Gibson read Matthew Gibson.

On page 479. Brown. For Abraham read Absalom.

On page 480. Buchanan, Wm. G. Error in record corrected in Ira White record.

On page 529. Deming, Benj. F., b. Sept. 4, 1827, read 1857.

On page 533. Douglass, Barton M. For "border" read "Andes."

On pages 575, 576. Henderson. For Charles T., b. May 23, 1824, read May 3
1824.

On Page 613. Ladd. For Daniel Child read Childs.

On page 671. Reid, David B, For Canoe read Casco.

On page 684. Ross. For Wm. Scott of Barton read Boston.

On page 688. Scott, Rev. Orange. For b. Bradford, read Brookfield.

On page 690. Shepard. For 1874 read 1894.

On page 694. Smith, Hiram. The record of his 2d dau. was not given the editor, and the omission was not observed until after the sheet was printed. The record should read. i. Lucy A., etc. ii. Mary, m. E. E. Johnson of Bradford, d. 1878, leaving a dau. Lizzie, who m. Frank R. Jenkins of Penn Yan, N. Y.

On page 699. Stevens, John. Read viii. Mary Jane m. 2d, Nov. 4, 1872, Franklin Farrington of Brandon, who d. June 30, 1892.

On page 719, Thrall, in 2d line of record read "ordained" a Congregational minister.